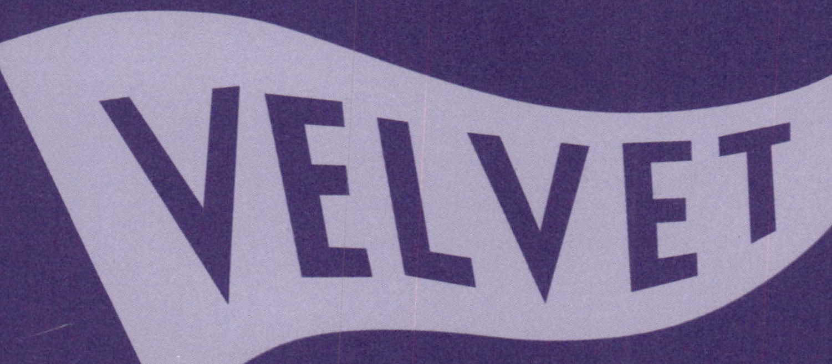

TONE

RECORD
CORP.

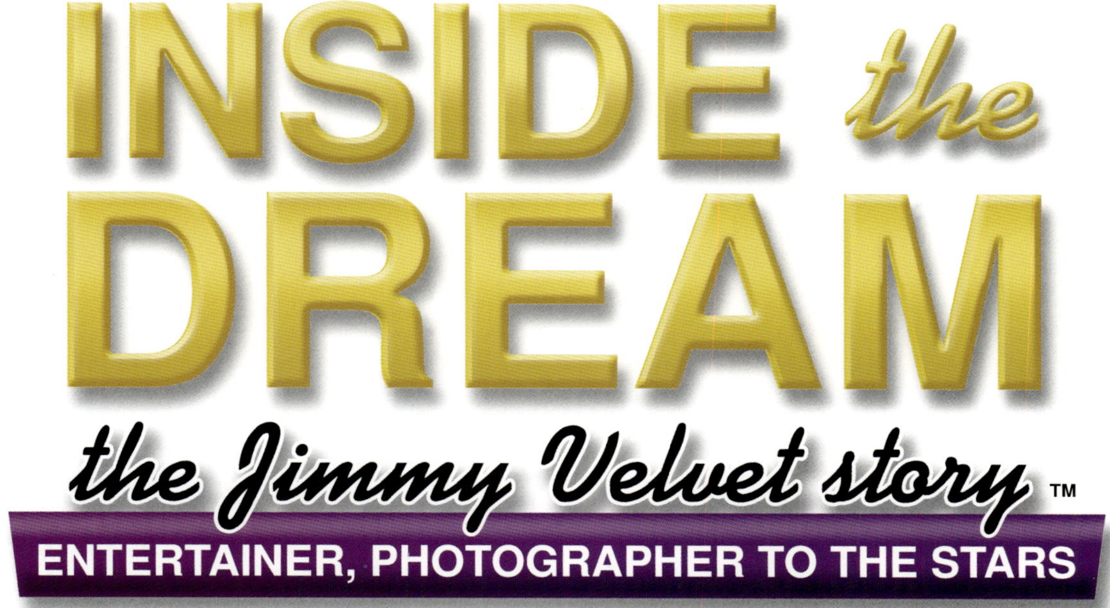

1st Printing

Edited by Leesa Griffin

Legends and Superstars Publications™
PO Box 1146, Hendersonville, TN 37077 USA

For information about special discounts for bulk purchases,
please contact Legends and Superstars Publications™ via email:
info@insidethedream.net or visit us on the web: www.insidethedream.net

Library of Congress Cataloging-n-Publication Data
Velvet, Jimmy

ISBN 978-0-9795111-0-3

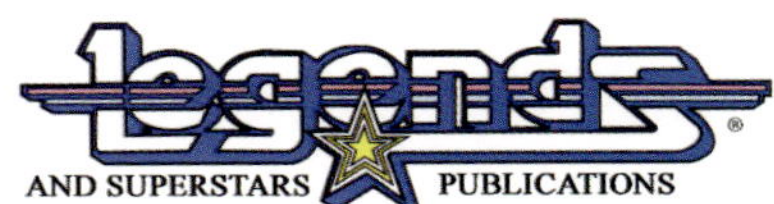

Acknowledgements

I've been told for years by so many people that I should tell my life story through my photos as the story by itself would seem like fiction. I am deeply grateful to the many people who have made this book possible:

My wife Robin, the love of my life, for knowing me better than I know myself. Thank you for your unconditional love, faith and strength in helping me see this through and never giving up when things got rough. I love you.

To Rocket Roese, my best friend and partner in this project. Your all inspiring energy, unwavering faith, love and support kept the wind beneath my wings to keep this project alive. This book would still be just a dream without you.

Kimmy & Steven Sculli who inspired me to put my best foot forward by sending me equipment to bring the negatives to life so this story could be told. You've stuck by me through the best and worst times. I thank you from the bottom of my heart for your friendship and generosity.

Eddie Ray, my buddy, for keeping me on the right path with countless hours of professional advice. You've been a faithful friend through it all.

To Gary Bridges, you've been like a son to me. Thanks for all your encouragement and for always believing in me.

Daniel Johnson who showed me how to look at the glass half full, never half empty and making me realize that at my age great things can still be accomplished.

LeesaBeth, for the time spent researching, your critique, patience and creative talents. You are amazing.

David Pinkston, my brother in Christ. Thank you for the many hours you put forth teaching me how to use the necessary equipment for developing this book. You have been my guardian angel.

To the members of the Blvd Design Studio from Belmont University who did the outstanding layout of this project. The team members: Jamie Browder, Jessi Menish, Lacy Clark, Katie Turner, Lucy Kane, and Kristin Armstrong.

To Kevin Johnson, for your artistic genius. You helped breathe new life into some fond memories. God has truly blessed you with a special talent. Thank you for your friendship, time and love for this project.

To the most important being in my life which is my Heavenly Father, my Lord and Master, Jesus Christ. His love sustains me. Through Him all things are possible.

I have learned to be content whatever the circumstances. I know what it is to be in need, and I know what it is to have plenty. I have learned the secret of being content in any and every situation, whether well fed or hungry, whether living in plenty or in want. I can do everything through him, who gives me strength.

Philippians 4:11-13

From my first meeting with Elvis throughout my career as an entertainer, Inside the Dream is a chronicle of amazing stories. If told without pictures, it would seem to be a fairytale. In my mind I was never a major star; just barely big enough to tour with the best of my day.

I was blessed to have worked with just about every star you could name, and for some unknown reason, I always had my camera. In the early days of rock n' roll we did not have the "paparazzi." The news media thought rock n' roll was a fad. So, I took thousands of photos throughout the years.

They sat in boxes until someone offered to buy the negatives to do a book. However, they just did not have the stories to go with the pictures. I bought the negatives back, and Inside the Dream was born.

In scanning the negatives, I found so many that I have decided to issue this first book as a coffee table photo book with well over a thousand unpublished photos. I hope you enjoy the stories told by these pictures. In the meantime, I will continue to write, in more detail, the stories that go with them, to be released in future publications.

At present, I live in Tennessee with my wife, Robin. We have 11 children: Shari Kay, Jimmy, Linda, Scott, Candida, Christi, Angie, Tim, Leesa, Mark and Jake. Our calendar is full with 20 Grandchildren and 4 Great Grandchildren, spending time with family, friends and serving our Lord. I'm still performing and appear at special engagements signing photos, CD's and records and still offer my services as a photographer and entertainer.

Sit back, relax, and enjoy. May God bless you,

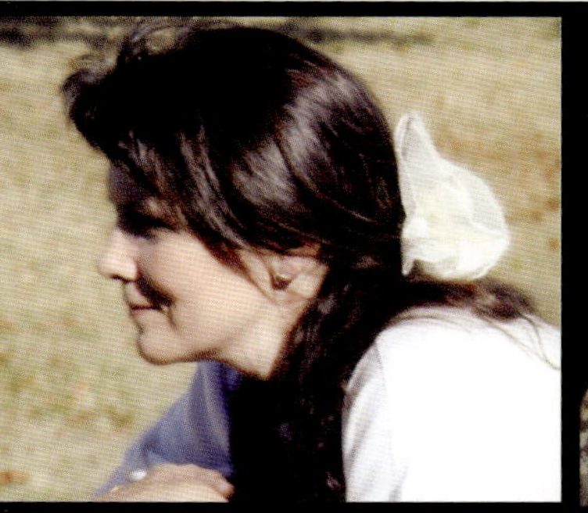

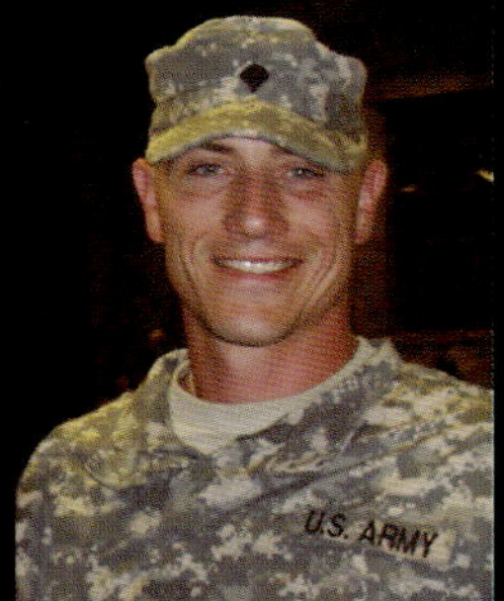

Our son Tim,
now serving in Iraq

We are so proud of
our family hero.

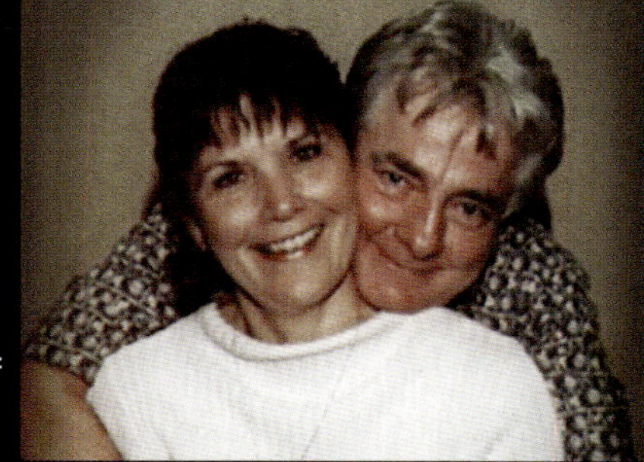

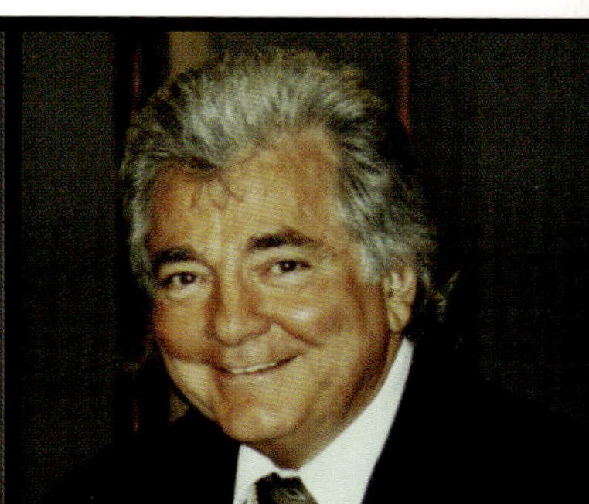

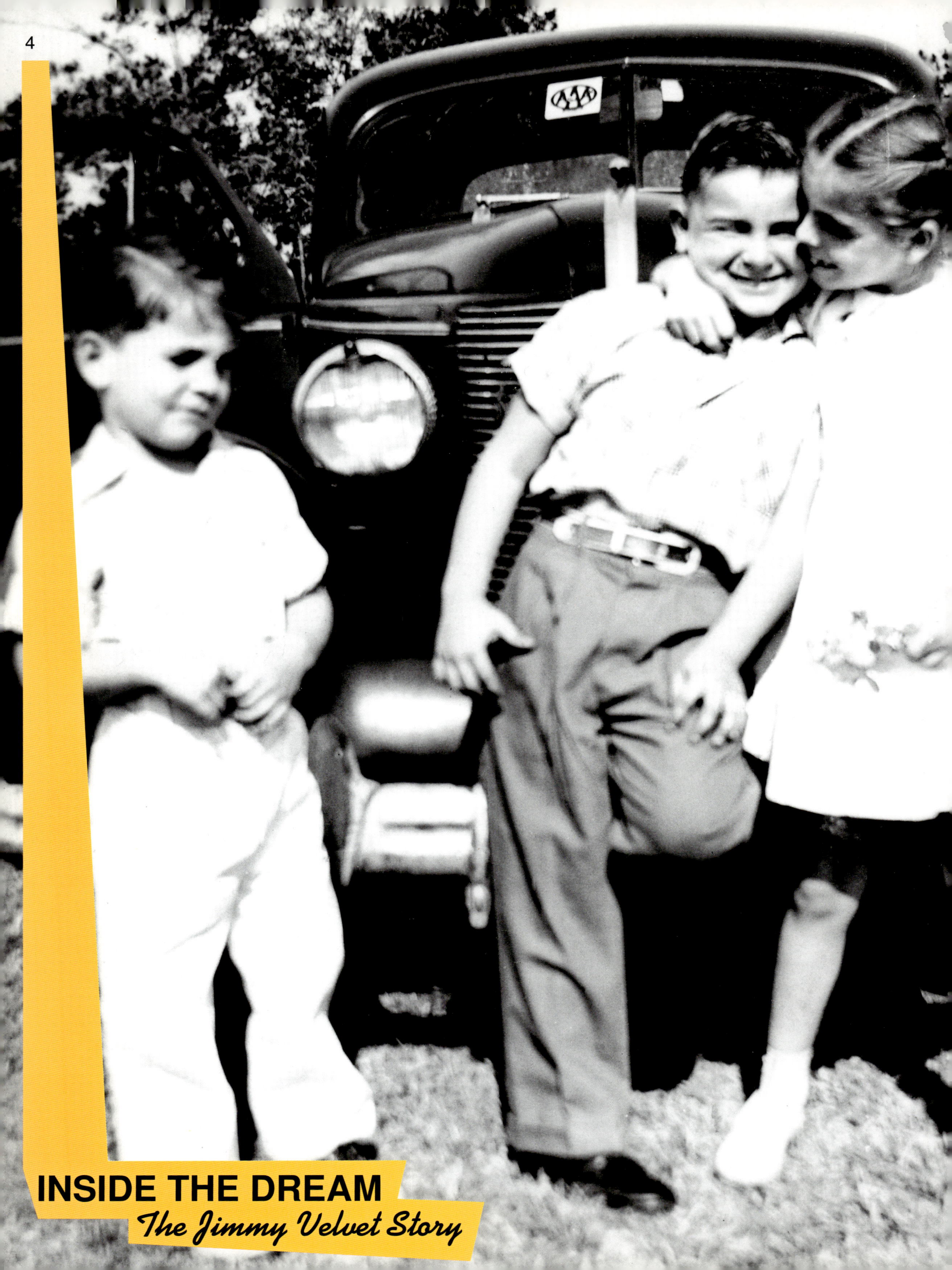

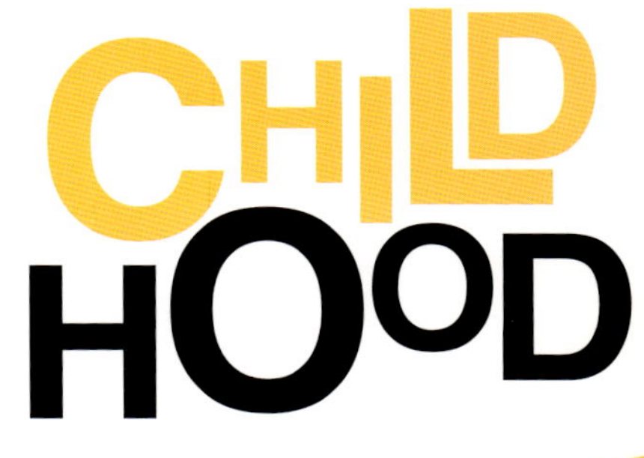

It all started on October 19, 1939 in Jacksonville, Florida at St. Vincent's Hospital where I was born to John & Jacqueline Tennant. My brother Johnny was already three years old and my sister Jolene was two (Jolene was actually born in Maine. We always said she was the Maine-E-Ack of the family).

My family moved to Hollywood, Florida when I was still a baby. My dad had been discharged from the Navy and my mother was discharged from the Army. They both served in WWII. My dad took a job as head chef at the Hollywood Beach Hotel and we lived on Cleveland Street. When I was 10 months old my dad built a child size boat for me and entered me (and my boat) into the baby contest where I won 1st place as the prettiest baby in Hollywood. That's me sitting in the boat with my Loving Cup Award.

At age three my life took a near fatal hit. My brother, sister and a few of their friends were playing a game of cowboys and Indians. They had me stand on a chair beneath a tree and put a rope around my neck (yes, the rope was also tied on the tree branch). While whooping and hollering around the tree they kicked the chair out from under my feet and I was left dangling as they continued to play. My mother happened to be standing at the kitchen sink looking out the window and saw my face in a nice shade of blue hanging from the tree branch. She rushed to get me out of the noose, and she saved my life. My sister still takes credit for helping me with my singing career by strengthening my vocal chords by hanging me from the tree! As a child I did sing a lot, mostly to myself and always while riding my tricycle up and down the street. My favorite song at the time was "That Old Black Magic".

We spent many of our summers in Williamsville, Virginia at my paternal grandparents' home. My grandmother was wonderful and my grandfather, Papa Daddy, was a gruff mountain man and was hard on us. Williamsville had two general stores just a hop, skip and a jump from my grandparents' house. Our favorite hangout there was Marshall's.

My parents' divorced when I was about four. During my growing up days my mother would visit us every couple of years. Sometimes she would take us away only to leave us abandoned somewhere. The Salvation Army or Traveler's Aide Society would locate my maternal grandmother (Bammie) and get us back to her safe and sound. One time we were as far away as Ocean City, New Jersey, another time was Richmond, Virginia. I loved my mother very much and she was the most beautiful woman I'd ever seen. Nobody ever did tame my mother, and wild as she was, I always missed her.

Later, while we were still little children, I wasn't quite of school age, my brother Johnny and I were put into a Catholic school for boys where I was often beaten. One day I asked my brother why I was always getting beaten. Johnny's reply: "Because you deserved it. You talk too much and you don't sit still." Looking back, it was probably true. At some point during this time Bammie came to the school and we took the train back to her house in Jacksonville, Florida. There she and my grandfather raised us. Their names were Georgia and Charles Giddings but we called them Bammie & Paka. They lived in a very small shotgun-style house and made the back porch into a bedroom for us kids. The house was nestled on 40 acres of farmland. Along with all that land, of course, came chores. We certainly had to earn our keep but were grateful to do so. My grandparents were strict, yet loving and it was their example and teachings that lead me to become a Christian at the age of six. When I was seven my grandmother would make me sing solos at church and sing in the choir. I was scared half out of my wits. Later, I was asked to appear now and again on the Toby Dowdy Show which later became the Johnny Tillotson Show. Johnny and I have remained friends.

By age twelve I was working three jobs. Starting at 5:00 am I started my farm chores: Milking the cows, slopping the pigs and feeding the chickens. When I finished my farm chores I ran my paper route, then after school and on Saturday's I delivered groceries for Jax Meat Market (I didn't earn a salary there, just tips).

When I was a teenager my mother rented a garage apartment on Dellwood Avenue in Jacksonville. My sister Jolene and I moved in with her for a few months. It was at that time that Johnny Tillotson introduced me to a nice family who happened to live down the street from us: John & Mae Axton and their son Hoyt. I became quite close to them. Mr. Axton was my coach in school and Mrs. Axton "Mama Mae" was my substitute English teacher. She was also a show promoter. Their son Hoyt became an actor and starred in the hit movie The Gremlins. He was also a singer and song writer, and the mastermind who penned Three Dog Night's "Joy to the World." By the way, Mama Mae (with Tommy Durdin) wrote: "Heartbreak Hotel" along with many other hits.

My Mother never stayed in one place very long. When she left the garage apartment, my sister and I went back to Bammie & Paka's. At the beginning of that summer (I was 15) my dad happened to call. We rarely heard from Dad except at Christmas and at birthday time when he sent a card with a five-dollar bill enclosed. I was surprised that he called to offer me a job at the Oceanside Hotel in Magnolia, Massachusetts as a Salad Chef. I would even be given a room to stay in while working there. I accepted the position, my Dad picked me up and we drove up to Massachusetts together. It was the longest stretch of time that I ever spent with him. My job was to open the big #10 cans of fruit, pour off the juice and make fancy salads with the fruit. I couldn't imagine throwing out the good juice so I poured the juice into one gallon-sized glass jugs to take back to my grandmother at the end of the summer. I stored the jugs in my hotel room and they took up nearly half the space in my room. One day while I was down in the kitchen working, someone announced that a huge explosion just took place in one of the hotel rooms. Turns out it was my room. Those full glass jugs with juice had fermented, exploded and made one big mess! There was juice and shards of glass everywhere from the ceiling to the floor, on the walls and in the bed. It was awful and smelled like a brewery. My Dad accused me of making wine and fired me on the spot. I went home with a broken heart overflowing with good intentions, and no juice for Bammie to put up for the winter.

Evidently, God had something else in store for me. Soon after my return home, I discovered that Mae Axton was promoting a show at the Gator Bowl with Hank Snow and the Carter Family. Mrs. Axton, knowing how badly I wanted to see the show but couldn't afford to go, got me in backstage. I was talking with a guitar player who didn't appear much older than I was. He was an interesting guy and after about a full hour of conversation he extended out his right hand for a handshake and said, "Oh, by the way, my name is Elvis Presley." My first thought was, "...strange name."... He went on stage and stole the show. The police couldn't control the crowd. It was at that moment I knew I wanted to be an entertainer. I was turning 16 and Elvis was 20. We exchanged phone numbers, stayed in touch and we remained friends until Elvis' untimely death in 1977.

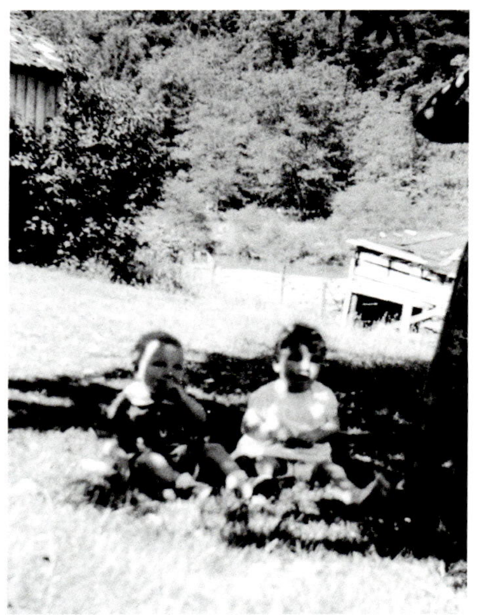

Me & my sister, Jolene

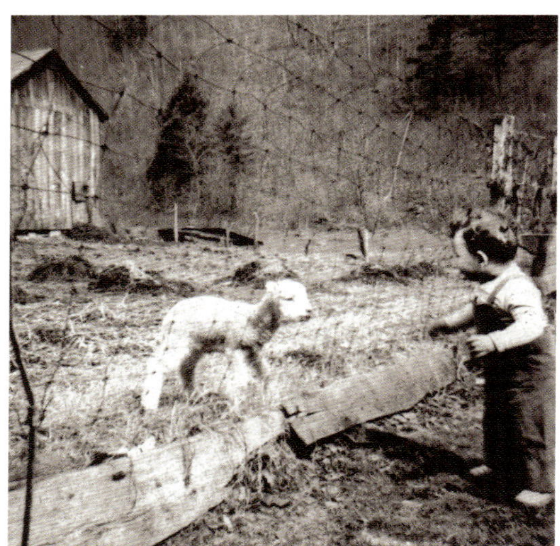

In Virgina, me with my lamb "Lambchops"

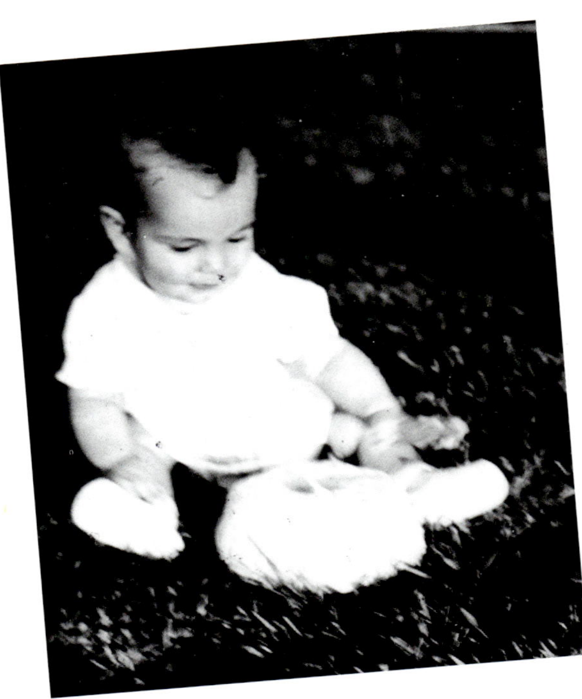

My first birthday, October 19, 1940

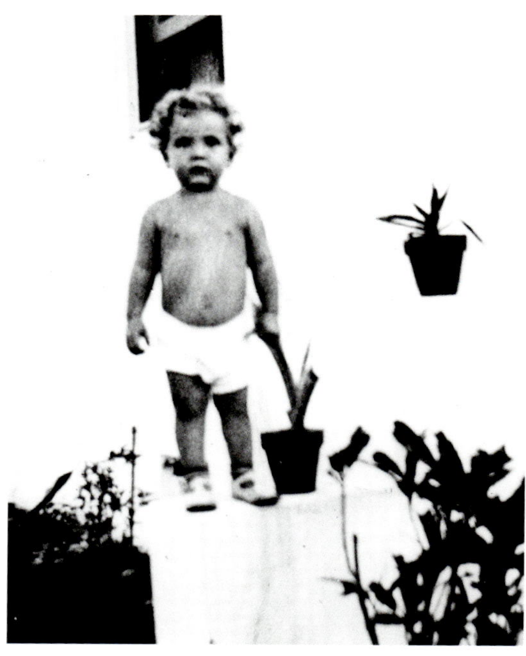

I had long blonde curls until they were cut, they never came back

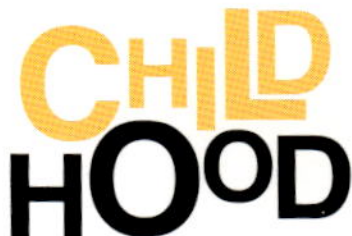

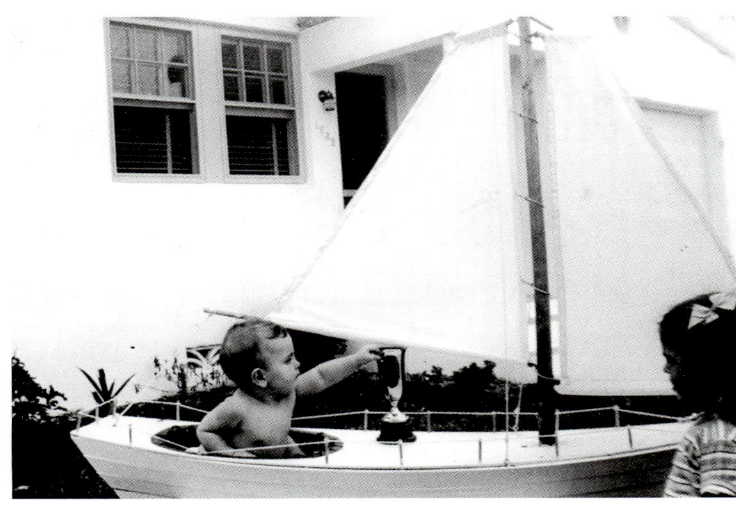

Me with my loving cup and Jolene

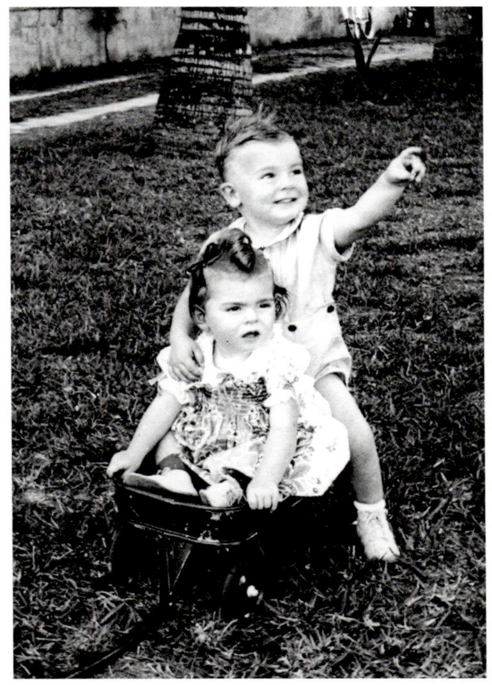

Jolene & Johnny

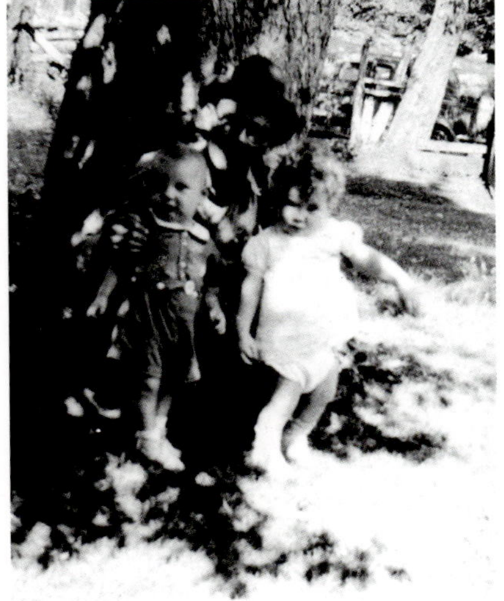

Me & Jolene with "Papa Daddy"

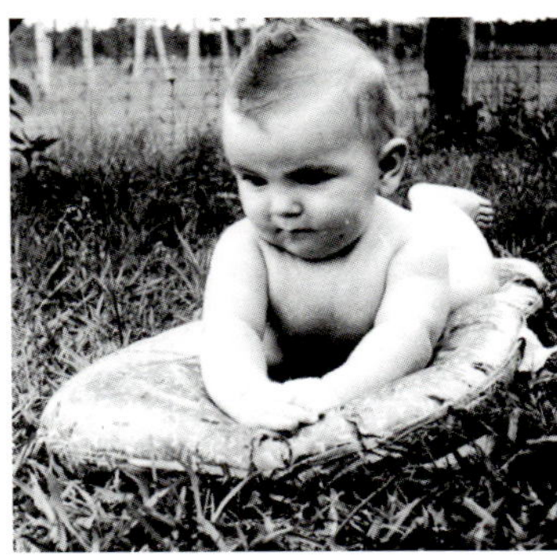

This would be me

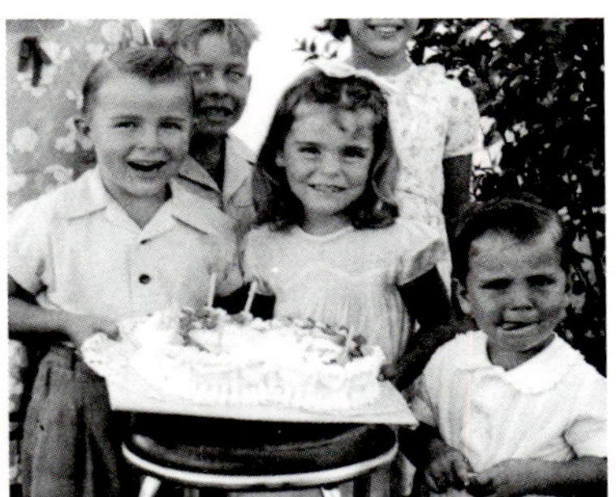

Johnny, Jolene & Me

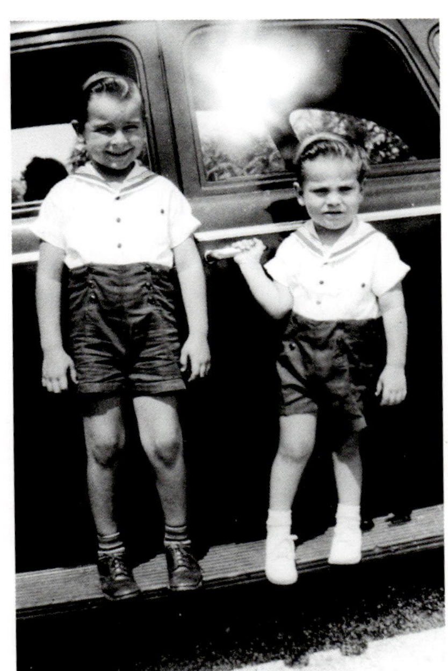

Johnny & Me

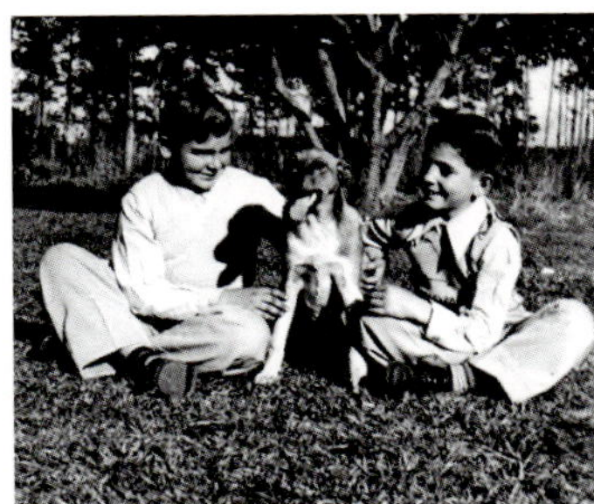

Johnny, Me, & Shep

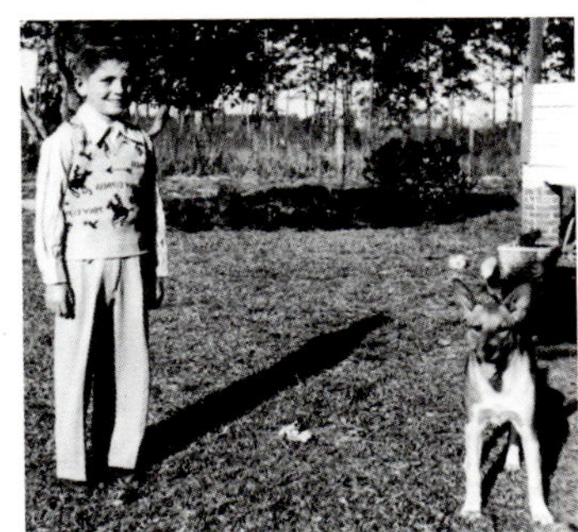

Me with Shep

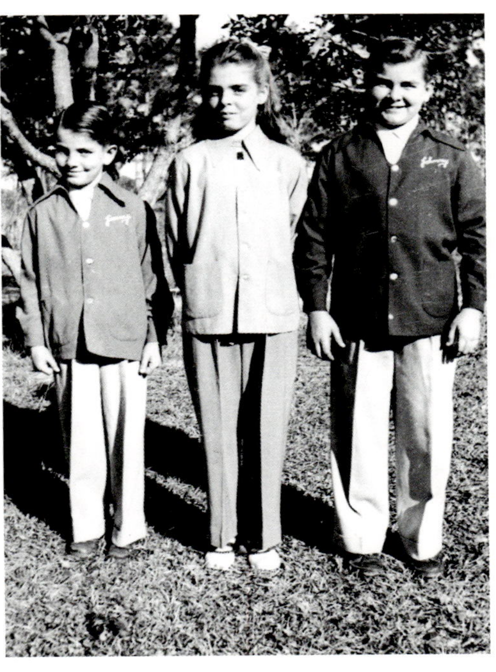

Me, Jolene, and Johnny

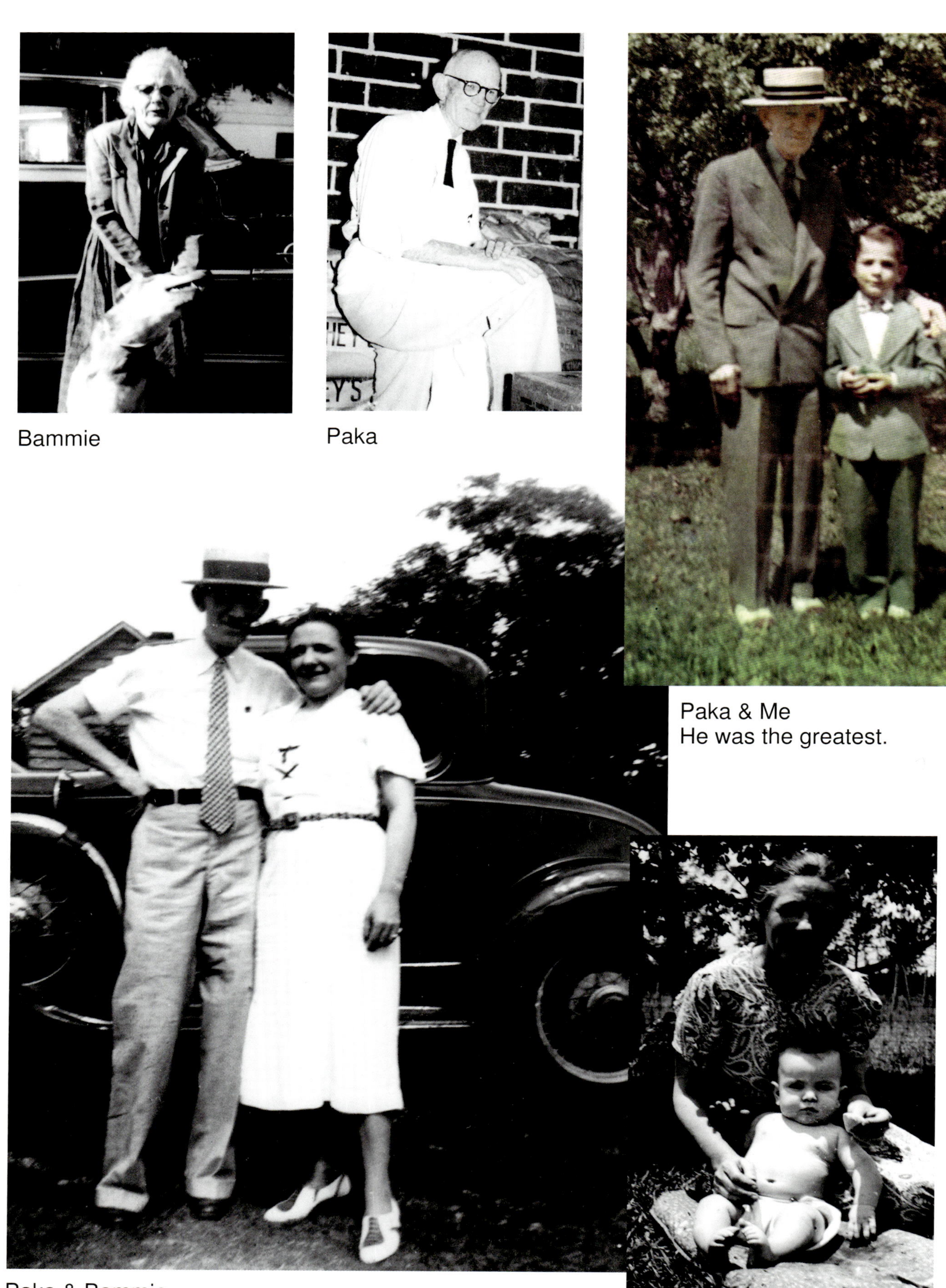

Bammie

Paka

Paka & Me
He was the greatest.

Paka & Bammie

Bammie & Me

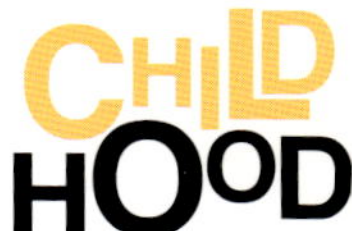

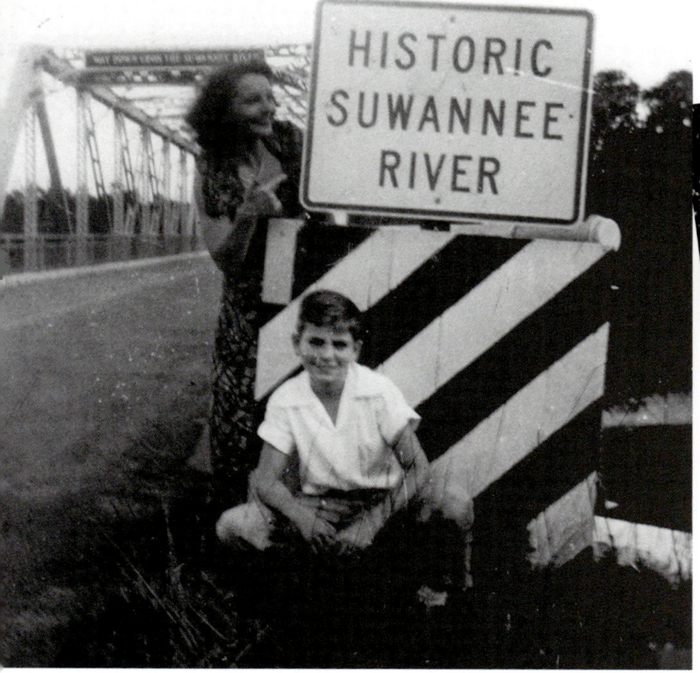

My mother and I on a rare visit. We went to Steven Foster Memorial and of course it was "Way down upon the Suwannee River."

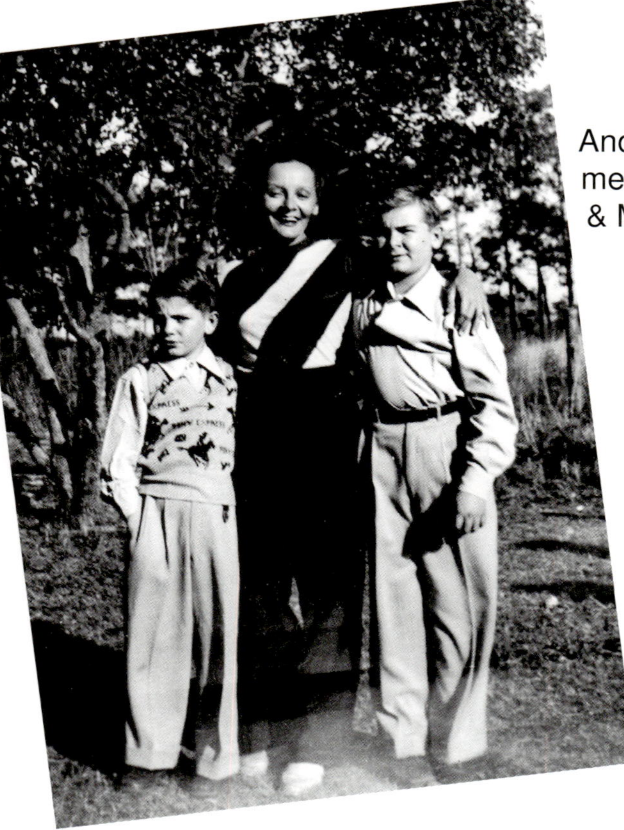

Another rare visit, me, Johnny, & Mother

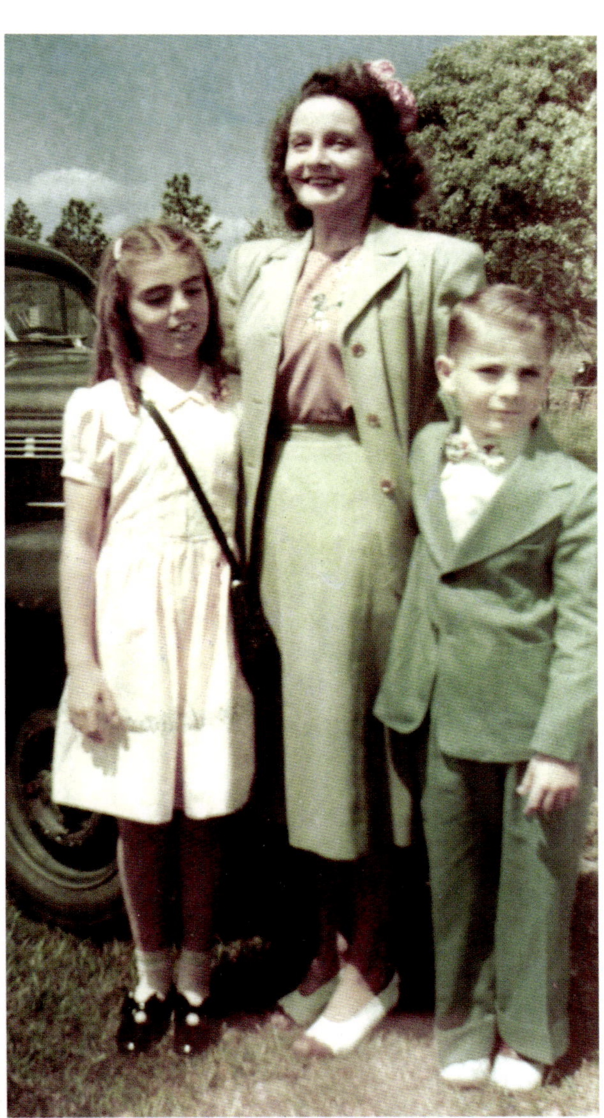

One of my mother's visits with Jolene and I

My mother, "Jackie," so pretty, I loved her so much.

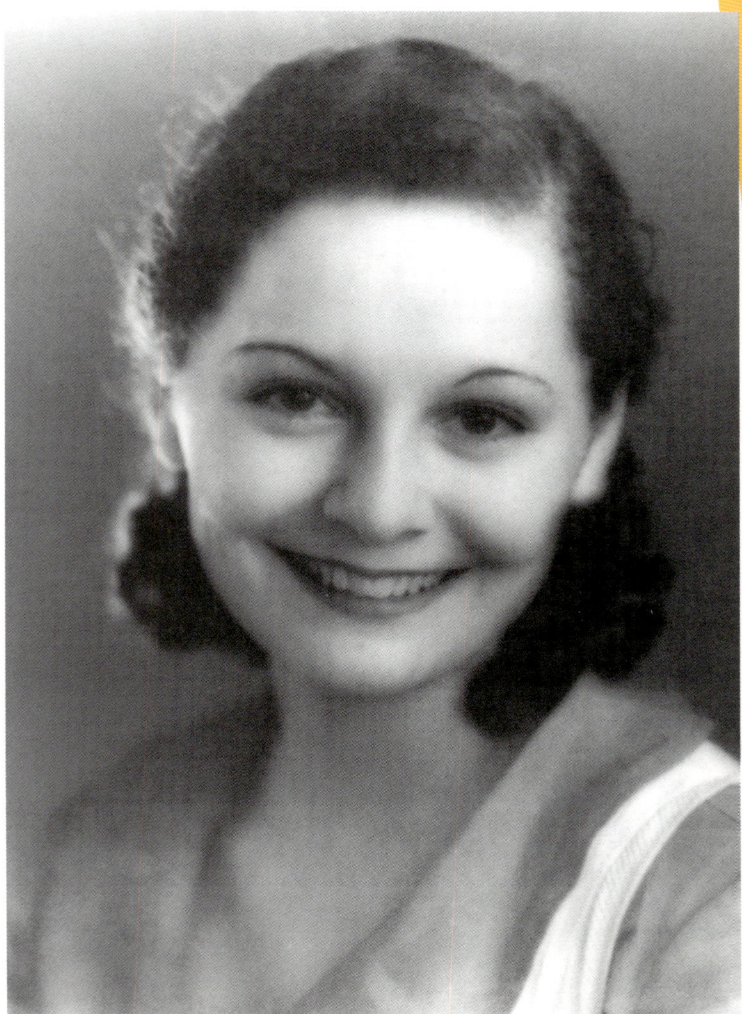

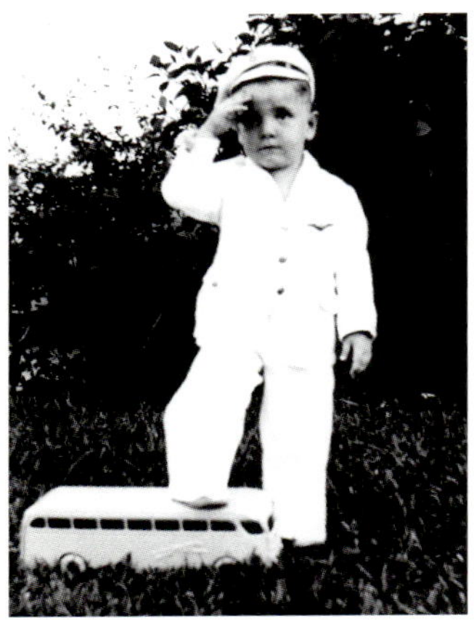

My Greyhound bus was always with me.

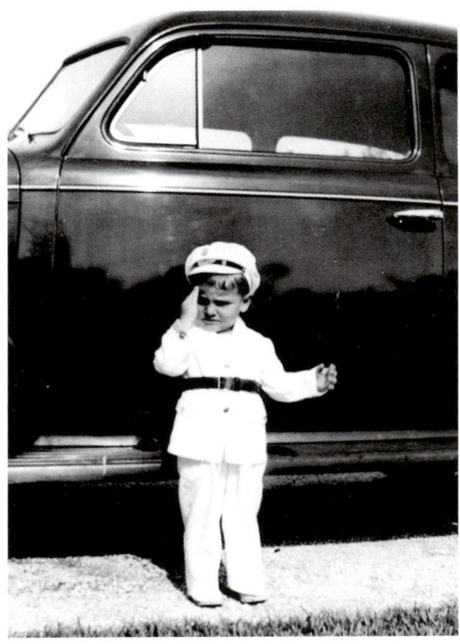

I was told that I was nicknamed "Lou" because my last name was Tennant so I would salute when they called me "lieutenant."

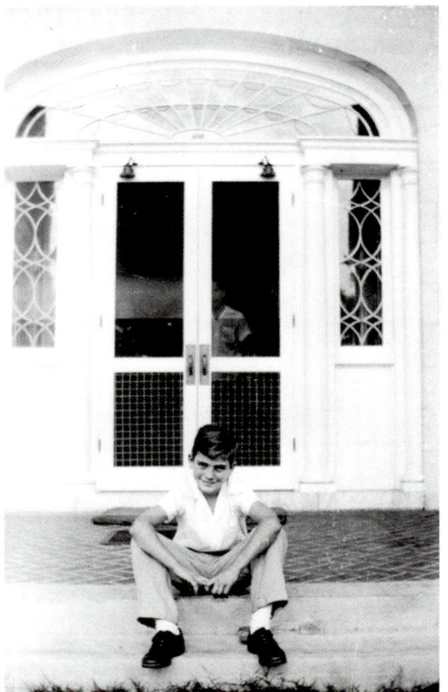

Me at the Steven Foster Memorial

Various pictures of my childhood

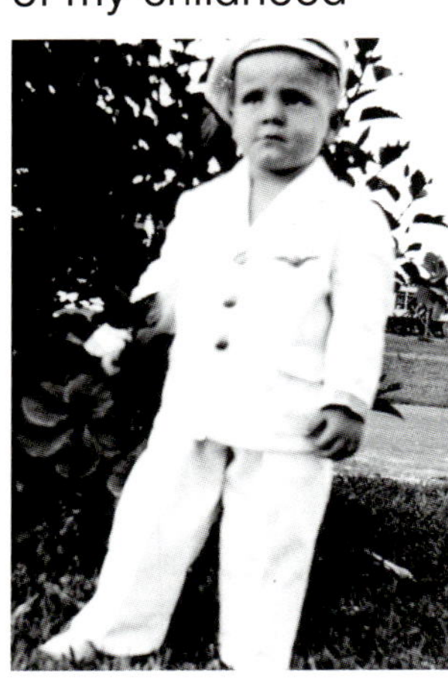

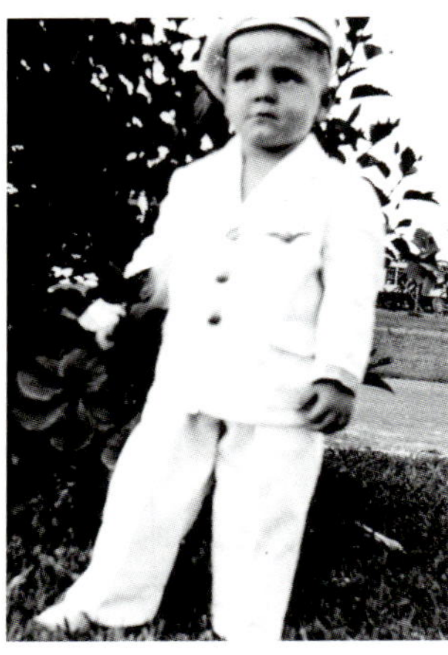

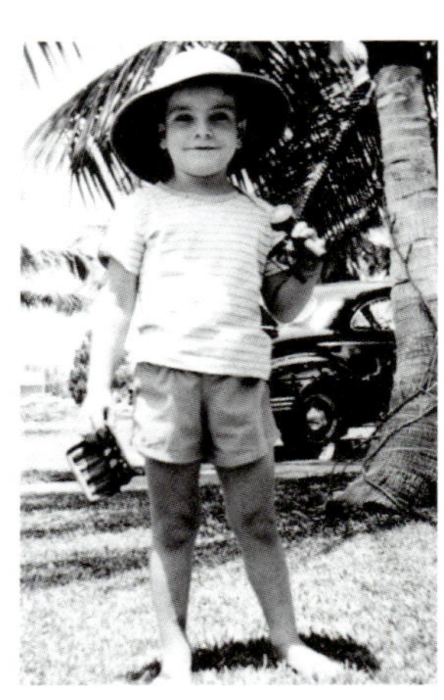

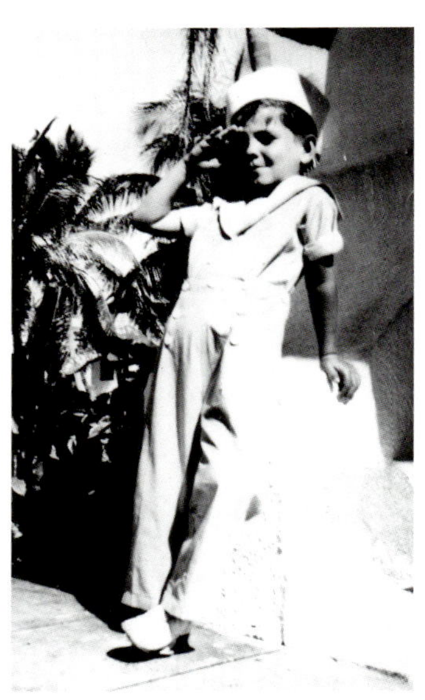

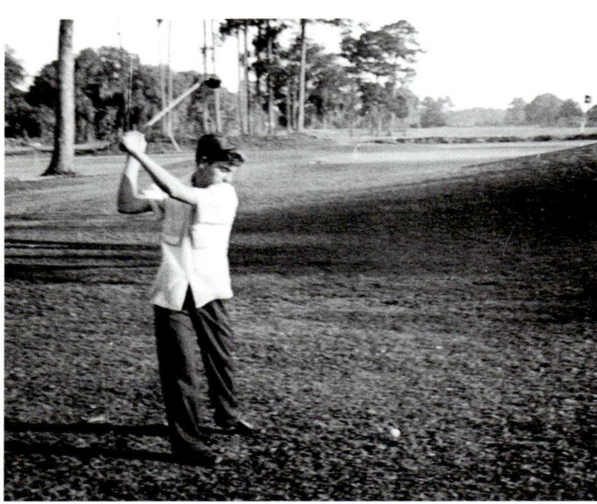

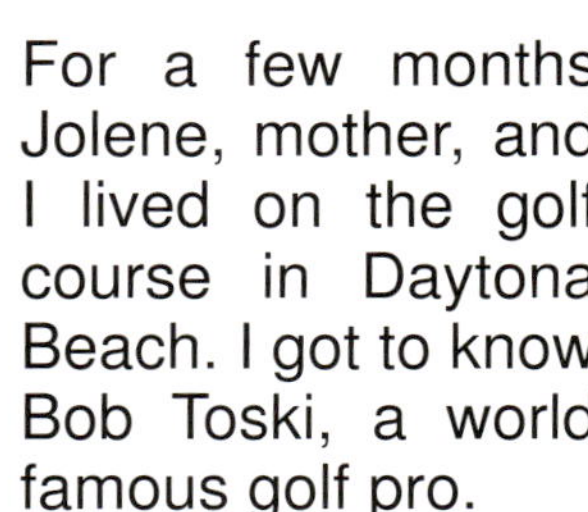

For a few months Jolene, mother, and I lived on the golf course in Daytona Beach. I got to know Bob Toski, a world famous golf pro.

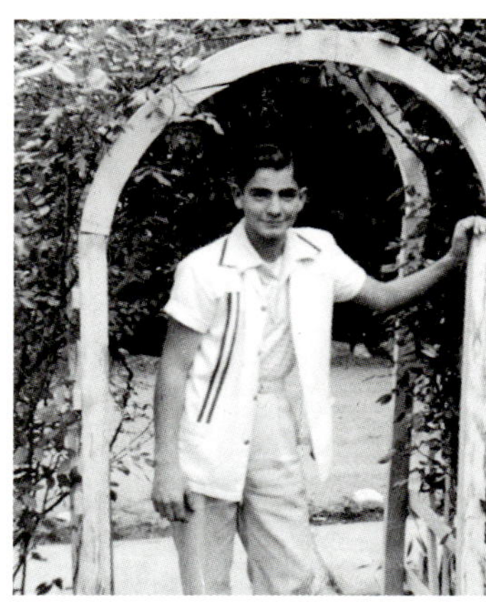

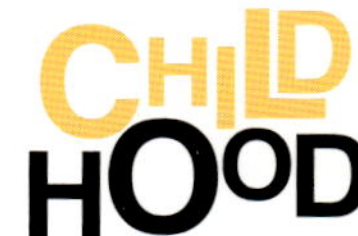

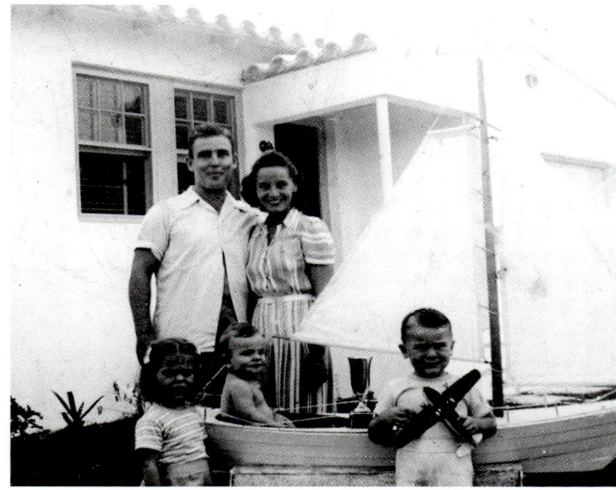

My dad "John Tennant," mother "Jackie," Jolene, and Johnny. I'm in the boat.

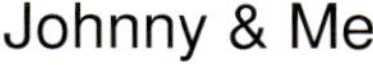
Johnny & Me

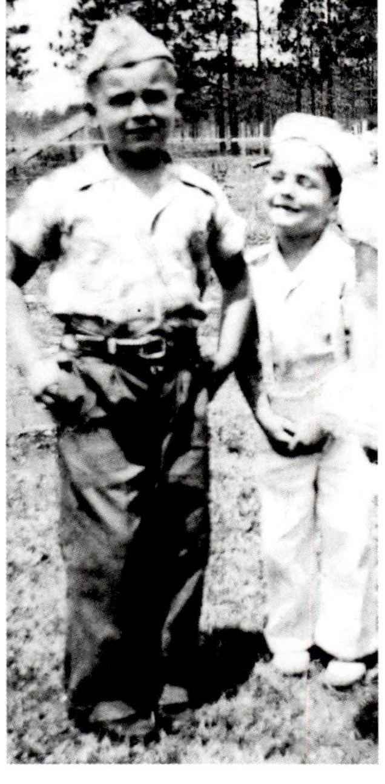

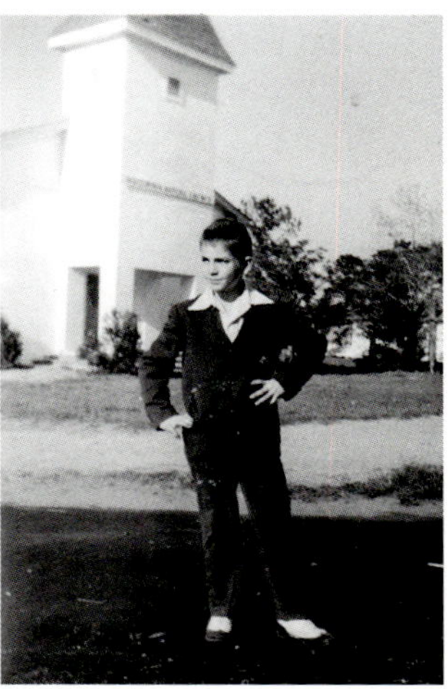

Macedonia Baptist Church

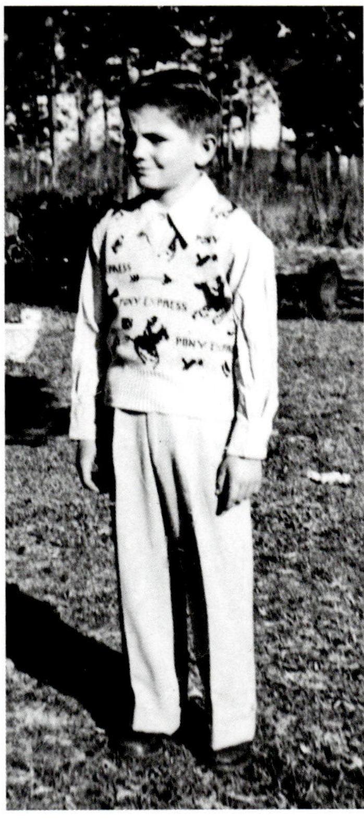

My Pony Express sweater

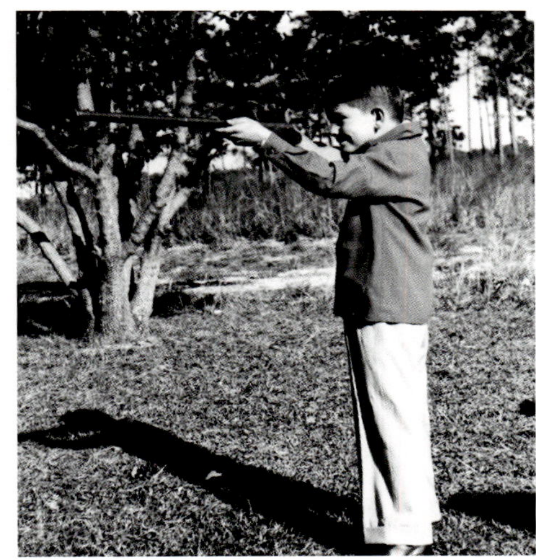

My first 22

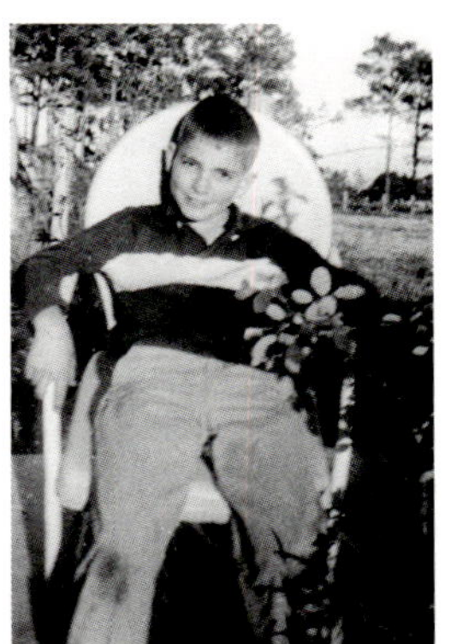

Some elementary school photos

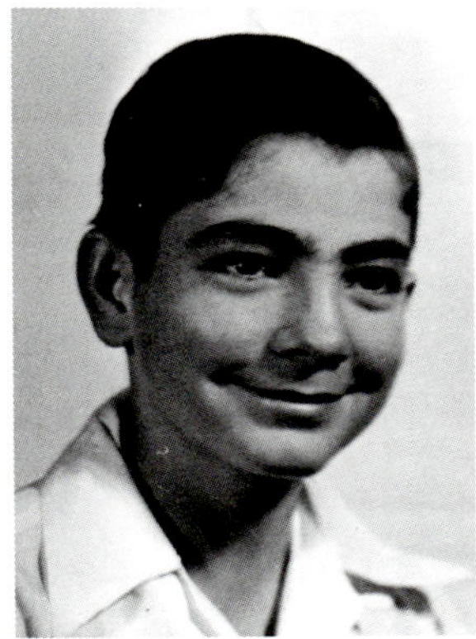

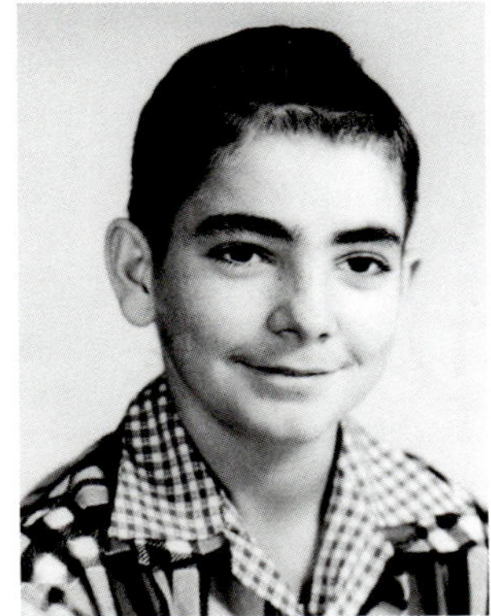

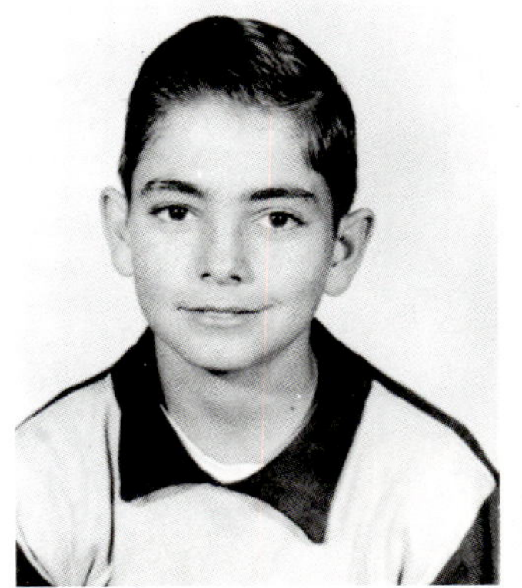

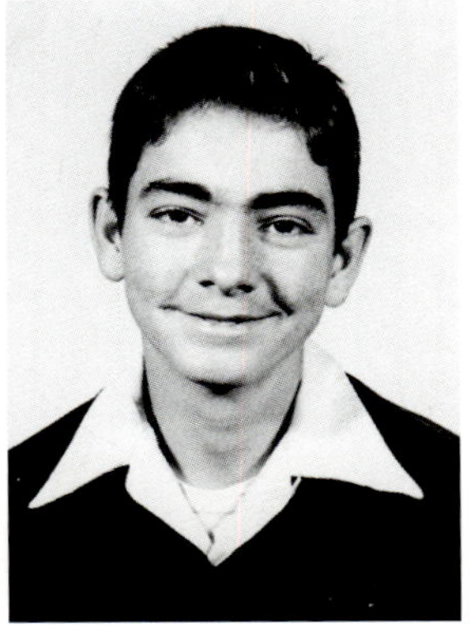

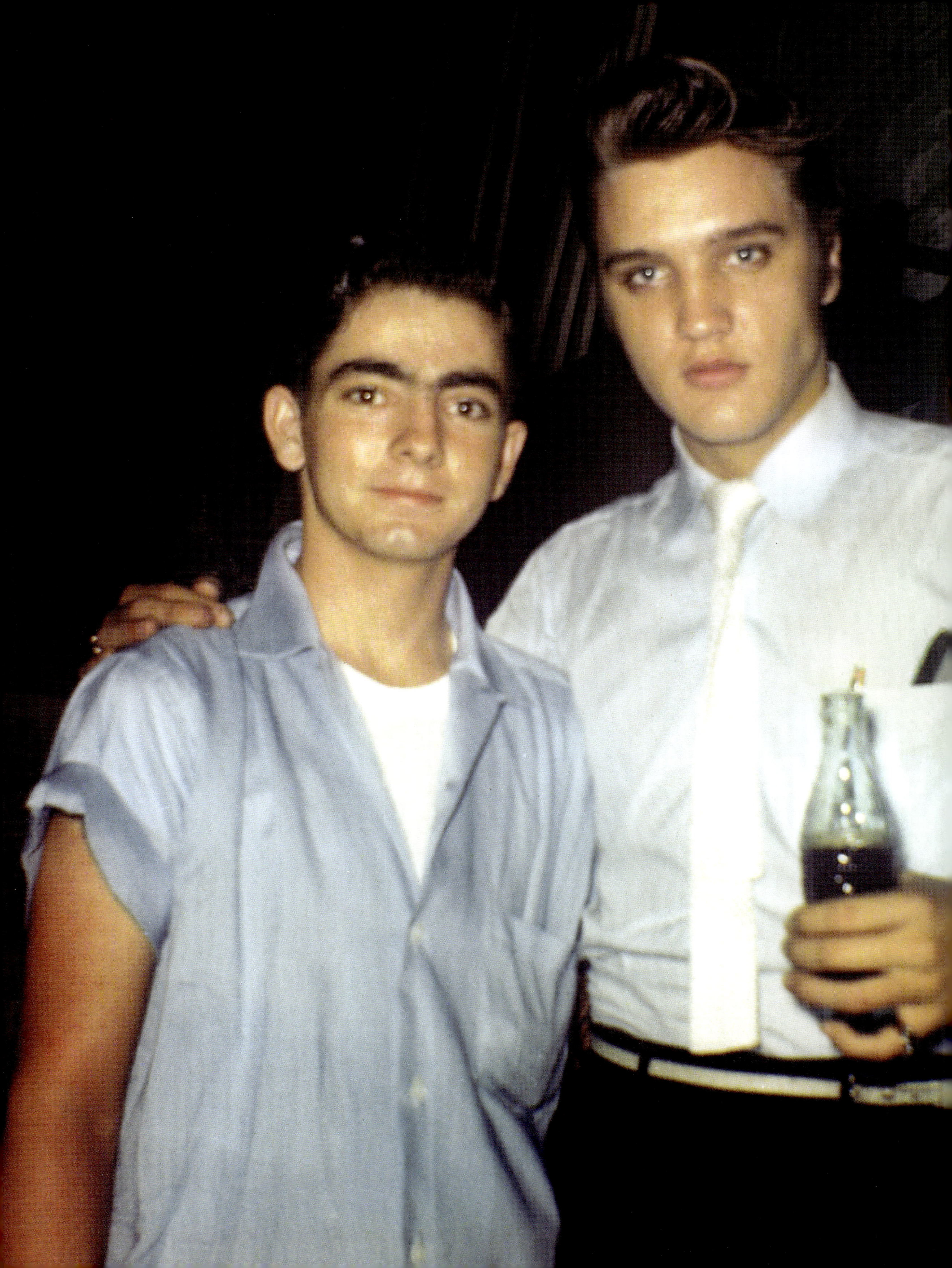

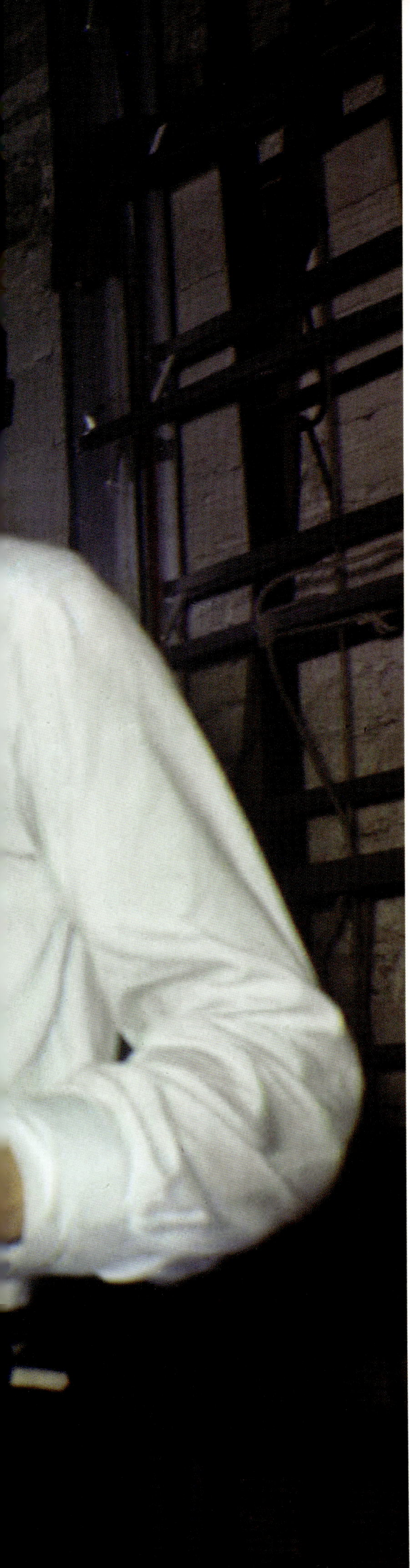

the 1950s

In August of 1956, Elvis invited me to go on tour with him. There were several dates, but I could only attend three of them: Miami, Jacksonville and New Orleans. In September I quit school and Elvis invited me to go with him to Tupelo. Next are the series of events from this time.

While in Miami, the girls (fans) wrote all over Elvis' Lincoln in lipstick. He traded that car in for a white, 1956 Lincoln Mark II. Part of Elvis' crew left for the next show. Elvis and I, with a few others, stopped off to meet my Dad at his beautiful home, the "Lazy T Ranch" in Hollywood, Florida (T for Tennant). My Dad wouldn't let us in the house but cooked us great burgers on the grill. He thought we were hoodlums with our sideburns. Imagine that! I was staying to visit with my Dad for a couple of days and the guys were leaving for Daytona or Tampa. Before they left, Elvis gave me a "Backstage Anytime" pass. Elvis had a rubber stamp with red ink and he would stamp a pass on a plain white business card that read: *Elvis Presley Show: This is to admit bearer backstage at anytime*. Below was a signature line and the date. He stamped and signed the pass and told me he was leaving the date open so I could use the pass anytime, anywhere. The guys headed north. During that trip Elvis got a speeding ticket in Ft. Lauderdale. Two days later I went back to Jacksonville and used my card to get into the Florida Theater (where my sister had once been an usherette). This was also the first time I used a camera. I bought a "Brownie Hawkeye" and one roll of color film, which, at that time, was something brand new for consumers. These great photos were made with that camera.

I remember on the first day of the show, Elvis upset the Juvenile Judge with his gyrations on stage. Judge Marion Gooding ordered him not to move on stage during his performance on the second and final night of the show. Elvis had a rough time toning down his show but he managed. I remember him singing a new song, "I Want You, I Need You, I Love You" with his finger moving. He sang a line that he made up, interjecting, "'Cause I can't sing when I'm standing still," and he cut loose and the house went wild! He ran for the stage door and headed for New Orleans. Yes, the judge was very upset. The next night was spent in New Orleans and after that I headed for home.

Six weeks later, September 26, 1956, I joined Elvis and his parents in Tupelo, Mississippi for the Mississippi - Alabama, Fair and Dairy show. This was my first meeting with Vernon and Gladys Presley. I had one roll of color film and a new camera. I took five photos of Elvis on stage and six photos backstage with his parents. These are the only known color photos of the famous Tupelo concert. It was a great time. Six months passed and I didn't see Elvis again until March of 1957, because on October 19, 1956, I joined the Air Force.

Elvis and I still kept in touch now and again. One of those times was while I was stationed at Mitchell Air Force Base in Hempstead, Long Island, New York. Elvis invited me to The Arena in Philadelphia. I rode the train to the show, where I took three or four photos and was honored when we met Dick Clark for the first time. I truly realized God's grace as a wonderful part of my life was opening up. While thinking back to how devastated I was when my Dad fired me, I knew how different my life would have been if he had kept me employed. I never would have met Elvis, and because of the friendship I shared with Elvis, many doors opened to me over the next fifty years.

On my 17th birthday I enlisted in the Air Force. One day later, on October 20, 1956, I was sent to Lackland Air Force Base, San Antonio, Texas, for basic training. During that time, I was caught smoking. I was ordered to dig a grave six foot long and three feet wide and four foot deep in the middle of the night in the cold October weather. Once that was accomplished, I was ordered to bury the cigarette and cover it up with the dirt from the freshly dug hole. After I completed the order, the instructor asked, "Which way was the label pointing?" I replied, "Straight up Sir!", and the instructor shouted back, "Dig it up and prove it!" Needless to say, I never had another cigarette after that (which was probably a good thing if I wanted to have a singing career). After basic training I was sent to Keesler AFB in Biloxi, Mississippi to be trained as a Radar Operator. Then I was assigned to Mitchell AFB, Hempstead, Long Island, New York. One evening while I was in New York City, I decided I wanted to see where Marilyn Monroe lived. In uniform, I walked down Sutton Place to see her home. In passing, I saw Marilyn and one of her girlfriends. My jaw dropped down to my knees as she walked by me. I had my camera with me and froze as she said, "Hello sweetie," and kept walking. I turned to watch her and she turned around and asked, "Did you want to take a picture, sweetie?" I said, "Yes Ma'am," and snapped a picture. WOW!!!

During this time of enlistment, I entered an Air Force talent show named Tops In Blue. A fantastic group from a Pittsburgh Air Force Base won. There were five guys in the group, soon to be known as the Del-Vikings. They had two major hits with "Come Go with Me" and "Whispering Bells." In July of 1957, I had started to sing more often, and was so blessed to meet and work with many known stars of this great era. Alan Freed had a big summer festival in New York before I was scheduled to leave for Fukeoka, Japan. I was stationed in Japan for just three months when the Air Force offered "early-outs" and I jumped on the offer so I could get started on the career I had always dreamed about.

I was processed out of the Air Force in Oakland, California in November of 1957. I booked my first tour with two friends I met earlier in the year with Alan Freed: Chuck Berry and Lloyd Price. We did two shows, one in San Jose and one in San Francisco. I remember riding in Chuck's Coupe deVille with his guitars and wardrobe filling the back seat. Lloyd rode shotgun and I was in the middle. What a scary ride; Chuck drove like a bat outta Hades!

I wound up in Hollywood and stayed for a couple of weeks at Dick Dale's house, at 11125 S. Wilton Place. Dick's father, Richard Monsour, let me put his address on my first publicity photo. I sent out publicity photos and was still trying to find a place to live. I ran into Tennessee Ernie Ford (known song: "16 Tons"), who introduced me to a music publisher at Hollywood and Vine. Her name was Betty Martin, Dean Martin's former wife. Through Betty I got to know her and Dean's four children: Craig, Claudia, Gail and Dina. The kids were living with Dean and his 2nd wife, Jeannie, at 601 Mountain Drive. I remember you could look out of Dean's bedroom window and see Debbie Reynolds' pool and house next door on Loma Vista Drive. A lot was going on at the time. It was early 1958 and Dean and Jeannie let me stay with them for awhile. I remember how impressed I was over their table coasters that looked like records made of gold and silver. The master bedroom had the most beautiful cabinets of mesh and glass. Dean and Jeannie also included me when they took weekend drives to some ranch with a name over the gate. One evening, Dean had come home for dinner still wearing a western outfit from the studio. He had on a hat, gun, and boots while filming Rio Bravo with John Wayne and Rick Nelson. Dean let me try them on and we took photos of me, Craig, and Dean wearing them. I had a crush on Claudia but I never did tell her how crazy I was about her. Craig and I tried our hand at singing as a duo but this effort failed. Dean was in the process of opening his restaurant on Sunset, named Dino's. It became famous for the filming of the TV series 77 Sunset Strip (which, by the way, was not the restaurant's address). Ed "Kookie" Byrnes became famous for combing his hair at the door as the parking attendant. "Kookie, Kookie, Lend Me Your Comb" later became a famous song.

Dean and Jeannie were so good to me. I was a young nobody. I was allowed to use Dean's black T-Bird as my own and sometimes I would drive Craig to school at Beverly Hills High. I met one of Craig's classmates and truly fell in love with this beautiful Jewish girl. Her name was Connie Freed. I often spent the night at her home in Beverly Hills, always on the couch. After a few months went by, Connie's father took me to dinner to talk about Connie and me. He felt that Connie and I were getting too serious and he asked me to break up with her because I wasn't Jewish. I reluctantly agreed and ended up heartbroken. I told Dean and Jeannie about this and Dean tried to help me with a new start by calling his friend, the President of NBC, Leo Durocher. (Leo is most noted for his baseball career and was inducted into the Baseball Hall of Fame in 1994). Leo called me and offered me a job as a page at NBC. I accepted, but before starting my job I wanted to go home. I still wasn't over my breakup with Connie. I talked to Dean and Jeannie about wanting to take a trip back home in the used Chrysler I had just bought. Dean graciously gave me credit cards to travel with and told me to sign his name, Dean Martin, on the receipts. He said if there was any trouble; just call him or Jeannie at home. Well, I was nearly back home in Hollywood, Florida, and filled up my gas tank at a Texaco station in Ft. Lauderdale. I signed the name "Dean Martin" on the receipt, as I had done all the way from California. The station attendant looked at me suspiciously and called the Broward County Sheriff's department to take me in. I explained what Dean had told me to do and gave them Dean's private home number. Instead of dialing the number I gave them, they called information in Beverly Hills and got Dean's office number. Nobody there knew me so they assumed that I stole the credit cards. They finally listened to me when I insisted they call Dean's office back to confirm the private number. They asked how I got Dean's private number and I explained that we were friends. They dialed the number and Jeannie answered the phone. Thank goodness! She told them the story and then asked them to put me on the phone. She told me that Dean was going to open at the Fontainebleau in Miami Beach and he would love to visit.

After this ordeal at the Sheriff's office, the officer invited me to dinner at his home and to spend the night. The next morning I left for home. Some time had passed and I called Dean at the hotel and he met me in the lobby. I had my two year old nephew, Darryl, with me at the time. We all went up to Dean's suite. While Dean and I were talking, Darryl crawled over to a wall socket and got shocked. He started to scream and Dean's fatherly instincts kicked in to high gear and he grabbed Darryl, sweeping him away from the wall. I'll never forget the tears that welled up in Dean's eyes (and Darryl's too, for that matter).

I'm sure Darryl didn't know what he was just saved from and was wondering why Dean grabbed him up into his arms. I truly love Dean's entire family. Dean and Jeannie also had three children together, Dino, Ricci and Gina.

In 1958, I recorded "The Witness," flipside, "Giggle Wiggle." It was on Thunder Records label, a local Florida hit. I then decided to go back to Hollywood, California where I recorded "Blue Velvet," flipside "Because of You" for Music City Records at Gold Star Studios. There I also recorded "Go Little Go Cat," flipside "Spark Plug" for Challenge Records with the Champs (of "Tequila" fame), also at Gold Star Studios. After that I decided to go back to Florida, where I began opening for many big-name acts including Buddy Holly, The Everly Brothers, Bill Haley, Roy Orbison, Johnny Cash, Danny and the Juniors, and Marty Robbins. During this time, Marty Robbins took me to Nashville to record for him. I cut four sides. I never asked for a copy of the tape, and sadly, time has passed and I don't remember what the recordings were. Marty was a really good friend to me and a great man in so many ways. Once I was in Nashville, that's pretty much where I knew I wanted to stay: Music City, USA.

My first recordings, "The Witness" and "Giggle Wiggle" 1958 - Thunder Records

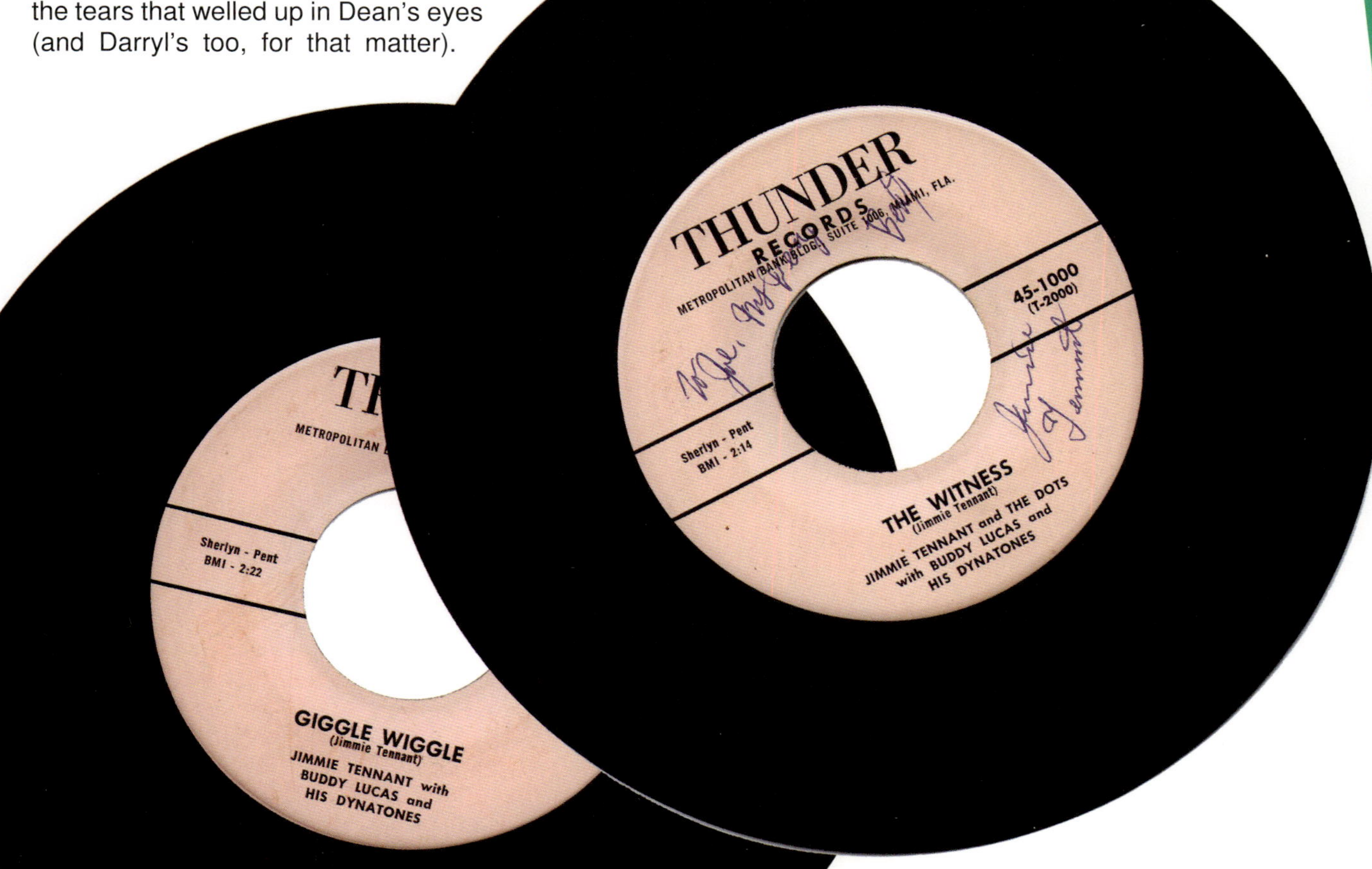

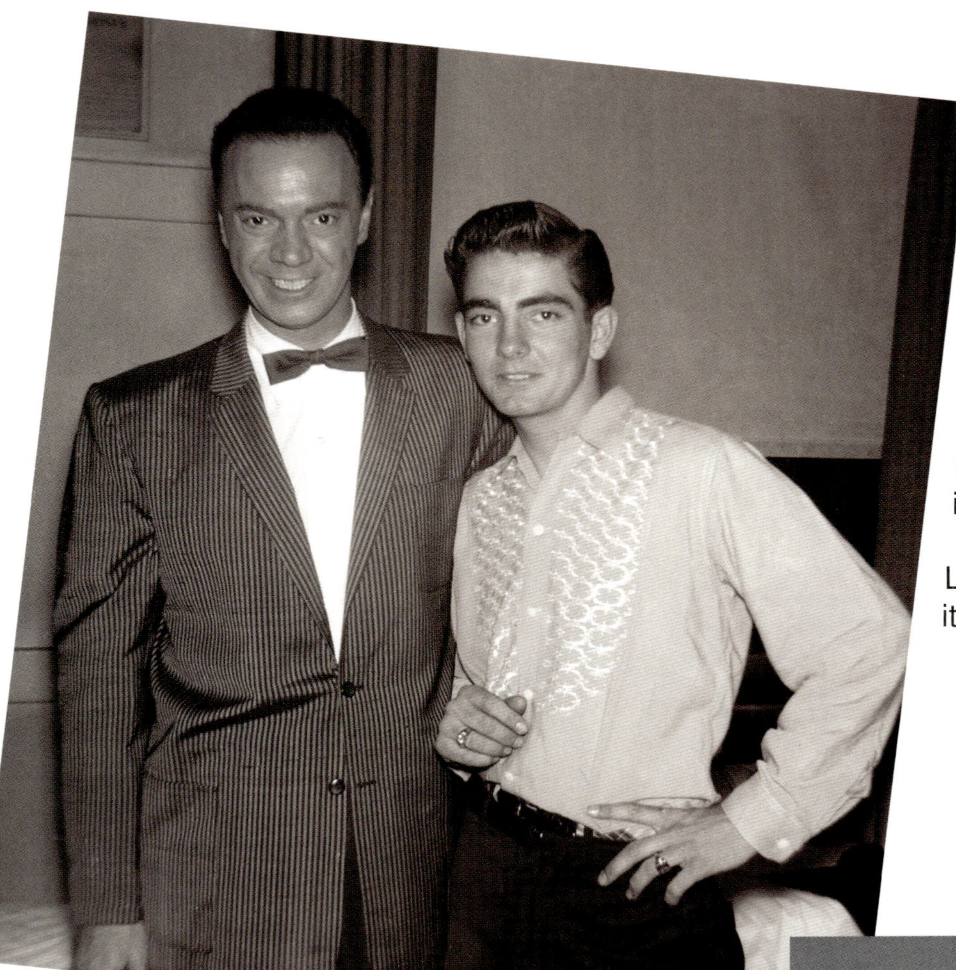

Alan Freed

Originally called "The High Priest of Rock n' Roll" and "The Pied Piper," he was named "King of Rock n' Roll in 1956.

Later the throne went to Elvis where it stays today.

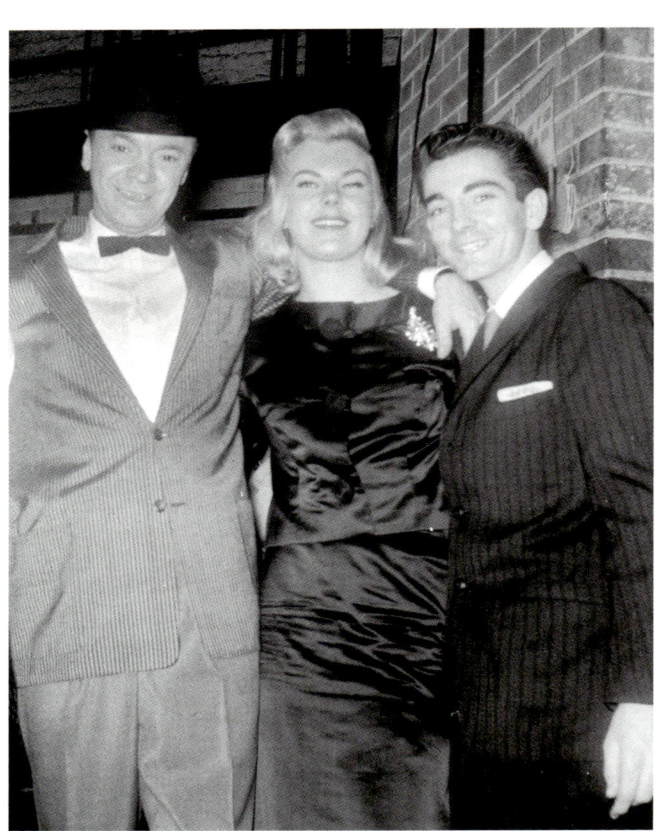

Alan Freed and his wife

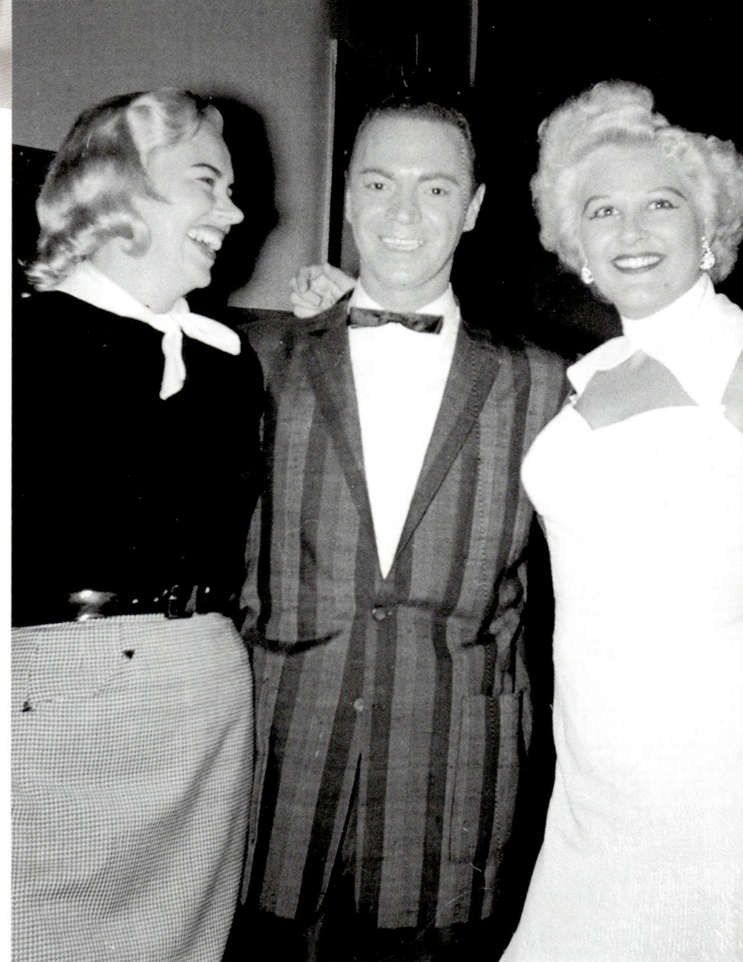

Alan and the Castle Sisters

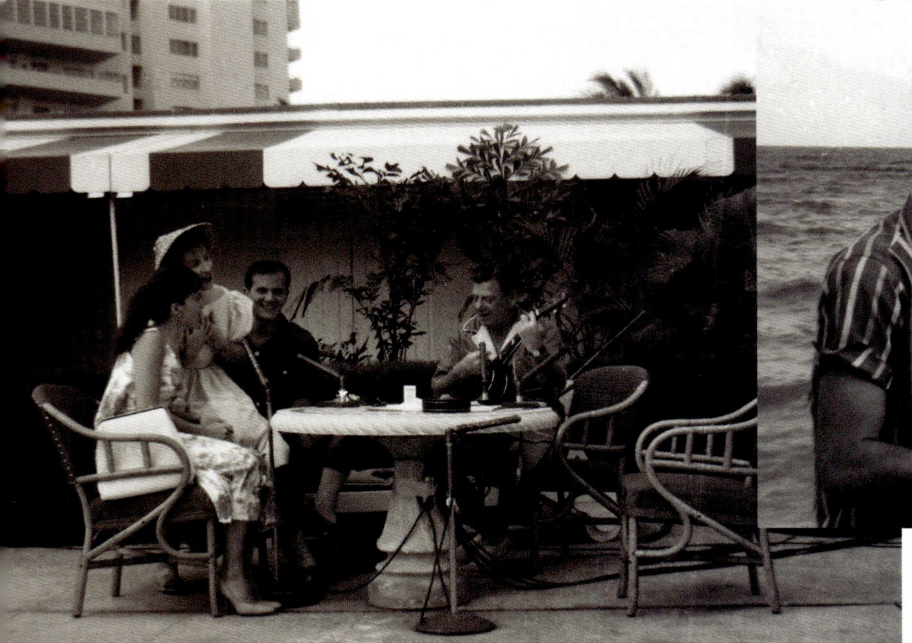

Shirley Boone, Carmela Quinn, Pat Boone and Arthur Godfrey live from Miami Beach, 1958
The Arthur Godfrey Show

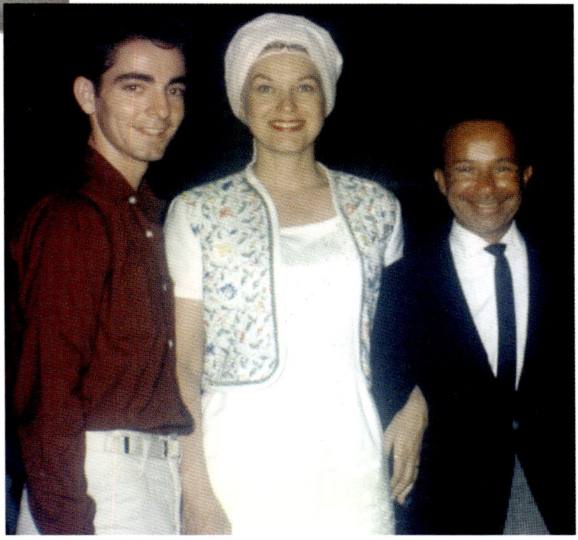

Jane Morgan and Little Jackie Heller

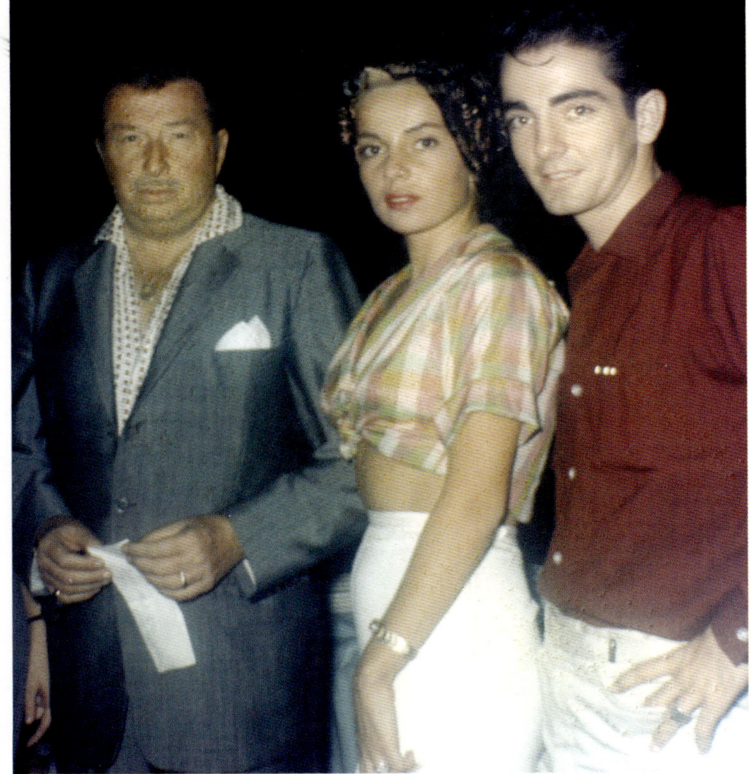

Xavier Cugart and Abby Lane
Miami Beach 1958

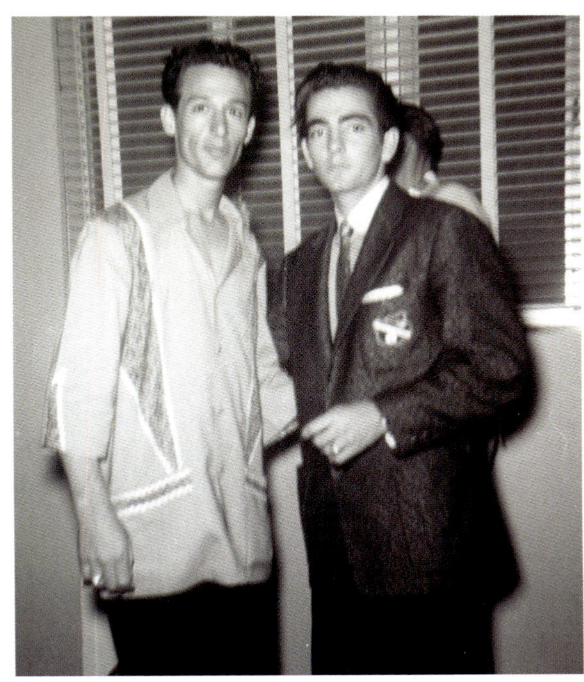

Dave Burgess- "The Champs"

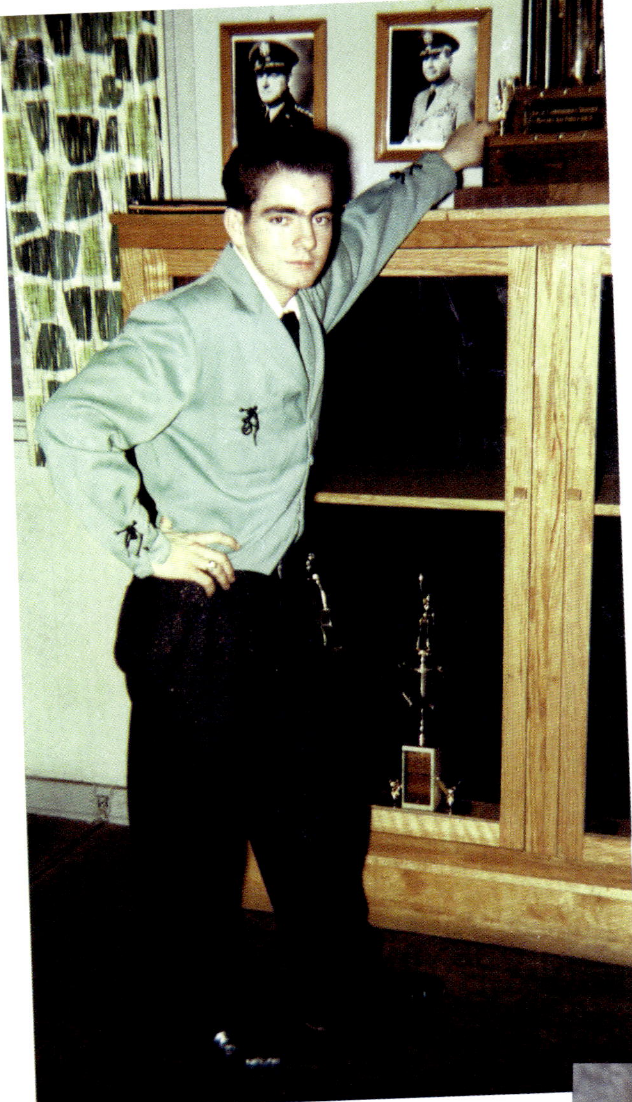

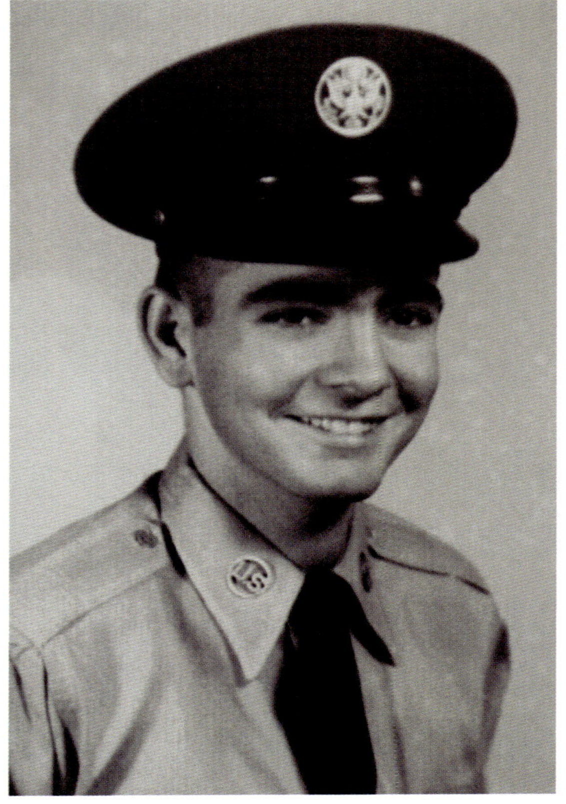

Jimmy Velvet in the
UNITED STATES AIR FORCE
1956-1957

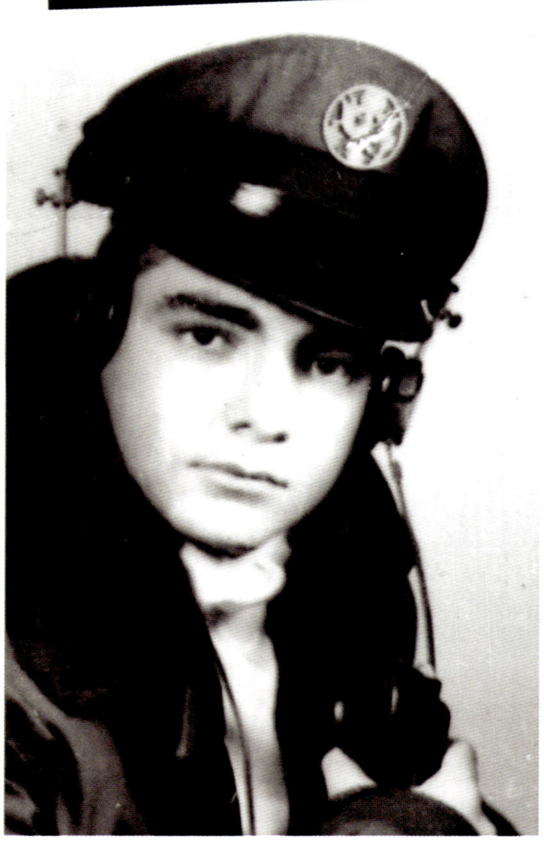

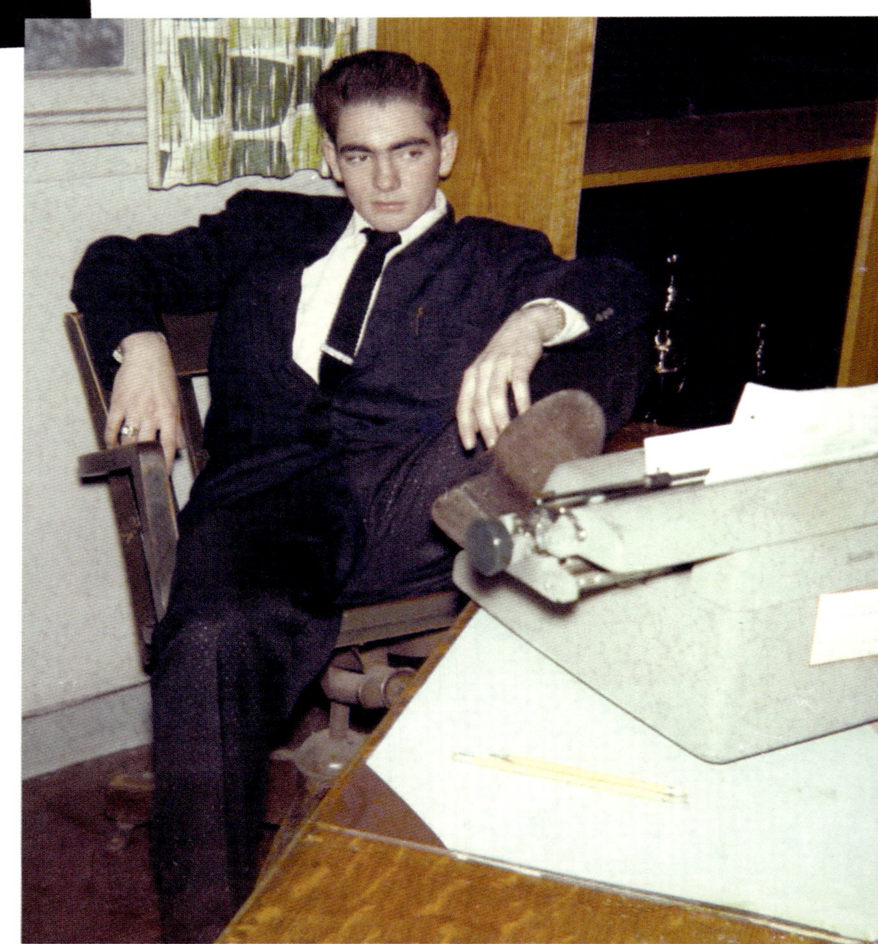

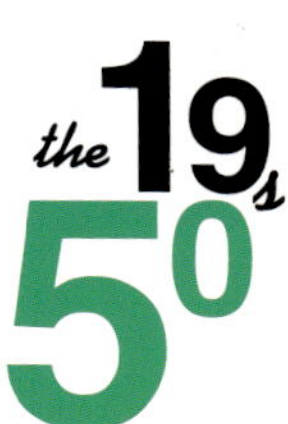

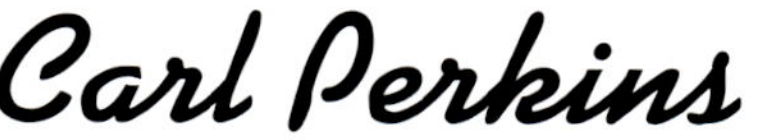

Carl Perkins

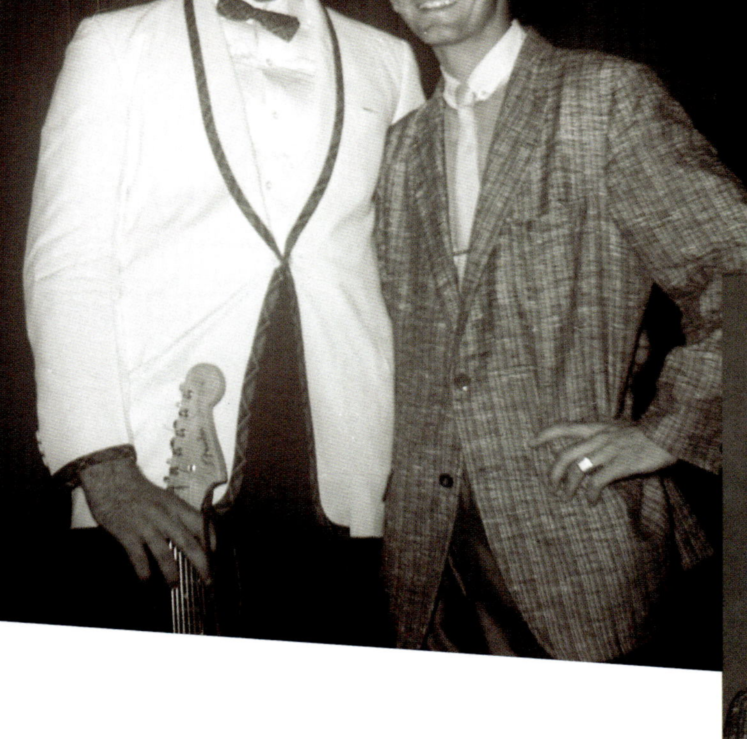

Johnny Cash

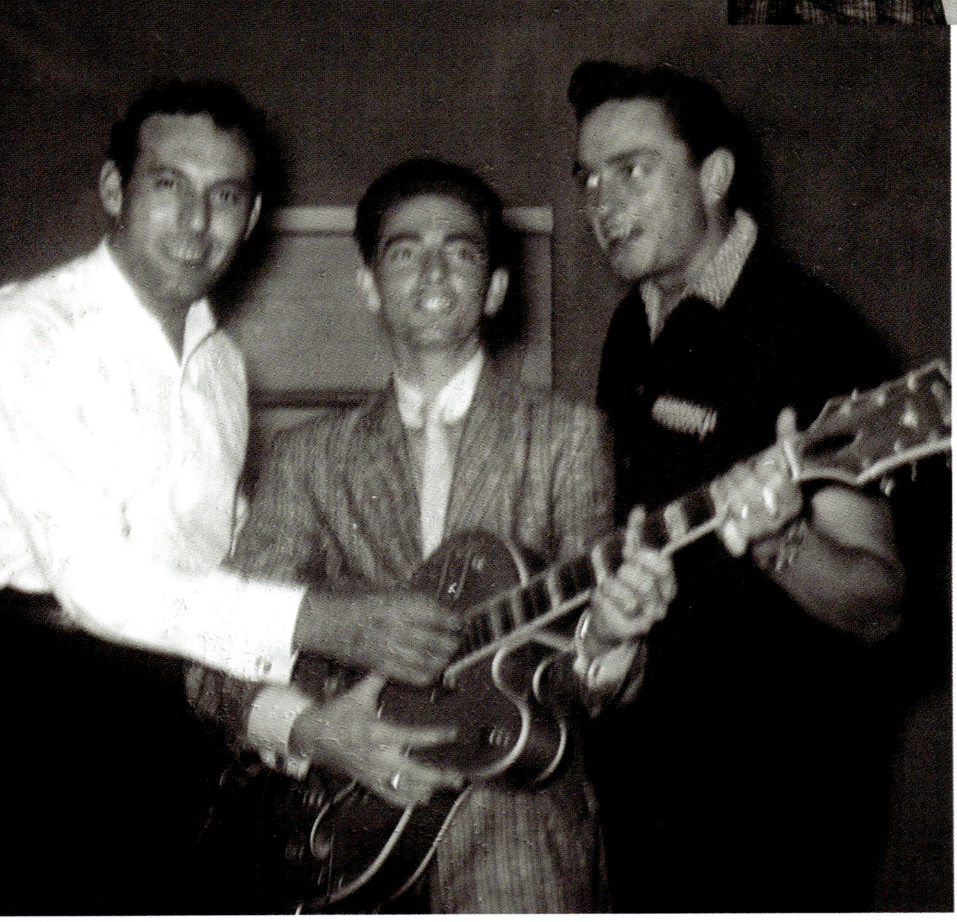

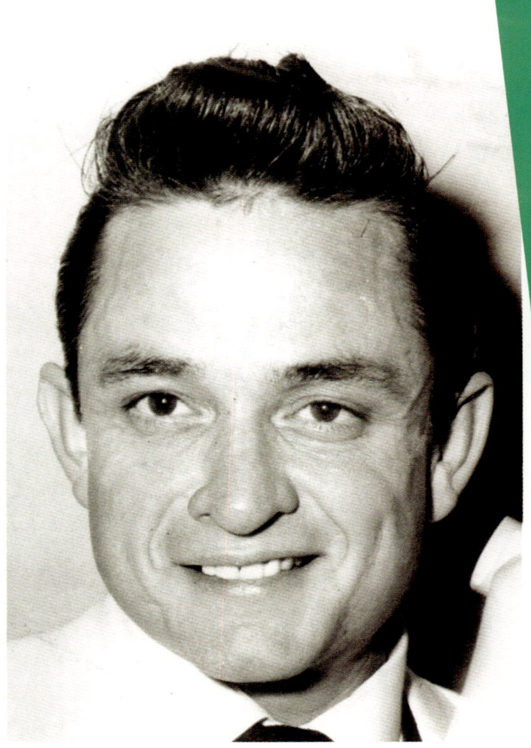

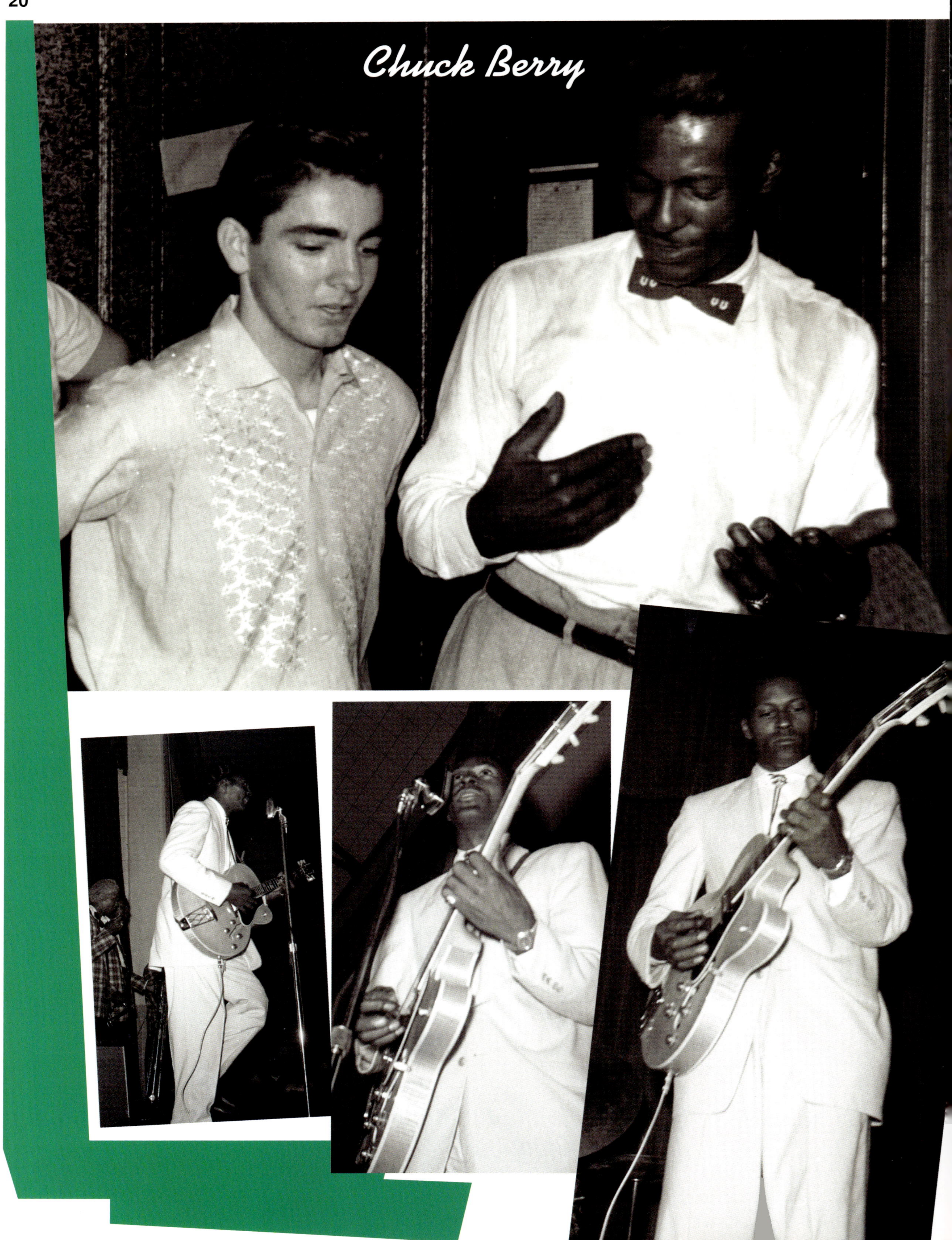
Chuck Berry

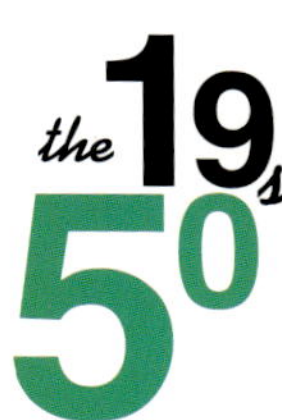

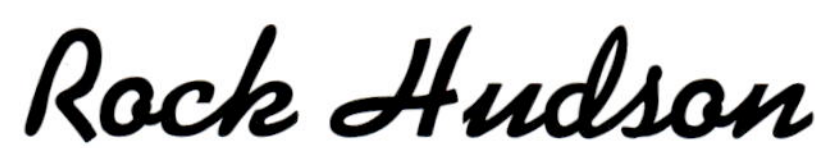

Rock Hudson

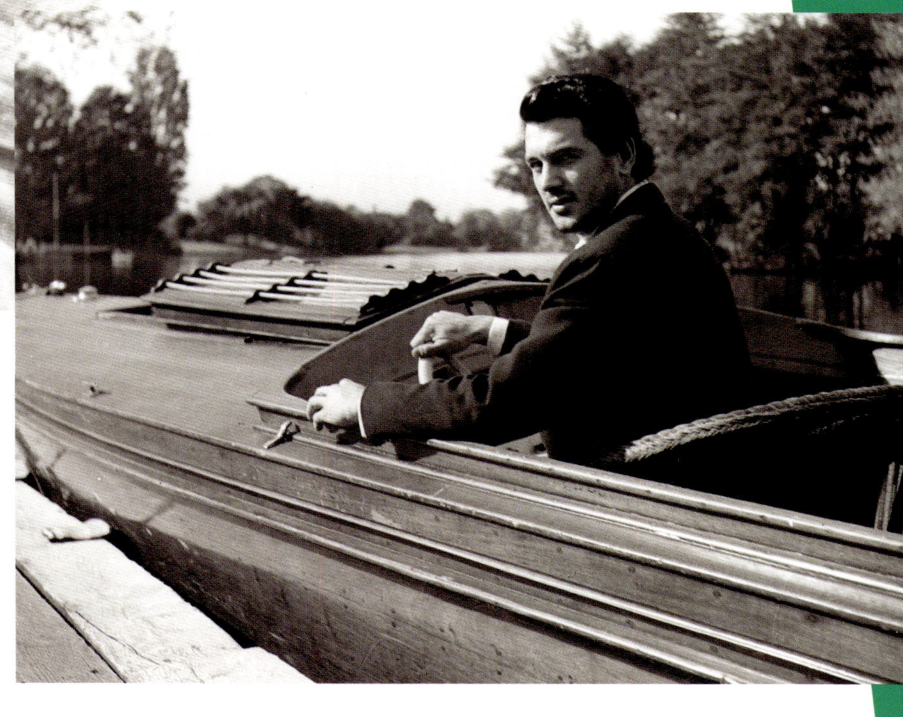

Johnnie Ray

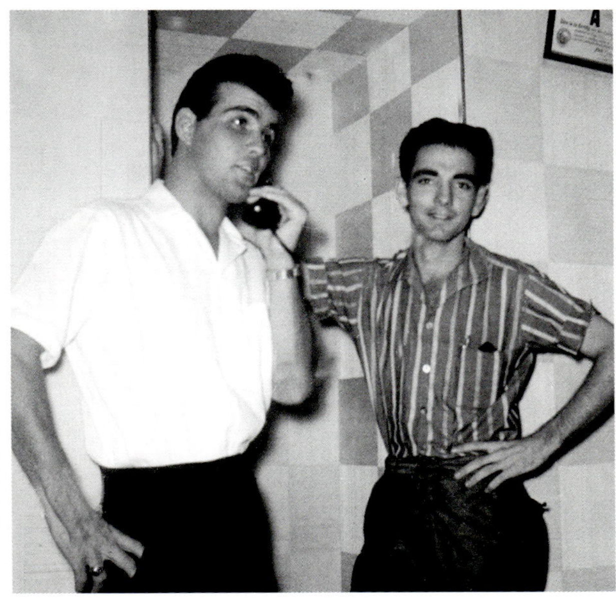

Billy Crash Craddock

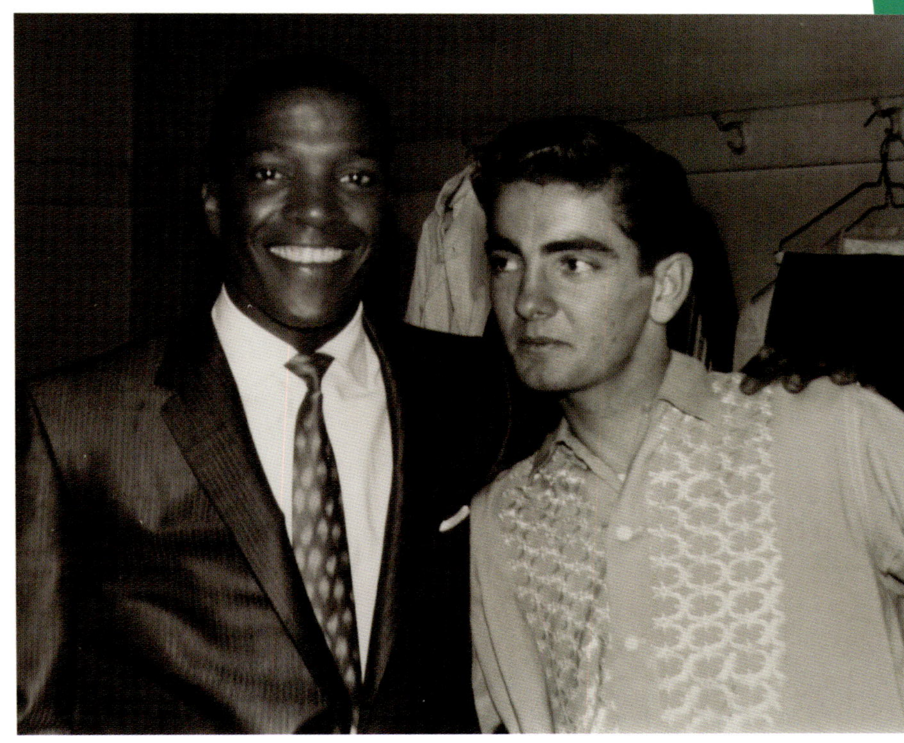

Clyde McPhatter, former lead singer of The Drifters and The Dominoes

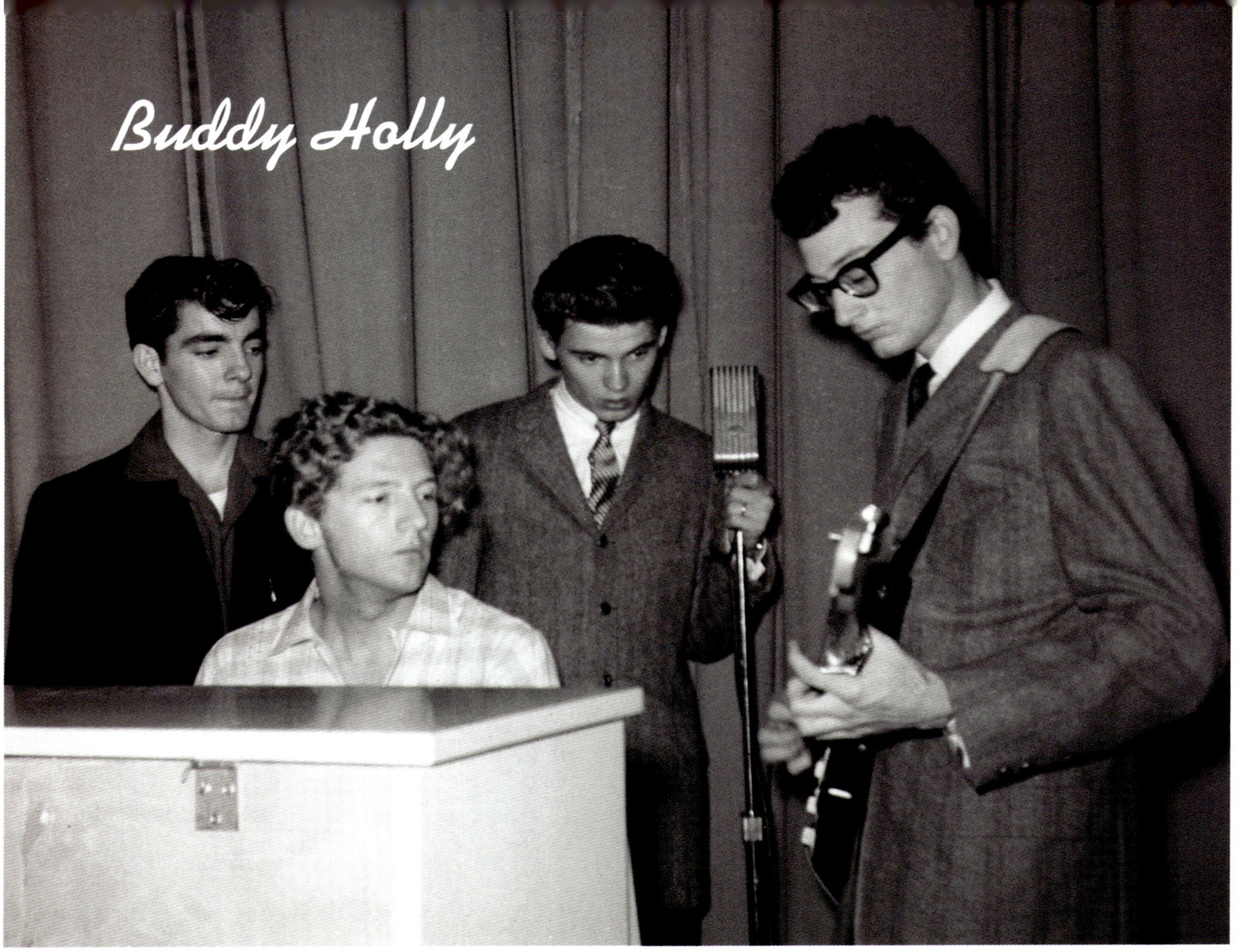

Buddy Holly

Jerry Lee Lewis, Don Everly, Buddy Holly

Buddy Holly and The Everly Brothers

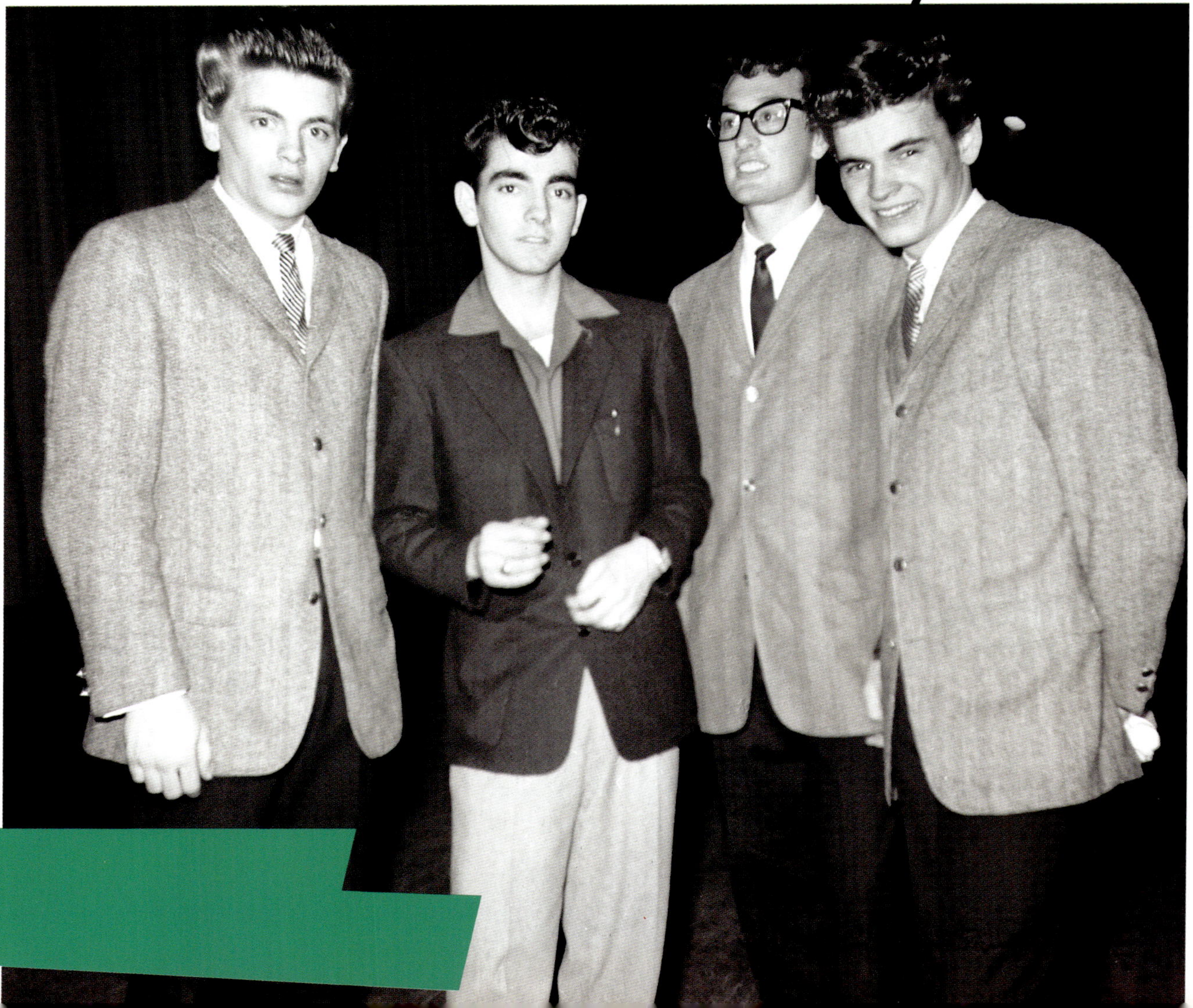

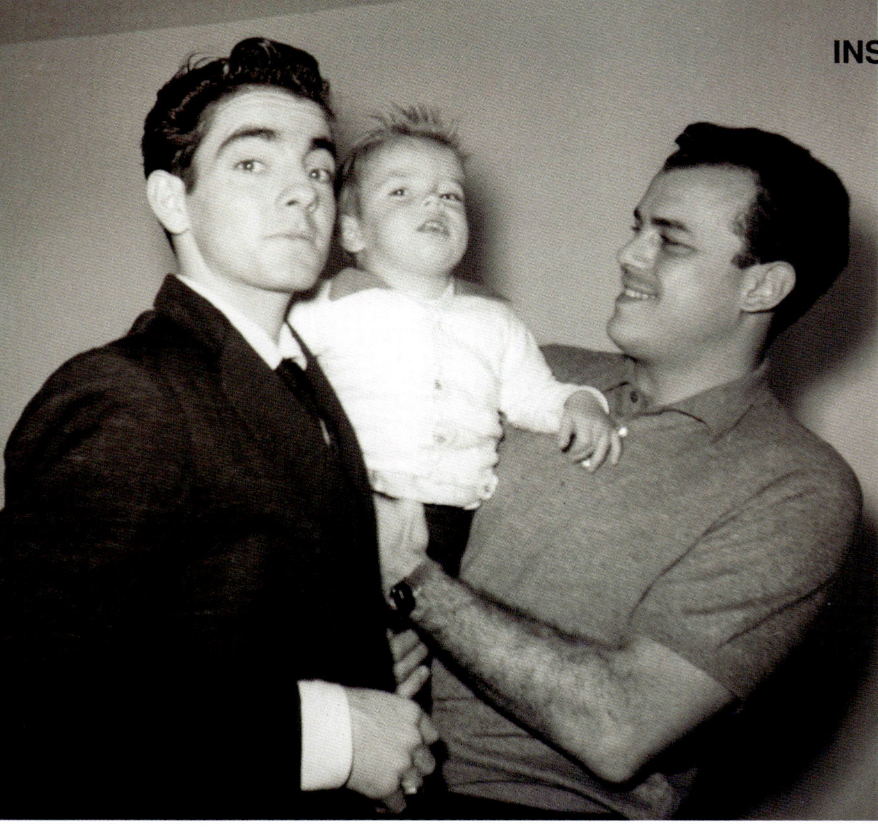

Me, Darryl, and Julius LaRosa

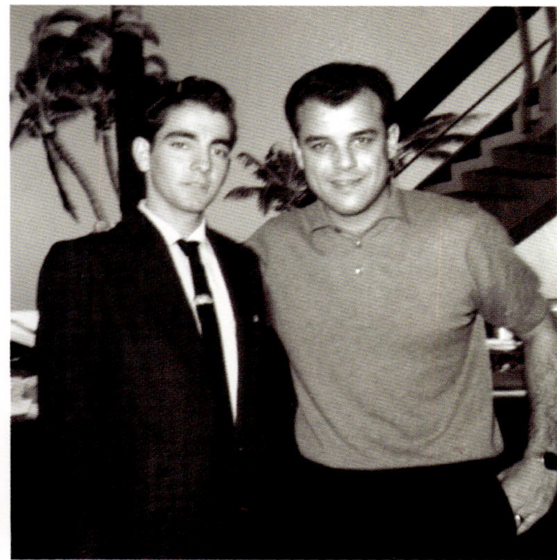

Julius LaRosa

Louis Lymon

Louis was Frankie Lymon's younger brother. At the age of 12, Louis Lymon and the Teenchords had a hit record: Too Young (1957) and I Found Out Why (1958)

Frankie Lymon and Jodie Sands

Connie Francis

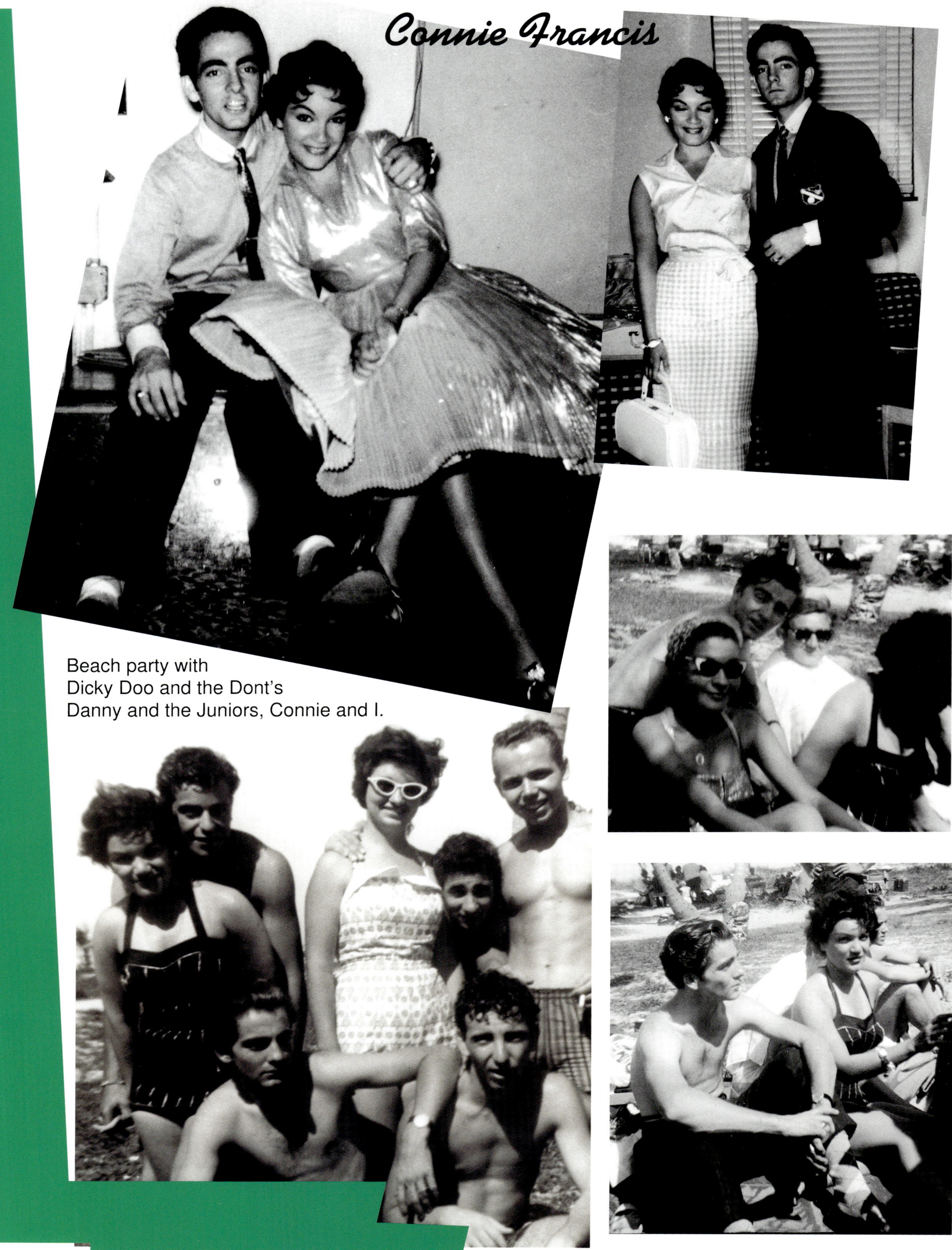

Beach party with
Dicky Doo and the Dont's
Danny and the Juniors, Connie and I.

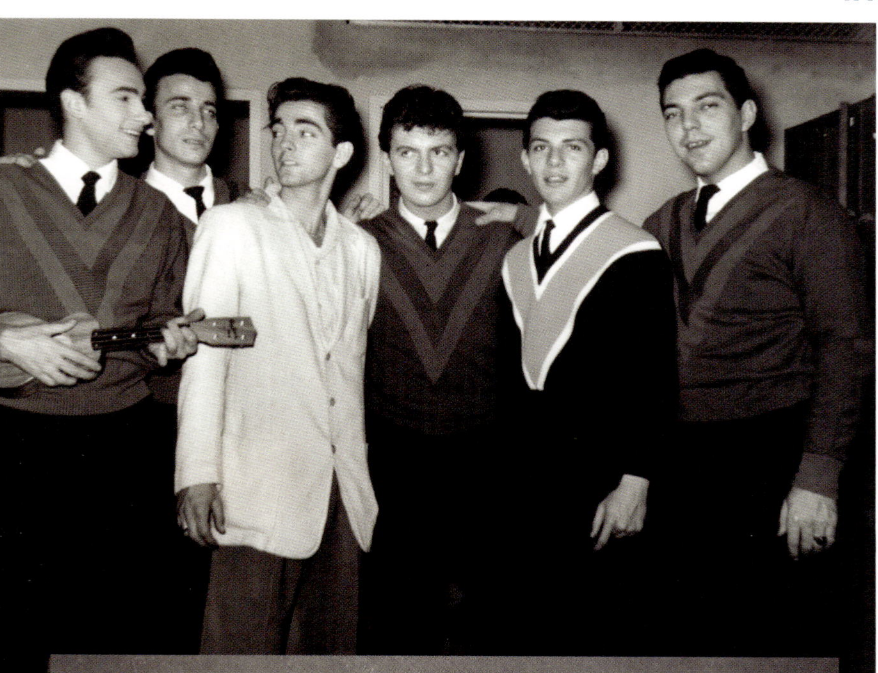

Dion and the Belmonts

Angelo D'Aleo
Fred Milano
Carlo Mastrangelo
with

Frankie Avalon

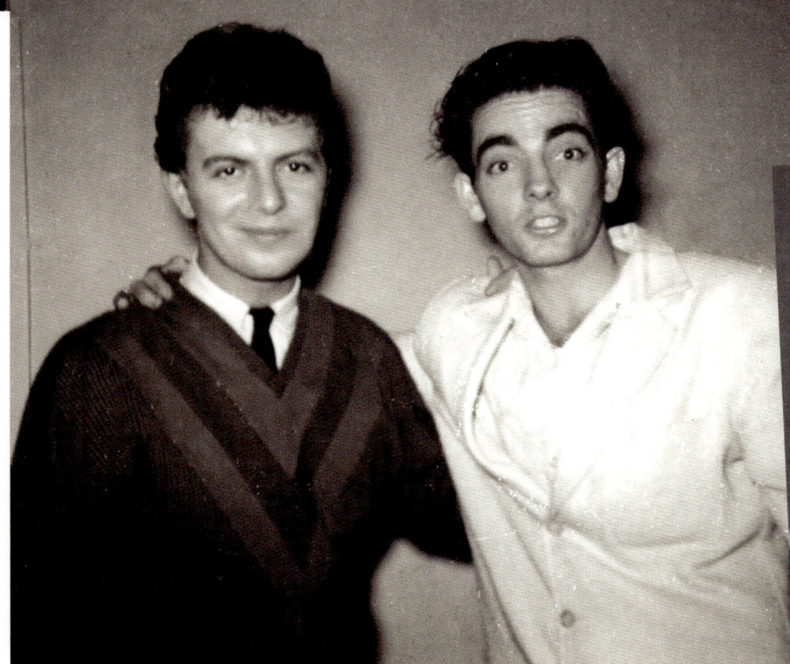

Dion DiMucci

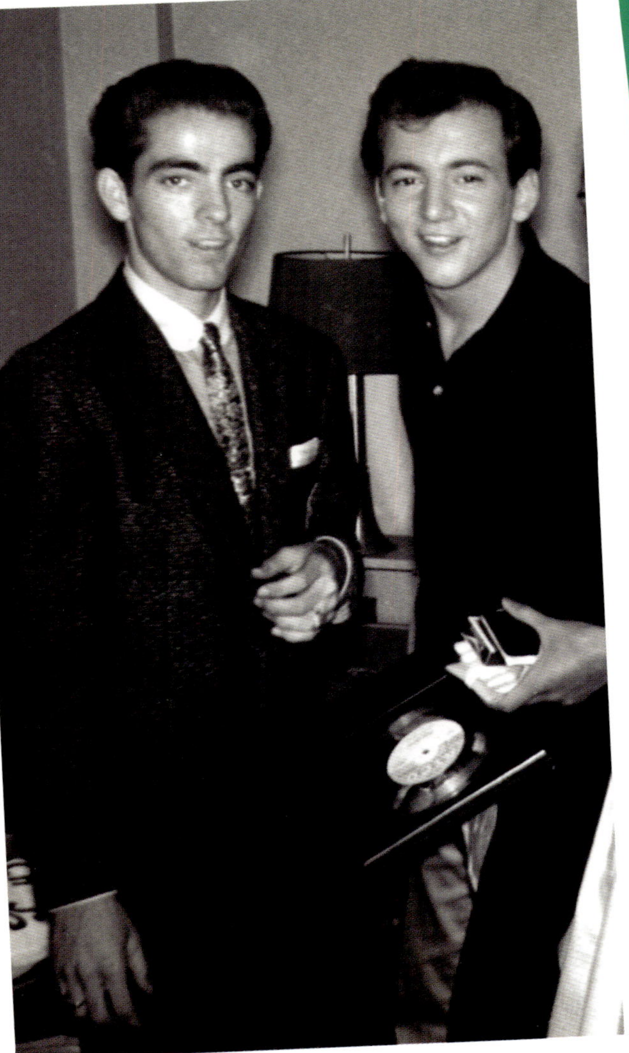

Bobby Darin, Judy and Jimmy

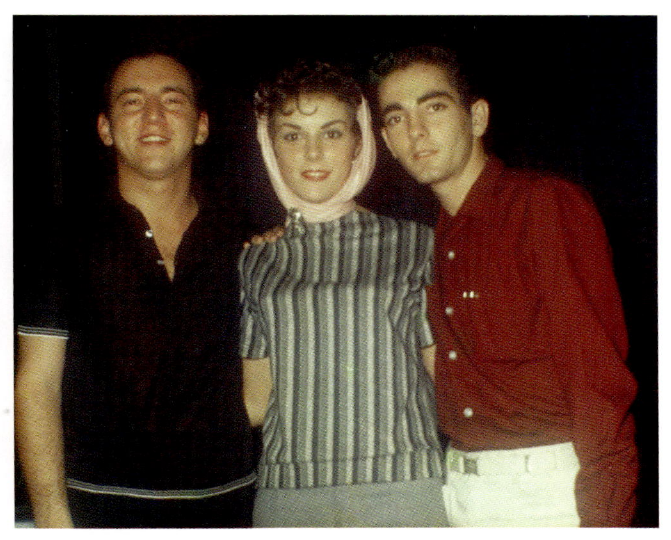

Bobby Darin

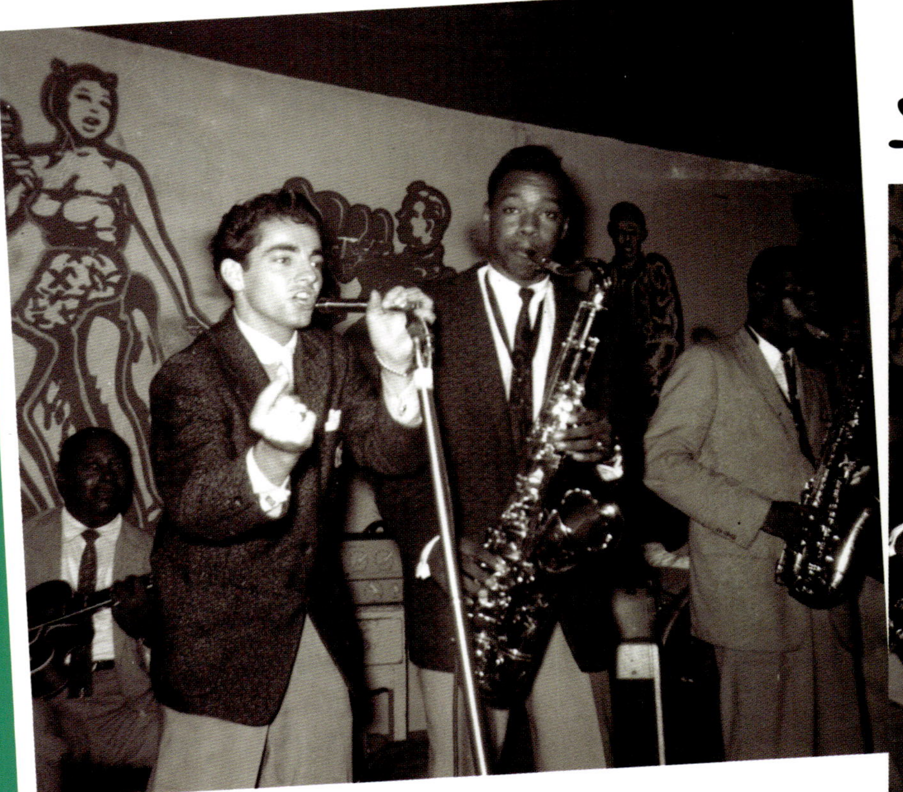

Davy Jones and me on stage 1958

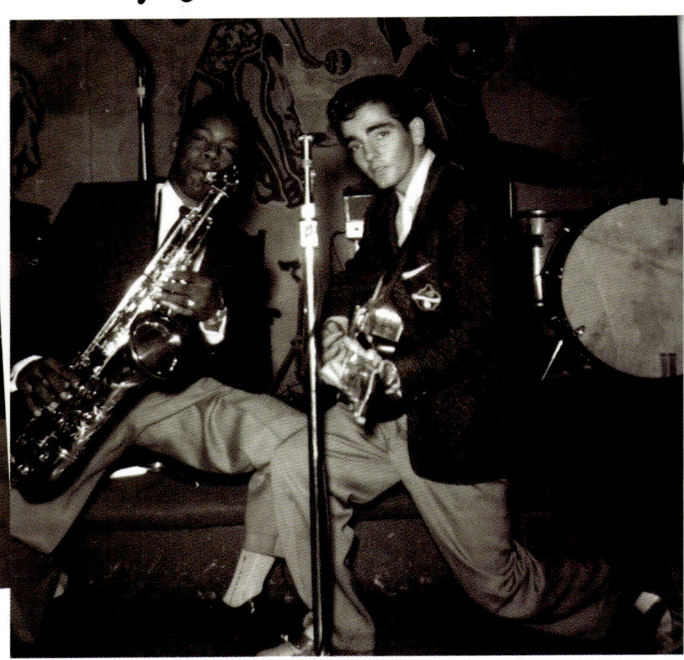

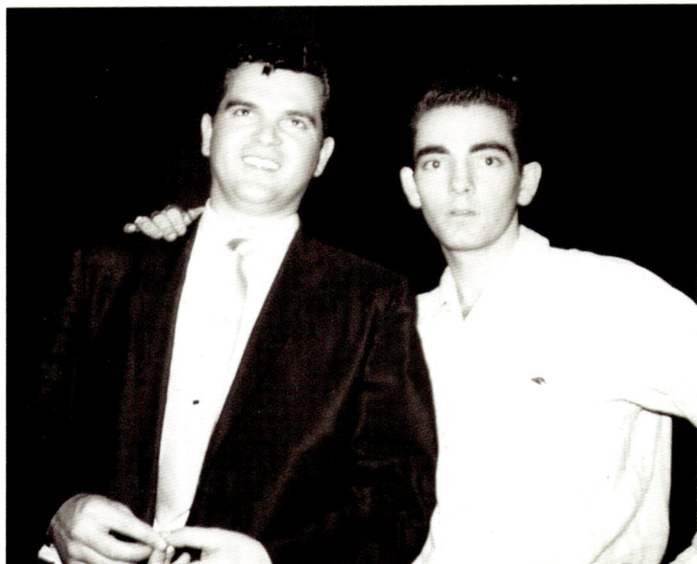

Conway Twitty

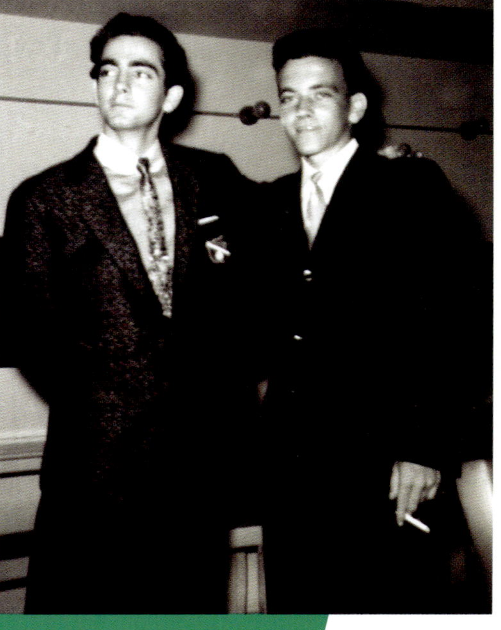

Rudy Vallee
and Chef John Tennant, my dad

Danny Rapp
from Danny and the Juniors

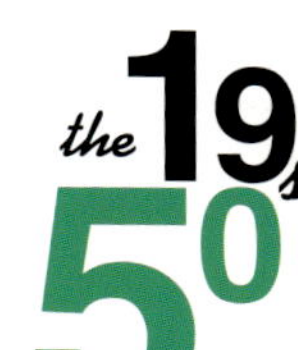

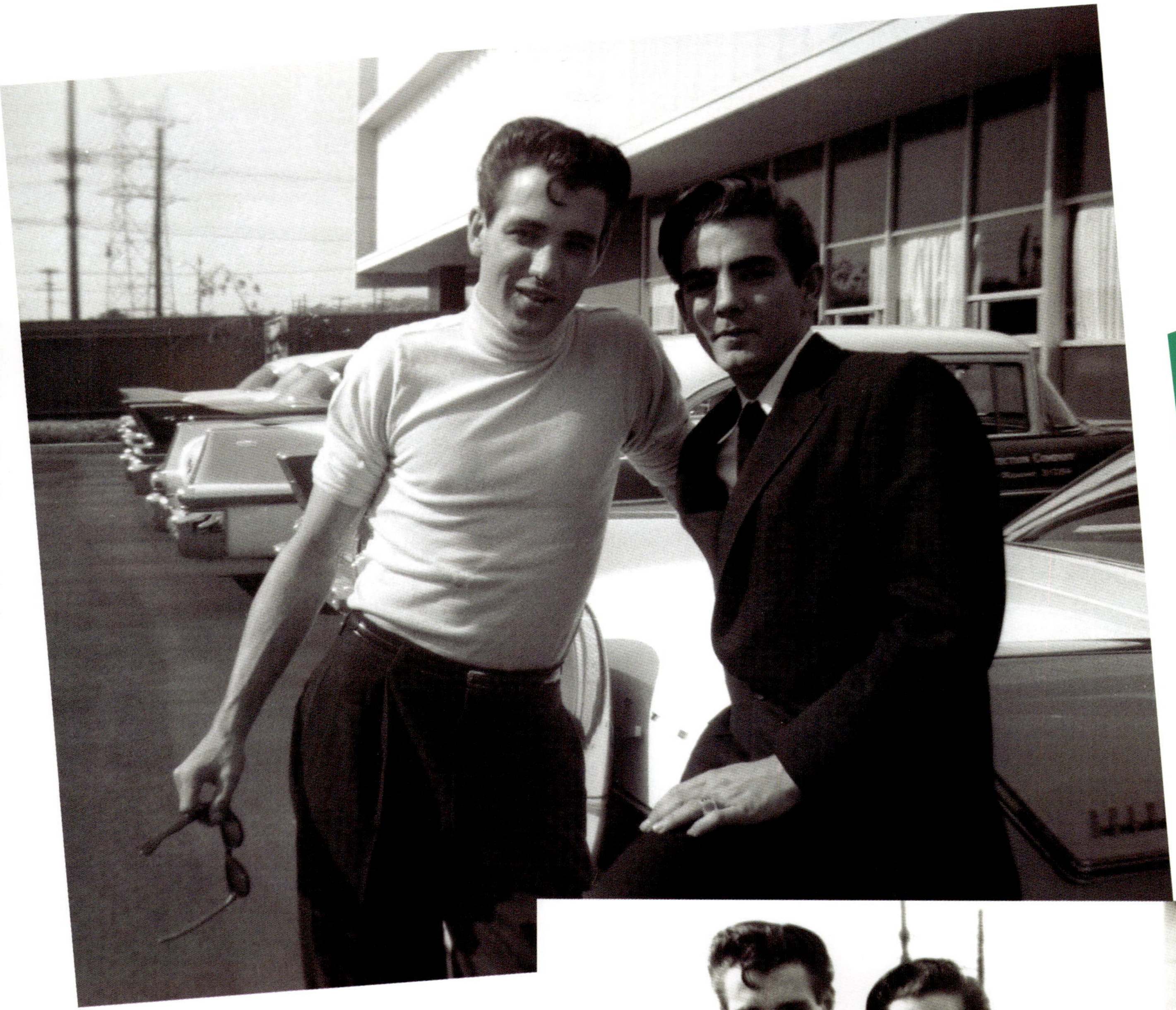

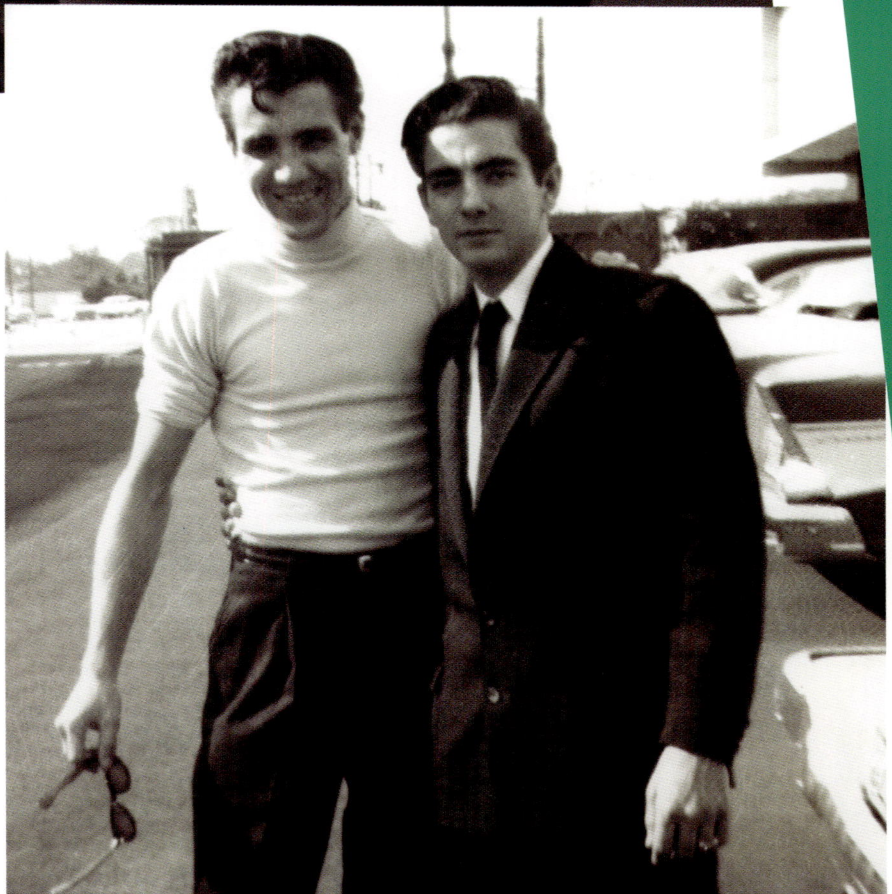

Jimmie Rodgers

Hits: "Honeycomb" and
"Kisses Sweet Than Wine"
At NBC in Burbank

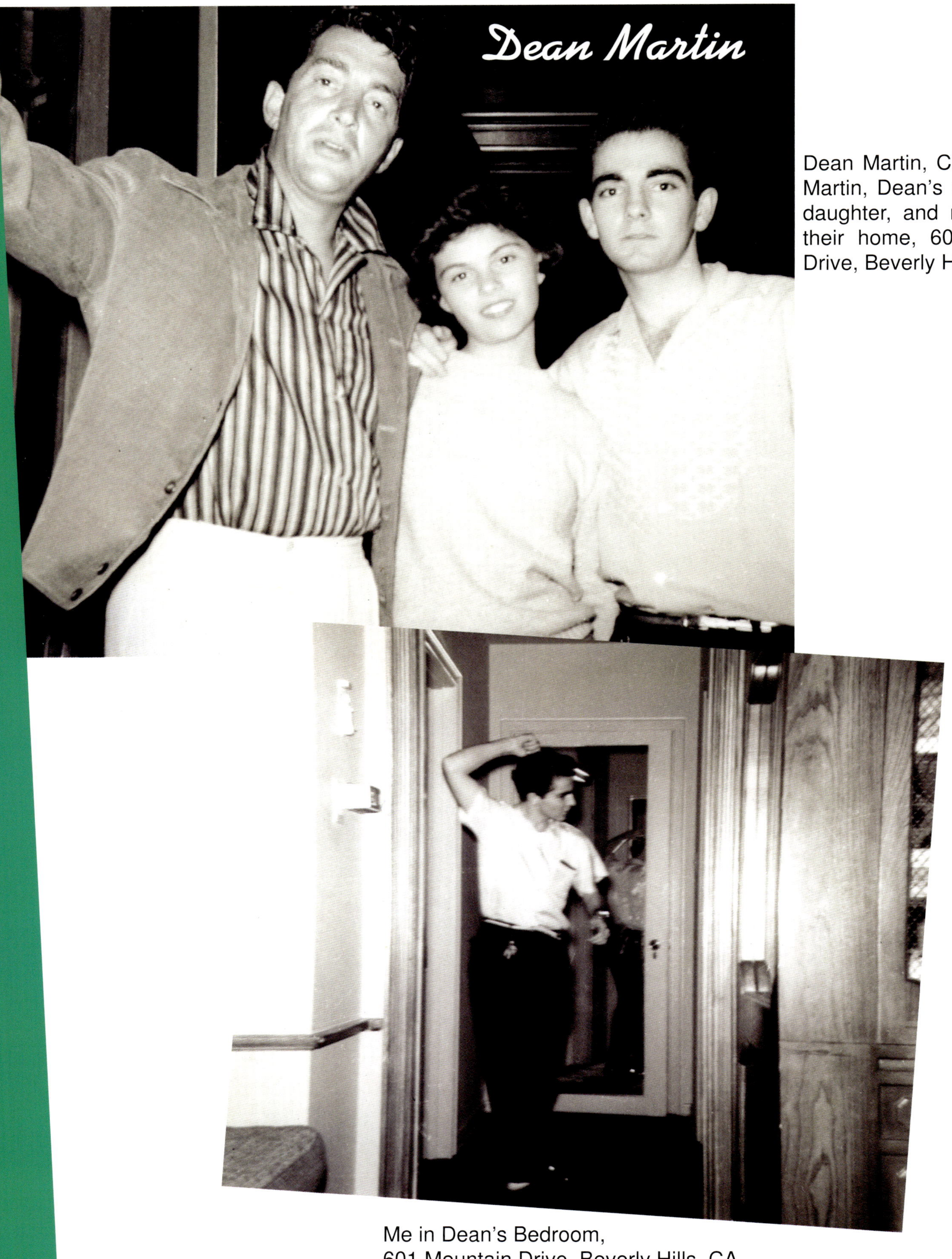

Dean Martin, Claudia Martin, Dean's oldest daughter, and me at their home, 601 Mt. Drive, Beverly Hills

Me in Dean's Bedroom,
601 Mountain Drive, Beverly Hills, CA

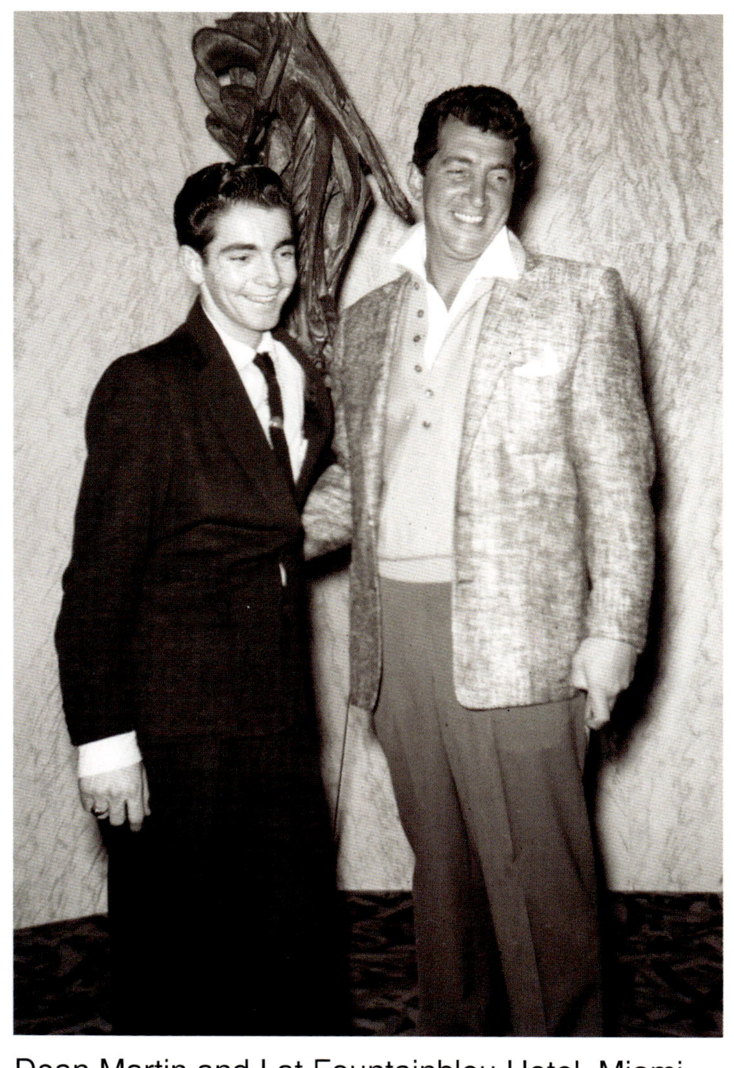

Dean Martin and I at Fountainbleu Hotel, Miami Beach

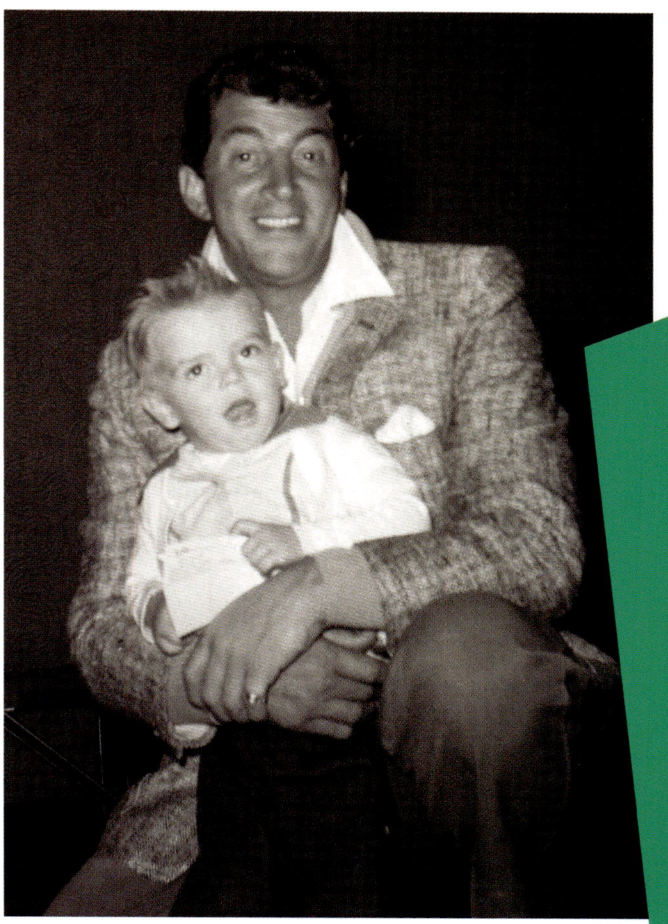

Dean with my nephew, Darryl Donkle

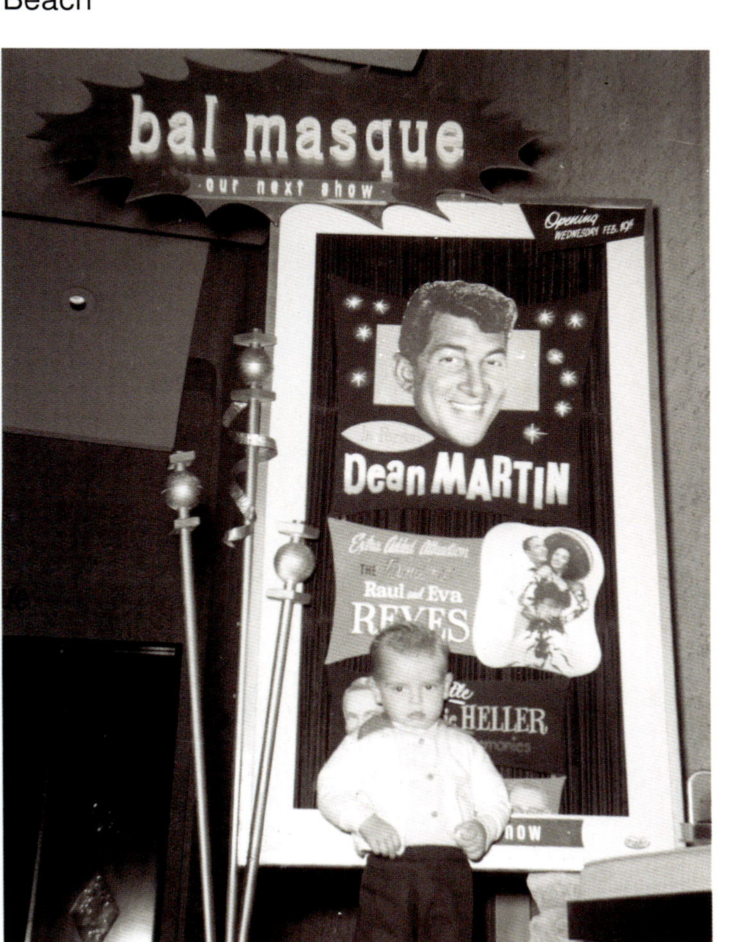

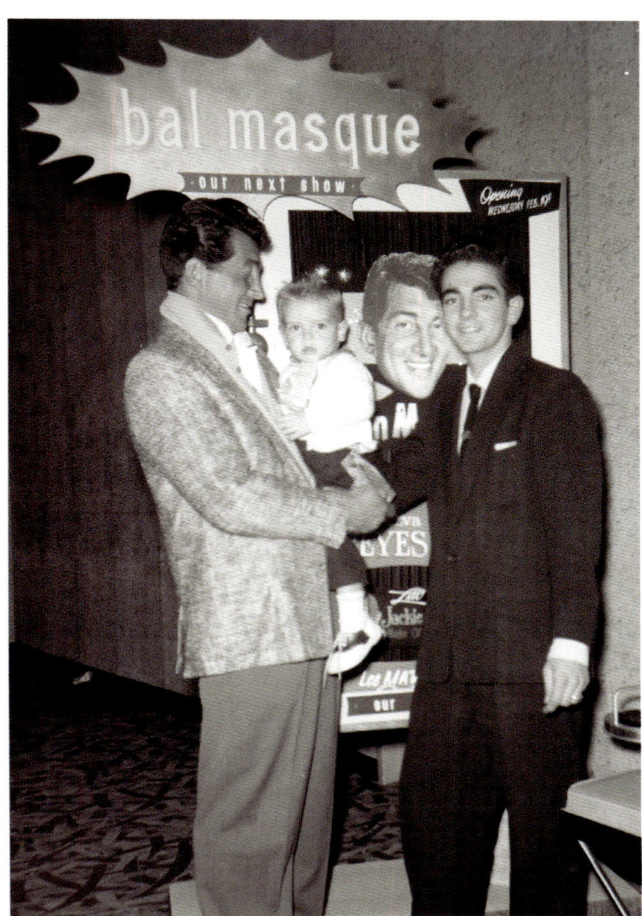

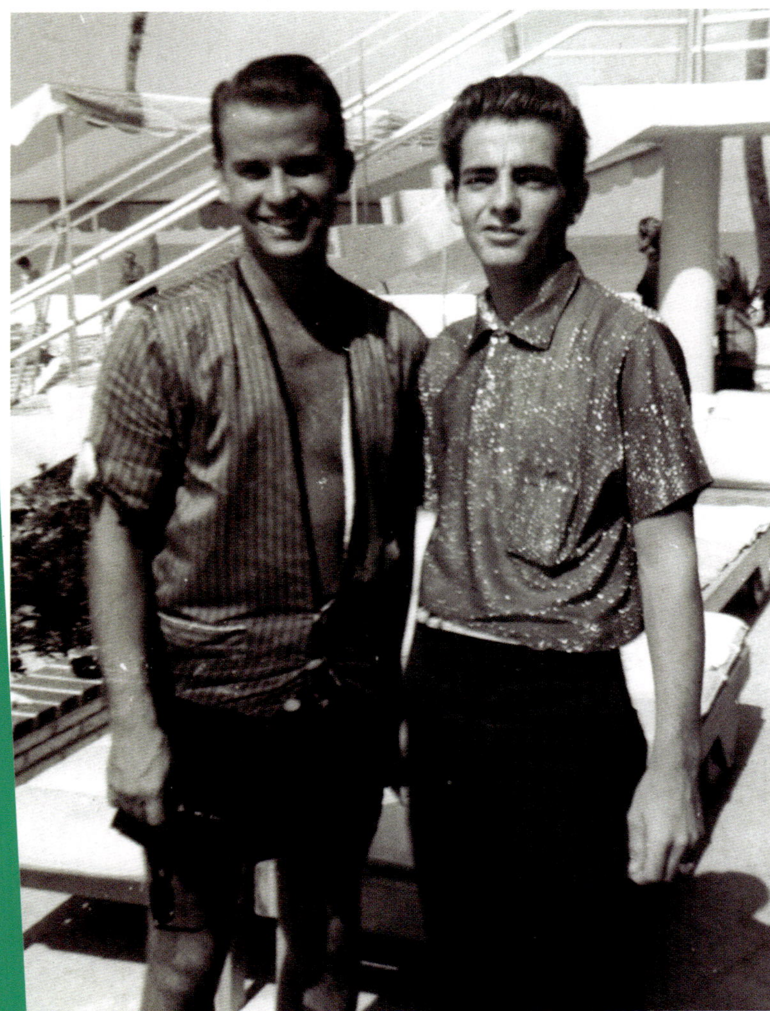

Dick Clark

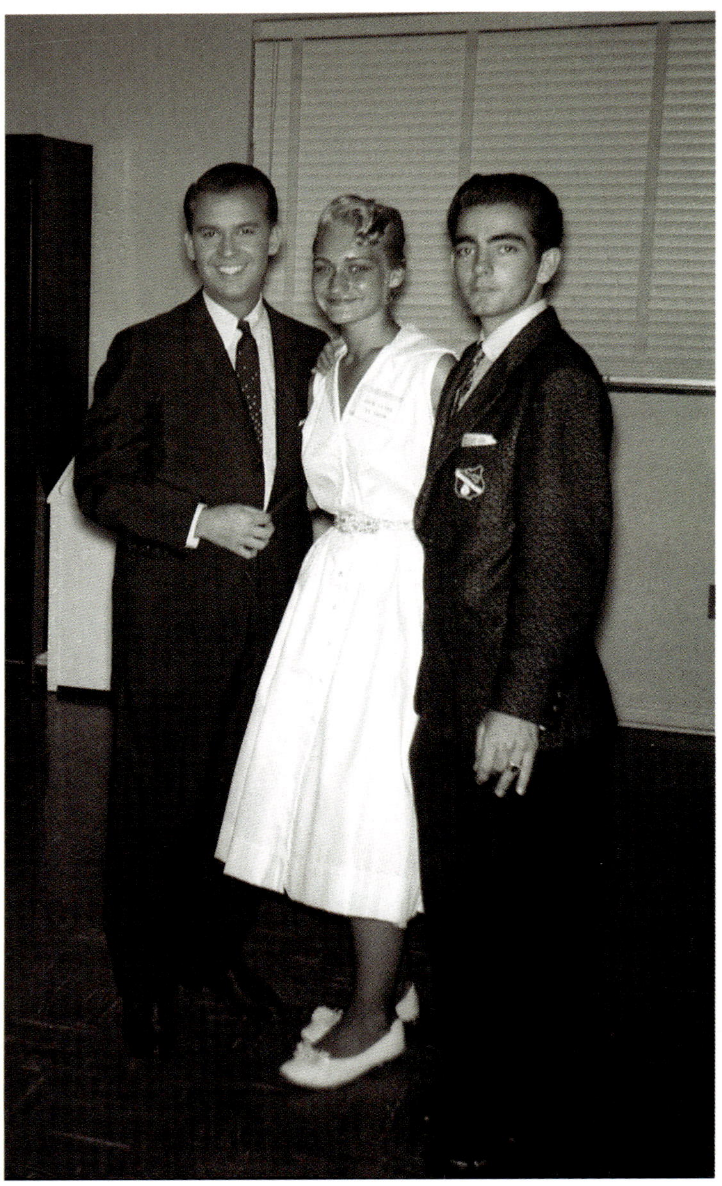

Dick Clark and Gail Smith

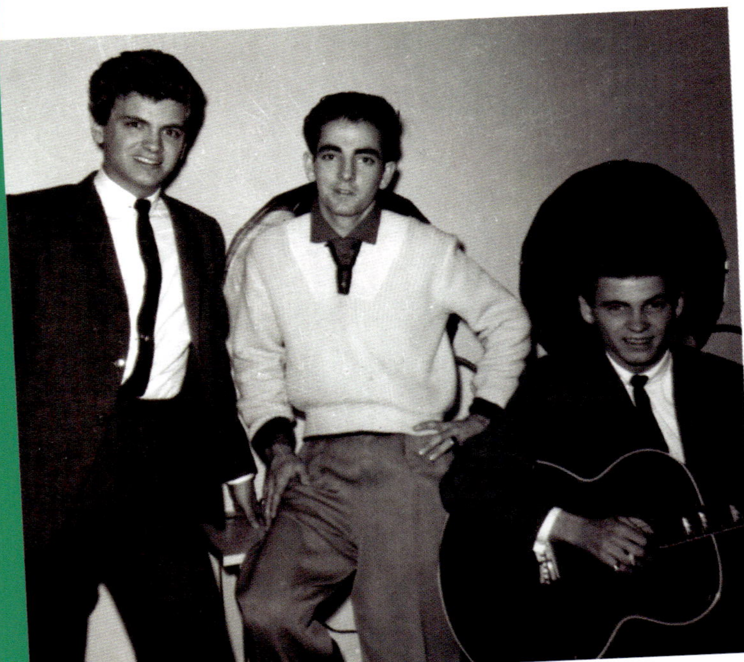

The Everly Brothers

Don and Phil

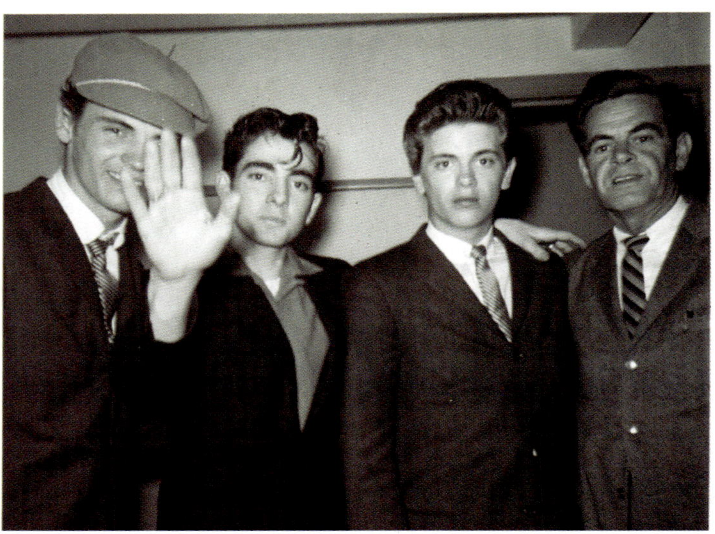

The Everly Brothers
with Dad, Ike

Fabian

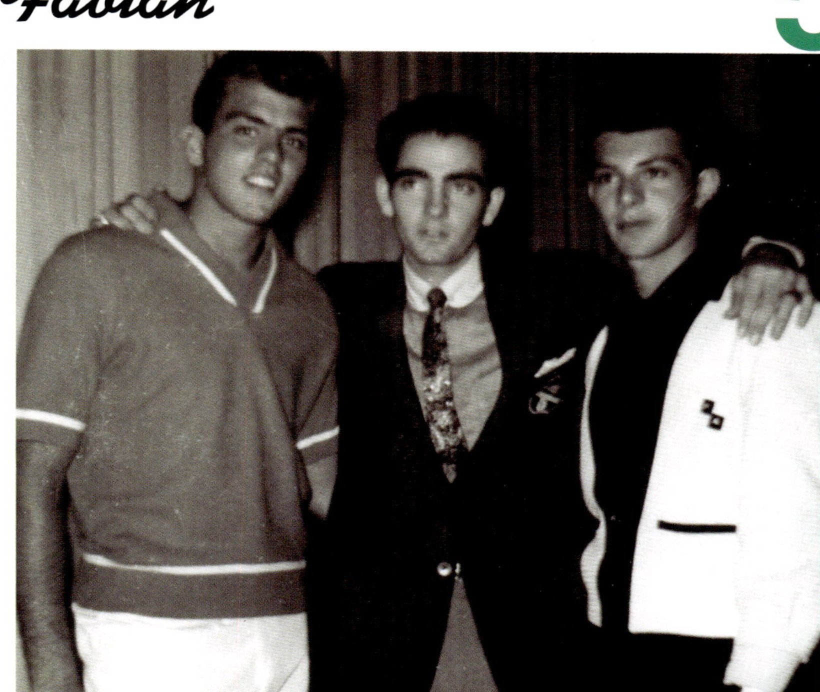

Frankie Avalon

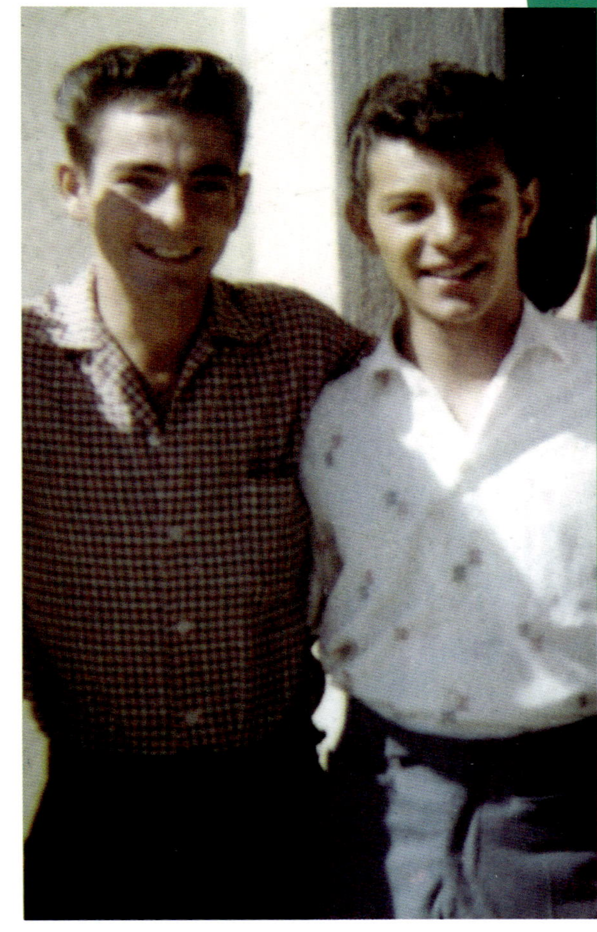

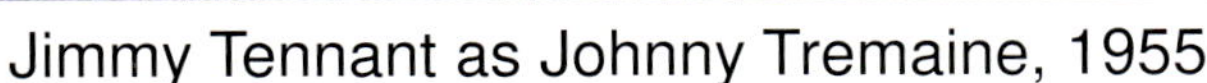
Jimmy Tennant as Johnny Tremaine, 1955

Jerry Lee Lewis

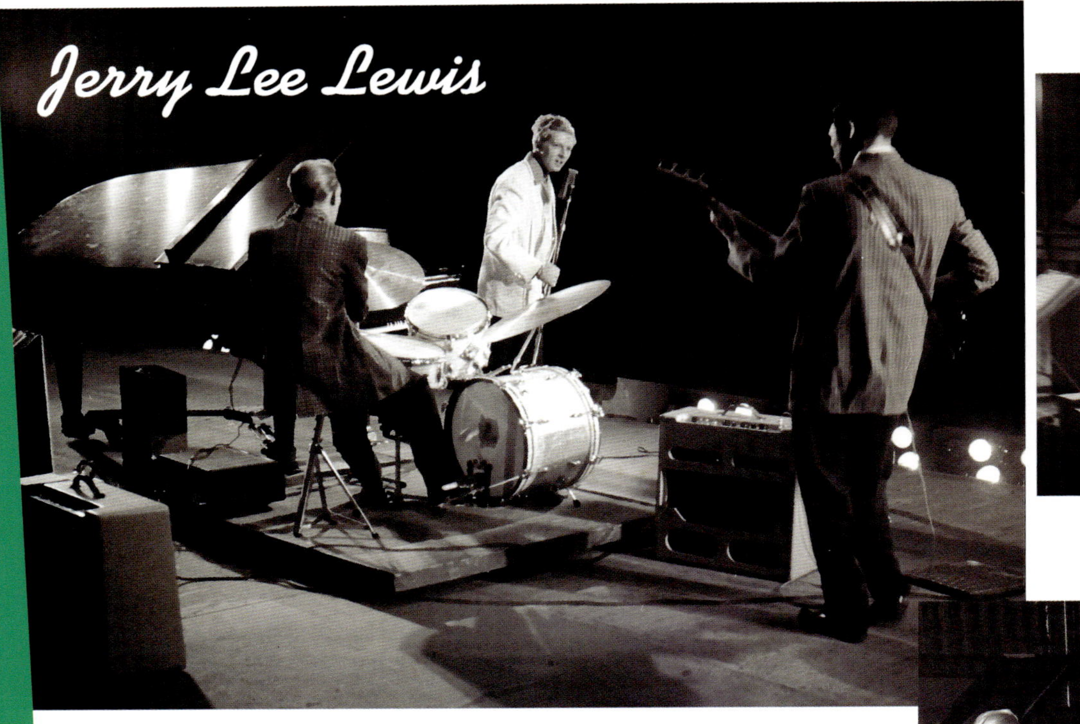

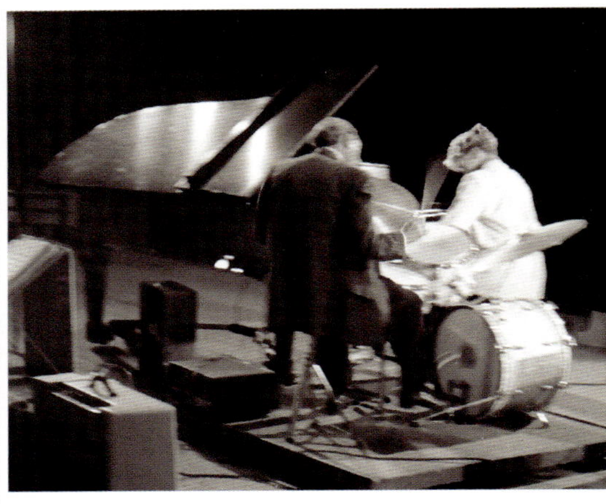

Jerry Lee, myself and J.W. Whitten

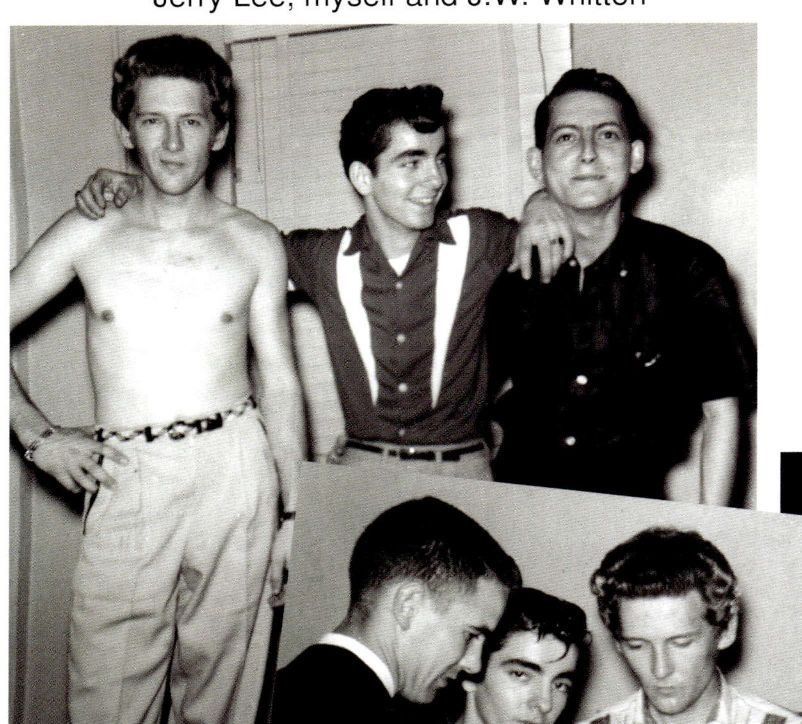

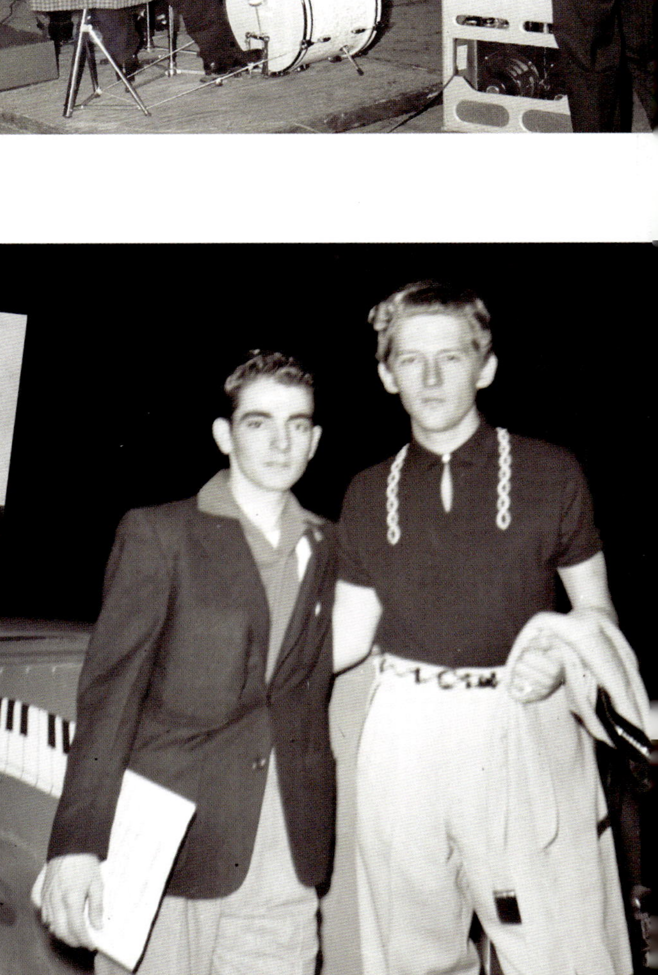

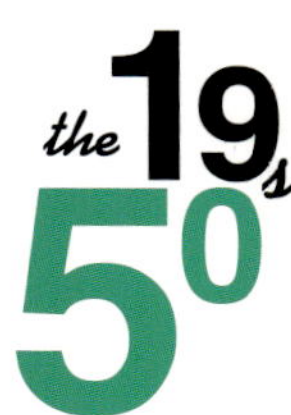

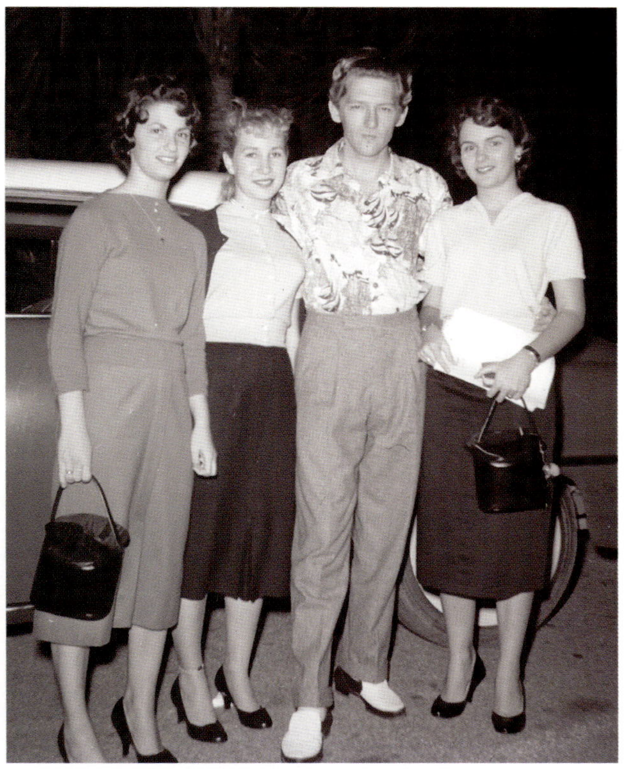

Jerry Lee Lewis with some of his fans

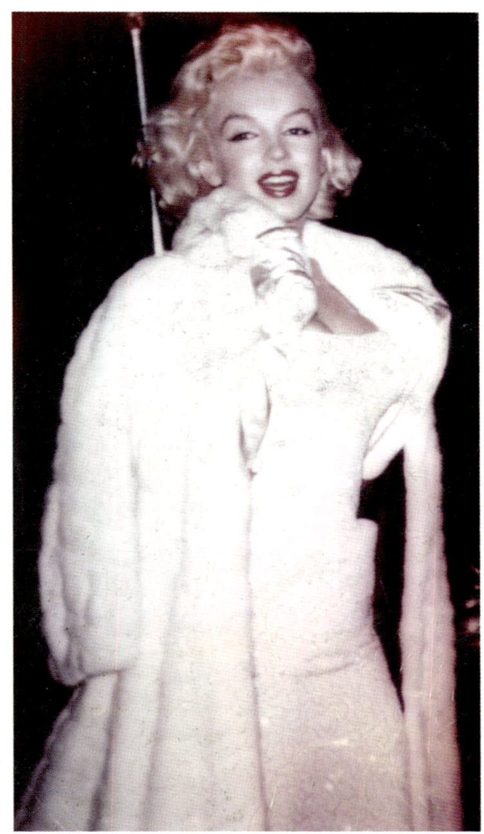

Marilyn Monroe

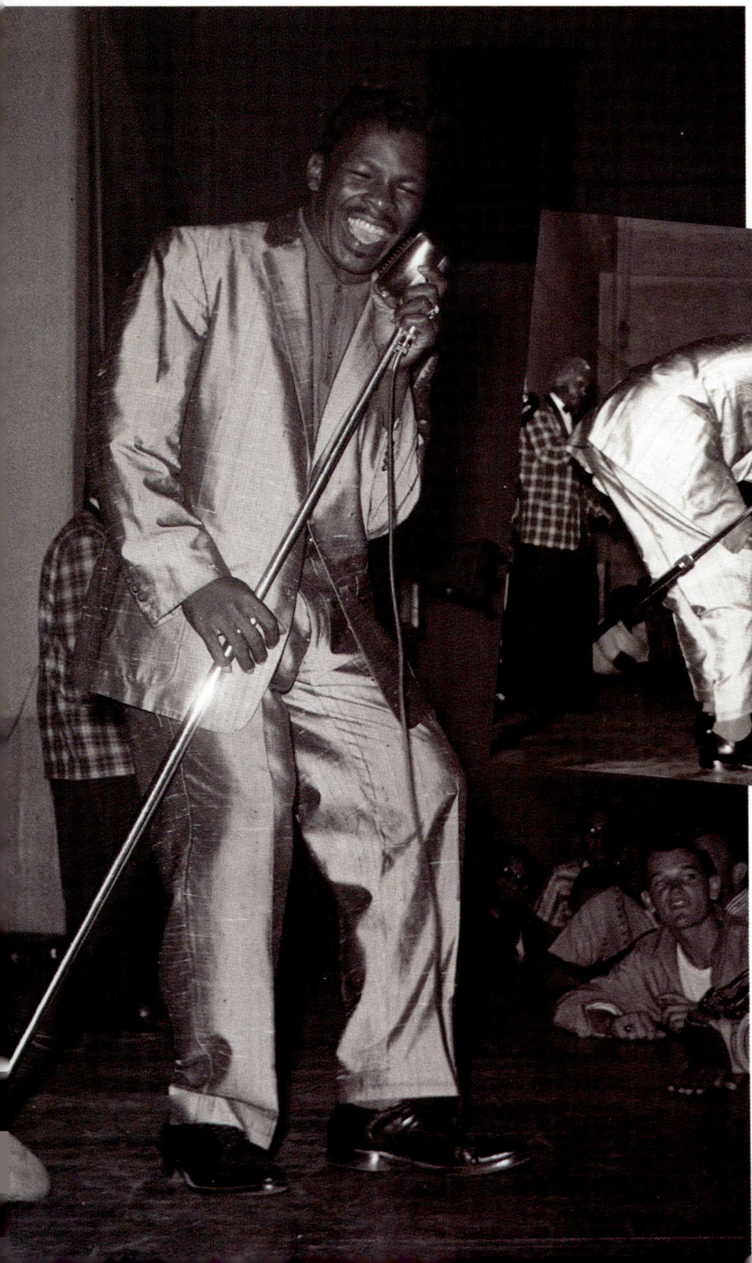

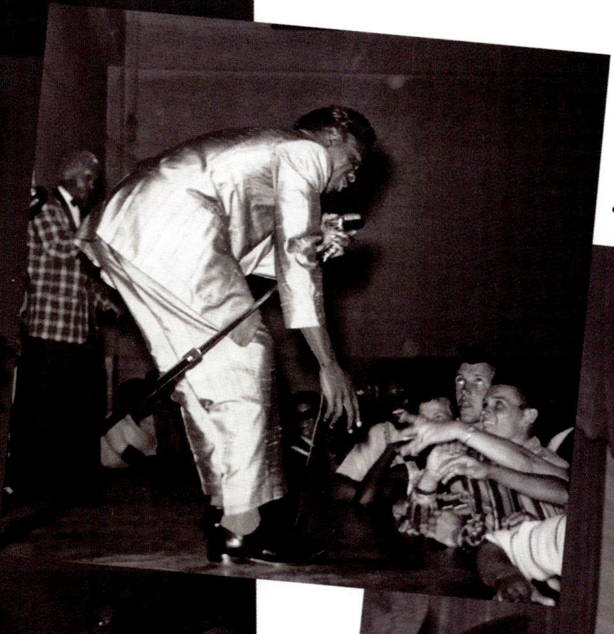

Lloyd Price

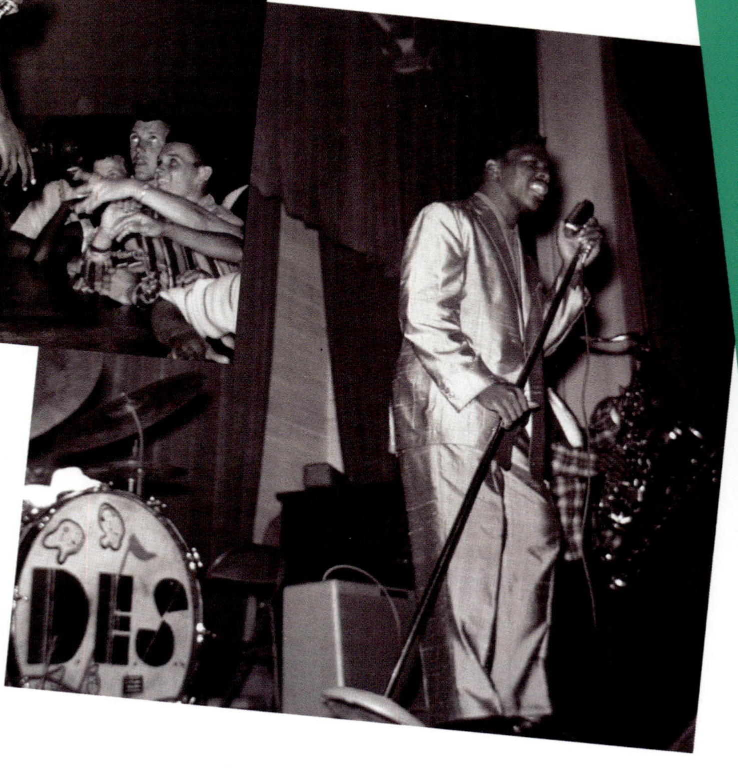

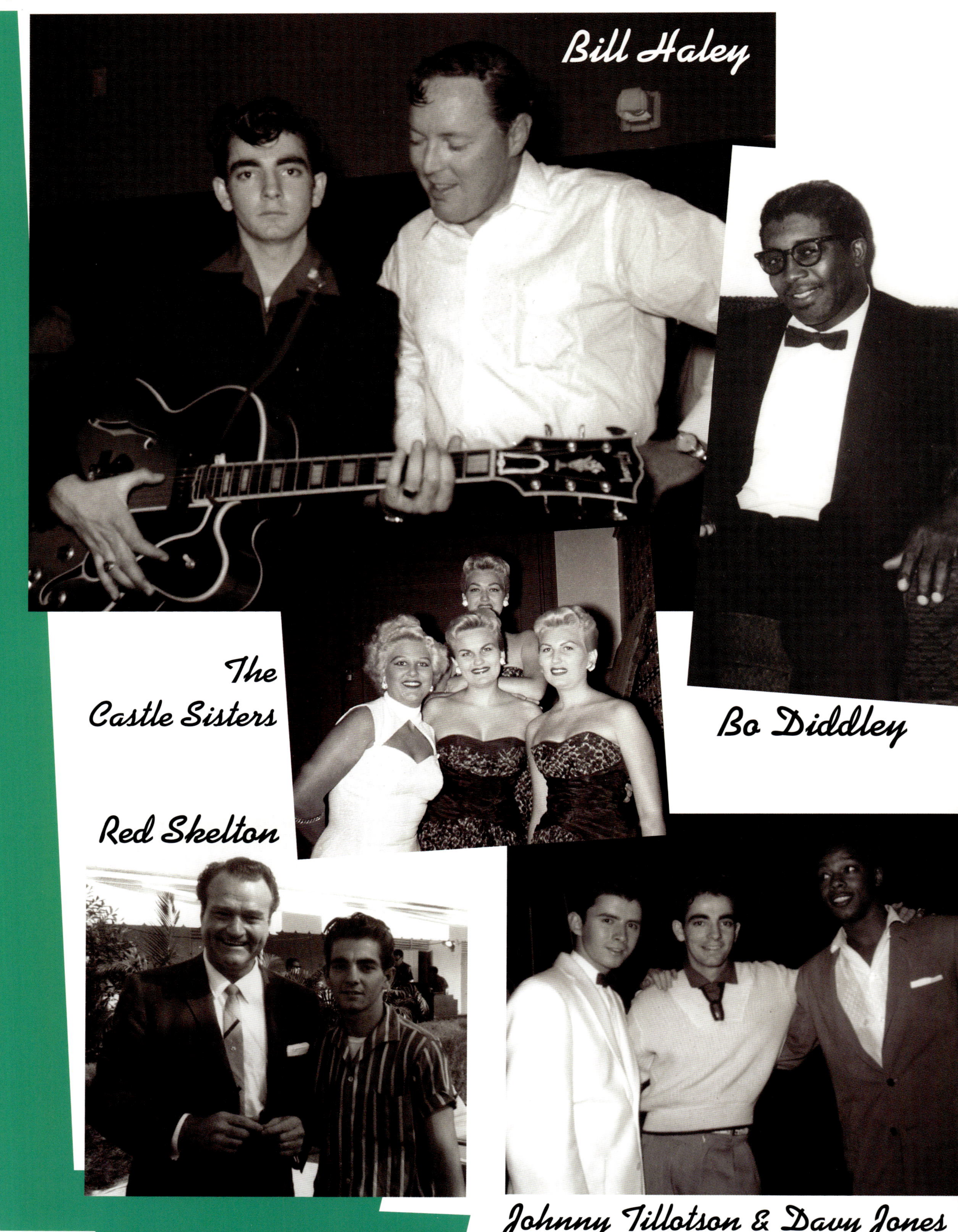

Bill Haley

The Castle Sisters

Bo Diddley

Red Skelton

Johnny Tillotson & Davy Jones

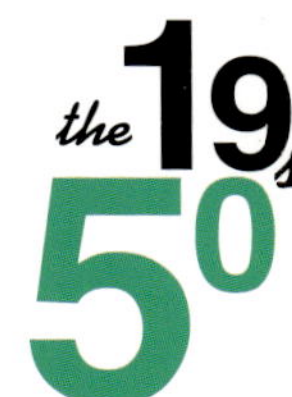

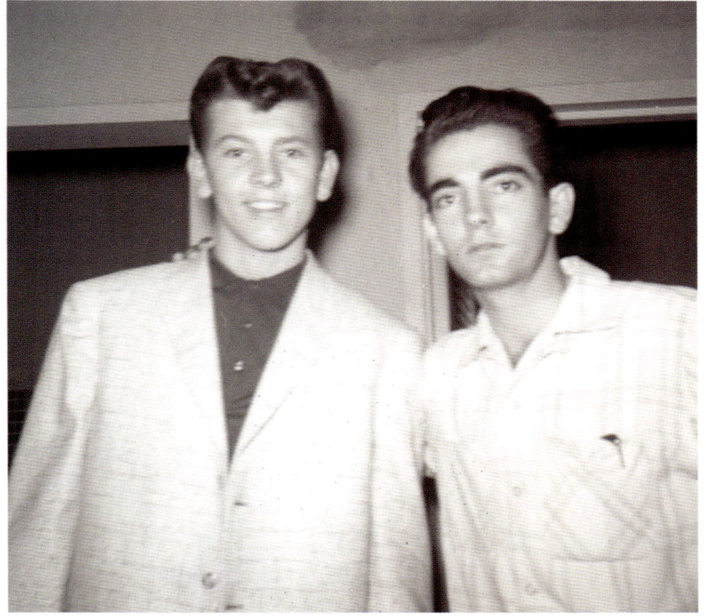

Jimmy Clanton

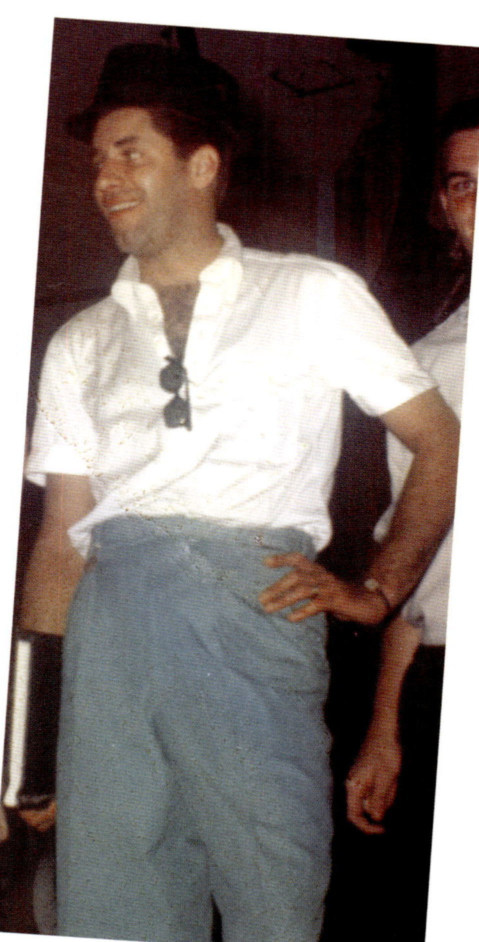

Jerry Lewis

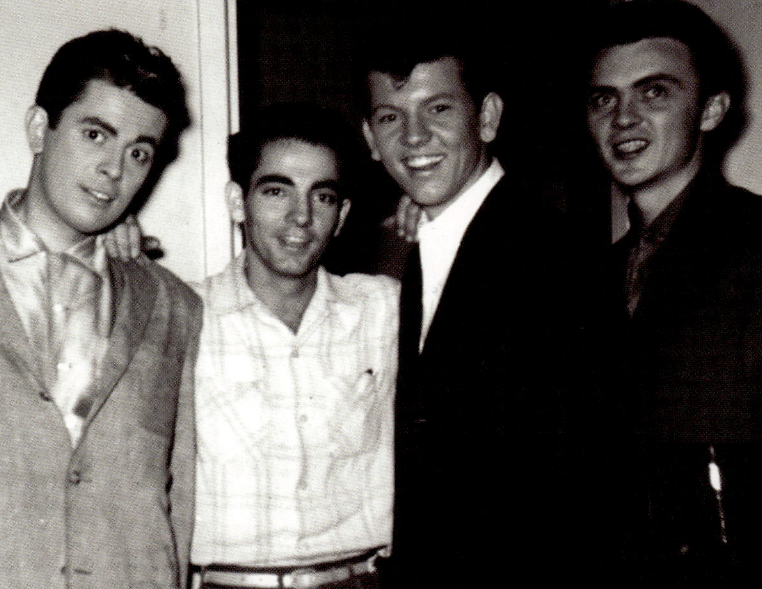

Jimmy Clanton and I with the Esquires

Teddy Randazzo

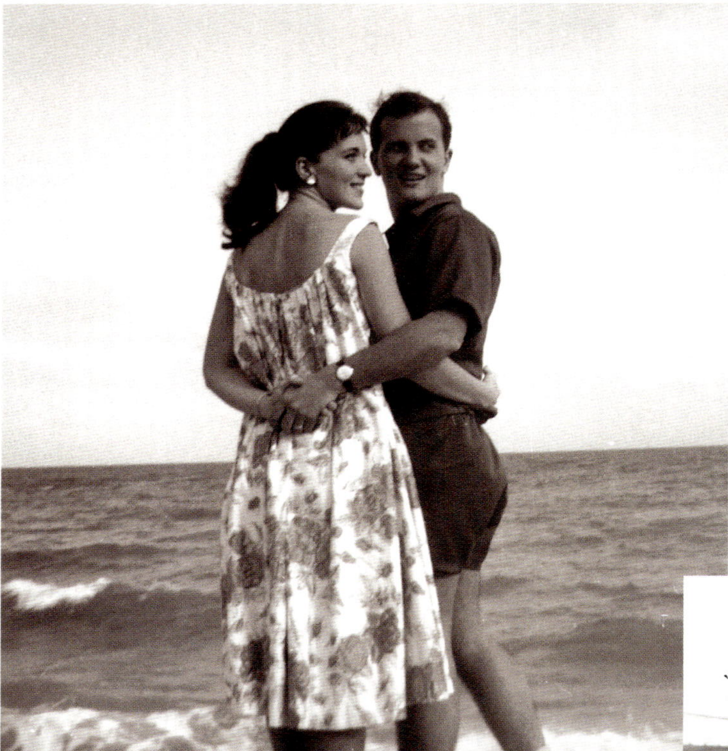

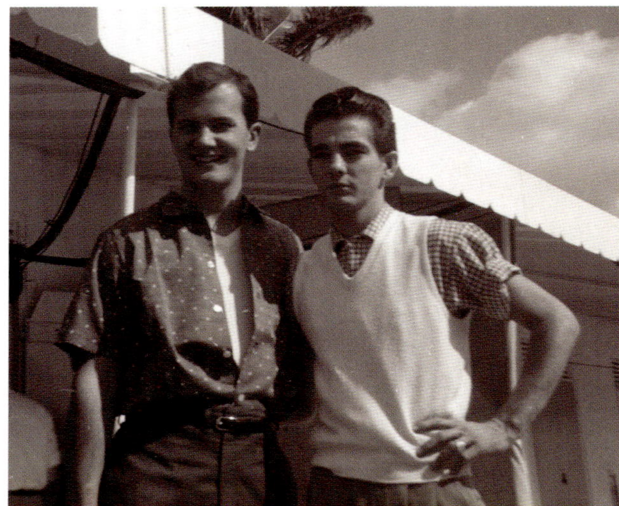

Pat Boone

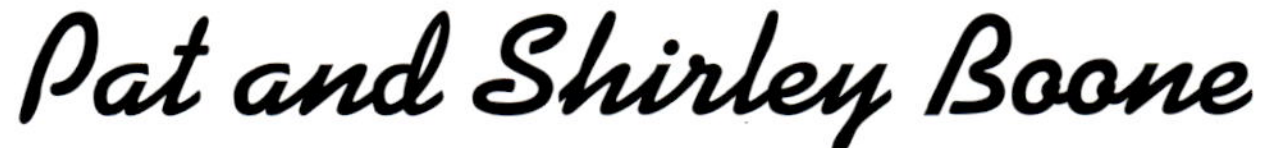

Pat and Shirley Boone

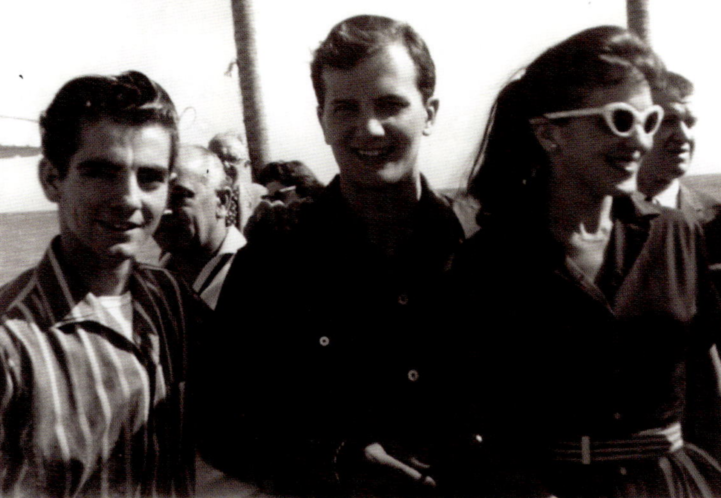

Me with Pat and Shirley Boone

Linda Laurie
Hit: "Ambrose"

To Jimmie
All the success you certainly deserve. I know you'll do it – Linda Laurie

LINDA LAURIE

Maurice Seymour N.Y.

Personal Manager
LOU STALLMAN
New York City

The Royal Teens

Bob Gaudio, Bill Crandall, Billy Dalton,
Tom Austin and Joe Pesci

Marty Robbins

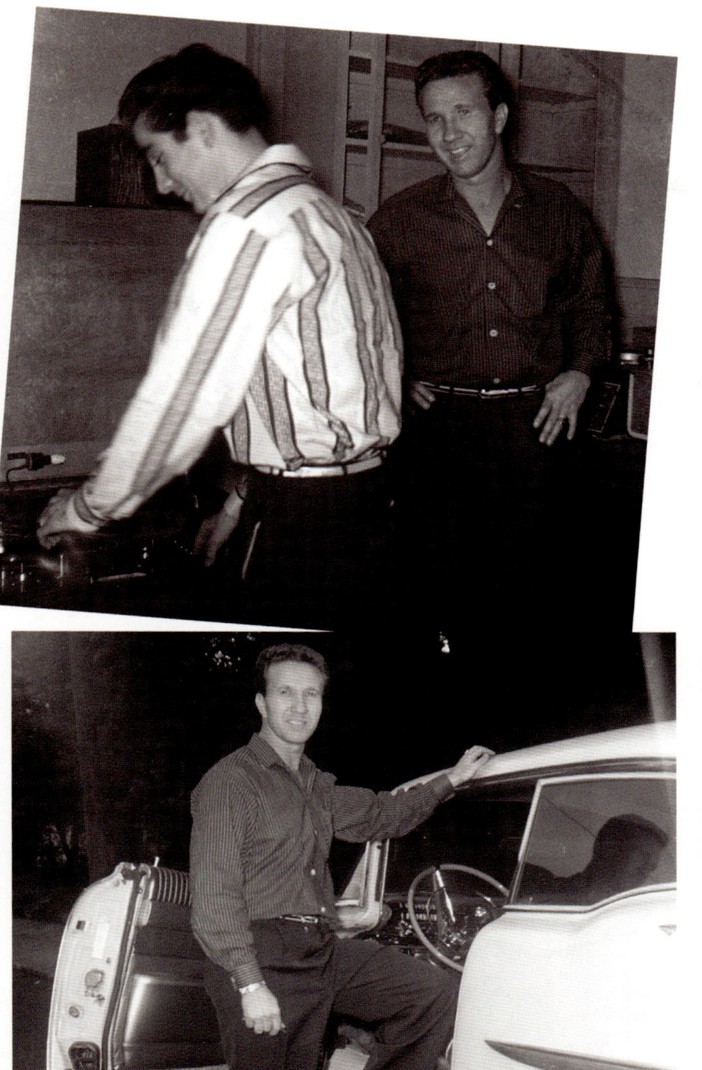

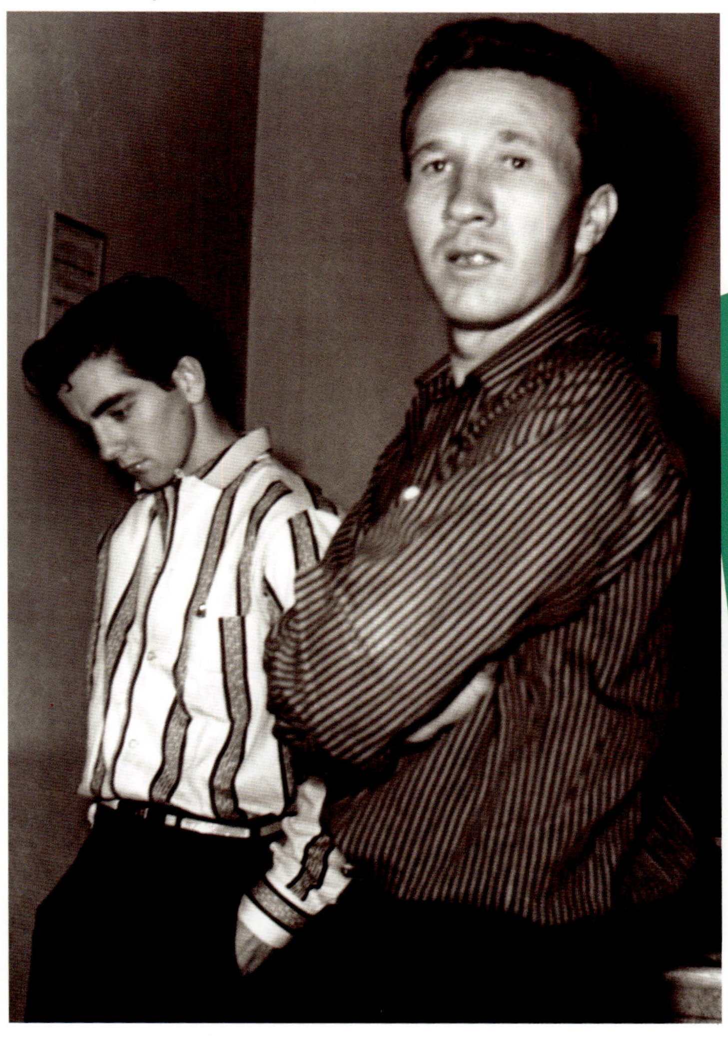

The above photos show Marty and I at his recording studio working on some of my earlier recordings.

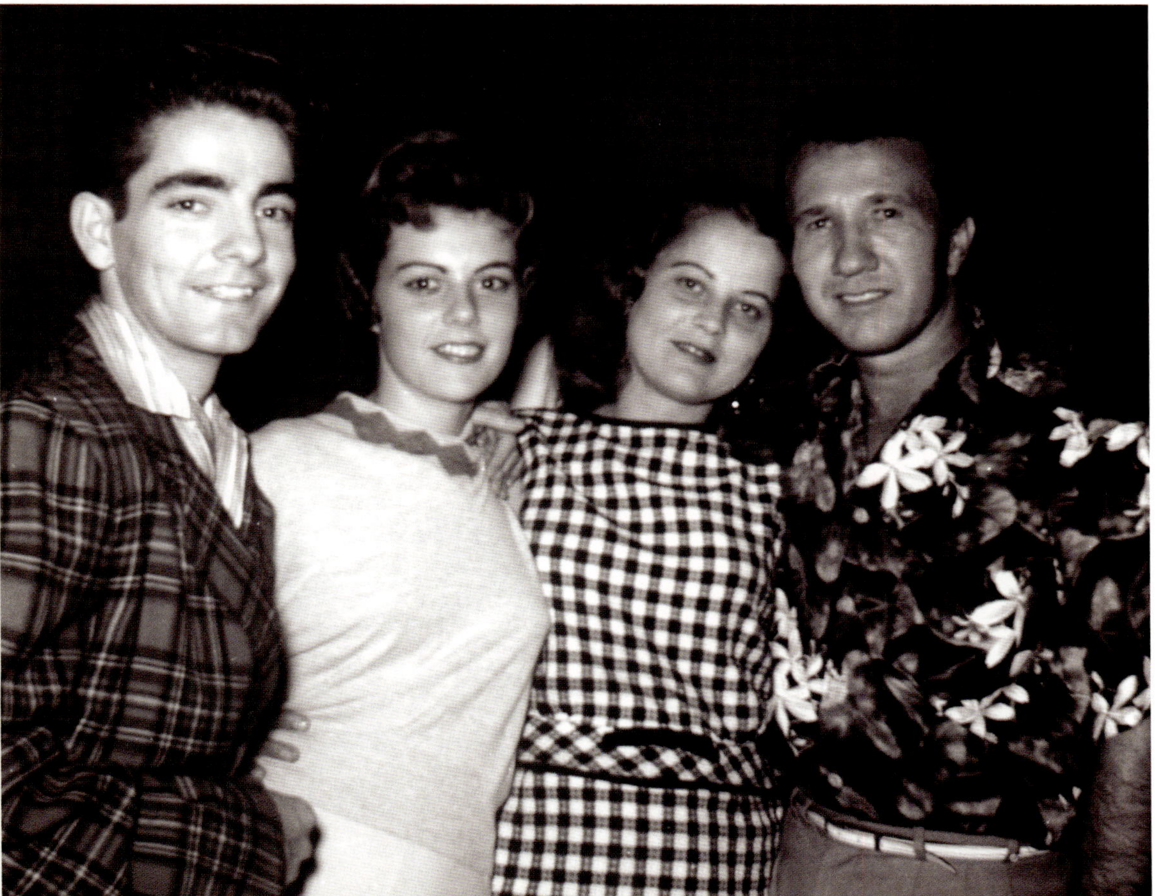

Backstage at the Ryman Auditorium, 1959

Graceland 1957

Elvis' Mother, Gladys Presley, at Graceland- 1957

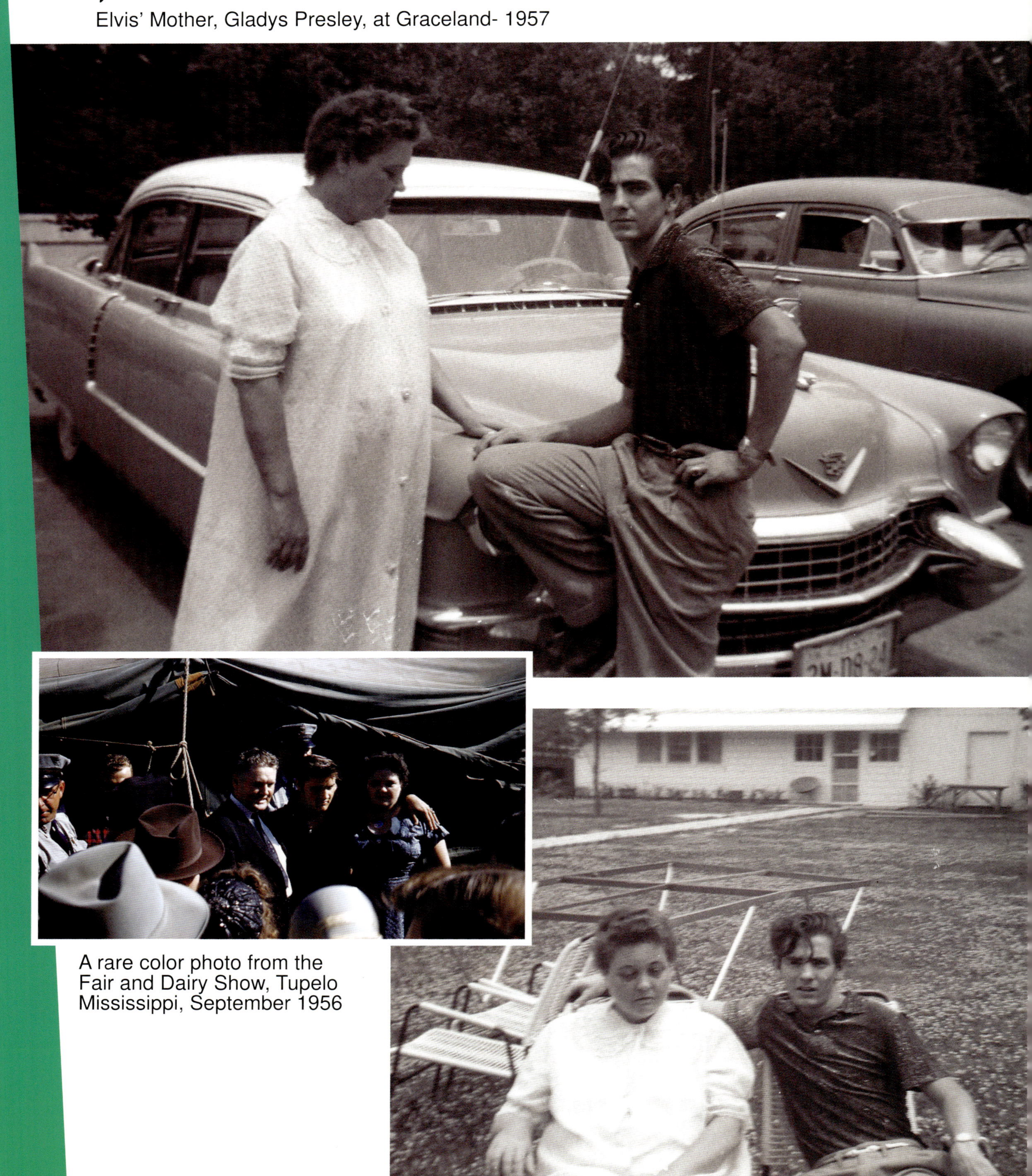

A rare color photo from the Fair and Dairy Show, Tupelo Mississippi, September 1956

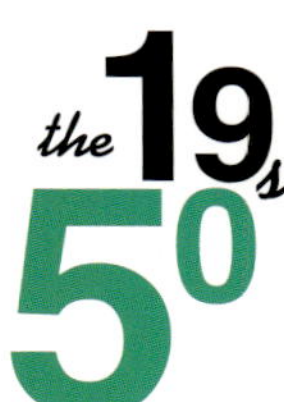

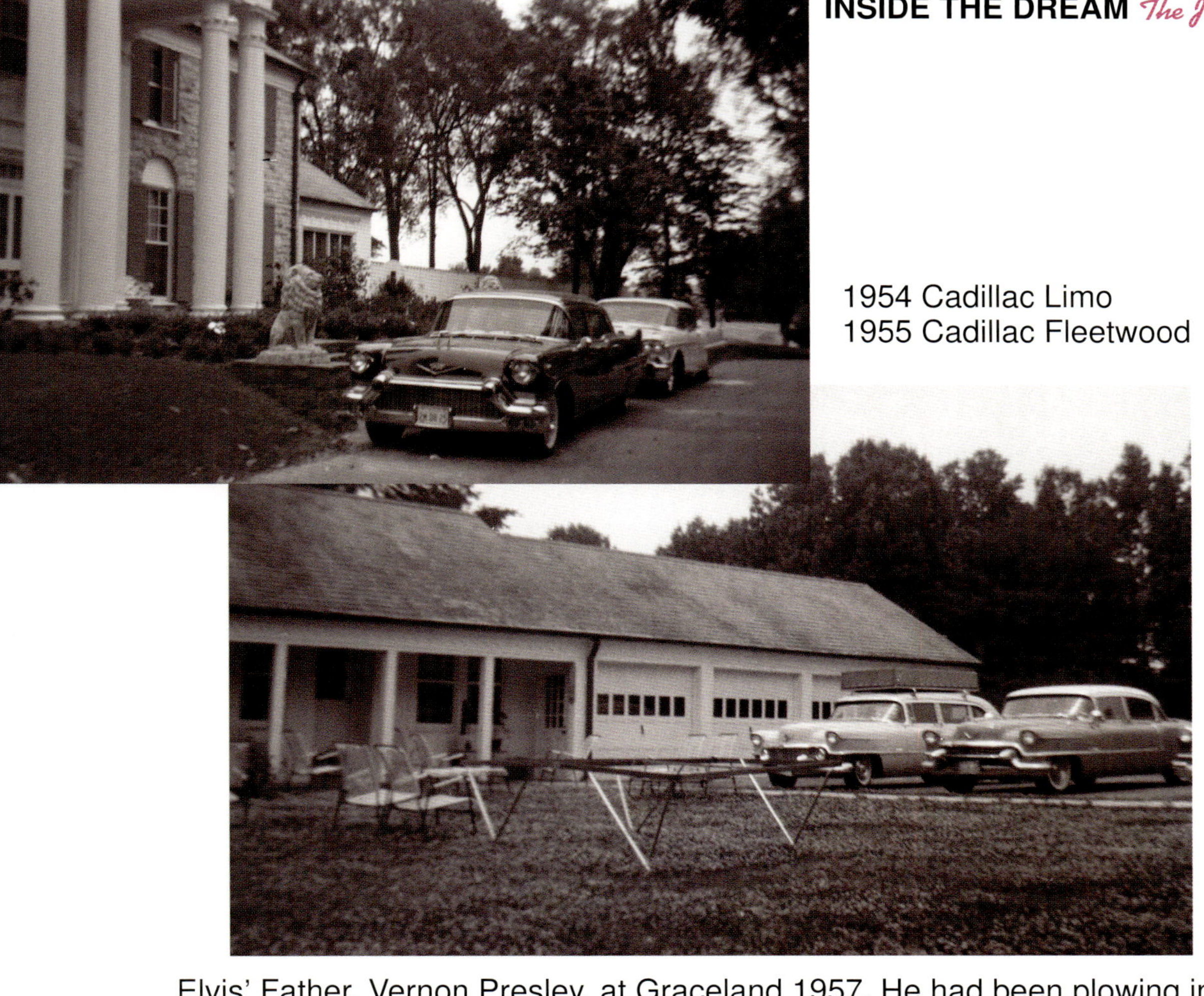

1954 Cadillac Limo
1955 Cadillac Fleetwood

Elvis' Father, Vernon Presley, at Graceland 1957. He had been plowing in the front yard with a mule and plow before this photo was taken.

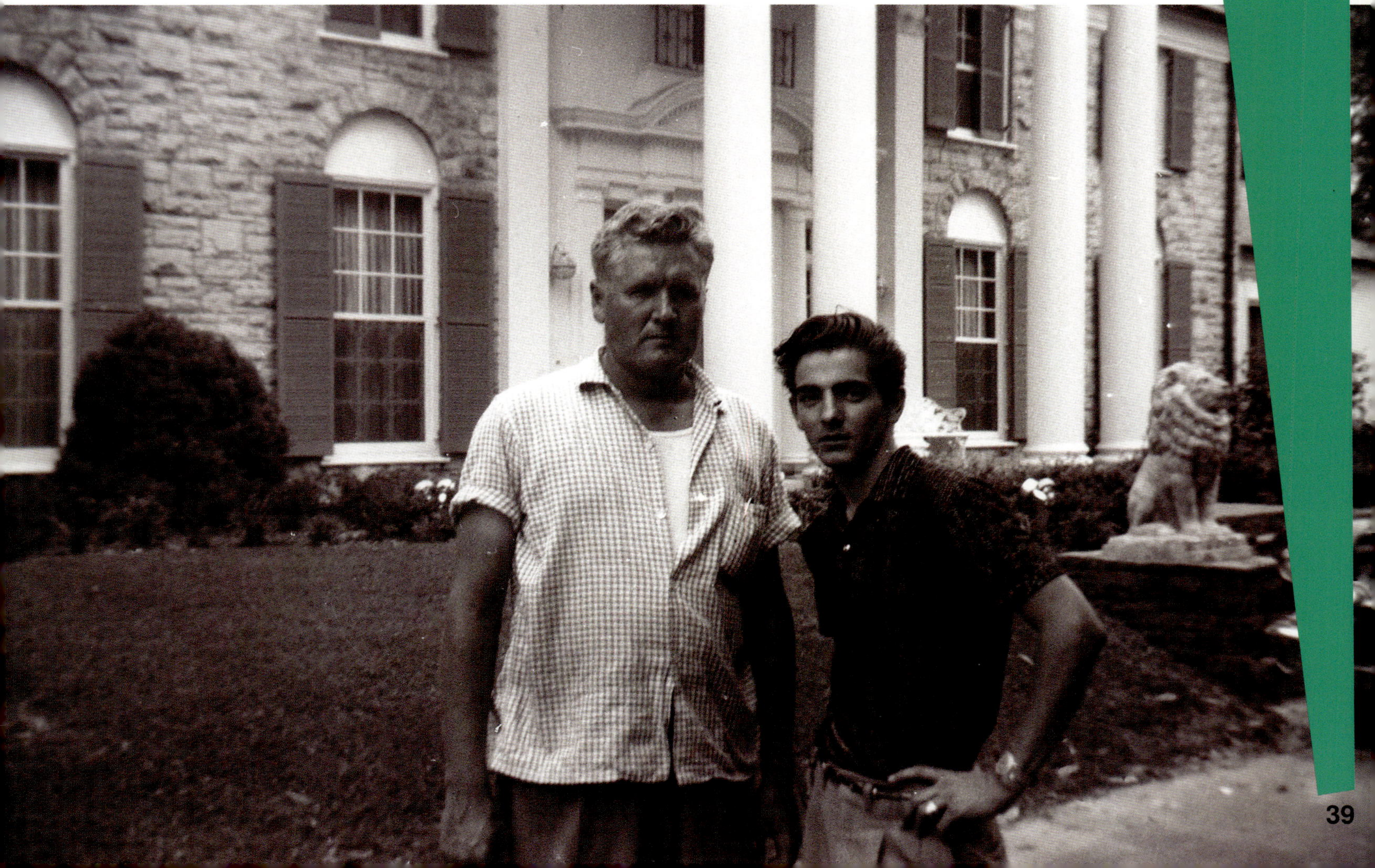

Elvis Presley

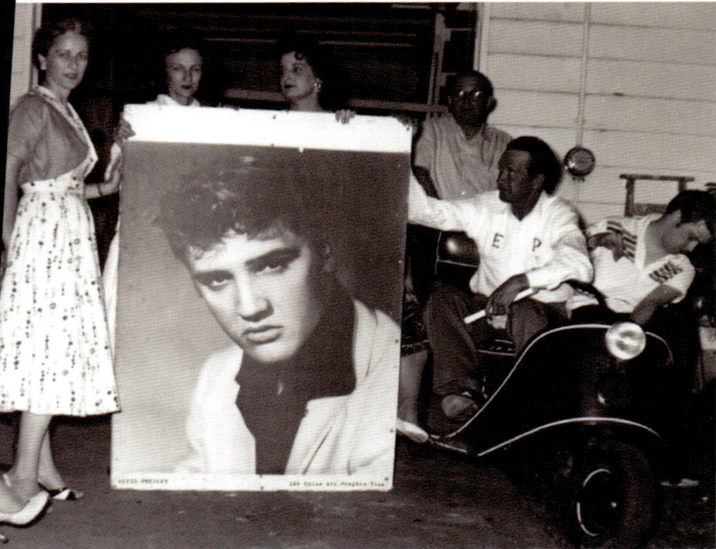

Aunt Loraine Smith, Uncle Travis Smith, and Gary Pepper (President of Elvis' Fan Club 1950s-1960s)

Elvis on the movie set with three of Dean Martin's daughters, Gail, Dina and Claudia

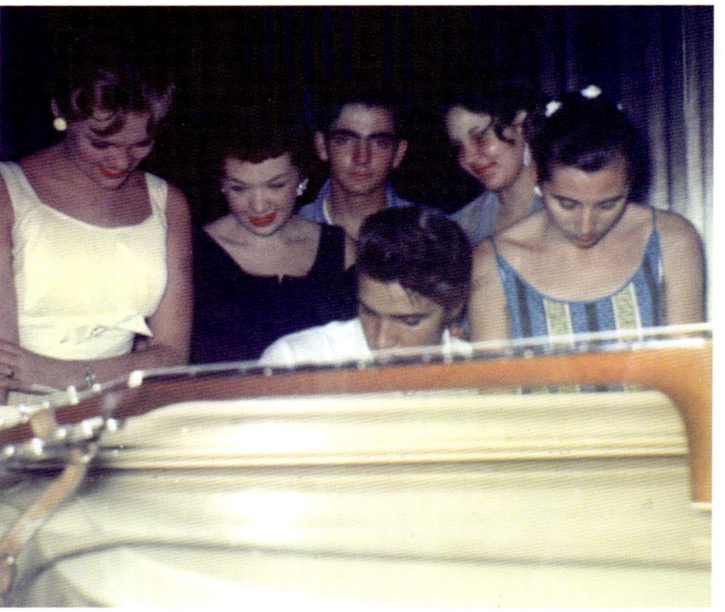

1956 Jacksonville, FL That's me behind the girls

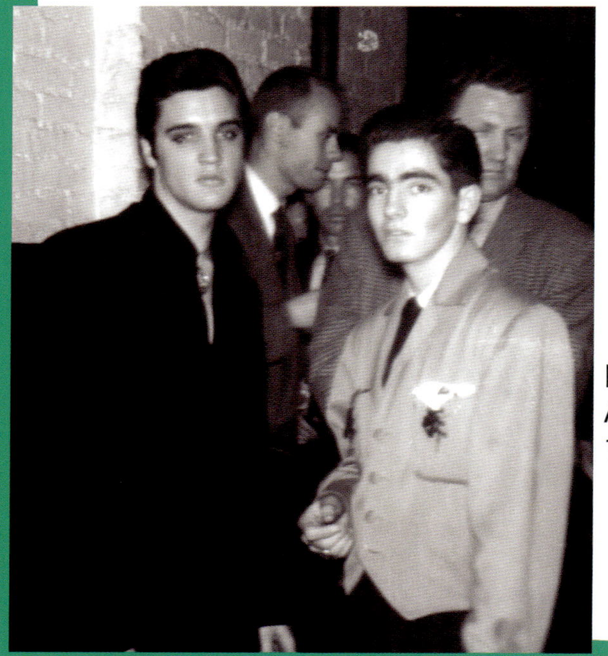

Philadelphia Arena, March 1957

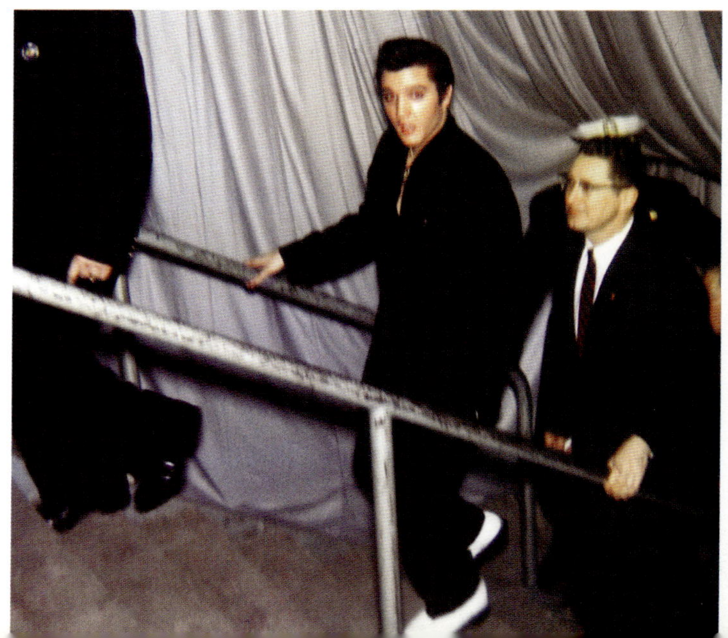

Uncle Vester Presley

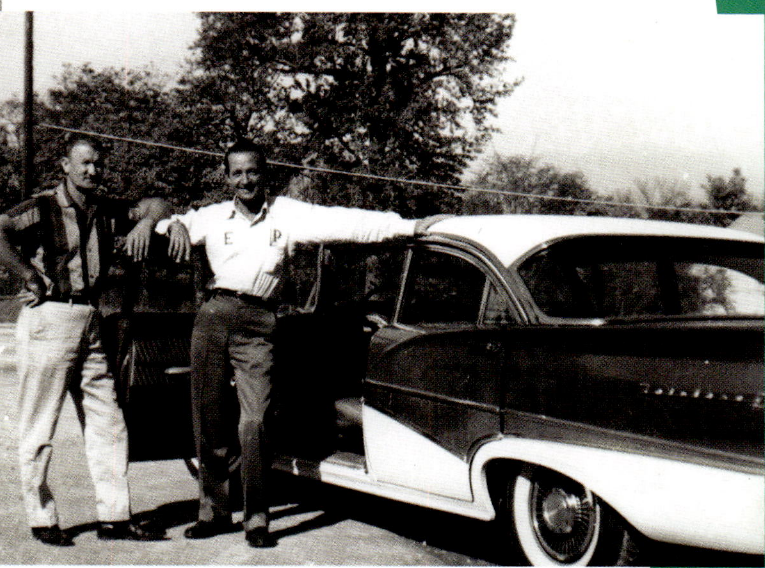

Uncle Vester Presley and Uncle Travis Smith

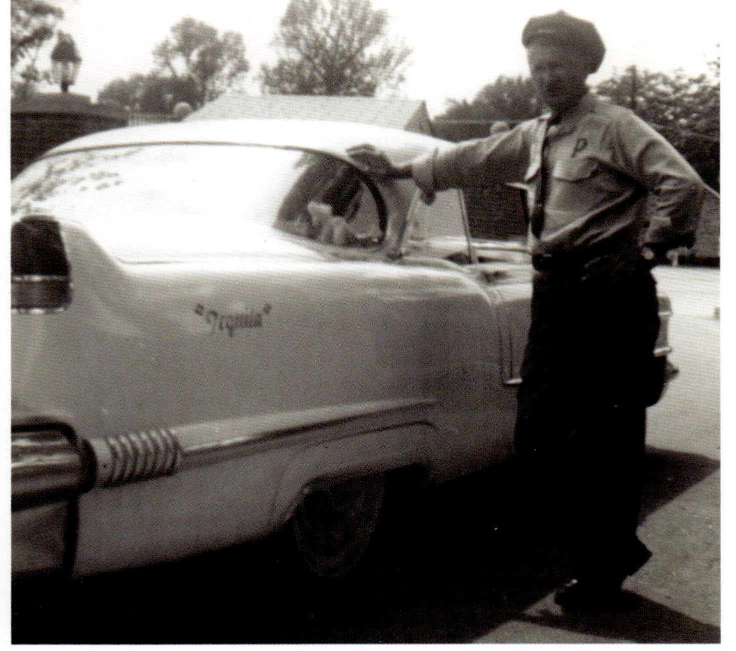

Uncle Vester Presley
Me leaving Graceland

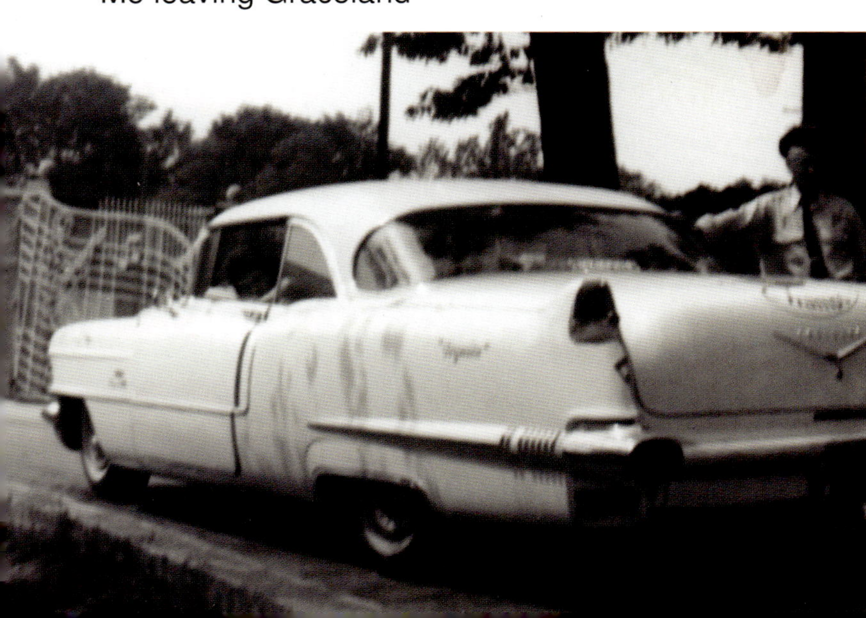

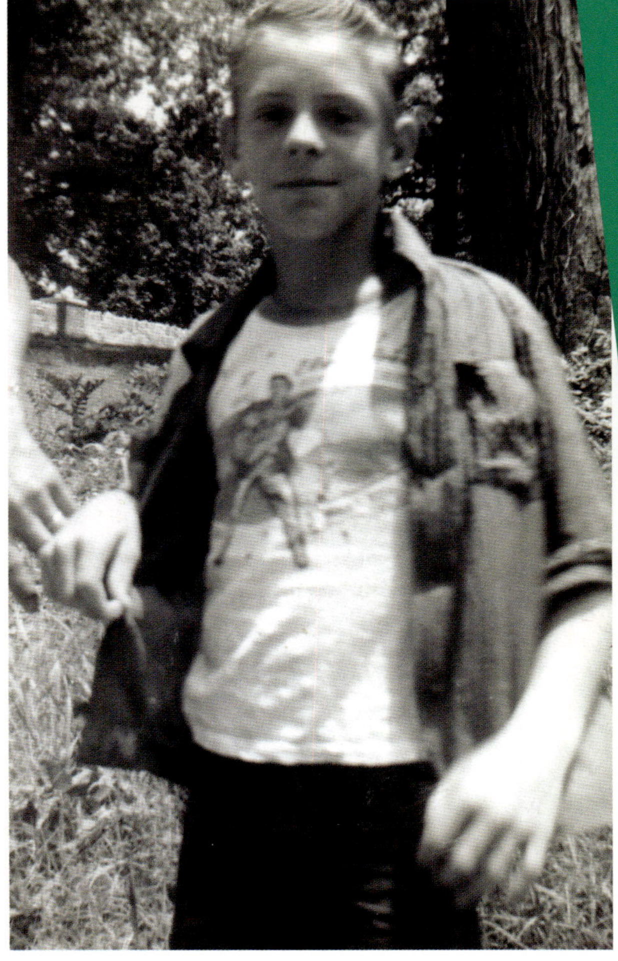

Billy Smith, Elvis' first cousin

Florida Theater
August 11, 1956

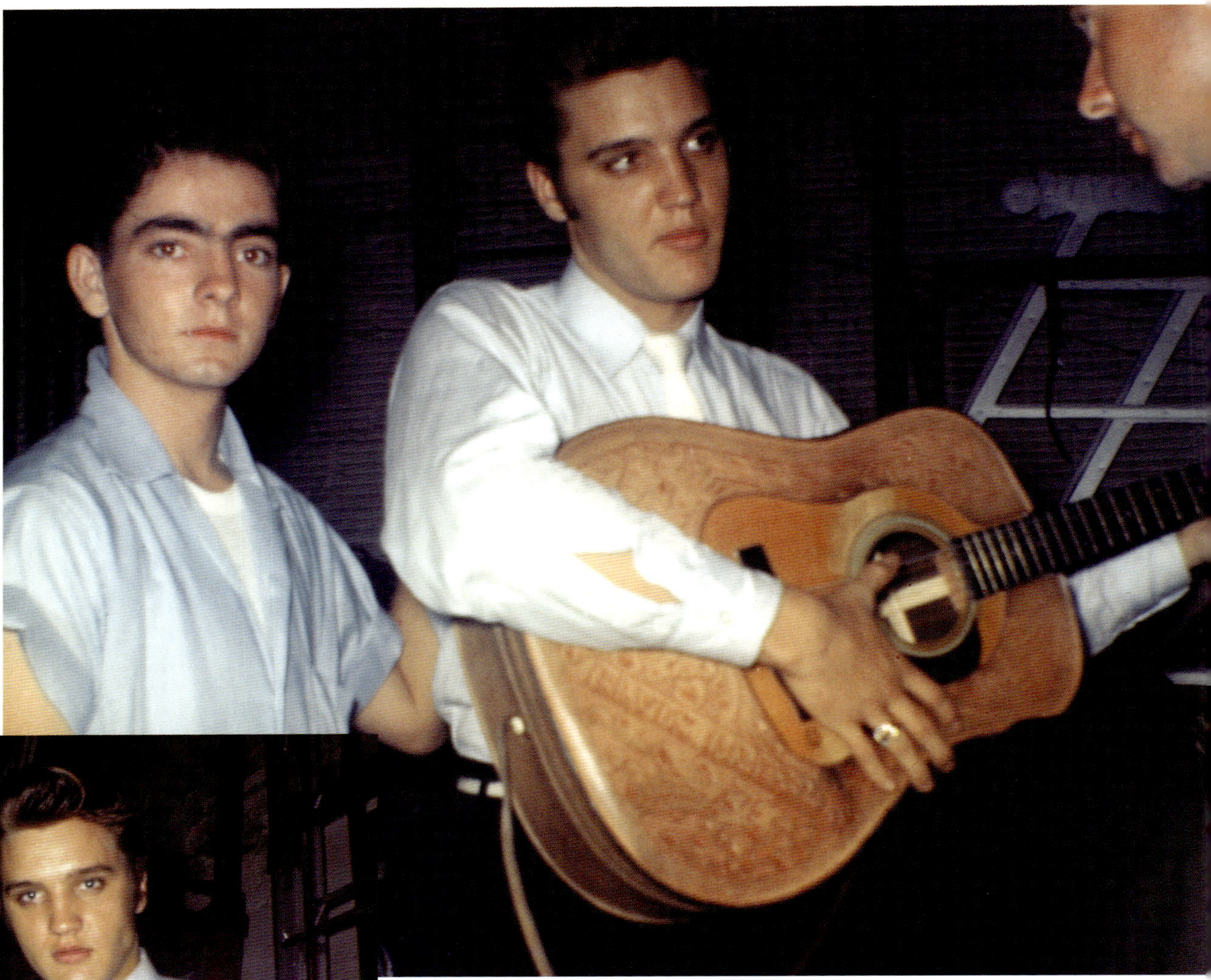

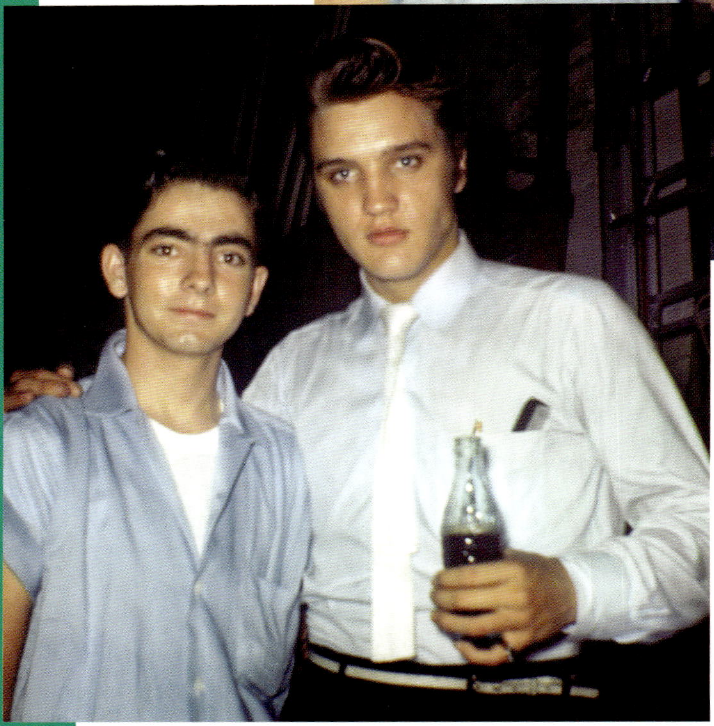

This was the first time I used a camera. I bought a "Brownie Hawkeye" and one roll of color film, which, at that time, was something brand new for consumers. These great photos were made with that camera.

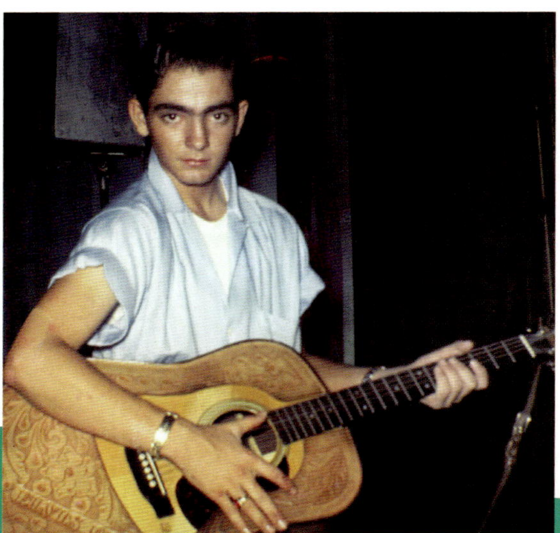

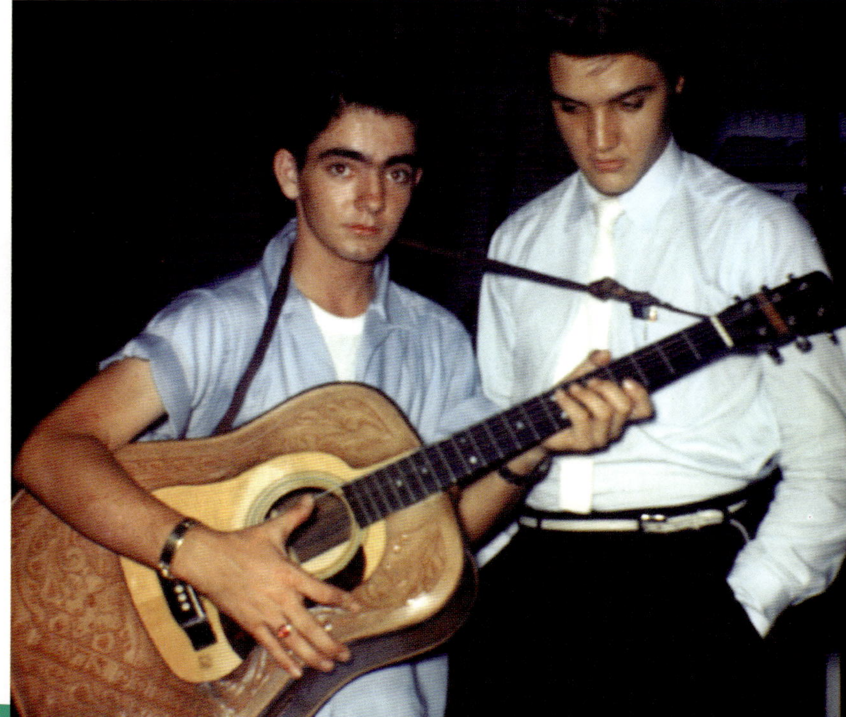

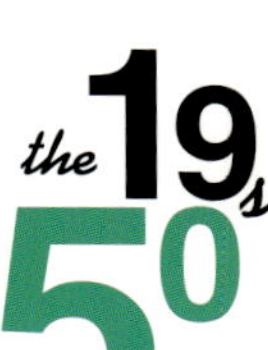

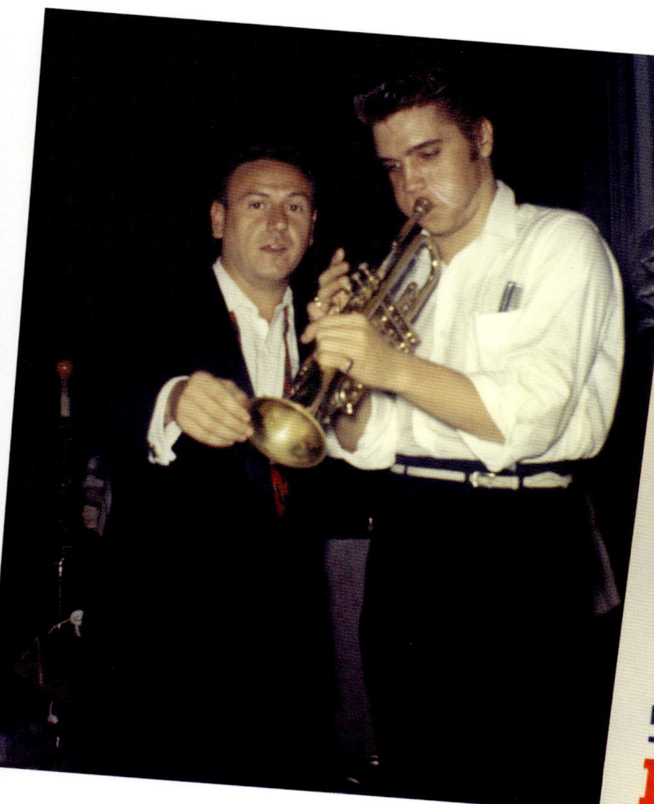

Phil Maraquin

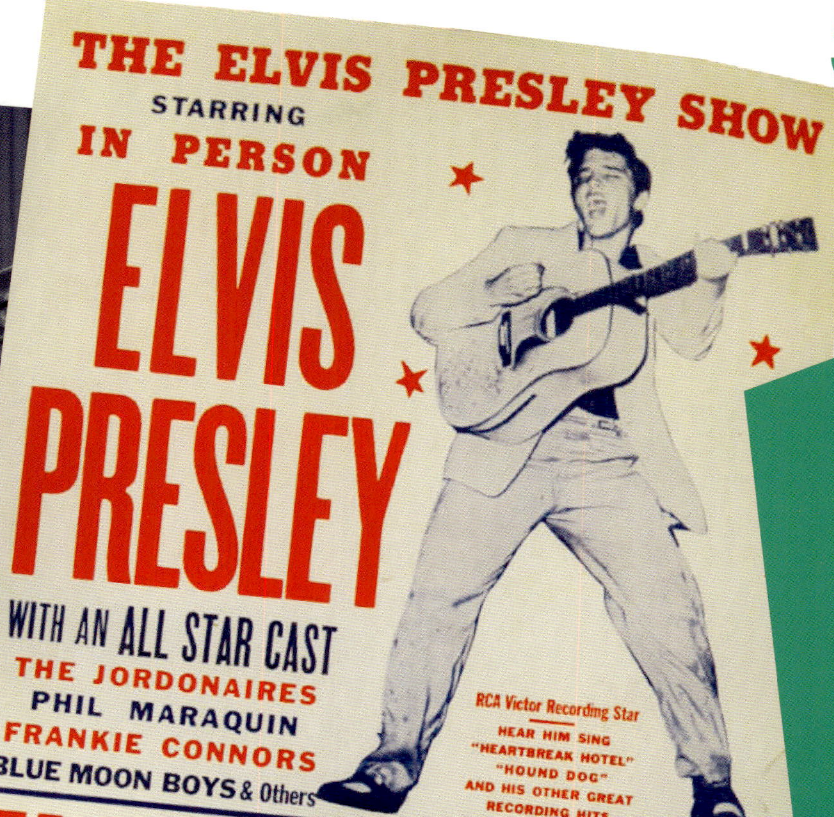

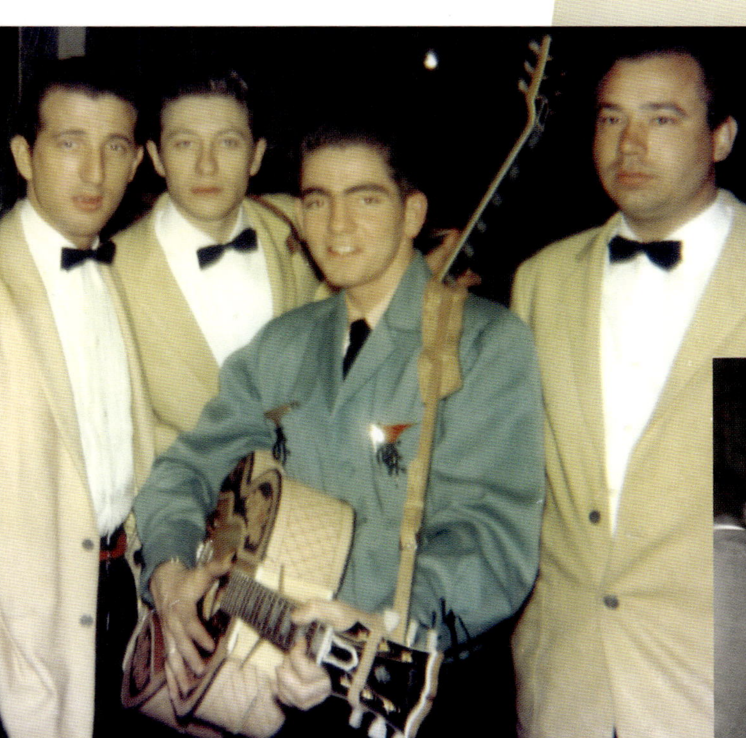

DJ Fontana, Scotty Moore, Me with Elvis' guitar, and Bill Black - 1957

This is Elvis' Gibson J200

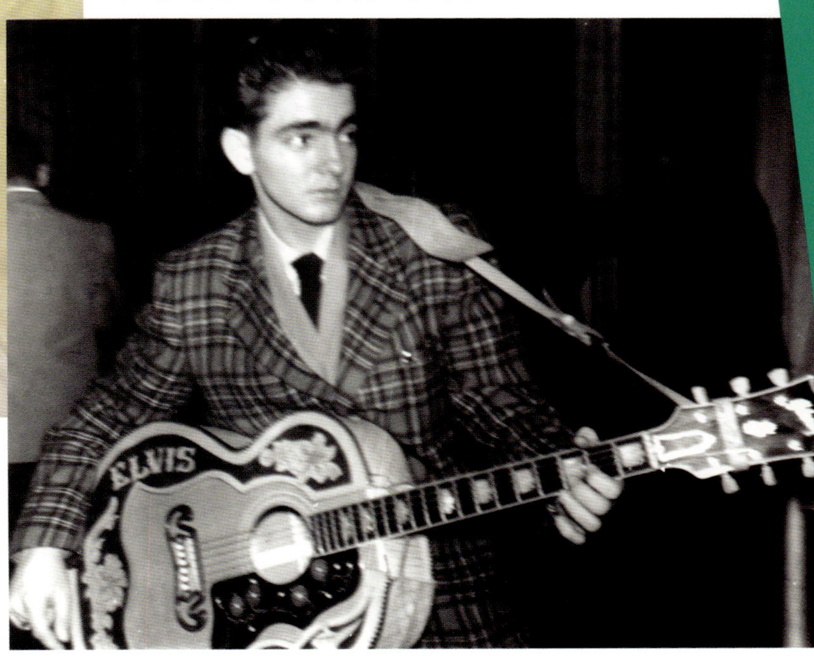

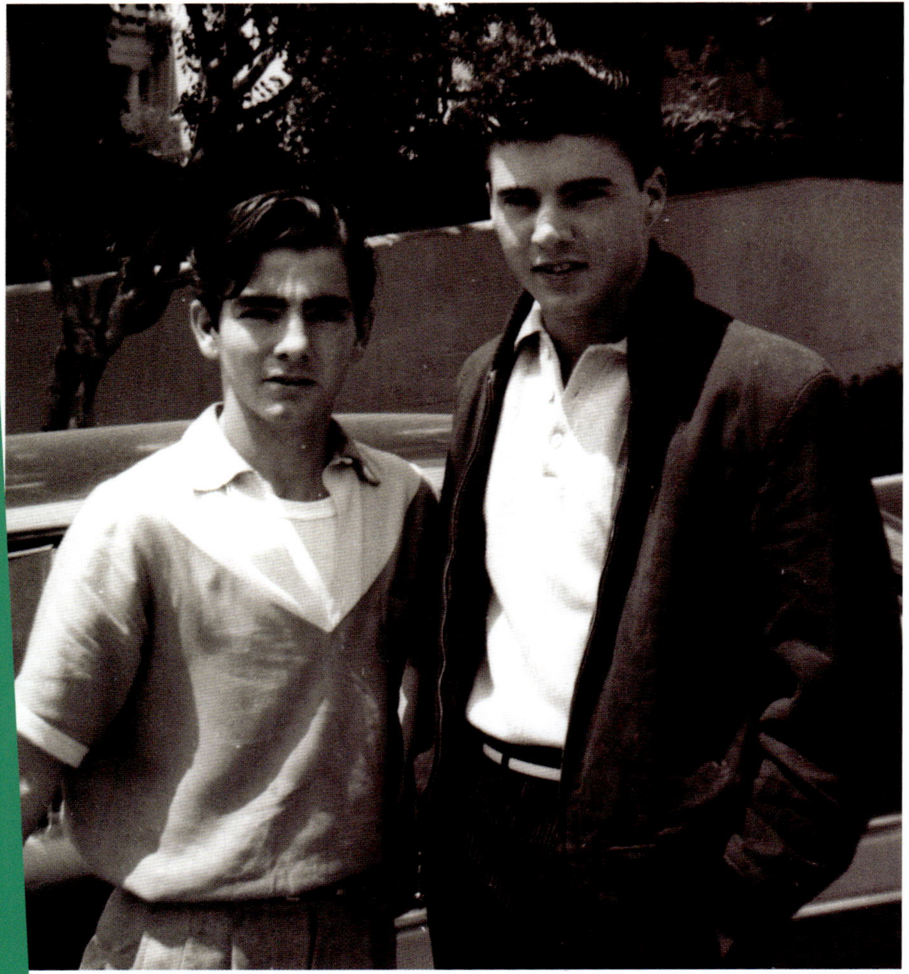

Rick Nelson in 1957

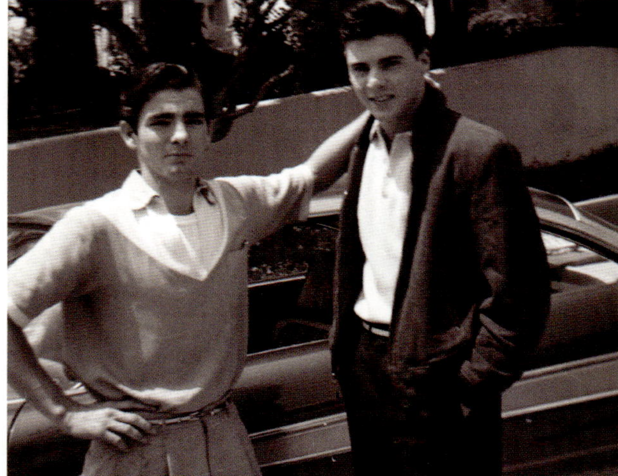

Rick's 1957 Plymouth Fury

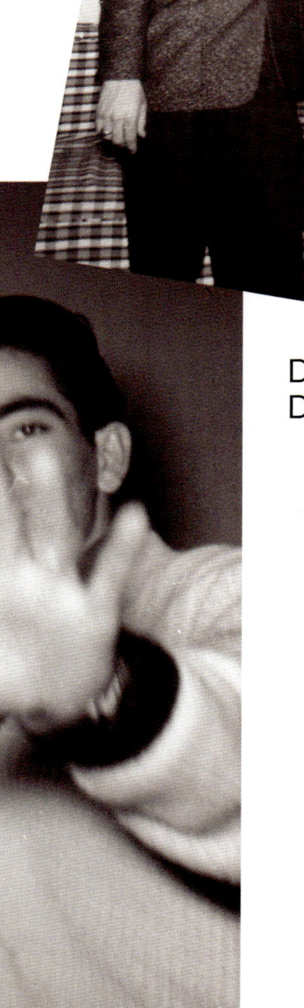

Dicky Doo of
Dicky Doo and the Don'ts

Billie Spang and *Tracy Pendarvis*

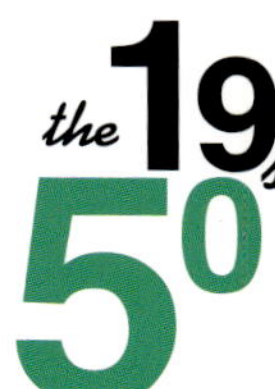

Jimmy Velvet The Early Days

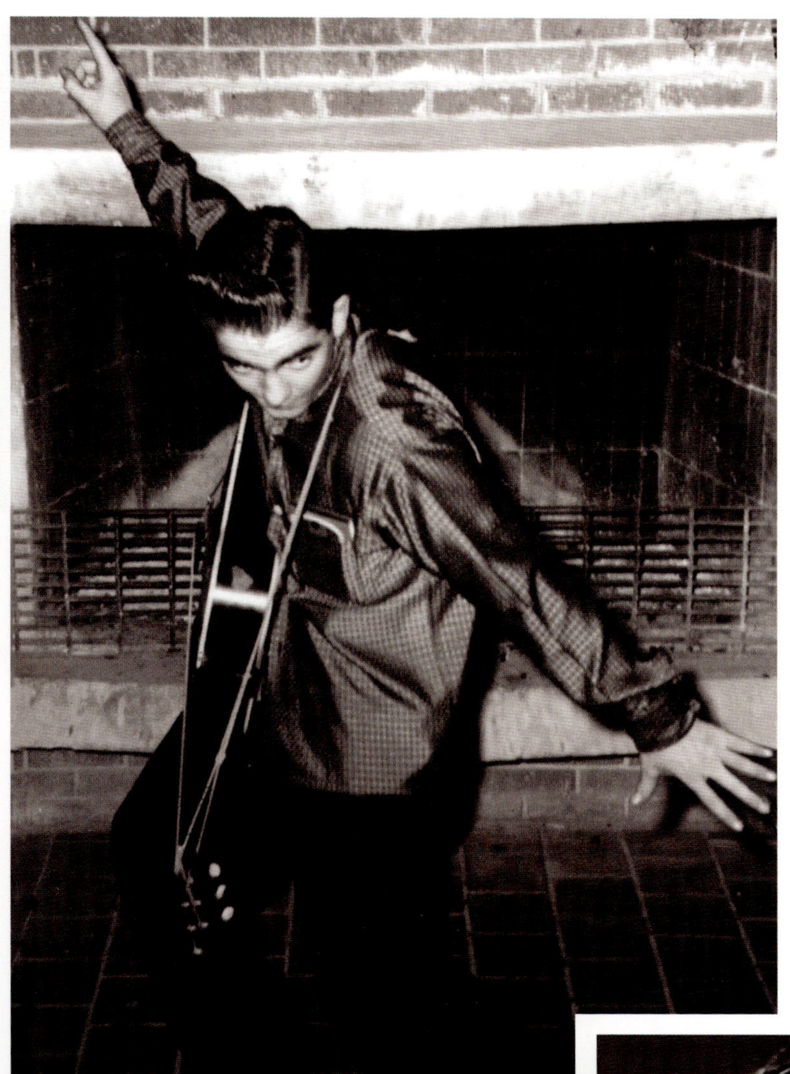

My first promo photo.
Thanks to my friend,
Richard Monsour

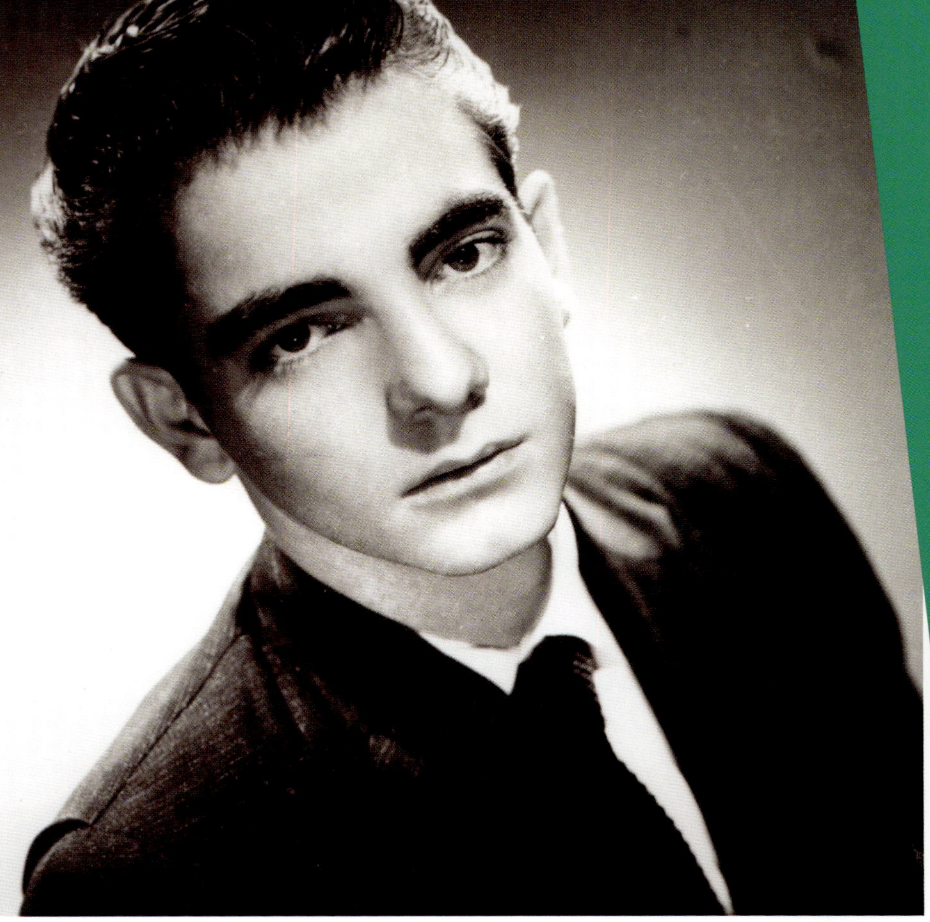

11125 South Wilton Place
Los Angeles, CA

JIMMIE TENNANT

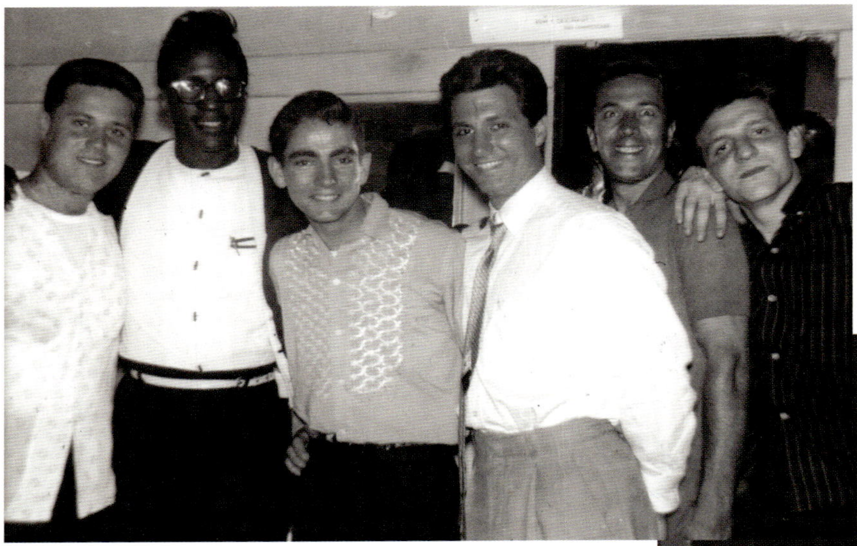

Laverne Baker

Screamin' Jay Hawkins
with Teddy Randazzo
and The 3 Chuckles

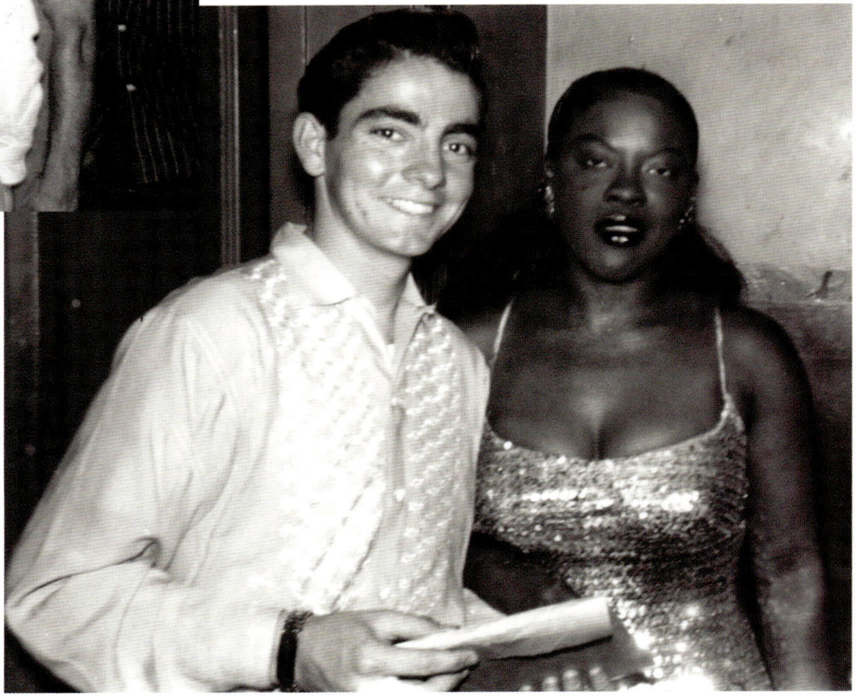

A few of my Cadillacs
in the late 50's

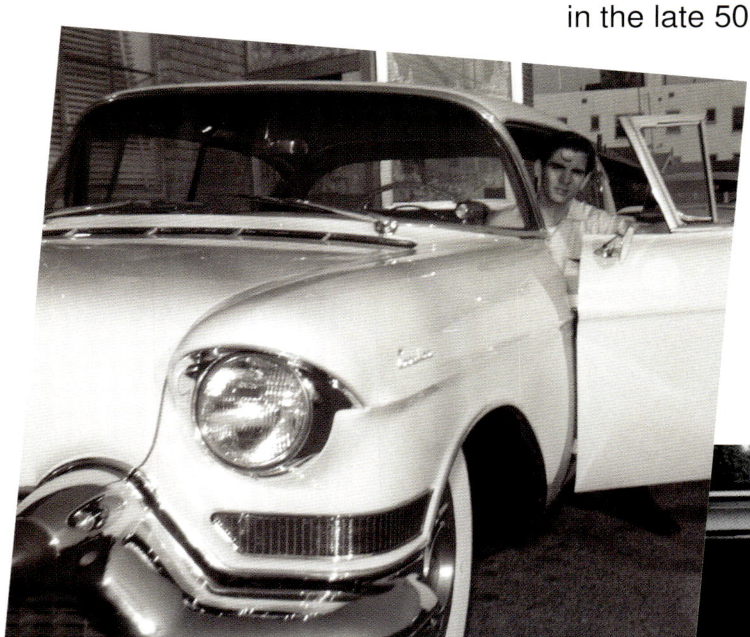

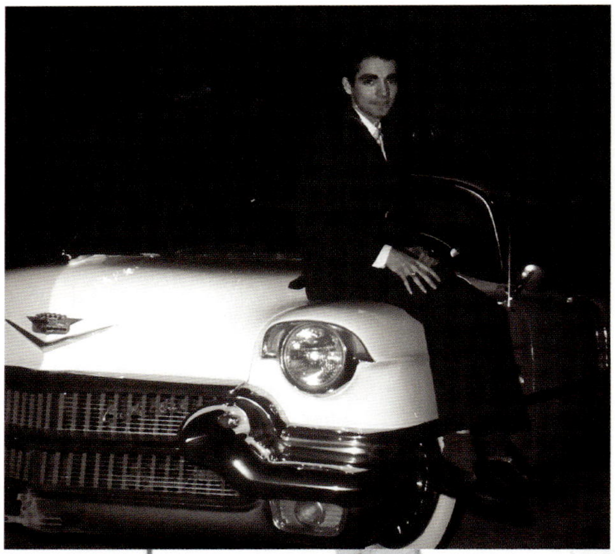

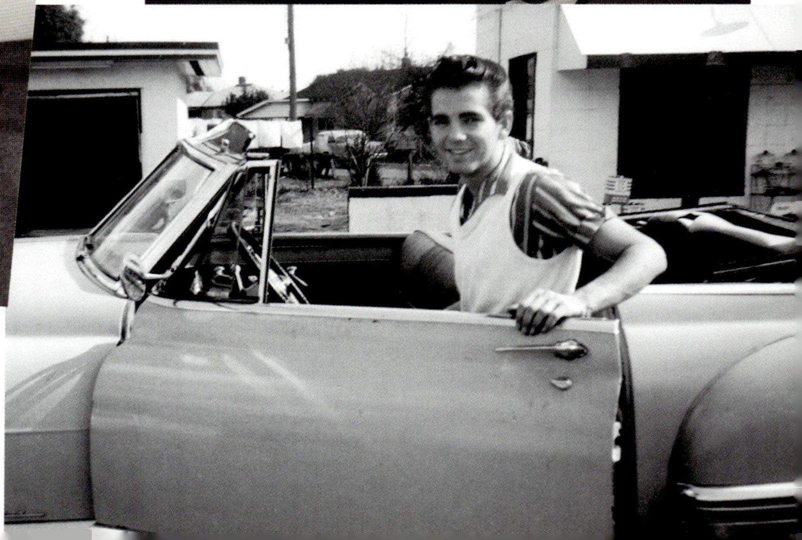

1958 on tour

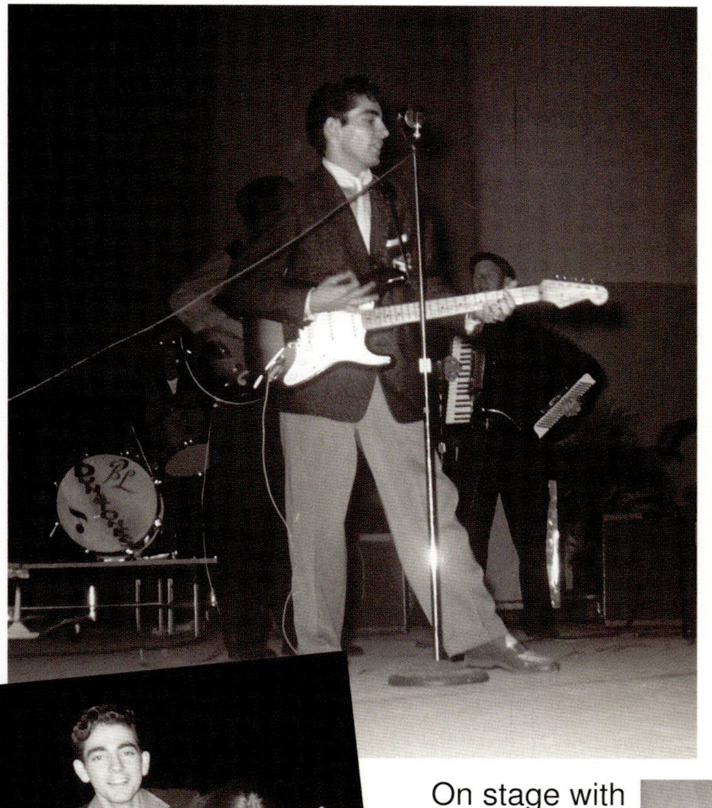

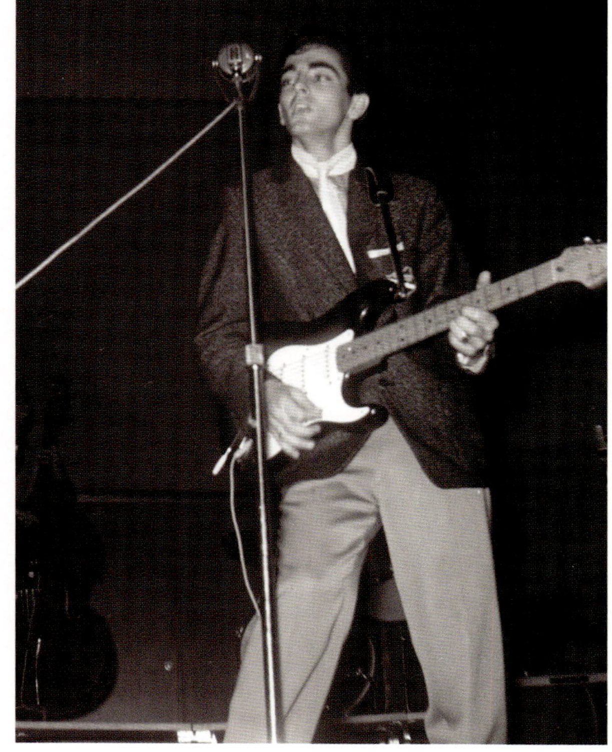

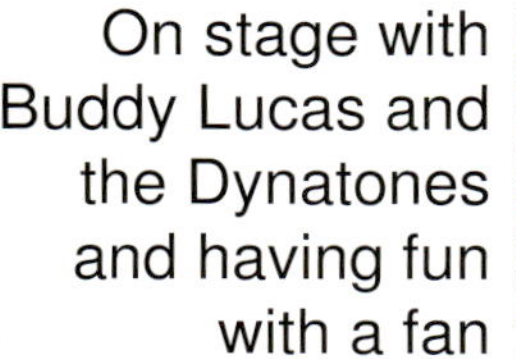

On stage with Buddy Lucas and the Dynatones and having fun with a fan

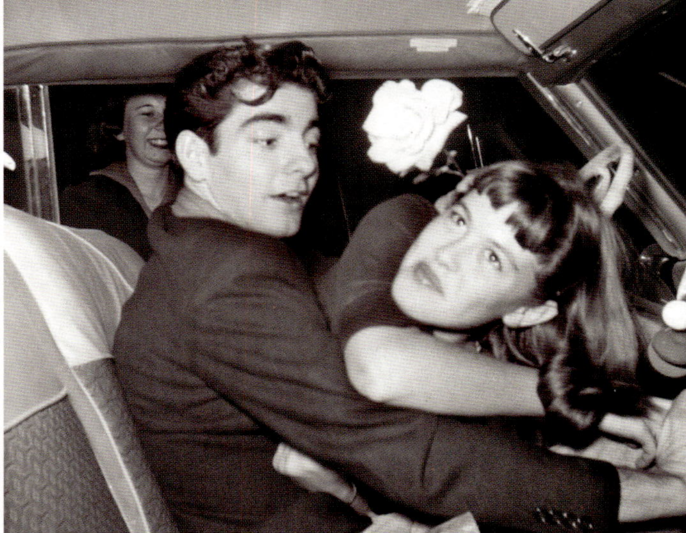

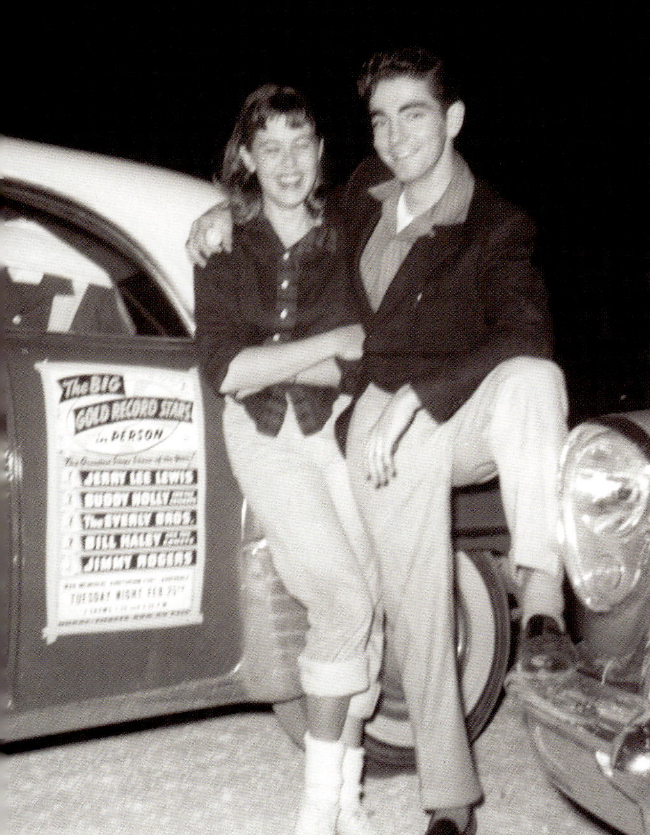

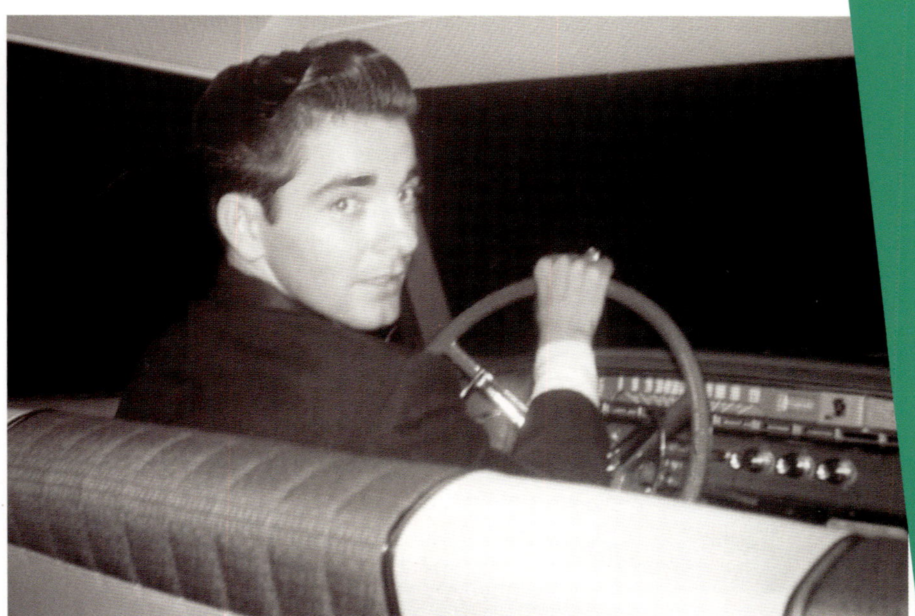

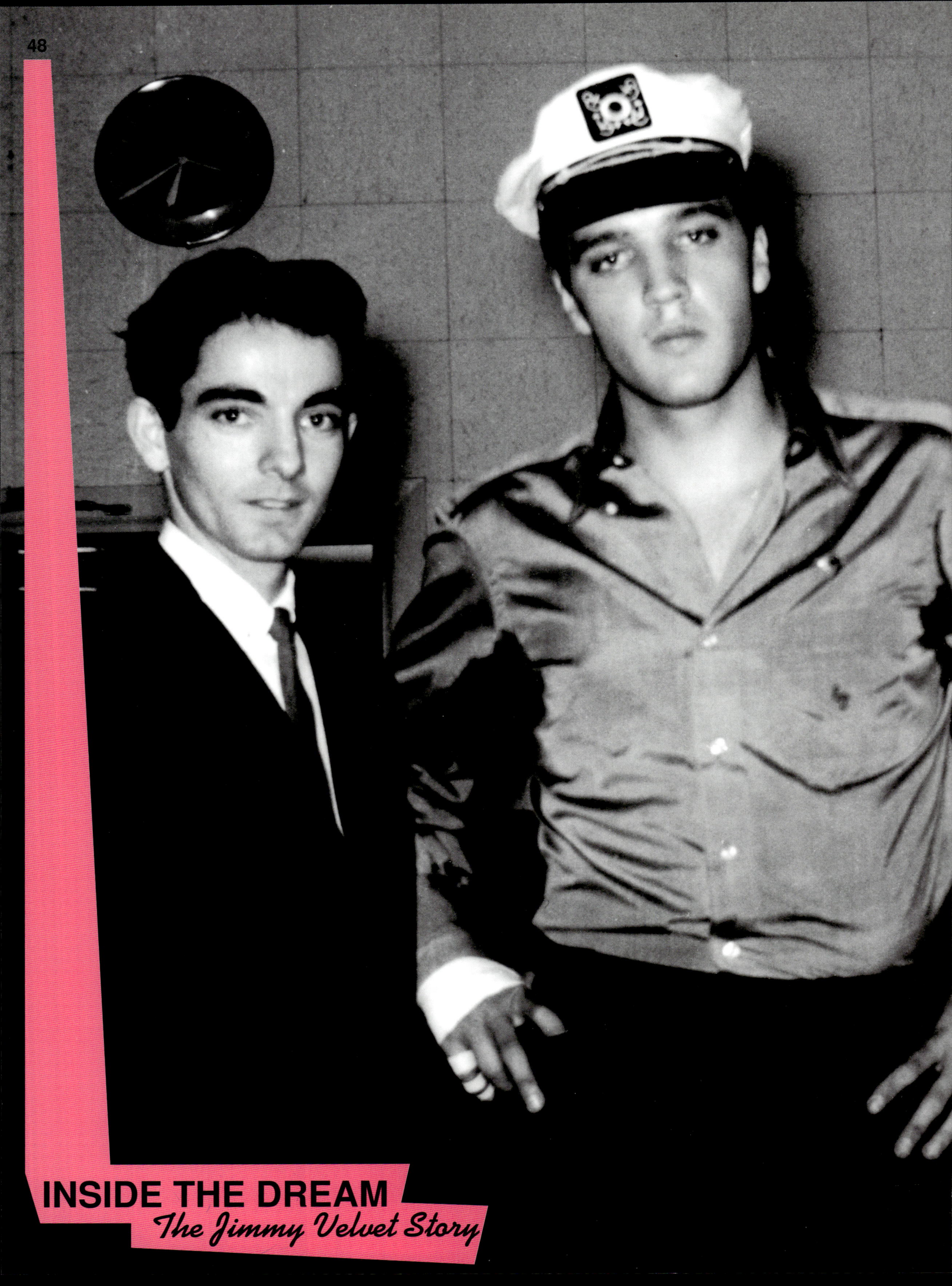

INSIDE THE DREAM
The Jimmy Velvet Story

the 1960s

I was starting the decade as a 20 year old who was determined to be a star. The 1960's were a most amazing time for this farm boy. This is also the time frame of my life when I legally had my name changed from Jimmy Tennant to Jimmy Velvet. I had a band named The Velvet-Tones and things were off to a good start. Meanwhile I made investments in Dallas and opened a fast food restaurant, Jimbo's Drive-In. I was also booking Jimmy Reed tours. One night Jimmy Reed became ill and his manager sent me a telegram saying that Jimmy would not be completing the tour. I lost everything at that point and went back to Jacksonville to my grandmother's home where I started to play shows again.

A couple of months went by and I met a man whom I will always cherish, Ray Curran. He was the manager of a country club in Jacksonville. I was playing a show at the club and the teenage girls really seemed to love my music, which impressed Ray. I'll never forget one night that Ray walked up to me and said that I needed to start recording again. While talking to me he counted out $100-dollar bills, handed them to me and told me to return to Nashville and cut a hit. I called Bill Justis to arrange the music and get prices from AFM (Musicians Union) and I hired the best Nashville offered: The Jordanaires, Prissy Reed, Chet Atkins, Jerry Reed, Kelso Herston, Jerry Kennedy, "Pig" Harcus and The Brenton Banks String Section. I recorded with them at RCA Studio B with Bill Porter as the Engineer.

While I waited to get a record deal, I worked at Shoneys on Thompson Lane in Nashville to save up some money. My manager decided to release the song "We Belong Together" on our own label but he spelled my name wrong using an "i" instead of an "e", Velvit. I quickly noted the error and we changed it for the next pressing. My name change became legal in 1965 right at the beginning of a Dick Clark Tour that I was on.

"We Belong Together" quickly became a big hit and flew to the top of the charts. It was #1 on the charts in Jacksonville for 5 weeks, #1 in Columbia, South Carolina for 17 weeks, and #1 in Baltimore for 5 weeks, just to name a few. I received many offers for the rights to release the single and chose to go with ABC Paramount. I was so excited to call Ray and tell him the great news. He informed me that he had just leased the song to Witch Records in Chicago. A court battle ensued, and ABC's Larry Newton and Felton Jarvis (A& R Director) had to go to court in Miami to fight for the rights against Witch Records. Witch won and I lost a major hit. My heart sank.

Soon I recorded "To The Aisle" (also at RCA Studio B) and ABC's Felton Jarvis produced it. I remember while I was recording, Fats Domino walked in. We talked for a while and even took pictures together.

At the end of one of my tours with Jay and The Americans, I bought a nightclub in Jamestown, NY, which was located inside the Hotel Jamestown. I named the club "The Jimmy Velvet Room" but later sold it back to the hotel to move to Hollywood, CA to work for Filmways at General Service Studios. I worked under Tommy Oliver and Dick Brown. Dick was Ava Gabor's husband. Filmways produced many top TV shows such as: Beverly Hillbillies, Petticoat Junction, Green Acres, Double Life of Henry Fife, The Addams Family and Mister Ed. I got to know all the cast and crews; it was an exciting time.

Next, my friend Tony Ferra, his wife and I developed a partnership for a USA Tour, Hollywood Cavalcade of Stars. I was the headliner; although, shortly after the tour began, one of the acts became instantly famous and their record went to #1. The act was Buffalo Springfield and the hit was "For What It's Worth". The members of the group were Stephen Stills, Neil Young, Richie Furay, Bruce Palmer, Dickie Davis, and Dewey Martin. The group later became Crosby, Stills, Nash, and Young. Dewey and I were old friends from Nashville where he was Faron Young's drummer and worked the Grand Ole Opry with Patsy Cline, Carl Perkins, Roy Orbison, and many more. The last show of this tour in 1966 was in Huntsville, Alabama. I loved it there, so I bought a house and built another lounge at a local mall. The lounge was The Velvet Room. I lived in Huntsville and continued to tour. Life was grand, as exciting and new opportunities kept coming. In 1967 I produced the Happening '67 Show for Dick Clark Productions. In 1969 I moved to Memphis for a while, then returned to Hollywood, CA for some tours.

During the 60's I worked with so many notable artists. I recorded two of my hits at Sam Phillips Studio: "It's Almost Tomorrow" and "Teen Angel". When I think back to Sam I remember this story: A couple of years earlier I was in Nashville on what is now known as Music Row. It was 10:15pm and I saw a three story house on fire. I heard a lady calling, "HELP! HELP!" I rushed into the house where I found that the voice was actually that of a mynah bird. I grabbed the cage and put the bird outside and made such a commotion alerting everyone on the 1st and 2nd floor. Sadly, I wasn't able to reach the 3rd floor where the owner of the house lived and she died that night. Her family was very grateful to me for trying to rescue everyone and offered me a monetary gift (which I refused), but when they offered me "Inky" the mynah bird, I couldn't refuse. The next night I was out with Sam and Judd Phillips, Jack "Cowboy" Clements, Billy Sherrill and Sally Wilbourn in Printers Alley, downtown Nashville. I brought Inky with me and Sam went nuts over him. I gave Inky to Sam. This bird could carry on whole conversations, not just mimic. Sam built Inky his own room at Sam's Memphis home and Inky was always king. During this time I was helping to build the Sam C. Phillips Studio in the Cumberland Lodge Building in Nashville, Tennessee.

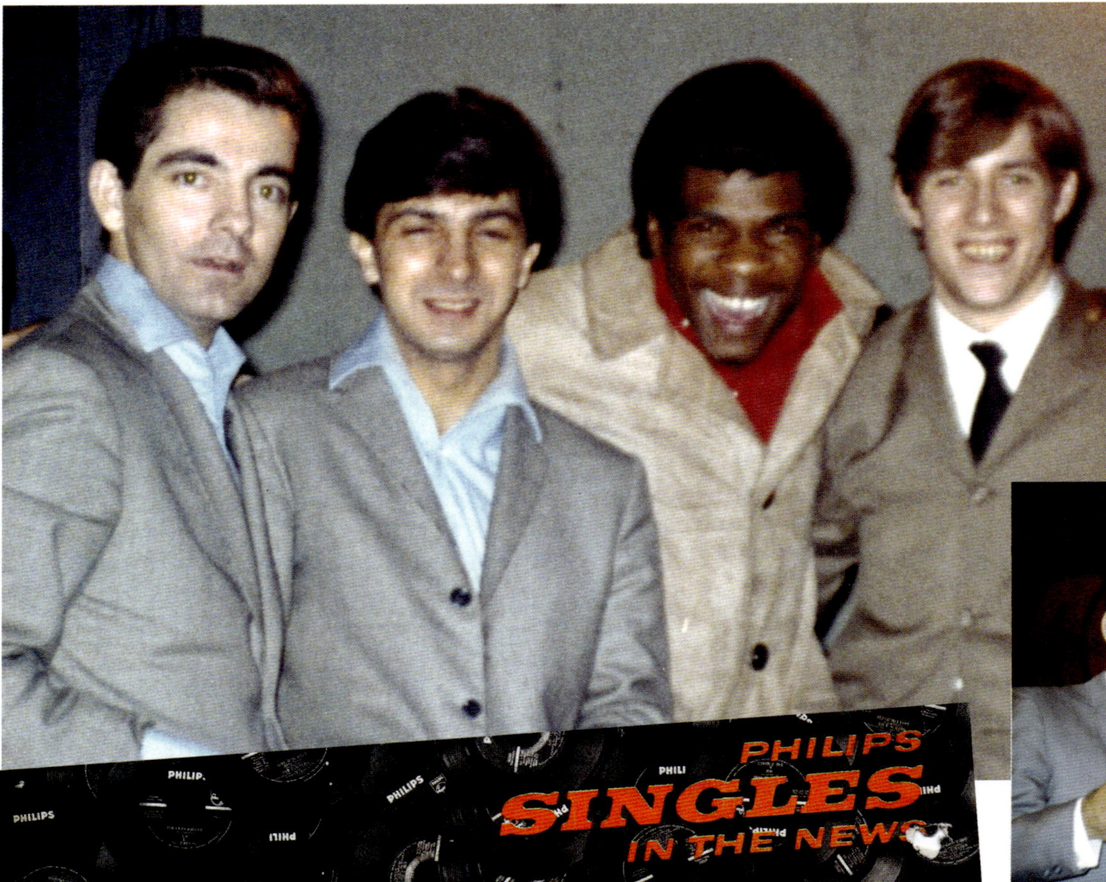

Billy Preston

Me, Gene, and Gare
with Billy Preston

PHILIPS
SINGLES IN THE NEWS

May 5, 1965

WE'RE GETTING THERE --- PLEASE STAY WITH IT

"IT'S ALMOST TOMORROW

BY: JIMMY VELVET - #40285

WCBS	-	NEW YORK, NEW YORK
WCAO	-	BALTIMORE, MARYLAND
WAMS	-	WILMINGTON, DELAWARE
WITH	-	BALTIMORE, MARYLAND
WCHA	-	CHAMBERSBURG, PA.
WIZE	-	SPRINGFIELD, OHIO
KBOX	-	DALLAS, TEXAS
WDRC	-	HARTFORD, CONNECTICUT
KNUZ	-	HOUSTON, TEXAS
KTSA	-	SAN ANTONIO, TEXAS
WKY	-	OKLAHOMA CITY, OKLA.
KELP	-	EL PASO, TEXAS
WQAM	-	MIAMI, FLORIDA
WHOO	-	ORLANDO, FLORIDA
KLIV	-	SAN JOSE, CALIFORNIA
WOLF	-	SYRACUSE, NEW YORK
WHYN	-	SPRINGFIELD, MASS.
KMAK	-	FRESNO, CALIFORNIA
KNAK	-	SALT LAKE CITY, UTAH
WFOM	-	MARIETTA, GEORGIA
KIMN	-	DENVER, COLORADO
WPDQ	-	JACKSONVILLE, FLA.
WNDR	-	SYRACUSE, NEW YORK
WHOT	-	YOUNGSTOWN, OHIO
WQXI	-	ATLANTA, GEORGIA
WICE	-	PROVIDENCE, R. I.
WBZ	-	BOSTON, MASSACHUSETTS
KLAC	-	LOS ANGELES, CALIF.
KOGO	-	SAN DIEGO, CALIF.
KYOK	-	HOUSTON, TEXAS
WOKY	-	MILWAUKEE, WISCONSIN
WIP	-	PHILADELPHIA, PA.
WGH	-	NEWPORT NEWS, VA.
WEED	-	ROCKY MOUNT, N. C.
WMCA	-	NEW YORK, NEW YORK
WORC	-	WORCESTER, MASS.
WIBG	-	PHILADELPHIA, PA.
WLAN	-	LANCASTER, PA.
WDXY	-	SUMTER, SOUTH CAROLINA
WNOE	-	NEW ORLEANS, LOUISIANA
KLIF	-	DALLAS, TEXAS
KOLE	-	PORT ARTHUR, TEXAS
KAYC	-	BEAUMONT, TEXAS
KONO	-	SAN ANTONIO, TEXAS
KELI	-	TULSA, OKLAHOMA
WHSL	-	WILMINGTON, N. C.
WFUN	-	MIAMI, FLORIDA
WLCY	-	ST. PETERSBURG, FLA.
WWDC	-	WASHINGTON, D. C.
WACK	-	NEWARK, NEW YORK
WICC	-	BRIDGEPORT, CONN.
KMBY	-	MONTEREY, CALIF.
WSGN	-	BIRMINGHAM, ALABAMA
KDKA	-	PITTSBURGH, PA.
KMPC	-	LOS ANGELES, CALIF.
WCAU	-	PHILADELPHIA, PA.
WSAY	-	ROCHESTER, NEW YORK
WBBQ	-	AUGUSTA, GEORGIA
WLAY	-	SHEFFIELD, ALABAMA
WKAP	-	ALLENTOWN, PA.
WMEX	-	BOSTON, MASSACHUSETTS
KAPT	-	SALEM, OREGON
KNOK	-	FORT WORTH, TEXAS
WSB	-	ATLANTA, GEORGIA
WAKR	-	AKRON, OHIO
WPEN	-	PHILADELPHIA, PA.
WBAX	-	WILKES-BARRE, PA.
KILT	-	HOUSTON, TEXAS

PHILIPS RECORDS • 35 EAST WACKER DRIVE • CHICAGO, ILLINOIS 60601

Casey Casem

and I on the Shebang TV Show

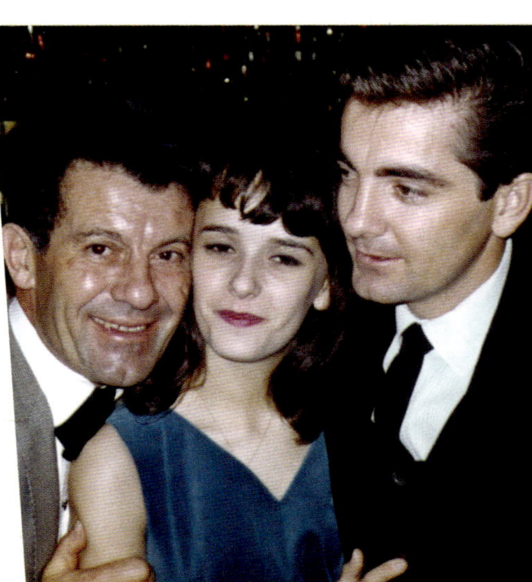

Tony Ferra, Pam
Newland, and Jimmy
Velvet

"Its Almost Tommorrow"
Breaking Nationwide May 5, 1965

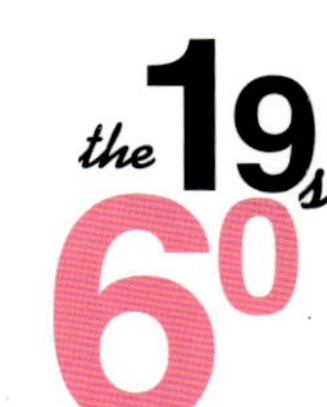

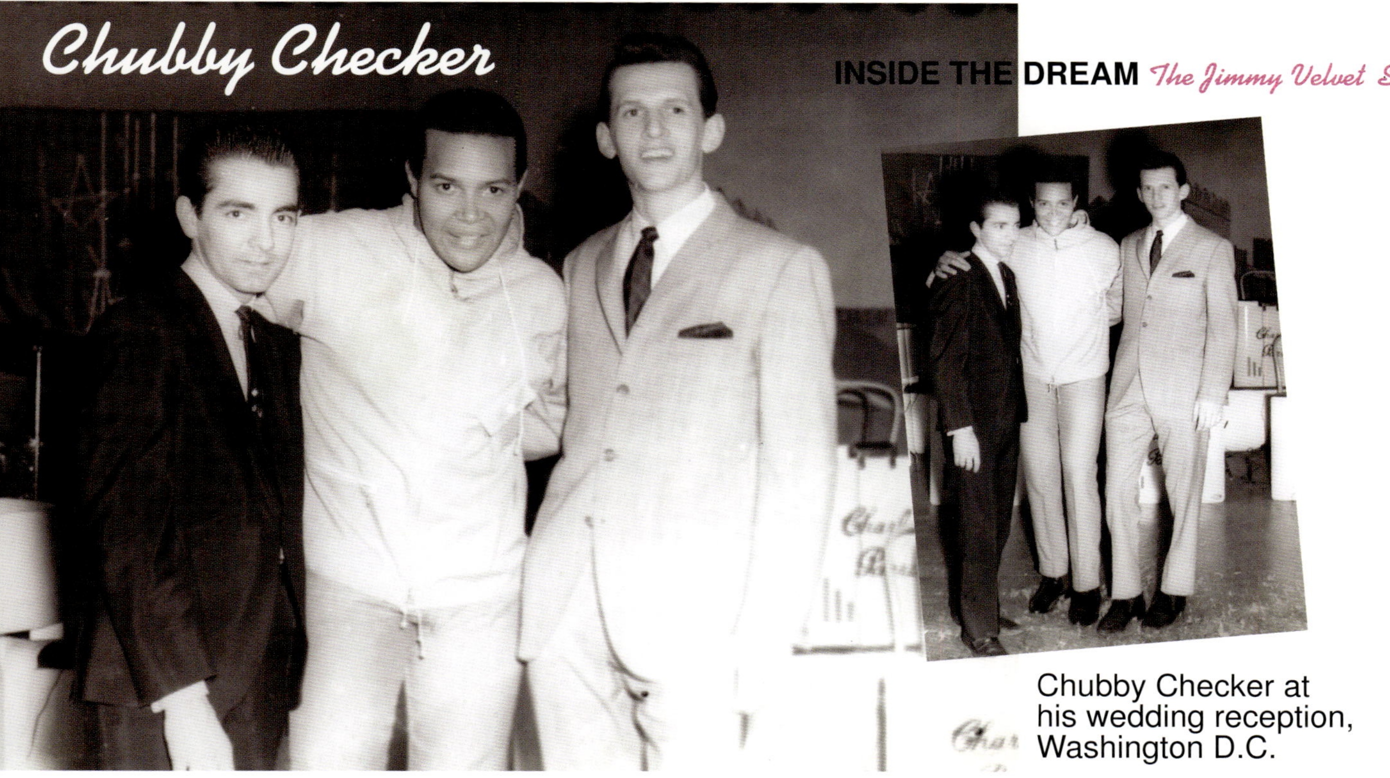

Chubby Checker at his wedding reception, Washington D.C.

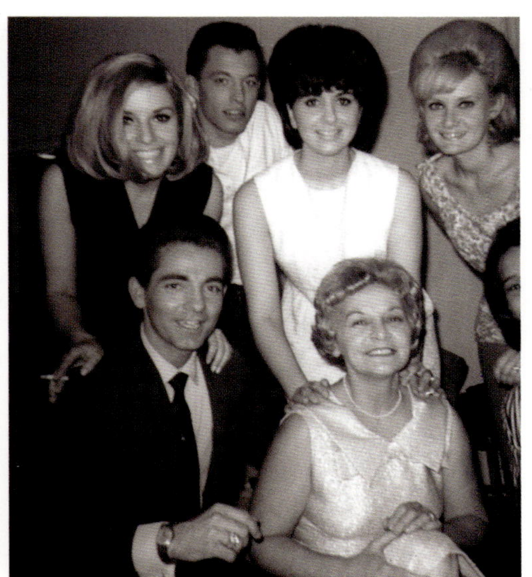

The Angels, Barry Darvell, my mother and I.

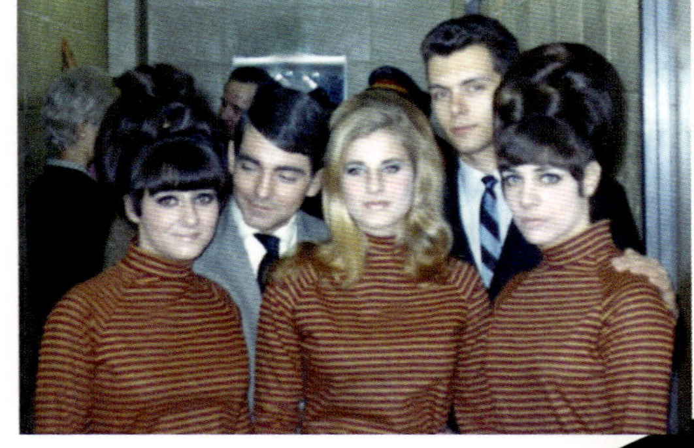

"The Angels" Jersey Girls I loved working with these girls.

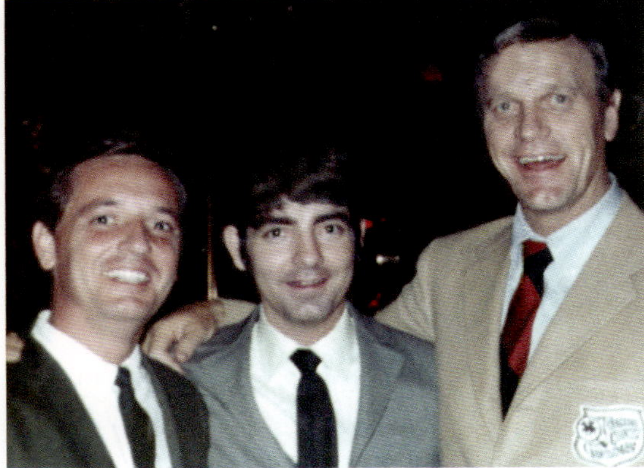

Amon Carter Evans and Eddy Arnold

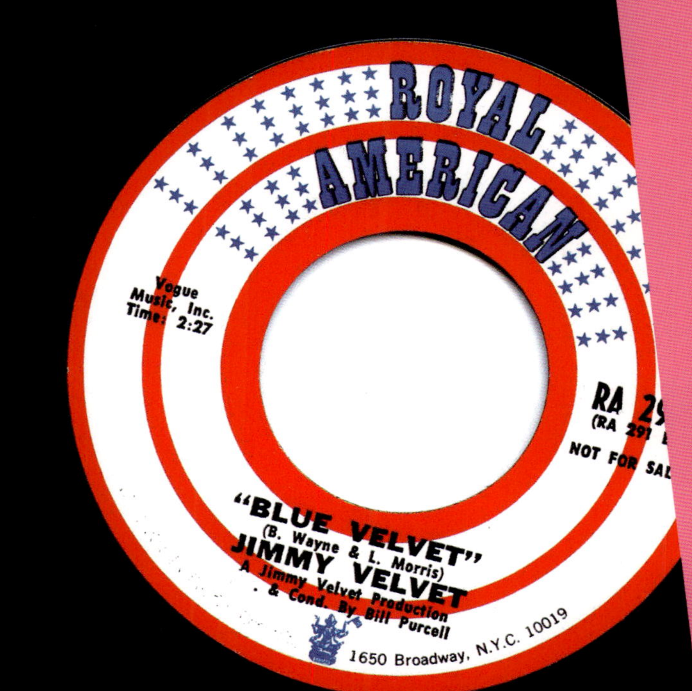

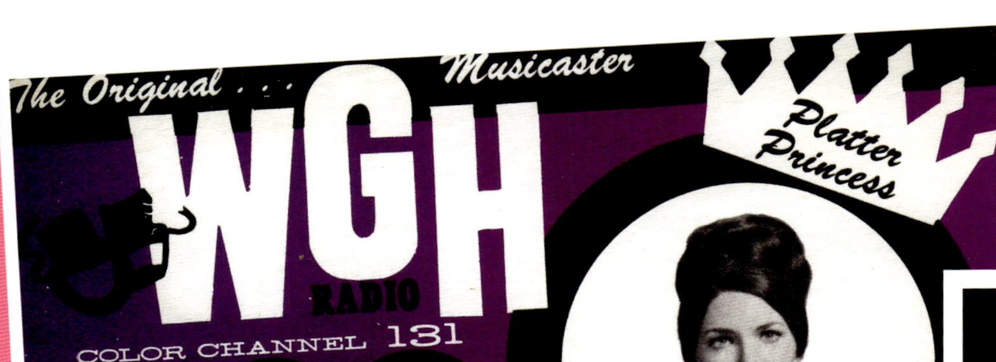

"It's Almost Tommorrow" #22
Norfolk, VA Beach

THE ORIGINAL OFFICIAL **TOP THIRTY**

1. HELP ME RHONDA . . . . The Beach Boys
2. TICKET TO RIDE/YES IT IS . . . . . The Beatles
3. SHE'S ABOUT A MOVER . . . Sir Douglas Quintet
4. LAND OF A THOUSAND DANCES . . . . Cannibal & The Headhunters
5. I'LL NEVER FIND ANOTHER YOU . The Seekers
6. CAST YOUR FATE TO THE WIND . . . . Sounds Orchestral
7. x COUNT ME IN . . . . Gary Lewis & The Playboys
8. WOOLY BULLY . . . . Sam The Sham
9. BABY THE RAIN MUST FALL . . Glen Yarbrough
10. REELIN & ROCKIN . . . . Dave Clark Five
11. BACK IN MY ARMS AGAIN . . . . . . The Supremes
12. CRYING IN THE CHAPEL . . . . . . Elvis Presley
13. JUST A LITTLE . . . . The Beau Brummels
14. ENGINE, ENGINE # 9 . . . . Roger Miller
15. SILHOUETTES . . . . Herman's Hermits
16. I KNOW A PLACE . . . . Petula Clark
17. IT'S NOT UNUSUAL . . . . Tom Jones
18. I'LL BE DOGGONE . . . . Marvin Gaye
19. TRUE LOVE WAYS . . . . Peter & Gordon
20. MRS. BROWN YOU GOT A LOVELY DAUGHTER . . . . Herman's Hermits
21. CONCRETE & CLAY . . . . Eddie Rambeau
22. x IT'S ALMOST TOMORROW . . . . . . Jimmy Velvet
23. x IT'S PARADISE . . . . The Showmen
24. x IT'S GONNA BE ALRIGHT . . . . Gerry & The Pacemakers
25. IKO IKO . . . . Dixie Cups
26. QUEEN OF THE HOUSE . . . . Jody Miller
27. THREE O'CLOCK IN THE MORNING . . . . Bert Kaempfert
28. DO THE FREDDIE . . . . Freddie & The Dreamers
29. YOU WERE MADE FOR ME . . . . Freddie & The Dreamers
30. x LAST CHANCE TO TURN AROUND . Gene Pitney

WGH FEATURED FIVE ALBUMS

THE BEACH BOY'S TODAY . . . . . . The Beach Boys
THIS DIAMOND RING . . . Gary Lewis & The Playboys
GIRL HAPPY . . . . Elvis Presley
RETURN OF ROGER MILLER . . . . Roger Miller
INTRO. HERMAN'S HERMITS . . . . Herman's Hermits

x Denotes Former Wax To Watch

WGH RADIO
Pulse Rated No. 1 - - 7 Consecutive Years
Norfolk. . . Portsmouth. . . Newport News
Hampton. . . Virginia Beach. . . Chesapeake

May 23, 1965

wax to watch PICKED BY

"Cara Mia"
by
Jay & The Americans

Dick L

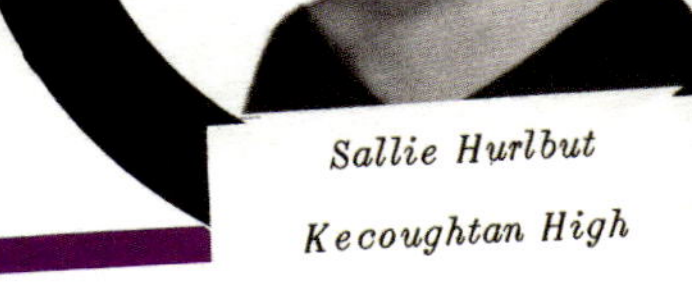

Sallie Hurlbut
Kecoughtan High

BERRY AND TILLOTSON HEADLINE NEXT BIG SHOW

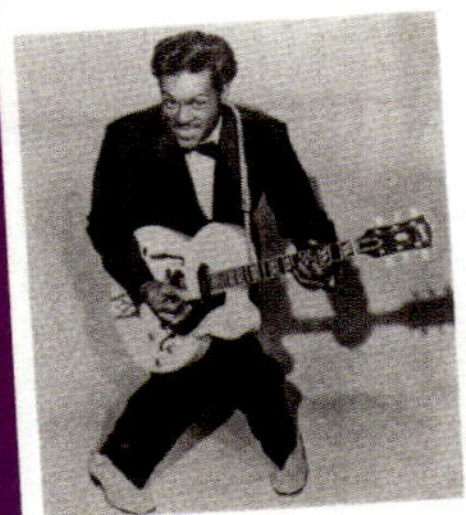

CHUCK BERRY and JOH NY TILLOTSON will l the next troop of stars i the Virginia Beach DC for WGH on SATURD MAY 29th. The Big Me ial Day Weekend show also include THE ANG THE ORLONS, JI VELVET, BARRY D VELL and many more.

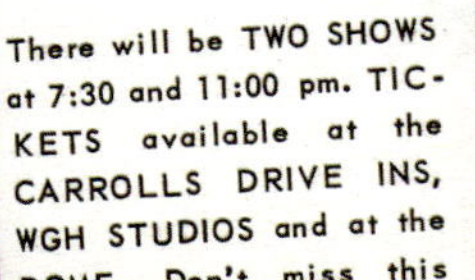

There will be TWO SHOWS at 7:30 and 11:00 pm. TICKETS available at the CARROLLS DRIVE INS, WGH STUDIOS and at the DOME. Don't miss this

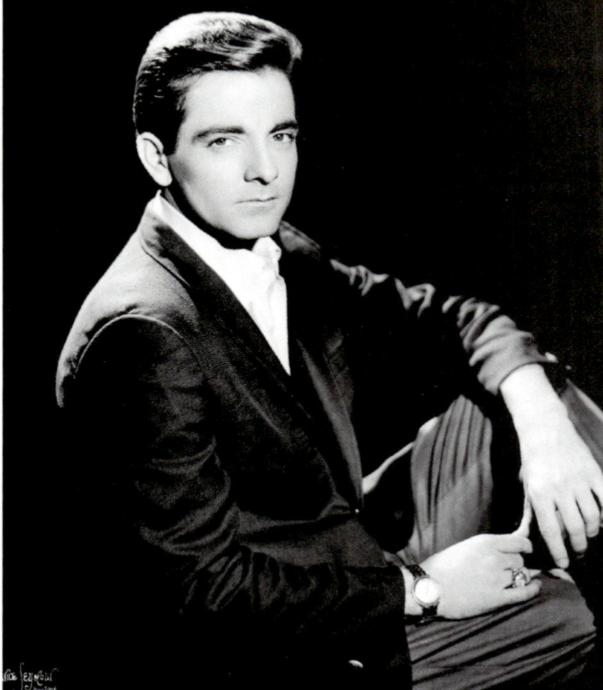

JIMMY VELVET

Personal Direction
SAM GONDON

Exclusive Management
WILLIAM MORRIS AGENCY

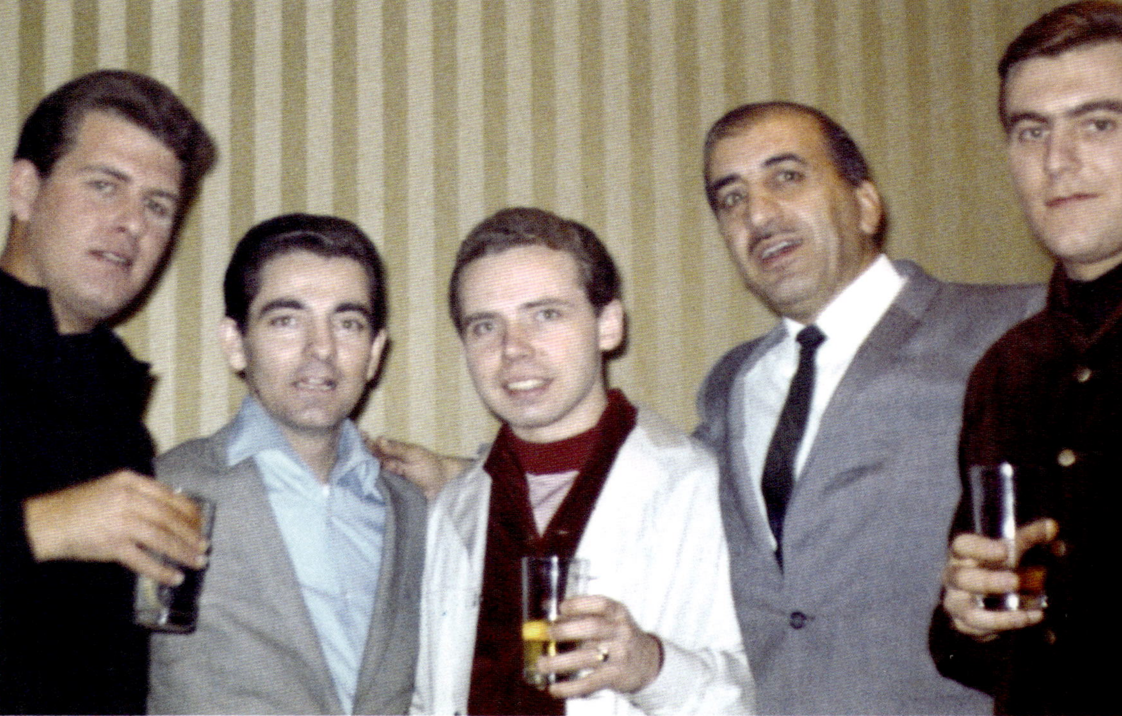

Len Berry, myself, Barry White, Dave White and Ray Gilmour

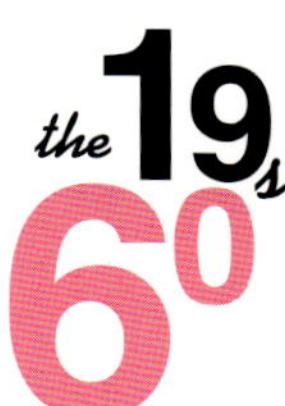

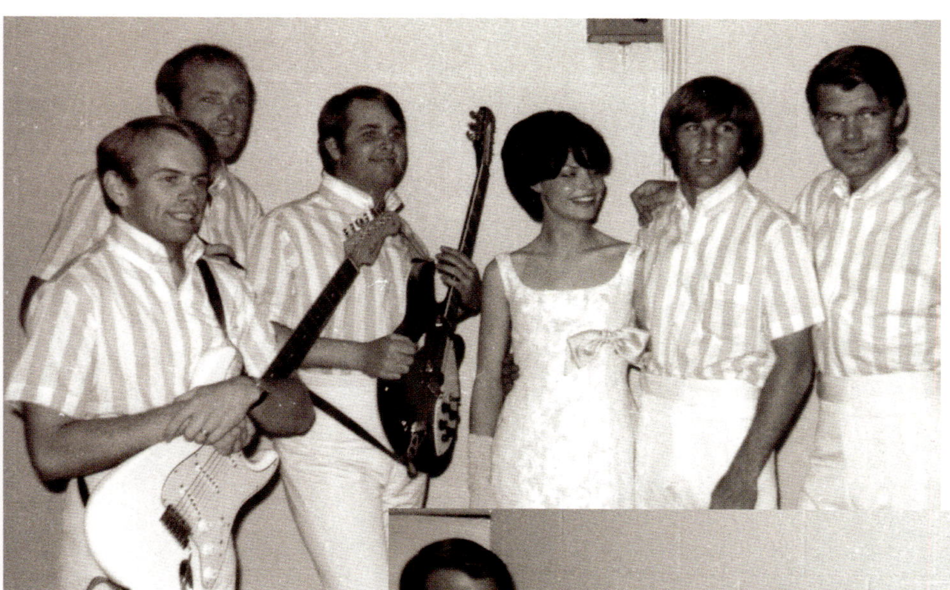

Beach Boys with
Glen Campbell

Glen Campbell,
Al Jardine, Carl Wilson,
Pam, Dennis WIlson,
Me and Mike Love

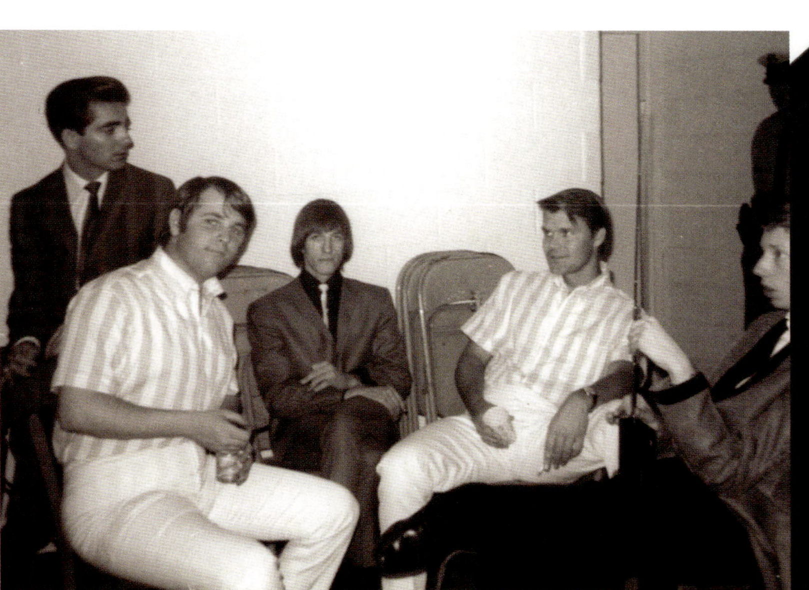

Me, Carl Wilson, Glen Campbell.
Back Seated: Doug Sham "Sir
Douglas Quintet"

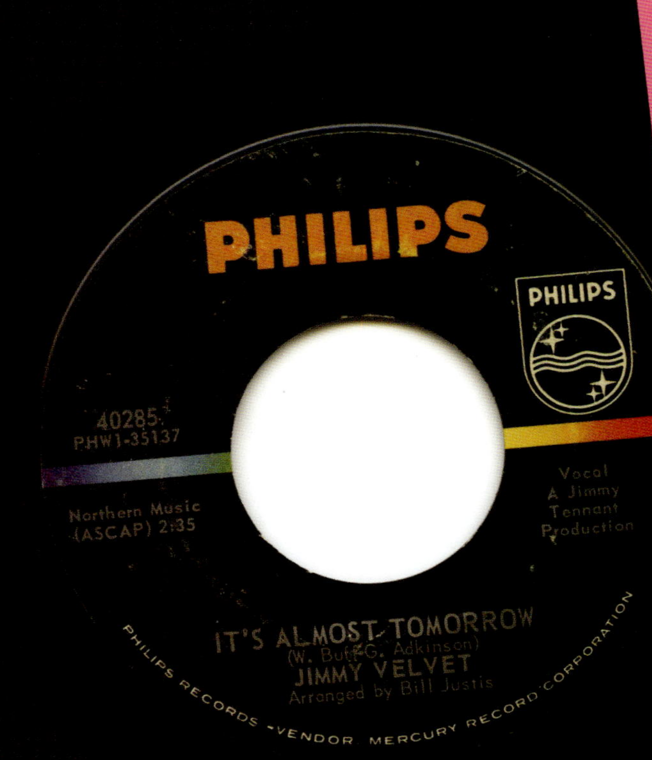

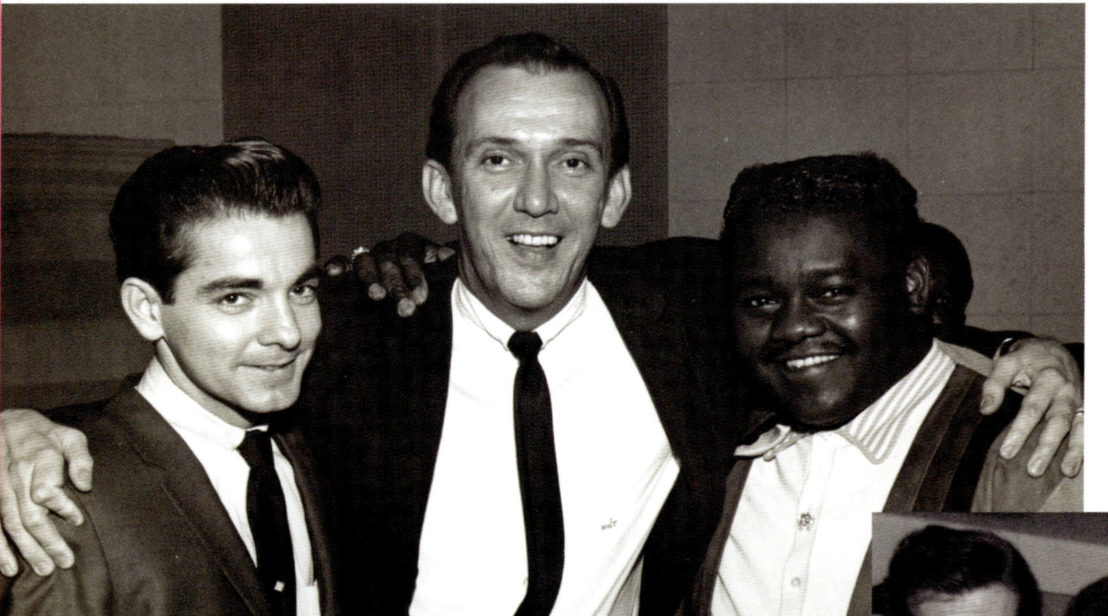

Hugh Jarrett and Fats Domino

Fats Domino

came to visit me at my recording session, 1963 RCA Studio B. Hugh Jarrett was one of The Jordanaires and a D.J. at WPLO in Atlanta.

George Hamilton and Diane

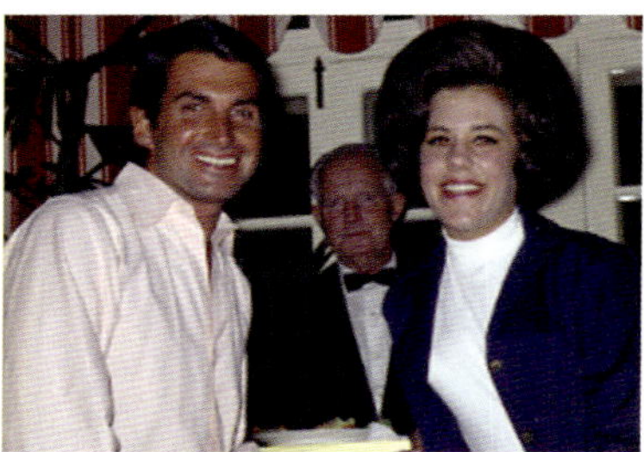

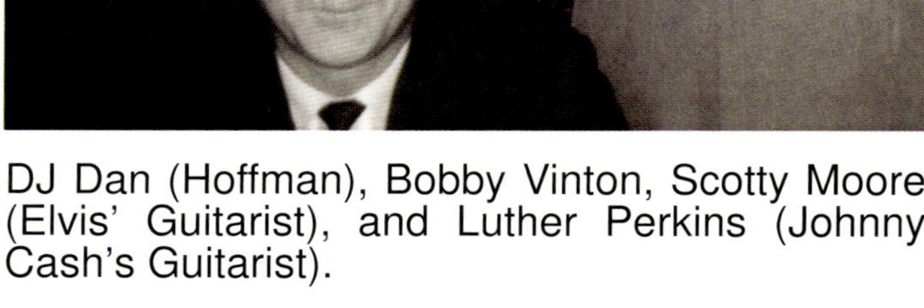

DJ Dan (Hoffman), Bobby Vinton, Scotty Moore (Elvis' Guitarist), and Luther Perkins (Johnny Cash's Guitarist).

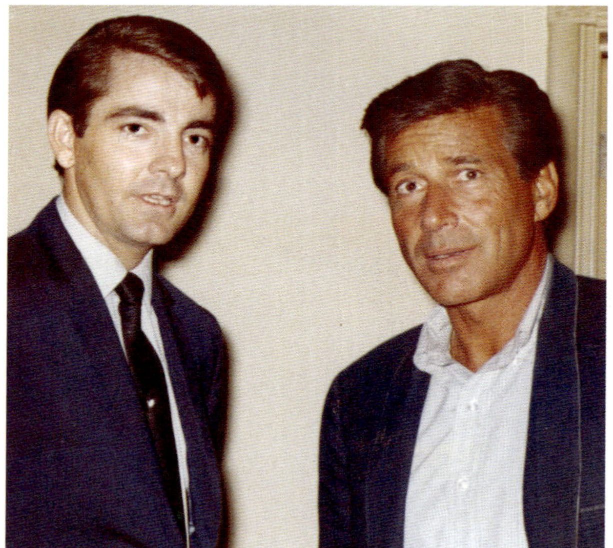

Efrem Zimbalist, Jr.

Eddie Hodges

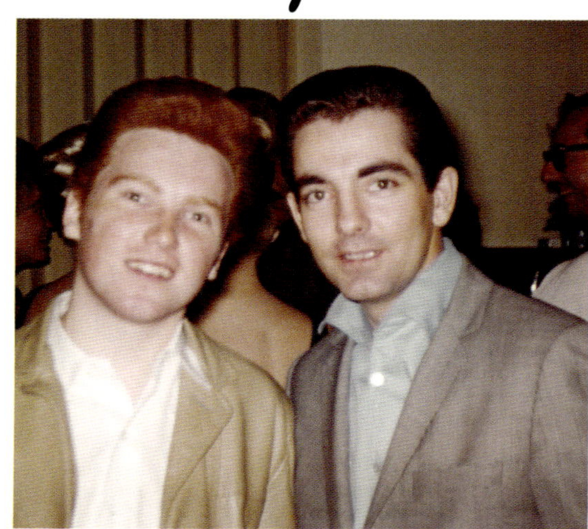

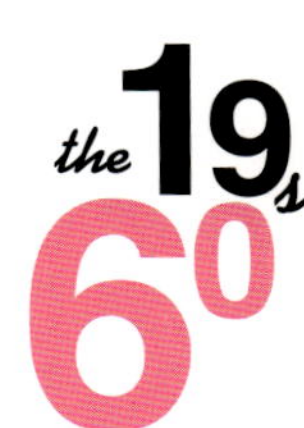

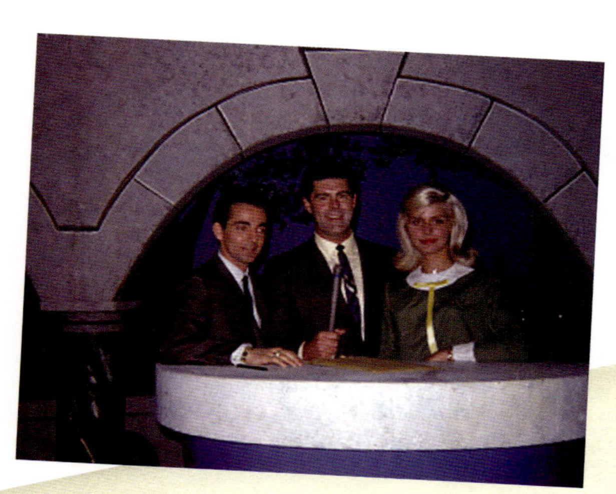

Bob Braun TV Show
Cincinatti, Ohio

dick clark productions
345 WEST 58TH STREET, NEW YORK, NEW YORK
TELEPHONE: 765-2550

May 19,1965

Sam Gordon
25 Ehrbar Ave.
Mt. Vernon,
N.Y.

Dear Sam,

Don't forget, California taping has been set up for June 2nd for Brian and Velvet. They should be there on June 1st and call Roz at the office.

Regards,

Tim Tormey

TT/bh

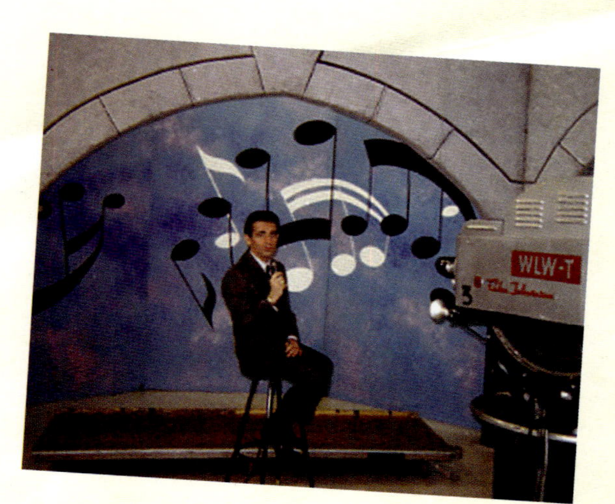

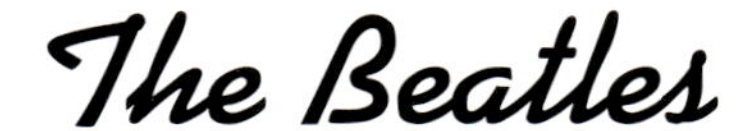

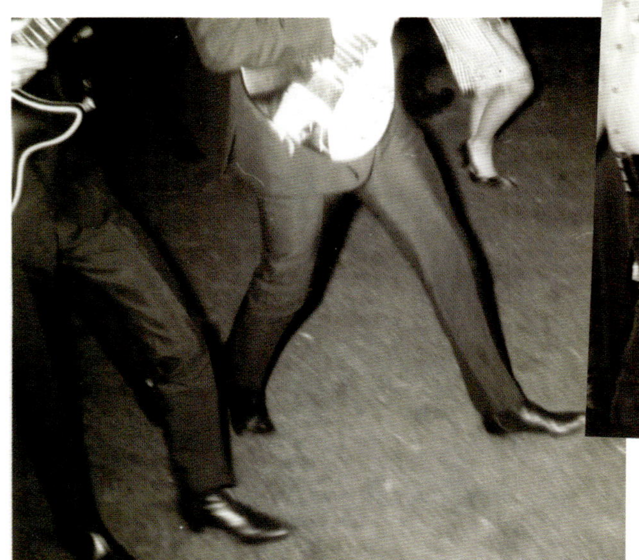

A fan bumped me while I was taking this photo and that is why I only got their feet.

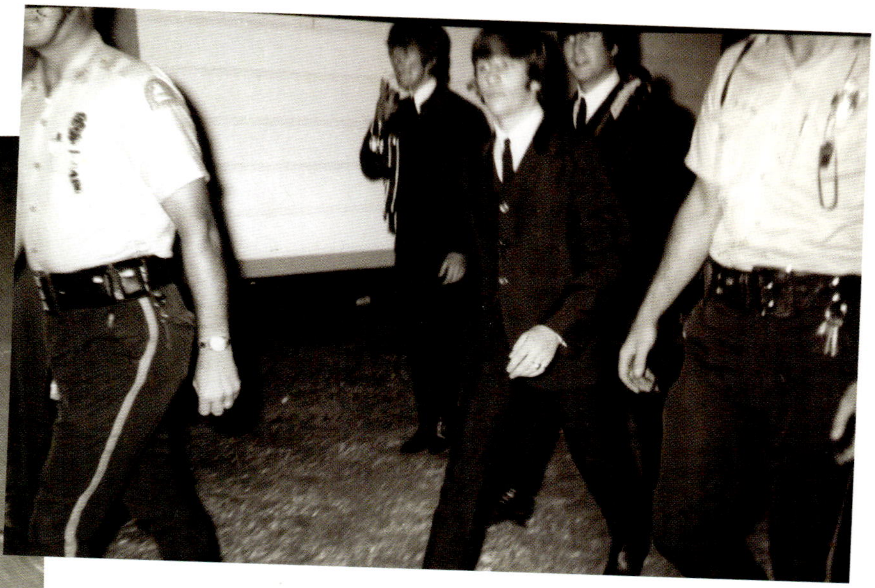

I met The Beatles in 1964 at the Gator Bowl. I only took two photos.

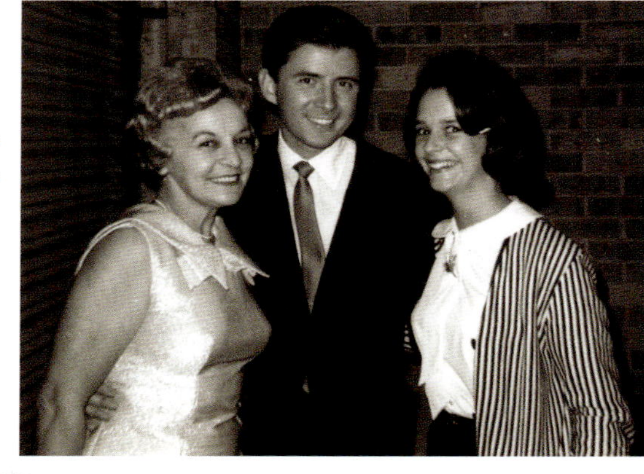

My mother and Pam with Johnny Tillotson. I grew up with Johnny.

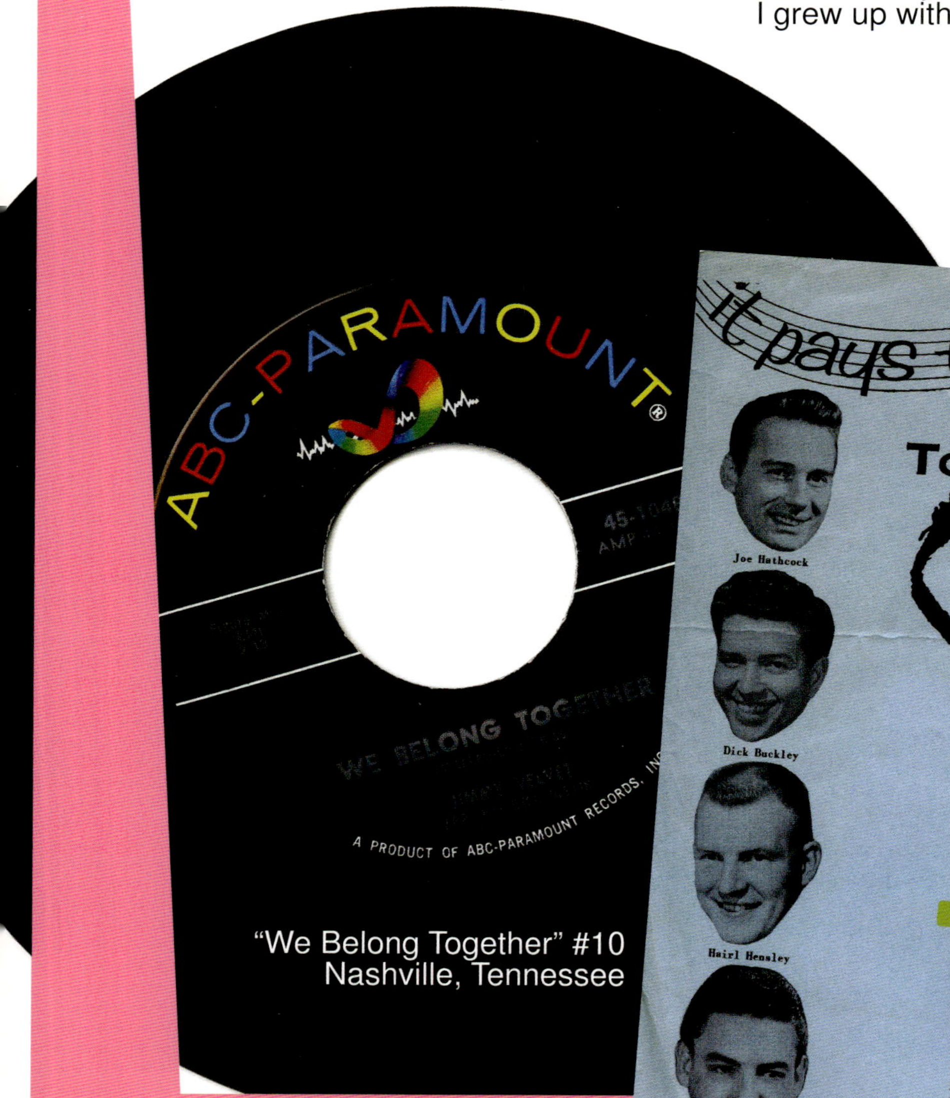

ABC-PARAMOUNT

WE BELONG TOGETHER

A PRODUCT OF ABC-PARAMOUNT RECORDS, INC.

"We Belong Together" #10
Nashville, Tennessee

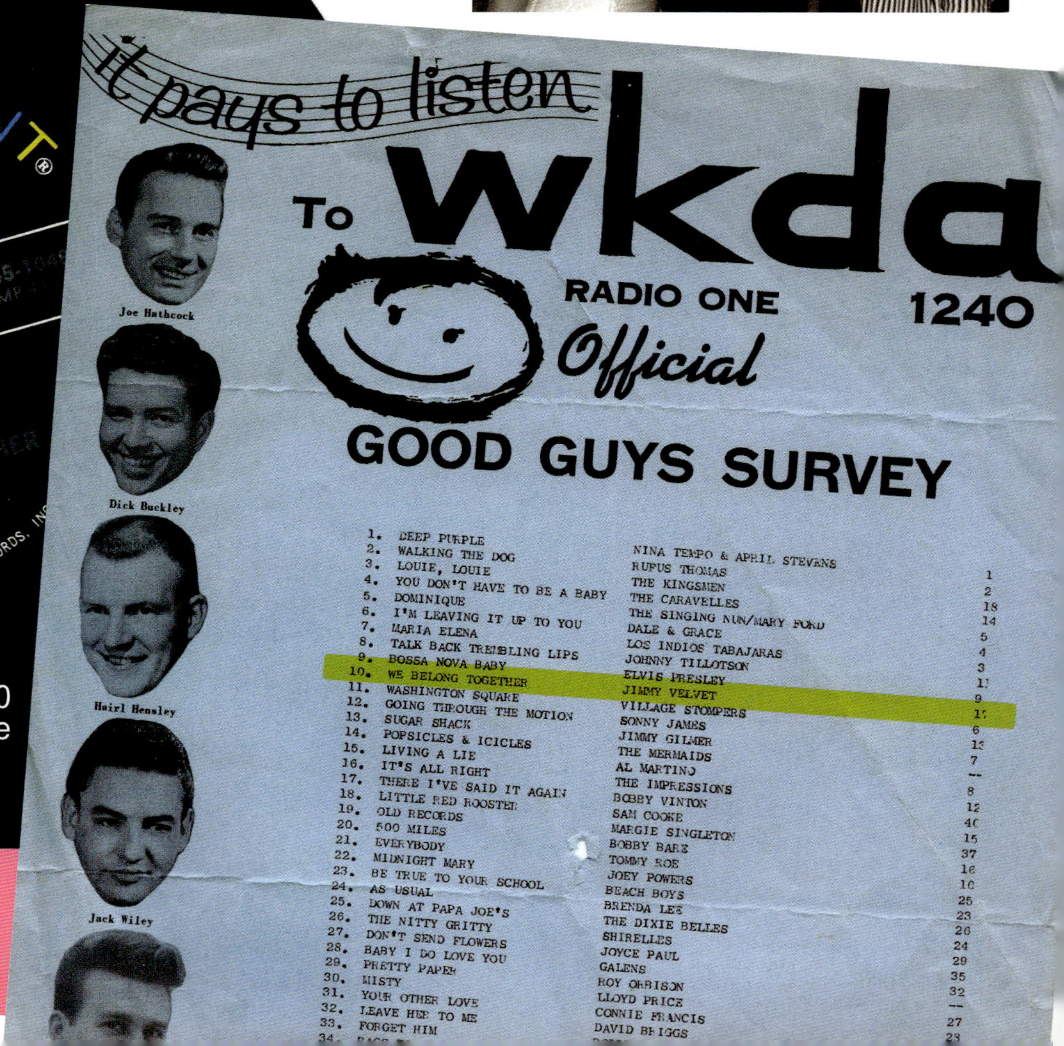

it pays to listen

To wkda

RADIO ONE 1240

Official

GOOD GUYS SURVEY

Joe Hathcock

Dick Buckley

Hairl Hensley

Jack Wiley

1.	DEEP PURPLE	NINA TEMPO & APRIL STEVENS	1
2.	WALKING THE DOG	RUFUS THOMAS	2
3.	LOUIE, LOUIE	THE KINGSMEN	18
4.	YOU DON'T HAVE TO BE A BABY	THE CARAVELLES	14
5.	DOMINIQUE	THE SINGING NUN/MARY FORD	5
6.	I'M LEAVING IT UP TO YOU	DALE & GRACE	4
7.	MARIA ELENA	LOS INDIOS TABAJARAS	3
8.	TALK BACK TREMBLING LIPS	JOHNNY TILLOTSON	1[illegible]
9.	BOSSA NOVA BABY	ELVIS PRESLEY	9
10.	WE BELONG TOGETHER	JIMMY VELVET	1[illegible]
11.	WASHINGTON SQUARE	VILLAGE STOMPERS	6
12.	GOING THROUGH THE MOTION	SONNY JAMES	1[illegible]
13.	SUGAR SHACK	JIMMY GILMER	7
14.	POPSICLES & ICICLES	THE MERMAIDS	--
15.	LIVING A LIE	AL MARTINO	8
16.	IT'S ALL RIGHT	THE IMPRESSIONS	12
17.	THERE I'VE SAID IT AGAIN	BOBBY VINTON	40
18.	LITTLE RED ROOSTER	SAM COOKE	15
19.	OLD RECORDS	MARGIE SINGLETON	37
20.	500 MILES	BOBBY BARE	16
21.	EVERYBODY	TOMMY ROE	10
22.	MIDNIGHT MARY	JOEY POWERS	25
23.	BE TRUE TO YOUR SCHOOL	BEACH BOYS	23
24.	AS USUAL	BRENDA LEE	26
25.	DOWN AT PAPA JOE'S	THE DIXIE BELLES	24
26.	THE NITTY GRITTY	SHIRELLES	29
27.	DON'T SEND FLOWERS	JOYCE PAUL	35
28.	BABY I DO LOVE YOU	GALENS	32
29.	PRETTY PAPER	ROY ORBISON	--
30.	MISTY	LLOYD PRICE	27
31.	YOUR OTHER LOVE	CONNIE FRANCIS	23
32.	LEAVE HER TO ME	DAVID BRIGGS	
33.	FORGET HIM		
34.			

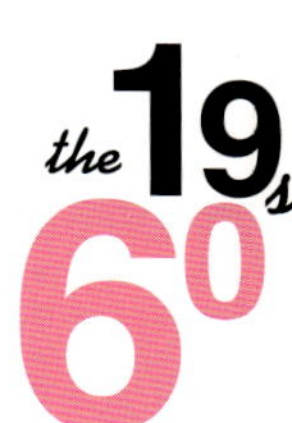

The Beverly Hillbillies

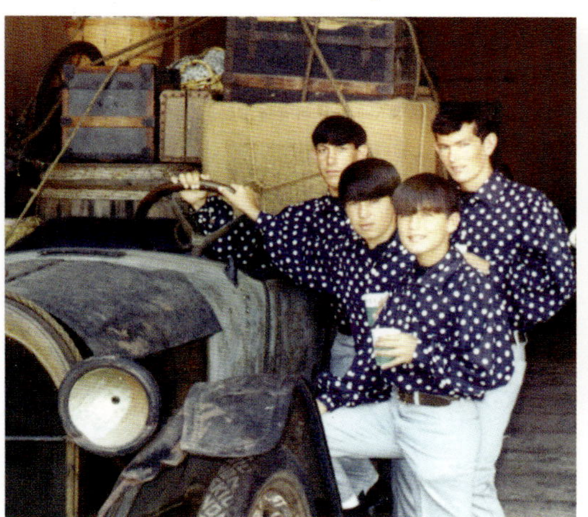

The Beverly Hillbillie's Oldsmobile Truck

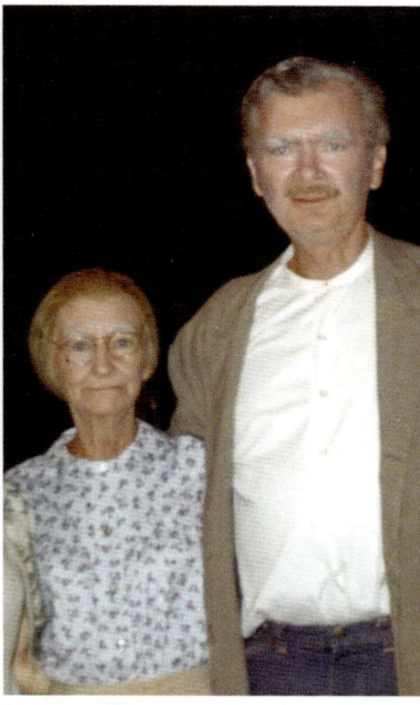

Irene Ryan and Buddy Epsen

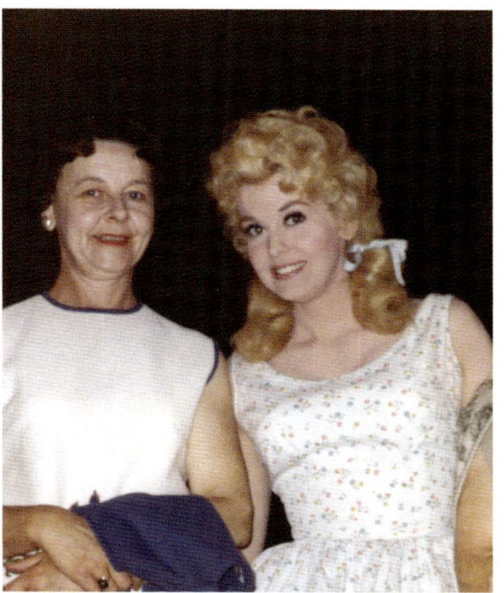

Donna Douglas

Righteous Brothers

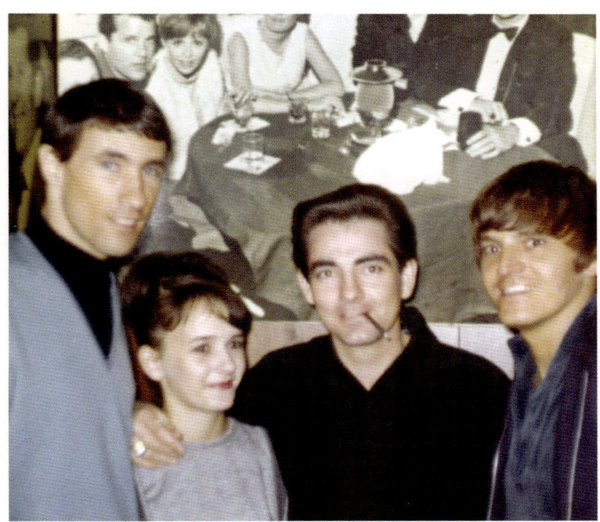

Bill Medley, Pam, Jimmy, and Joey Page

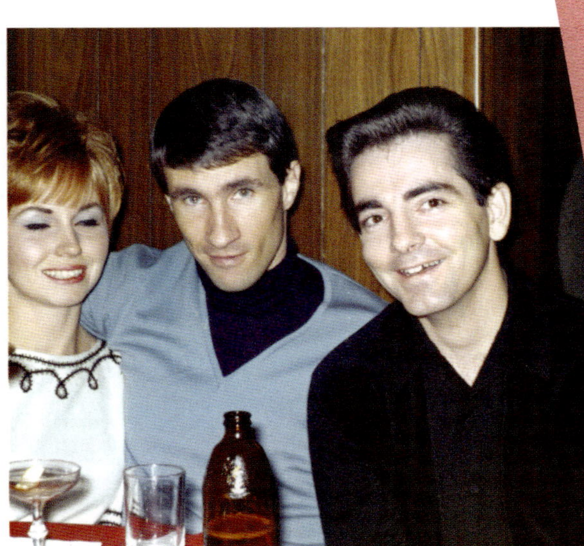

Karen and Bill Medley

See The Big

JIMMY VELVET SHOW

National Guard Armory

SCOTTSBORO, ALABAMA

2 Big Shows: 3:00 AND 8:00 P. M.

Sat. Jan. 2, 1965

TICKETS ON SALE AT KEN'S RECORD SHOP AND ALL MEMBERS OF THE RESCUE SQUAD.

ADVANCE TICKETS $1.00 — TICKETS AT DOOR $1.25

SPONSORED BY

SCOTTSBORO RESCUE SQUAD

Bob Hope

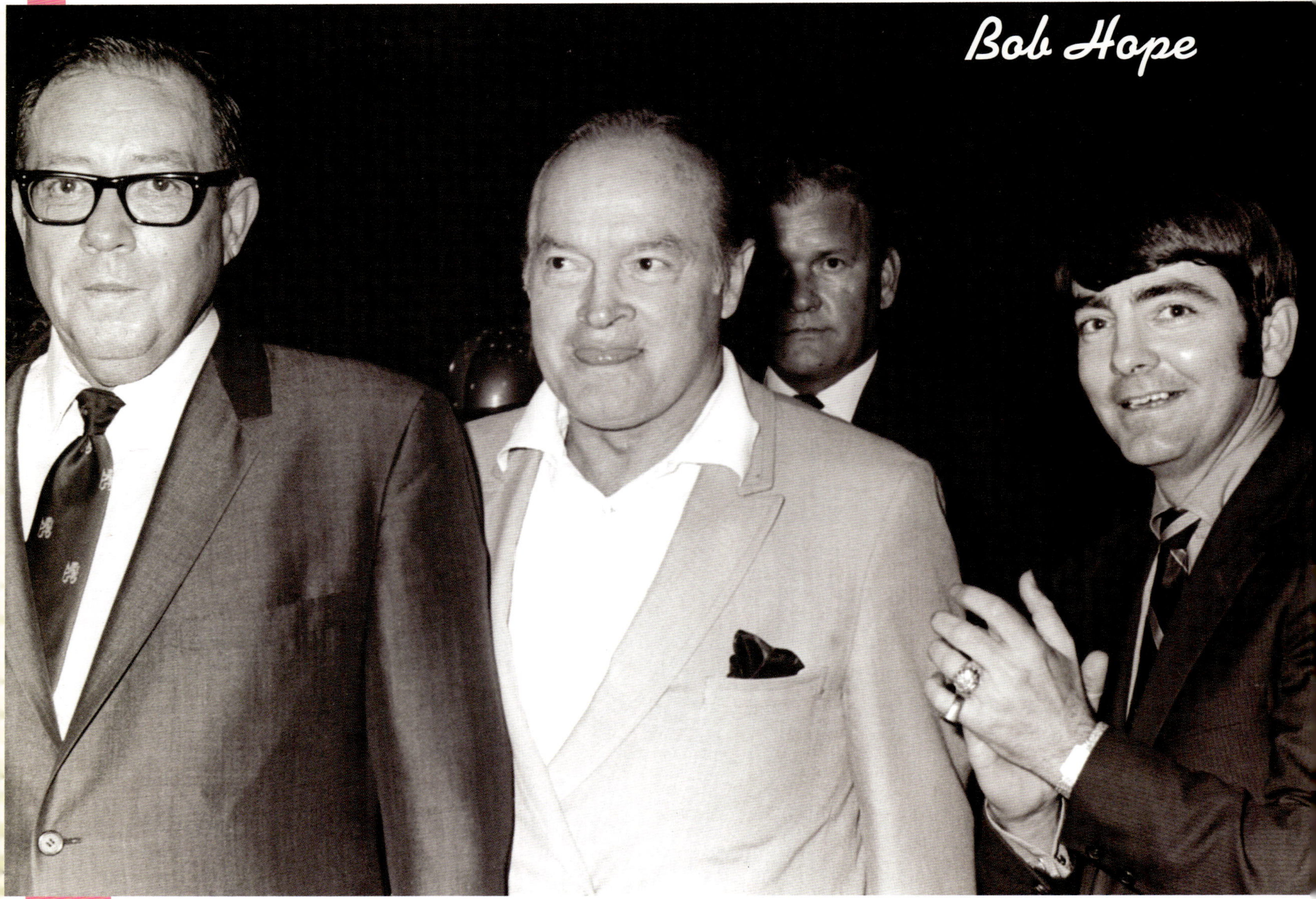

Gov. John Bell Williams, Bob Hope and I

In 1969 I Performed with Bob Hope to raise funds for Hurricane Camile Victims in Jackson, Mississippi

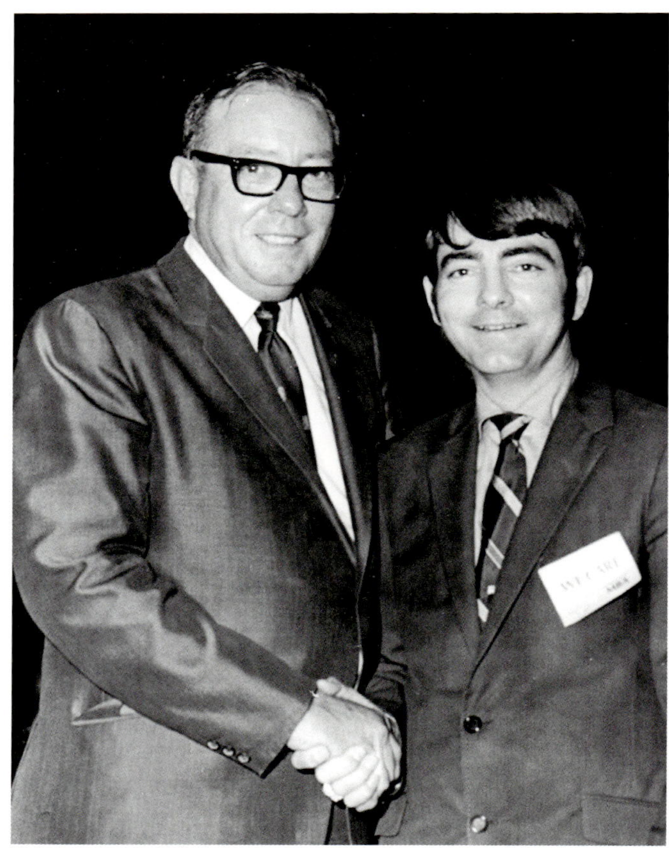

Governor John Bell Williams of Mississippi

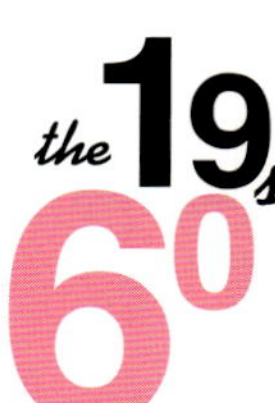

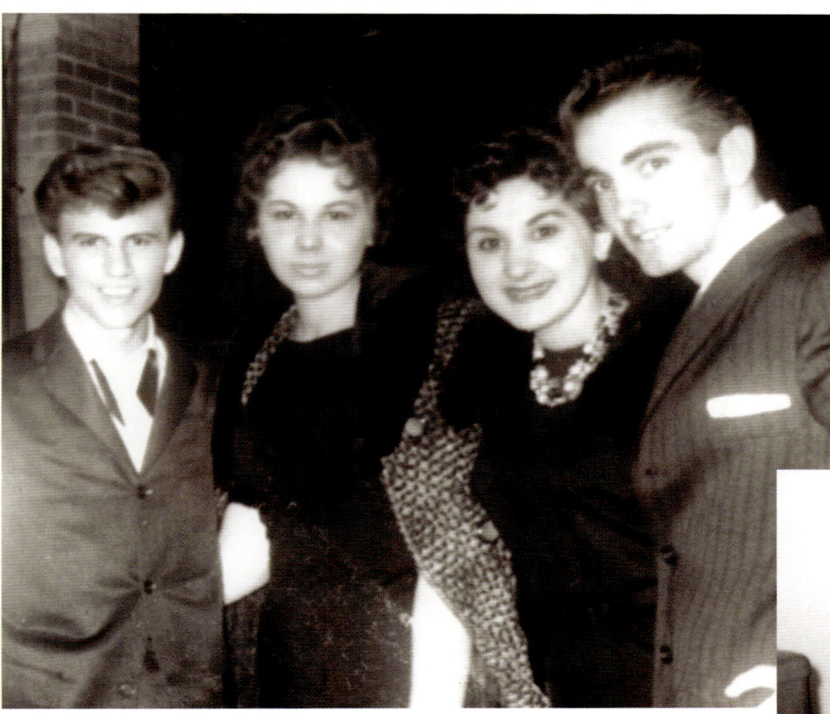

Bobby Rydell, Connie Denave, her niece and I

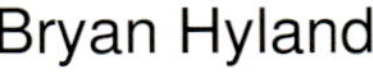

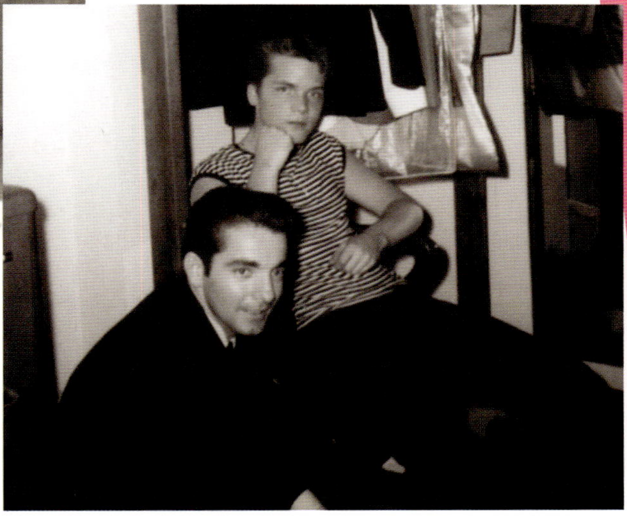

Bryan Hyland

Cannibal and The Headhunters

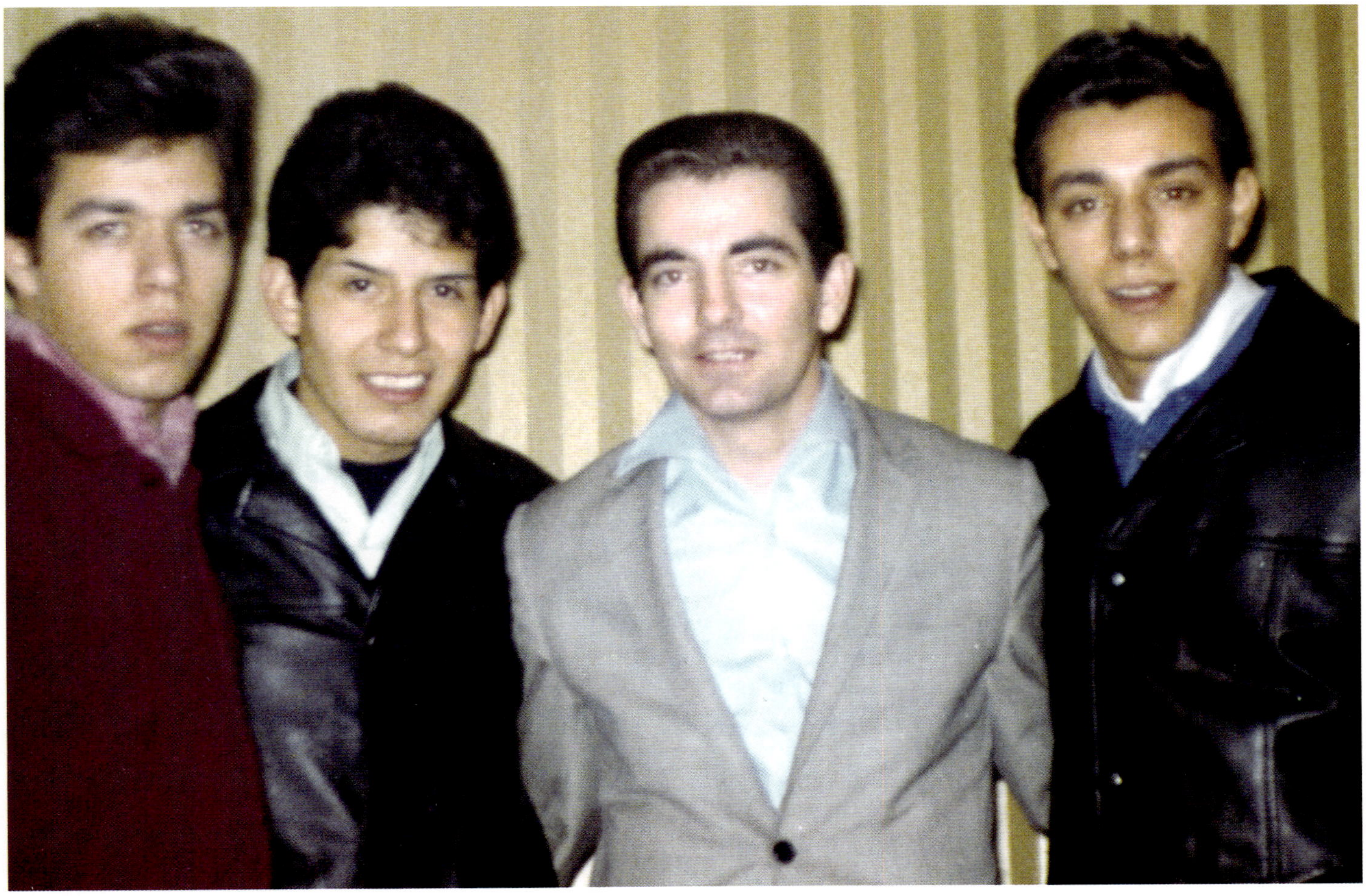

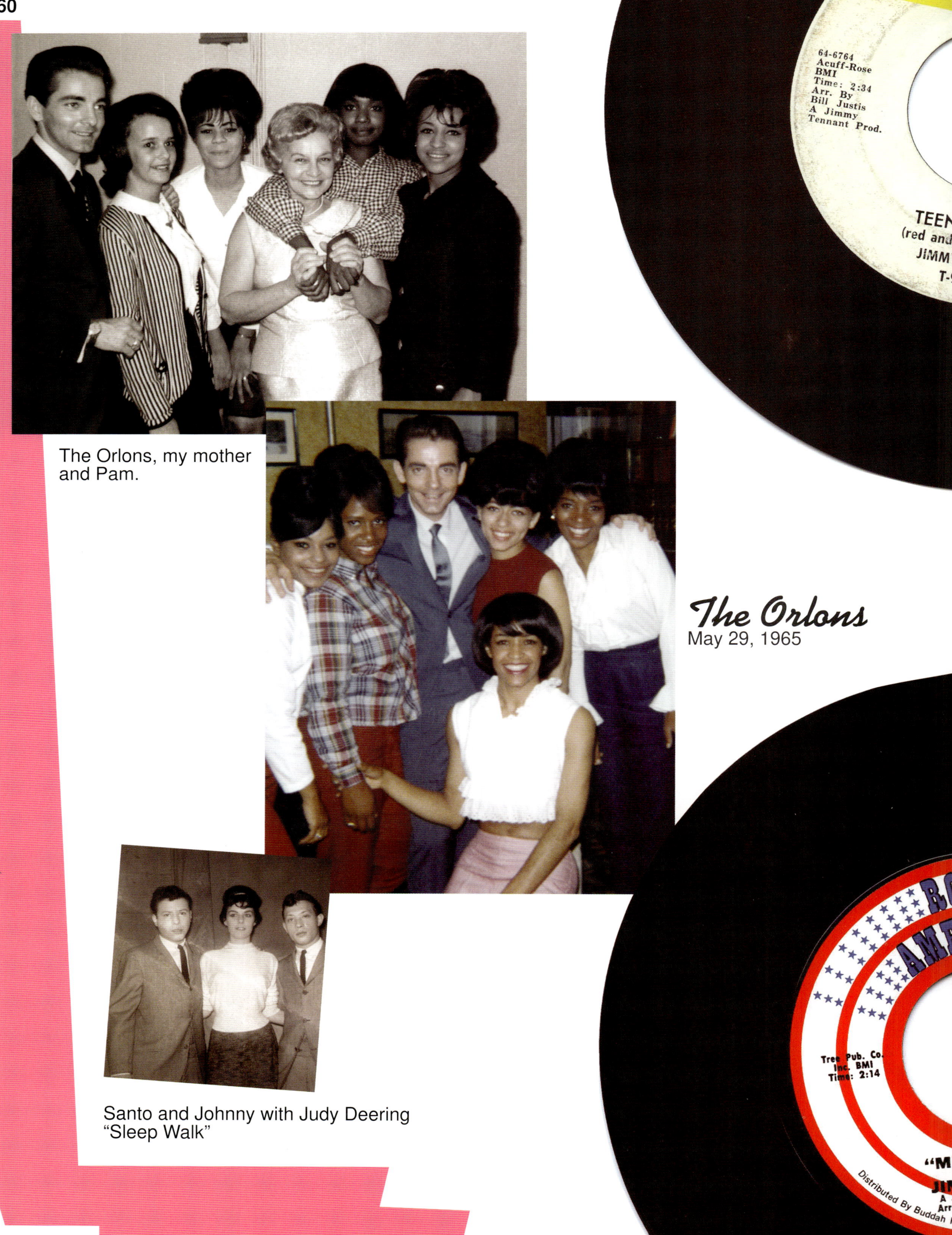

The Orlons, my mother and Pam.

The Orlons
May 29, 1965

Santo and Johnny with Judy Deering
"Sleep Walk"

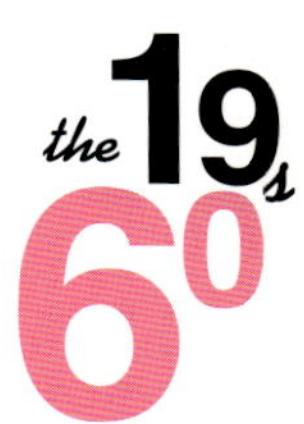

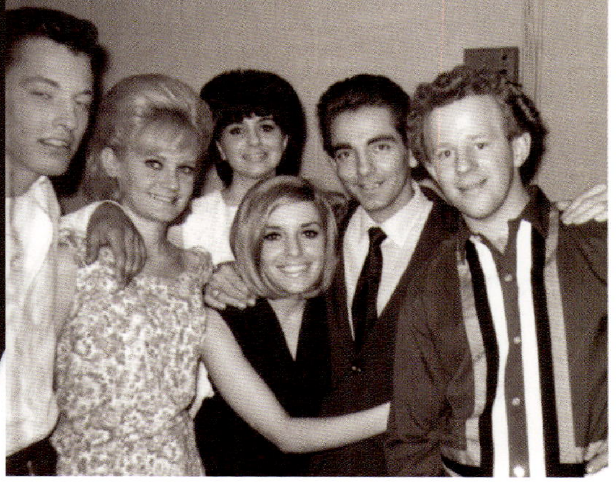

Barry Darvell and The Angels (Halo's), Joey Welz, and I

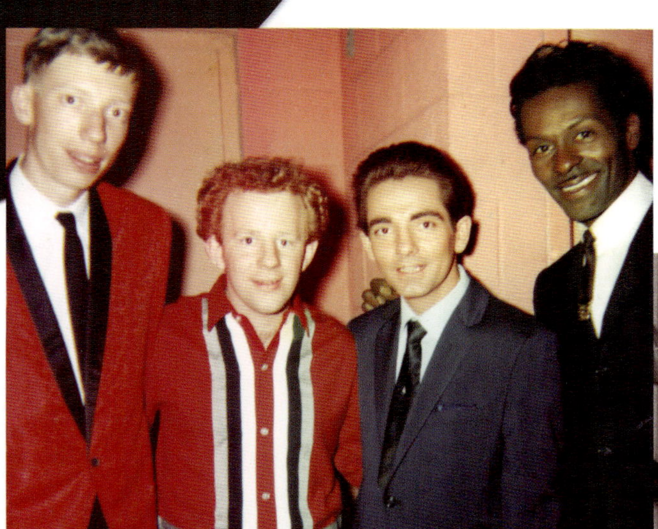

Gene Loving
Joey Welz
Chuck Berry
WGH Radio Virgina Beach

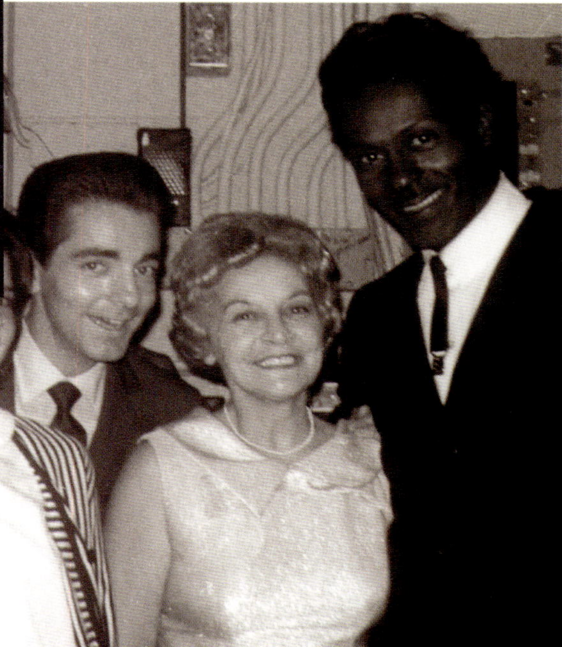

Chuck Berry
and mom

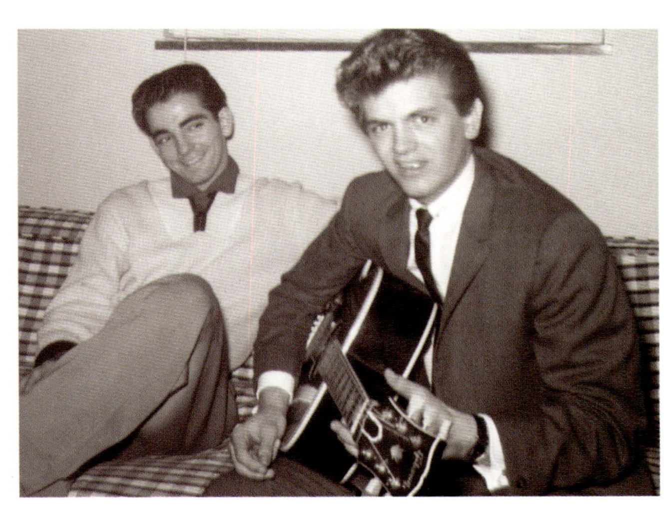

Phil Everly

dick clark | 9125 SUNSET BOULEVARD, LOS ANGELES, CAL
CRestview 8-0311

Dear Jimmy . . . .

Thanks very much for working with us on "Where The Action Is". As you've probably gathered by now, we're proud of our show. With luck, we will be presenting you in a most interesting fashion. The acceptance of your appearance on "Where The Action Is" is just as important to us as it is to you as an artist.

In your travels about the country and during the course of any radio, television or press interviews, we would sincerely appreciate your mentioning your appearance on the show. "Where The Action Is" is seen daily, Monday through Friday on ABC-TV at 2:00 P.M.

Thanks again for joining us.

Sincerely,

Dick

DICK CLARK
DICK CLARK PRODUCTIONS

DC/hc

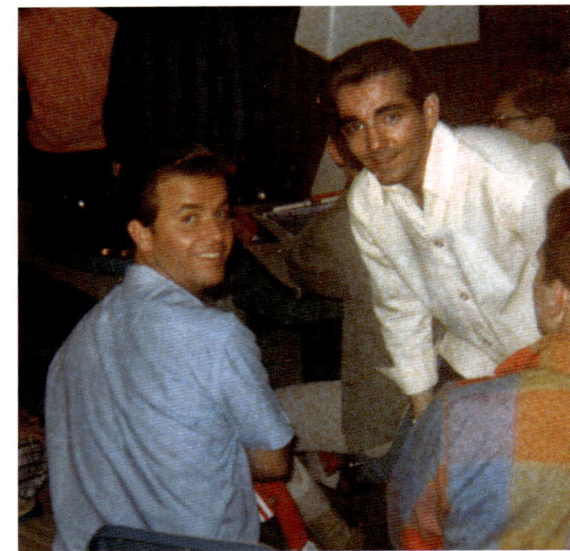

Dick Clark and I on "Where the Action Is"

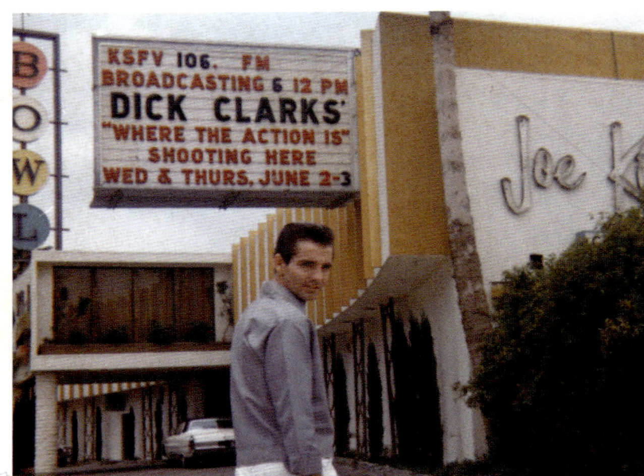

Getting ready to shoot, 1965.

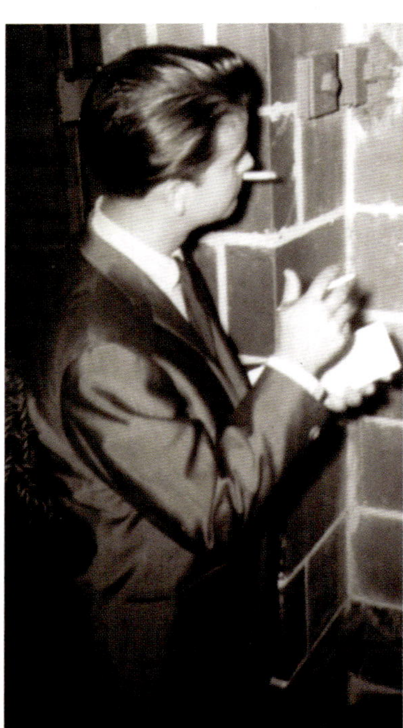

Dick Clark

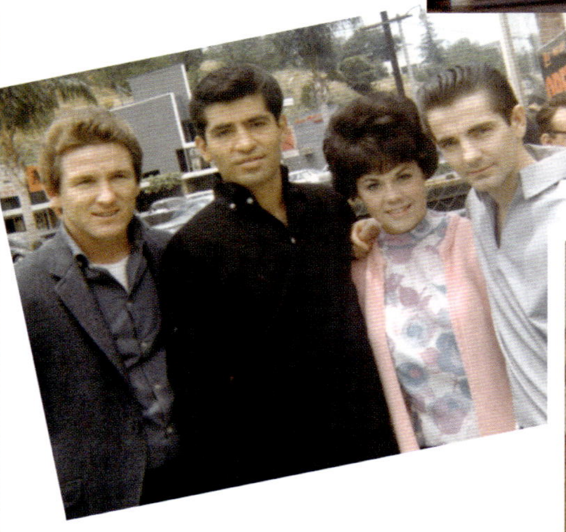

Jimmy Cross, Steve Alaimo, Linda Scott and I.

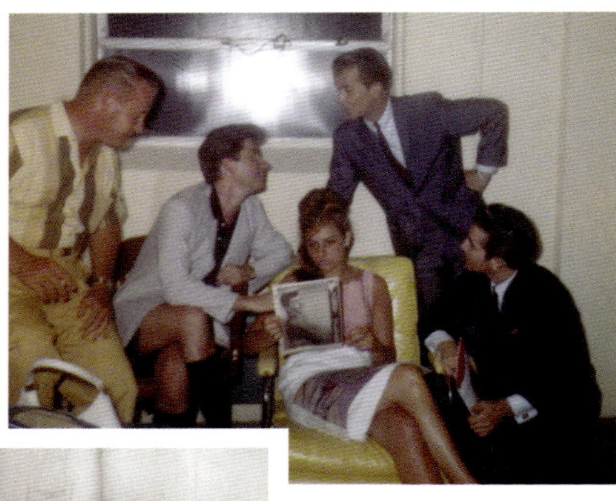

Jack Heyward, Johnny Tillotson, and his wife, Dick Clark and I

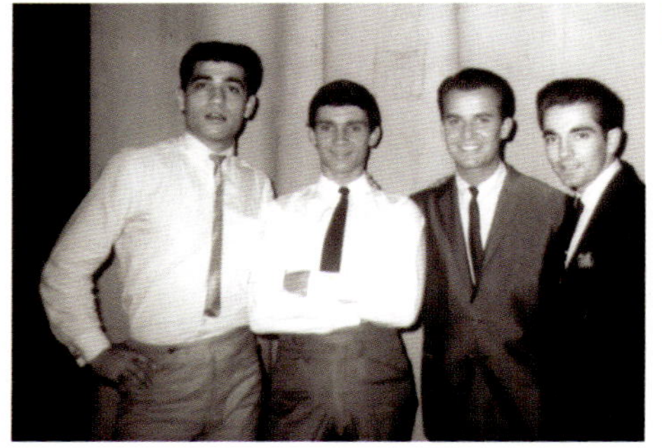

Steve Alaimo, Gene Pitney, Dick Clark, and I.

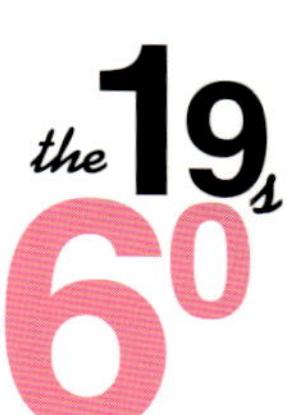

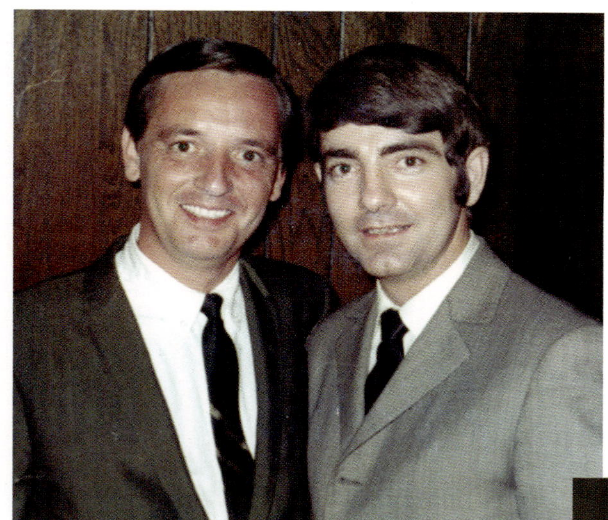

Amon Carter Evans

Eddie Cochran
Billy Crash Craddock
Jackie Wilson and
Johnny Restivo

Robin Seymour TV Show
Detroit with me and Eddie Rambeau
"Concrete and Clay"

Elvis Presley

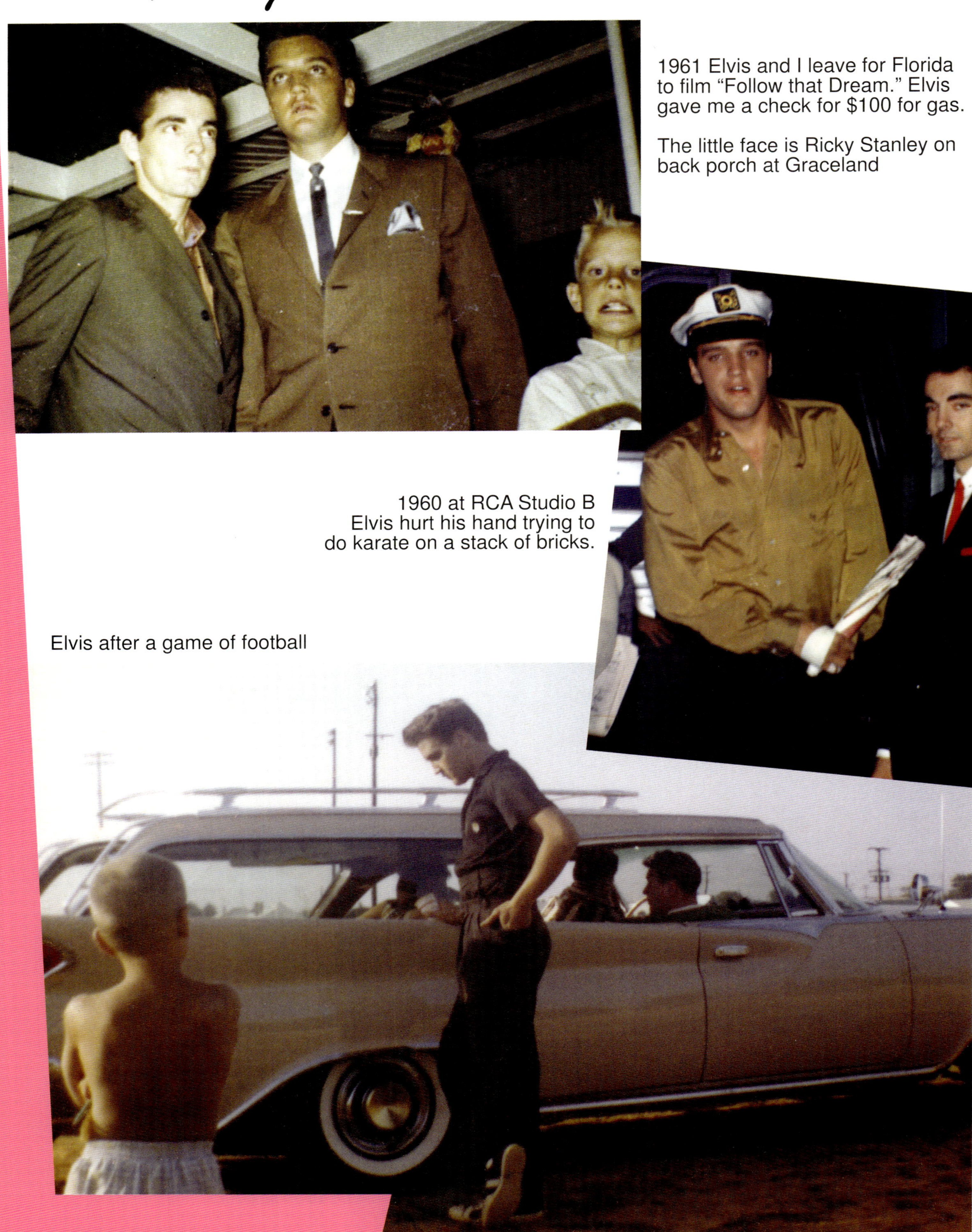

1961 Elvis and I leave for Florida to film "Follow that Dream." Elvis gave me a check for $100 for gas.

The little face is Ricky Stanley on back porch at Graceland

1960 at RCA Studio B
Elvis hurt his hand trying to
do karate on a stack of bricks.

Elvis after a game of football

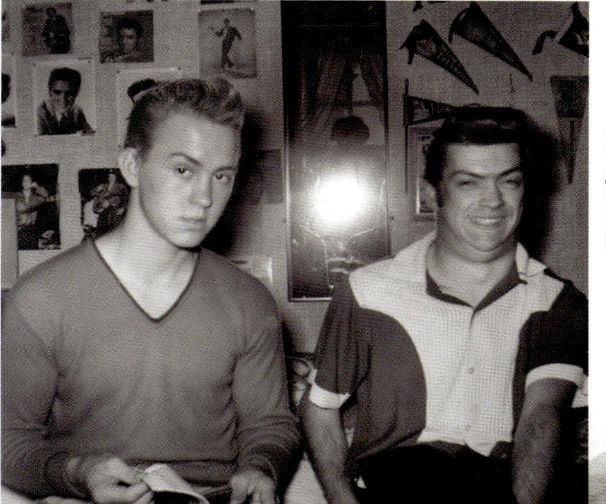

Elvis' 1st cousin, Bobby Smith, and Gary Pepper (President of Elvis Fan Club). Bobby looked so much like Elvis.

Elvis' Aunt Loraine Smith, wife of Travis Smith and mother to Bobby and Billy Smith at Graceland, 1960

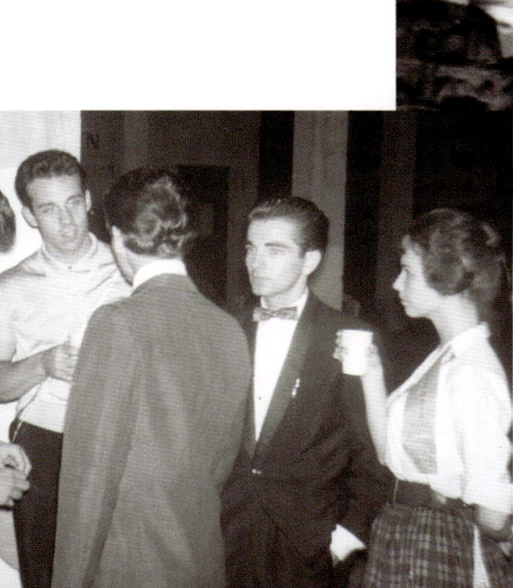

Everly Brothers, Jack Scott, and Nancy.

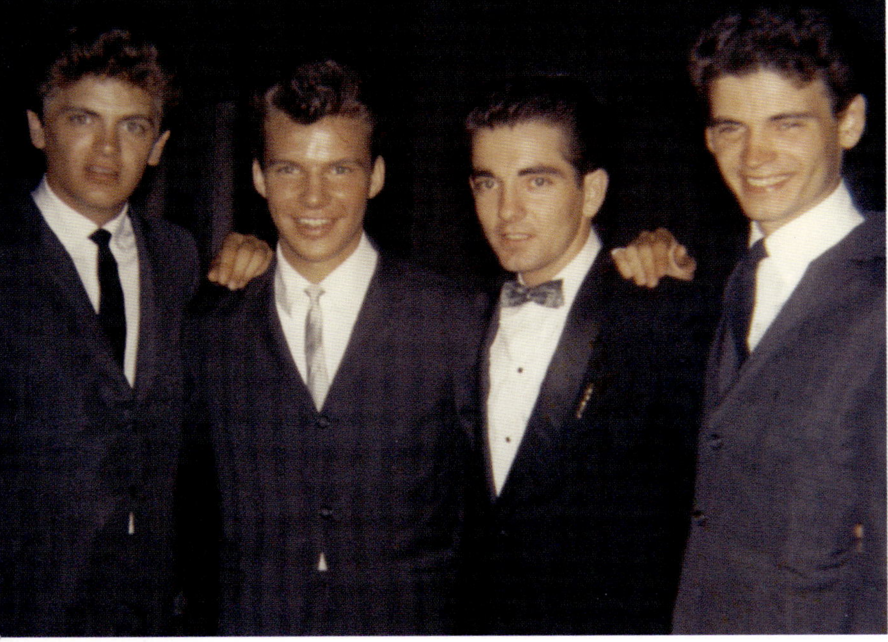

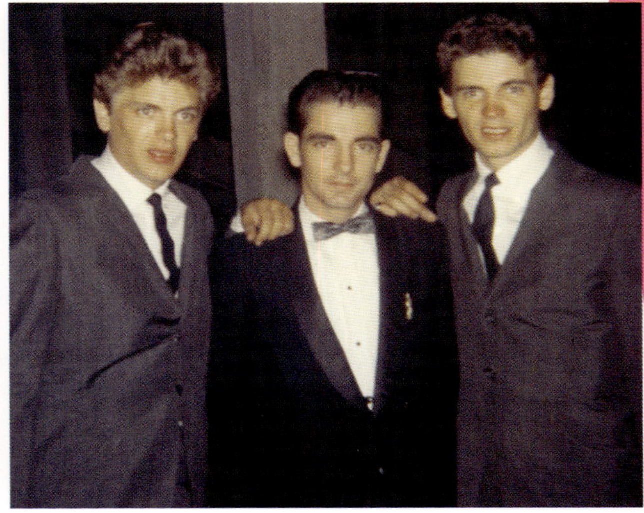

A great show. Bobby Vee, The Everly Brothers and Me.

Vernon Presley

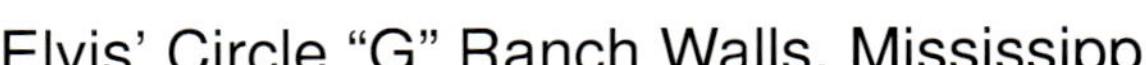

Elvis' Circle "G" Ranch Walls, Mississippi

One Sunday, right after church, we headed down to the Circle "G" and Vernon caught two fish.

Me at Graceland

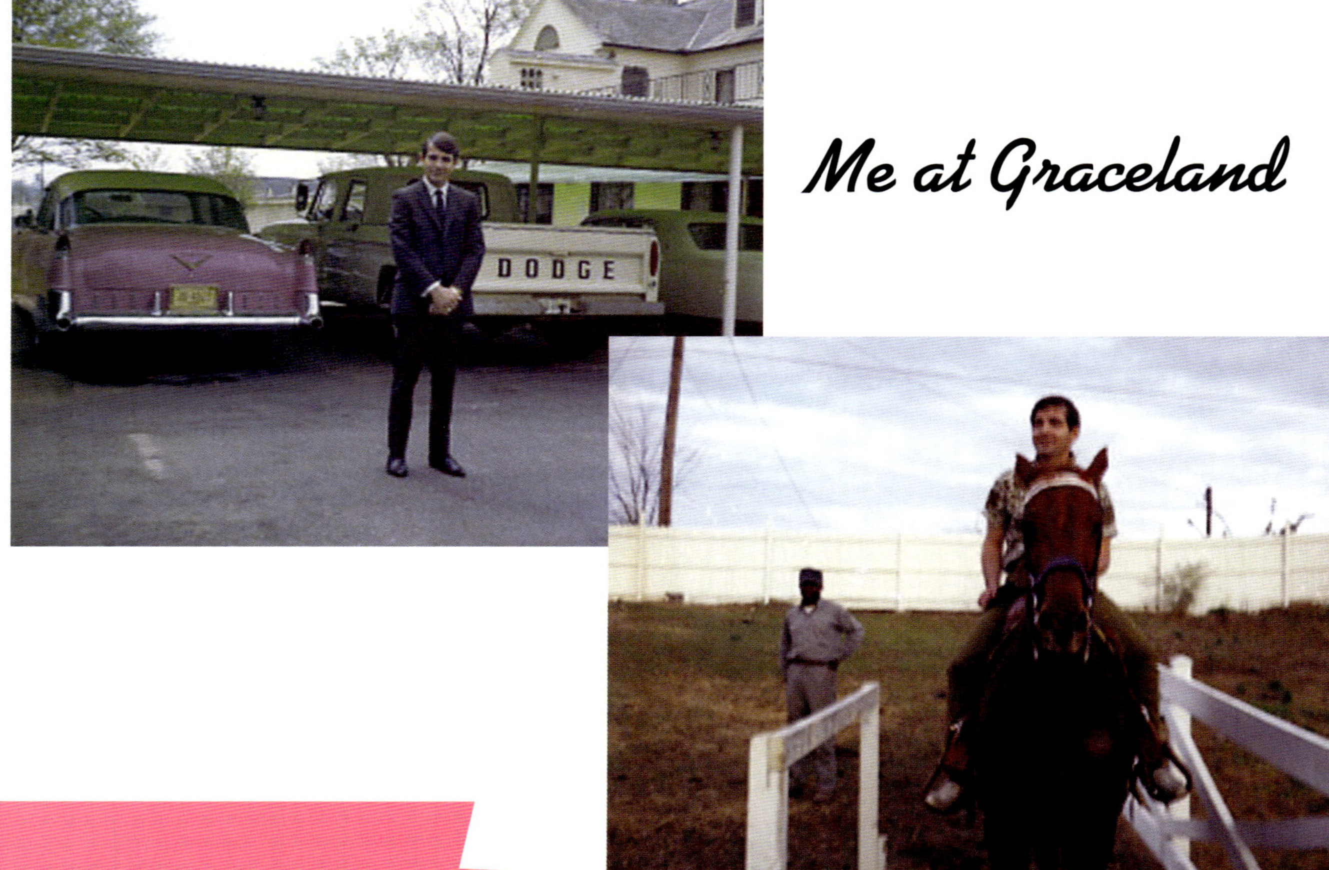

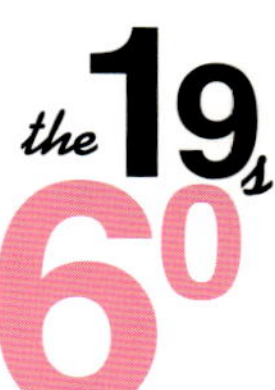

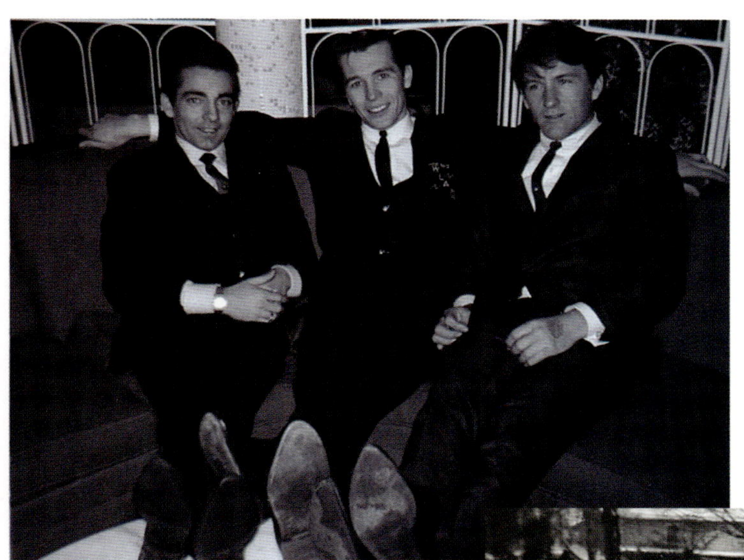

Jimmy Cross and I visiting my friend, Chuck Raymond, at WLAN Radio, Lancaster, Pennsylvania

Jimmy Cross and I at a Cemetery in Virginia "I Want My Baby Back"

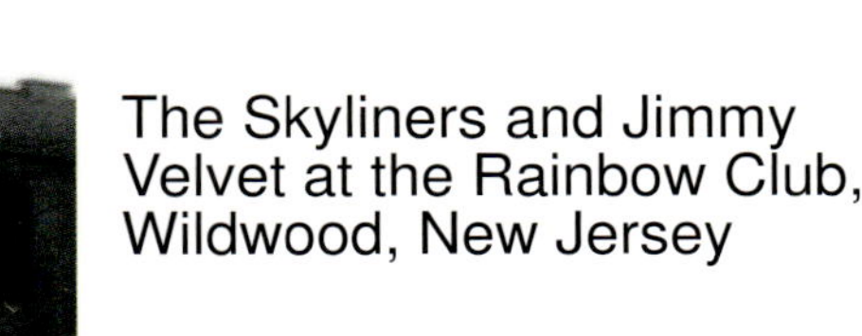

The Skyliners and Jimmy Velvet at the Rainbow Club, Wildwood, New Jersey

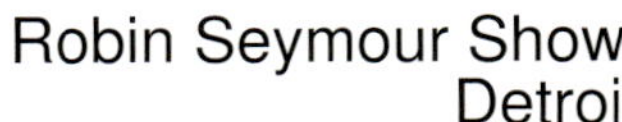

Robin Seymour Show, Detroit

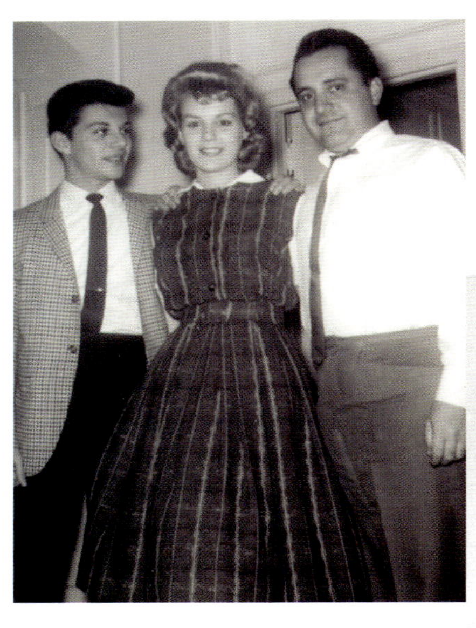

Frankie Avalon

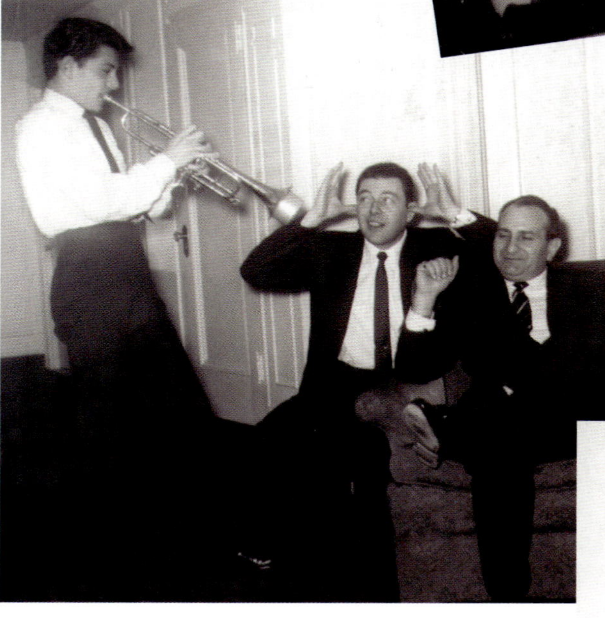

Warwick Hotel, New York City 1960
Frankie Avalon, Bob Marcucci, Judy Deering and I

Judy and I with

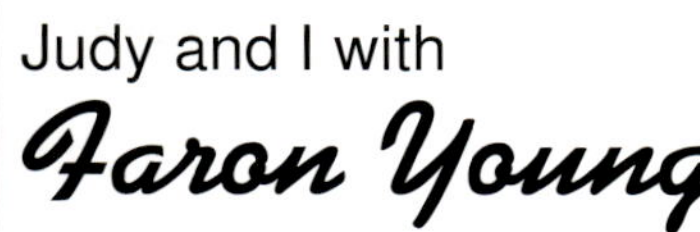

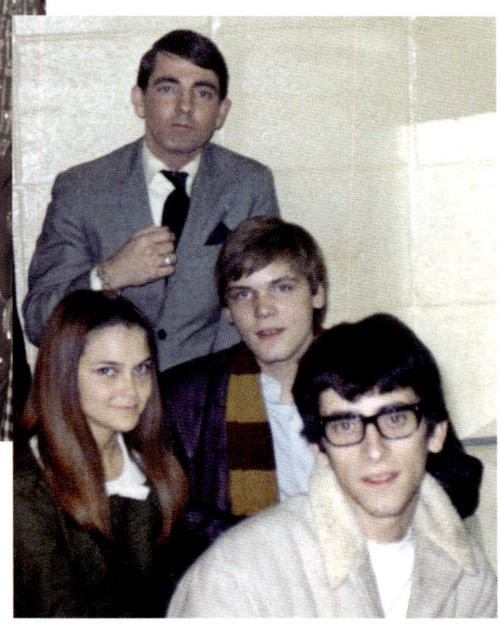

Baltimore Show with

Bryan Hyland
Gary Lewis

Joey Page
Glen Campbell

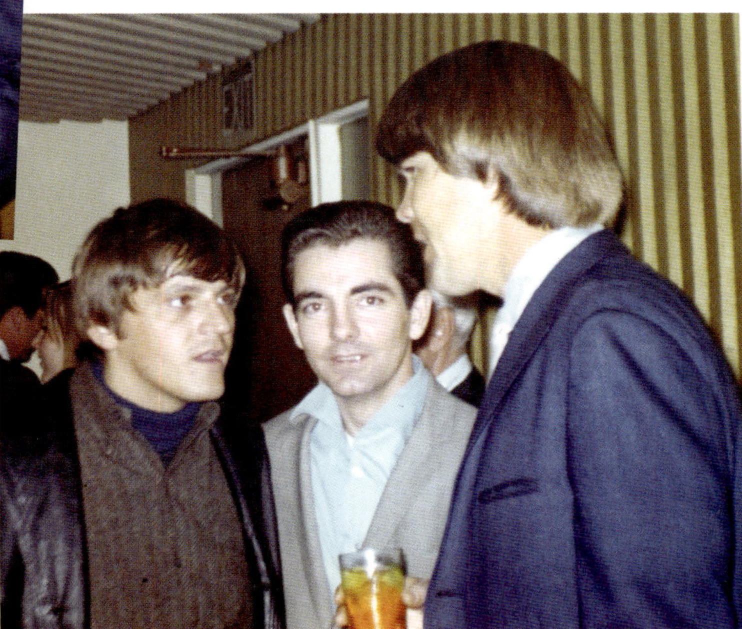

Joey and Glen in Hollywood

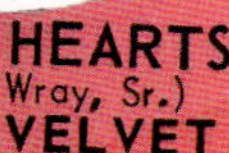

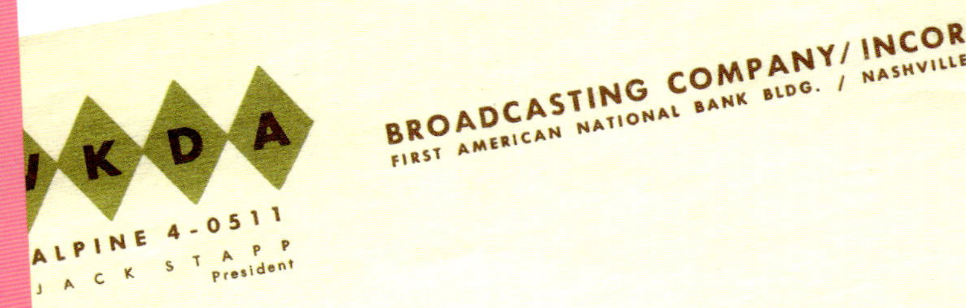

January 21, 1964

Mr. Jimmy Velvet
2712 Hartford Drive
Nashville, Tennessee

Dear Jimmy:

Our party at Tennessee Preparatory School was an overwhelming success...how could it have been otherwise? It was one of those special occasions that happens all too rarely in show business.

The sheer delight of this deserving and enthusiastic audience was inspiring to behold, and the performance you gave was certainly richly deserving of their delight.

We feel proud and privileged to have been associated with that performance and we want to thank you for helping to make the party both successful and memorable. We hope you enjoyed the party as much as we did.

With applause and appreciation,

WKDA GOOD GUYS

GG/djh

1240 KILOCYCLES

WKDA Radio note when I appeared with Brenda Lee, Ray Stevens and others for fund raiser for Tennessee Prepatory Schools.

Mark Dinning
Bobby Vee
Gene Pitney
Merline Garner
Jack Scott

Bobby Goldsboro, Gene Pitney, me, and Dobie Gray

George Hamilton

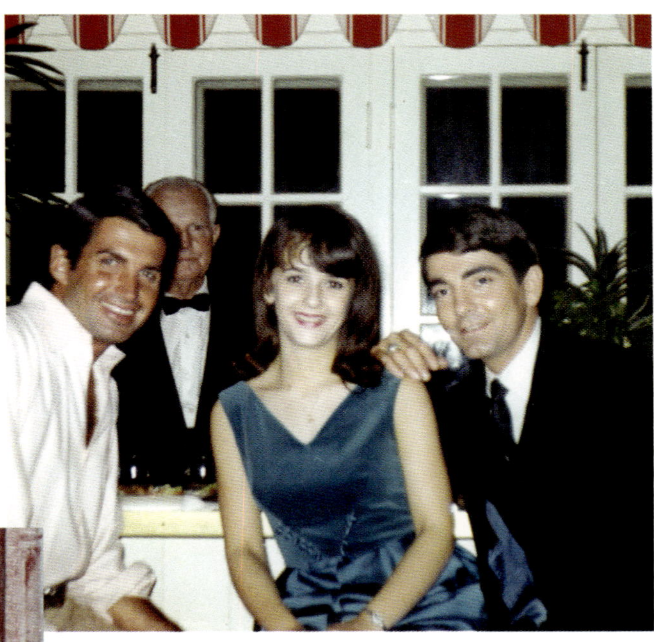

George Hamilton, Pam, and I at his Beverly Hills Home

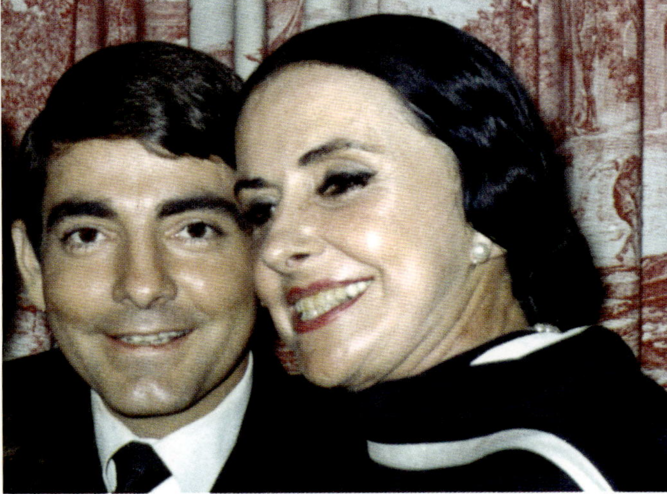

George Hamilton's Mother, Ann Hamilton Spaulding

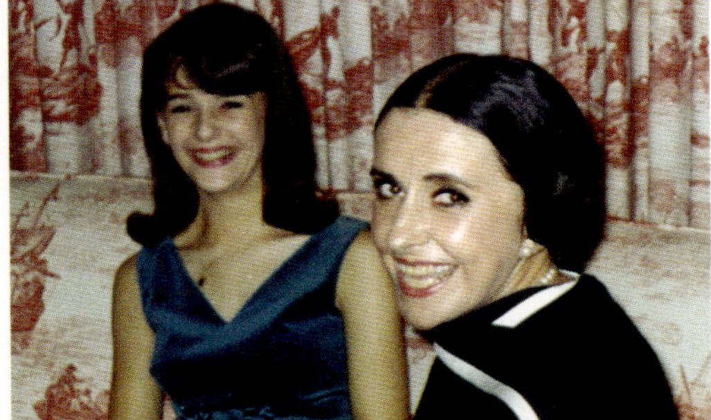

Pam and Ann

WKNR KEENER13.COM The Home of the Legend

WKNR, DETROIT, MI
Survey for week ending Wednesday June 9, 1965

TW	TITLE	ARTIST	LW
1.	Mr Tambourine Man	Byrds	2
2.	I Can't Help Myself	Four Tops	1
3.	Baby Im Yours	Barbara Lewis	12
4.	Seventh Son	Johnny Rivers	10
5.	Yes Im Ready	Barbara Mason	13
6.	A Little Bit of Heaven	Ronnie Dove	24
7.	For Your Love	Yardbirds	11
8.	What The World Needs Now	Jackie DeShannon	17
9.	Cara Mia	Jay & The Americans	27
10.	Voodoo Women	Bobby Goldsboro	7
11.	This Little Bird	Marianne Faithful / Nashville Teens	
12.	Before & After	Chad & Jeremy	18
13.	Crying in the Chapel	Elvis Presley	6
14.	I Still Love You	Jeff Berry	
15.	Last Chance to Turn Around	Gene Pitney	
16.	Just a Little	Beau Brummels	
17.	Help Me Rhonda	Beach Boys	
18.	Back in My Arms Again	Supremes	
19.	Oo Wee Baby I Love You	Fred Hughes	
20.	It's Almost Tomorrow	Jimmy Velvet	
21.	Laurie	Dickie Lee	
22.	Satisfaction	Rolling Stones	
23.	You Turn Me On	Ian Whitcomb	
24.	You Really Know How To Hurt A Guy	Jan & Dean	
25.	I'll Keep Holding On	Marvelettes	
26.	Girl Come Running	Four Seasons	
27.	Remember Me	Dean Martin	
28.	Catch the Wind	Donovan	
29.	Happy Feet Time	Montclairs	
	nderful World	Herman's Hermits	
	irl Little Girl	Tino & Revlons	

WKNR Detroit, MI

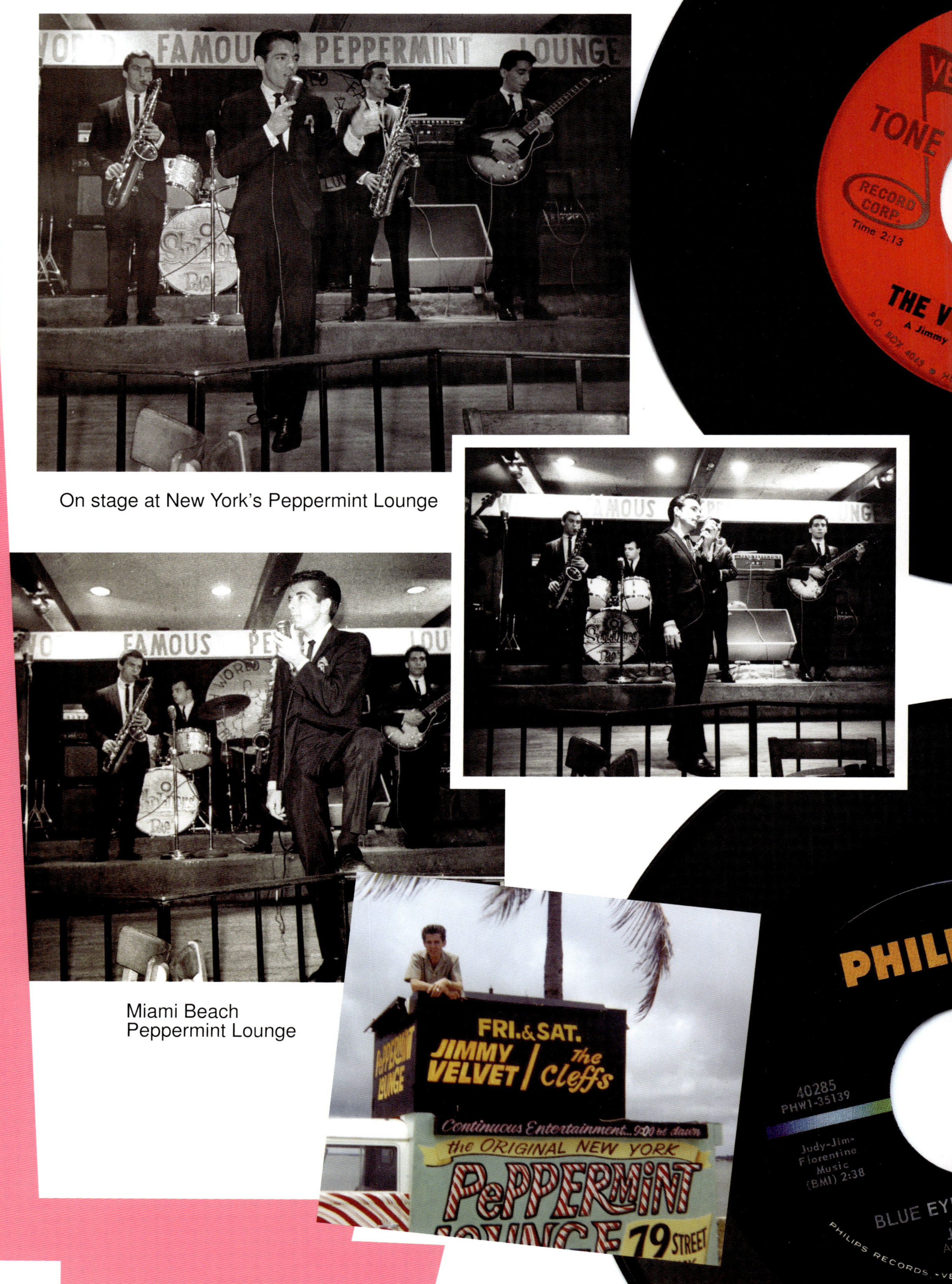

On stage at New York's Peppermint Lounge

Miami Beach Peppermint Lounge

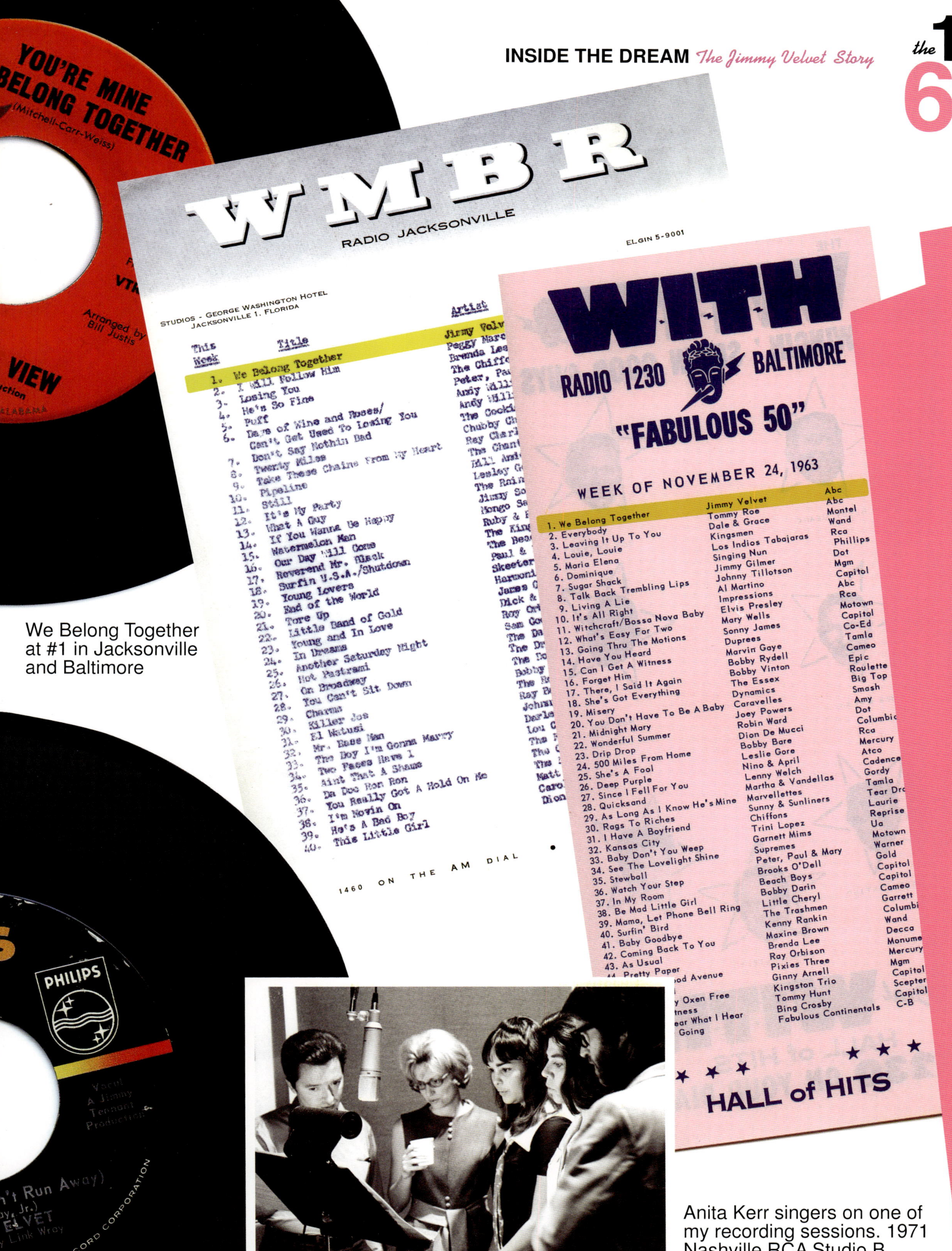

WMBR

RADIO JACKSONVILLE

ELGIN 5-9001

STUDIOS - GEORGE WASHINGTON HOTEL
JACKSONVILLE 1. FLORIDA

This Week | Title

1. We Belong Together
2. I Will Follow Him
3. Losing You
4. He's So Fine
5. Puff
6. Days of Wine and Roses/
Can't Get Used To Losing You
Don't Say Nothin Bad
7. Twenty Miles
8. Take These Chains From My Heart
9. Pipeline
10. Still
11. It's My Party
12. What A Guy
13. If You Wanna Be Happy
14. Watermelon Man
15. Our Day Will Come
16. Reverend Mr. Black
17. Surfin U.S.A./Shutdown
18. Young Lovers
19. End of the World
20. Tore Up
21. Little Band of Gold
22. Young and In Love
23. In Dreams
24. Another Saturday Night
25. Hot Pastrami
26. On Broadway
27. You Can't Sit Down
28. Charms
29. Killer Joe
30. El Watusi
31. Mr. Bass Man
32. The Boy I'm Gonna Marry
33. Two Faces Have I
34. Aint That A Shame
35. Da Doo Ron Ron
36. You Really Got A Hold On Me
37. I'm Movin On
38. He's A Bad Boy
39. This Little Girl
40.

Artist

Jimmy Velv
Peggy Marc
Brenda Lee
The Chiffo
Peter, Pa
Andy Will
Andy Will
The Cooki
Chubby Ch
Ray Charl
The Chant
Bill And
Lesley G
The Rain
Jimmy So
Mongo Sa
Ruby & R
The King
The Bea
Paul &
Skeeter
Harmoni
James G
Dick &
Roy Or
Sam Co
The Da
The Dr
The Do
Bobby
The Re
Ray B
Johnn
Darle
Lou C
The F
The C
The
Matt
Caro
Dion

1460 ON THE AM DIAL

WITH

RADIO 1230 BALTIMORE

"FABULOUS 50"

WEEK OF NOVEMBER 24, 1963

1. We Belong Together	Jimmy Velvet	Abc
2. Everybody	Tommy Roe	Abc
3. Leaving It Up To You	Dale & Grace	Montel
4. Louie, Louie	Kingsmen	Wand
5. Maria Elena	Los Indios Tabajaras	Rca
6. Dominique	Singing Nun	Phillips
7. Sugar Shack	Jimmy Gilmer	Dot
8. Talk Back Trembling Lips	Johnny Tillotson	Mgm
9. Living A Lie	Al Martino	Capitol
10. It's All Right	Impressions	Abc
11. Witchcraft/Bossa Nova Baby	Elvis Presley	Rca
12. What's Easy For Two	Mary Wells	Motown
13. Going Thru The Motions	Sonny James	Capitol
14. Have You Heard	Duprees	Co-Ed
15. Can I Get A Witness	Marvin Gaye	Tamla
16. Forget Him	Bobby Rydell	Cameo
17. There, I Said It Again	Bobby Vinton	Epic
18. She's Got Everything	The Essex	Roulette
19. Misery	Dynamics	Big Top
20. You Don't Have To Be A Baby	Caravelles	Smash
21. Midnight Mary	Joey Powers	Amy
22. Wonderful Summer	Robin Ward	Dot
23. Drip Drop	Dion De Mucci	Columbic
24. 500 Miles From Home	Bobby Bare	Rca
25. She's A Fool	Leslie Gore	Mercury
26. Deep Purple	Nino & April	Atco
27. Since I Fell For You	Lenny Welch	Cadence
28. Quicksand	Martha & Vandellas	Gordy
29. As Long As I Know He's Mine	Marvellettes	Tamla
30. Rags To Riches	Sunny & Sunliners	Tear Dro
31. I Have A Boyfriend	Chiffons	Laurie
32. Kansas City	Trini Lopez	Reprise
33. Baby Don't You Weep	Garnett Mims	Ua
34. See The Lovelight Shine	Supremes	Motown
35. Stewball	Peter, Paul & Mary	Warner
36. Watch Your Step	Brooks O'Dell	Gold
37. In My Room	Beach Boys	Capitol
38. Be Mad Little Girl	Bobby Darin	Capitol
39. Mama, Let Phone Bell Ring	Little Cheryl	Cameo
40. Surfin' Bird	The Trashmen	Garrett
41. Baby Goodbye	Kenny Rankin	Columbi
42. Coming Back To You	Maxine Brown	Wand
43. As Usual	Brenda Lee	Decca
44. Pretty Paper	Ray Orbison	Monume
ood Avenue	Pixies Three	Mercury
l	Ginny Arnell	Mgm
y Oxen Free	Kingston Trio	Capitol
tness	Tommy Hunt	Scepter
ear What I Hear	Bing Crosby	Capitol
Going	Fabulous Continentals	C-B

HALL of HITS

We Belong Together at #1 in Jacksonville and Baltimore

Anita Kerr singers on one of my recording sessions. 1971 Nashville RCA Studio B

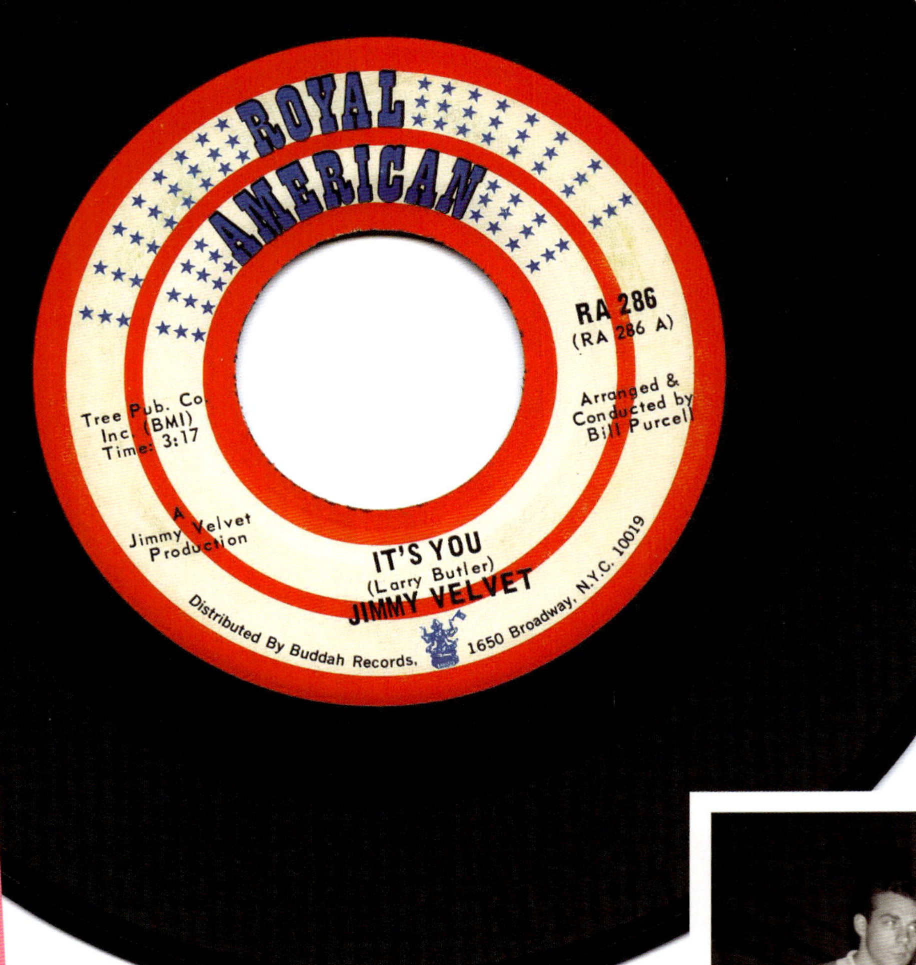

Jack Scott

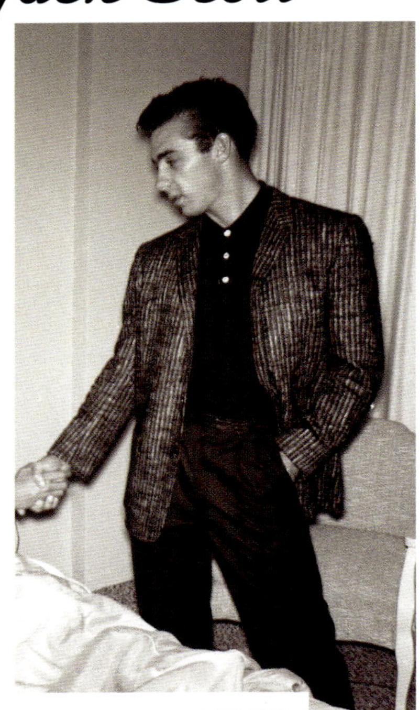

Jack Scott and Bill Brennen

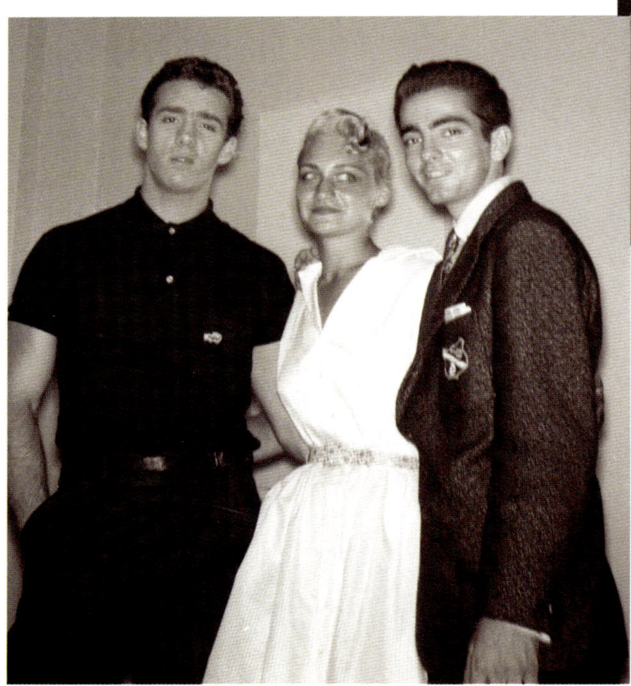

Jack and Gail Smith

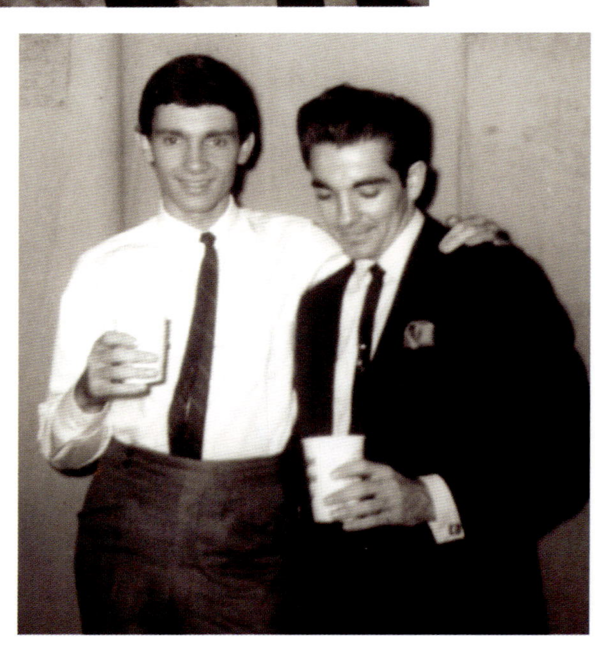

Gene Pitney and I

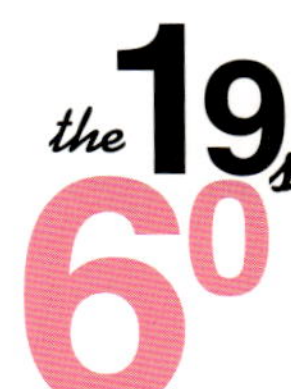

James Brown

The tour with James Brown was fantastic. What an entertainer!

With us was Phillips Records promotion man and his wife.

"It's Almost Tomorrow" was #11. WHYN Radio Chart Springfeild, MA

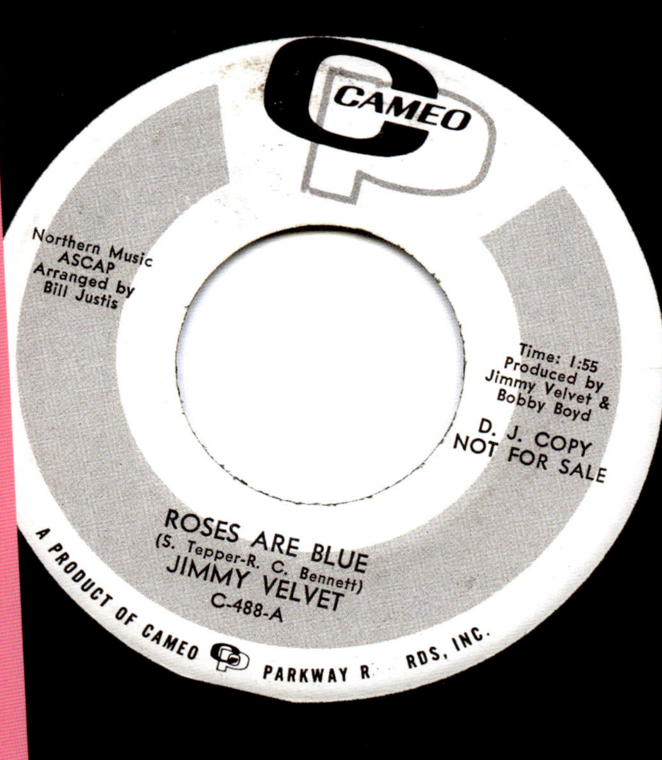

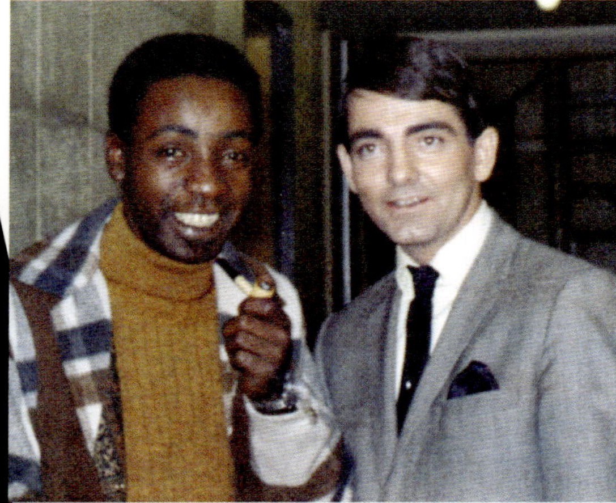

Jerry Butler

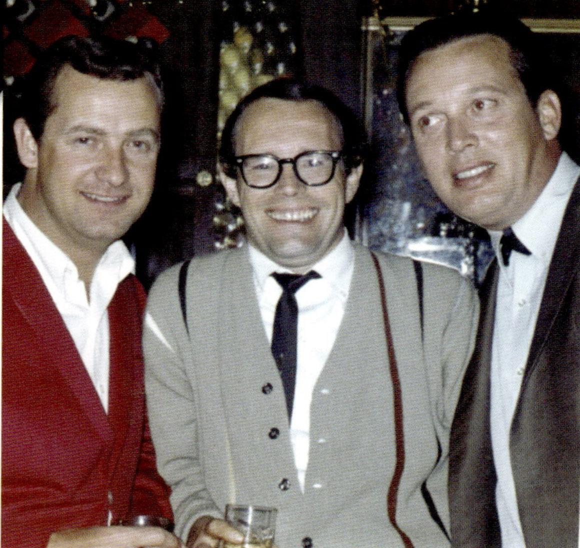

2 of LA's top DJ's and Jerry Wallace

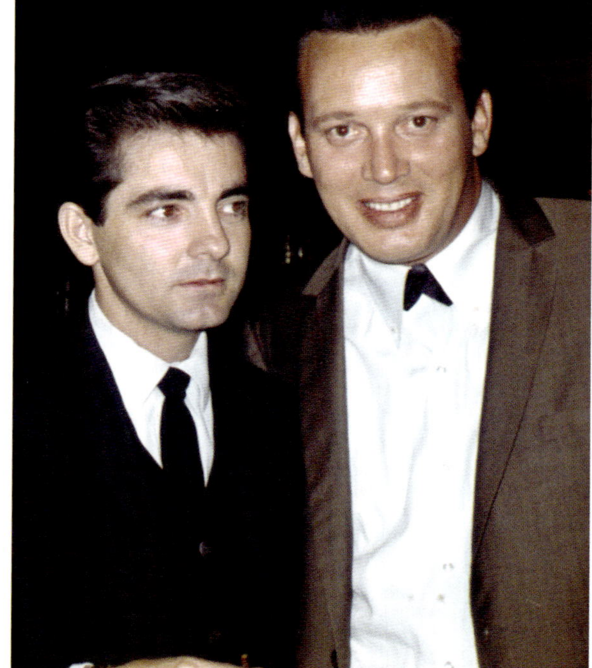

Jerry Wallace

"Primrose Lane"

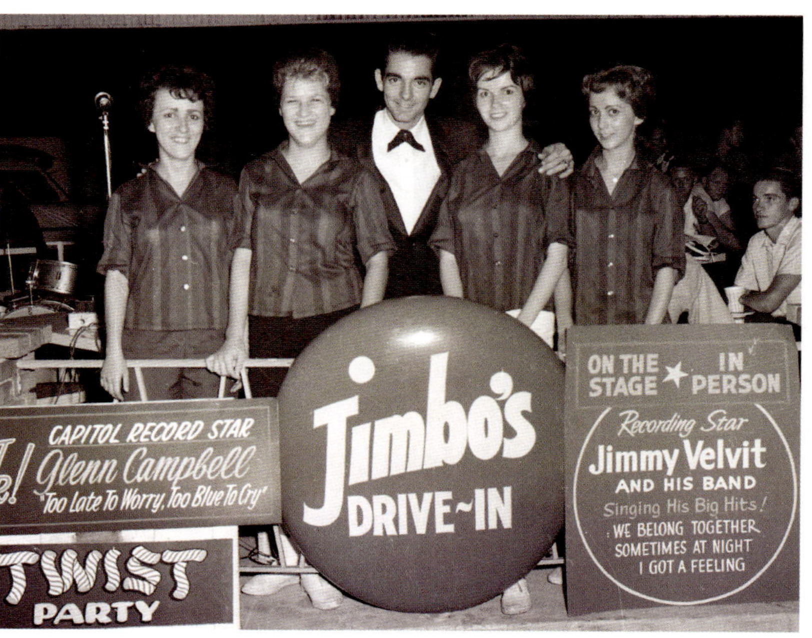

Opening of my drive-in in Dallas, TX 1960. Glen Campbell and Johnny Crawford attended

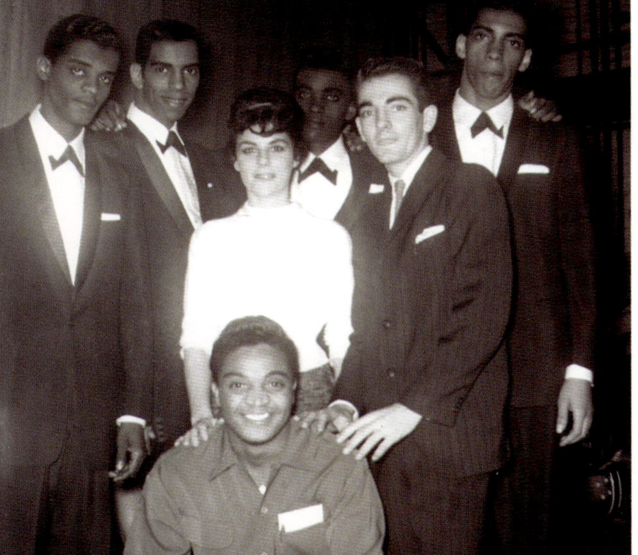

Jackie Wilson

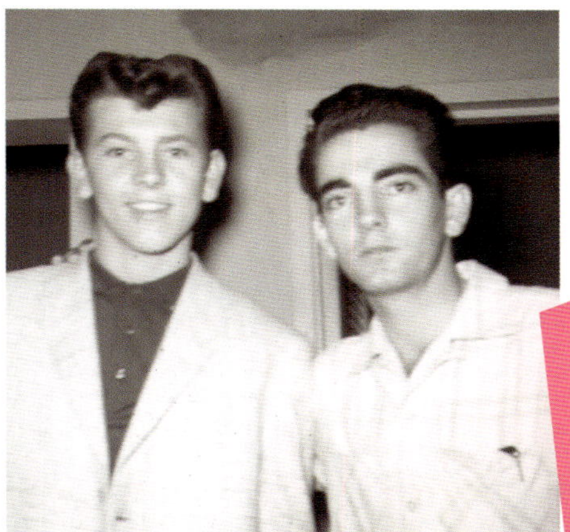

Jimmy Clanton

Jimmy Dean

Don Law, President of Columbia Records, Stonewall Jackson, Columbia Artist, and Jimmy Dean before he made his fortune making sausage. Johnny Cash shot this photo with my camera. We were on our way to the premier of Johnny's new movie "Five Minutes to Live."

July 9, 1969

Mr. Johnny Velvet
P O Box 5070
Huntsville, Alabama 35805

dick clark

Dear Johnny:

Just a note to let you we had to reschedule your inter-view. We had it set to be inserted into one of the shows we taped on June 29th but we were unable to do so.

We will inform you at another time of an air date for your segment.

Thank you.

Sincerely,

Ed Yates
Ed Yates
Producer/Director
AMERICAN BANDSTAND

EY:bb

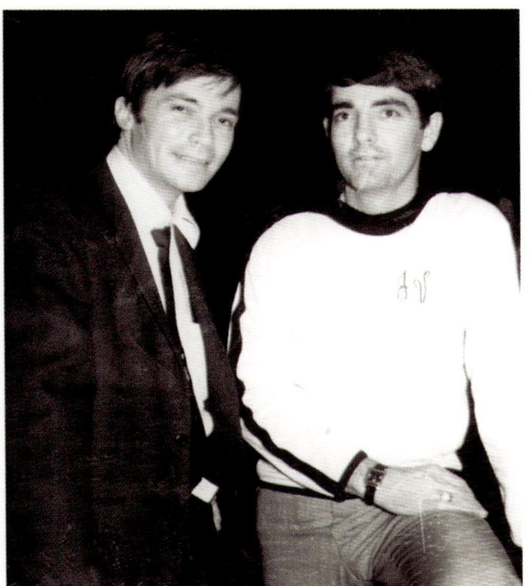

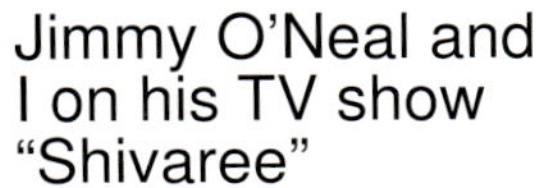

Jimmy O'Neal and I on his TV show "Shivaree"

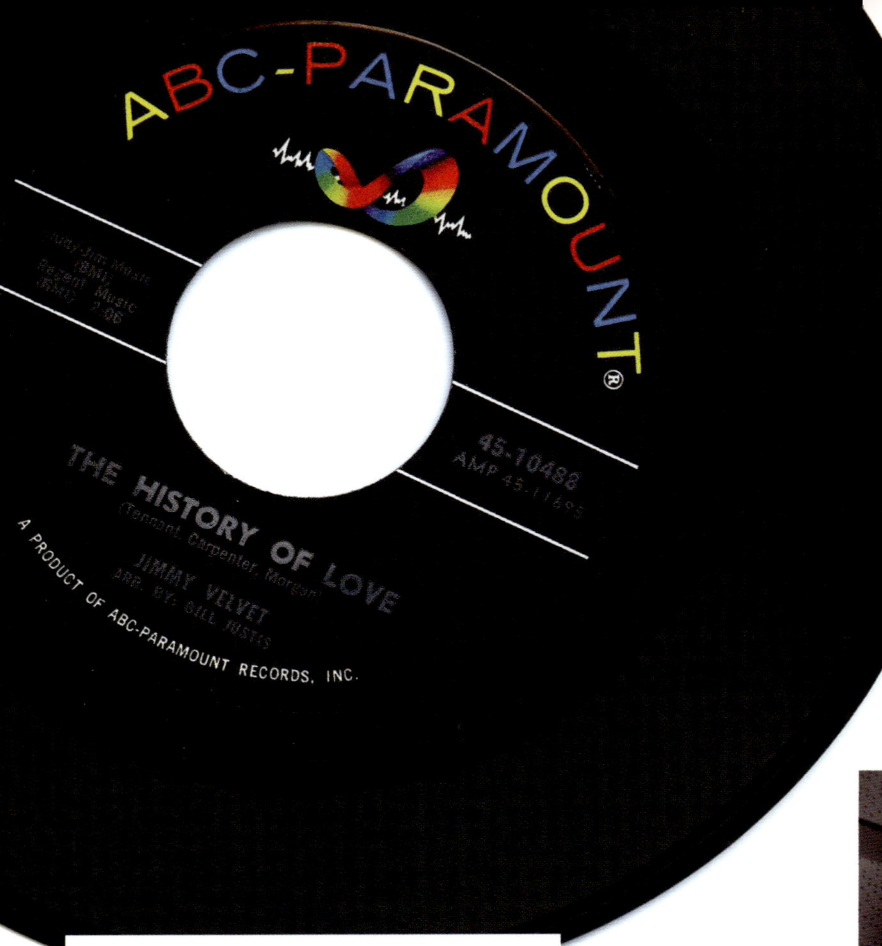
ABC-PARAMOUNT®
Regent Music
(BMI)
45-10488
AMP 45-11695
THE HISTORY OF LOVE
(Tennant, Carpenter, Morgan)
JIMMY VELVET
ARR. BY: BILL JUSTIS
A PRODUCT OF ABC-PARAMOUNT RECORDS, INC.

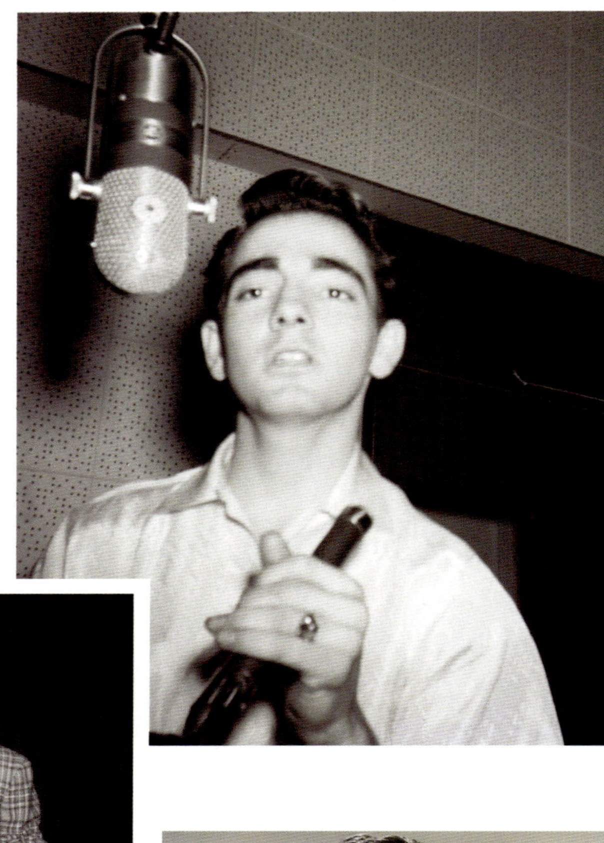

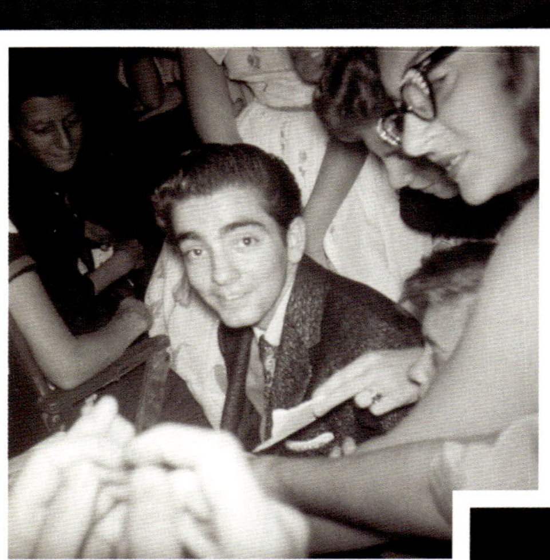

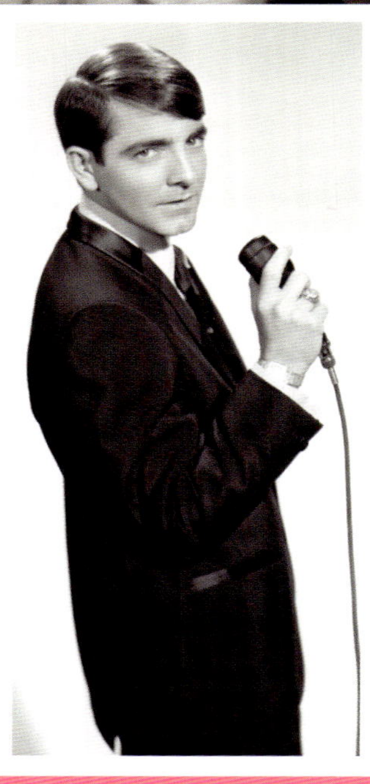

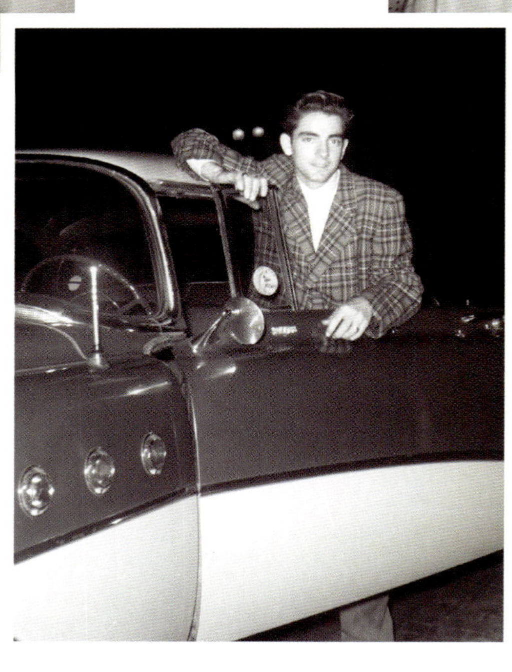

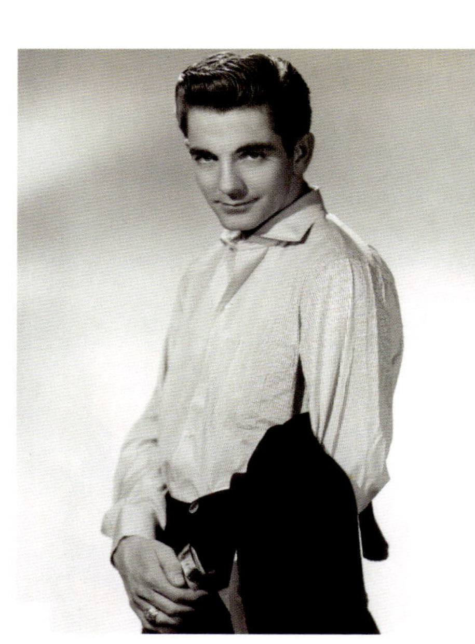

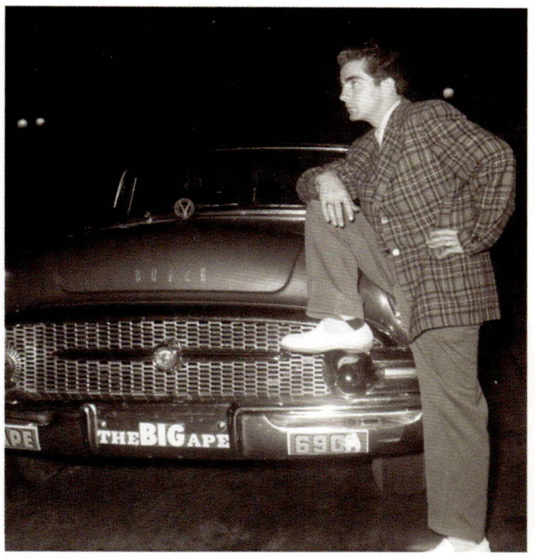

This plaid coat was given to me by Elvis in Philadelphia Arena, March 1957.

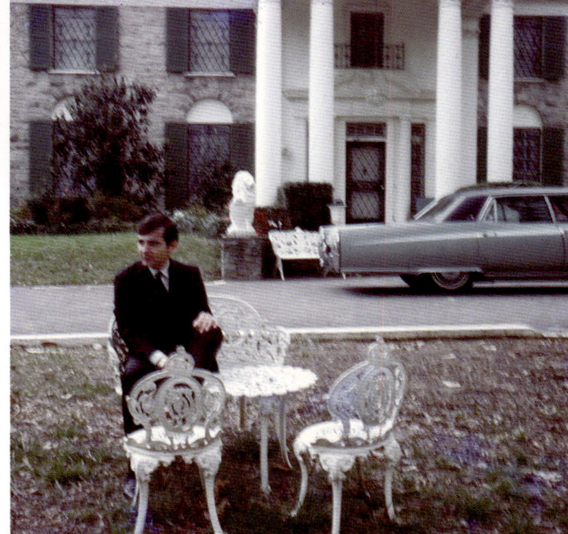

1968 at Graceland

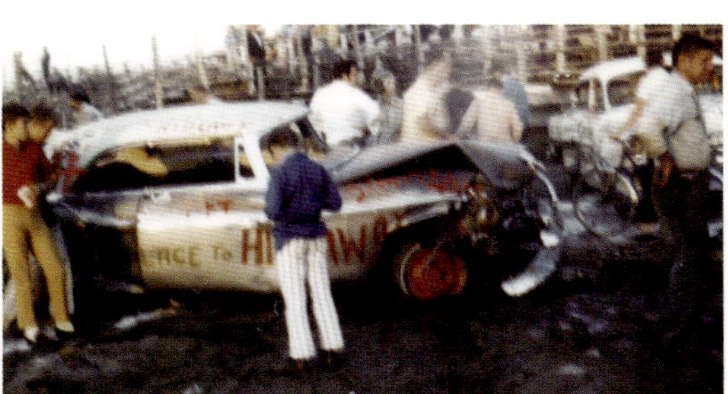

My #444 at Riverside Race Track 1969

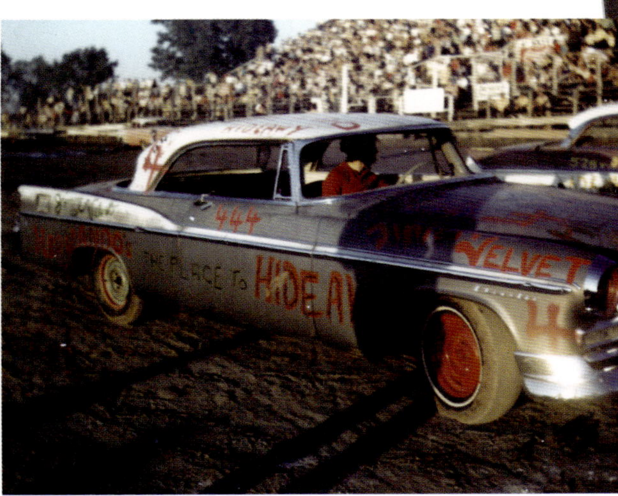

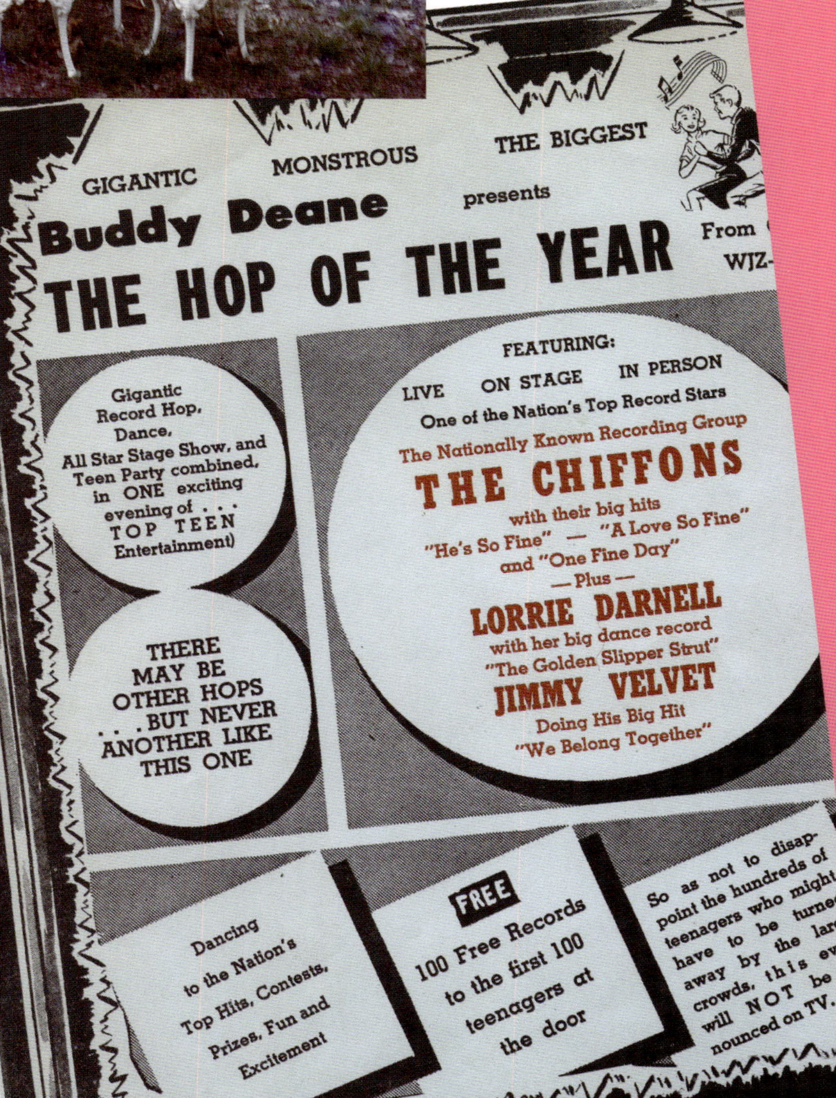

GIGANTIC MONSTROUS THE BIGGEST

Buddy Deane presents From WJZ-

THE HOP OF THE YEAR

Gigantic Record Hop, Dance, All Star Stage Show, and Teen Party combined, in ONE exciting evening of . . . TOP TEEN Entertainment)

THERE MAY BE OTHER HOPS . . . BUT NEVER ANOTHER LIKE THIS ONE

FEATURING:
LIVE ON STAGE IN PERSON
One of the Nation's Top Record Stars
The Nationally Known Recording Group
THE CHIFFONS
with their big hits
"He's So Fine" — "A Love So Fine"
and "One Fine Day"
— Plus —
LORRIE DARNELL
with her big dance record
"The Golden Slipper Strut"
JIMMY VELVET
Doing His Big Hit
"We Belong Together"

Dancing to the Nation's Top Hits, Contests, Prizes, Fun and Excitement

FREE
100 Free Records to the first 100 teenagers at the door

So as not to disappoint the hundreds of teenagers who might have to be turned away by the large crowds, this event will NOT be announced on TV.

THE ONLY HOP OF ITS KIND THIS YEAR IN THIS ENTIRE AREA
DON'T MISS IT!

Bankert's Restaurant Rec. Hall
Littlestown, Pa.

Saturday, Oct.
8:00 to 11:00 p.m.
of Admission $1.00

The Hop of the Year
Baltimore, MD

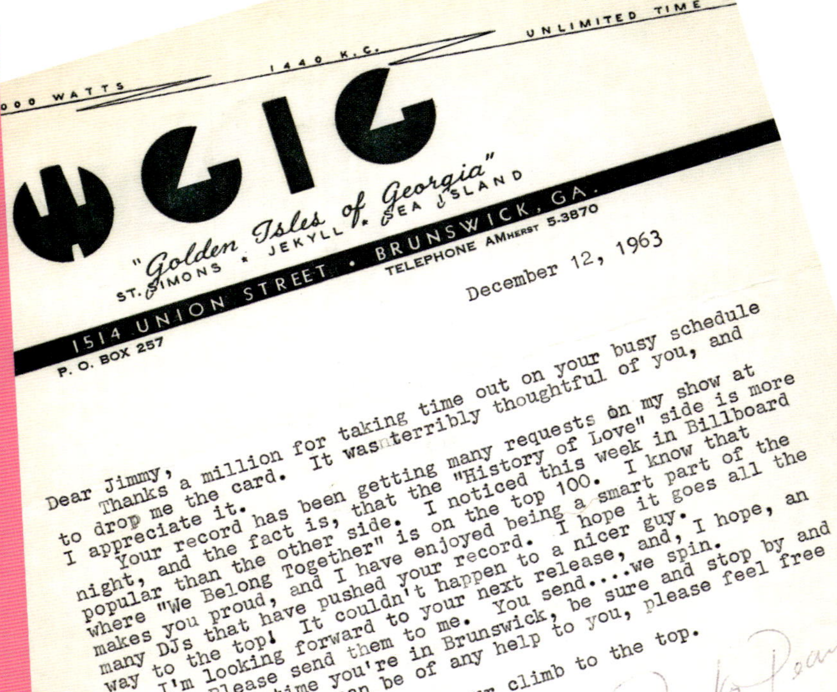

WGIG

1000 WATTS 1440 K.C. UNLIMITED TIME

"Golden Isles of Georgia"

ST. SIMONS • JEKYLL • SEA ISLAND

1514 UNION STREET • BRUNSWICK, GA.

P. O. BOX 257 TELEPHONE AMHERST 5-3870

December 12, 1963

Dear Jimmy,

Thanks a million for taking time out on your busy schedule to drop me the card. It was terribly thoughtful of you, and I appreciate it.

Your record has been getting many requests on my show at night, and the fact is, that the "History of Love" side is more popular than the other side. I noticed this week in Billboard where "We Belong Together" is on the top 100. I know that makes you proud, and I have enjoyed being a smart part of the many DJs that have pushed your record. I hope it goes all the way to the top! It couldn't happen to a nicer guy.

I'm looking forward to your next release, and, I hope, an album. Please send them to me. You send....we spin.

The next time you're in Brunswick, be sure and stop by and see me. And if I can be of any help to you, please feel free to call on me.

Lots of luck to you on your climb to the top.

We're Growing In Glynn

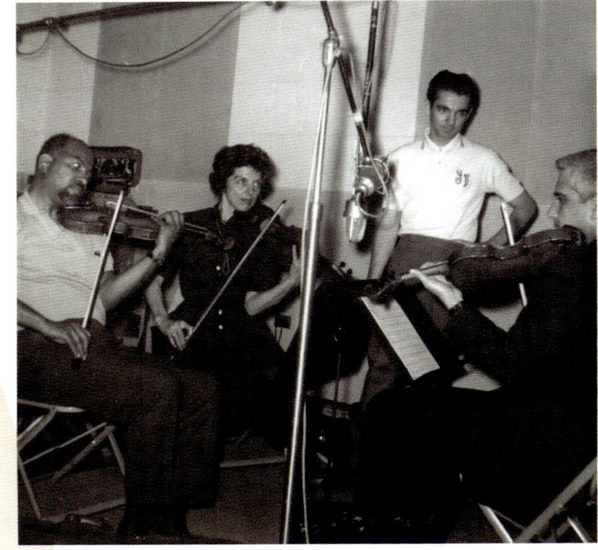

Brenton Banks String Section

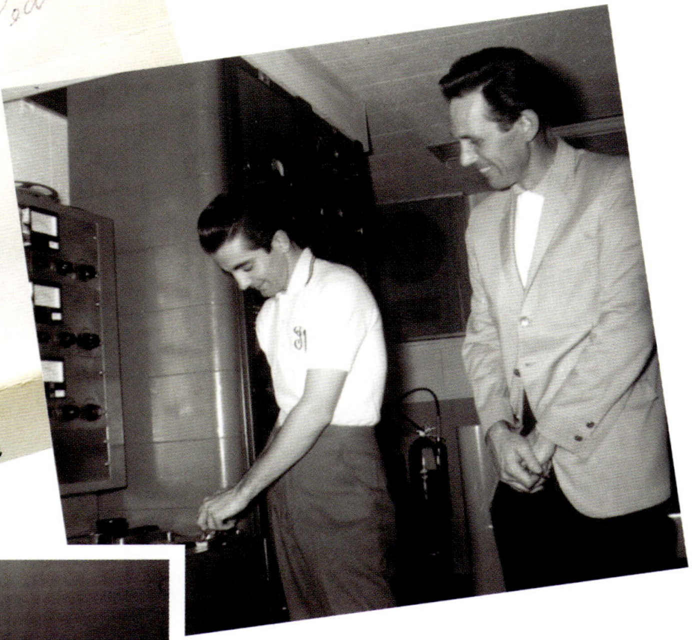

Chet Atkins
RCA Studio B 1962

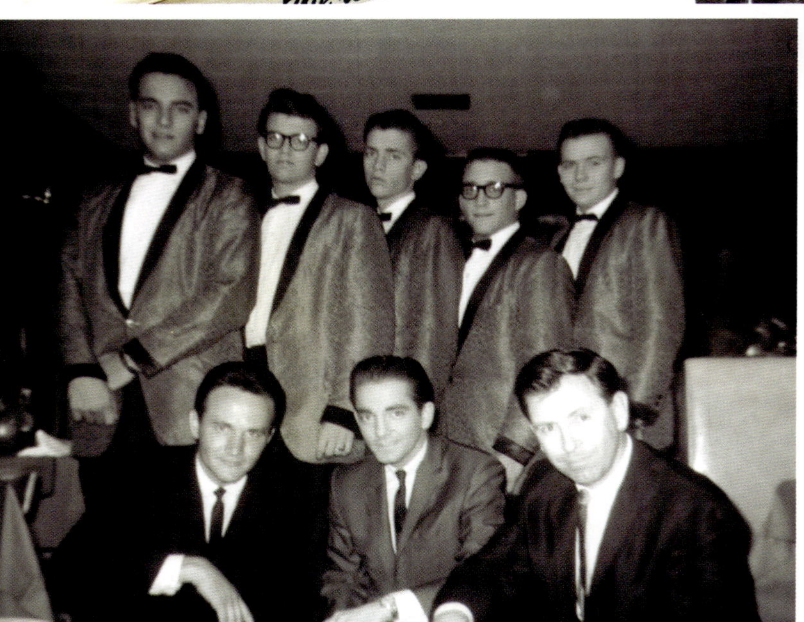

My show in Nashville with my band "The Teakwoods" and Roger Miller (left) and Bill Purcell my arranger 1964

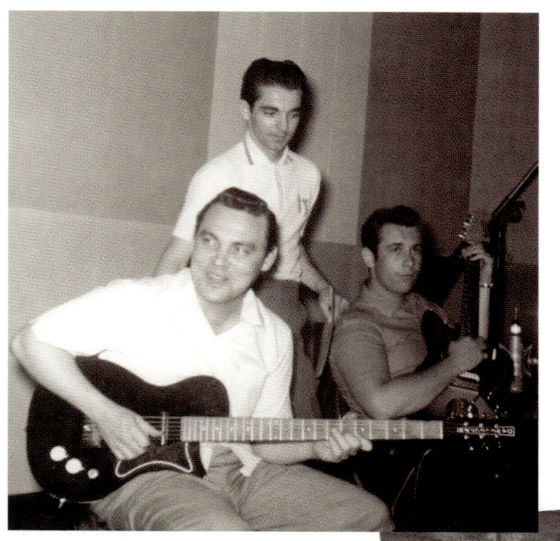

Recording my 2nd biggest hit “We Belong Together” in RCA Studio B, 1962
Arranger: Bill Justis

Jerry Kennedy, Kelso Herston, and Jerry Reed on guitars

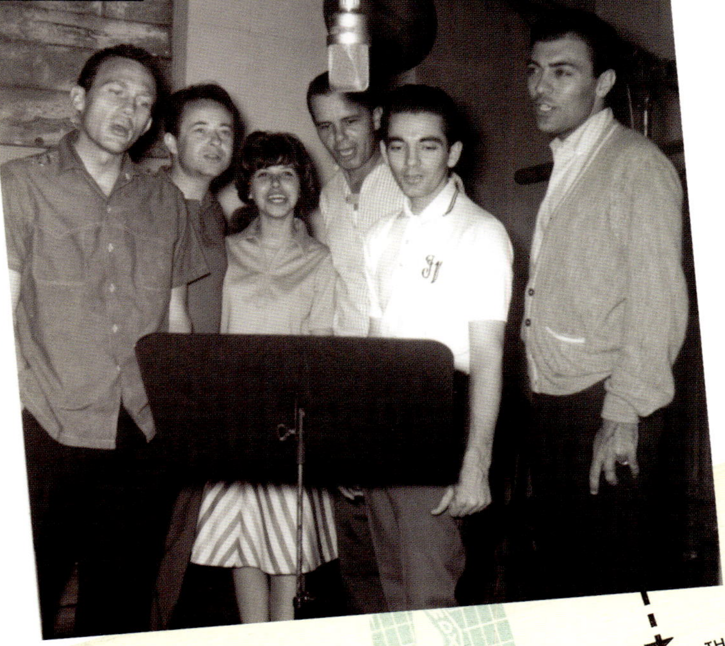

The Jordanaires and Prissy Reed on vocal back up. Hoyt Hawkins, Gordon Stoker, Neal Matthews, and Ray Walker.

WDXY RADIO ANOTHER OF THE GOOD THINGS ABOUT SUMTER

P.O. BOX 1269 • 814 BOULEVARD RD. • SUMTER, S. C.

March 31st

JIMMY VELVET
BOX 7338
ASHVILLE, TENN

DEAR JIMMY;

First off, many thanks for your mailing of your latest single. Second off let me say this is one of the greatest records I have heard in quite some time.

We have had immediate first day action on it and predict hot requests and heavy sales here in South Carolina. ITS ALMOST TOMORROW is a #1 recording Jimmy and the best of luck to you on it.

Please keep us on your mailing list for new releases and I will add your name to the WDXY TUNEDEX for weekly mailing from this end. (Enclosed sample survey).

WDXY has just boosted its power and we are now un-sur passed in the state. Hope we can help you out.

Best of everything,

Dick Reus

Dick Reus
Music Dir

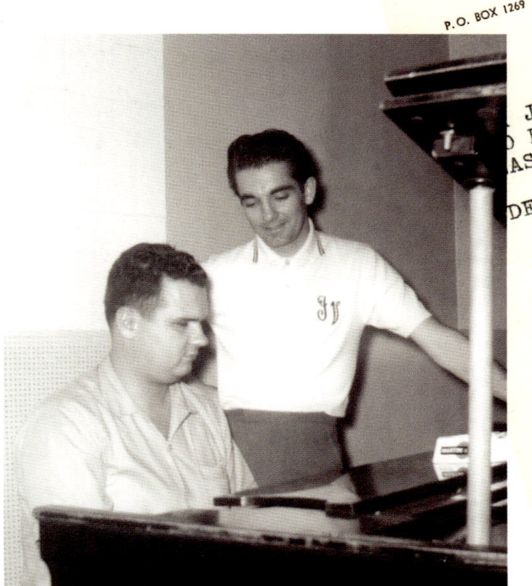

Pig Harcus on Piano

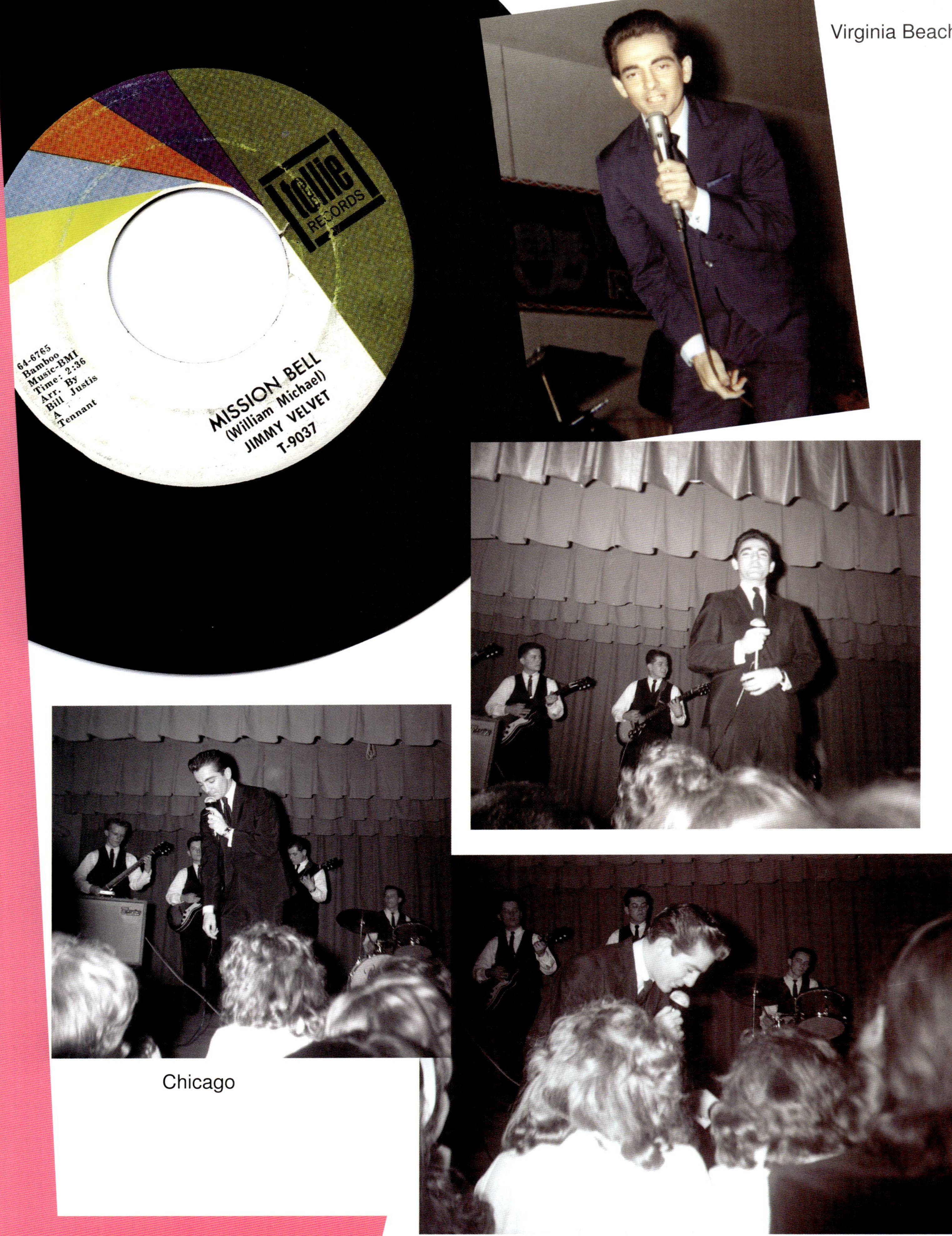

Virginia Beach

Chicago

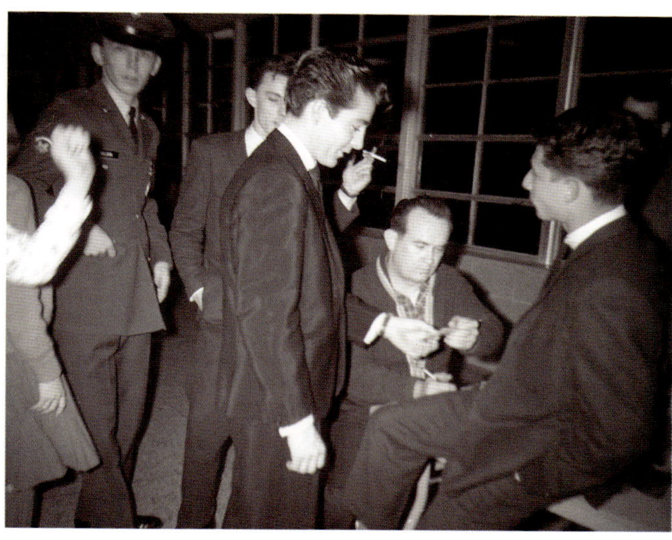

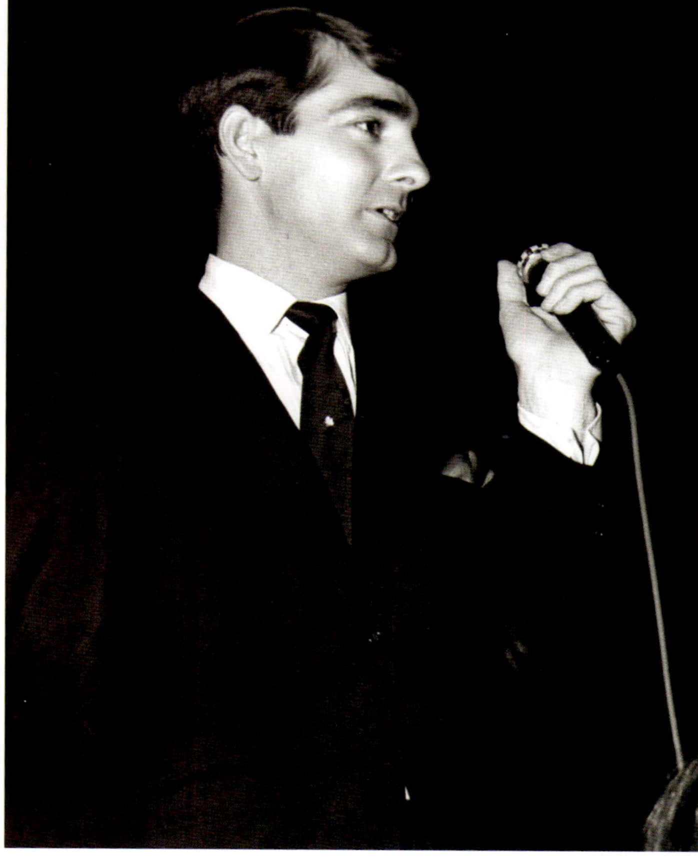

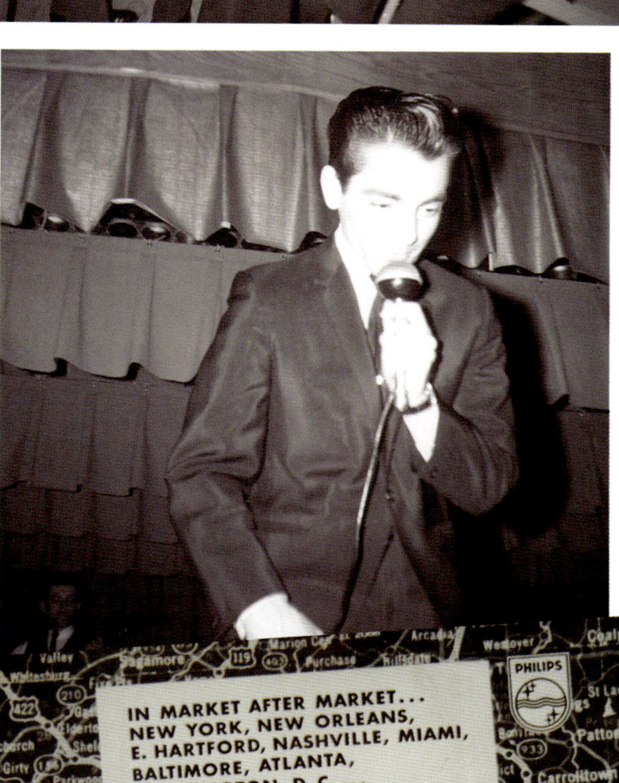

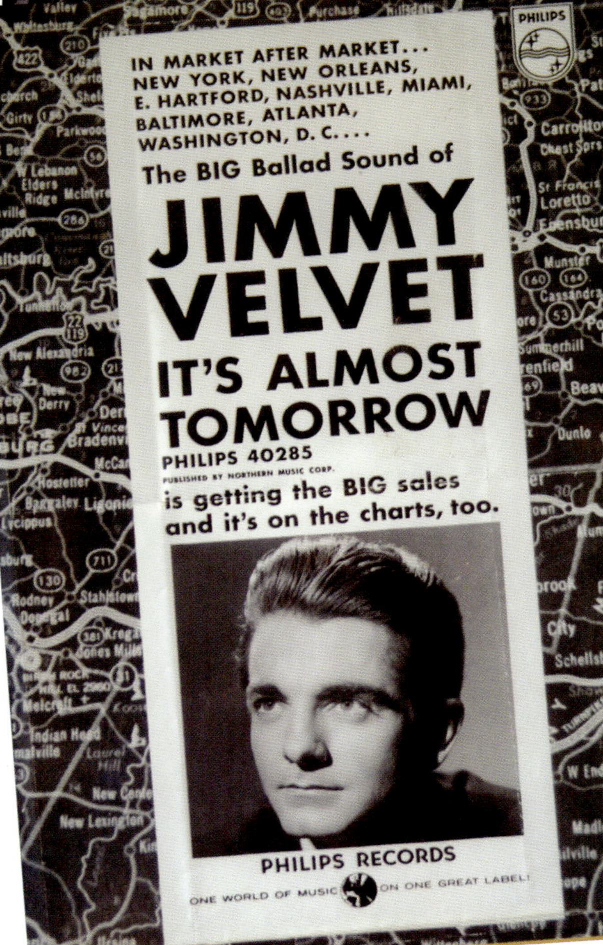
IN MARKET AFTER MARKET...
NEW YORK, NEW ORLEANS,
E. HARTFORD, NASHVILLE, MIAMI,
BALTIMORE, ATLANTA,
WASHINGTON, D. C....
The BIG Ballad Sound of
JIMMY
VELVET
IT'S ALMOST
TOMORROW
PHILIPS 40285
is getting the BIG sales
and it's on the charts, too.
PHILIPS RECORDS
ONE WORLD OF MUSIC ON ONE GREAT LABEL!
PHILIPS

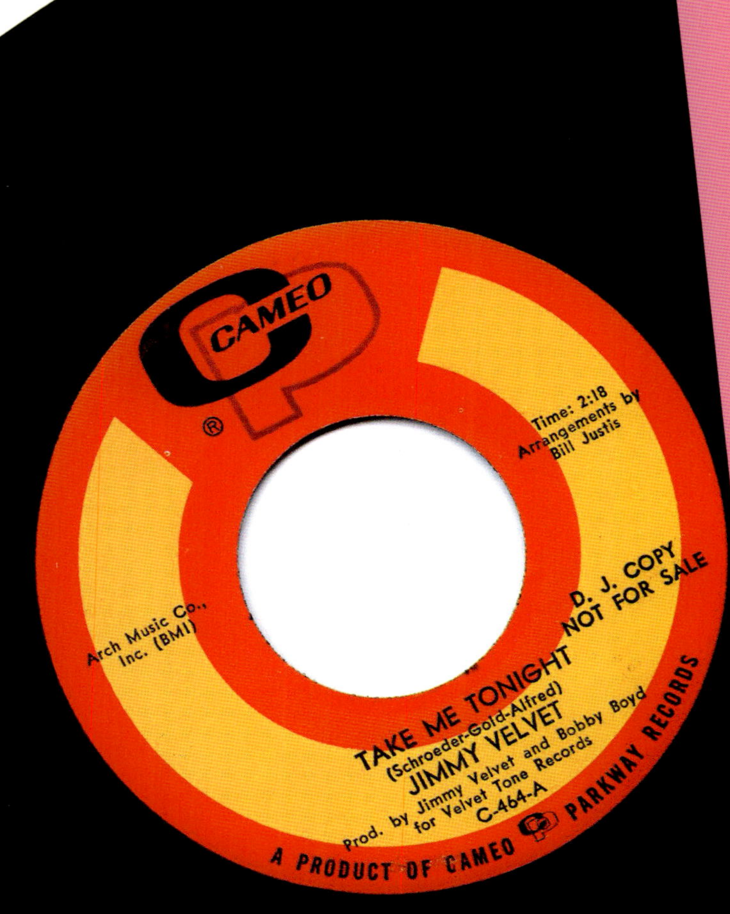
CAMEO
Time: 2:18
Arrangements by
Bill Justis
Arch Music Co.,
Inc. (BMI)
D. J. COPY
NOT FOR SALE
TAKE ME TONIGHT
(Schroeder-Gold-Alfred)
JIMMY VELVET
Prod. by Jimmy Velvet and Bobby Boyd
for Velvet Tone Records
C-464-A
A PRODUCT OF CAMEO PARKWAY RECORDS

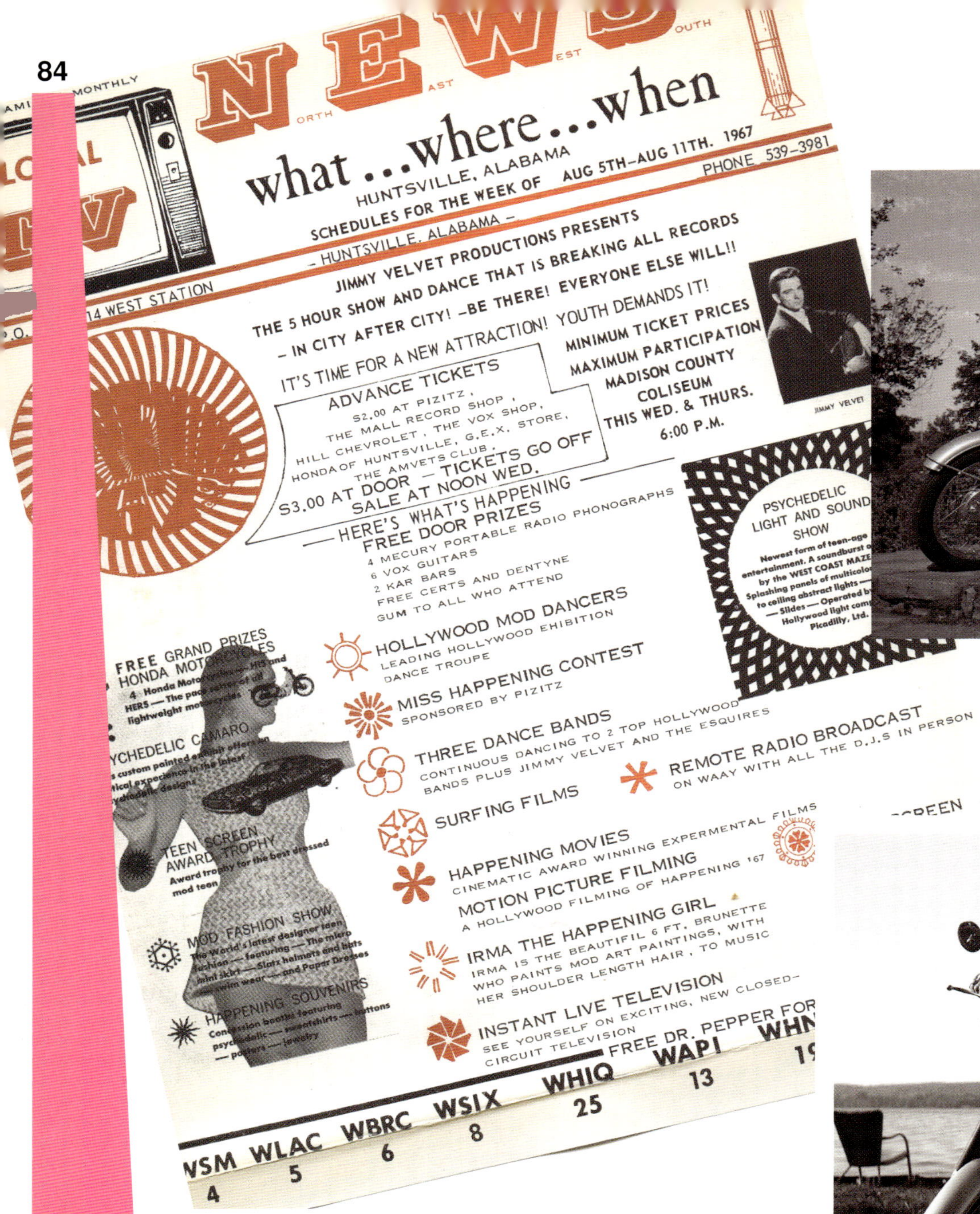

MONTHLY

NEWS

what ...where...when

HUNTSVILLE, ALABAMA

SCHEDULES FOR THE WEEK OF AUG 5TH–AUG 11TH. 1967

PHONE 539-3981

– HUNTSVILLE, ALABAMA –

14 WEST STATION

JIMMY VELVET PRODUCTIONS PRESENTS

THE 5 HOUR SHOW AND DANCE THAT IS BREAKING ALL RECORDS – IN CITY AFTER CITY! –BE THERE! EVERYONE ELSE WILL!!

IT'S TIME FOR A NEW ATTRACTION! YOUTH DEMANDS IT!

MINIMUM TICKET PRICES
MAXIMUM PARTICIPATION
MADISON COUNTY
COLISEUM
THIS WED. & THURS.
6:00 P.M.

JIMMY VELVET

ADVANCE TICKETS
$2.00 AT PIZITZ, THE MALL RECORD SHOP, HILL CHEVROLET, THE VOX SHOP, HONDA OF HUNTSVILLE, G.E.X. STORE, THE AMVETS CLUB.
$3.00 AT DOOR — TICKETS GO OFF SALE AT NOON WED.

— HERE'S WHAT'S HAPPENING —

FREE DOOR PRIZES
4 MECURY PORTABLE RADIO PHONOGRAPHS
6 VOX GUITARS
2 KAR BARS
FREE CERTS AND DENTYNE GUM TO ALL WHO ATTEND

PSYCHEDELIC LIGHT AND SOUND SHOW

FREE GRAND PRIZES
HONDA MOTORCYCLES

PSYCHEDELIC CAMARO

HOLLYWOOD MOD DANCERS
LEADING HOLLYWOOD EXHIBITION DANCE TROUPE

MISS HAPPENING CONTEST
SPONSORED BY PIZITZ

THREE DANCE BANDS
CONTINUOUS DANCING TO 2 TOP HOLLYWOOD BANDS PLUS JIMMY VELVET AND THE ESQUIRES

REMOTE RADIO BROADCAST
ON WAAY WITH ALL THE D.J.S IN PERSON

SURFING FILMS

TEEN SCREEN AWARD TROPHY

HAPPENING MOVIES
CINEMATIC AWARD WINNING EXPERMENTAL FILMS

MOTION PICTURE FILMING
A HOLLYWOOD FILMING OF HAPPENING '67

MOD FASHION SHOW

IRMA THE HAPPENING GIRL
IRMA IS THE BEAUTIFIL 6 FT. BRUNETTE WHO PAINTS MOD ART PAINTINGS, WITH HER SHOULDER LENGTH HAIR, TO MUSIC

HAPPENING SOUVENIRS

INSTANT LIVE TELEVISION
SEE YOURSELF ON EXCITING, NEW CLOSED–CIRCUIT TELEVISION

FREE DR. PEPPER FOR

WSM 4 WLAC 5 WBRC 6 WSIX 8 WHIQ 25 WAPI 13 WHN

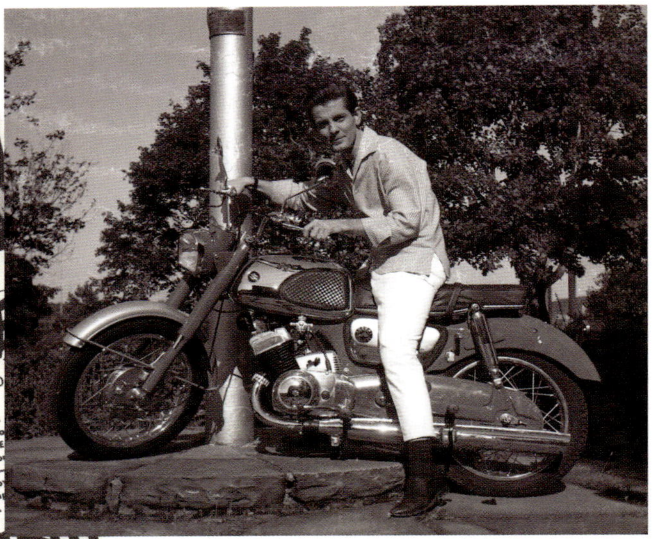

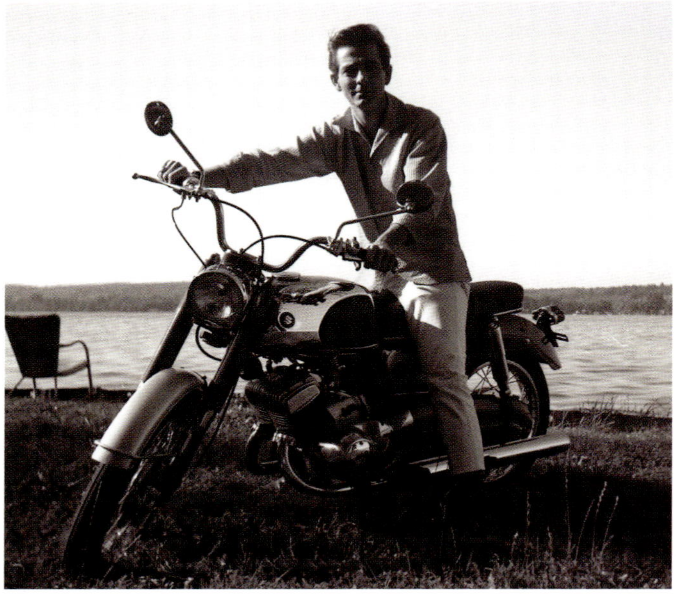

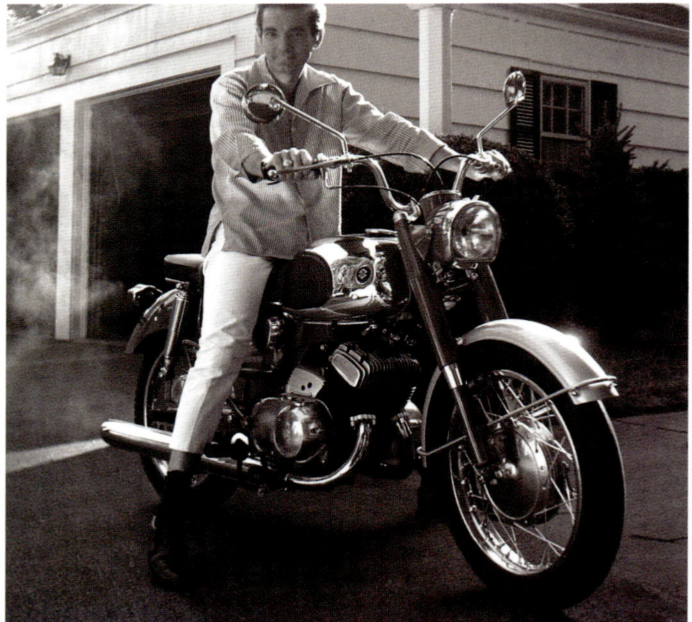

I use to get free Suzuki's to pose on them for advertisements.

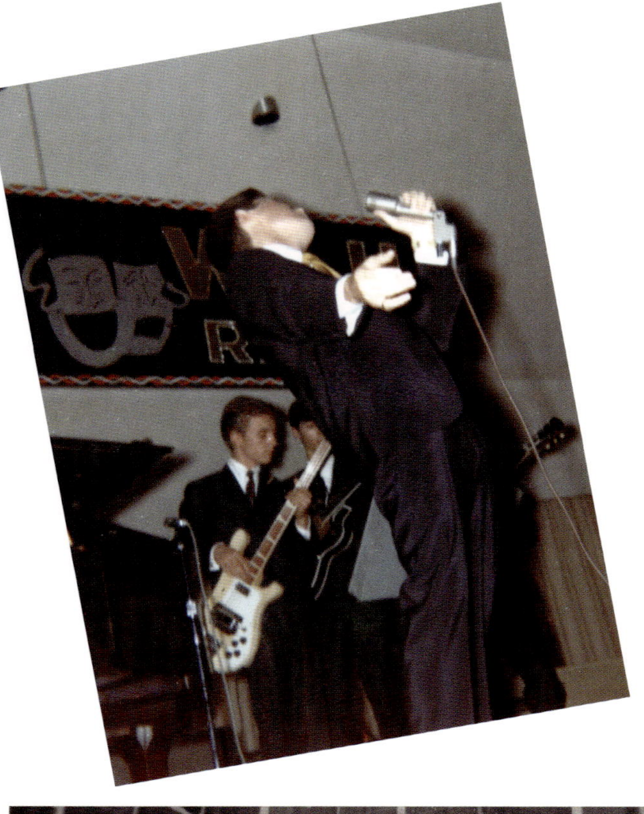

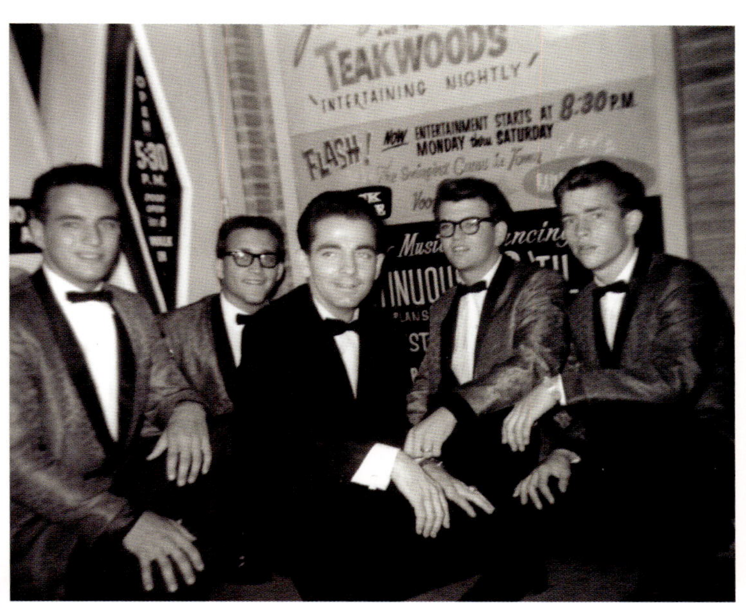

Jimmy Velvet and *The Teakwoods*
1964

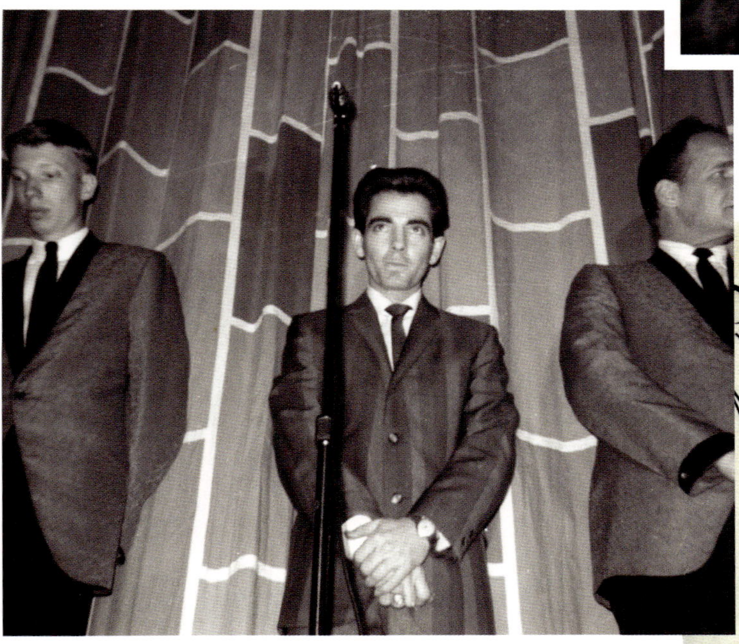

Gene Loving, WGH Norfolk

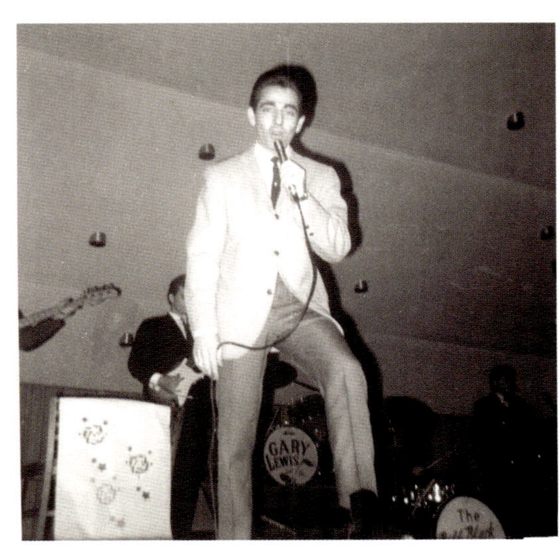

On stage with the "Bill Black Combo"

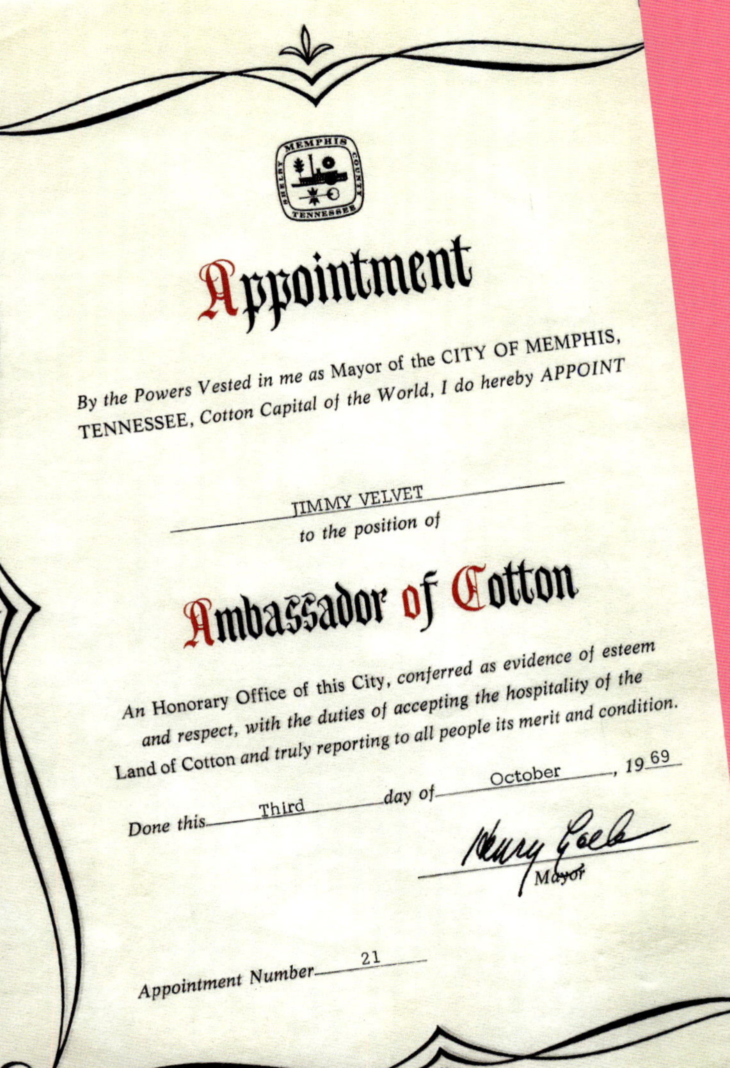

MEMPHIS SHELBY COUNTY TENNESSEE

Appointment

By the Powers Vested in me as Mayor of the CITY OF MEMPHIS, TENNESSEE, Cotton Capital of the World, I do hereby APPOINT

JIMMY VELVET

to the position of

Ambassador of Cotton

An Honorary Office of this City, conferred as evidence of esteem and respect, with the duties of accepting the hospitality of the Land of Cotton and truly reporting to all people its merit and condition.

Done this Third day of October, 1969

Henry Loeb
Mayor

Appointment Number 21

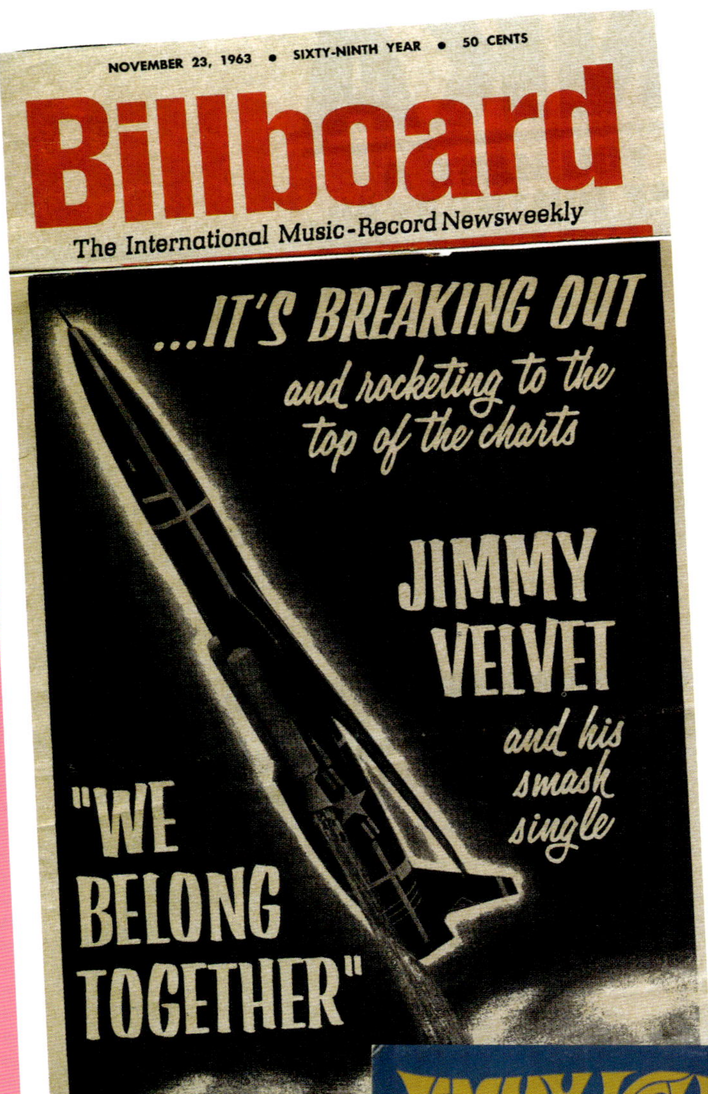

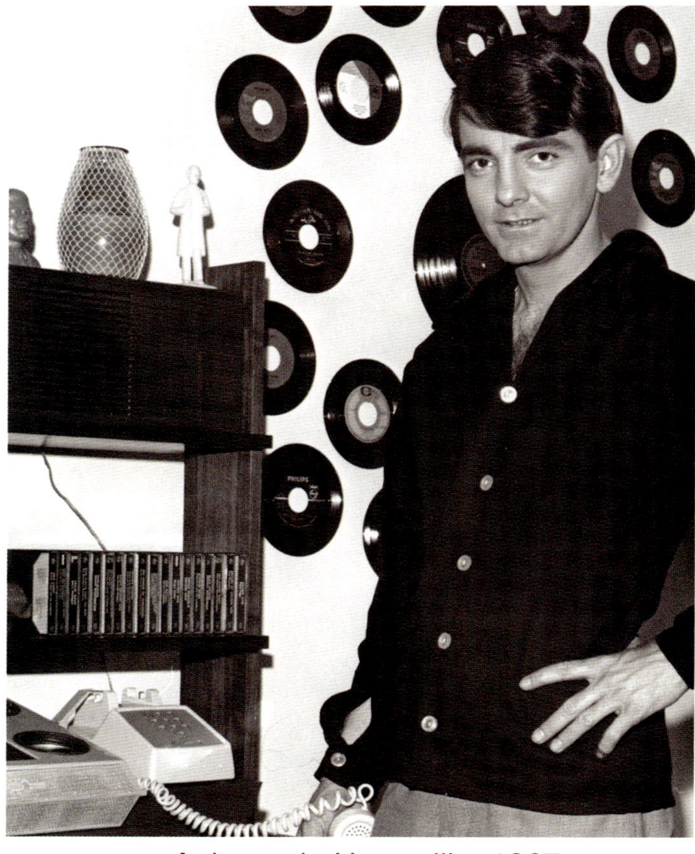
At home in Huntsville, 1967

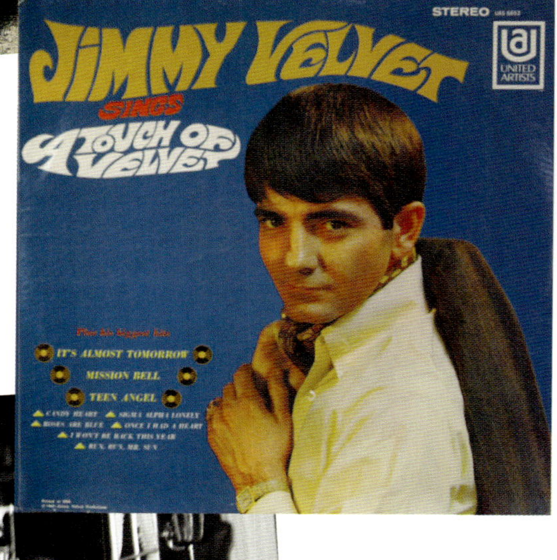

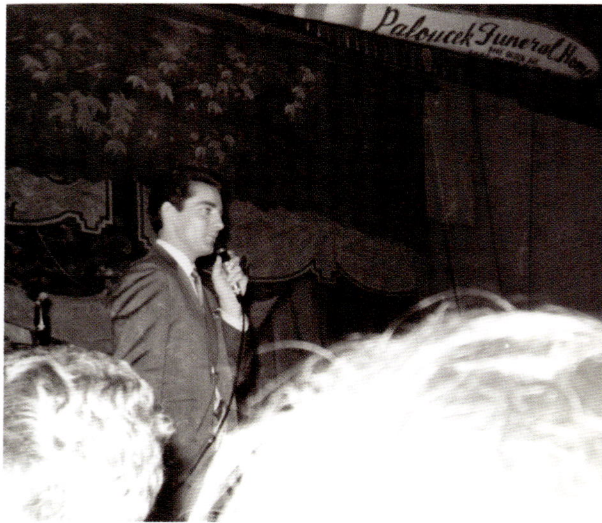

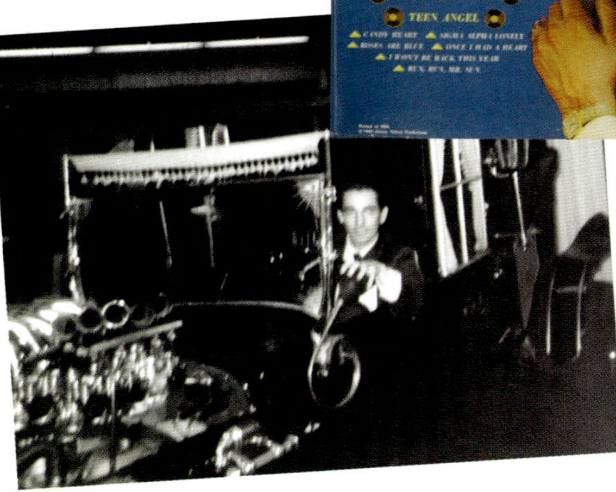
Portland, OR
Teen Age Worlds Fair
Dick Clark Tour

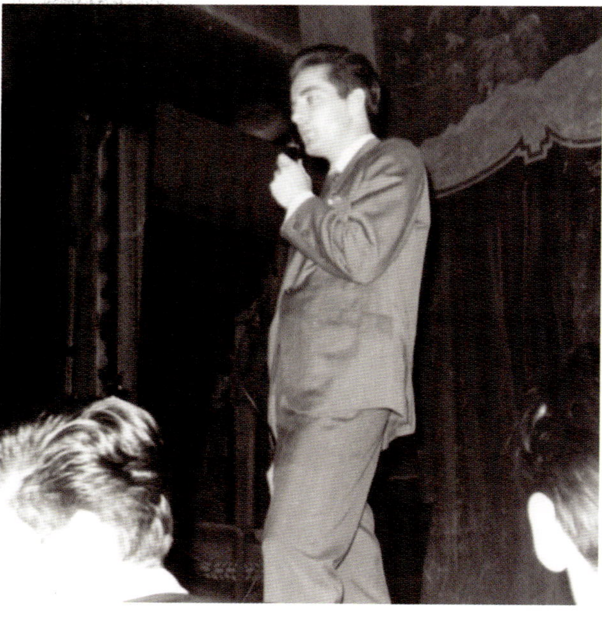
Dick Clark Tour
Chicago, IL

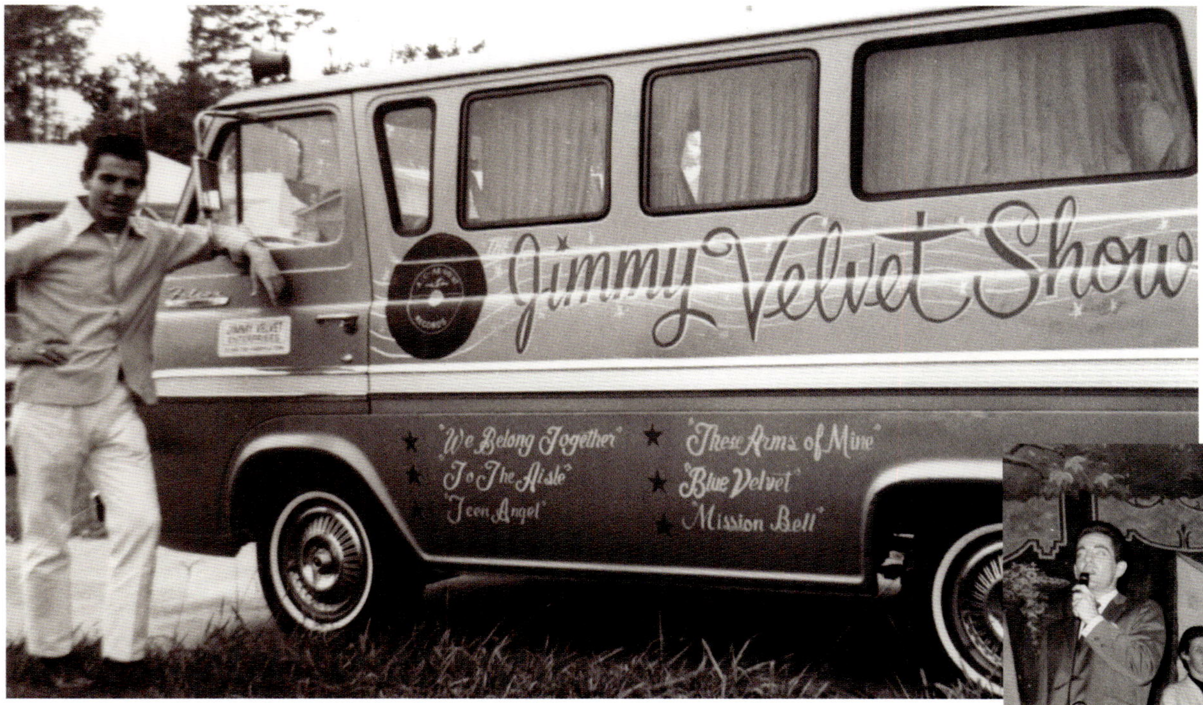

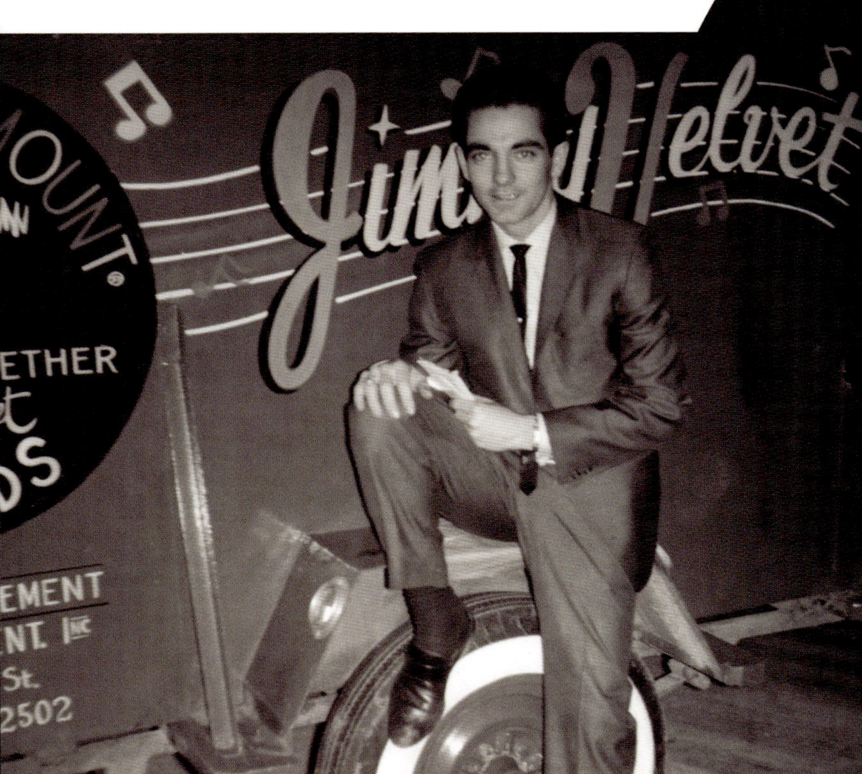
Jimmy Velvet
OUNT.
ETHER
EMENT
2502

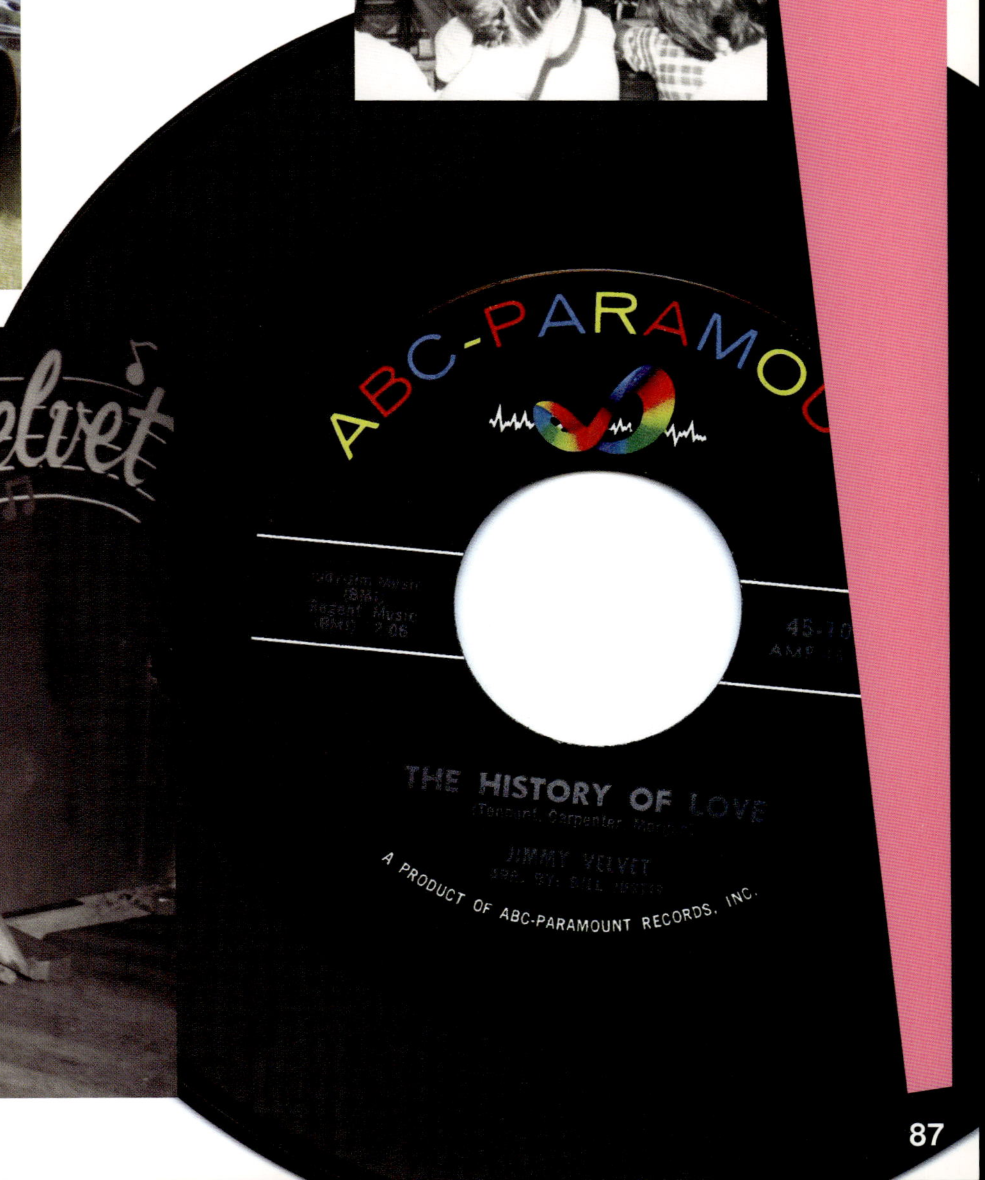

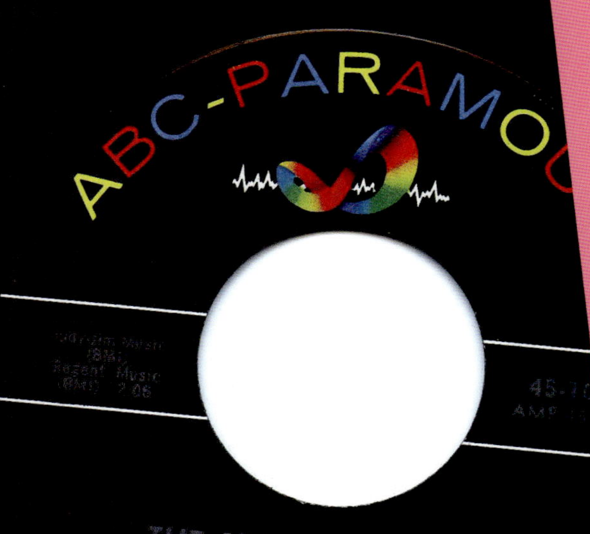
ABC-PARAMOU

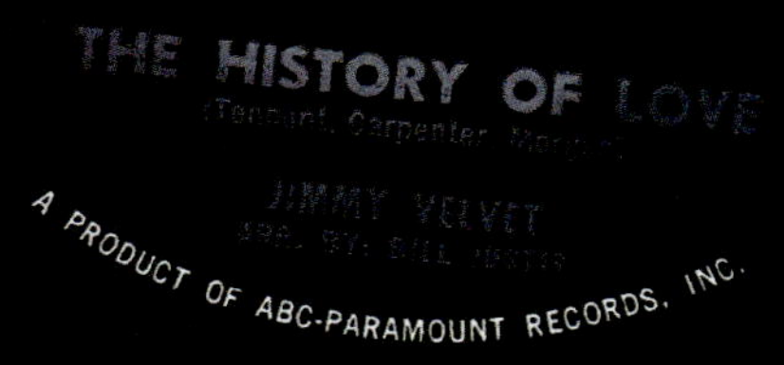
THE HISTORY OF LOVE
JIMMY VELVET
A PRODUCT OF ABC-PARAMOUNT RECORDS, INC.

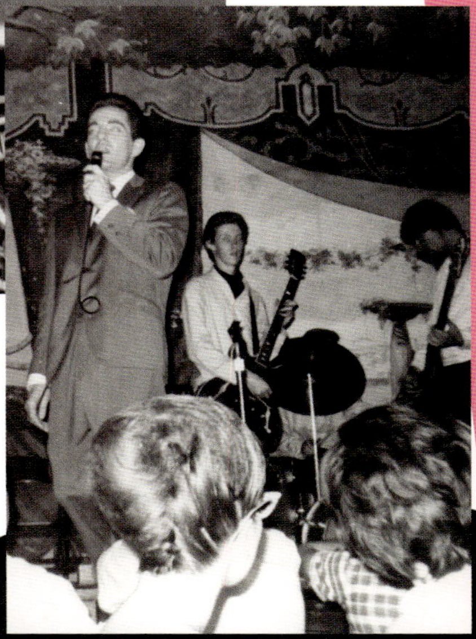

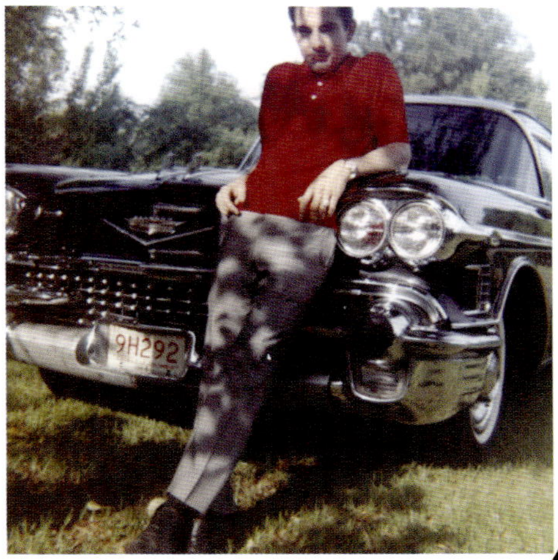

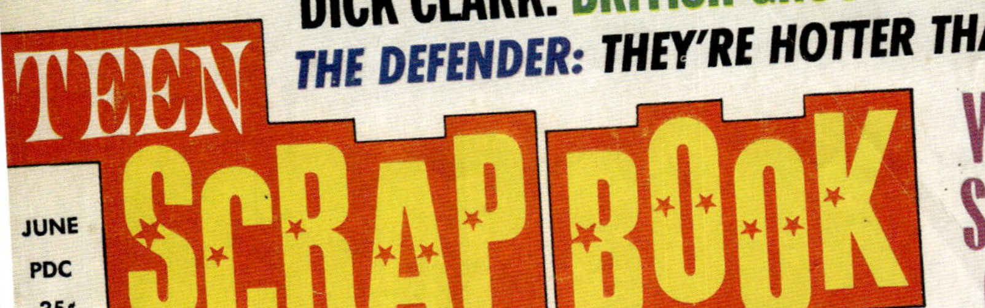

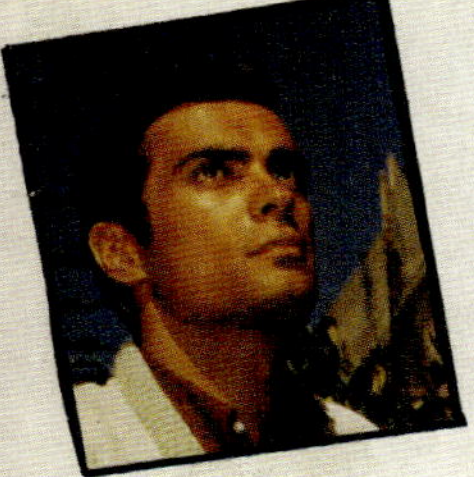

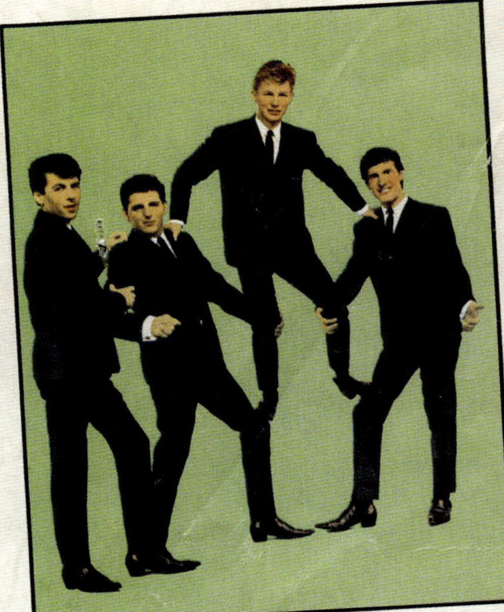

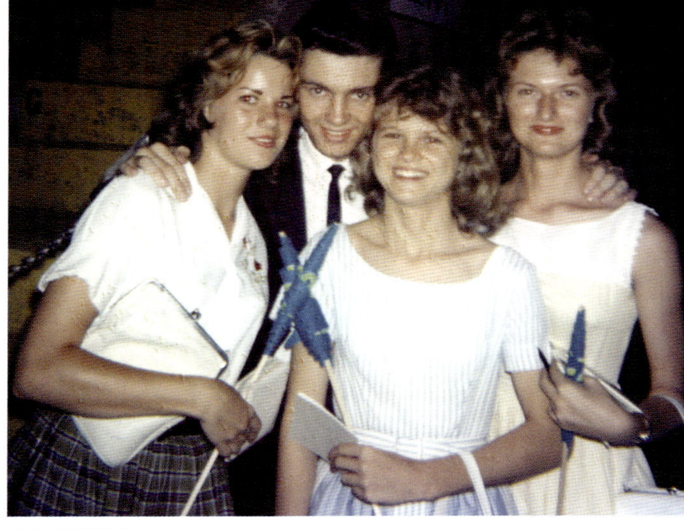

Gene Pitney and fans

Me with my band " The Teakwoods" 1964

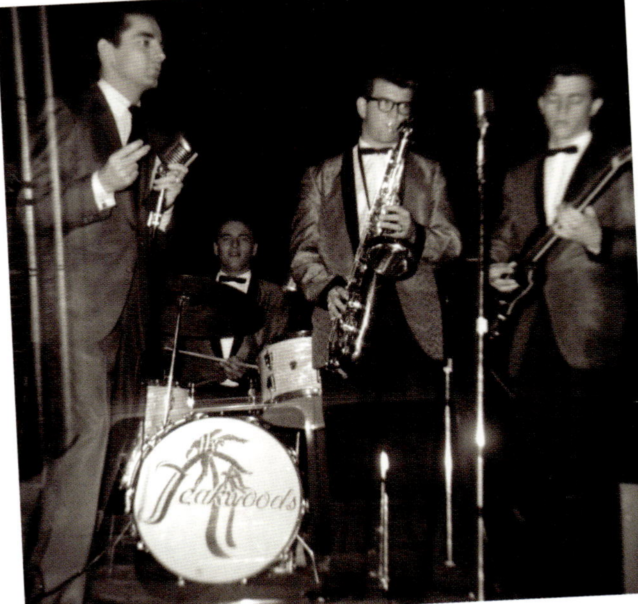

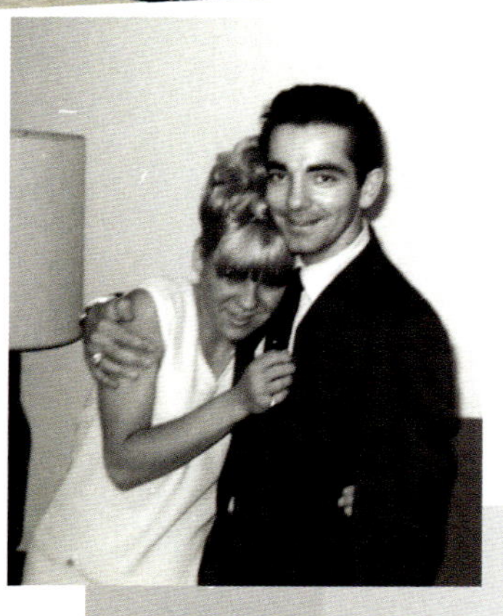

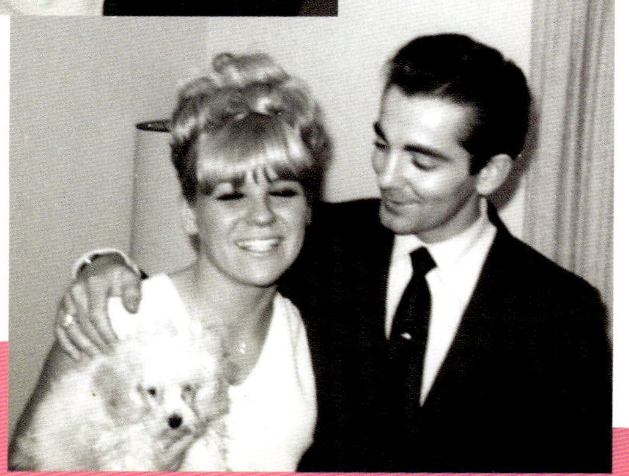

My dear friend

Lauren Chapin

and my dog Bell Butt in Hollywood, 1965. Lauren was "Kathy" on "Father Knows Best". We are still best friends."

Kitt and Kory

Kitt and Kory on Noel Ball Show 1960

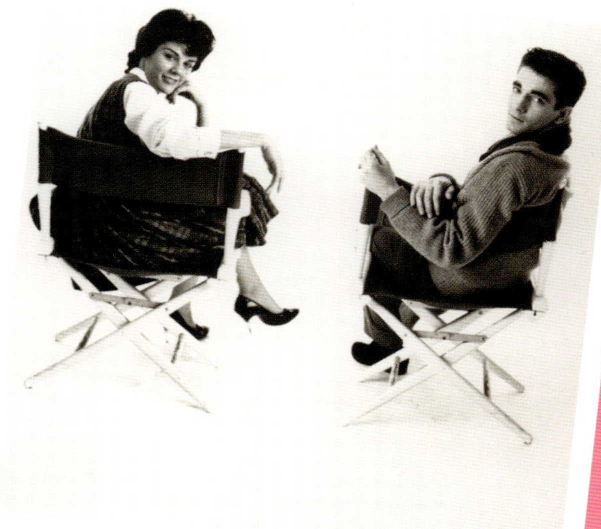

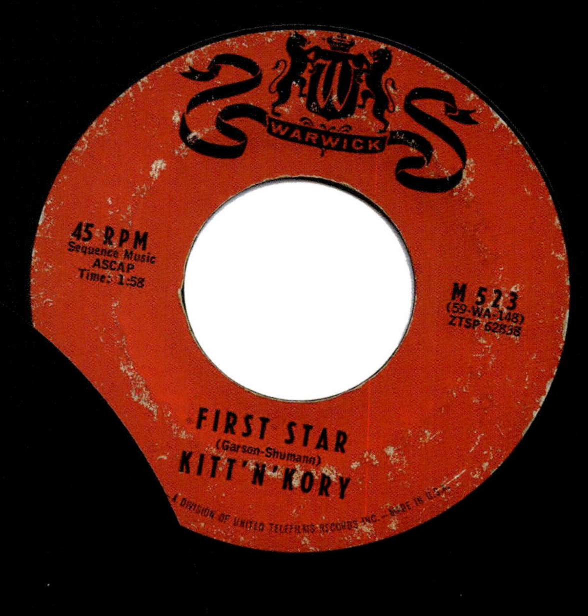

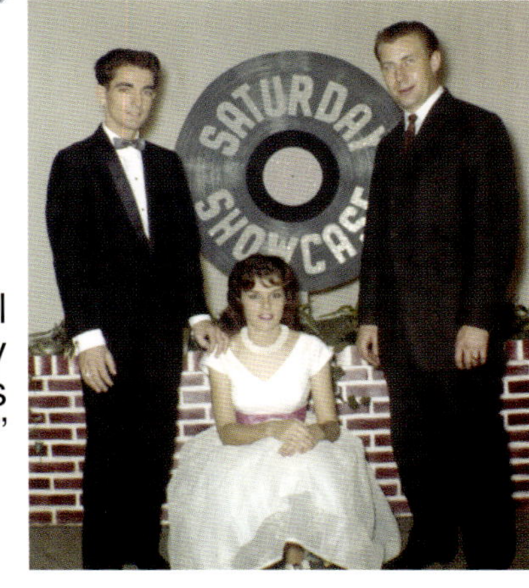

Kitt N' Kory on Noel Ball's Saturday Showcase. Judy was "Kitt" and I was "Kory"

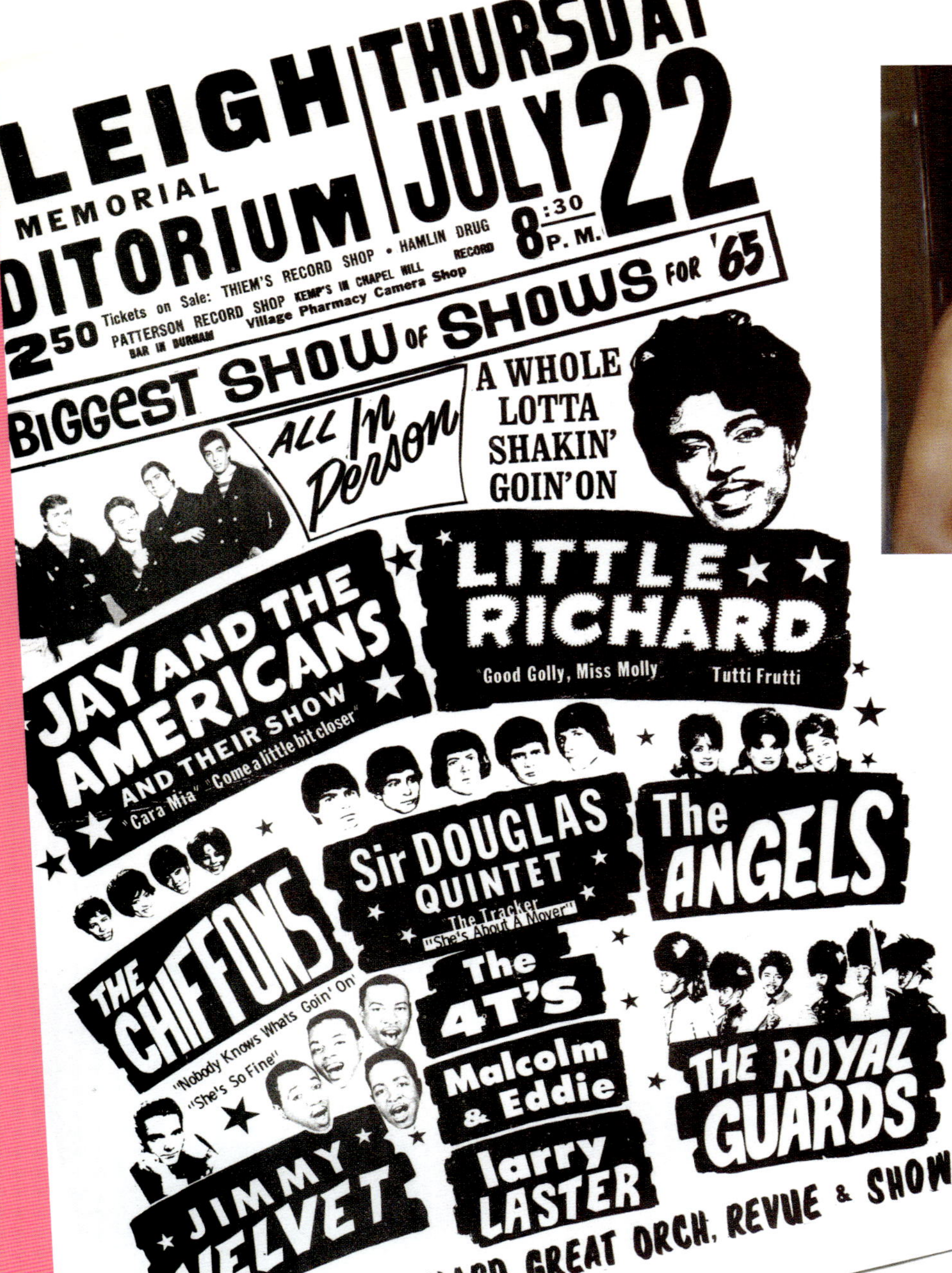

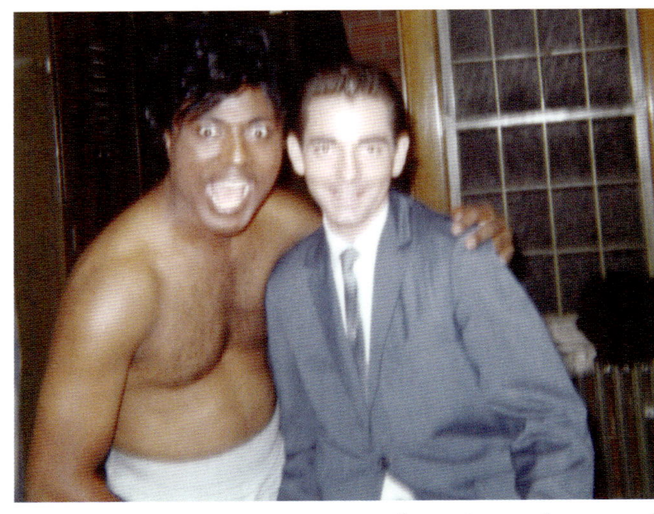

Little Richard

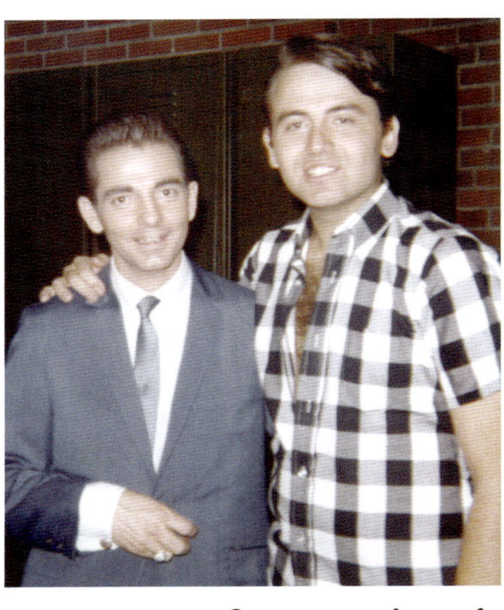

Jay Black

1965 on tour with all of the above. 6 weeks with this crew was a hoot and a ton of fun

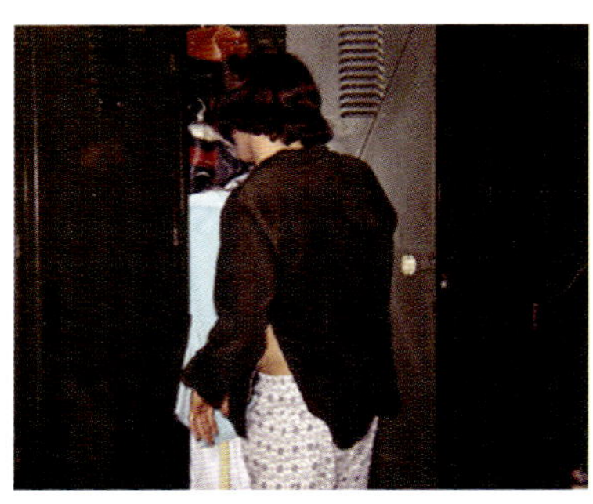

"Augie" Sir Douglas

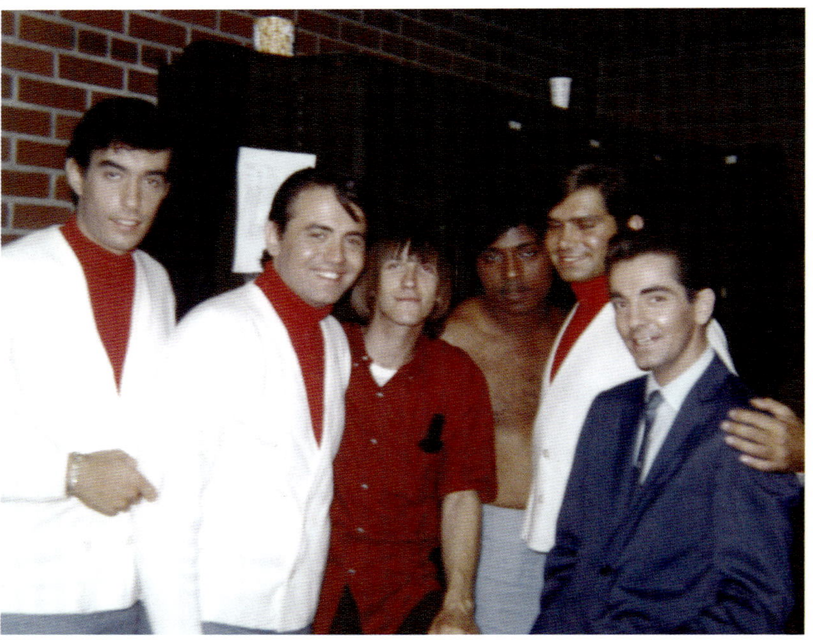

Jay and the Americans and Sir Douglas

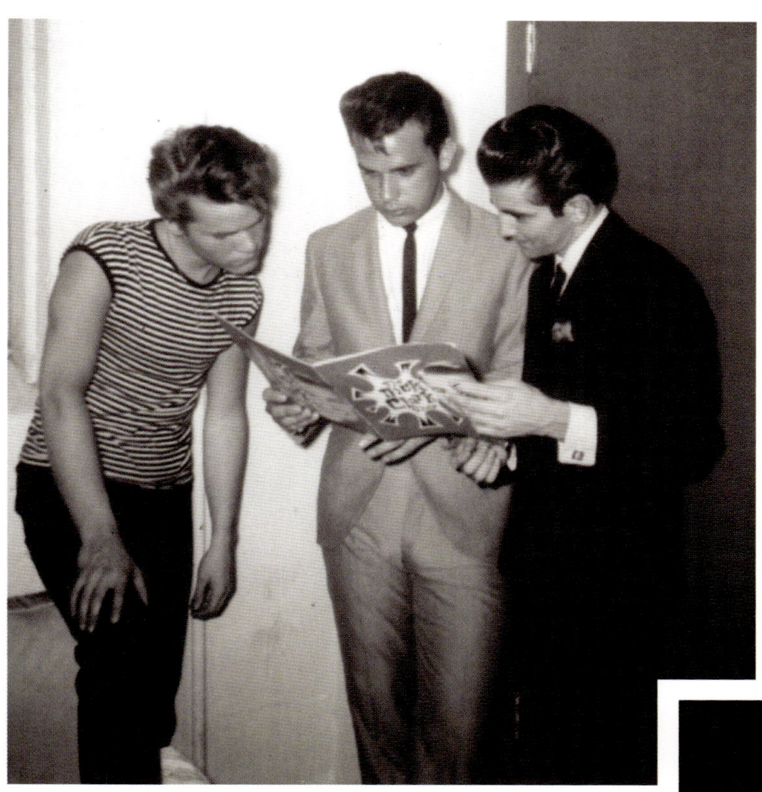

Bryan Hyland

Lou Christie

Luther Perkins
Johnny Cash's Guitar Player

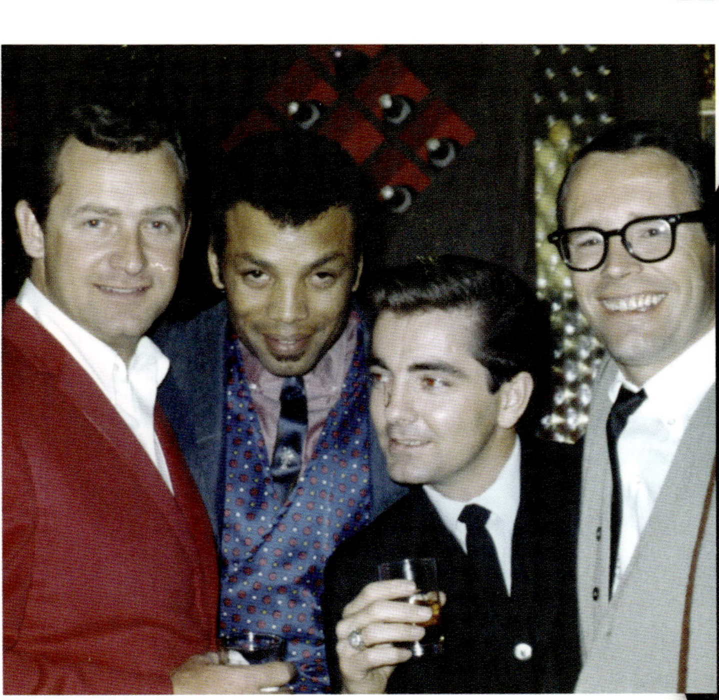

Jewel Akens "Birds and the Bees"

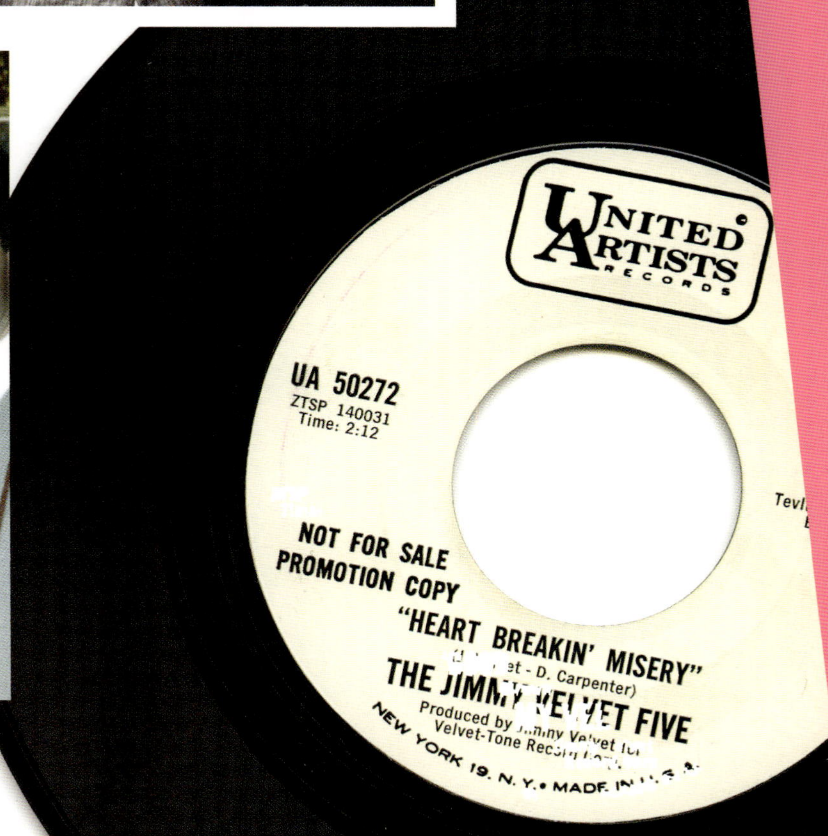

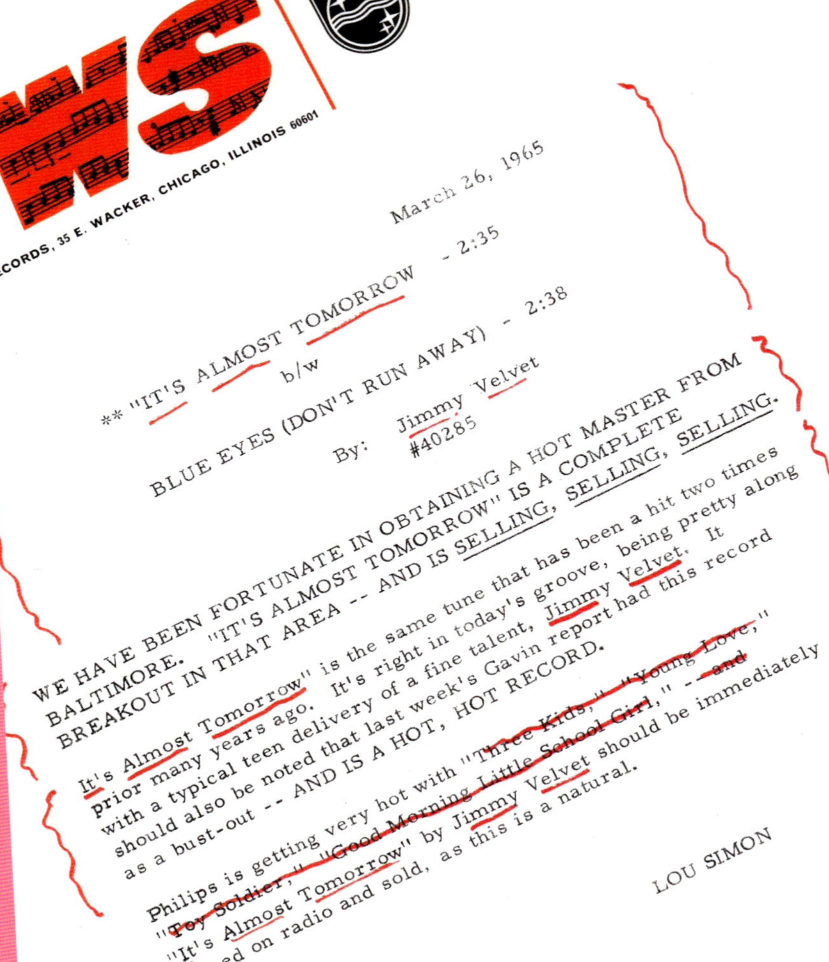

RECORDS, 35 E. WACKER, CHICAGO, ILLINOIS 60601

March 26, 1965

** "IT'S ALMOST TOMORROW - 2:35

b/w

BLUE EYES (DON'T RUN AWAY) - 2:38

By: Jimmy Velvet

#40285

WE HAVE BEEN FORTUNATE IN OBTAINING A HOT MASTER FROM BALTIMORE. "IT'S ALMOST TOMORROW" IS A COMPLETE BREAKOUT IN THAT AREA -- AND IS SELLING, SELLING, SELLING.

It's Almost Tomorrow" is the same tune that has been a hit two times prior many years ago. It's right in today's groove, being pretty along with a typical teen delivery of a fine talent, Jimmy Velvet. It should also be noted that last week's Gavin report had this record as a bust-out -- AND IS A HOT, HOT RECORD.

Philips is getting very hot with "Three Kids," "Young Love," "Toy Soldier," "Good Morning Little School Girl," -- and "It's Almost Tomorrow" by Jimmy Velvet should be immediately placed on radio and sold, as this is a natural.

LOU SIMON

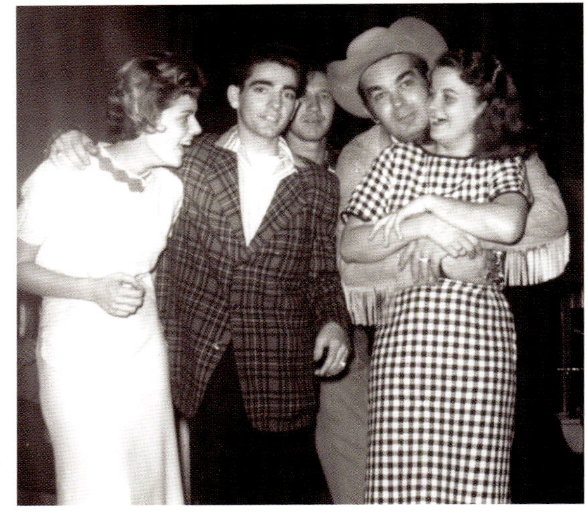

Judy, me, Marty, Tex and his girl.

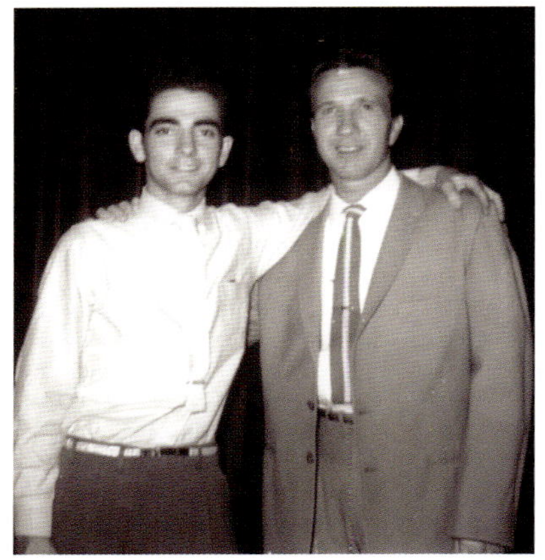

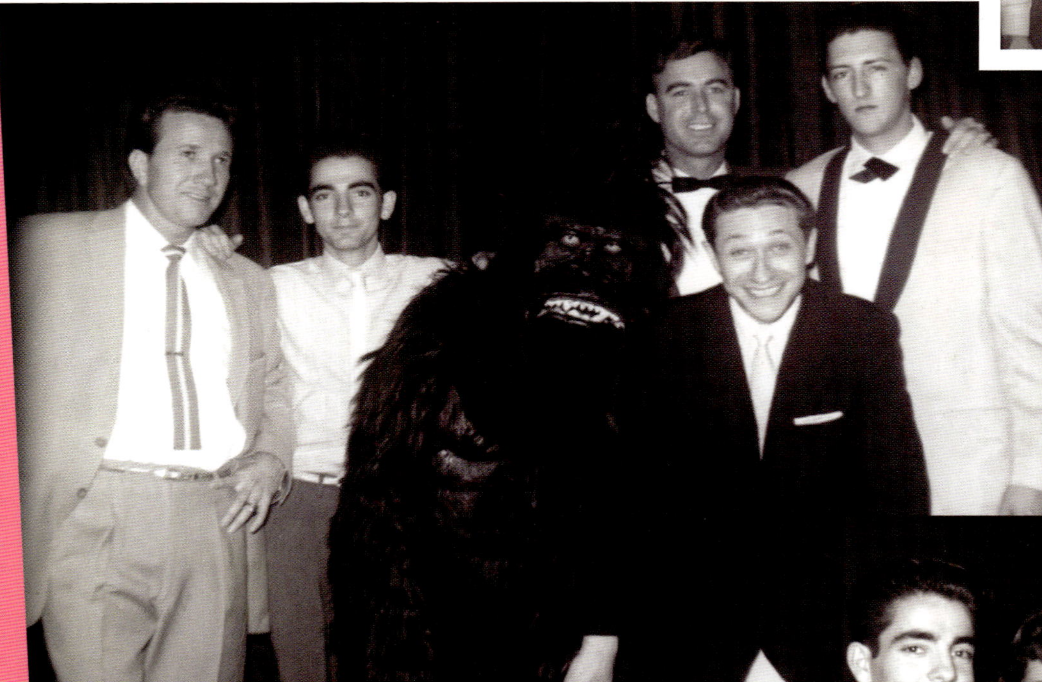

Me, Marty Robbins, Johnny Horton, Thomas Wayne, Scotty Moore, and the "Big Ape" WAPE Show

Marty Robbins

Me, Judy, her friend and Marty in Nashville

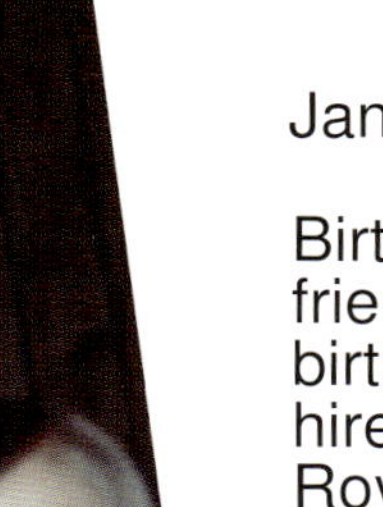

Janet Evan's Birthday

Birthday party for a very special friend, Janet Evans. It was her 17th birthday. Her dad, Amon Evans hired Perry Como, The Platters, Roy Hamilton, and Eddy Arnold for the party

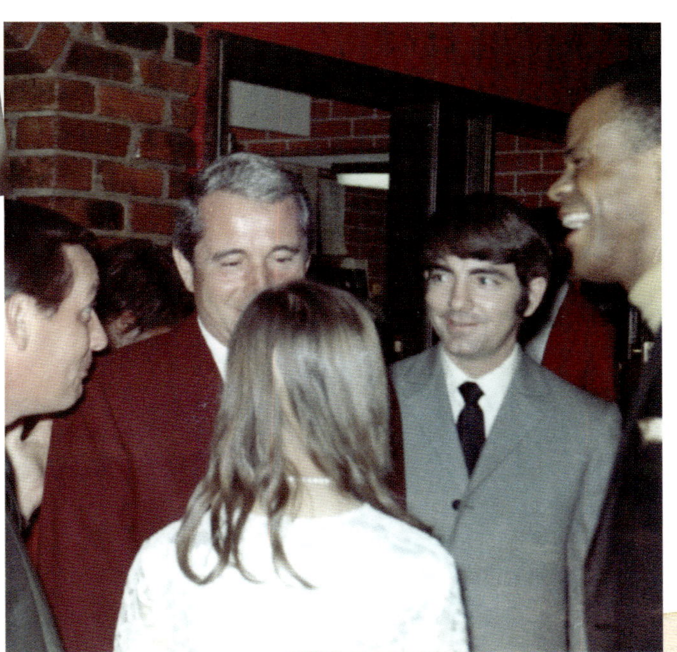

Perry Como, Herbert Reed, The Platters' bass singer and Janet

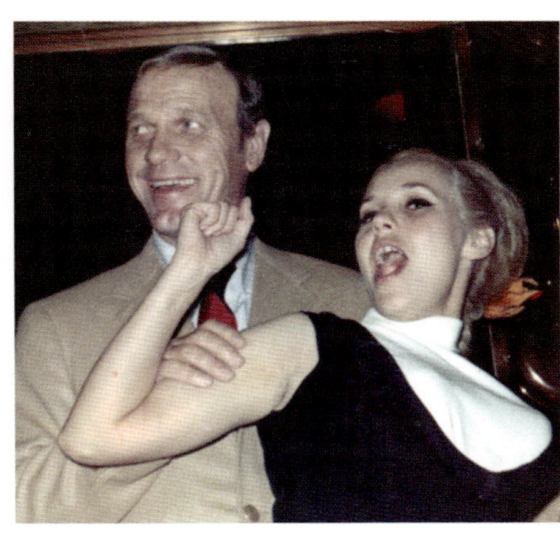

Eddy Arnold and server

COUNTRY MUSIC SURVEY

913 18th Avenue, South, Nashville, Tennessee, 37203
(615 — 242-3515)

Monday - June 9 - 1969 - Issue Twelve

RECORD OF THE WEEK: "ONE HAS MY NAME"-Jerry Lee Lewis (Smash) Jerry's just moving on out there. Make room topside.

COUNTRY MUSIC PICK: "IT'S YOU"-Jimmy Velvet (Royal American) It's been a long, long time between records for Jimmy Velvet. And this one is a MONSTER!

NEWCOMER PICK: "SAN FRANCISCO IS A LONELY TOWN"-Ben Peters (Liberty) Peters has penned himself one fine piece of material. A hit tune.

TOP 50

...ES PEOPLE PLAY-F.Weller (Col)
...JUN BABY-H.Williams,Jr. (MGM)
...nging My Song-T.Wynette (Epc)
...R. WALKER-B.J.Spears (Cap)
...Gave Me A Mountain-J.Bush (Stp)
...RUNNING BEAR-S.James (Cap)
... I LOVE YOU MORE-C.Twitty (Dec)
... TWO WORLDS COLLIDE-J.Reeves (RCA)
...) Please Don't Go-E.Arnold (RCA)
...) I'll Share My World-G.Jones (Mus)
...6) Never Was A Time-J.C.Riley (Plan)
...13) Back To Birmingham-L.Ashley (Ash)
...17) ONE MORE MILE-D.Dudley (Mrc)
...(18) I'M A DRIFTER-B.Goldsboro (UA)
...(11) Lincoln Park Inn-B.Bare (RCA)
...(24) OLD FAITHFUL-M.Tillis (Kap)
...(19) Why You Been Gone-J.Darrell (UA)
...8.(22) SMOKY PLACES-B.Walker (Mon)
...19.(31) ONE HAS MY NAME-J.L.Lewis (Sma)
20.(20) Too Much Of A Man-A.Hardin (Col)
*21.(32) STATUE OF A FOOL-J.Greene (Dec)
22.(23) W. Va. Woman-B.E.Wheeler (UA)
*23.(28) BE GLAD-D.Reeves (UA)
24.(12) Sweetheart Of The Year-R.Price (Col)
25.(29) Good Deal Lucille-C.Smith (Col)
*26.(34) LEAVE MY DREAM ALONE-W.Mack (Dec)
27.(8) Woman Of The World-L.Lynn (Dec)
28.(30) Heaven Below-J.W.Ryles (Col)
*29.(43) JOHNNY B. GOODE-B.Owens (Cap)
*30.(38) DON'T LET ME-L.G. & J.L.Lewis (Sma)
*31.(36) I'M A GOOD MAN-J.Reno (Dot)
32.(33) Solitary-D.Gibson (RCA)
*33.(45) SAND & SHOVELS-W.Jennings (RCA)
34.(35) Truck Stop-J.Smith (ABC)
*35.(42) ALL FOR THE LOVE-C.King (Col)
36.(41) Spring-C.Hart (Metro)
37.(40) Man Away From Home-V.Trevor (R.Am.)
*38.(47) WHERE'S THE PLAYGROUND-G.Campbell (C...
39.(14) My Life-B.Anderson (Dec)
*40.(46) I'M DYNAMITE-Peggy Sue (Dec)
41.(26) When We Tried-J.Howard (Dec)
42.(21) Big Man-D.Mullins (Plan)
43.(44) This Generation-H.Cargill (Mon)
44.(49) Let's Put Our Worlds-C.Louvin (Cap)
*45.(--) ALL I HAVE TO OFFER-C.Pride (RCA)
46.(50) Make It Rain-B.Mize (Imp)
*47.(--) I'M NOT THROUGH-J.Glaser (RCA)
48.(--) Upstairs In Bedroom-B.Wright (Dec)
49.(--) Cut Across Shorty-N.Stuckey (RCA)
50.(--) All Night Long-C.Smith (Kap)

SALES

My Grass Is Green-R.Drusky (Mrc)
Big Wind-P.Wagoner(RCA)
Take Out The Garbage-Tubb, Lynn (Dec)
Until Something Better-B.Lewis (UA)
Don't Give Me A Chance-C.Gray (Dec)
...ham Blues-J.Barlow (Dot)
... Sanders (Imp)

You Comb Her Hair-C.Potter (Dot)
White Cloud/Beloved-D.Rodgers (Col)
Everybody Wants-E.Bruce (Mon)
Strawberry Farms-T.T.Hall (Mrc)
Daddy-D.Parton (RCA)
Boo Dan-J.Newman (Dec)
Rome Wasn't Built-H.Snow (RCA)

ACTION

Once More-L.Williams (Hick)
... Luman (Hick)

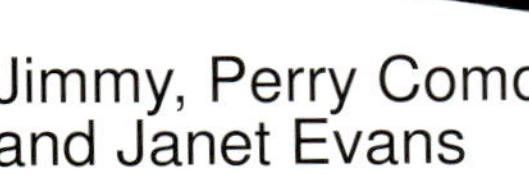

Jimmy, Perry Como and Janet Evans

Natalie Wood's Surprise Party

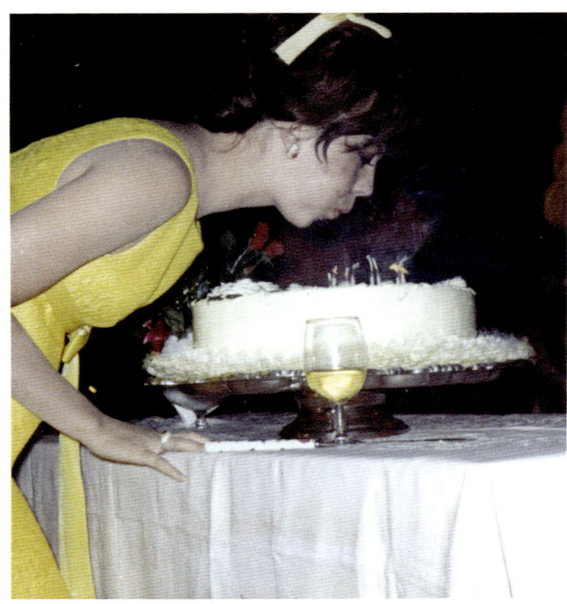

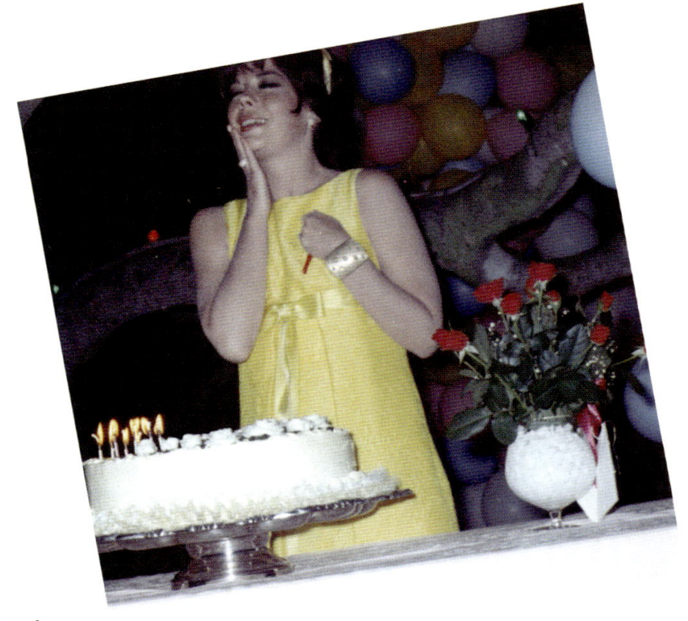

We threw this fantastic surprise party for Natalie at her home while she was filming "Penelope." We filled the pool with balloons and placed her presents on the diving board. The cake had trick candles. Natalie was gorgeous. Her sister, Lana, and her dad, Nick, planned it. I was honored to be invited. Tuesday Weld was pregnant. Ryan O'Neal was with Lana.

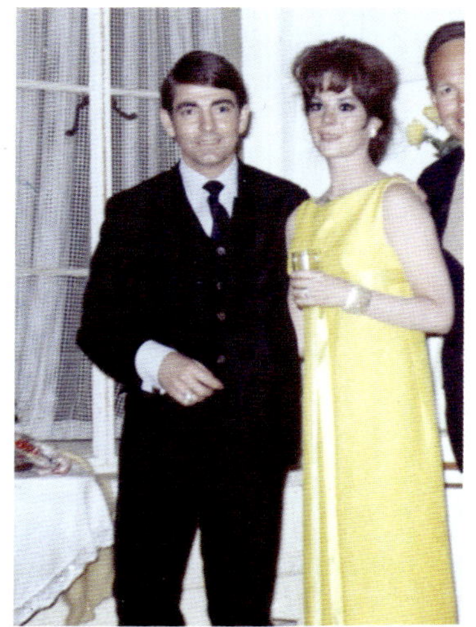

Me and Natalie

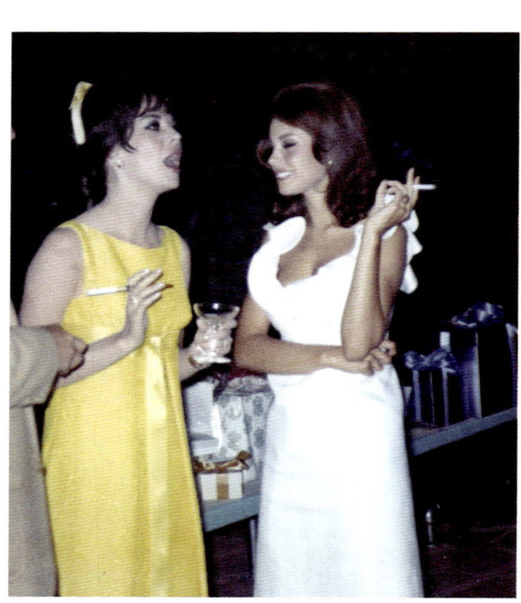

Natalie and Lana

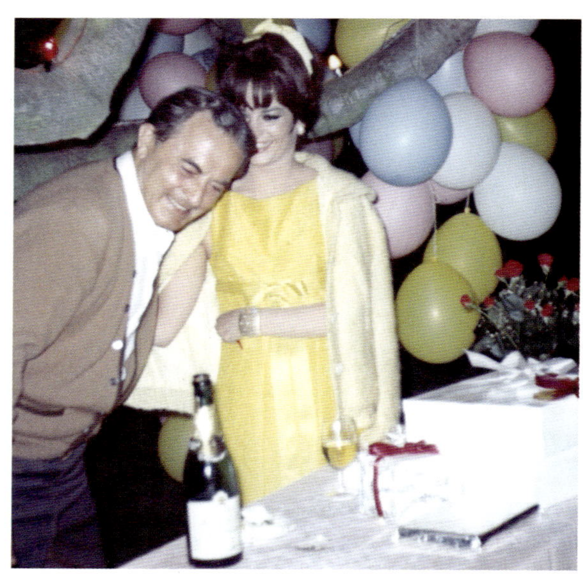

Natalie and her dad, Nick

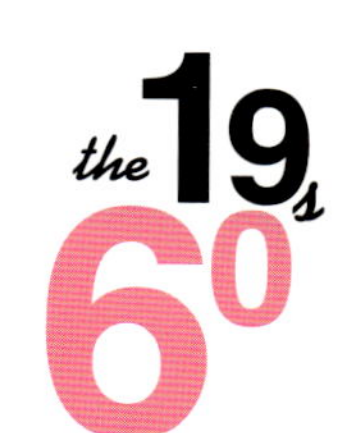

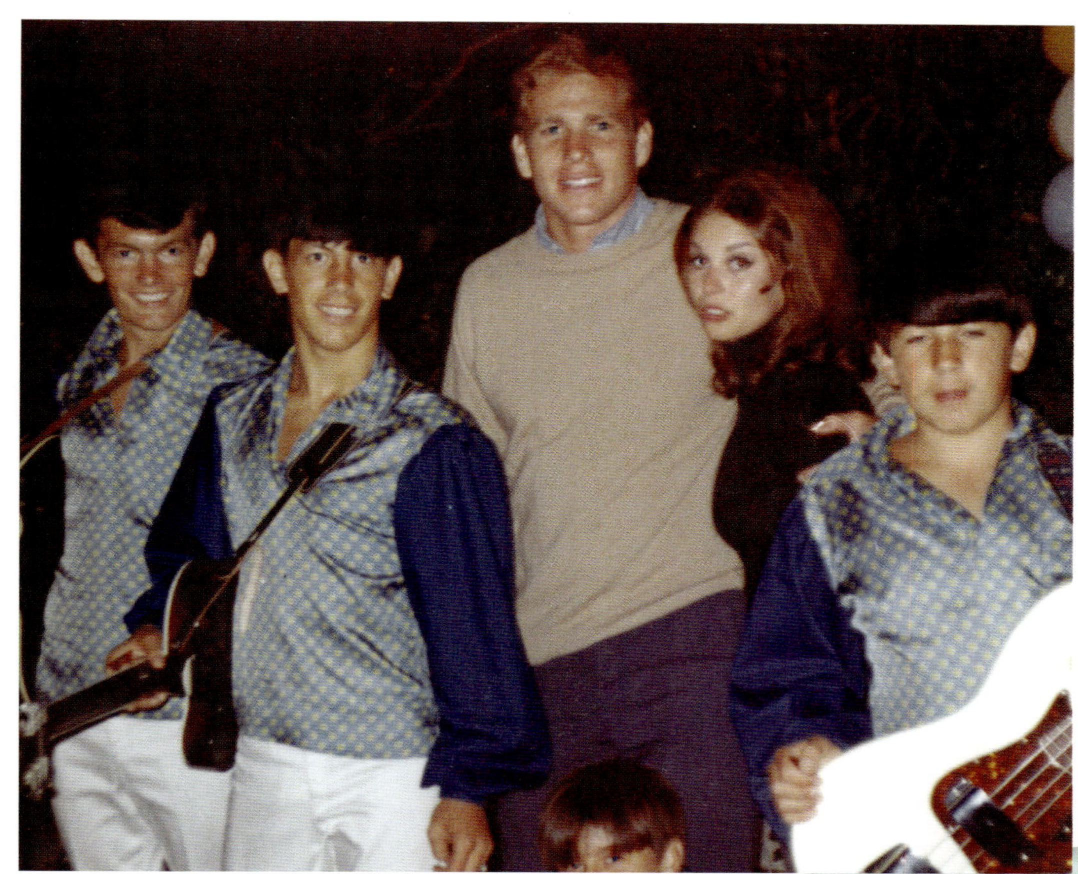

Ryan O'Neal

and Lana Wood at Natalie Woods Birthday Party. The band was from Arkansas.

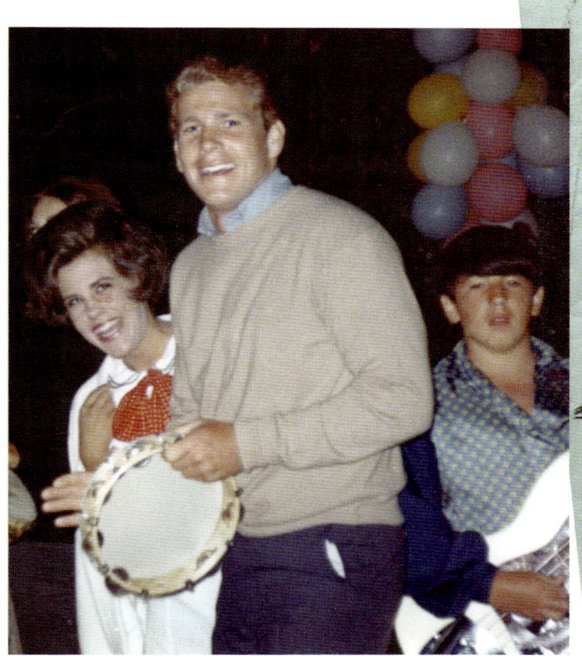

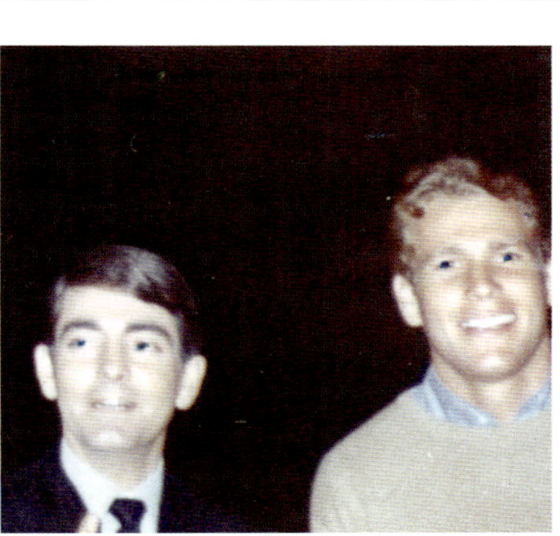

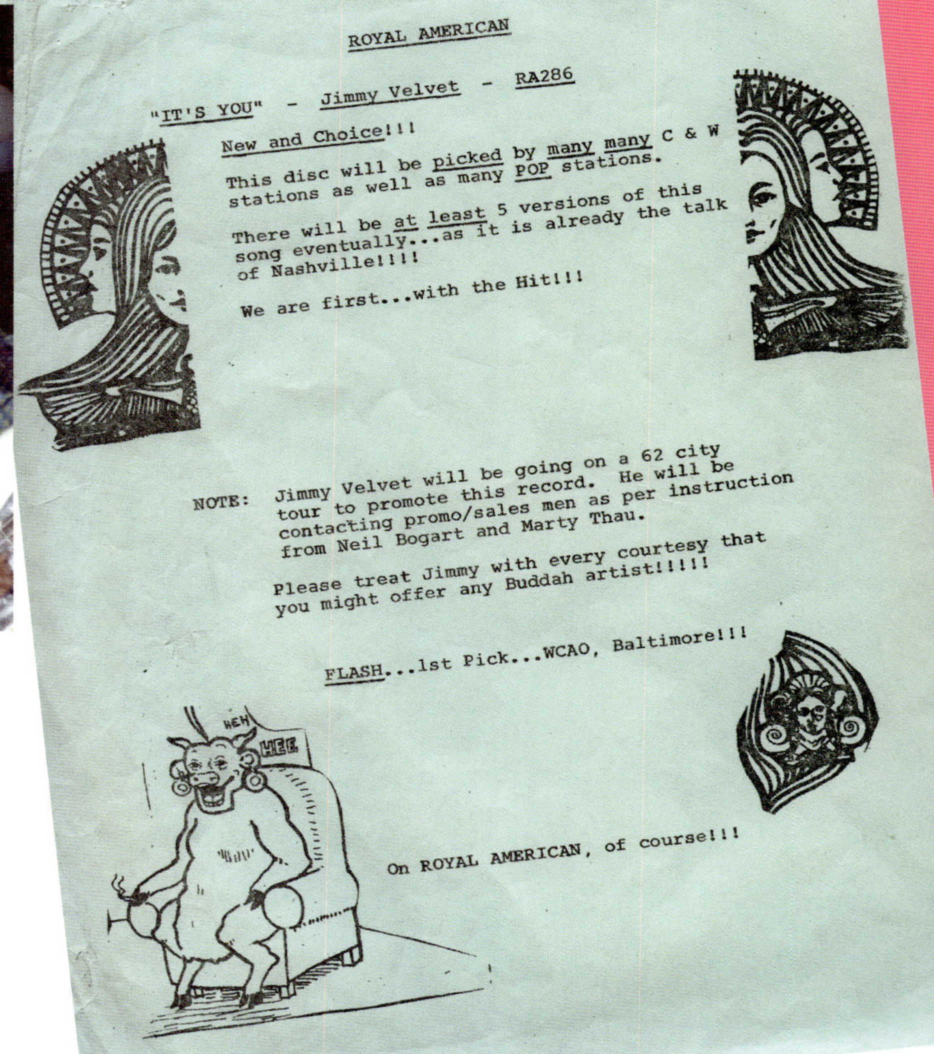

ROYAL AMERICAN

"IT'S YOU" - Jimmy Velvet - RA286

New and Choice!!!

This disc will be picked by many many C & W stations as well as many POP stations.

There will be at least 5 versions of this song eventually...as it is already the talk of Nashville!!!!

We are first...with the Hit!!!

NOTE: Jimmy Velvet will be going on a 62 city tour to promote this record. He will be contacting promo/sales men as per instruction from Neil Bogart and Marty Thau.

Please treat Jimmy with every courtesy that you might offer any Buddah artist!!!!!

FLASH...1st Pick...WCAO, Baltimore!!!

HEH HEE

On ROYAL AMERICAN, of course!!!

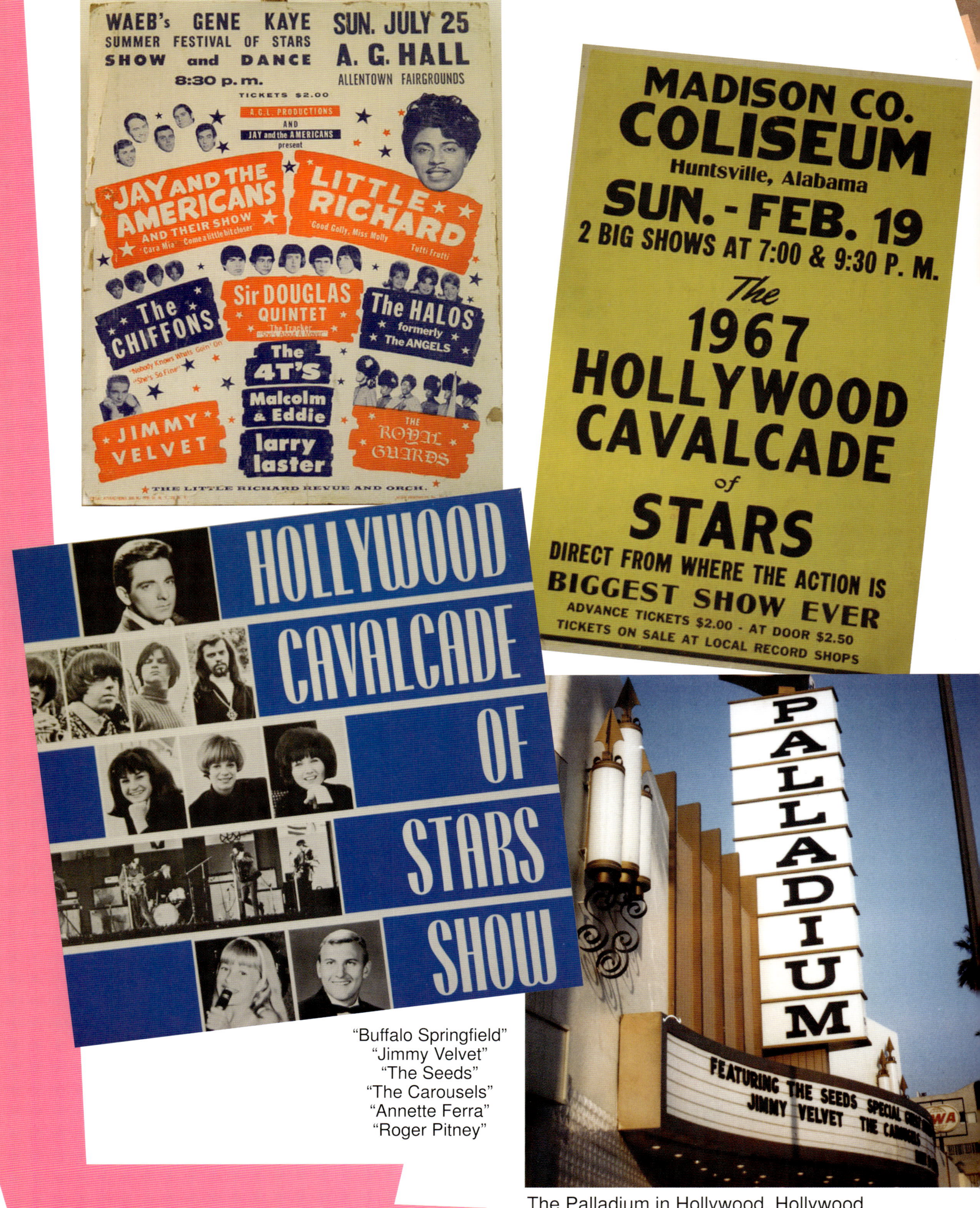

"Buffalo Springfield"
"Jimmy Velvet"
"The Seeds"
"The Carousels"
"Annette Ferra"
"Roger Pitney"

The Palladium in Hollywood. Hollywood Cavalcade of Stars Tour

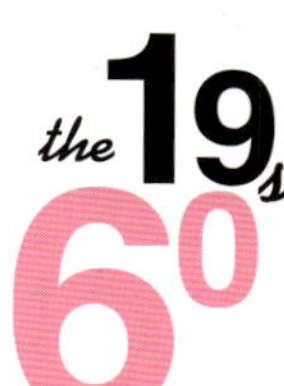

ngratulations to
LIAM H. WEAVER
nner of Car No. 2
in
WQAM's
latest
THREE CAR GIVE-AWAY
★
WQAM's THIRD MUSTANG
in less than a year will be
given away May 22nd
LISTEN AND WIN ON
WQAM!

WQA 560

FABULOUS
56 SURVEY
FOR WEEK ENDING MAY 15, 1965

This WQAM survey is a true, accurate and unbiased account of record popularity, based upon sales reports, juke box plays and telephone requests.

WQAM DJ's

TED CLARK
LEE SHERWOOD

W Q A M FABULOUS 56 SURVEY

Last Week
5 1. HELP ME RHONDA (1st wk)
2 2. Cast Your Fate
1 3. Tiger A Go Go
3 4. Ticket/Yes It Is
4 5. Count Me In
9 6. I Can't Explain
23 7. Wooly Bully
8 8. Never Find Another
18 9. Almost Tomorrow
6 10. Mrs. Brown
15 11. It's Not Unusual
10 12. Tired of Waiting
7 13. Silhouettes
13 14. Gonna be Alright

BEACH BOYS
Sounds Orchestral
Buzz & Bucky
Beatles
Gary Lewis
The Who
Sam The Sham
Seekers
Jimmy Velvet
Herman's Hermits
Tom Jones
Kinks
Herman's Hermits
Gerry-Pacemakers

FOR WEEK ENDING MAY 15, 1965

Last Week
45 31. Back in Your Arms
34 32. The Entertainer
35 33. It's Growing
** 34. Voodoo Woman
39 35. Concrete & Clay
40 36. Dream on Dreamer
24 37. King of the Road
** 38. I'll be Doggone
44 39. Made for Me
** 40. Last Chance
43 41. He's the One for Me
47 42. Just a Little
** 43. L-O-N-E-L-Y
48 44. She's Lost You

Supre
Tony C
Temptat
Bobby Gold
Unit 4/Ra
Perr
Roger
Marv
Freddie-D
Gen
Tamm
Beau
Bol

WQAM DJ's

TED CLARK
LEE SHERWOOD
CHARLIE MURDOCK
JIM DUNLAP
BILL WINTERS
RICK SHAW
ROBY YONGE

W Q A M FABULOUS 56 SURVEY

Last Week
3 1. TIGER A GO GO
2 2. Cast Your Fate
1 3. Ticket/Yes It Is
4 4. Count Me In
24 5. Help Me Rhonda
5 6. Mrs. Brown
9 7. Silhouettes
7 8. Never Find Another
12 9. I Can't Explain
6 10. Tired of Waiting
16 11. Minute You're Gone
8 12. Game of Love
19 13. Gonna Be Alright
10 14. She's About a Mover
21 15. It's Not Unusual
11 16. Telling You Now
13 17. Last Time
25 18. Almost Tomorrow
17 19. I Know a Place
14 20. Stop in Name of Love
18 21. Race is On
23 22. Once in my Life
47 23. Wooly Bully
15 24. King of the Road
22 25. Shotgun
28 26. True Love Ways
29 27. Teach Me Tiger
26 28. 1000 Dances
34 29. Rain Must Fall
35 30. Just in Case

BUZZ & BUCKY
Sounds Orchestral
Beatles
Gary Lewis
Beach Boys
Herman's Hermits
Herman's Hermits
Seekers
The Who
Kinks
Cliff Richard
Wayne Fontana
Gerry-Pacemakers
Sir Douglas
Tom Jones
Freddie-Dreamers
Rolling Stones
Jimmy Velvet
Petula Clark
Supremes
Jack Jones
Righteous Brothers
Sam the Sham
Roger Miller
Junior Walker
Peter & Gordon
April Stevens
Headhunters
Glenn Yarbrough
Legends

FOR WEEK ENDING MAY

Last Week
31 31. Roses & Roses
33 32. I'll be Doggone
42 33. Do the Freddie
43 34. The Entertainer
46 35. It's Growing
20 36. Birds & Bees
36 37. In the Meantime
39 38. Hurting Each Other
** 39. Concrete & Clay
48 40. Dream on Dreamer
** 41. Crying in the C
41 42. Clapping Hands
50 43. He's the One f
** 44. Made for Me
** 45. Back in Your
49 46. Without You
** 47. Just a Littl
** 48. She's Lost Y
** 49. Ooo Baby Ba
** 50. Iko Iko

SHERWOOD Voodoo
CLARK L-O-N-E
DUNLAP Break
MURDOCK Now th
SHAW Reeli
ALLEN Price

INTRODUCING
** New to L

Miami, FL

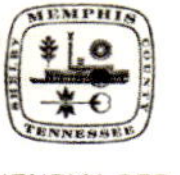

HENRY LOEB
MAYOR

City of Memphis
Tennessee

October 2,1969

Mr. Jimmy Velvet
PO Box 16411
Memphis, Tennessee 38116

Dear Jimmy:

I enjoyed meeting you today and thanks so much for the record which we all appreciated at our house.

The kids knew you and were proud of the autographed copy.

As per your request, and with best wishes to you that it will bring you much good luck and good fortune, enclosed is a "key to the city."

I am also asking my secretary to enclose a certificate to you with this letter. As you move ahead in life, keep Memphis and Memphians in mind.

Sincerely,

Henry Loeb

HL:vsw

encl

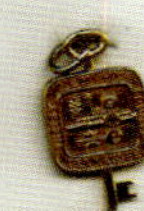

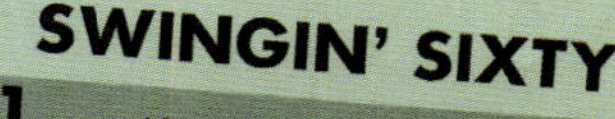

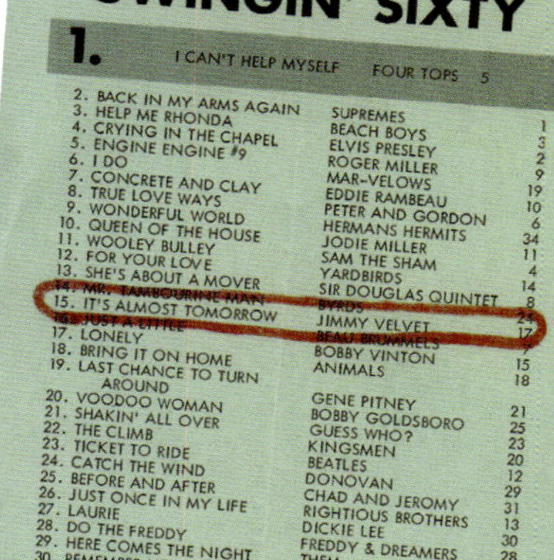

SWINGIN' SIXTY

1. I CAN'T HELP MYSELF — FOUR TOPS — 5

2. BACK IN MY ARMS AGAIN
3. HELP ME RHONDA
4. CRYING IN THE CHAPEL
5. ENGINE ENGINE #9
6. I DO
7. CONCRETE AND CLAY
8. TRUE LOVE WAYS
9. WONDERFUL WORLD
10. QUEEN OF THE HOUSE
11. WOOLEY BULLEY
12. FOR YOUR LOVE
13. SHE'S ABOUT A MOVER
14. MR. TAMBOURINE MAN
15. IT'S ALMOST TOMORROW
16. JUST A LITTLE
17. LONELY
18. BRING IT ON HOME
19. LAST CHANCE TO TURN AROUND
20. VOODOO WOMAN
21. SHAKIN' ALL OVER
22. THE CLIMB
23. TICKET TO RIDE
24. CATCH THE WIND
25. BEFORE AND AFTER
26. JUST ONCE IN MY LIFE
27. LAURIE
28. DO THE FREDDY
29. HERE COMES THE NIGHT
30. REMEMBER ME
31. SEVENTH SON
32. BLACK FOREST
33. BE MY GIRL
34. LITTLE LONELY ONE

SUPREMES
BEACH BOYS
ELVIS PRESLEY
ROGER MILLER
MAR-VELOWS
EDDIE RAMBEAU
PETER AND GORDON
HERMANS HERMITS
JODIE MILLER
SAM THE SHAM
YARDBIRDS
SIR DOUGLAS QUINTET
BYRDS
JIMMY VELVET
BEAU BRUMMELS
BOBBY VINTON
ANIMALS
GENE PITNEY
BOBBY GOLDSBORO
GUESS WHO?
KINGSMEN
BEATLES
DONOVAN
CHAD AND JEROMY
RIGHTIOUS BROTHERS
DICKIE LEE
FREDDY & DREAMERS
THEM
DEAN MARTIN
JOHNEY RIVERS
HORST JANKOWSKI
ROYAL LANCERS
TOM JONES

1 3 2 9 19 10 6 34 11 4 14 8 23 17 7 15 18 21 25 23 20 12 29 31 13 30 28 33 35 50 36 38 41

35. HUSH HUSH SWEET CHARLOTTE
36. IS THIS WHAT I GET?
37. GIVE US YOUR BLESSING
38. IT'S WONDERFUL
39. I'VE BEEN LOVING YOU TOO LONG
40. TOO MANY RIVERS
41. I'LL KEEP HOLDING ON
42. AND I LOVE HIM
43. I LOVE YOU SO
44. YES I'M READY
45. TELL HER
46. YOU REALLY KNOW HOW TO HURT A GUY
47. CARA, MIA
48. A WORLD OF OUR OWN
49. I'M BRANDED
50. WHAT'S HE DOING IN MY WORLD?
51. LIPSTICK TRACES
52. EVERYBODY PHILLY
53. A LITTLE BIT OF HEAVEN
54. KEEP ON TRYING
55. MARIE
56. FROM THE BOTTOM OF MY HEART
57. IN HOLLYWOOD
58. WHEN A BOY FALLS IN LOVE
59. BOOMERANG
60. OO WEE BABY - I LOVE YOU

PA
RO
SH
OV
OTI
BREN
MAR
ESTH
BOBB
BARBA
FRANK
JAN A
JAY AN
SEEKERS
LINK W
EDDY AR
O'JAYS
CITATION
RONNIE D
BOBBY VEE
BACHELOR
MOODY BL
DOBIE GRAY
SAM COOKE
JUNIOR WAL
FRED HUGHES

FEATURE ALBUM
TOM JONES — IT'S NOT UNUSUAL

From **ENTERTAINMENT CENT**
Bob Dettrey — Gap Fire Hall/Royal Lancers
Chuck Raymond — McCaskey Post Prom/Respectables — 12:3

WAAY TOP 40 — WEEK ENDING MAY 30

POS.	TITLE	ARTIST
1	Get Back/Flip	Beatles
2	More Today Than Yesterday	Spiral Staircase
3	These Eyes	Guess Who
4	Heather Honey	Tommy Roe
5	Everyday With You Girl	Classic IV
6	I've Been Hurt	Bill Deal
7	The Boxer	Simon & Garfunkel
8	Goodbye	Mary Hopkins
9	Cherry Wine	Tommy James
10	Day Is Done	Peter, Paul & Mary
11	Bad Moon Rising	Creedence Clearwater
12	Let Me	Paul Revere
13	Hawaii 5-0	Ventures
14	Too Busy Thinking About My Baby	Marvin Gaye
15	Sorry Suzanne	Hollies
16	One	3 Dog Night
17	What Is a Man	4 Tops
18	Special Delivery	1910 Fruitgum Co.
19	Grazin In The Grass	Friends of Distinction
	Love	Mercy
	Pretty World	Sergio Mendes
	Good Morning Star Shine	Oliver
	Morning Girl	Neon Philharmonic
	Hush A Bye	Jay & The Americans
25	Where's The Playground Suzie	Glen Campbe
26	It's Never To Late	Steppenwolf
27	Listen to The Band/Flip	Monkees
28	I Could Never Lie To You	New Colony
29	Pinball Wizard	Who
30	See	Rascals
31	Hurt So Bad	Lettermen
32	Israelites	Desmond Del
33	April Fools	Dion Warwic
34	Time Is Tight	Booker T
35	Hair	Cowsills
36	Son of A Travelin Man	Ed Ames
37	Imagine The Swan	Zombies
38	Go Away Little Girl/Young Girl	Tokens
39	Friend, Woman, Lover & Wife	O.C. Smith
40	Earth Angel	Vogues

PICK HIT ✱

t's You — Jimmy Velvet

HOT I

Get your seeds from the WAAY participating GOURD SPONSORS and GROW YOUR VERY GOURD. It may win you $100. Listen THE PROS for details

Huntsville, AL

SWINGIN' SIXTY

1. COME SEE ABOUT ME — SUPREMES — 2

2. DOWNTOWN
3. I FEEL FINE/SHE'S A WOMAN
4. GOIN' OUT OF MY HEAD
5. THE JERK
6. YOU'VE LOST THAT LOVIN' FEELIN'
7. LOVE POTION NUMBER 9
8. THE WEDDING
9. SHA LA LA
10. MR. LONELY
11. KEEP SEARCHIN'
12. THOU SHALT NOT STEAL
13. ANYWAY YOU WANT IT
14. MOUNTAIN OF LOVE
15. AMEN
16. PROMISED LAND
17. INTO SOMETHING GOOD
18. TOO MANY FISH IN THE SEA
19. TEEN ANGEL
20. HOW SWEET IT IS
21. TIME IS ON MY SIDE
22. DEAR HEART
23. OH NO, NOT MY BABY
24. BOOM BOOM
25. RINGO
26. WILD ONE
27. I'LL BE THERE
28. SINCE I DON'T HAVE YOU
29. LOVIN' PLACE
30. DON'T FORGET I STILL LOVE YOU
31. DO-WACKA-DO
32. WATCH OUT SALLY
33. SOMETIMES I WONDER

PETULA CLARK
BEATLES
LITTLE ANTHONY
LARKS
RIGHTIOUS BROTHERS
SEARCHERS
JULIE ROGERS
MANFRED MANN
BOBBY VINTON
DEL SHANNON
DICK & DEEDE
DAVE CLARK FIVE
JOHNEY RIVERS
IMPRESSIONS
CHUCK BERRY
HERMANS HERMITS
MARVALETTES
JIMMY VELVET
MARVIN GAYE
ROLLING STONES
ANDY, JACK & HENRY
MAXINE BROWN
ANIMALS
LORNE GREENE
MARTHA & VANDELLAS
GERRY & PACEMAKERS
CHUCK JACKSON
GALE GARNETT
BOBBI MARTIN
ROGER MILLER
DIANE RENAY
MAJOR LANCE

41 1 4 3 40 11 13 7 5 30 16 6 10 14 29 8 18 20 25 15 22 24 27 12 28 57 31 35 39 36 32 44

37. ONE MORE TIME
38. YOU'RE NOBODY TILL SOMEBODY LOVES YOU
39. THE 81
40. SMILE
41. JOLLY GREEN GIANT
42. COLD WALLS
43. GIVE HIM A GREAT BIG KISS
44. I'M GONNA LOVE YOU TOO
45. LET'S LOCK THE DOOR
46. HAWAII TATTOO
47. MAYBE
48. WHITE CLIFFS OF DOVER
49. THE IN CROWD
50. SOMEWHERE IN YOUR HEART
51. I CAN'T STOP
52. WHAT NOW
53. HAVE YOU LOOKED INTO YOUR HEART
54. I WANT YOU TO BE MY BABY
55. THE NAME GAME
56. RUN RUN RUN
57. LOVE ME, LOVE ME
58. LAUGH LAUGH
59. ODE TO THE LITTLE BROWN SHACK
60. LITTLE BELL

RAY CHARLES SINGE
DEAN MARTIN
CANDY & KISSES
B.EVERETT & J.BUTLE
KINGSMEN
KIT KATS
SHANGRI-LA'S
HULLABALLOOS
JAY & AMERICANS
WAIKIIS
SHANGRI-LA'S
RALEIGH & COUPONS
DOBIE GREY
FRANK SINATRA
HONEYCOMBS
GENE CHANDLER
JERRY VALE
EXCITERS
SHIRLEY ELLIS
GESTURES
PIXIES THREE
BEAU BRUMMELS
BILLY ED WHEELER
DIXIE CUPS

FEATURE ALBUM
YOU'VE LOST THAT LOVIN' FEELIN' — RIGHTIOUS BROTHERS

New Dimension Hop Lineup

Fred Klein	Silver Springs/7 Dwarfs	8:30 - 11:30 Fri.
Bob Dettrey	Lafayette Fire Hall/Emeralds	8:30 - 11:30 Fri.
Chuck Raymond	1035 Teen Club/Invictas	8 - 11 Sat.
Fred Klein	Schoeneck Fire Co./Tangents	8 - 11 Sat.
Kenn Allan	Lititz Rec. Center/X-Men	8:30 - 11:30 Sat.
Chuck Raymond	220 Teen Spot/El Dantes	8 - 11 Sun.

Lancaster, PA

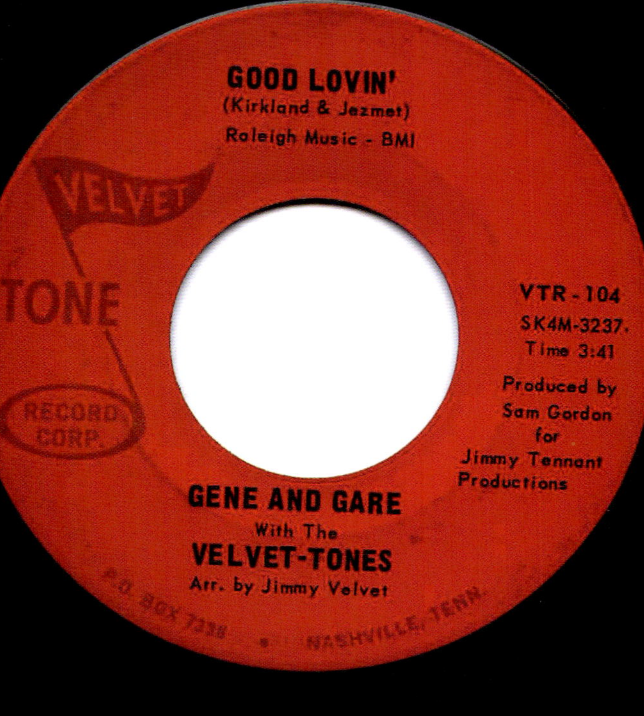

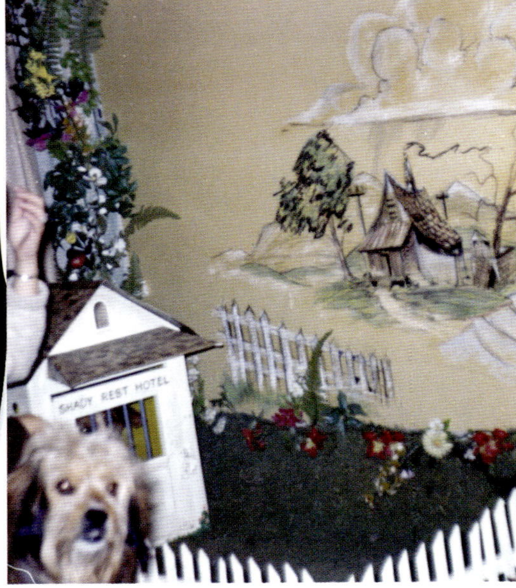

I was with Filmways for a while in the 60's and got to know most of the stars at "General Service Studios." I worked for Dick Brown, Ava Gabor's Husband. Filmways had many hit shows including:
"Beverly Hillbillies"
"Petticoat Junction"
"Green Acres"
"Double Life of Henry Fife"
"Addam's Family"
"Mr. Ed"
"George Burns Show"

"Higgins" was also "Benji"

Linda Henning- Betty Jo
Lori Saunders- Bobbie Jo
Gunilla Hutton- Billie Jo
Bea Benaderet, Pam Newland and Bellbutt

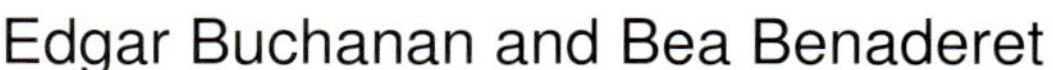

Edgar Buchanan and Bea Benaderet

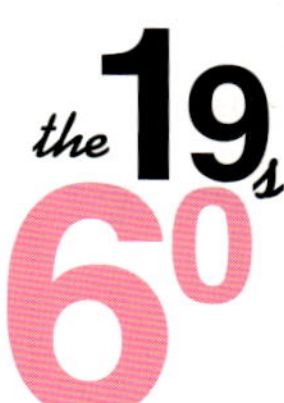

The Platters

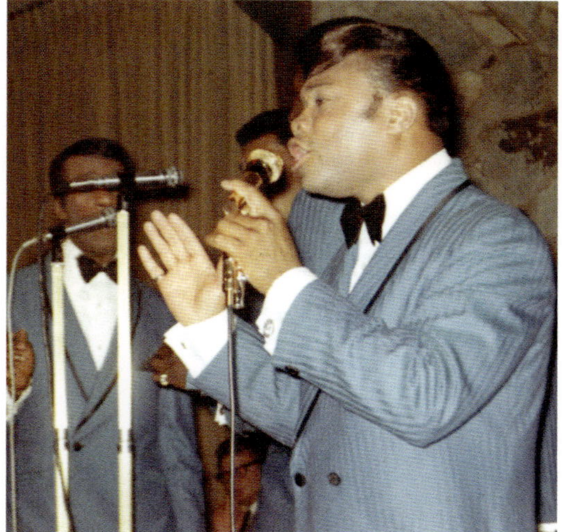

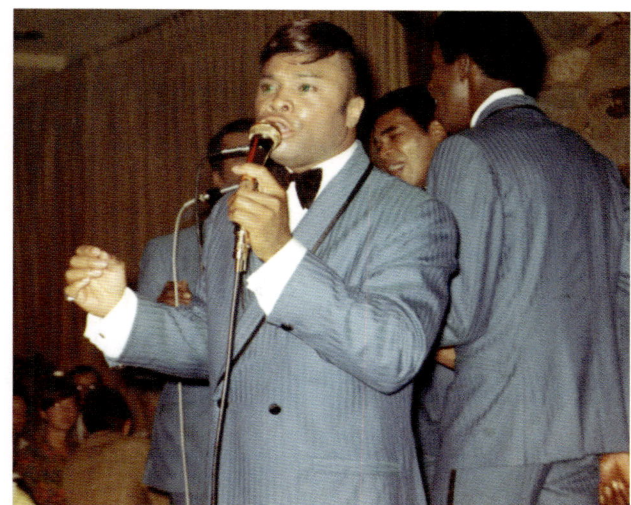

Sonny Turner. We are still good friends.

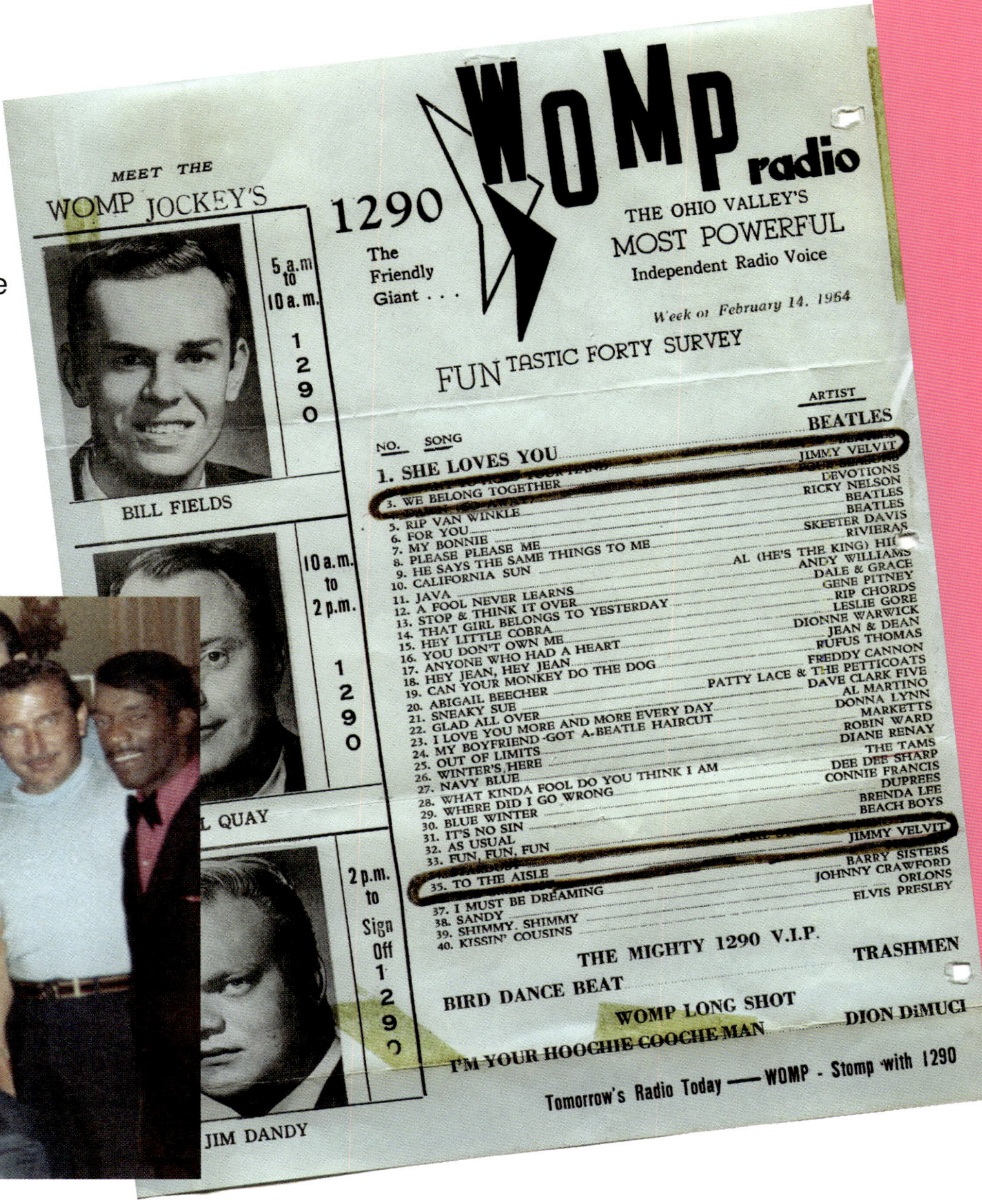

WOMP Ohio
I had two songs on the charts at the same time- "We Belong Together" was at #3 and "To the Aisle"was heading up at #35. February 14, 1964

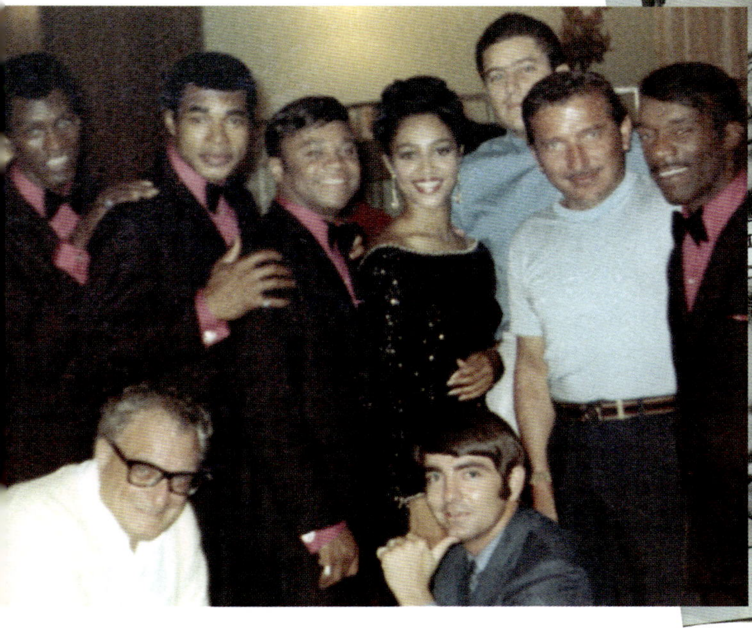

MEET THE WOMP JOCKEY'S

5 a.m. to 10 a.m. 1290 — BILL FIELDS

10 a.m. to 2 p.m. 1290 — L QUAY

2 p.m. to Sign Off 1290 — JIM DANDY

1290 The Friendly Giant . . .

WOMP radio

THE OHIO VALLEY'S MOST POWERFUL Independent Radio Voice

Week of February 14, 1964

FUN TASTIC FORTY SURVEY

NO. SONG

1. SHE LOVES YOU
3. WE BELONG TOGETHER
5. RIP VAN WINKLE
6. FOR YOU
7. MY BONNIE
8. PLEASE PLEASE ME
9. HE SAYS THE SAME THINGS TO ME
10. CALIFORNIA SUN
11. JAVA
12. A FOOL NEVER LEARNS
13. STOP & THINK IT OVER
14. THAT GIRL BELONGS TO YESTERDAY
15. HEY LITTLE COBRA
16. YOU DON'T OWN ME
17. ANYONE WHO HAD A HEART
18. HEY JEAN, HEY JEAN
19. CAN YOUR MONKEY DO THE DOG
20. ABIGAIL BEECHER
21. SNEAKY SUE
22. GLAD ALL OVER
23. I LOVE YOU MORE AND MORE EVERY DAY
24. MY BOYFRIEND -GOT A-BEATLE HAIRCUT
25. OUT OF LIMITS
26. WINTER'S HERE
27. NAVY BLUE
28. WHAT KINDA FOOL DO YOU THINK I AM
29. WHERE DID I GO WRONG
30. BLUE WINTER
31. IT'S NO SIN
32. AS USUAL
33. FUN, FUN, FUN
35. TO THE AISLE
37. I MUST BE DREAMING
38. SANDY
39. SHIMMY, SHIMMY
40. KISSIN' COUSINS

ARTIST

BEATLES
JIMMY VELVIT
DEVOTIONS
RICKY NELSON
BEATLES
BEATLES
SKEETER DAVIS
RIVIERAS
AL (HE'S THE KING) HI
ANDY WILLIAMS
DALE & GRACE
GENE PITNEY
RIP CHORDS
LESLIE GORE
DIONNE WARWICK
JEAN & DEAN
RUFUS THOMAS
FREDDY CANNON
PATTY LACE & THE PETTICOATS
DAVE CLARK FIVE
AL MARTINO
DONNA LYNN
MARKETTS
ROBIN WARD
DIANE RENAY
THE TAMS
DEE DEE SHARP
CONNIE FRANCIS
DUPREES
BRENDA LEE
BEACH BOYS
JIMMY VELVIT
BARRY SISTERS
JOHNNY CRAWFORD
ORLONS
ELVIS PRESLEY

THE MIGHTY 1290 V.I.P.

BIRD DANCE BEAT — TRASHMEN

WOMP LONG SHOT

I'M YOUR HOOCHIE COOCHIE MAN — DION DiMUCI

Tomorrow's Radio Today — WOMP - Stomp with 1290

The Platters (Herbert Reed, Sonny Turner, Johnny Rodgers, Sandra Dawn, and Ron Austin), and their musical director and writer "Buck Ram"

Box MAY 22ND 1965

RADIO ACTIVE CHART

...y of key radio stations in all important markets throughout the country to determine by percentage of th...
...ng which releases are being added to station play lists this week for the first time and also the degree of c...
...tion combining previous reports. Percentage figures on left indicate how many of the stations reporting t...
...have added the following titles to their play list for the first time. Percentage figures on right include to...
...left plus the percentage title received in prior week or weeks. (SURVEY COMPLETED TO MAY 12...

...% OF STATIONS ...DING TITLES TO PROG. SCHED. THIS WEEK	TITLE — ARTIST — LABEL	TOTAL % OF STATIONS TO HA... ADDED TITLES T... PROG. SCHED. TO DATE
60%	Wonderful World—Herman's Hermits—MGM	88%
50%	I'm The One Who Loves You—Dean Martin—Reprise	50%
45%	Before And After—Chad & Jeremy—Columbia	45%
40%	I Can't Help Myself—Four Tops—Motown	75%
38%	Is This What I Get For Loving You—Ronettes—Philles	38%
35%	Bring It On Home To Me—Animals—MGM	78%
33%	You Really Know How To Hurt A Guy—Jan & Dean—Liberty	33%
31%	Mr. Tambourine Man—Byrds—Columbia	81%
30%	Too Many Rivers—Brenda Lee—Decca	30%
28%	Tell Her (You Love Her Every Day)—Frank Sinatra—Reprise	28%
27%	He's Gonna Be Fine Fine Fine—Ikettes—Modern	27%
19%	Bring A Little Sunshine—Vic Dana—Dolton	19%
18%	Engine, Engine #9—Roger Miller—Smash	96%
17%	Tears Keep Falling—Jerry Vale—Columbia	60%
16%	A Walk In The Black Forest—Horst Jankowski—Mercury	94%
16%	Hush, Hush Sweet Charlotte—Patti Page—Columbia	52%
15%	I've Been Loving You Too Long—Otis Redding—Volt	40%
14%	Here Comes The Night—Them—Parrot	25%
14%	Three O'Clock In The Morning—Lou Rawls—Capitol	13%
13%	Break Up—Del Shannon—Amy	23%
12%	The Climb—Kingsmen—Wand	55%
11%	It's Almost Tomorrow—Jimmy Velvet—Philips	87%
11%	It's Wonderful To Be In Love—Ovations—Gold Wax	24%
10%	Oo Wee Baby, I Love You—Fred Hughes—VeeJay	10%

"It's Almost Tomorrow" recieved 87% of stations playing it in 1965

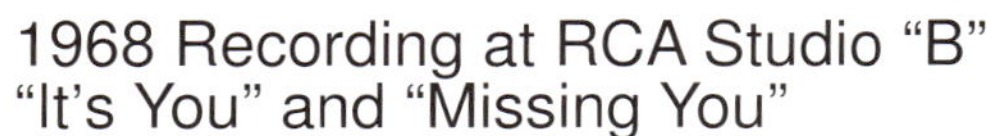

1968 Recording at RCA Studio "B"
"It's You" and "Missing You"

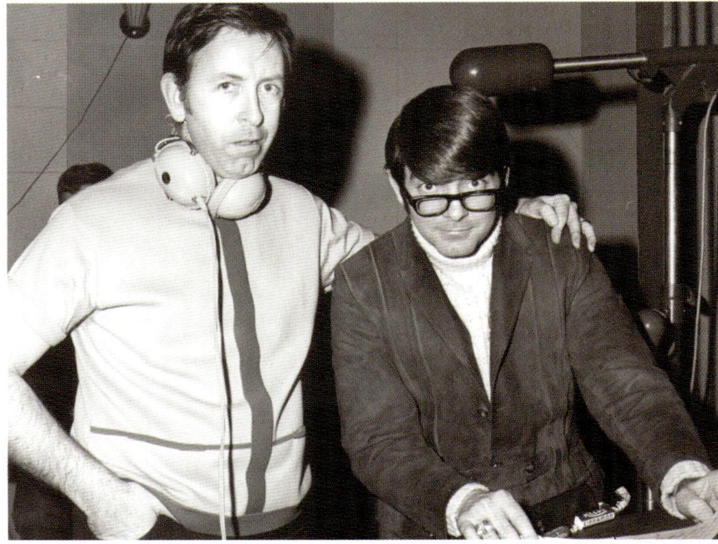

Bill Purcell-Arranger

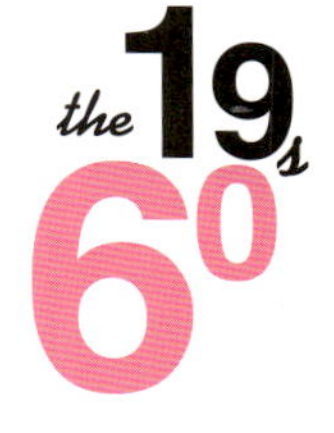

Bill Purcell

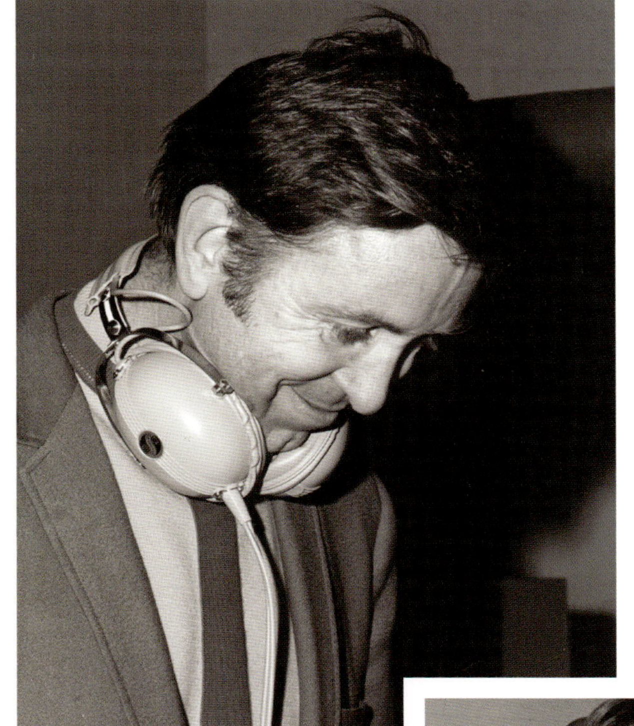

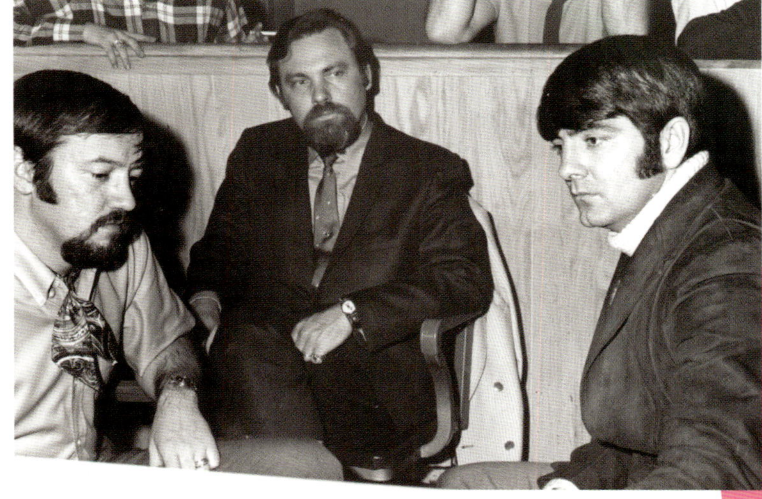

My brother in law, "Larry Butler" was a major writer and producer for Kenny Rogers, Tina Turner, and Johnny Cash just to name a few of his artists.

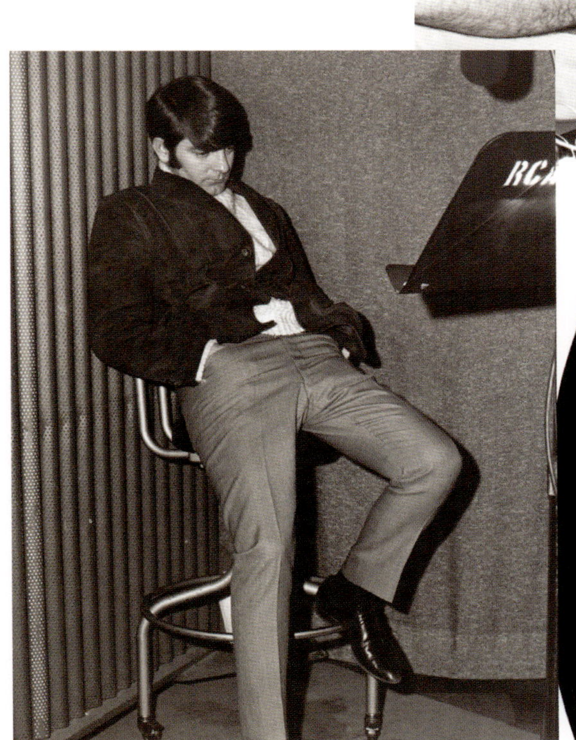

Listening to the playback of "It's You" Written by Larry Butler

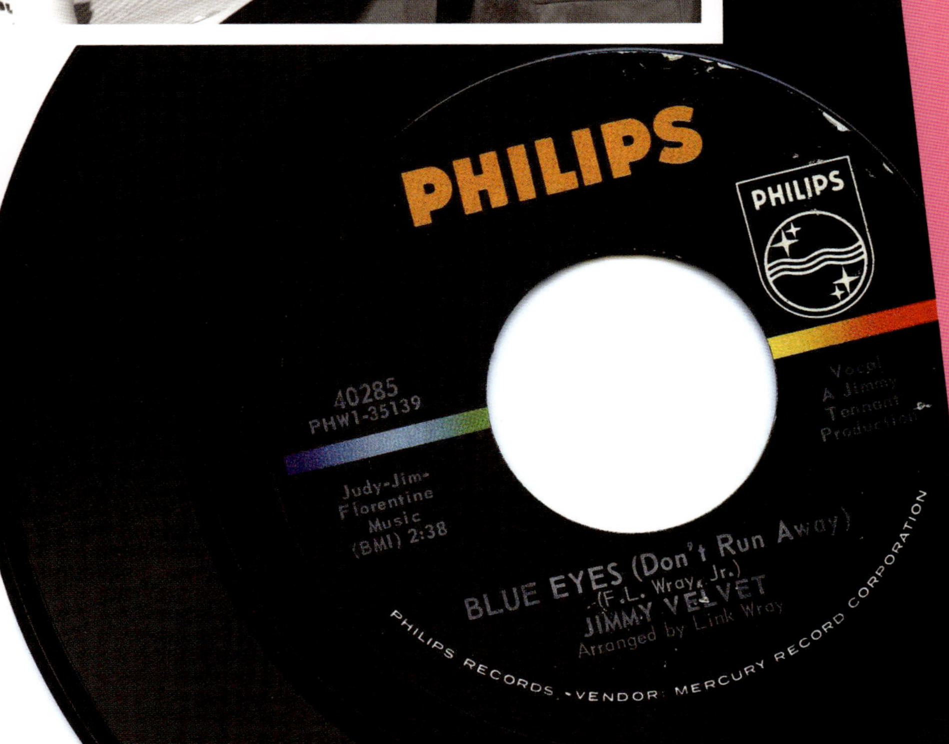

Rocky Marciano

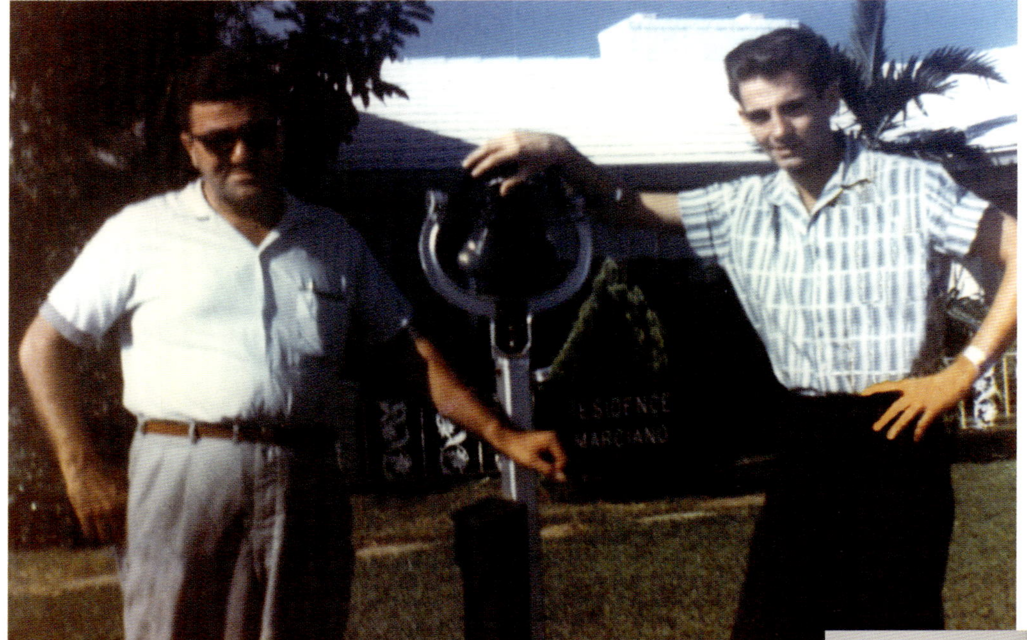

I met Rocky Marciano and his wife, Barbara, through Ed Sullivan. Rocky invited me to his Ft. Lauderdale home. The mailbox says "Residence Marciano."

WLAN - Lancaster, PA
Christmas 1963
"We Belong Together" #1

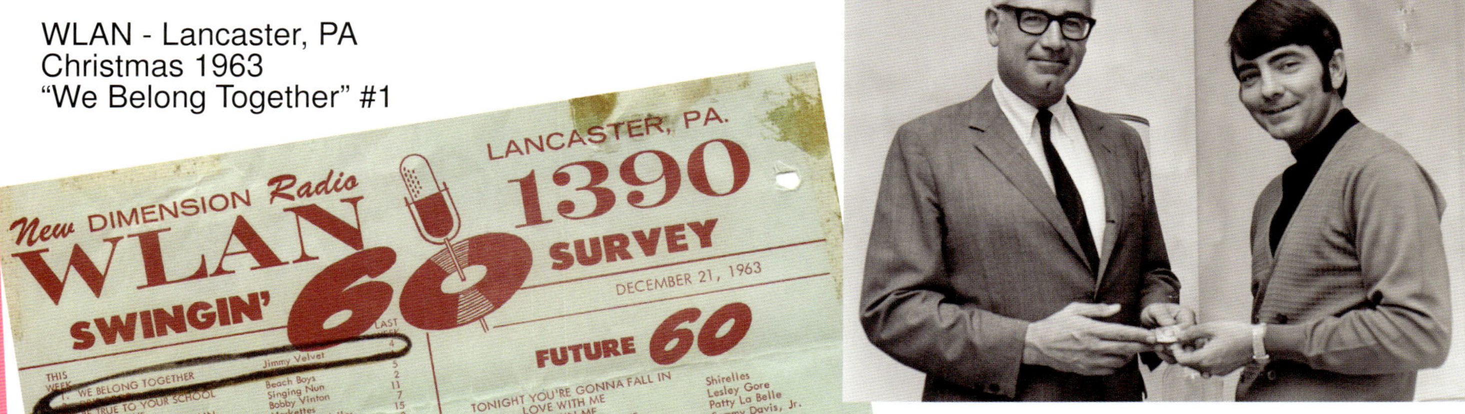

New DIMENSION Radio WLAN 1390 LANCASTER, PA.

SWINGIN' 60 SURVEY

DECEMBER 21, 1963

THIS WEEK			LAST WEEK
1.	WE BELONG TOGETHER	Jimmy Velvet	4
2.	[illegible]		
3.	BE TRUE TO YOUR SCHOOL	Beach Boys	5
4.	DOMINIQUE	Singing Nun	2
5.	THERE I'VE SAID IT AGAIN	Bobby Vinton	11
6.	OUTER LIMITS	Markettes	7
7.	QUICKSAND	Martha Vandellas	15
8.	TURN AROUND	Dick & Dee Dee	8
9.	LODDY LO/HOOKA TOOKA	Chubby Checker	9
10.	LOUIE LOUIE	Kingsmen	6
11.	OH WHAT A NIGHT FOR LOVE	Roy Tyson	10
12.	TALK BACK TREMBLIN' LIPS	Johnny Tillotson	12
13.	BOSSA NOVA BABY	Elvis Presley	3
14.	I ADORE HIM/THANK YOU AND GOOD NIGHT	Angles	
15.	CAN I GET A WITNESS	Marvin Gaye	14
16.	HAVE YOU HEARD	Duprees	16
17.	POPSICLES & ICICLES	Murmaids	13
18.	AS USUAL	Brenda Lee	20
19.	SINCE I FELL FOR YOU	Lenny Welch	22
20.	MIDNIGHT MARY	Joey Powers	24
21.	BOY NEXT DOOR	Secrets	23
22.	GOTTA TRAVEL ON	Timi Yuro	27
23.	YOU DON'T HAVE TO BE A BABY TO CRY	Caravelles	19
24.	AS LONG AS I KNOW HE'S MINE	Marvalettes	28
25.	WONDERFUL SUMMER	Robin Ward	29
26.	BABY DON'T YOU WEEP	Garnett Mims	33
27.	WIVES AND LOVERS	Jack Jones	38
28.	FORGET HIM	Bobby Rydell	36
29.	BON-DOO-WAH	Orlons	34
30.	LIPSTICK PAINT A SMILE ON ME	Demetrius Tapp	37
31.	PRETTY PAPER	Roy Orbison	42
32.	DAWN	David Rockingham Trio	40
33.	DRAG CITY	Jan & Dean	41
34.	YOUNG WINGS CAN FLY	Ruby & Romantics	39
35.	I GOTTA DANCE TO KEEP FROM CRYING	Miracles	43
36.	COLD COLD WINTER/442 GLENWOOD AVE.	Pixies Three	44
37.	IT'S ALL IN THE GAME	Cliff Richard	47
38.	GIRLS GROW UP FASTER THAN BOYS	Cookies	52
39.	STEWBALL	Peter, Paul & Mary	48
40.	BABY I LOVE YOU	Ronettes	49
41.	SOME WHERE	Tymes	53
42.	THAT LUCKY OLD SUN	Ray Charles	56
43.	RAGS TO RICHES	Sunny & Sunliners	51
44.	WHISPERING	Tempo & Stevens	50
45.	TODAY'S TEARDROPS	Rick Nelson	-
46.	PLEASE	Frank Ifield	57
47.	THAT BOY JOHN/HANKY PANKY	Raindrops	55
48.	SHE'S GOT EVERYTHING	Essex	58
49.	KANSAS CITY	Trini Lopez	60
50.	SWANEE RIVER	Ace Canon	-
51.	MISERY	Dynamics	59
52.	THE NITTY GRITTY	Shirley Ellis	30
53.	WHEN THE LOVE LIGHT STARTS SHINING	Supremes	-
54.	DAISEY PETAL PICKIN'	Jimmy Gilmer	-
55.	NIGHT RIDER	Dick Dale	-
56.	ALLY ALLY OXEN FREE	Kingston Trio	-
57.	I CAN'T STOP TALKING ABOUT YOU	Steve & Edie	-
58.	ANYONE WHO HAD A HEART	Dionne Warwick	-
59.	HEY LITTLE COBRA	Rip Chords	-
60.	COME DANCE WITH ME	Jay & Americans	-

FUTURE 60

TONIGHT YOU'RE GONNA FALL IN LOVE WITH ME	Shirelles
YOU DON'T OWN ME	Lesley Gore
YOU'LL NEVER WALK ALONE	Patty La Belle
THE SHELTER OF YOUR ARMS	Sammy Davis, Jr.
PROMISES	Ray Peterson
THAT'S ME	Pat Boone
WHO CARES	Fats Domino
SNAP YOUR FINGERS	Barbara Lewis
THE IMPOSSIBLE HAPPENED	Peggy March
BE MY GIRL	Lettermen

NEW DIMENSION SOUNDS OF CHRISTMAS

THE TWELVE GIFTS OF CHRISTMAS	Allan Sherman
LITTLE ST. NICK	Beach Boys
HOLIDAY HOOTENANNY	Paul & Paula
WHITE CHRISTMAS	Andy Williams
ROCKIN' AROUND THE CHRISTMAS TREE	Brenda Lee
DO YOU HEAR WHAT I HEAR	Bing Crosby
AN OLD CHRISTMAS CARD	Jim Reeves
LITTLE DRUMMER BOY	Someone Chorale
SILENT NIGHT	Jackie Wilson
JINGLE BELL ROCK	Bobby Helms
SANTA'S COMING IN A WHIRLEY BIRD	Pat Boone
THAT'S WHAT I WANT FOR CHRISTMAS	Nancy Wilson
A CHRISTMAS LOVE	Johnny Kaye
CHRISTMAS TIME	Jan Bradley
WHAT CAN I GIVE HIM	Jack Halloran Singers
A SOALIN'	Peter, Paul & Mary
SLEIGH RIDE	Ronettes
IT'S CHRISTMAS EVE & WE'RE ALONE	Cathy Tippins
LONELY CHRISTMAS	Orioles
SANTS SANTA	Rocky Fellers
SILVER BELLS	Bing Crosby
WHAT IS A SANTA CLAUSE	Stan Kenton
LITTLE MARY CHRISTMAS	Adrienne

NEW DIMENSION HOP LINE-UP

Ron Beach	1035 Teen Club	8:00 - 11:00 Sat.
Fred Klein	Schoeneck Fire Hall	8:00 - 11:00 Sat.
Kenn Allan	Lititz Rec. Center	8:30 - 11:30 Sat
Bob Dettrey	T-Bird Inn	9:00 - 1:00 Sun

FROM THE FABULAS FIVE
MERRY CHRISTMAS AND HAPPY NEW YEAR

DETTREY DICK CLARK FRED KLEIN CHUCK RAYMOND LARRY

Receiving honorary police chief badge from Jackson, MS police chief in 1969. I got the badge for Elvis' collection. He gave it back to me in 1973

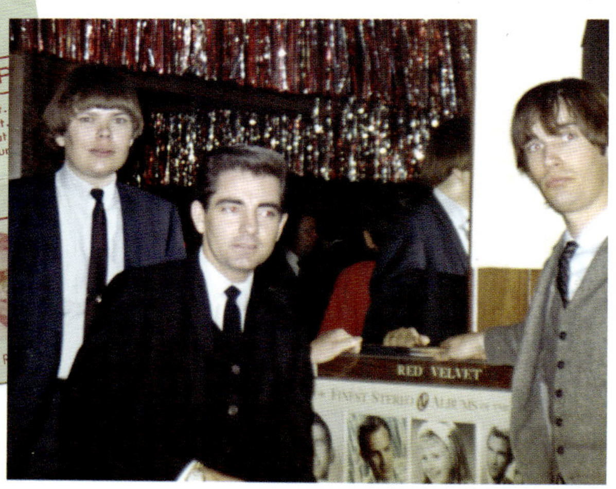

The Yardbirds and Eric Clapton at "Red Velvet"

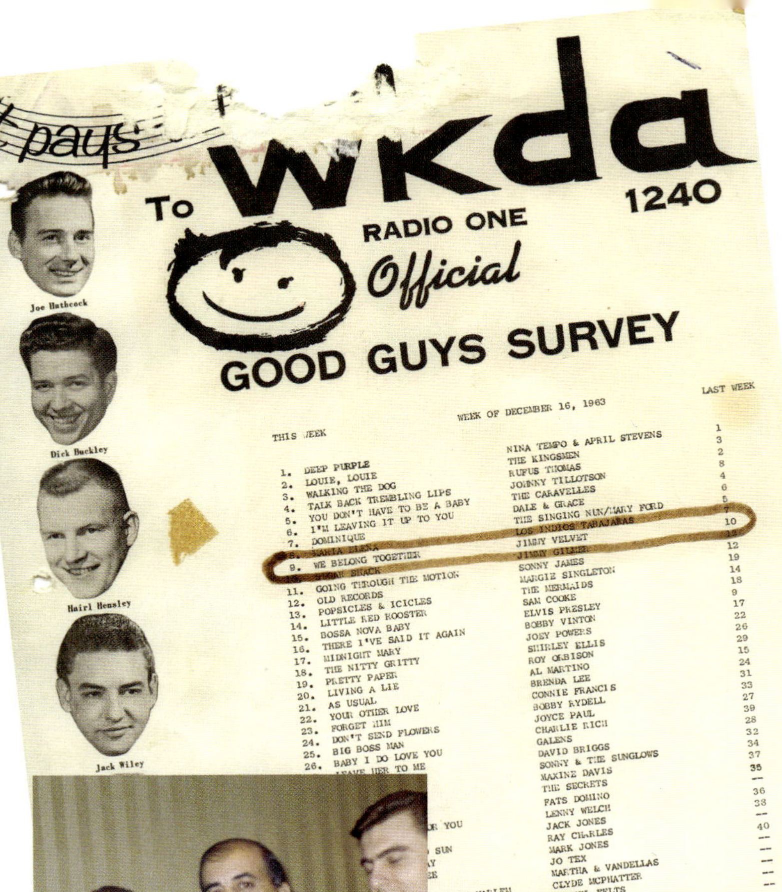

it pays To WKDA 1240

RADIO ONE Official

GOOD GUYS SURVEY

WEEK OF DECEMBER 16, 1963

THIS WEEK			LAST WEEK
1.	DEEP PURPLE	NINO TEMPO & APRIL STEVENS	1
2.	LOUIE, LOUIE	THE KINGSMEN	3
3.	WALKING THE DOG	RUFUS THOMAS	2
4.	TALK BACK TREMBLING LIPS	JOHNNY TILLOTSON	8
5.	YOU DON'T HAVE TO BE A BABY	THE CARAVELLES	4
6.	I'M LEAVING IT UP TO YOU	DALE & GRACE	6
7.	DOMINIQUE	THE SINGING NUN/MARY FORD	5
8.	MARIA ELENA	LOS INDIOS TABAJARAS	7
9.	WE BELONG TOGETHER	JIMMY VELVET	10
10.	SUGAR SHACK	JIMMY GILMER	13
11.	GOING THROUGH THE MOTION	SONNY JAMES	12
12.	OLD RECORDS	MARGIE SINGLETON	19
13.	POPSICLES & ICICLES	THE MERMAIDS	14
14.	LITTLE RED ROOSTER	SAM COOKE	18
15.	BOSSA NOVA BABY	ELVIS PRESLEY	9
16.	THERE I'VE SAID IT AGAIN	BOBBY VINTON	17
17.	MIDNIGHT MARY	JOEY POWERS	22
18.	THE NITTY GRITTY	SHIRLEY ELLIS	26
19.	PRETTY PAPER	ROY ORBISON	29
20.	LIVING A LIE	AL MARTINO	15
21.	AS USUAL	BRENDA LEE	24
22.	YOUR OTHER LOVE	CONNIE FRANCIS	31
23.	FORGET HIM	BOBBY RYDELL	33
24.	DON'T SEND FLOWERS	JOYCE PAUL	27
25.	BIG BOSS MAN	CHARLIE RICH	39
26.	BABY I DO LOVE YOU	GALENS	28
	LEAVE HER TO ME	DAVID BRIGGS	32
		SONNY & THE SUNGLOWS	34
		MAXINE DAVIS	37
		THE SECRETS	35
		FATS DOMINO	—
	...R YOU	LENNY WELCH	36
		JACK JONES	38
	...SUN	RAY CHARLES	—
	...Y	MARK JONES	40
	...E	JO TEX	—
		MARTHA & VANDELLAS	—
	...EART OF HARLEM	CLYDE MCPHATTER	—
	...OVE	MARVEL FELTS	—
	...HERRY	DALE WARD	—

...EEK - YONDER COMES A SUCKER - JOE BARRY

...CORD - OLD RECORDS

... SHIRT FOR CHRISTMAS AT WKDA ...

Nashville, TN

Direct From Ch. 13, WJZ-TV

Buddy Deane presents:

The Hop of The YEAR

A Gigantic Record Hop, Dance
All Star Stage Show, and Teen Party
Combined in ONE Exciting Evening
of Top Teen Entertainment
There may be Other Hops
But never Another Like This

Featuring Live, On Stage, In Person

The Nationally Known Recording Group

The Chiffons

"HE'S SO FINE" WITH THEIR BIG HITS "A LOVE SO FINE" AND "ONE FINE DAY"

PLUS

Lorrie Darnell

WITH HER BIG DANCE RECORD "THE GOLDEN SLIPPER STRUT"

Jimmy Velvet

DOING HIS BIG HIT "WE BELONG TOGETHER"

Sat. October 26, 1963

8:00 to 11:00 p. m. (Promptly)

Bankert's Rest. Rec. Hall

LITTLESTOWN, Pennsylvania

Admission

Dave White, Ray Gilmour, and Len Berry

WITH

RADIO 1230 BALTIMORE

"FABULOUS 50"

WEEK OF MARCH 8, 1964

1. She Loves You	The Beatles	Swan
2. I Want To Hold Your Hand / Flip	The Beatles	Capitol
3. Please Please Me / Flip	The Beatles	Vee Jay
4. Java	Al Hirt	Rca
5. Dawn	Four Seasons	Phillips
6. Hello Dolly	Louis Armstrong	Kapp
7. Fun, Fun, Fun	Beach Boys	Capitol
8. I Love You More Everyday	Al Martino	Capitol
9. Kissin' Cousins	Elvis Presley	Rca
10. Navy Blue	Dianne Renay	20th
11. Look Homeward Angel	The Monarchs	Sound Stage
12. Stay	Four Seasons	Vee Jay
13. My Heart Belongs To You	Bobby Vinton	Epic
14. I Wish You Love	Gloria Lynn	Everest
15. To The Aisle	Jimmy Velvet	Abc
16. Castles In The Sand	Steve Wonder	Tamla
17. Good News	Sam Cooke	Rca
18. Can Your Monkey Do The Dog	Rufus Thomas	Stax
19. Stockholme	Lawrence Welke	Dot
20. A Fool Never Learns	Andy Williams	Columbia
21. California Sun	Riverias	Rivera
22. What Kind Of Fool	The Tams	Abc
23. Live Wire	Martha And Vandellas	Gordy
24. He's A Good Guy	Marvelettes	Tamla
25. I Can't Stand It	Soul Sisters	Sue
26. Shelter Of Her Arms	Sammy Davis, Jr.	Reprise
27. Money	Kingsmen	Wand
28. Going Back To Louisiana	Bruce Channel	Le Cam
29. Go Tell It To The Mountain	Peter, Paul & Mary	Warner
30. Needles And Pins	Searchers	Kapp
31. Twistand Shout	The Beatles	Tollie
32. My Bonnie	The Beatles	Mgm
33. Baltimore	Sonny James	Capitol
34. Penetration	Pyramids	Best
35. I Dig The Way You Do Things	Temptations	Gordy
36. Glad All Over	Dave Clark Five	Epic
37. Stardust	Nino And April	Atco
38. MyBoyfriend Got A Beatle Haircut	Donna Lynn	Capitol
39. Baby, Don't You Cry	Ray Charles	Abc
40. I'm Not Going To Work Today	Boothog Pefferly	Sound Stage
41. We Love You Beatles	The Carefrees	London
42. Hi-Heel Sneakers	Tommy Tucker	Checker
43. Forever	Pete Drake	Smash
44. Mexican Drummer Boy	Tiajuana Brass	A & M
45. There Is A Meeting Here Tonight	Joe And Eddie	Crescendo
46. Think	Brenda Lee	Decca
47. Sha La La	Shirelles	Scepter
48. You Are A Wonderful One	Marvin Gaye	Tamla
49. Crooked Little Man	Serendipity Singers	Phillips
50. Rip Van Winkle	The Devotions	Roulette

★ ★ ★ ★ ★ ★ ★ ★

HALL of HITS

WFEC—1400 on Y...

presents

SECOND ANNIVERSARY

at

ZEMBO TEMPLE, Harr...

TUESDAY, JULY 20—8...

Tickets $2.00-$2.50-$3.00

ON SALE AT: Sears Ticket Office, Korvette's
Caplans Record Shop
Colonial Park Plaza Camp Hill Shoppin...

JAY AND THE AMERICANS
AND THEIR SHOW
"Cara Mia"
"Come A Little Bit Closer"

LITT... RICHA...
"Good Golly, Mis...
"Tutti Frutt...

The CHIFFONS "Nobody Knows What's Go... "She So Fine"

Sir DOUGLAS QUINTET "The Trac... "She's About A ...

The HALOS Formerly THE ANGELS

also

JIMMY VELVET ● THE ROYAL GUARDS

and the 4 T's, Malcom & Eddie, Larry Laster

and THE LITTLE RICHARD ... and ORCHESTRA...

FRI. OCT. 28

TEEN PRODUCTIONS, INC.

PRESENT

BIG BATTLE OF BANDS

STARRING

THE CONCORDS "BYE BABY, BYE BYE"

THE 4th DIMENSIONS

THE MARCELLS

PLUS

JIMMY VELVET "WE BELONG TOGETHER"

THE SHOREMEN WYNWOOD RECORDS

THE TITANS

GLEN BURNIE ARMORY

W.C.A.O.

M.C. ALAN FIELD

FREE RECORDS & ALBUMS

NO ONE ADMITTED OVER AGE 20

ADMISSION $1.75

Baltimore, MD

Velvet Prospects

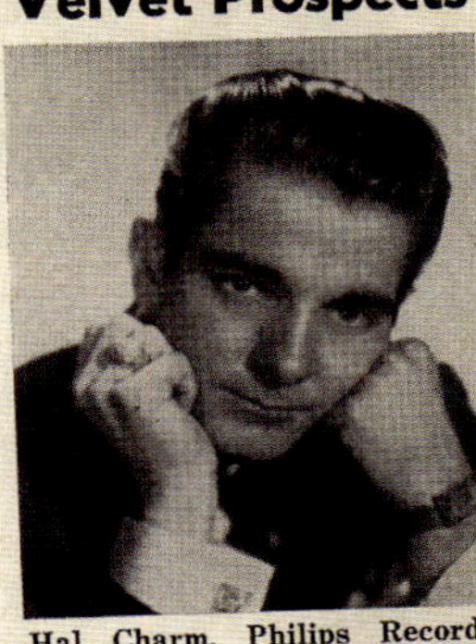

Hal Charm, Philips Records promo man in Baltimore, recently heard Jimmy Velvet's (above) Velvet Tone Record Corp. single, "It's Always Tomorrow," and was instrumental in getting the hit possibility out on Philips. After two days in release, Baltimore had or-

Dick Clark Tour Summer 1965

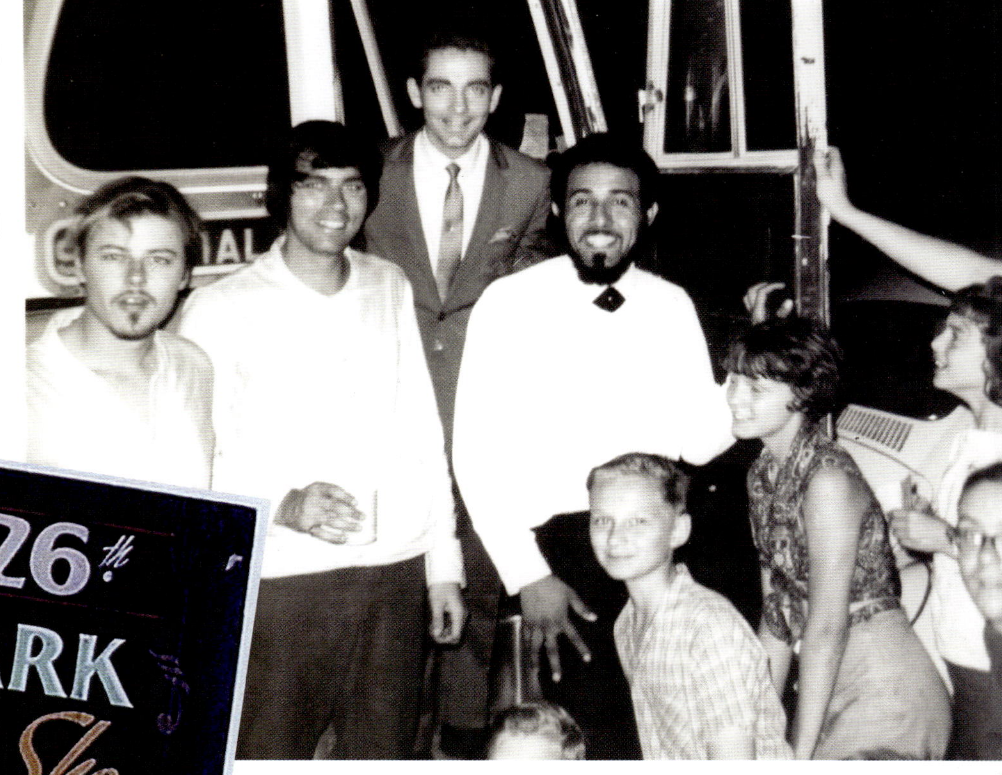

Sam the Sham and The Pharaohs
The Ikettes
Tony Clark
Jimmy Velvet

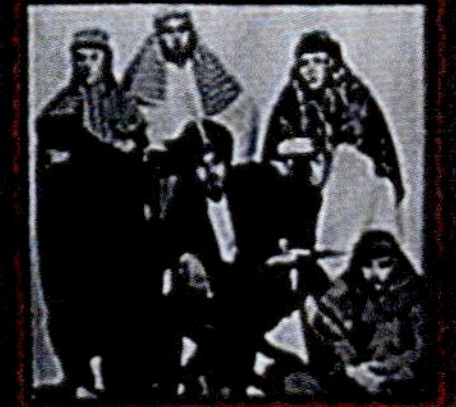

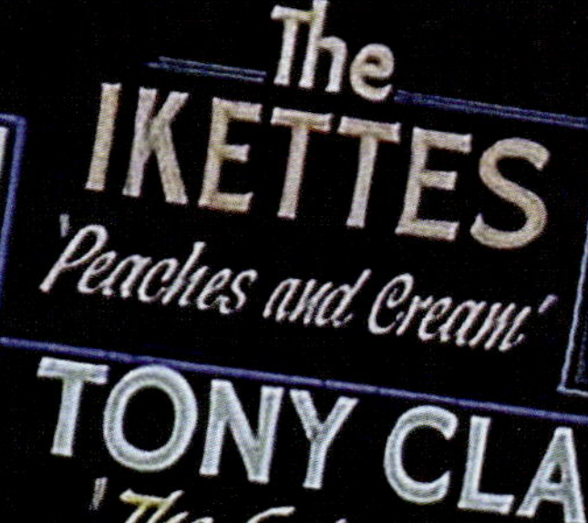

Dick Clark Tour. Someone put my name as Johnny instead of Jimmy.

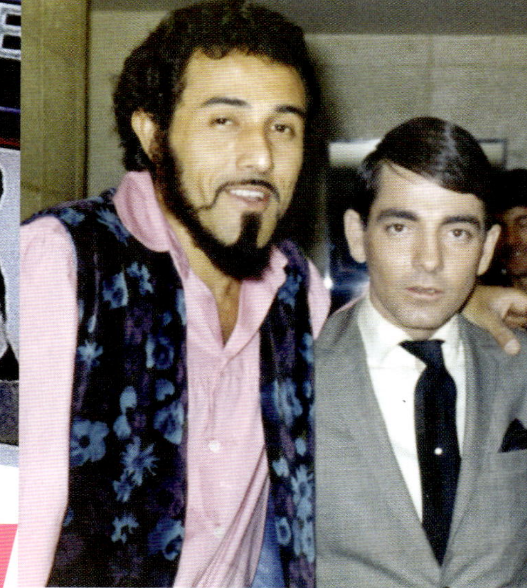

Sam the Sham

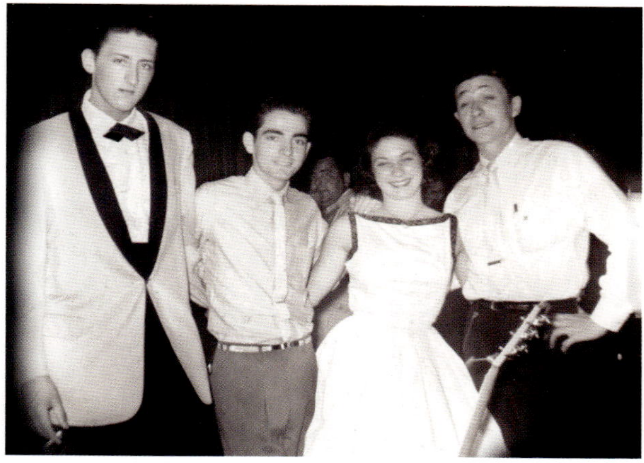

Thomas Wayne
Donna and Scotty Moore

Sir Douglas Quintet

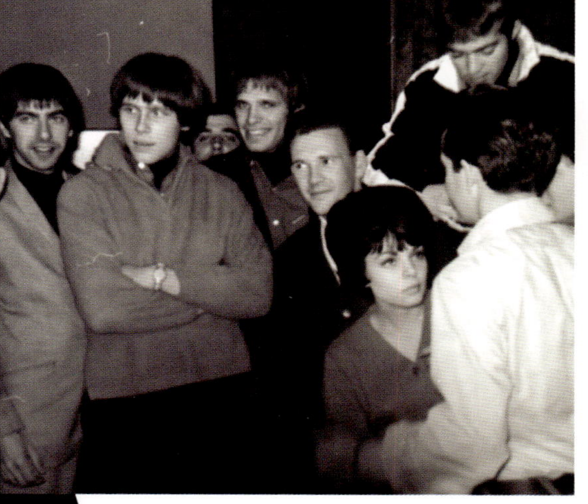

Sonny Limbo, Dale Ward, and The Famed Rocks.

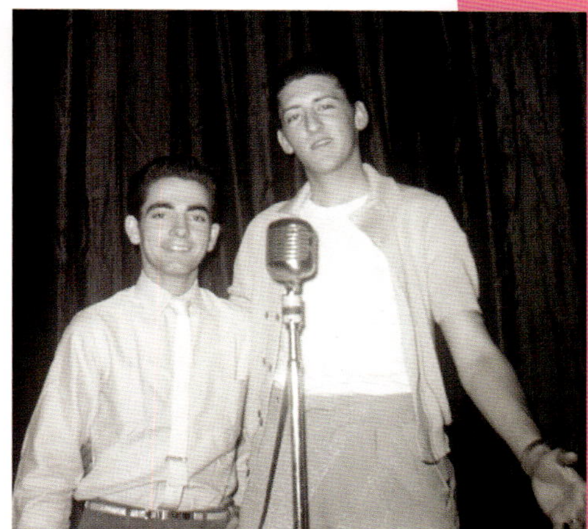

Thomas Wayne

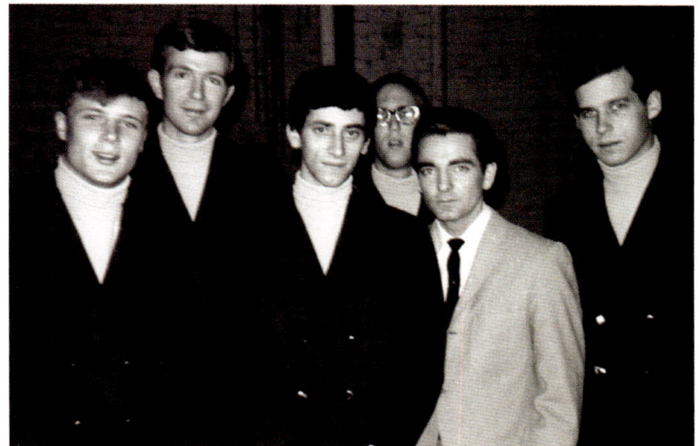

Gary Lewis, The Playboys

Vernon Presley's Birthday Party 1968

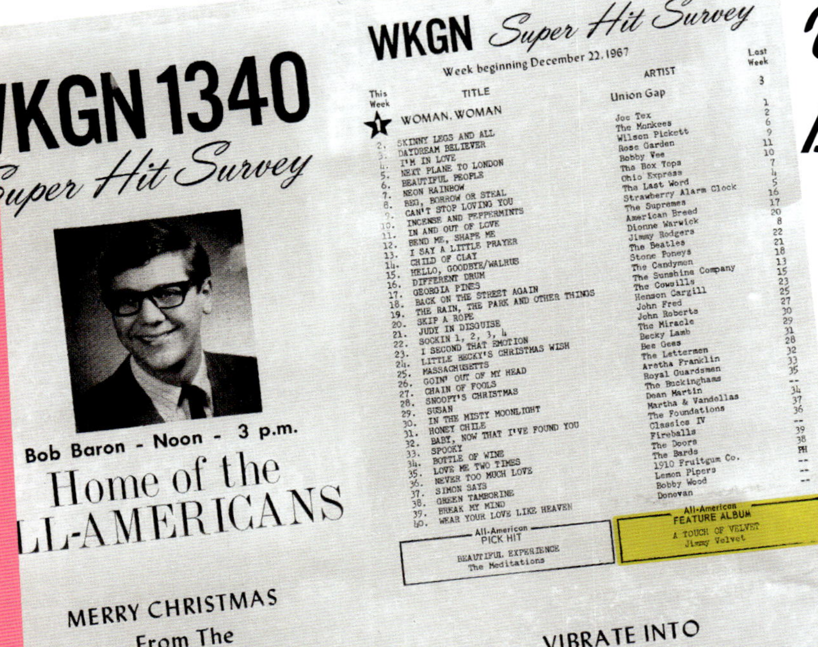

WKGN 1340

Super Hit Survey

Bob Baron - Noon - 3 p.m.

Home of the ALL-AMERICANS

MERRY CHRISTMAS From The "ALL AMERICANS"

WKGN Super Hit Survey

Week beginning December 22, 1967

This Week	TITLE	ARTIST	Last Week
1	WOMAN, WOMAN	Union Gap	3
2.	SKINNY LEGS AND ALL	Joe Tex	1
3.	DAYDREAM BELIEVER	The Monkees	2
4.	I'M IN LOVE	Wilson Pickett	6
5.	NEXT PLANE TO LONDON	Rose Garden	9
6.	BEAUTIFUL PEOPLE	Bobby Vee	11
7.	NEON RAINBOW	The Box Tops	10
8.	BEG, BORROW OR STEAL	Ohio Express	7
9.	CAN'T STOP LOVING YOU	The Last Word	4
10.	INCENSE AND PEPPERMINTS	Strawberry Alarm Clock	5
11.	IN AND OUT OF LOVE	The Supremes	16
12.	BEND ME, SHAPE ME	American Breed	17
13.	I SAY A LITTLE PRAYER	Dionne Warwick	20
14.	CHILD OF CLAY	Jimmy Rodgers	8
15.	HELLO, GOODBYE/WALRUS	The Beatles	22
16.	DIFFERENT DRUM	Stone Poneys	21
17.	GEORGIA PINES	The Candymen	18
18.	BACK ON THE STREET AGAIN	The Sunshine Company	13
19.	THE RAIN, THE PARK AND OTHER THINGS	The Cowsills	15
20.	SKIP A ROPE	Henson Cargill	23
21.	JUDY IN DISGUISE	John Fred	25
22.	SOCKIN 1, 2, 3, 4	John Roberts	27
23.	I SECOND THAT EMOTION	The Miracle	30
24.	LITTLE BECKY'S CHRISTMAS WISH	Becky Lamb	29
25.	MASSACHUSETTS	Bee Gees	31
26.	GOIN' OUT OF MY HEAD	The Lettermen	28
27.	CHAIN OF FOOLS	Aretha Franklin	32
28.	SNOOPY'S CHRISTMAS	Royal Guardsmen	33
29.	SUSAN	The Buckinghams	35
30.	IN THE MISTY MOONLIGHT	Dean Martin	--
31.	HONEY CHILE	Martha & Vandellas	34
32.	BABY, NOW THAT I'VE FOUND YOU	The Foundations	37
33.	SPOOKY	Classics IV	36
34.	BOTTLE OF WINE	Fireballs	--
35.	LOVE ME TWO TIMES	The Doors	39
36.	NEVER TOO MUCH LOVE	The Bards	38
37.	SIMON SAYS	1910 Fruitgum Co.	PH
38.	GREEN TAMBORINE	Lemon Pipers	--
39.	BREAK MY MIND	Bobby Wood	--
40.	WEAR YOUR LOVE LIKE HEAVEN	Donovan	--

All-American PICK HIT
BEAUTIFUL EXPERIENCE
The Meditations

All-American FEATURE ALBUM
A TOUCH OF VELVET
Jimmy Velvet

VIBRATE INTO '68 WITH THE FUN VIBRATIONS ON WKGN 1340

Album Pick Up of the Week
WKGN Radio, Knoxville
"A Touch of Velvet"

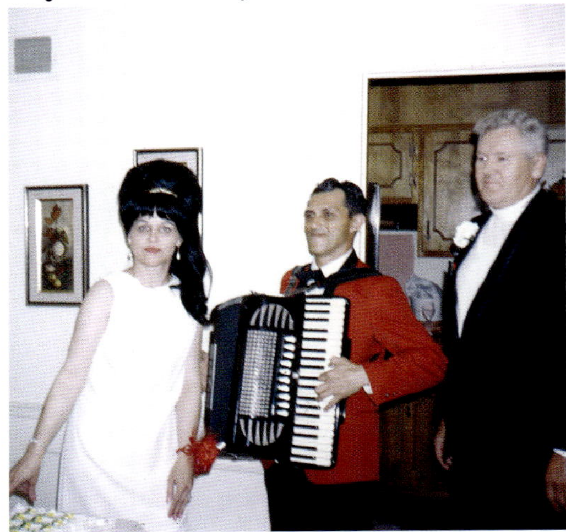

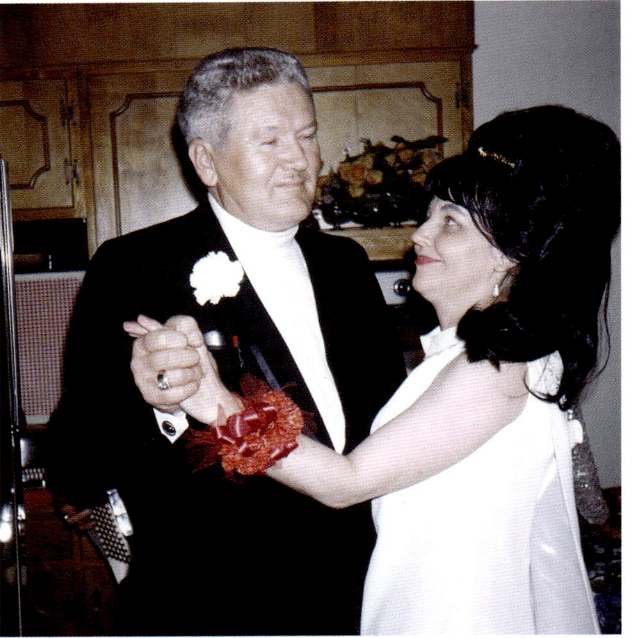

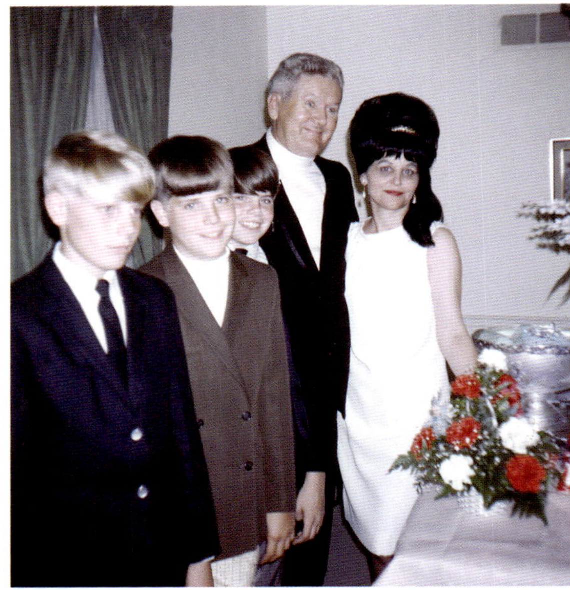

Rick, David, Billy, Vernon and Dee

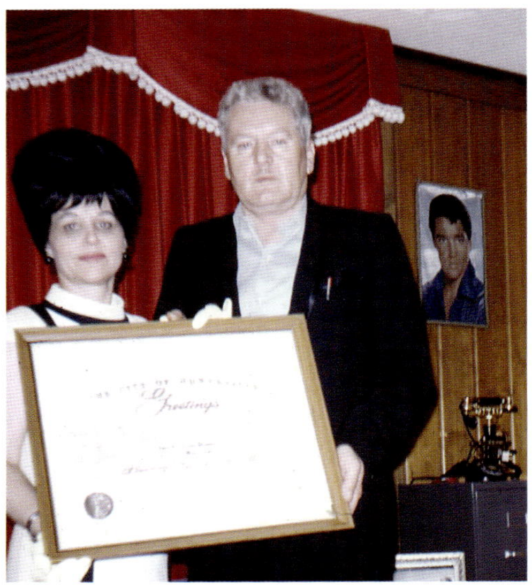

Dee and Vernon. Honorary citizen of Huntsville, AL, which I gave to Vernon.

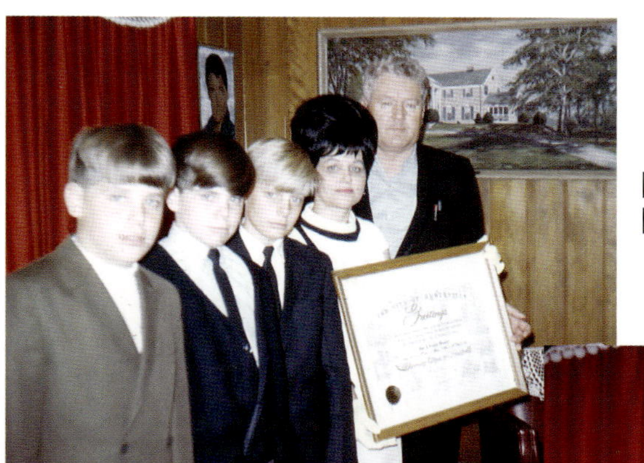

David, Billy, Rick, Dee and Vernon

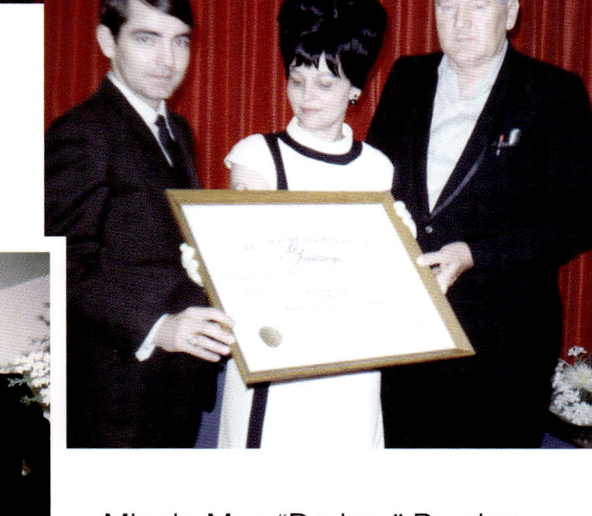

Me, Dee and Vernon

Minnie Mae "Dodger" Presley, Evis' Grandmother

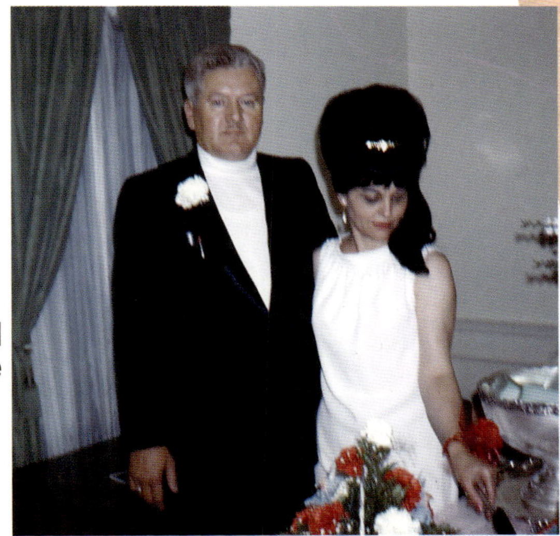

Vernon and Dee

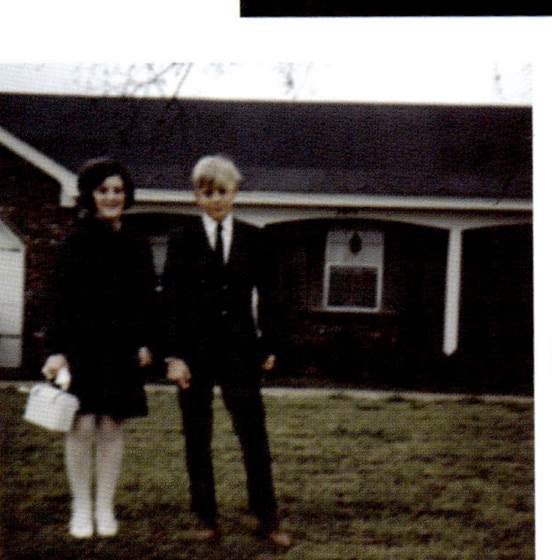

Rick and his date

IT'S OFFICIAL! KAY-KIS, NUMBER ONE RADIO 99, IS YOUR OFFICIAL "BEATLE-APPROVED STATION" SERVING NORTHERN CALIFORNIA. DIAL RADIO 99 EVERY DAY!

K-KIS DIAL 99

'Million Dollar Music Survey'

The Official Contra Costa-Solano-Napa County Report

FEBRUARY 15 — FEBRUARY 21, 1964

1. LITTLE BOYS AND GIRLS .... Ron Freschi
2. I NEED YOUR LOVE .... Jack Wayne, Jr.
3. HOOT HOOT NIGHT OWL .... The Aubry Twins
4. LONELY AVENUE .... The Crickets
5. THE ROAD I'M ON / HOOCHIE COOCHIE MAN .... Dion
6. TALK TO ME BABY .... Frank Sinatra
7. BABY, DON'T CRY / MY HEART .... Roy Charles
8. TO THE AISLE .... Jimmy Velvet
9. BLUE TEARDROPS .... Jimmy Le Fever
10. SEARCHIN' .... Ace Canno
11. GIRL FROM SPANISH TOWN .... Marty Robbins
12. DANCE ON, LITTLE GIRL .... Thurston Harris
13. LAST NIGHT I HAD THE STRANGEST DREAM .... Kingston Trio
14. LONELY DAYS OF WINTER .... Frankie Laine
15. HEIMAT DEINE STERNE .... The Blue Boys

K-KIS FEATURE ALBUMS

1. MEET THE BEATLES .... The Beatles
2. INTRODUCING, THE BEATLES .... The Beatles
3. BEAUTY AND THE BEARD .... Al Hirt and Ann Margare
4. HIS GREATEST HITS .... Rusty Drape
5. VINCE GAURALDI, BOLA SETE AND FRIENDS .... Fantasy Record
6. KISSIN' COUSINS .... Elvis Presley Soundtrack Albu
7. 500 MILES AWAY FROM HOME .... Bobby Ba
8. WONDERFUL SUMMER .... Robin Wa
9. FORGET HIM .... Bobby Ryd
10. NEED TO BELONG .... Jerry Butl

K-KIS "SOUND" CITIZENS

BUD ZUMWALT — LES BEIGEL — BOBBY LEE — BILL PLUMM
OLLIE FREEMAN — GARY MARSHALL — LARRY ICKES

K-KIS — COMMAND RADIO — DIAL 9

(Printed by Ben Franklin at Monument Printing) 15

San Diego #8
K-KIS Radio
February 21, 1964
"To the Aisle"

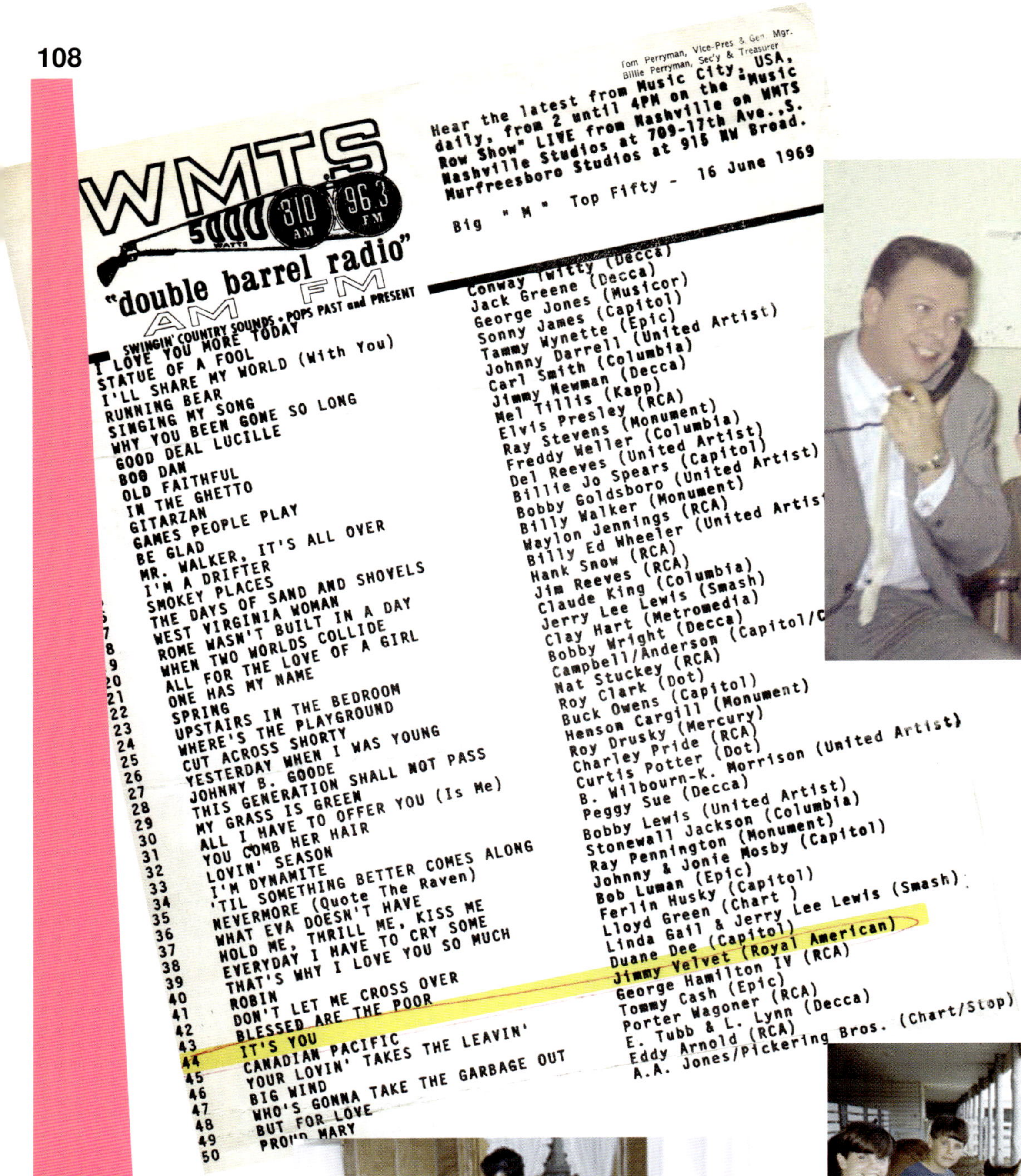

Tom Perryman, Vice-Pres & Gen. Mgr.
Billie Perryman, Sec'y & Treasurer

WMTS 5000 WATTS 810 AM 96.3 FM

"double barrel radio" AM FM

SWINGIN' COUNTRY SOUNDS • POPS PAST and PRESENT

Hear the latest from Music City, USA, daily, from 2 until 4PM on the "Music Row Show" LIVE from Nashville on WMTS Nashville Studios at 709-17th Ave., S. Murfreesboro Studios at 915 NW Broad.

Big " M " Top Fifty - 16 June 1969

	I LOVE YOU MORE TODAY	Conway Twitty (Decca)
	STATUE OF A FOOL	Jack Greene (Decca)
	I'LL SHARE MY WORLD (With You)	George Jones (Musicor)
	RUNNING BEAR	Sonny James (Capitol)
	SINGING MY SONG	Tammy Wynette (Epic)
	WHY YOU BEEN GONE SO LONG	Johnny Darrell (United Artist)
	GOOD DEAL LUCILLE	Carl Smith (Columbia)
	BOO DAN	Jimmy Newman (Decca)
	OLD FAITHFUL	Mel Tillis (Kapp)
	IN THE GHETTO	Elvis Presley (RCA)
	GITARZAN	Ray Stevens (Monument)
	GAMES PEOPLE PLAY	Freddy Weller (Columbia)
	BE GLAD	Del Reeves (United Artist)
	MR. WALKER, IT'S ALL OVER	Billie Jo Spears (Capitol)
	I'M A DRIFTER	Bobby Goldsboro (United Artist)
	SMOKEY PLACES	Billy Walker (Monument)
	THE DAYS OF SAND AND SHOVELS	Waylon Jennings (RCA)
	WEST VIRGINIA WOMAN	Billy Ed Wheeler (United Artis
	ROME WASN'T BUILT IN A DAY	Hank Snow (RCA)
20	WHEN TWO WORLDS COLLIDE	Jim Reeves (RCA)
21	ALL FOR THE LOVE OF A GIRL	Claude King (Columbia)
22	ONE HAS MY NAME	Jerry Lee Lewis (Smash)
23	SPRING	Clay Hart (Metromedia)
24	UPSTAIRS IN THE BEDROOM	Bobby Wright (Decca)
25	WHERE'S THE PLAYGROUND	Campbell/Anderson (Capitol/C
26	CUT ACROSS SHORTY	Nat Stuckey (RCA)
27	YESTERDAY WHEN I WAS YOUNG	Roy Clark (Dot)
28	JOHNNY B. GOODE	Buck Owens (Capitol)
29	THIS GENERATION SHALL NOT PASS	Henson Cargill (Monument)
30	MY GRASS IS GREEN	Roy Drusky (Mercury)
31	ALL I HAVE TO OFFER YOU (Is Me)	Charley Pride (RCA)
32	YOU COMB HER HAIR	Curtis Potter (Dot)
33	LOVIN' SEASON	B. Wilbourn-K. Morrison (United Artist)
34	I'M DYNAMITE	Peggy Sue (Decca)
35	'TIL SOMETHING BETTER COMES ALONG	Bobby Lewis (United Artist)
36	NEVERMORE (Quote The Raven)	Stonewall Jackson (Columbia)
37	WHAT EVA DOESN'T HAVE	Ray Pennington (Monument)
38	HOLD ME, THRILL ME, KISS ME	Johnny & Jonie Mosby (Capitol)
39	EVERYDAY I HAVE TO CRY SOME	Bob Luman (Epic)
40	THAT'S WHY I LOVE YOU SO MUCH	Ferlin Husky (Capitol)
41	ROBIN	Lloyd Green (Chart)
42	DON'T LET ME CROSS OVER	Linda Gail & Jerry Lee Lewis (Smash)
43	BLESSED ARE THE POOR	Duane Dee (Capitol)
44	IT'S YOU	Jimmy Velvet (Royal American)
45	CANADIAN PACIFIC	George Hamilton IV (RCA)
46	YOUR LOVIN' TAKES THE LEAVIN'	Tommy Cash (Epic)
47	BIG WIND	Porter Wagoner (RCA)
48	WHO'S GONNA TAKE THE GARBAGE OUT	E. Tubb & L. Lynn (Decca)
49	BUT FOR LOVE	Eddy Arnold (RCA)
50	PROUD MARY	A.A. Jones/Pickering Bros. (Chart/Stop)

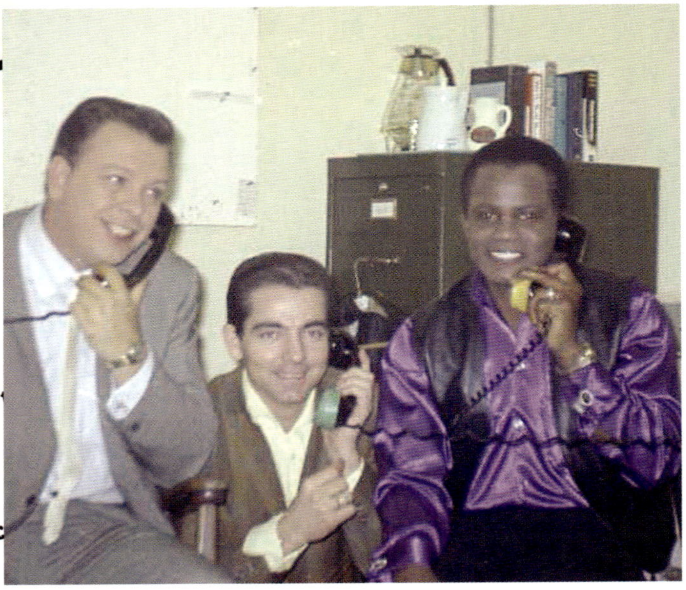

Billy Strange and Joe Tex

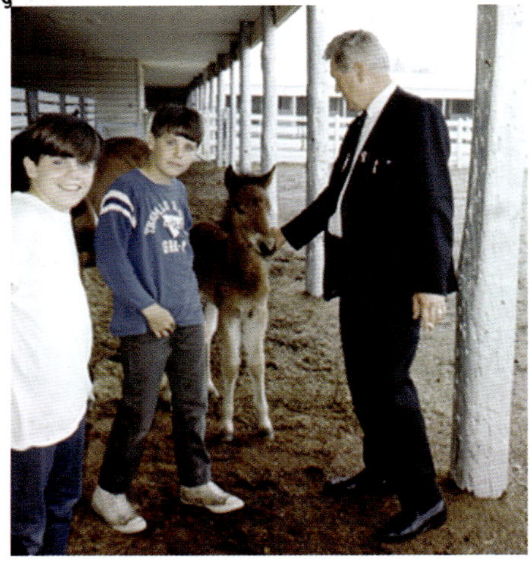

Vernon and the boys at Elvis' circle "G" ranch in Walls, MS

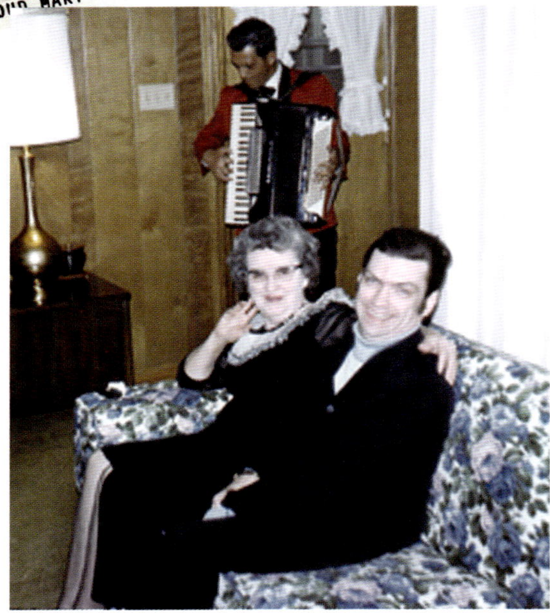

Mrs. Pepper and her son Gary, Elvis Fan Club President.

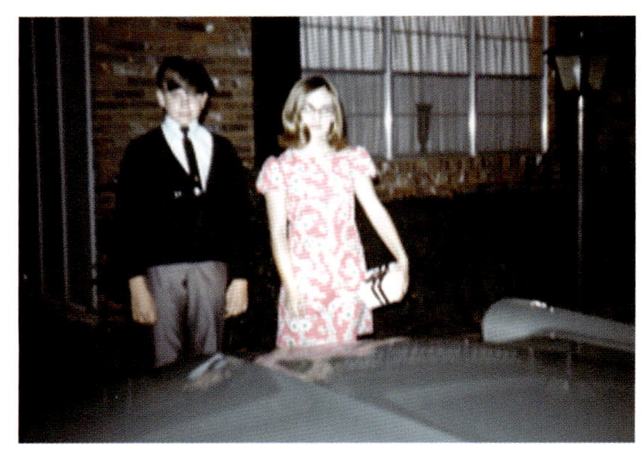

Billy and his date

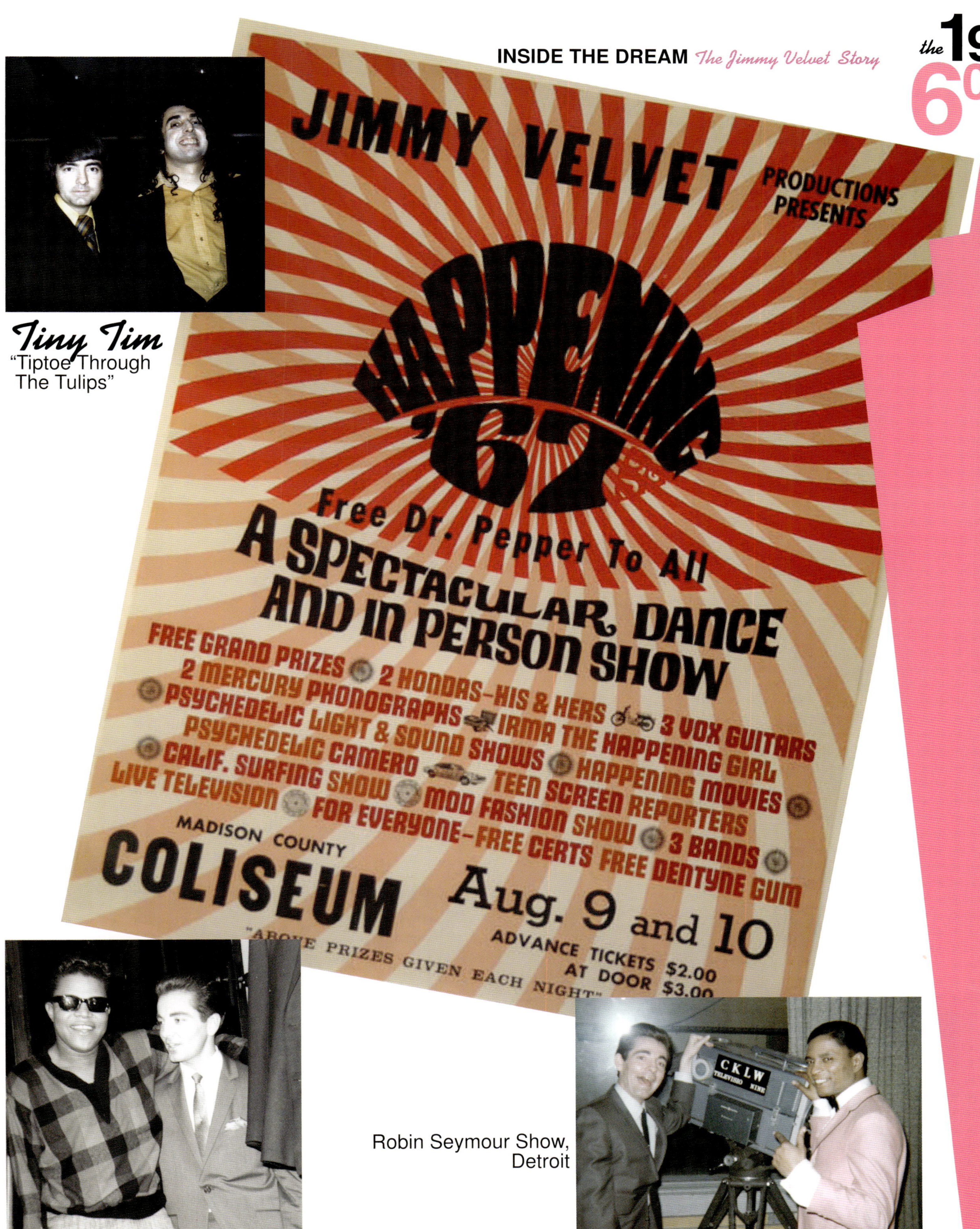

Tiny Tim
"Tiptoe Through The Tulips"

Robin Seymour Show, Detroit

Tony Clark and I on the Dick Clark Tour his hit was, "The Entertainer"

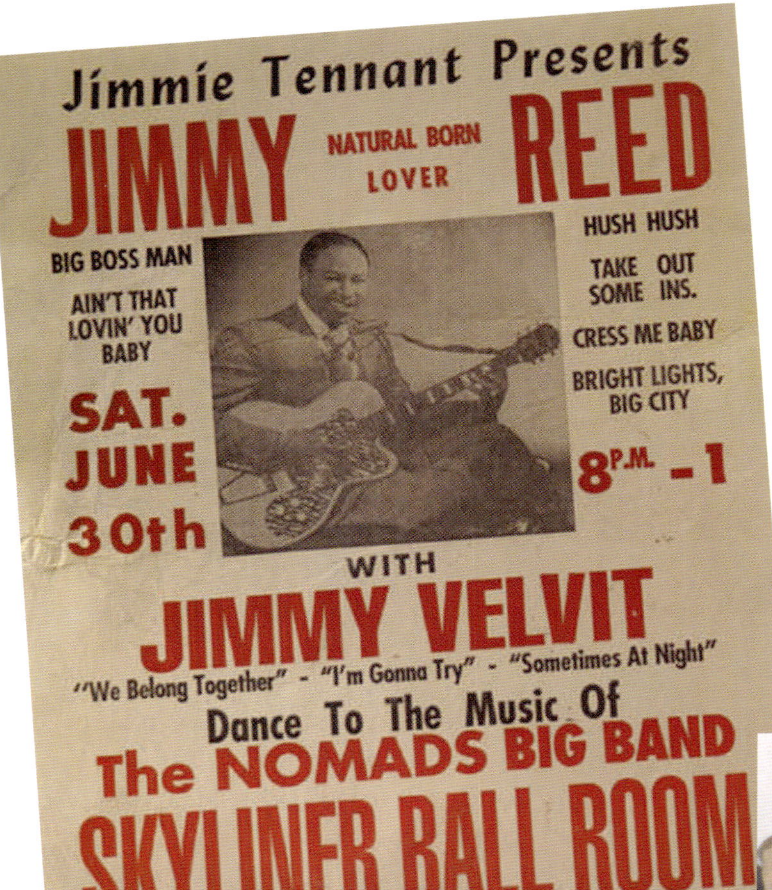

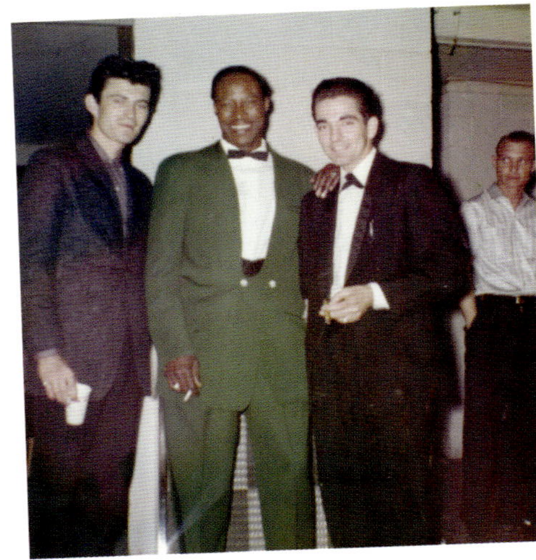

Jimmy Reed and I at a show in Lubbock, TX

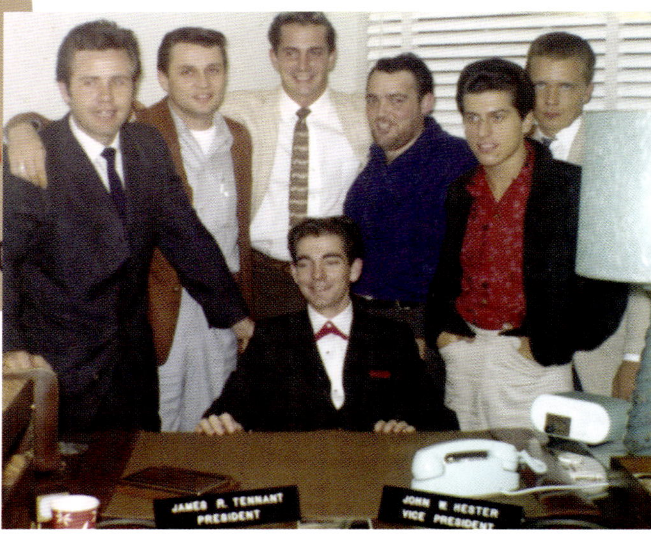

My Nashville Office in 1960 notice dark haired boy next to me thats Johnny Ramastella later known as Johnny Rivers

WAPE DJ Bobby Dee on right and Mrs. Dee, Johnny Horton, and Thomas Wayne. Johnny's biggest hit "Battle of New Orleans." Thomas Wayne's was "Tragedy." Thomas was "Thomas Wayne Perkins," Johnny Cash's guitar player Luther Perkins brother.

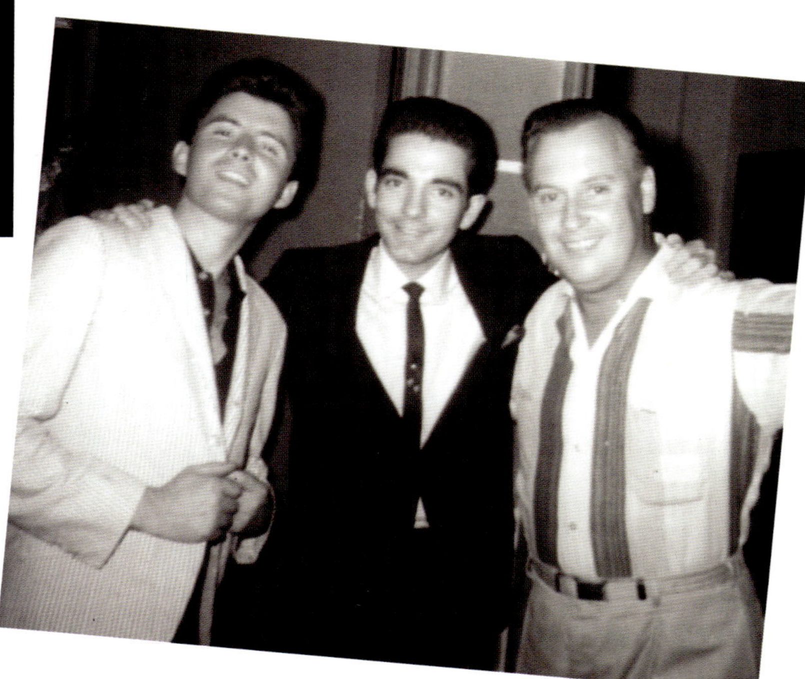

Johnny Tillotson and Jack Heyward

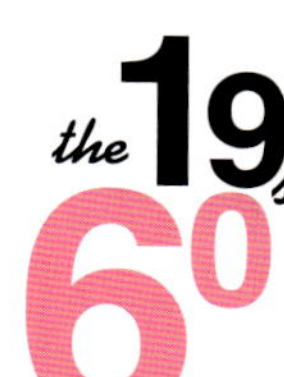

Columbia, SC WNOK Chart "We Belong Together" #7 and "To the Aisle" #3. "We Belong Together was #1 in Columbia for 17 weeks. November '63- February '64.

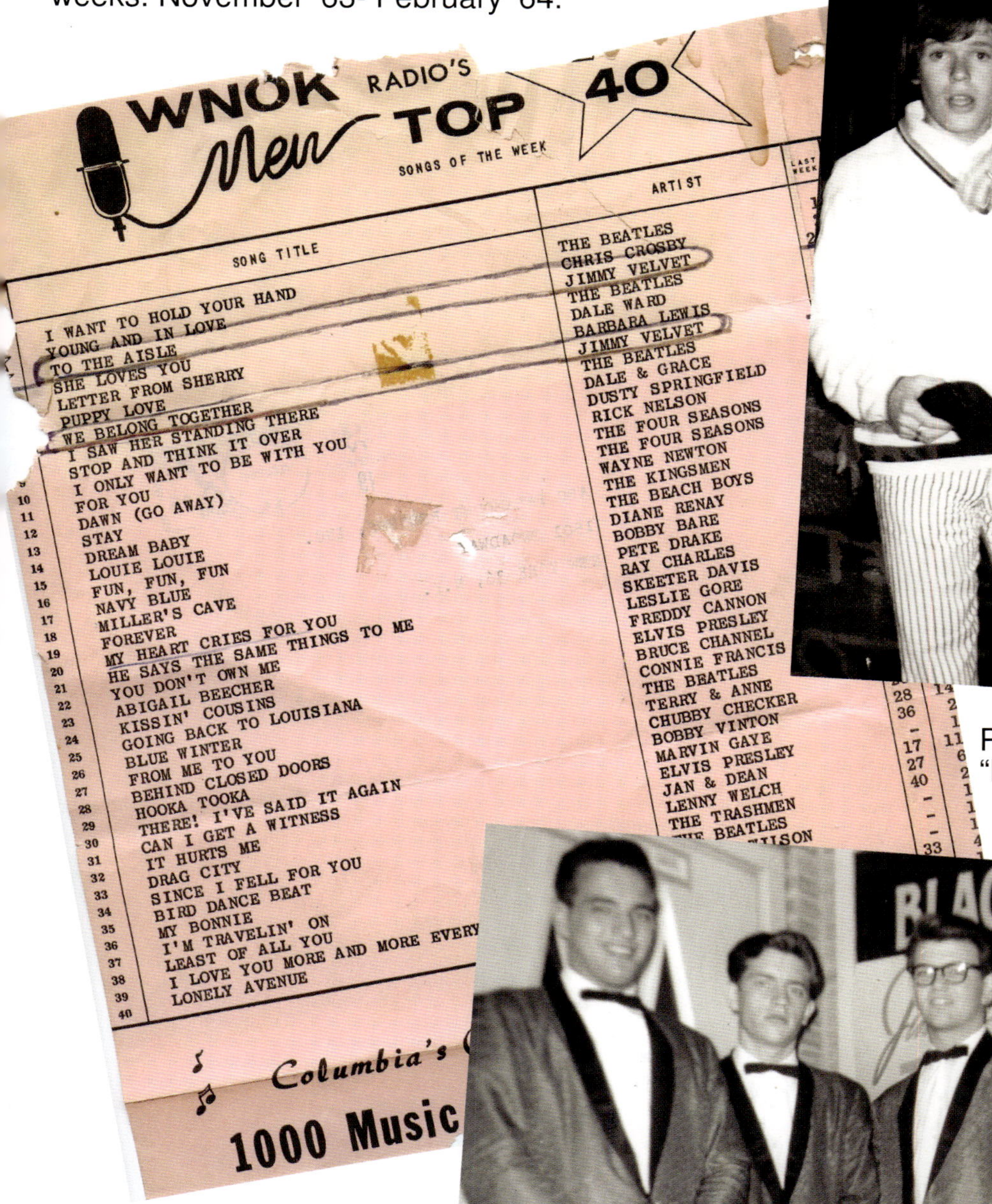

WNOK RADIO'S New TOP 40 SONGS OF THE WEEK

	SONG TITLE	ARTIST
1	I WANT TO HOLD YOUR HAND	THE BEATLES
2	YOUNG AND IN LOVE	CHRIS CROSBY
3	TO THE AISLE	JIMMY VELVET
4	SHE LOVES YOU	THE BEATLES
5	LETTER FROM SHERRY	DALE WARD
6	PUPPY LOVE	BARBARA LEWIS
7	WE BELONG TOGETHER	JIMMY VELVET
8	I SAW HER STANDING THERE	THE BEATLES
9	STOP AND THINK IT OVER	DALE & GRACE
10	I ONLY WANT TO BE WITH YOU	DUSTY SPRINGFIELD
11	FOR YOU	RICK NELSON
12	DAWN (GO AWAY)	THE FOUR SEASONS
13	STAY	THE FOUR SEASONS
14	DREAM BABY	WAYNE NEWTON
15	LOUIE LOUIE	THE KINGSMEN
16	FUN, FUN, FUN	THE BEACH BOYS
17	NAVY BLUE	DIANE RENAY
18	MILLER'S CAVE	BOBBY BARE
19	FOREVER	PETE DRAKE
20	MY HEART CRIES FOR YOU	RAY CHARLES
21	HE SAYS THE SAME THINGS TO ME	SKEETER DAVIS
22	YOU DON'T OWN ME	LESLIE GORE
23	ABIGAIL BEECHER	FREDDY CANNON
24	KISSIN' COUSINS	ELVIS PRESLEY
25	GOING BACK TO LOUISIANA	BRUCE CHANNEL
26	BLUE WINTER	CONNIE FRANCIS
27	FROM ME TO YOU	THE BEATLES
28	BEHIND CLOSED DOORS	TERRY & ANNE
29	HOOKA TOOKA	CHUBBY CHECKER
30	THERE! I'VE SAID IT AGAIN	BOBBY VINTON
31	CAN I GET A WITNESS	MARVIN GAYE
32	IT HURTS ME	ELVIS PRESLEY
33	DRAG CITY	JAN & DEAN
34	SINCE I FELL FOR YOU	LENNY WELCH
35	BIRD DANCE BEAT	THE TRASHMEN
36	MY BONNIE	THE BEATLES
37	I'M TRAVELIN' ON	...WILSON
38	LEAST OF ALL YOU	
39	I LOVE YOU MORE AND MORE EVERY	
40	LONELY AVENUE	

Columbia's ...

1000 Music ...

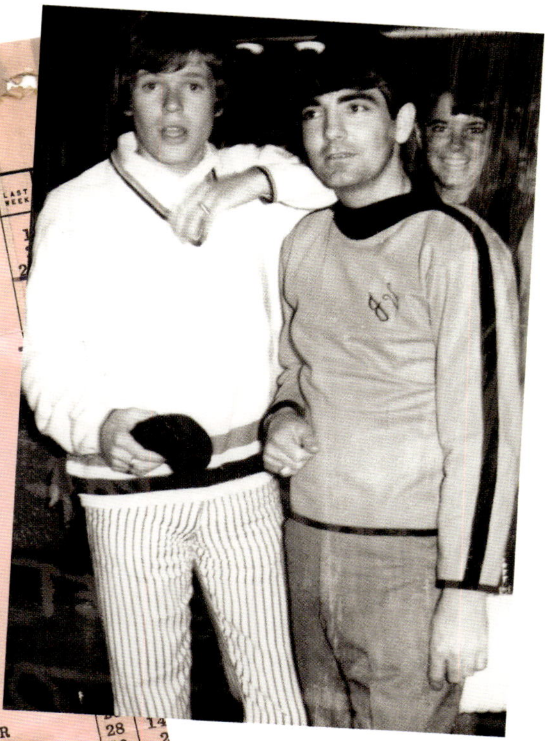

Peter Noone of "Herman's Hermits"

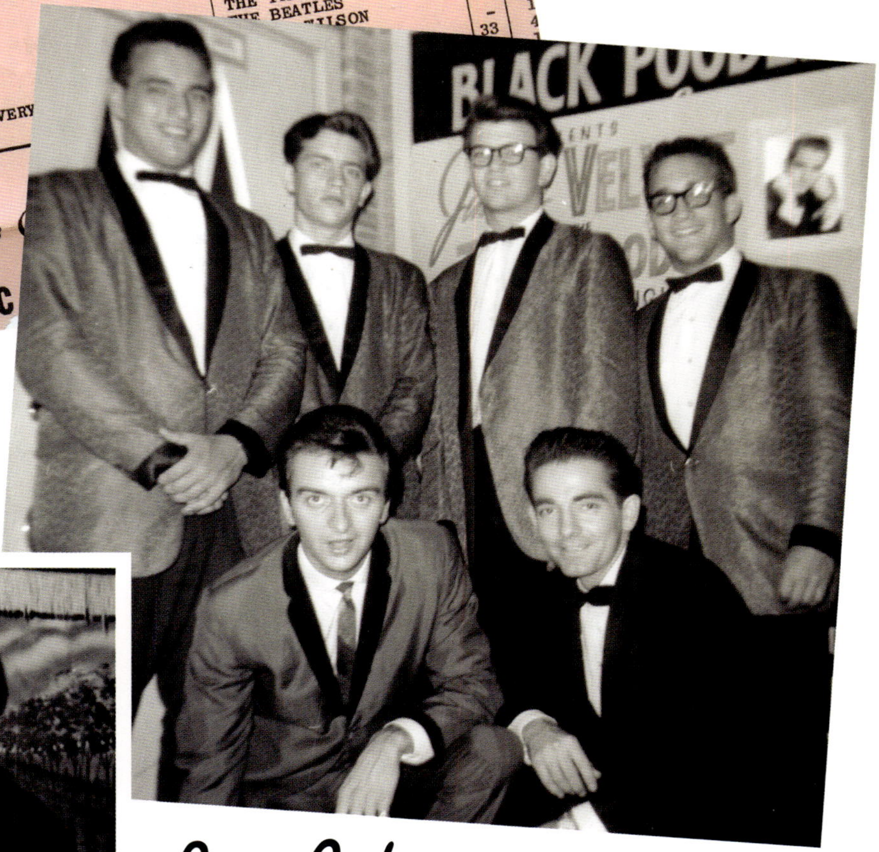

Ray Peterson

My band and I at the show with my friend of many years, Ray Peterson. Ray had so many great hits:
"Tell Laura I Love Her"
"Corina. Corina"
"Goodnight My Love"

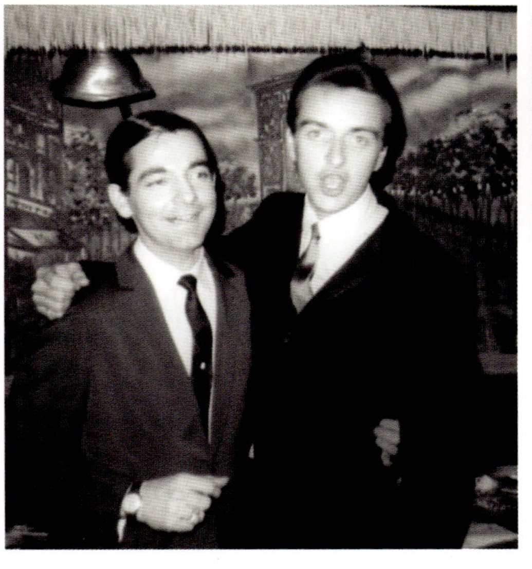

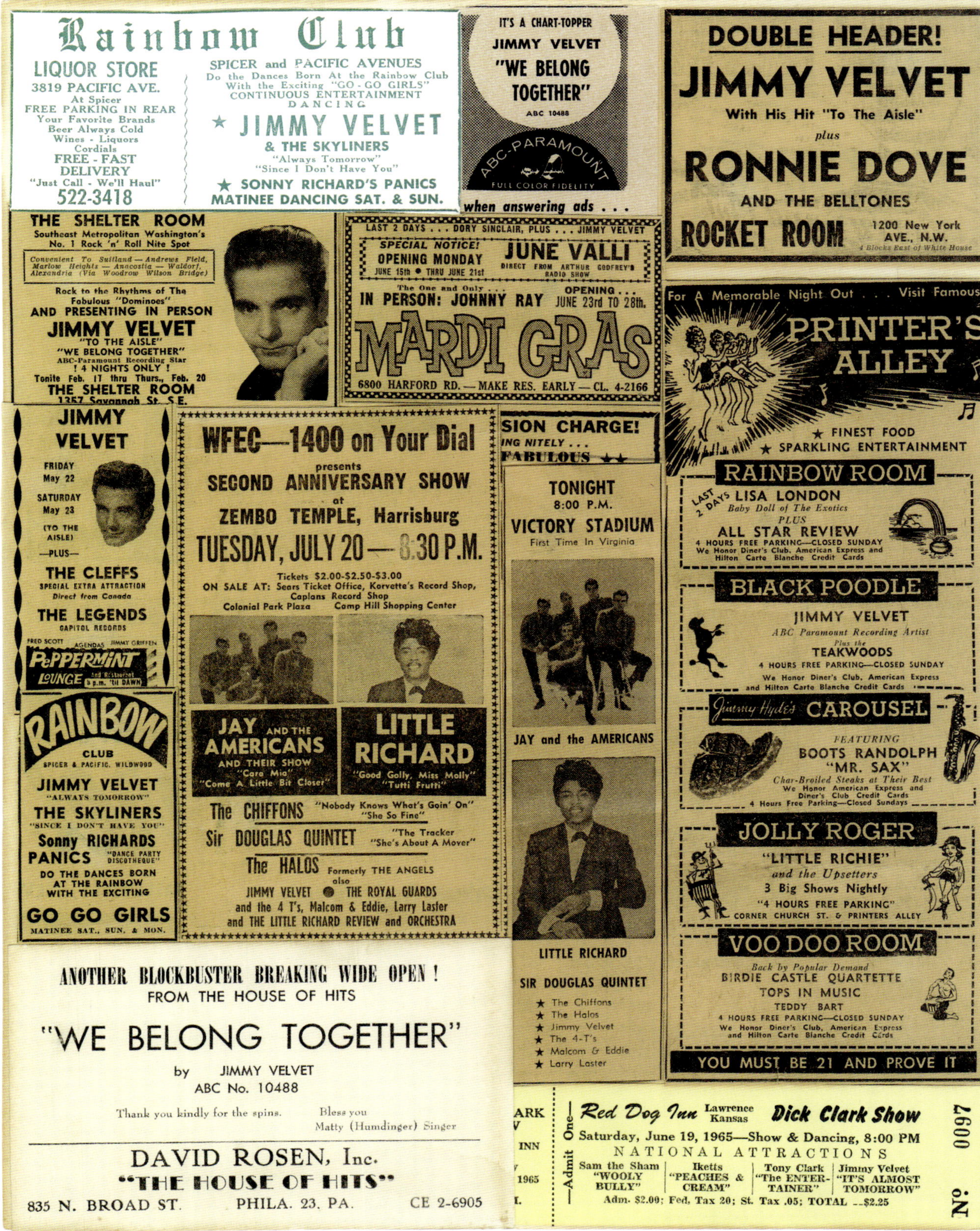

Rainbow Club
LIQUOR STORE
3819 PACIFIC AVE.
At Spicer
FREE PARKING IN REAR
Your Favorite Brands
Beer Always Cold
Wines - Liquors
Cordials
FREE - FAST DELIVERY
"Just Call - We'll Haul"
522-3418
SPICER and PACIFIC AVENUES
Do the Dances Born At the Rainbow Club
With the Exciting "GO - GO GIRLS"
CONTINUOUS ENTERTAINMENT
DANCING
★ JIMMY VELVET
& THE SKYLINERS
"Always Tomorrow"
"Since I Don't Have You"
★ SONNY RICHARD'S PANICS
MATINEE DANCING SAT. & SUN.
IT'S A CHART-TOPPER
JIMMY VELVET
"WE BELONG TOGETHER"
ABC 10488
ABC-PARAMOUNT
FULL COLOR FIDELITY
when answering ads . . .
DOUBLE HEADER!
JIMMY VELVET
With His Hit "To The Aisle"
plus
RONNIE DOVE
AND THE BELLTONES
ROCKET ROOM
1200 New York AVE., N.W.
THE SHELTER ROOM
Southeast Metropolitan Washington's No. 1 Rock 'n' Roll Nite Spot
Rock to the Rhythms of The Fabulous "Dominoes"
AND PRESENTING IN PERSON
JIMMY VELVET
"TO THE AISLE"
"WE BELONG TOGETHER"
ABC-Paramount Recording Star
! 4 NIGHTS ONLY !
Tonite Feb. 17 thru Thurs., Feb. 20
THE SHELTER ROOM
LAST 2 DAYS . . . DORY SINCLAIR, PLUS . . . JIMMY VELVET
SPECIAL NOTICE!
OPENING MONDAY
JUNE 15th THRU JUNE 21st
JUNE VALLI
DIRECT FROM ARTHUR GODFREY'S RADIO SHOW
The One and Only . . .
IN PERSON: JOHNNY RAY
OPENING . . . JUNE 23rd TO 28th.
MARDI GRAS
6800 HARFORD RD. — MAKE RES. EARLY — CL. 4-2166
For A Memorable Night Out . . . Visit Famous
PRINTER'S ALLEY
★ FINEST FOOD
★ SPARKLING ENTERTAINMENT
JIMMY VELVET
FRIDAY May 22
SATURDAY May 23
(TO THE AISLE)
—PLUS—
THE CLEFFS
SPECIAL EXTRA ATTRACTION
Direct from Canada
THE LEGENDS
CAPITOL RECORDS
PePPERMiNT LOUNGE
WFEC—1400 on Your Dial
presents
SECOND ANNIVERSARY SHOW
at
ZEMBO TEMPLE, Harrisburg
TUESDAY, JULY 20 — 8:30 P.M.
Tickets $2.00-$2.50-$3.00
Colonial Park Plaza
Camp Hill Shopping Center
JAY AND THE AMERICANS
AND THEIR SHOW
"Cara Mia"
"Come A Little Bit Closer"
LITTLE RICHARD
"Good Golly, Miss Molly"
"Tutti Frutti"
The CHIFFONS
"Nobody Knows What's Goin' On"
"She So Fine"
Sir DOUGLAS QUINTET
"The Tracker"
"She's About A Mover"
The HALOS
Formerly THE ANGELS
also
JIMMY VELVET ● THE ROYAL GUARDS
and the 4 T's, Malcom & Eddie, Larry Laster
and THE LITTLE RICHARD REVIEW and ORCHESTRA
SION CHARGE!
ING NITELY . . .
FABULOUS
TONIGHT
8:00 P.M.
VICTORY STADIUM
First Time In Virginia
JAY and the AMERICANS
LITTLE RICHARD
SIR DOUGLAS QUINTET
★ The Chiffons
★ The Halos
★ Jimmy Velvet
★ The 4-T's
★ Malcom & Eddie
★ Larry Laster
RAINBOW ROOM
LAST 2 DAYS LISA LONDON
Baby Doll of The Exotics
PLUS
ALL STAR REVIEW
BLACK POODLE
JIMMY VELVET
ABC Paramount Recording Artist
Plus the
TEAKWOODS
4 HOURS FREE PARKING—CLOSED SUNDAY
Jimmy Hyde's CAROUSEL
FEATURING
BOOTS RANDOLPH
"MR. SAX"
Char-Broiled Steaks at Their Best
JOLLY ROGER
"LITTLE RICHIE"
and the Upsetters
3 Big Shows Nightly
"4 HOURS FREE PARKING"
CORNER CHURCH ST. & PRINTERS ALLEY
VOO DOO ROOM
Back by Popular Demand
BIRDIE CASTLE QUARTETTE
TOPS IN MUSIC
TEDDY BART
YOU MUST BE 21 AND PROVE IT
RAINBOW CLUB
SPICER & PACIFIC, WILDWOOD
JIMMY VELVET
"ALWAYS TOMORROW"
THE SKYLINERS
"SINCE I DON'T HAVE YOU"
Sonny RICHARDS PANICS
"DANCE PARTY DISCOTHEQUE"
DO THE DANCES BORN AT THE RAINBOW WITH THE EXCITING
GO GO GIRLS
MATINEE SAT., SUN. & MON.
ANOTHER BLOCKBUSTER BREAKING WIDE OPEN!
FROM THE HOUSE OF HITS
"WE BELONG TOGETHER"
by JIMMY VELVET
ABC No. 10488
Thank you kindly for the spins.
Bless you
Matty (Humdinger) Singer
DAVID ROSEN, Inc.
"THE HOUSE OF HITS"
835 N. BROAD ST.
PHILA. 23, PA.
CE 2-6905
Admit One
Red Dog Inn Lawrence Kansas
Dick Clark Show
Saturday, June 19, 1965—Show & Dancing, 8:00 PM
NATIONAL ATTRACTIONS
Sam the Sham "WOOLY BULLY"
Iketts "PEACHES & CREAM"
Tony Clark "The ENTER-TAINER"
Jimmy Velvet "IT'S ALMOST TOMORROW"
Adm. $2.00; Fed. Tax 20; St. Tax .05; TOTAL $2.25
No 0097

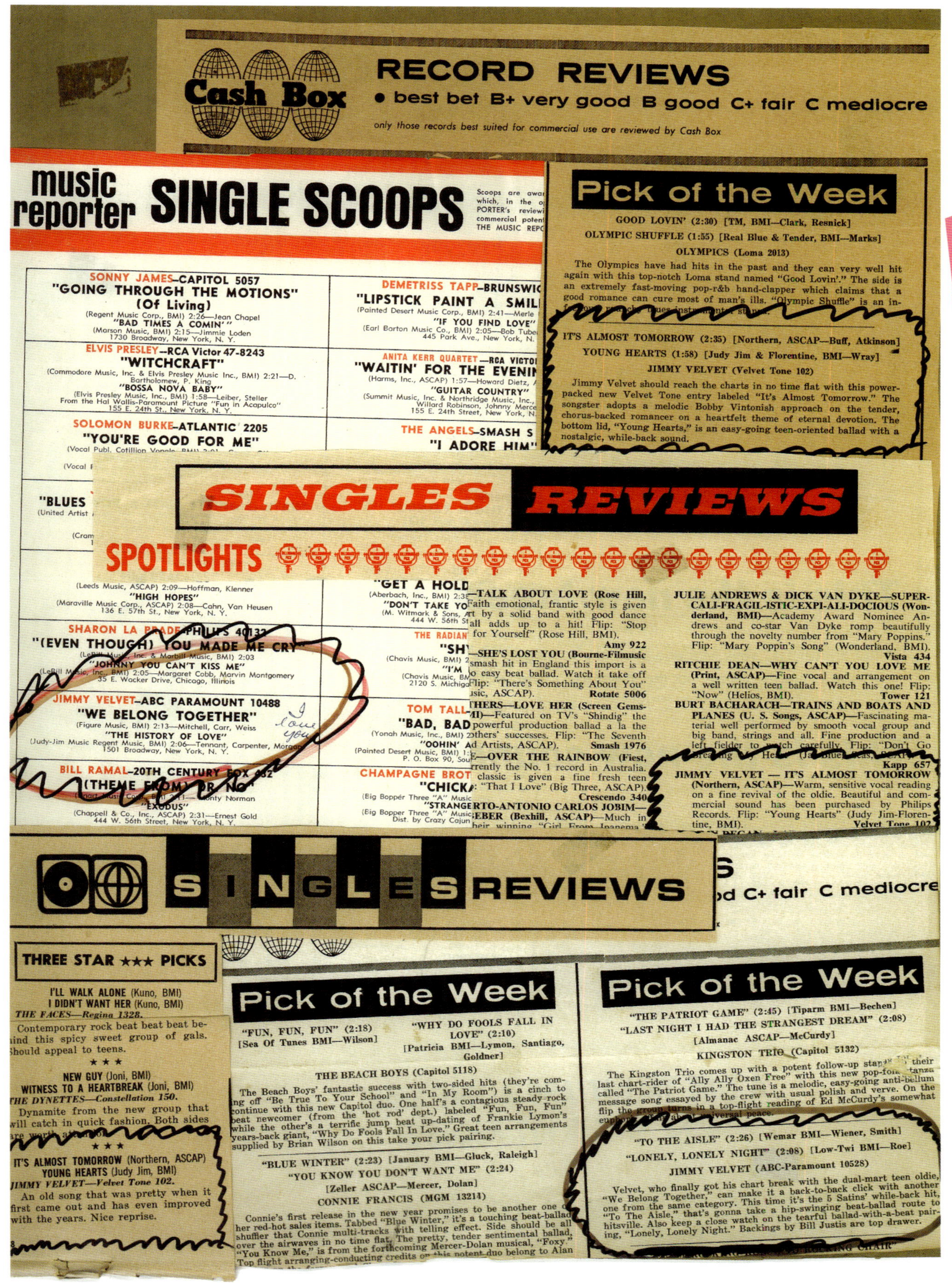

Cash Box
RECORD REVIEWS
● best bet B+ very good B good C+ fair C mediocre
only those records best suited for commercial use are reviewed by Cash Box

music reporter SINGLE SCOOPS

SONNY JAMES—CAPITOL 5057
"GOING THROUGH THE MOTIONS" (Of Living)
(Regent Music Corp., BMI) 2:26—Jean Chapel
"BAD TIMES A COMIN'"
(Marson Music, BMI) 2:15—Jimmie Loden
1730 Broadway, New York, N. Y.

ELVIS PRESLEY—RCA Victor 47-8243
"WITCHCRAFT"
(Commodore Music, Inc. & Elvis Presley Music Inc., BMI) 2:21—D. Bartholomew, P. King
"BOSSA NOVA BABY"
(Elvis Presley Music, Inc., BMI) 1:58—Leiber, Stoller
From the Hal Wallis-Paramount Picture "Fun in Acapulco"
155 E. 24th St., New York, N. Y.

SOLOMON BURKE—ATLANTIC 2205
"YOU'RE GOOD FOR ME"

DEMETRISS TAPP—BRUNSWIC
"LIPSTICK PAINT A SMIL
(Painted Desert Music Corp., BMI) 2:41—Merle
"IF YOU FIND LOVE"
(Earl Barton Music Co., BMI) 2:05—Bob Tuber
445 Park Ave., New York, N.

ANITA KERR QUARTET—RCA VICTOR
"WAITIN' FOR THE EVENIN
(Harms, Inc., ASCAP) 1:57—Howard Dietz,
"GUITAR COUNTRY"
(Summit Music, Inc. & Northridge Music, Inc., Willard Robinson, Johnny Merce
155 E. 24th Street, New York, N.

THE ANGELS—SMASH
"I ADORE HIM"

Pick of the Week

GOOD LOVIN' (2:30) [TM, BMI—Clark, Resnick]
OLYMPIC SHUFFLE (1:55) [Real Blue & Tender, BMI—Marks]
OLYMPICS (Loma 2013)

The Olympics have had hits in the past and they can very well hit again with this top-notch Loma stand named "Good Lovin'." The side is an extremely fast-moving pop-r&b hand-clapper which claims that a good romance can cure most of man's ills. "Olympic Shuffle" is an in-

IT'S ALMOST TOMORROW (2:35) [Northern, ASCAP—Buff, Atkinson]
YOUNG HEARTS (1:58) [Judy Jim & Florentine, BMI—Wray]
JIMMY VELVET (Velvet Tone 102)

Jimmy Velvet should reach the charts in no time flat with this power-packed new Velvet Tone entry labeled "It's Almost Tomorrow." The songster adopts a melodic Bobby Vintonish approach on the tender, chorus-backed romancer on a heartfelt theme of eternal devotion. The bottom lid, "Young Hearts," is an easy-going teen-oriented ballad with a nostalgic, while-back sound.

SINGLES REVIEWS
SPOTLIGHTS

"BLUES"
(United Artist

(Leeds Music, ASCAP) 2:09—Hoffman, Klenner
"HIGH HOPES"
(Maraville Music Corp., ASCAP) 2:08—Cahn, Van Heusen
136 E. 57th St., New York, N. Y.

SHARON LA PRADE—PHILIPS 40132
"(EVEN THOUGH) YOU MADE ME CRY"
"JOHNNY YOU CAN'T KISS ME"
(LeBill Music, Inc., BMI) 2:05—Margaret Cobb, Marvin Montgomery
35 E. Wacker Drive, Chicago, Illinois

JIMMY VELVET—ABC PARAMOUNT 10488
"WE BELONG TOGETHER"
(Figure Music, BMI) 2:13—Mitchell, Carr, Weiss
"THE HISTORY OF LOVE"
(Judy-Jim Music Regent Music, BMI) 2:06—Tennant, Carpenter, Morgan
1501 Broadway, New York, N. Y.

I love you

BILL RAMAL—20TH CENTURY FOX
"(THEME FROM) EXODUS"
(Chappell & Co., Inc., ASCAP) 2:31—Ernest Gold
444 W. 56th Street, New York, N. Y.

"GET A HOLD
(Aberbach, Inc., BMI)
"DON'T TAKE YO
(M. Witmark & Sons,
444 W. 56th St.

THE RADIAN
"SH
(Chavis Music, BMI)
"I'M
(Chavis Music, BMI)
2120 S. Michigan

TOM TALL
"BAD, BAD
(Yonah Music, Inc., BMI)
"OOHIN'
(Painted Desert Music, BMI)
P. O. Box 90,

CHAMPAGNE BROT
"CHICK
(Big Bopper Three "A" Music
(Big Bopper Three "A" Music
Dist. by Crazy Cajun

—TALK ABOUT LOVE (Rose Hill, Faith emotional, frantic style is given rt by a solid band with good dance all adds up to a hit! Flip: "Stop for Yourself" (Rose Hill, BMI). Amy 922

—SHE'S LOST YOU (Bourne-Filmusic smash hit in England this import is a o easy beat ballad. Watch it take off Flip: "There's Something About You" usic, ASCAP). Rotate 5006

THERS—LOVE HER (Screen Gems-MI)—Featured on TV's "Shindig" the powerful production ballad a la the others' successes. Flip: "The Seventh Artists, ASCAP). Smash 1976

—OVER THE RAINBOW (Fiest, rrently the No. 1 record in Australia. classic is given a fine fresh teen "That I Love" (Big Three, ASCAP). Crescendo 340

RTO-ANTONIO CARLOS JOBIM—EBER (Bexhill, ASCAP)—Much in

JULIE ANDREWS & DICK VAN DYKE—SUPER-CALI-FRAGIL-ISTIC-EXPI-ALI-DOCIOUS (Wonderland, BMI)—Academy Award Nominee Andrews and co-star Van Dyke romp beautifully through the novelty number from "Mary Poppins." Flip: "Mary Poppin's Song" (Wonderland, BMI). Vista 434

RITCHIE DEAN—WHY CAN'T YOU LOVE ME (Print, ASCAP)—Fine vocal and arrangement on a well written teen ballad. Watch this one! Flip: "Now" (Helios, BMI). Tower 121

BURT BACHARACH—TRAINS AND BOATS AND PLANES (U. S. Songs, ASCAP)—Fascinating material well performed by smooth vocal group and big band, strings and all. Fine production and a left fielder to watch carefully. Flip: "Don't Go Kapp 657

JIMMY VELVET — IT'S ALMOST TOMORROW (Northern, ASCAP)—Warm, sensitive vocal reading on a fine revival of the oldie. Beautiful and commercial sound has been purchased by Philips Records. Flip: "Young Hearts" (Judy Jim-Florentine, BMI). Velvet Tone 102

SINGLES REVIEWS

THREE STAR ★★★ PICKS

I'LL WALK ALONE (Kuno, BMI)
I DIDN'T WANT HER (Kuno, BMI)
THE FACES—Regina 1328.
Contemporary rock beat beat beat behind this spicy sweet group of gals. Should appeal to teens.

★ ★ ★

NEW GUY (Joni, BMI)
WITNESS TO A HEARTBREAK (Joni, BMI)
THE DYNETTES—Constellation 150.
Dynamite from the new group that will catch in quick fashion. Both sides

★ ★ ★

IT'S ALMOST TOMORROW (Northern, ASCAP)
YOUNG HEARTS (Judy Jim, BMI)
JIMMY VELVET—Velvet Tone 102.
An old song that was pretty when it first came out and has even improved with the years. Nice reprise.

Pick of the Week

"FUN, FUN, FUN" (2:18) [Sea Of Tunes BMI—Wilson]
"WHY DO FOOLS FALL IN LOVE" (2:10) [Patricia BMI—Lymon, Santiago, Goldner]
THE BEACH BOYS (Capitol 5118)

The Beach Boys' fantastic success with two-sided hits (they're coming off "Be True To Your School" and "In My Room") is a cinch to continue with this new Capitol duo. One half's a contagious steady rock beat newcomer (from the 'hot rod' dept.) labeled "Fun, Fun, Fun" while the other's a terrific jump beat up-dating of Frankie Lymon's years-back giant, "Why Do Fools Fall In Love." Great teen arrangements supplied by Brian Wilson on this take your pick pairing.

"BLUE WINTER" (2:23) [January BMI—Gluck, Raleigh]
"YOU KNOW YOU DON'T WANT ME" (2:24) [Zeller ASCAP—Mercer, Dolan]
CONNIE FRANCIS (MGM 13214)

Connie's first release in the new year promises to be another one of her red-hot sales items. Tabbed "Blue Winter," it's a touching beat-ballad shuffler that Connie multi-tracks with telling effect. Side should be all over the airwaves in no time flat. The pretty, tender sentimental ballad, "You Know Me," is from the forthcoming Mercer-Dolan musical, "Foxy." Top flight arranging-conducting credits

Pick of the Week

"THE PATRIOT GAME" (2:45) [Tiparm BMI—Bechen]
"LAST NIGHT I HAD THE STRANGEST DREAM" (2:08) [Almanac ASCAP—McCurdy]
KINGSTON TRIO (Capitol 5132)

The Kingston Trio comes up with a potent follow-up to their last chart-rider of "Ally Ally Oxen Free" with this new pop-folk stanza called "The Patriot Game." The tune is a melodic, easy-going anti-bellum message song essayed by the crew with usual polish and verve. On the flip the group turns in a top-flight reading of Ed McCurdy's somewhat

"TO THE AISLE" (2:26) [Wemar BMI—Wiener, Smith]
"LONELY, LONELY NIGHT" (2:08) [Low-Twi BMI—Roe]
JIMMY VELVET (ABC-Paramount 10528)

Velvet, who finally got his chart break with the dual-mart teen oldie, "We Belong Together," can make it a back-to-back click with another one from the same category. This time it's the 5 Satins' while-back hit, "To The Aisle," that's gonna take a hip-swinging beat-ballad route to hitsville. Also keep a close watch on the tearful ballad-with-a-beat pairing, "Lonely, Lonely Night." Backings by Bill Justis are top drawer.

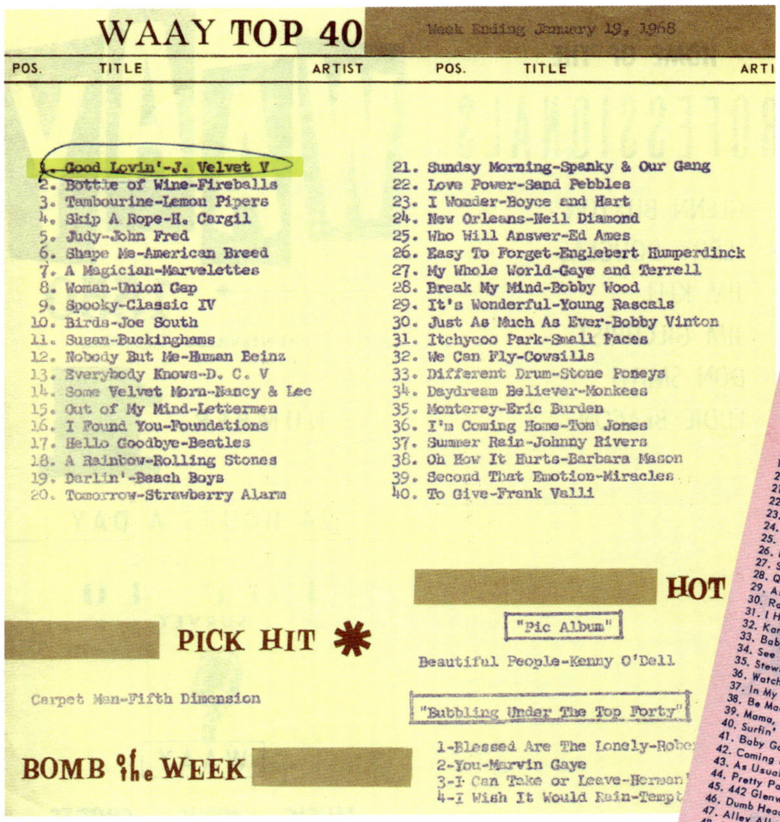

WAAY TOP 40

Week Ending January 19, 1968

POS.	TITLE – ARTIST	POS.	TITLE – ARTIST
1.	Good Lovin'-J. Velvet V	21.	Sunday Morning-Spanky & Our Gang
2.	Bottle of Wine-Fireballs	22.	Love Power-Sand Pebbles
3.	Tambourine-Lemon Pipers	23.	I Wonder-Boyce and Hart
4.	Skip A Rope-H. Cargil	24.	New Orleans-Neil Diamond
5.	Judy-John Fred	25.	Who Will Answer-Ed Ames
6.	Shape Me-American Breed	26.	Easy To Forget-Englebert Humperdinck
7.	A Magician-Marvelettes	27.	My Whole World-Gaye and Terrell
8.	Woman-Union Gap	28.	Break My Mind-Bobby Wood
9.	Spooky-Classic IV	29.	It's Wonderful-Young Rascals
10.	Birds-Joe South	30.	Just As Much As Ever-Bobby Vinton
11.	Susan-Buckinghams	31.	Itchycoo Park-Small Faces
12.	Nobody But Me-Human Beinz	32.	We Can Fly-Cowsills
13.	Everybody Knows-D. C. V	33.	Different Drum-Stone Poneys
14.	Some Velvet Morn-Nancy & Lee	34.	Daydream Believer-Monkees
15.	Out of My Mind-Lettermen	35.	Monterey-Eric Burden
16.	I Found You-Foundations	36.	I'm Coming Home-Tom Jones
17.	Hello Goodbye-Beatles	37.	Summer Rain-Johnny Rivers
18.	A Rainbow-Rolling Stones	38.	Oh How It Hurts-Barbara Mason
19.	Darlin'-Beach Boys	39.	Second That Emotion-Miracles
20.	Tomorrow-Strawberry Alarm	40.	To Give-Frank Valli

HOT

"Pic Album"

Beautiful People-Kenny O'Dell

PICK HIT ✱

Carpet Man-Fifth Dimension

"Bubbling Under The Top Forty"

1-Blessed Are The Lonely-Robe
2-You-Marvin Gaye
3-I Can Take or Leave-Horsem
4-I Wish It Would Rain-Tempt

BOMB of the WEEK

Huntsville, AL

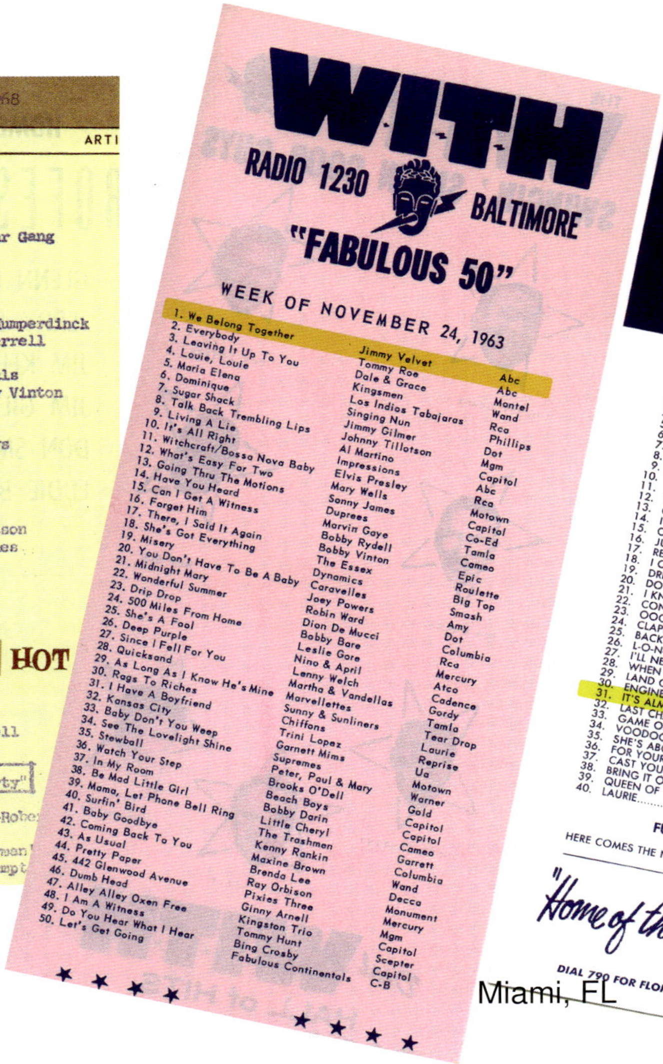

WITH RADIO 1230 BALTIMORE "FABULOUS 50"

WEEK OF NOVEMBER 24, 1963

1.	We Belong Together	Jimmy Velvet	Abc
2.	Everybody	Tommy Roe	Abc
3.	Leaving It Up To You	Dale & Grace	Montel
4.	Louie, Louie	Kingsmen	Wand
5.	Maria Elena	Los Indios Tabajaras	Rca
6.	Dominique	Singing Nun	Phillips
7.	Sugar Shack	Jimmy Gilmer	Dot
8.	Talk Back Trembling Lips	Johnny Tillotson	Mgm
9.	Living A Lie	Al Martino	Capitol
10.	It's All Right	Impressions	Abc
11.	Witchcraft/Bossa Nova Baby	Elvis Presley	Rca
12.	What's Easy For Two	Mary Wells	Motown
13.	Going Thru The Motions	Sonny James	Capitol
14.	Have You Heard	Duprees	Co-Ed
15.	Can I Get A Witness	Marvin Gaye	Tamla
16.	Forget Him	Bobby Rydell	Cameo
17.	There, I Said It Again	Bobby Vinton	Epic
18.	She's Got Everything	The Essex	Roulette
19.	Misery	Dynamics	Big Top
20.	You Don't Have To Be A Baby	Caravelles	Smash
21.	Midnight Mary	Joey Powers	Amy
22.	Wonderful Summer	Robin Ward	Dot
23.	Drip Drop	Dion De Mucci	Columbia
24.	500 Miles From Home	Bobby Bare	Rca
25.	She's A Fool	Leslie Gore	Mercury
26.	Deep Purple	Nino & April	Atco
27.	Since I Fell For You	Lenny Welch	Cadence
28.	Quicksand	Martha & Vandellas	Gordy
29.	As Long As I Know He's Mine	Marvelletes	Tamla
30.	Rags To Riches	Sunny & Sunliners	Tear Drop
31.	I Have A Boyfriend	Chiffons	Laurie
32.	Kansas City	Trini Lopez	Reprise
33.	Baby Don't You Weep	Garnett Mims	Ua
34.	See The Lovelight Shine	Supremes	Motown
35.	Stewball	Peter, Paul & Mary	Warner
36.	Watch Your Step	Brooks O'Dell	Gold
37.	In My Room	Beach Boys	Capitol
38.	Be Mad Little Girl	Bobby Darin	Capitol
39.	Mama, Let Phone Bell Ring	Little Cheryl	Cameo
40.	Surfin' Bird	The Trashmen	Garrett
41.	Baby Goodbye	Kenny Rankin	Columbia
42.	Coming Back To You	Maxine Brown	Wand
43.	As Usual	Brenda Lee	Decca
44.	Pretty Paper	Ray Orbison	Monument
45.	442 Glenwood Avenue	Pixies Three	Mercury
46.	Dumb Head	Ginny Arnell	Mgm
47.	Alley Alley Oxen Free	Kingston Trio	Capitol
48.	I Am A Witness	Tommy Hunt	Scepter
49.	Do You Hear What I Hear	Bing Crosby	Capitol
50.	Let's Get Going	Fabulous Continentals	C-B

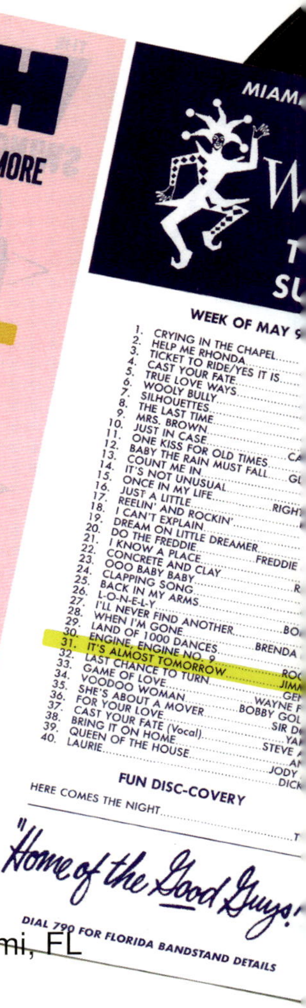

MIAMI

WEEK OF MAY 9

1.	CRYING IN THE CHAPEL	
2.	HELP ME RHONDA	
3.	TICKET TO RIDE/YES IT IS	
4.	CAST YOUR FATE	
5.	TRUE LOVE WAYS	
6.	WOOLY BULLY	
7.	SILHOUETTES	
8.	THE LAST TIME	
9.	MRS. BROWN	
10.	JUST IN CASE	
11.	ONE KISS FOR OLD TIMES	CA
12.	BABY THE RAIN MUST FALL	GL
13.	COUNT ME IN	
14.	IT'S NOT UNUSUAL	
15.	ONCE IN MY LIFE	
16.	JUST A LITTLE	RIGHT
17.	REELIN' AND ROCKIN'	
18.	I CAN'T EXPLAIN	
19.	DREAM ON LITTLE DREAMER	
20.	DO THE FREDDIE	
21.	I KNOW A PLACE	FREDDIE
22.	CONCRETE AND CLAY	
23.	OOO BABY BABY	
24.	CLAPPING SONG	R
25.	BACK IN MY ARMS	
26.	L-O-N-E-L-Y	
27.	I'LL NEVER FIND ANOTHER	BO
28.	WHEN I'M GONE	
29.	LAND OF 1000 DANCES	BRENDA
30.	ENGINE, ENGINE NO. 9	
31.	IT'S ALMOST TOMORROW	ROC
32.	LAST CHANCE TO TURN	JIMM
33.	GAME OF LOVE	GE
34.	VOODOO WOMAN	WAYNE F
35.	SHE'S ABOUT A MOVER	BOBBY GOL
36.	FOR YOUR LOVE	SIR D
37.	CAST YOUR FATE (Vocal)	YA
38.	BRING IT ON HOME	STEVE A
39.	QUEEN OF THE HOUSE	AN
40.	LAURIE	JODY
		DICK

FUN DISC-COVERY

HERE COMES THE NIGHT .... T

"Home of the Good Guys!"

DIAL 790 FOR FLORIDA BANDSTAND DETAILS

Miami, FL

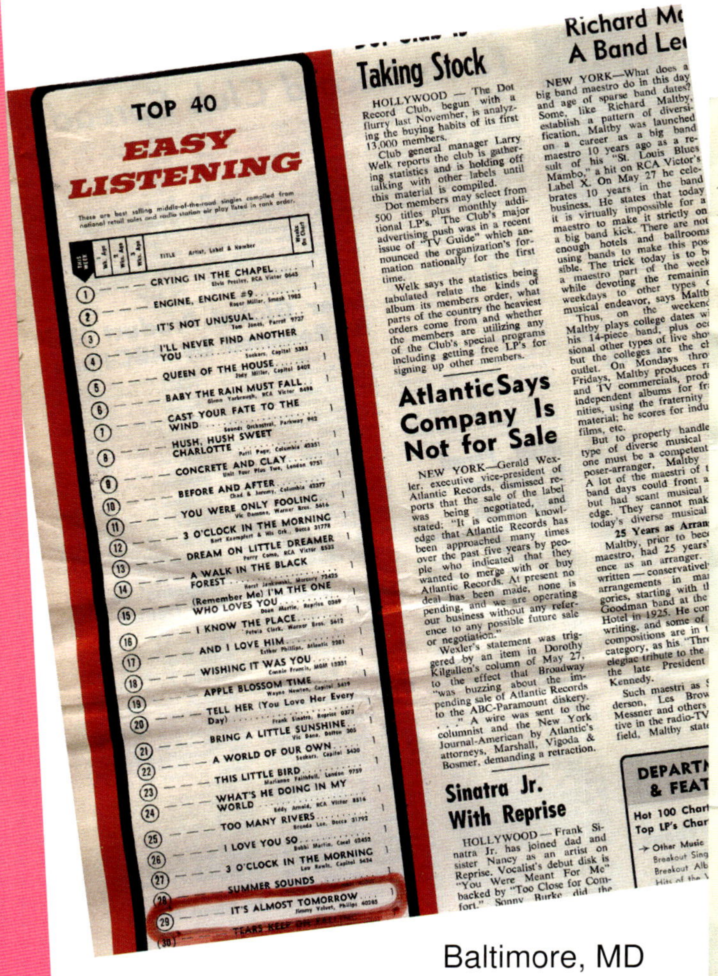

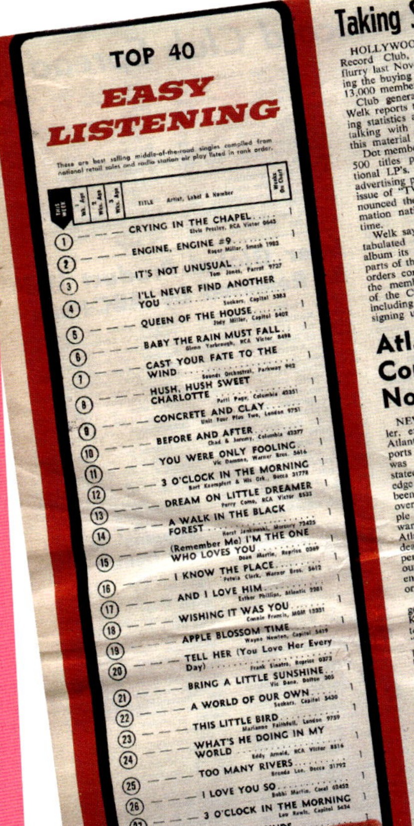

TOP 40 EASY LISTENING

These are best selling middle-of-the-road singles compiled from national retail sales and radio station air play listed in rank order.

THIS WEEK	1 Wk. Ago	2 Wks. Ago	3 Wks. Ago	TITLE Artist, Label & Number	Weeks On Chart
1	—	—	—	CRYING IN THE CHAPEL — Elvis Presley, RCA Victor 0643	1
2	—	—	—	ENGINE, ENGINE #9 — Roger Miller, Smash 1983	1
3	—	—	—	IT'S NOT UNUSUAL — Tom Jones, Parrot 9737	1
4	—	—	—	I'LL NEVER FIND ANOTHER YOU — Seekers, Capitol 5383	1
5	—	—	—	QUEEN OF THE HOUSE — Jody Miller, Capitol 5402	1
6	—	—	—	BABY THE RAIN MUST FALL — Glenn Yarbrough, RCA Victor 8498	1
7	—	—	—	CAST YOUR FATE TO THE WIND — Sounds Orchestral, Parkway 942	1
8	—	—	—	HUSH, HUSH SWEET CHARLOTTE — Patti Page, Columbia 43251	1
9	—	—	—	CONCRETE AND CLAY — Unit Four Plus Two, London 9751	1
10	—	—	—	BEFORE AND AFTER — Chad & Jeremy, Columbia 43277	1
11	—	—	—	YOU WERE ONLY FOOLING — Vic Damone, Warner Bros. 5616	1
12	—	—	—	3 O'CLOCK IN THE MORNING — Bert Kaempfert & His Ork., Decca 31778	1
13	—	—	—	DREAM ON LITTLE DREAMER — Perry Como, RCA Victor 8533	1
14	—	—	—	A WALK IN THE BLACK FOREST — Horst Jankowski, Mercury 72425	1
15	—	—	—	(Remember Me) I'M THE ONE WHO LOVES YOU — Dean Martin, Reprise 0369	1
16	—	—	—	I KNOW THE PLACE — Petula Clark, Warner Bros. 5612	1
17	—	—	—	AND I LOVE HIM — Esther Phillips, Atlantic 2281	1
18	—	—	—	WISHING IT WAS YOU — Connie Francis, MGM 13331	1
19	—	—	—	APPLE BLOSSOM TIME — Wayne Newton, Capitol 5419	1
20	—	—	—	TELL HER (You Love Her Every Day) — Frank Sinatra, Reprise 0373	1
21	—	—	—	BRING A LITTLE SUNSHINE — Vic Dana, Dolton 305	1
22	—	—	—	A WORLD OF OUR OWN — Seekers, Capitol 5430	1
23	—	—	—	THIS LITTLE BIRD — Marianne Faithfull, London 9759	1
24	—	—	—	WHAT'S HE DOING IN MY WORLD — Eddy Arnold, RCA Victor 8516	1
25	—	—	—	TOO MANY RIVERS — Brenda Lee, Decca 31792	1
26	—	—	—	I LOVE YOU SO — Bobbi Martin, Coral 62452	1
27	—	—	—	3 O'CLOCK IN THE MORNING — Lou Rawls, Capitol 5424	1
28	—	—	—	SUMMER SOUNDS	
29	—	—	—	IT'S ALMOST TOMORROW — Jimmy Velvet, Philips 40285	1
30	—	—	—	TEARS KEEP ON FALLING	

Taking Stock

HOLLYWOOD — The Dot Record Club, begun with a flurry last November, is analyzing the buying habits of its first 13,000 members.

Club general manager Larry Welk reports the club is gathering statistics and is holding off talking with other labels until this material is compiled.

Dot members may select from 500 titles plus monthly additional LP's. The Club's major advertising push was in a recent issue of "TV Guide" which announced the organization's formation nationally for the first time.

Welk says the statistics being tabulated relate the kinds of album its members order, what parts of the country the heaviest orders come from and whether the members are utilizing any of the Club's special programs including getting free LP's for signing up other members.

Atlantic Says Company Is Not for Sale

NEW YORK—Gerald Wexler, executive vice-president of Atlantic Records, dismissed reports that the sale of the label was being negotiated, and stated: "It is common knowledge that Atlantic Records has been approached many times over the past five years by people who indicated that they wanted to merge with or buy Atlantic Records. At present no deal has been made, none is pending, and we are operating our business without any reference to any possible future sale or negotiation."

Wexler's statement was triggered by an item in Dorothy Kilgallen's column of May 27, to the effect that Broadway "was buzzing about the impending sale of Atlantic Records to the ABC-Paramount diskery. . . ." A wire was sent to the columnist and the New York Journal-American by Atlantic's attorneys, Marshall, Vigoda & Bosmer, demanding a retraction.

Sinatra Jr. With Reprise

HOLLYWOOD — Frank Sinatra Jr. has joined dad and sister Nancy as an artist on Reprise. Vocalist's debut disk is "You Were Meant For Me" backed by "Too Close for Comfort." Sonny Burke did the

Richard Ma… A Band Le…

NEW YORK—What does a big band maestro do in this day and age of sparse band dates? Some, like Richard Maltby, establish a pattern of diversification. Maltby was launched on a career as a big band maestro 10 years ago as a result of his "St. Louis Blues Mambo," a hit on RCA Victor's Label X. On May 27 he celebrates 10 years in the band business. He states that today it is virtually impossible for a maestro to make it strictly on a big band kick. There are not enough hotels and ballrooms using bands to make this possible. The trick today is to be a maestro part of the week while devoting the remainin… weekdays to other types o… musical endeavor, says Maltb…

Thus, on the weekend Maltby plays college dates wi… his 14-piece band, plus occ… sional other types of live sho… but the colleges are the ch… outlet. On Mondays thro… Fridays, Maltby produces ra… and TV commercials, prod… independent albums for fra… nities, using the fraternity … material; he scores for indu… films, etc.

But to properly handle … type of diverse musical … one must be a competent … poser-arranger, Maltby … A lot of the maestri of t… band days could front a… but had scant musical … edge. They cannot mak… today's diverse musical …

25 Years as Arran…

Maltby, prior to beco… maestro, had 25 years' … ence as an arranger. … written — conservativel… arrangements in mar… gories, starting with th… Goodman band at the … Hotel in 1925. He con… writing, and some of … compositions are in t… category, as his "Thre… elegiac tribute to the … the late President … Kennedy.

Such maestri as S… derson, Les Brow… Messner and others … tive in the radio-TV … field, Maltby state…

DEPARTM… & FEAT…

Hot 100 Chart
Top LP's Char…
→ Other Music …
Breakout Sing…
Breakout Alb…
Hits of the W…

Baltimore, MD

RADIO BALTIMORE WCAO Radio Highlights

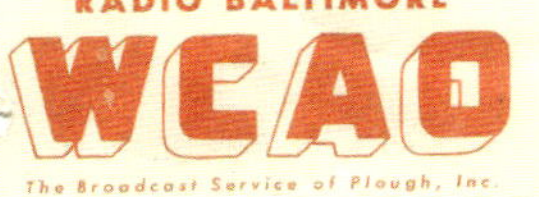

The Broadcast Service of Plough, Inc.

THIS WK			LAST WK	WKS LSTD	LABEL
3	WE BELONG TOGETHER	JIMMY VELVET	4	6	ABC
4	THERE I SAID IT AGAIN	BOBBY VINTON	30	3	EPIC
5	[illegible]	DYNAMICS	8	4	BIG
6	LEAVING IT UP TO YOU	DALE AND GRACE	1	10	MONT
7	TALK BACK TREMBLING LIPS	JOHNNY TILLOTSON	6	5	MGM
8	QUICKSAND	MARTHA-VANDELLAS	9	4	GORD
9	MARIA ELENA	LOS INDIOS TABAJARAS	3	6	RCA
10	SINCE I FELL FOR YOU	[illegible]	12	4	CAD
11	FORGET HIM	[illegible] RYDELL	15	4	CAMEO
12	LIVING A LIE	AL MARTINO	11	7	CAP
13	MIDNIGHT MARY	JOEY POWERS	7	5	AMY
14	SURFIN' BIRD	TRASHMEN	23	2	GARR
15	DON'T HAVE TO BE A BABY	CARAVELLES	14	4	SMASH
16	LOVELIGHT STARTS SHINING	SUPREMES	24	3	MOT
17	DRIP DROP	DION DIMUCI	16	5	COL
18	EVERYBODY	TOMMY ROE	13	7	ABC
19	HAVE YOU HEARD	DUPREES	19	6	COED
20	MARVELOUS TOY	CHAD MITCHELL TRIO	40	2	MERC
21	AS LONG AS I KNO HE'S MINE	MARVELETTES	21	6	TAMLA
22	PRETTY PAPERS	ROY ORBISON	33	2	MONU
23	442 GLENWOOD AVENUE	PIXIES THREE	36	2	MERC
24	YOU'RE GOOD FOR ME	SOLOMON BURKE	22	6	ATL
25	BABY DON'T YOU WEEP	MIMMS-ENCHANTERS	25	4	UA
26	KANSAS CITY	TRINI LOPEZ	27	3	REPR
27	RAGS TO RICHES	SUNNY-SUNLINERS	30	3	TD
28	IMPOSSIBLE HAPPENED	PEGGY MARCH	28	4	RCA
29	NEED TO BELONG	JERRY BUTLER	26	6	VJ
30	DO YOU HEAR WHAT I HEAR	BING CROSBY	—	1	CAP
31	GOTTA DANCE TO KEEP	MIRACLES	29	3	TAMLA
32	AS USUAL	BRENDA LEE	—	1	DECCA
33	WATCH YOUR STEP	BROOKS O'DELL	34	2	GOLD
34	COMING BACK TO YOU	MAXINE BROWN	32	3	WAND
35	BE TRUE TO YOUR SCHOOL	BEACH BOYS	—	1	CAP
36	POPSICLES AND ICICLES	MURMAIDS	—	1	CHATT
37	I HAVE A BOYFRIEND	CHIFFONS	37	2	LAURI
38	FOR YOUR SWEET LOVE	CASCADES	38	2	RCA
39	DOO WAH DITTY	EXCITERS	39	2	
40	BOY NEXT DOOR	SECRETS	—	1	

WCAO DISCOVERY - LETTER FROM SHERRY - Dale Ward - Dot

ALBUMS

THE SINGING NUN - Phillips
IN THE WIND - Peter, Paul and Mary - Warner Bros.
PAINTED TAINTED ROSE - Al Martino - Capitol
BYE BYE BIRDIE - Sound Track - RCA

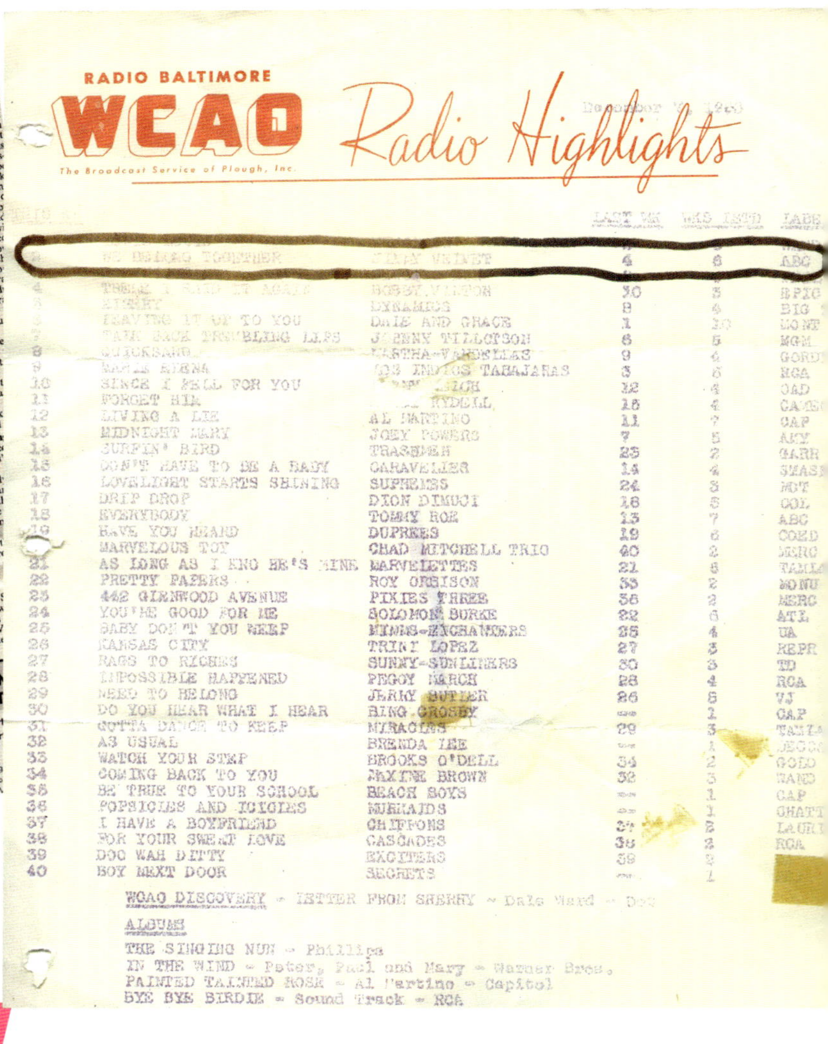

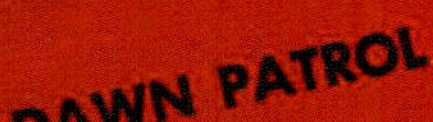

music reporter

as music reporter sees the

RECORD SCENE

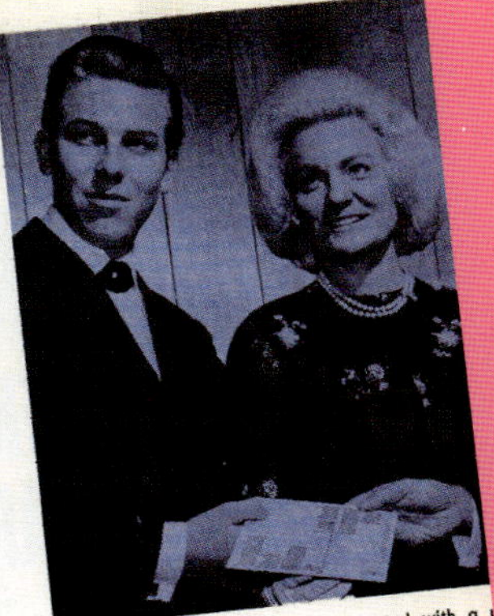

Hank Williams, Jr. (left) was hosted with a [illegible] signing of recording contract with MGM. A[illegible] mother-manager, Audrey Williams, and Arnol[illegible] Records, who came in from New York.

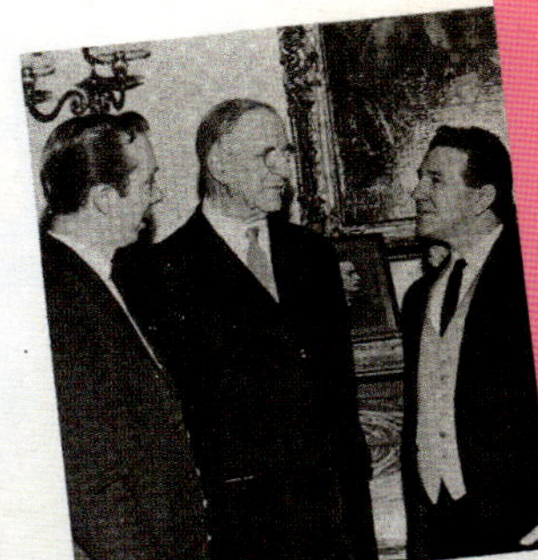

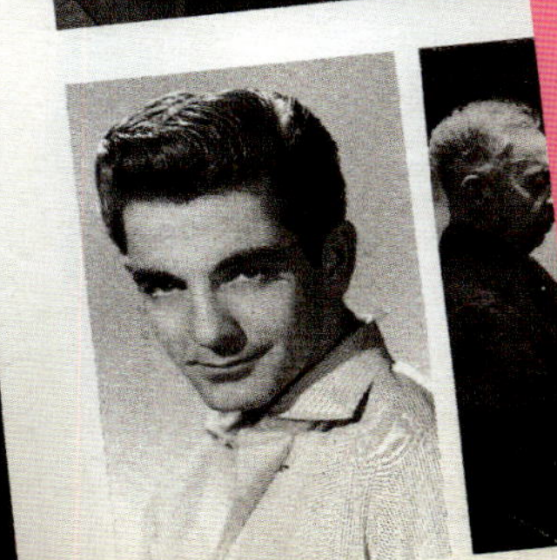

The Clancy Brothers and Tommy Makem, famed Irish folk-song group, are received by President De Valera, Ireland's head of state, at his residence. The visit was the high spot of the quartet's highly successful tour of Europe. Left to right are: Makem, President DeValera, Tom Liam and Pat Clancy.

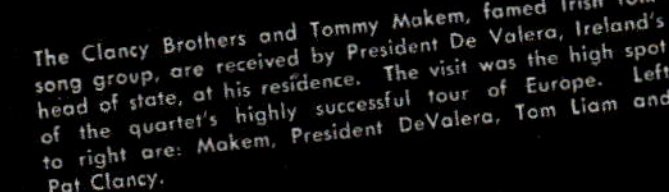

Jimmy Velvet, Music City recording artist, has a new single just released by ABC-Paramount, "To The Aisle" backed with "Lonely, Lonely, Heart", produced by the label's Nashville A&R rep., Felton Jarvis.

Artur Rubinstein, worlds famous pianist, has just re-inked a new long-termed pact with RCA-Victor. Rubinstein is 75 years old, but he's agile as ever, both in his fingers and concert plans. He'll give three recitals in New York Feb. 5-7, thereafter enters a recording program of 18 sessions, and later will do 100 concerts around the world.

Wilmington's Authentic Music Survey

NOVEMBER 23, 1963

WAMS JET SPEED NEWS 1380

TOP 30 tunes for the week Featured By "The Fabulous 5"

	TITLE	ARTIST	LAST WEEK
1.	I'm Leaving It Up To You	Dale & Grace	1
2.	Can I Get A Witness	Marvin Gaye	5
3.	You Lost The Sweetest Boy	Mary Wells	2
4.	It's All Right	The Impressions	3
5.	Hey Little Girl	Major Lance	6
6.	[illegible]	Solomon Burke	[illegible]
7.	We Belong Together	Jimmy Velvet	10
8.	[illegible]	The Four Pennies	[illegible]
9.	Deep Purple	N. Tempo/A.Stevens	4
10.	Walking the Dog	Rufus Thomas	19
11.	Dominique	The Singing Nun	16
12.	Cry To Me	Betty Harris	9
13.	Little Red Rooster	Sam Cooke	14
14.	Wild!	Dee Dee Sharp	7
15.	(Down At) Papa Joe's	The Dixiebelles	12
16.	The Cheerleader	Paul Petersen	21
17.	Baby Don't Y[illegible] Weep	Garnet Mimms	29
18.	Bossa Nova [illegible]	Elvis Presley	13
19.	As Long As I [illegible]now He's Mine	The Marvelettes	22
20.	Have You Hea[illegible]d	The Duprees	23
21.	Quicksand	Martha & The Vandellas	--
22.	Midnight Mary	Joey Powers	24
23.	Louie, Louie	The Kingsmen	--
24.	31 Flavors	The Shirelles	26
25.	I Adore Him	The Angels	25
26.	She's A Fool	Lesley Gore	28
27.	I Wonder What She's Doing	Barry & Tamerlanes	--
28.	Baby I Do Love You	The Galens	30
29.	Popsicles and Icicles	The Murmaids	--
30.	In My Room/Be True To School	The Beach Boys	--

WILLIE GAYLORD 5-9 A.M.

ROGER HOLMES 9 A.M.-1 P.M.

DEAN [illegible]R 1-4 P.M.

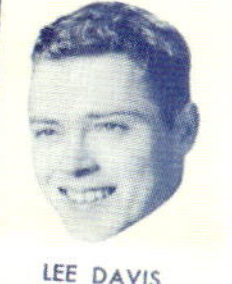

LEE DAVIS 4-8 P.M.

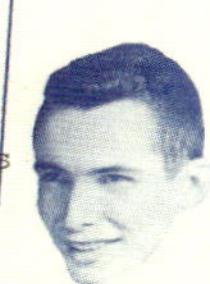

DAVE ELD[illegible]GE

WAMS PIKS OF THE WEEK

Natasha-Eric & Serenaders
Down South-The Lanas
Bluesette-Toots Thielemans
Queridita Mia-Keith Colley
Ronnie-Donna Lynn

WAMS SHOWCASE ALBUMS

Let Me Sing-Brenda Lee
The Routers Play 1963's Great Instrumental Hits
You're Mine You-George Chakiris

WAMS WAX TO WATCH

Memory Pain-Percy Mayfield
Letter From Sherry-Dale Ward
Son Of Rebel Rouser-Duane Eddy
Who Do You Love-Sapphires
If Love Is-The Echoes
Dumb Head-Ginny Arnell
Adios-D.Jenkins/Delighters

Wonderful

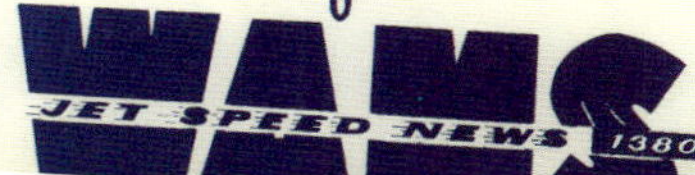

SURVEY PROVEN NO. 1

NEWS LIVE

THE NITE WATCH

Willmington, DE

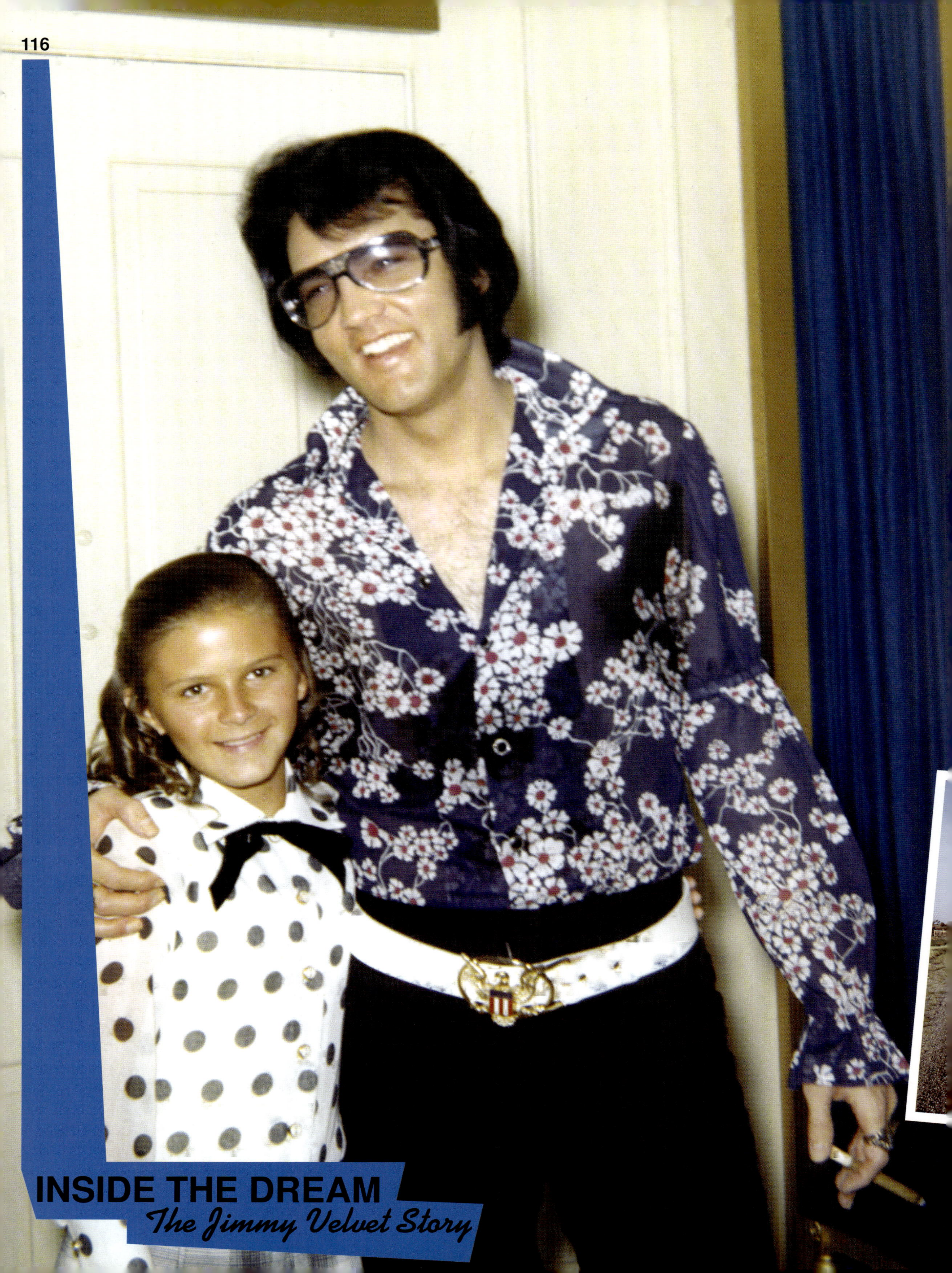

the 1970s

In the 1970's I lived in Franklin, TN, where I opened "Music City Amusements" and a dinner club on Music Row named the Glass Menagerie that seated 1200 people. I booked all types of entertainment from The Mills Brothers, The Glen Miller Orchestra, Frank Sinatra, Jr. to Canned Heat, Ronnie Dove, Sammi Smith, Beverly Bremers, The Diamonds, and Isaac Hayes. In 1973, Isaac had just won the Academy Award for "Shaft" and I had two sold-out shows. The club burned to the ground one week before his show was scheduled.

I had a small part in a Mickey Spillane mystery, The Delta Factor. I became friends with Christopher George and his wife, Lynda Day-George. They had been my guests a couple of times a few years later at The Glass Menagerie. Chris was once a chef and had his own restaurant. He also starred in the TV series, Rat Patrol. Other stars in The Delta Factor that I worked with were Yvette Mimimeux and Diane McBane.

On July 13, 1973, I was sworn in at the Shelby Country Sheriffs Department in Memphis, with Elvis Presley and his father Vernon. Vernon and I were made Captains and Elvis was Chief Deputy. Elvis had just bought a white Stutz that still had the drive-out tags on it.

I became the manager and producer of George Wallace, Jr., and produced his hit Missing You, written by my brother-in-law Larry Butler. My house was always open to various friends with whom I worked along the way. A regular guest was Vic Dana ("Red Roses for a Blue Lady"), and Robert Altman leased my home for Paul Newman and his wife, Joanne Woodward, while filming a movie in Tennessee.

One of the biggest turning points in my life was on June 1, 1978, when I opened the first Elvis Presley Museum with Vernon Presley's blessing. The museum was located directly across the street from Graceland.

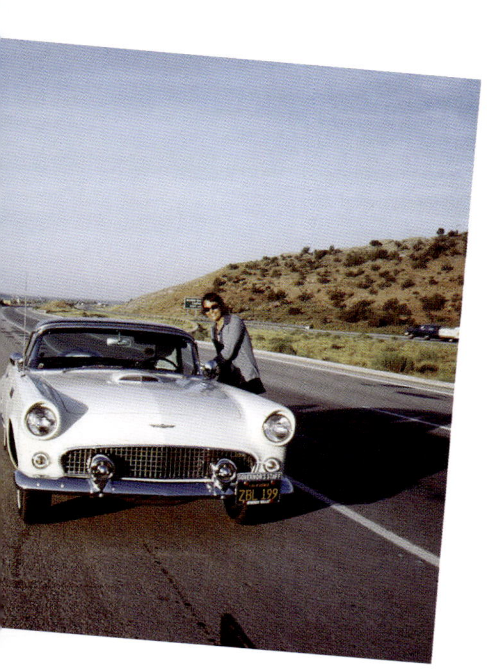

Henry Fonda's T-Bird

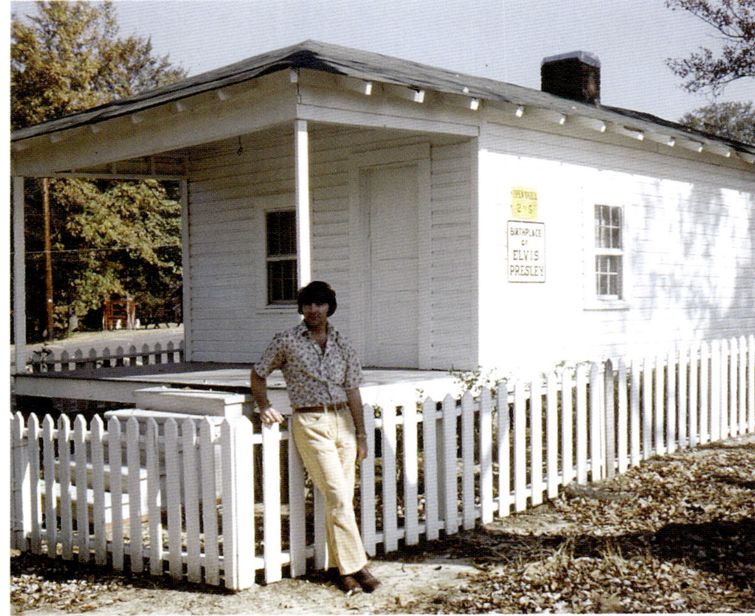

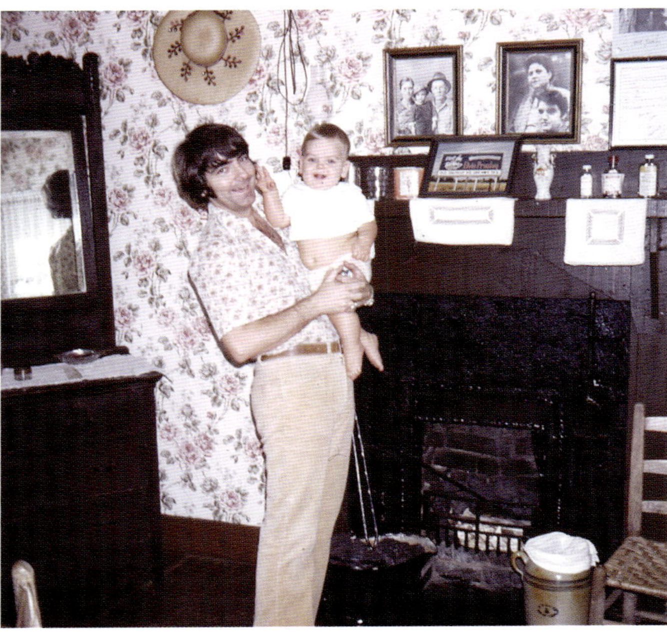

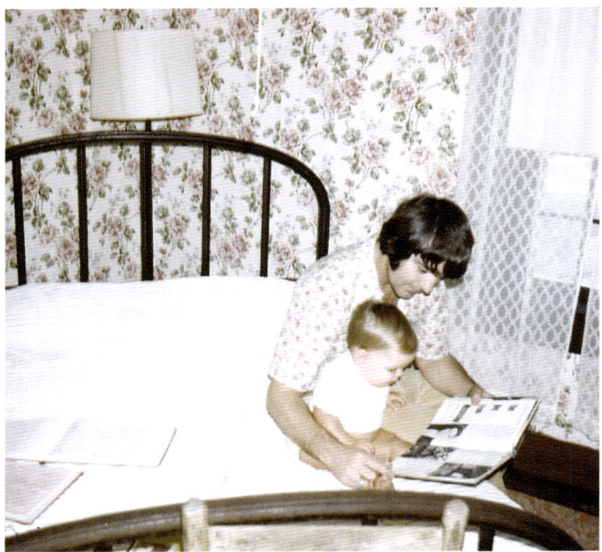

My son Scott and I in the Tupelo home where Elvis was born.

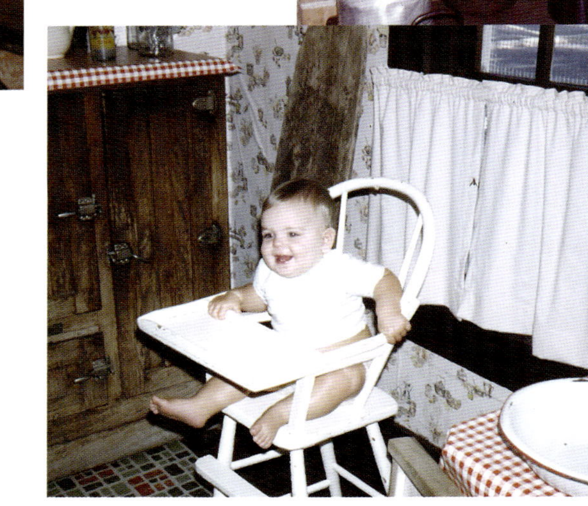

Elvis playing the Knabe Player Piano at the Hillcrest House in Truesdale Estates. The piano was Antique Green.

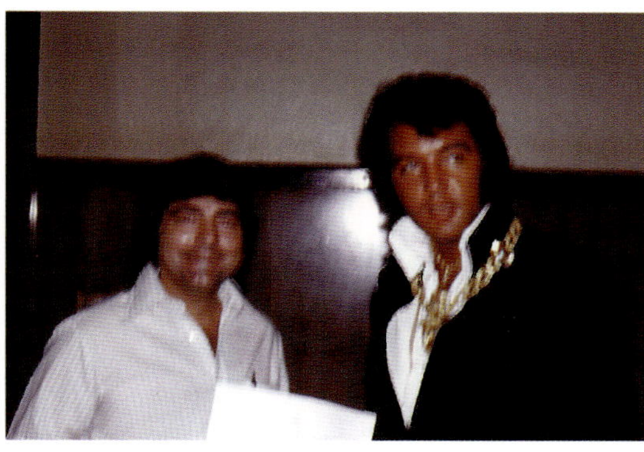

Elvis Presley

On July 13, 1973, Elvis, Vernon and I were sworn in as Deputies By Sheriff Roy "Skip" Nixon. Elvis looked the best ever. I on the other hand wasn't prepared. Vernon took this shot but as usual, he used his whole hand to press the button instead of his finger and blurred the photograph. Elvis was chief Deputy. Venon and I were Captains.

OFFICE OF

SHERIFF OF SHELBY COUNTY

COUNTY OF SHELBY,
State of Tennessee

By virtue of authority of law in me vested, I do hereby *appoint and constitute* James R. Velvet, *a Deputy Sheriff* under me, in and for the said County of Shelby, to do and perform such duties as are prescribed by law.

This *commission* to continue at my will.

Given under my hand, at office, in the Court House, in the City of Memphis, this the 13th day of July 1973

Roy C. Nixon
Sheriff of Shelby County.

STATE OF TENNESSEE,
County of Shelby

I do solemnly swear that I will support the Constitution of the United States, and the Constitution and Laws of the State of Tennessee; and that I will discharge the duties of the office of DEPUTY SHERIFF OF SHELBY COUNTY, TENNESSEE, to which I have been appointed, and which I am about to assume; and that I have not given, accepted, or knowingly carried a challenge, in writing or otherwise, to any person being a citizen of the State, or aided or abetted therein, since the adoption of the Constitution in 1835 and that I will not be guilty of either of these acts during my continuance in office: So help me God.

James R. Jimmy Velvet

Sworn to and subscribed before me, this 13th *day* of July 1973

Robert M. Gray Clerk.

D. C.

OFFICE OF

SHERIFF OF SHELBY COUNTY

COUNTY OF SHELBY,
State of Tennessee

By virtue of authority of law in me vested, I do hereby *appoint and constitute* Elvis Presley, *a Deputy Sheriff* under me, in and for the said County of Shelby, to do and perform such duties as are prescribed by law.

This *commission* to continue at my will.

Given under my hand, at office, in the Court House, in the City of Memphis, this the 13th day of July 1973

Roy C. Nixon
Sheriff of Shelby County.

STATE OF TENNESSEE,
County of Shelby

I do solemnly swear that I will support the Constitution of the United States, and the Constitution and Laws of the State of Tennessee; and that I will discharge the duties of the office of DEPUTY SHERIFF OF SHELBY COUNTY, TENNESSEE, to which I have been appointed, and which I am about to assume; and that I have not given, accepted, or knowingly carried a challenge, in writing or otherwise, to any person being a citizen of the State, or aided or abetted therein, since the adoption of the Constitution in 1835 and that I will not be guilty of either of these acts during my continuance in office: So help me God.

Elvis Presley

Sworn to and subscribed before me, this 13th *day* of July 1973

Robert M. Gray Clerk.

E. Hawkins D. C.

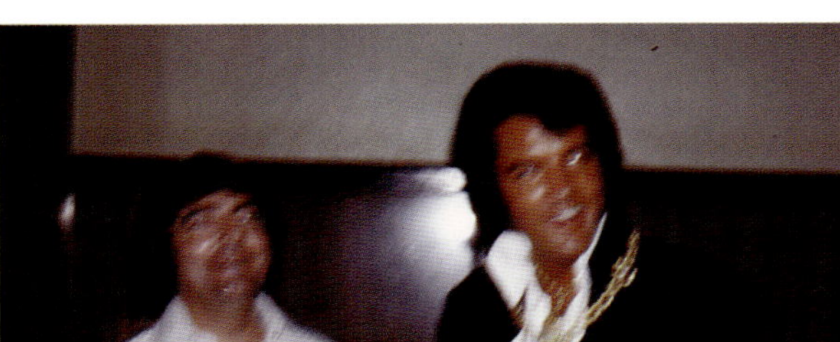

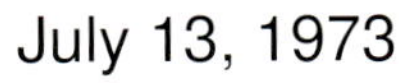

July 13, 1973

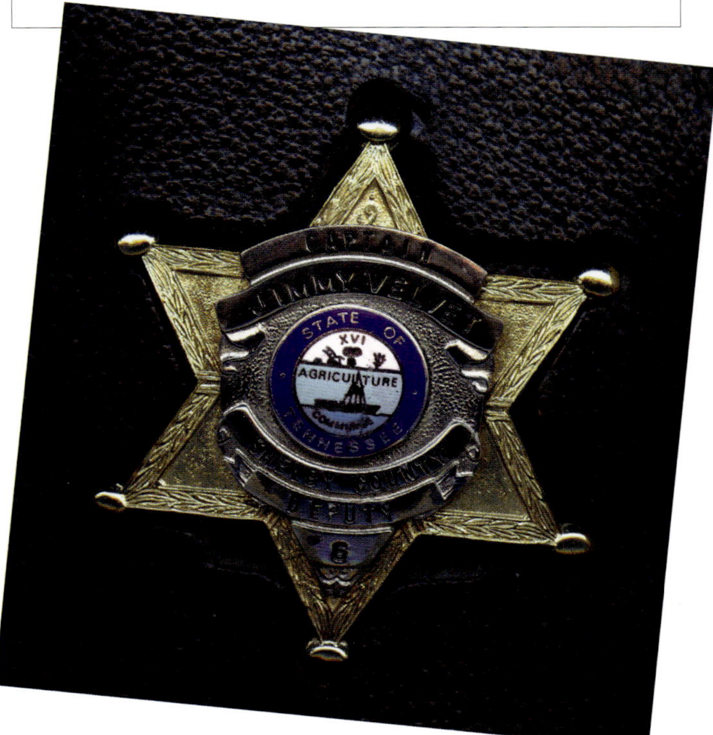

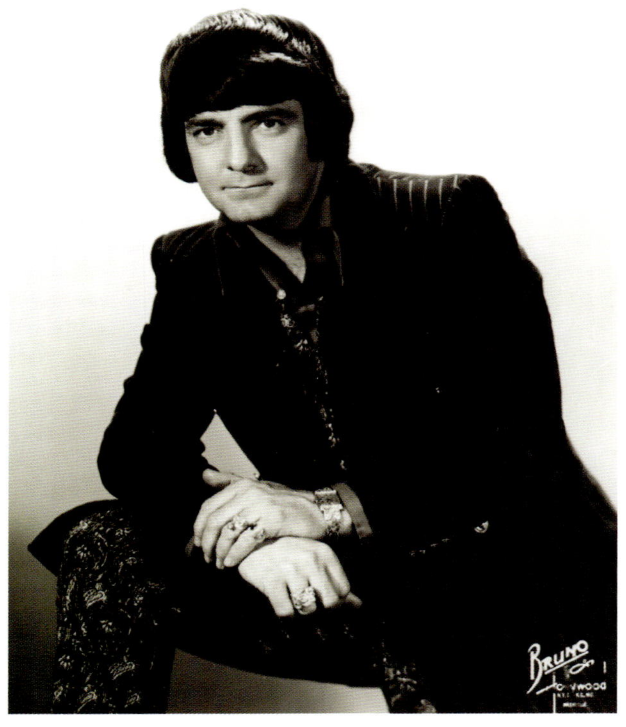

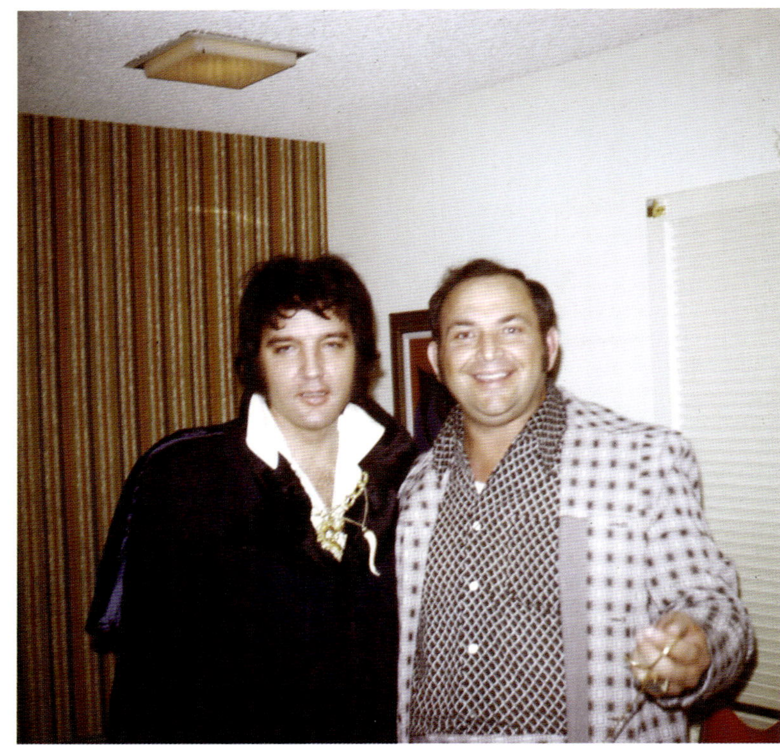

Elvis with Terry Upton wearing a black opal ring which Elvis had given to him that day. I later bought the ring from Terry.

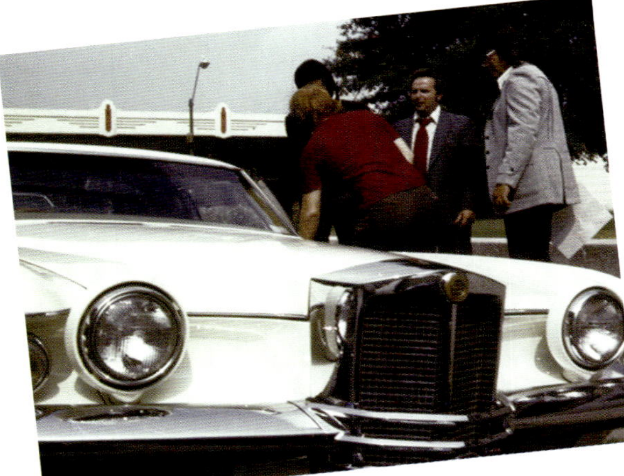

Red West, Roy Nixon, Sheriff, Elvis, and Sonny West 1973

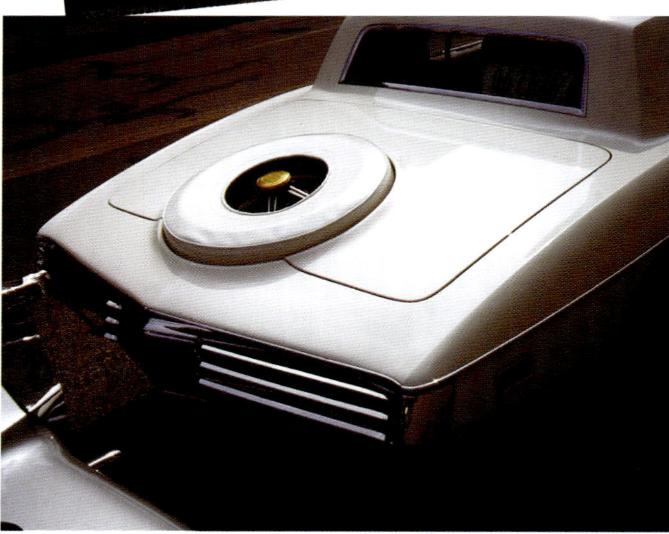

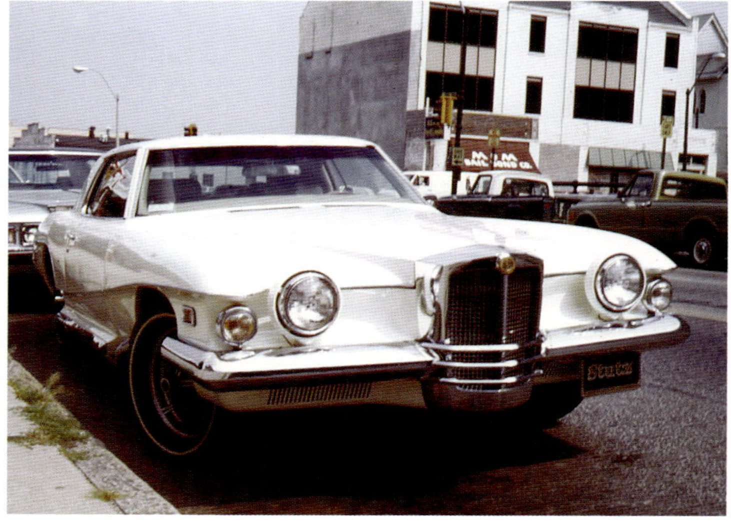

Elvis just got this new white stutz. It still had the drive out plates.

Secretariat

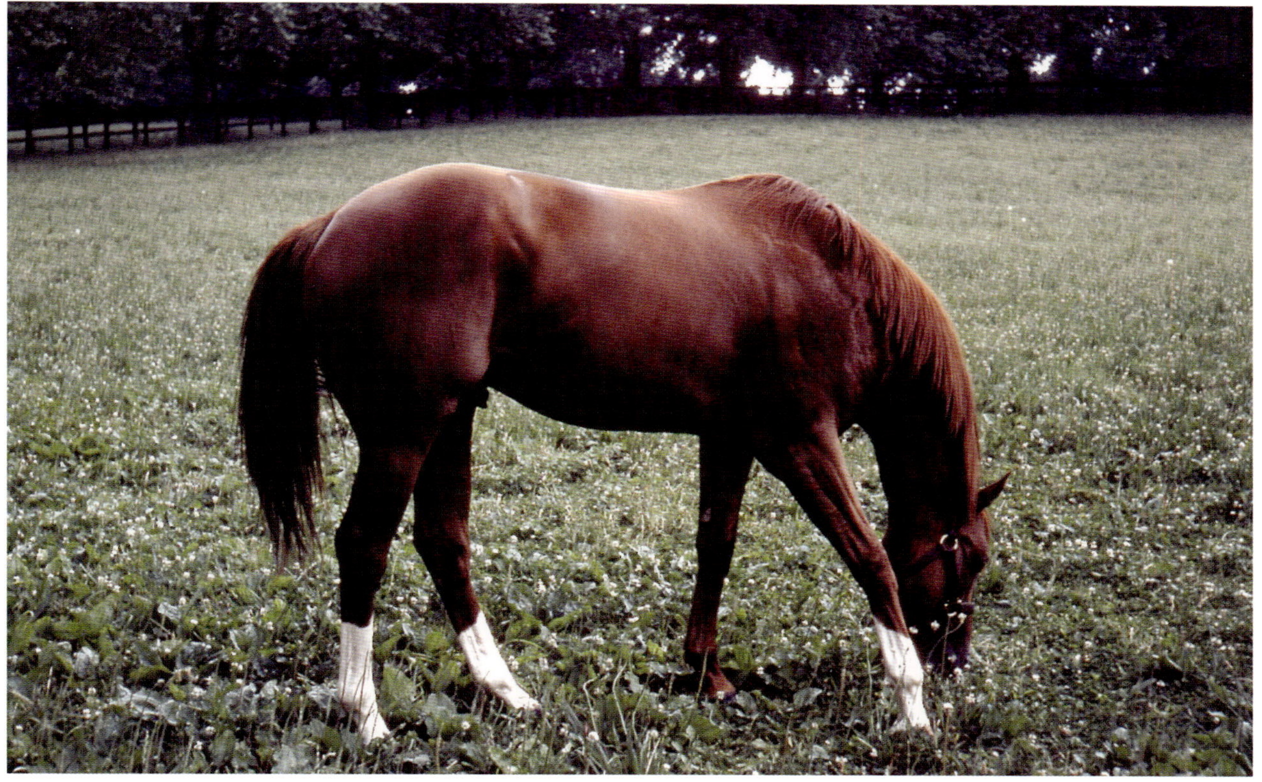

1973 Triple Crown winner and a delight to watch.

My mother, Jackie and I

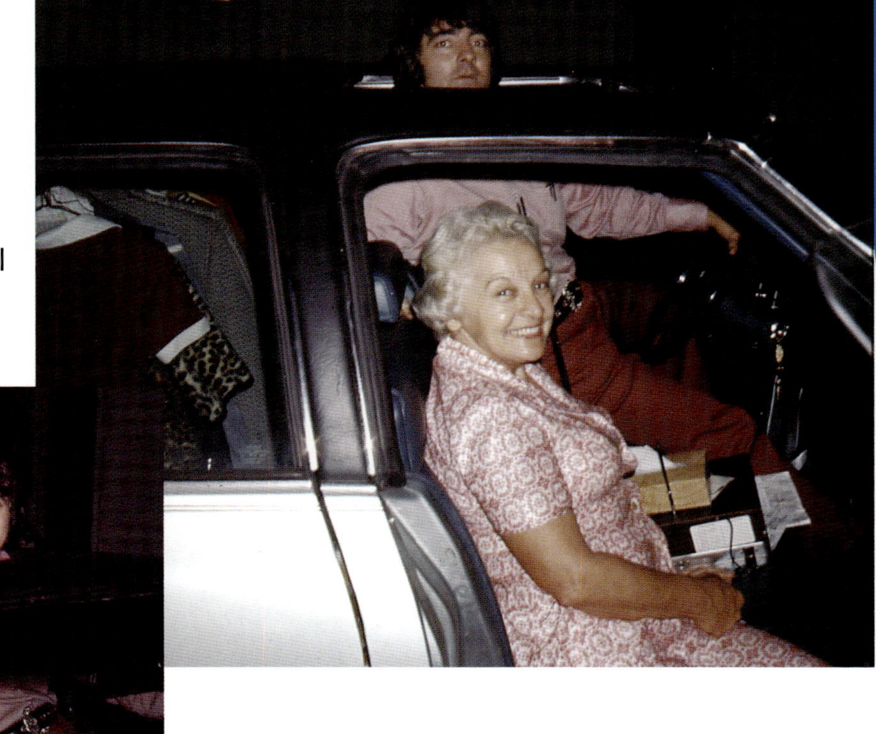

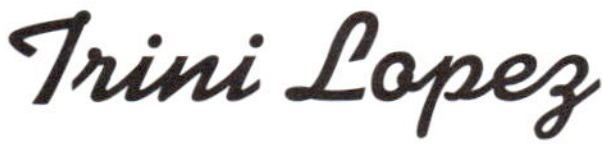

Trini Lopez

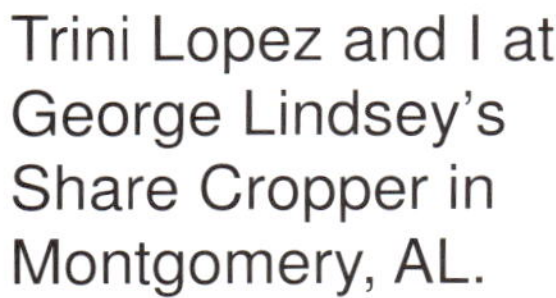

Trini Lopez and I at George Lindsey's Share Cropper in Montgomery, AL.

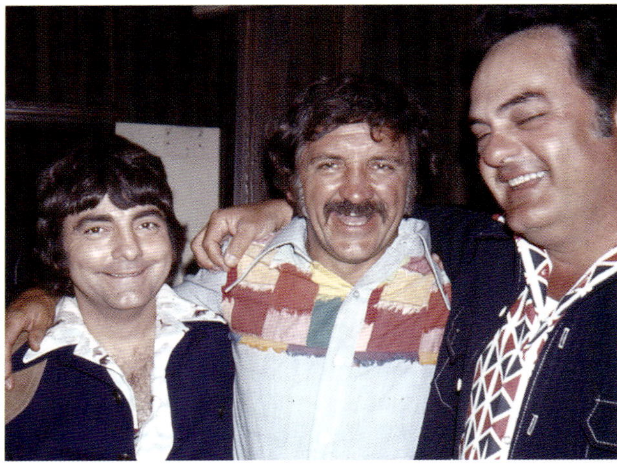

George "Goober" Lindsey

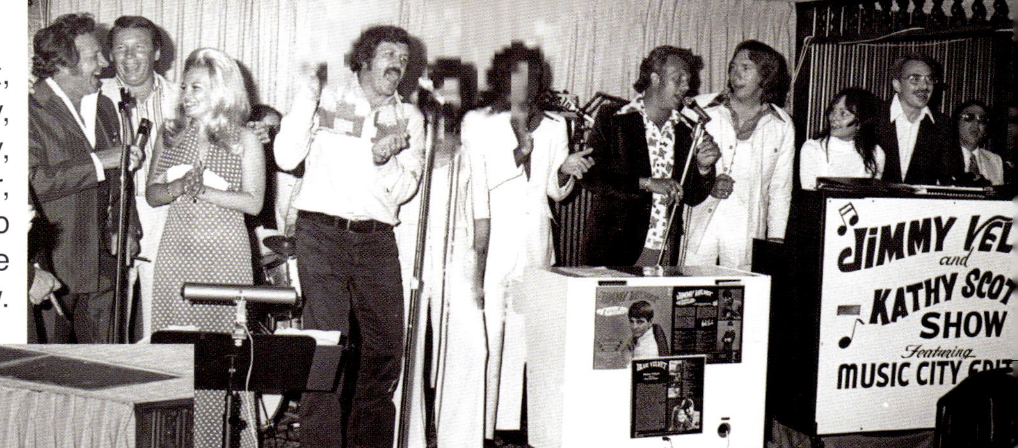

Ferlin Husky, Buck Trent, Melba Montgomery, George "Goober" Lindsey, Evel Knievel, Buddy Baker, Kathy Scott, and Jack Dodson who played Howard Sprague on the Andy Griffith Show.

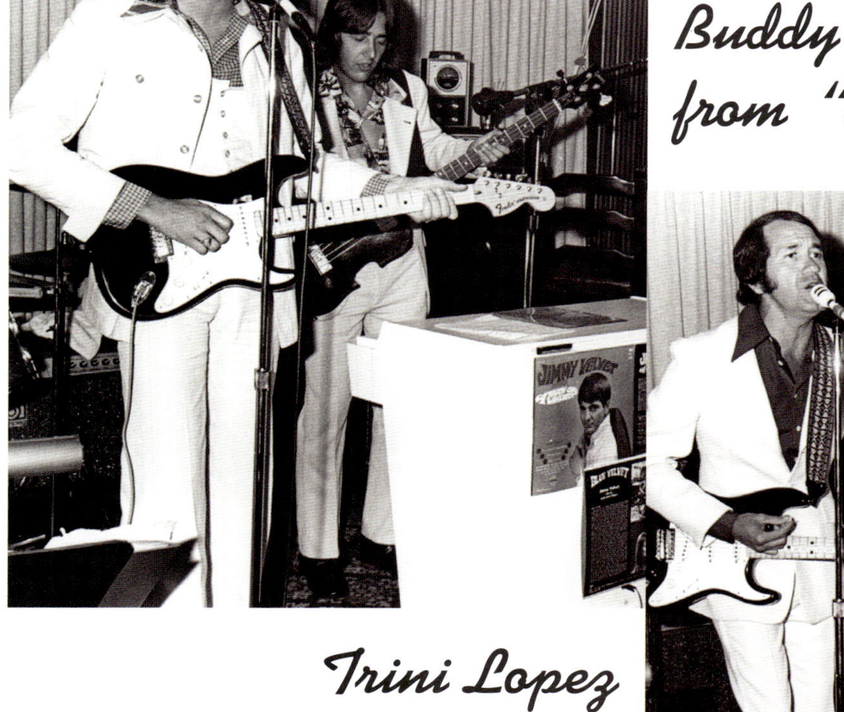

Buddy Baker from "Hee Haw"

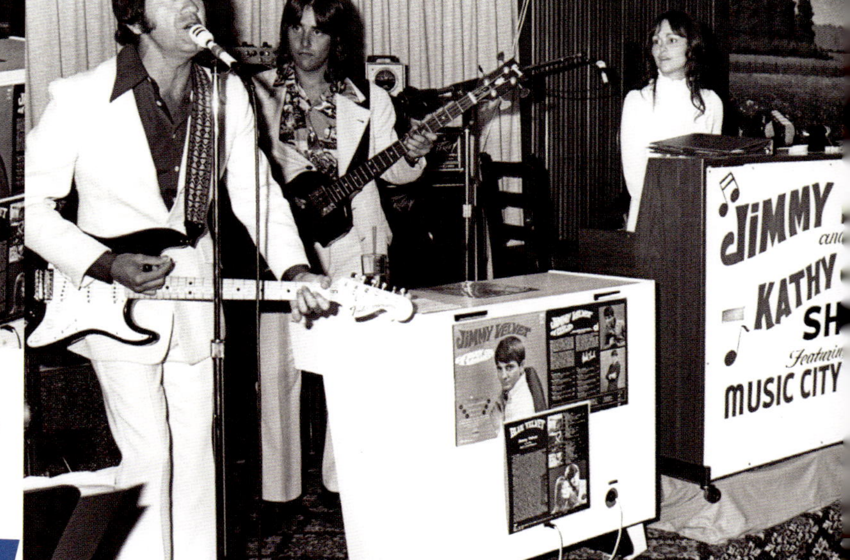

Trini Lopez

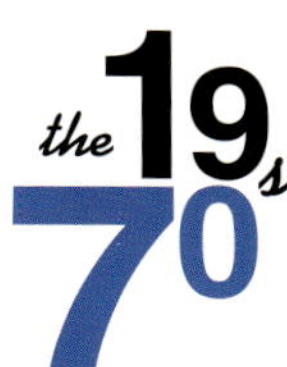

Evel Knievel

This is in Montgomery, AL. We were playing a celebrity golf tournament and I was appearing at George Lindsey's Share Cropper. All of the stars came and jammed with us that night. Evel amazed us all with his poetry and his art.

Evel with two of our kids Scott and Candida

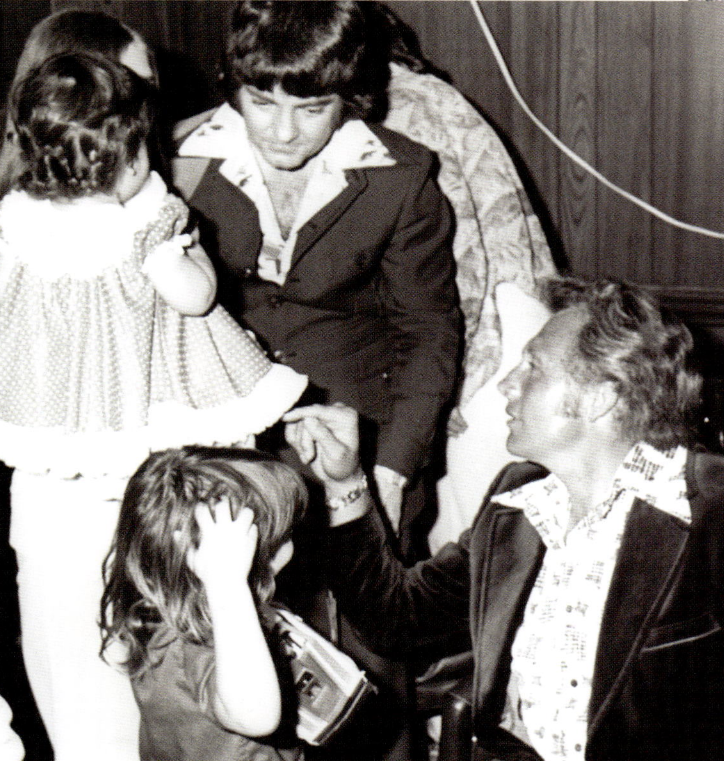

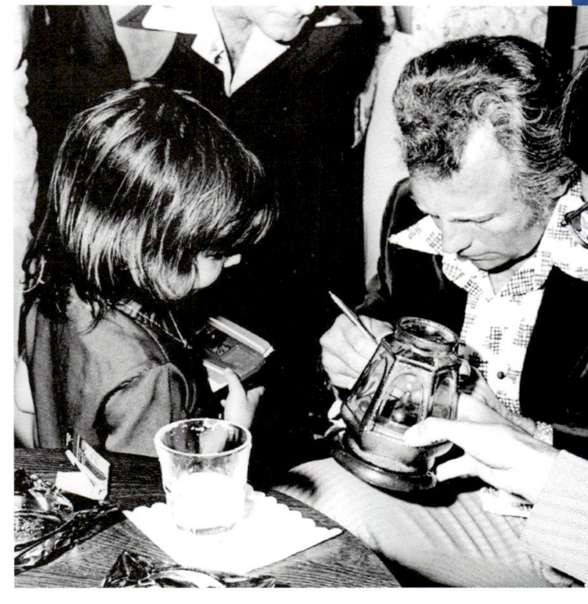

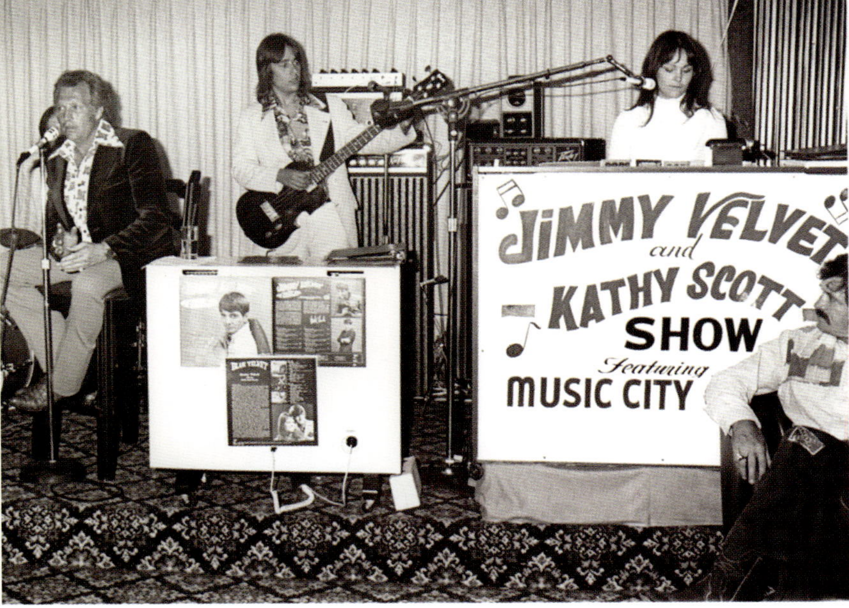

Evel Knievel, Bass Player, Kathy Scott, George Lindsey

Christopher George

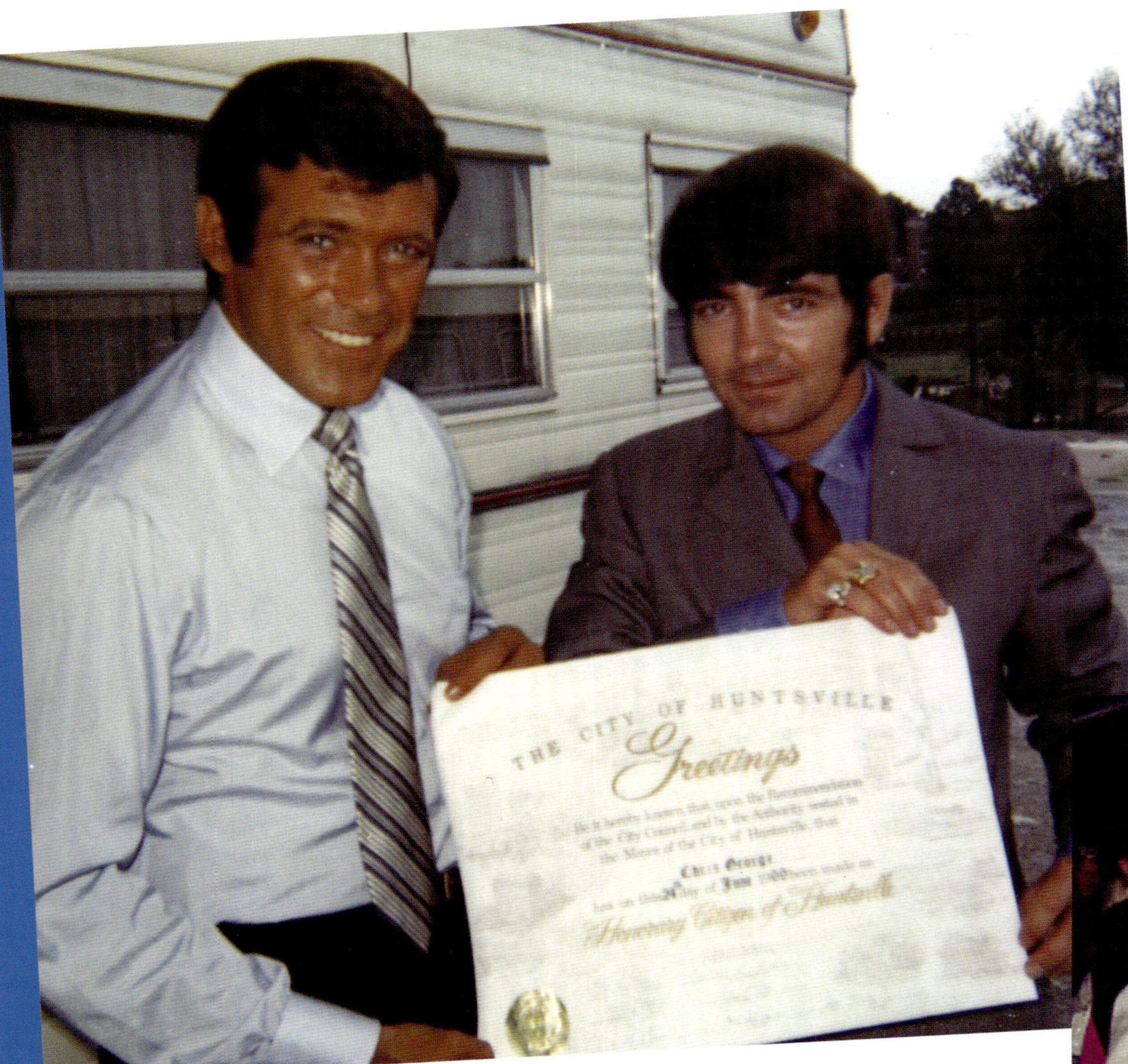

Christopher George and I on the movie set for Mickey Spillane's Delta Factor. My part was small. Chris was my favorite actor and star of Rat Patrol.

These shots are at my restaurant The Glass Menagerie on music row. Chris is with his wife Lynda Day George, co-star of Mission Impossible.

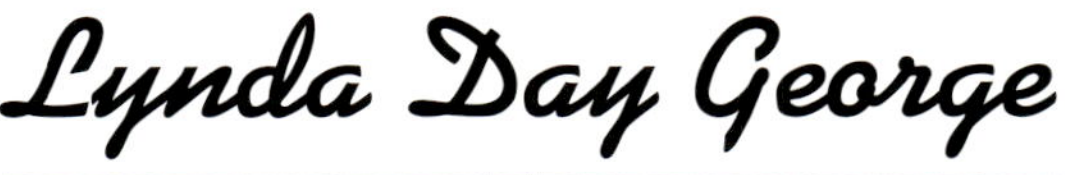

Lynda Day George

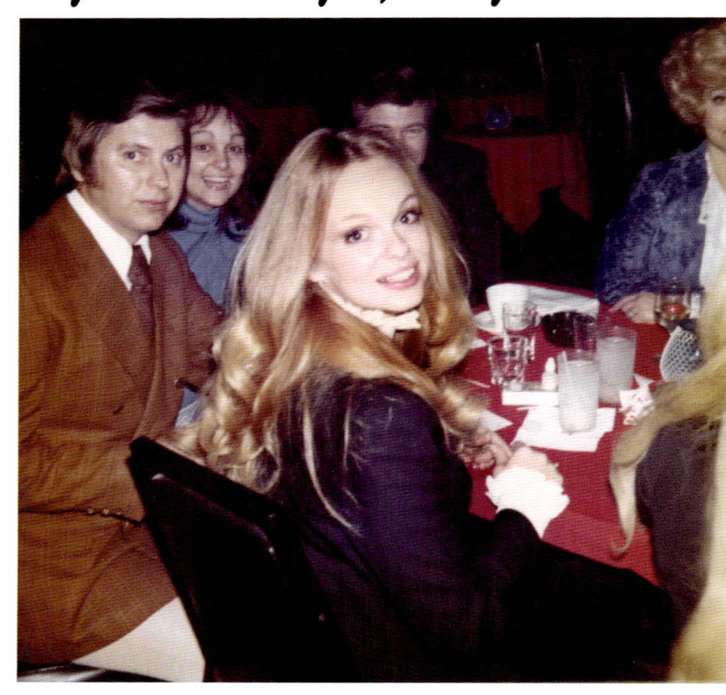

Mickey Spillane

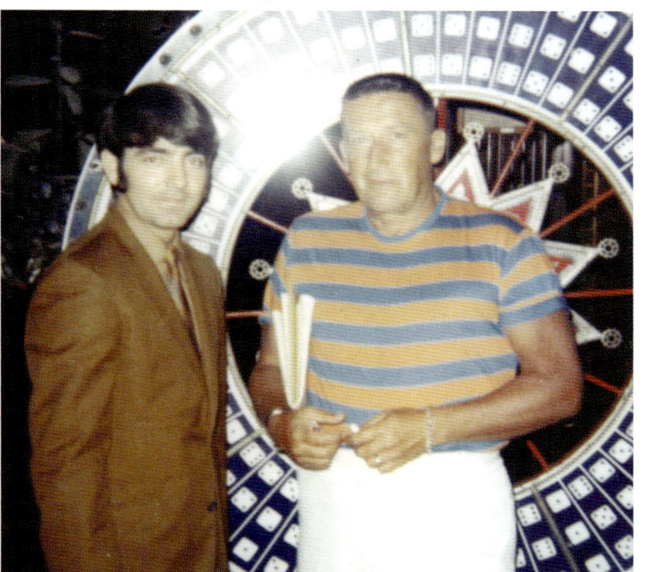

Mickey Spillane and I on set of Delta Factor, one of the many Mickey Spillane Mysteries.

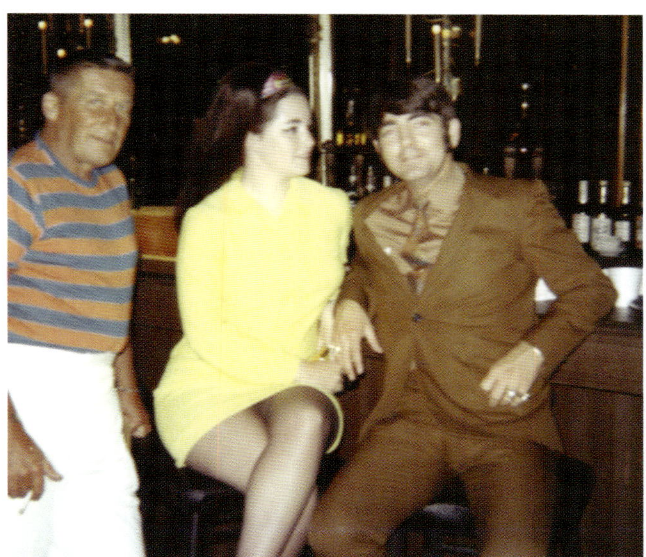

Delta Factor

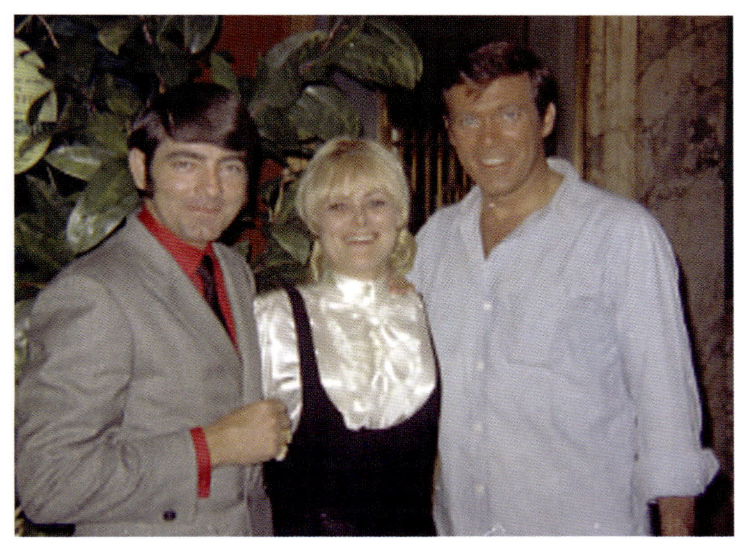

Diane McBain

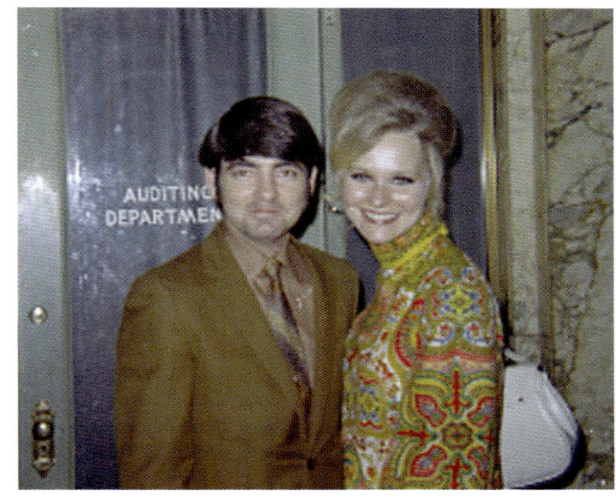

Yvette Mimieux

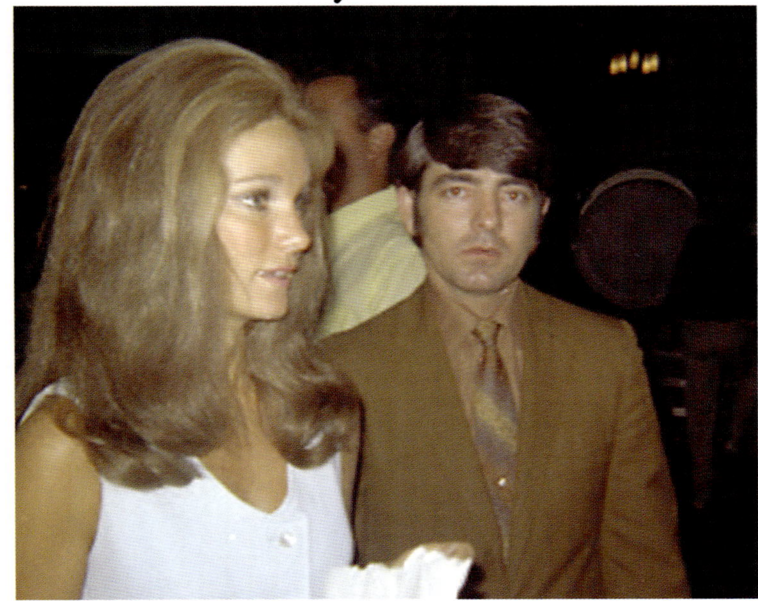

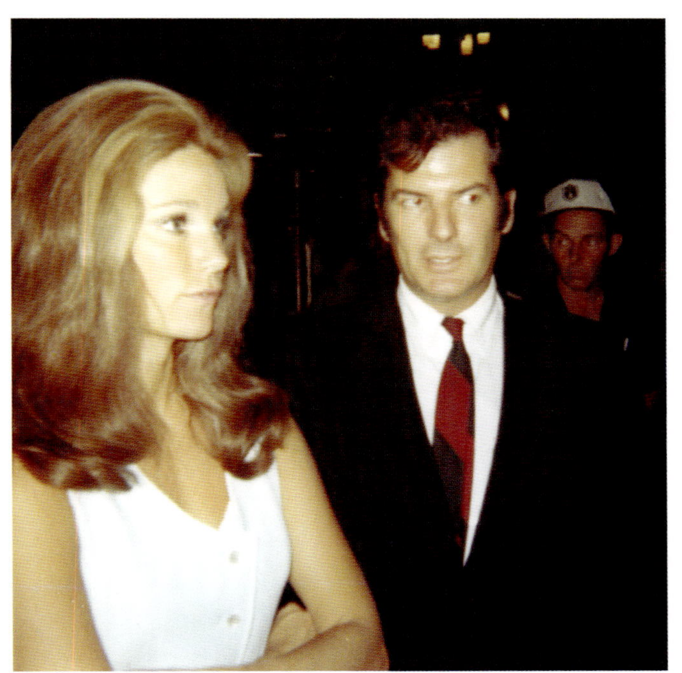

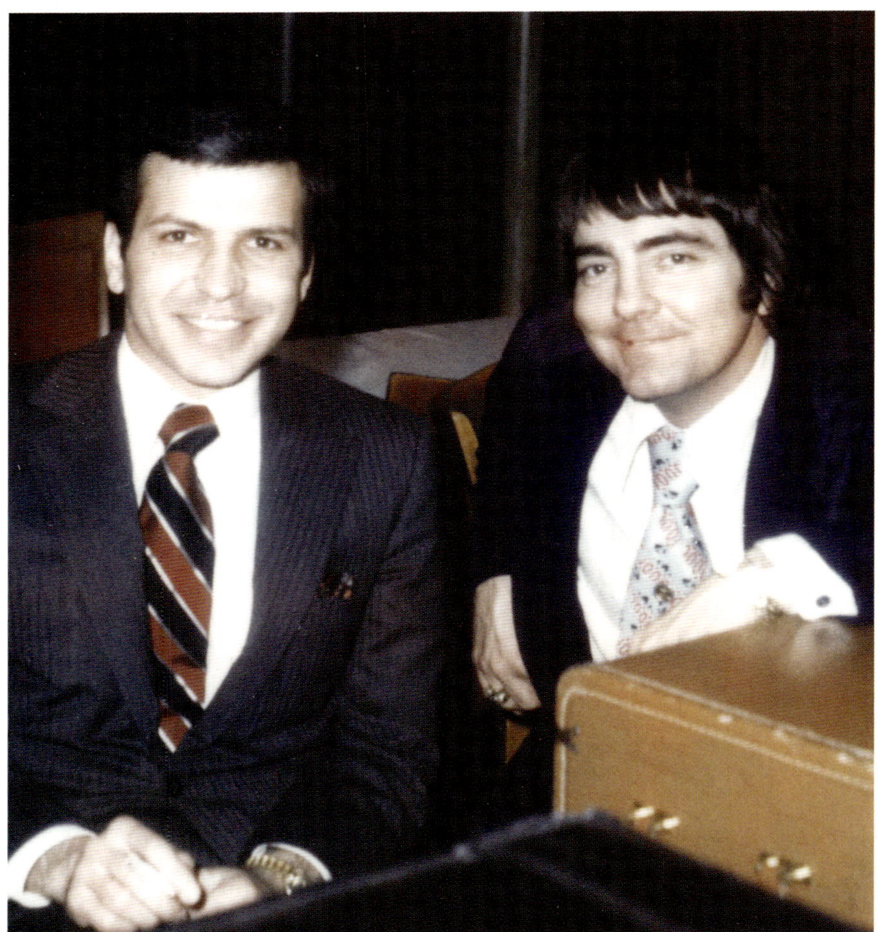

Frank Sinatra Jr.

Frank Sinatra Jr. and I at my restaurant on Music Row, The Glass Menagarie. I had a 1200 seat show room named Mr. Bojangles. It burned to the ground in 1973.

Frank had a sold-out show.

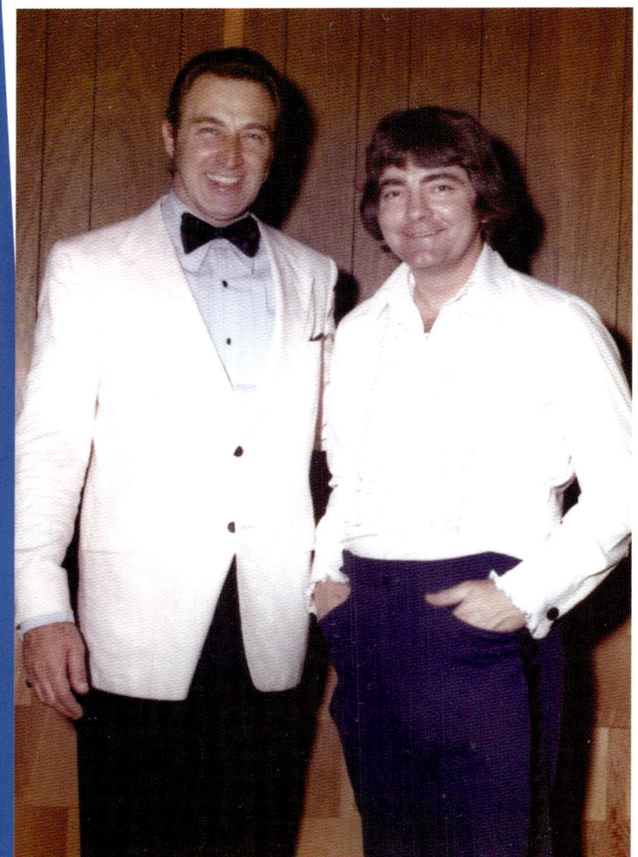

The Glenn Miller Orchestra

directed by Buddy DeFranco and Beverly Bremers.

Beverly stared on broadway in Hair and had the # 1 record Don't Say You Don't Remember. What a delight. What an Entertainer.

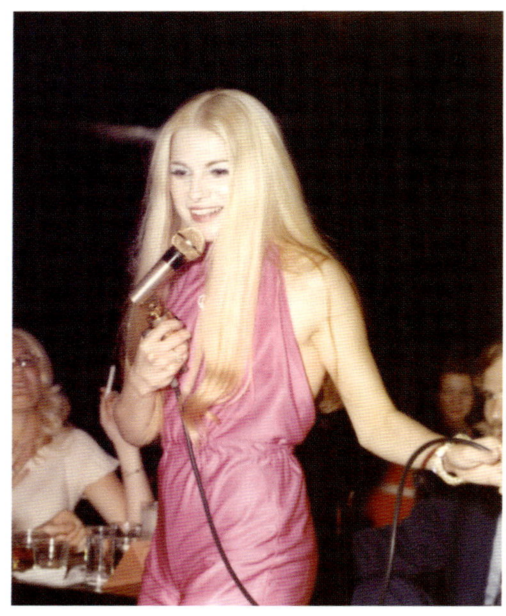

Beverly Bremers

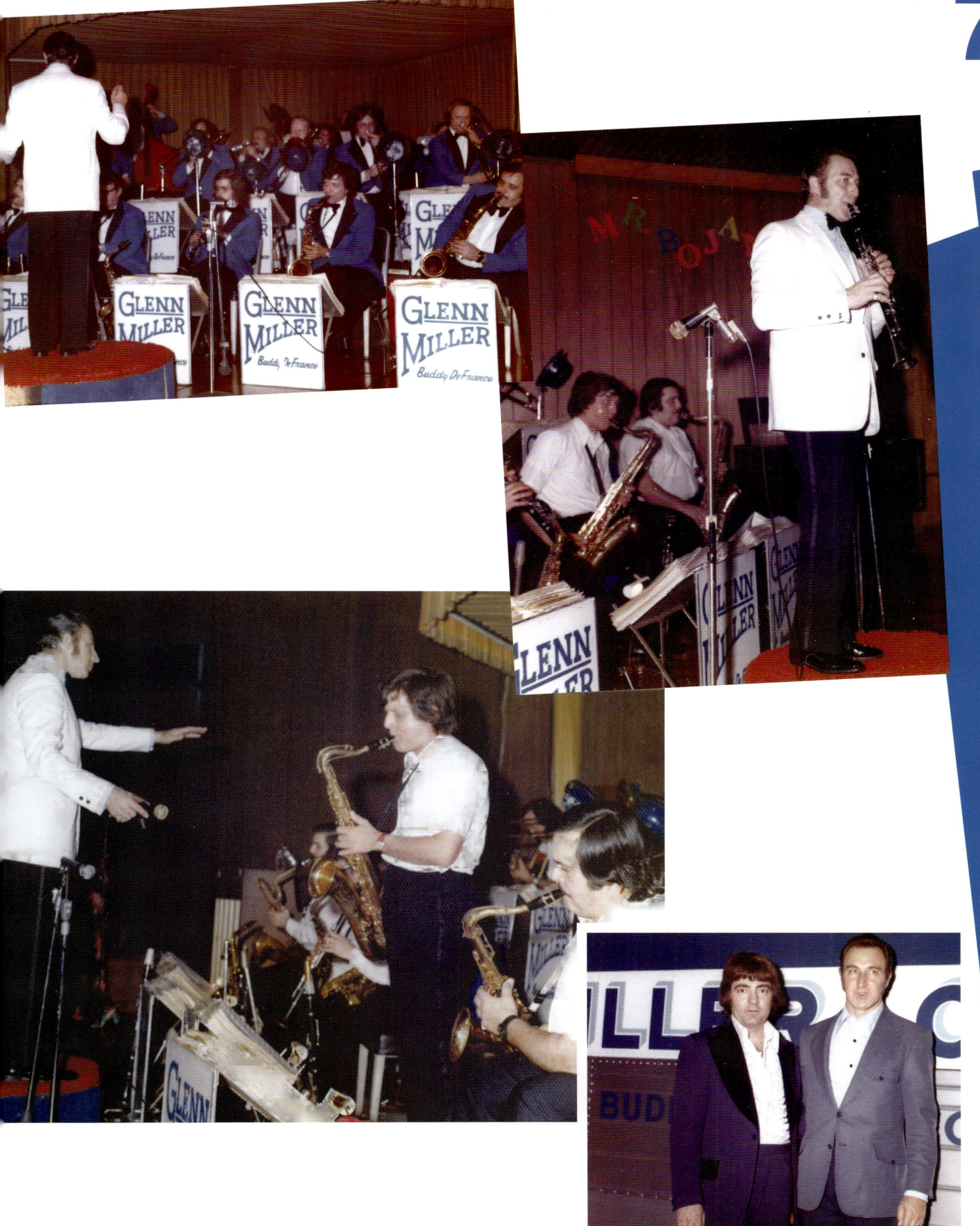

Buddy DeFranco and I by the
Glenn Miller tour bus.

Sammi Smith

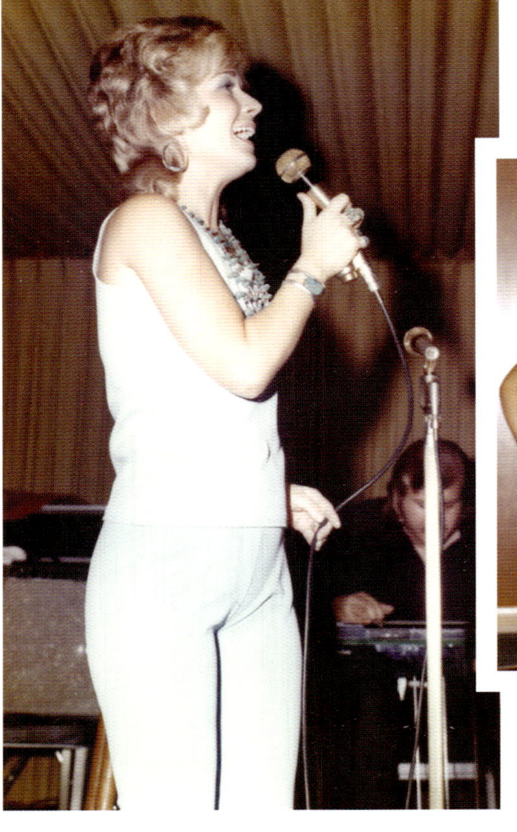

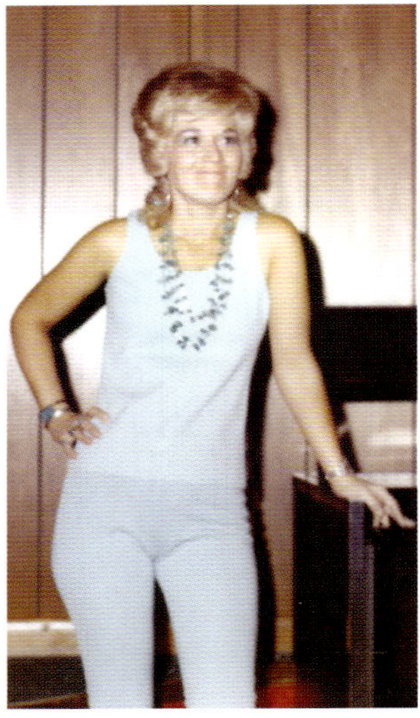

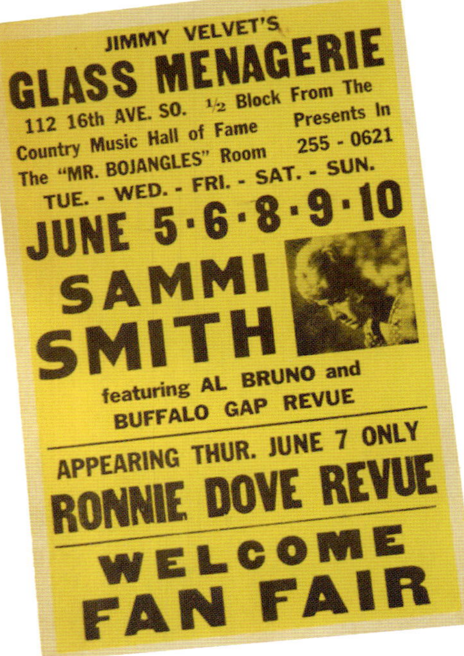

Sammi Smith in the Mr. Bojangles Room at the Glass Menagerie singing her #1 hit, Help Me Make It Through the Night by Kris Kristofferson.

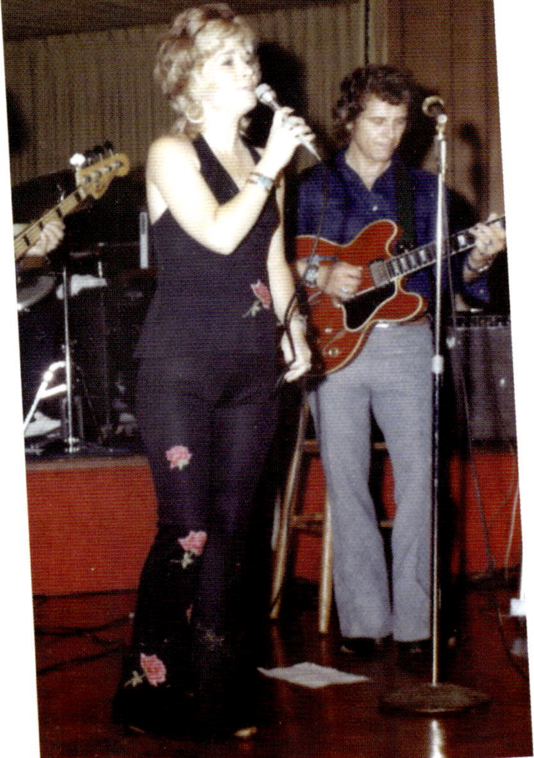

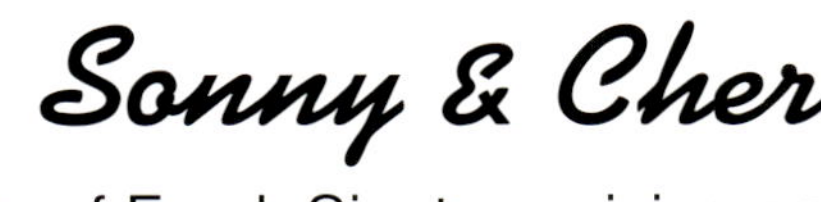

Sonny & Cher

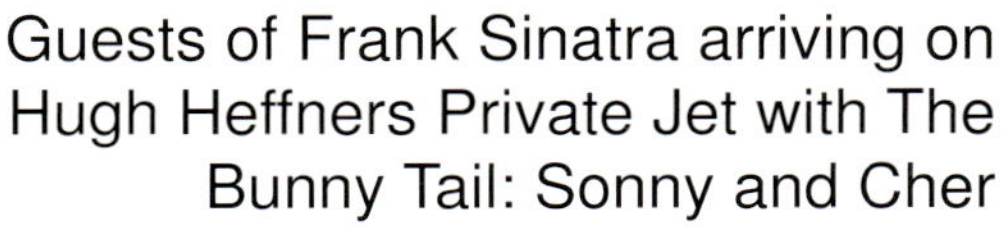

Guests of Frank Sinatra arriving on Hugh Heffners Private Jet with The Bunny Tail: Sonny and Cher

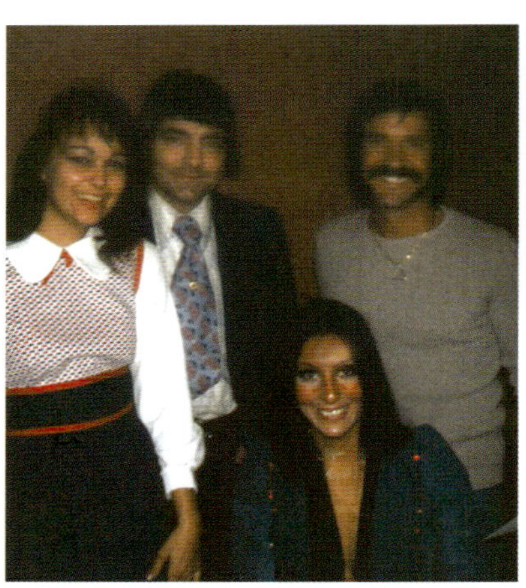

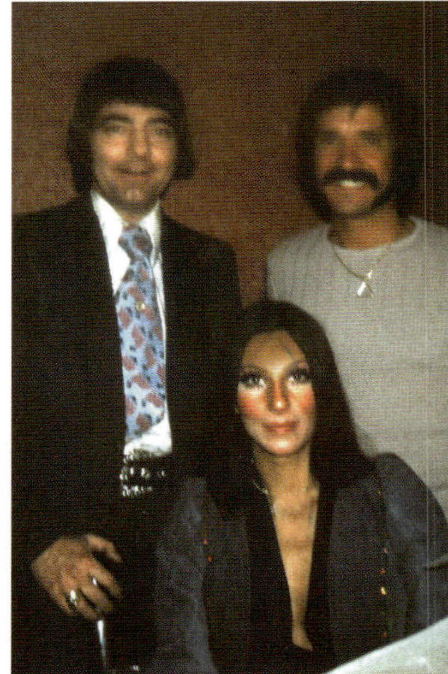

The Inkspots

1973

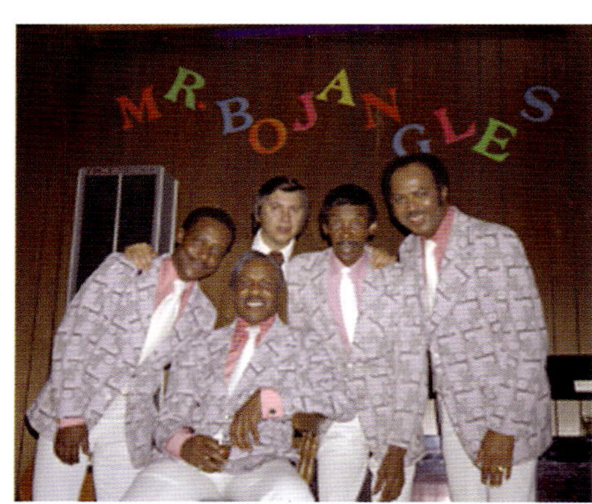

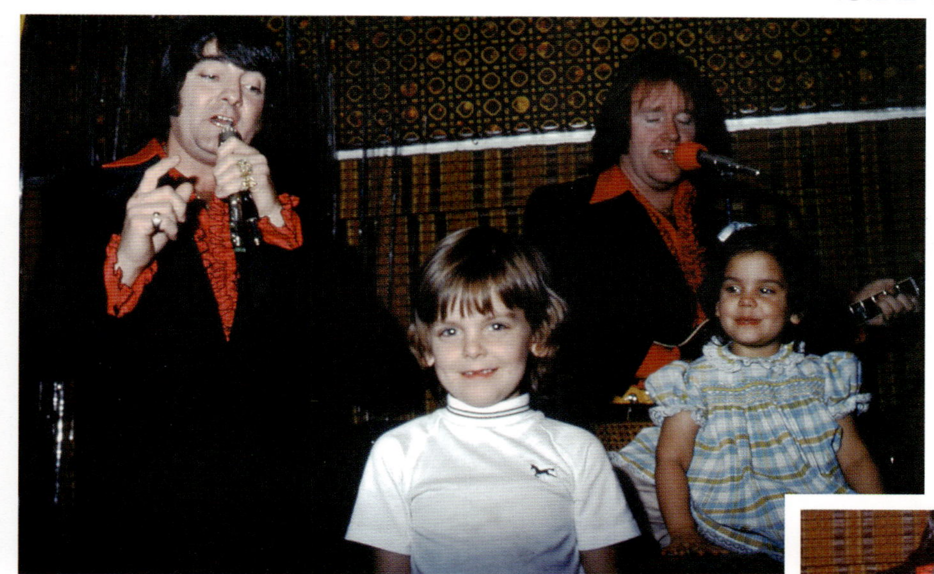

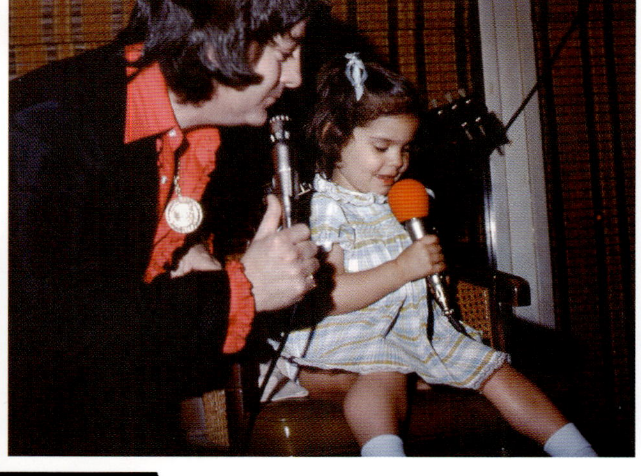

A highlight for me was to have my kids on stage with me. Above: Scott and Candida.

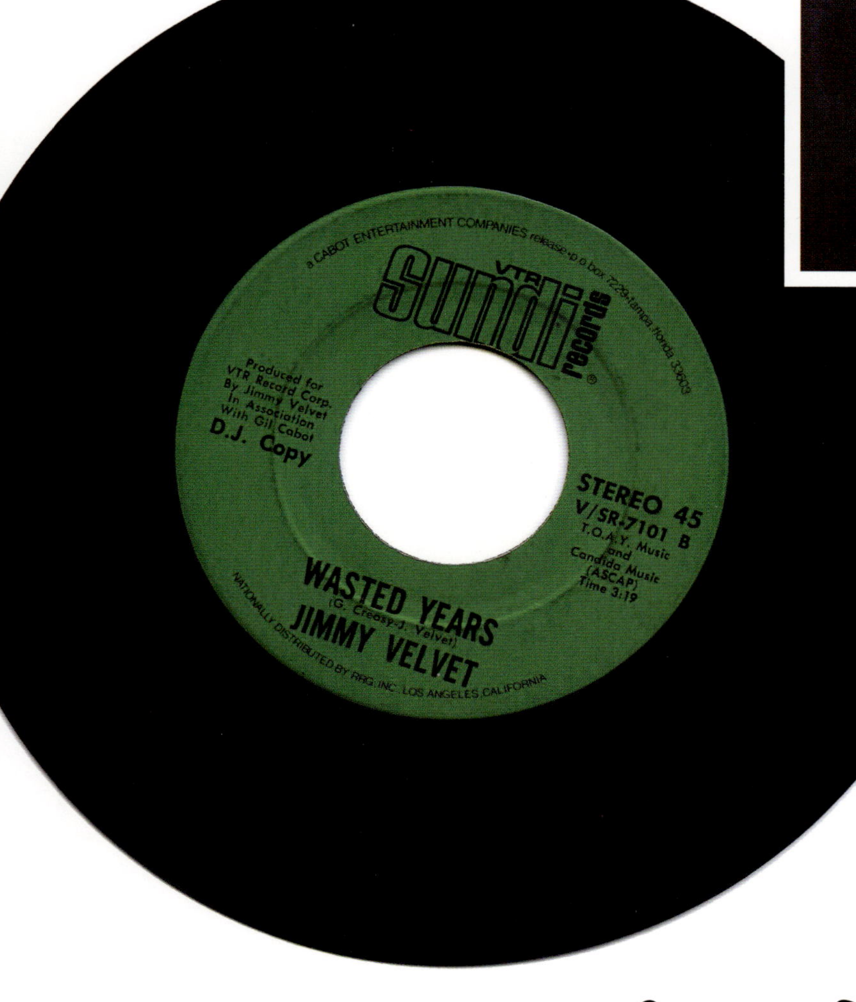

Ronnie Dove

Ronnie was a Glass Menagerie favorite and a young man whom I discovered in a bar on Charles St. in Baltimore "The Spa". I set him up with my arranger Bill Justis to record. He had many hits.

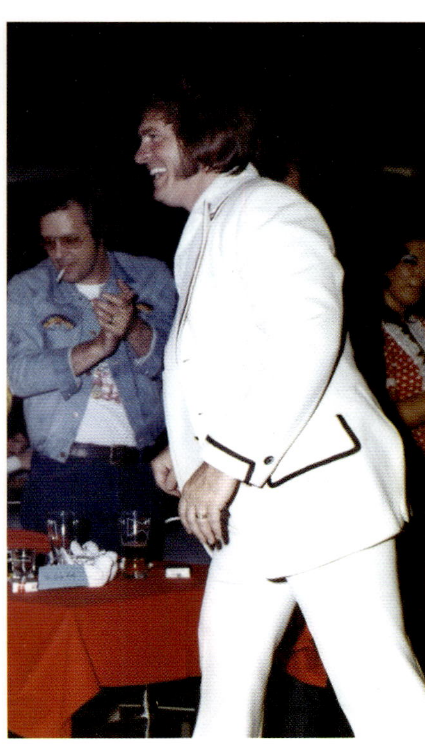

George Wallace Jr.

1971. This is George Wallace Jr. and I at "Cowboy" Jack Clement's studio in Nashville. I was the producer of his hit (which I was teaching him in this photo) Missing You. It was written by my brother-in-law Larry Butler. George finished college and went on to become the Alabama state controller. We spent many nights raiding the kitchen at the Governor's mansion.

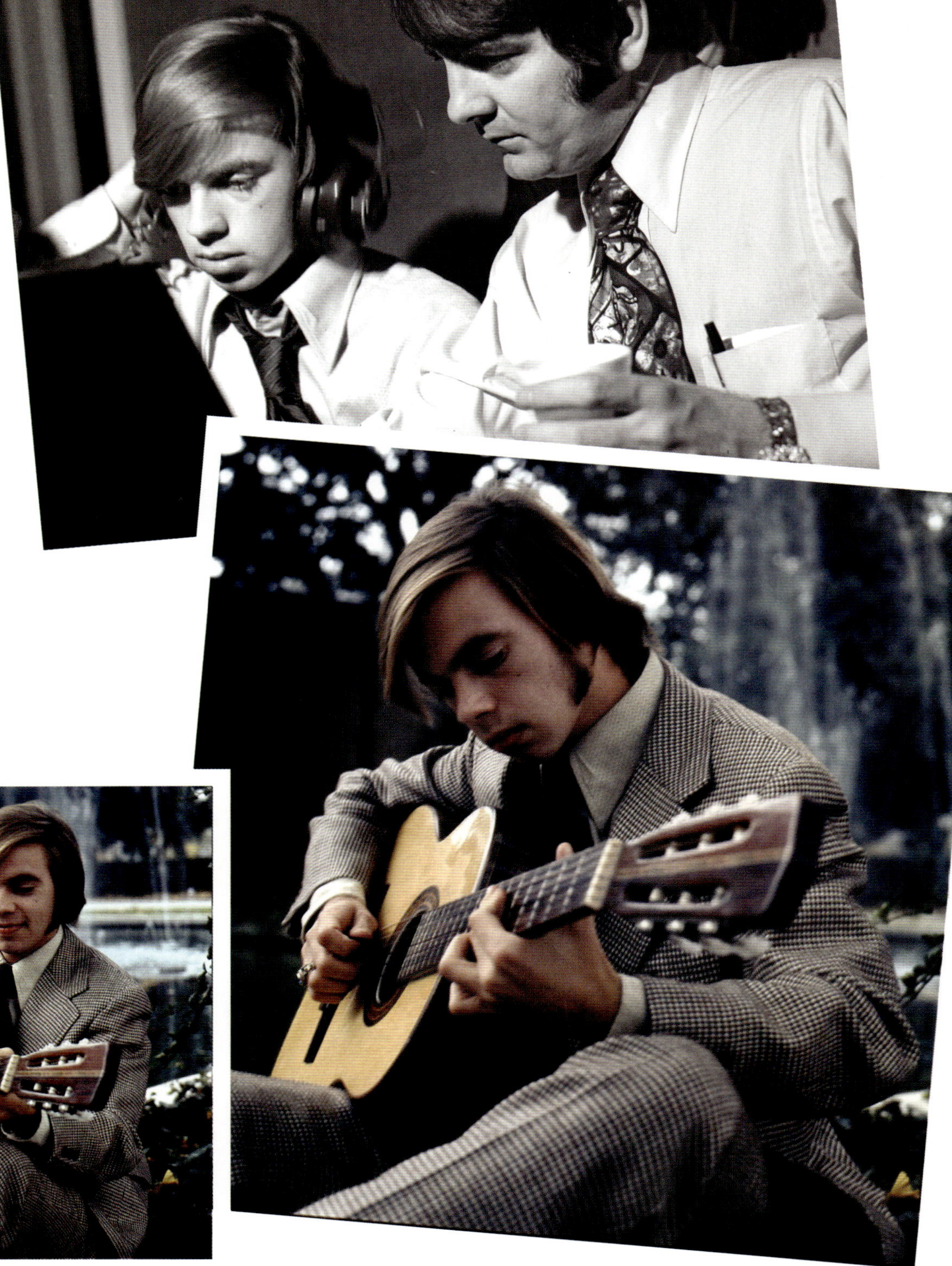

George Wallace in front of the old Country Music Hall of Fame.

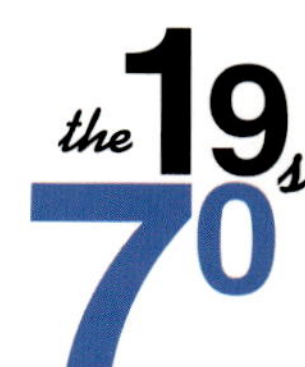

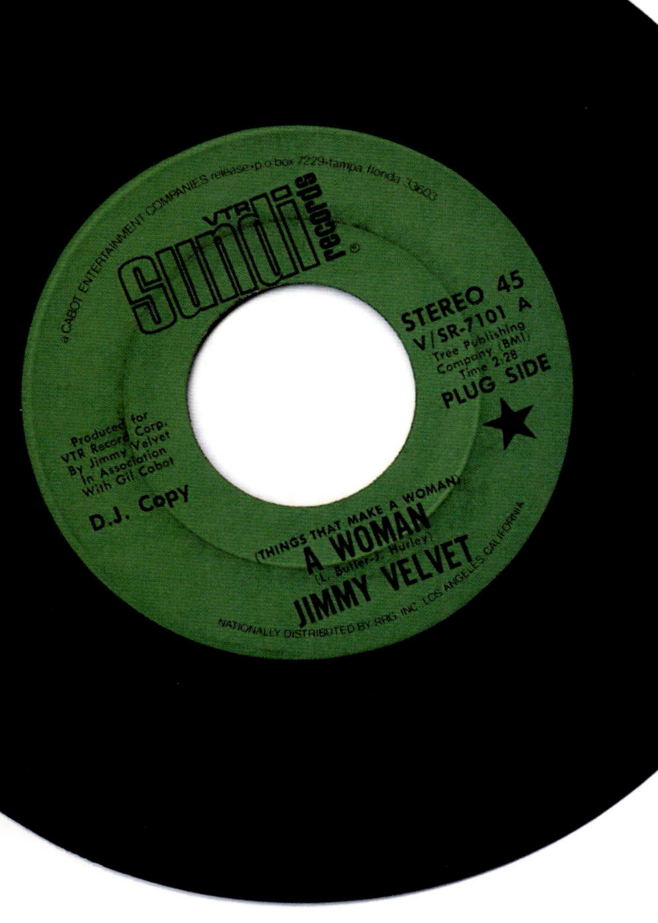

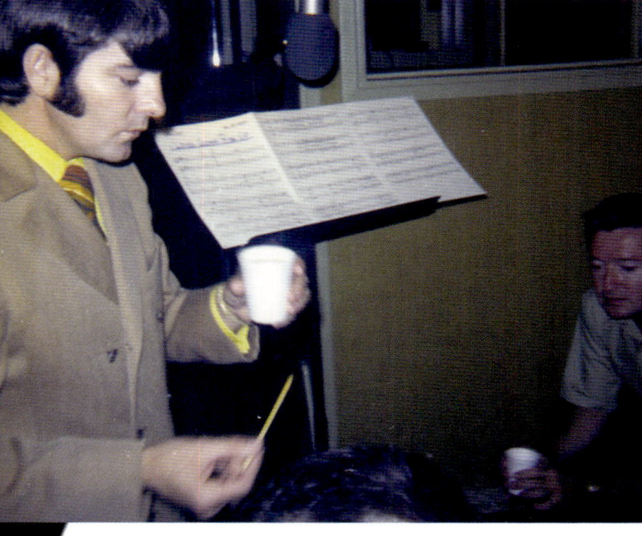

Here I am in session with Louis Nunnaly and Anita Kerr Singers.

Vic Dana

My friend and often house-guest Vic Dana. Vic had many hits including Red Roses for a Blue Lady.

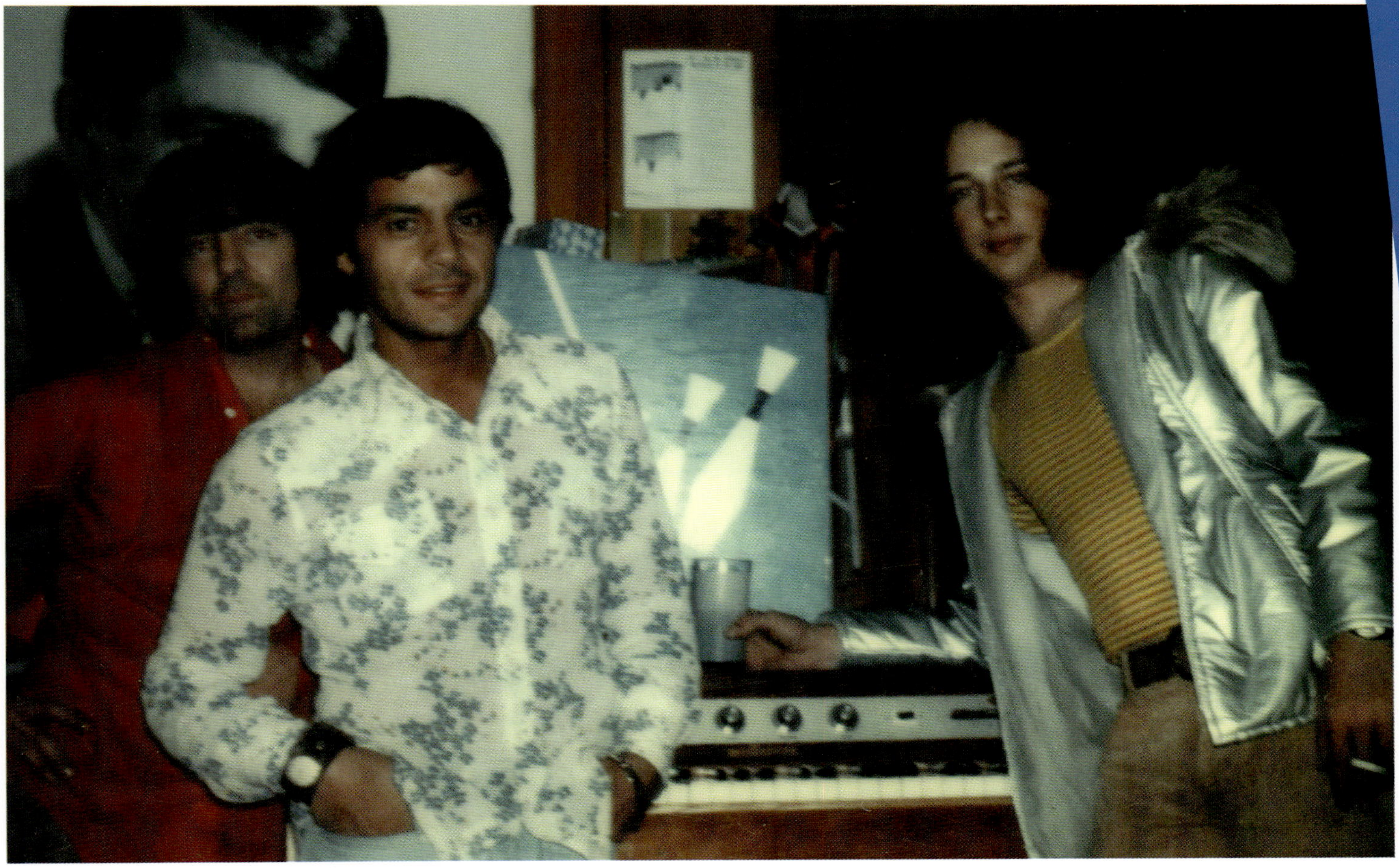

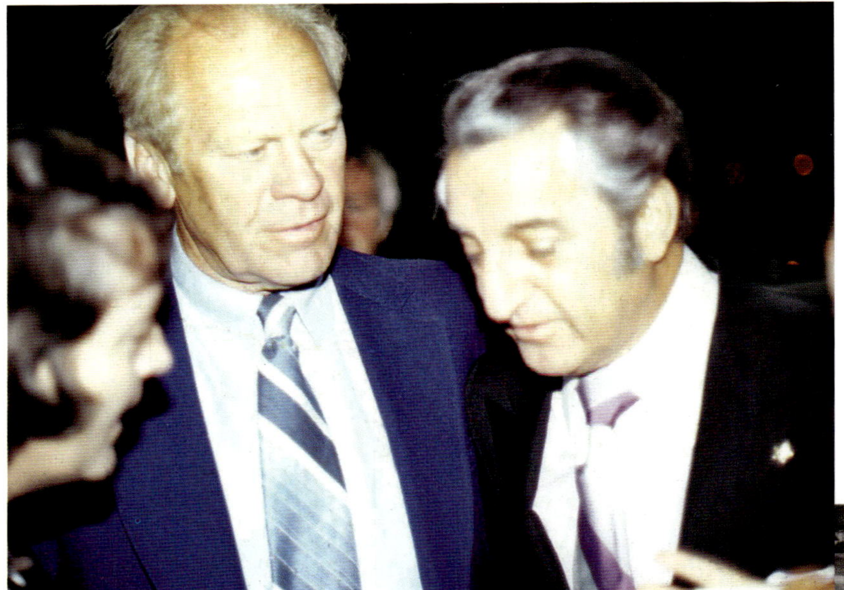

President, Gerald Ford and Danny Thomas

The Whittaker Family

This is a true life loving family: Thelma and John Whittaker with their 8 children. Far right seated: Johnny Whittaker. Famous and loved by all he was “Jody” on Famiily Affair.

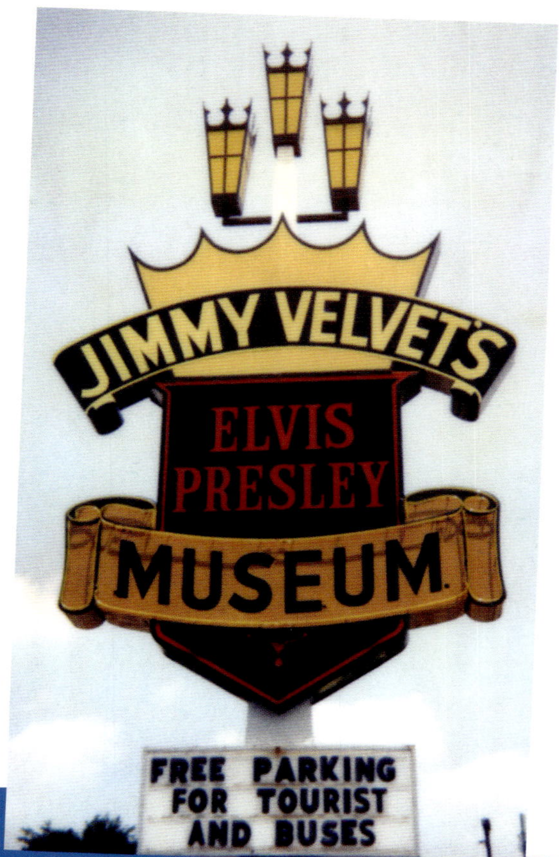

On June 1, 1978, I opened the first Elvis Presley Museum with Vernon Presley’s blessing. The museum was located directly across the street from Graceland.

Joe Higgins

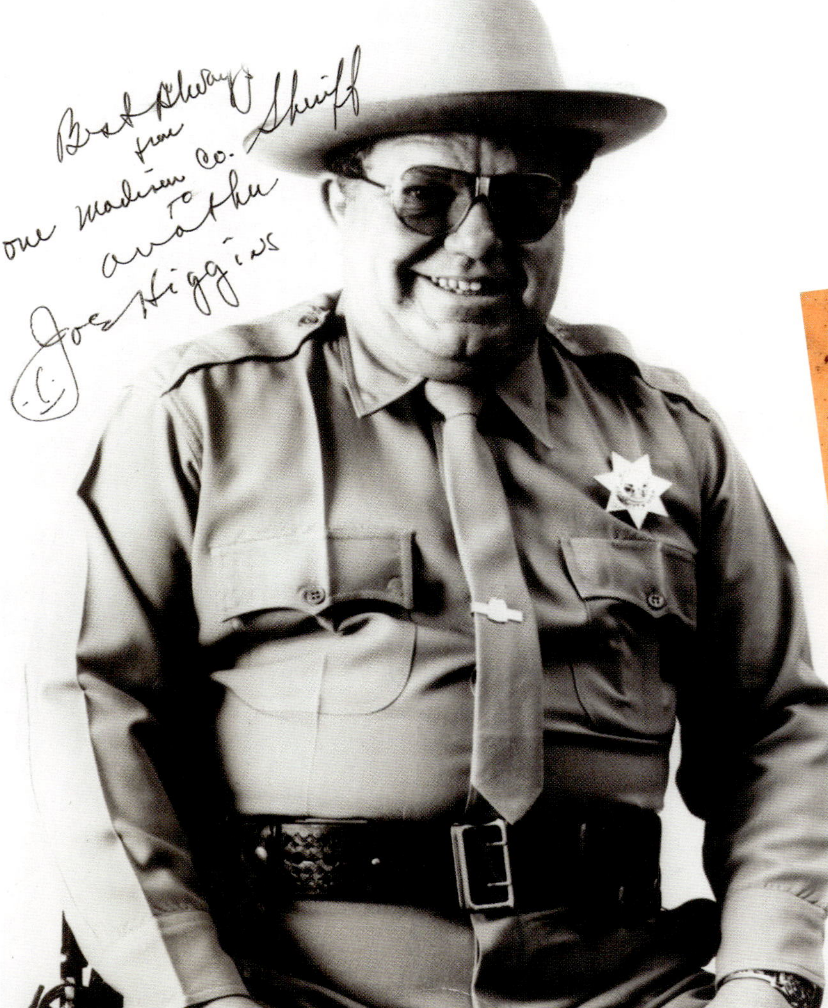

TV Sheriff Joe Higgins.
We both had Madison County Sheriff's Badges.

Law Enforcement Training Section • *M.I.S.C.*

CLASSIFICATION CARD

POLICE FIREARMS QUALIFICATION

THIS CARD EXPIRES ONE YEAR FROM DATE OF ISSUE

JIMMY VELVET EXPERT

COURSE OF FIRE **F.B.I.** DOUBLE ACTION

THIS IS TO CERTIFY THAT THE ABOVE HAS BEEN AWARDED THIS CLASSIFICATION CARD AS A RESULT OF RANGE SCORES OBTAINED THIS DATE.

L@ L@
DATE

These are a couple of the law enforcement badges that were presented to me over the years.

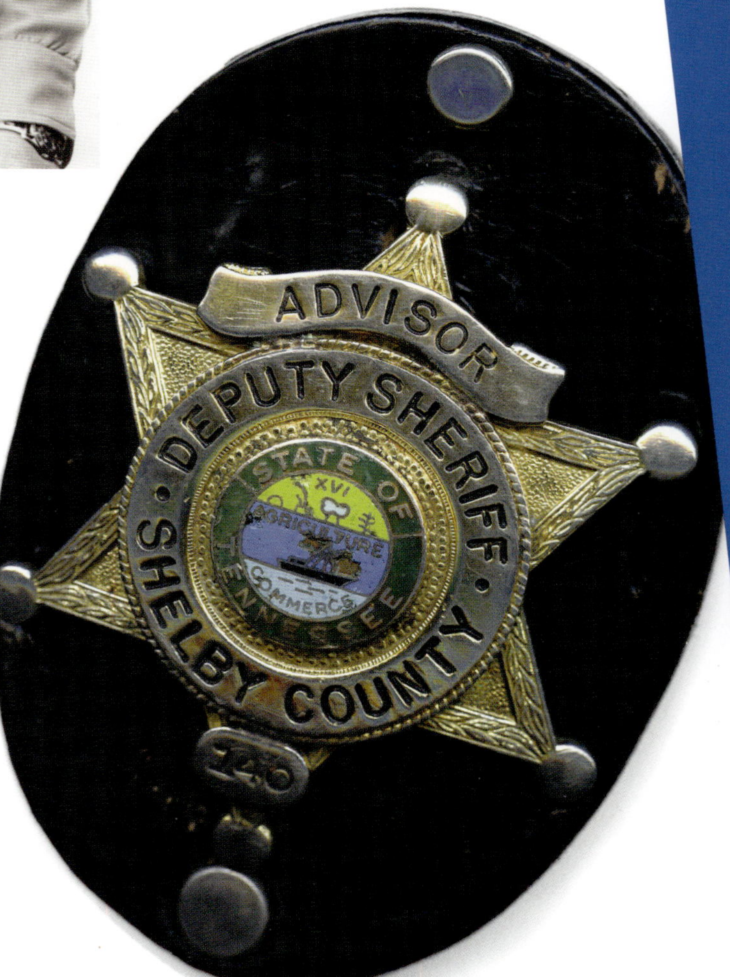

Shelby County DeputySheriff's Badge
presented by Gene Barksdale, 1979

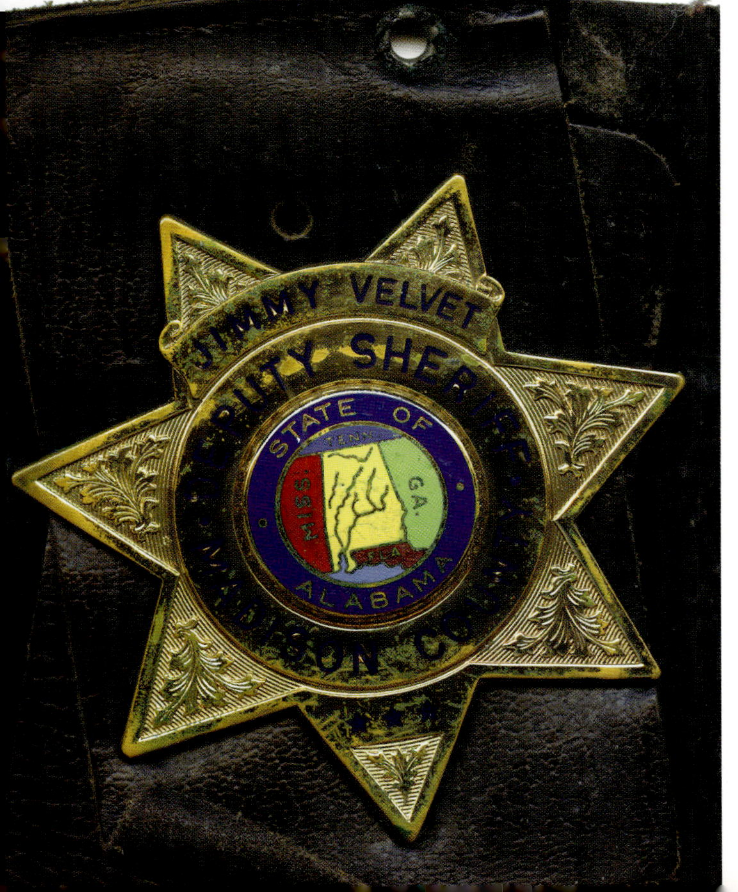

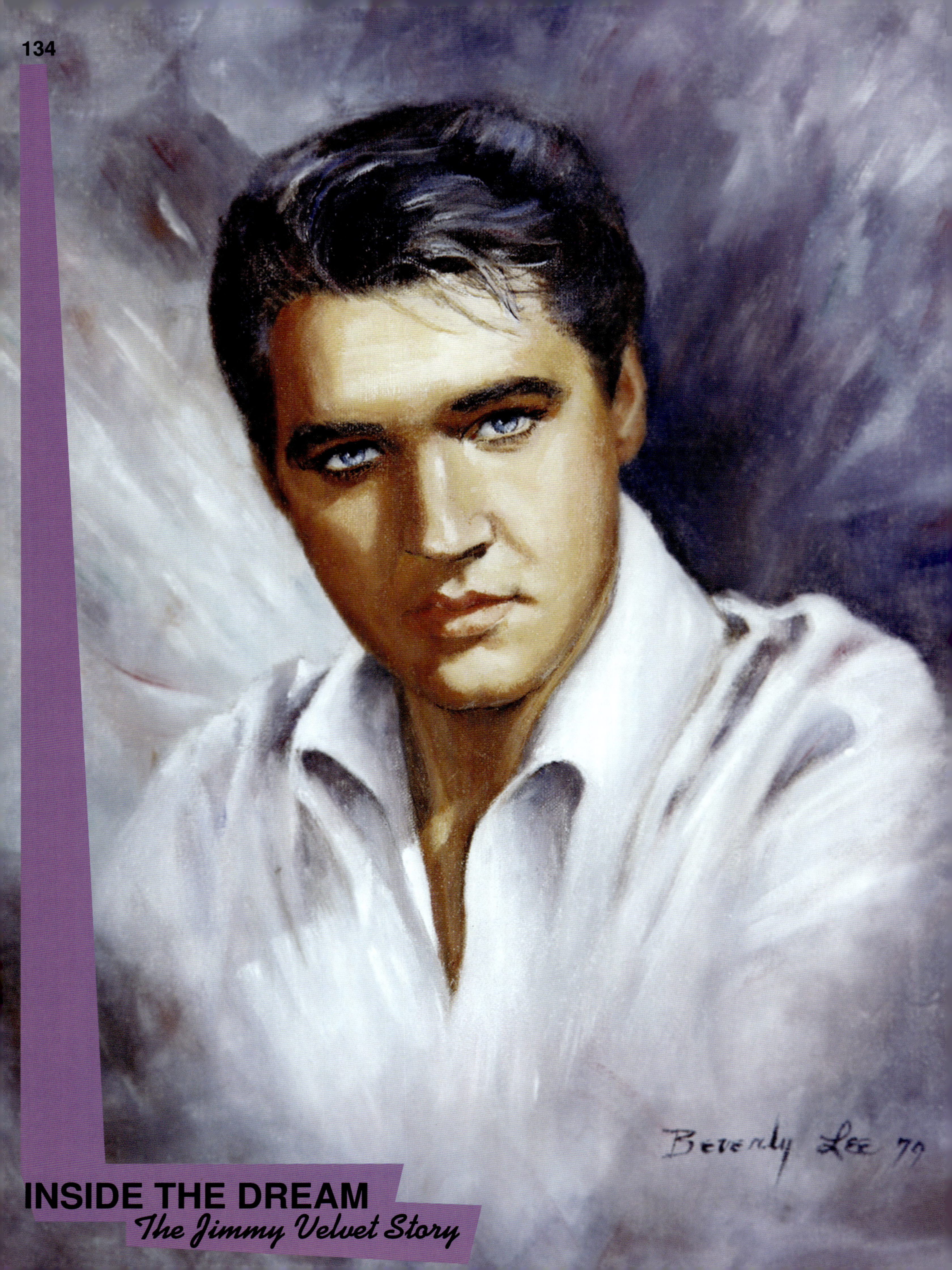

Throughout the 80's, I was busy running the Elvis Presley Museums. I opened the second museum in Honolulu in 1982. In 1984, I opened another museum in Orlando and another in Nashville in 1985. I also developed two mobile museums that toured the country and abroad, these exhibits were free to Elvis fans. Along with the museums I also owned two recording studios in Nashville: American Sound Studios.

I helped Warner-Brothers with Elvis-owned items for "This is Elvis." I opened another restaurant in downtown Nashville which was said by many to have been "ahead of its time." The name of the restaurant was Superstars Café. I displayed personal items owned by celebrities in the world of rock 'n roll, country music, movies, and TV. The great food was an added plus. Dick Clark and his wife Keri spent a day with my family in Nashville. When I picked them up at the airport, we went to Superstars. Dick loved all the entertainment history, especially a piano that had belonged to Jerry Lee Lewis (which Dick ended up buying from me).

After spending time at the restaurant, we went to the Elvis Presley Museum and then to my studios. It was a great time. Shortly after the visit, I received a heartwarming personal note from Dick and Keri about the visit we shared, making a special mention about having met my daughter Candida. It was a very special time.

It was in the 80's that I combined three of the Elvis Presley Museums for the greatest show ever. It was at the Showboat Hotel and Casino in Atlantic City. The live show consisted of Carl Perkins, Roy Orbison, The Jordanaires, Johnny Cash, Lucio, and most of Elvis' guys including George Kline, Alan Fortas, Richard Davis, DJ Fontana, and Scotty Moore. Somewhere in all of this, I also appeared on the Geraldo Show.

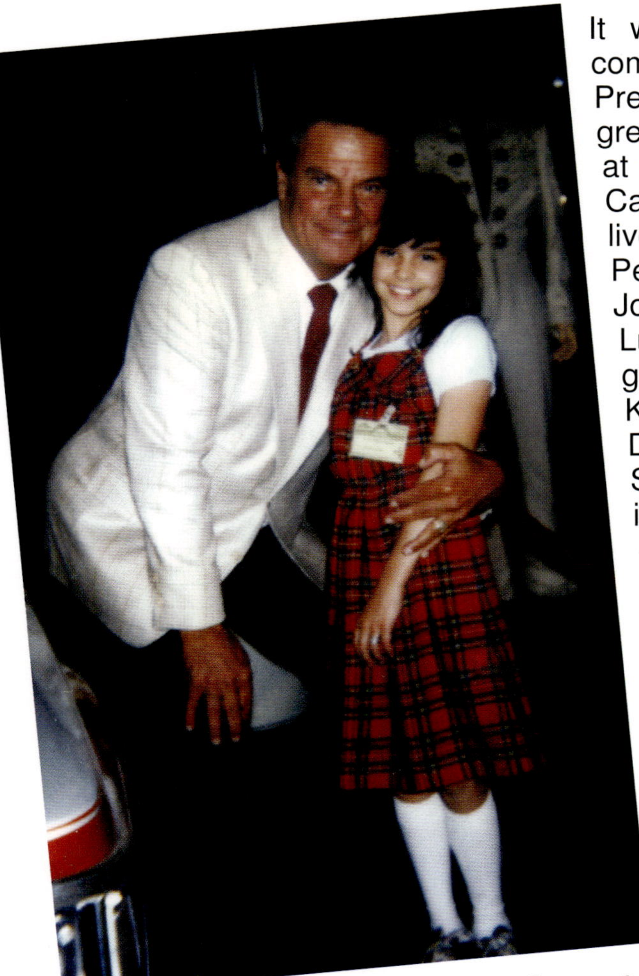

Bert Parks

Bert Parks and Candida Velvet

Gordon Stoker, The Jordanaires

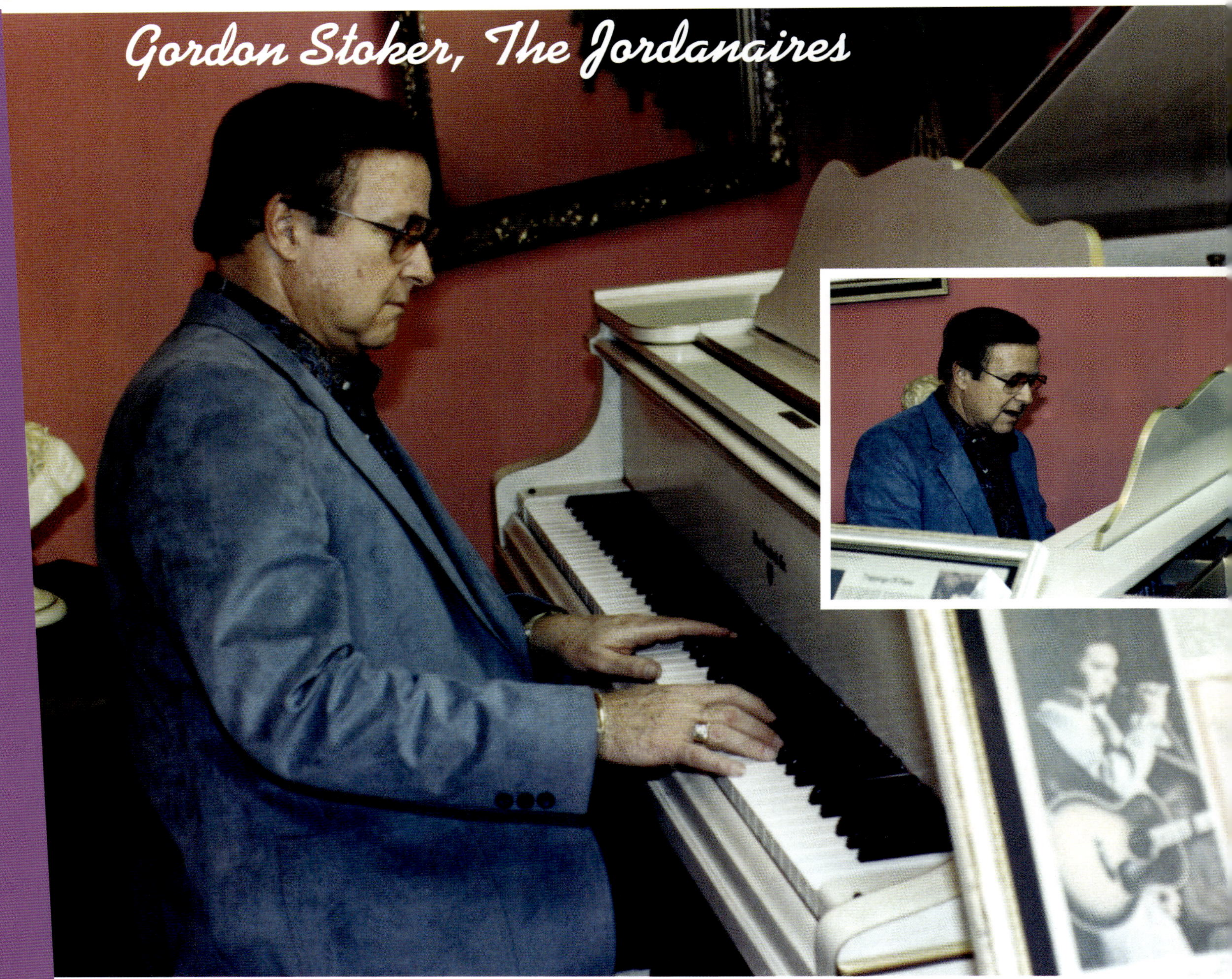

Gordon Stoker of The Jordanaires playing Elvis' Knabe piano at the Elvis Presley Museum in Orlando.

Joe Esposito

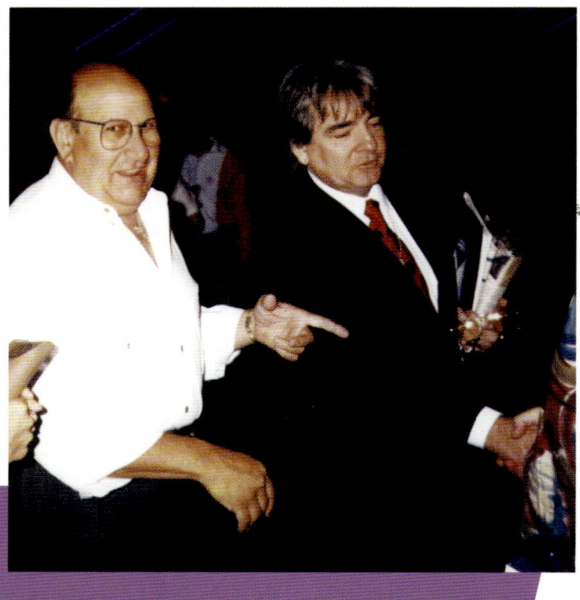

Elvis' Aunt Loraine Smith

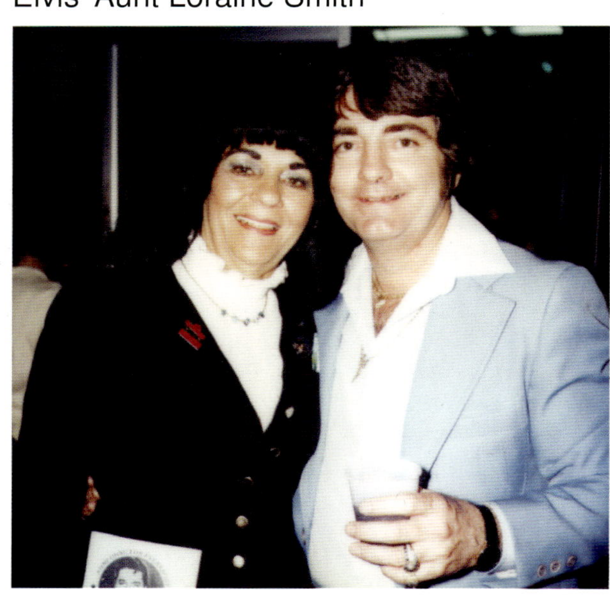

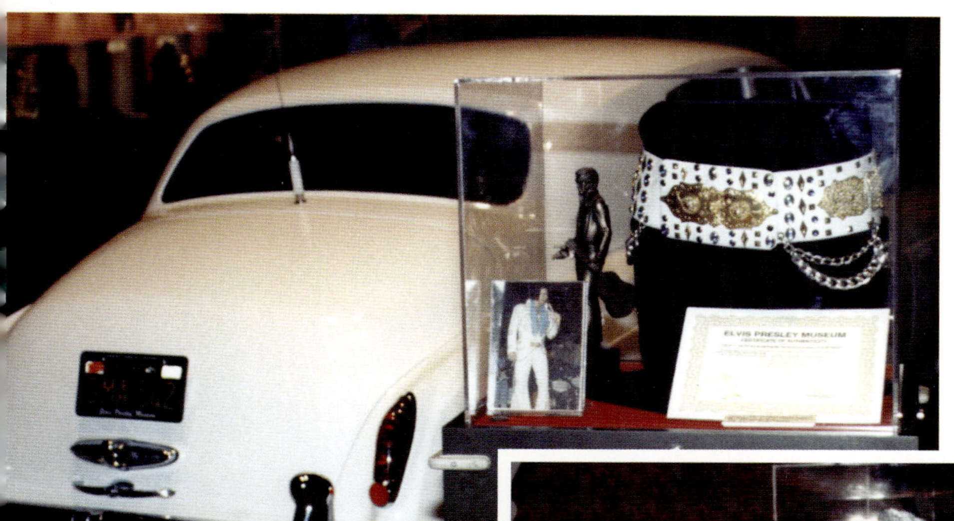

Elvis Presley Museum on tour in 1988 on Elvis's Birthday in Atlantic City, New Jersey.

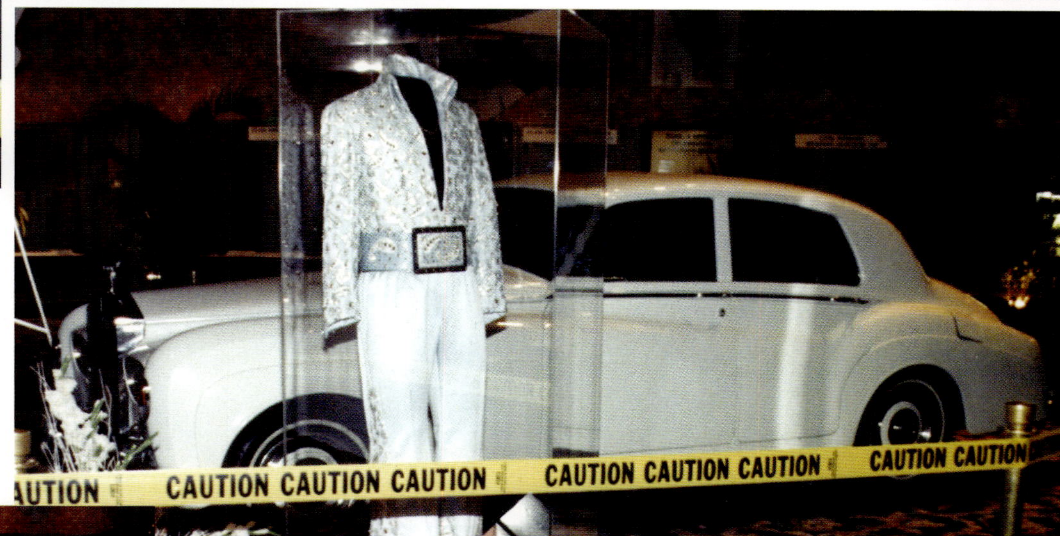

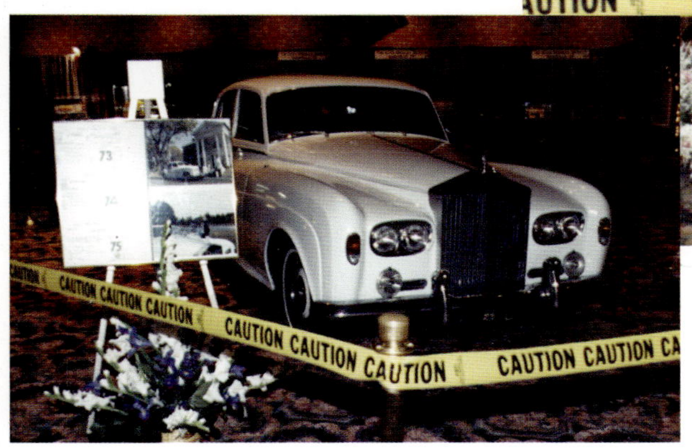

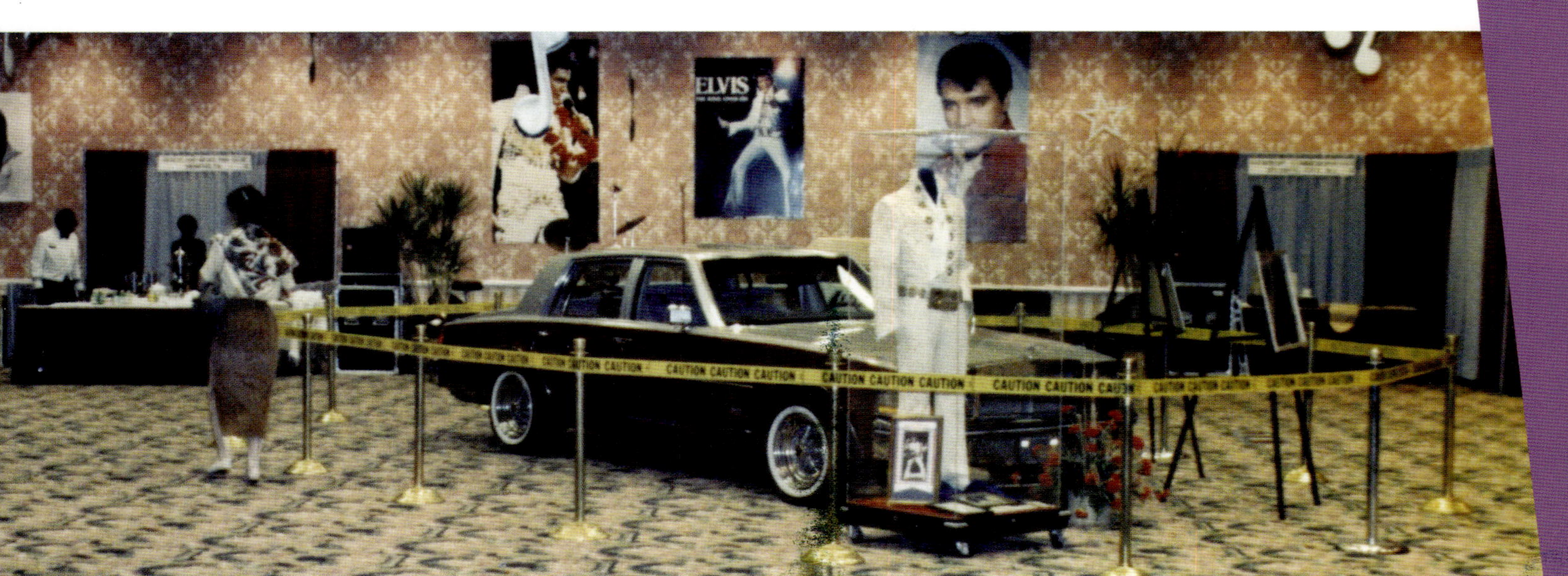

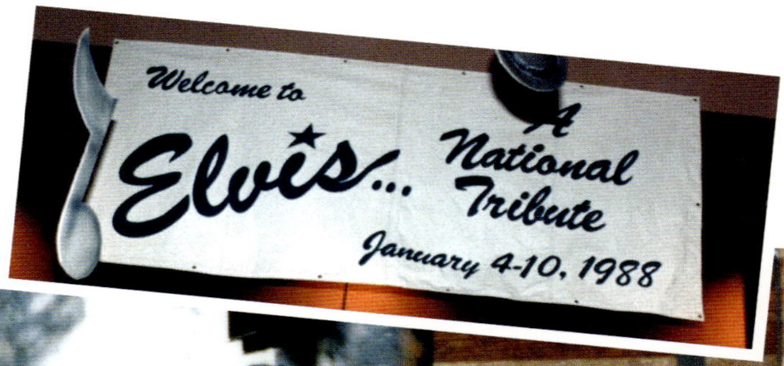

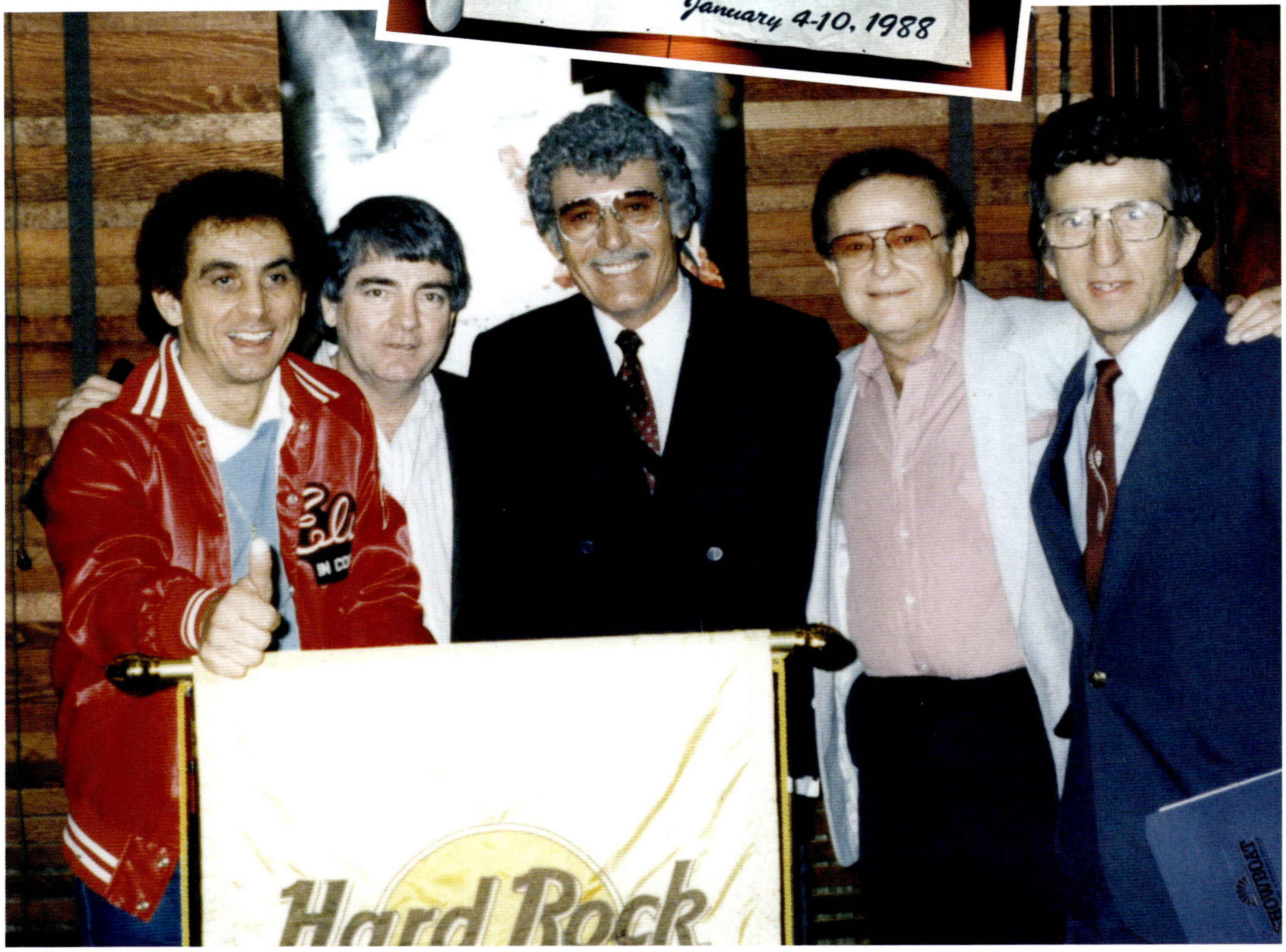

George Kline, Me, Carl Perkins, Gordon Stoker, D.J. Fontana
Promoting our show in Atlantic City at the showboat. We had our press conference at the Hard Rock Cafe in N.Y.C. The show was the greatest ever.

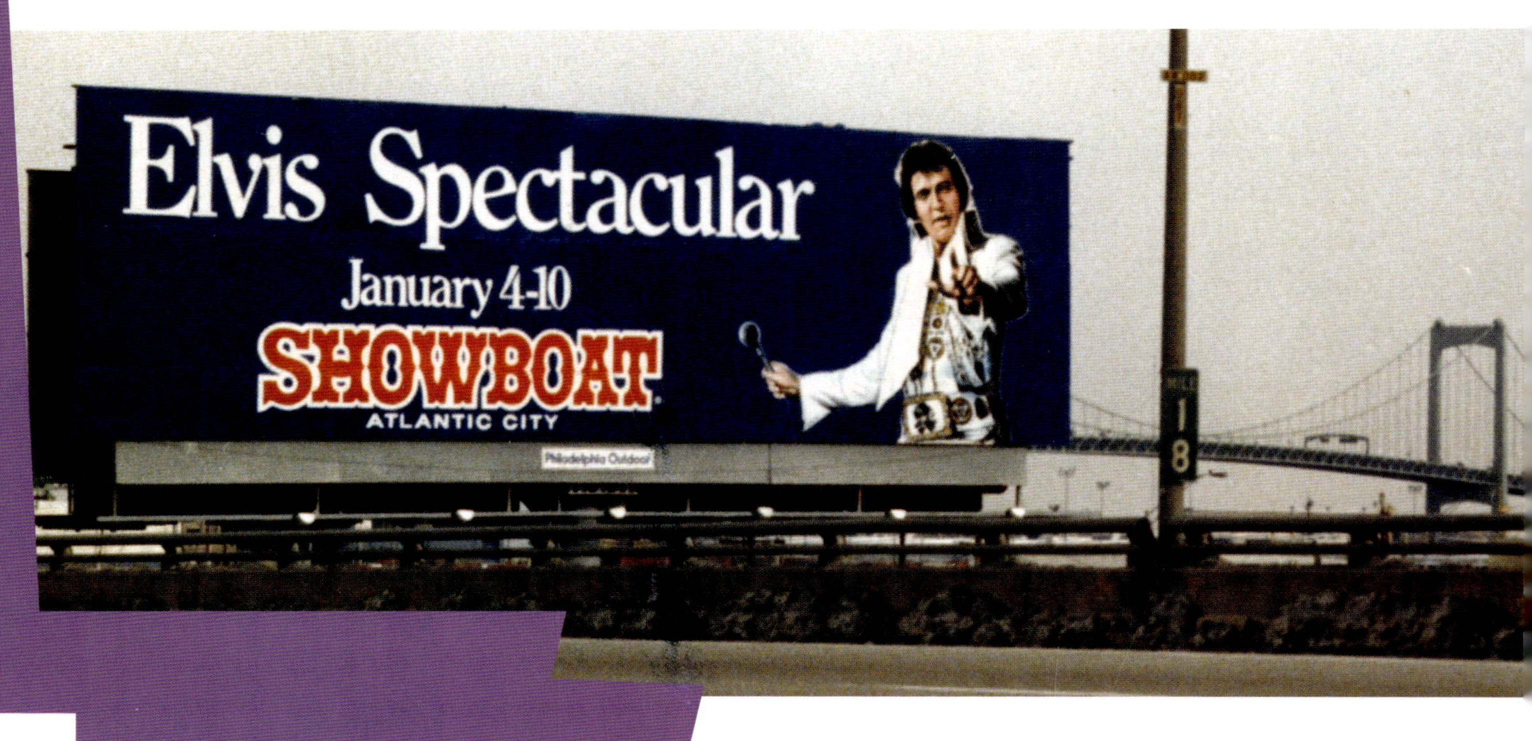

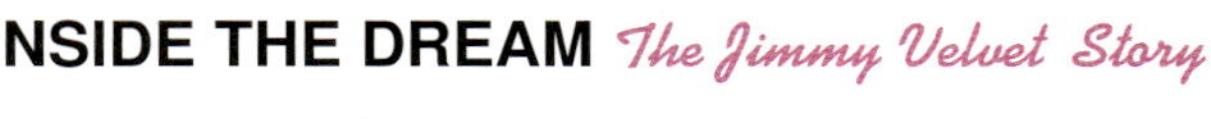

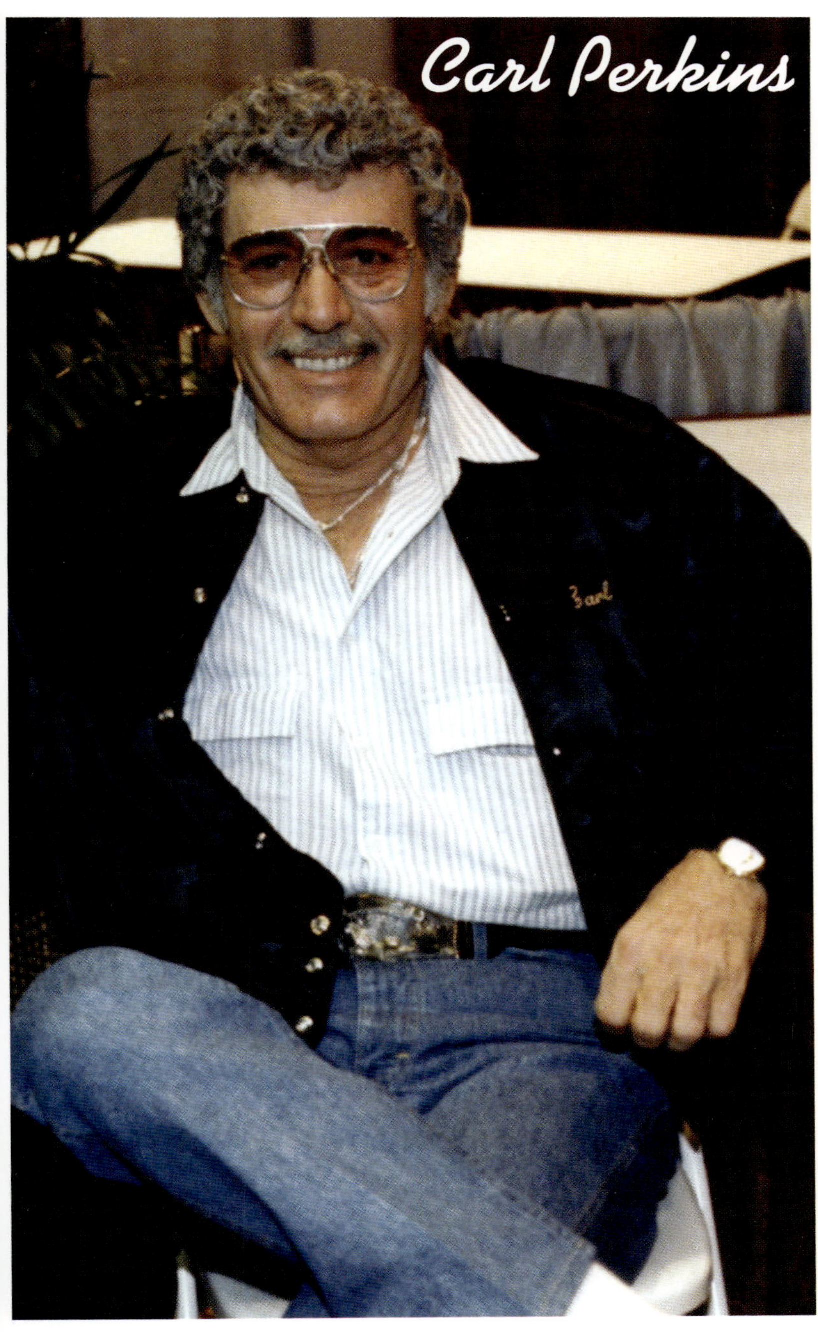

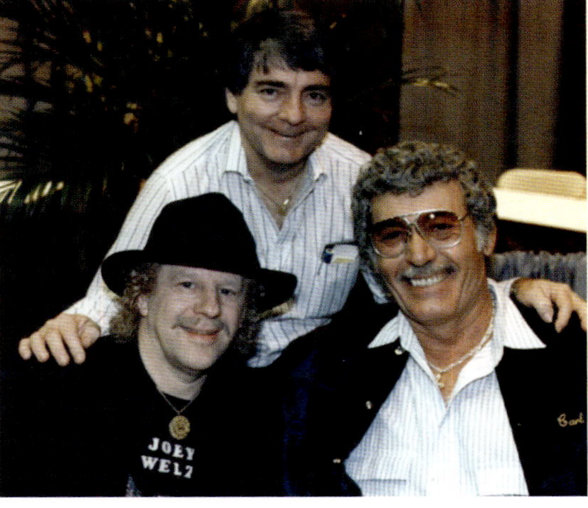

Joey Welz and Carl Perkins

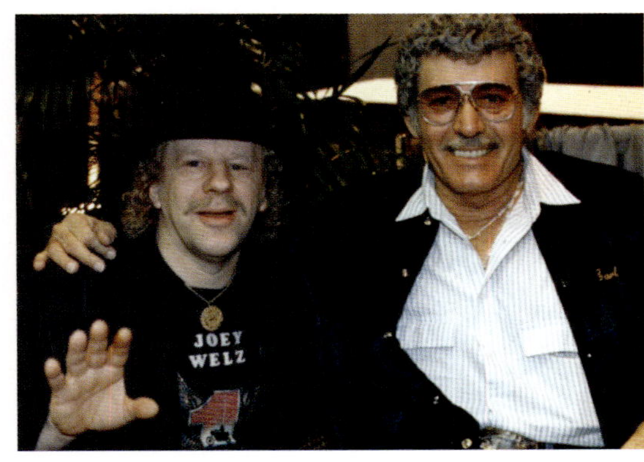

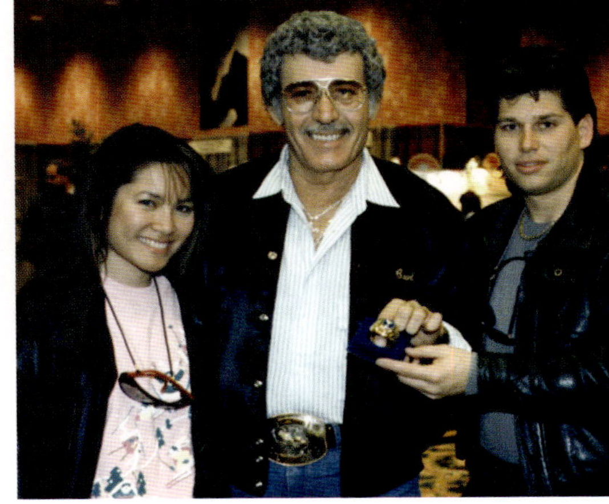

Alan Fortas, Joey Welz, Richard Davis, and Carl Perkins

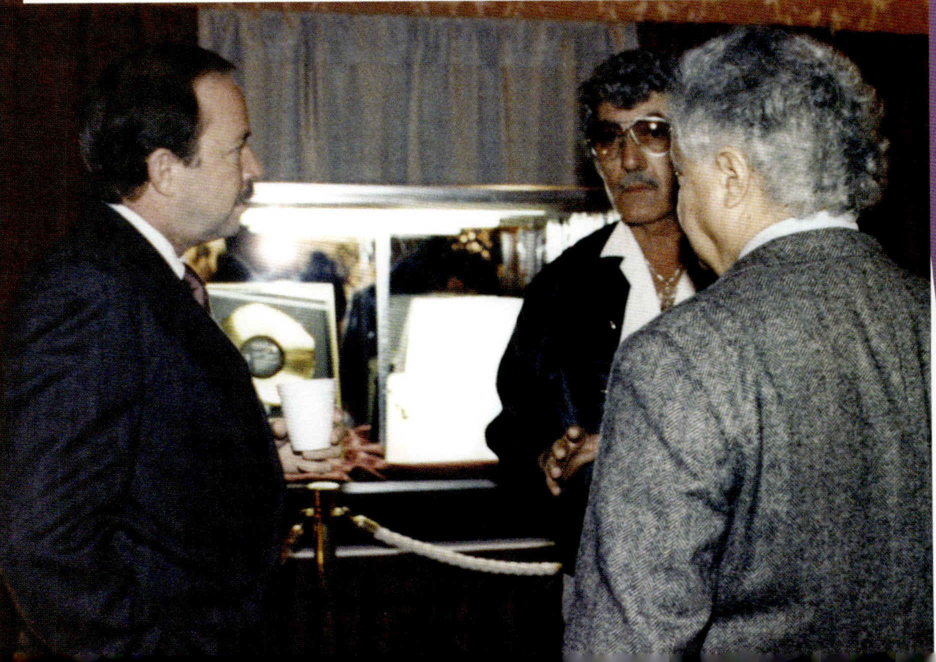

George Kline

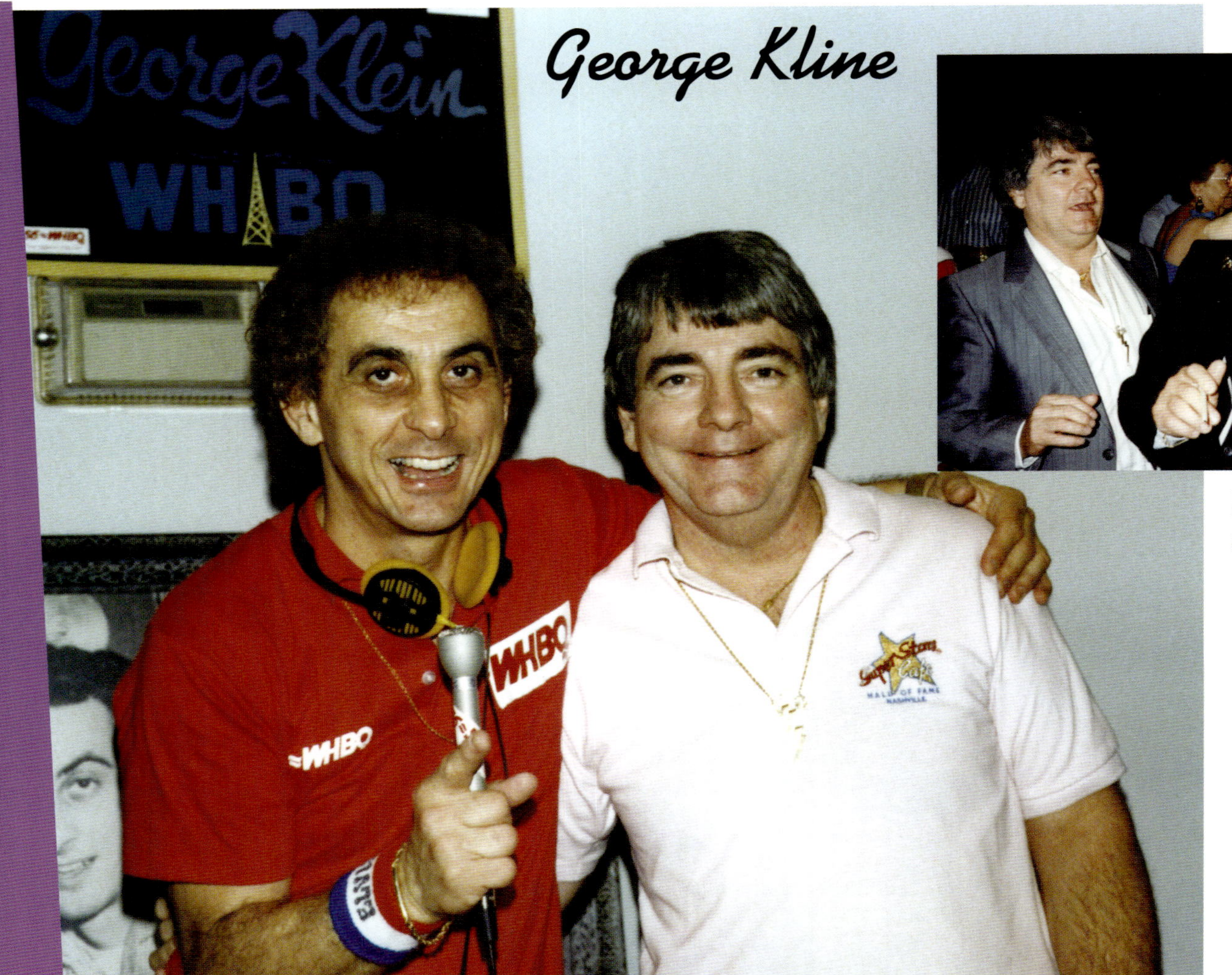

Me, George and Joanne

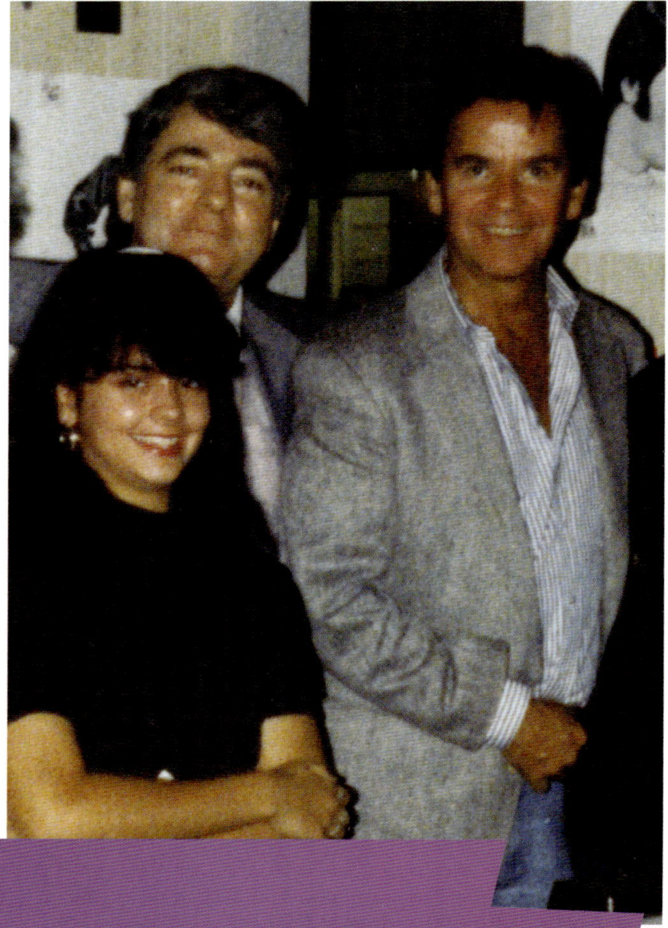

Dick Clark

Dick and Kari Clark spent the day with my family in 1989. Dick fell in love with my daughter, Candida (as a matter of speech of course).

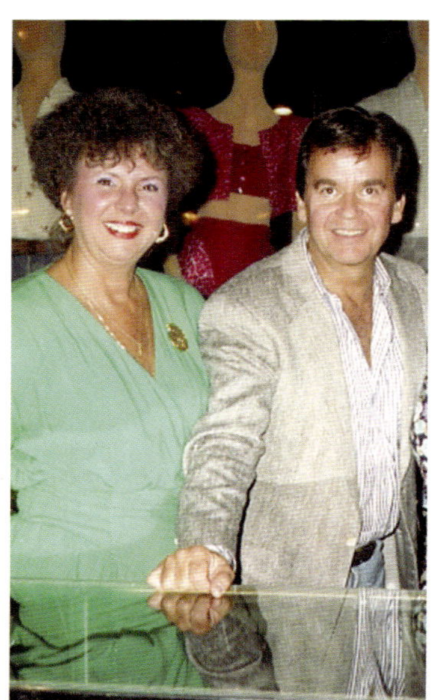

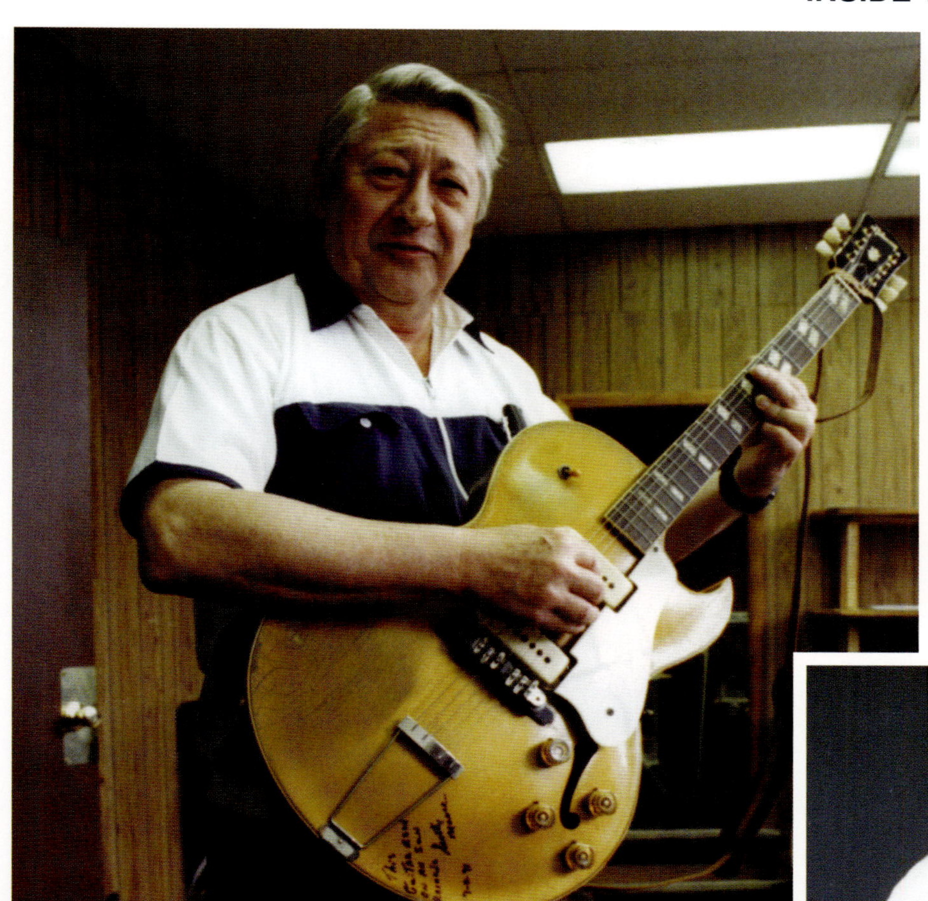

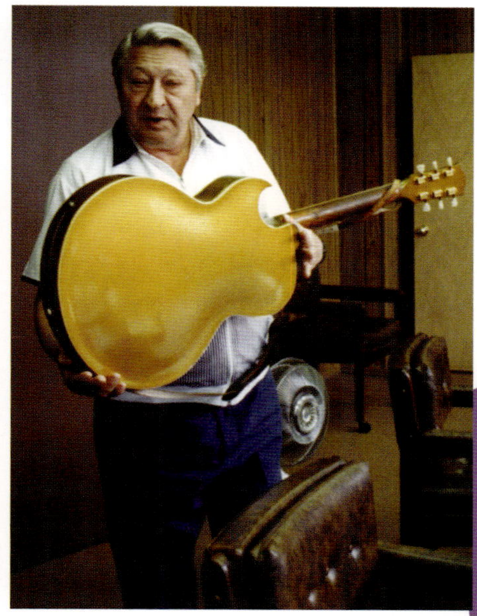

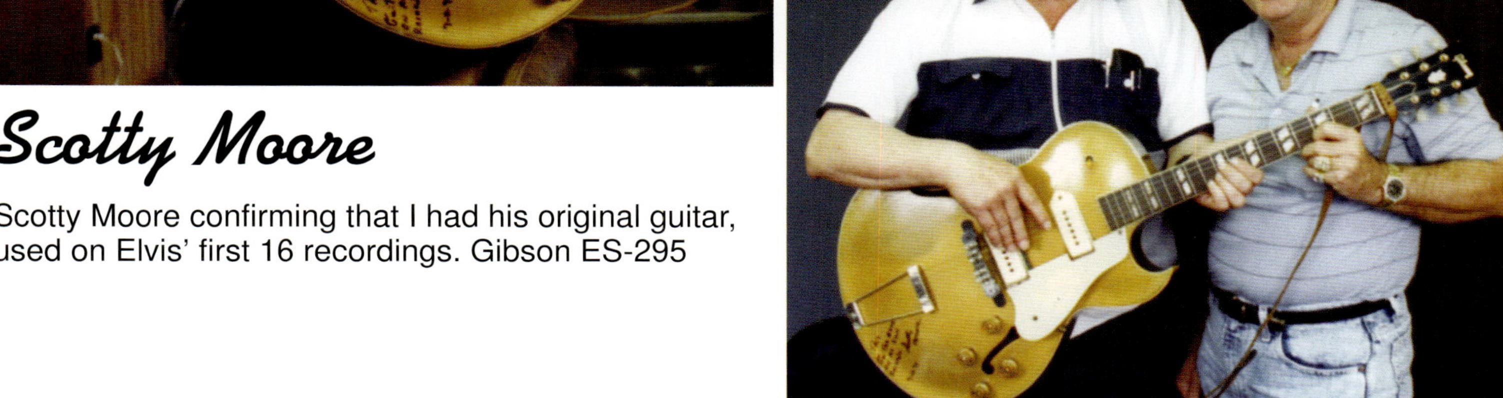

Scotty Moore

Scotty Moore confirming that I had his original guitar, used on Elvis' first 16 recordings. Gibson ES-295

Charly McClain

Charly McClain Country star. I bought Elvis' Rolls Royce from her that day.

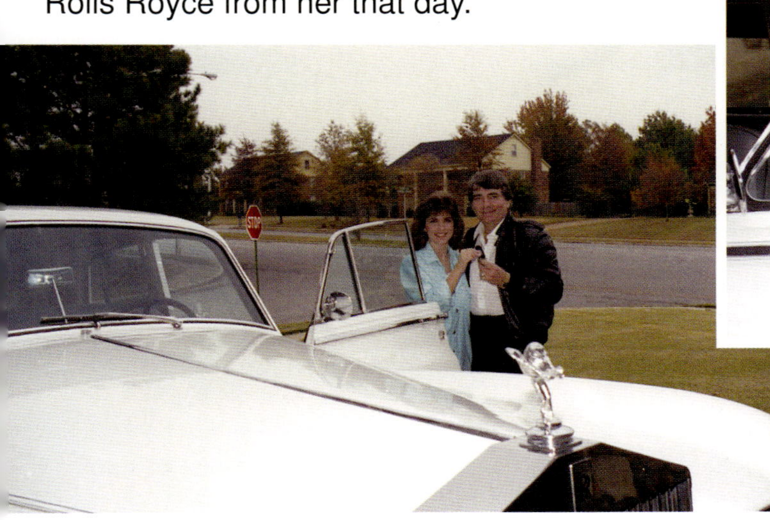

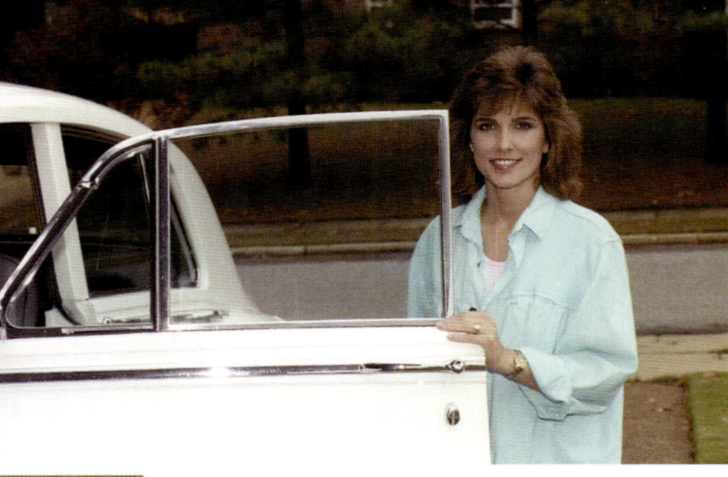

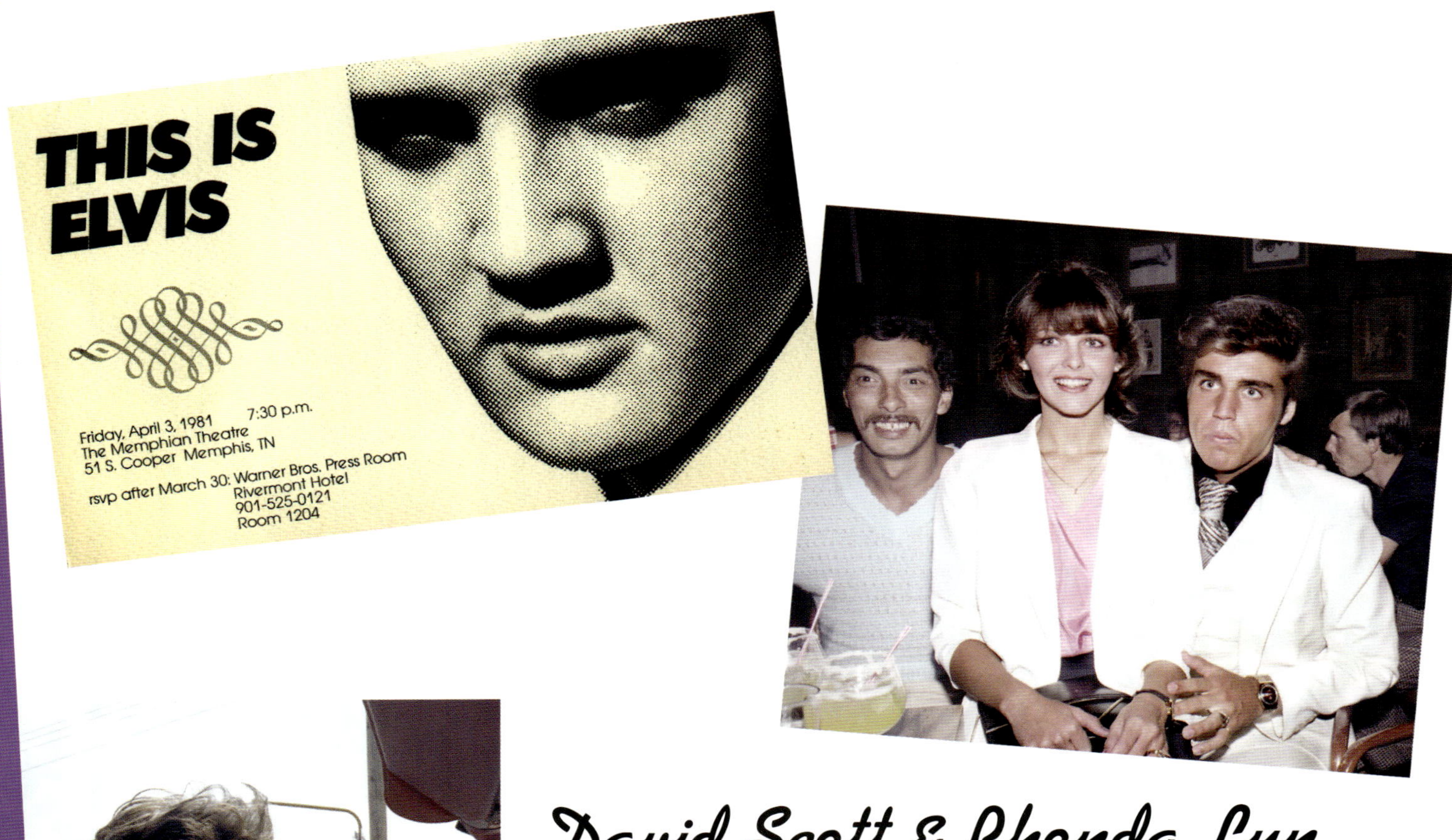

David Scott & Rhonda Lyn

(Elvis & Priscilla)

During the filming of "This Is Elvis" I became close with many of the Warner Brothers crew and stars. I furnished many of Elvis' personal items for the making of this movie. This 76' Cadillac convertible, jewelry, wardrobe, etc. Warner Brother's lost Elvis' lion ring on his bed at Graceland. "This Is Elvis" produced by David L. Wolper and directed by Malcom Leo and Andrew Solt.

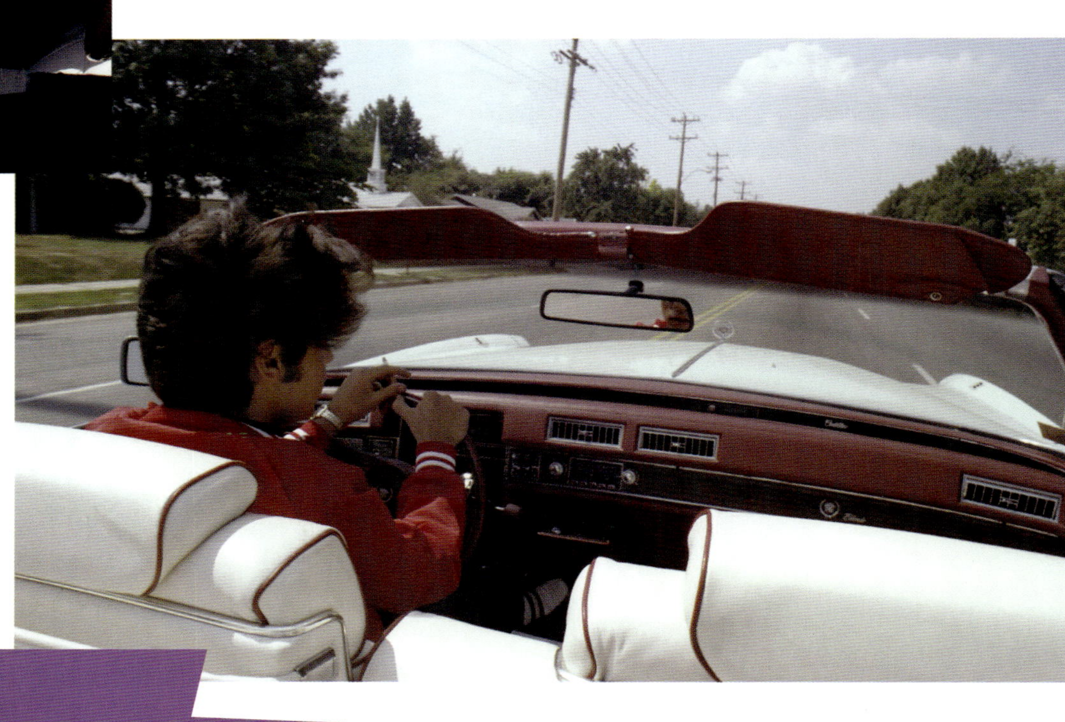

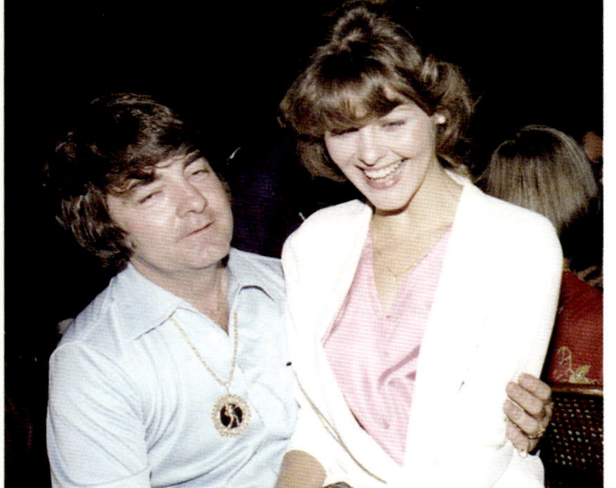

Rhonda Lyn who portrayed Priscilla in "This is Elvis."

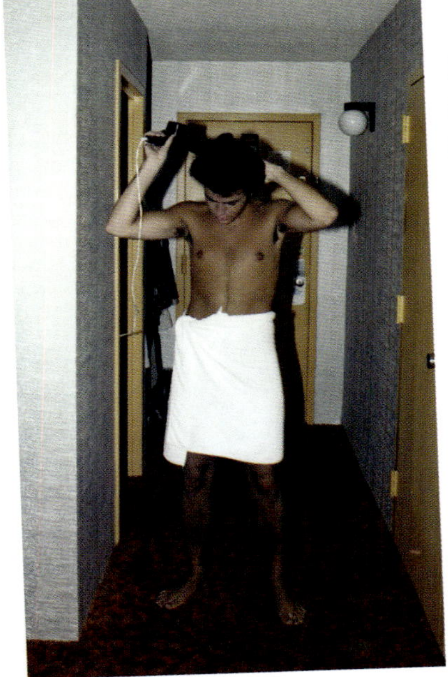

David fresh out of the shower.

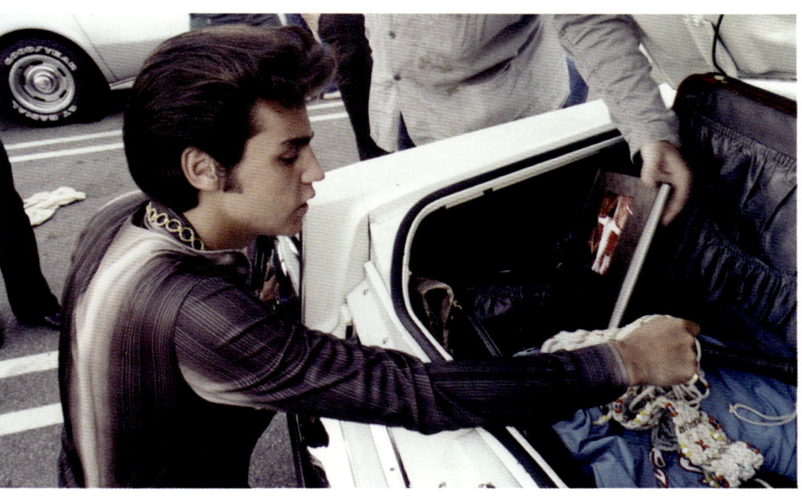

David Scott with items of Elvis for use in the film. I let David use Elvis' 76' Cadillac convertible while filming.

My friend Shirley Connell

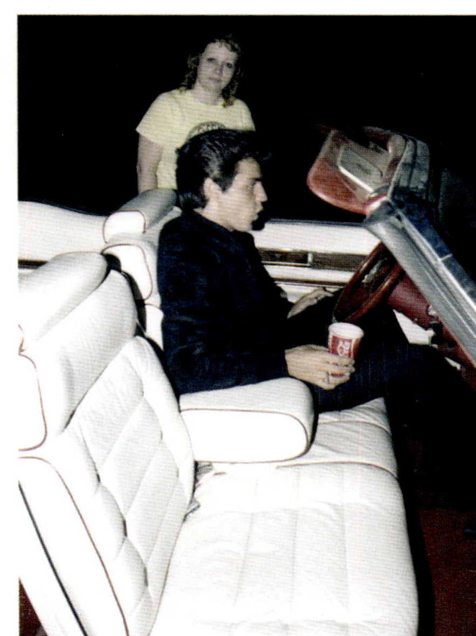

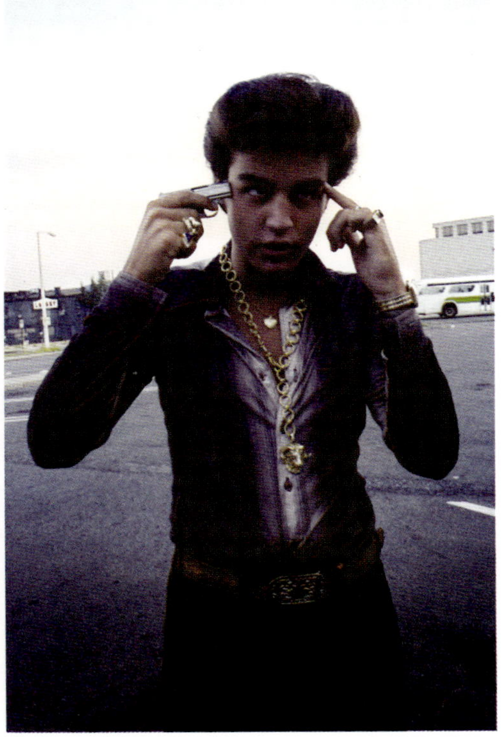

David with one of Elvis' guns. He said one day, "I'm going to shoot myself." And he did.

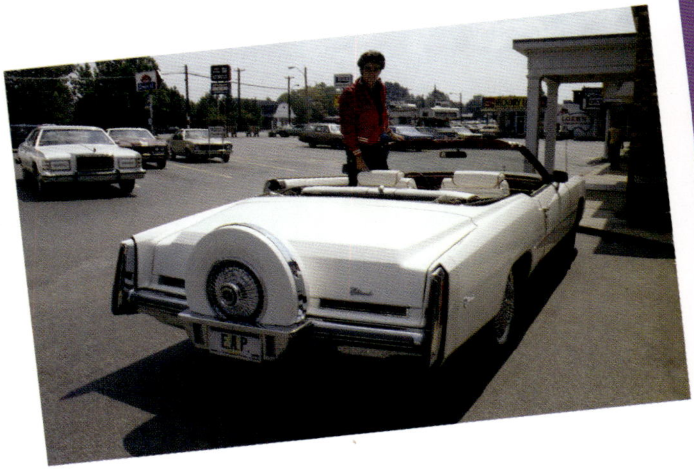

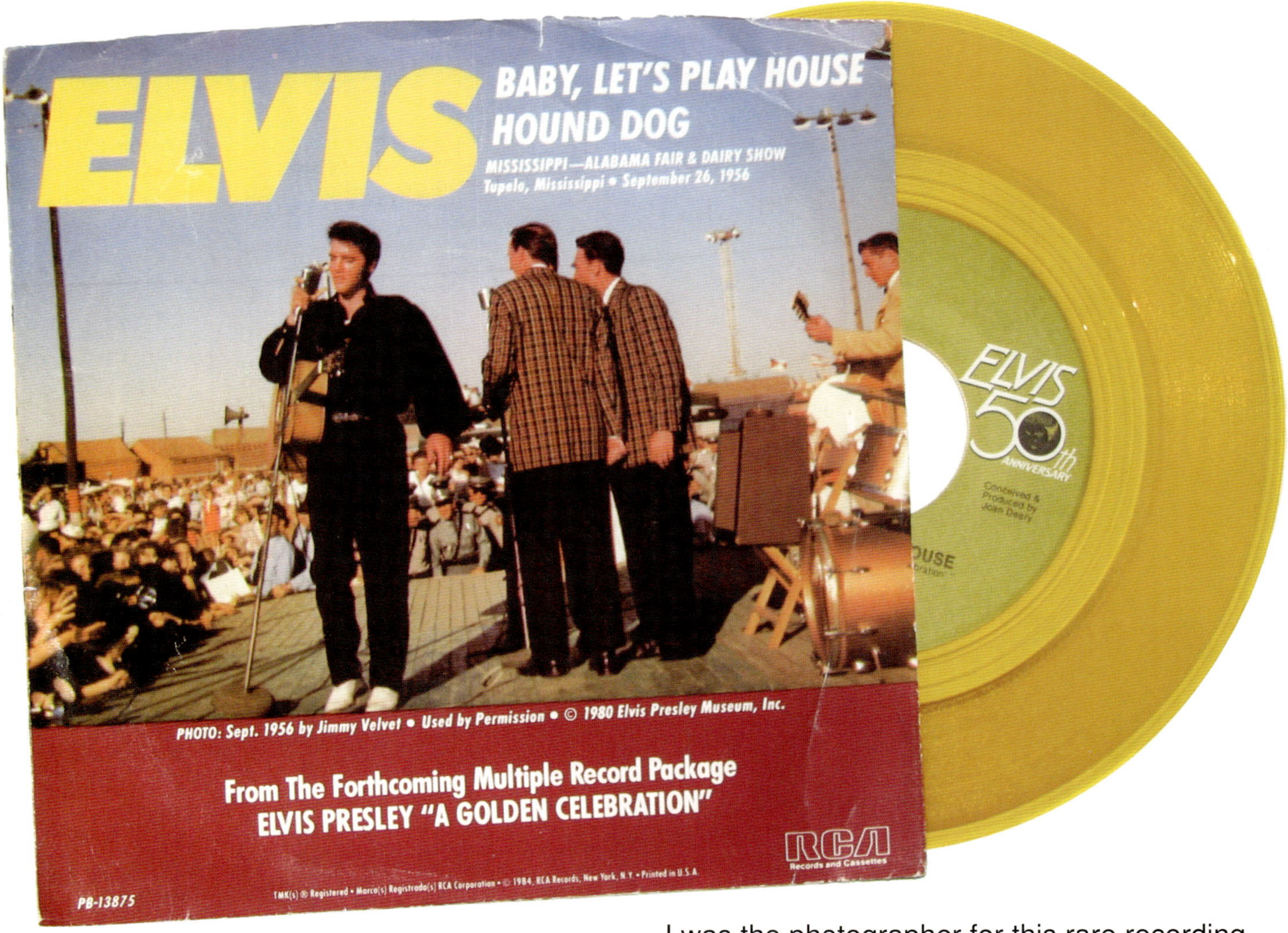

ELVIS

BABY, LET'S PLAY HOUSE
HOUND DOG

MISSISSIPPI—ALABAMA FAIR & DAIRY SHOW
Tupelo, Mississippi • September 26, 1956

PHOTO: Sept. 1956 by Jimmy Velvet • Used by Permission • © 1980 Elvis Presley Museum, Inc.

From The Forthcoming Multiple Record Package
ELVIS PRESLEY "A GOLDEN CELEBRATION"

RCA

PB-13875

I was the photographer for this rare recording. There were only 20,000 pressed and only sold in Tupelo and only for 1 day. I still have 500 copies. This is the rarest release of Elvis.

What a reunion: Charlie Hodge, Mark James, Jimmy Velvet, Aunt Loraine Smith, Marian Cocke, George Kline, Richard Davis, Eddie Fadel, Alan Fortas, Sam Phillips (seated).

Photo by: Sharon Kalmen

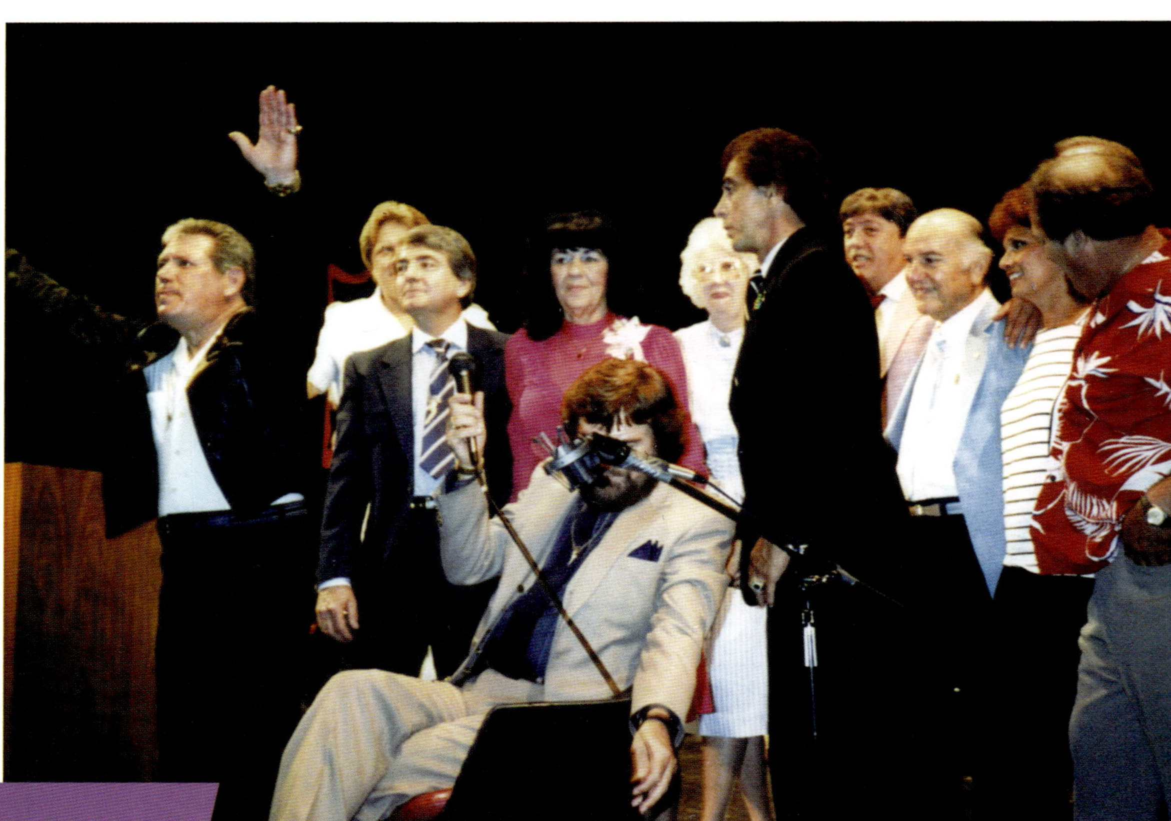

Ed Parker

King of Kenpo Karate
and good friend
Ed Parker

INTERNATIONAL 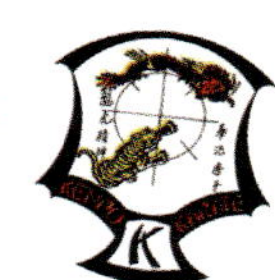 KENPO KARATE ASSOCIATION
1705 E. WALNUT ST. • PASADENA, CALIF. 91106 • (213) 682-2456

November 1, 1985

Mr. Jimmy Velvet
Corporate Headquarters
110 Poplar St.
Franklin, TN. 37064

Dear Jimmy,

Thank you for your check in the amount of $549.24. I still did not receive an answer concerning the decal that Elvis had placed on his guitar which was my Karate logo. I also have another of Elvis's gis (his karate uniform) in a case that might be good to display at one of your traveling museums. On the karate uniform is the patch (or logo) that Elvis used on his guitar. If this may be of interest to you, please write or call me at (213) 682-2456. There are items that could be sold along with the other paraphanelia that you are selling, but it is up to you to decide, Jim. Looking forward to hearing from you at your earliest convenience.

Respectfully,

Ed Parker

Ed Parker
President

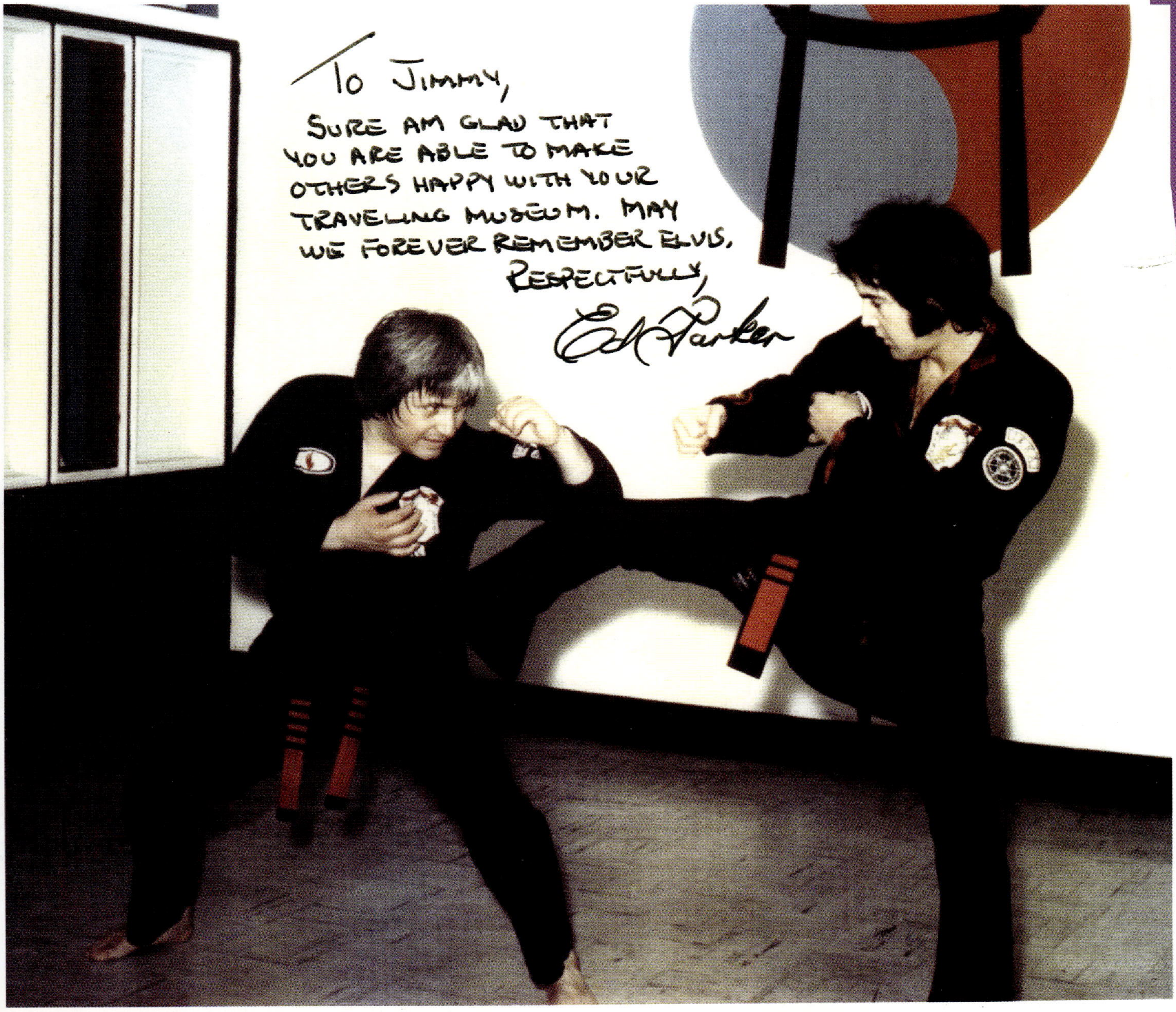

To Jimmy,
Sure am glad that you are able to make others happy with your traveling museum. May we forever remember Elvis,
Respectfully,
Ed Parker

Rick Nelson

Eric Hilliard Nelson
On tour, Reno, Nevada

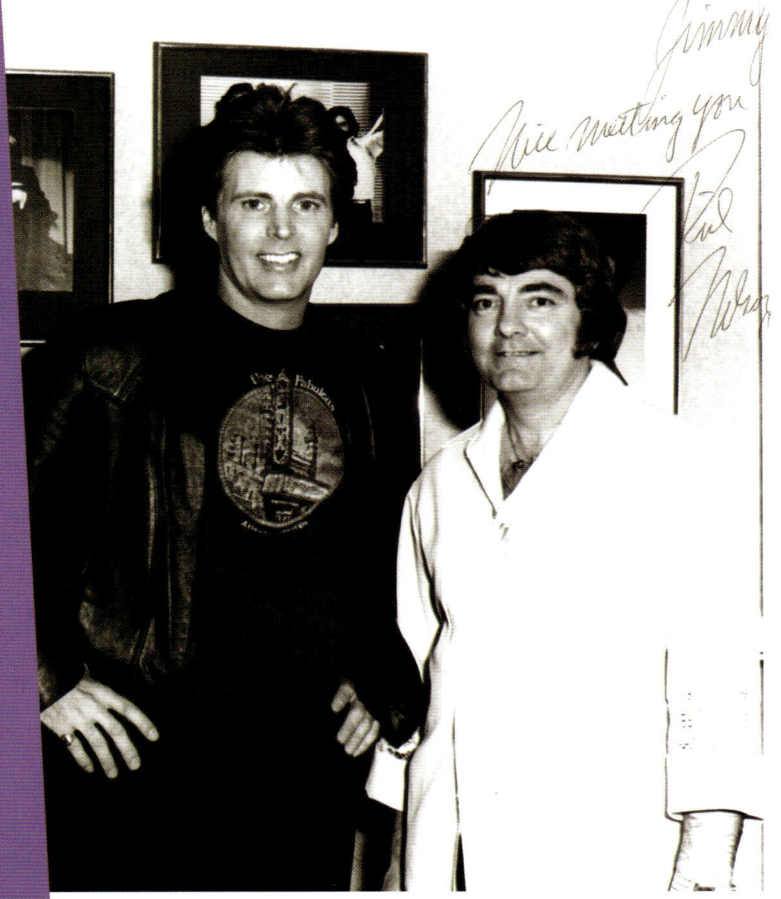

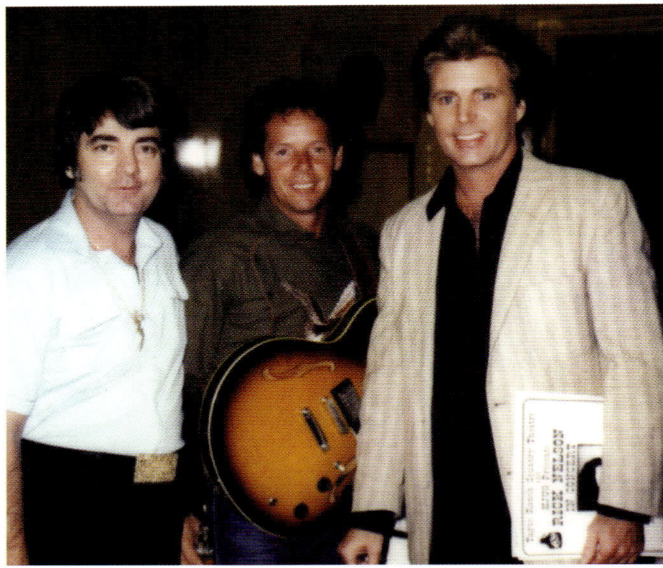

Me with Rick and his guitarist "Pat" we were all great friends.

Rick and Helen

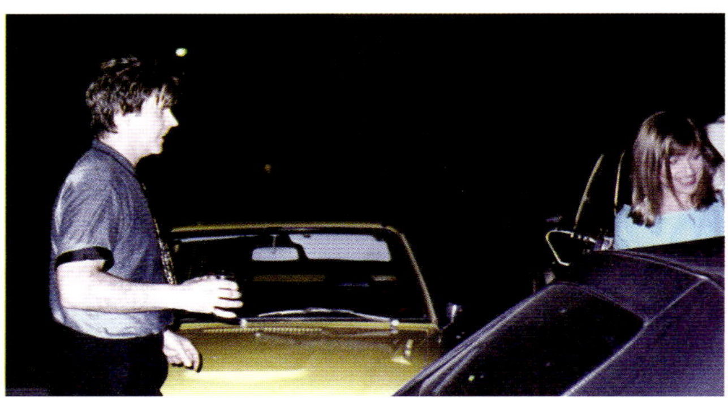

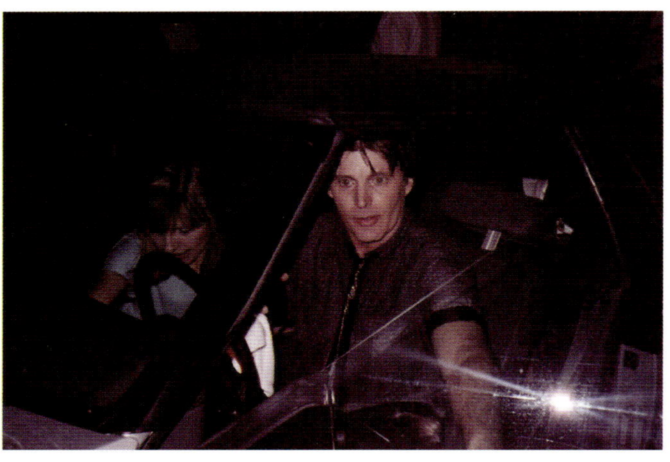

Greg McDonald

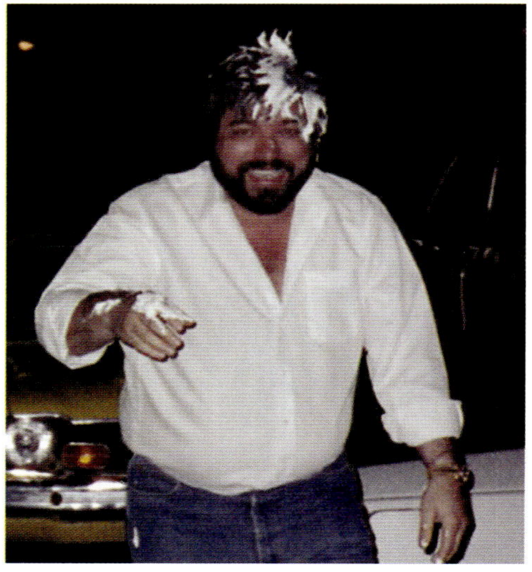

Rick Nelson's Birthday Party

Rick Nelson's birthday party in Orange County. His manager Greg McDonald got the worse mess of whip cream.

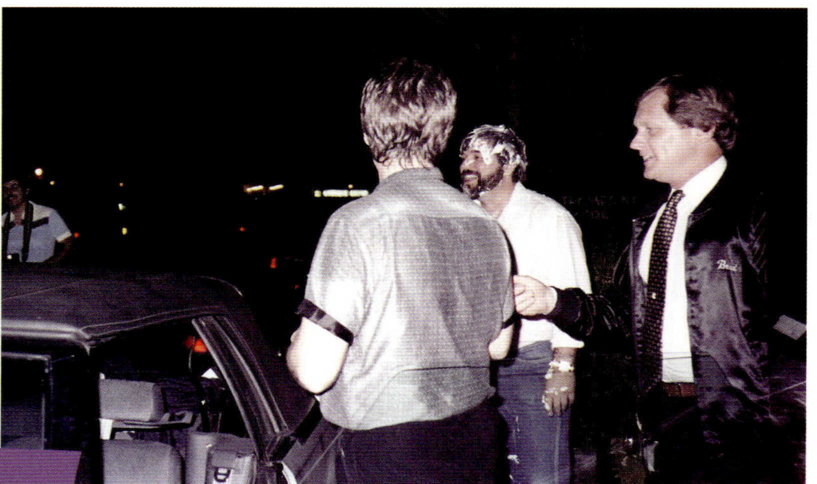

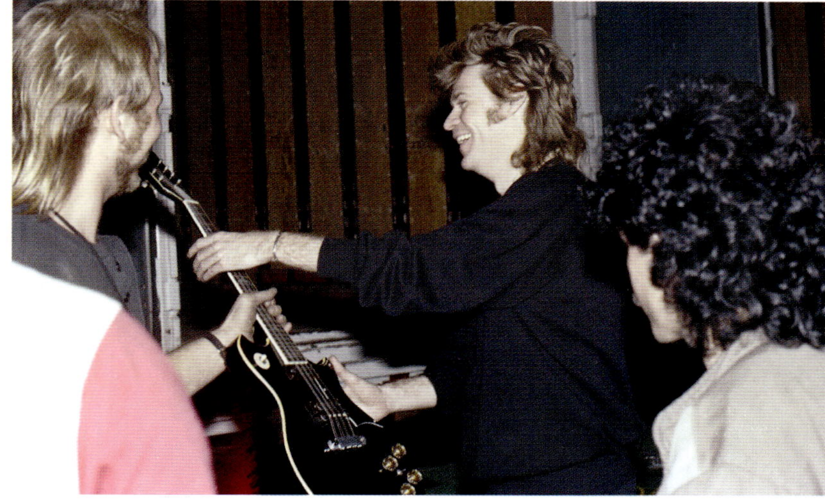

Hall and Oates

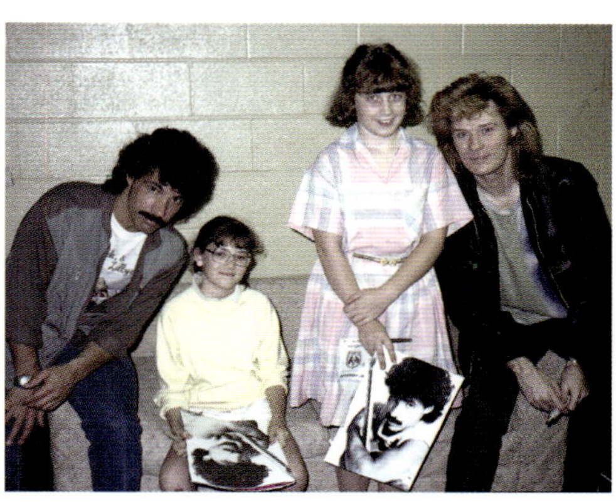

Funny Story...
Fred Smith, owner of Fed Ex was at my show in Memphis and told me that Fed Ex had lost a guitar that belonged to "Whole Oats". They had paid the insurance claim and had now found the guitar so I went to Fred's office the next day and picked it up. Years later, I was in Orlando and "Hall and Oates" were at the convention center, I presented the guitar to Daryl and he jumped with joy "My mando" he said. I photographed the whole thing. 2 years later, I was their guest in Memphis and presented them with Honorary citizen awards Daryl gave me the guitar, his "mando."

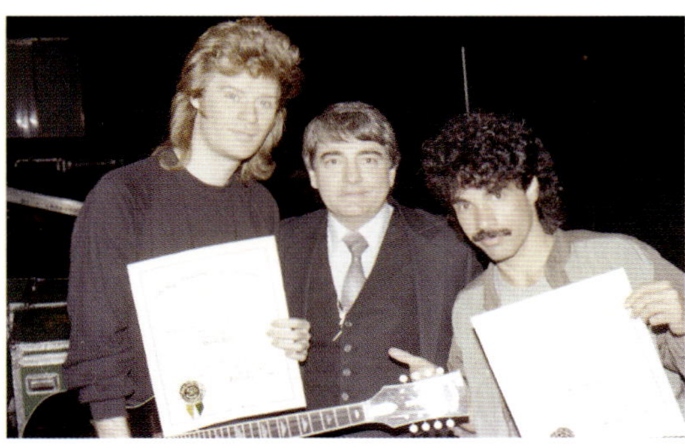

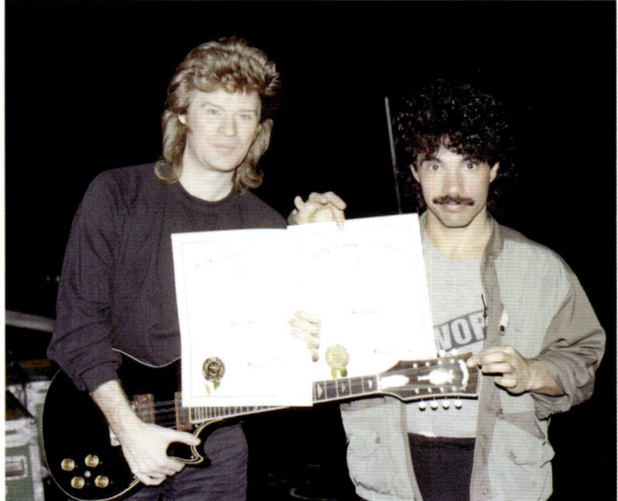

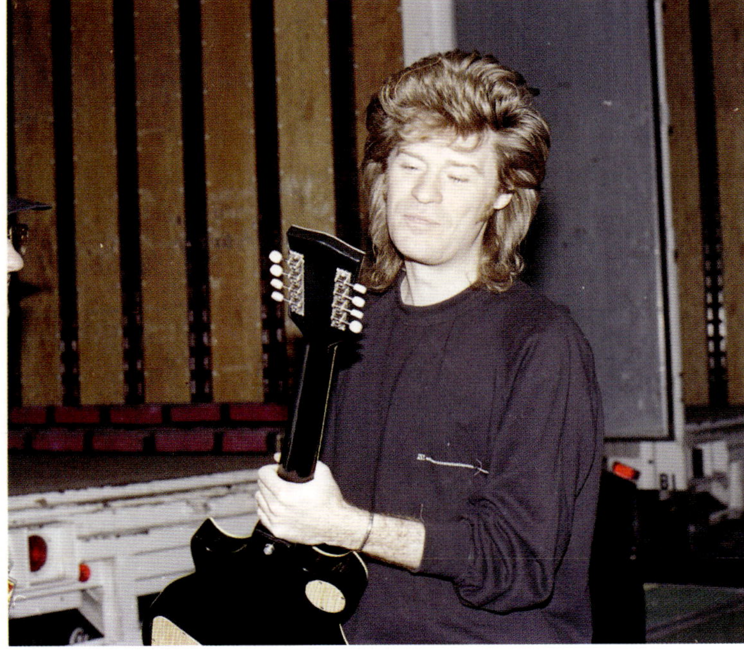

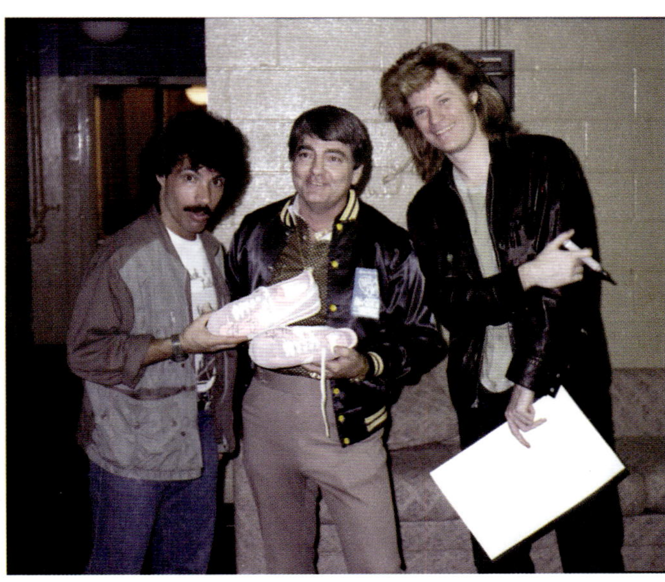

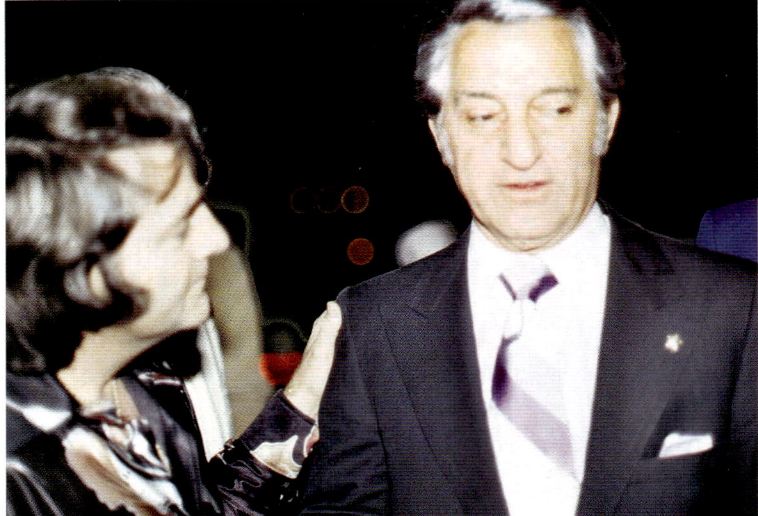

Danny Thomas

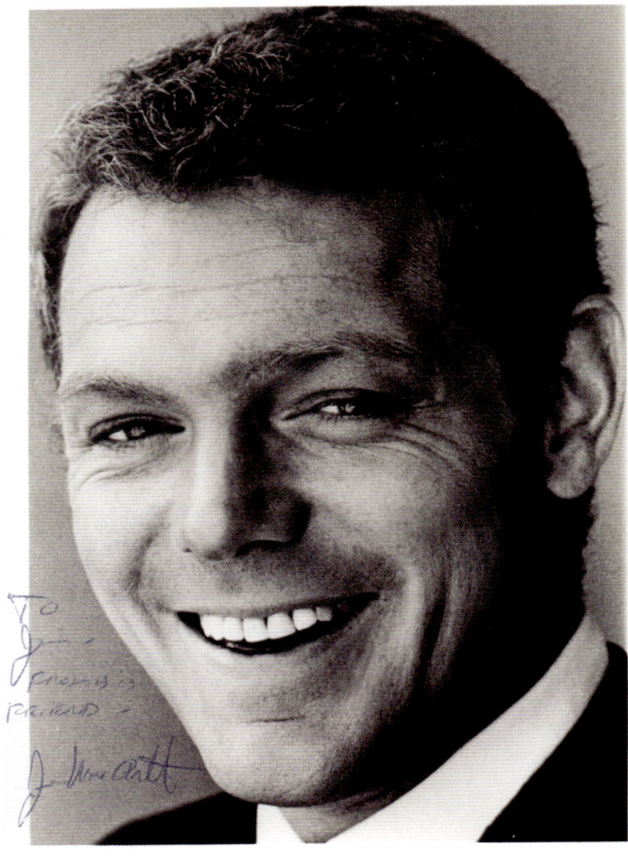

James MacArthur
Son of "Helen Hayes" "Dano" Hawaii 50

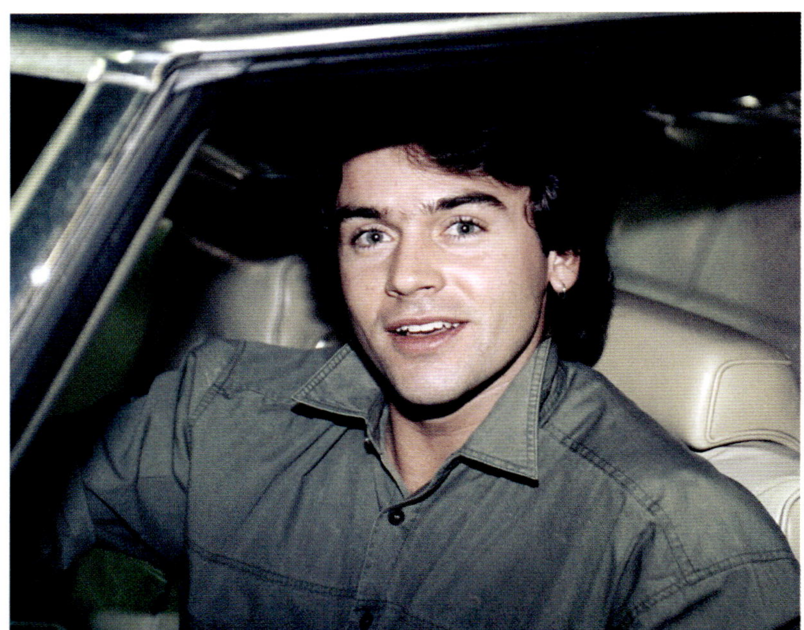

Kurt McKinney
General Hospital

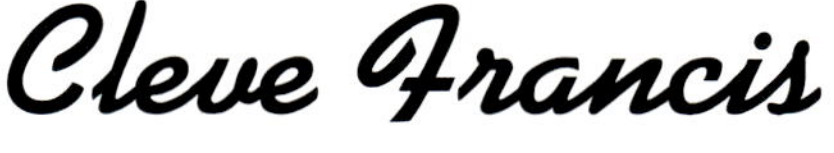

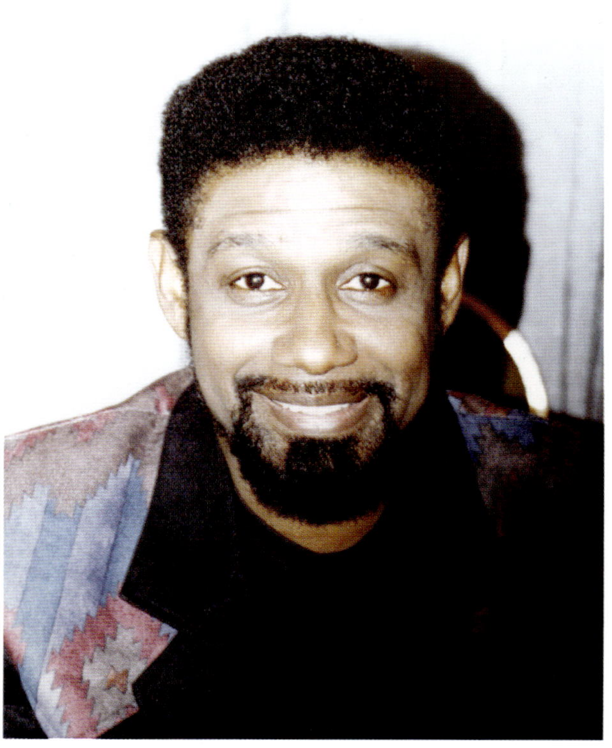

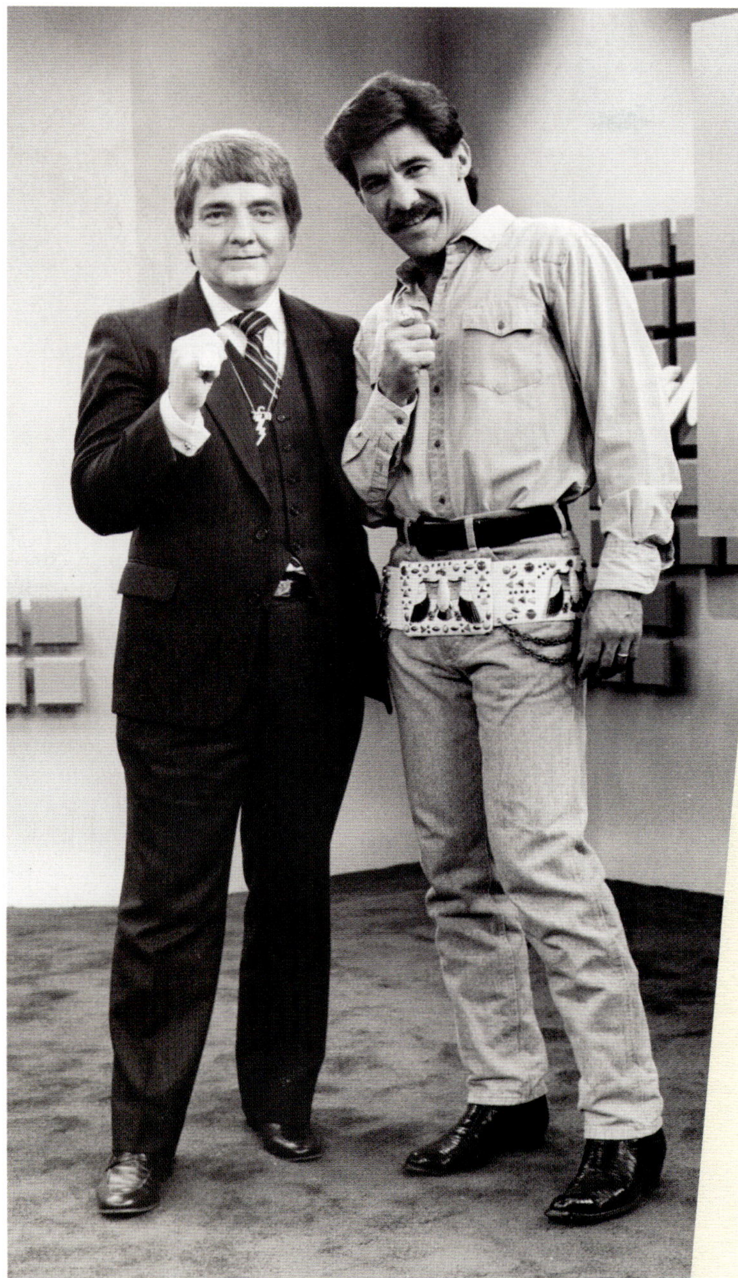

Geraldo

On the Geraldo Show
I'm wearing Elvis' jewlery
Geraldo is wearing Elvis' belt
and jewlery.

THE LIPPIN GROUP

A memo from Marisa Hanania Spitz

December 30, 1987

Jimmy:

Thanks for appearing on "Geraldo!"

As promised, enclosed are photos
from the show.

Best,

Marisa Hanania

MH/mg

enc.

501 Madison Avenue, 23rd Floor, New York, New York 10022
(212) 838-6140
8124 West Third Street, Los Angeles, California 90048
(213) 653-5910

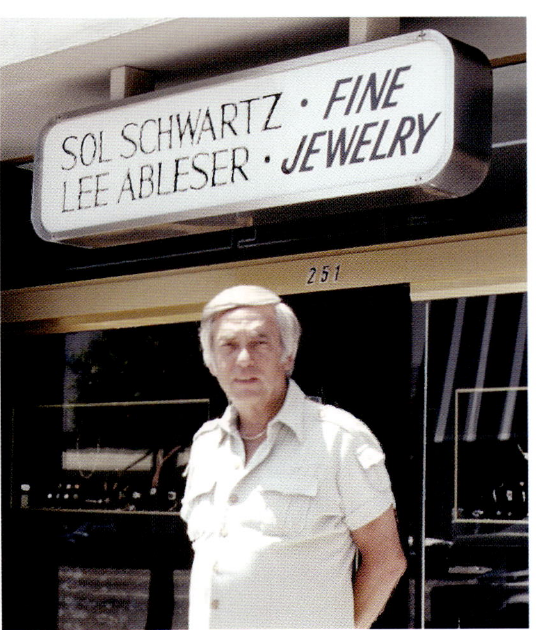

Sol Schwartz

Elvis' jeweler in Beverly Hills.
What a guy. We all love him
and Lee Ableser his partner.

Bert Parks

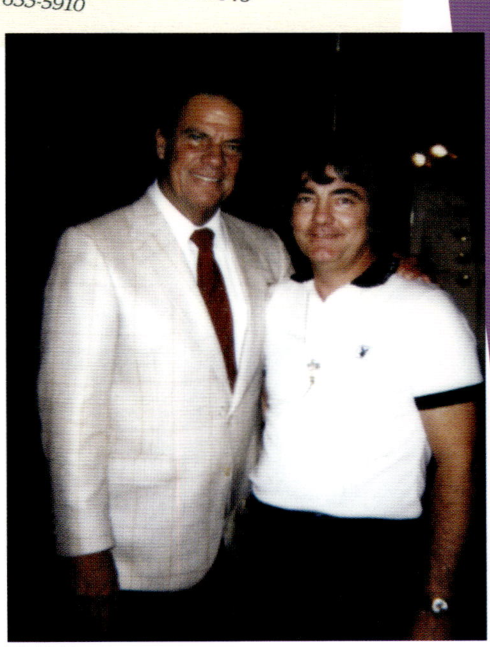

Pete Best

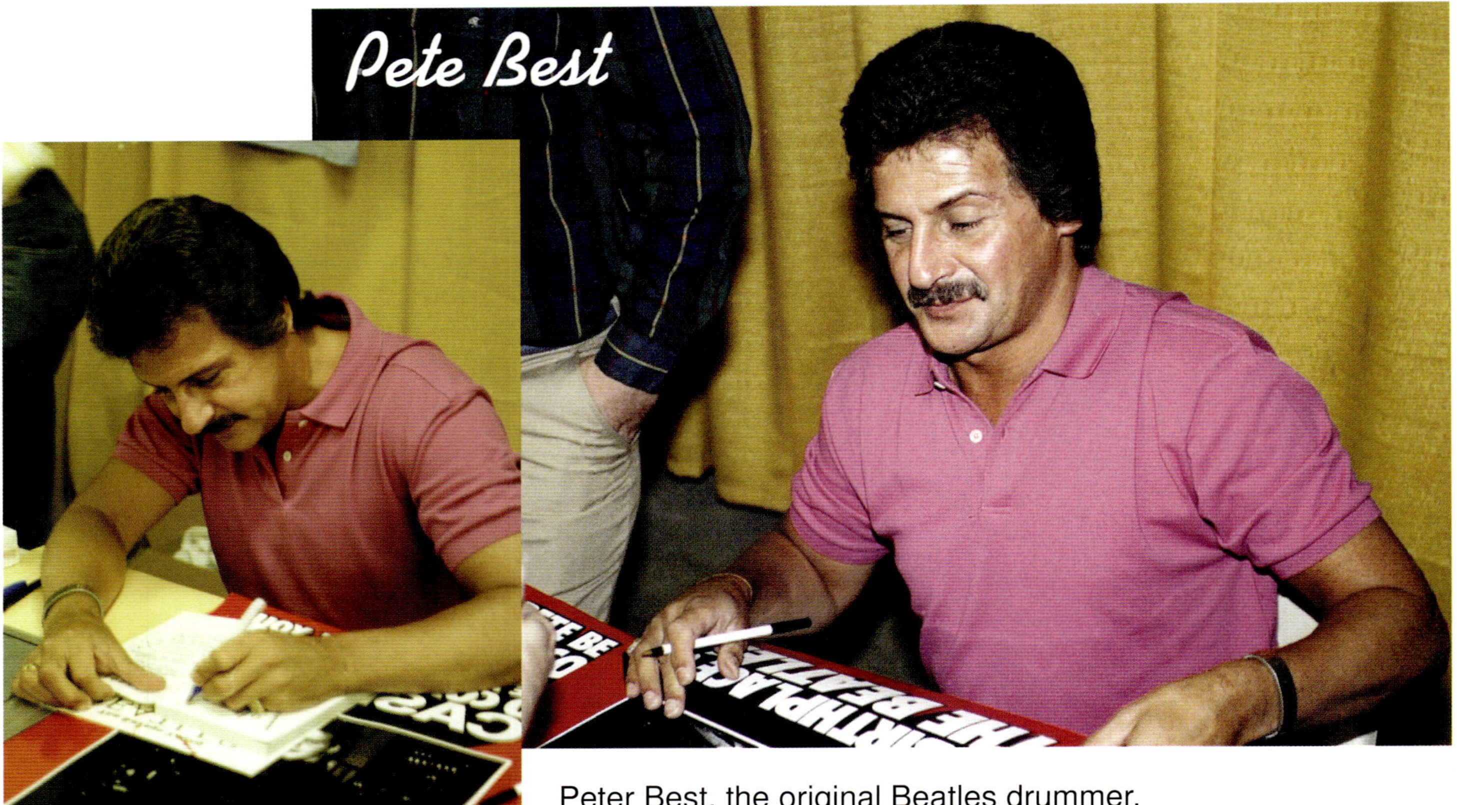

Peter Best, the original Beatles drummer.
Joined the Beatles in 1959.

Hank Ballard

The Midnighters

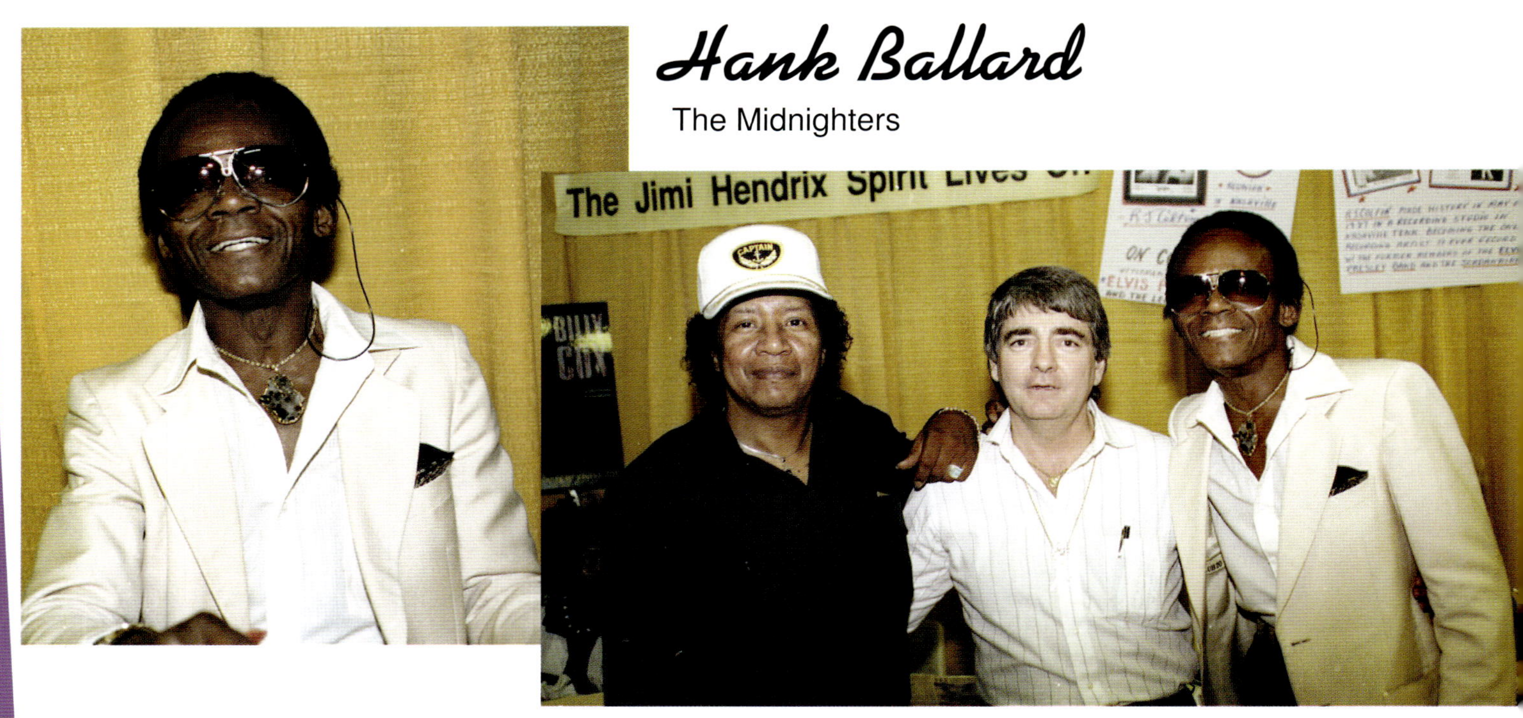

Ace Canon

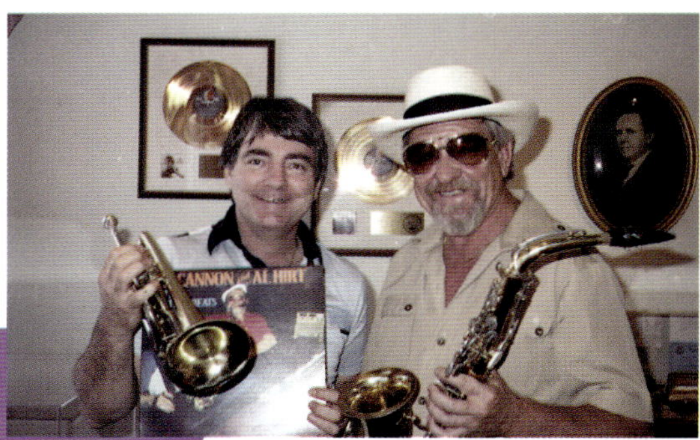

Linda Thompson and Bruce Jenner

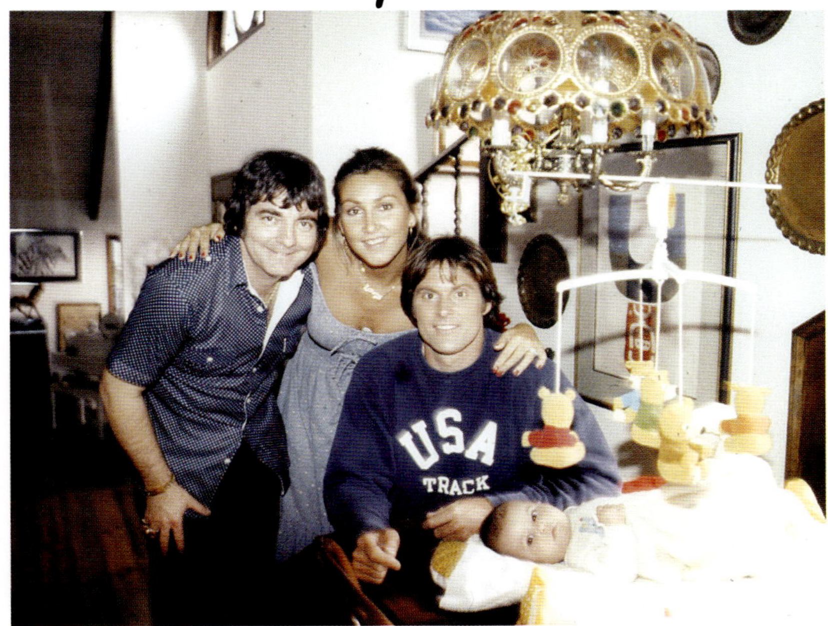

My special friend Linda Thompson Jenner and Bruce Jenner with baby Brandon at their Malibu home. Everyone always loved Linda, what a joy.

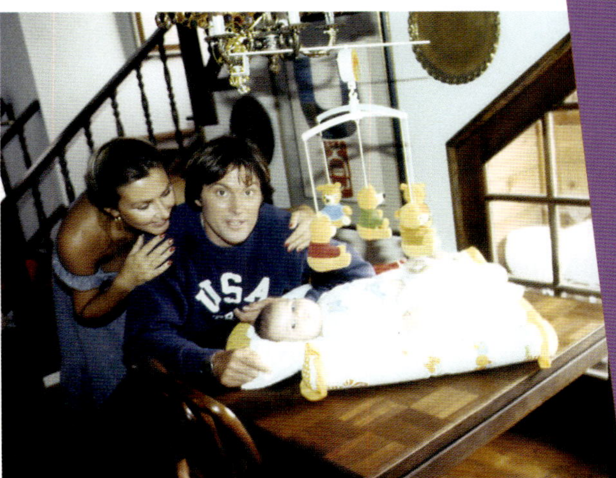

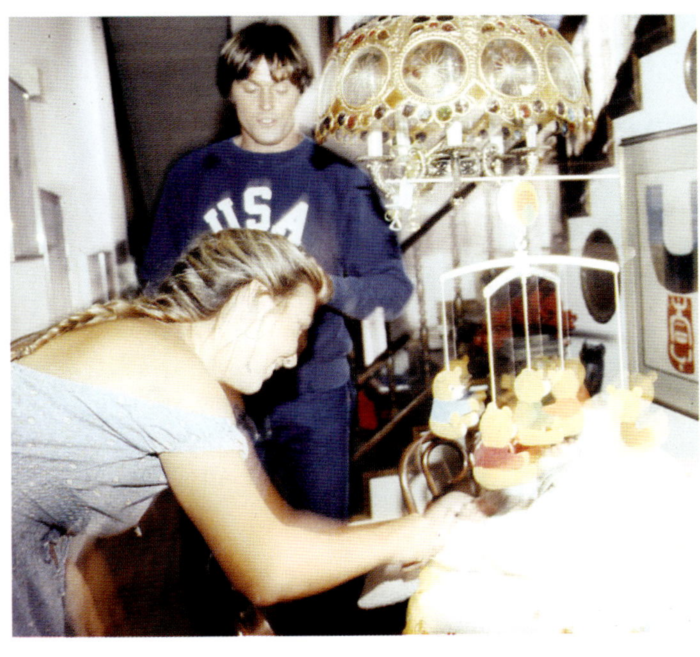

1972 Miss Tennessee, Linda wrote hit songs like "No Explanation" for the movie "Pretty Woman", nominated for Best Song Academy Award and Grammy for "I Have Nothing" Whitney Houston in the 1992 film "Bodygaurd." She cowrote with David Foster "The Flower of 'The Dream" official song of the 1996 Olympics.

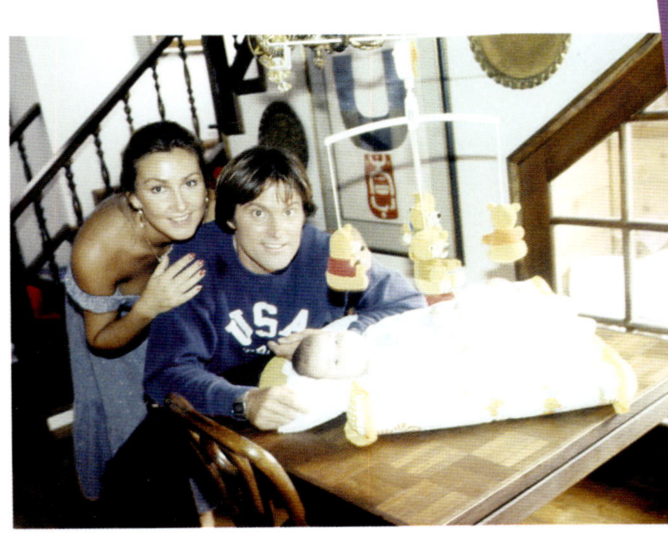

Jan and Dean

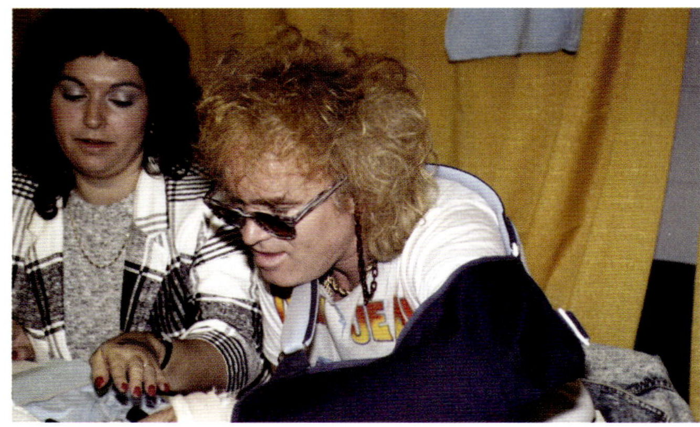

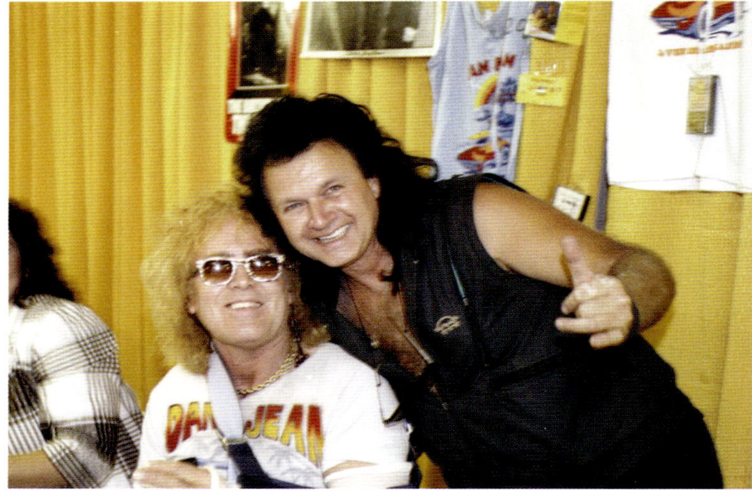

Dick and Jan Berry

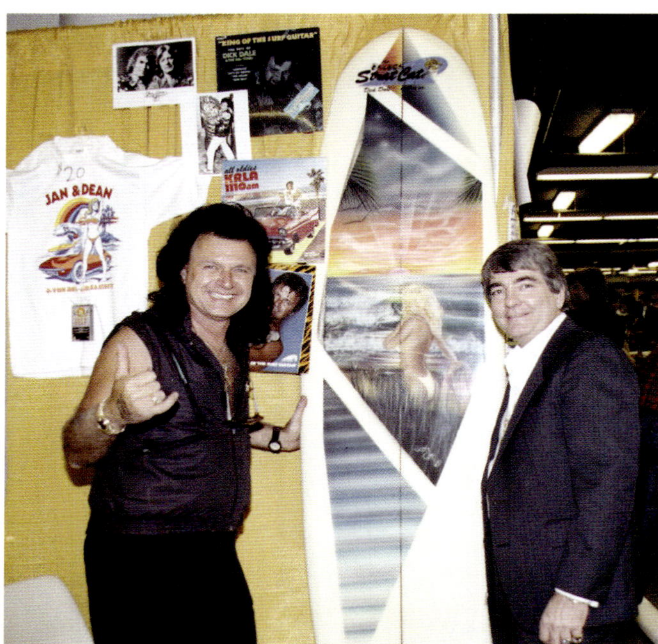

Dick Dale the King of the Surf Guitar

Dick Dale

Richard Anthony Monsour

When I first moved to Hollywood in 1957, I met Dick Dale and his family. The Monsours. They put me up for a while at their home at 11125 So. Wilton Pl. and his dad even helped me with my first professional photo.

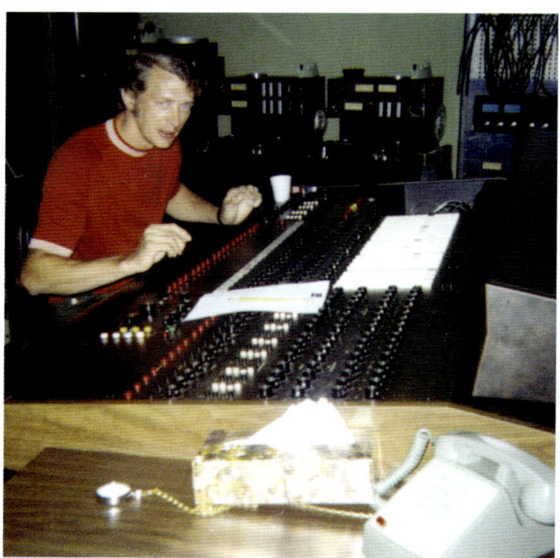

Jimmy Velvet's American Studios

Nigel Olsson

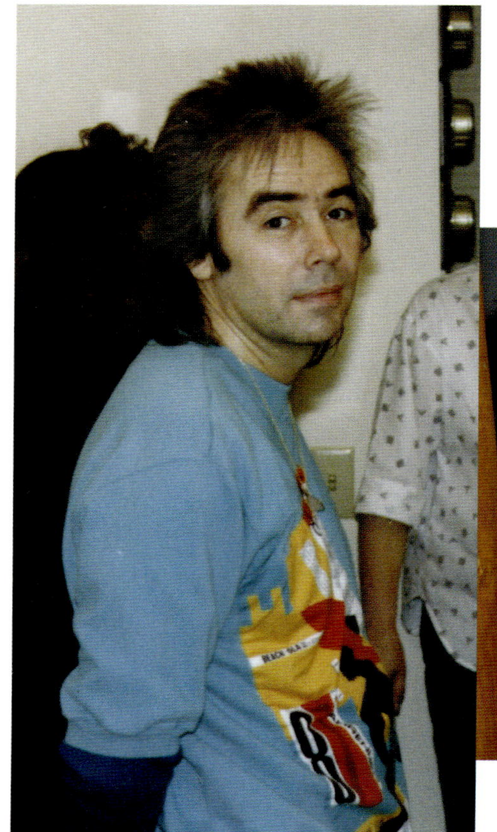

My nephew and Elton's drummer.

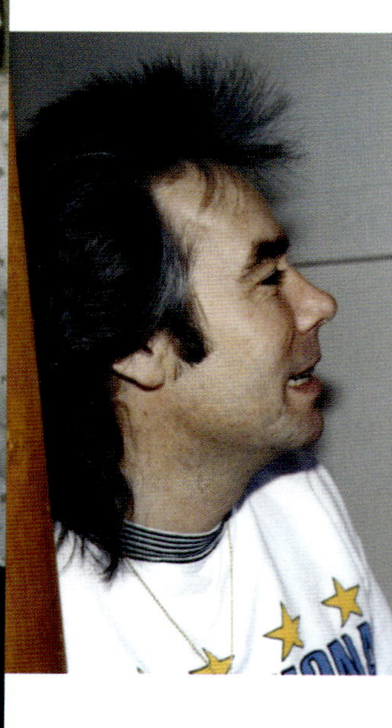

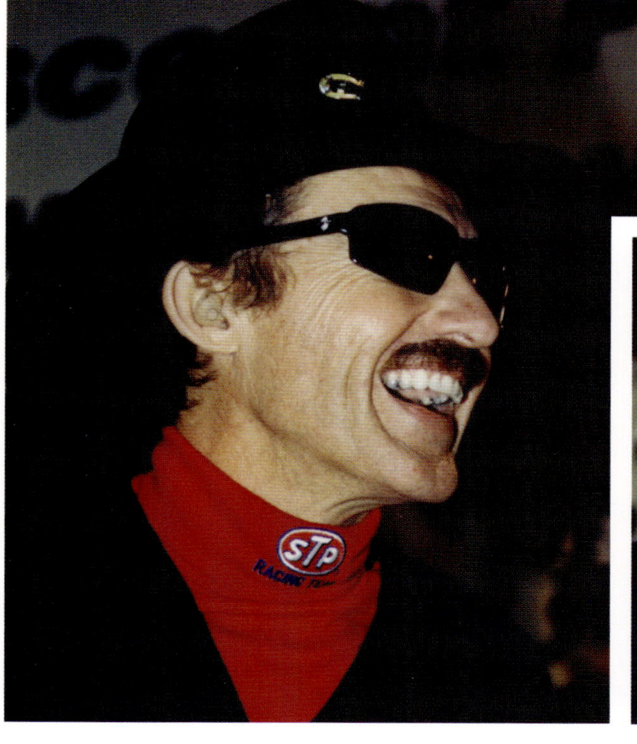

Richard Petty

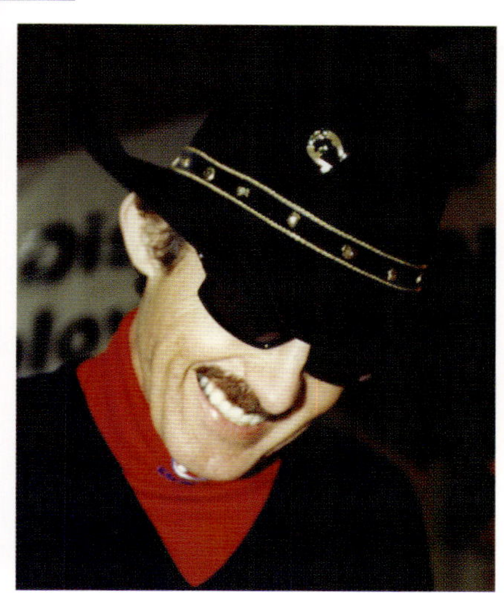

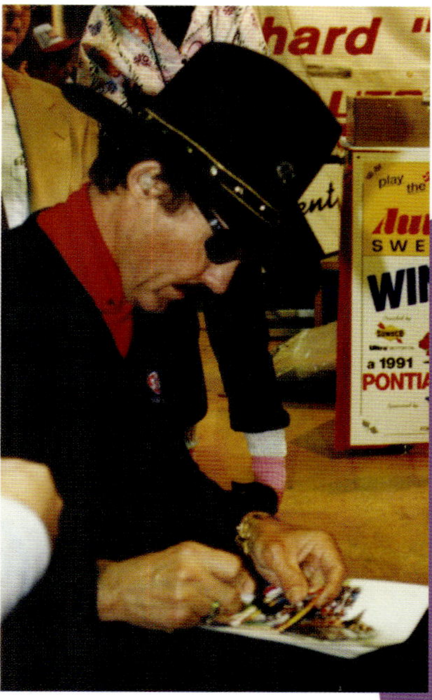

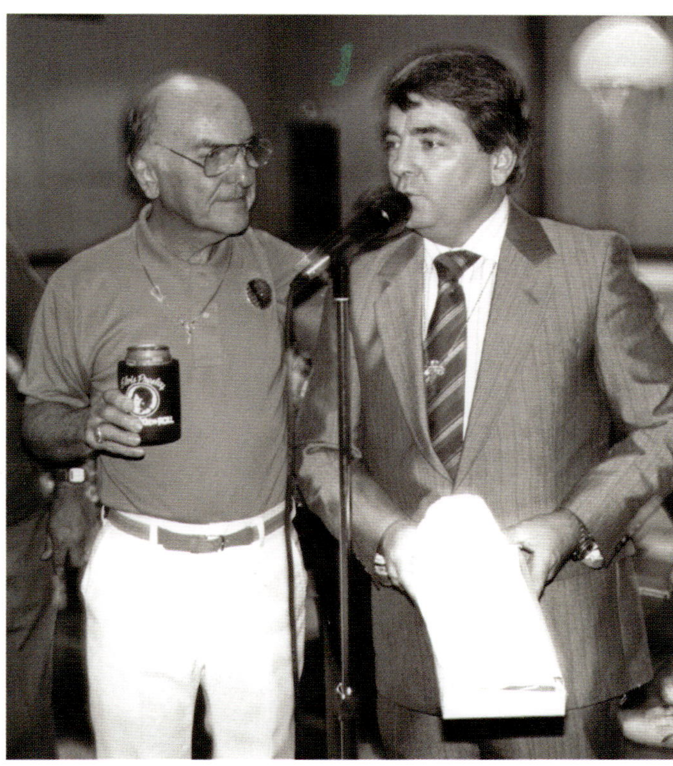

Eddie Fadel

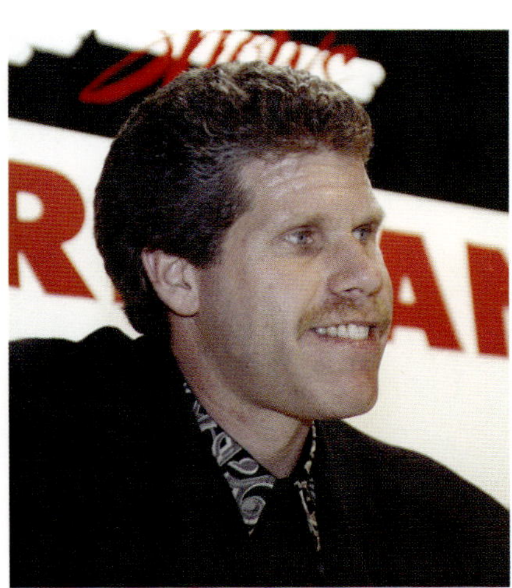

Ron Perlman

Beauty and the Beast, "Vincent"

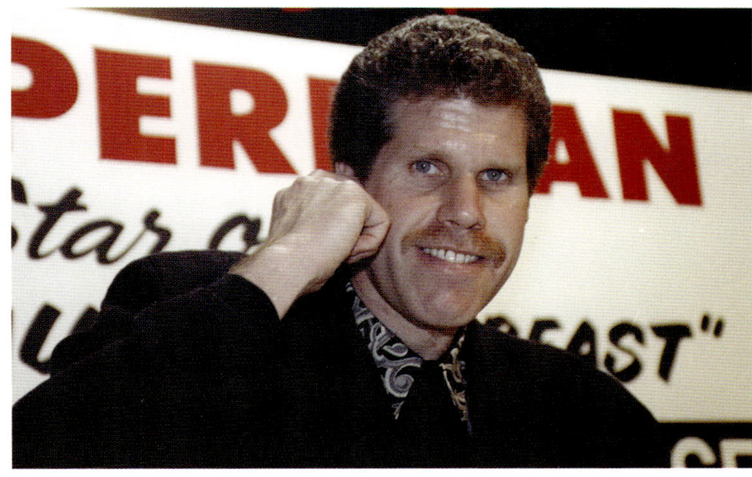

Walt Cunningham

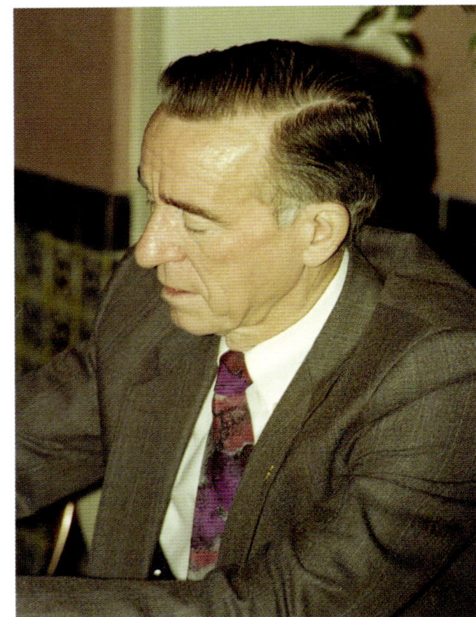

Ronnie Walt Cunningham
Apollo 7 October 11, 1968

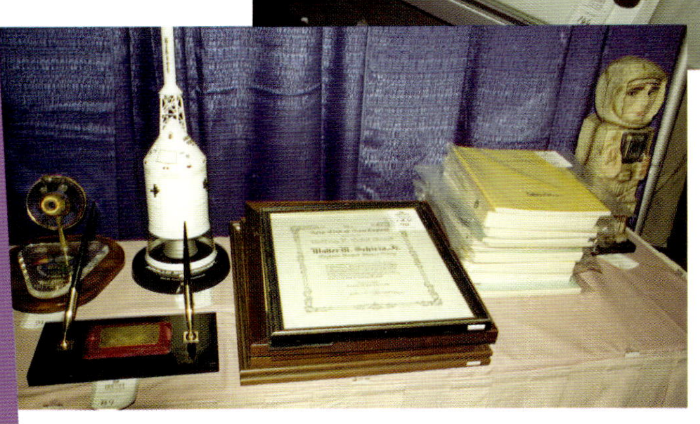

Pete Conrad

Charles "Pete" Conrad

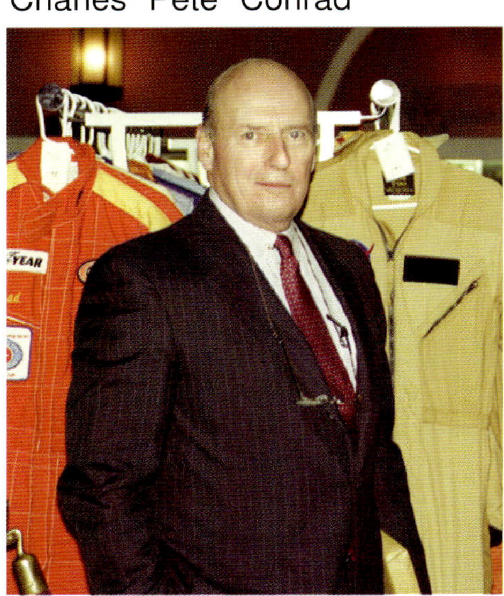

Col. Charles "Pete" Conrad was 3rd man to walk on the moon. Apollo 12 U.S. Astronauts Pete Conrad of Gemini 5 and II, Apollo 12 and Skylab 2.

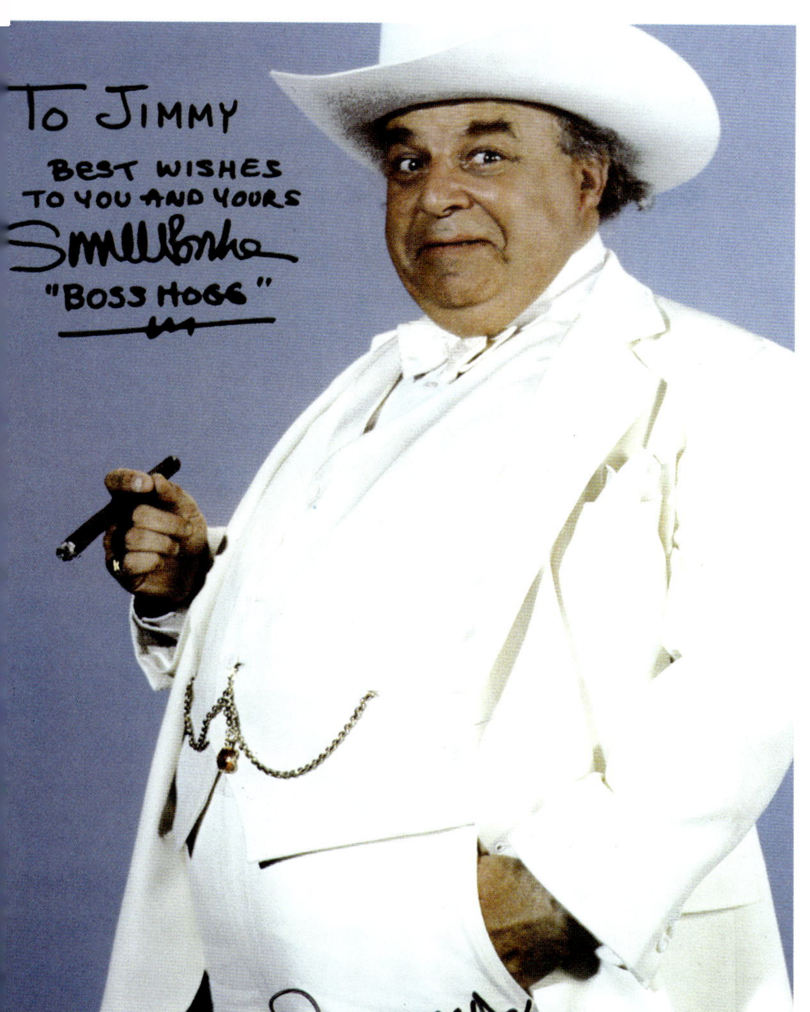

Sorrell Booke

"Boss Hogg" on The Dukes of Hazzard

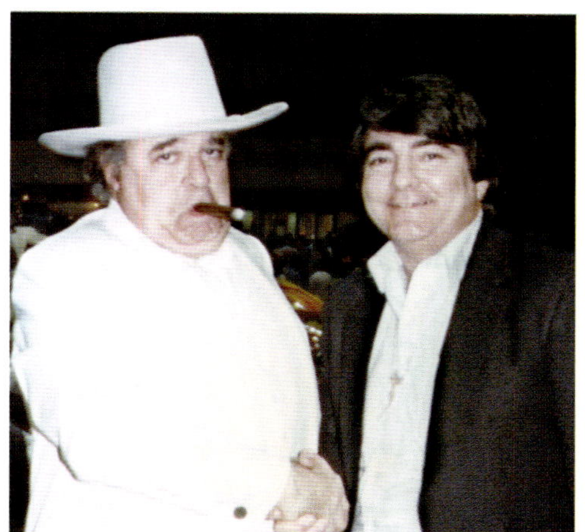

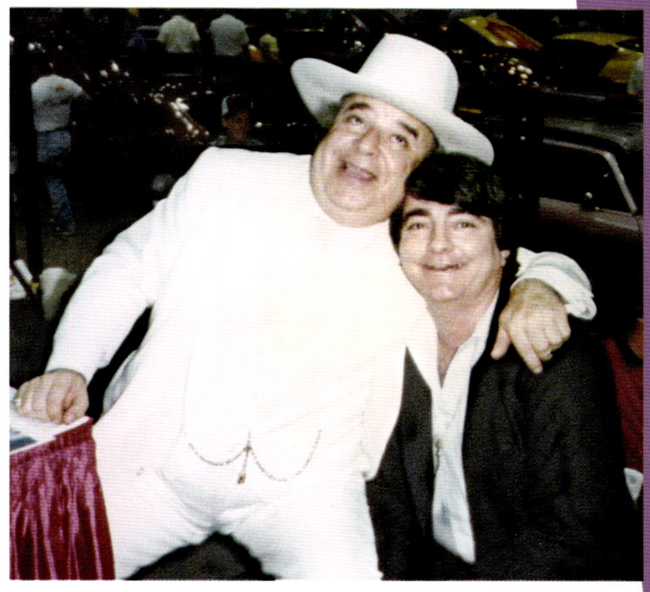

Otis Blackwell

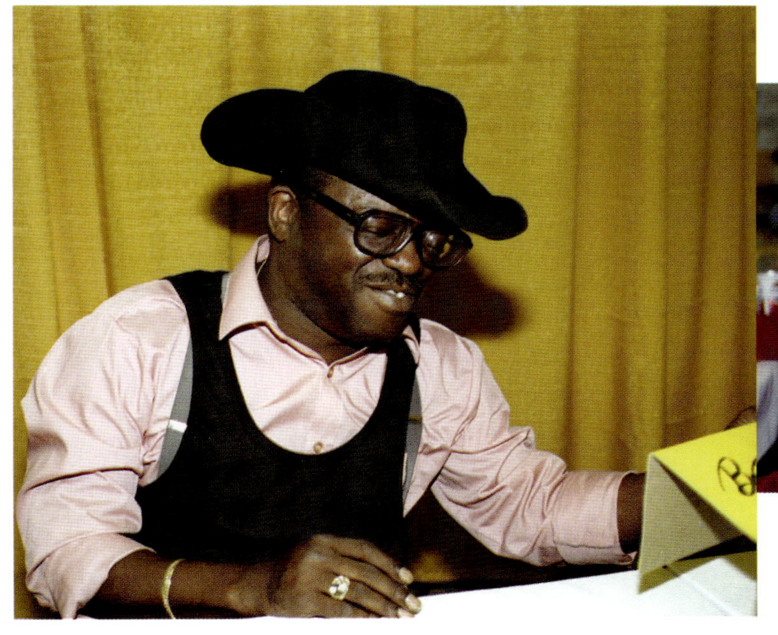

Otis wrote "Don't Be Cruel," "Fever," "Great Balls of Fire," "Breathless," "Handy Man," "Hey Little Girl." I miss him.

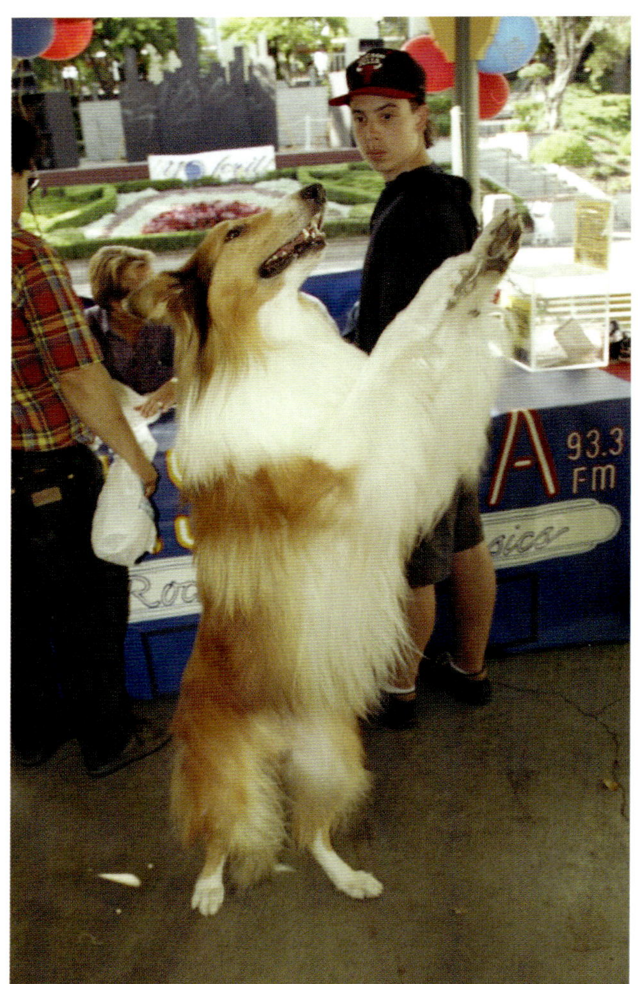

Lassie

"Lassie" My favorite star. I love him. Bob Weatherwax promised me a puppy. I'm waiting Bob.

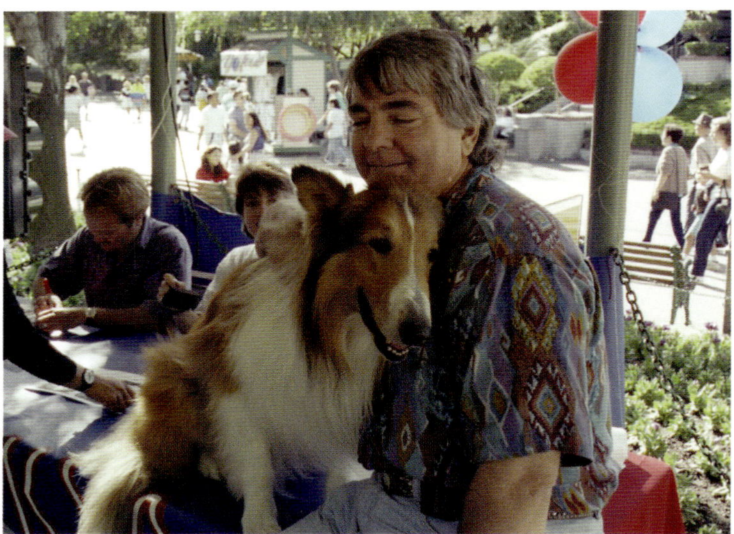

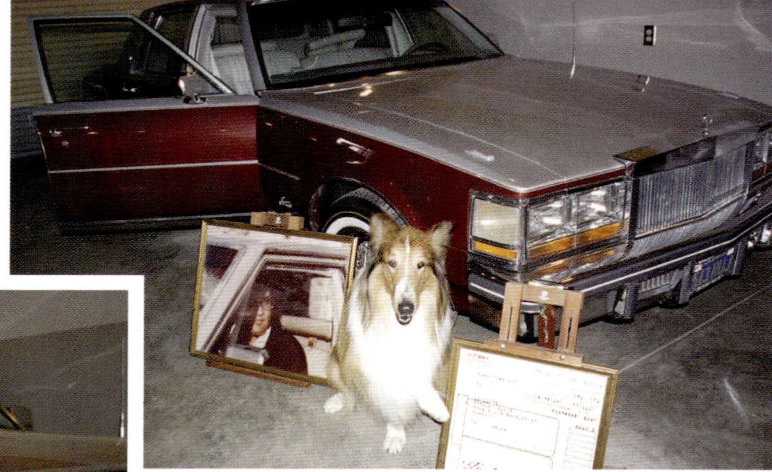

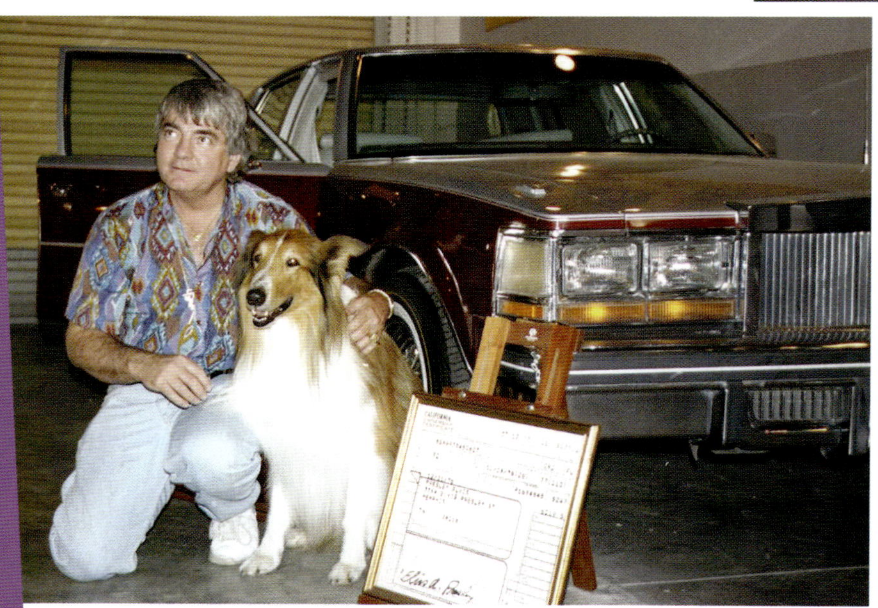

John Provost

Timmy on later Lassie shows.

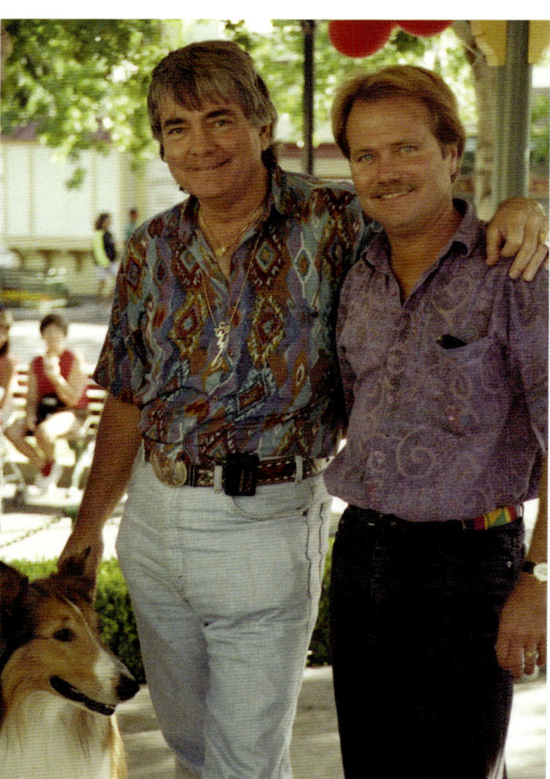

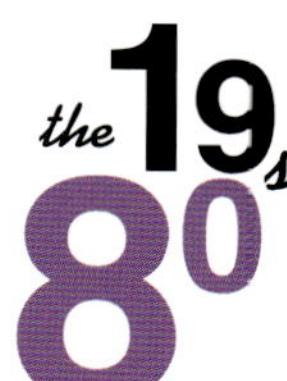

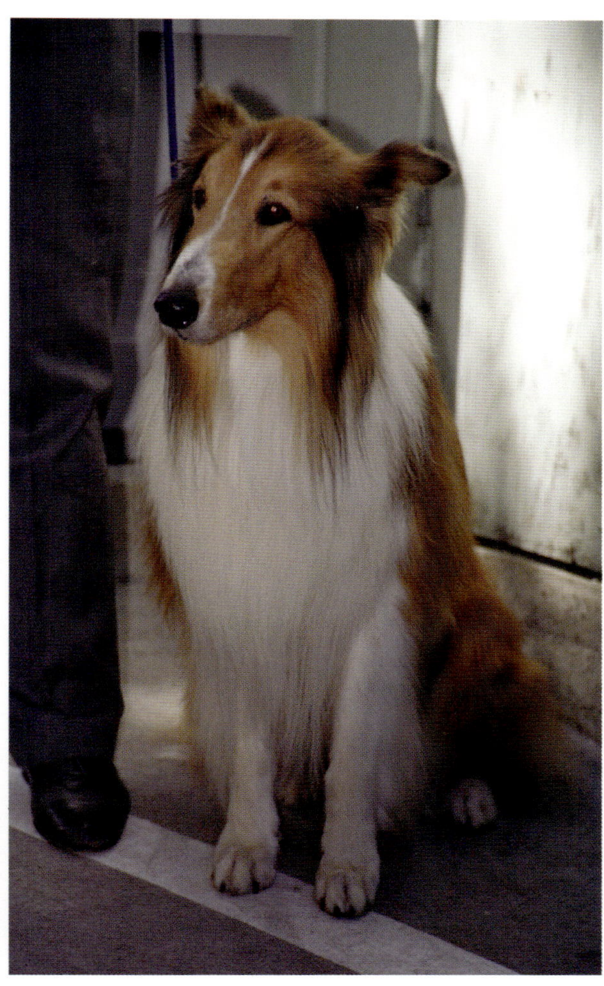

Trainer **Bob Weatherwax**

The small dog is "Mel Gibson."

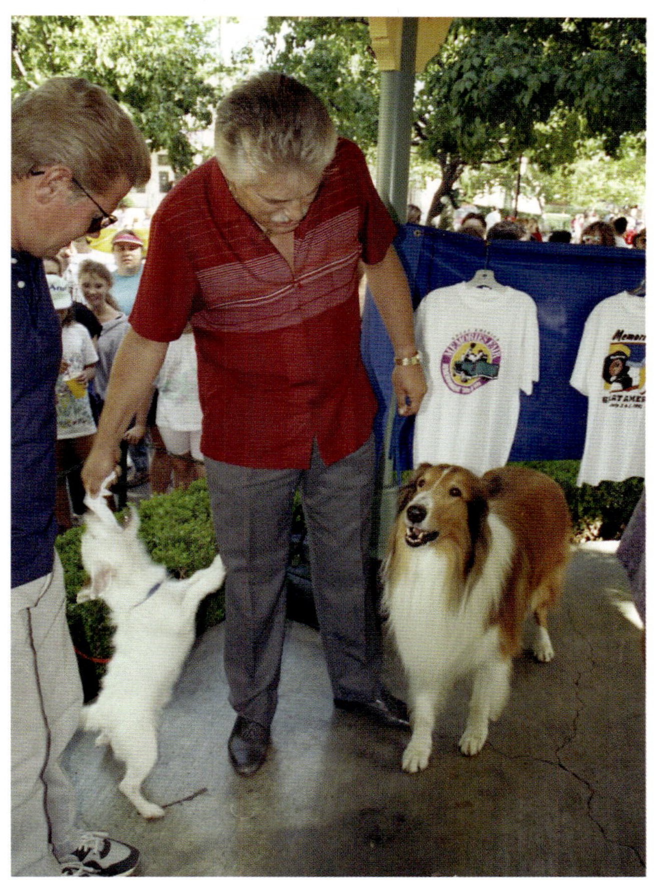

Lassie in Elvis' last Cadillac

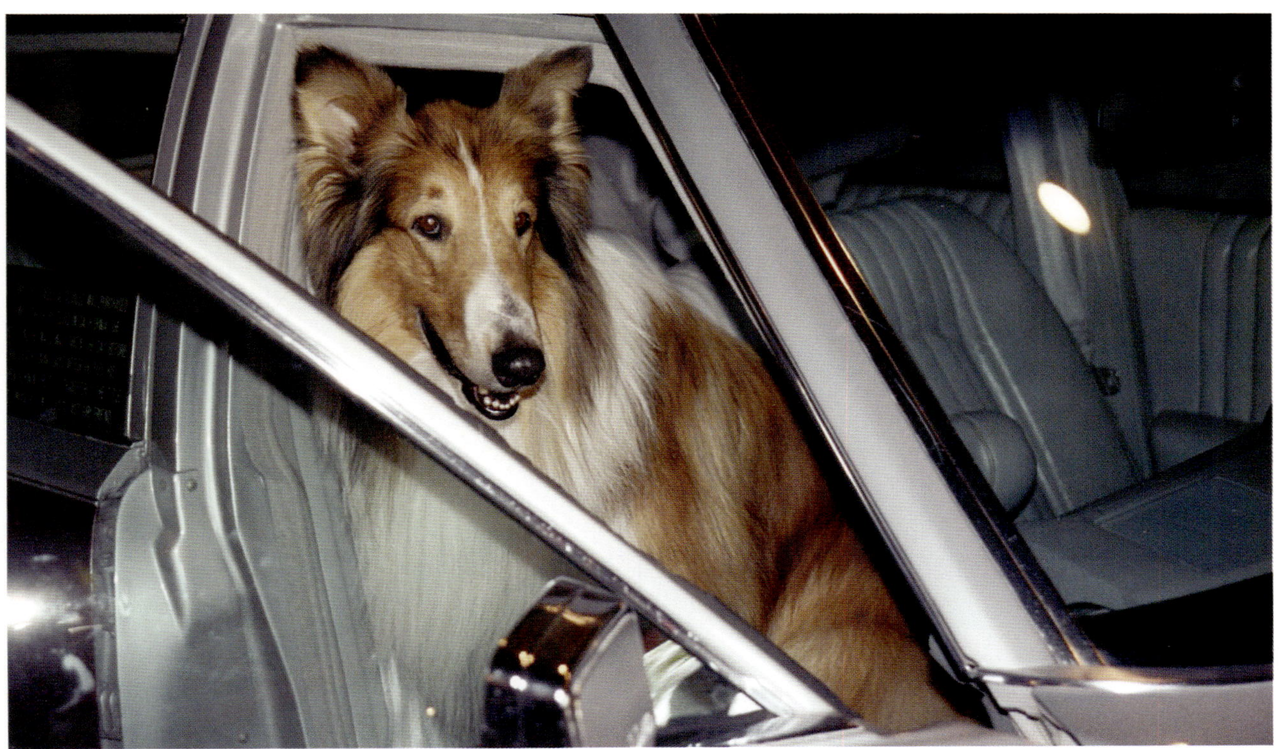

Jon Bon Jovi

Bobby Blotzer
of Ratt

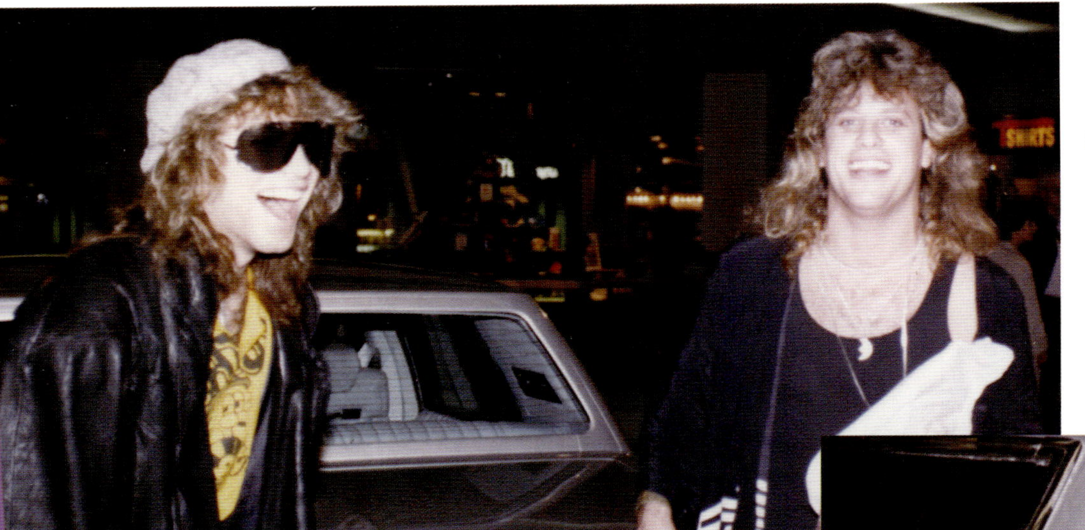

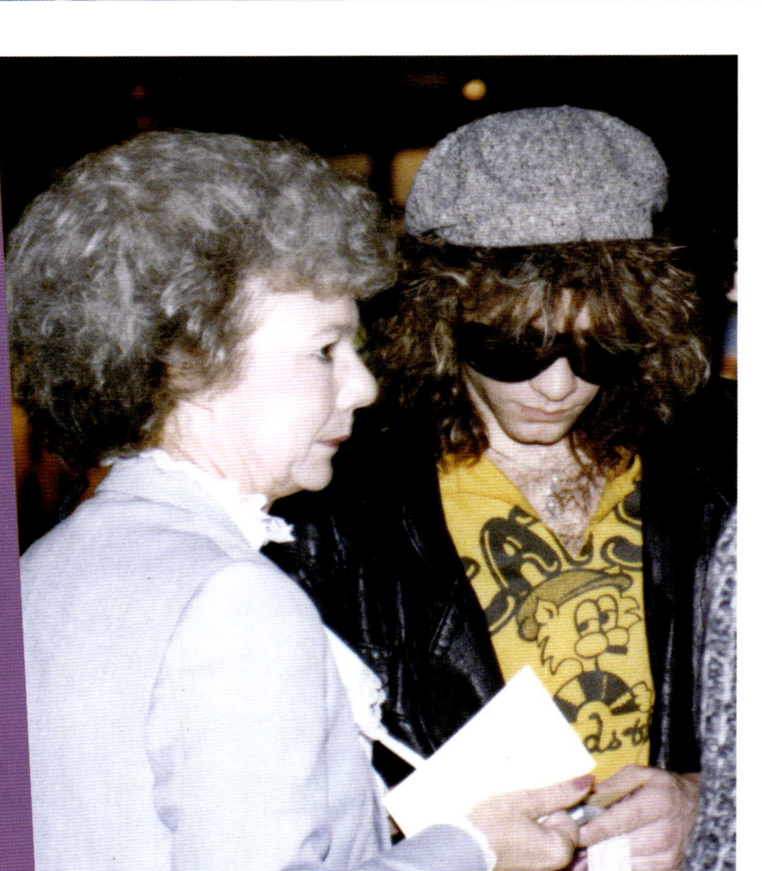

Wilma Wooten and Jon Bon Jovi

Bobby Blotzer in Elvis' last Cadillac

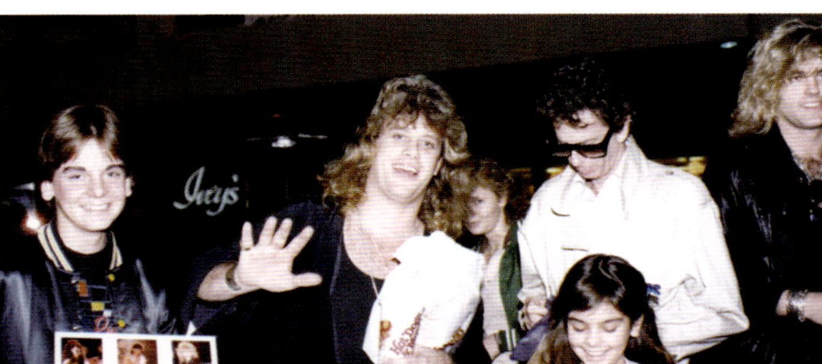

Scott, Bobby, Candida, and Robin Crosby

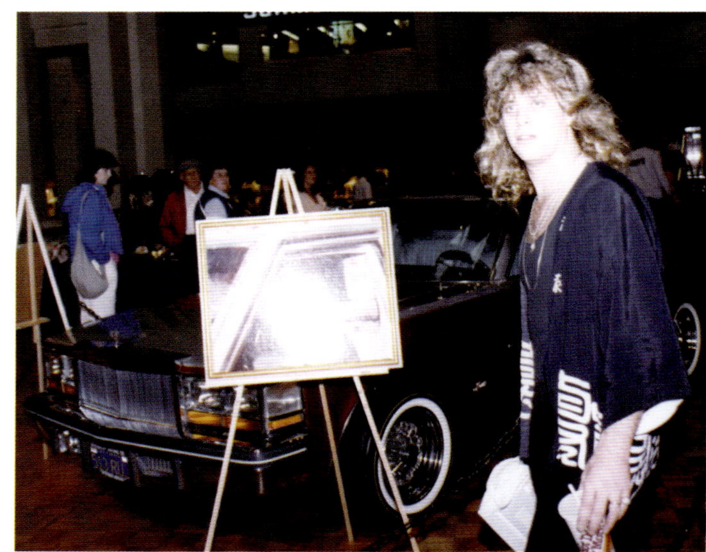

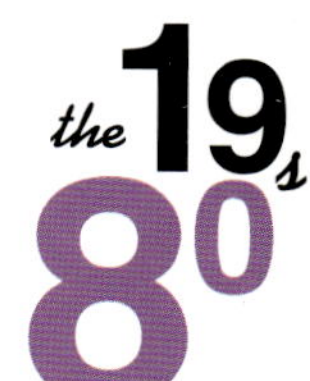

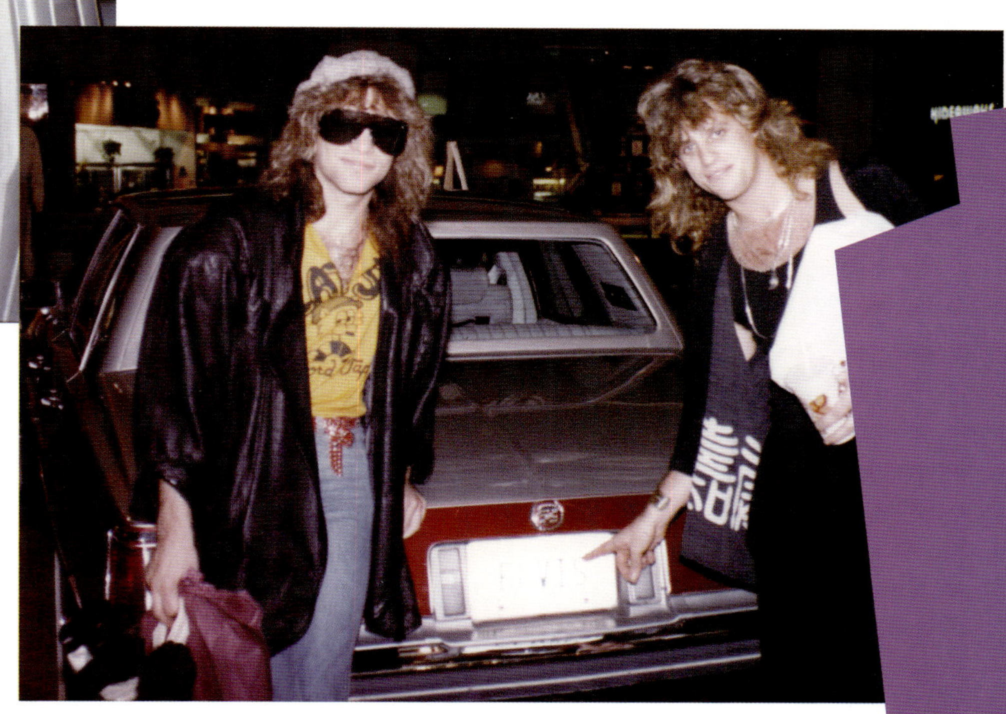

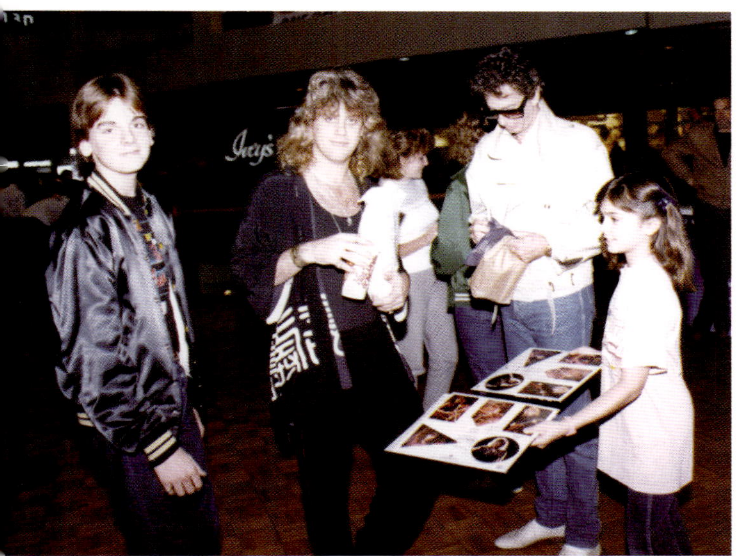

Scotty, Bobby, and Candida

Scott and Candida with

Robin Crosby

of Ratt

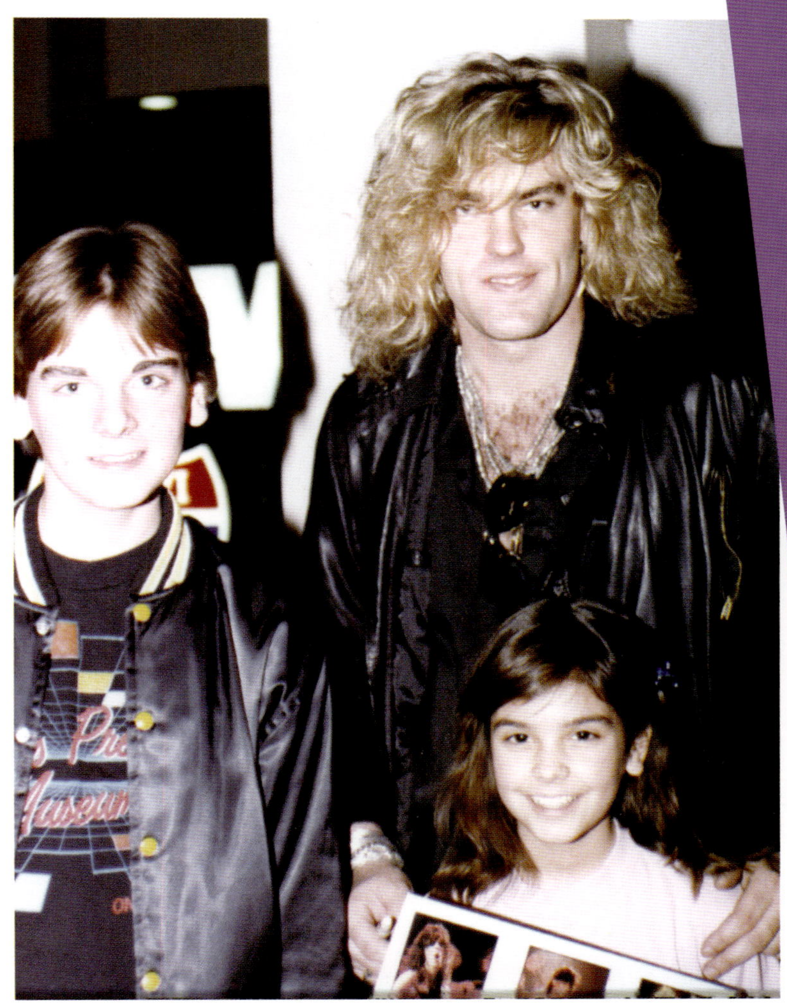

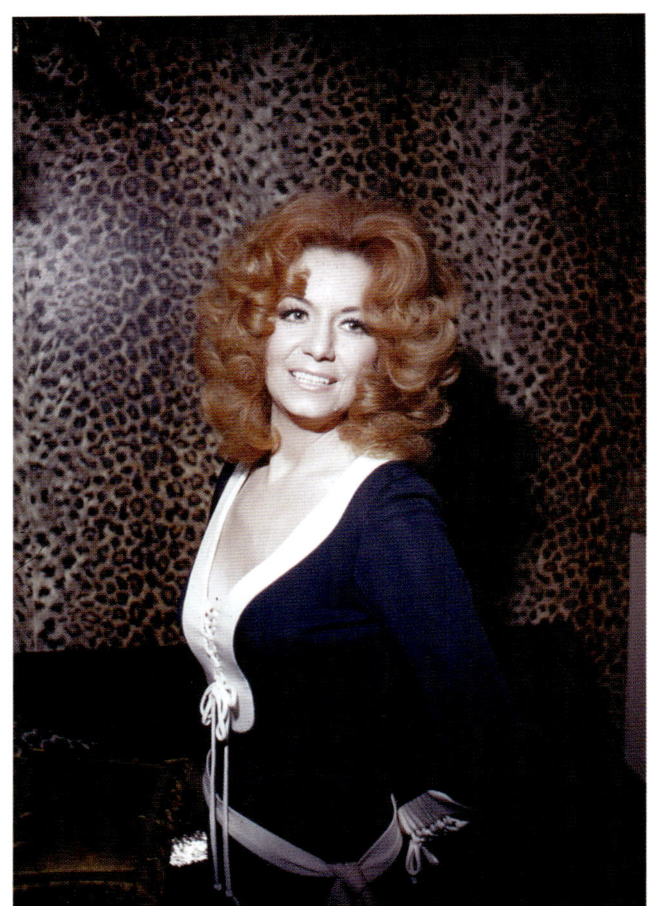

Dottie West

"Country Sunshine"

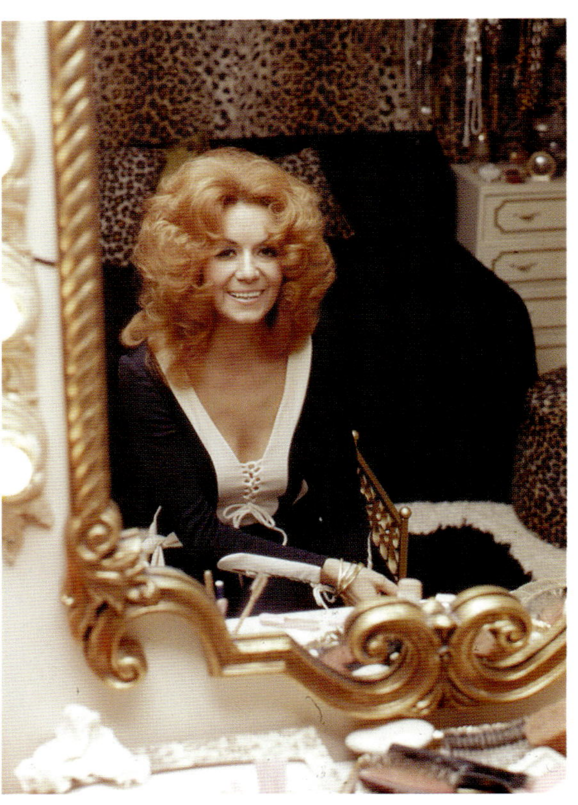

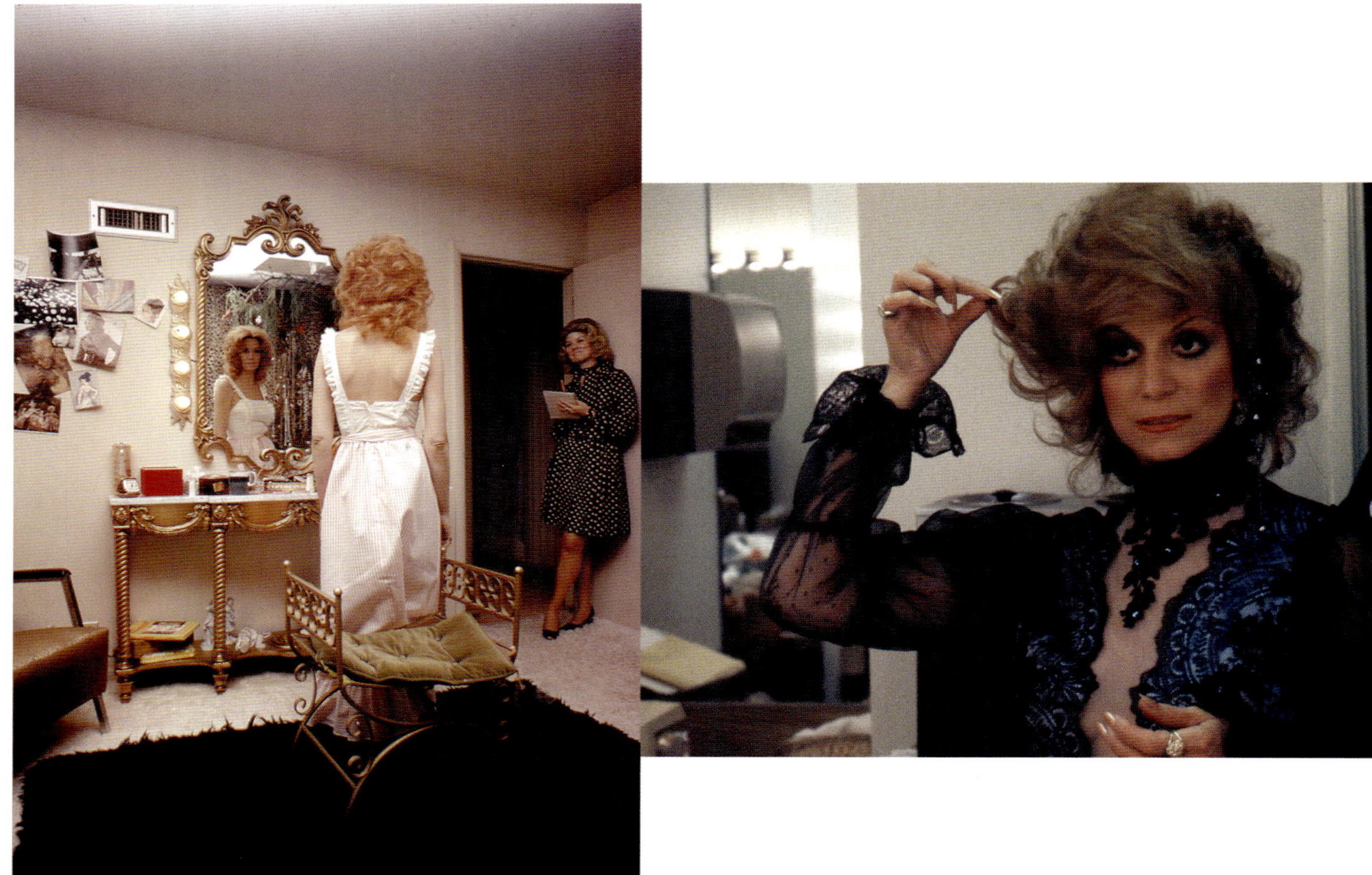

Barbara Mandrell

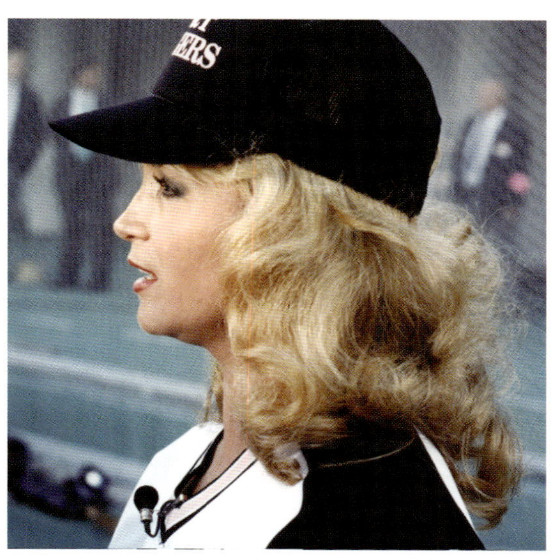

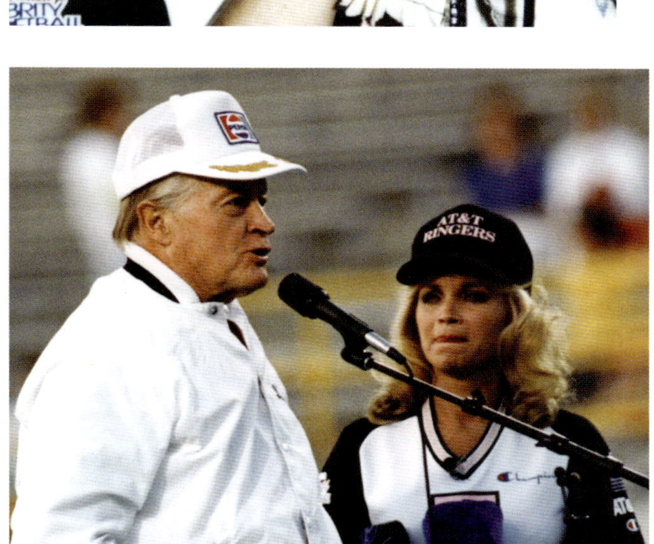

Bob Hope and Barbara Mandrell

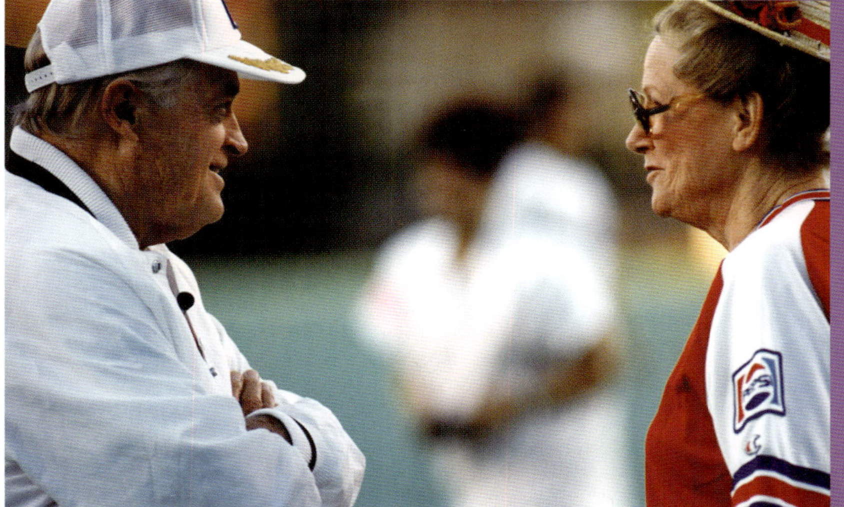

Bob Hope & Minnie Pearl

Lynn Swann

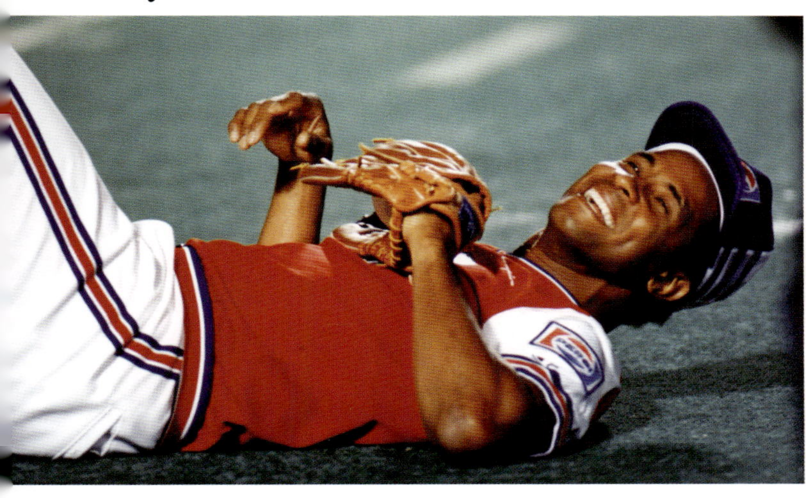

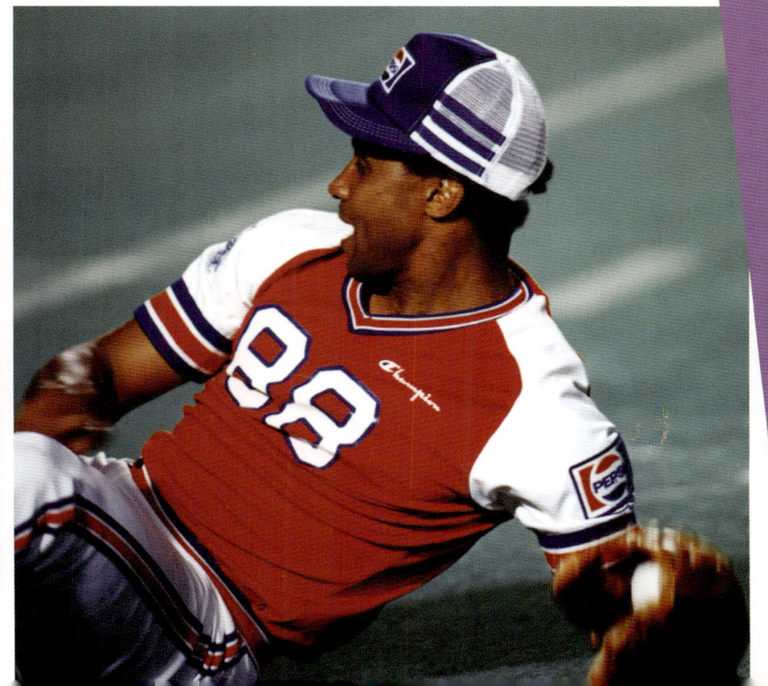

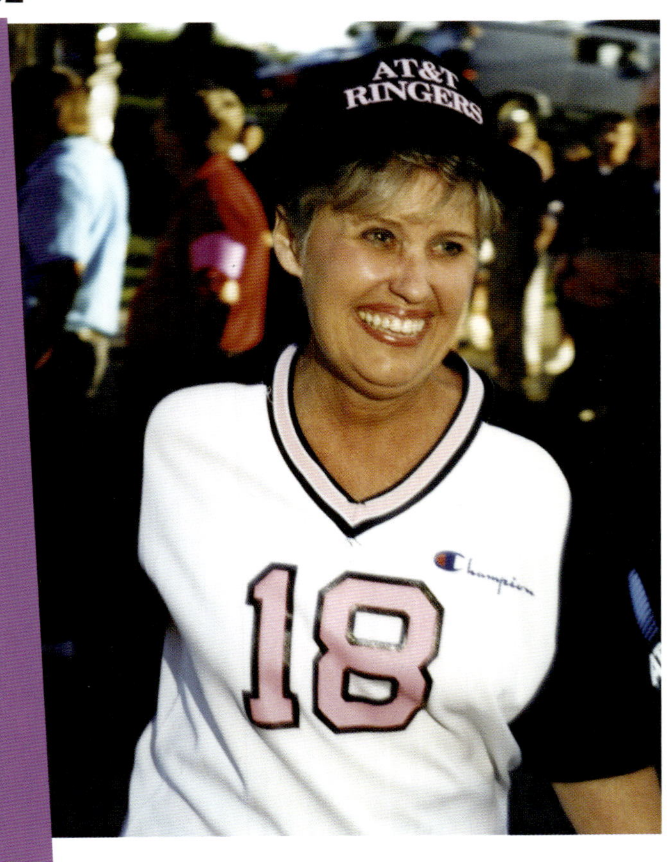

Erma Bombeck

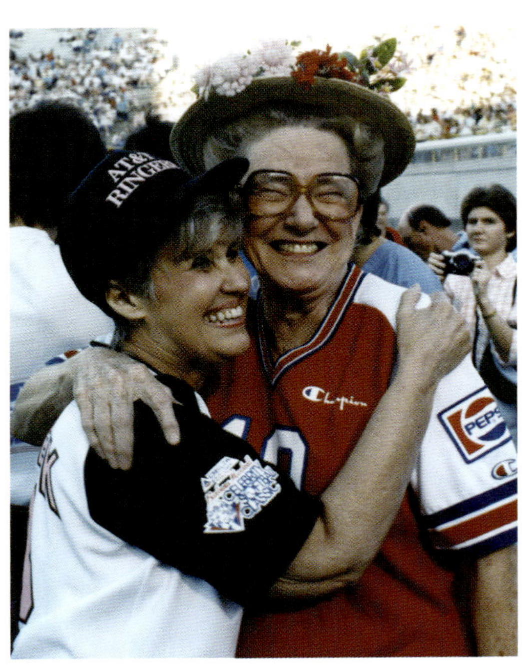

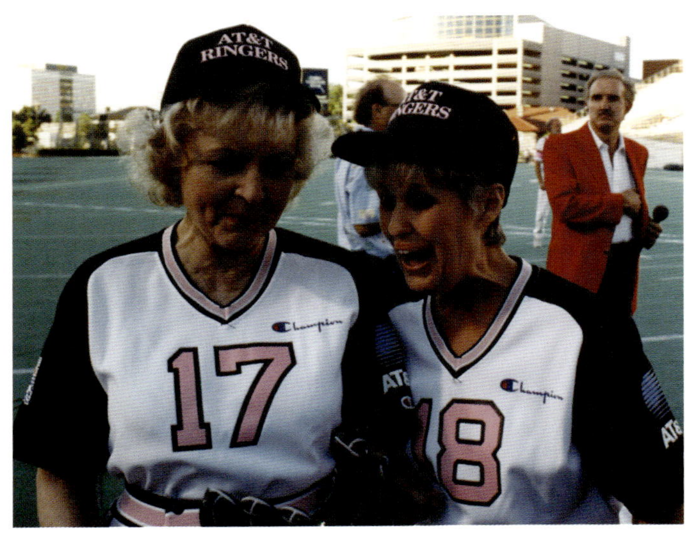

Betty White

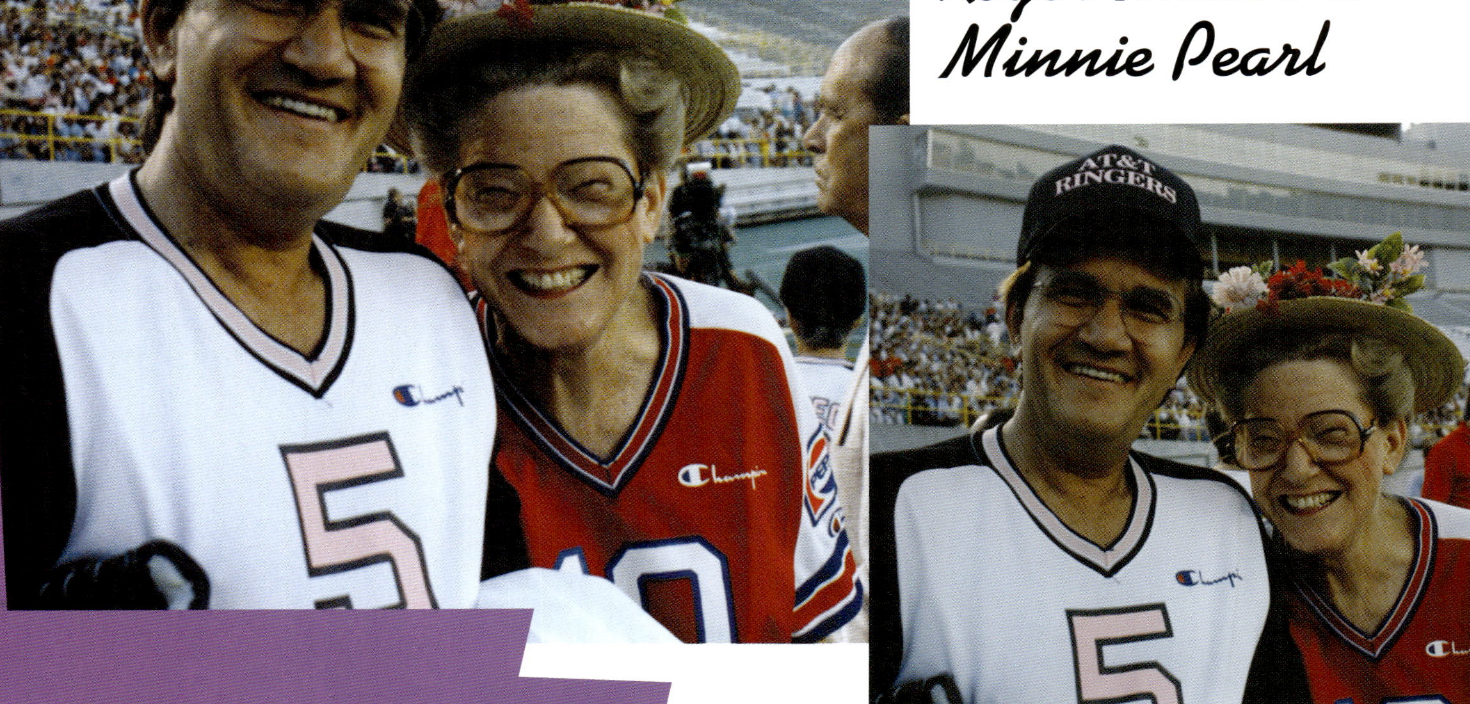

Roger Miller & Minnie Pearl

LL Cool J

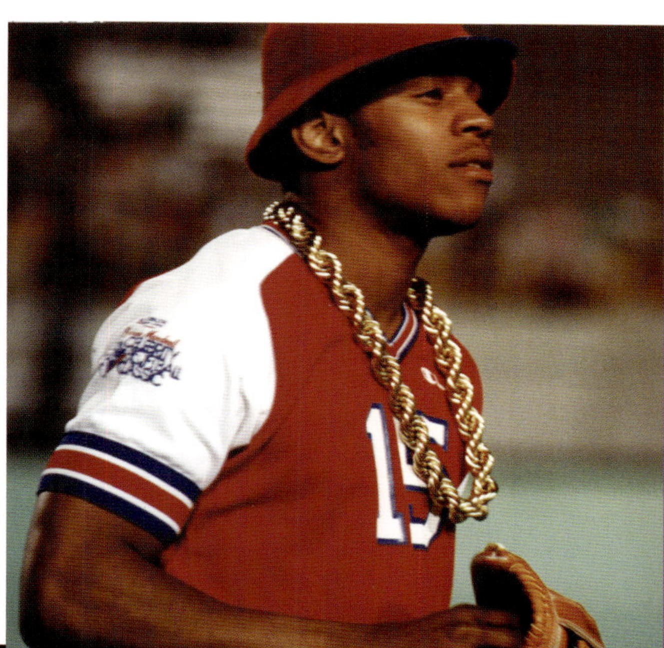

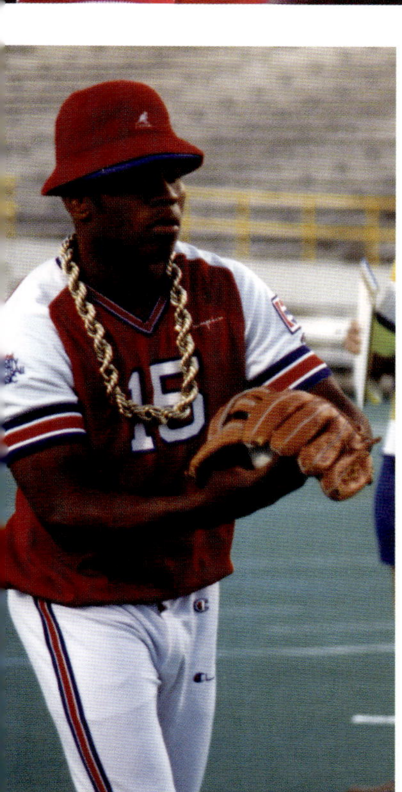

John Stamos

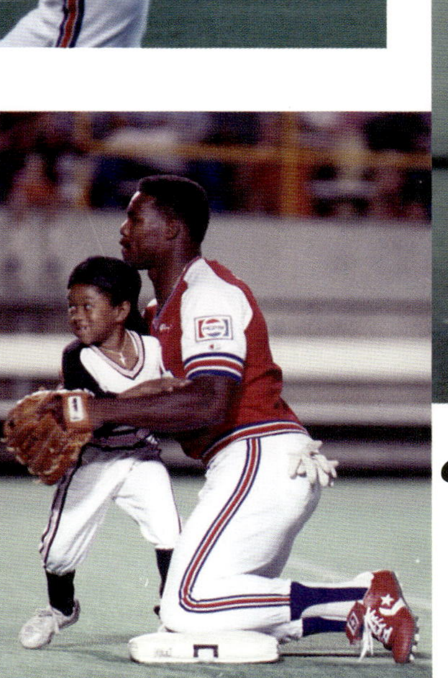

Emanuel Lewis

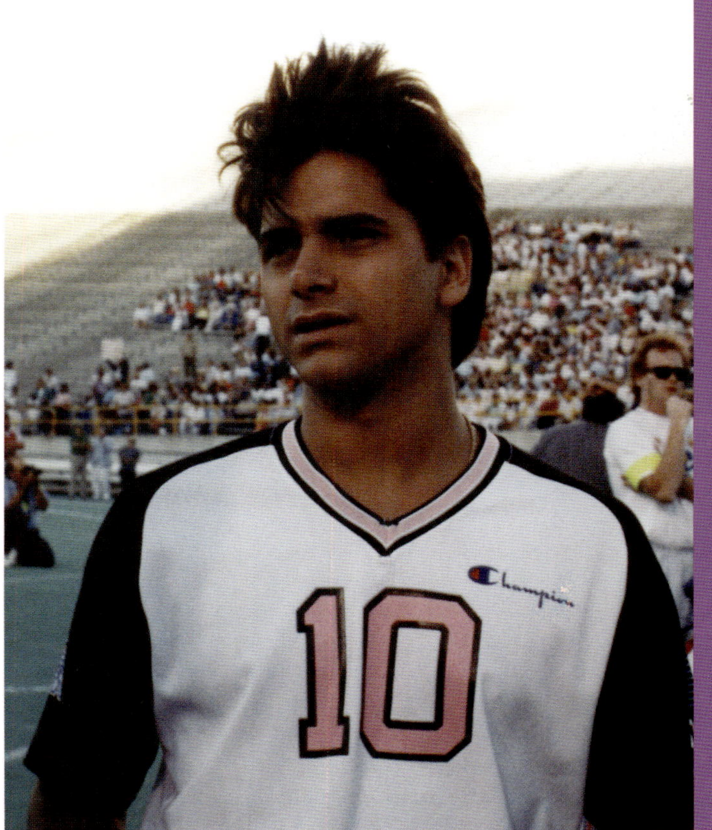

Oprah Winfrey

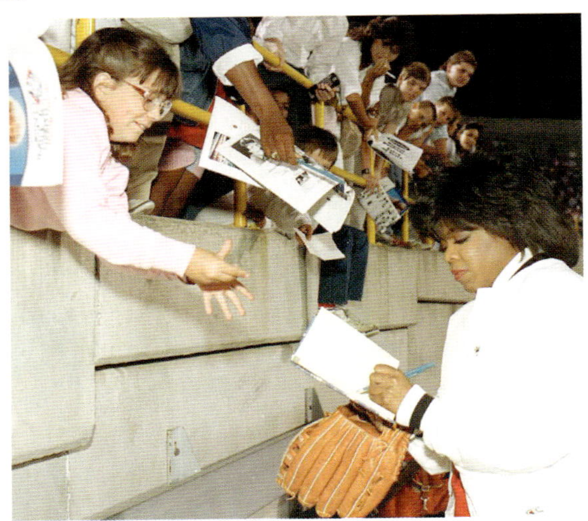

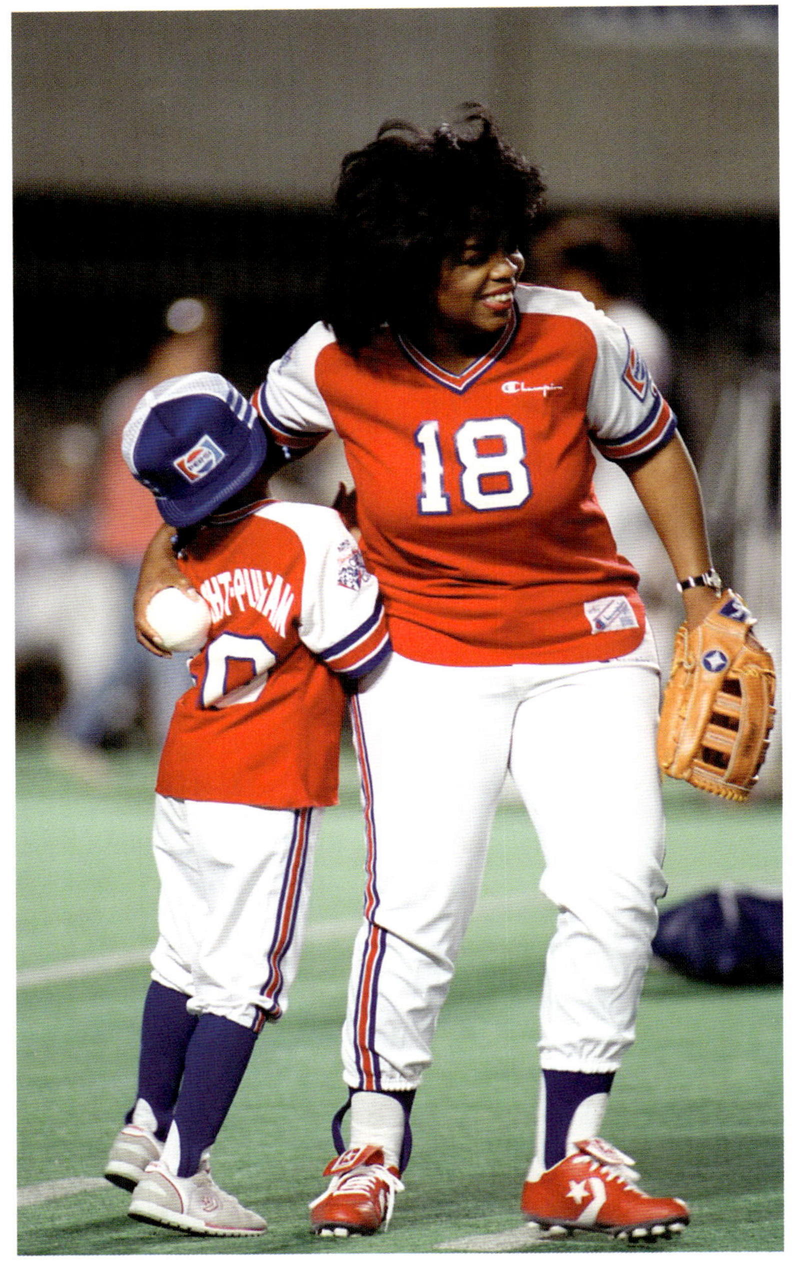

Oprah & Keshia

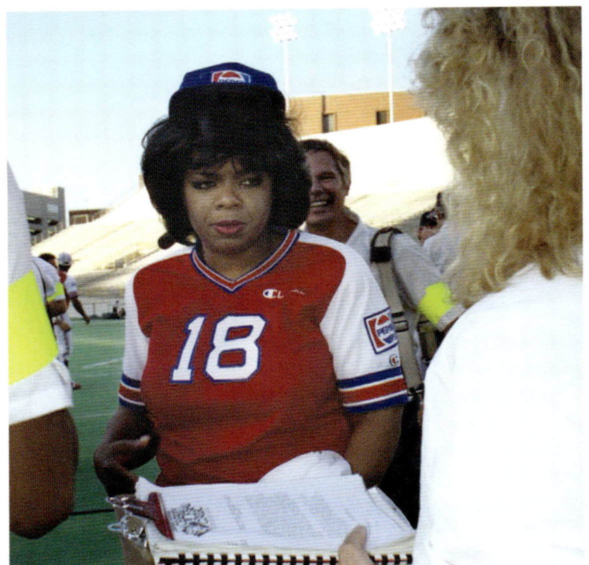

Louise Mandrell, Oprah, and the Statler Brothers

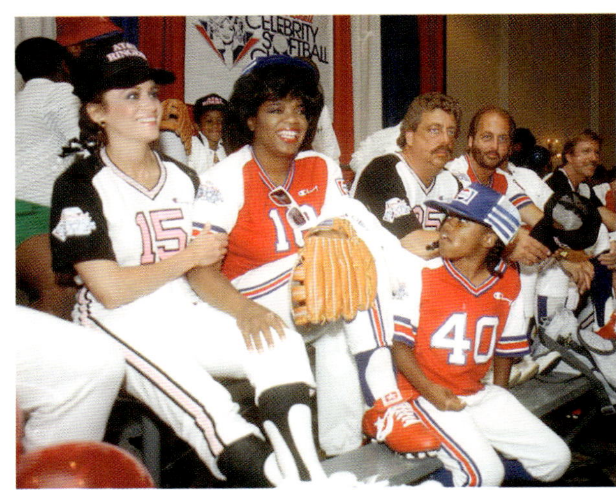

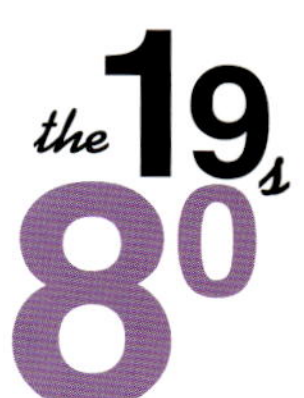

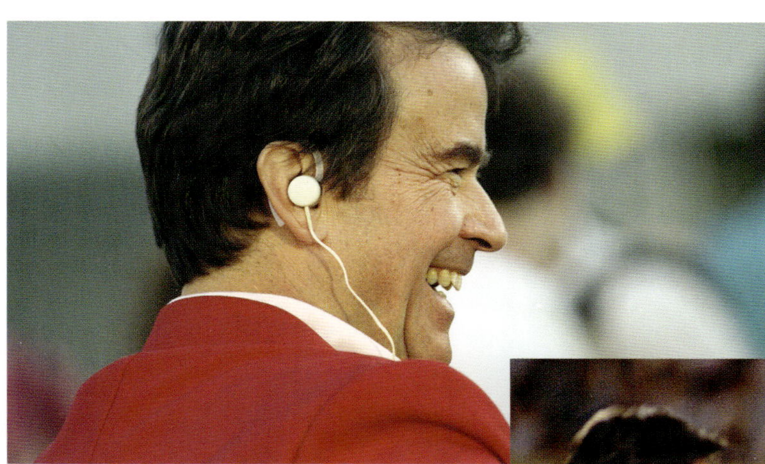

Dick Clark

Dick Clark, Roy Acuff, Oprah and Bob Hope

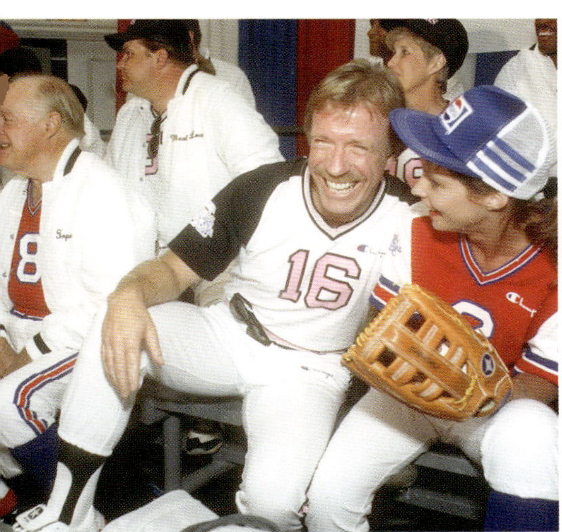

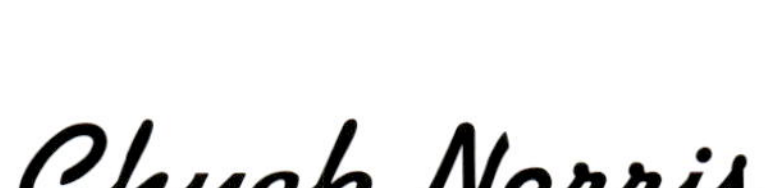

Chuck Norris

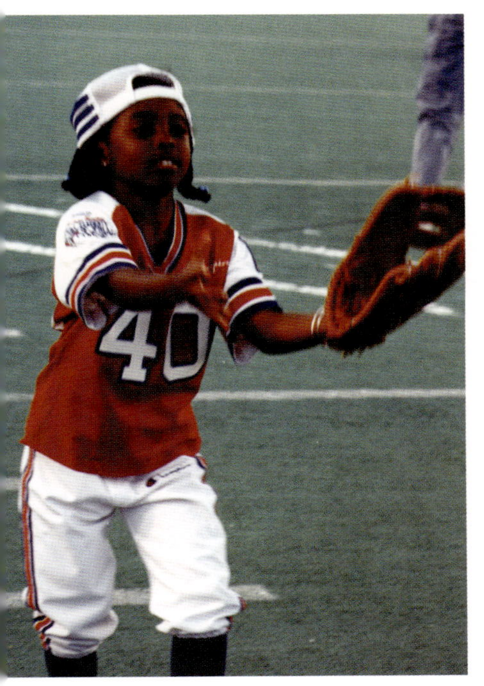

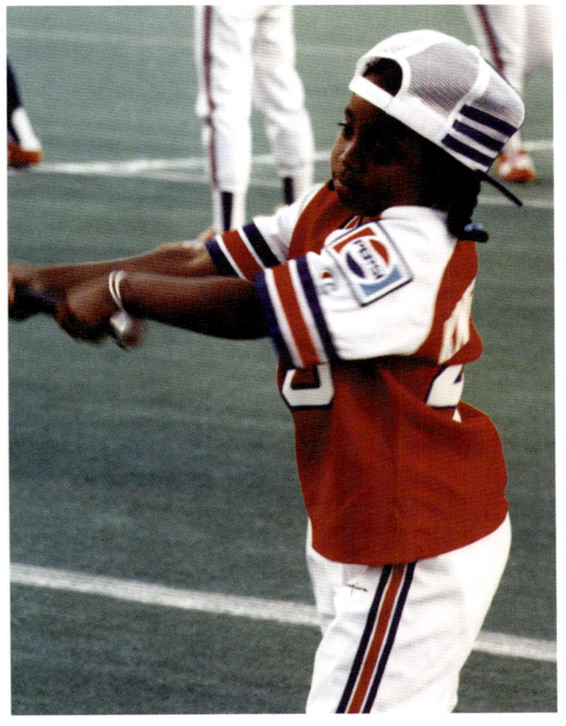

Keshia Knight-Pulliam

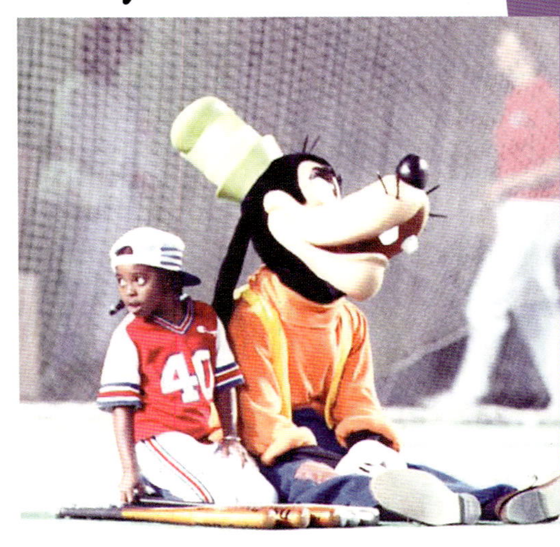

Wolfman Jack

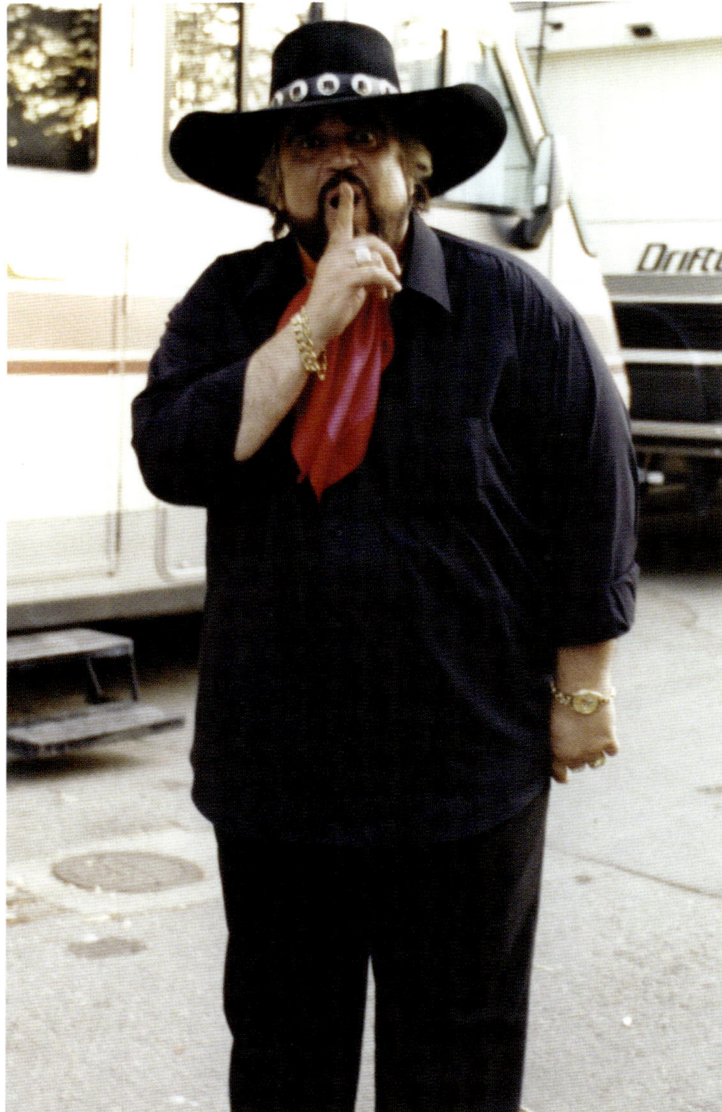

The Wolfman
Robert Weston Smith
"Wolfman Jack"

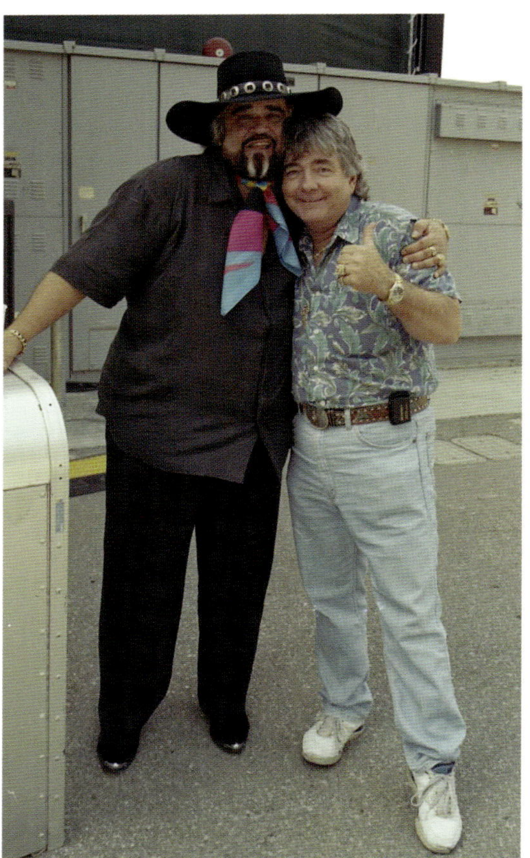

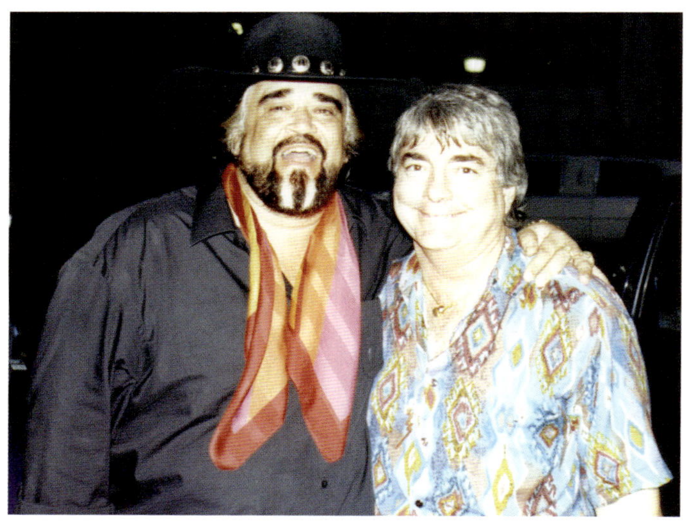

Wolfman Jack and I worked many shows together. He was a unique guy.

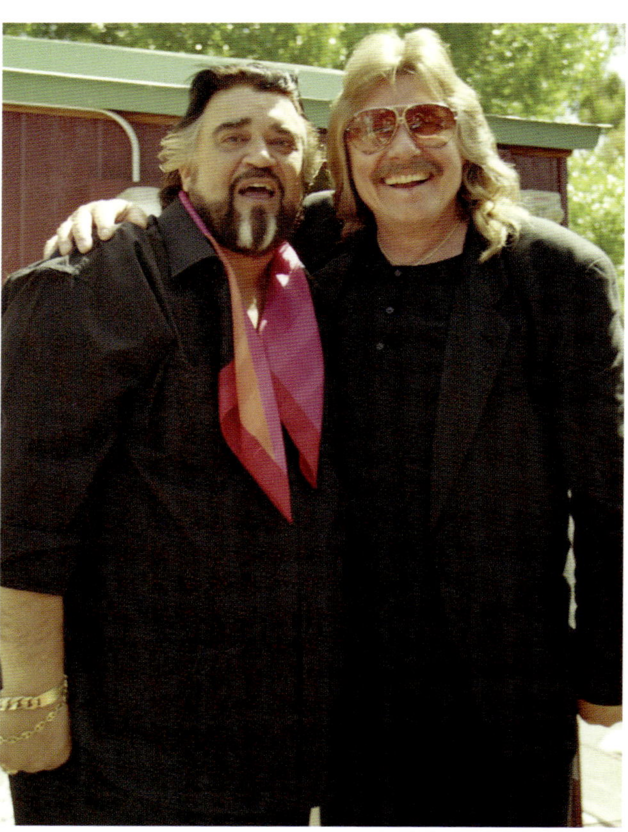

Wolf with Mark Lindsay

Freddie "Boom Boom" Cannon

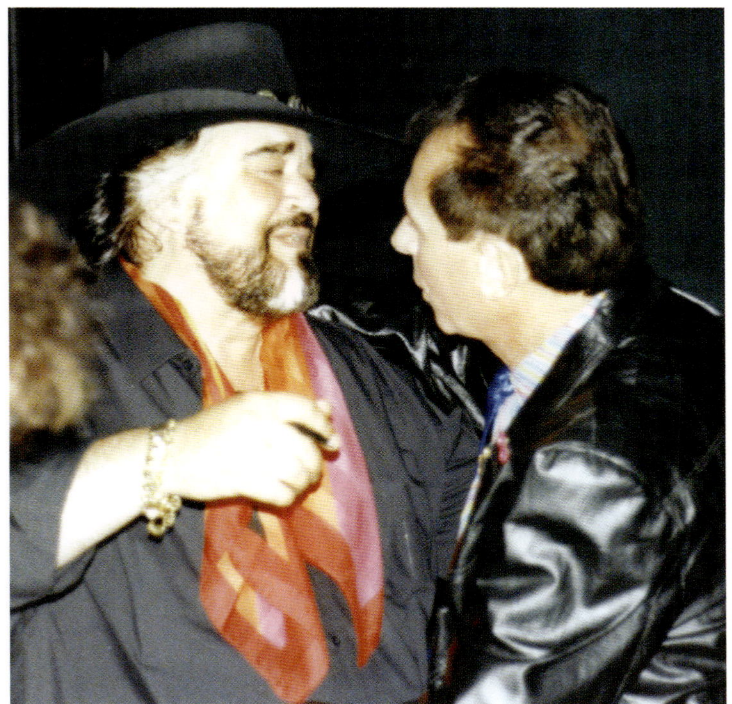

Wolf with Freddie "Boom Boom" Cannon

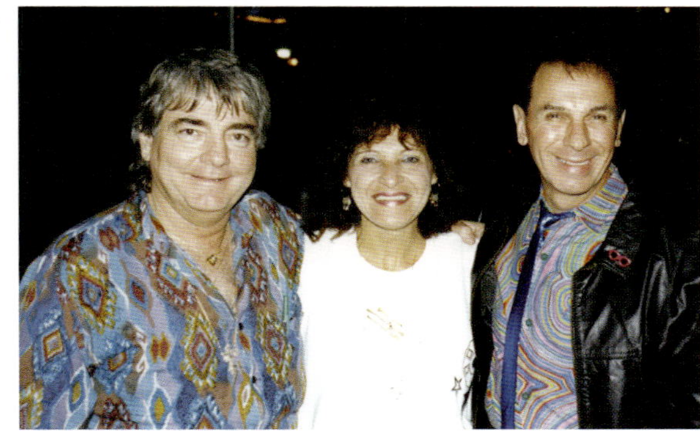

Freddie "Boom Boom" Cannon and his wife of many years.

Hoyt Axton

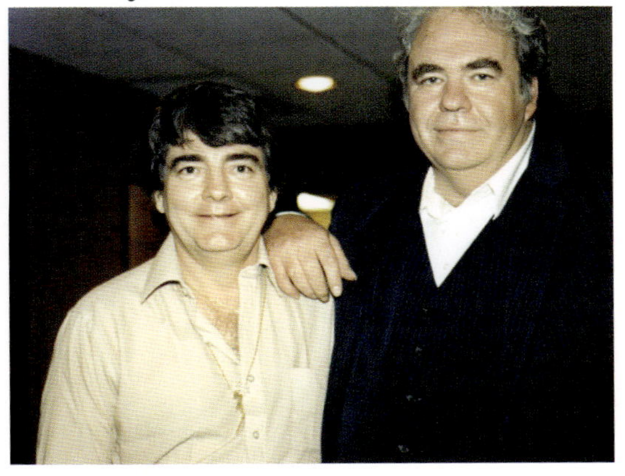

Bo Diddley

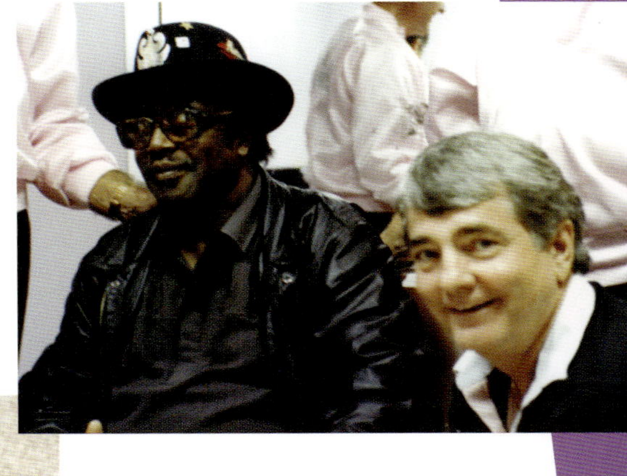

Rufus Thomas

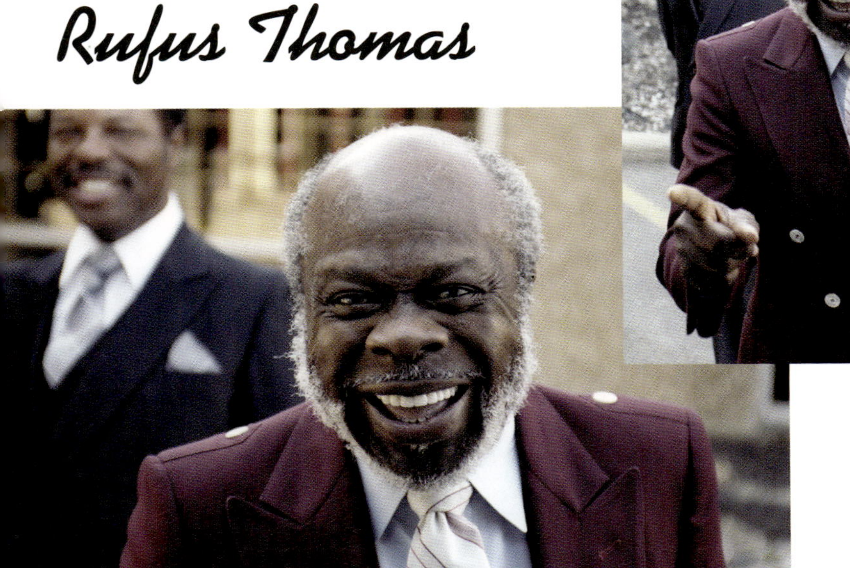

Memphis D.J. WDIA Radio, also great entertainer and funny man. His biggest hits "Walking the Dog" and "Do the Funky Chicken."

Bill Belew

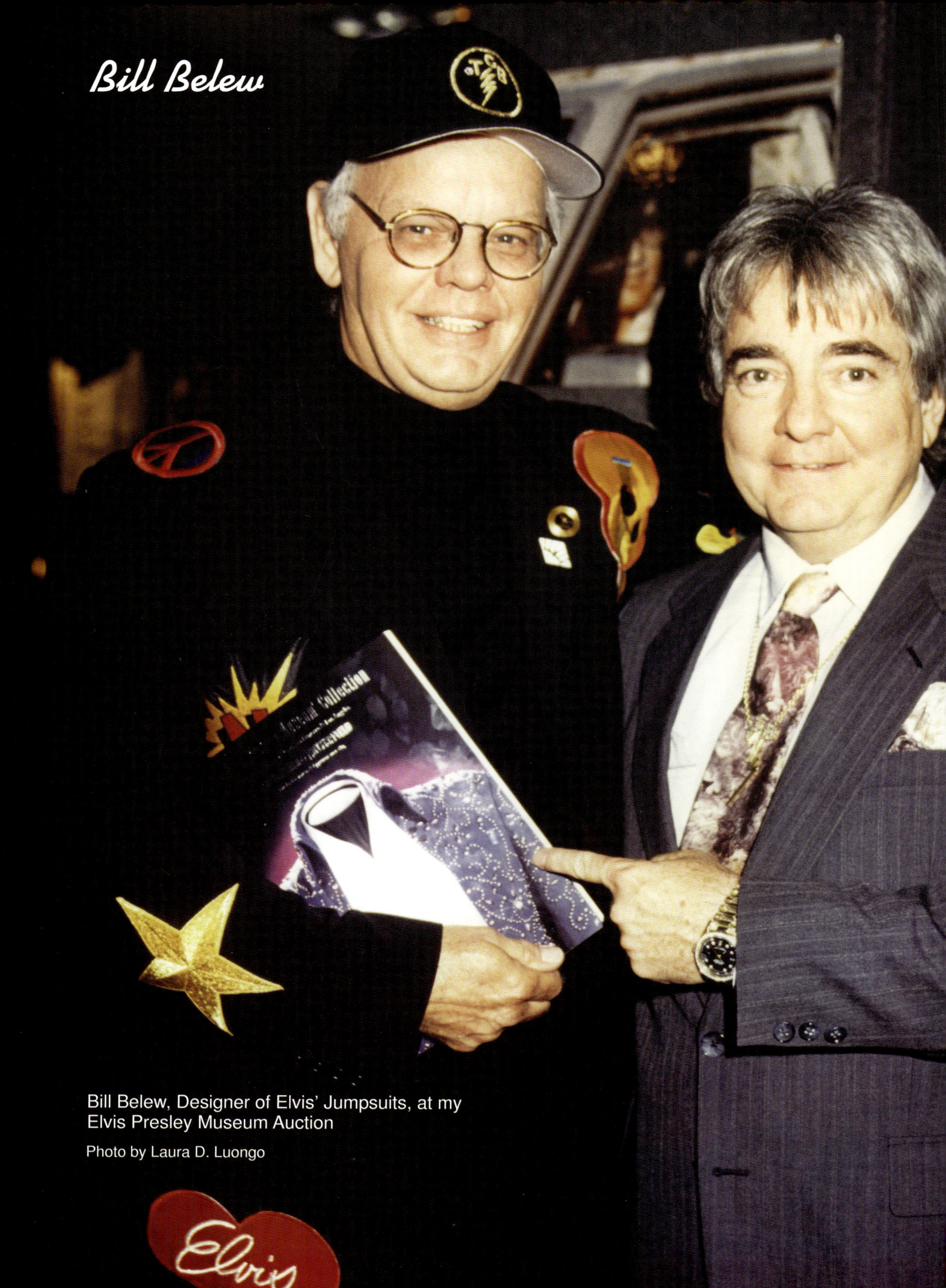

Bill Belew, Designer of Elvis' Jumpsuits, at my Elvis Presley Museum Auction

Photo by Laura D. Luongo

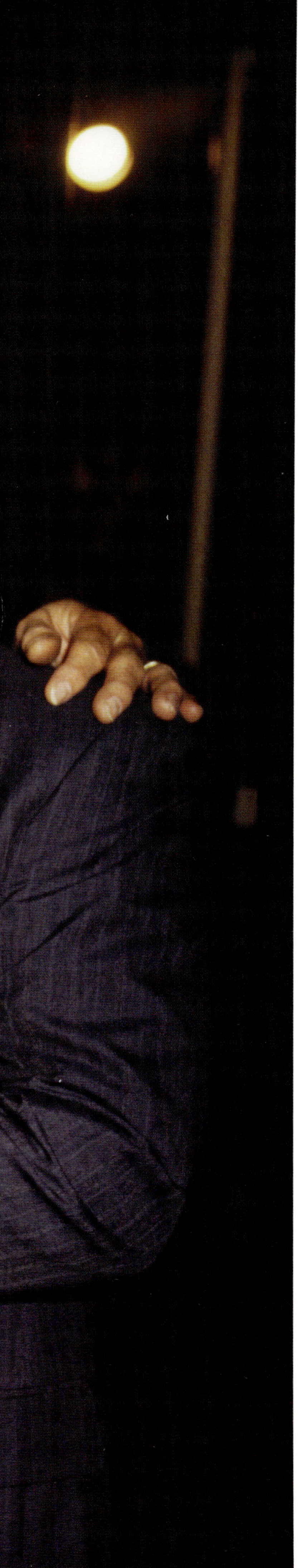

the 1990s

This was a tumultuous decade, but still had many good times. I attended Colonel Parker's 85th Birthday party at the Las Vegas Hilton. I met "Slash" of Guns and Roses and traded one of Elvis's guns that I owned for one of Slash's guitars and multi-platinum album award. During one of the tours, I was in Japan photographing the Emperor's enthronement. I went back to my hotel and happened to see Princess Diana and Prince Charles. It turned out that they were staying at the same hotel on the same floor I was. Princess Di was ever so gracious granting me permission to take a picture, and I was a nervous wreck as the camera wouldn't flash. I didn't have a fresh battery in the camera after taking so many photos at the enthronement. I'll never forget how kind and patient Princess Di was. The pictures didn't turn out well but I've included a few in the book anyway.

In 1992, I received a phone call from Nancy Jones (George Jone's wife) saying she and George would like to buy my farm which was located in Franklin, Tennessee. I think George was the only person I would sell it to. I was one of his biggest fans and we had somewhat of a history. One night in Memphis I let George borrow Elvis' white '76 Eldorado convertible that I owned and he wrecked it. Yes, it's the car pictured in the 1980's chapter of this book. I met with George and Nancy, we had fun haggling over a price for the farm which including some trading. They traded me their house in Lakeland, Florida including the contents, his "Possom" golf cart and his guitar shaped diamond ring. George also traded his red Jaguar Convertible with only 2,000 miles on it, his white Lexus with 2000 miles on it, his restored 1963 Ford Galaxy 500 convertible and a restored 1930 Studebaker. We finalized the deal by trading llamas, tractors, peacocks and guinnea hens. The Jones' still live there today, they're as special to me now as they were then.

My biggest endeavor was when I decided to auction over 600 pieces of Elvis Presley's personal effects. It was the most publicized celebrity auction in history. I toured the world with the news of the upcoming auction which was held in 1994 at the Las Vegas Hilton on June 18 & 19. I don't remember ever sleeping from my first thought of the auction to the last and final hammer price. The second day of the auction was clouded by the news covering the OJ Simpson Bronco chase, but it was still an outstanding auction of great success. I was on top of the world, financially, and that was about to change.

You've heard: "The Lord giveth and the Lord taketh away?" Well, it's very true. I didn't realize it at the time but I know now that it was a great blessing. I became so caught up in my business that I lost track of who I was and where I was in God's eyes. I was saved at the age of six but was lost most of my adult life. As life went on and I ventured into the entertainment industry, I lost sight of my life's purpose; I lost my focus on God. I never stopped believing in Him and always tried to be kind, generous, and helpful to others. Though I had been trampled on by many "friends" and others throughout my life, I never let it change my heart. What did change was my focus on giving to God and serving Him by tithing and attending church. I was caught up in over-indulging pleasures of houses, homes, cars, jewelry, and the "finer things in life." I would soon find out that the finer things in life are not "things." I lost the true meaning of life and fell into a big dark hole, losing it all. He got my attention in a big way. I'm being very honest when I say I am happier now that the burden of "stuff" has been lifted. Life has been a struggle, but I'm content and happier than I have ever been. There is truth in the adage, "The less you have, the less you have to worry about." The Lord will provide; keep the faith because He's real.

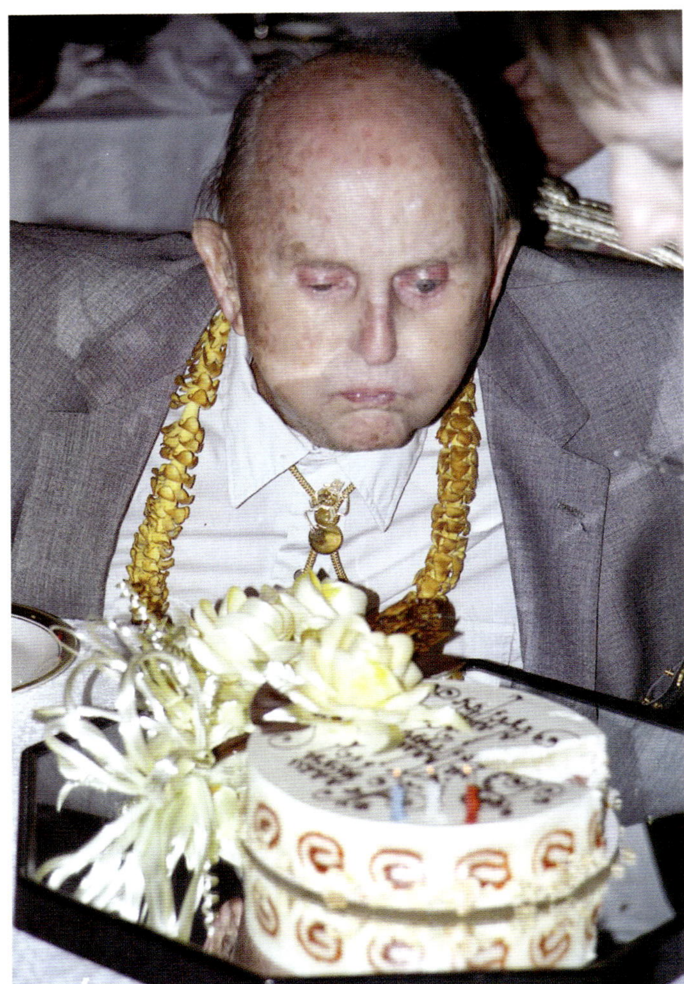

Col. Tom Parker

His 85th Birthday Party
at the Las Vegas Hilton, 1994

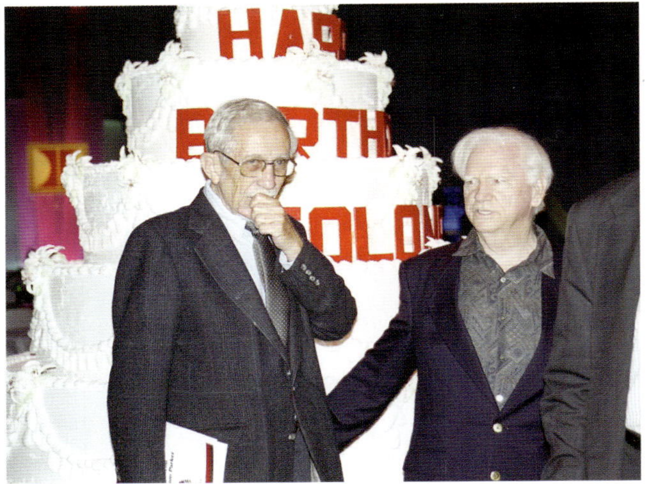

Tom Hewlett and Tom Diskin

The Col. and his wife with Hank Snow and his wife and Sam Phillips

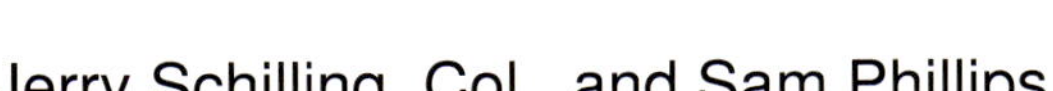

Jerry Schilling, Col., and Sam Phillips

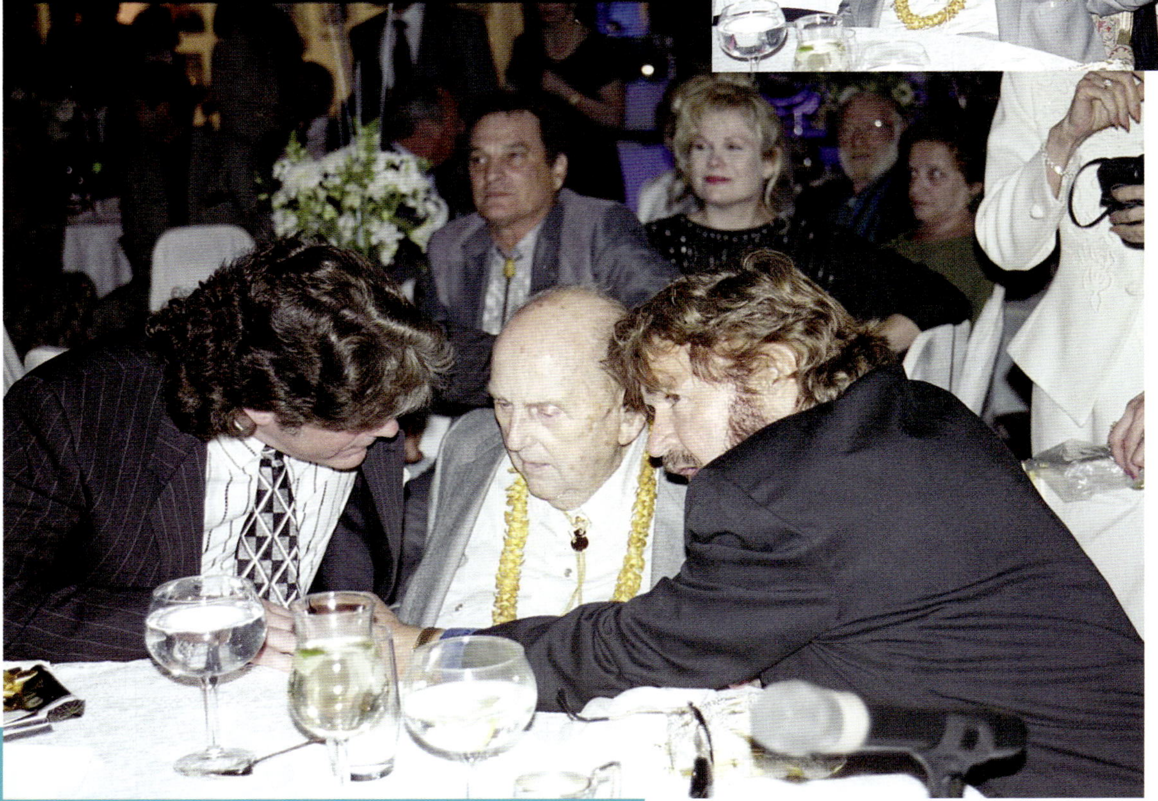

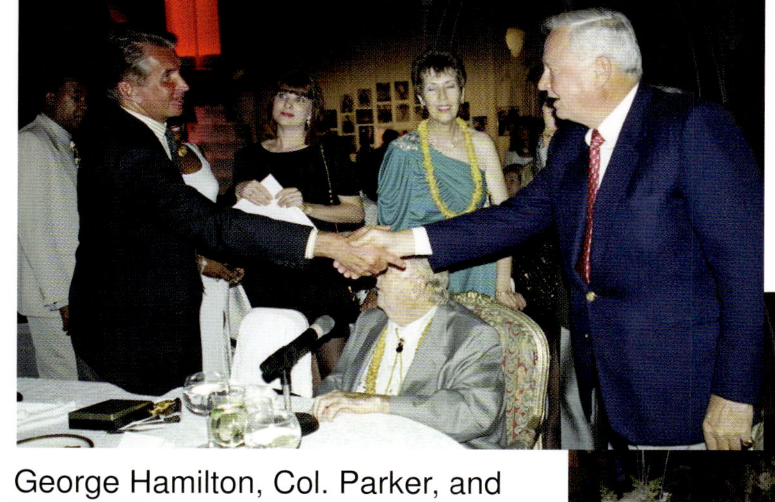

George Hamilton, Col. Parker, and Baron Hilton

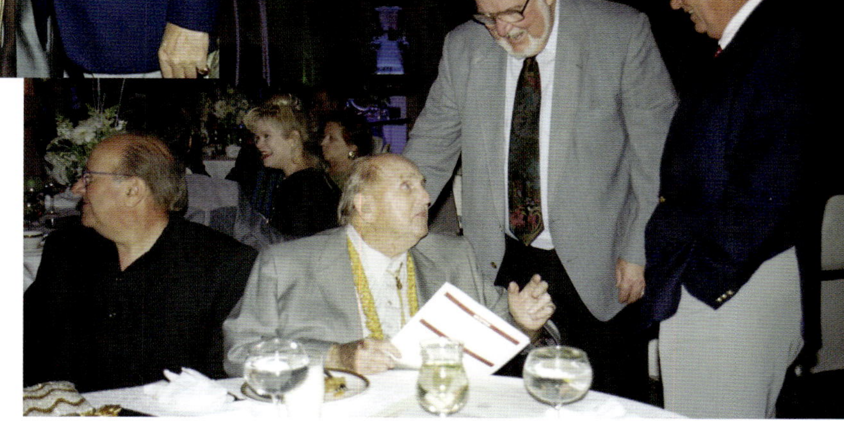

Joe Esposito, Col. Parker, and Baron Hilton

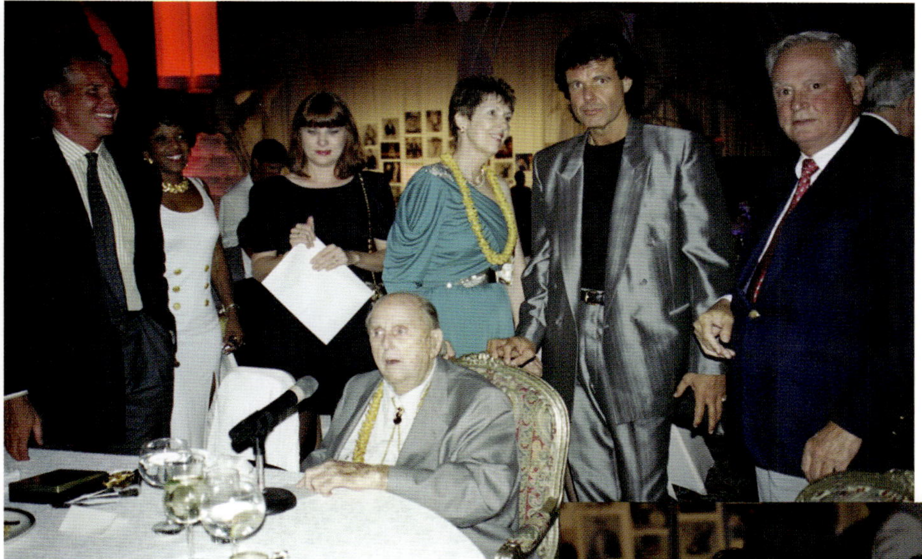

George Hamilton, Col. Parker, Mrs. Parker, and Baron Hilton

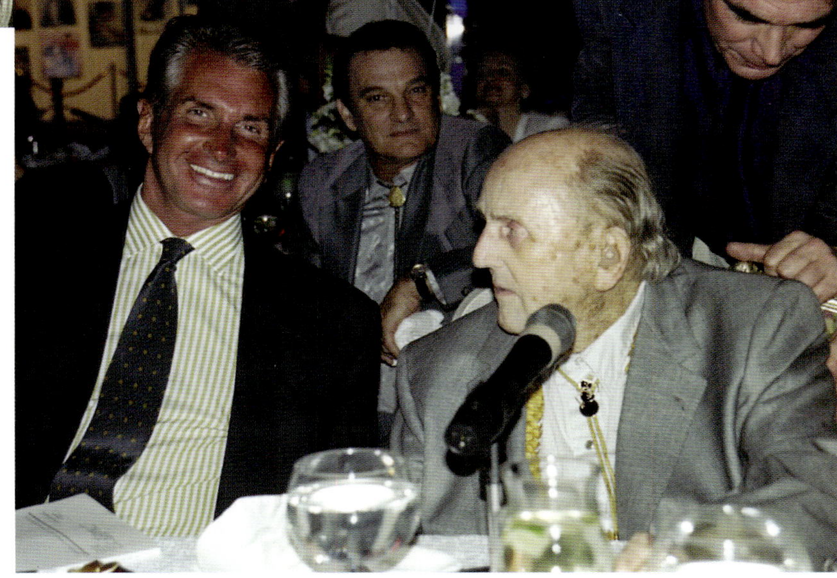

George Hamilton and Col. Parker

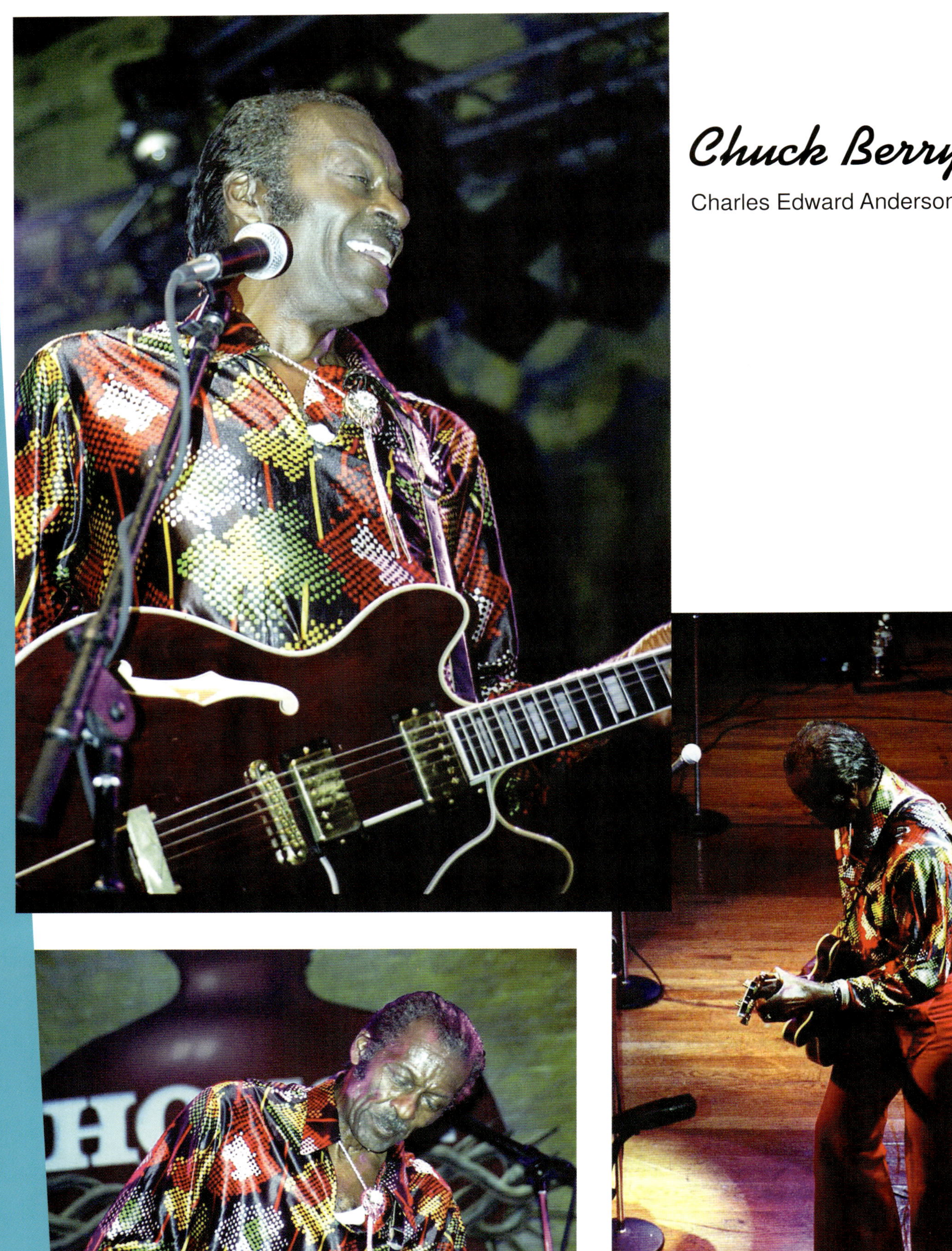

Chuck Berry

Charles Edward Anderson Berry

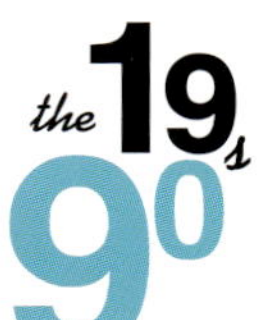

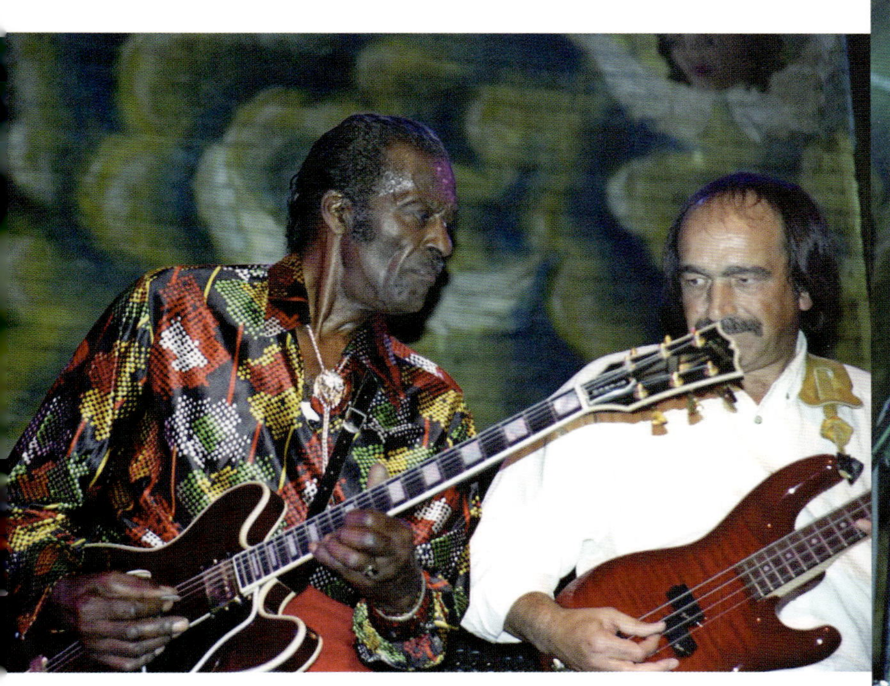

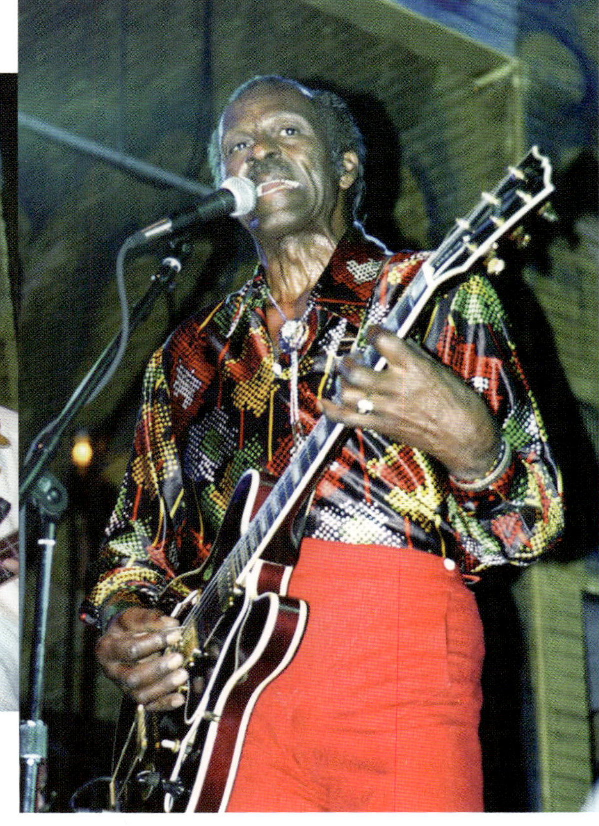

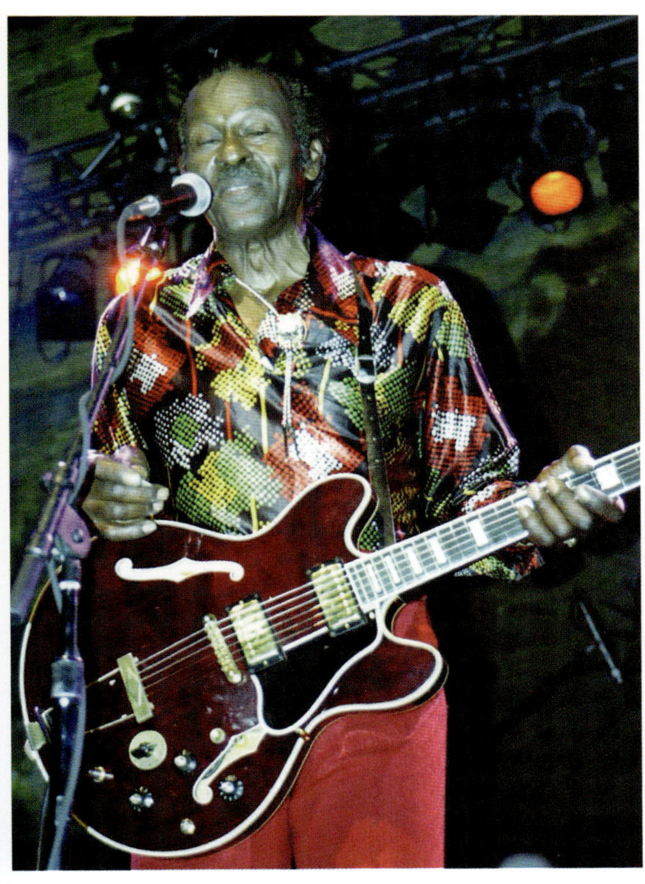

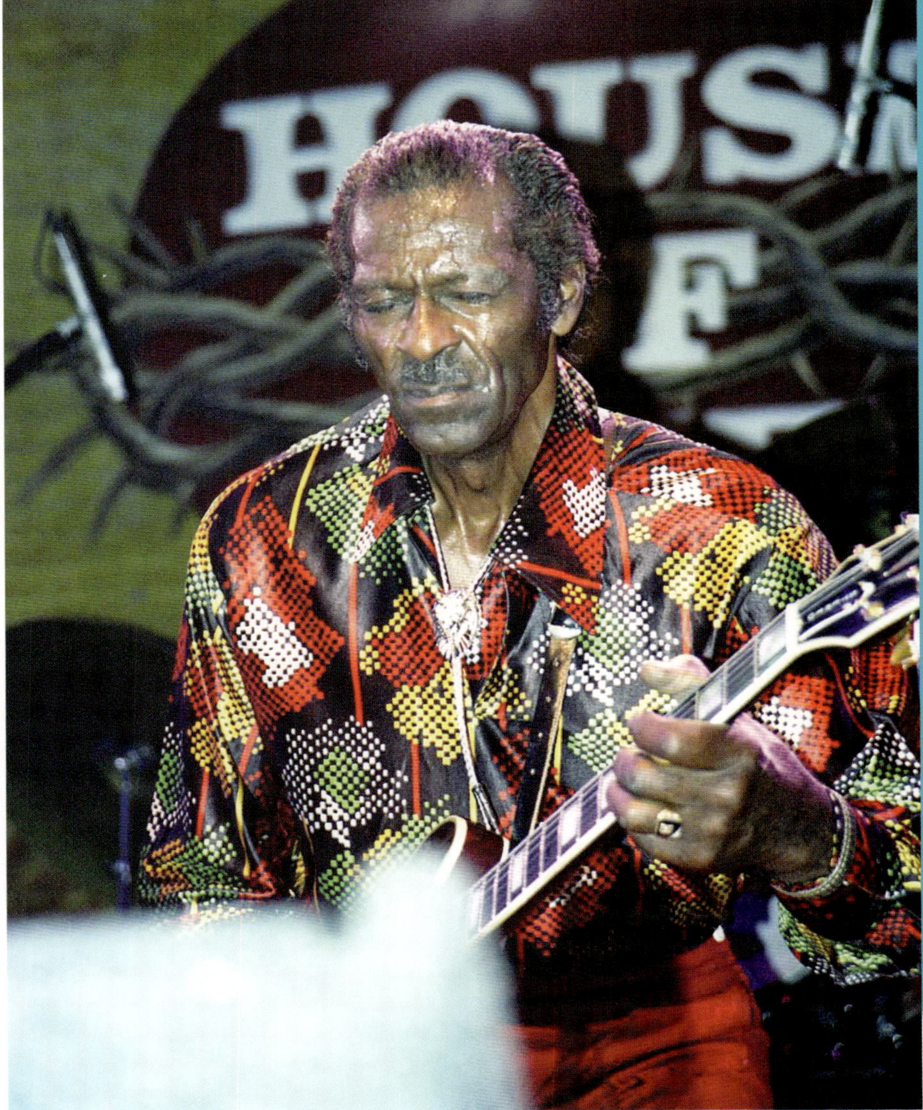

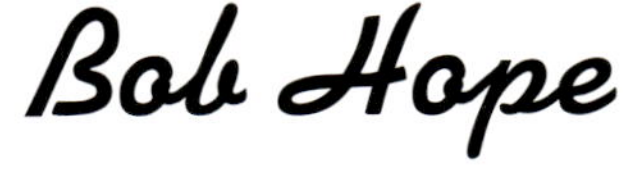

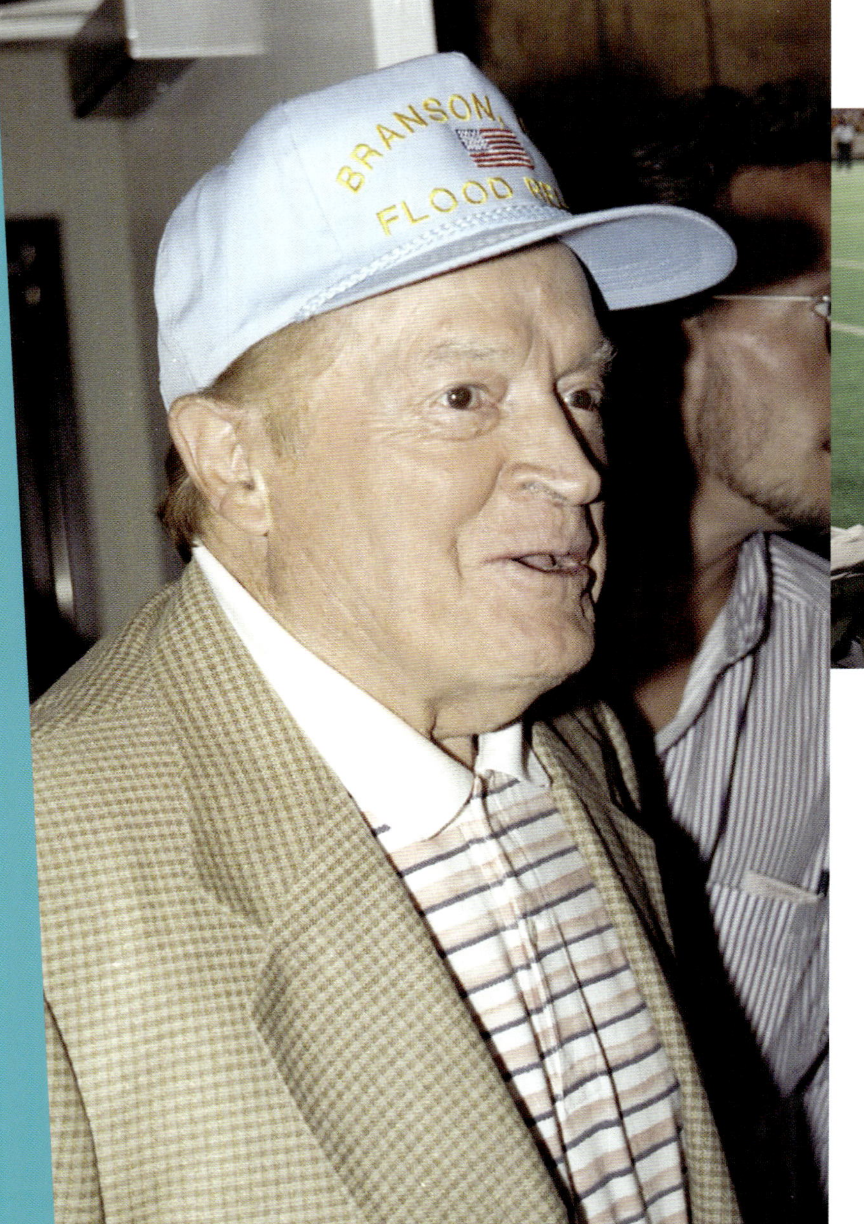

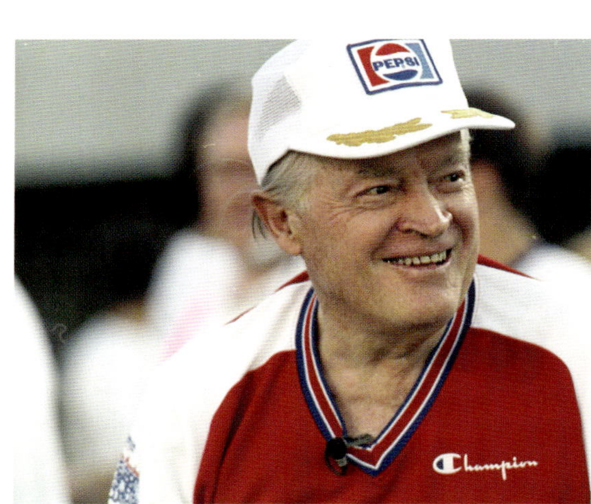

Joan Collins in London

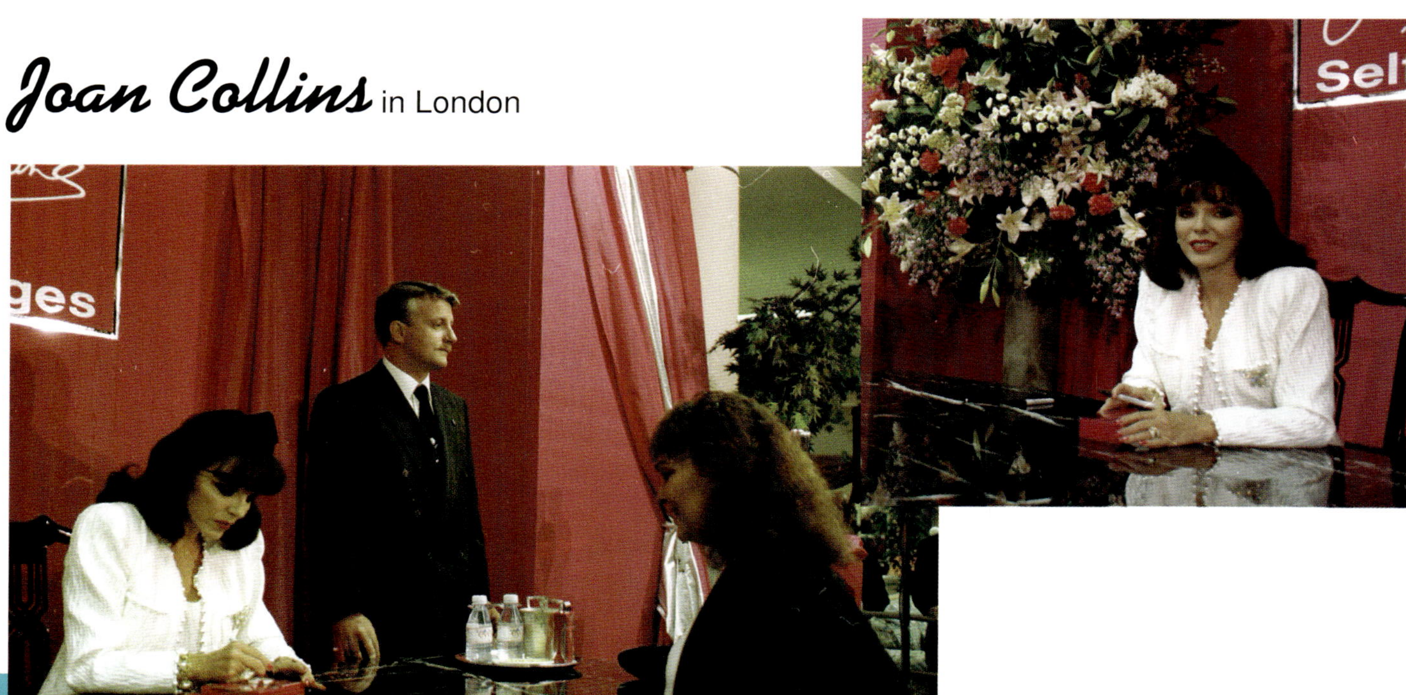

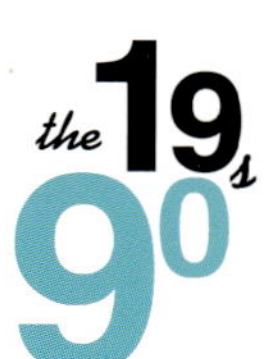

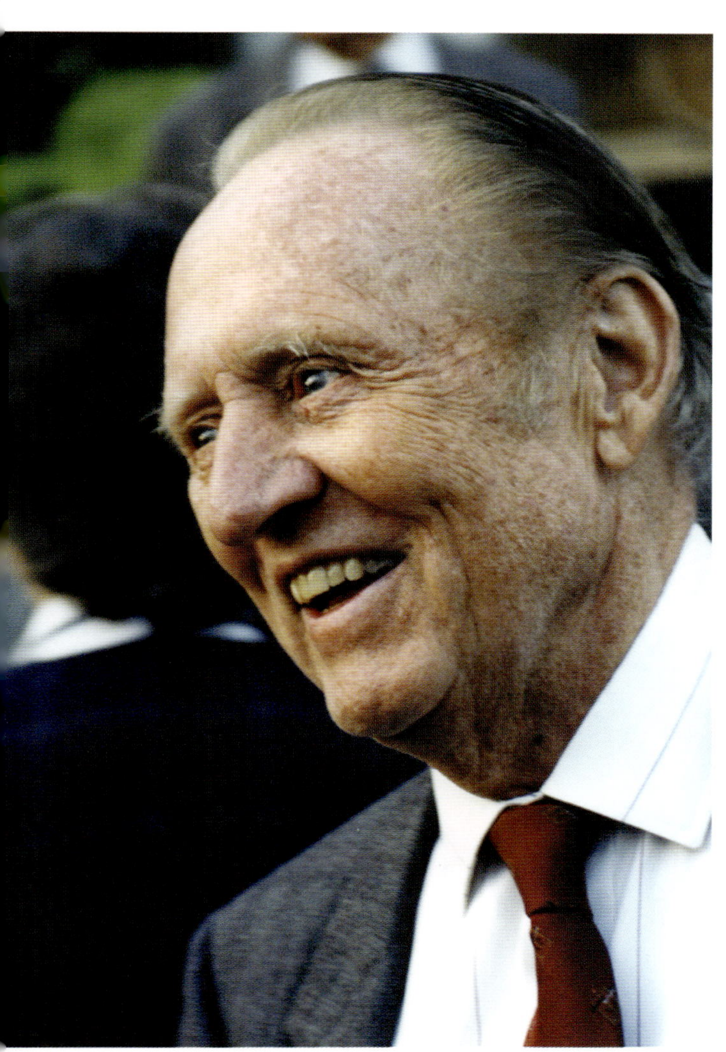

Art Linkletter

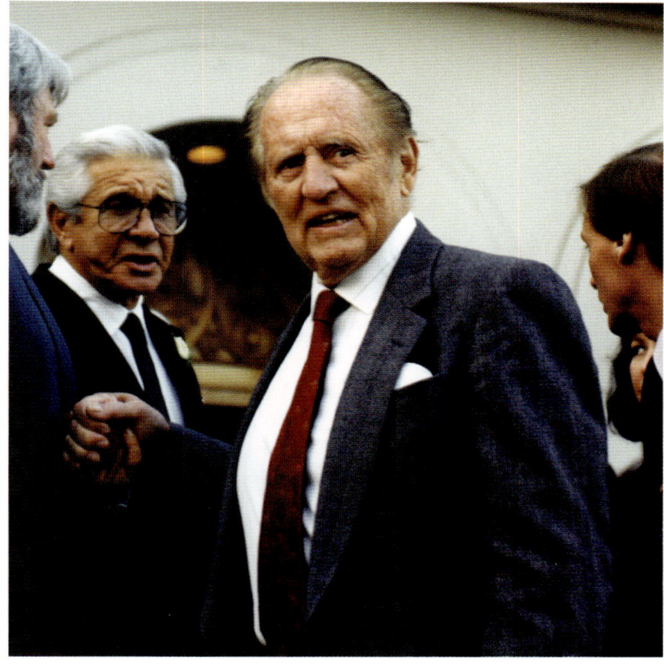

Jerry Mathers

Beaver from "Leave it to Beaver"

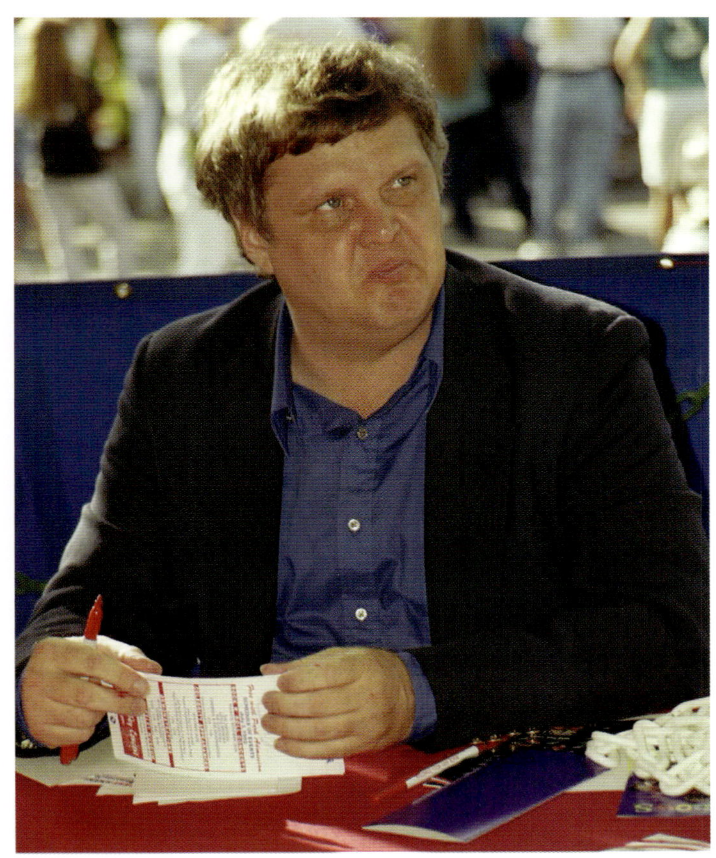

Anita Bryant

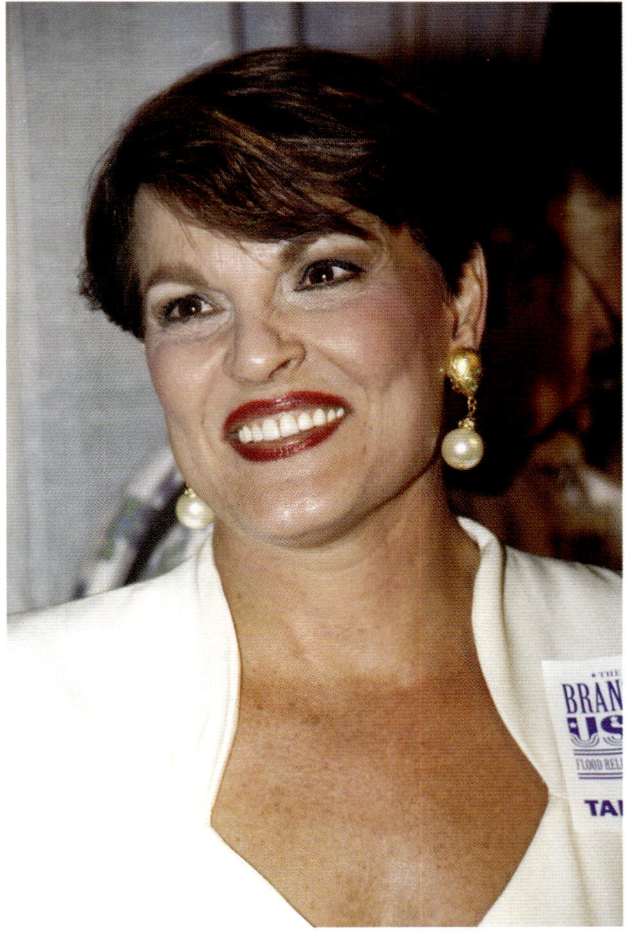

Billy Ray Cyrus

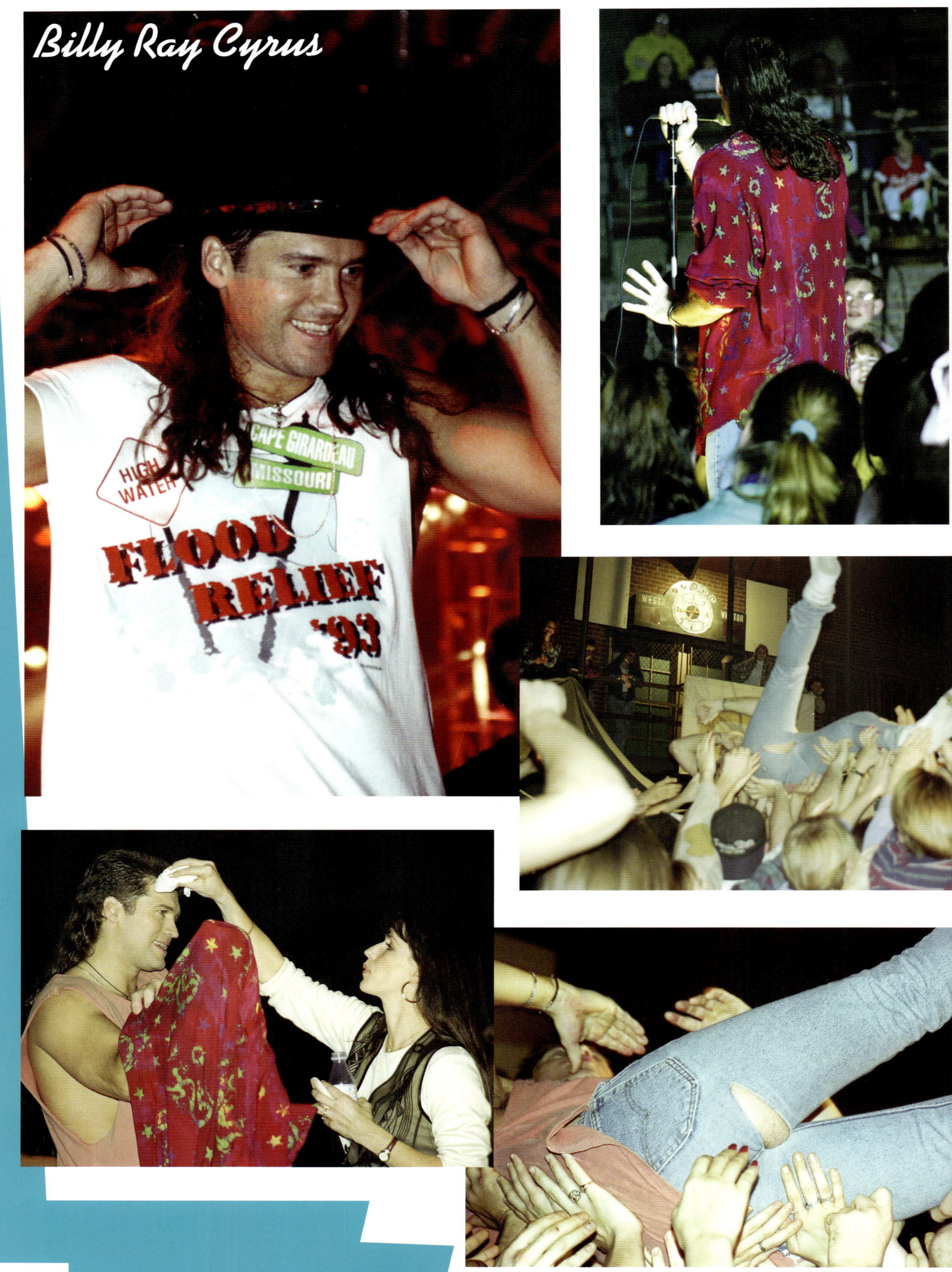

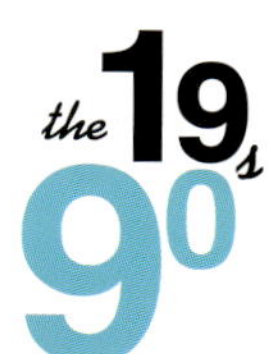

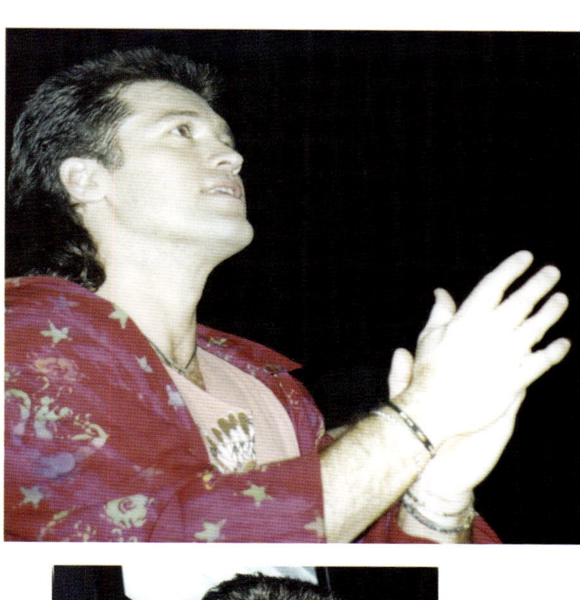

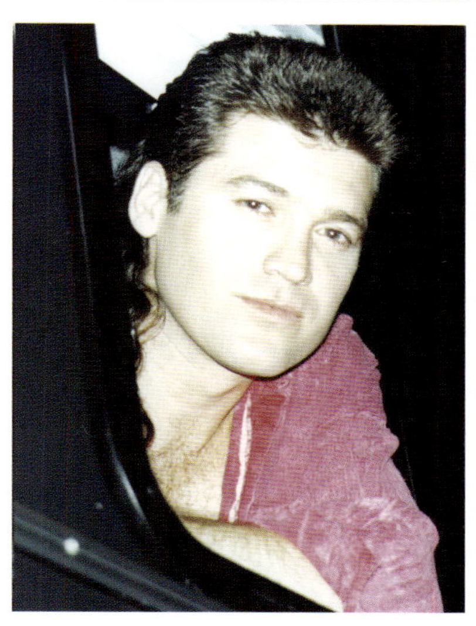

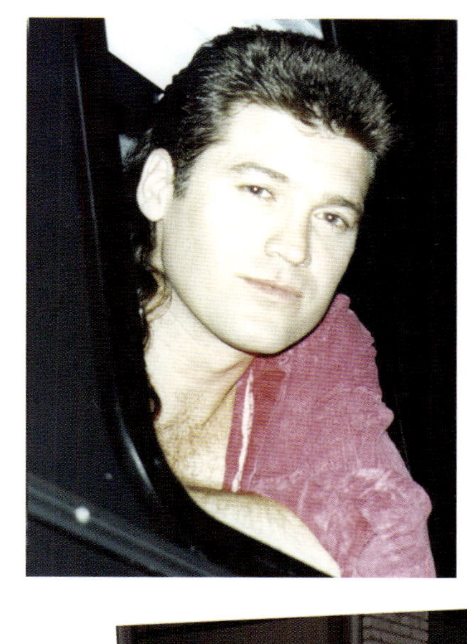

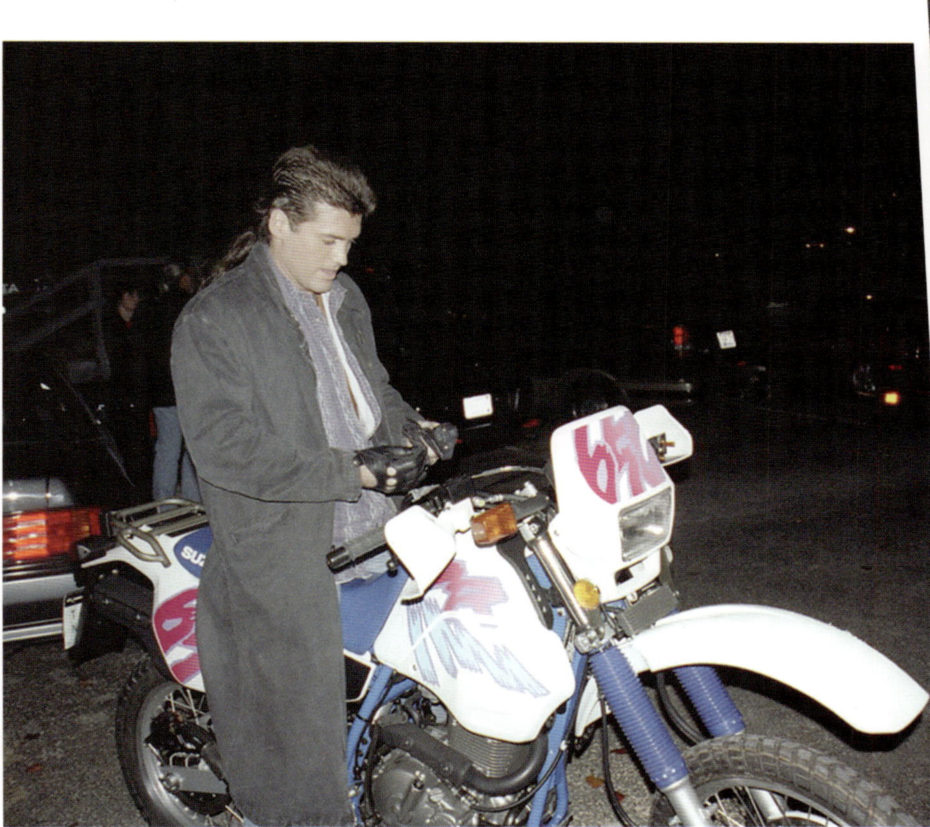

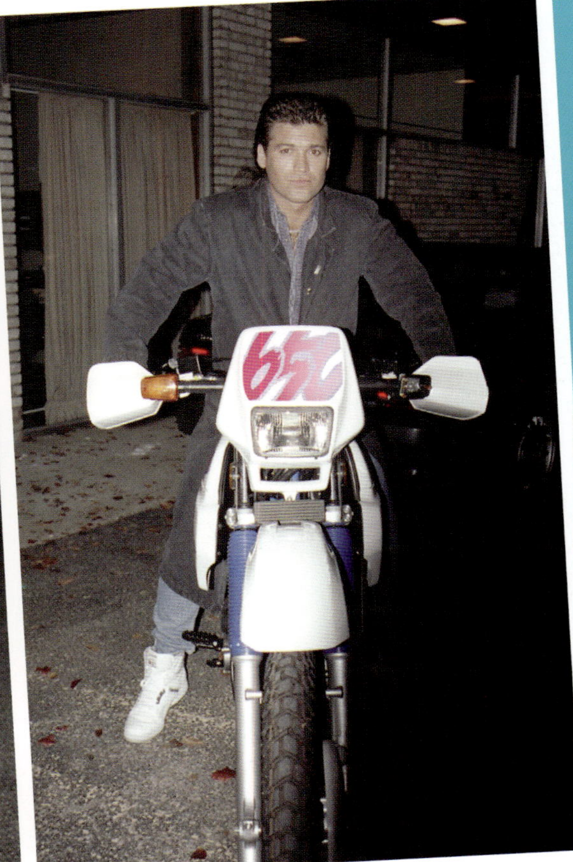

Doug Supernaw

I Don't Call Him Daddy

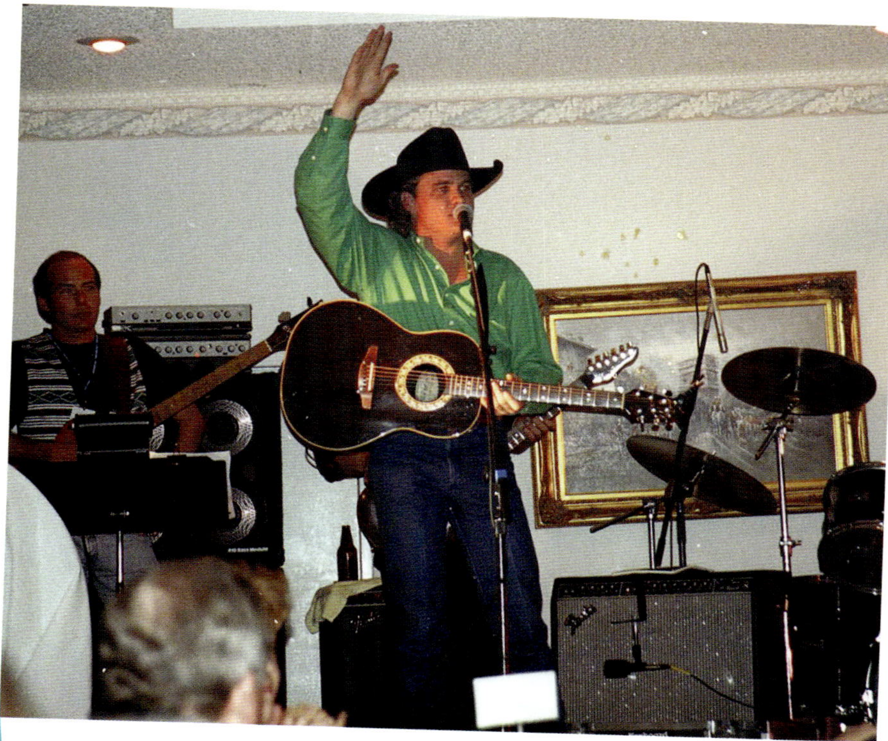

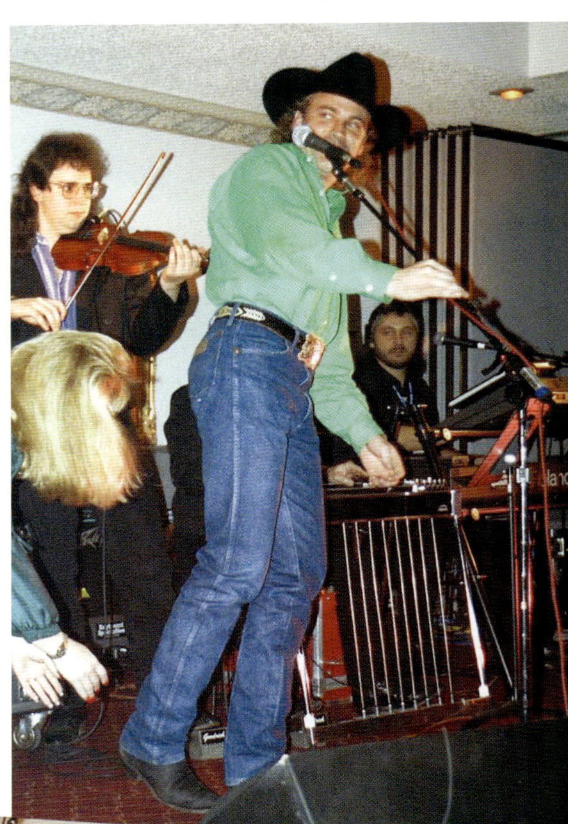

Auctioned all of his clothes for Charlie Daniels Charity. The girls took it all.

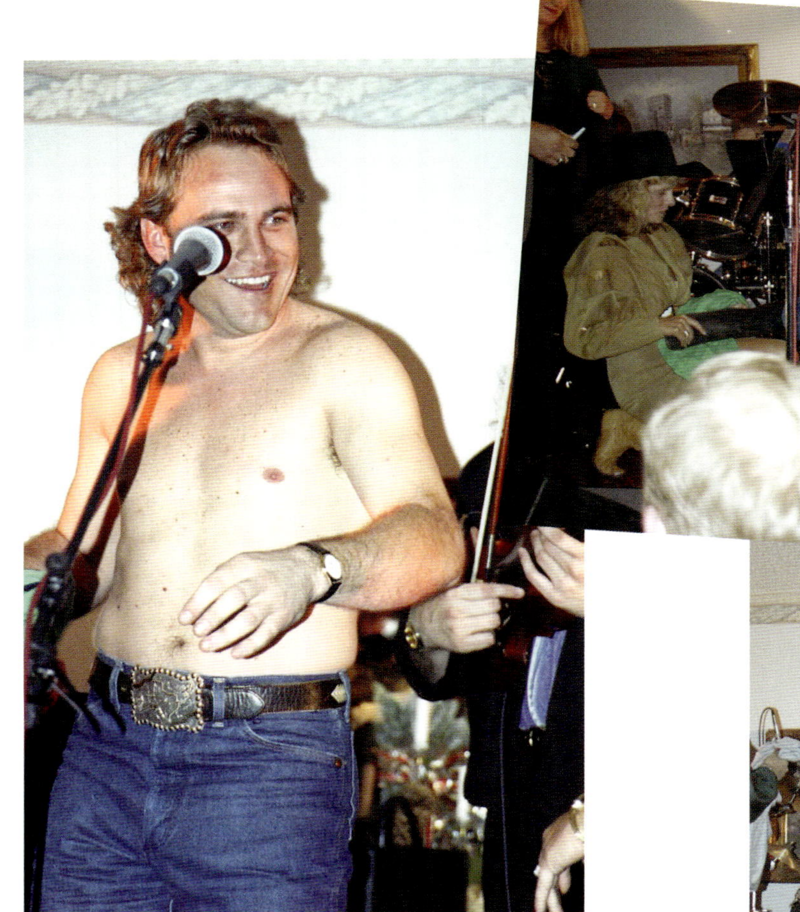

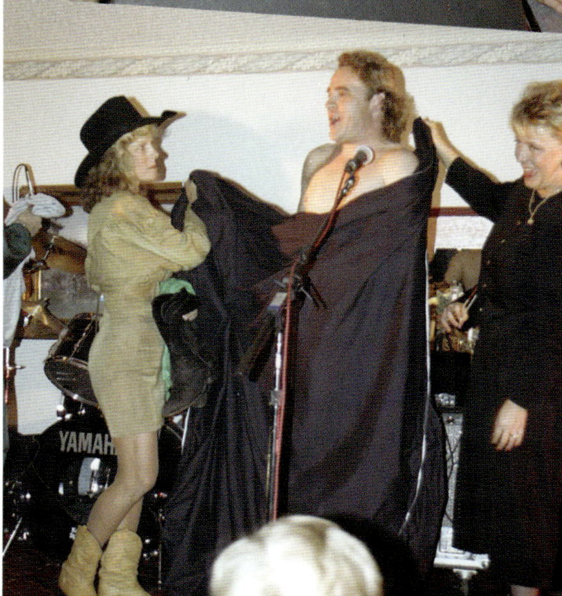

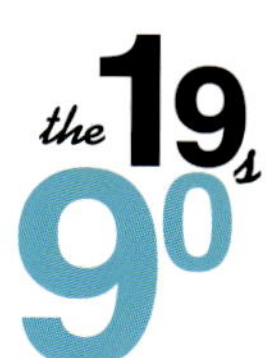

Doug Stone

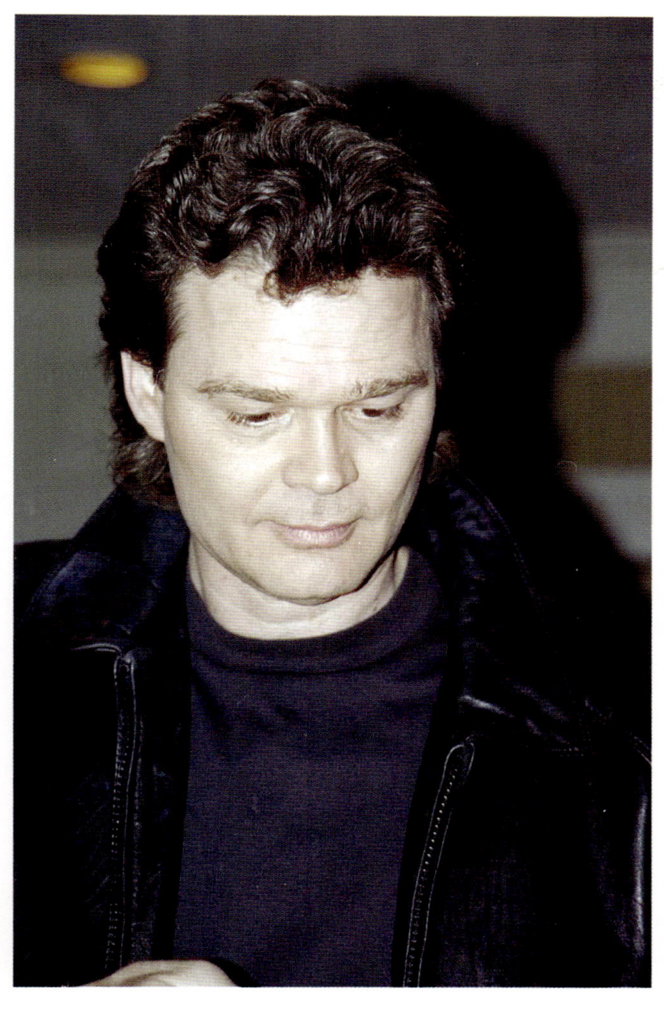

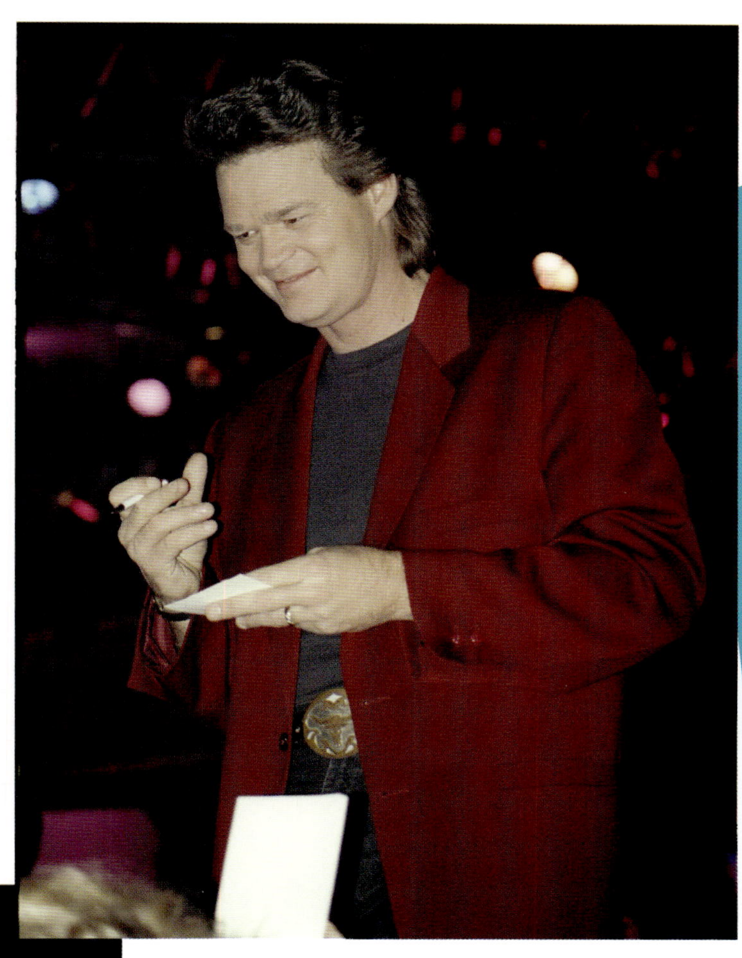

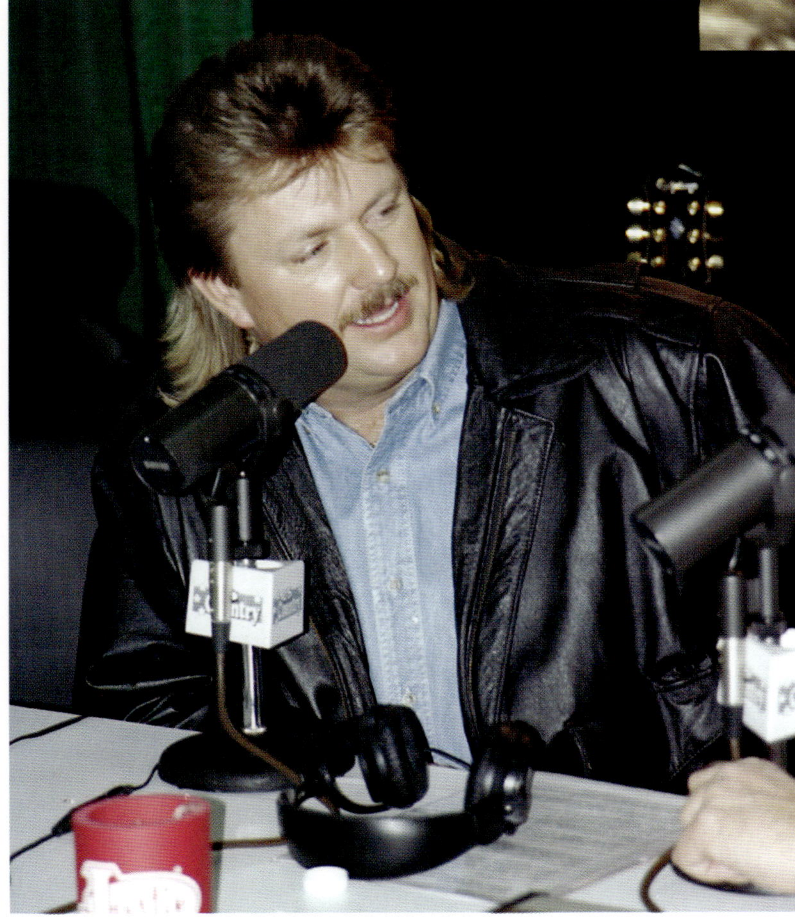

Joe Diffie

Alan Jackson

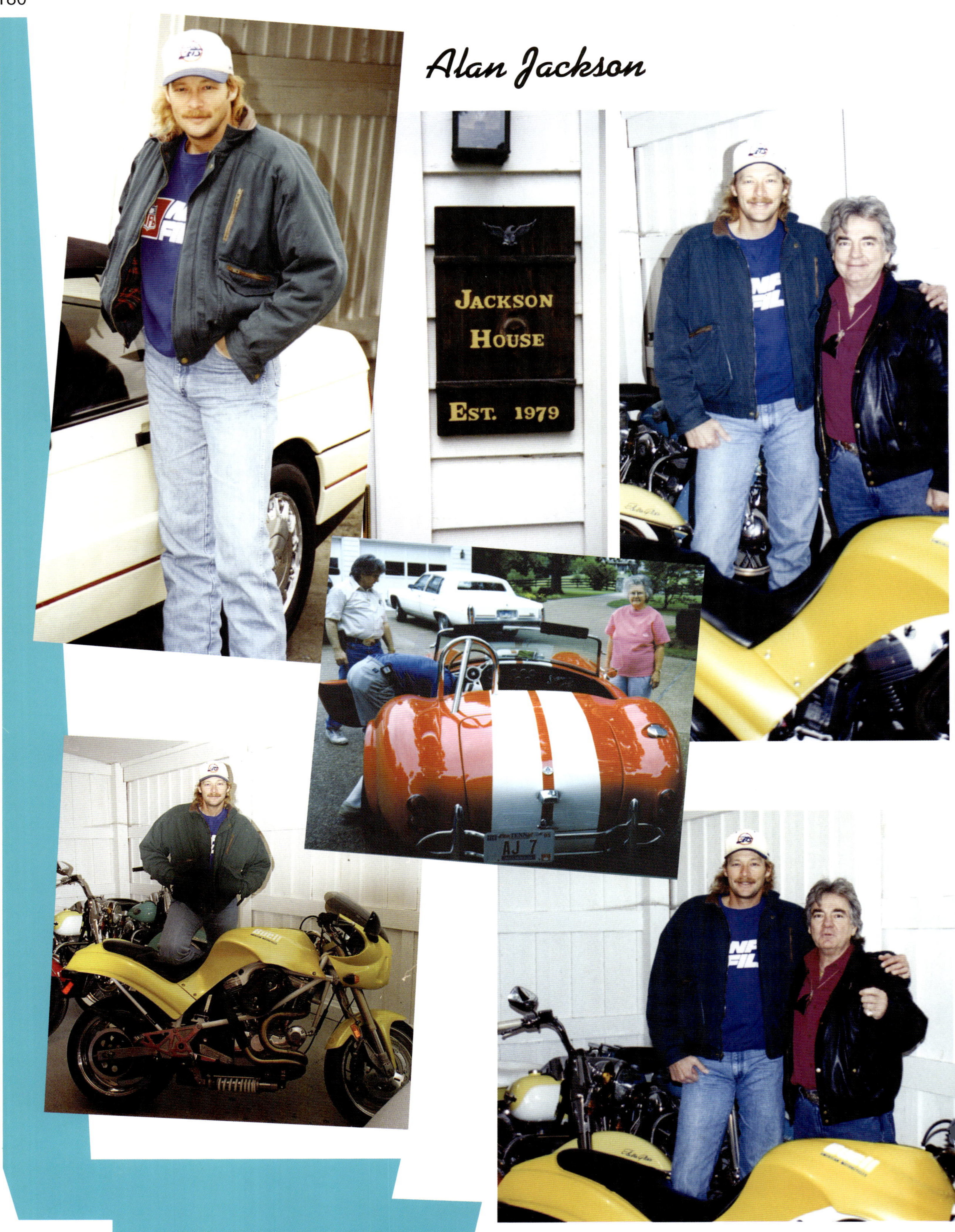

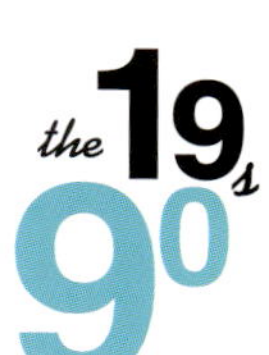

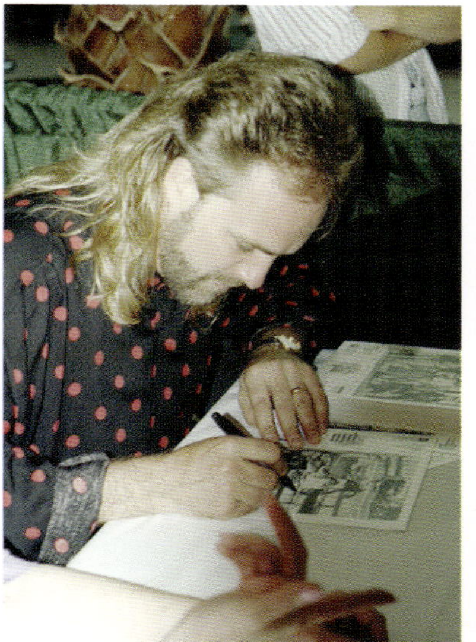

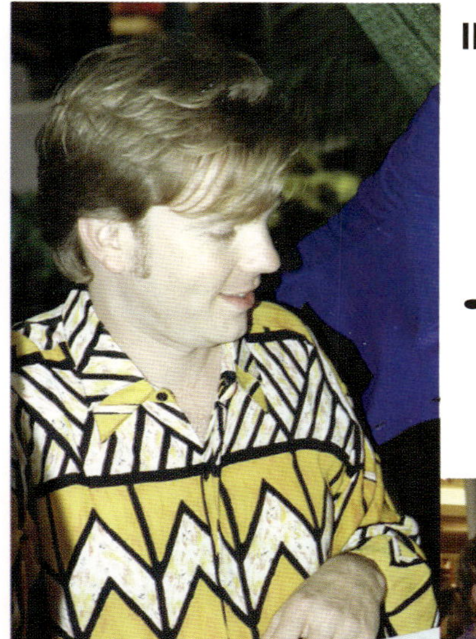

Little Texas

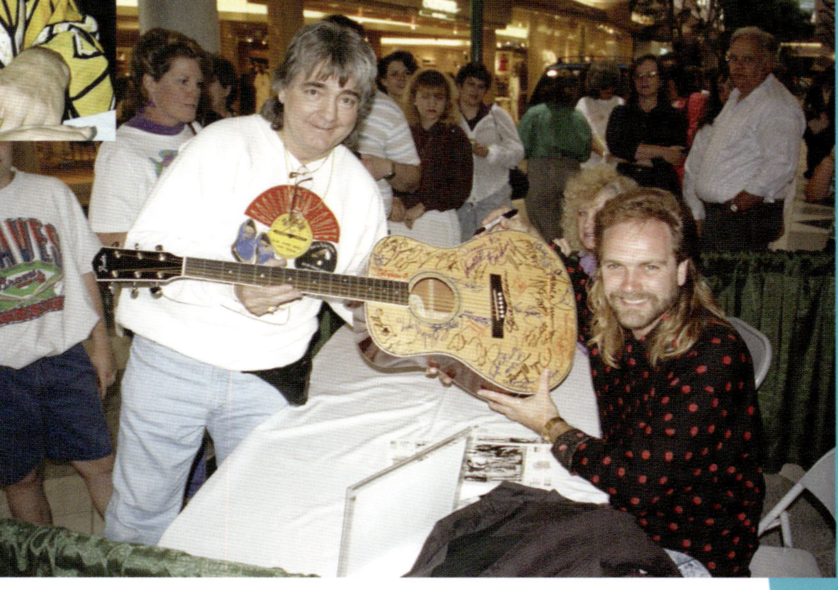

David Lee Murphy

Party Crowd
Dust on the Bottle

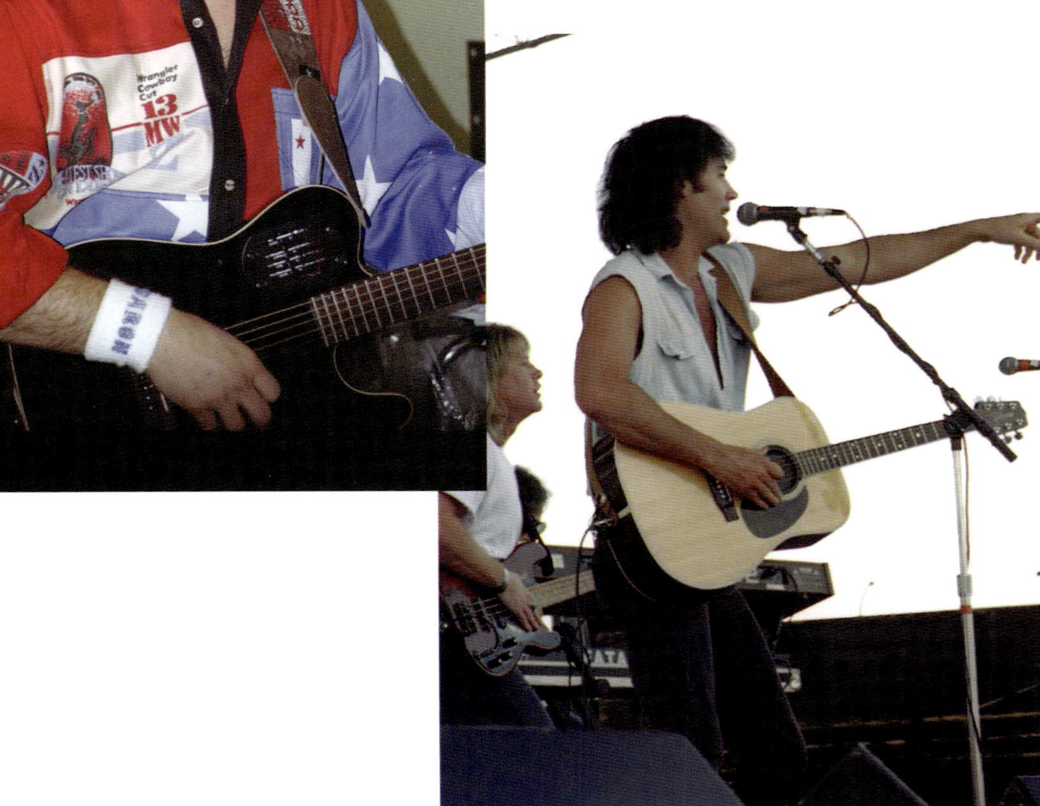

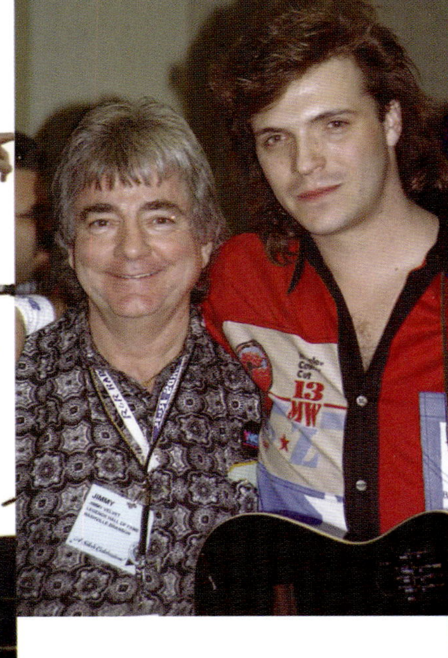

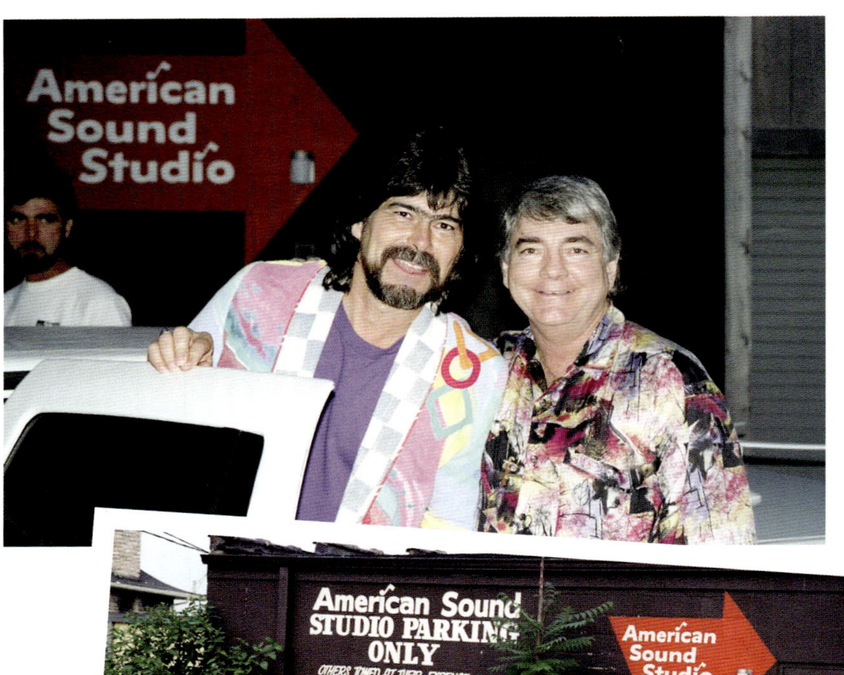

Alabama's **Randy Owen**

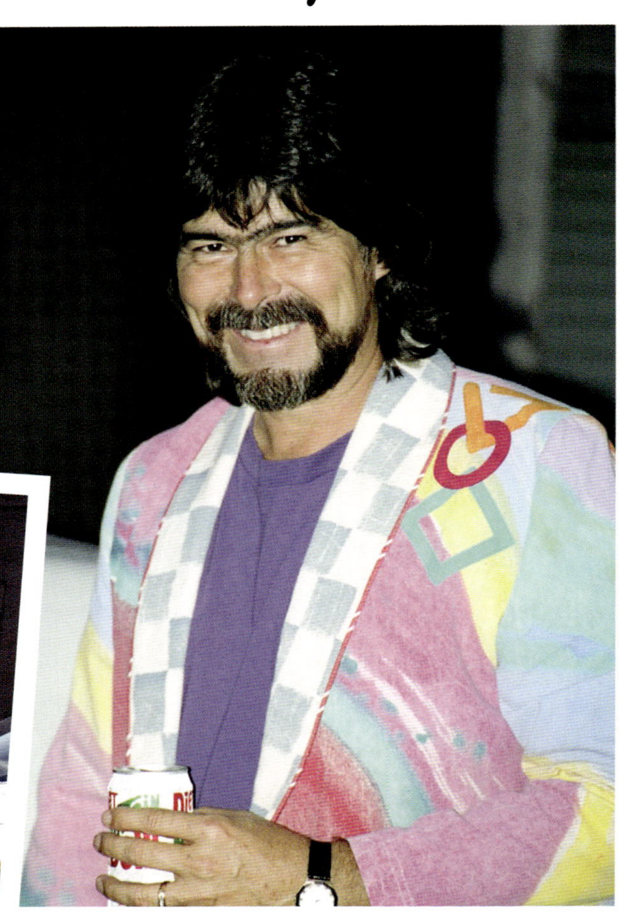

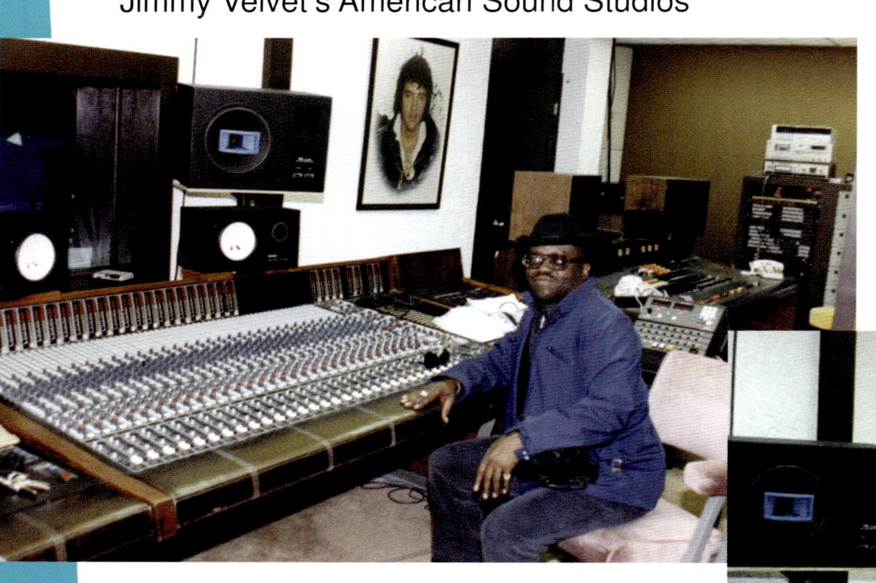

Jimmy Velvet's American Sound Studios

Otis Blackwell and Lucio

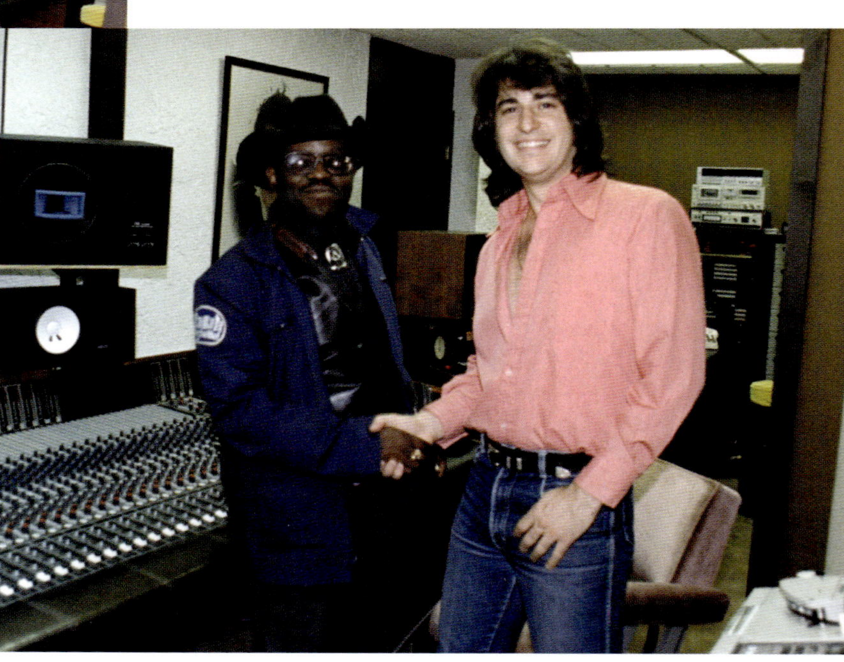

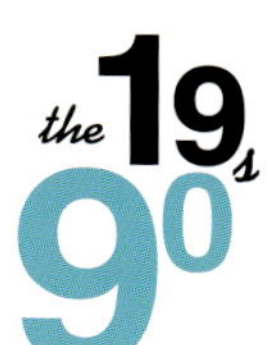

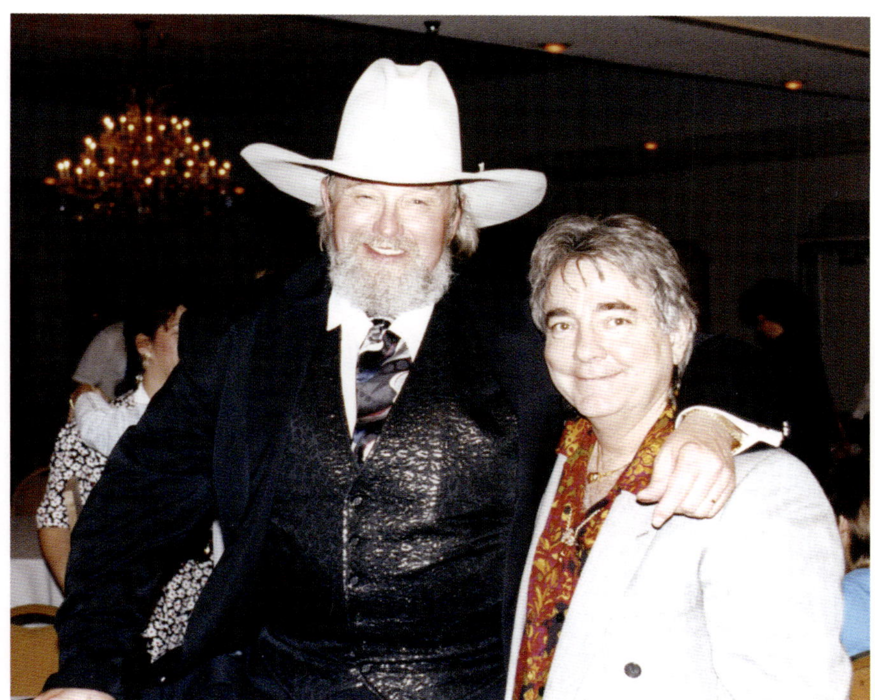

Charlie Daniels

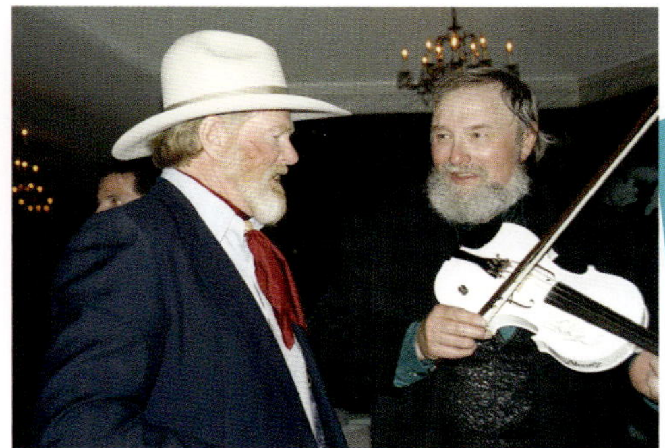

Charlie Daniels and Red Steagael

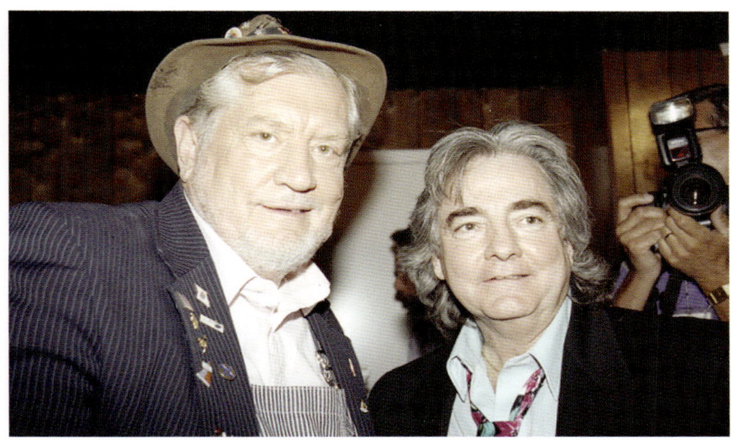

Boxcar Willie

Chris LeDoux

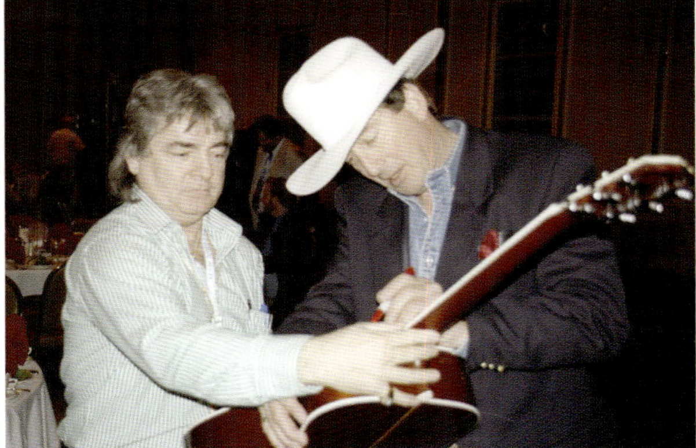

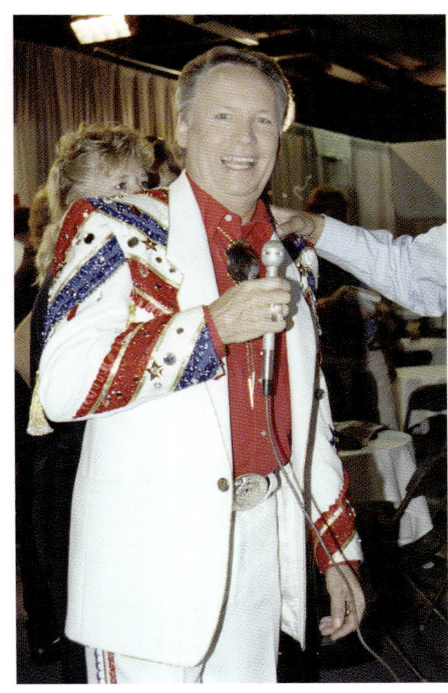

Buck Trent

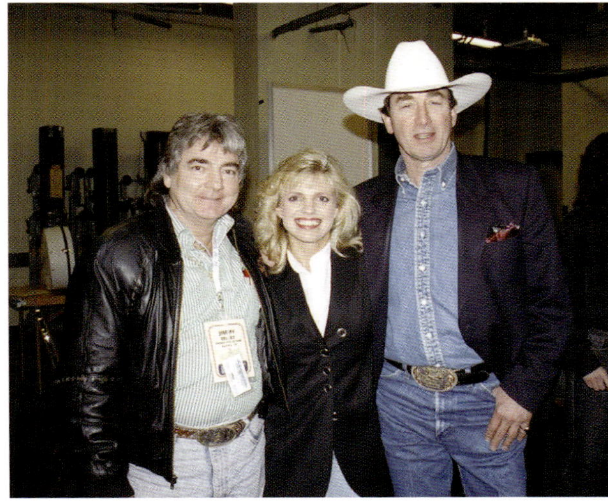

Jimmy, Joan Kennedy, and Chris LeDoux

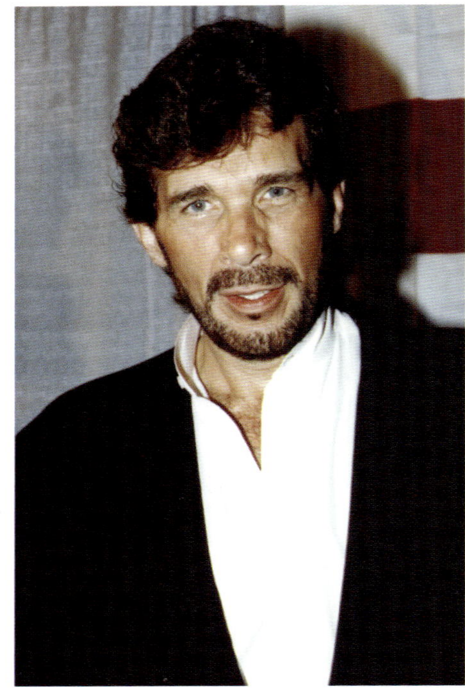

Eddie Rabbit

Ken Mellons

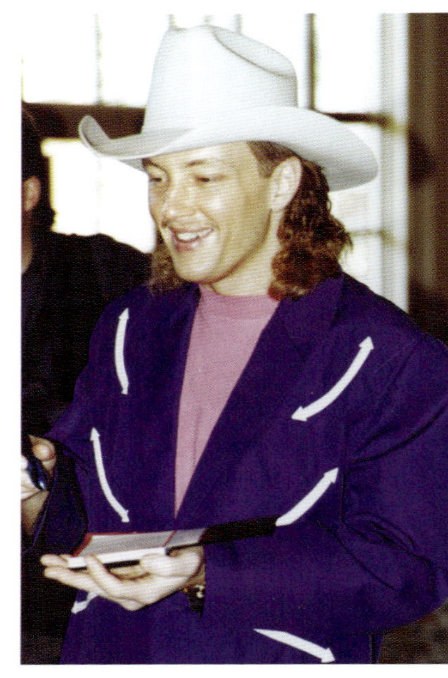

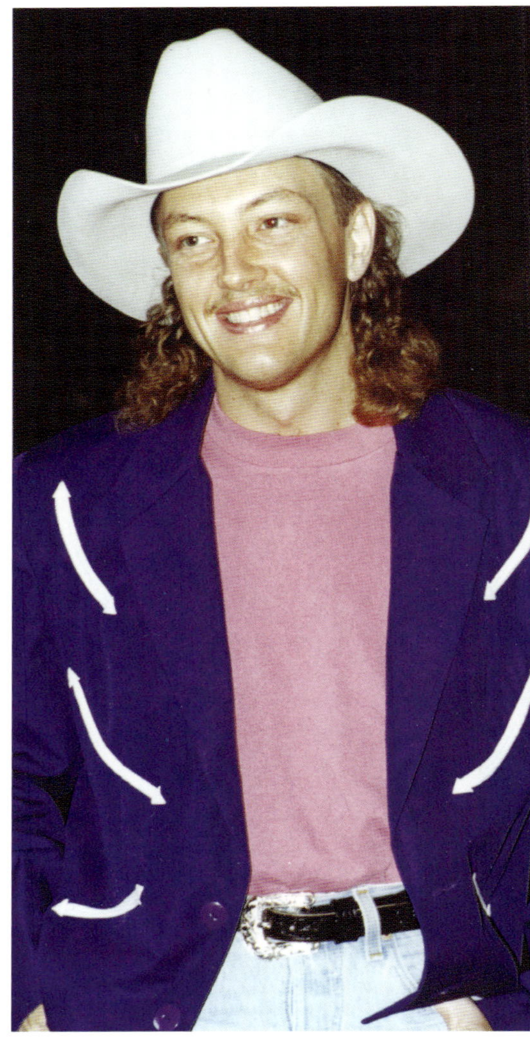

Linda Davis

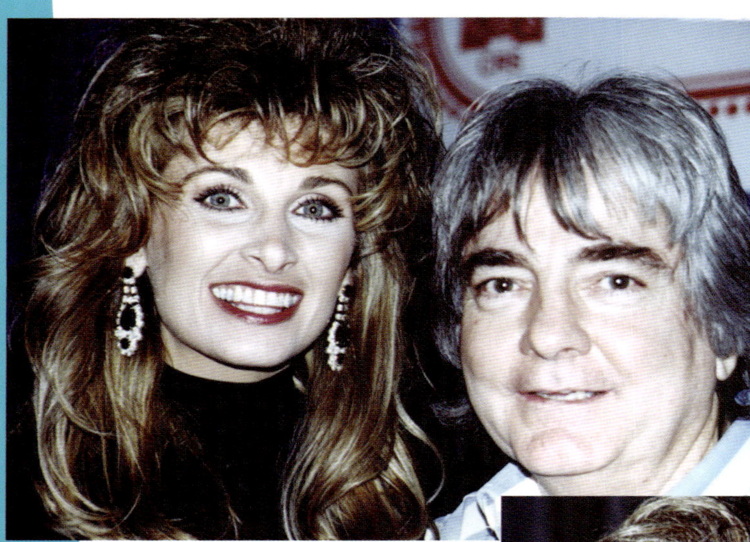

Clay Walker

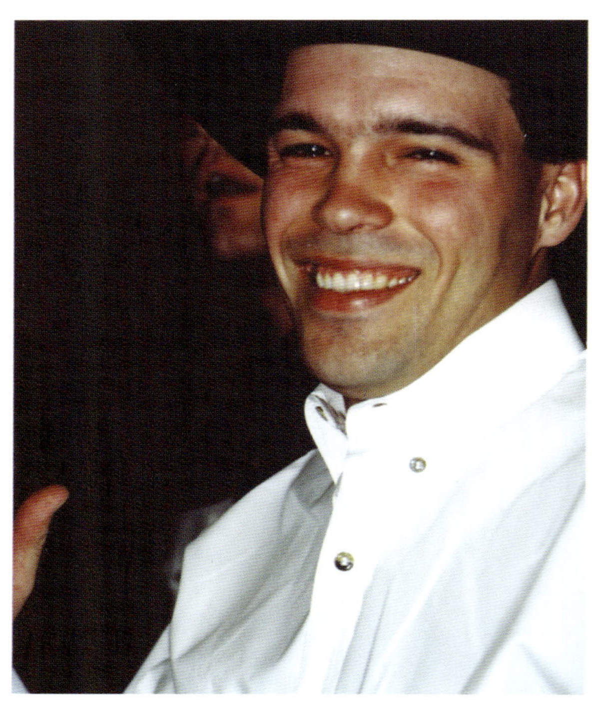

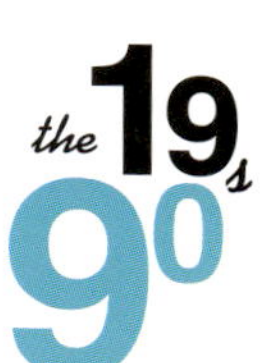

Neal McCoy

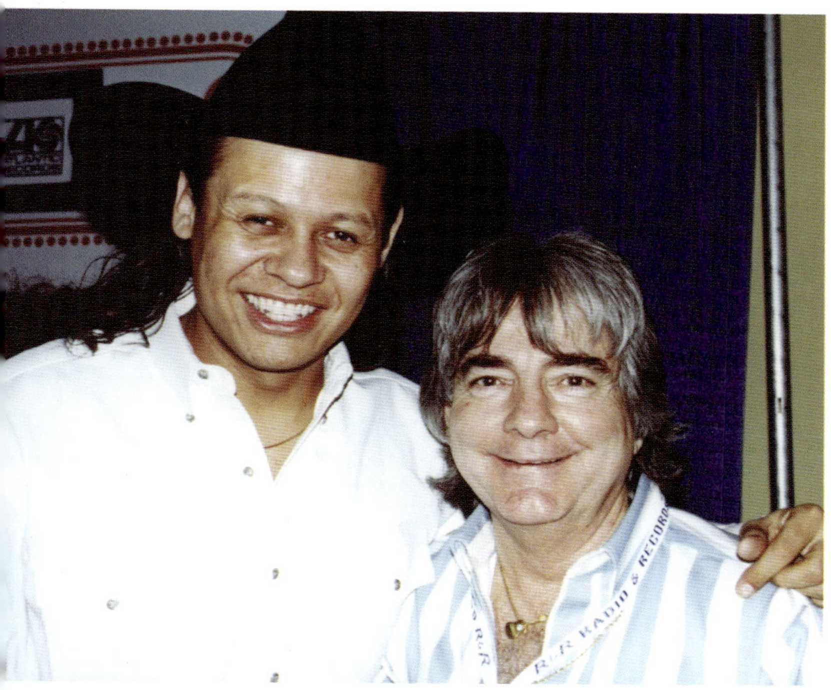

Gene Watson

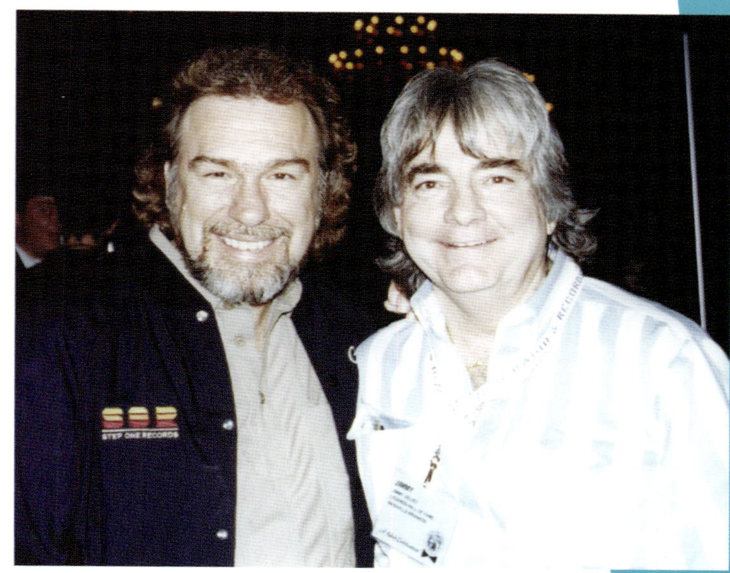

Sammy Kershaw

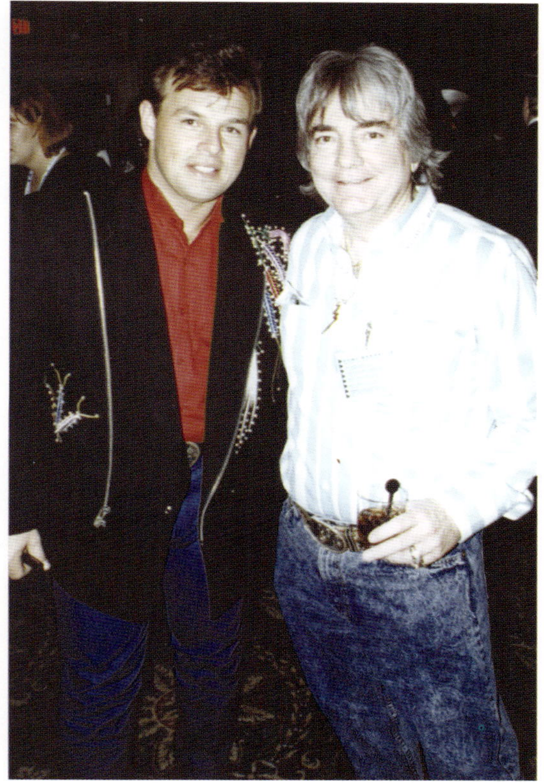

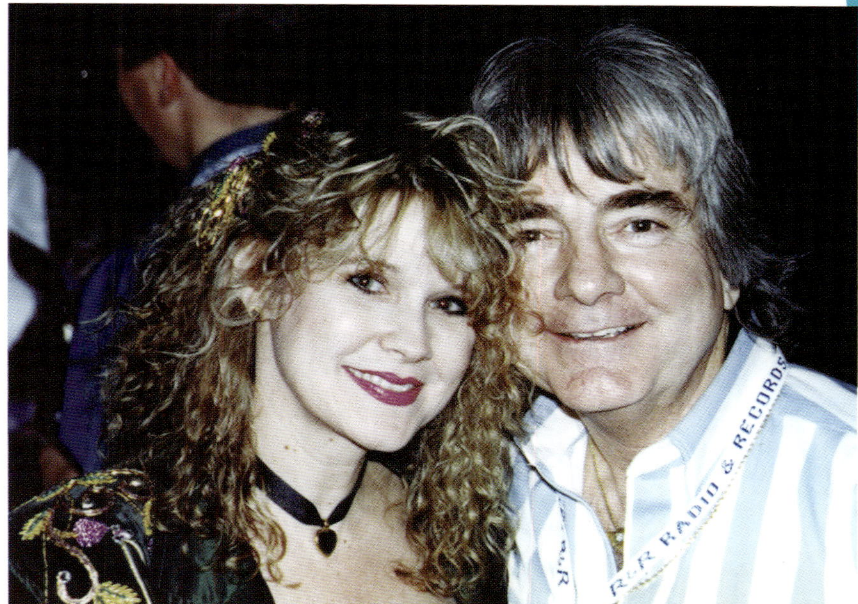

Becky Hobbs

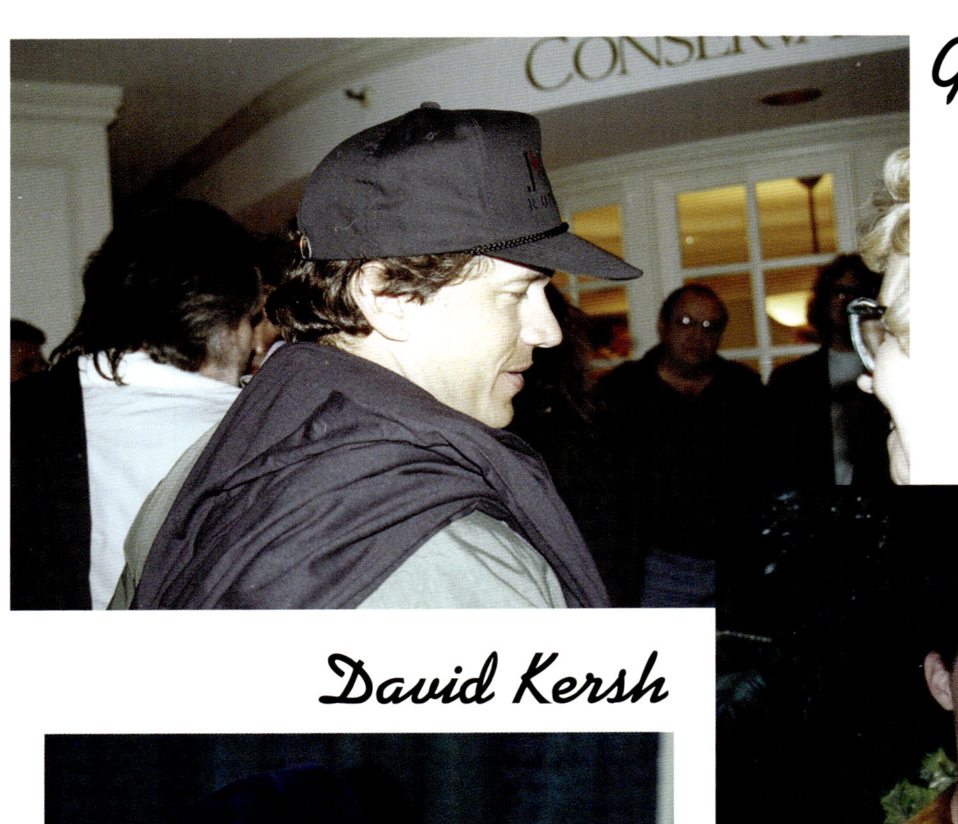

George Strait

David Kersh

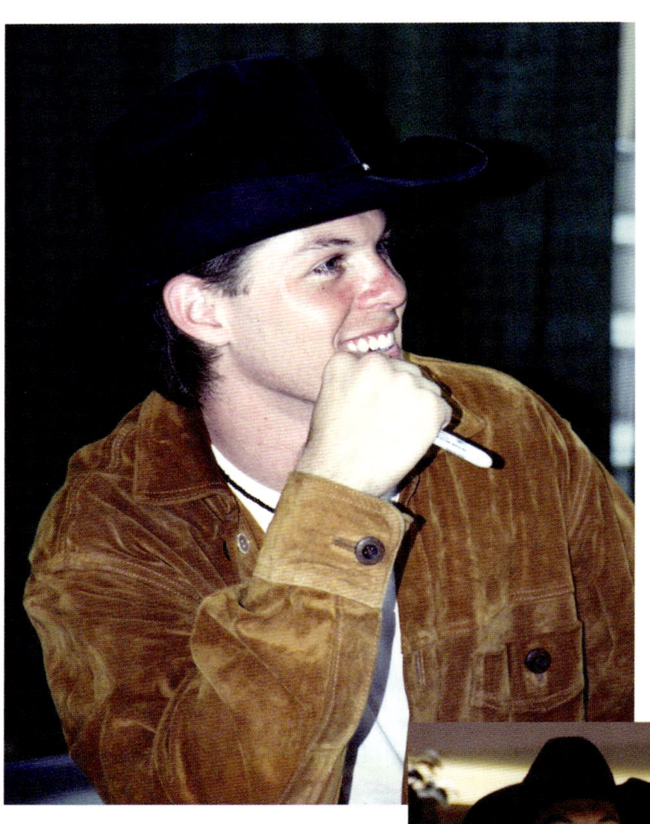

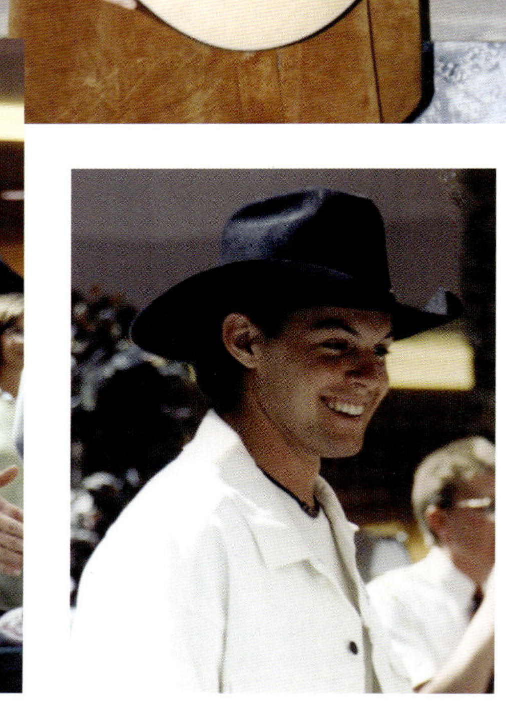

Crook and Chase

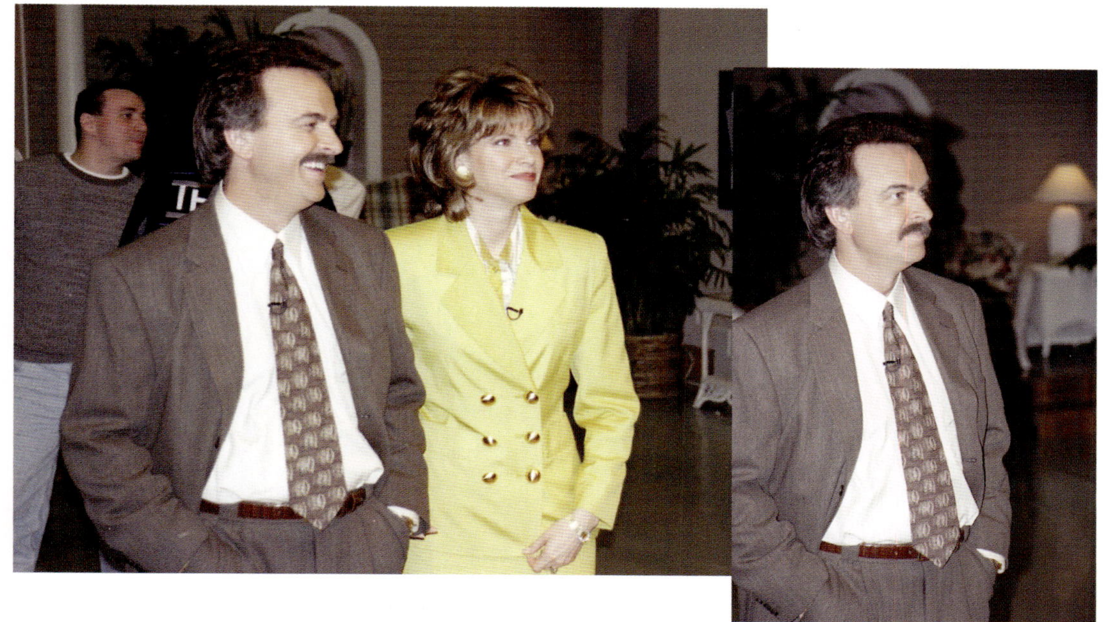

Charlie Chase

Mr. and Mrs. Freddie "Boom Boom" Cannon

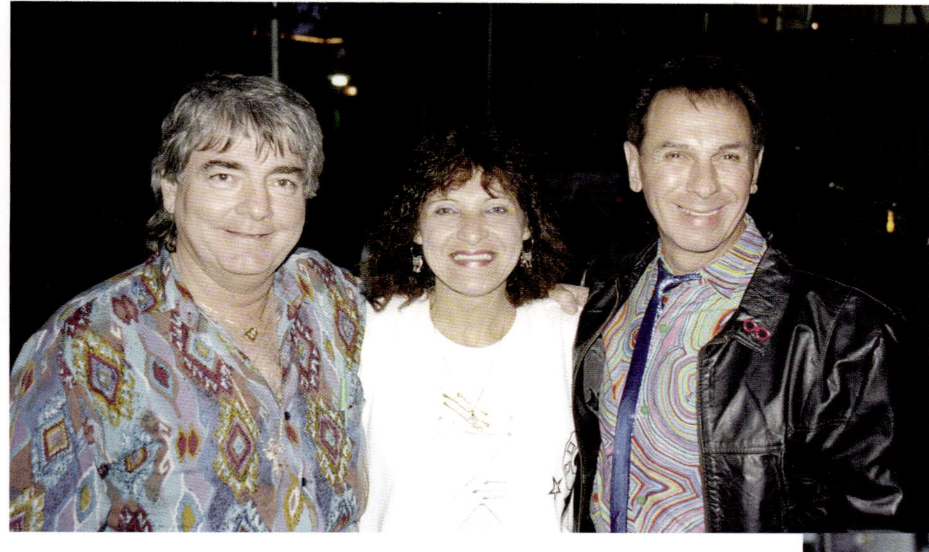

Deborah Allen

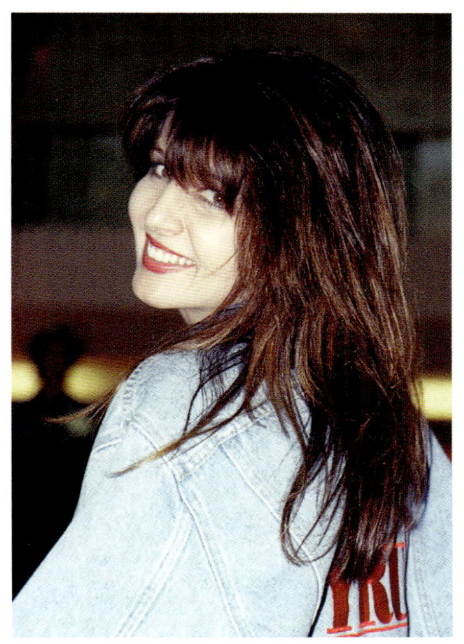

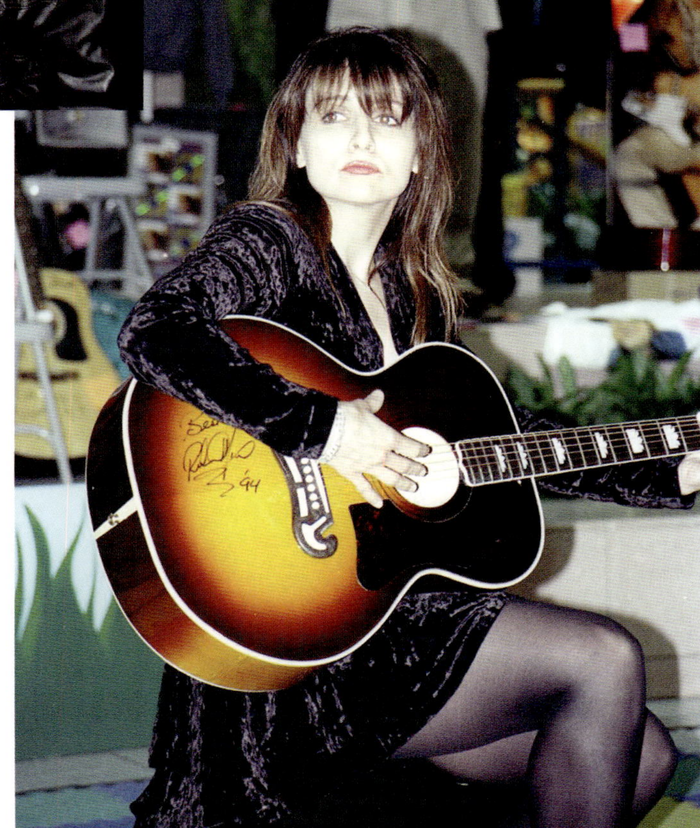

John Lee Hooker

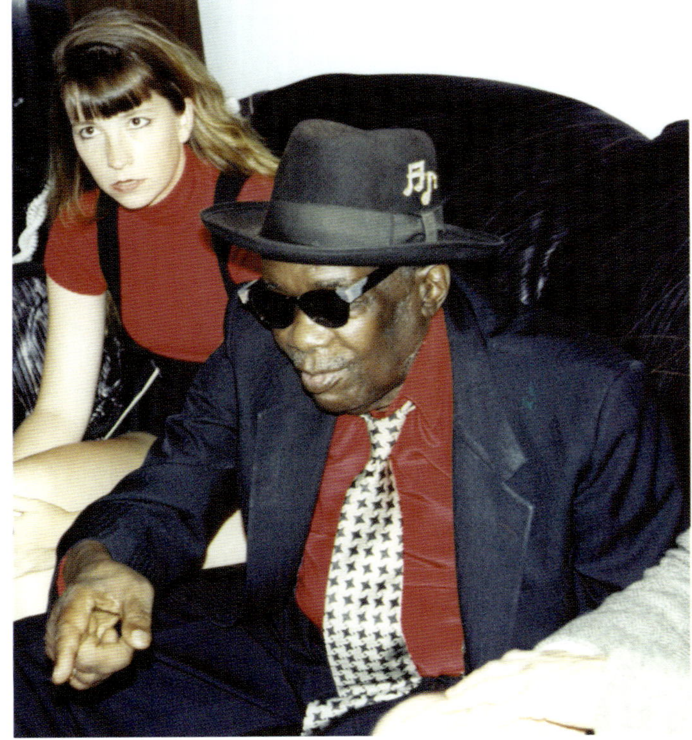

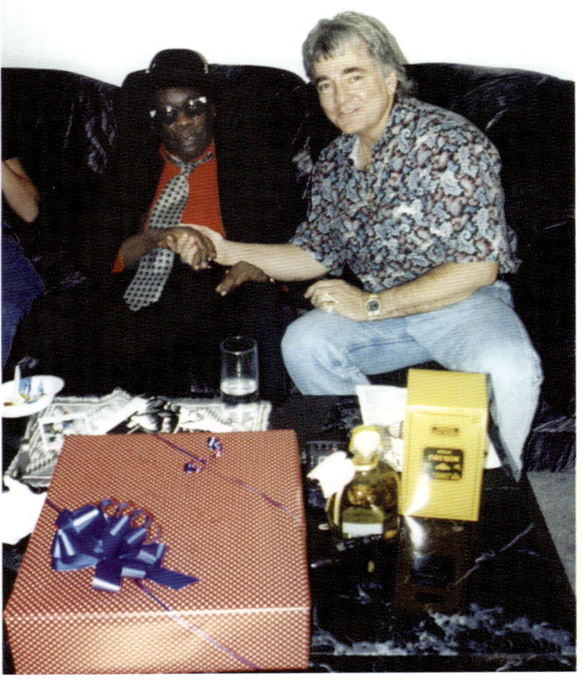

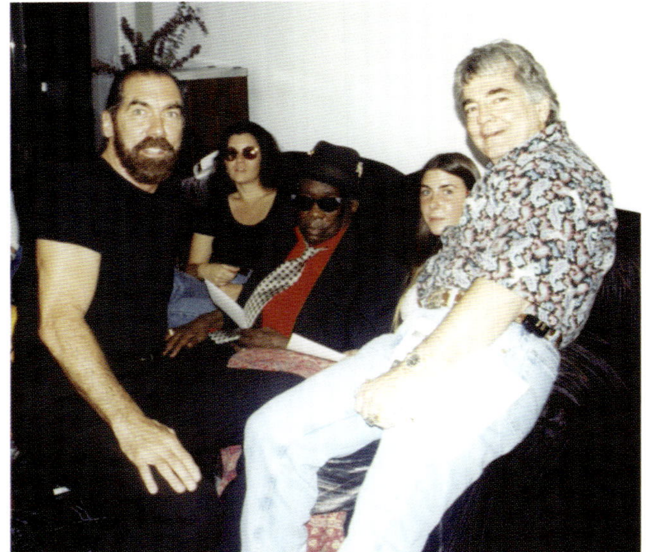

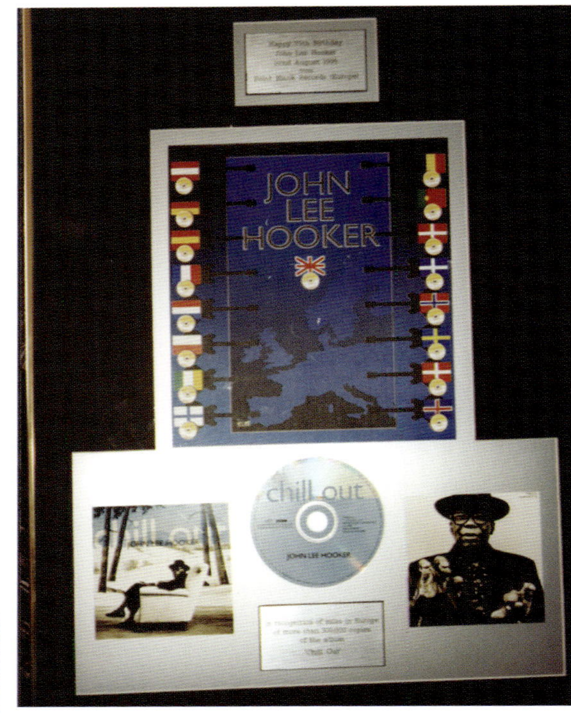

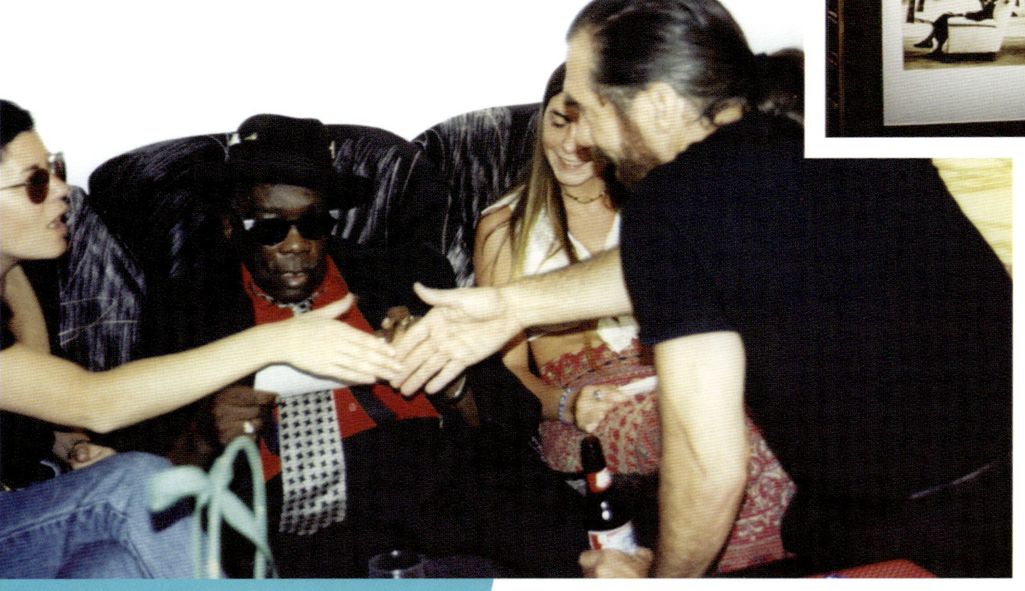

John Paul

Founder of Mitchell Hair Products

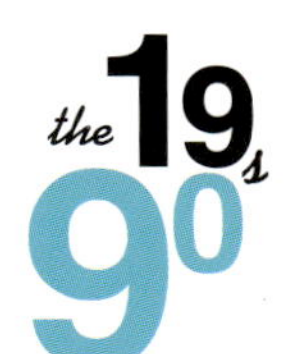

Bob Denver

Gilligan from "Gilligan's Island"

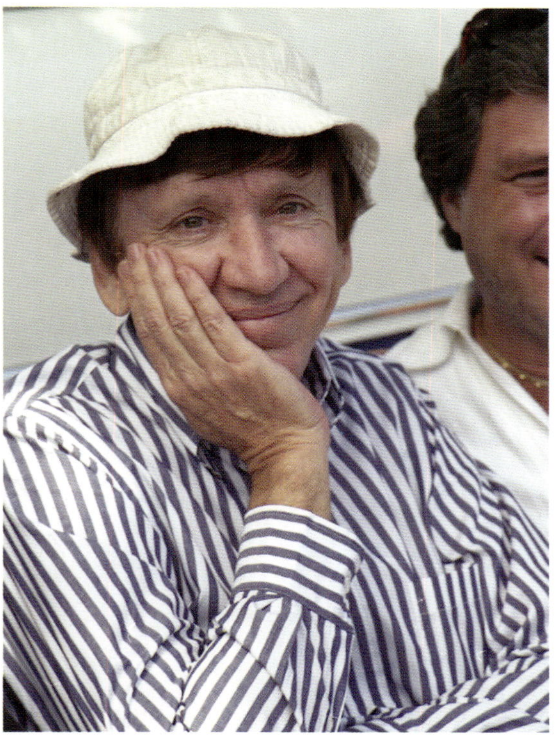

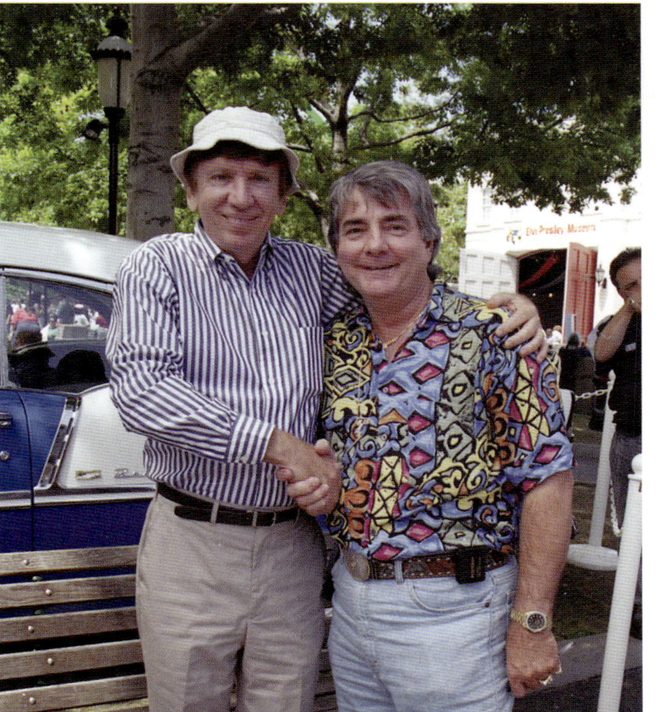

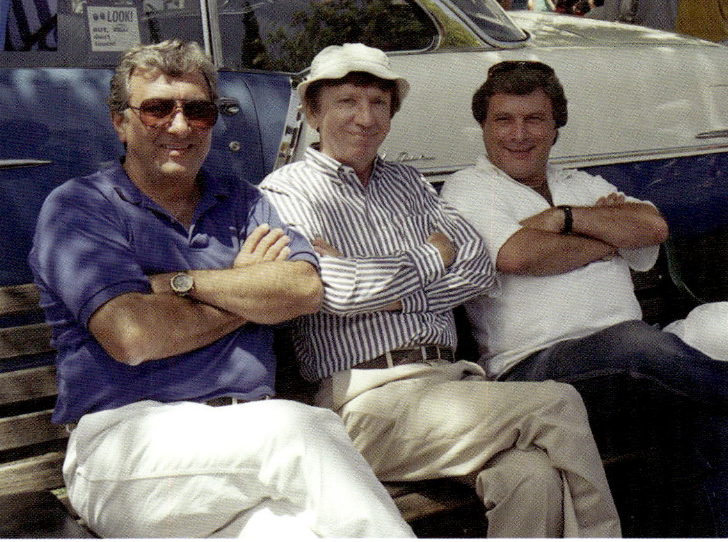

Richard Nader and Bob Denver

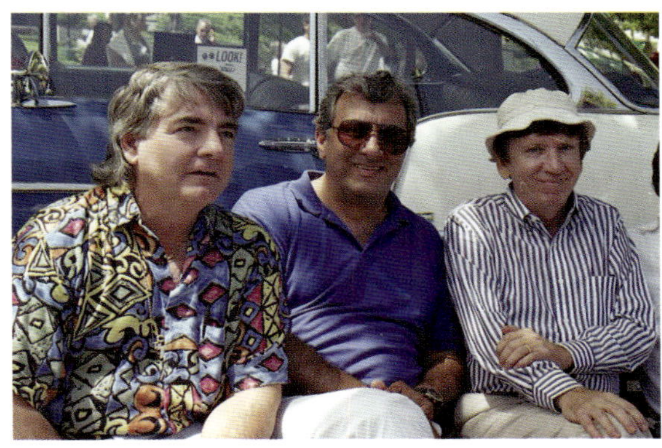

Bob Denver and I

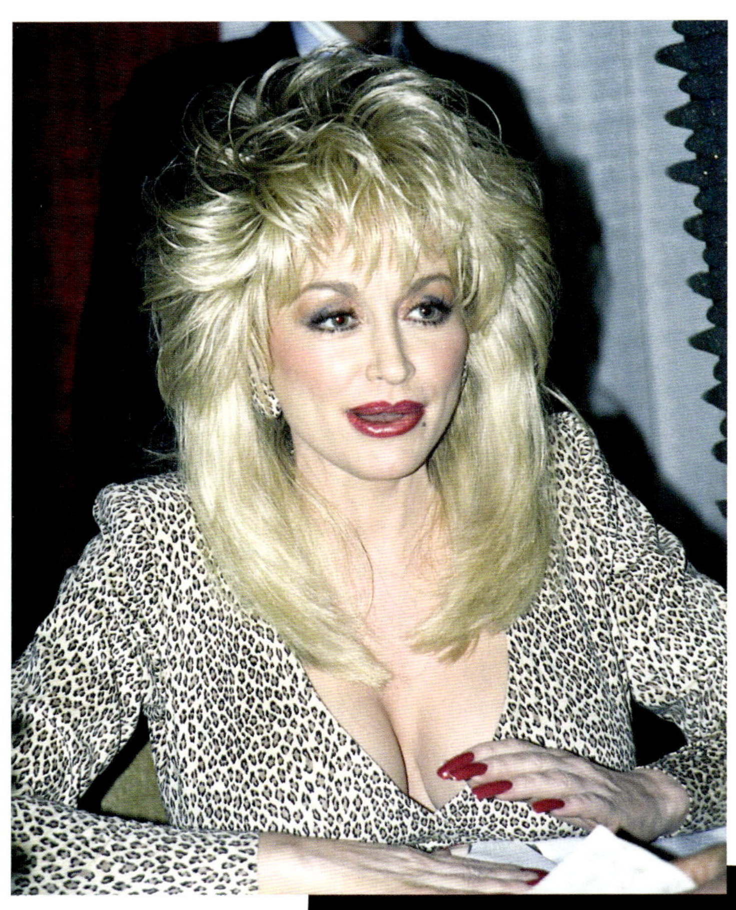

Dolly Parton

"Nuff said"

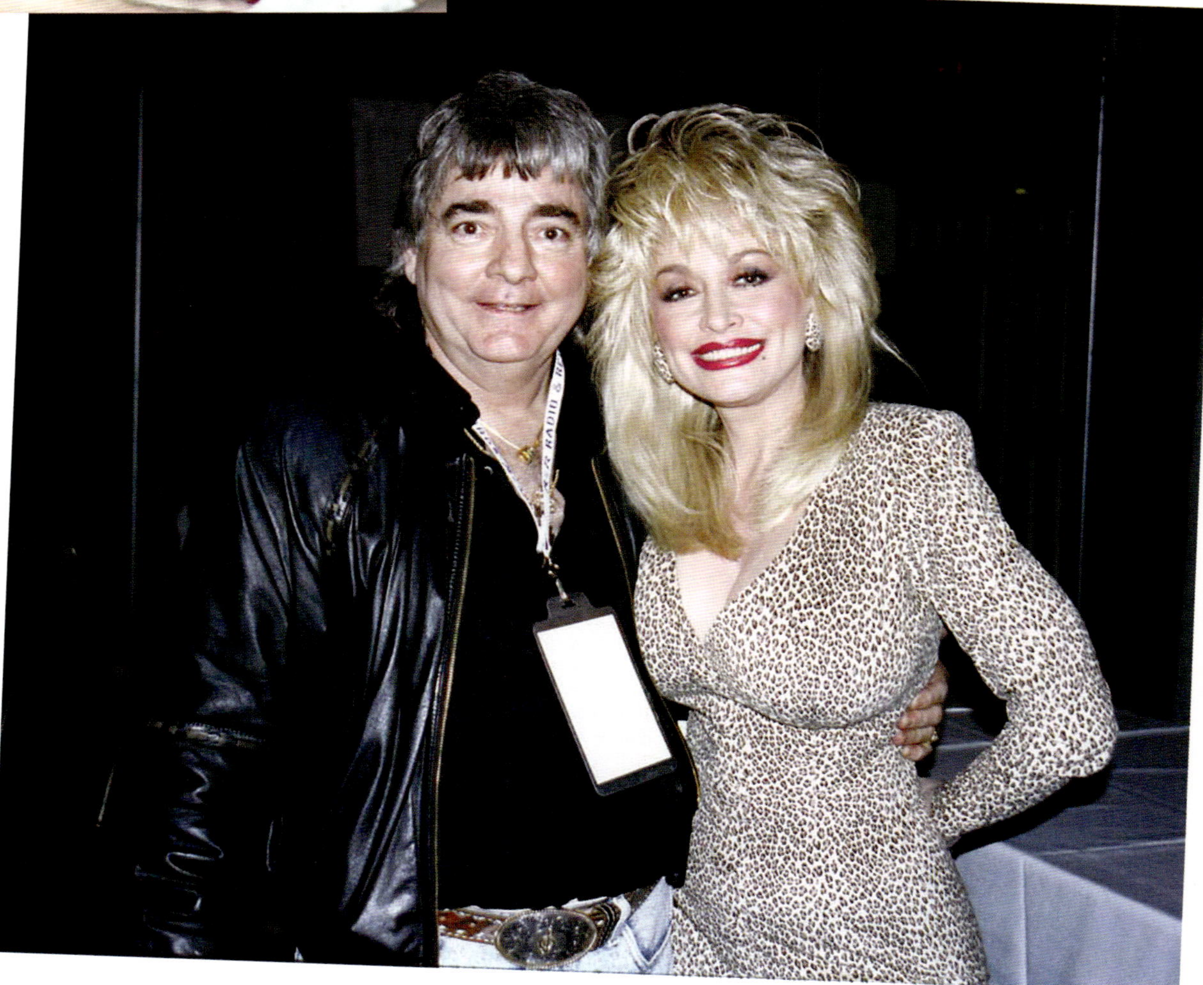

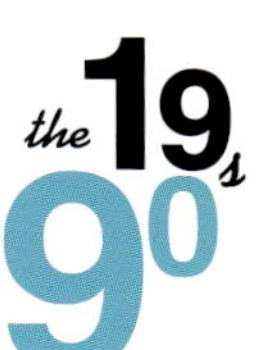
the 19
90
s

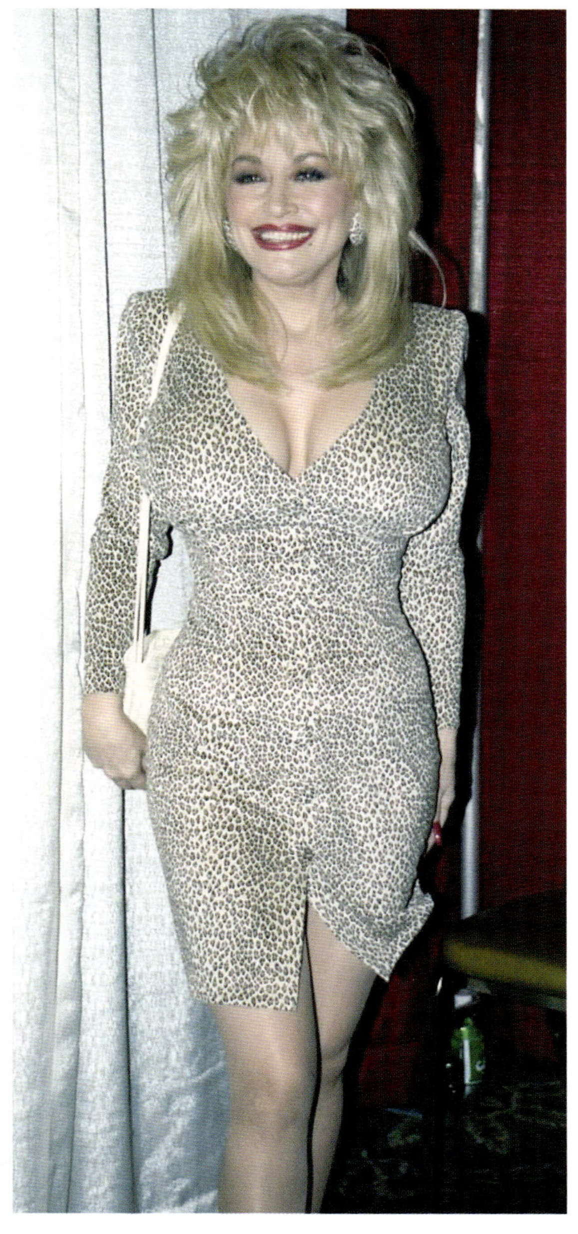

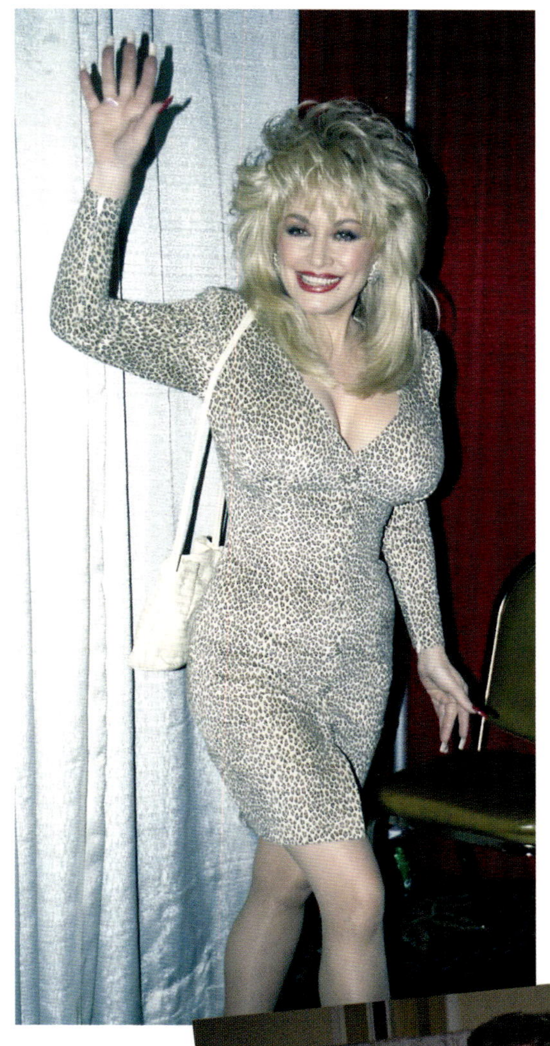

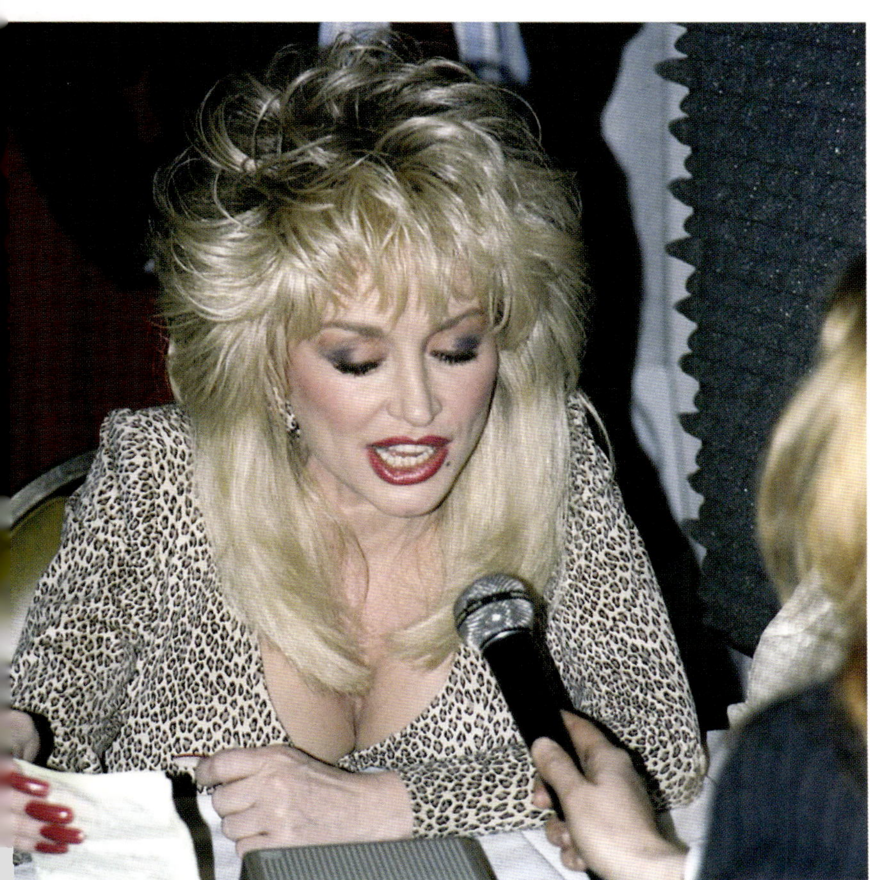

Dolly Parton

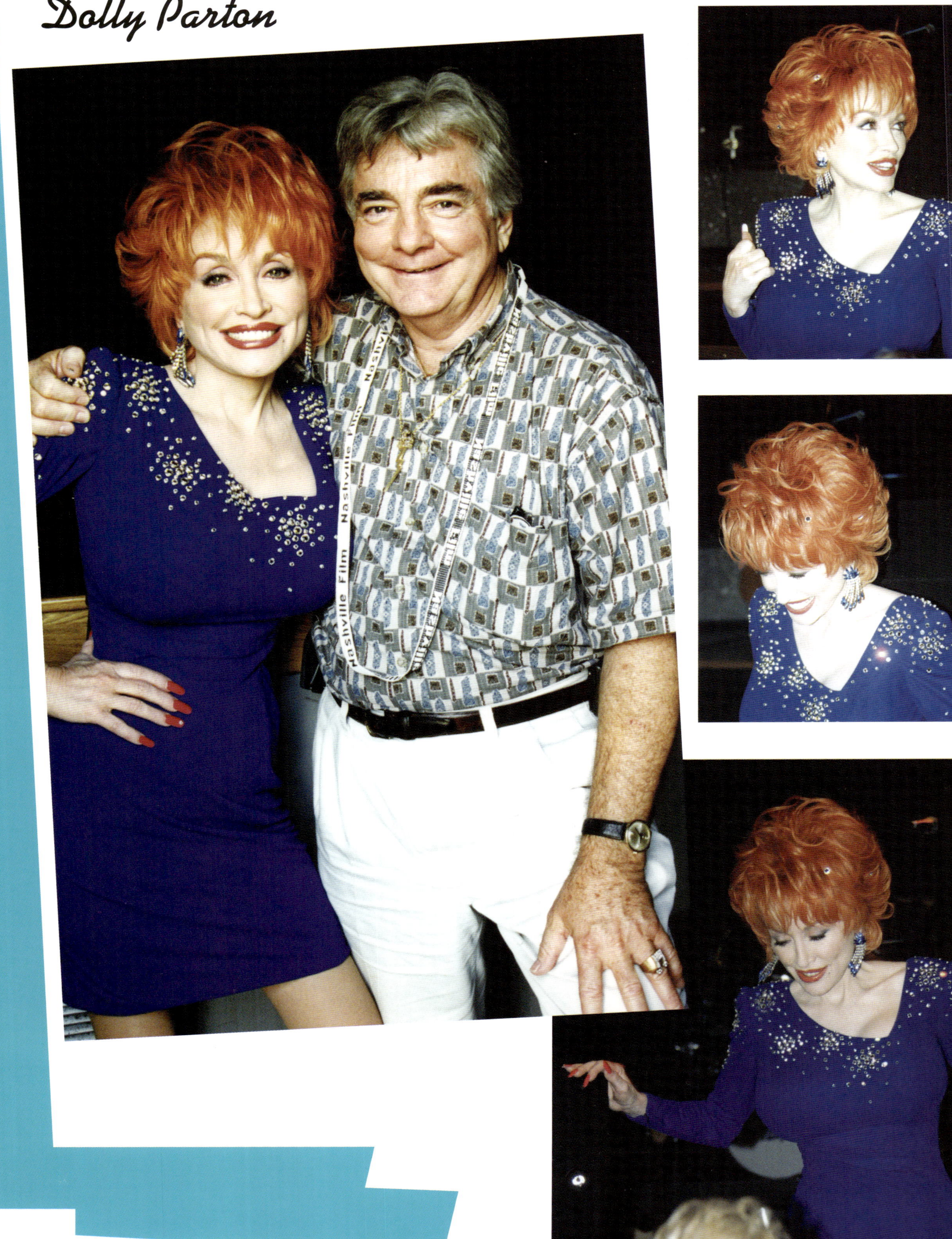

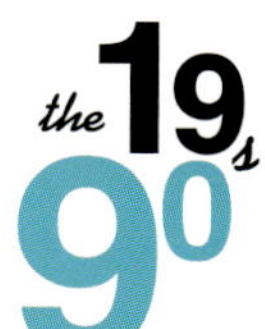

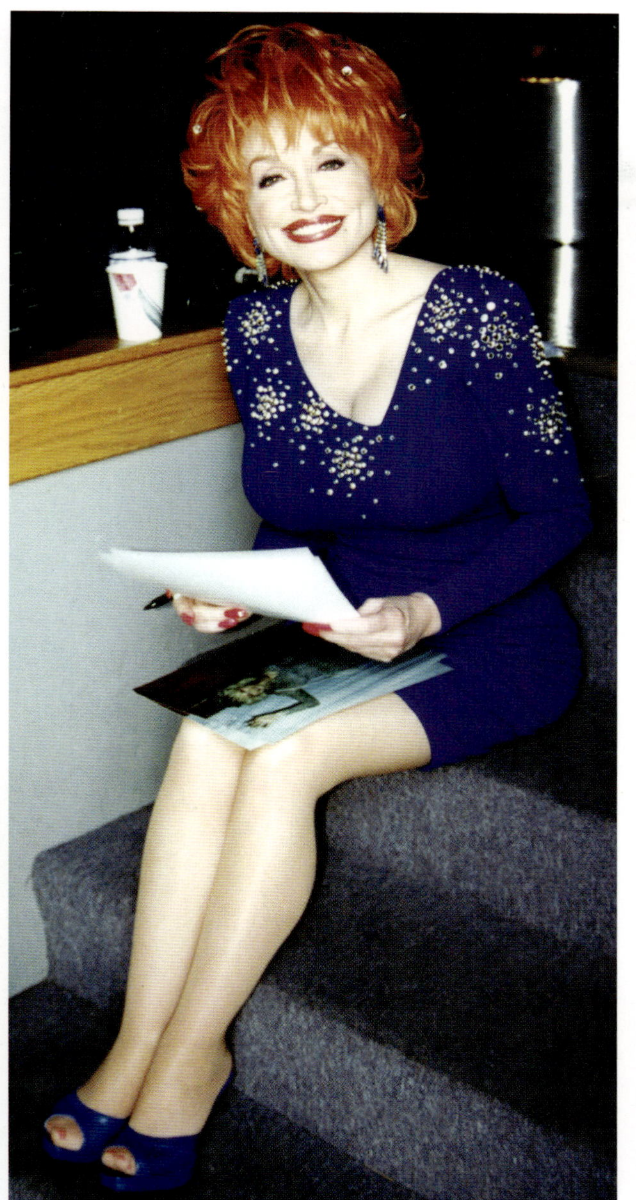

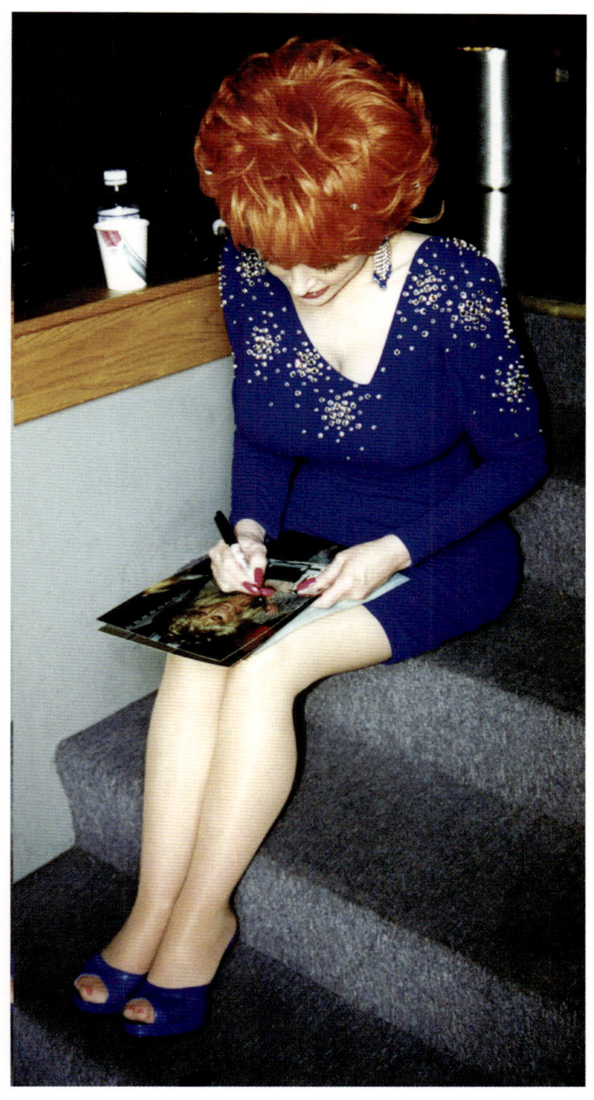

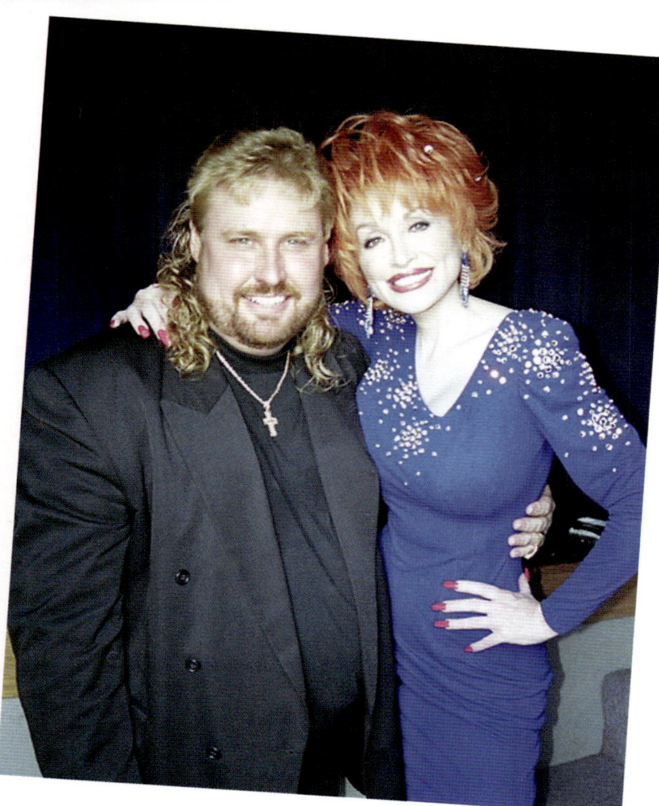

Dolly with my dear friend Gary Wayne Bridges

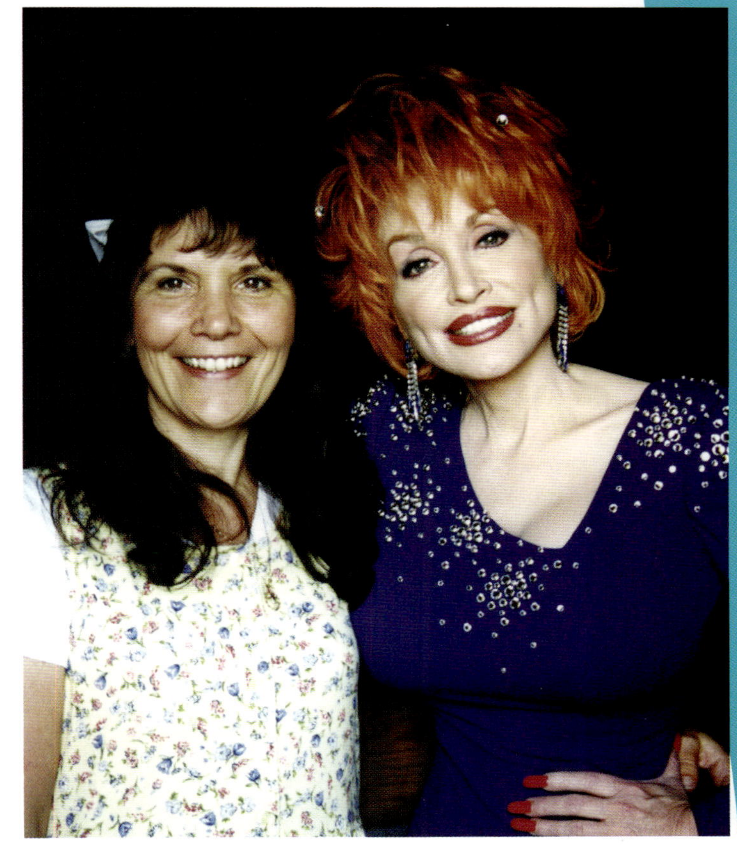

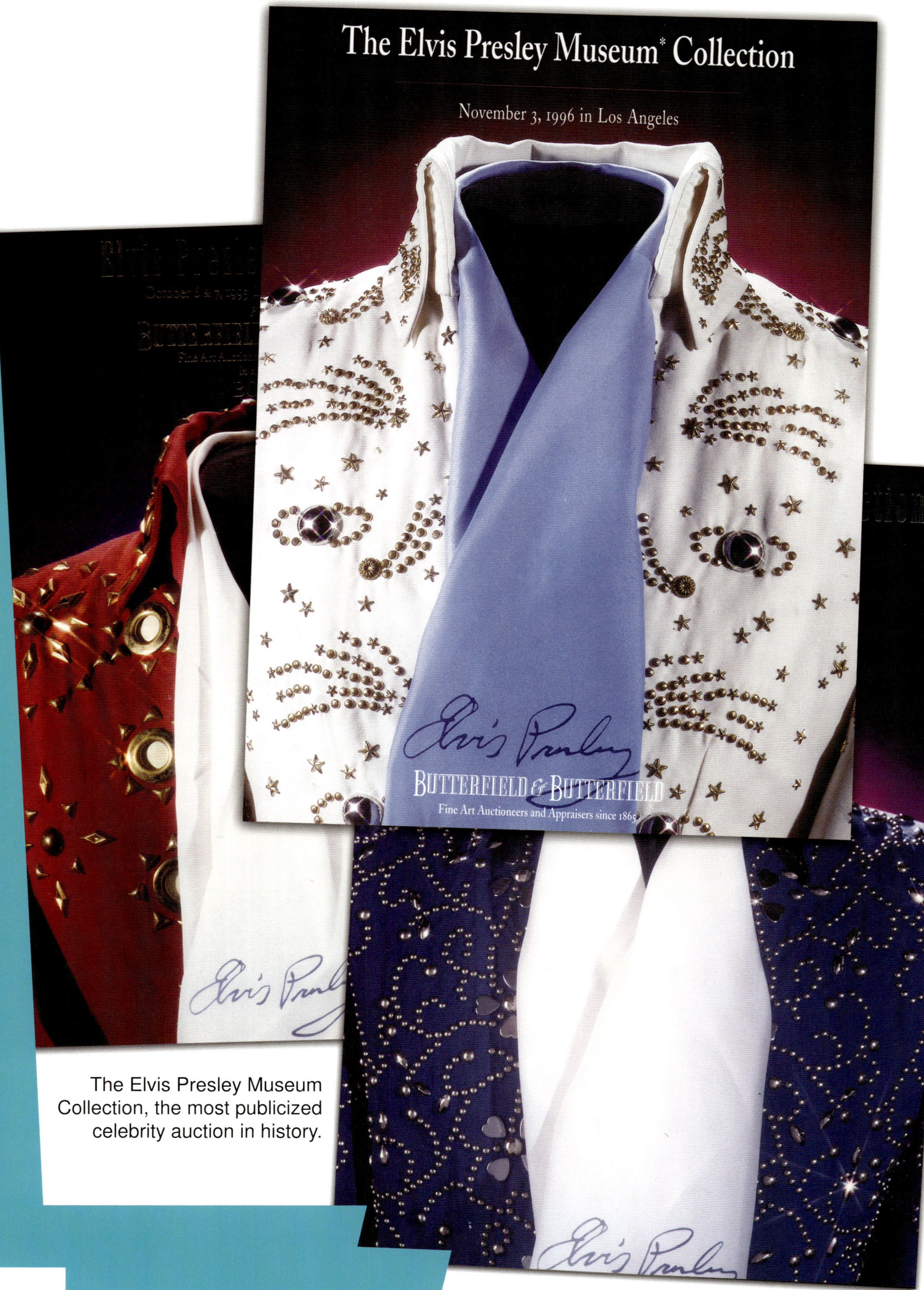

The Elvis Presley Museum Collection, the most publicized celebrity auction in history.

Elvis' American Express Card

Ferlin Husky

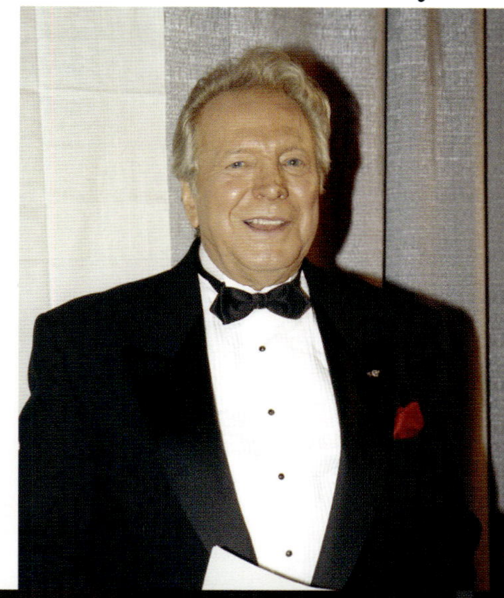

The Osmonds and Ross Perot

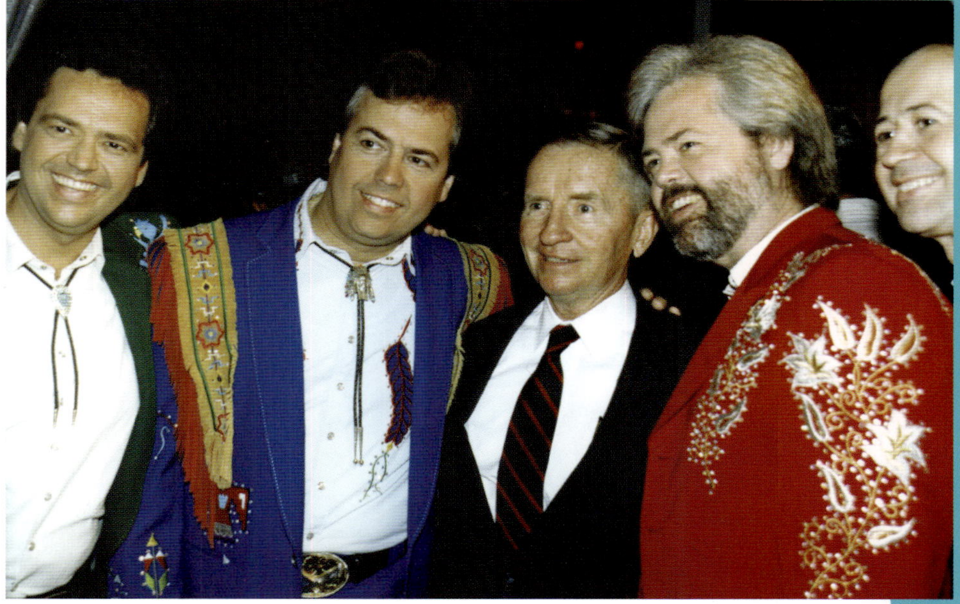

Greg McDonald
and his wife

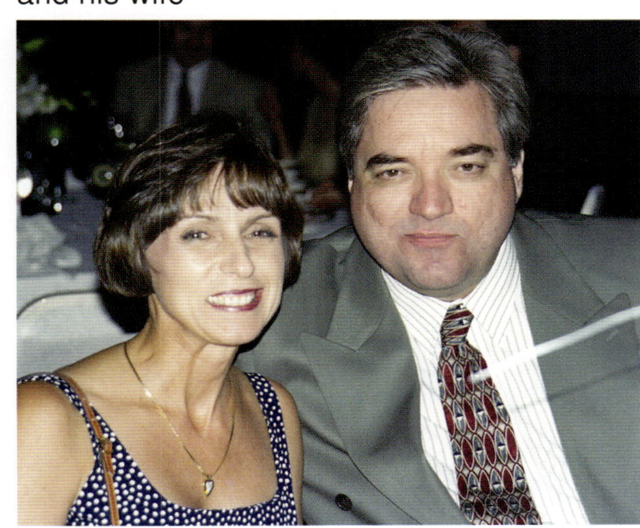

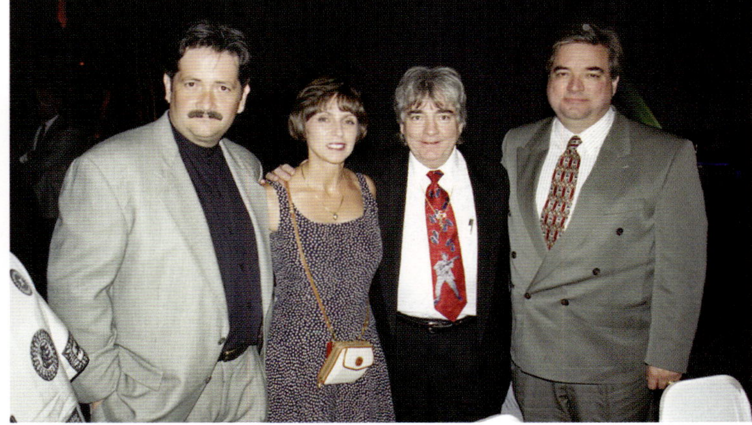

Greg is a very dear fiend.
He was Rick Nelson's manager, a close friend of Elvis and the Col., and he owned a music store in Palm Springs where Elvis would purchase equipment from him. He is now working with Universal Studios Orlando.

My buddy

Dan Haggerty

"Grizzly Adams"

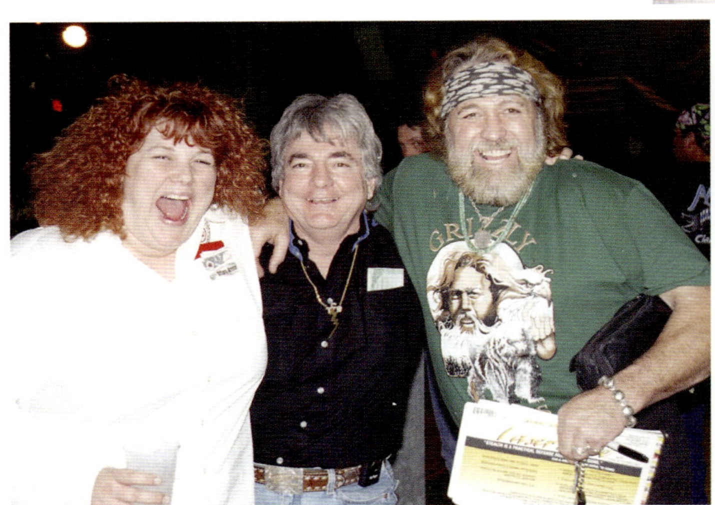

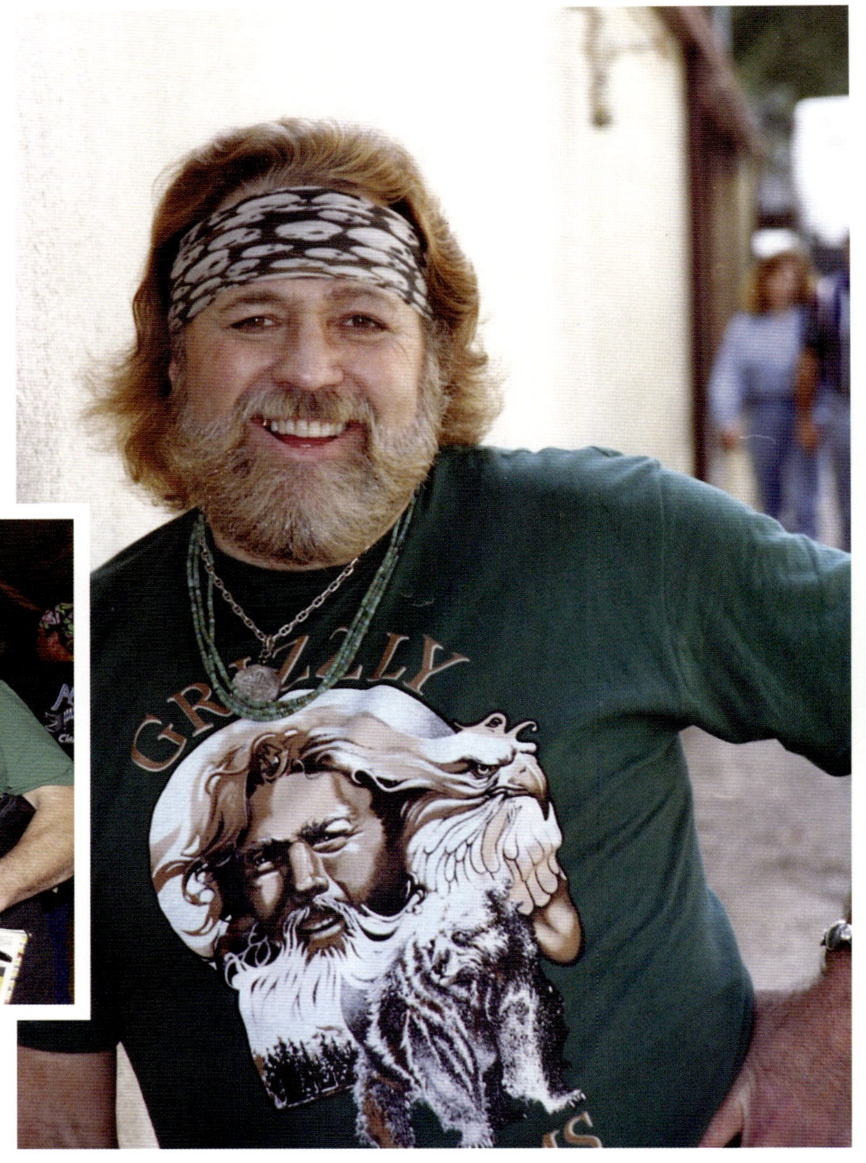

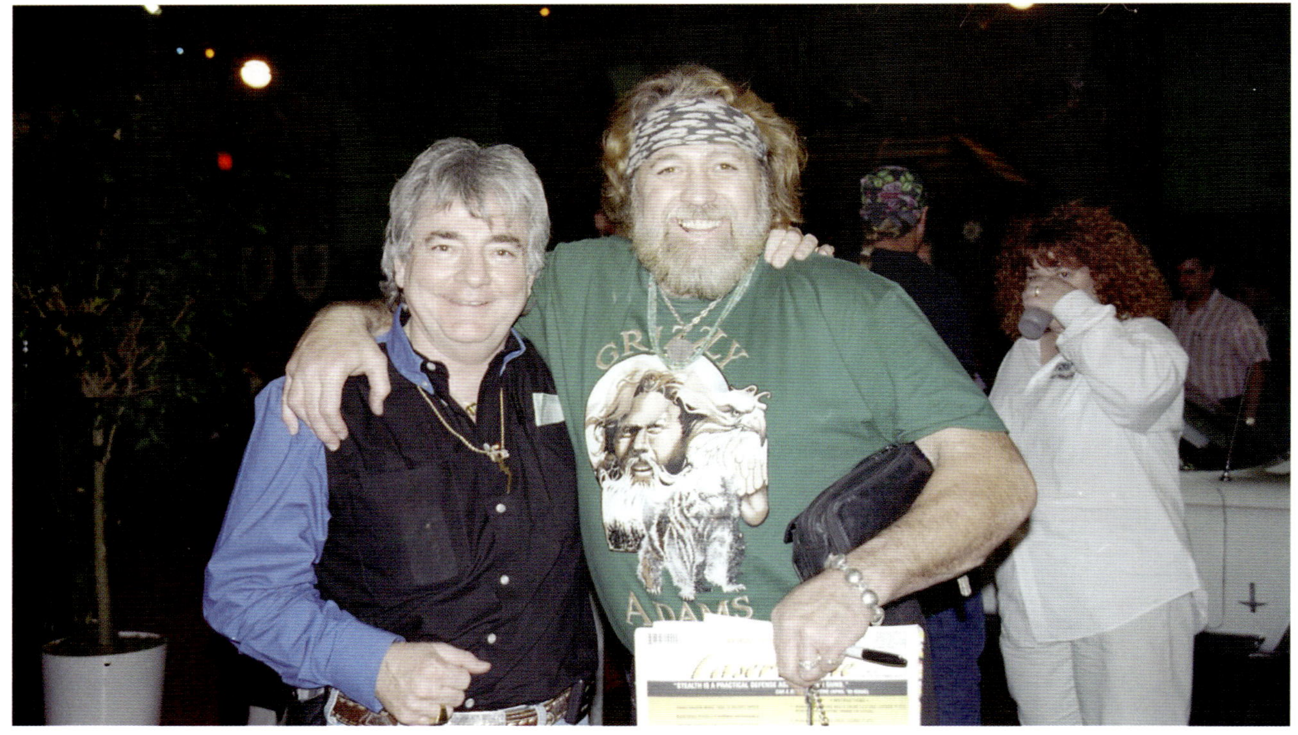

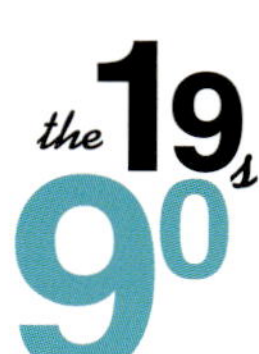

Clinton Gregory

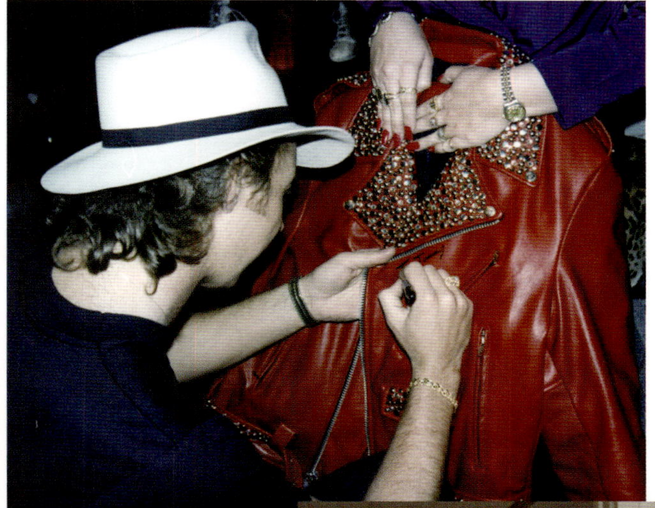

Confederate Railroad

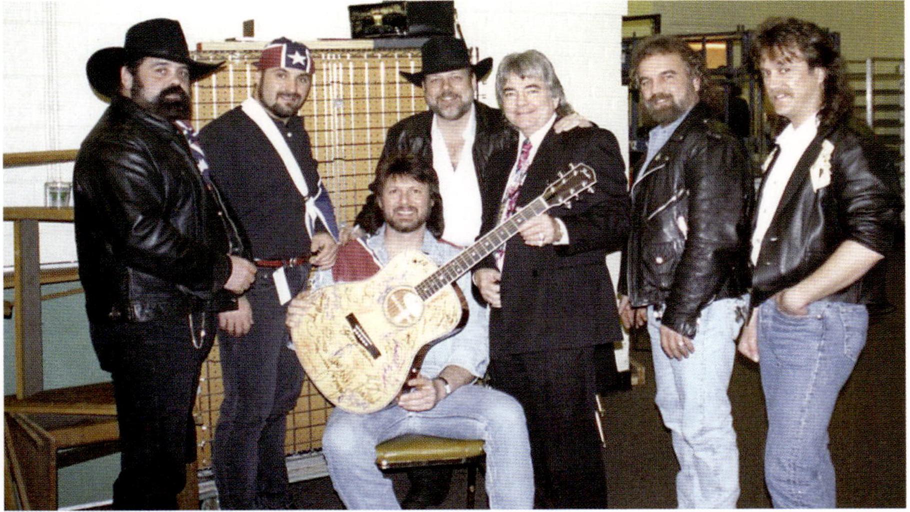

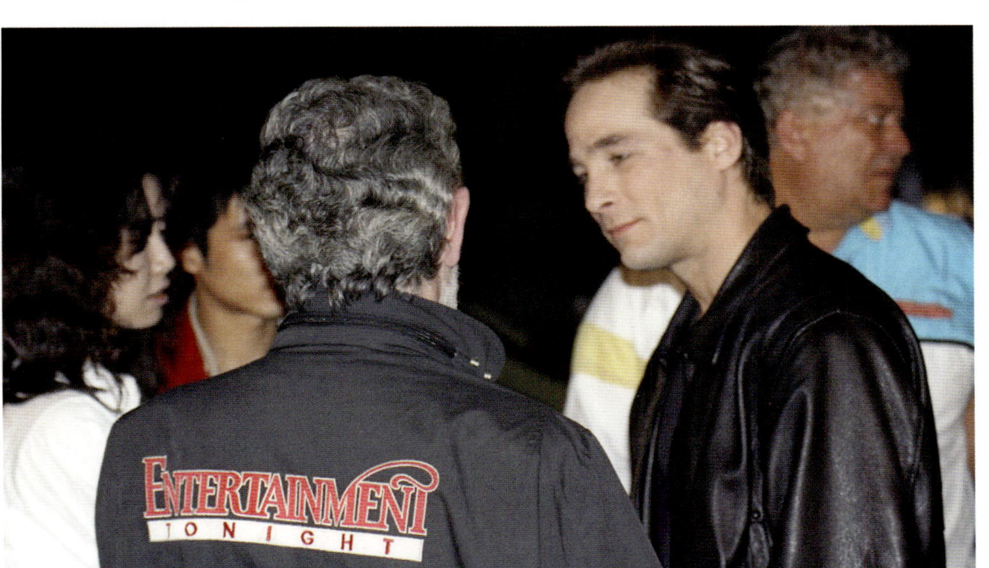

Clint Black

and Entertainment Tonight's Producer Dick Heard

Dick and Eddie Rabbit wrote "Kentucky Rain" for Elvis.

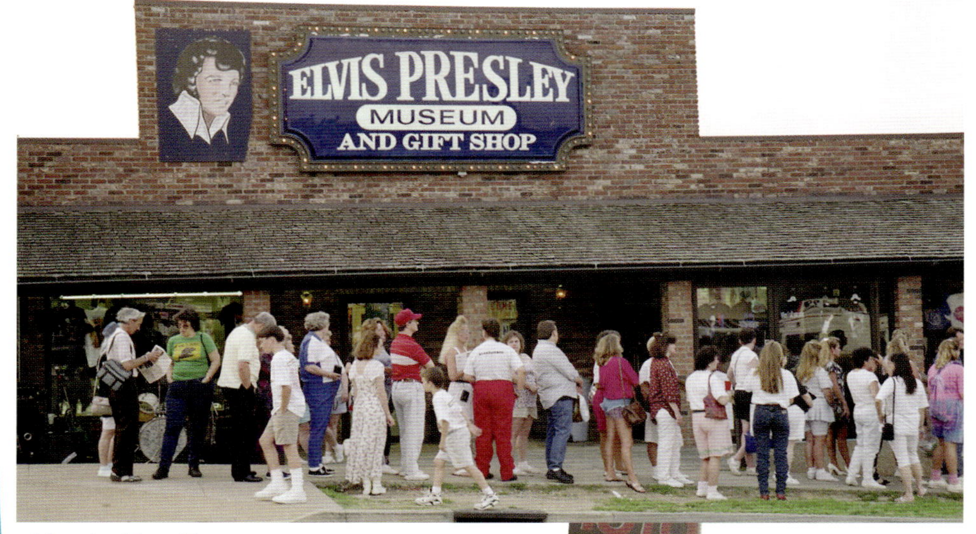

One of my 5 Elvis Presley Museums.
Others were in Memphis, Honolulu,
Orlando, and Branson.
Plus 2 road tours.

Nashville, Tennessee

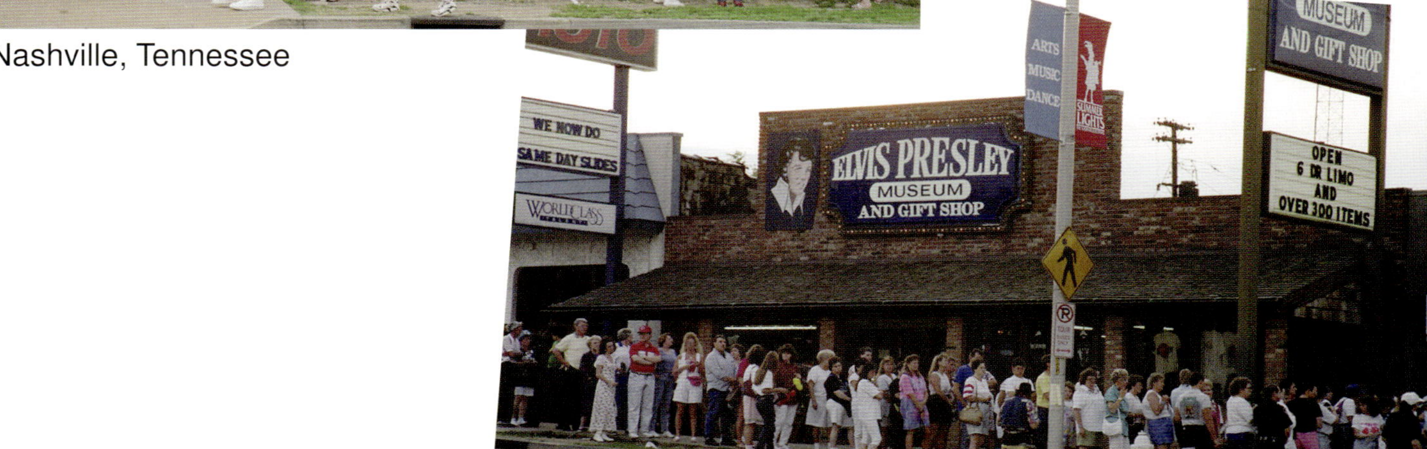

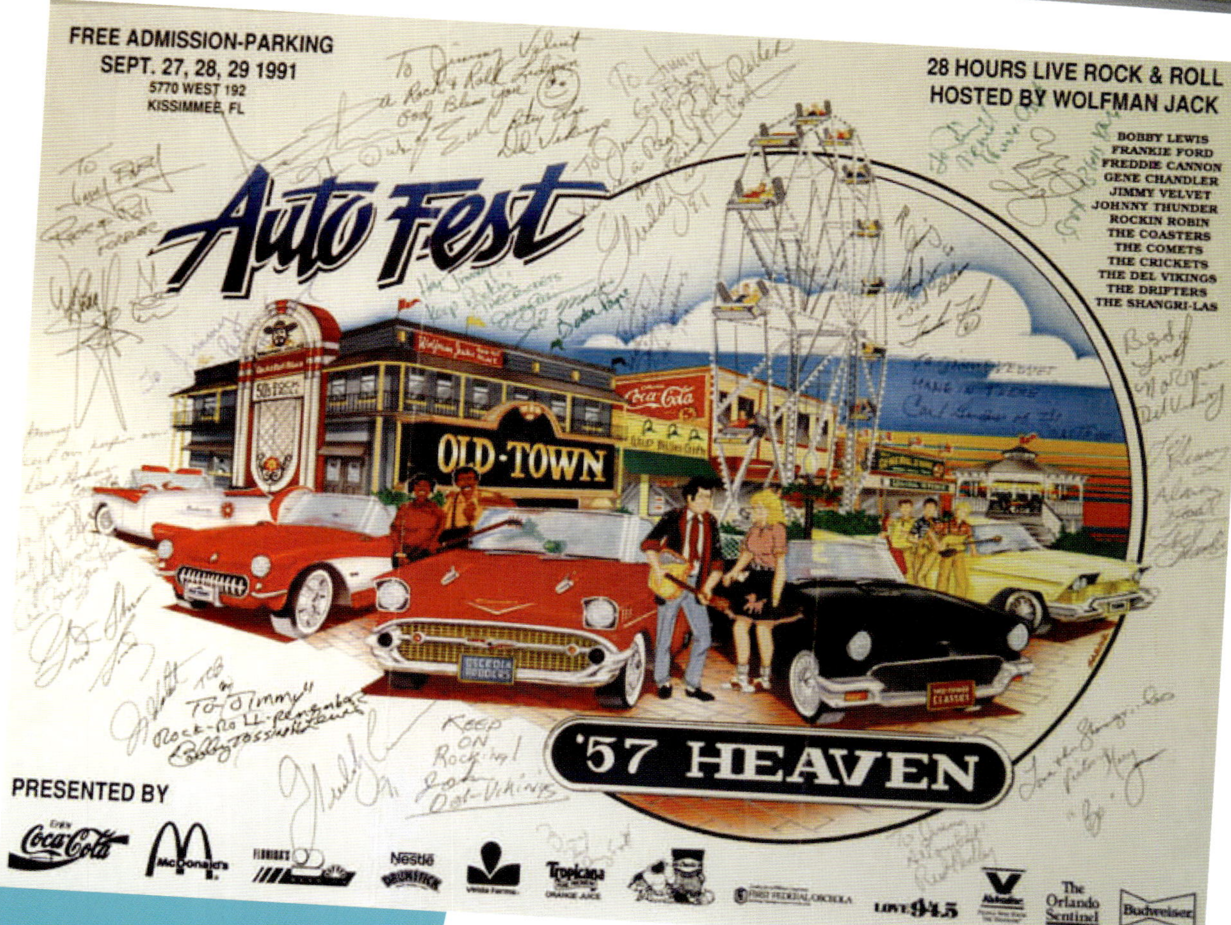

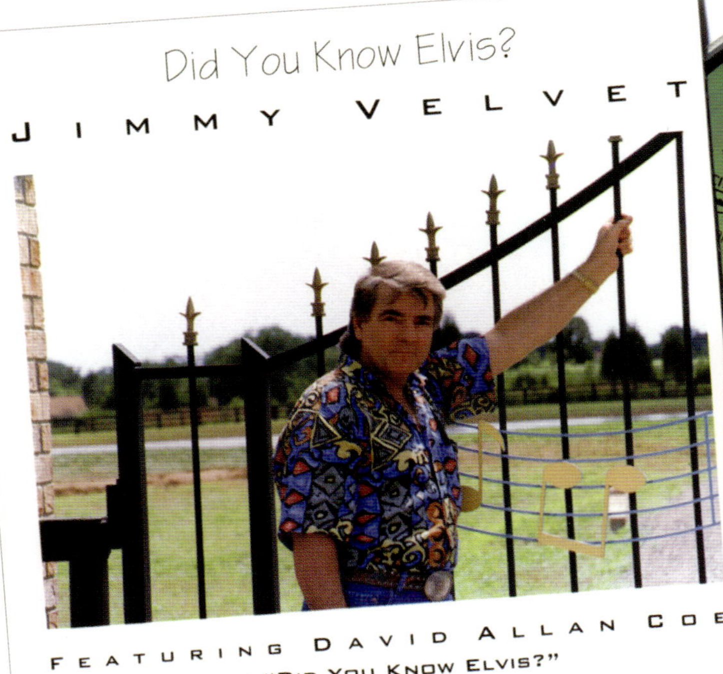

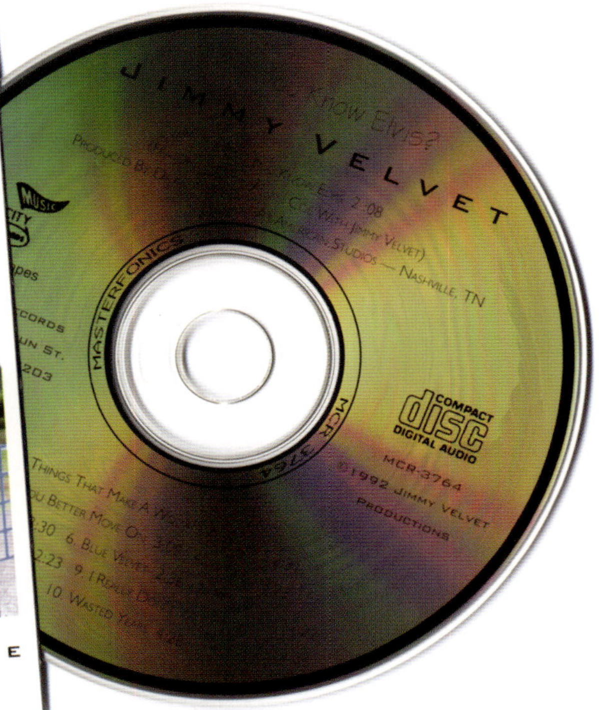

"Did You Know Elvis"
Hollywood Chart 1992 #8
David Allan Coe and Jimmy Velvet

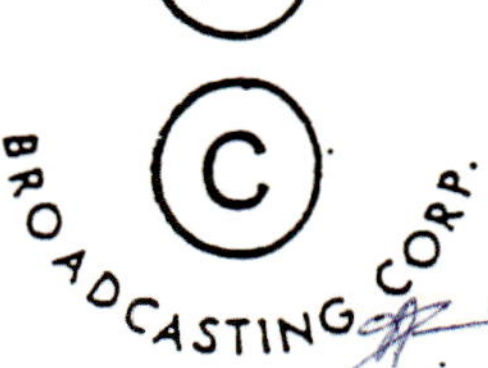

TRANS-AMERICAN BROADCASTING CORP.

T A B C

Shane Wilder
Program Director

P.O. BOX 3503
HOLLYWOOD, CALIF. 90078

818-508-1433

Oct. 9, 1992

TABC Hot Indie Country Playlist

1: 9-1-1-The Elwell Bros./West
2: Alcohol of Fame-The Wood Bros./K-Tel
3: Who needs it-Clinton Gregory/SOR
4: Excuse me lady-Rich Wilson/Missile
5: Need no trouble-Heartland Express/615
6: Betcha say that to all the girls-Adrianne/Rambo Star
7: Can I come home to you-The Bellamys/Bellamy
8: Did you know Elvis-Jimmy Velvet/Music City
9: Throwin' caution to the wind-Patti Savage/Trek
10: New Fool-Alison Kraus/Rounder
11: Take me South-Craig Morgan/MBS
12: Puerta Vallarta-Jess Lee/Music Line-Canada
13: Way down deep-Ruthie Steele/Trek
14: Eyes of Love-Judy Fields/Dreamwest
15: The reason I'm alone-Scooter Lee/Southern Tracks
16: Help I'm white and I can't get down-The Geezinslaws/SOR
17: You put the soul in the song-Jerry Raby/Stargem
18: Never be sorry-Marilyn/MBS
19: A salute to Kitty Wells-Keith Bradford/Crest
20: Still in love with you-Verna Charlton/Music Line-Canada
21: The memories still haunt my mind-Cousin Glenn/Stargem
22: Daddy don't live in heaven-Kimberly Summers/Staircase
23: Why don't we get it over-Jamie Harper/Starcut
24: Questions-The Sand Hill Gang/KSS
25: Cowboy Lady-Curt Powers/Musicland
26: If you ain't got me-Jason Cooper/Music Line-Canada
27: Wher'm I gonna live-Billy Ray Cyrus/Mercury
28: The Texas Two Step-Lucky Lee/Cannon
29: Take the keys to my heart-Susan Graham/BGE
30: Throwin' Stones-Cindy Astlin-Aud/615

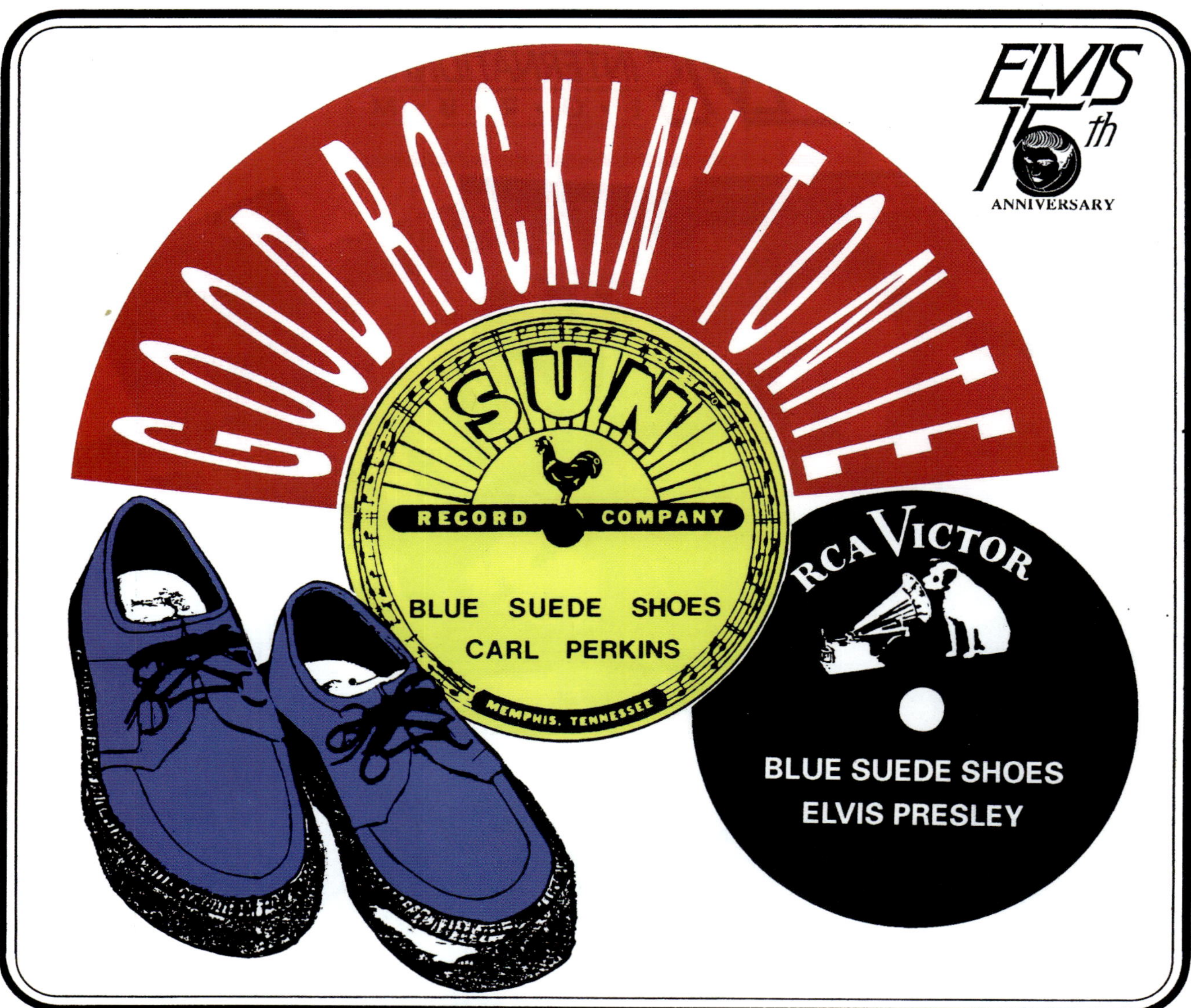

"GOOD ROCKIN' TONITE III"

CARL PERKINS **RONNIE McDOWELL**

JAMES BURTON

JORDANAIRES **D.J. FONTANA**

SUN RHYTHM SECTION

JIMMY VELVET **BILLY BOY ROCKA**

HOSTED BY
EDDIE FADAL AND JERRY OSBORNE

AUGUST 13TH, 1992
15TH ANNIVERSARY TRIBUTE
COOKS CONVENTION CENTER
MEMPHIS, TENNESSEE

MAKE CHECKS PAYABLE TO:
ELVIS INTERNATIONAL F·O·R·U·M

PO BOX 3373
THOUSAND OAKS, CA 91359
(805) 379-4012
Reserved Seating: $30/$25/$20

John Entwistle
in London
The Who

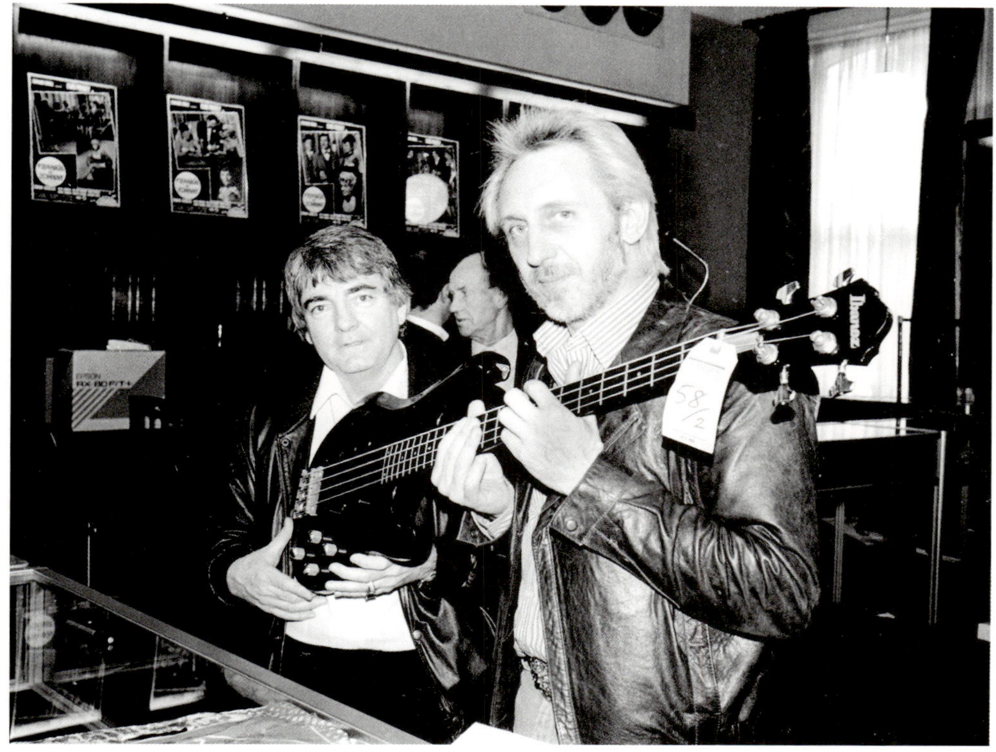

James Burton and Marty Stuart

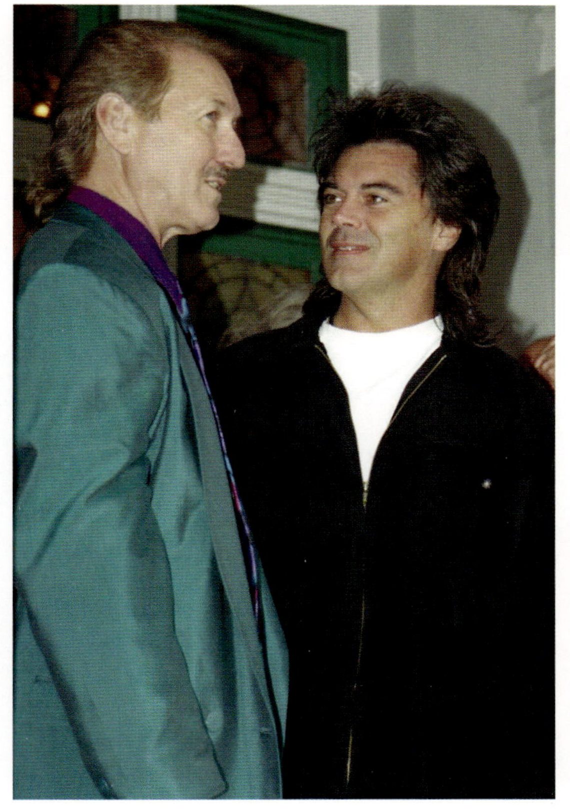

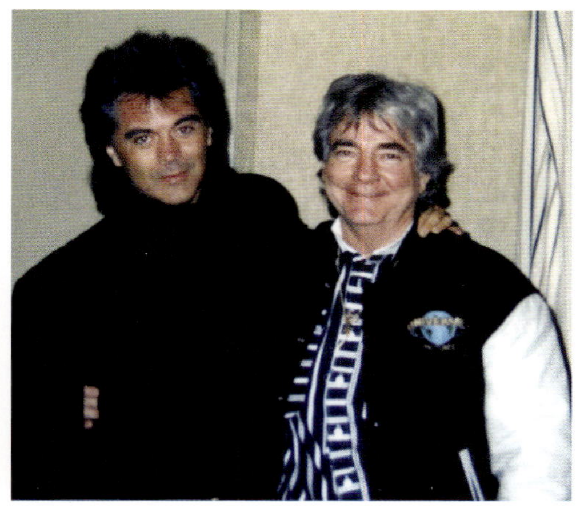

Ronnie McDowell

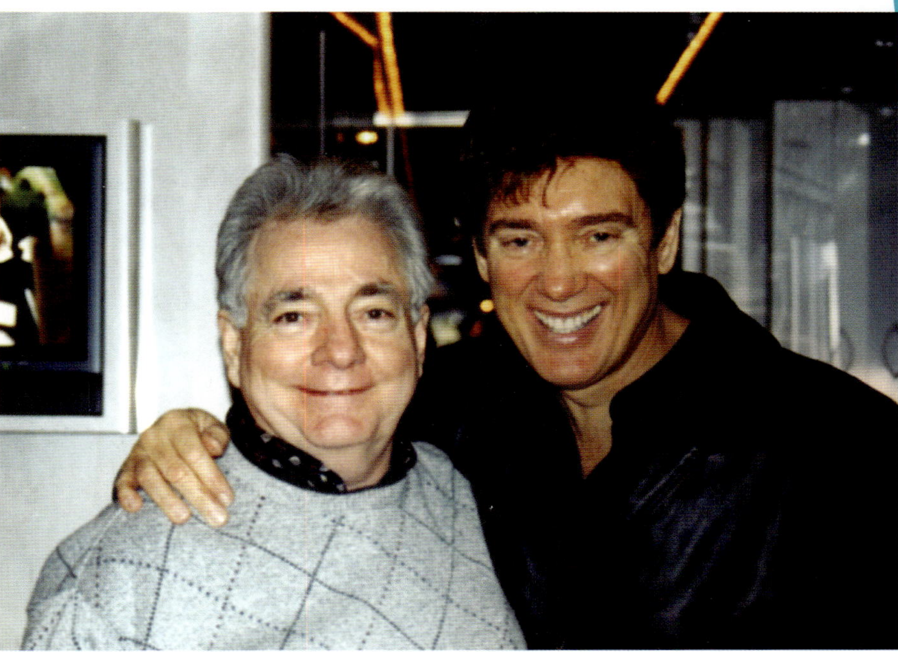

Emmy Lou Harris

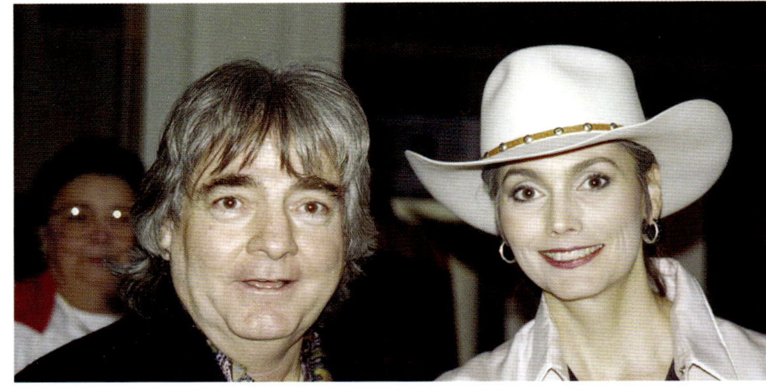

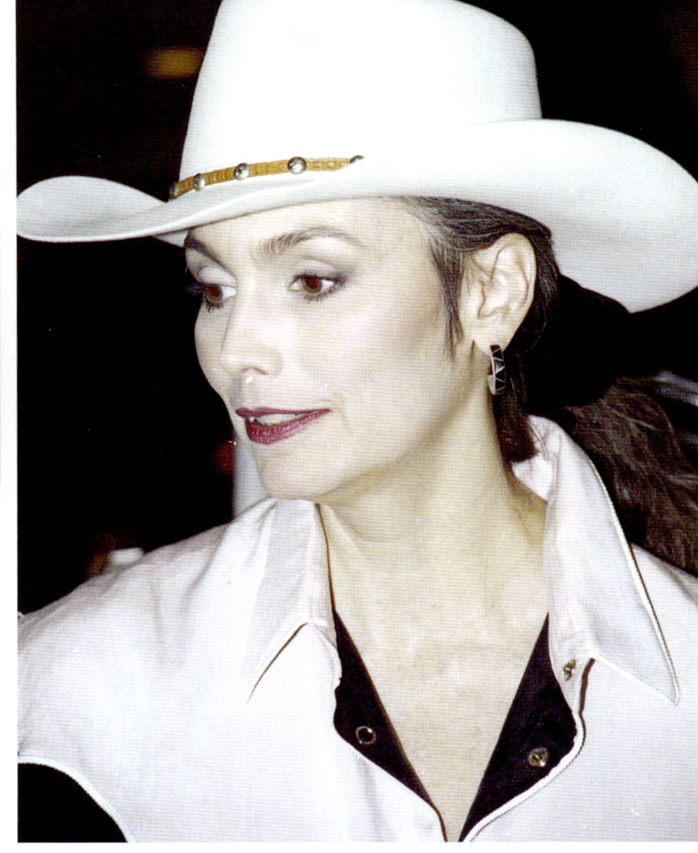

Faith Hill

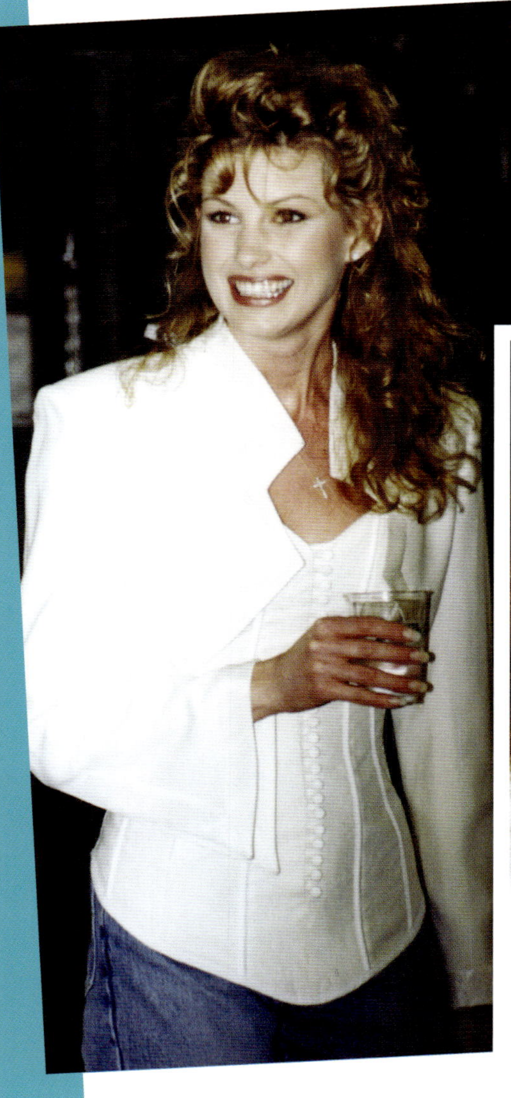

Faith Hill and Lari White

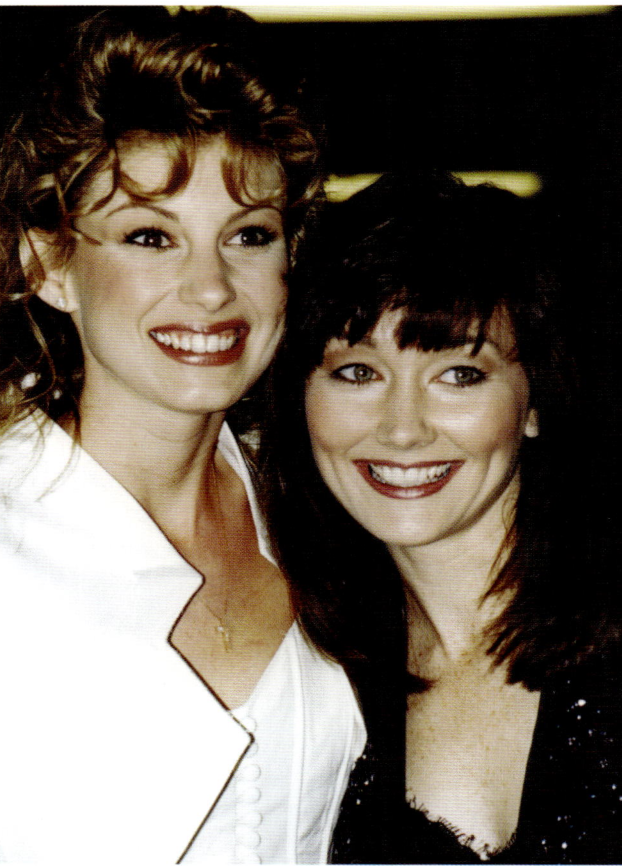

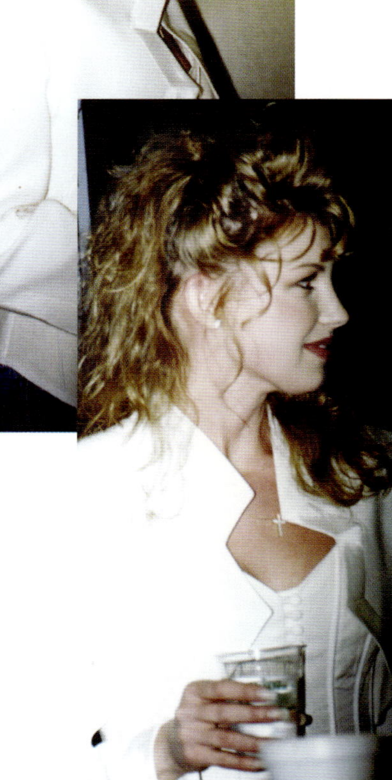

Garth Brooks

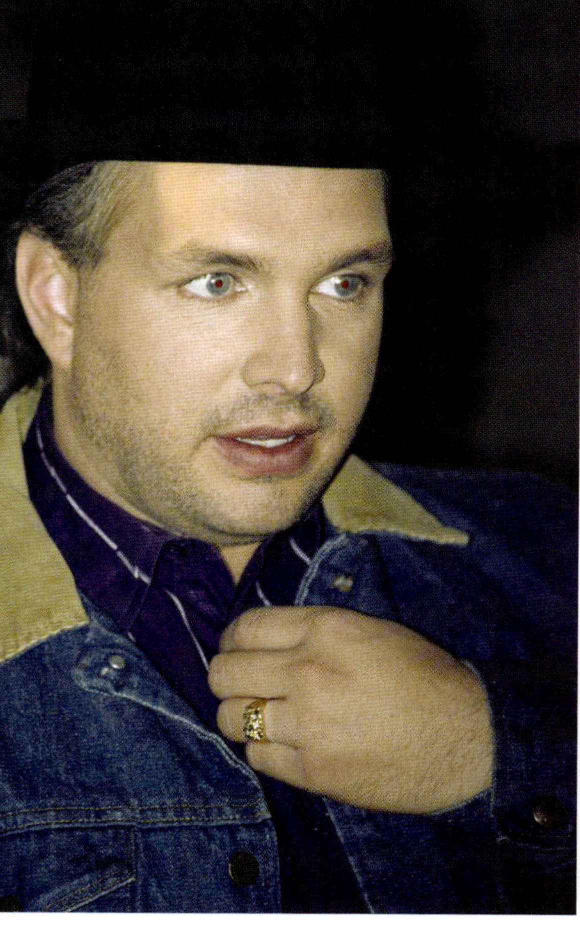

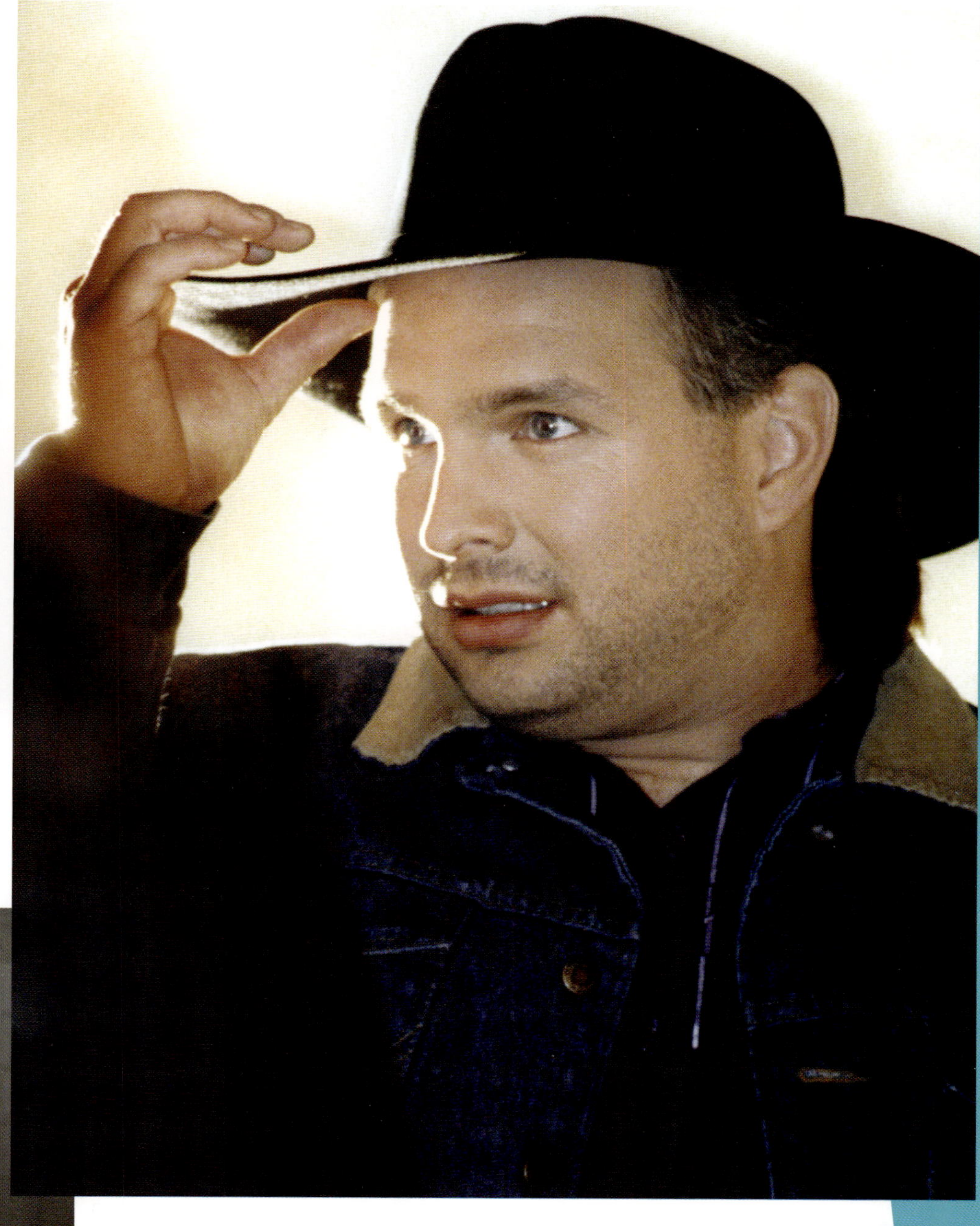

Garth's mom and dad

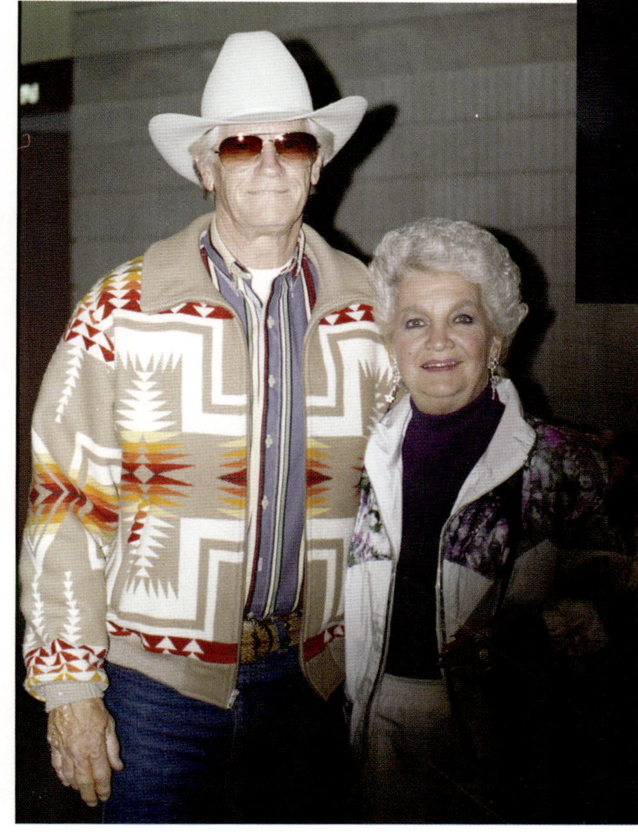

Garth's mom, "Colleen Carroll," was a very good country music artist on Capitol.

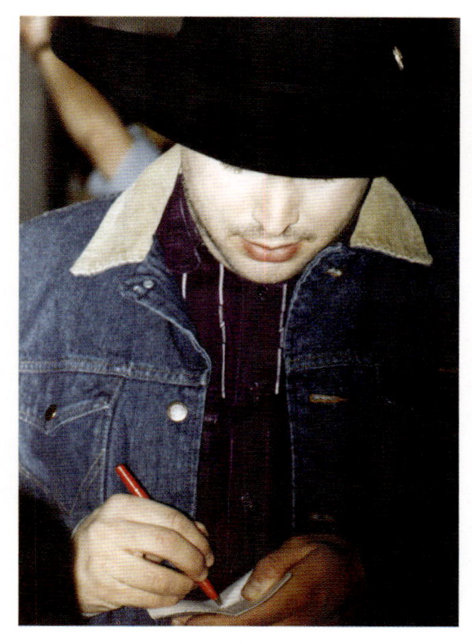

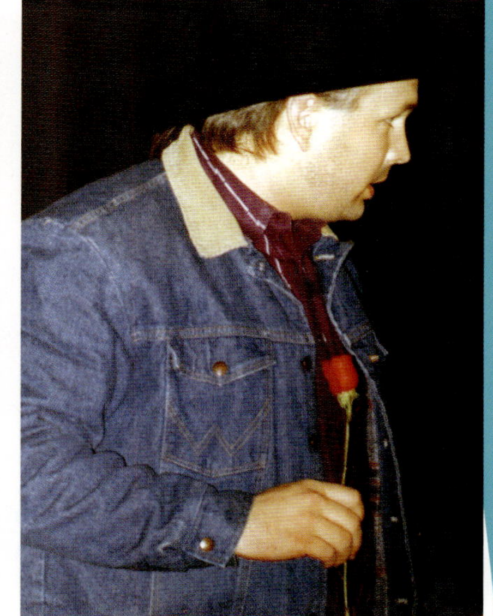

George Jones

A great part of my life.

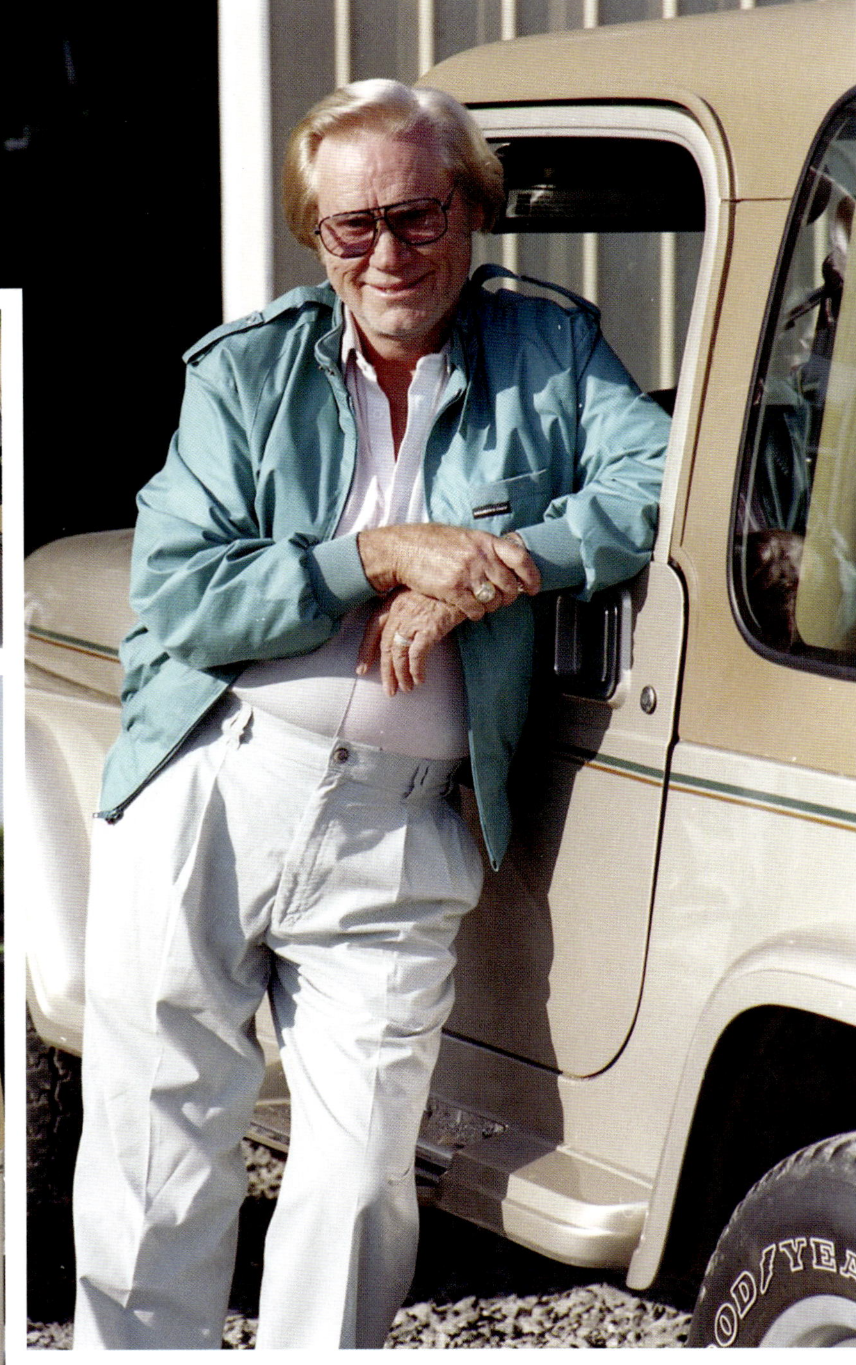

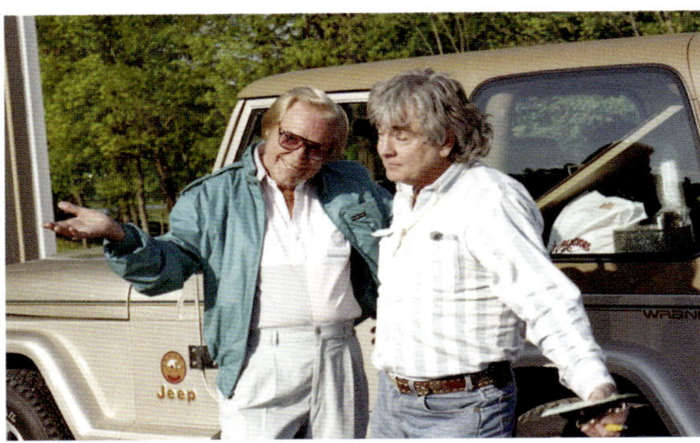

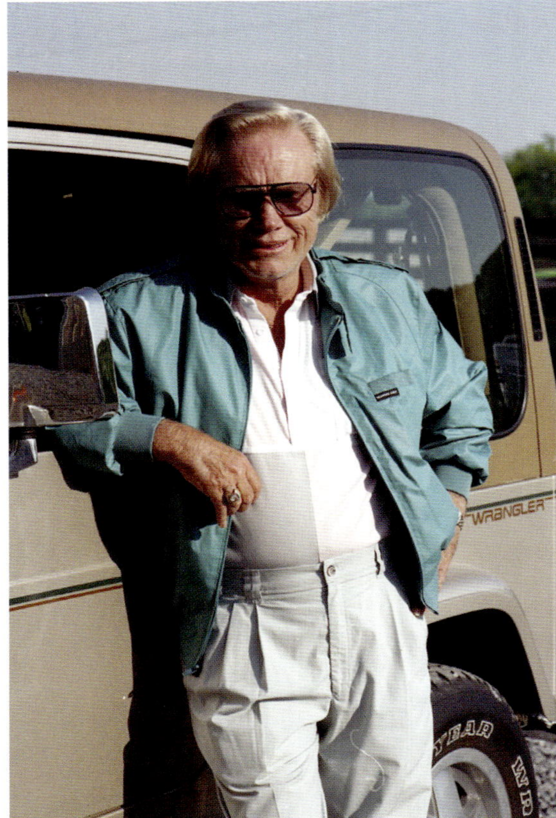

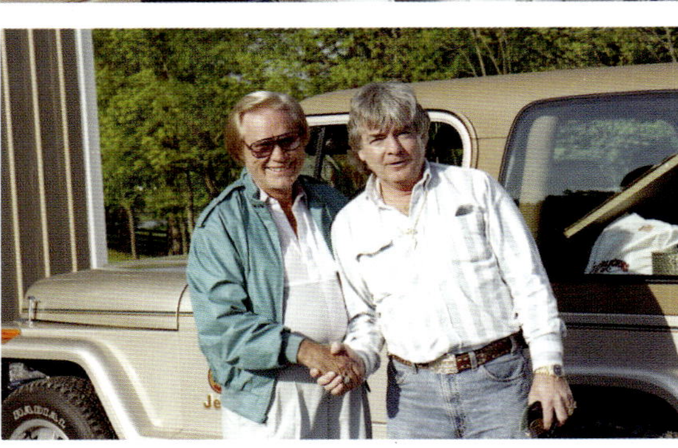

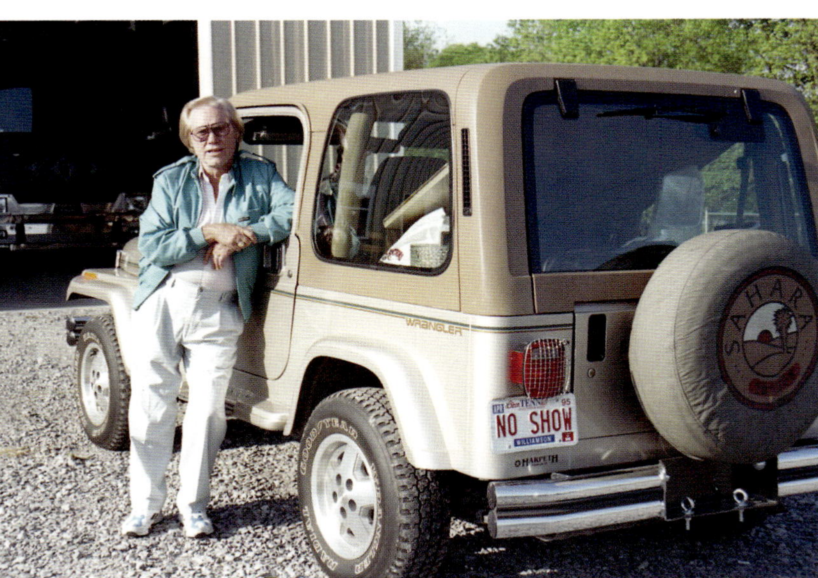

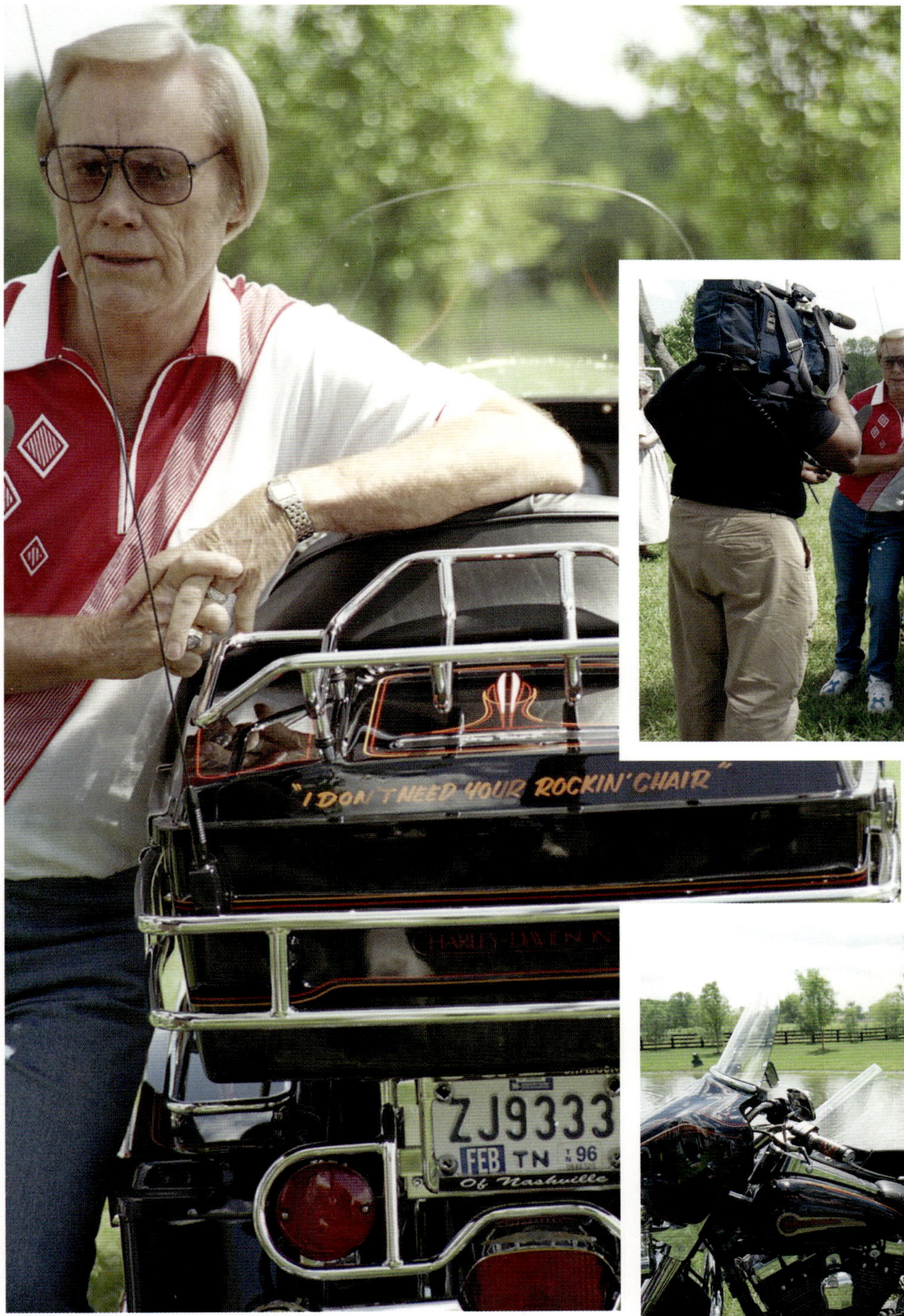

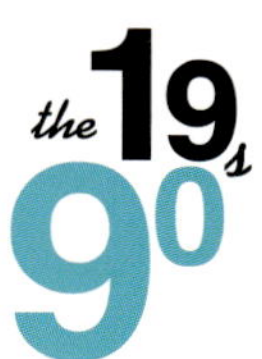

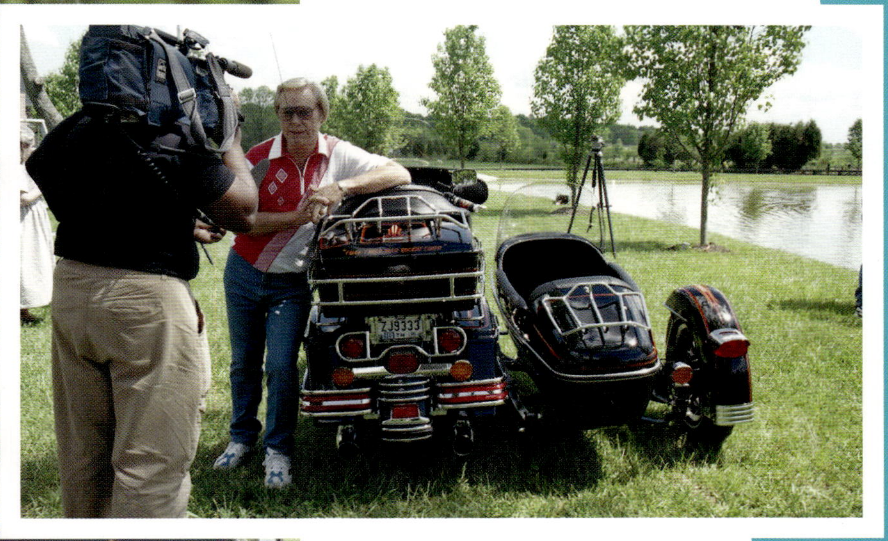

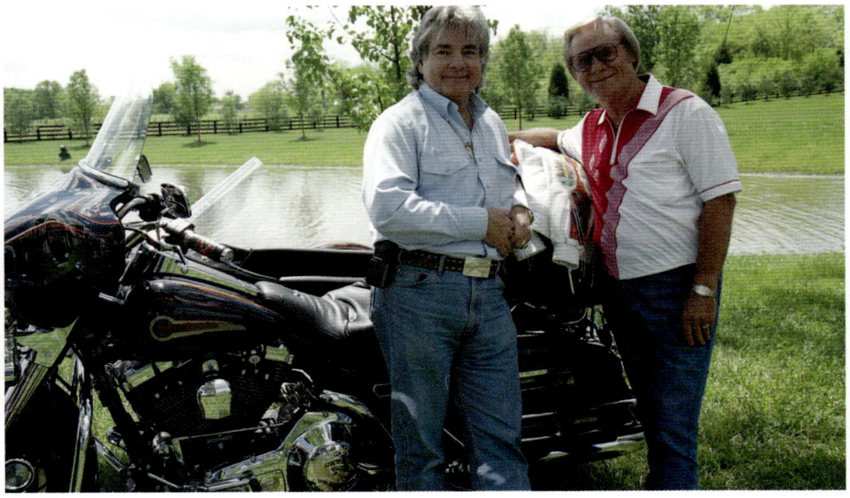

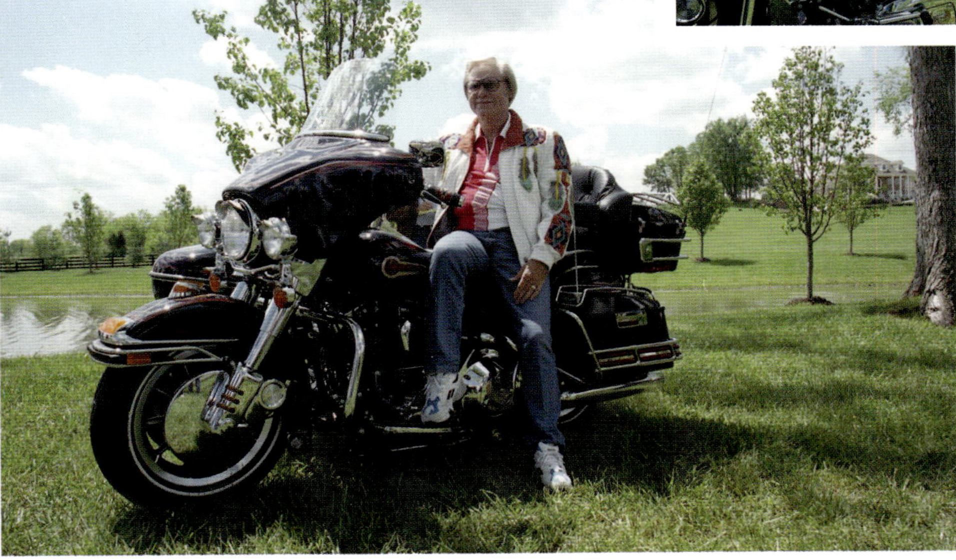

George Jones and his Harley.

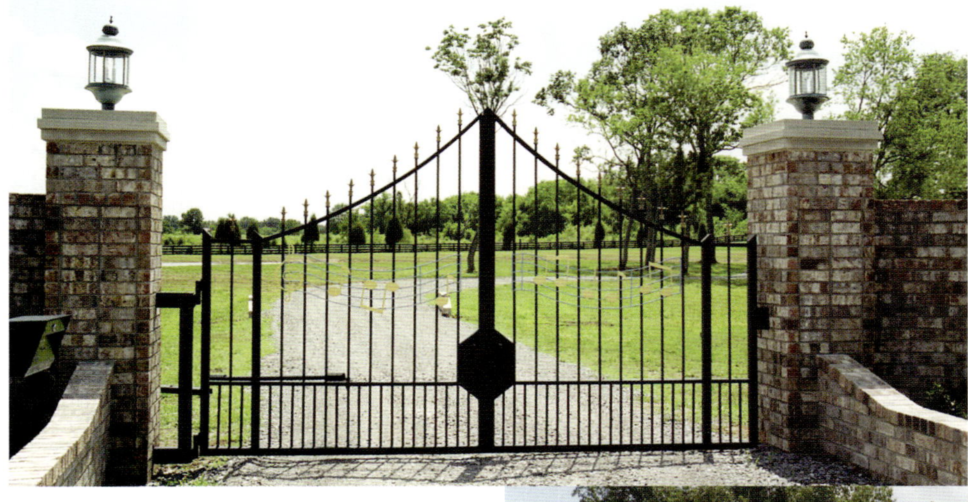

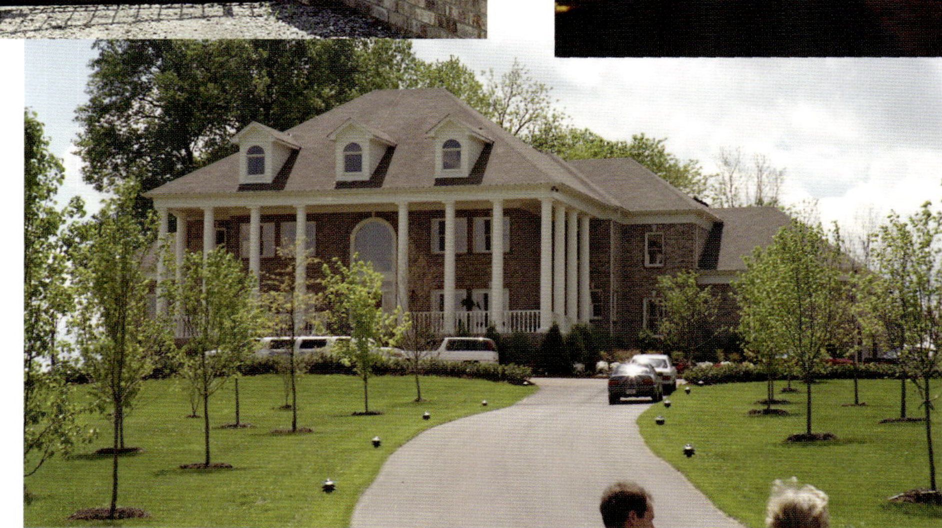

This was my farm and George and Nancy talked me into selling it to her and George. They still live here.

The front gates are on one of my CD's with "David Allan Coe."

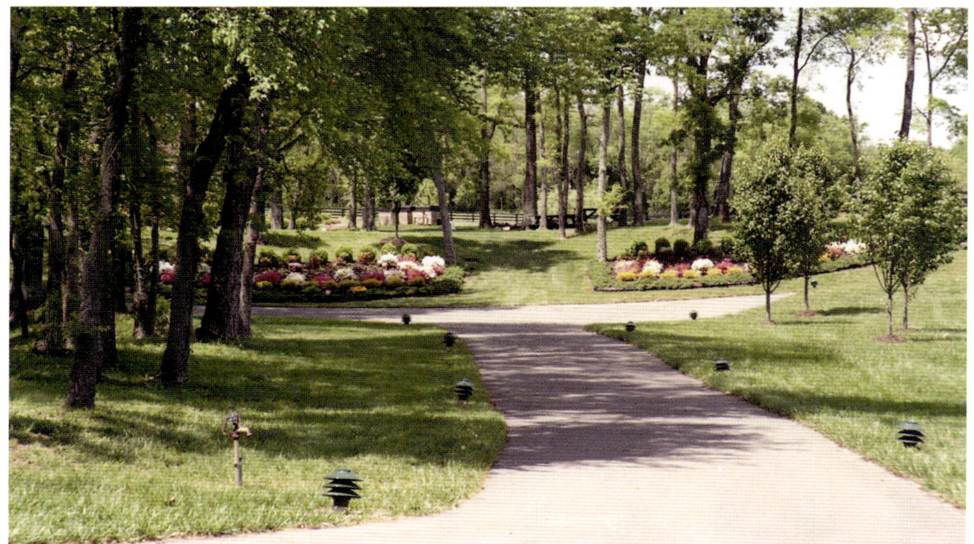

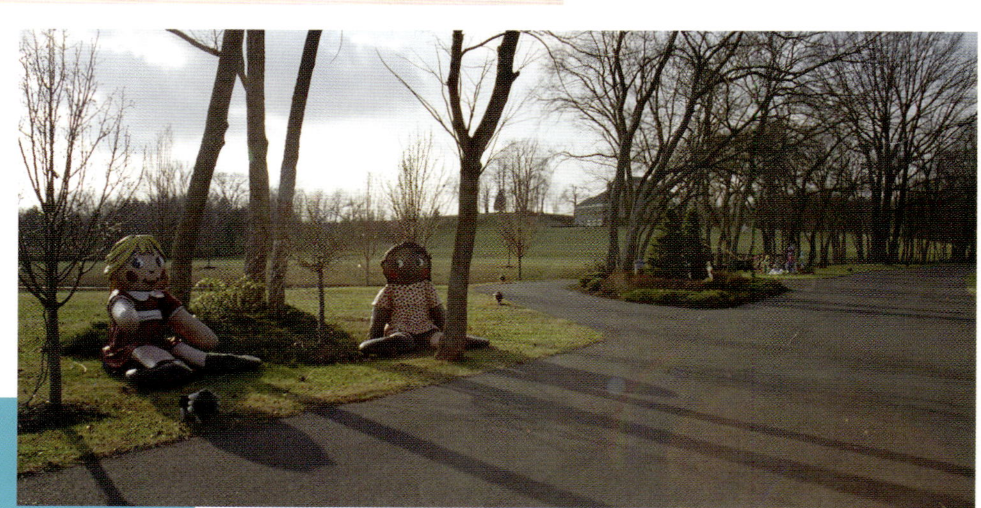

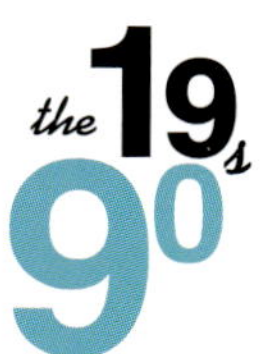

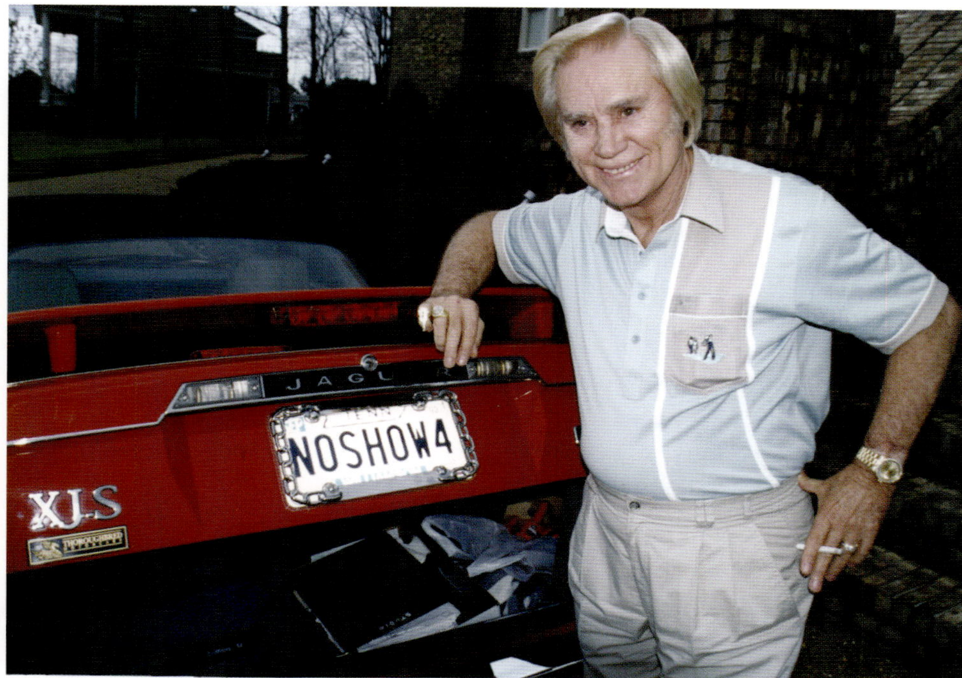

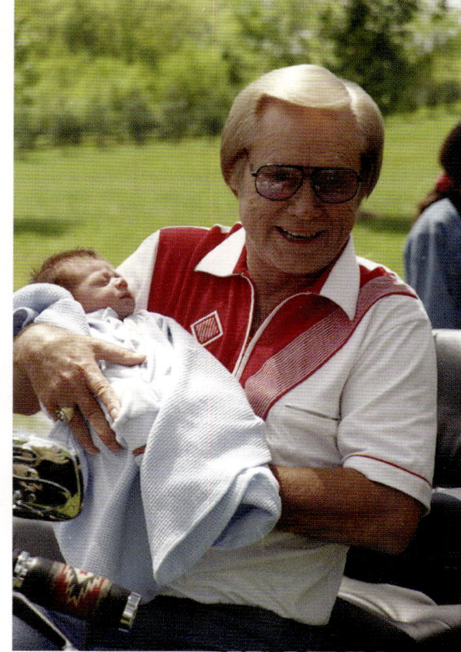

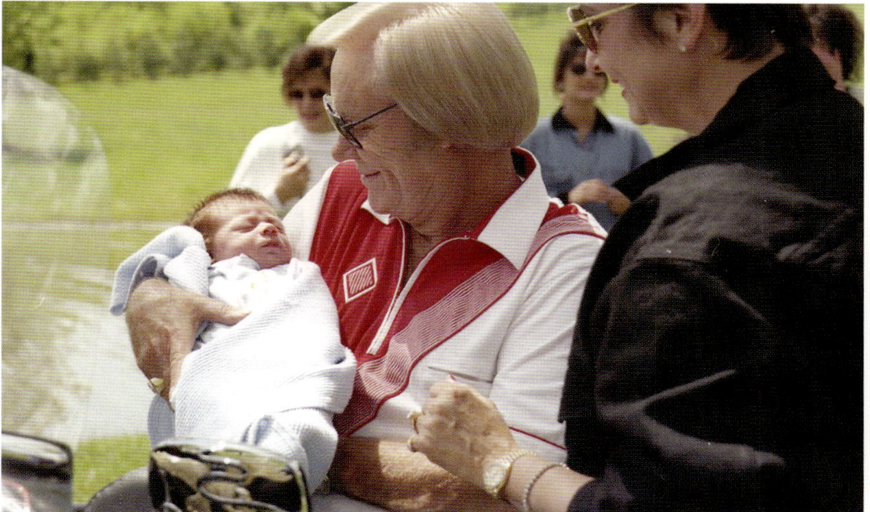

George, Nancy, and Grandbaby

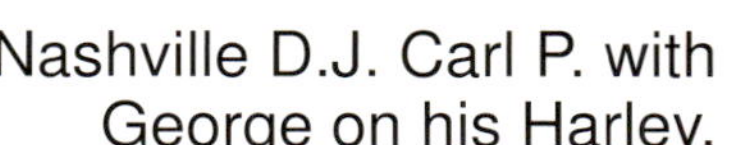

Nashville D.J. Carl P. with George on his Harley.

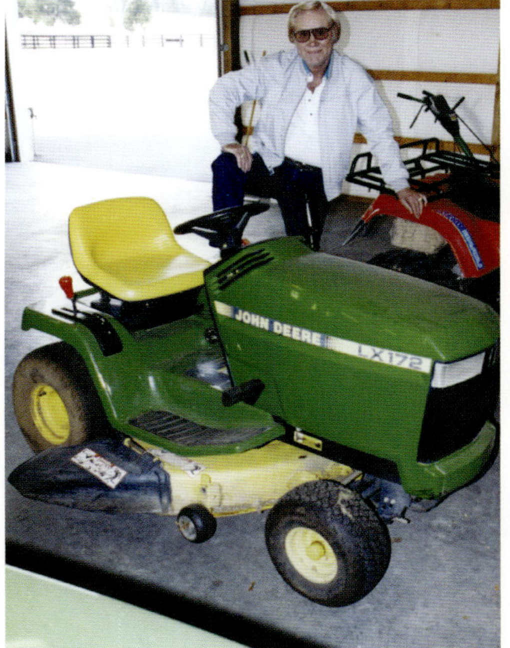

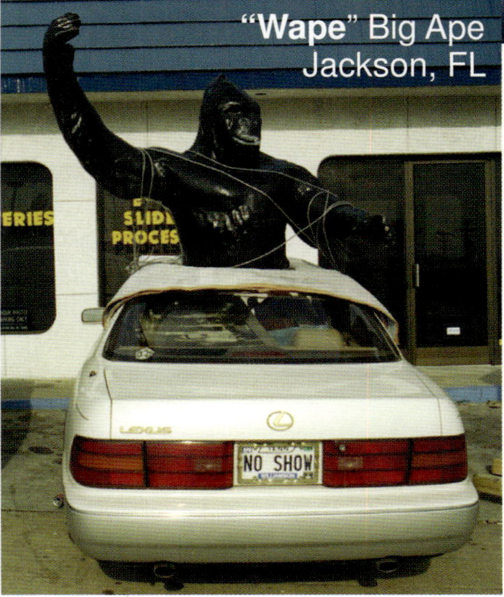

"Wape" Big Ape
Jackson, FL

I drove this Lexus from Jacksonville to George's house.

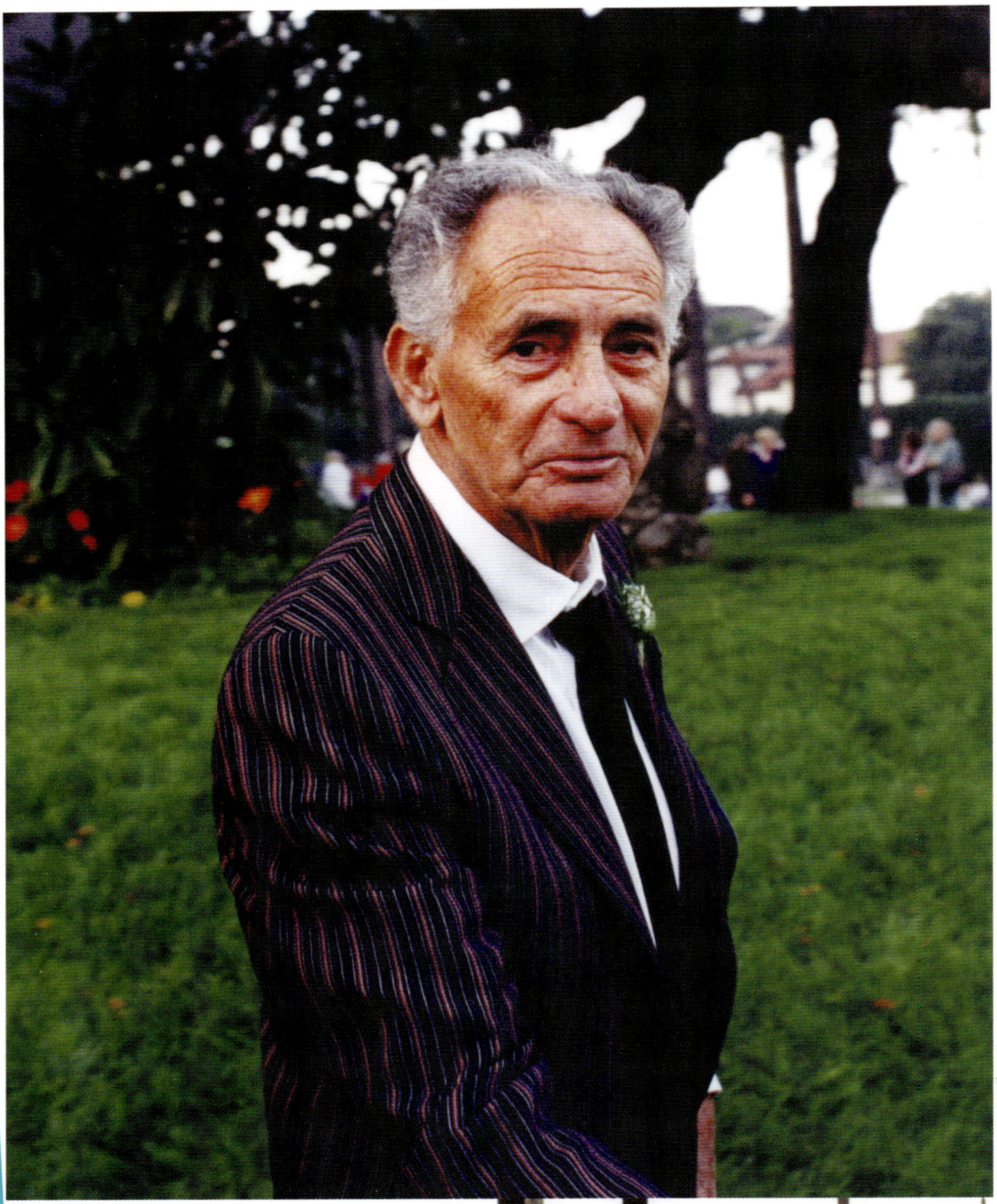

Joey Bishop

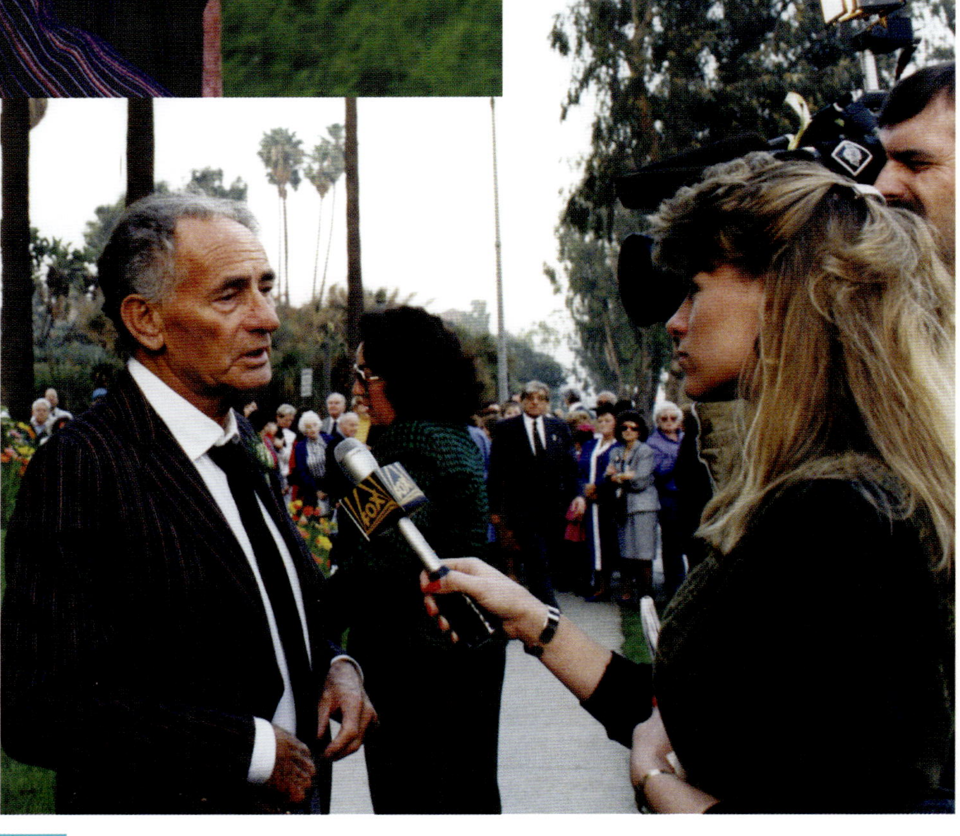

James Dean's Grave

Fairmount, Indiana

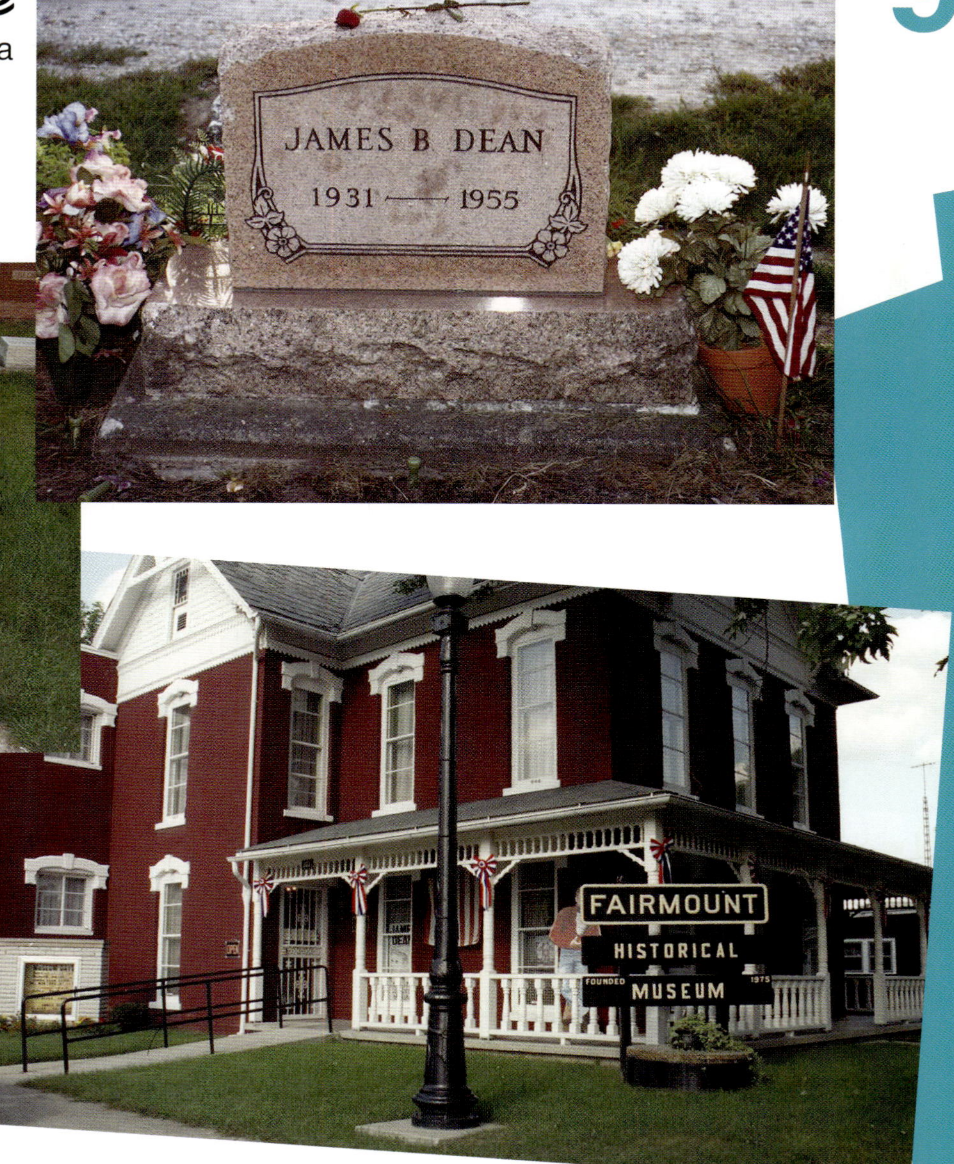

Andrew Solt and wife

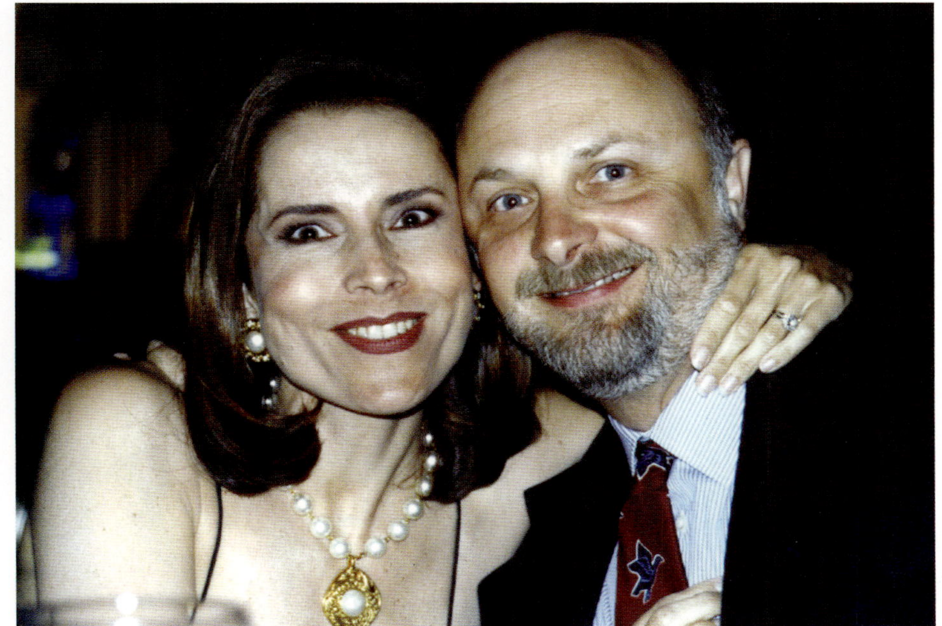

Joan Jett

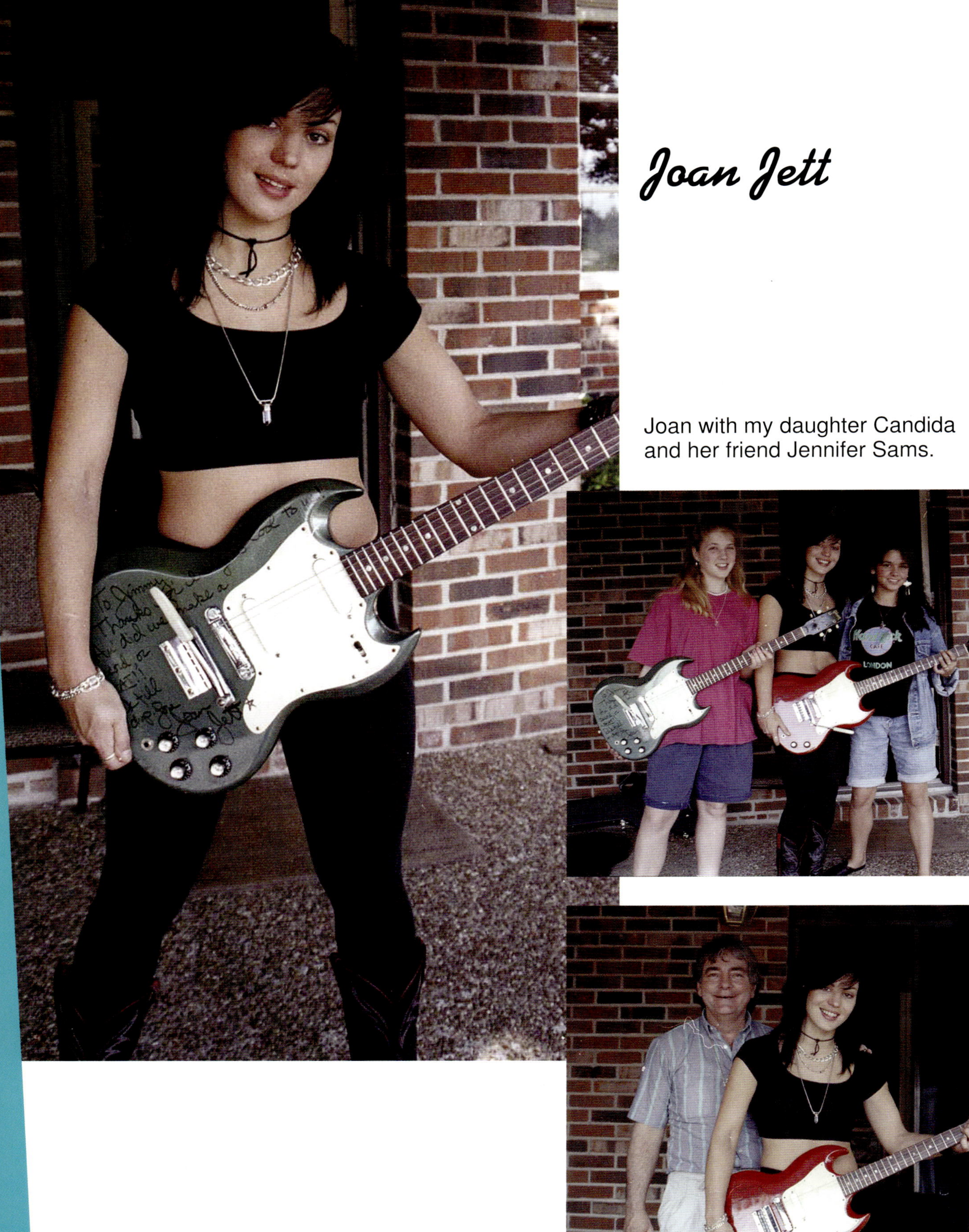

Joan with my daughter Candida and her friend Jennifer Sams.

She recorded at my studio for "Days of Thunder." She signed two guitars for me.

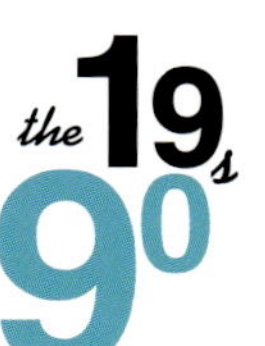

John Davidson

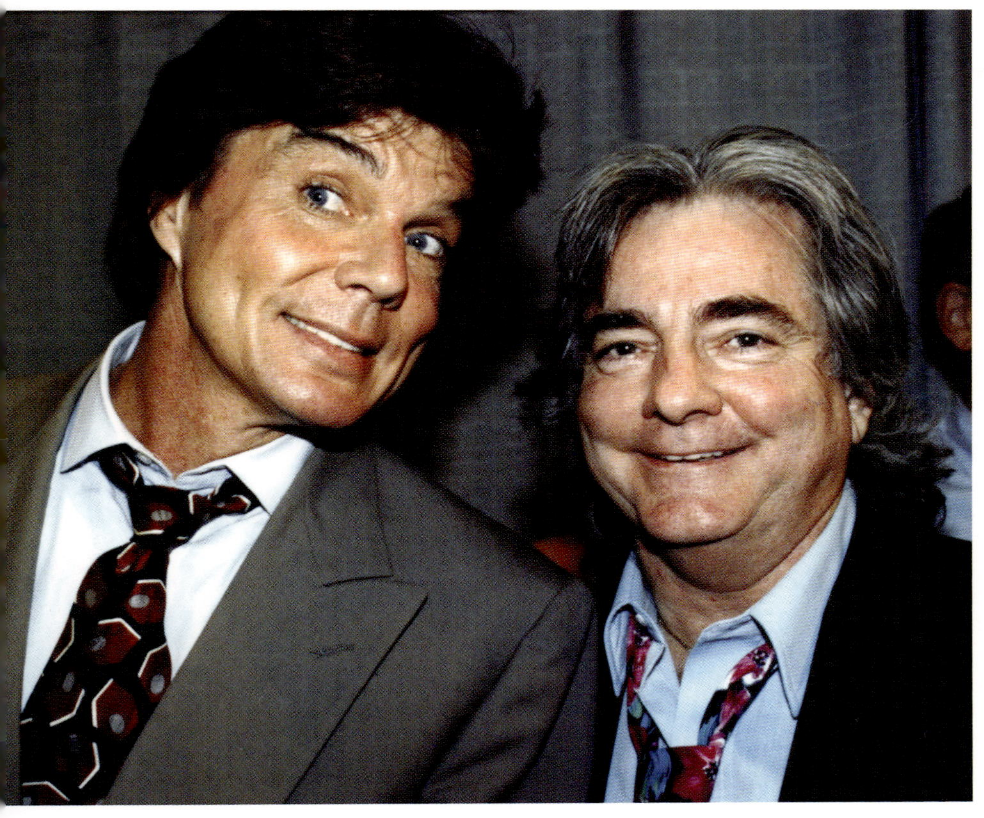

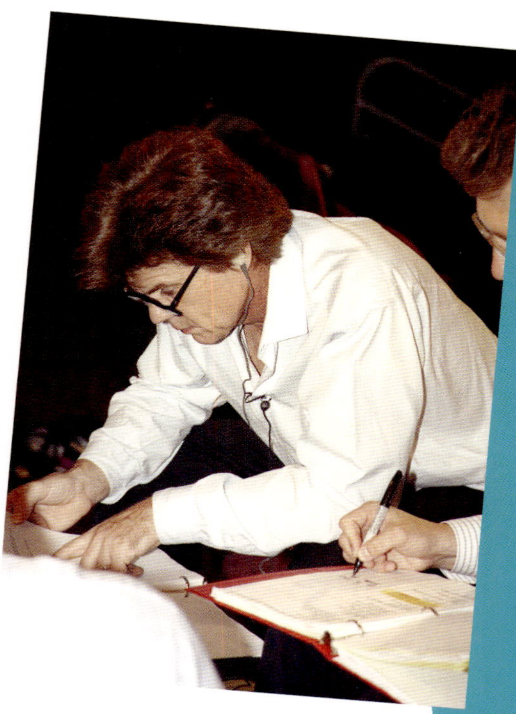

John Davidson planning show.

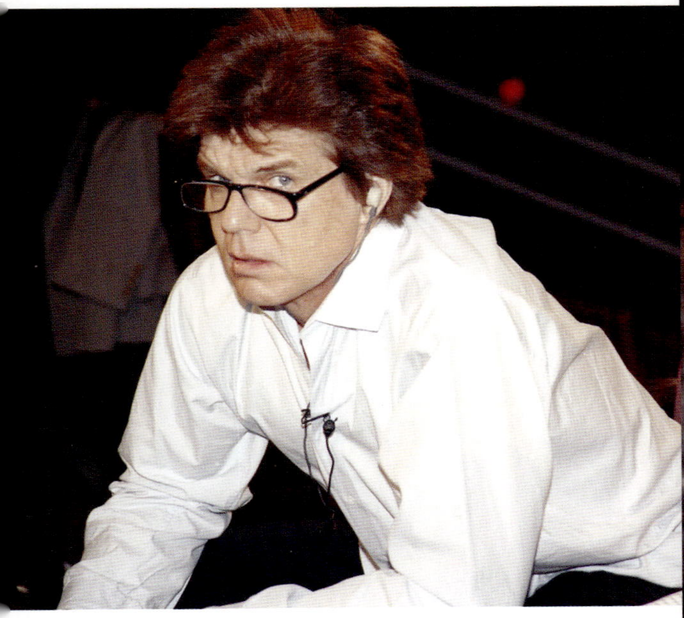

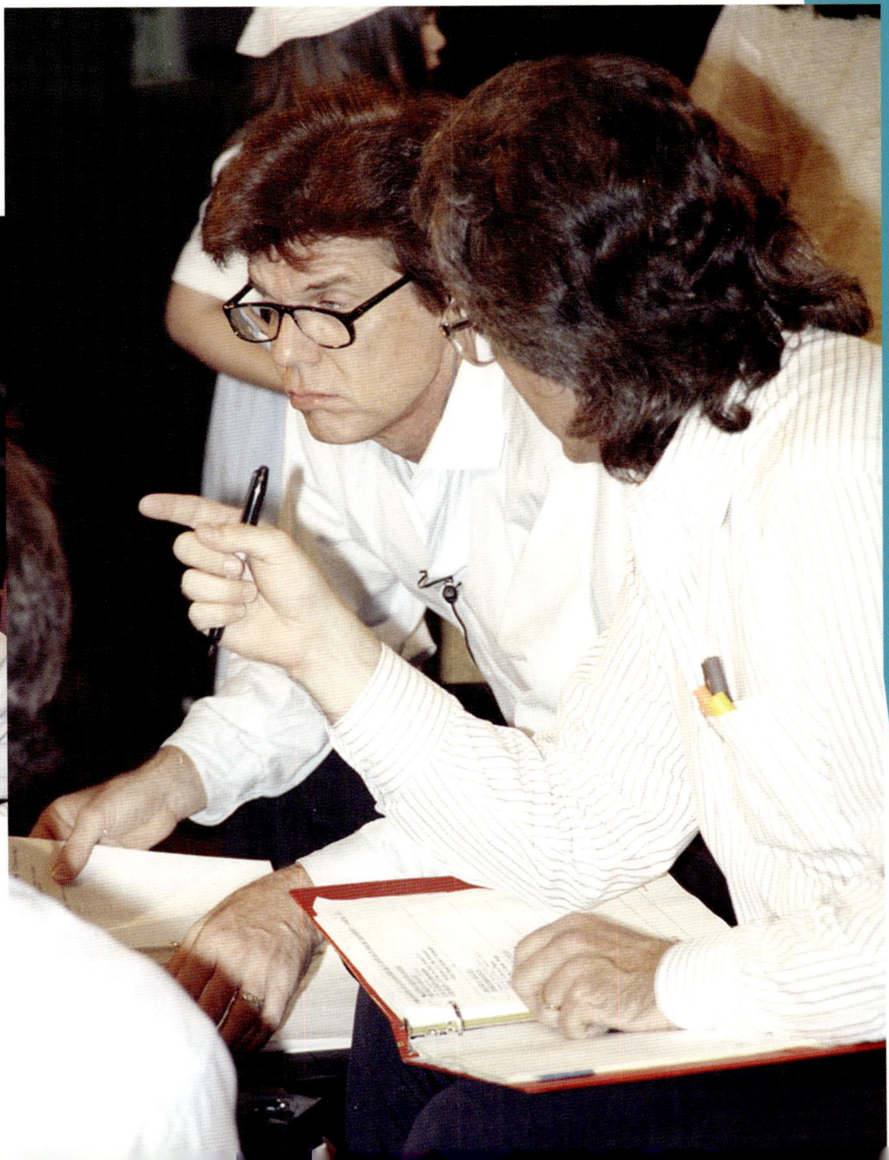

SLICK DOWN YOUR D.A., BRUSH BACK THAT PONYTAIL & DUST OFF THEM BLUE SUEDE SHOES...IT'S HERE!

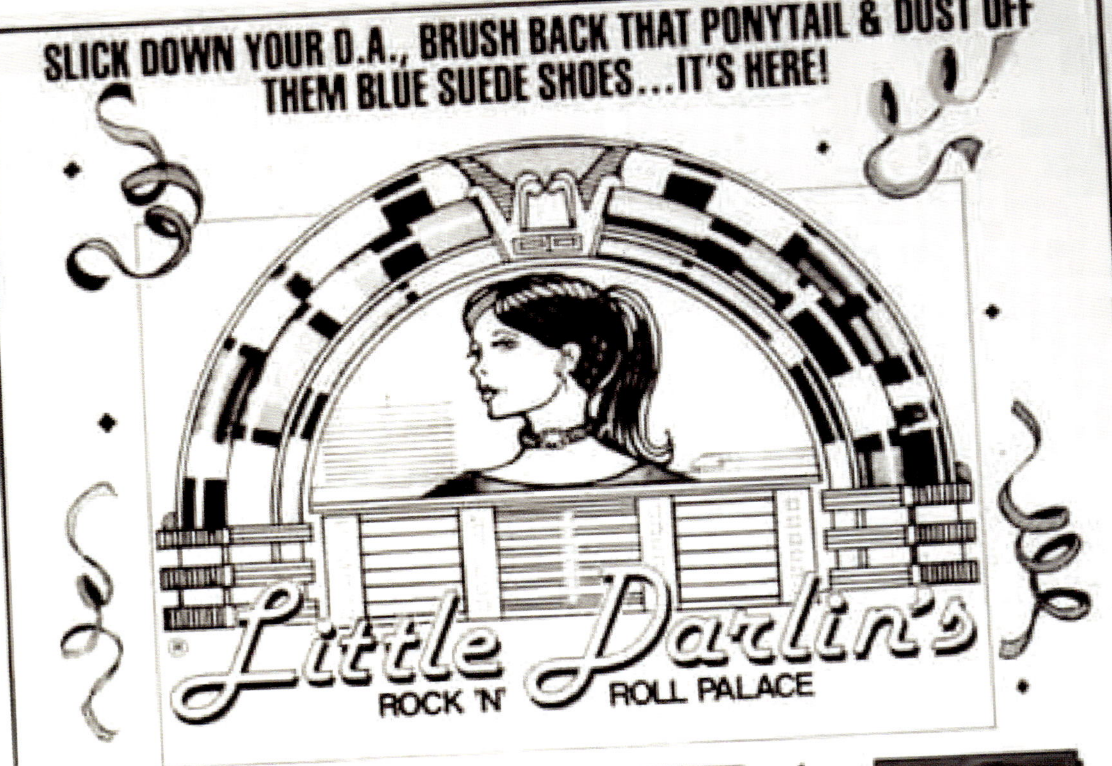

THE DIXIE CUPS
June 6-11
Chapel of Love

CHANNEL 6 SPECIAL
June 12

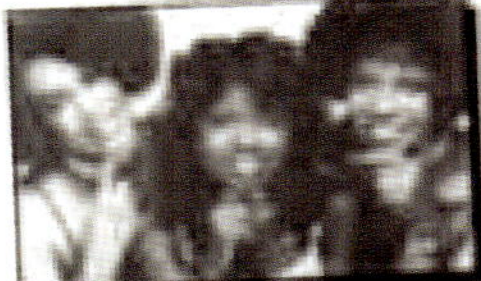

THE DIXIE CUPS
Chapel of Love

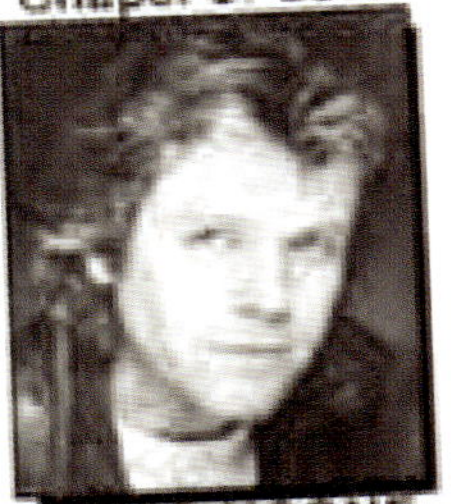

PETER NOONE
Henry the VIII

THE HOME OF THE

Living Legends of Rock n' Roll

Featuring
ROCKIN' ROBIN

Stroll back in time to experience a club unlike anything Orlando has seen before. Little Darlin's Rock 'N' Roll Palace is 8500 square feet of Dining, Dancing, Saddle Shoes, Poodle Skirts, Hoola Hoops and the world's greatest 50's stars, seven days a week. Walk past classic cars through a 24' juke box into another day and time. Rock, Roll and Remember at Little Darlin's Rock 'N' Roll Palace.

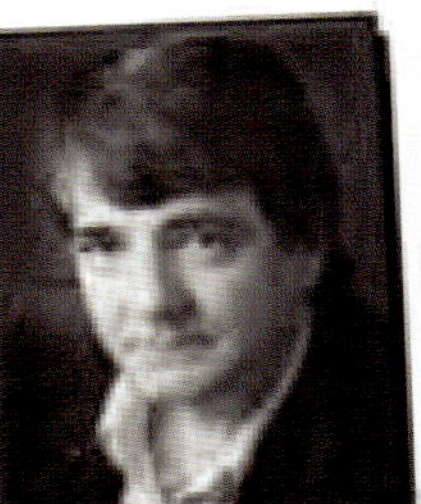

JIMMY VELVET
June 13-18
Blue Velvet

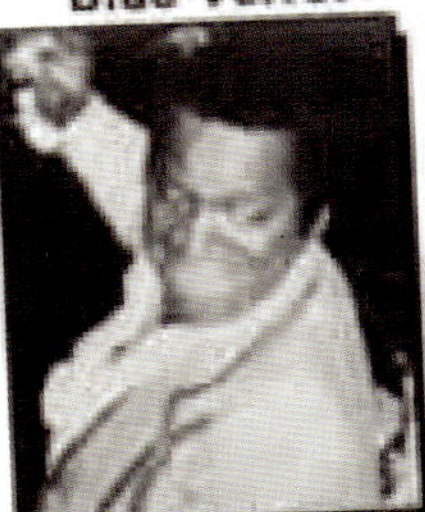

BOBBY LEWIS
June 20-25
Tossin & Turnin

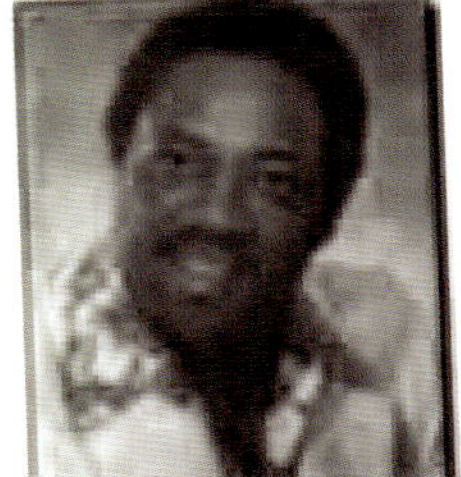

DEE CLARK
June 13-18
Raindrops

ENTERTAINMENT CHARGE EVENINGS

FAMILIES WELCOME

OLD TOWN

HIGHWAY 192
(One mile east of I-4)
KISSIMMEE, FLORIDA
396-6499
OPEN 12:00 NOON TO 2:00 A.M.

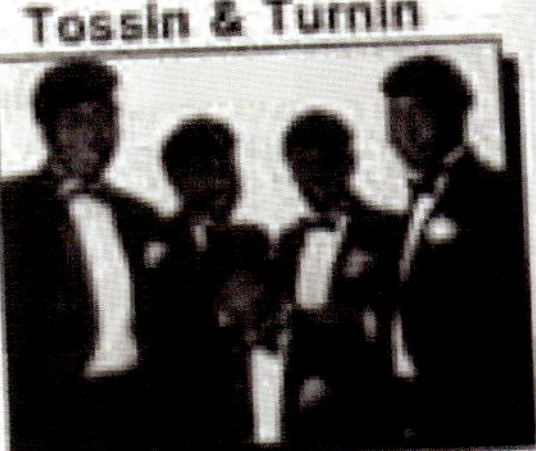

THE TAMS
June 27-July 2
What Kind of Fool Do You Think I Am?

Champagne Balloon Flights available

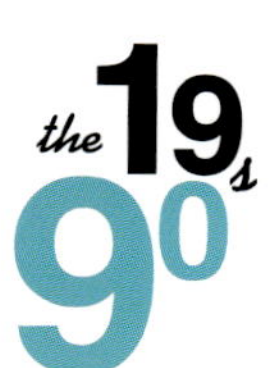

Angie Dickinson

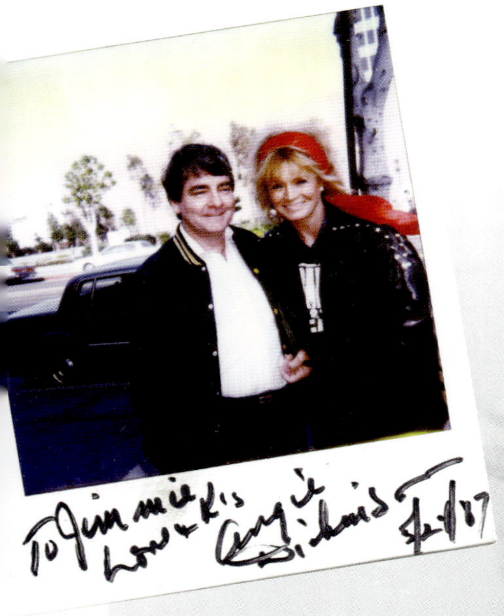

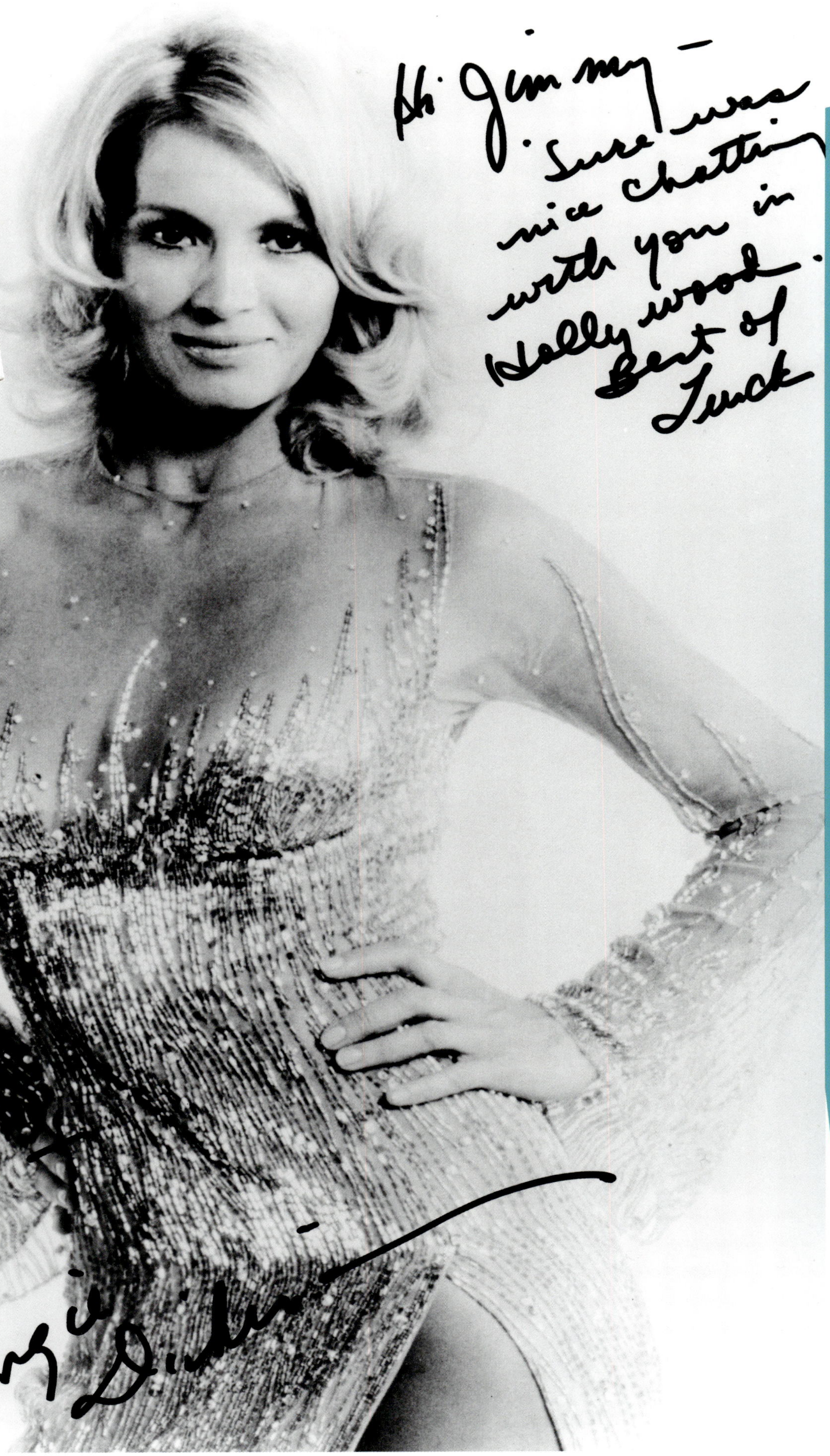

James Burton and Ronnie Dunn

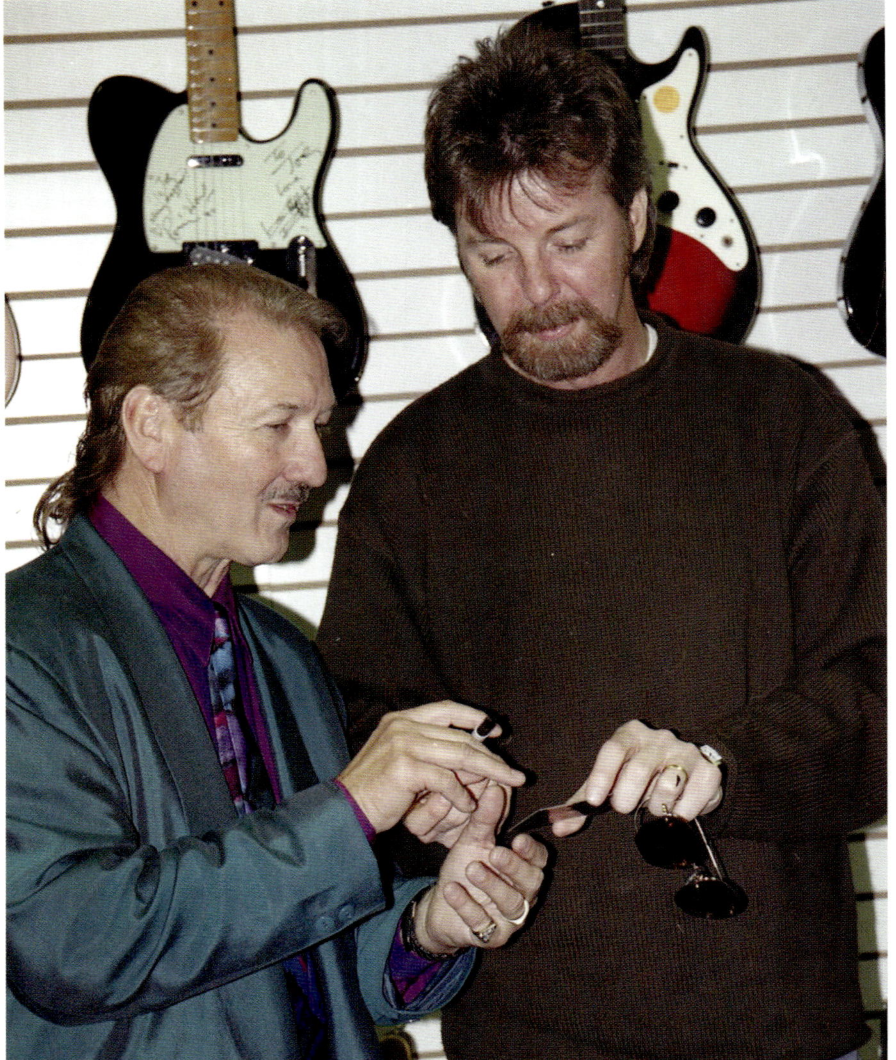

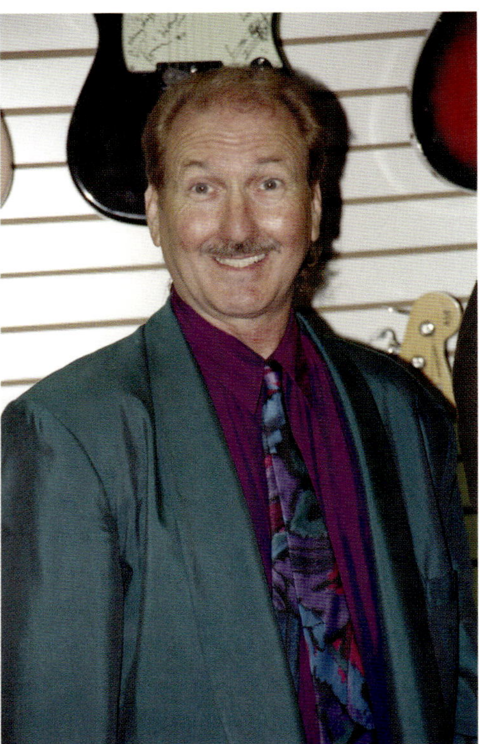

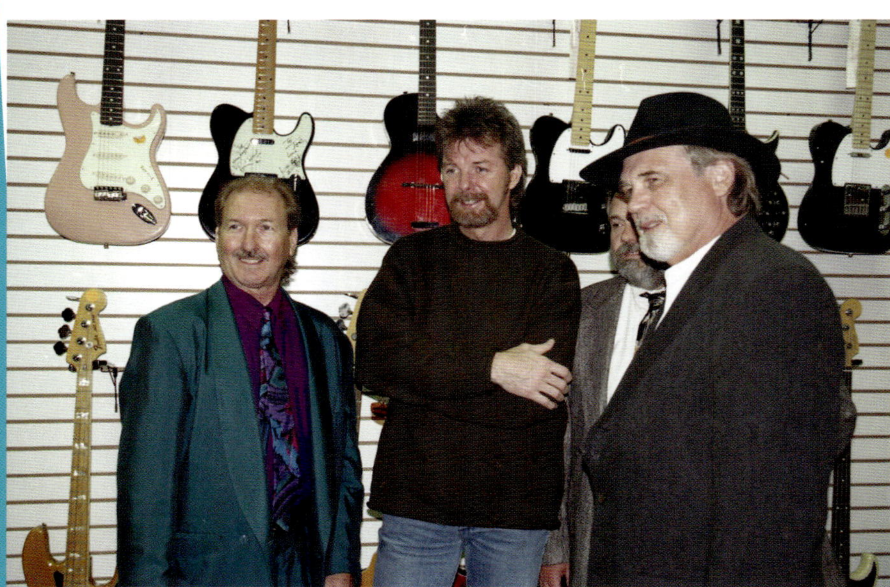

James Burton, Ronnie Dunn, and Duane Eddy

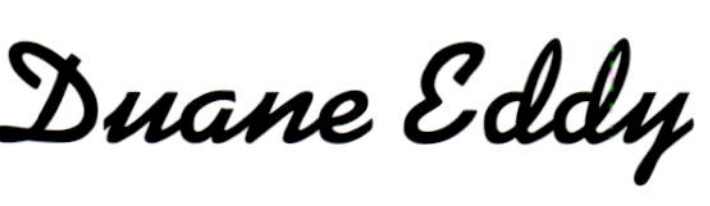

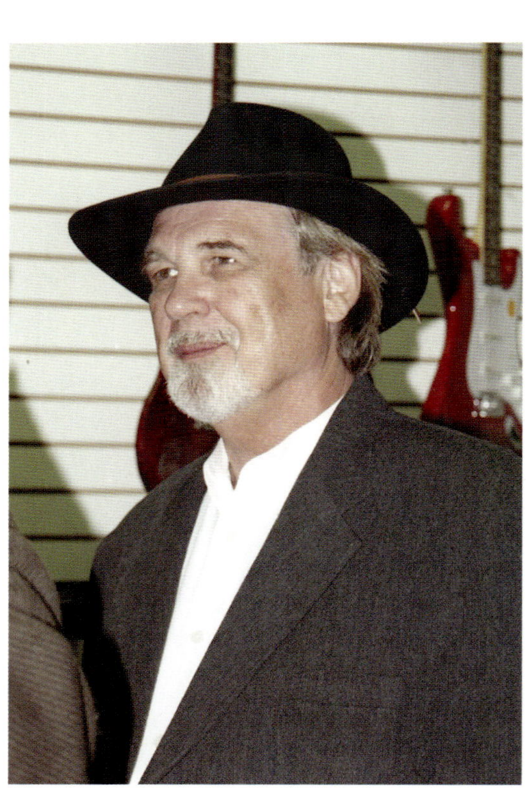

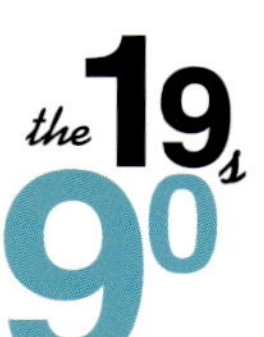

Billy Dean

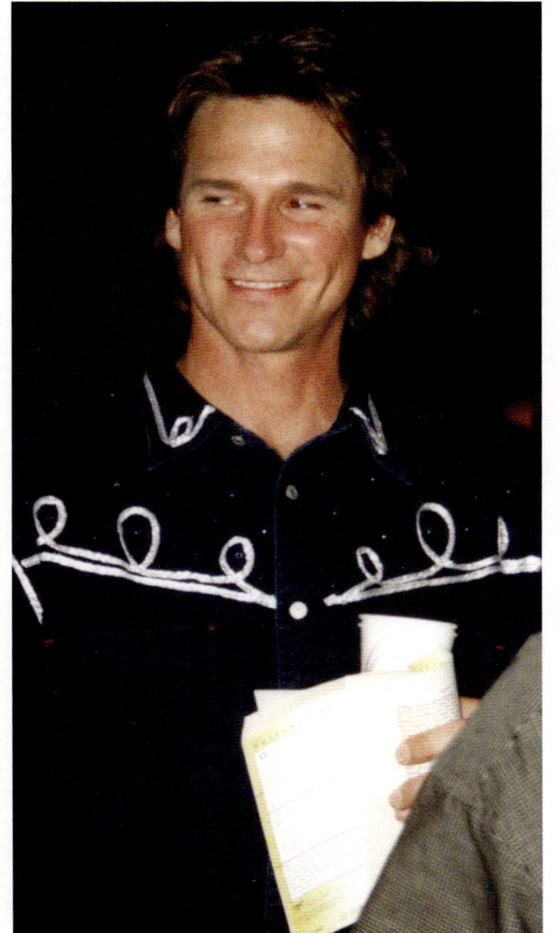

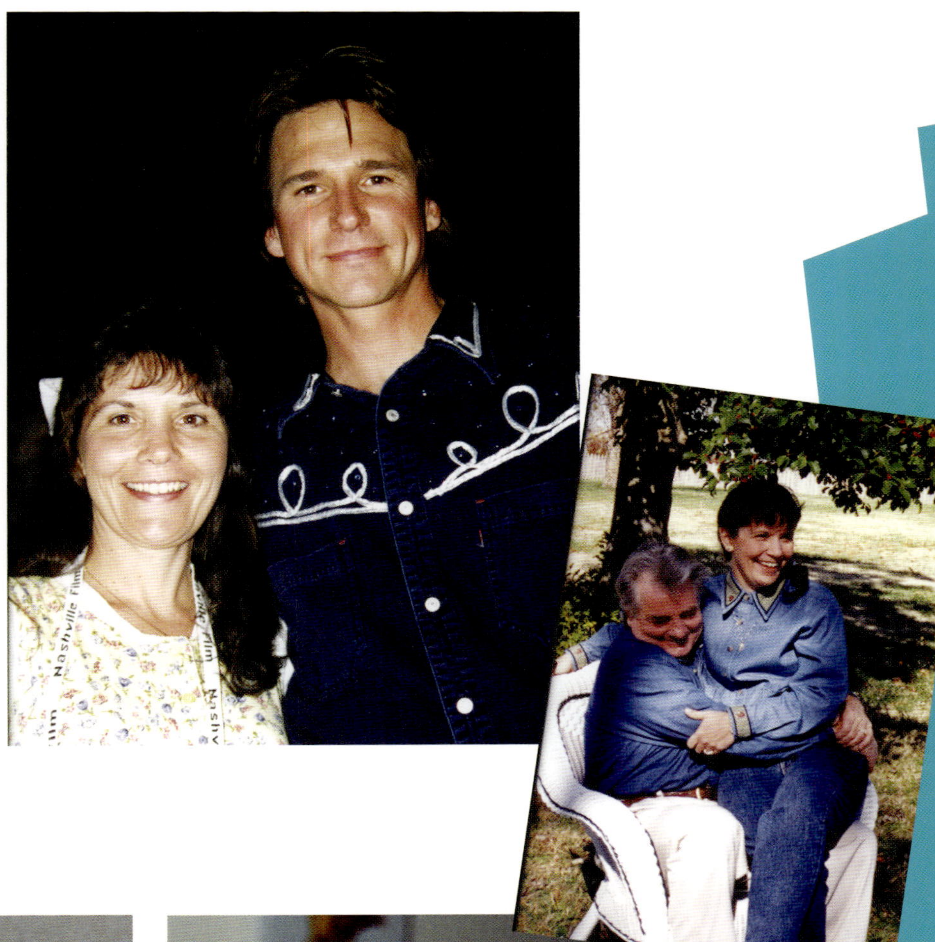

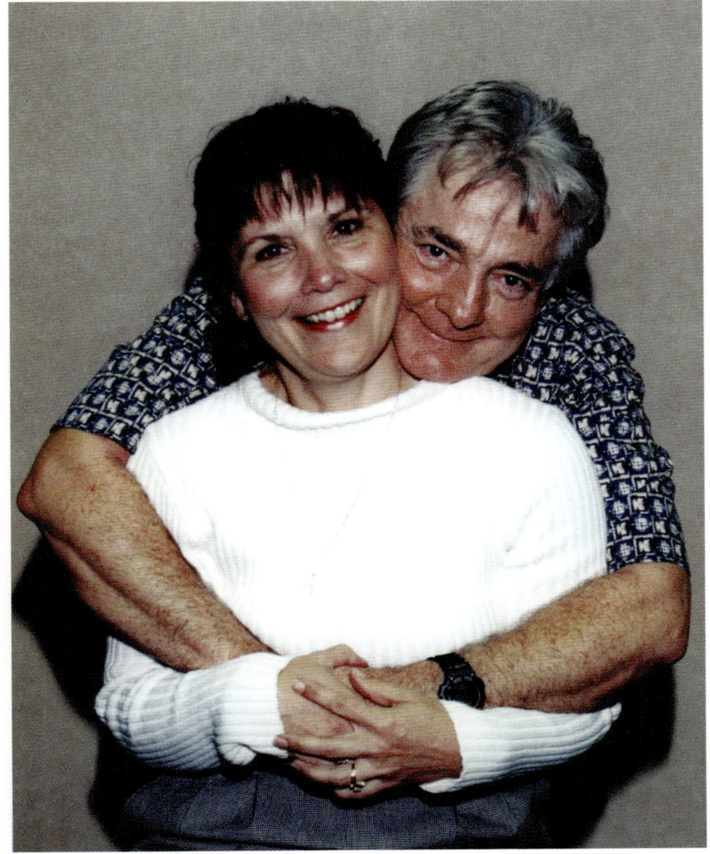

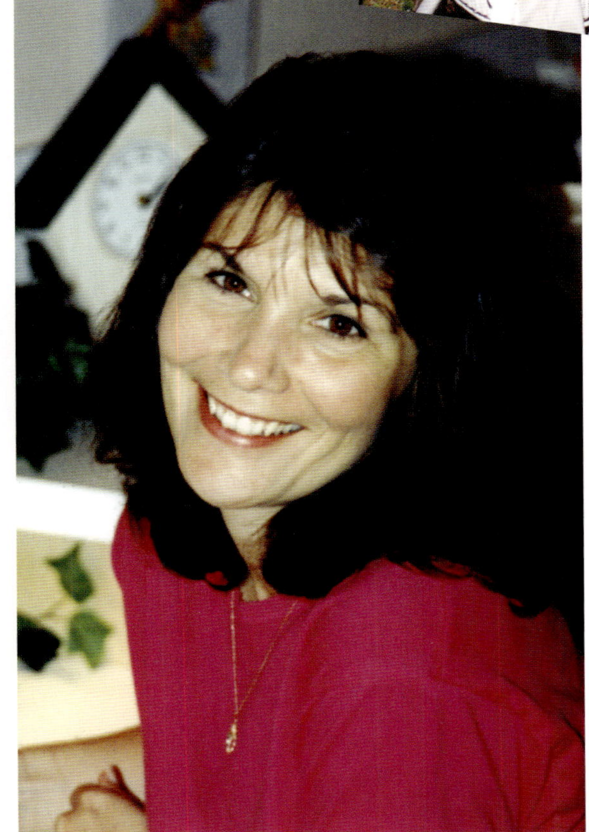

Robin, the love of my life

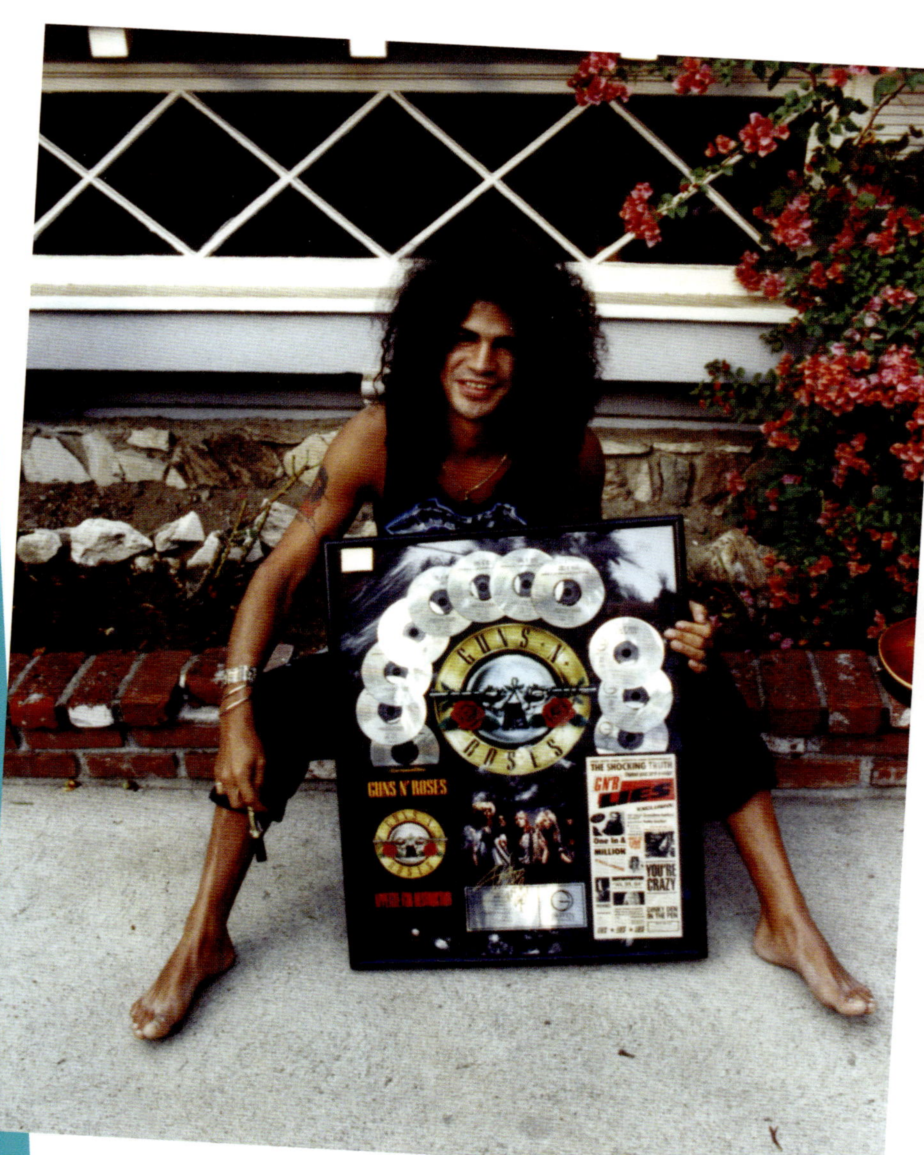

Slash

I traded him one of Elvis' guns for his guitar and this multi-platinum award for Guns N' Roses, now "Velvet Revolver."

Bobby Unser

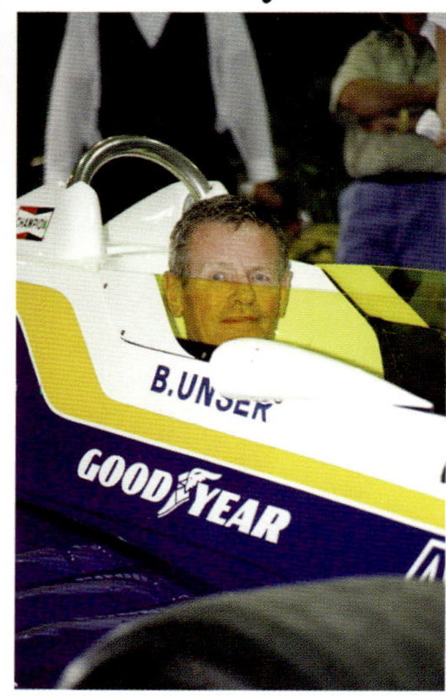

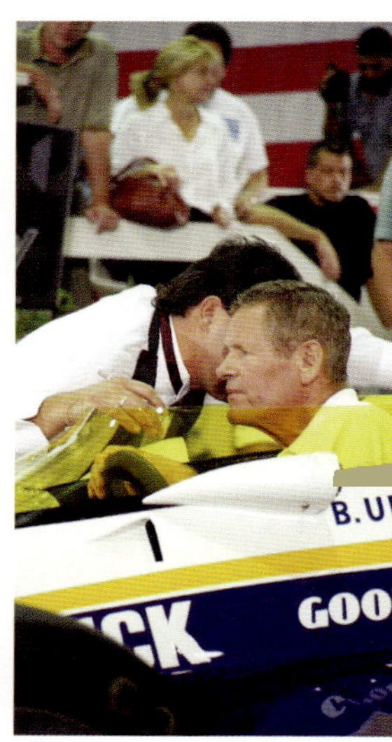

Waylon Jennings

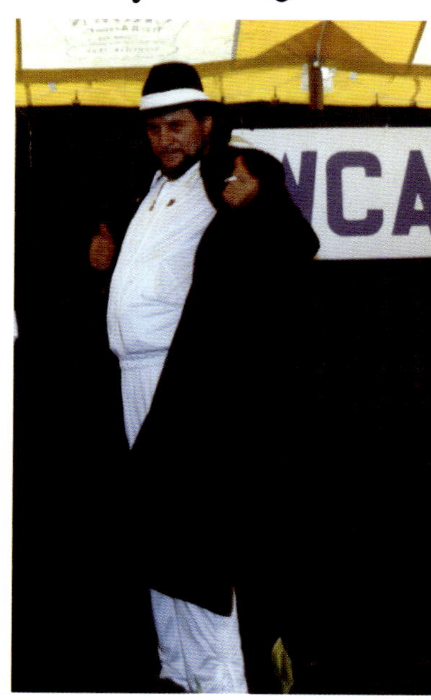

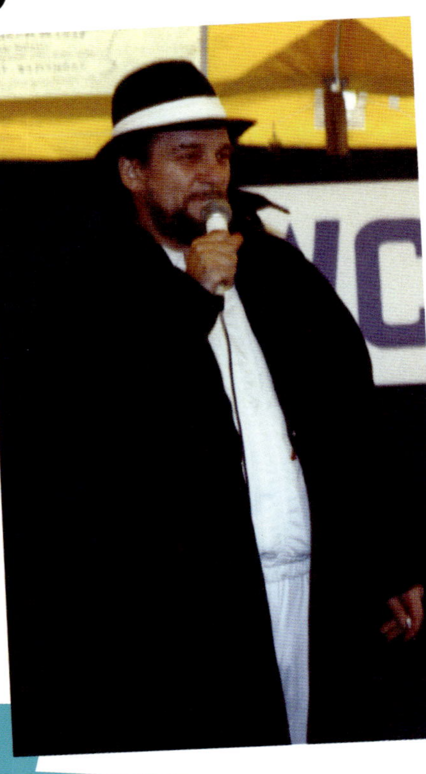

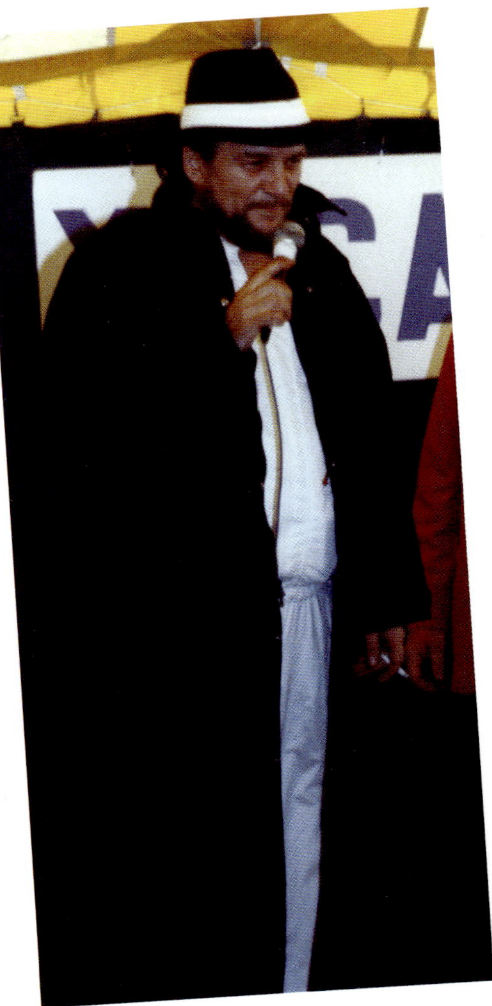

Johnny Cash

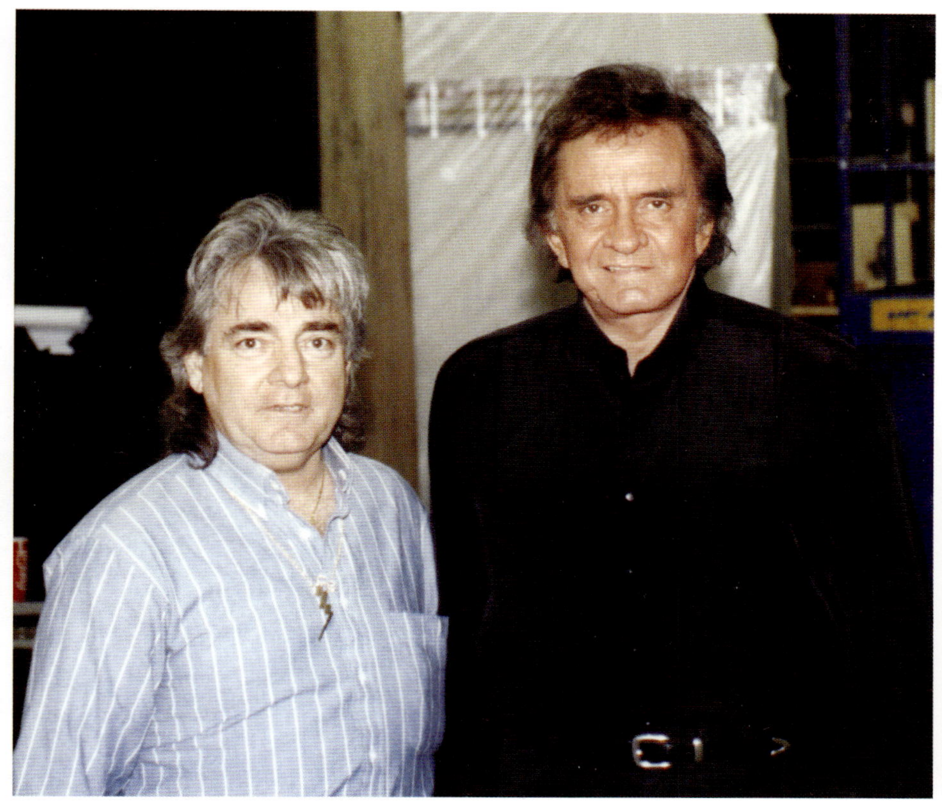

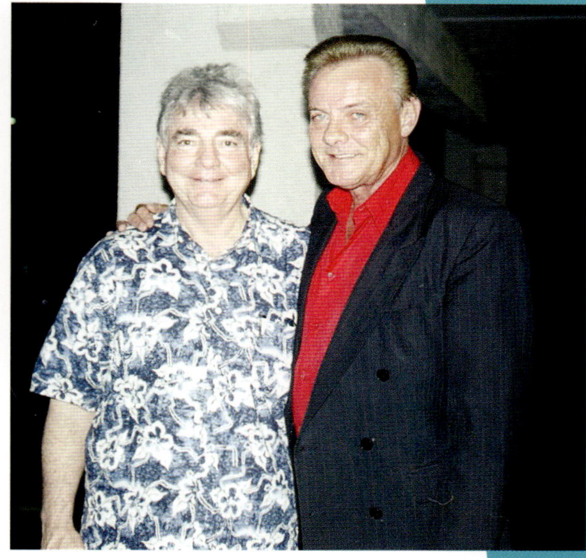

My 2nd Oldest Friend

George Elliott

since 1963

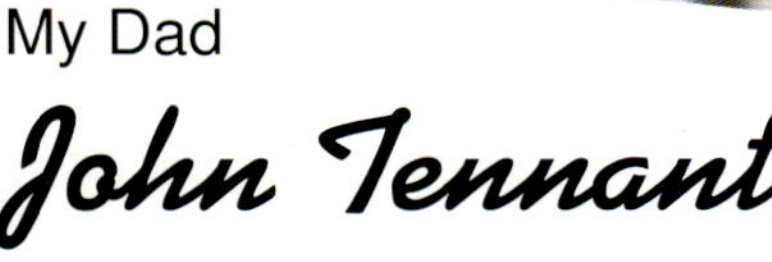

My Dad

John Tennant

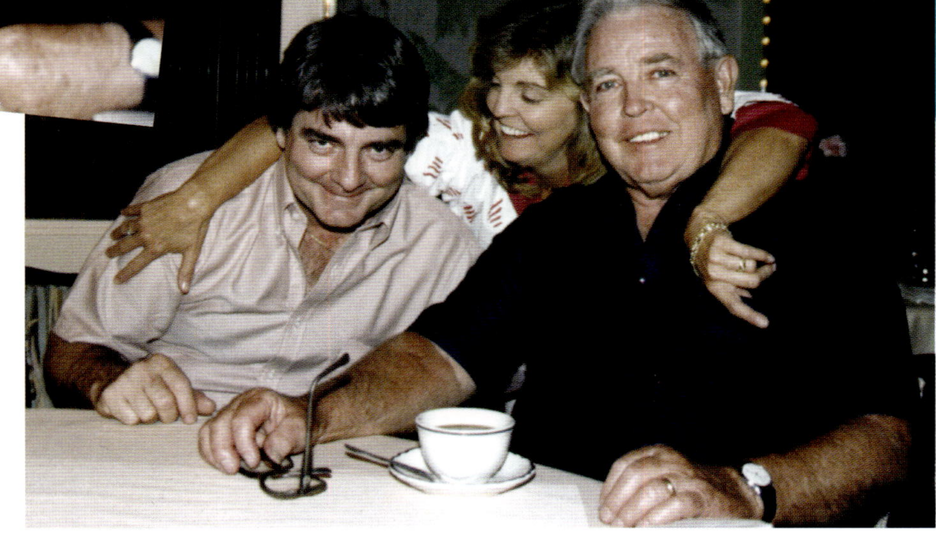

Me, Dad, and my sister Jolene

Kenny Rogers

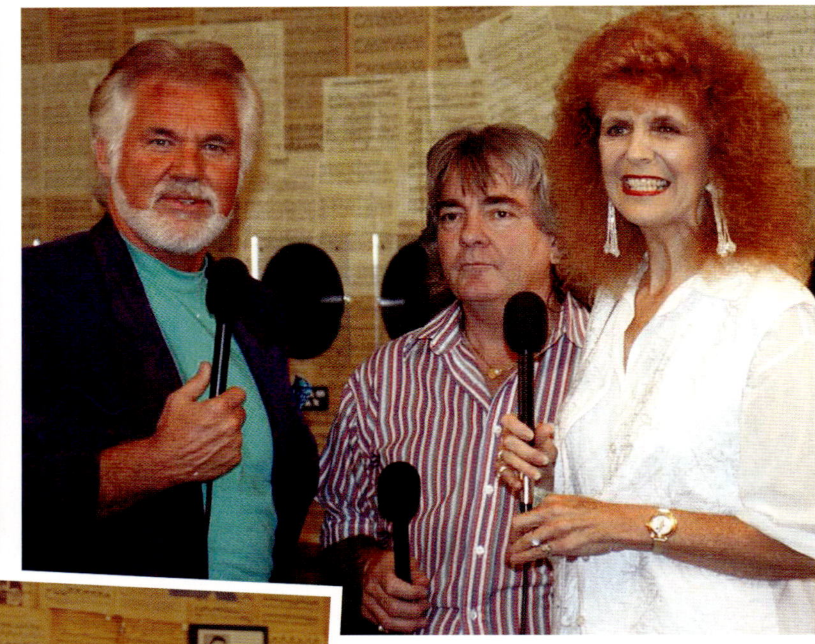

Kenny Rogers and Shelly West

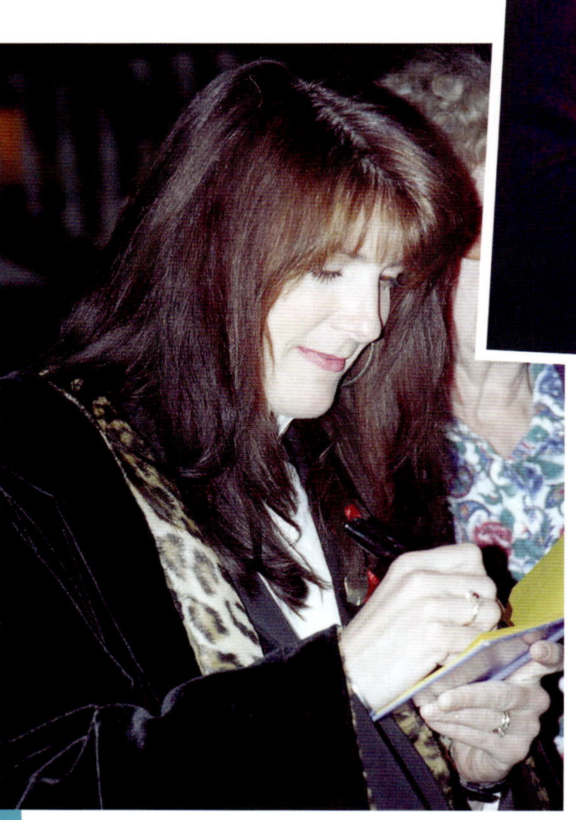

Kathy Mattea

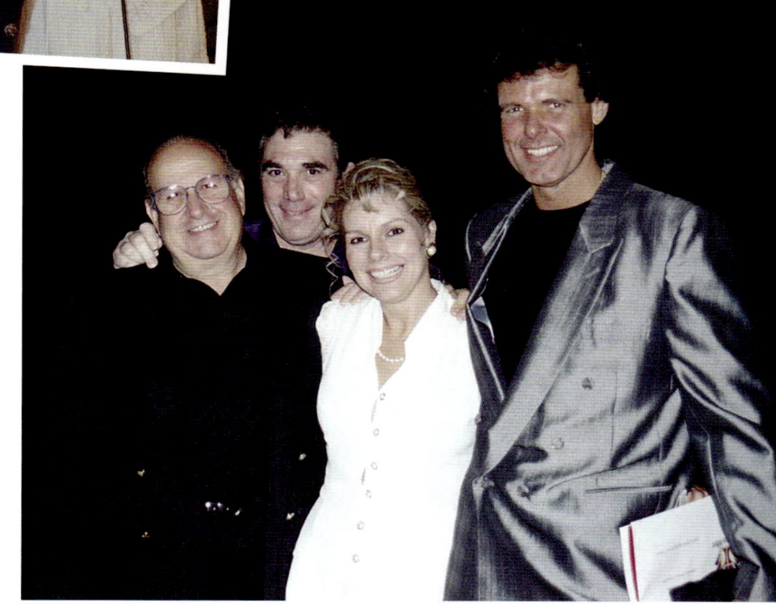

Joe Esposito, Malcolm Leo, Patsy Andersen, and Charlie Stickerod

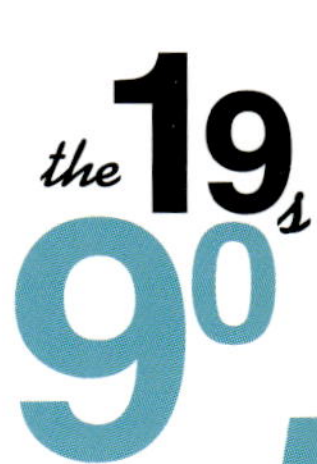

Lauren Chapin
at my Lakeland home.

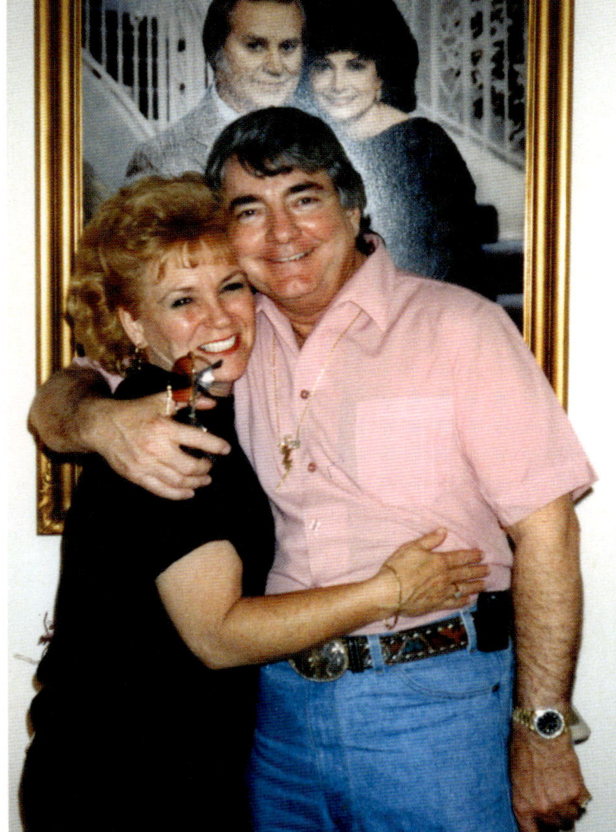

Lauren played Kathy "Kitten" Anderson in "Father Knows Best."

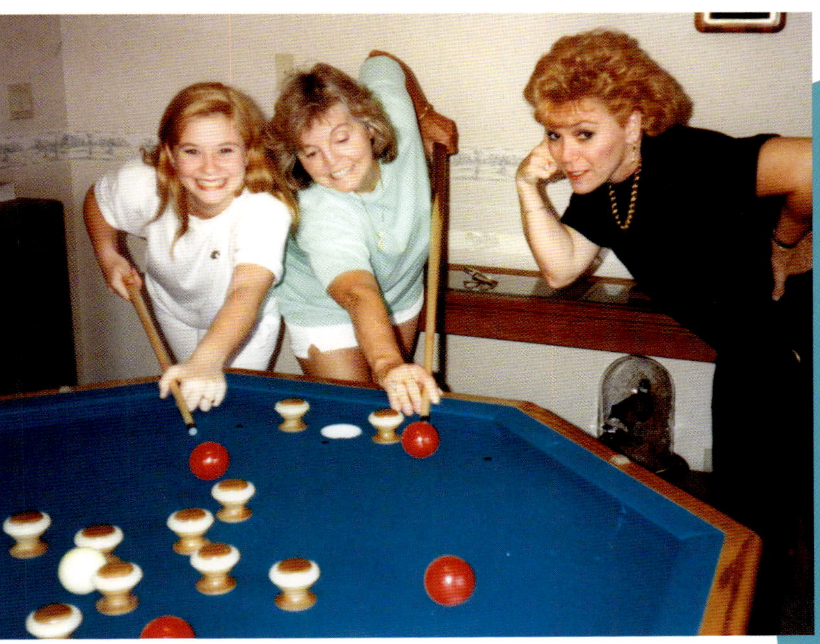

Summer Chapin, Jolene Kenyon and Lauren Chapin

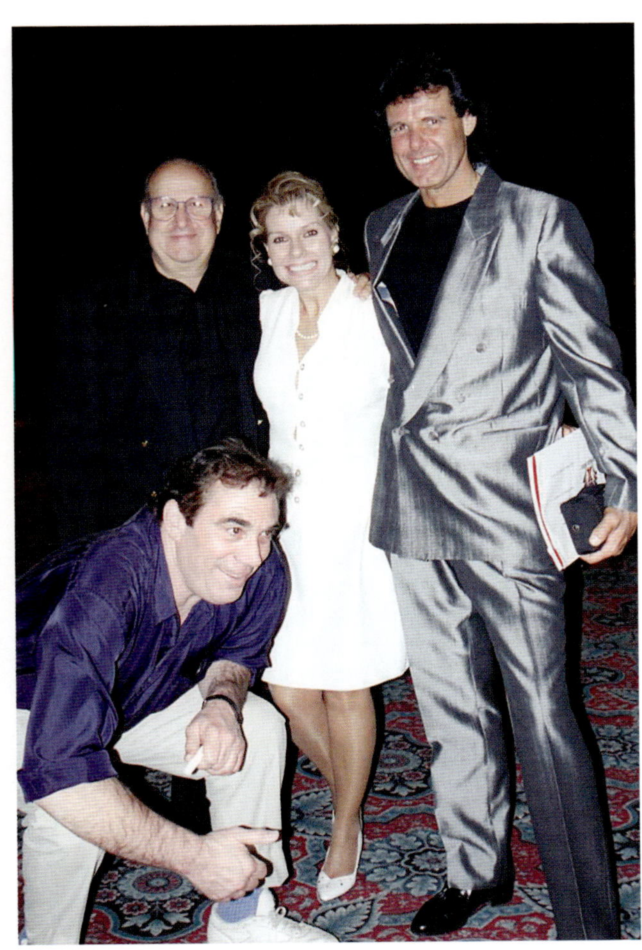

Malcolm Leo, Joe Esposito, Patsy Andersen, and Charlie Stickerod

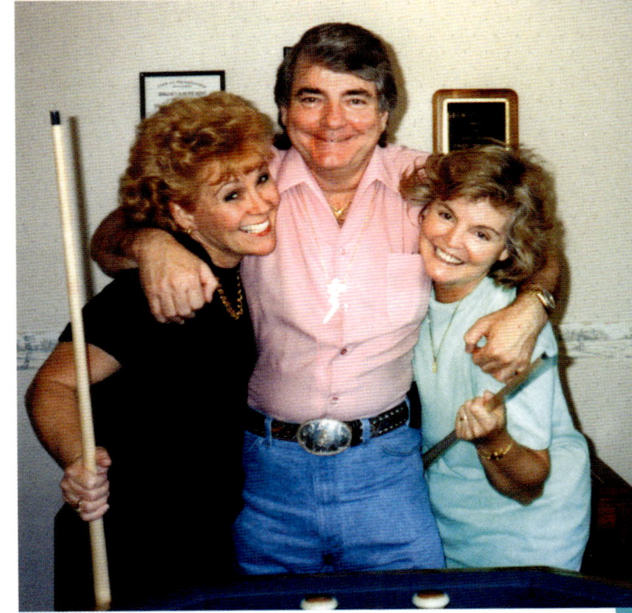

Lauren Chapin, Me, and my sister Jolene

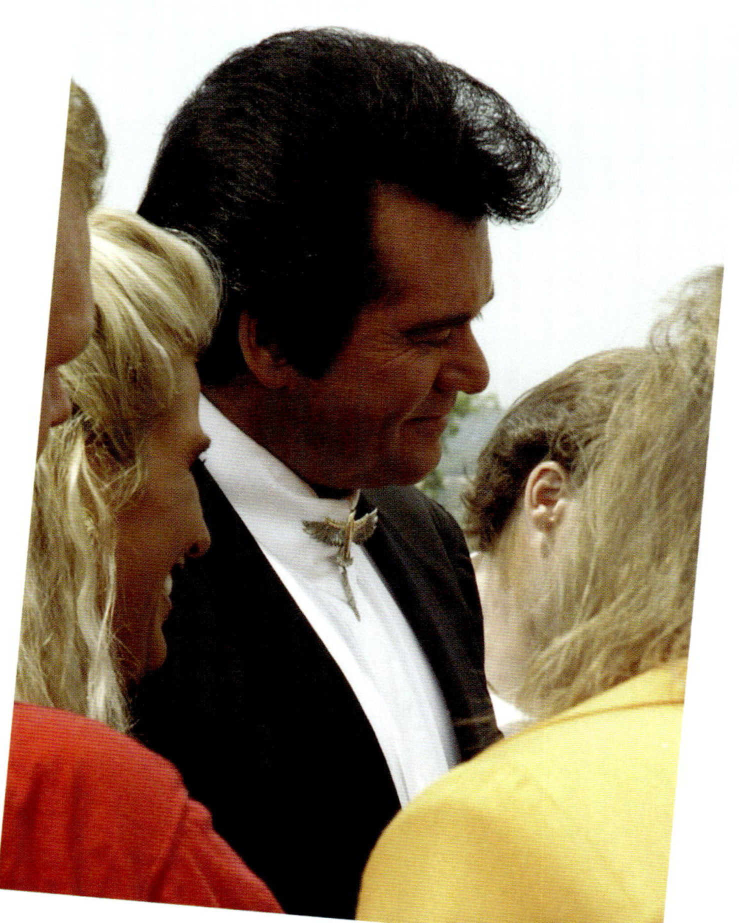

Wayne Newton

Mr. Las Vegas

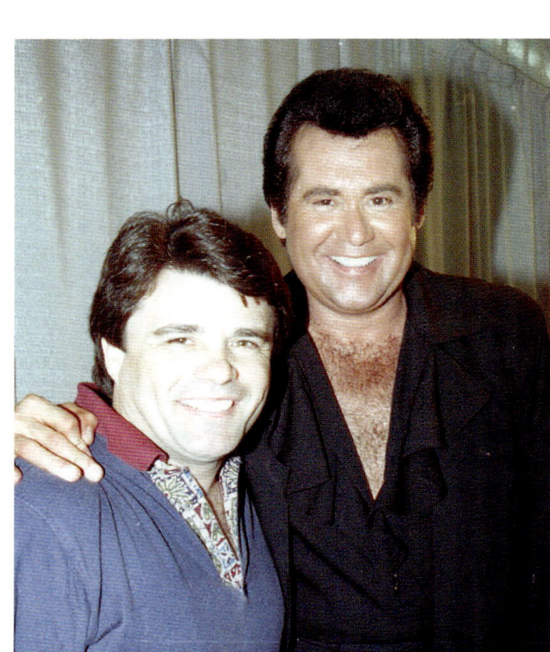

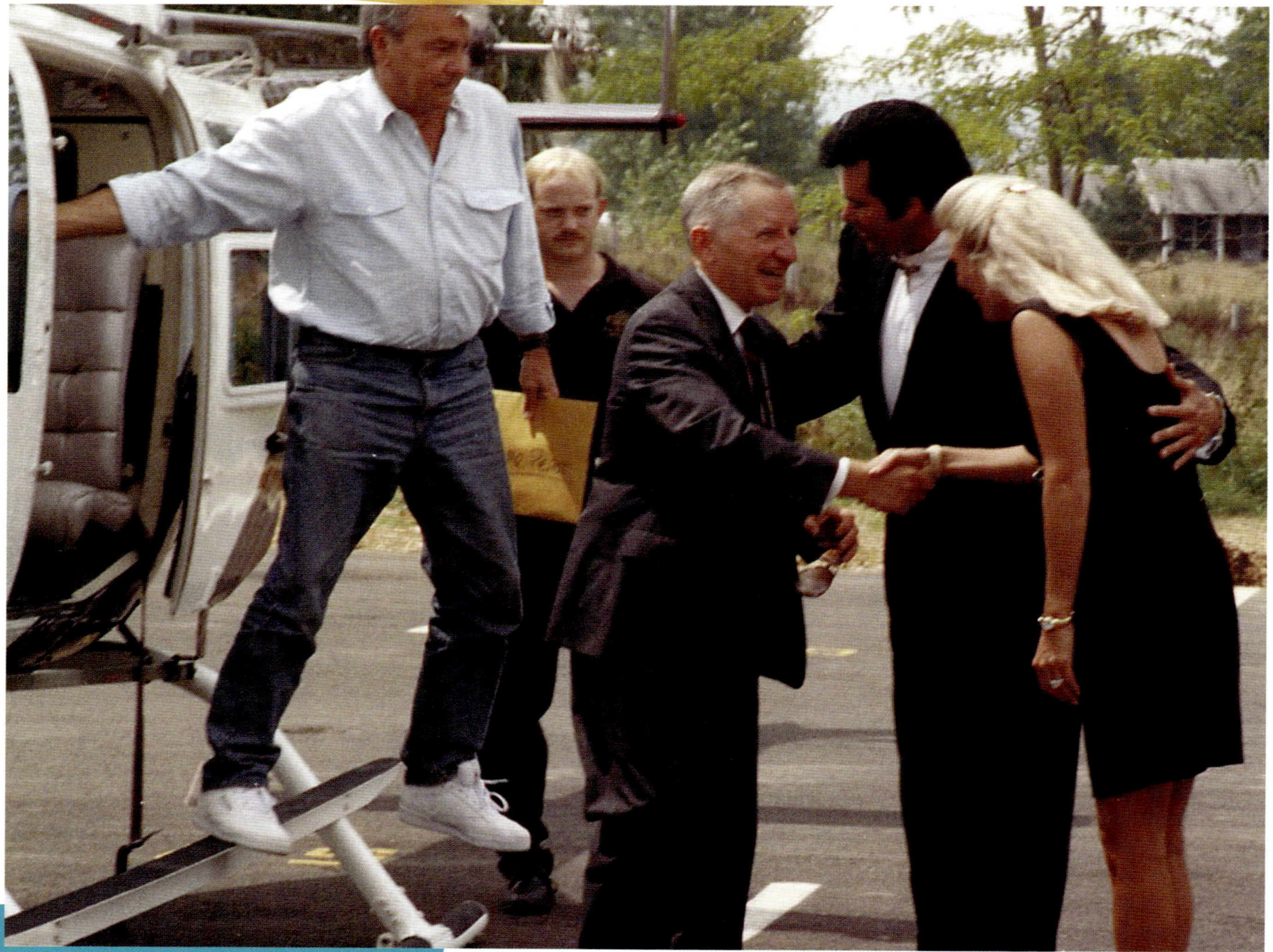

H. Ross Perot and Mr. & Mrs. Wayne Newton

Bill Dana

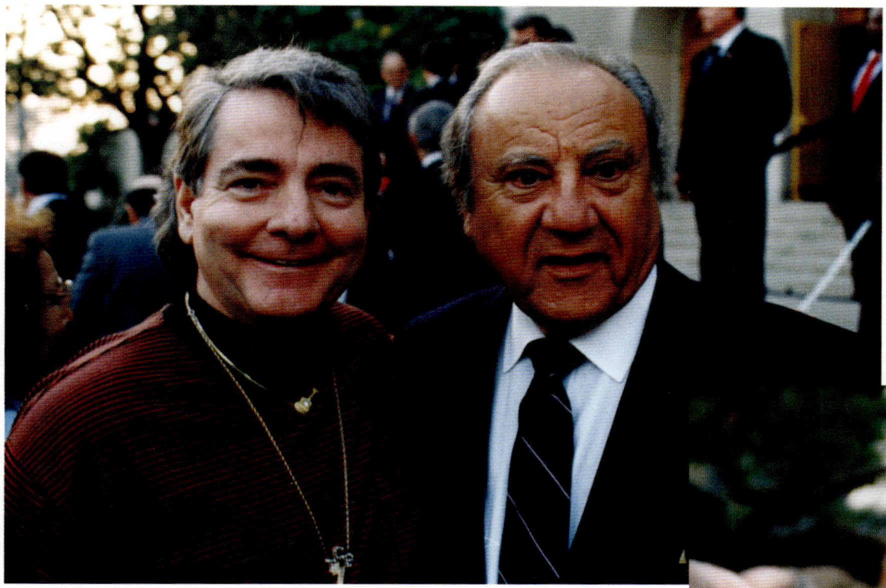

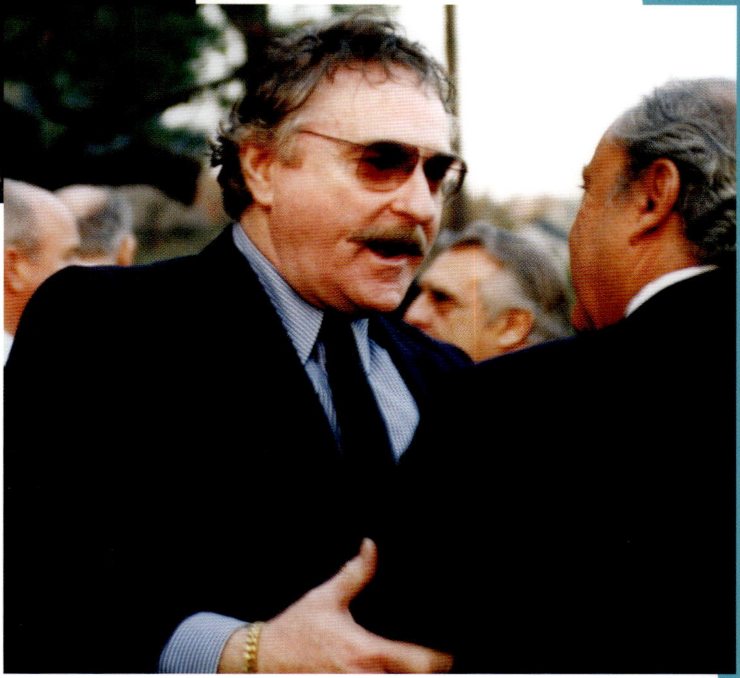

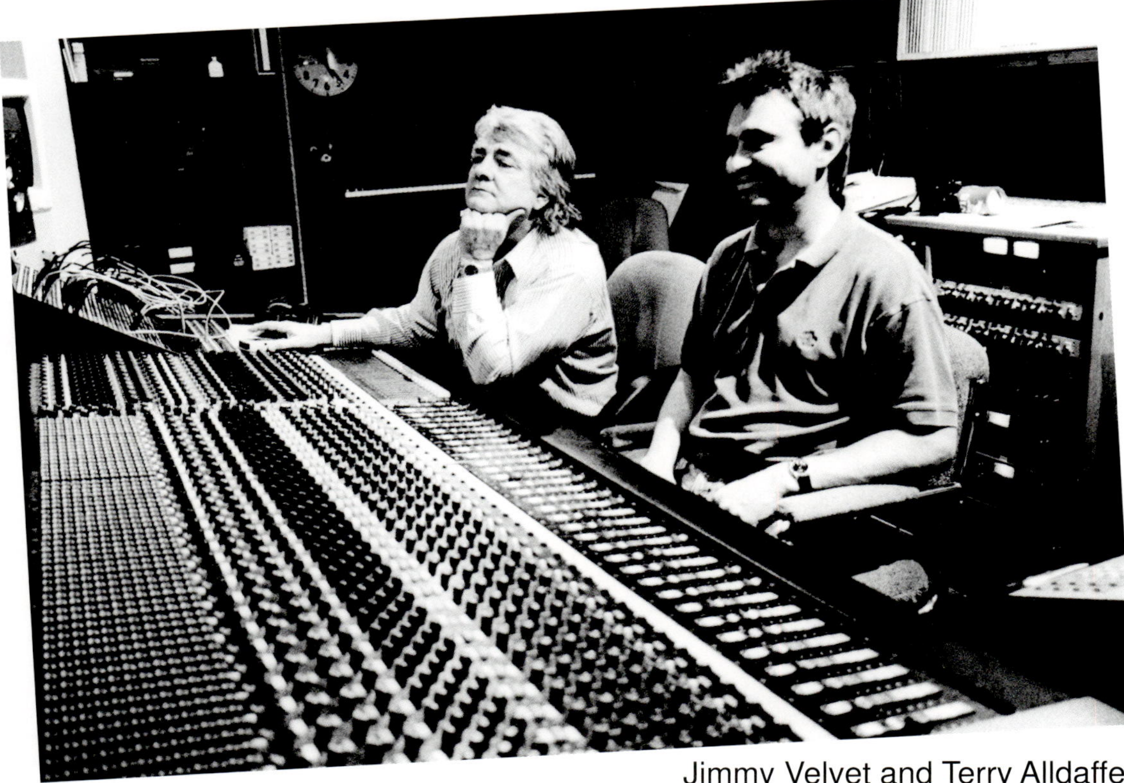

Jimmy Velvet and Terry Alldaffer
at Jimmy Velvet's American Studios.

Patrick Duffy & Larry Hagman

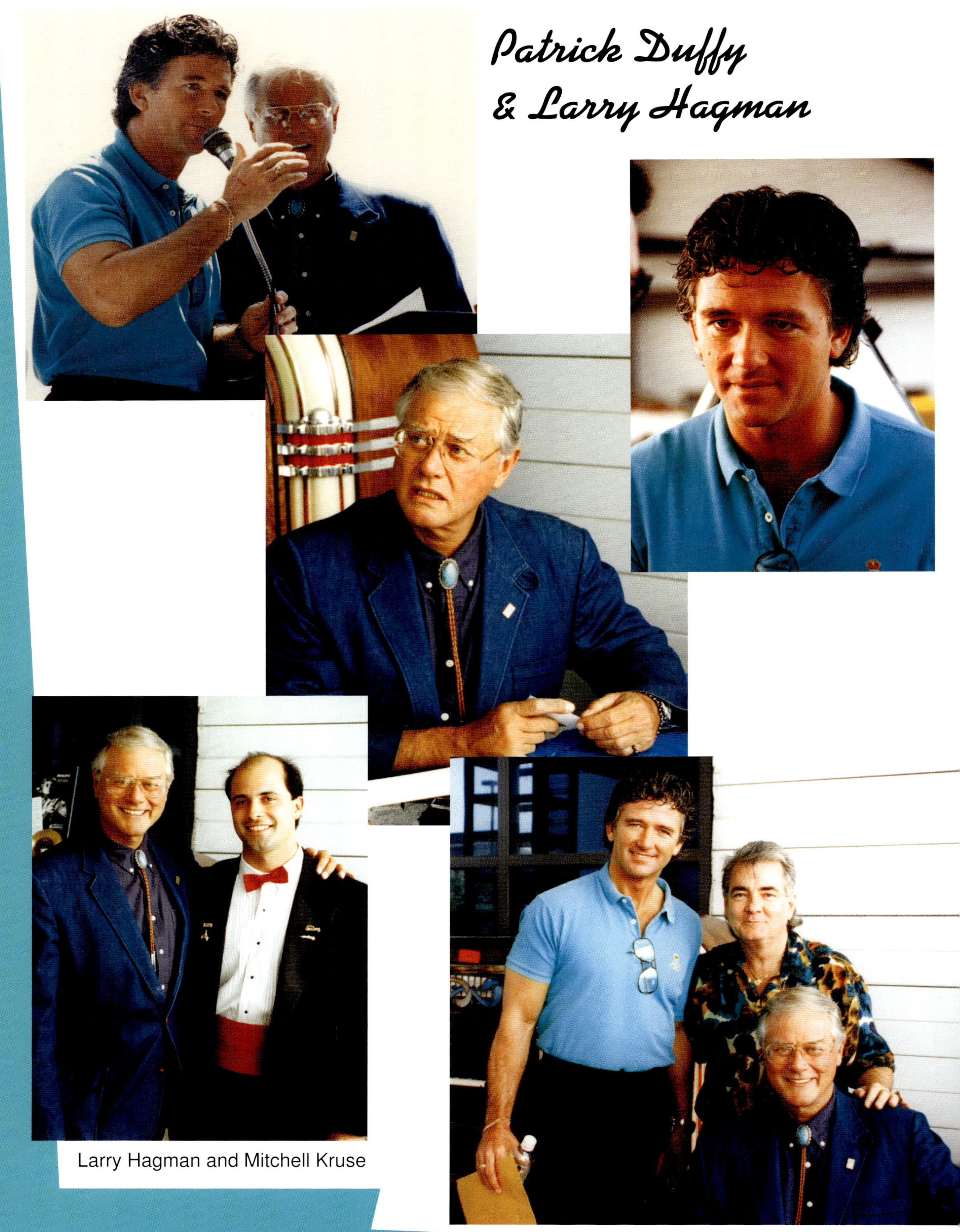

Larry Hagman and Mitchell Kruse

Patrick Duffy, Me and Larry Hagman

Little Richard

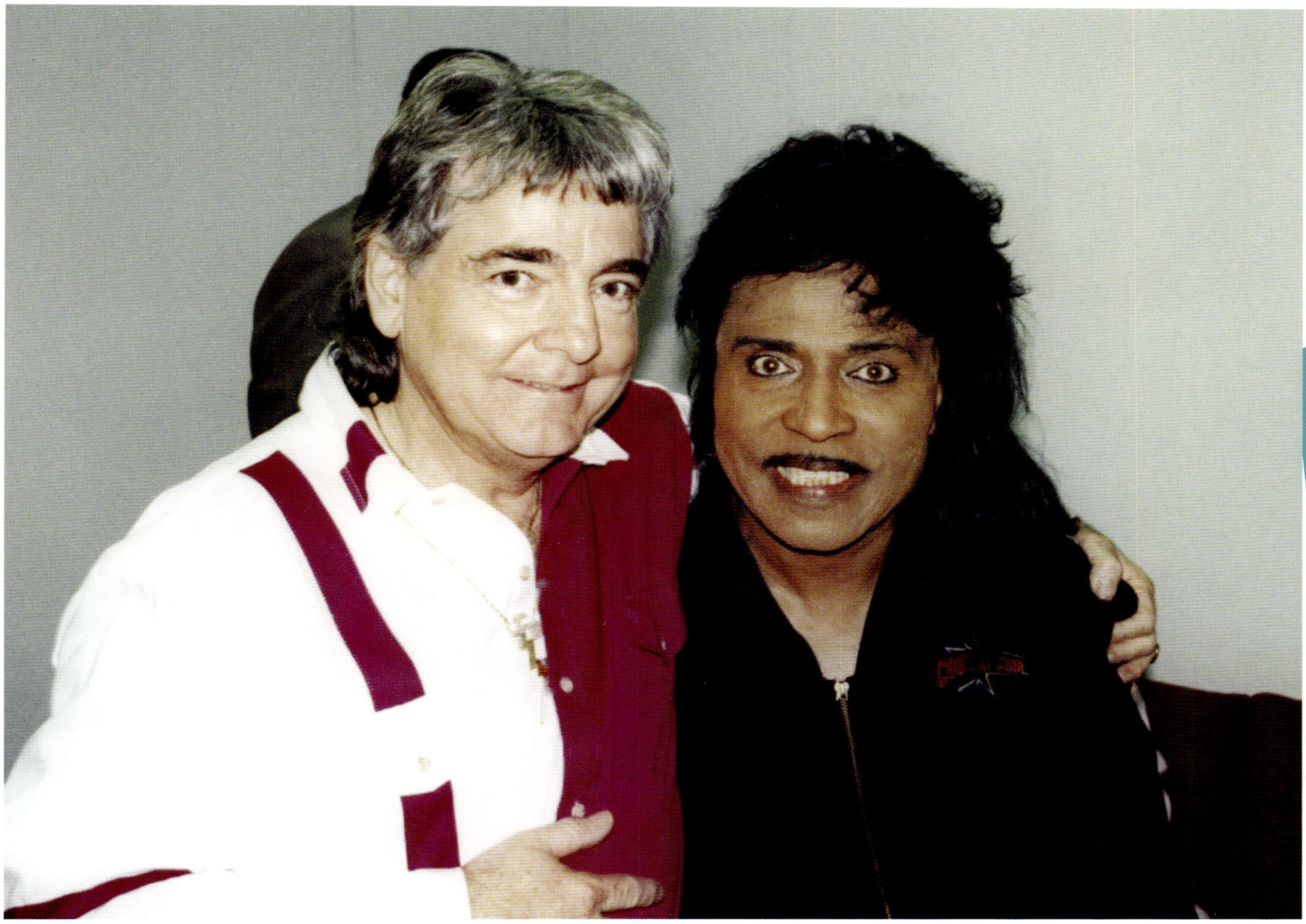

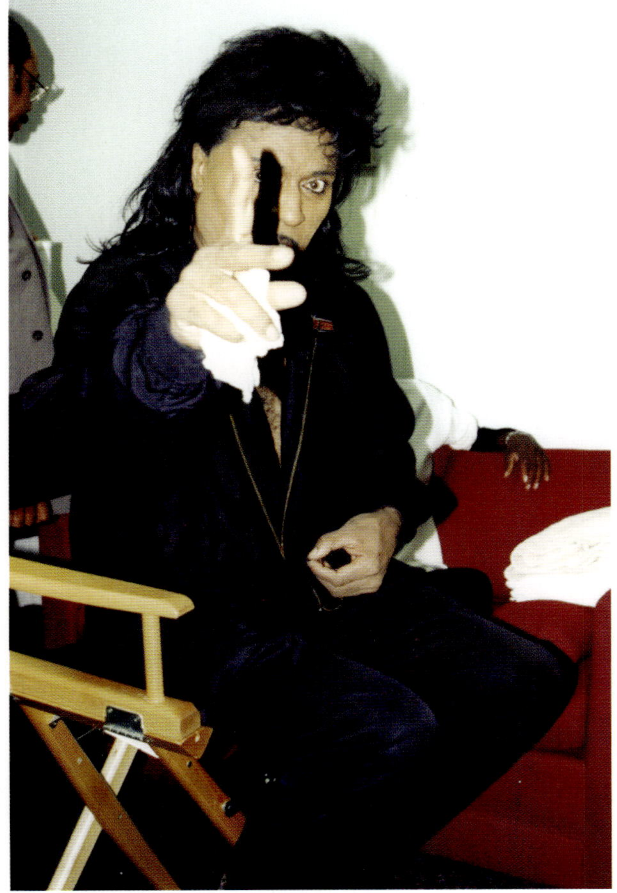

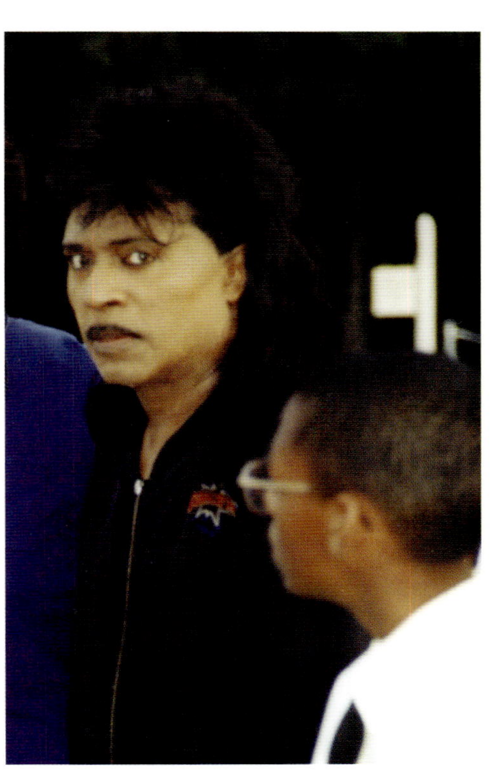

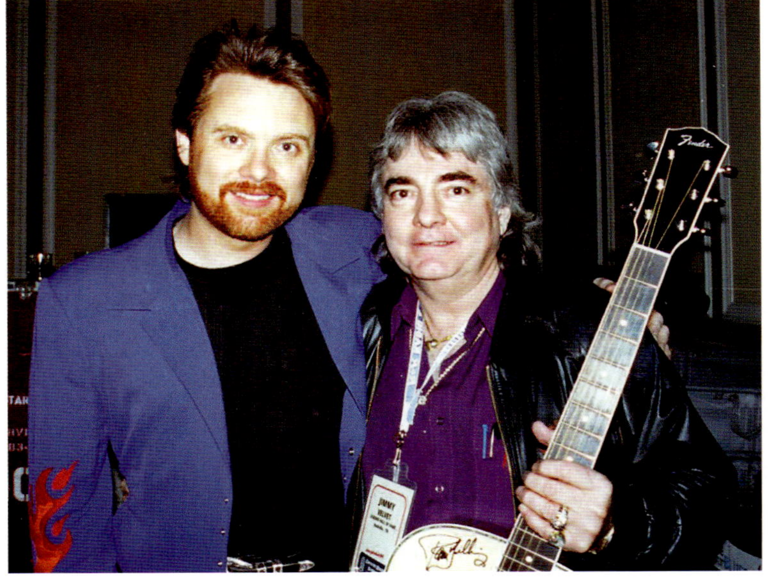

Lee Roy Parnell

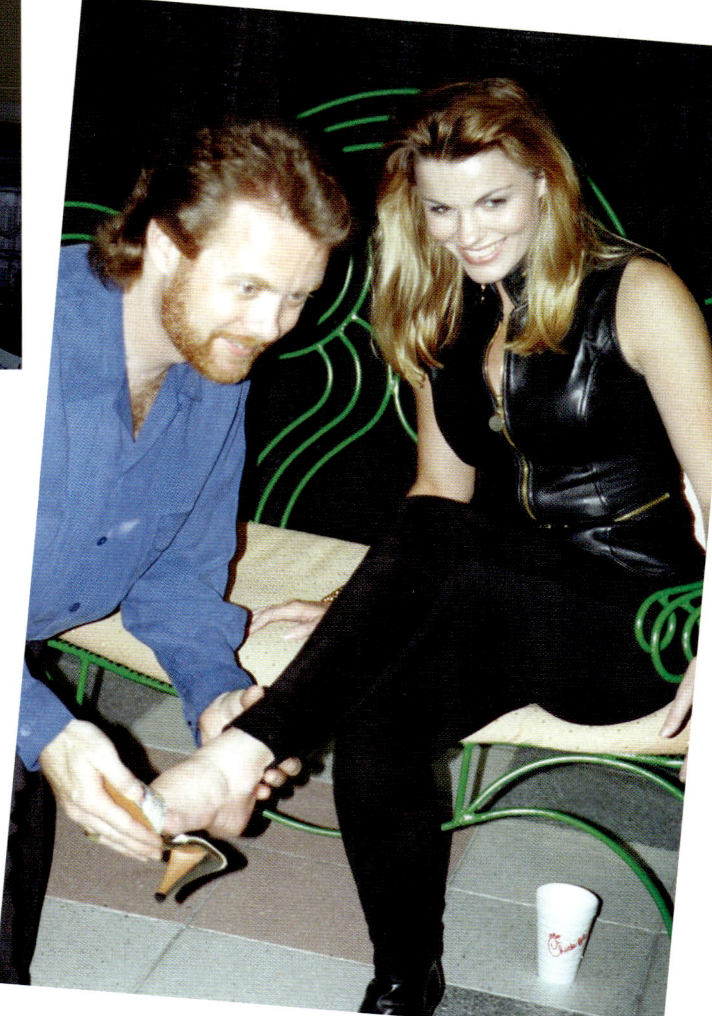

Leroy and Lisa Stuart

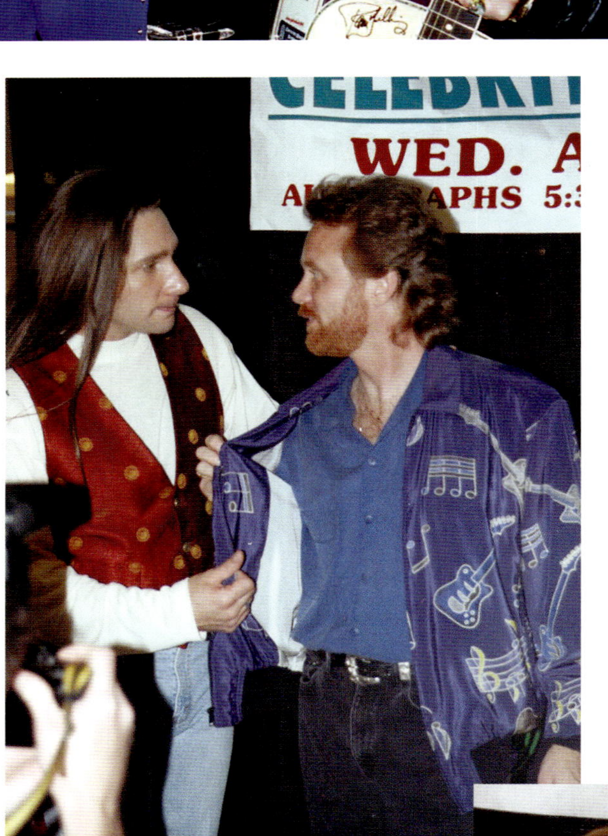

Little Texas Lee Roy Parnell

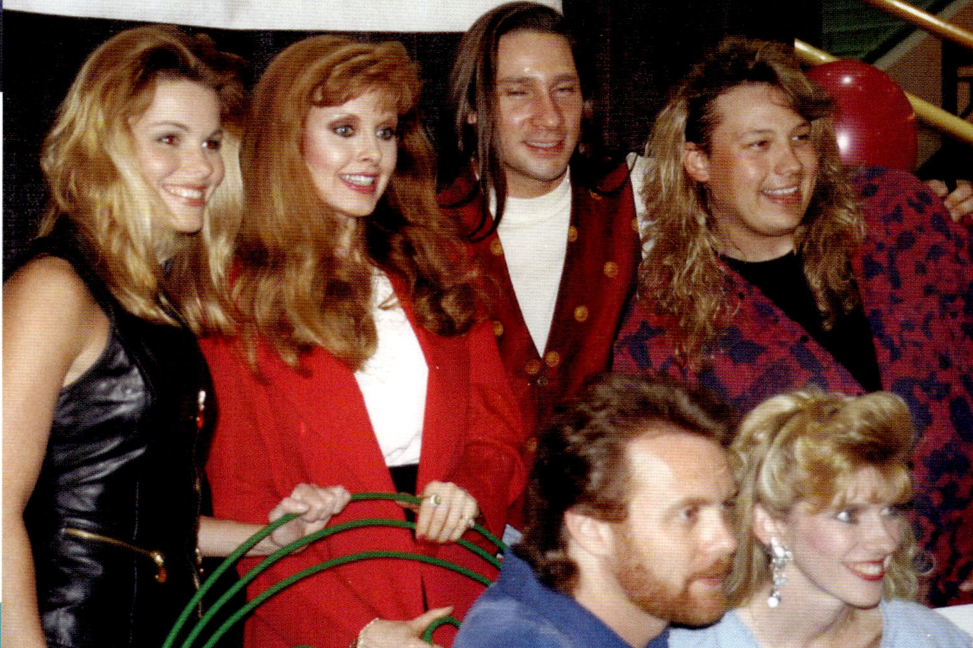

Lisa, Little Texas, Lee Roy Parnell

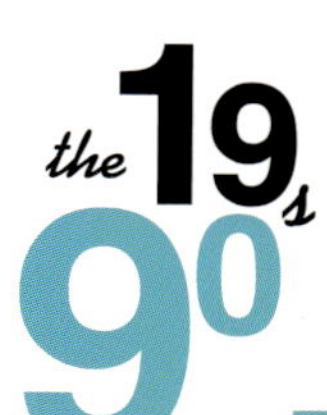

Little Texas

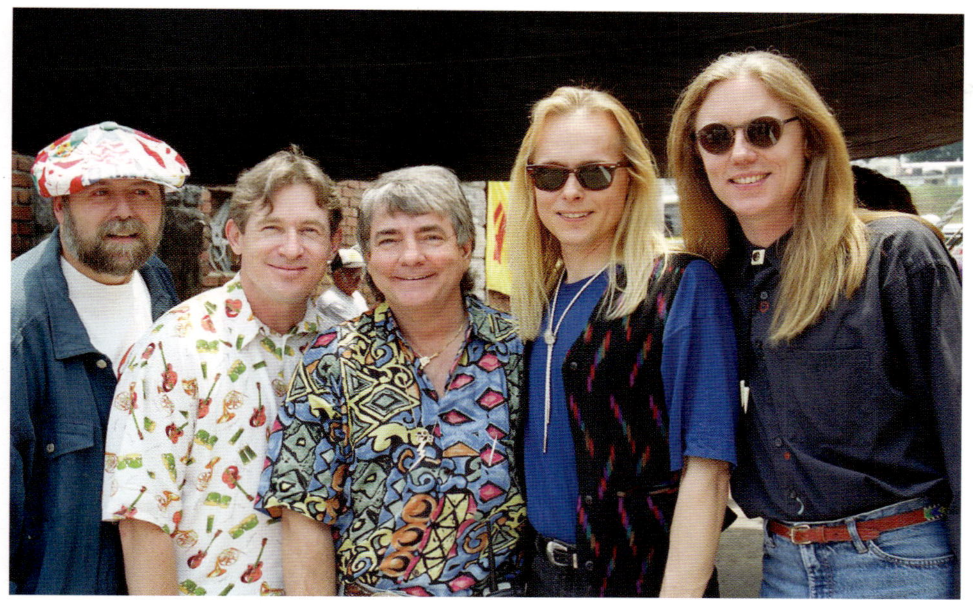

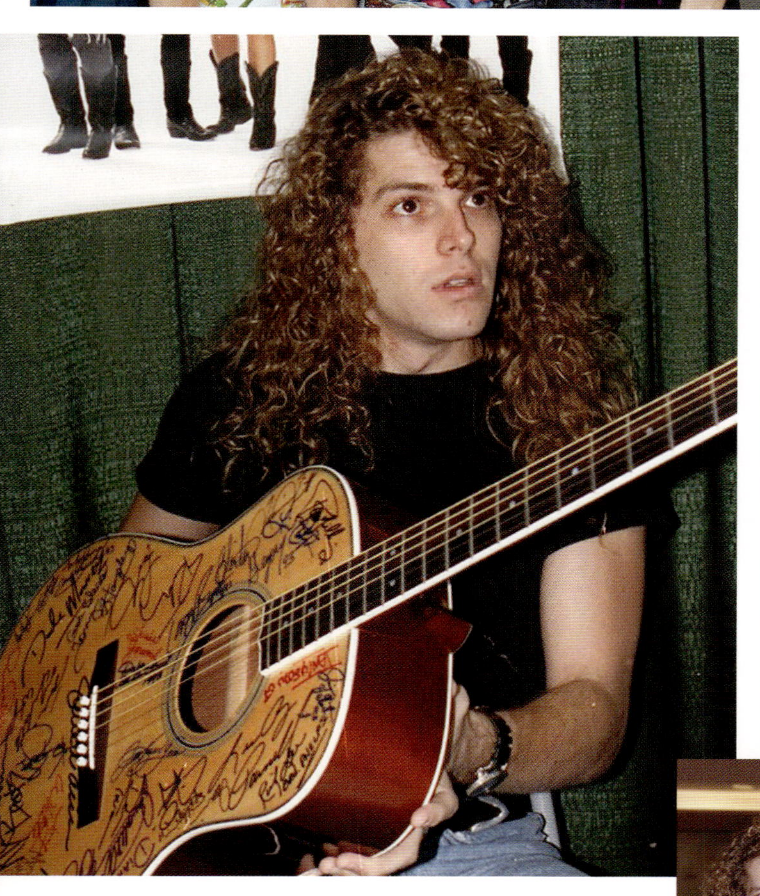

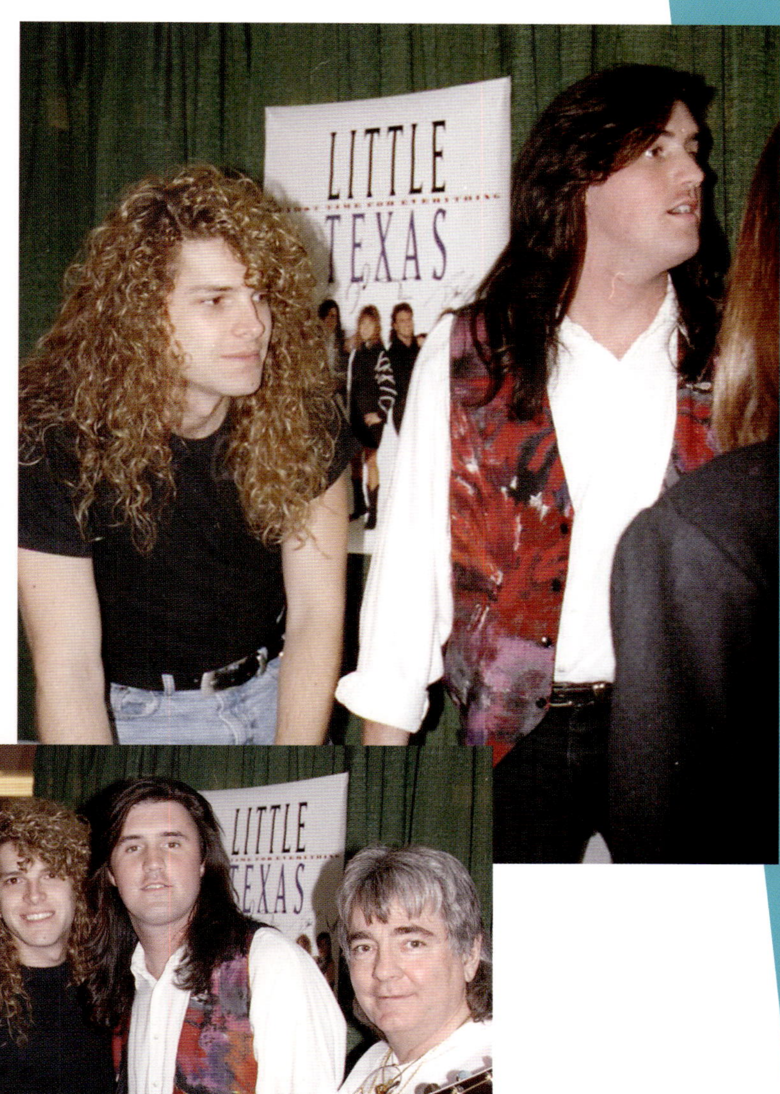

Little Texas

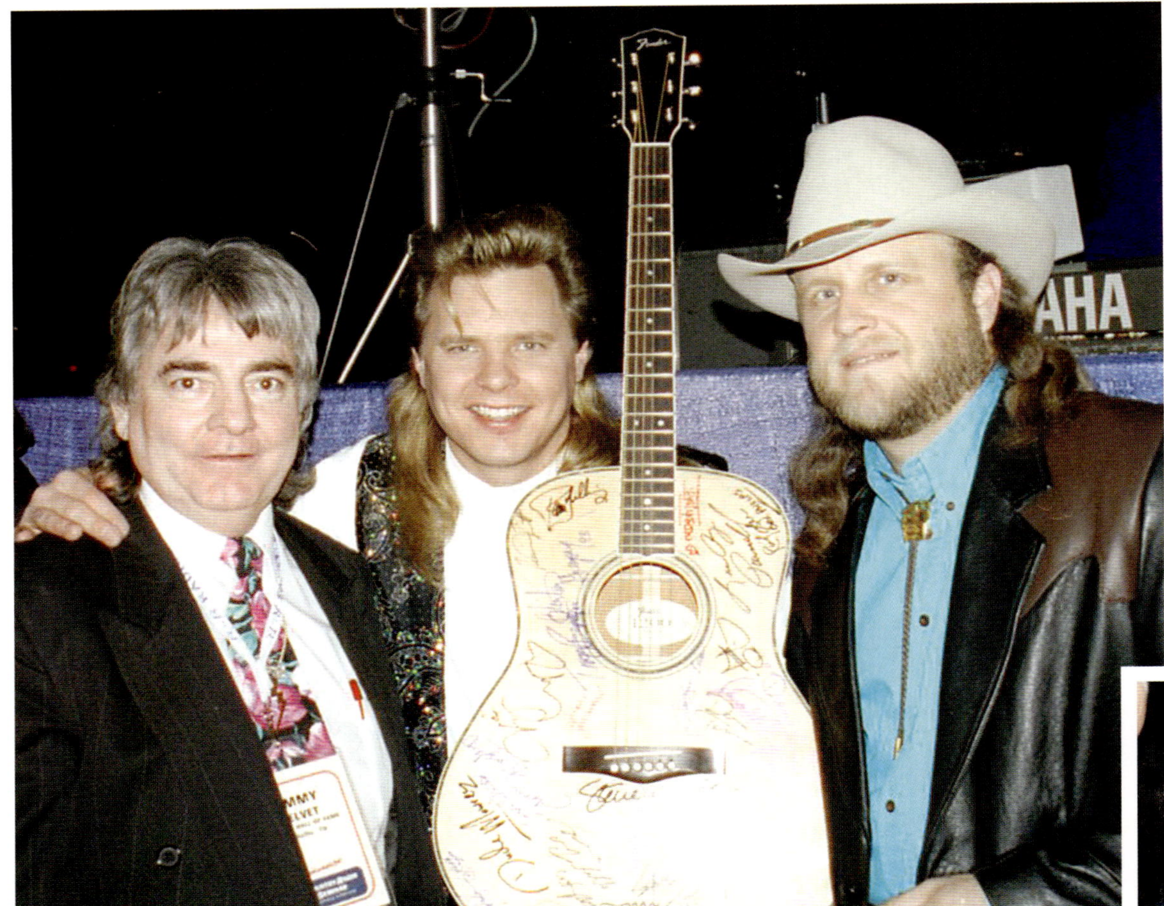

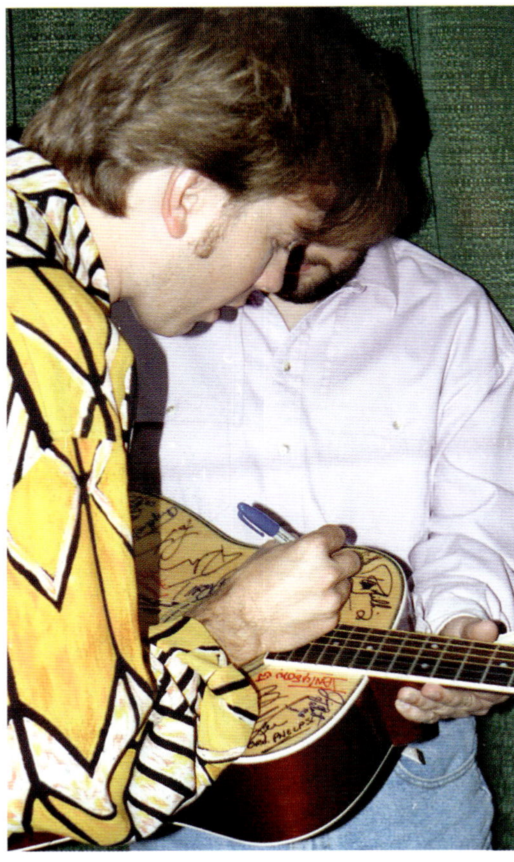

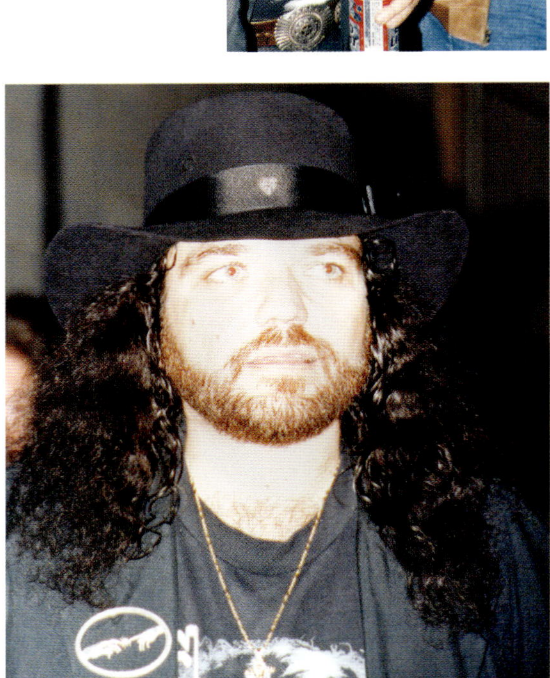

Gary Rossington of Lynyrd Skynyrd
and Rossington-Collins Band

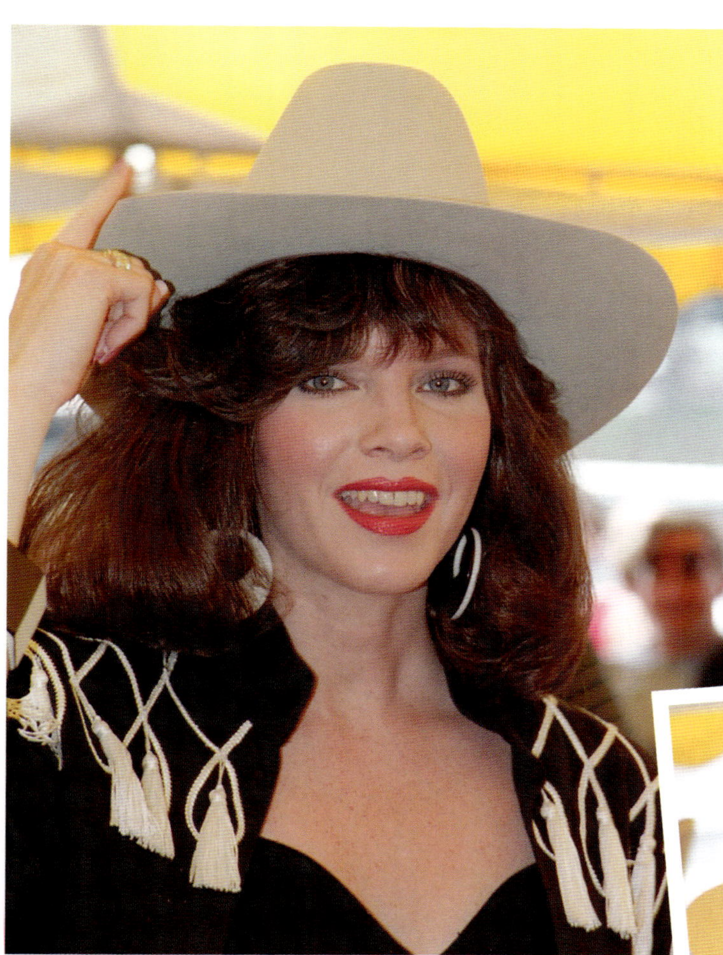

Lorianne Crook

What a doll and lots of fun

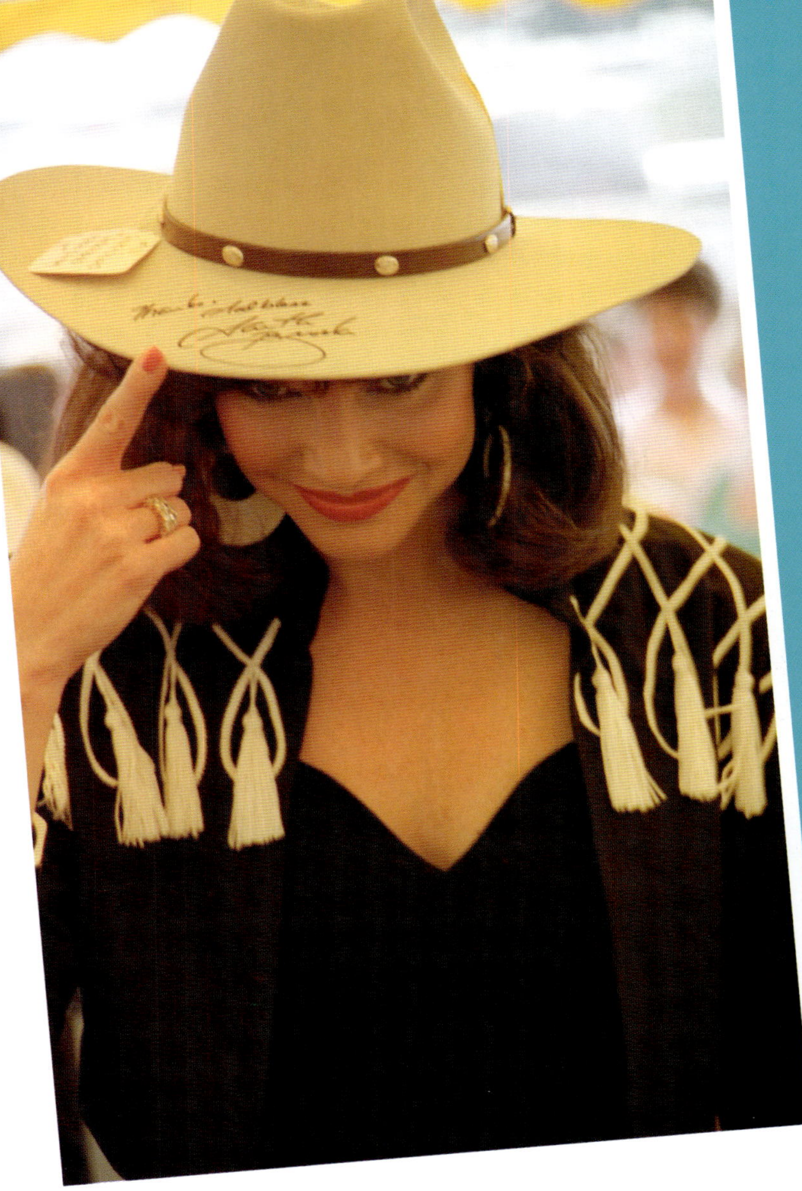

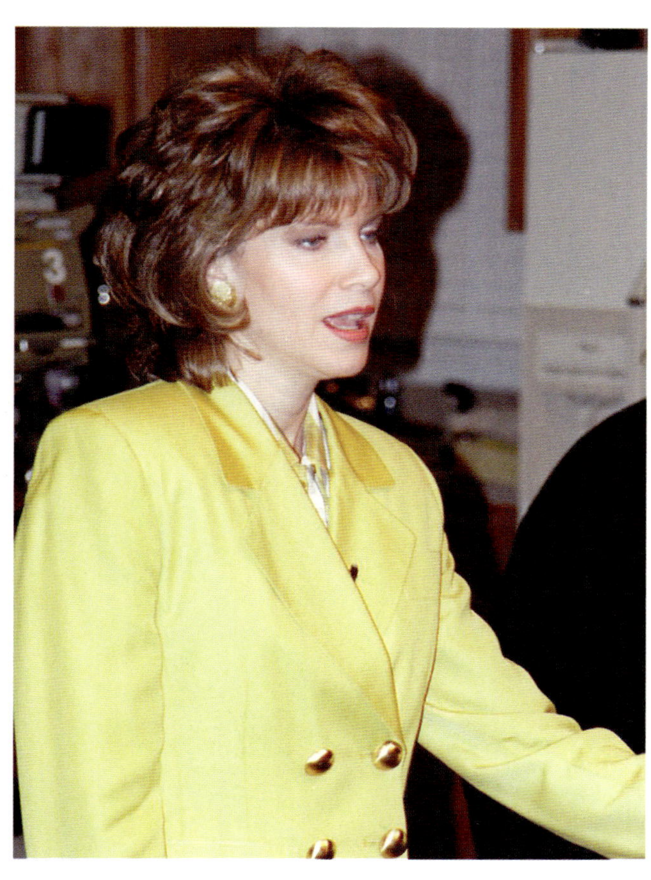

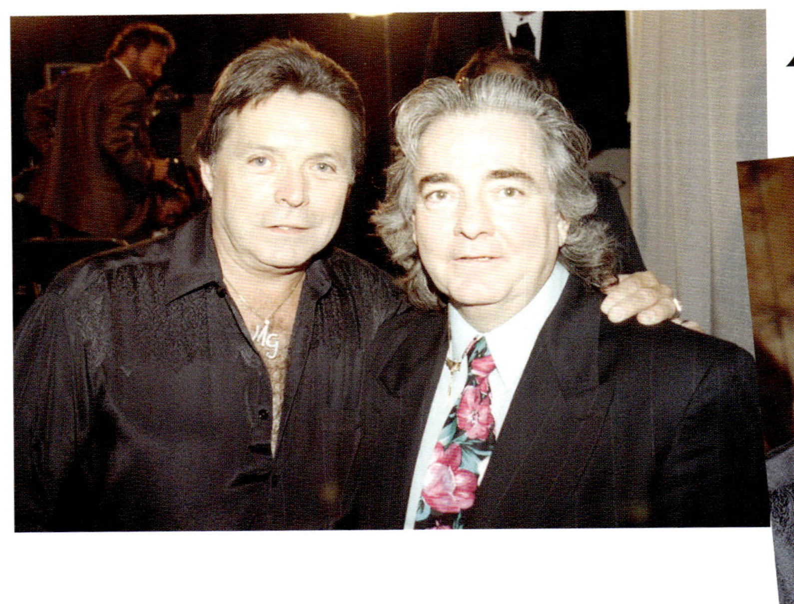

Mickey Gilley

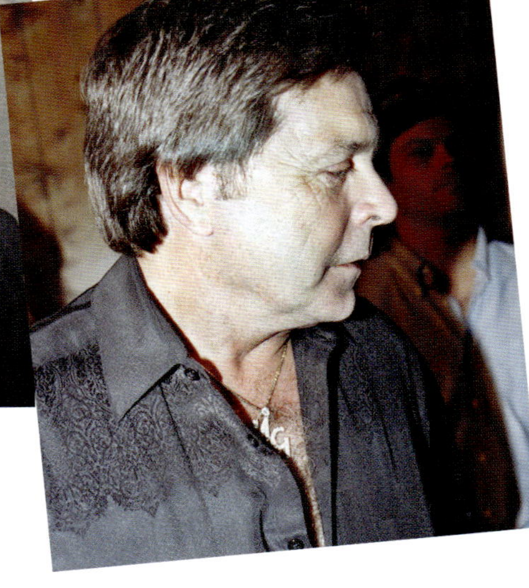

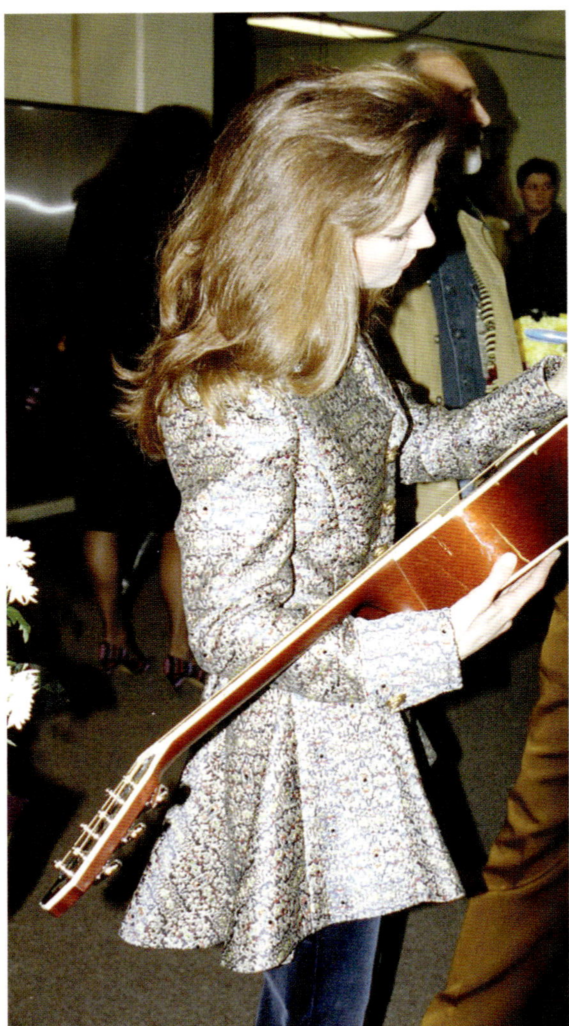

Martina McBride

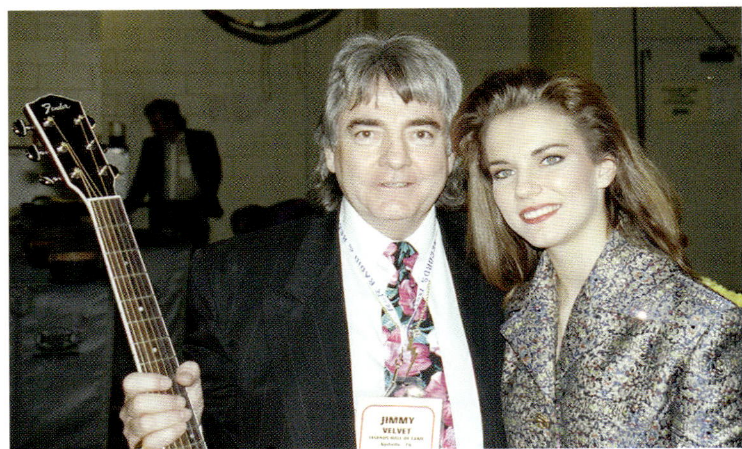

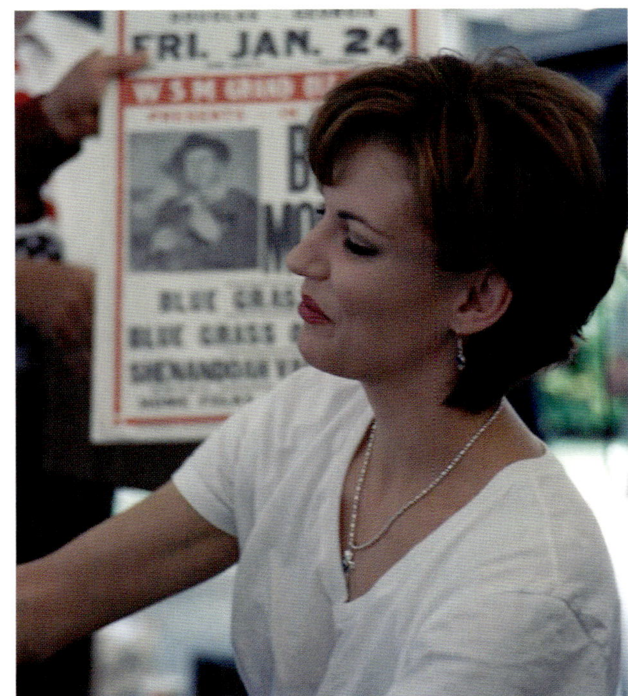

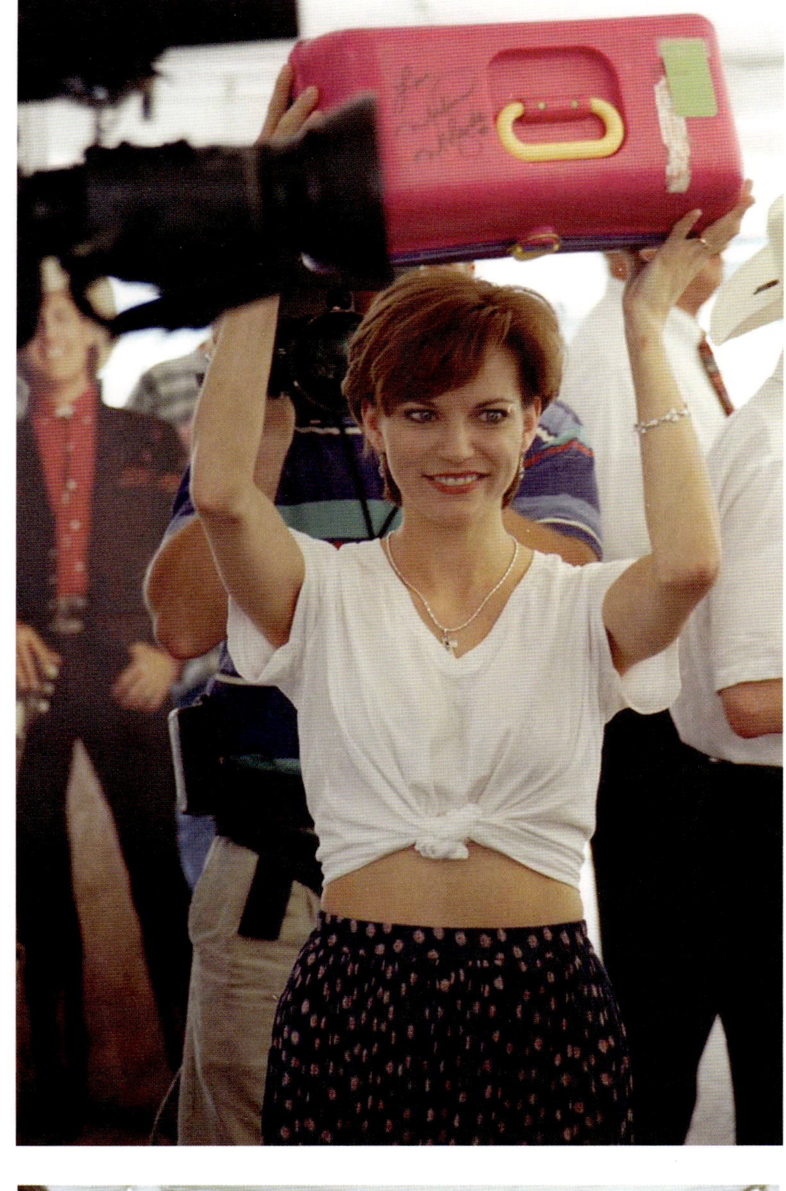

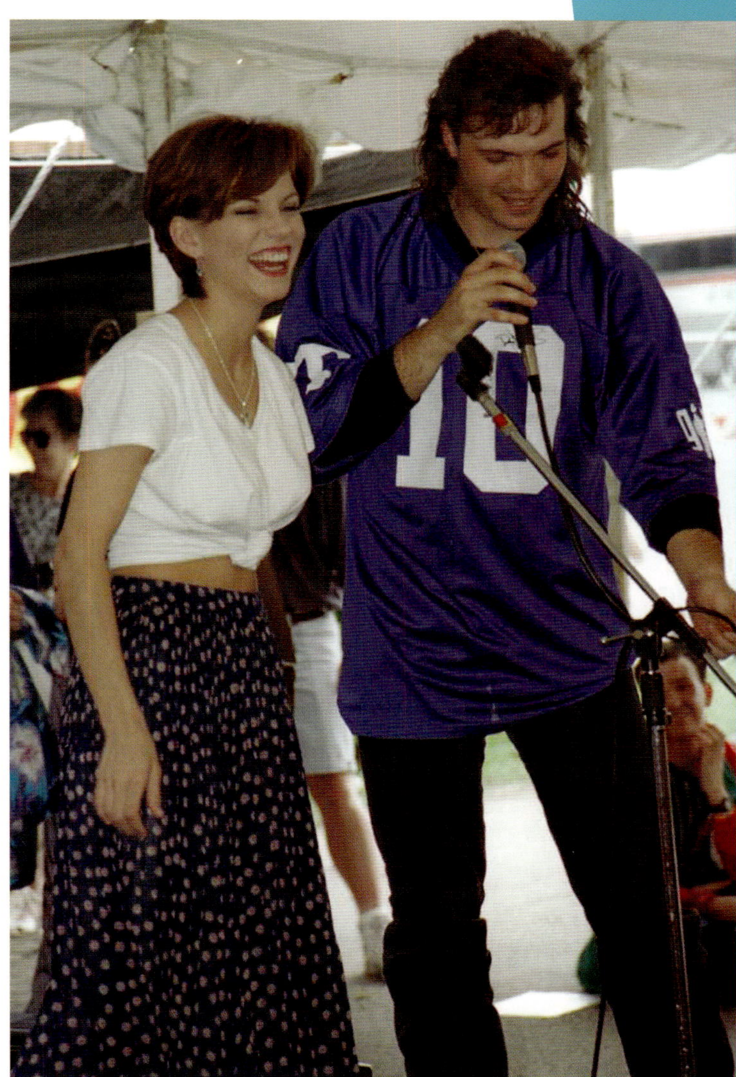

Martina and David Lee Murphy

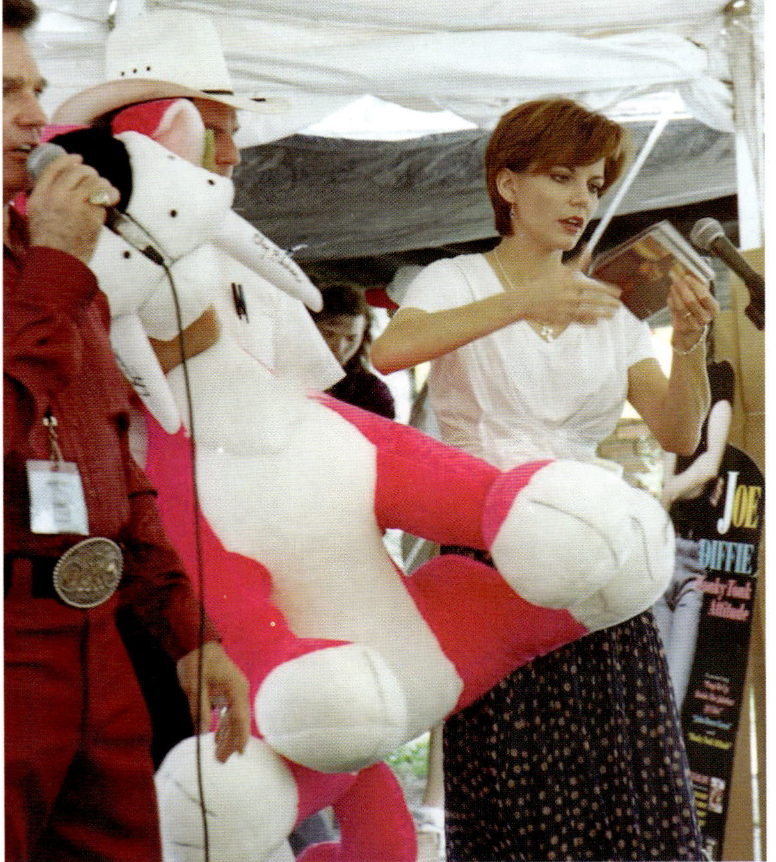

Mark Collie

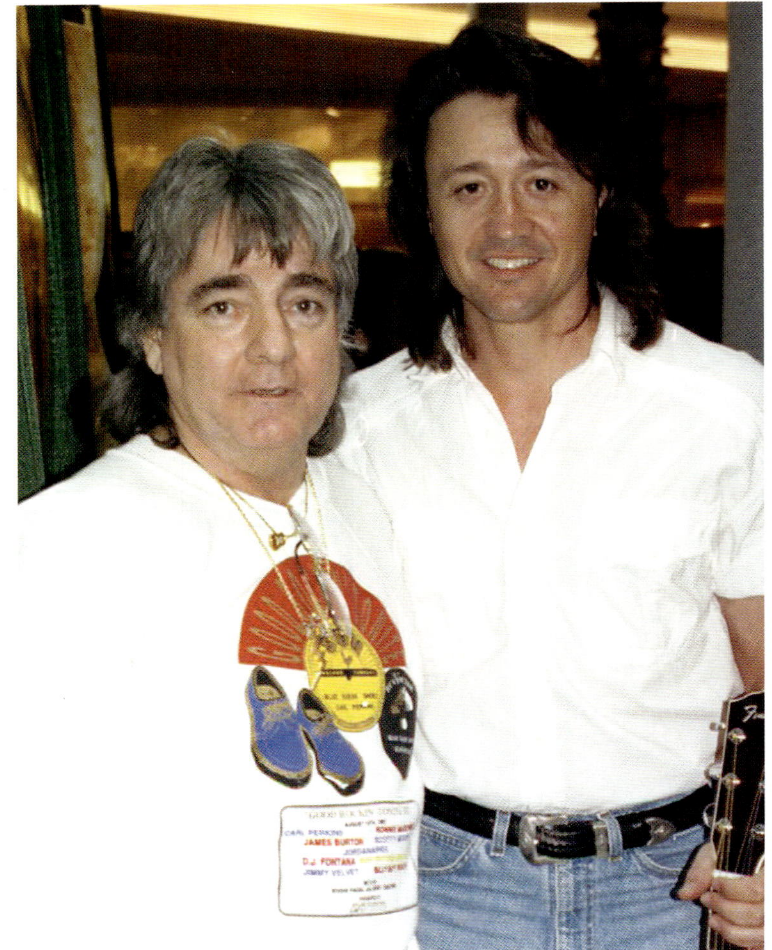

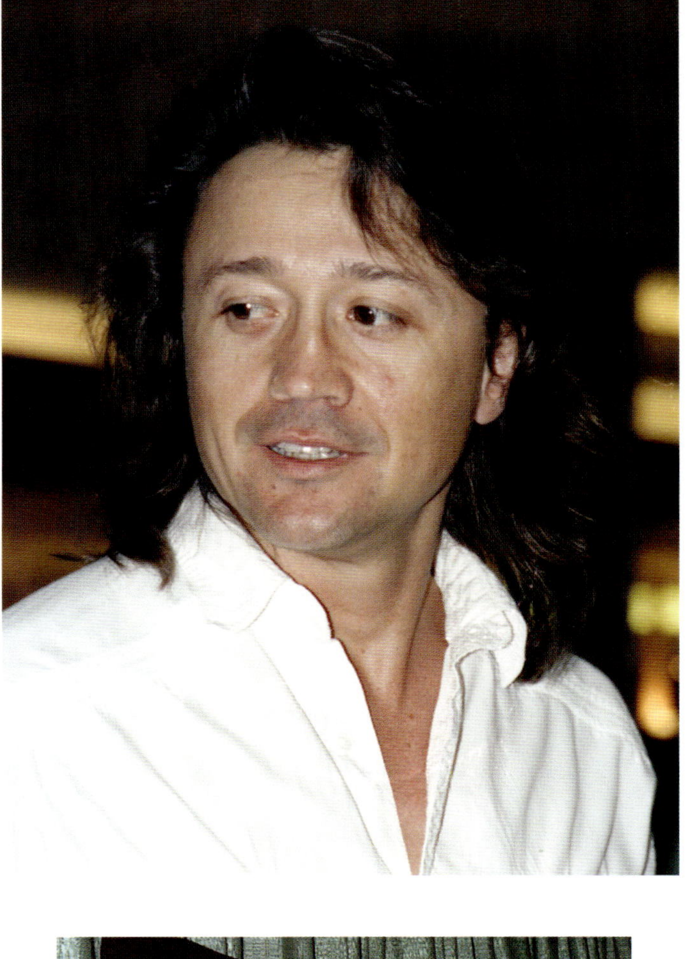

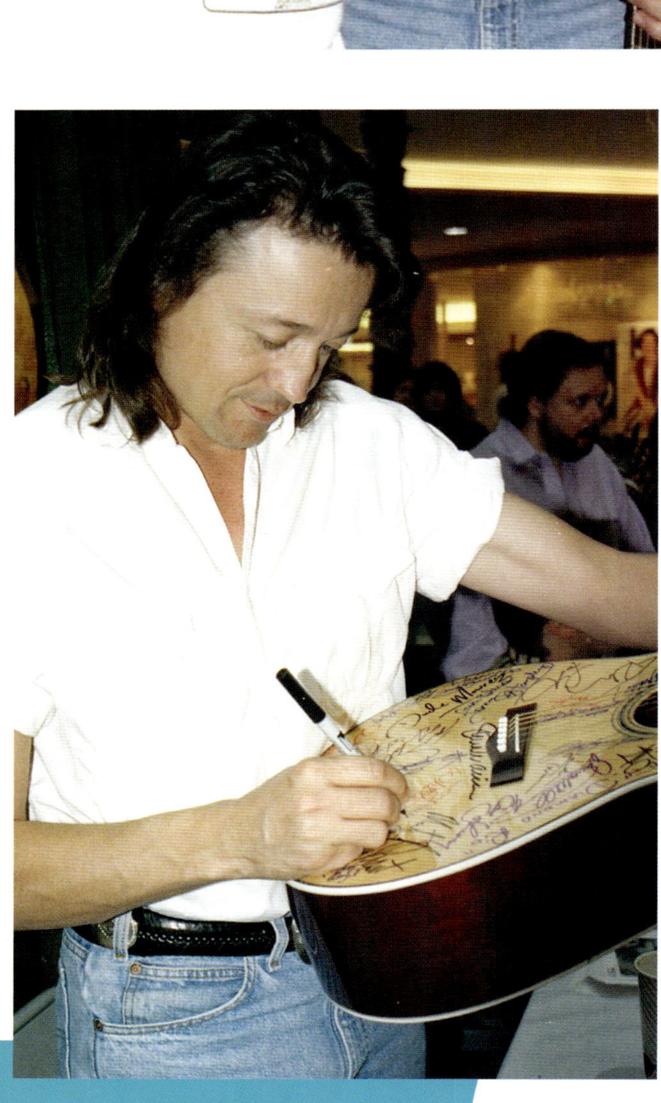

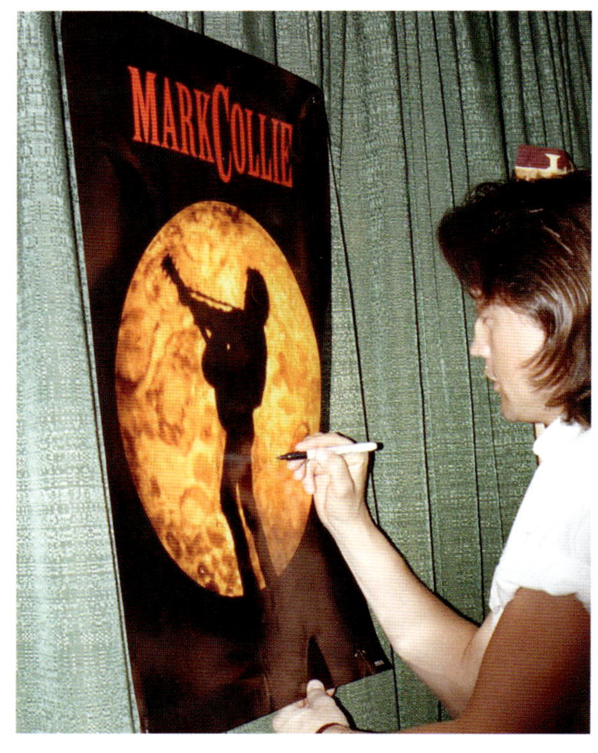

Marty Stuart

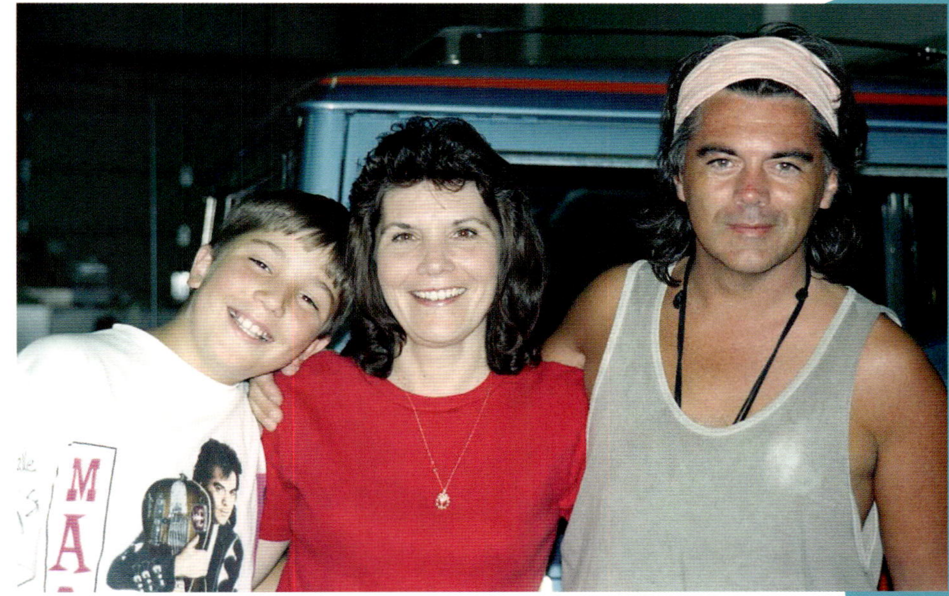

Jake, Robin, and Marty

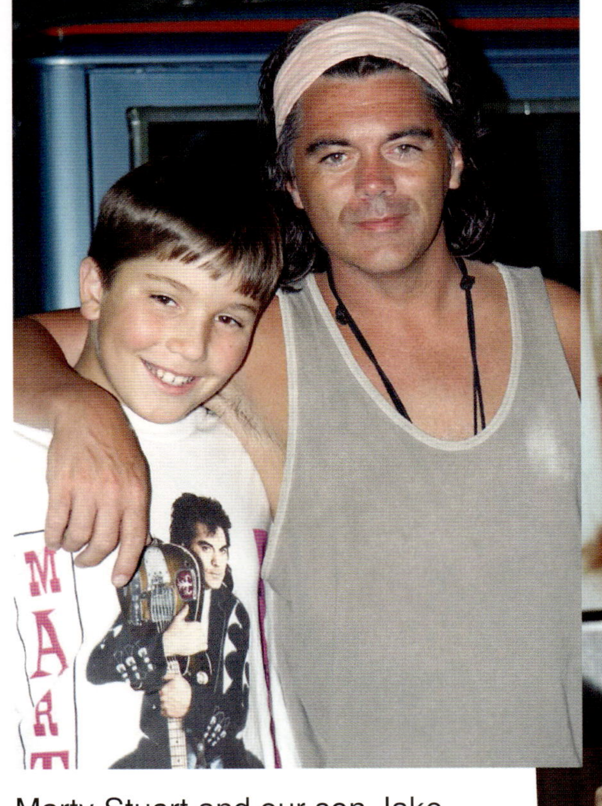

Marty Stuart and our son Jake

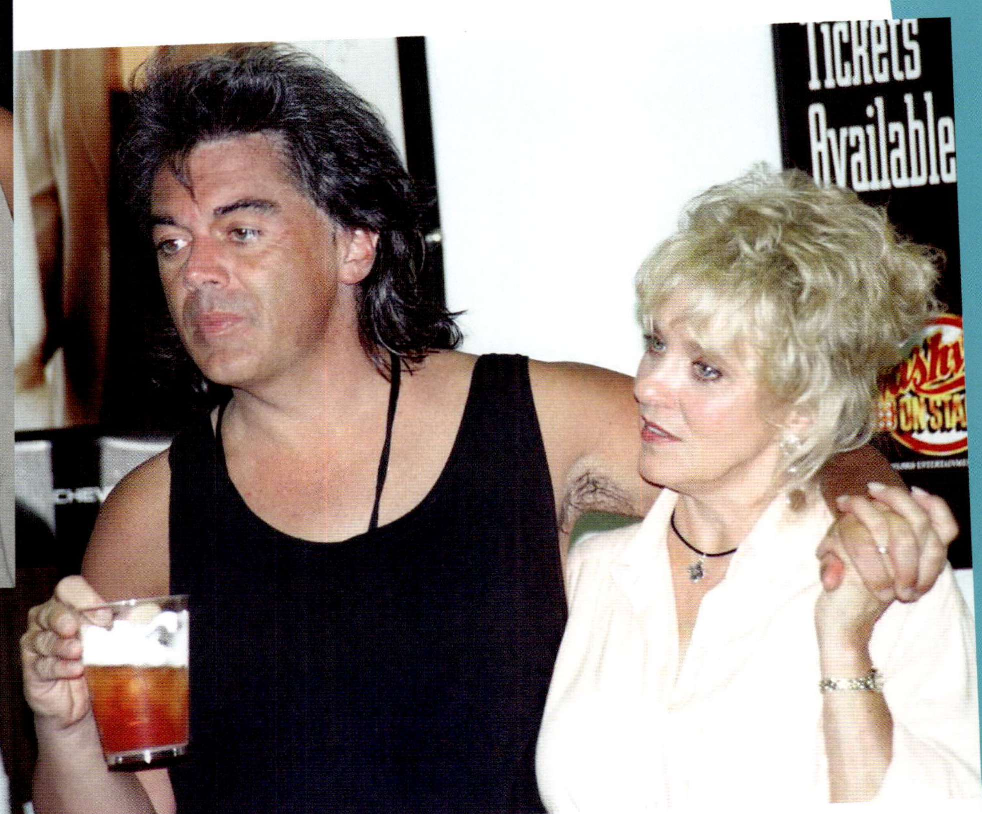

Marty and **Connie Smith**

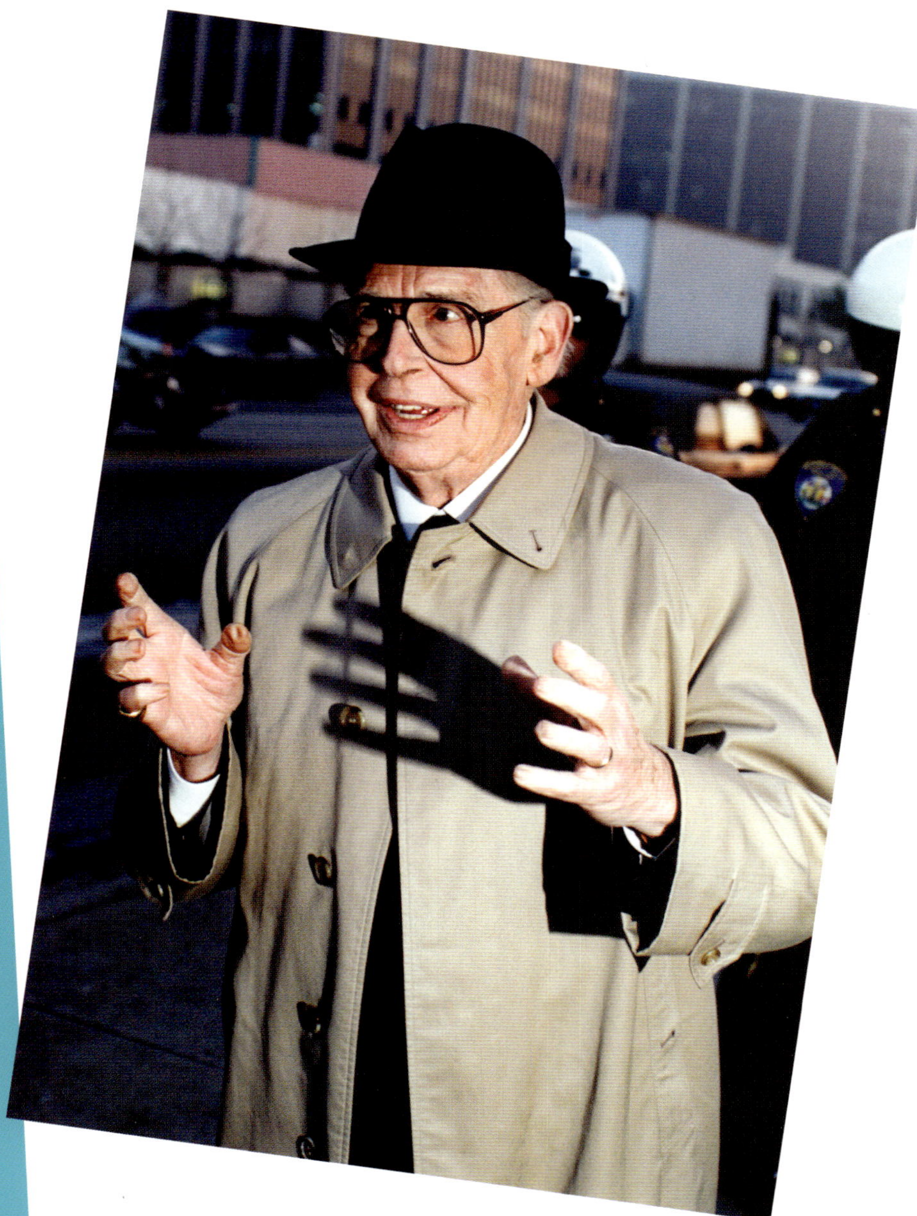

Milton Berle

"Uncle Miltie"

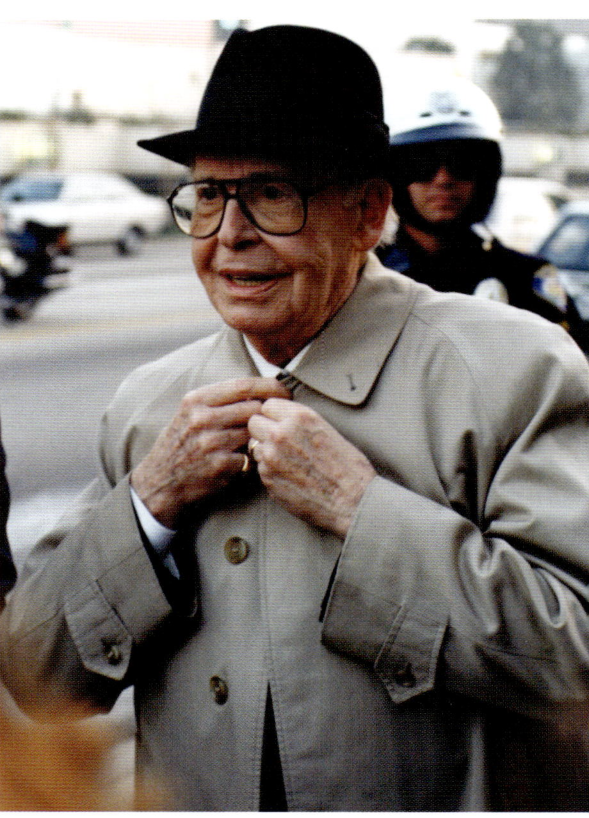

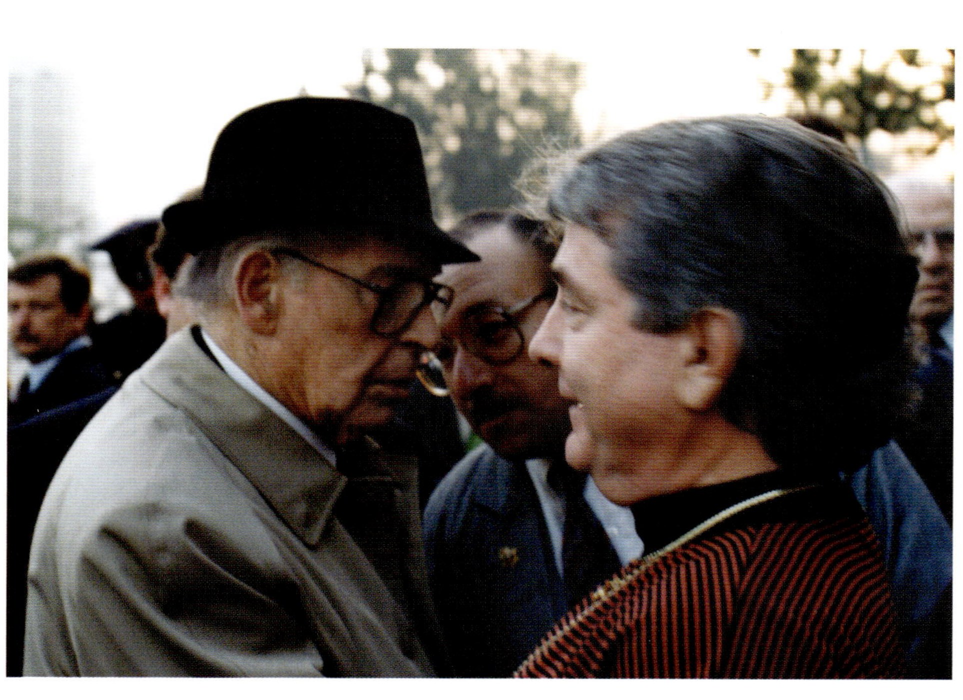

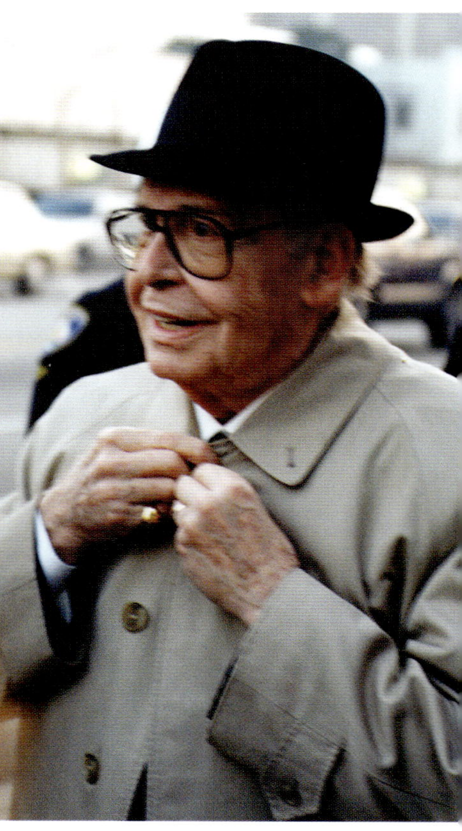

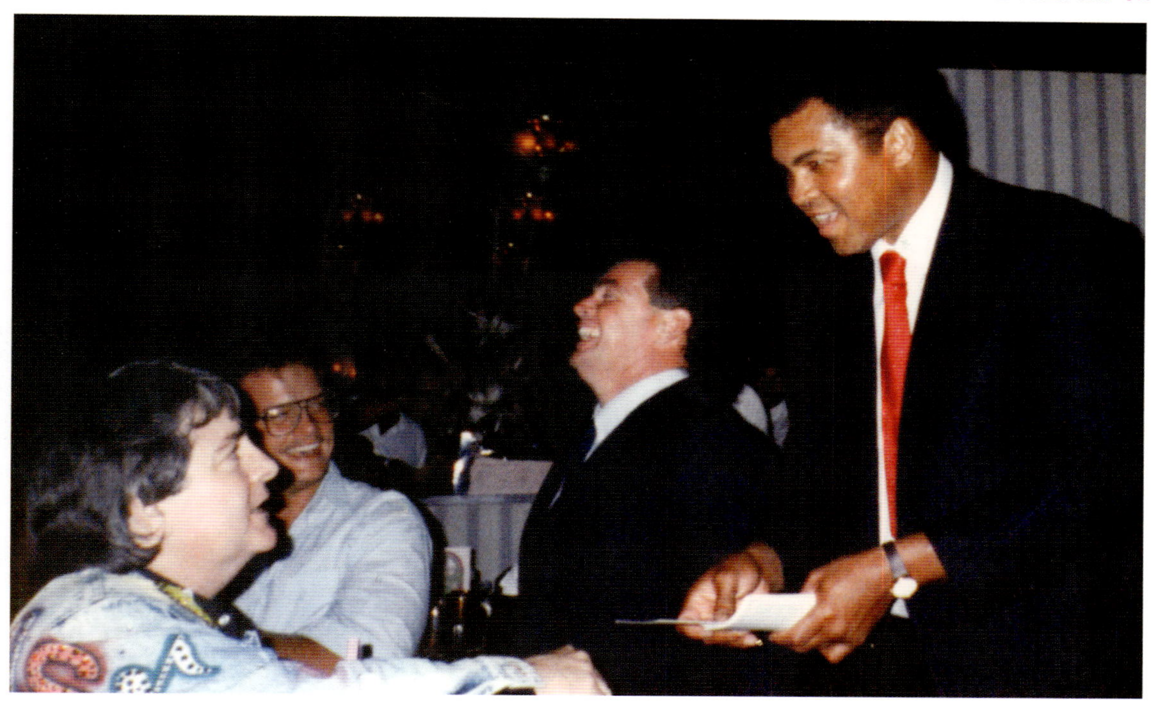

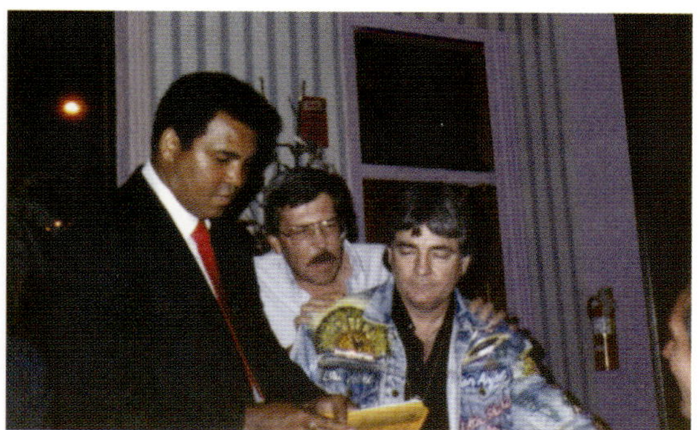

Muhammad Ali

I'm his #1 fan. He was fantastic as a singer, Cassius Clay, on his LP on Epic in the early 60's. The title: "I am the Greatest". He sang Rock N' Roll.

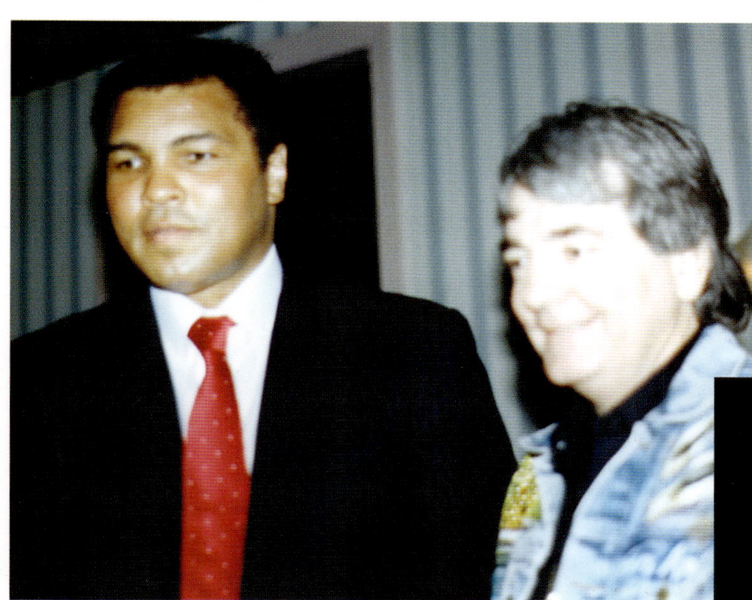

Sam Phillips

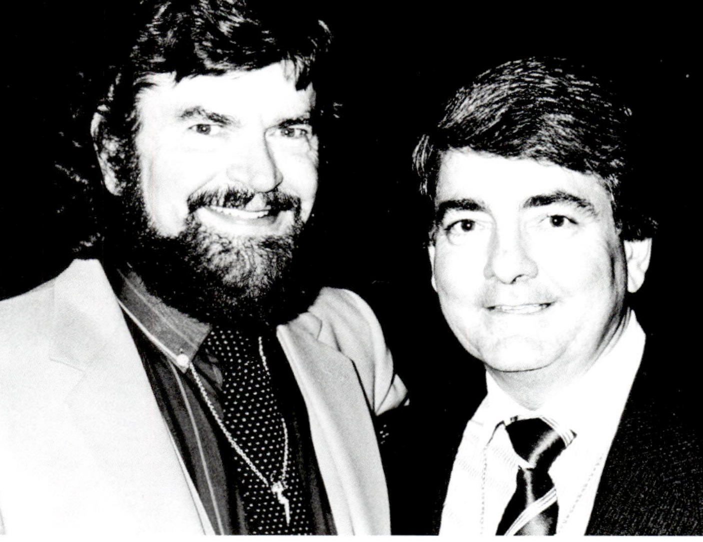

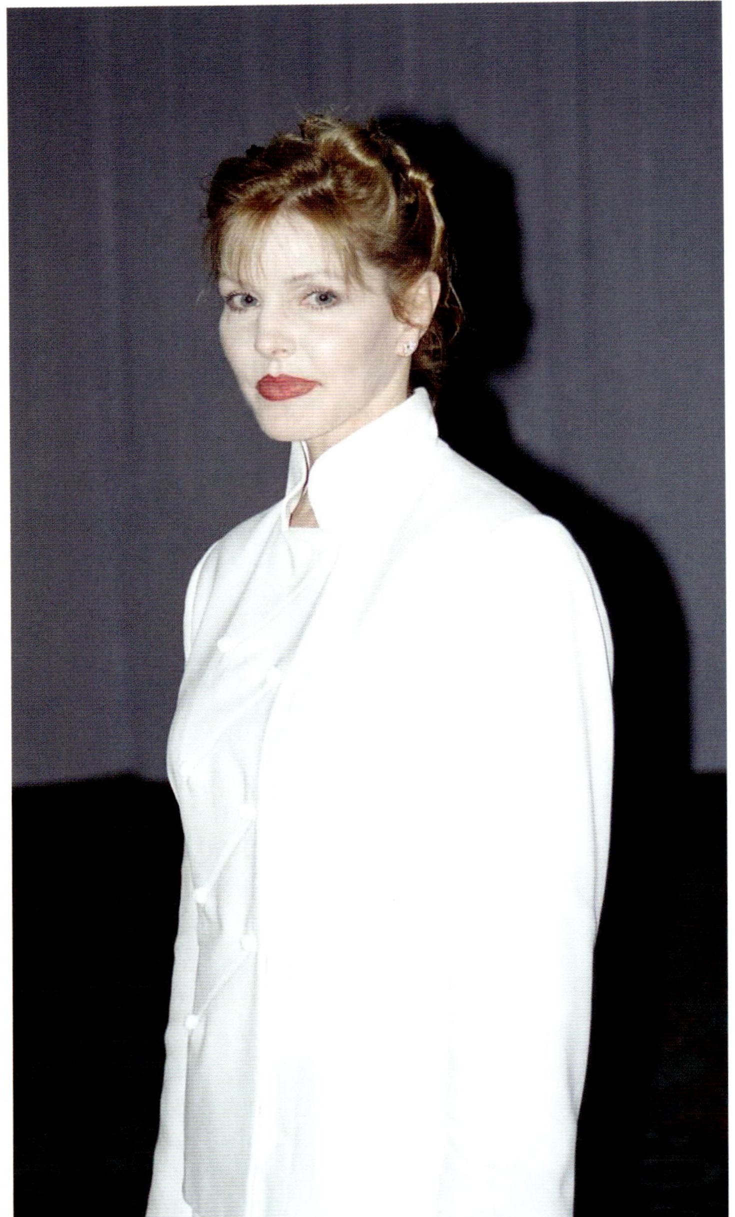

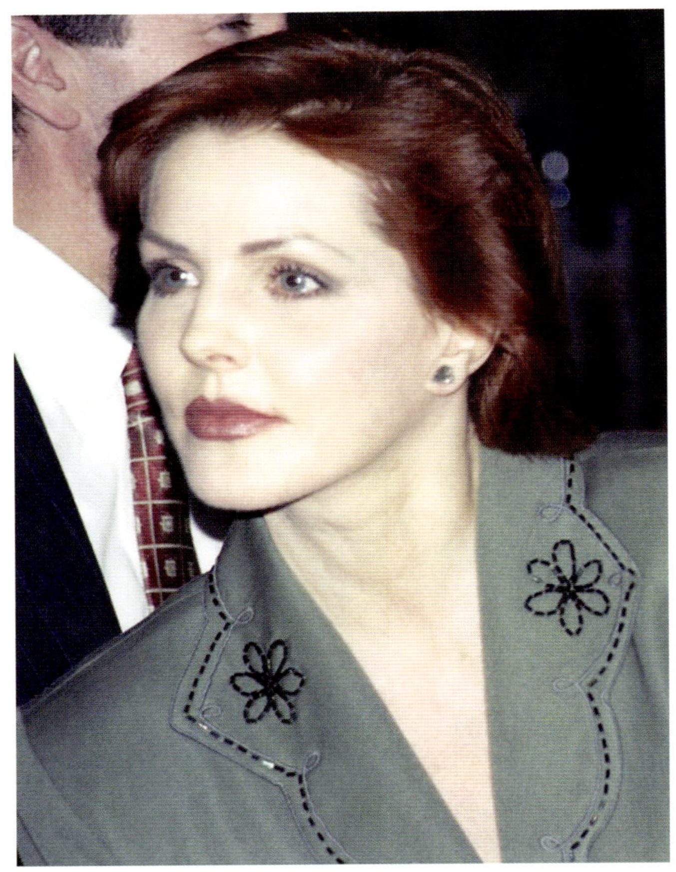

Priscilla Presley

Her mother married Paul Beaulieu (USAF officer) and her biological father was James Wagner.

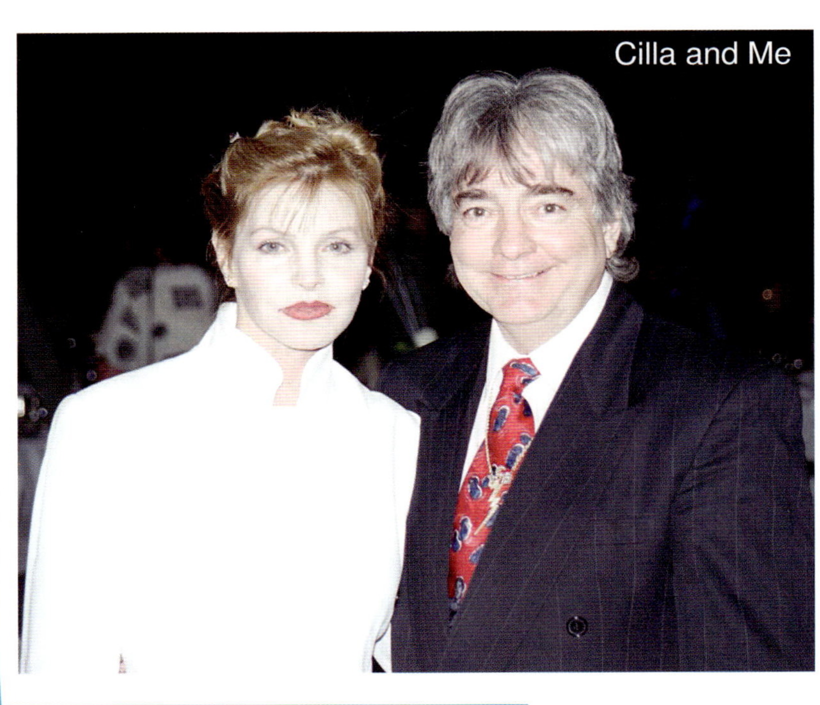

Cilla and Me

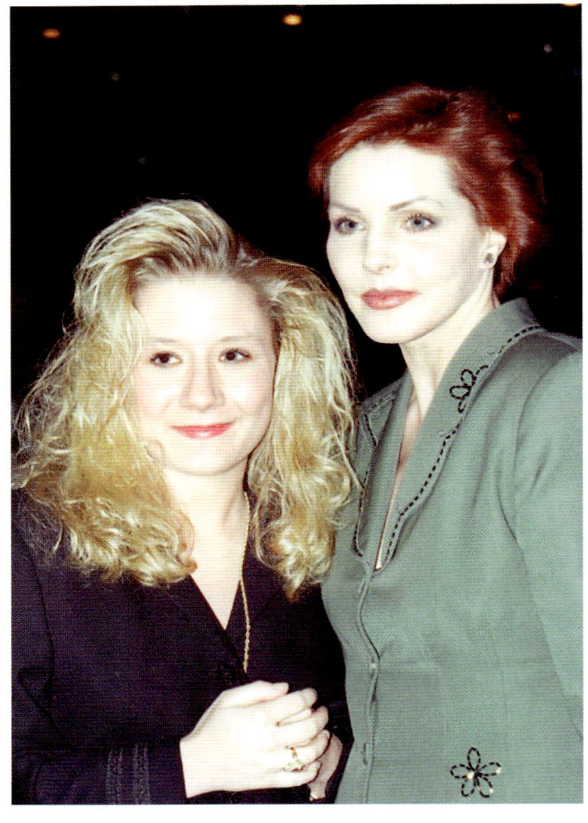

Darla Townes and Priscilla

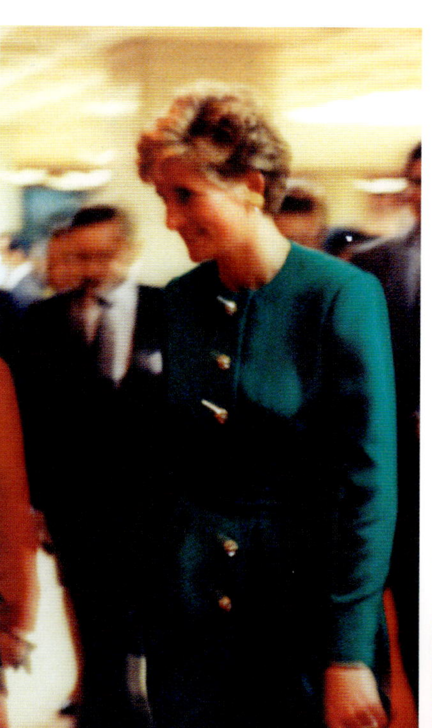

Princess Diana

My camera battery was dead but she was very kind to wait with me.

Princess Di in Tokyo after Emperor's enthrownment.

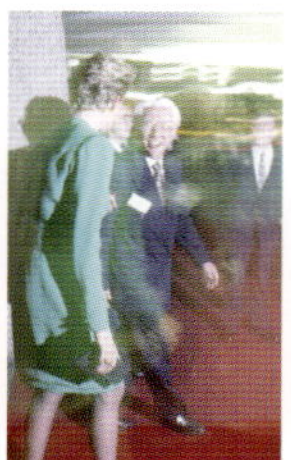

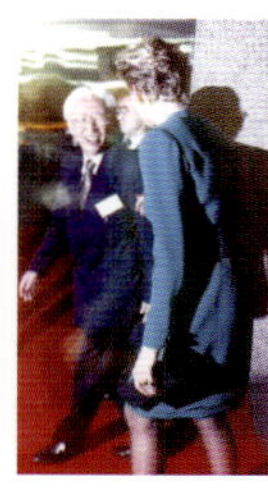

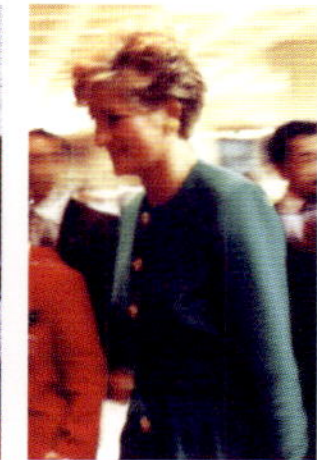

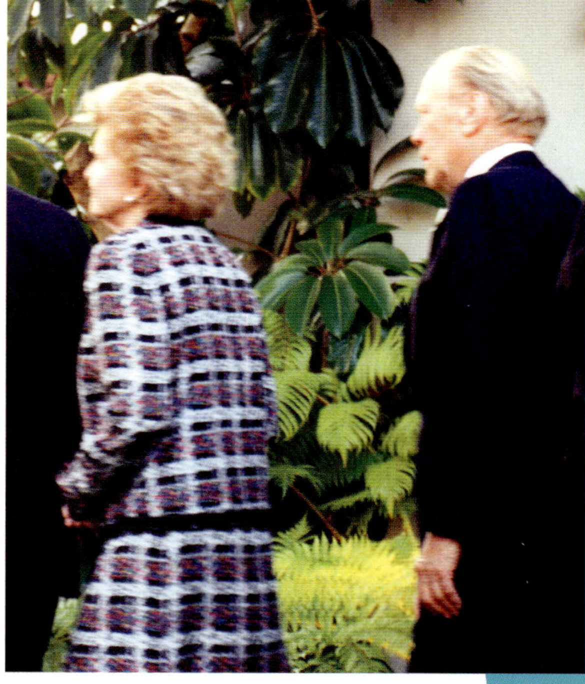

President and Mrs. Ford

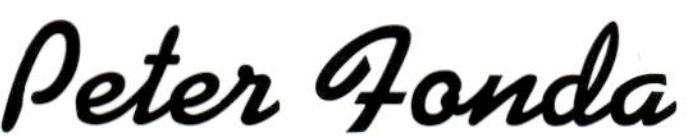

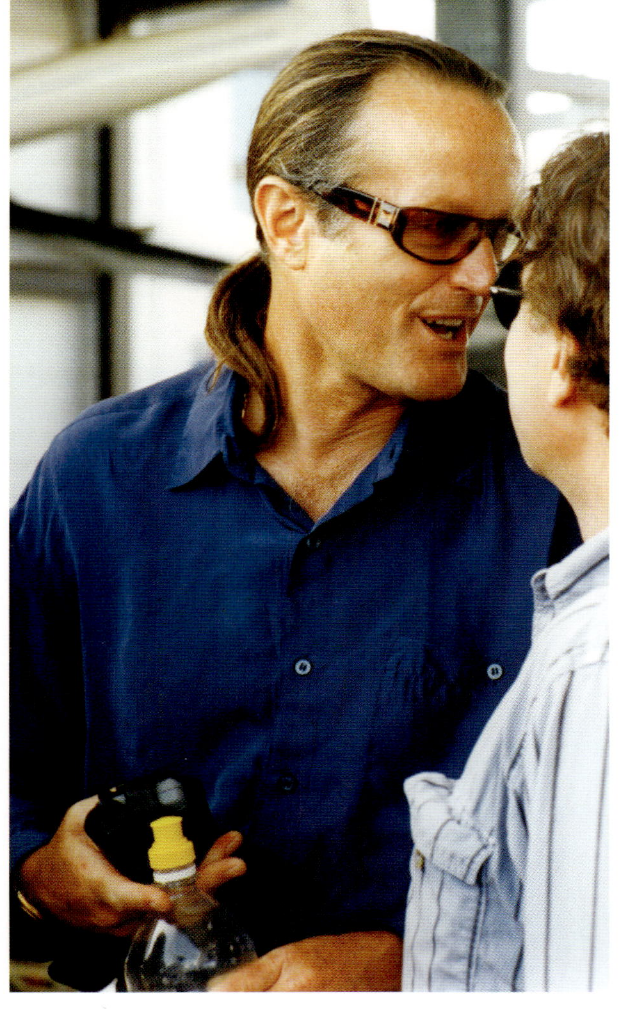

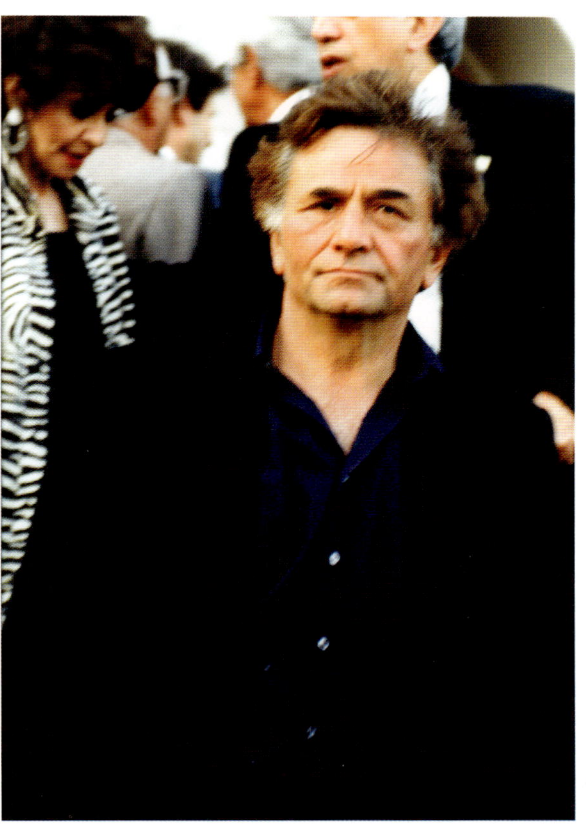

Peter Falk

Ross Perot

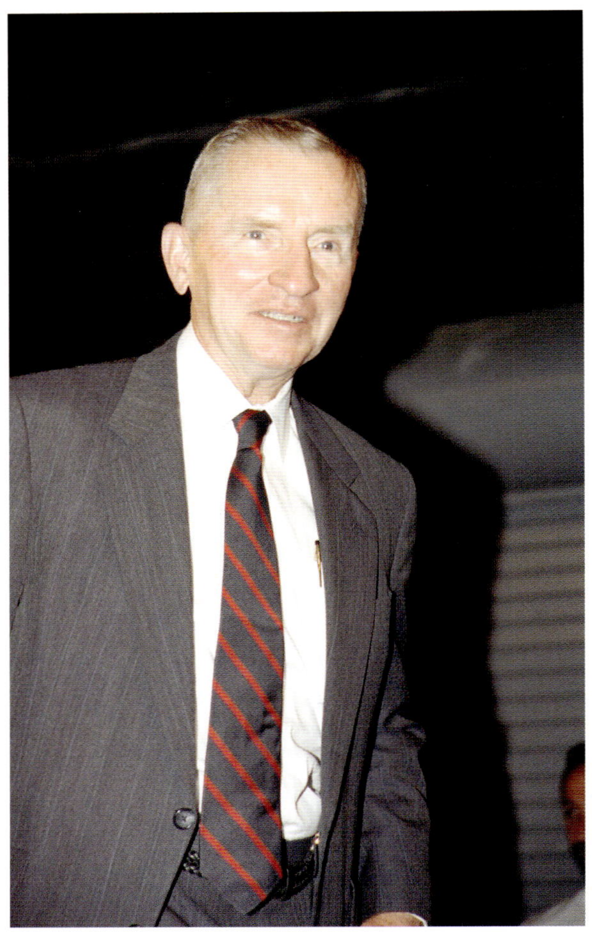

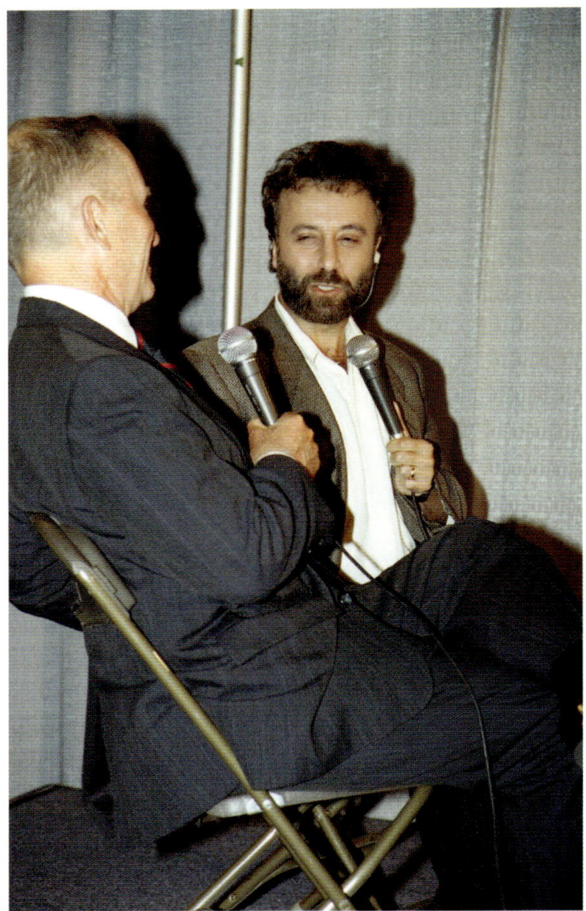

Mr. Perot and Yakov Smirnoff

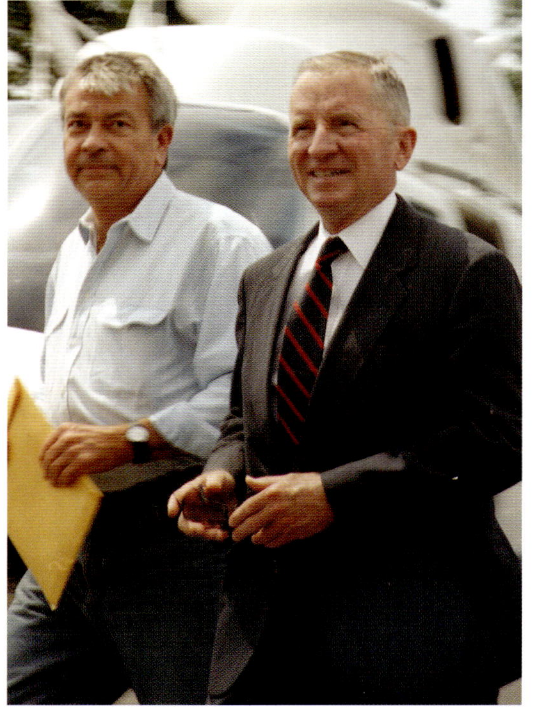

Mr. Perot and Tony Orlando

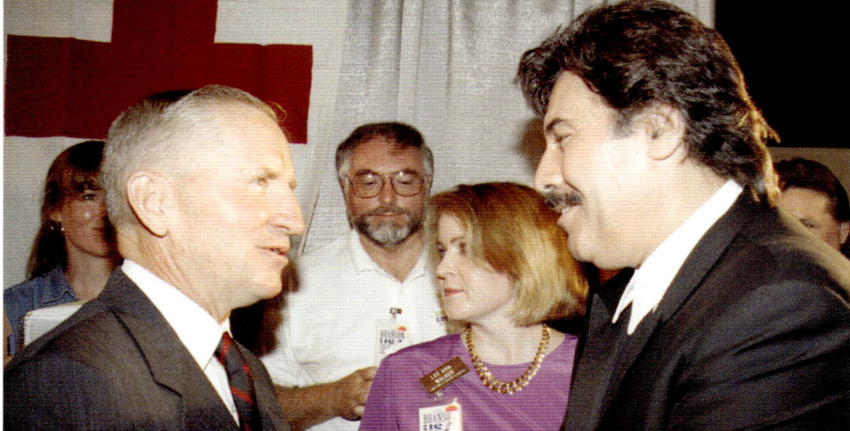

Yakov Smirnoff

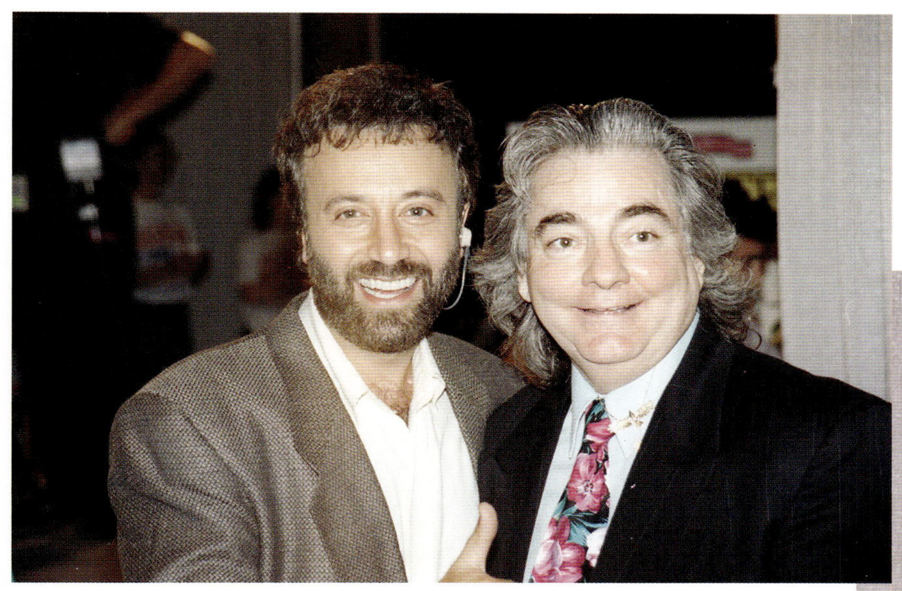

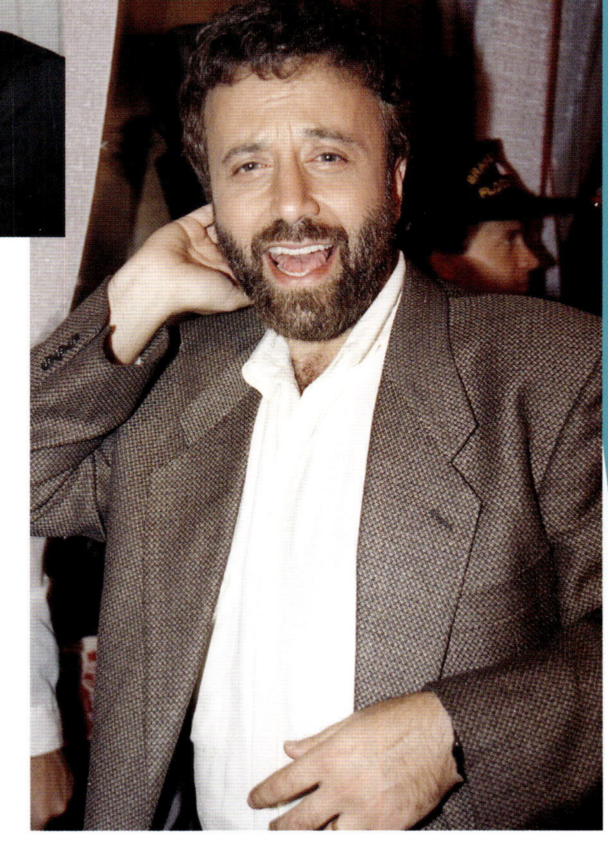

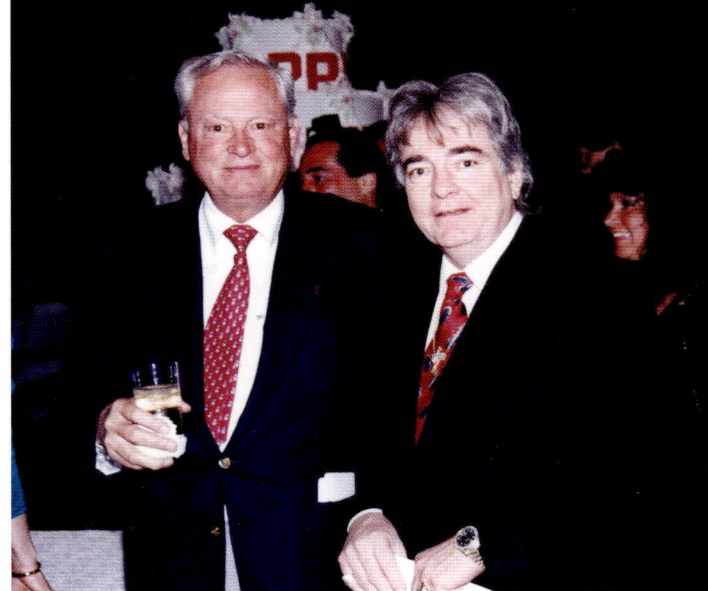

Baron Hilton and Me

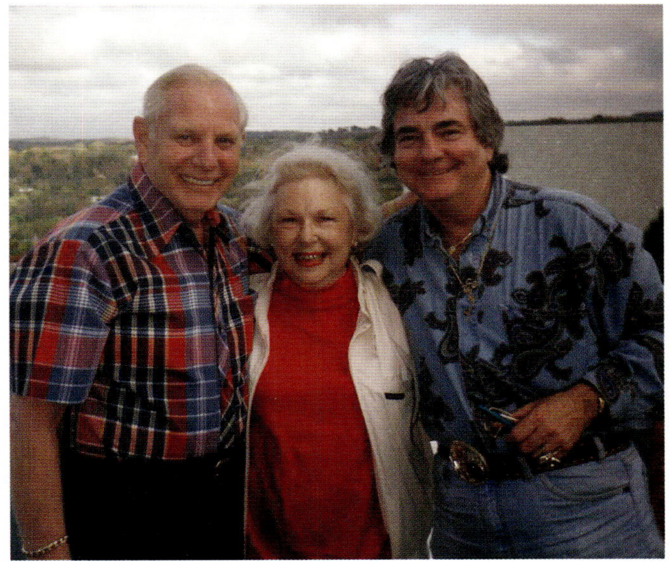

Mr. and Mrs. Lee Ableser
Elvis' Beverly Hills Jeweler at my Branson home.

Neal McCoy

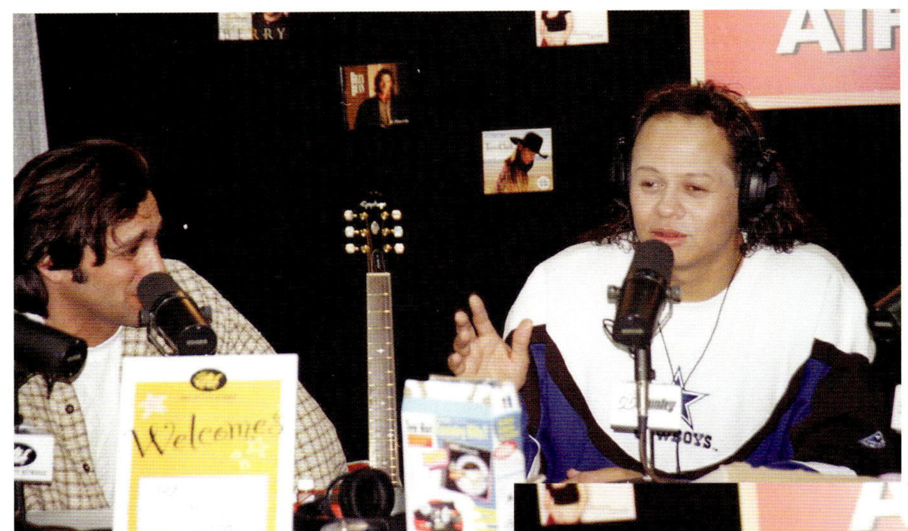

Joe Nichols and Neal McCoy

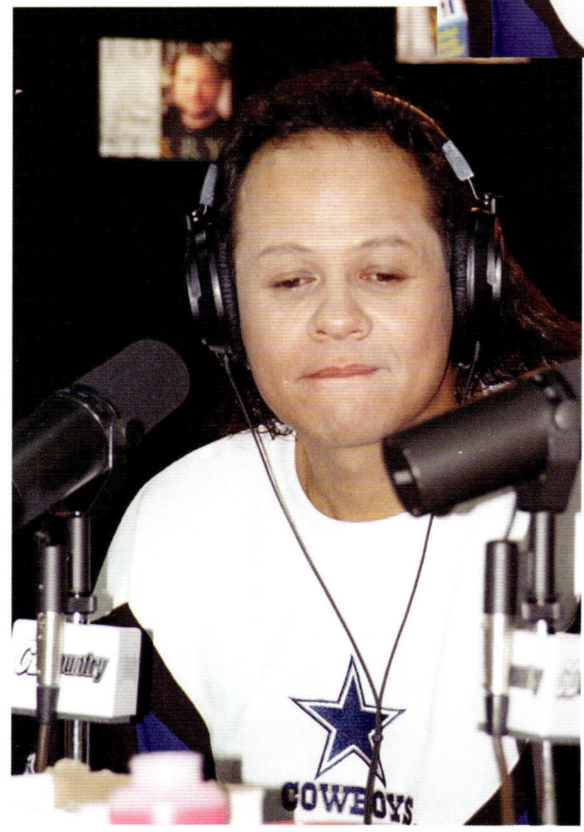

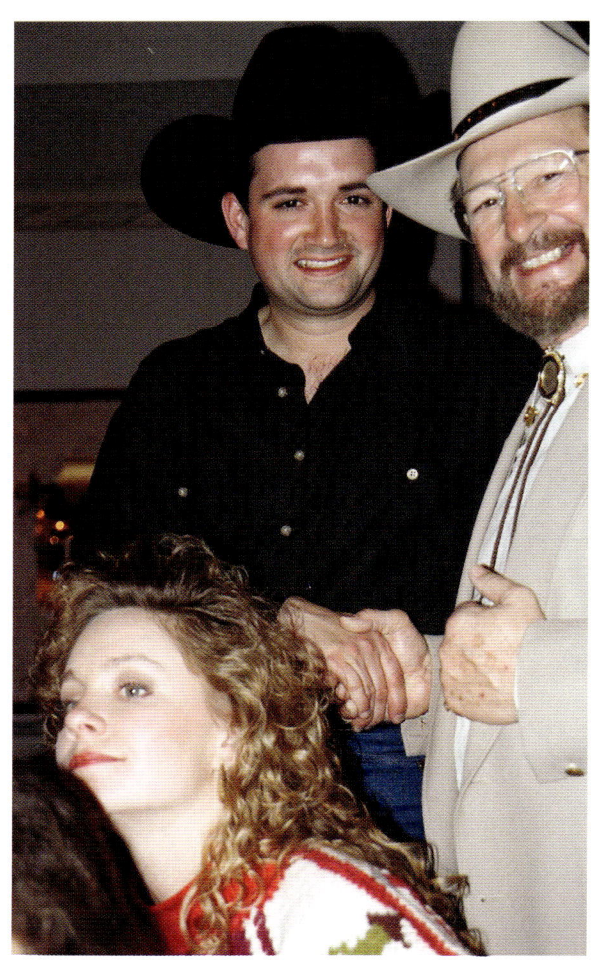

Mr. and Mrs. Tracy Byrd

Otis Blackwell

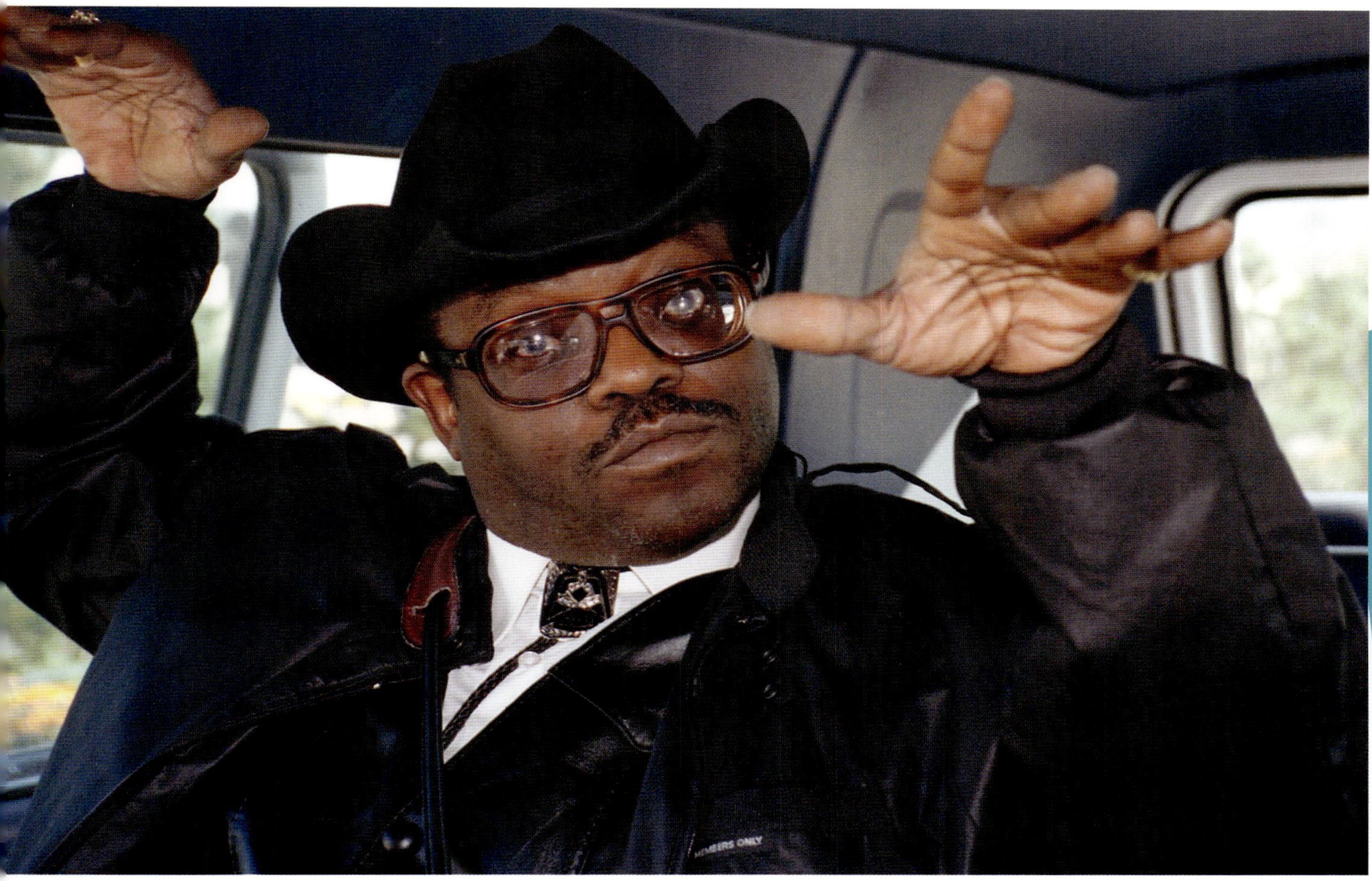

Otis wrote so many hits.
"Don't be Cruel"
"Return to Sender"
"Whole Lotta Shakin' Goin On"
"Greatest Balls of Fire"
"Handy Man"

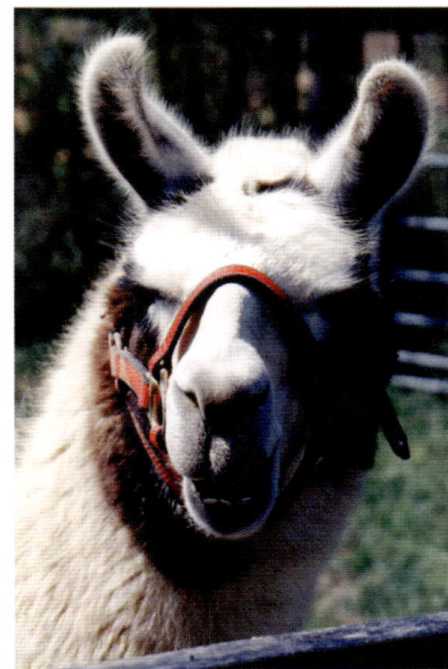

Oliver North

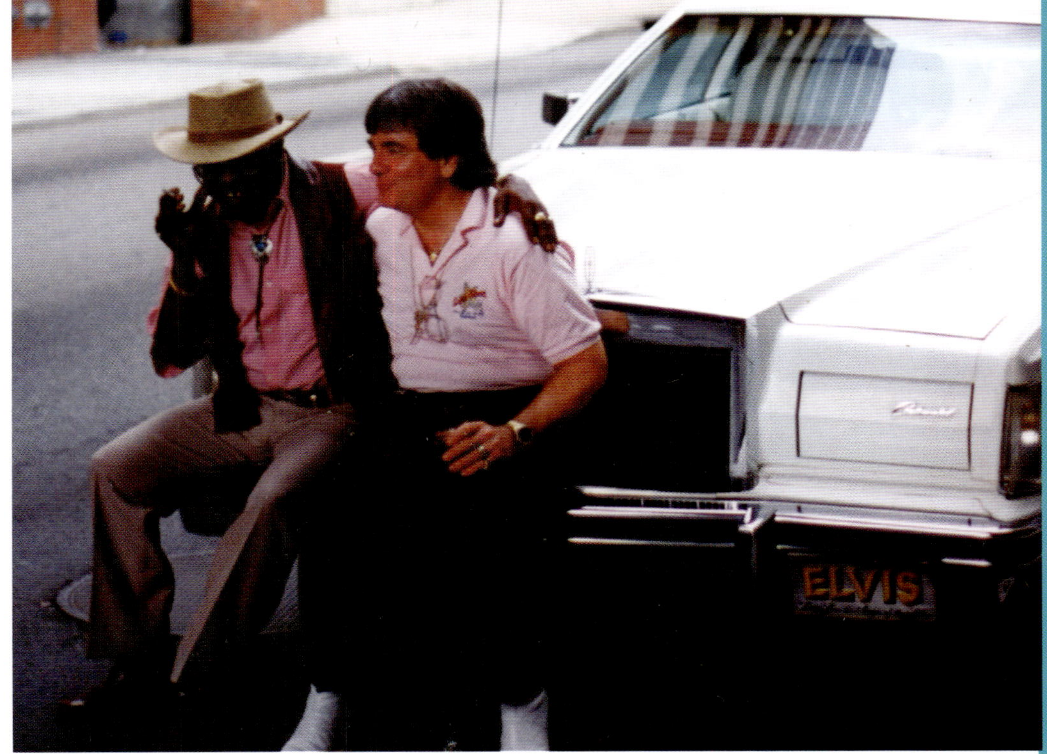

A close and dear friend to me.
Otis and I on Elvis' car

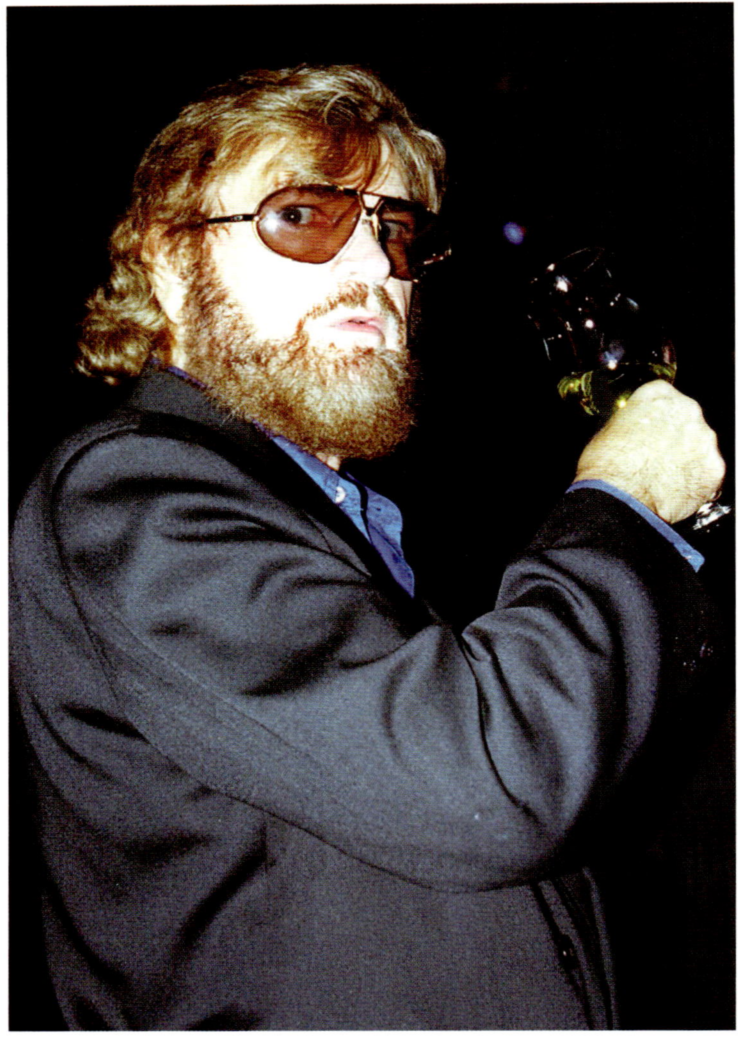

Sam C. Phillips

Rock N' Roll Legend, Sam C. Phillips Studio and Sun Records

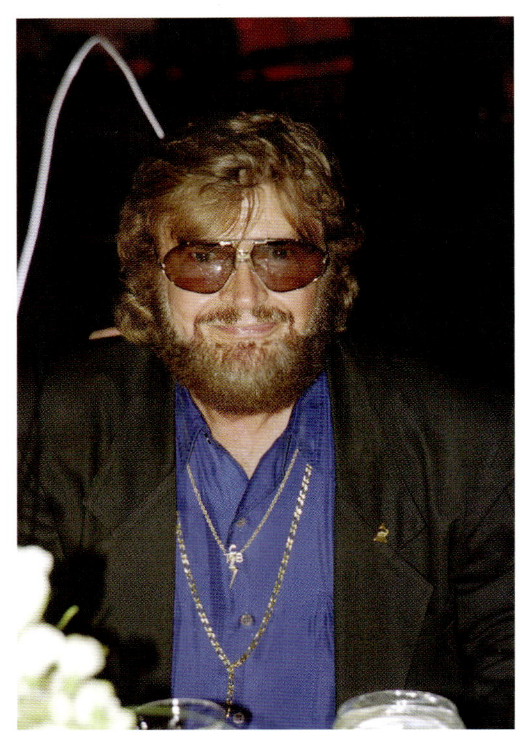

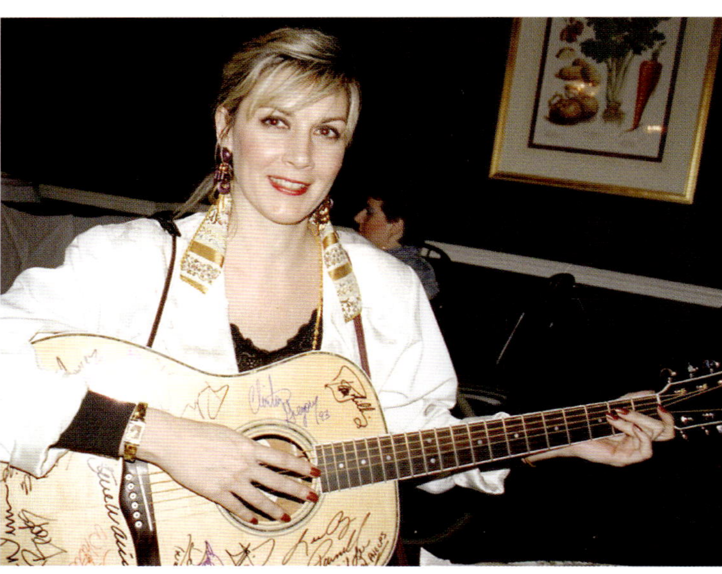

Patty Loveless

Pam Tillis

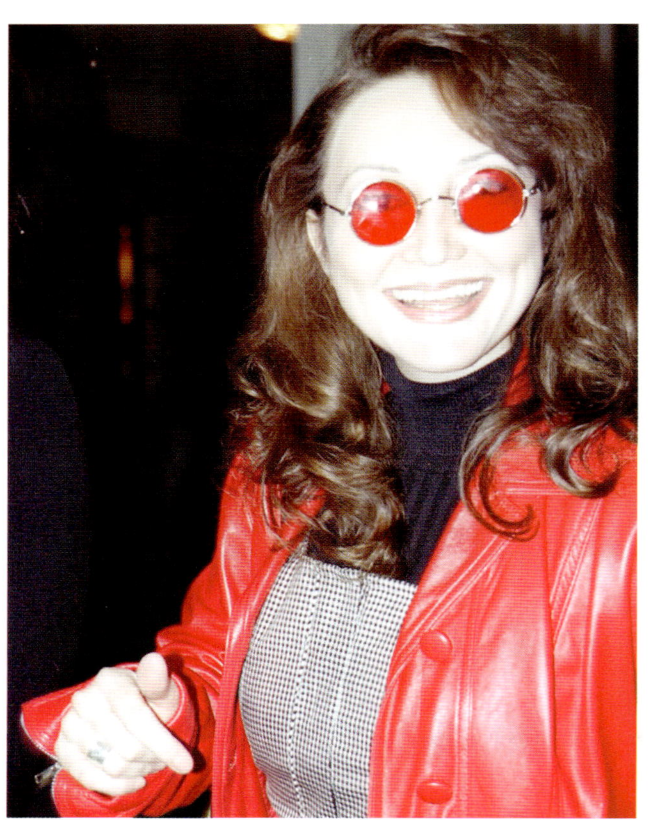

Paul Peterson

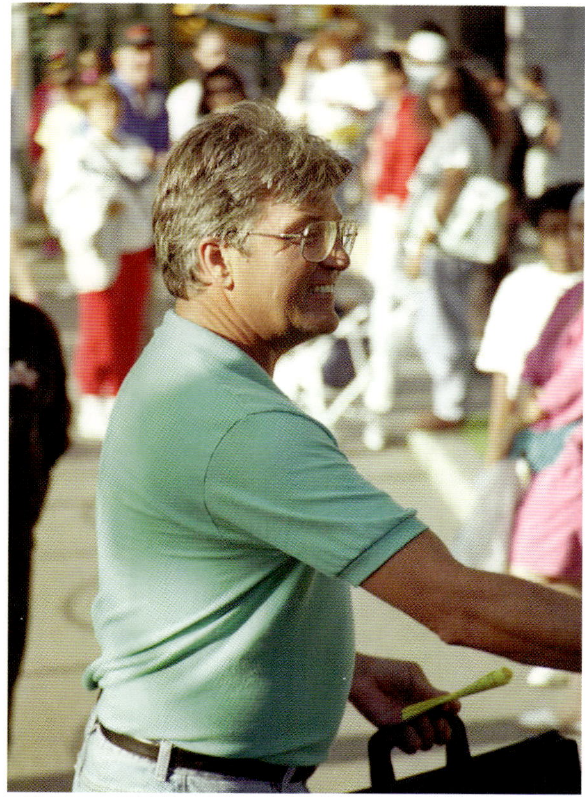

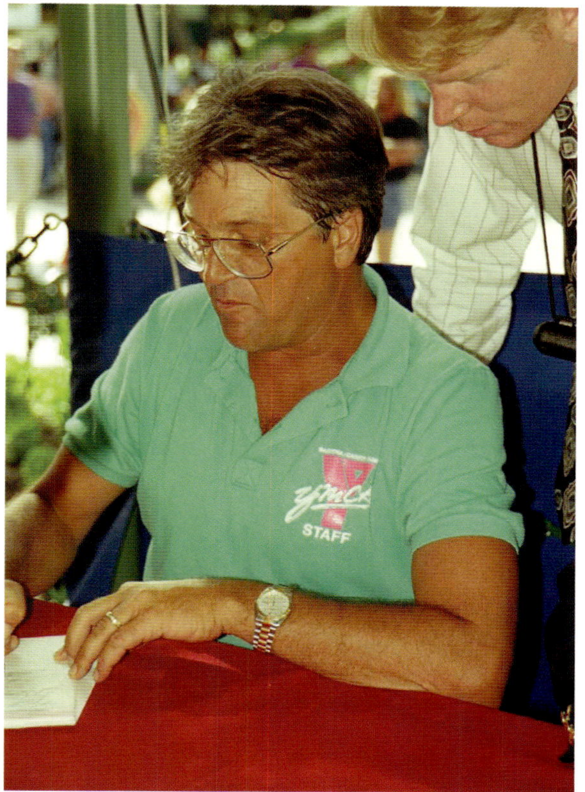

Paul Peterson from "Donna Reed Show"

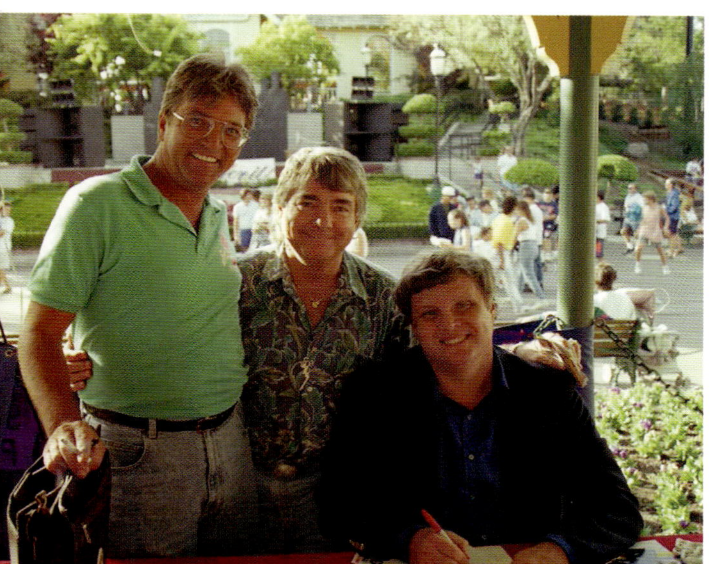

Paul Peterson, Jimmy, and Jerry Mathers (The Beaver from "Leave it to Beaver")

Wolfman Jack

Paul Revere and The Raiders with Mark Lindsay

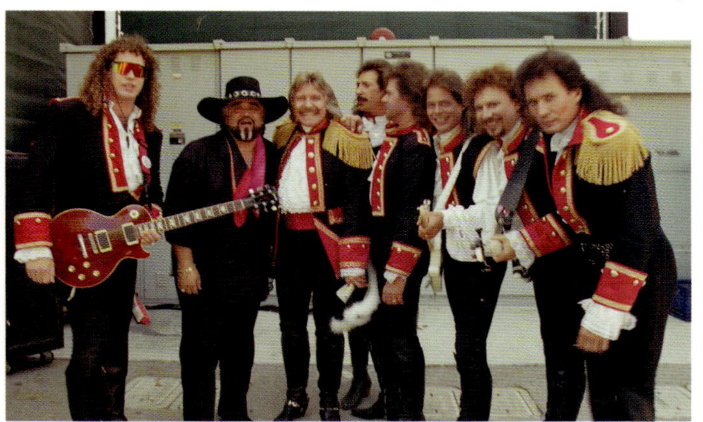

Paul Revere and the Raiders

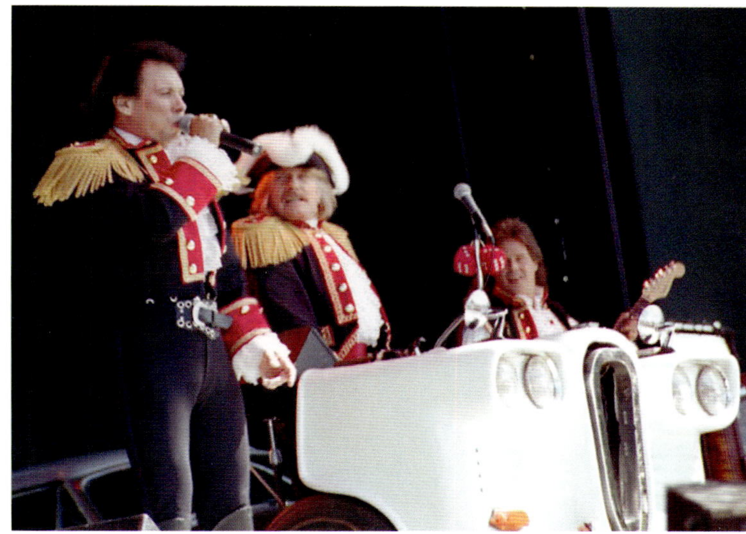

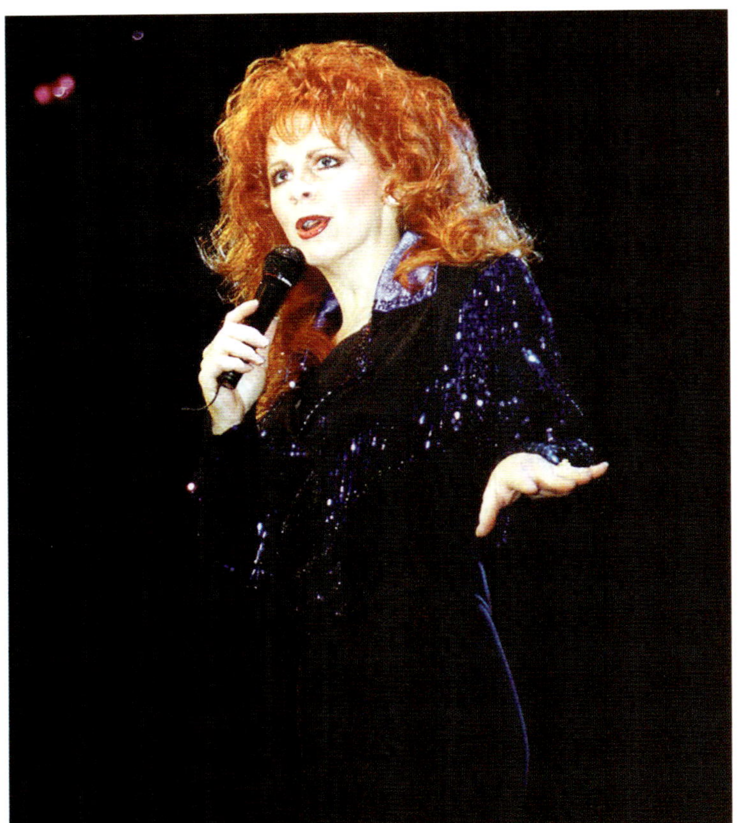

Reba

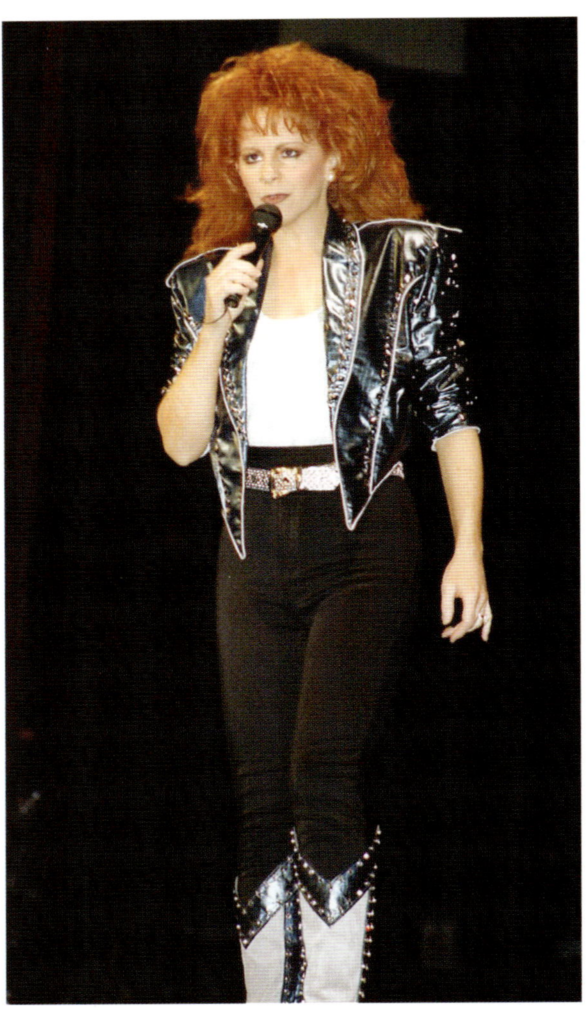

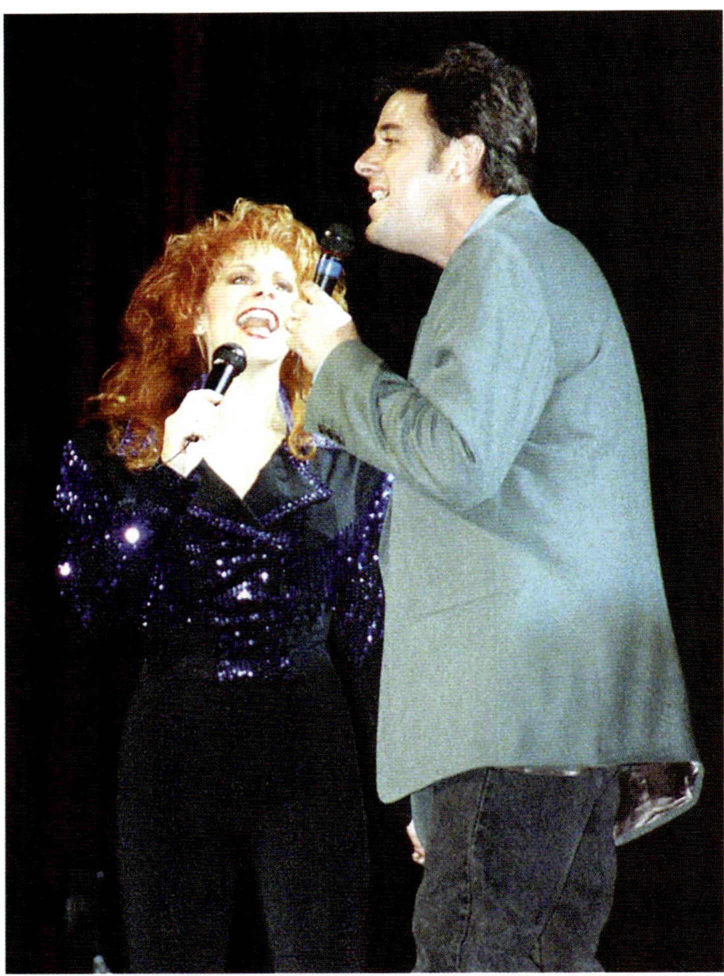

Reba and Vince

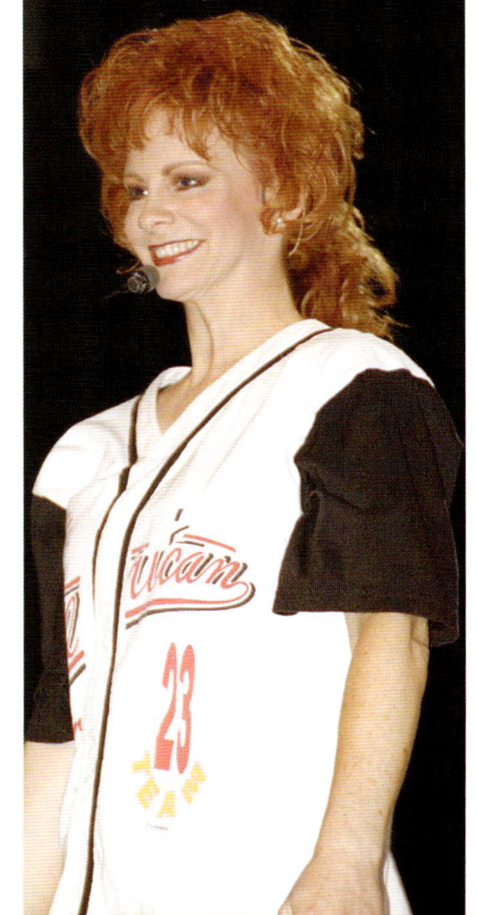

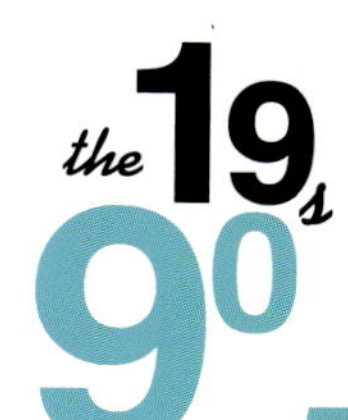

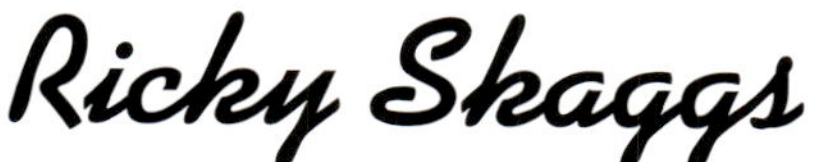

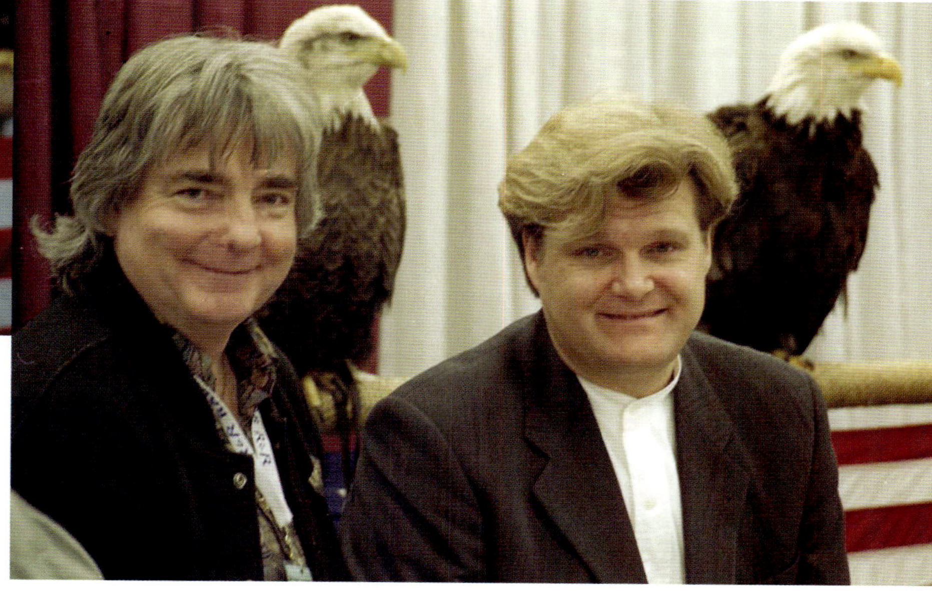

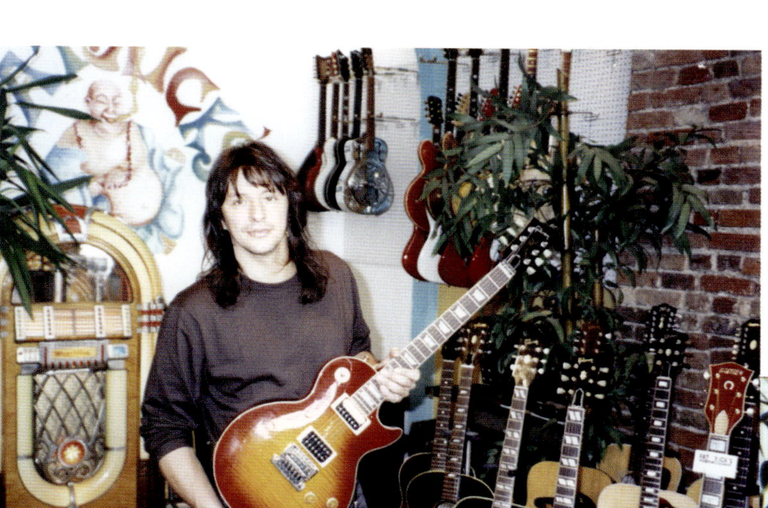

Richie Sambora

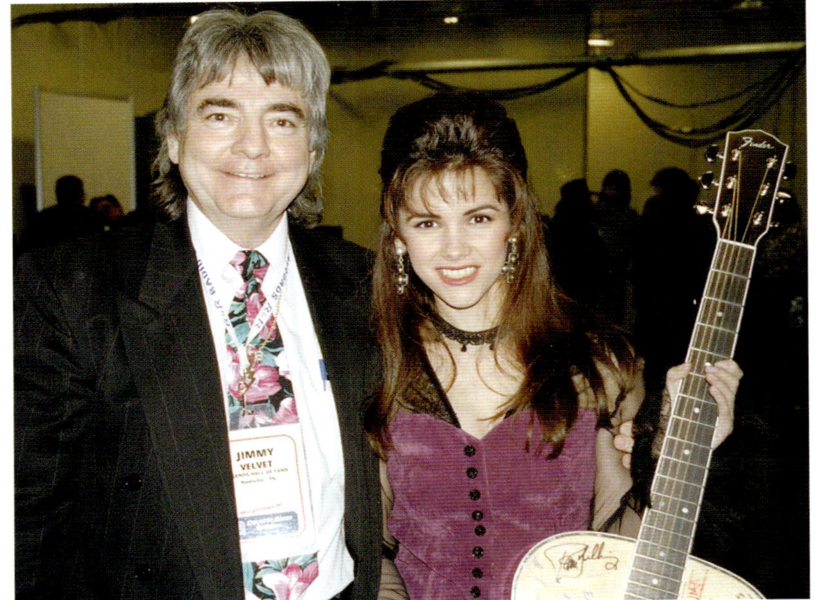

Rona Reeves

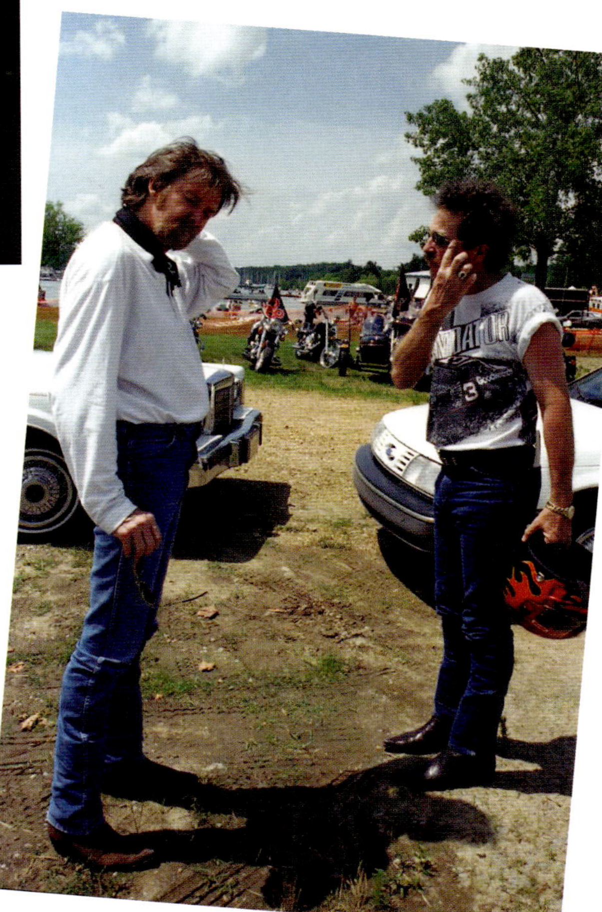

Ronnie and Kix

Brooks and Dunn

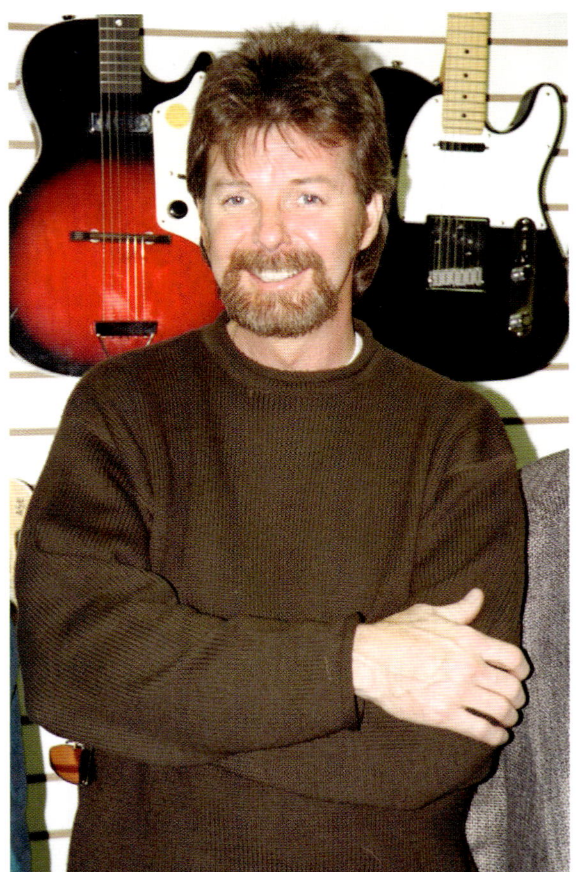

Ronnie Dunn

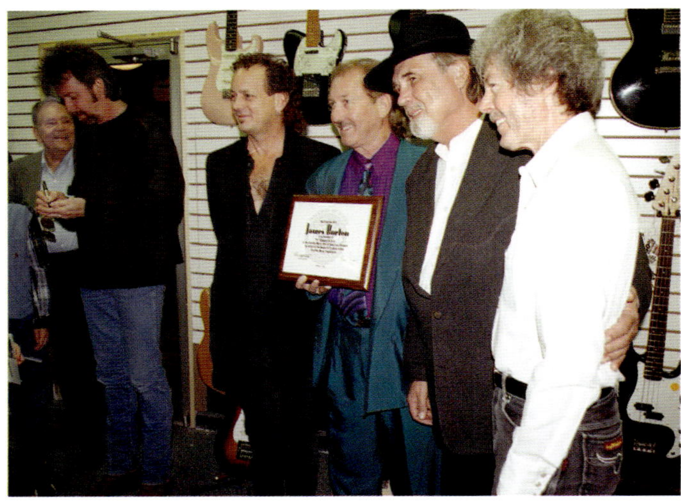

Ronnie Dunn, James Burton, Duane Eddy

The Lettermen

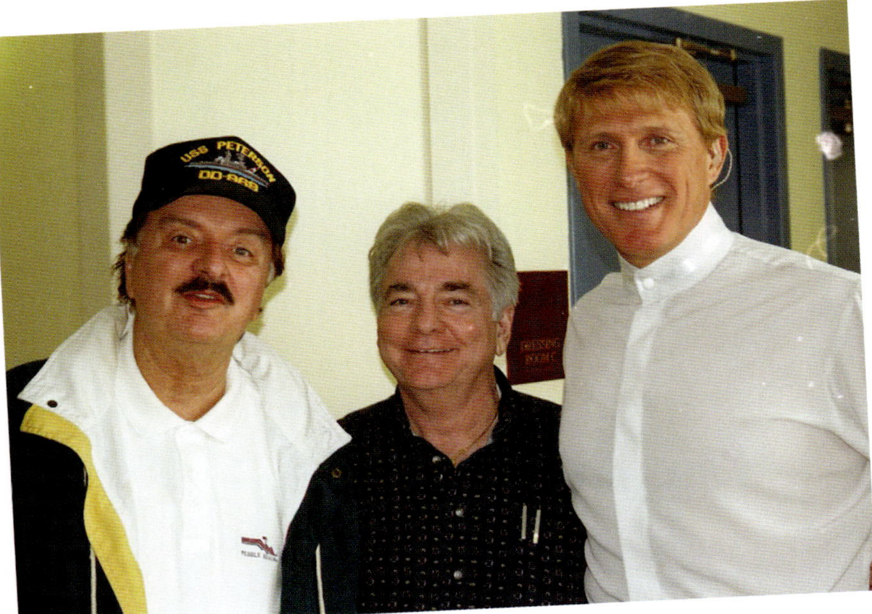

Ray Peterson, Jimmy, and Donovan Tea

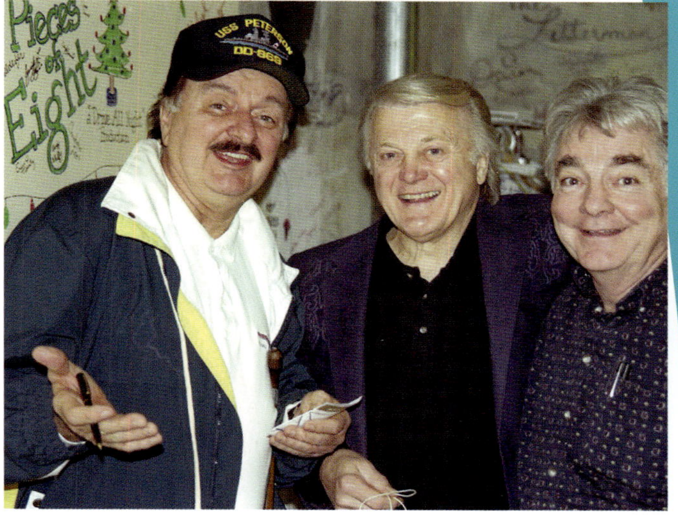

Ray, Tony Butala, and JV

Ray Peterson

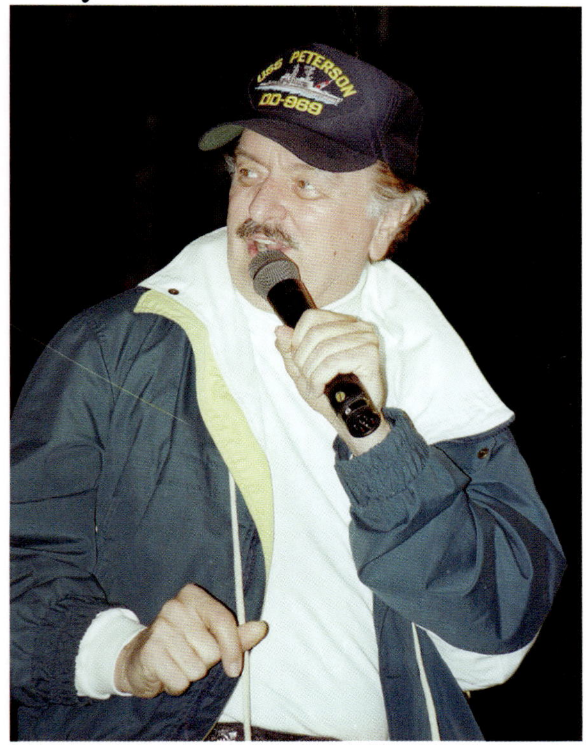

Ray was one of my dearest friends since 1960. We toured and also did TV appearances together many times. It broke my heart to lose him.

Randy Travis

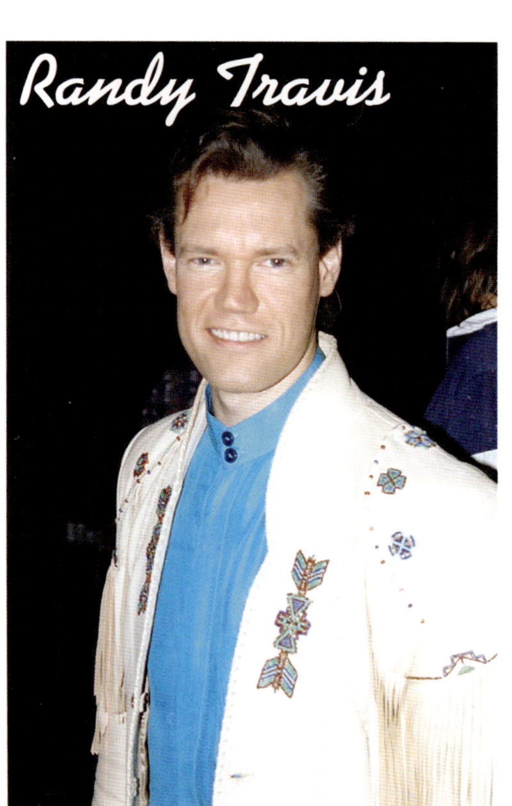

SHeDAISY

Kristyn Robyn, Kelsi Marie, Kassidy Lorriane

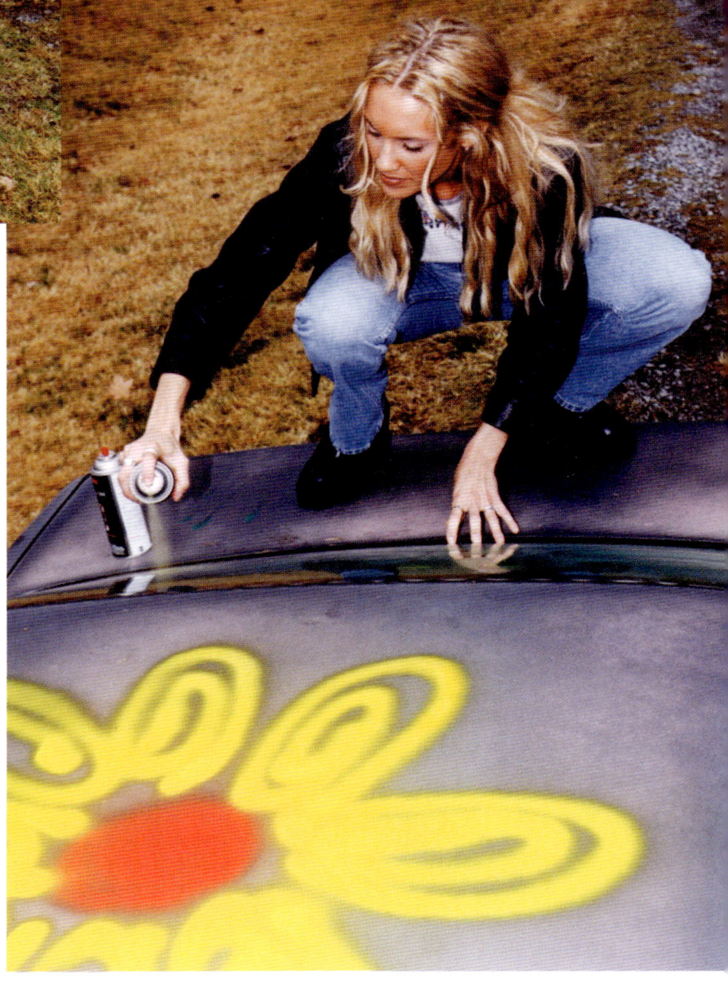

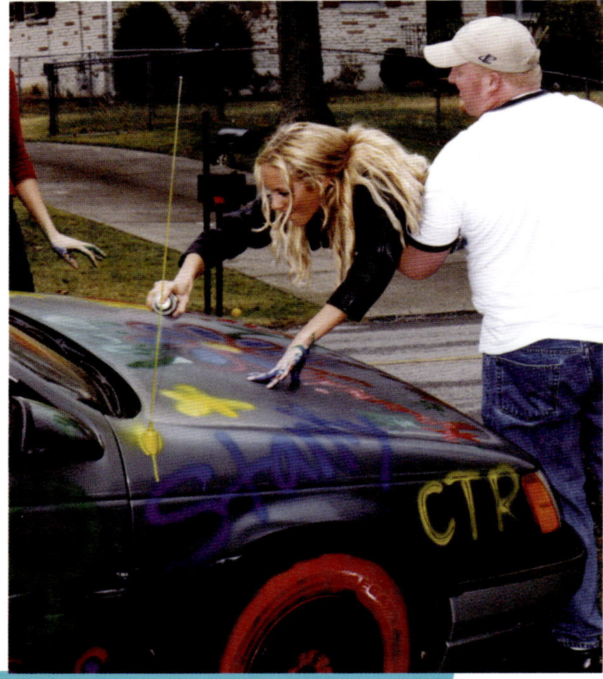

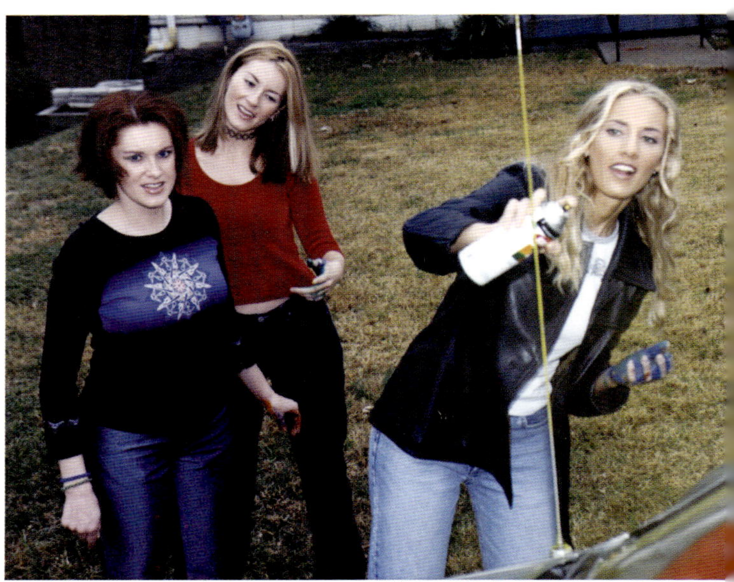

Osborn Sisters

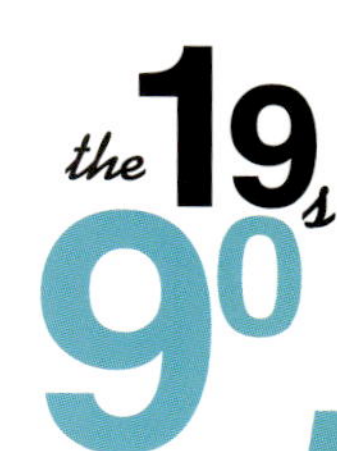

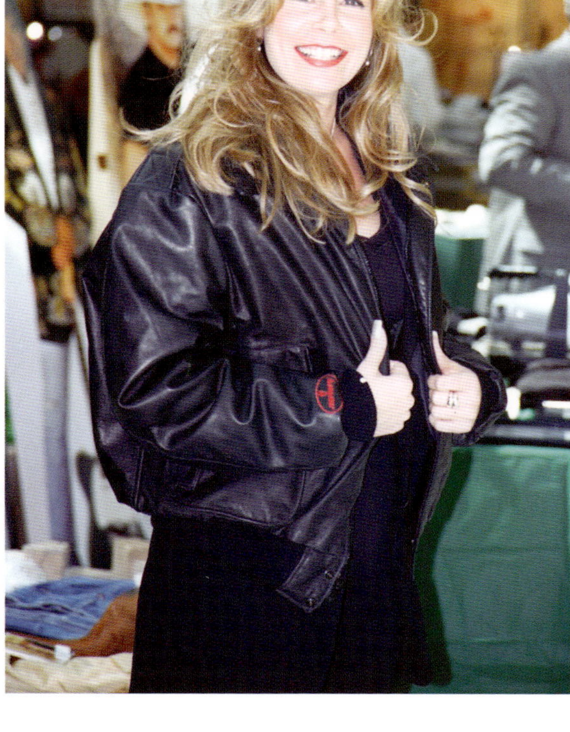

Stephanie Bentley

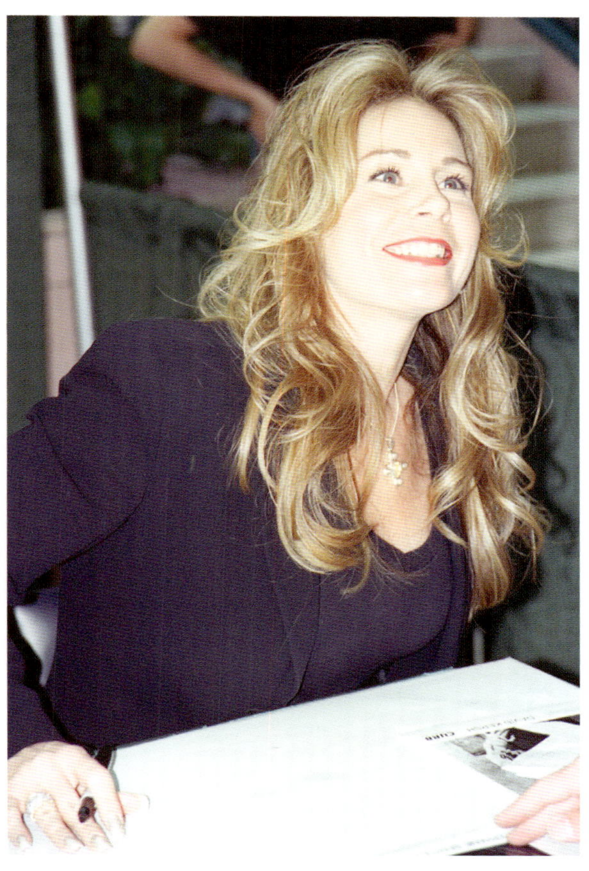

Steve Earle

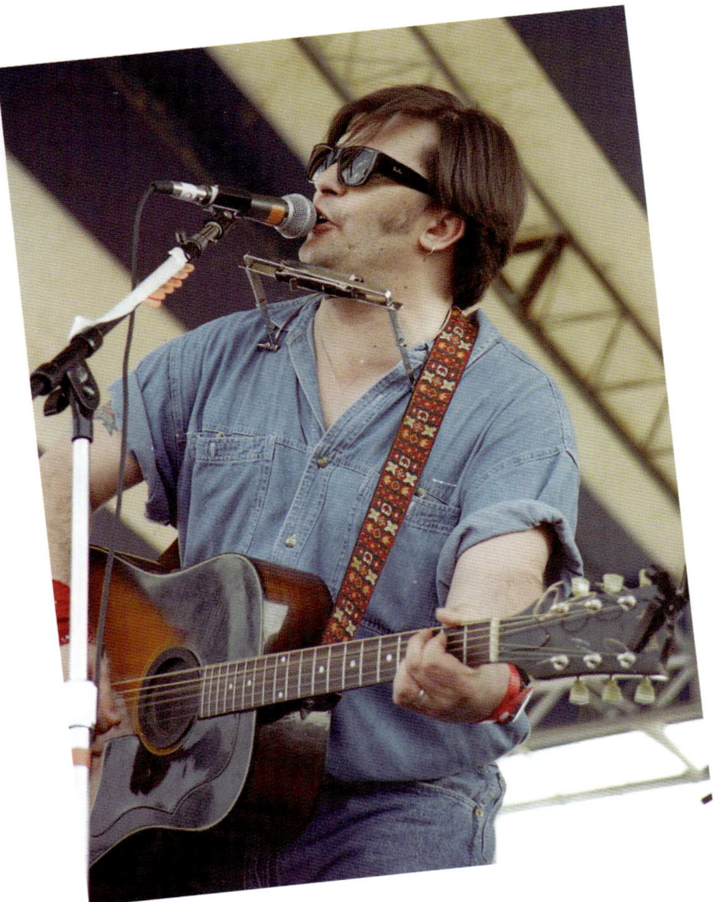

TG Shepherd

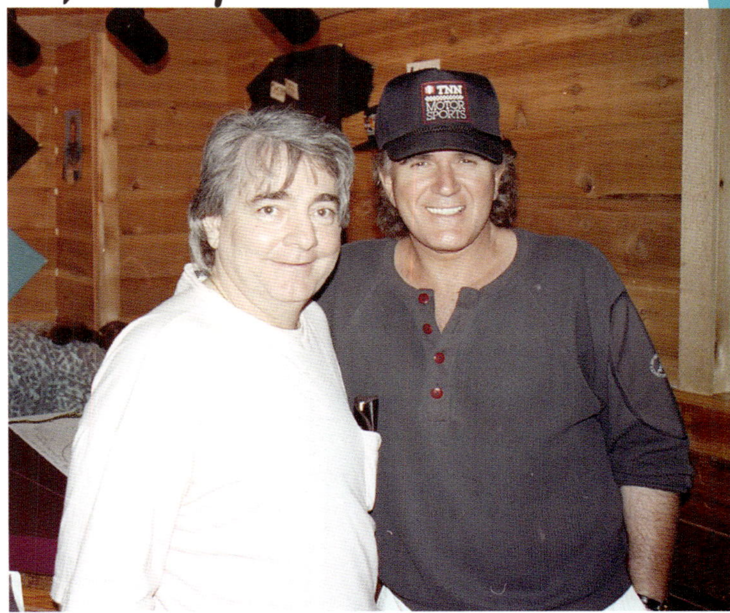

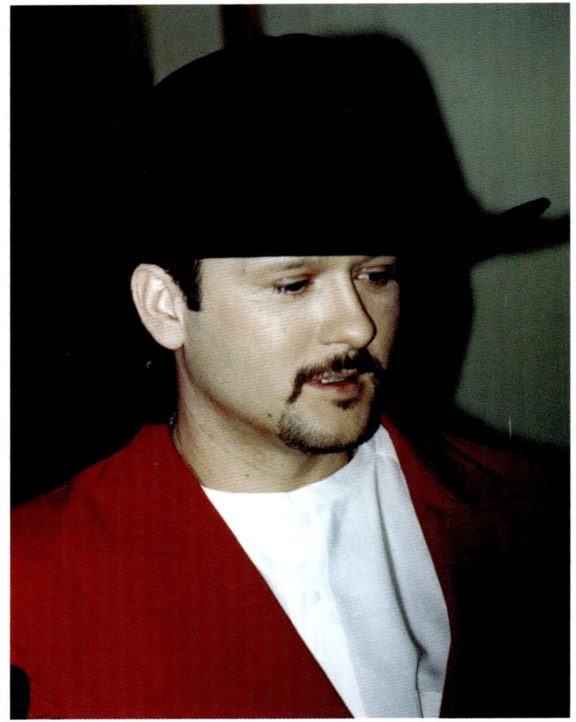

Tim McGraw

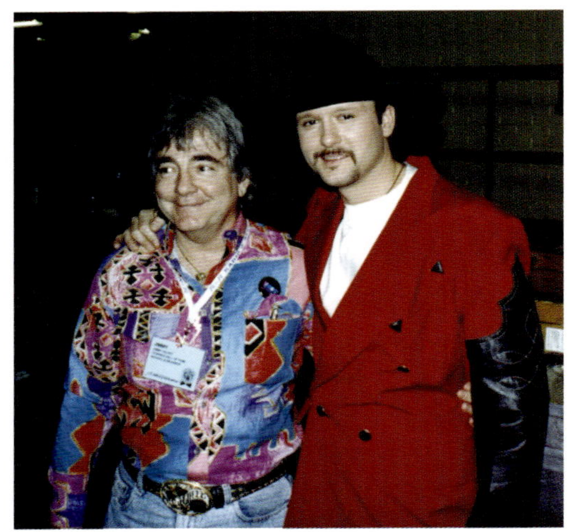

Trisha Yearwood

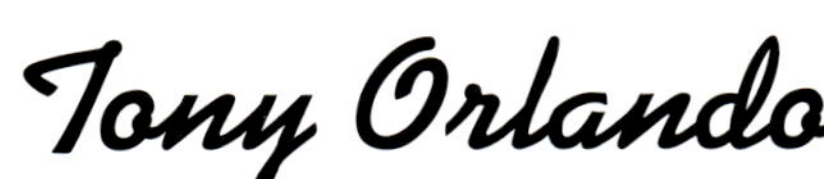

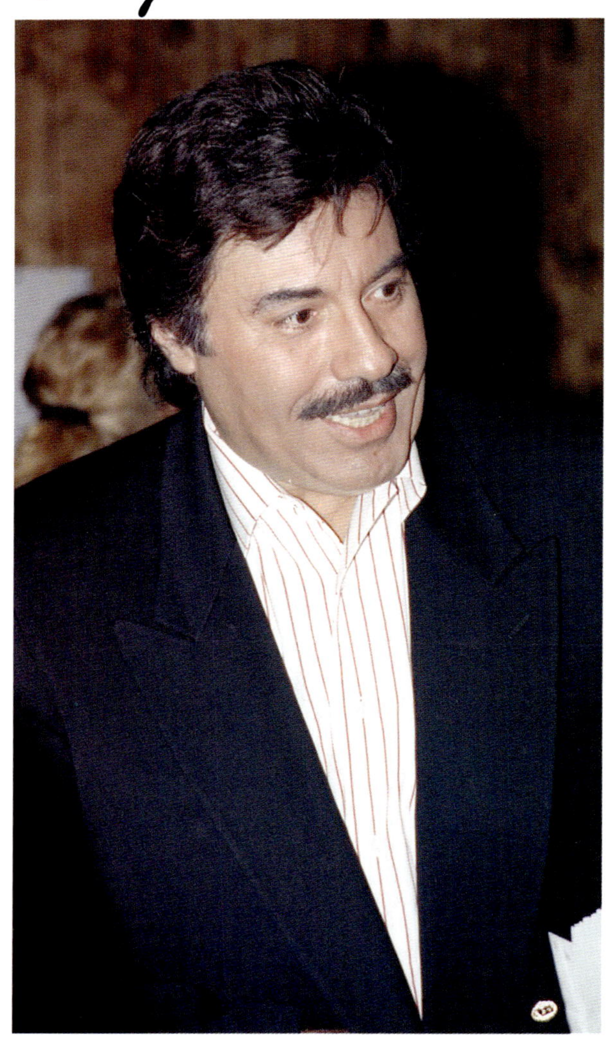

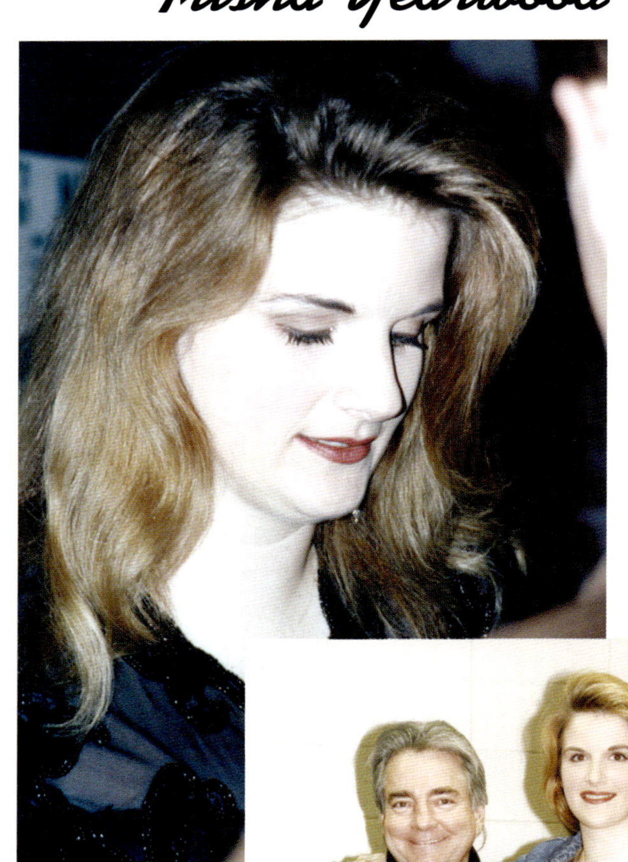

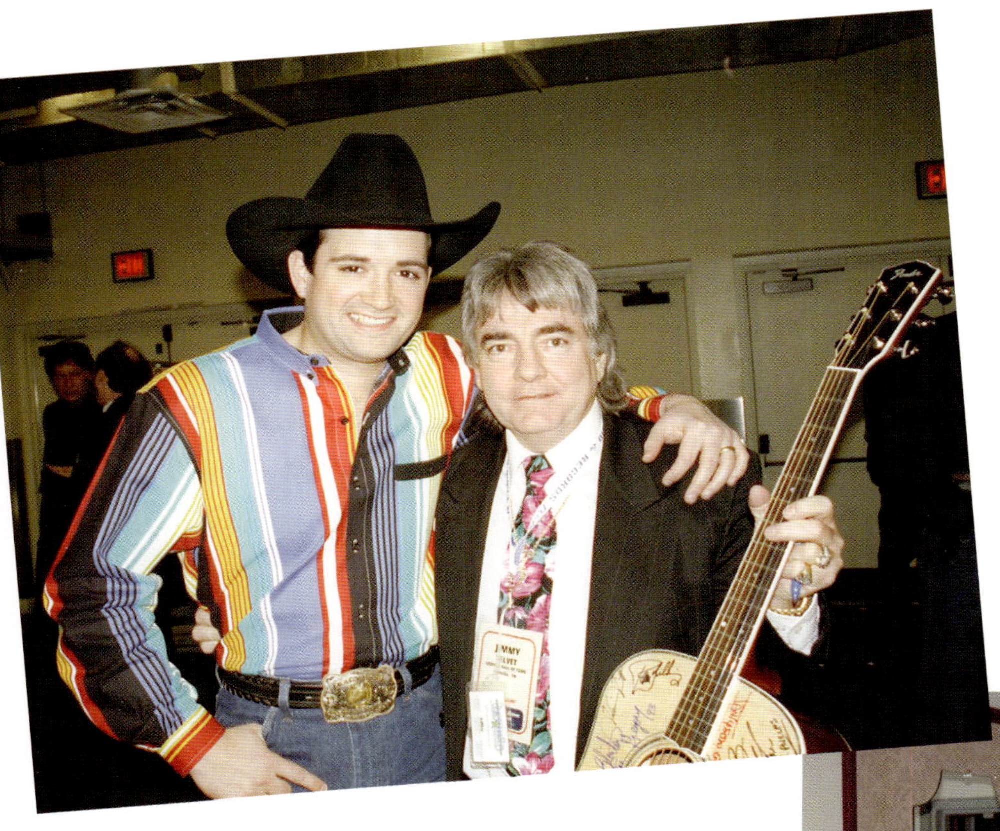

Tracy Byrd

Toby Keith

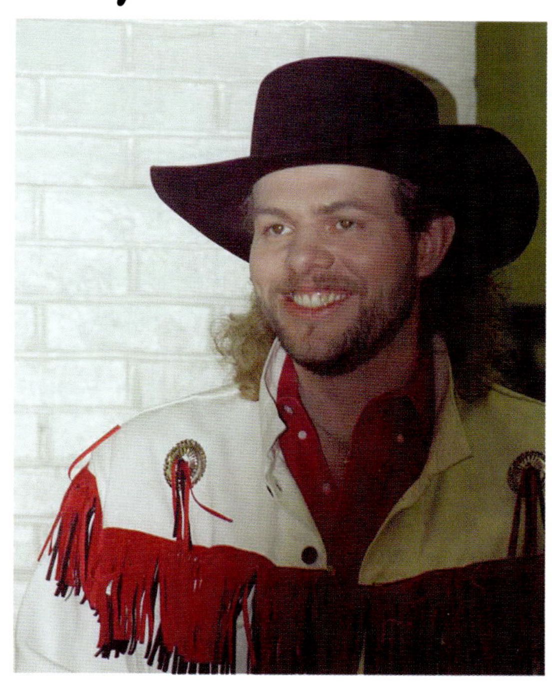

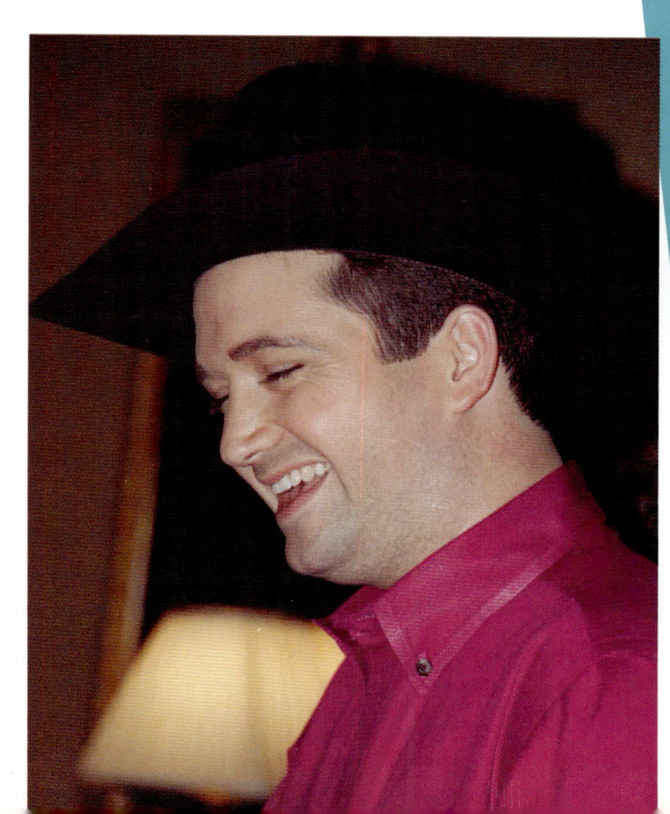

Travis Tritt

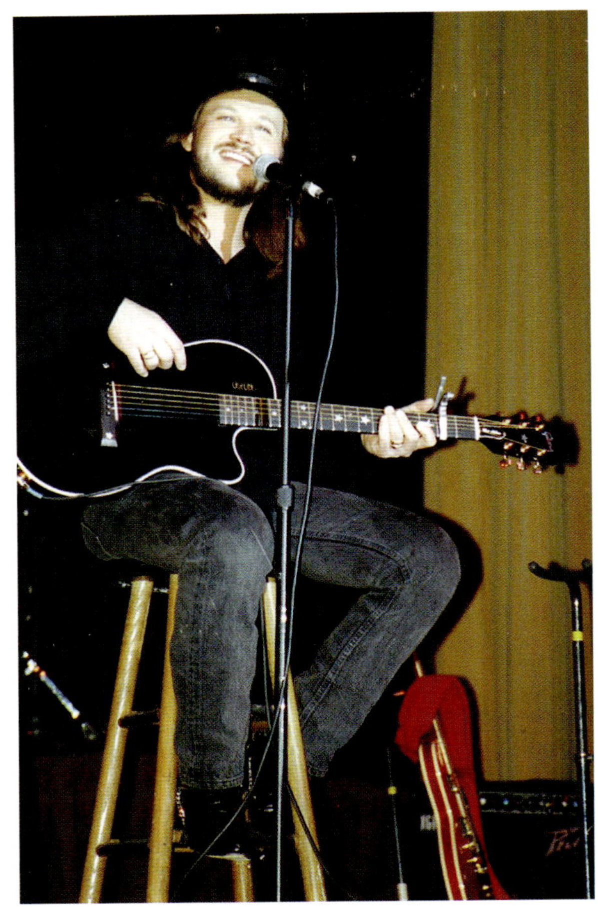

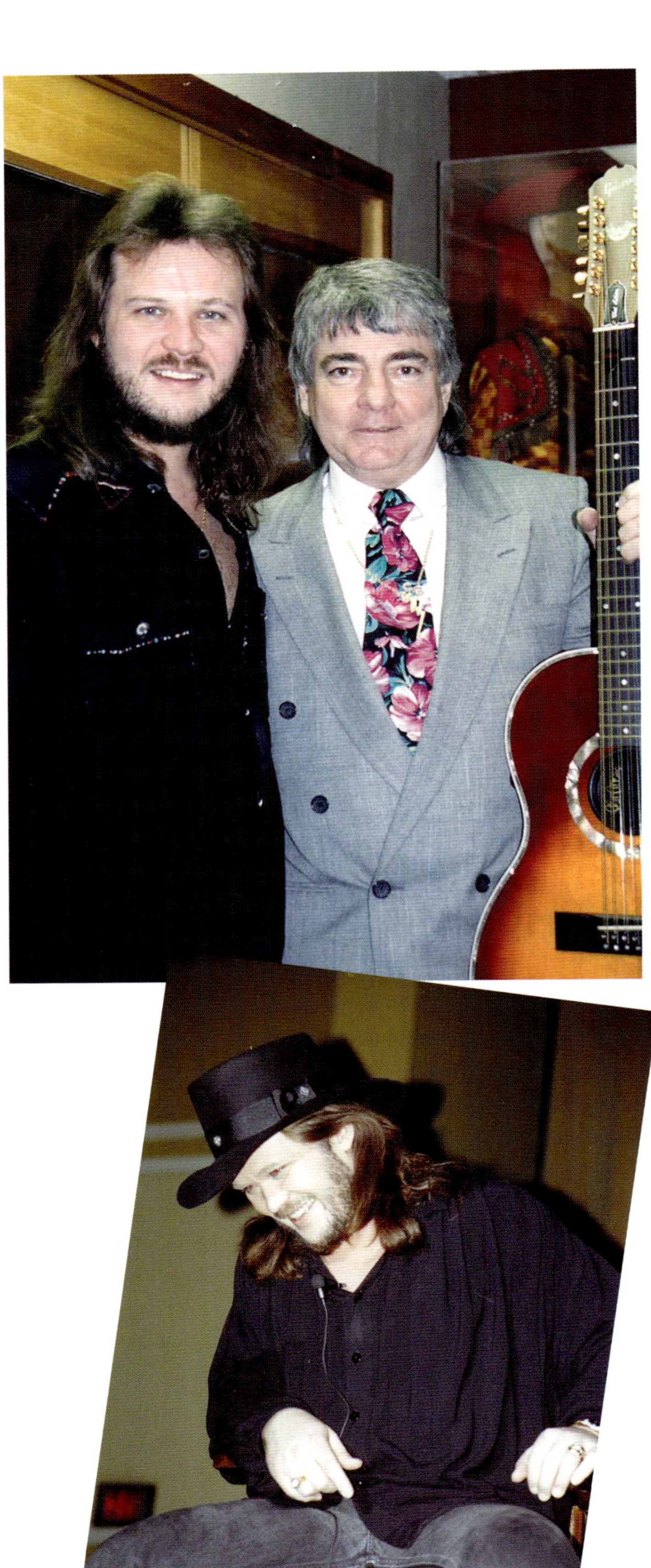

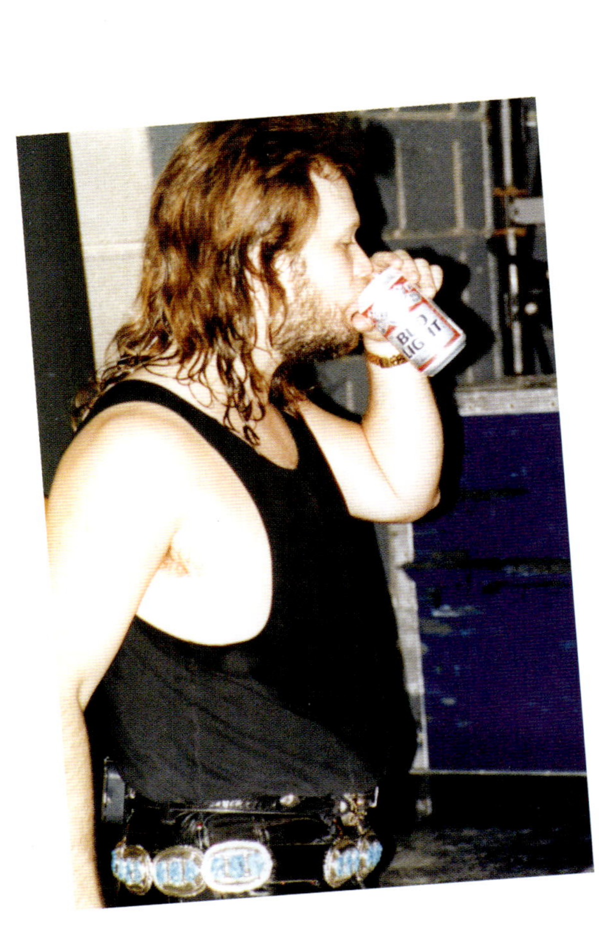

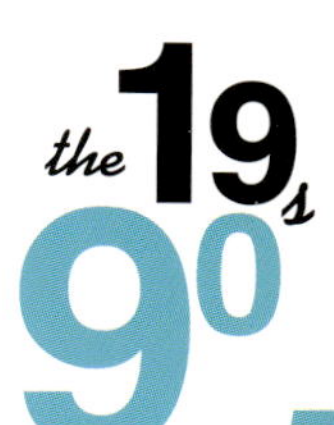

Vince Gill

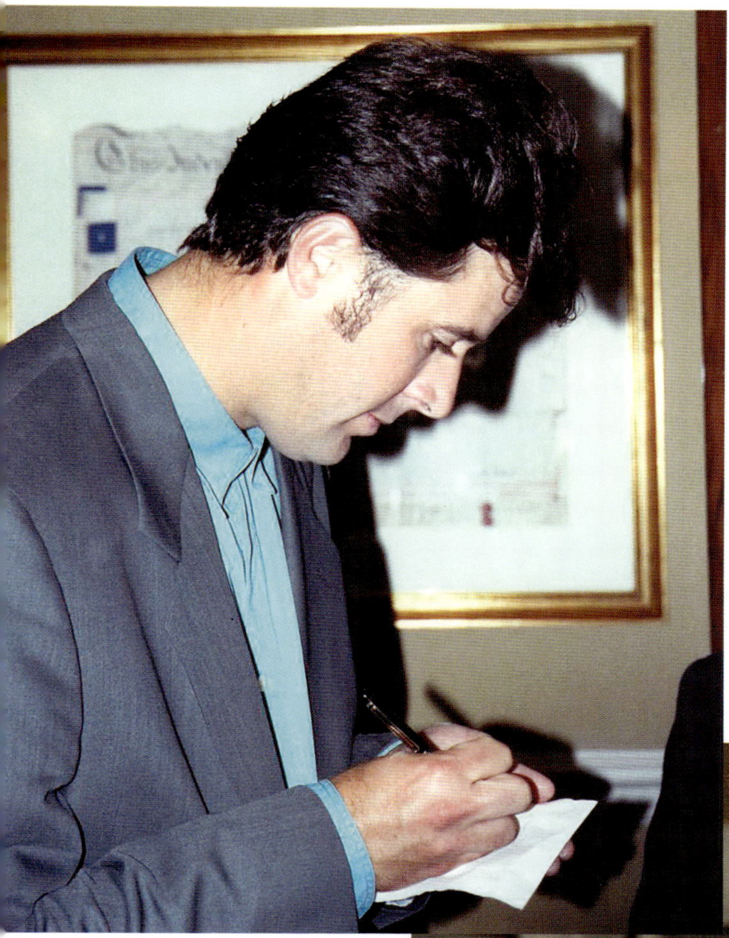

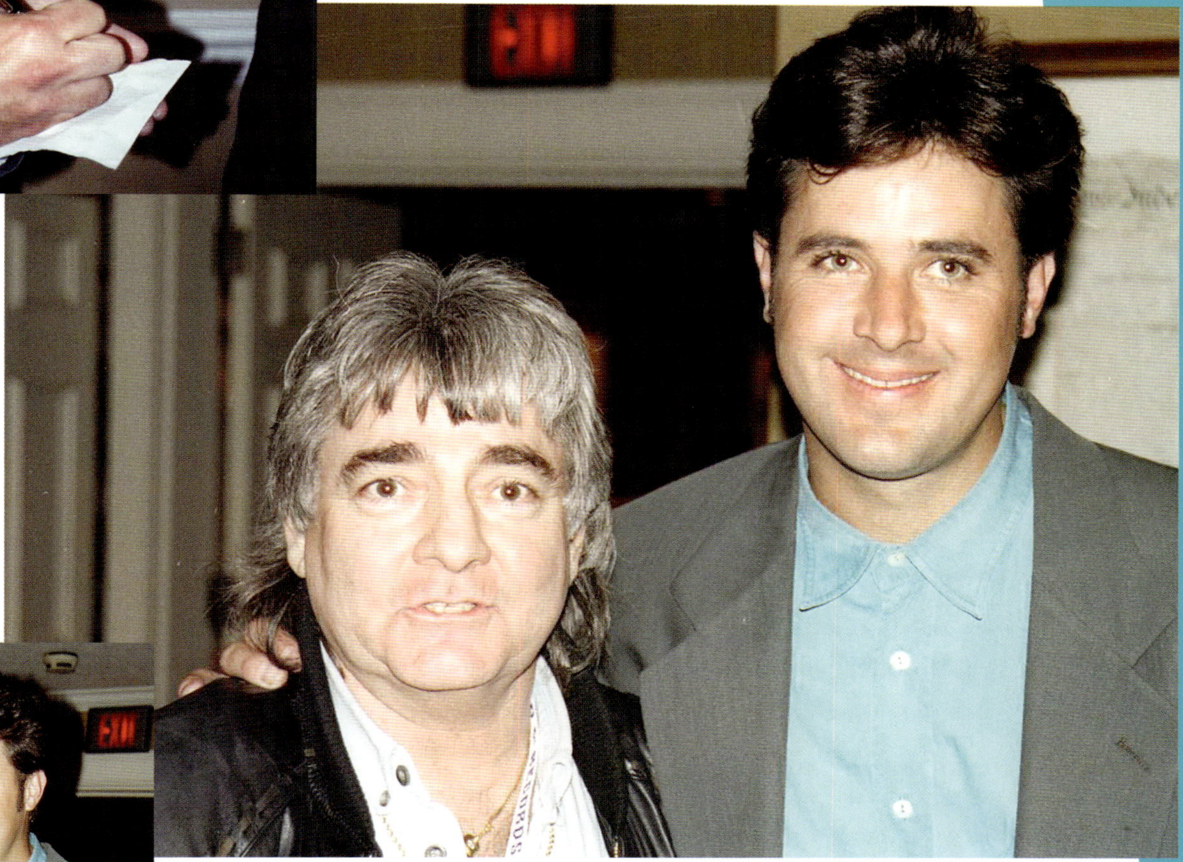

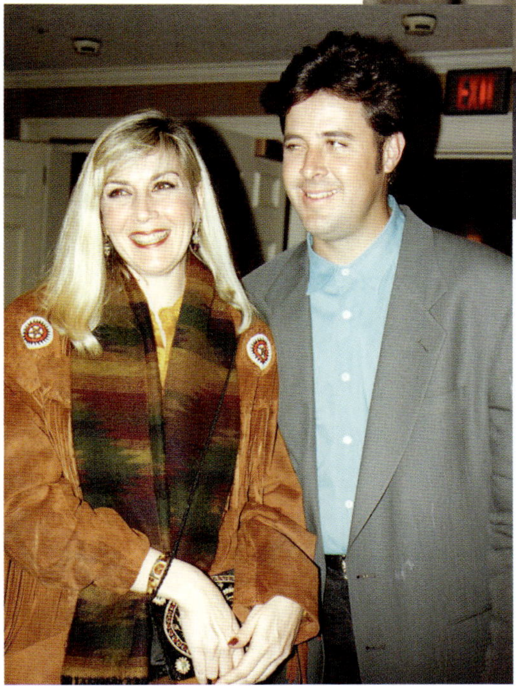

Janis and Vince

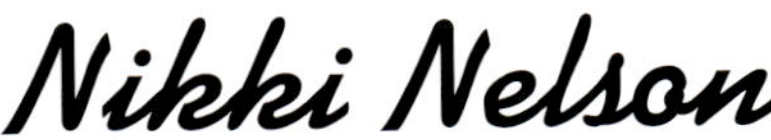

Nikki Nelson

Highway 101

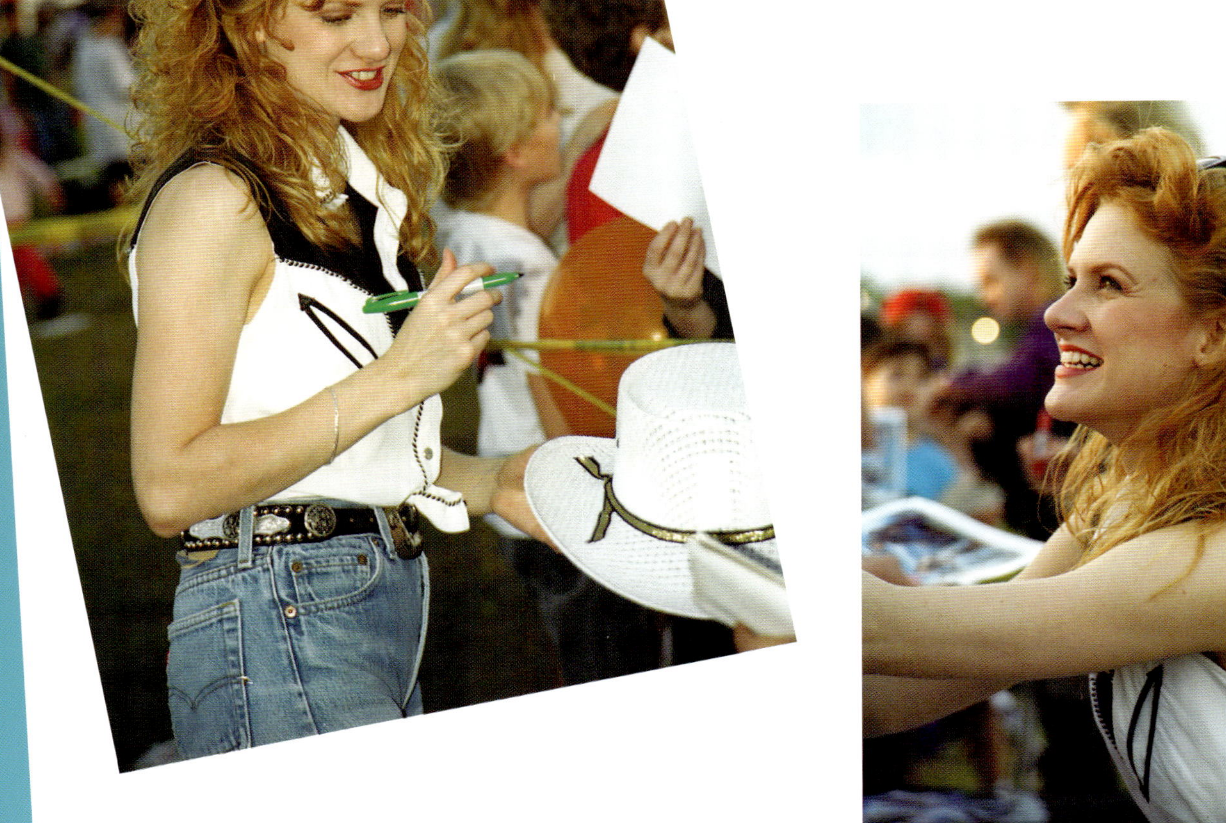

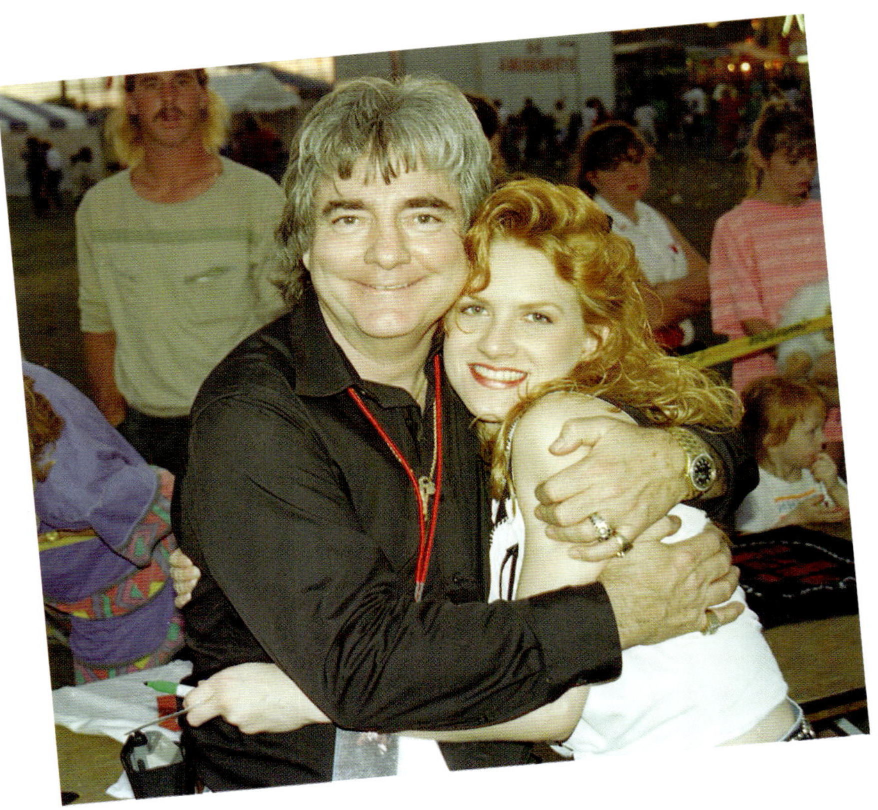

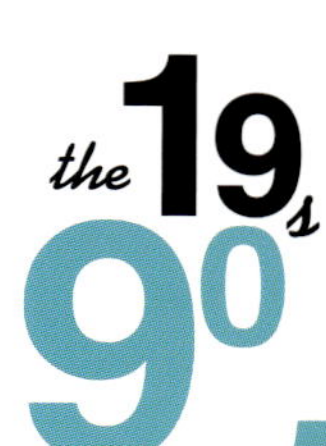

Mindy McCready

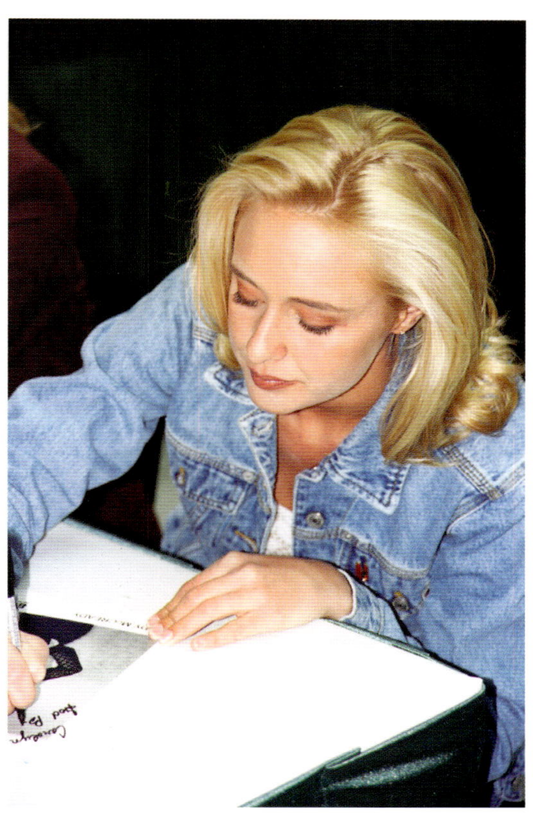

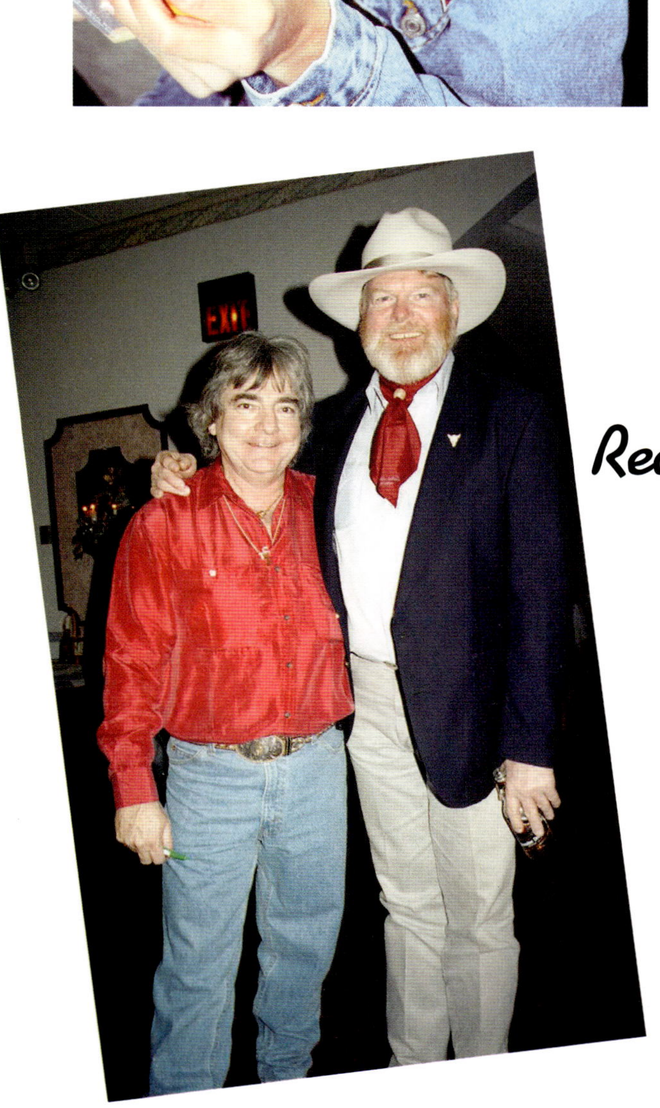

Red Steagael

Mel McDaniel

Country Singer and Song Writer

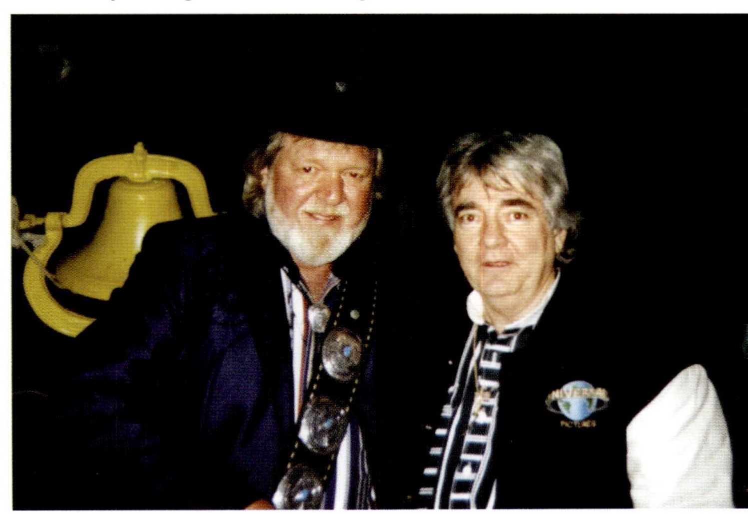

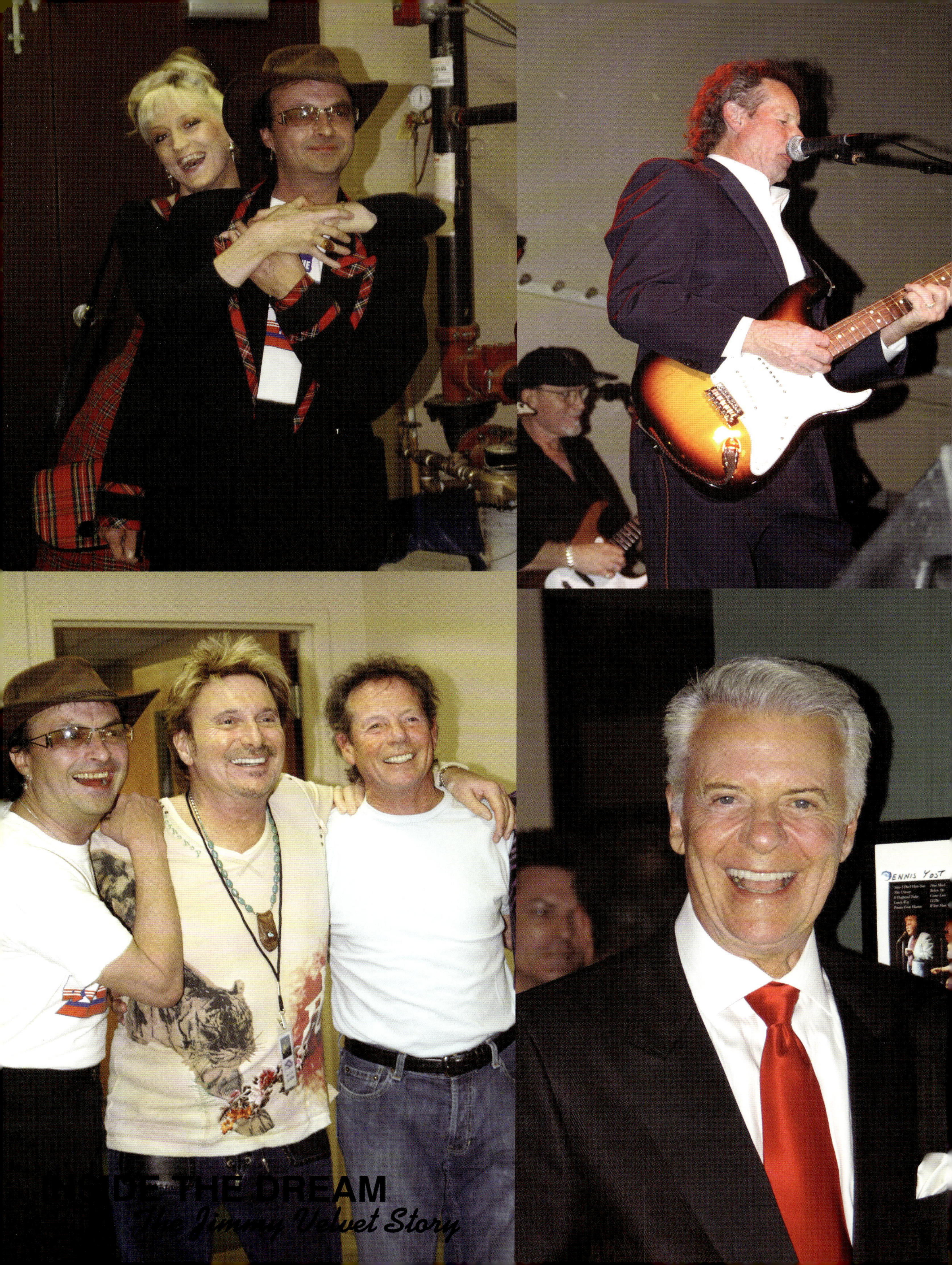

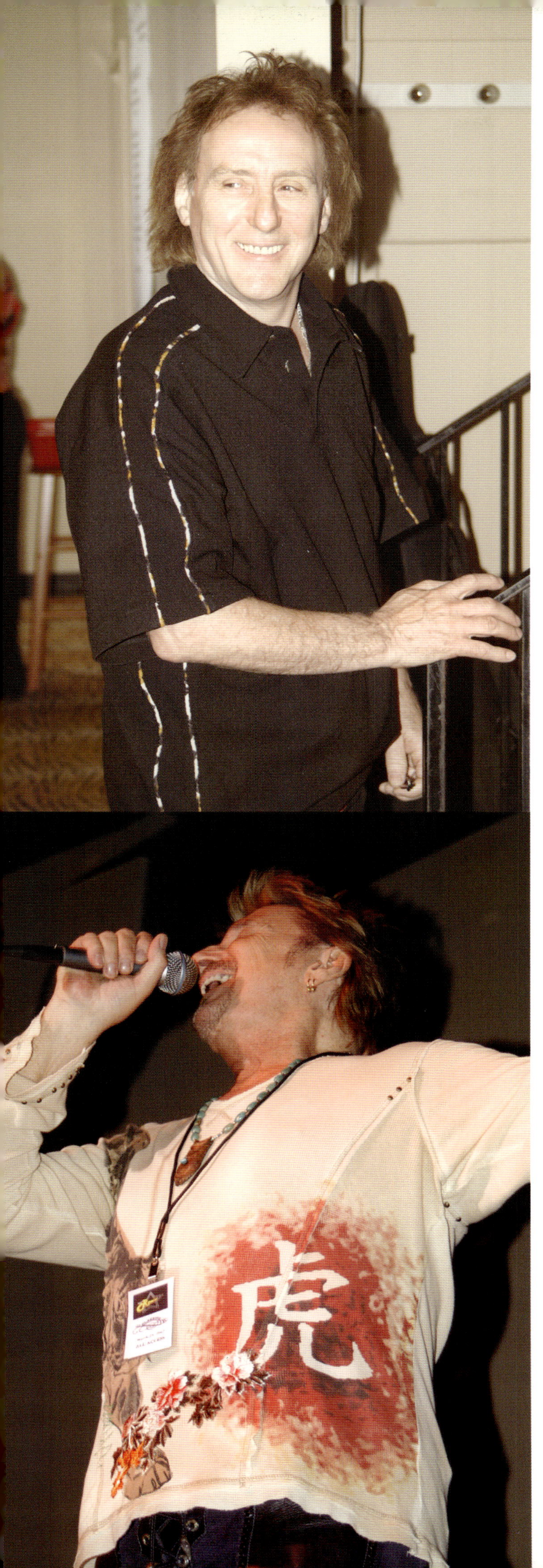

2000 on

This decade has been slower-paced, with the reshaping of my life after the closing of the museums and having had a financial setback. It's been quite a challenge trying to transform my life at my age.

I've been out and about, singing and performing with old friends from the "oldies" crowd, working in Las Vegas at photo signings and speaking engagements regarding entertainment history. I became involved with America Remembers, which sponsored tribute firearms. I met with Johnny Cash, George Jones, and Travis Tritt, and they all agreed to sign on and endorse a firearm named for them. I've also given some time to charity events.

This book has been my main focus since I was richly blessed to have recently regained my photo and negative archives. Unfortunately, due to the large volume of photos, there just wasn't enough time allowed for me to write a full volume just yet.

This is the final chapter, and I want to thank you for your interest in this book. It's been fun, and I hope that you've enjoyed the walk down memory lane as much as I have!

God's richest blessings to you and yours,

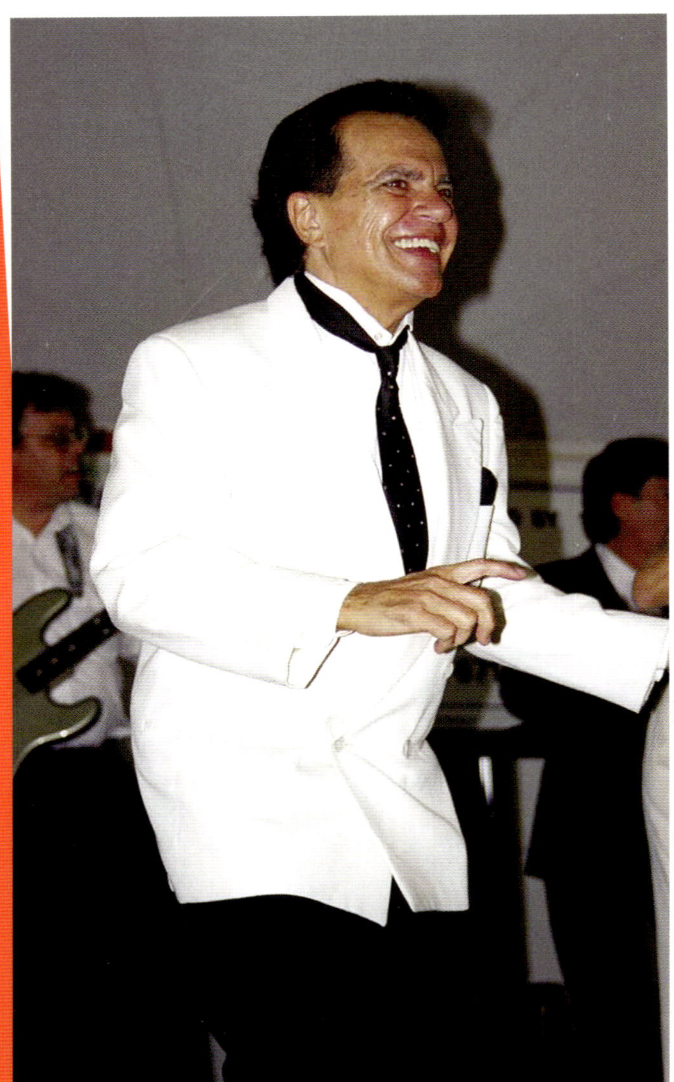

Joey Dee & the Starliters

Performing with his wife Lois
Peppermint Twist

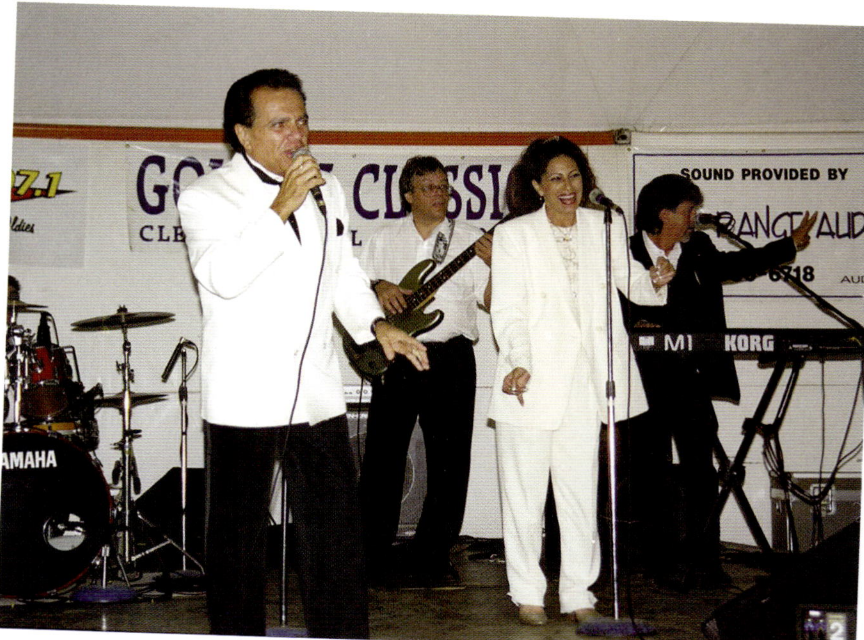

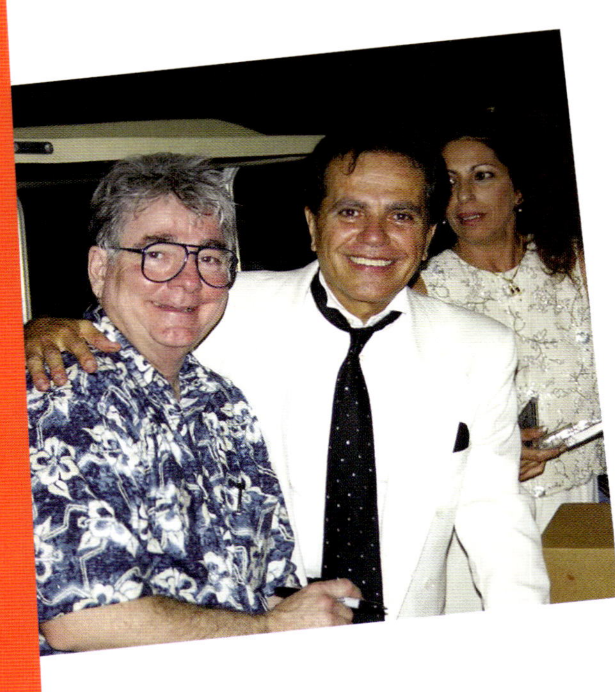

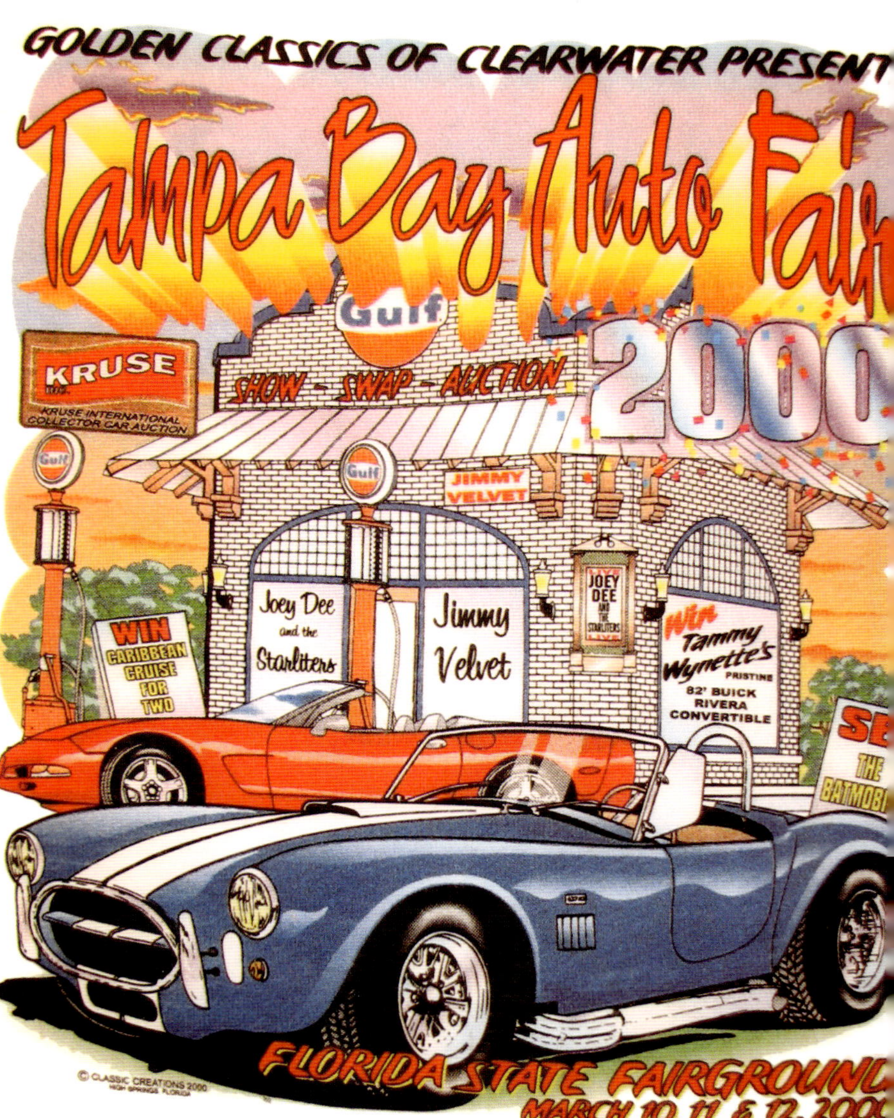

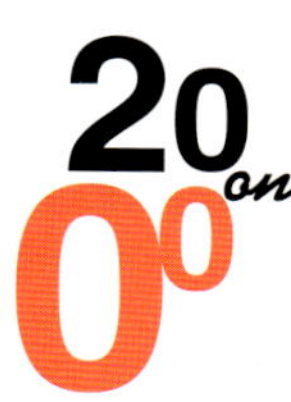

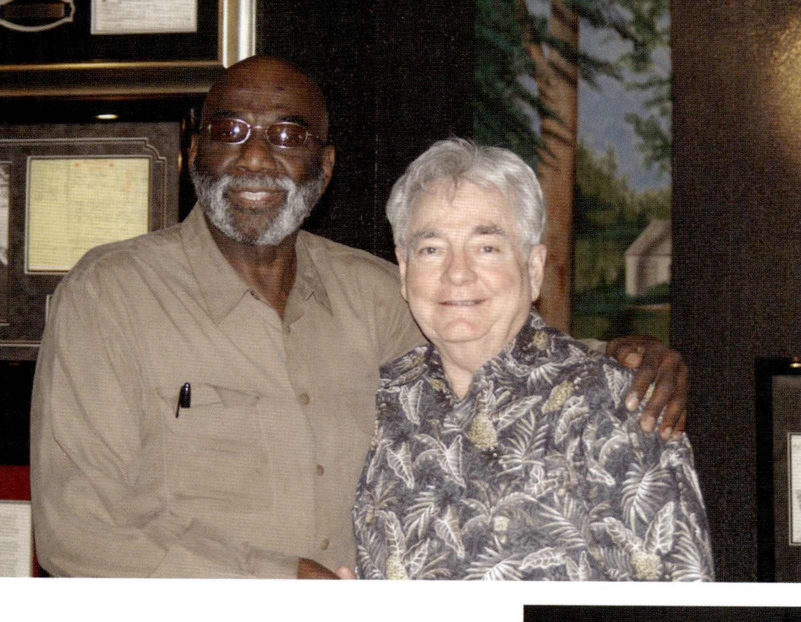

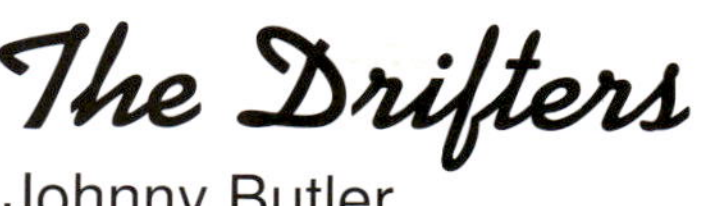

The Drifters

Johnny Butler

At the Tampa Bay Auto Fair with Dan's mom

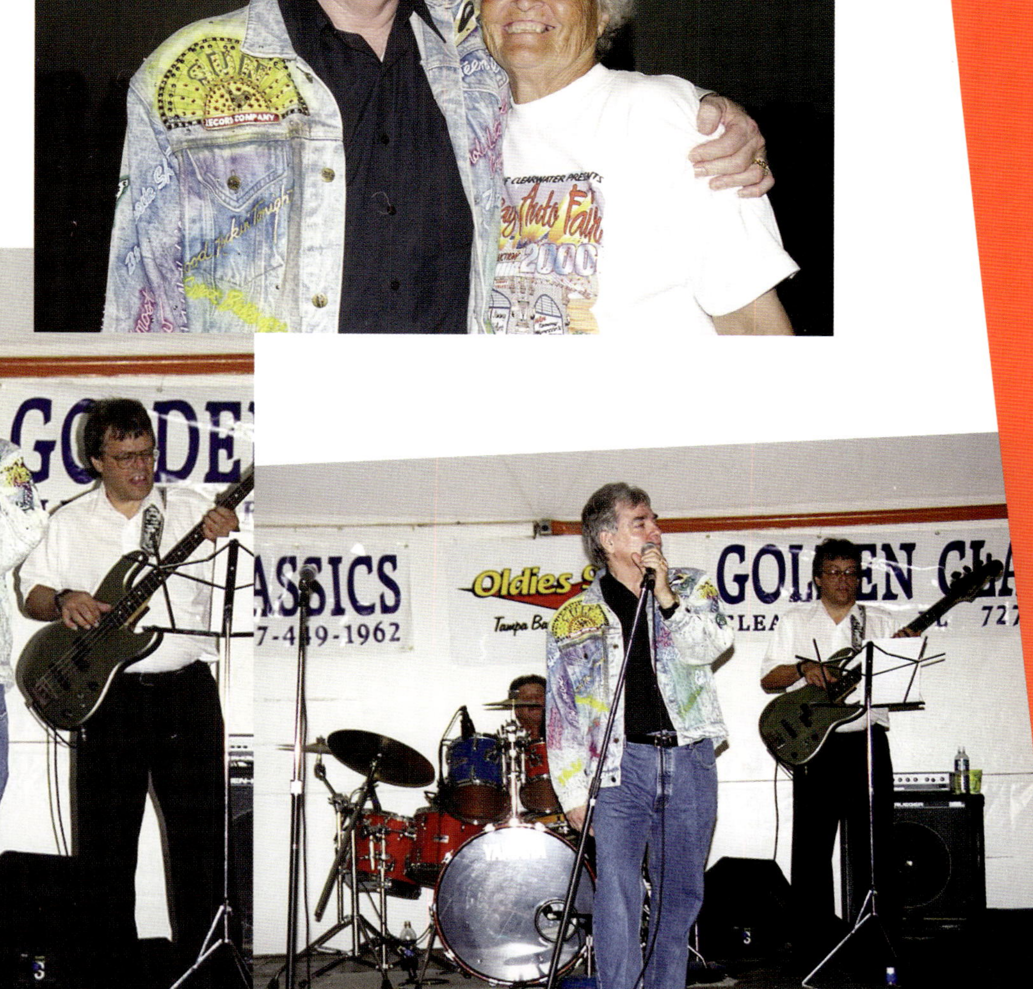

On stage at the Tampa Bay Auto Fair

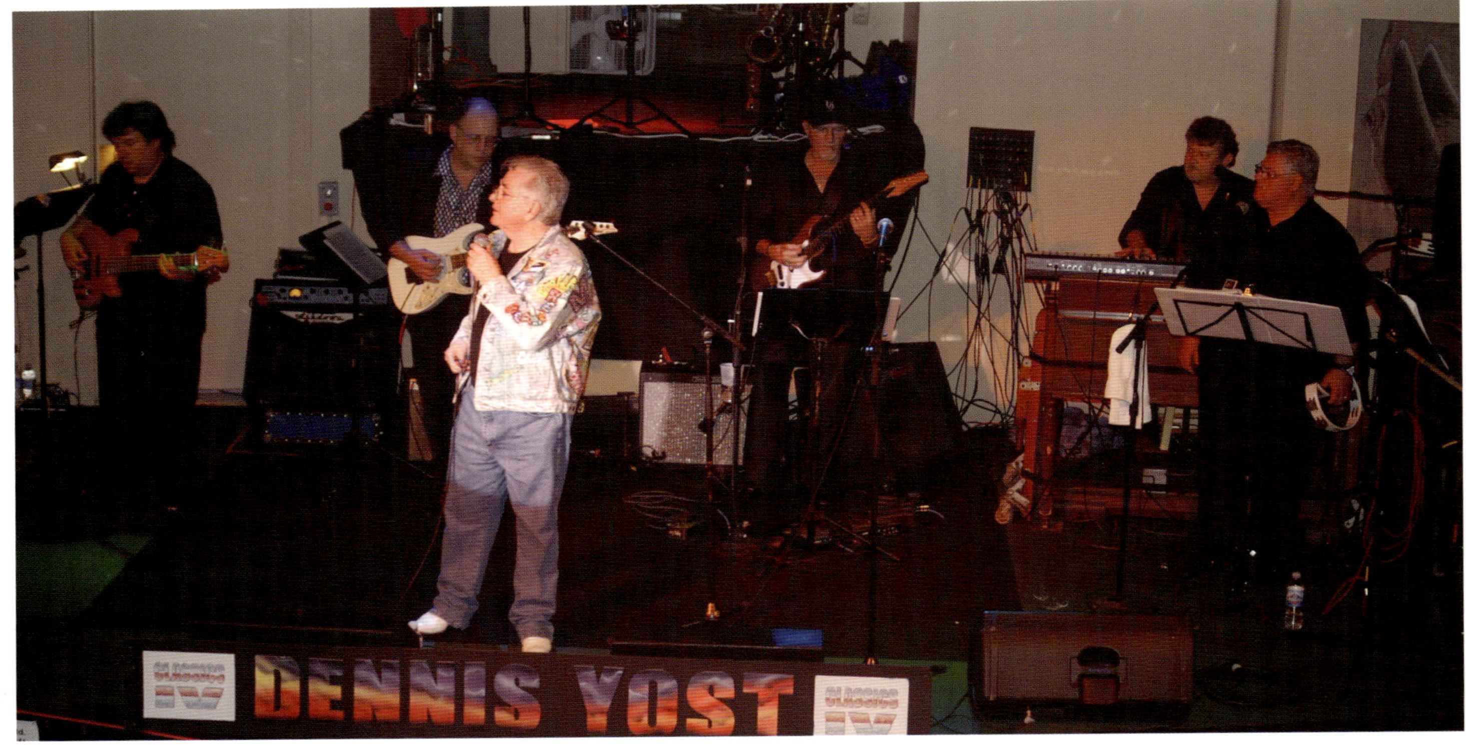

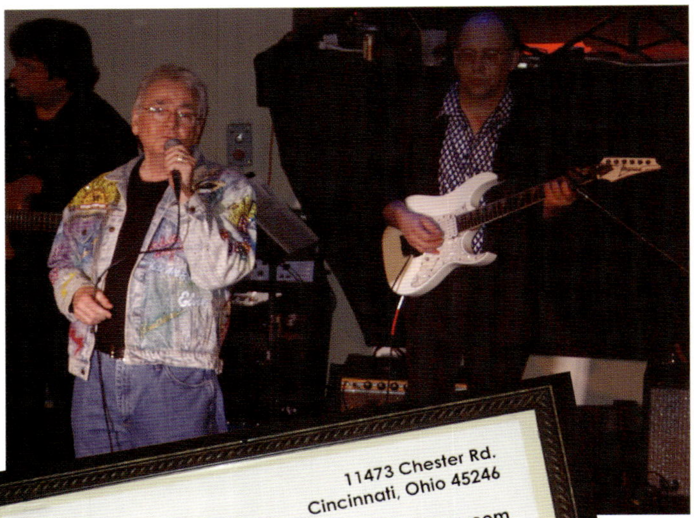

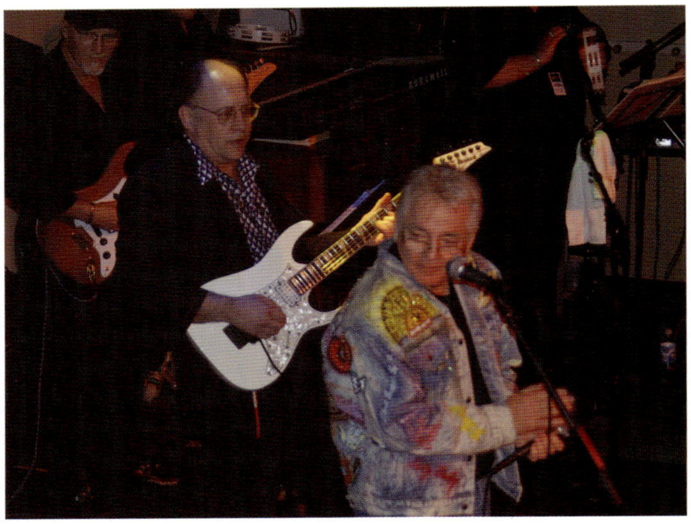

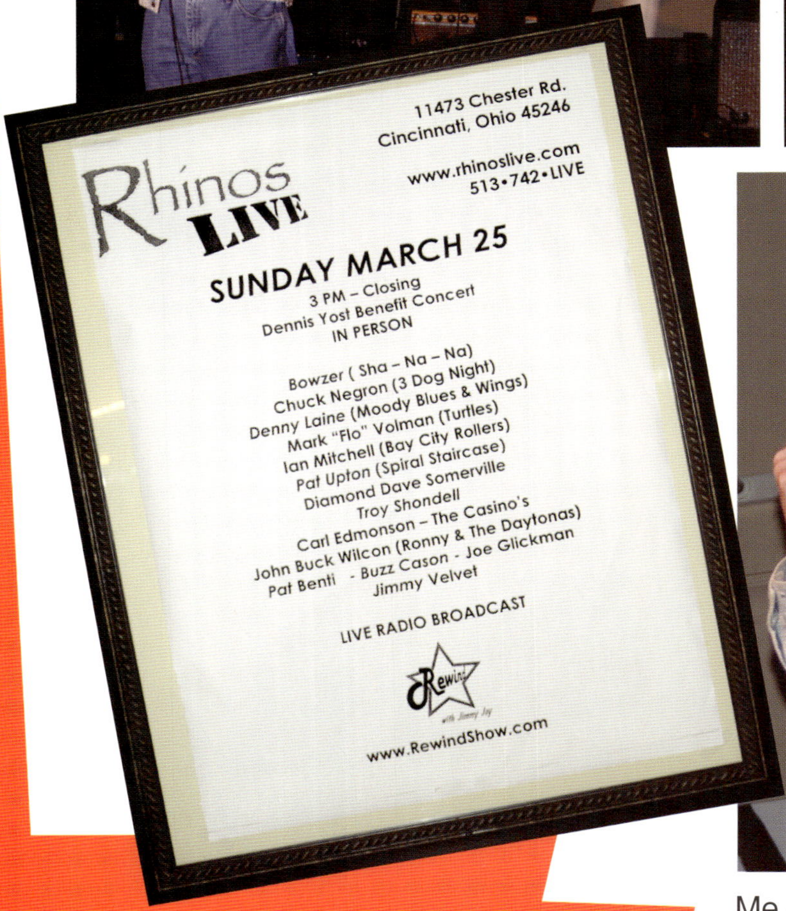

11473 Chester Rd.
Cincinnati, Ohio 45246

www.rhinoslive.com
513•742•LIVE

Rhinos LIVE

SUNDAY MARCH 25
3 PM – Closing
Dennis Yost Benefit Concert
IN PERSON

Bowzer (Sha – Na – Na)
Chuck Negron (3 Dog Night)
Denny Laine (Moody Blues & Wings)
Mark "Flo" Volman (Turtles)
Ian Mitchell (Bay City Rollers)
Pat Upton (Spiral Staircase)
Diamond Dave Somerville
Troy Shondell
Carl Edmonson – The Casino's
John Buck Wilcon (Ronny & The Daytonas)
Pat Benti - Buzz Cason - Joe Glickman
Jimmy Velvet

LIVE RADIO BROADCAST

Rewind

www.RewindShow.com

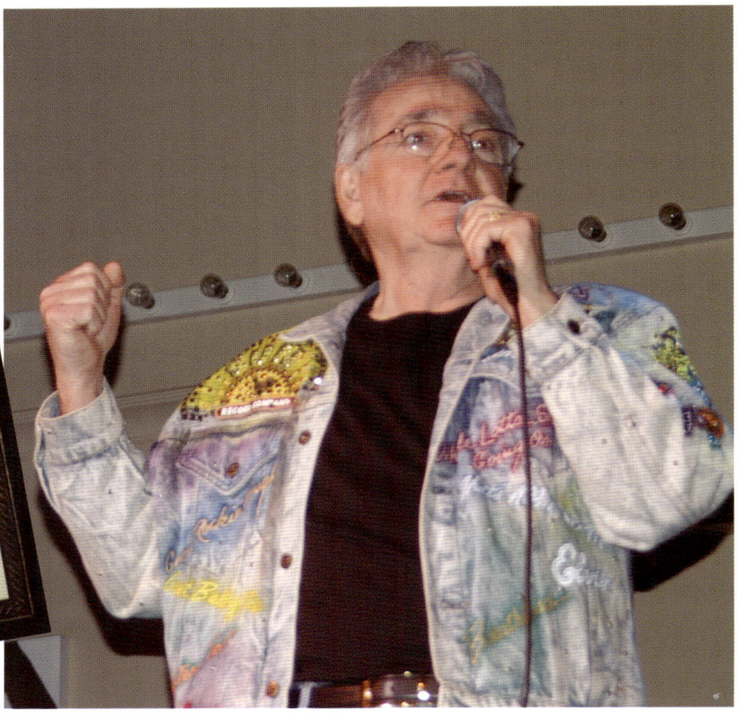

Me on stage March 25th 2007
Cincinnati, Ohio

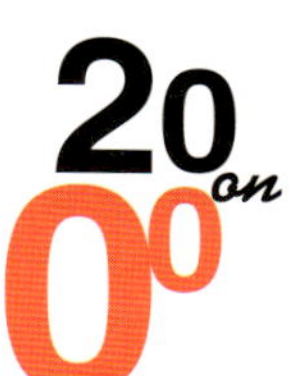

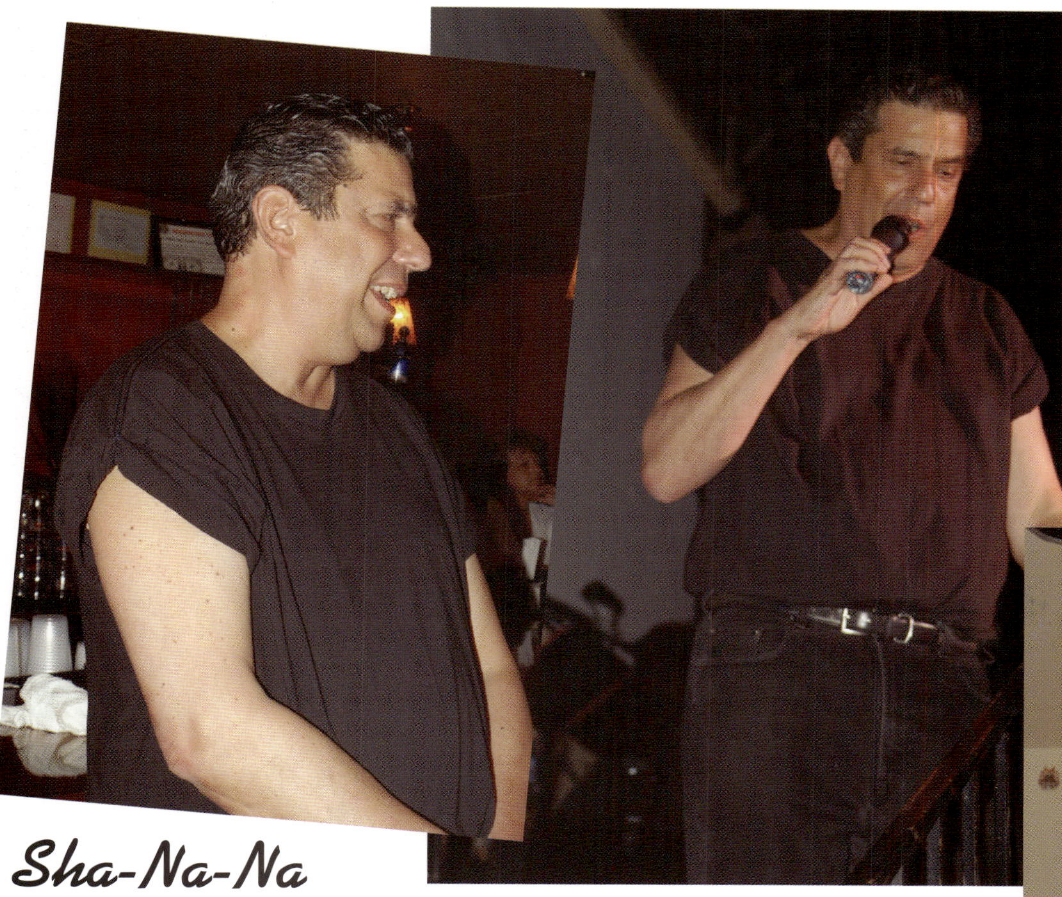

Sha-Na-Na
Jon "Bowzer" Bauman
"Goodnight Sweetheart"

Joe G
The Classics IV and
Zippity Doo Wop Band

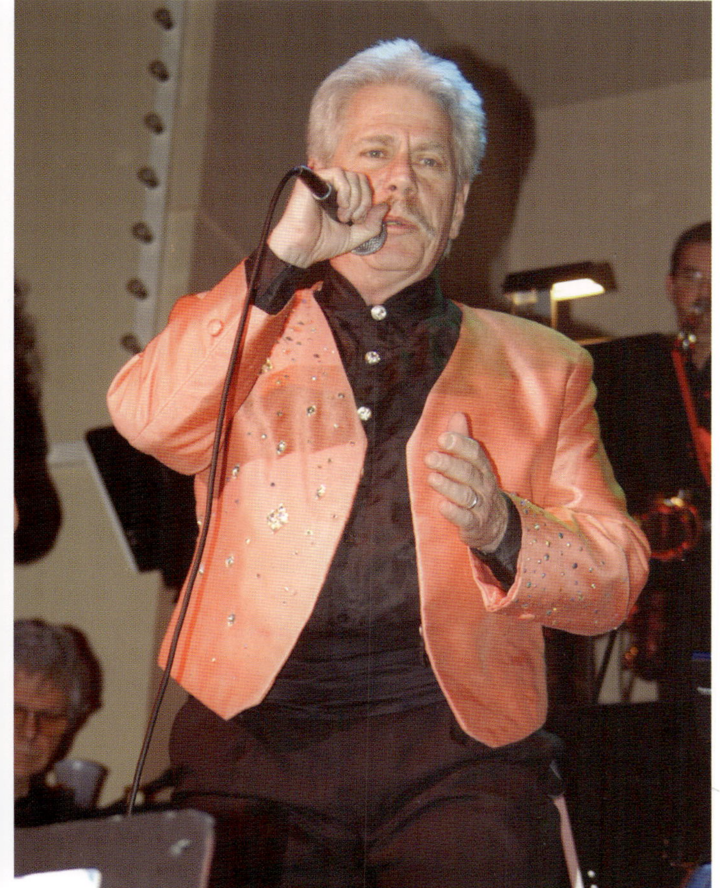

Jimmy Beaumont
The Skyliners
Pennies from Heaven
This I Swear
Since I Dont Have You

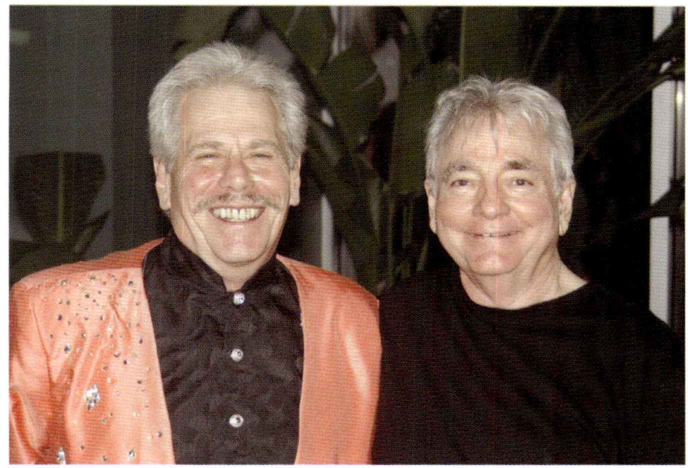

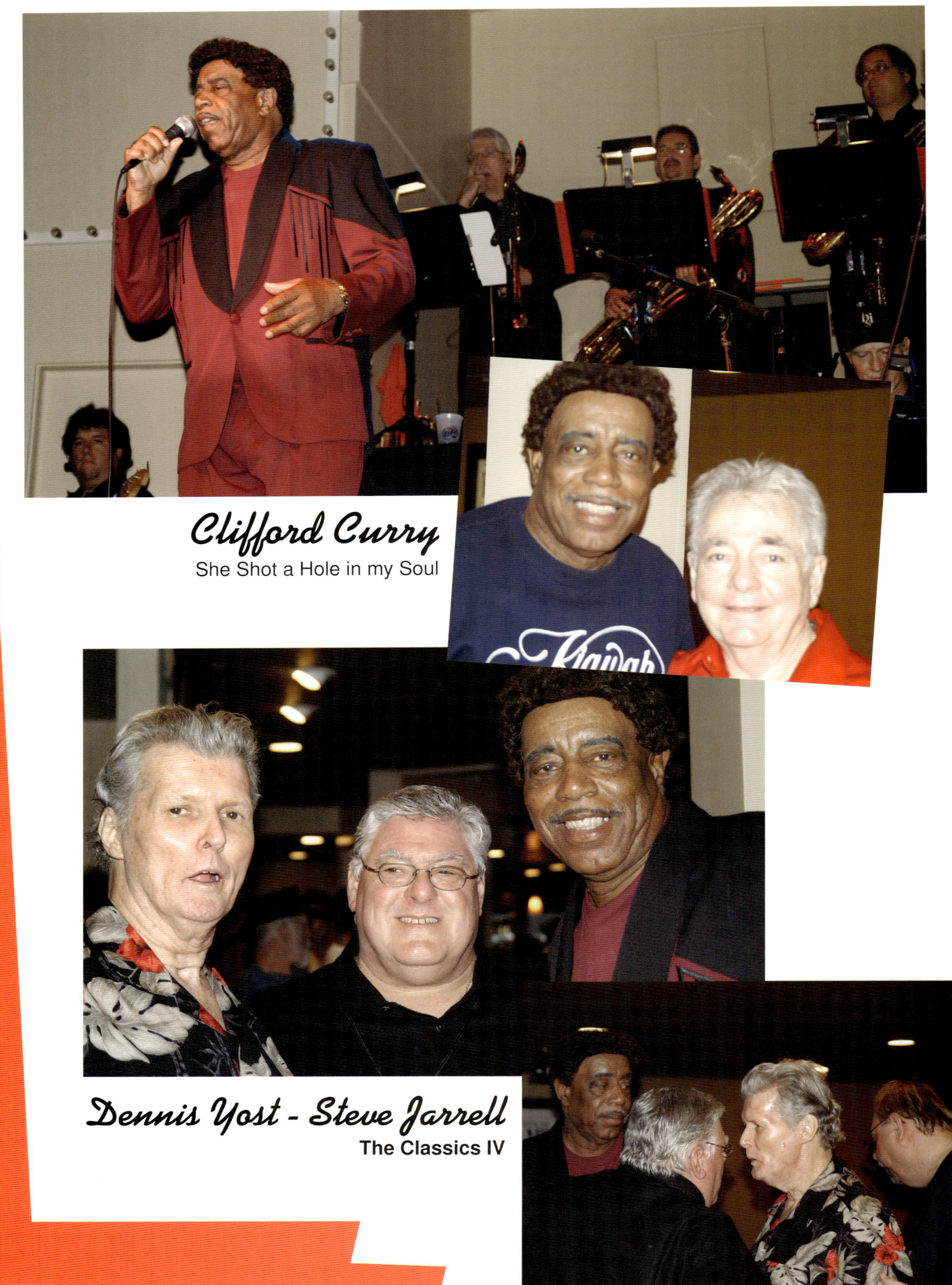

Clifford Curry

She Shot a Hole in my Soul

Dennis Yost - Steve Jarrell

The Classics IV

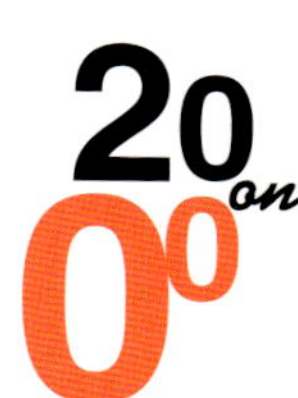

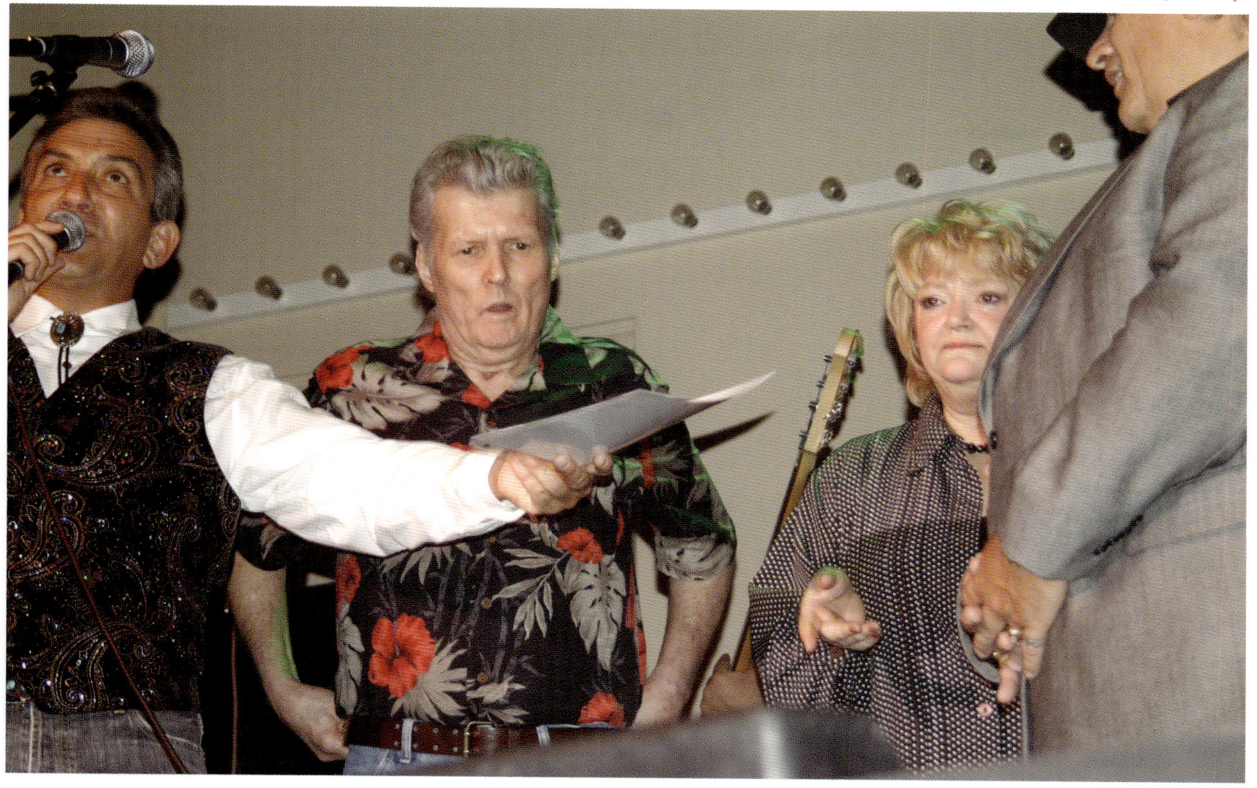

Dennis and Linda Yost

Spooky, Stormy, Traces, Everyday With You Girl

John "Bucky" Wilkin of Ronny and the Daytonas

Little GTO

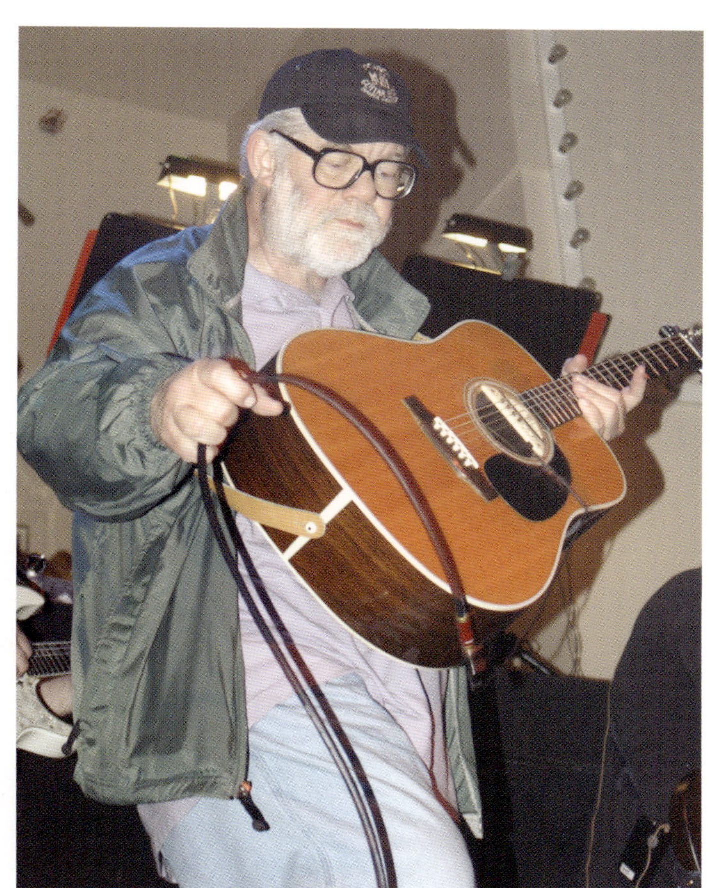

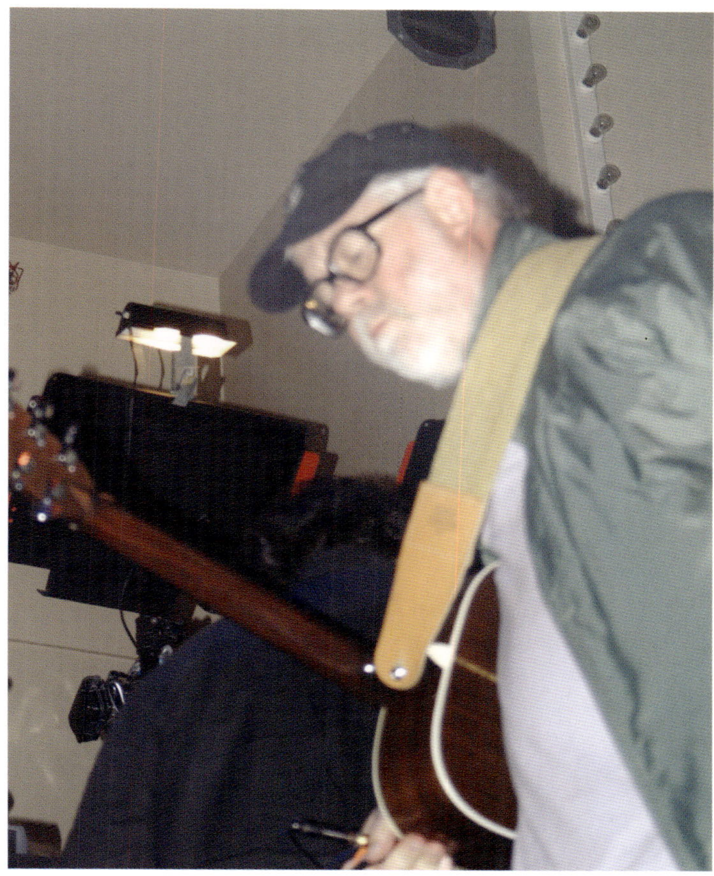

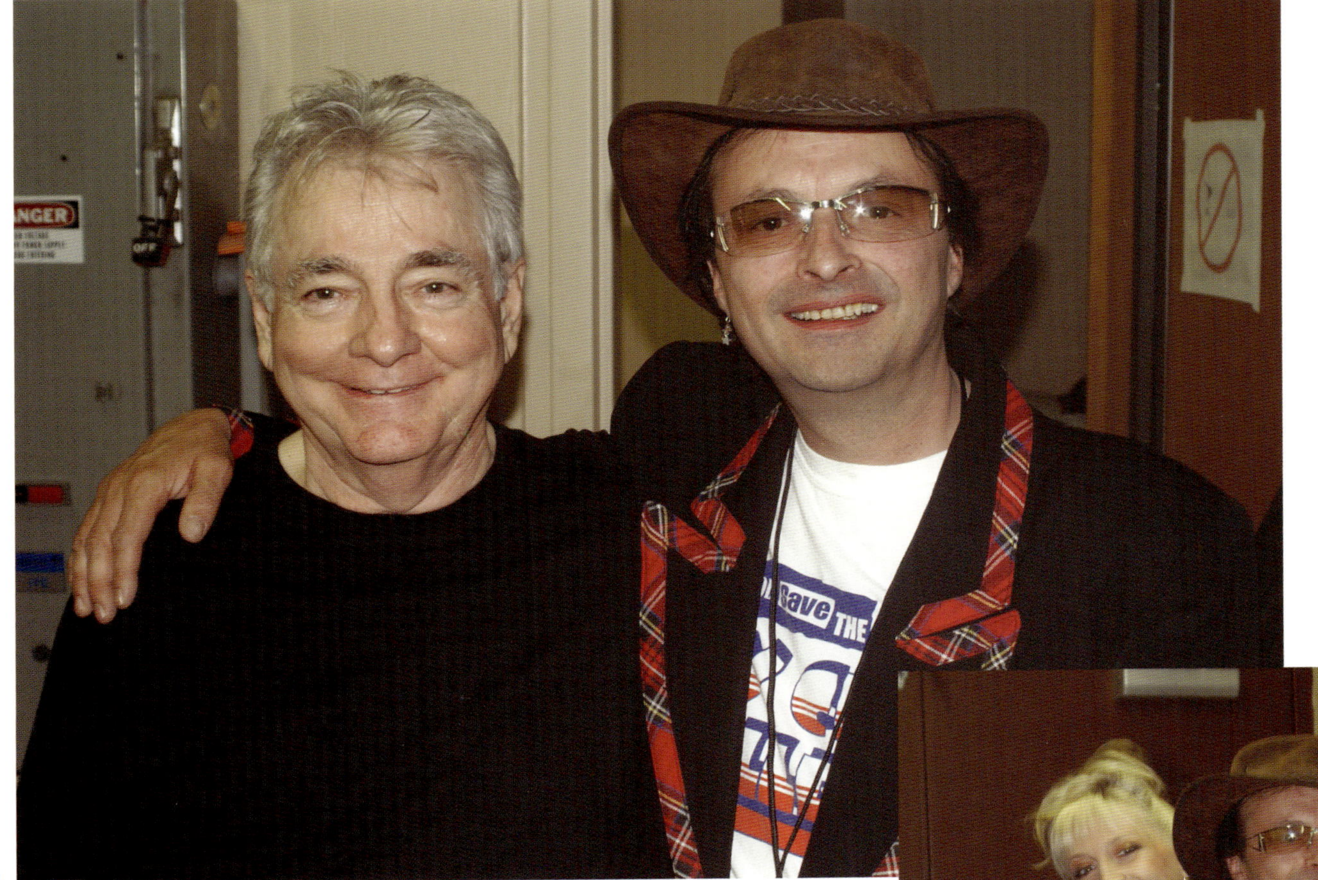

Ian Mitchell of the *Bay City Rollers*

Right: Wendy Ann and Ian
Doctor, Doctor
Saturday Night

Pat Benti
Ian Mitchell
Denny Laine
Chuck Negron
Jimmy J

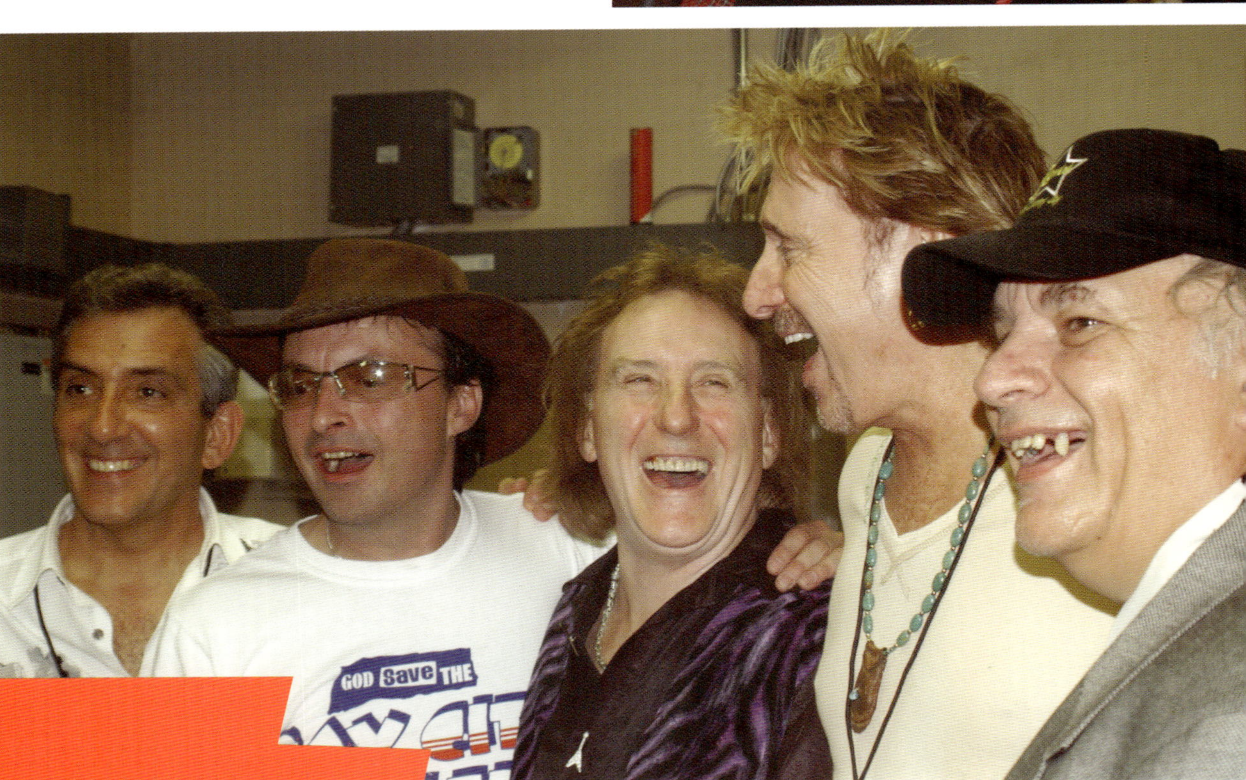

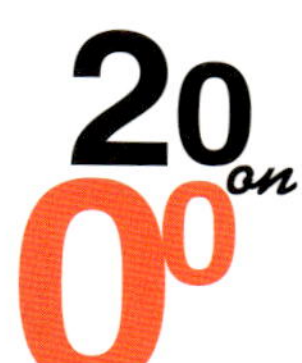

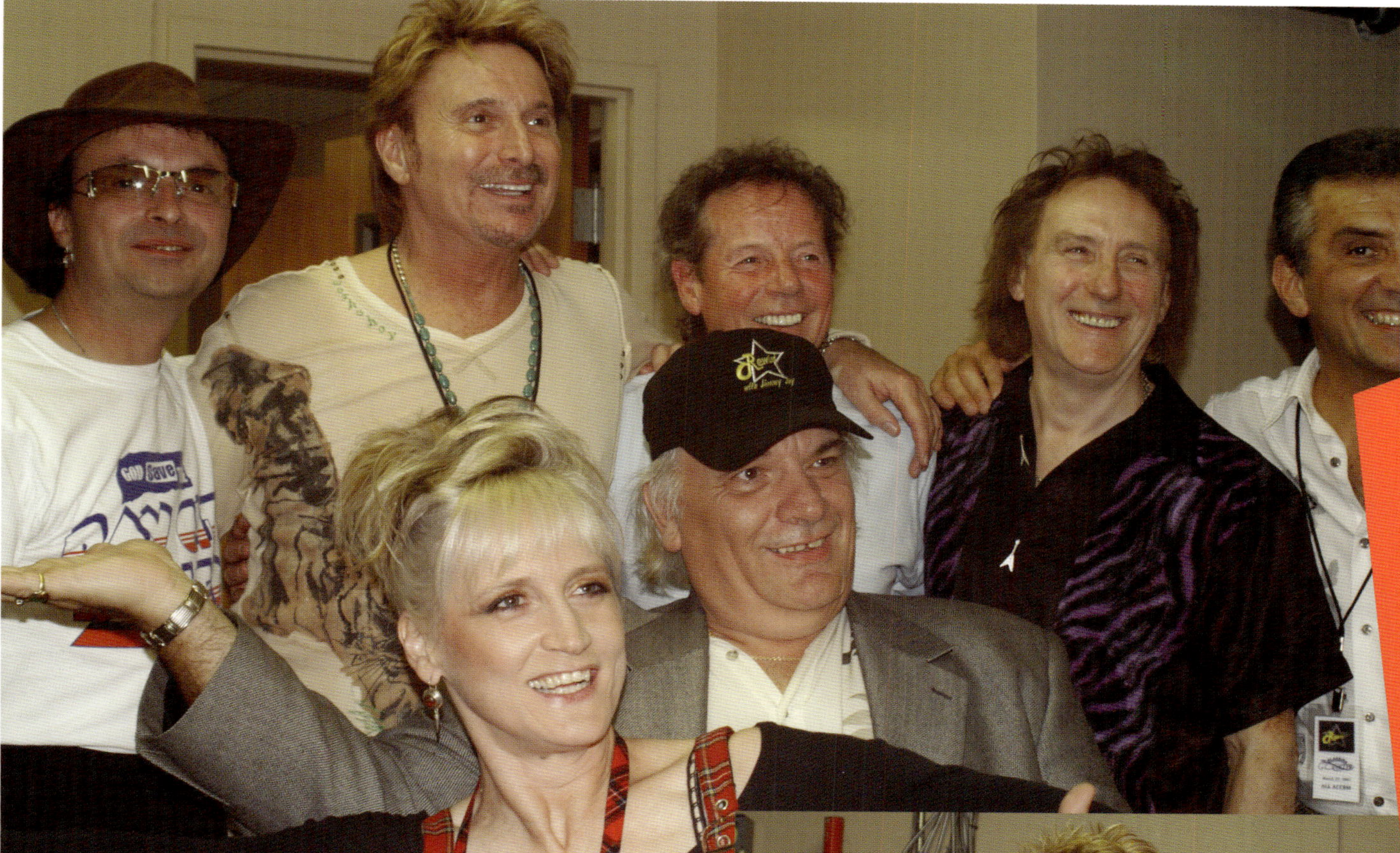

Top Row: Ian, Chuck, Pat, Denny, and Pat Benti
Bottom Row: Wendy Ann, Jimmy J

Ian, Chuck, Denny

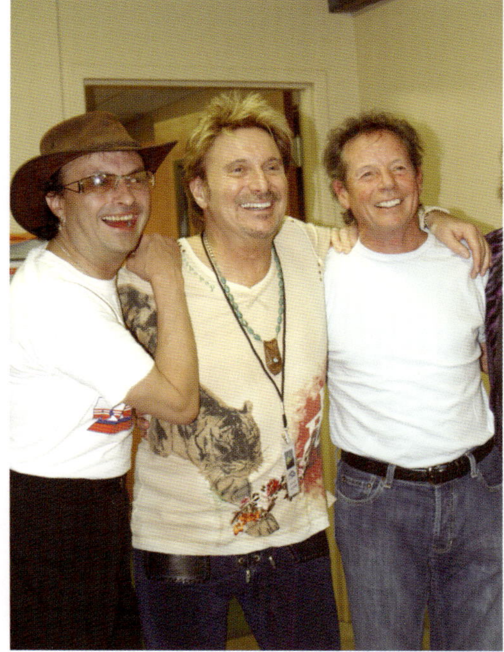

Ian, Chuck, Pat Upton

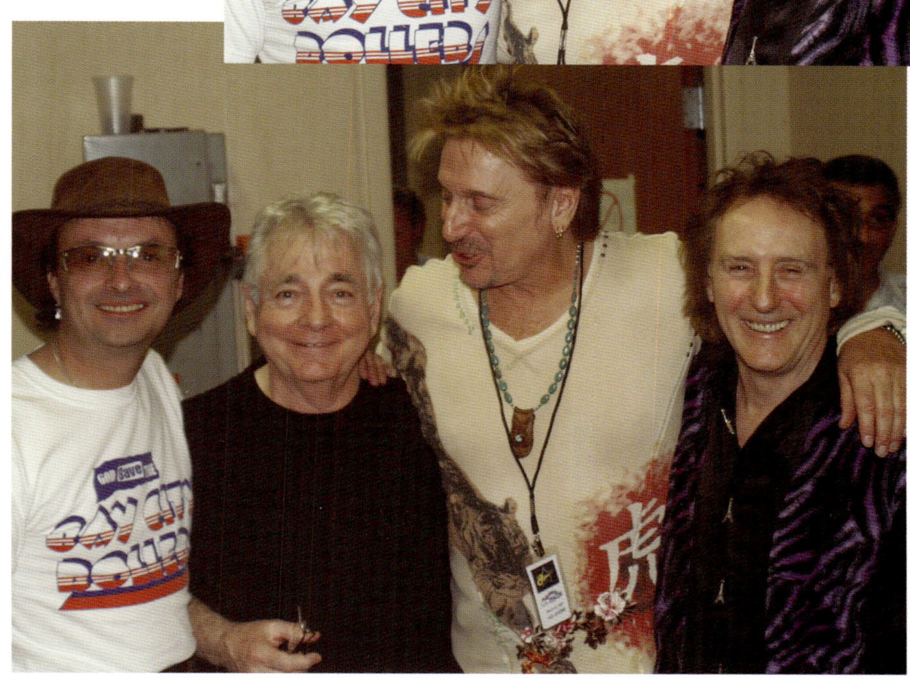

Ian, Me, Chuck, Denny

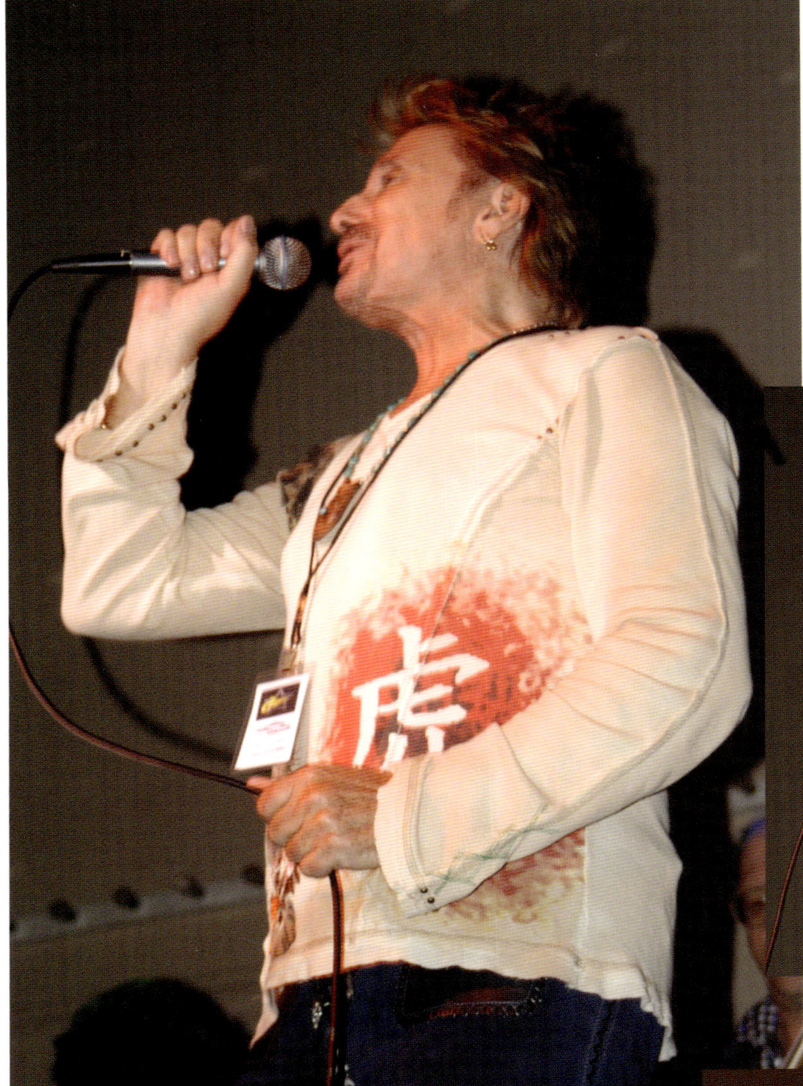

Chuck Negron

3 Dog Night
Joy to the World

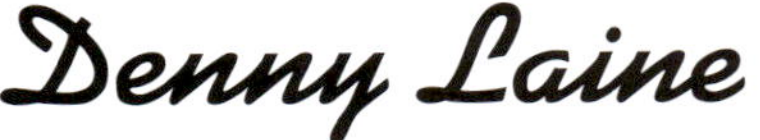

Denny Laine

Wings
Moody Blues
Band on the Run
Go Now
Time to Hide

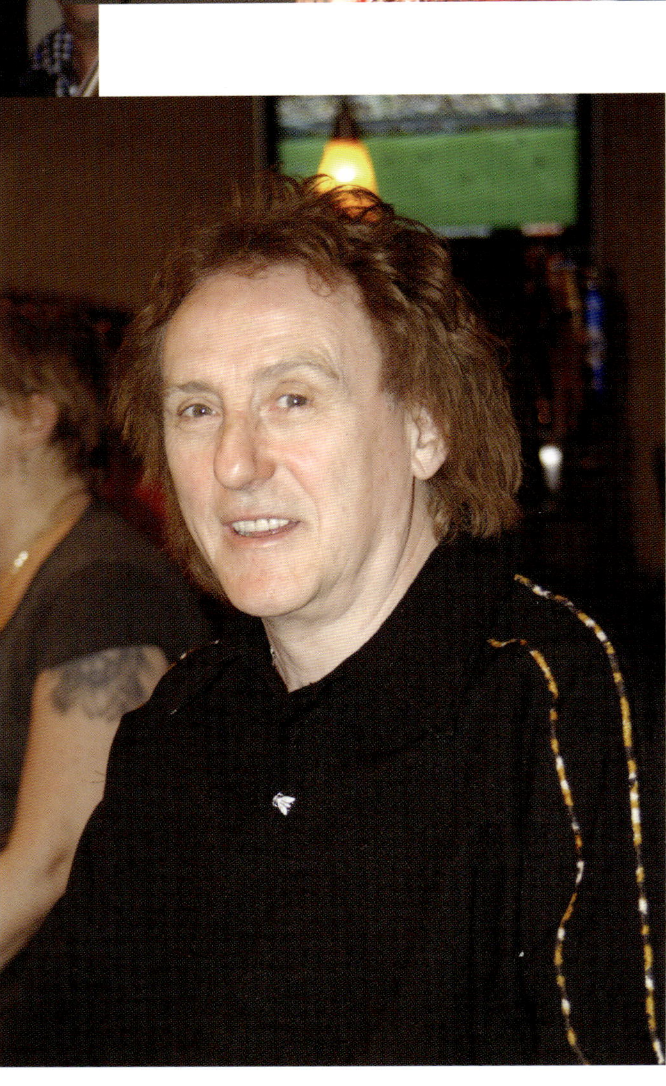

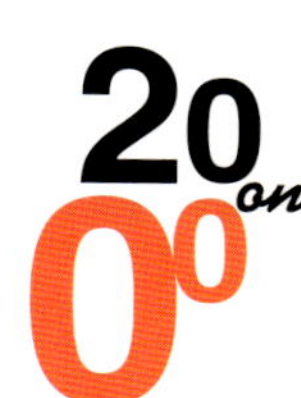

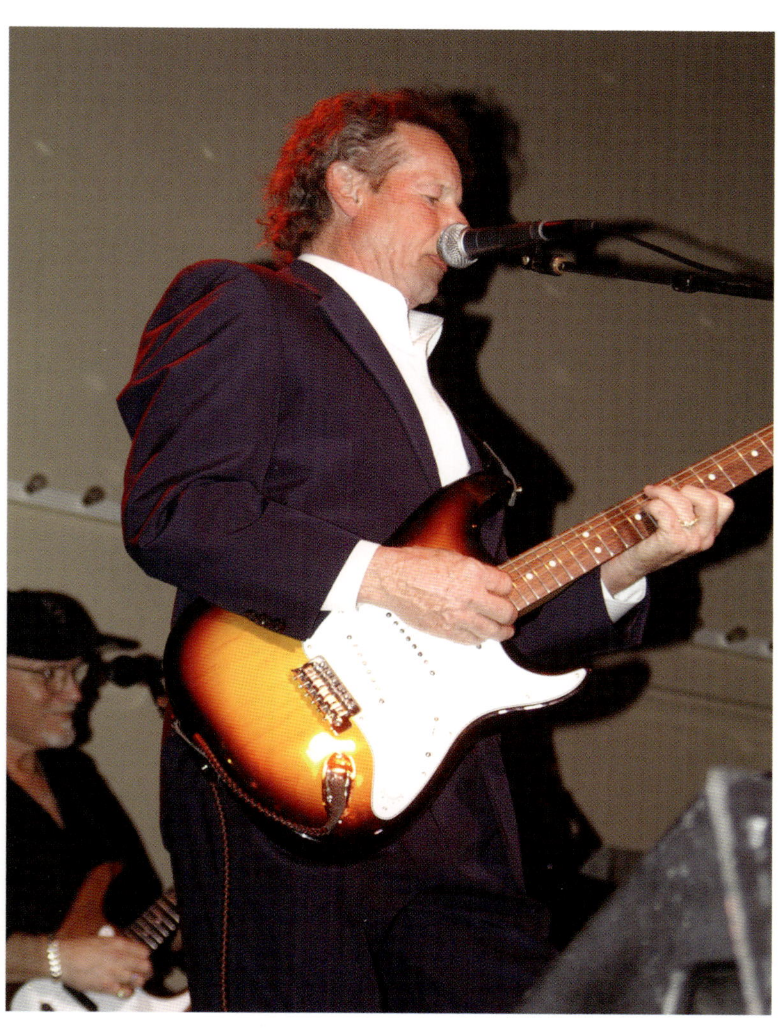

Pat Upton

Spiral Staircase
More Today Than Yesterday
Our Day Will Come
Since I Fell For You

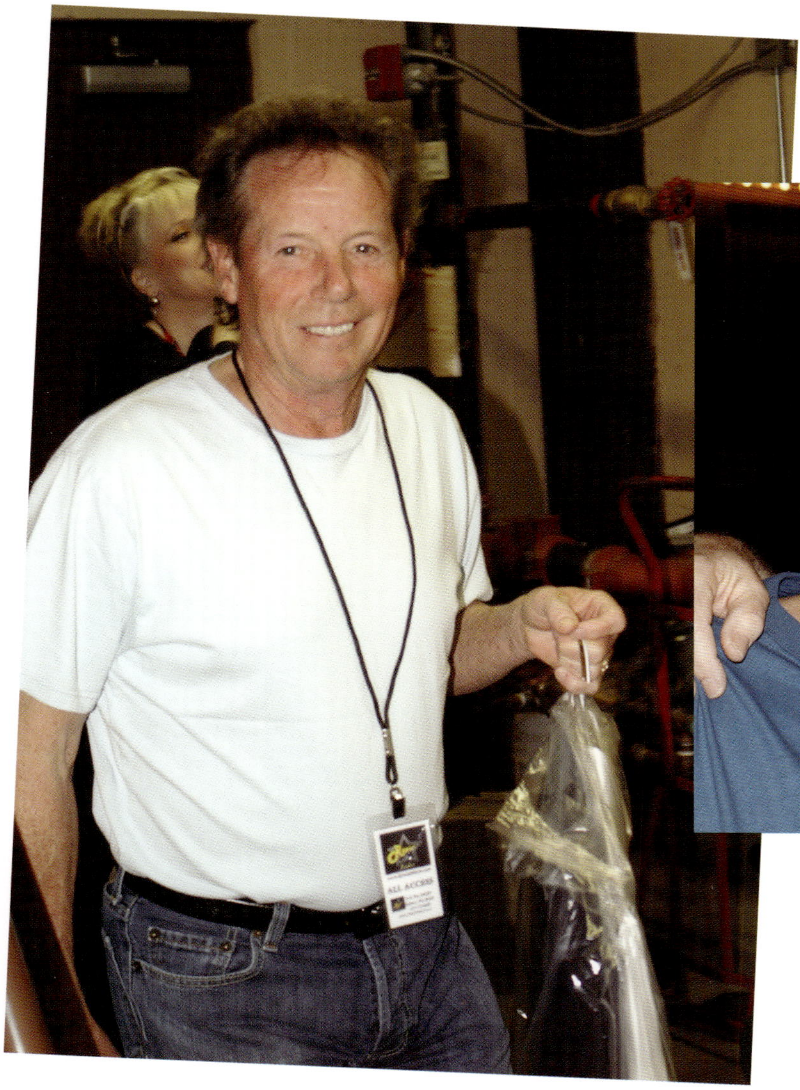

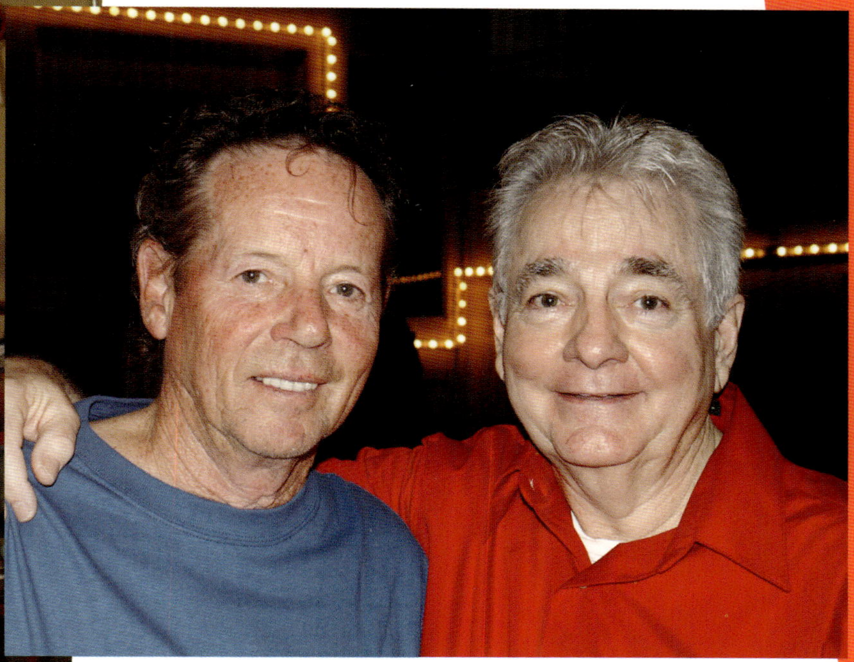

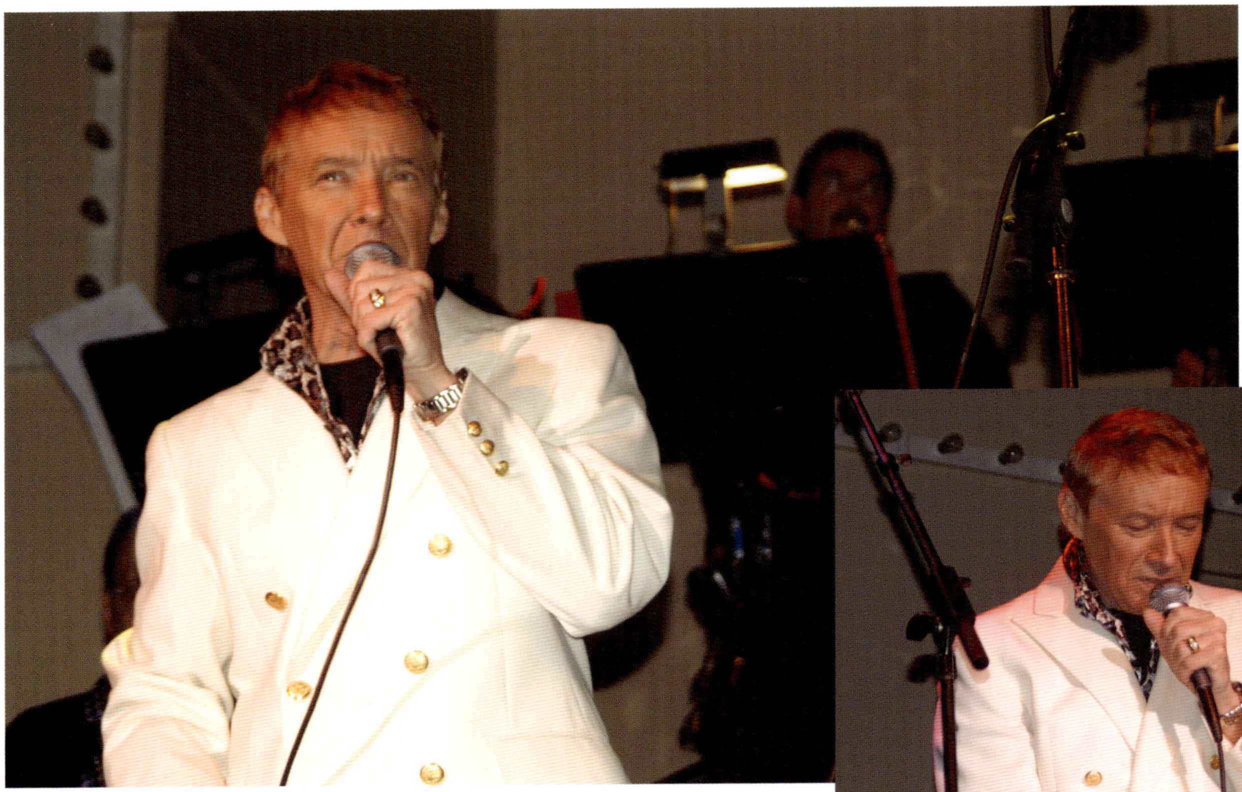

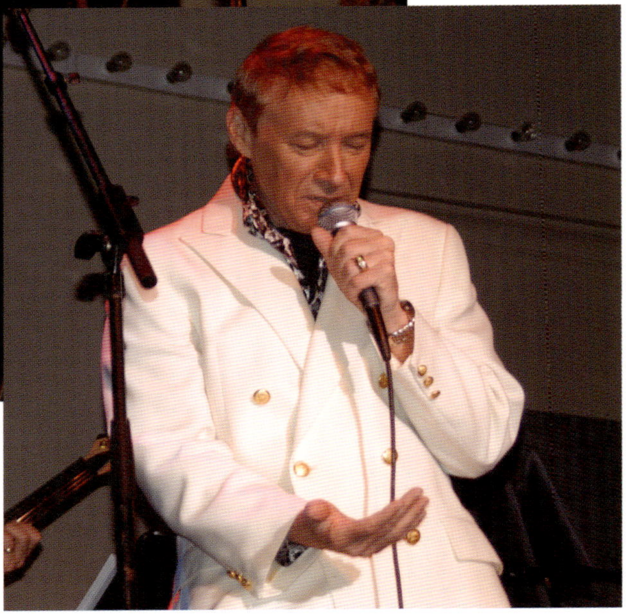

Troy Shondell

This Time We're Really Breaking Up
Slow Down
Treat Her Right

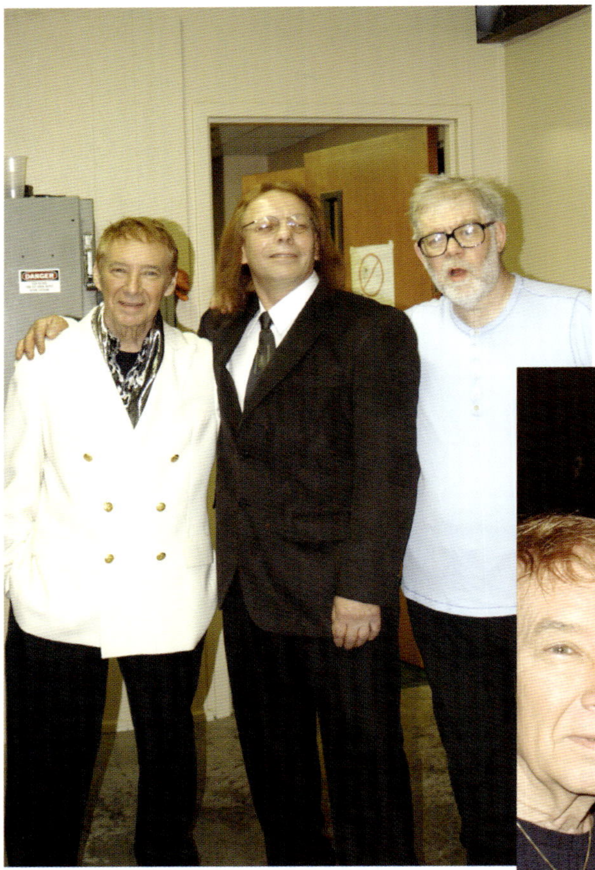

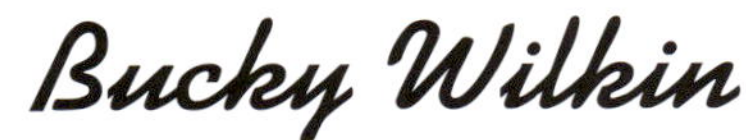

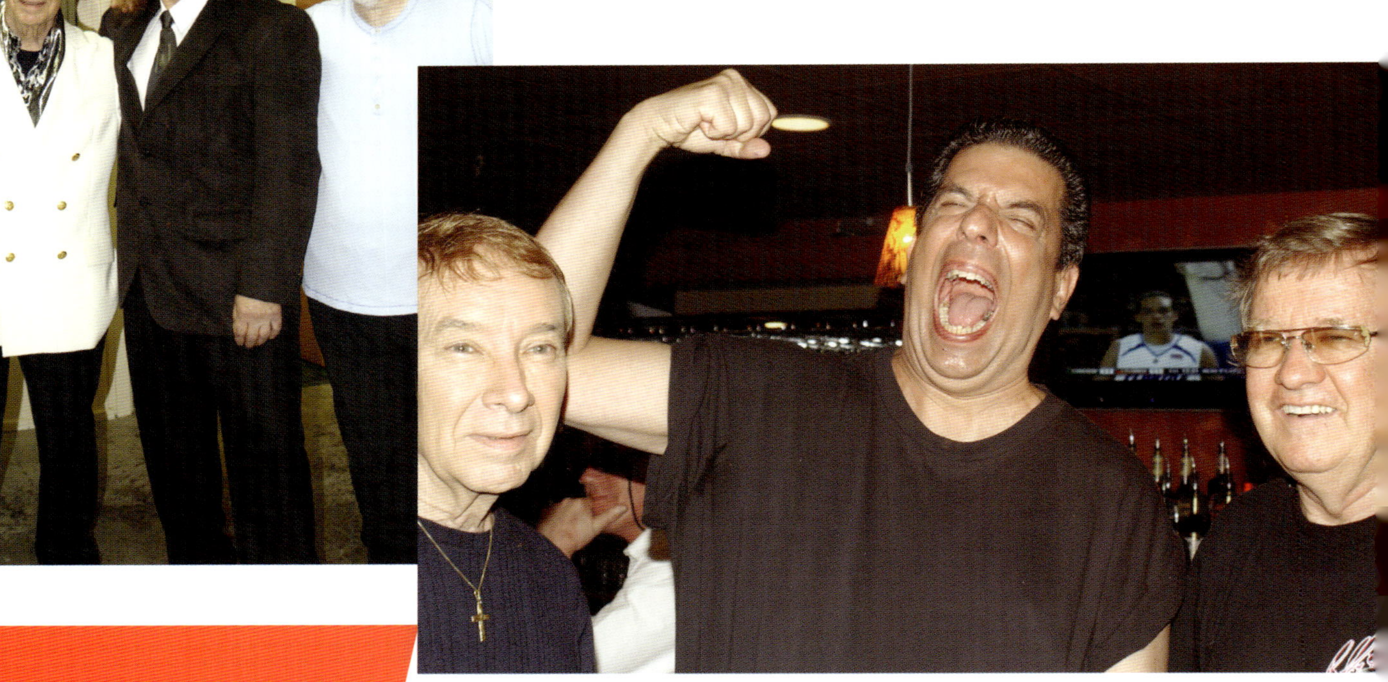

Troy Shondell and Jon "Bowzer" Bauman

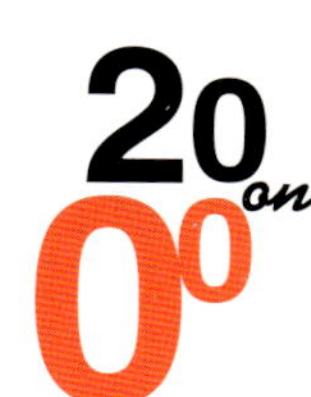

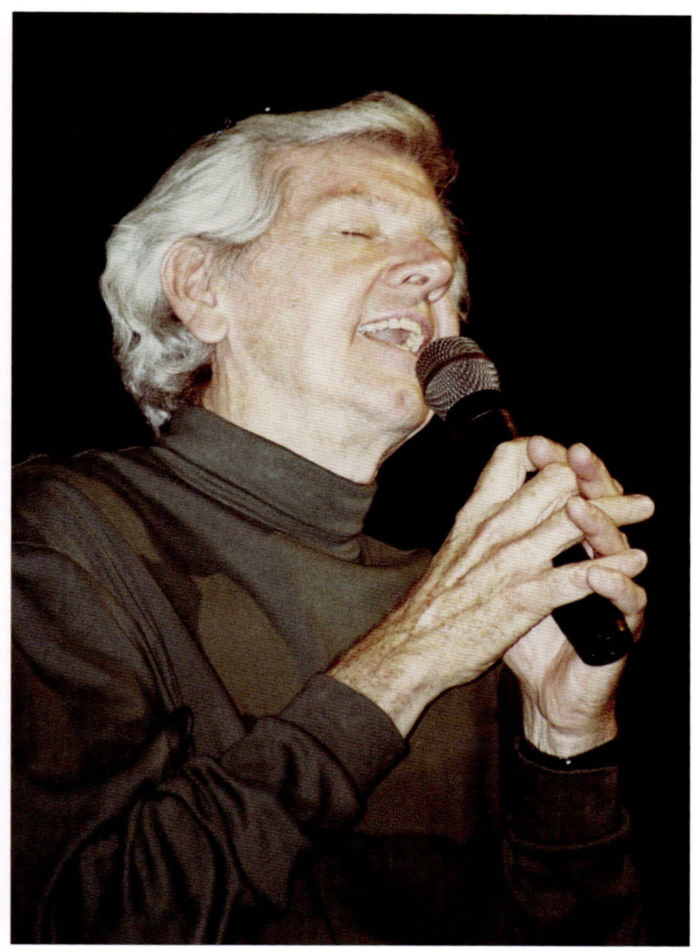

Jimmy Clanton

Just a Dream
Go Jimmy Go
Venus in Blue Jeans

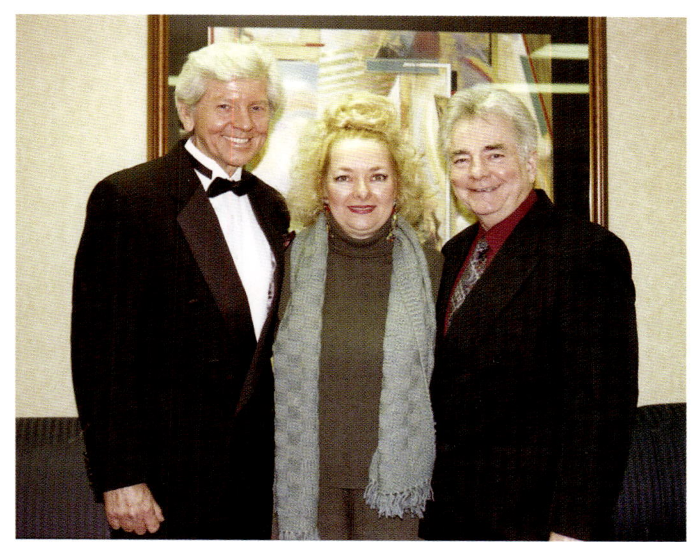

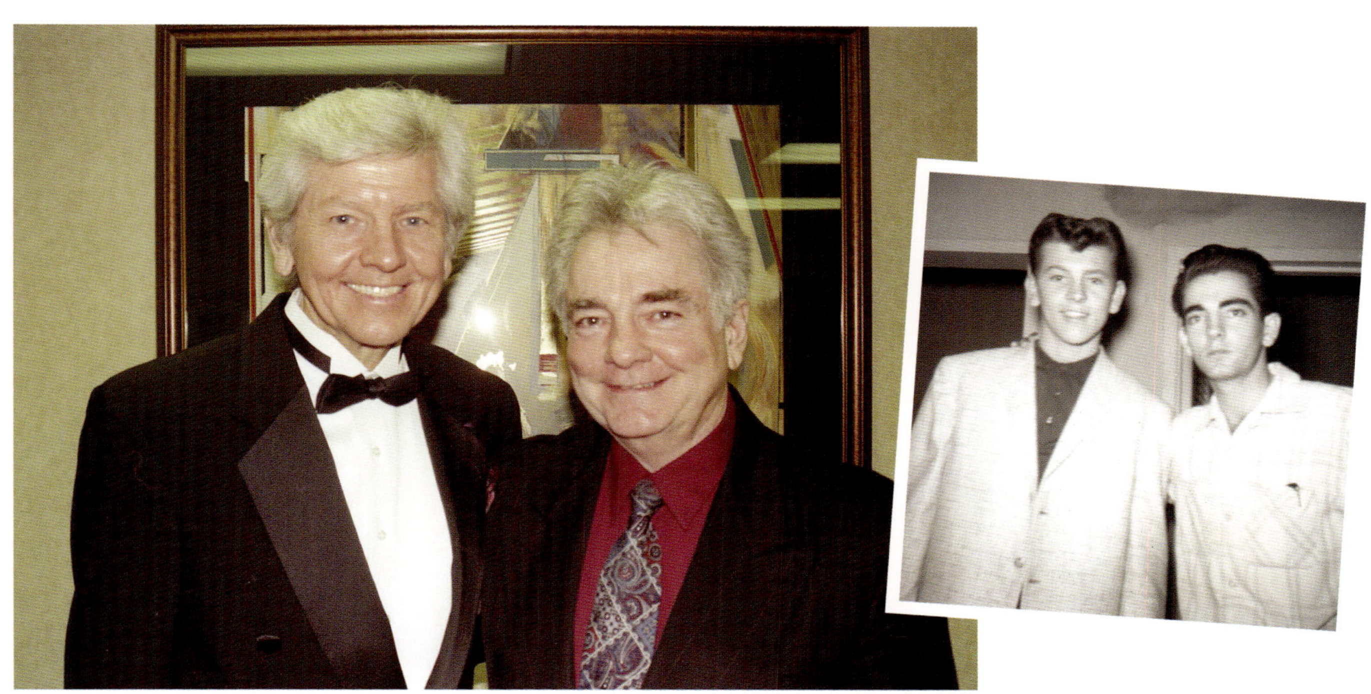

From 1958 to 2004, what a difference 46 years makes.
At least we both still have our hair even if it is “salt and pepper”.

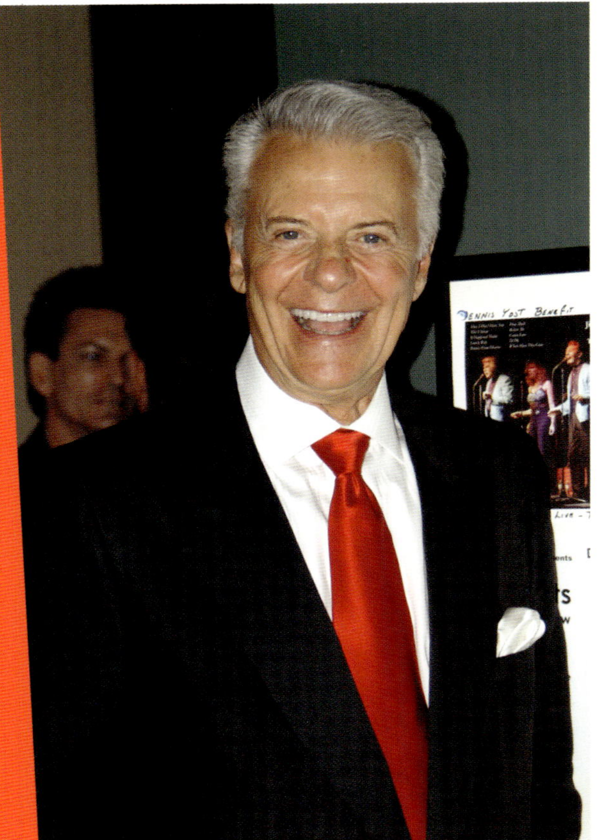

Dave Somerville and The Diamonds

Little Darlin
The Stroll
Church Bells May Ring
Walkin Along
One Summer Night

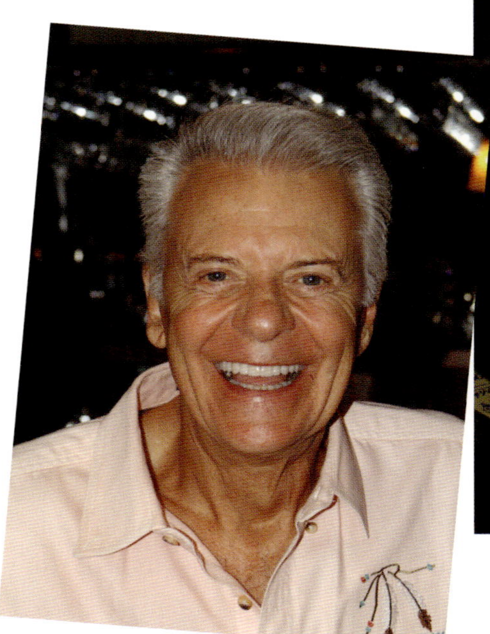

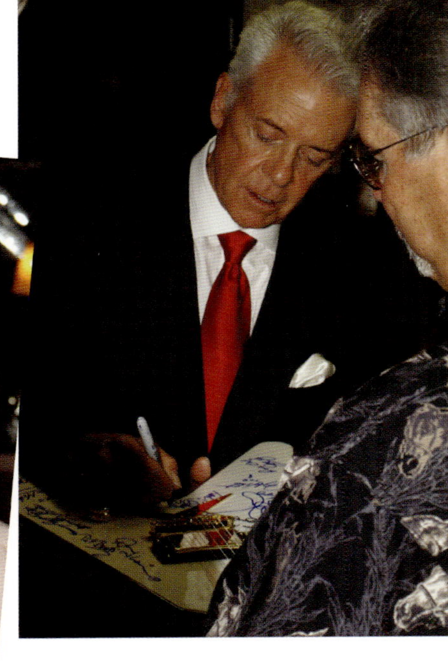

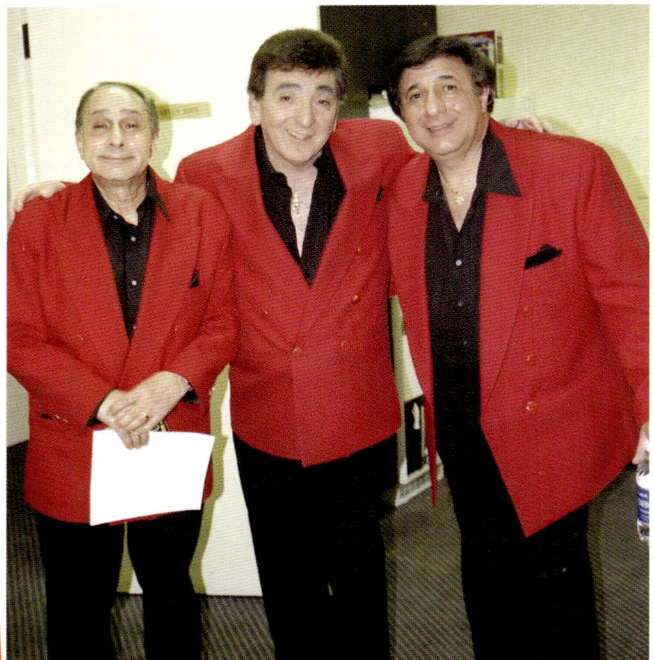

Danny and the Juniors

At The Hop, Rock and Roll Is Here To Stay

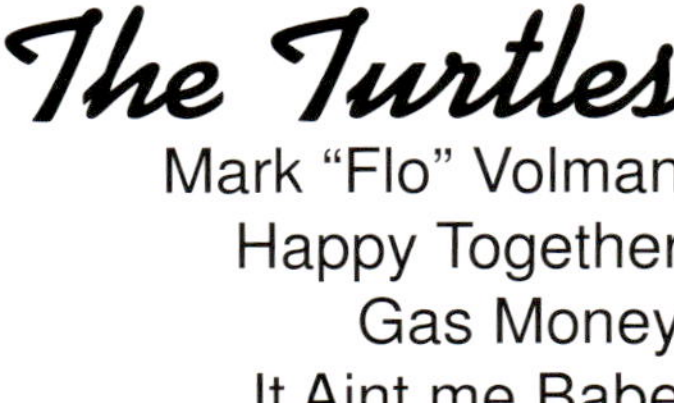

The Turtles

Mark "Flo" Volman
Happy Together
Gas Money
It Aint me Babe

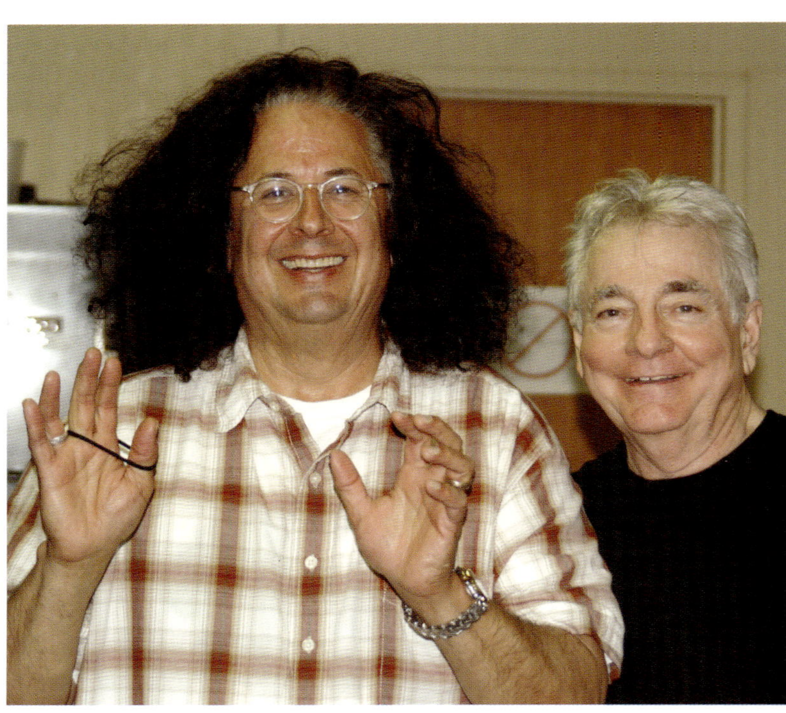

Charles Stanley

InTouch Ministries

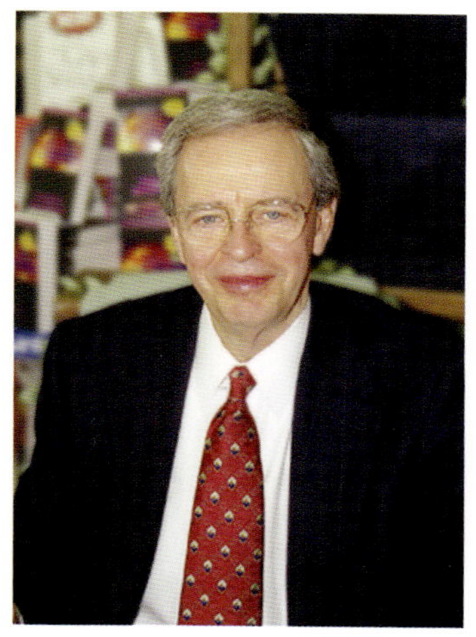

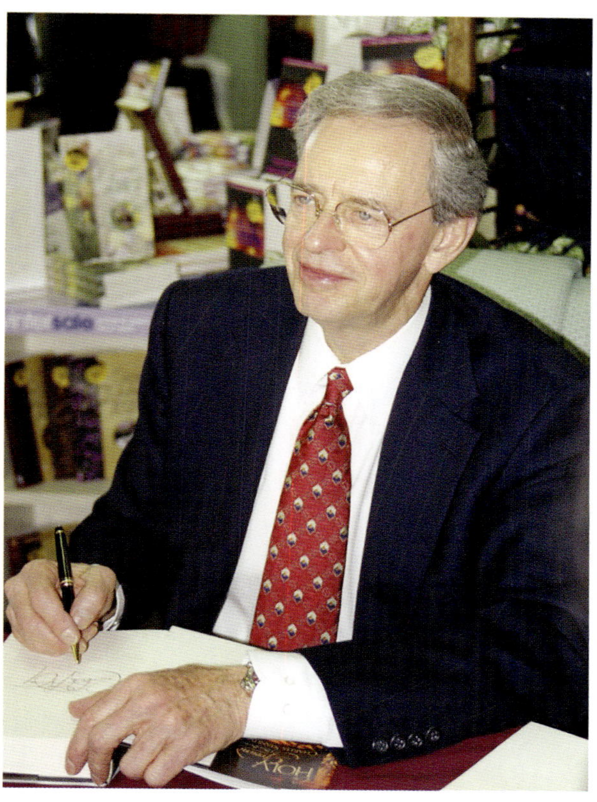

Three of my favorite teachers and pastors

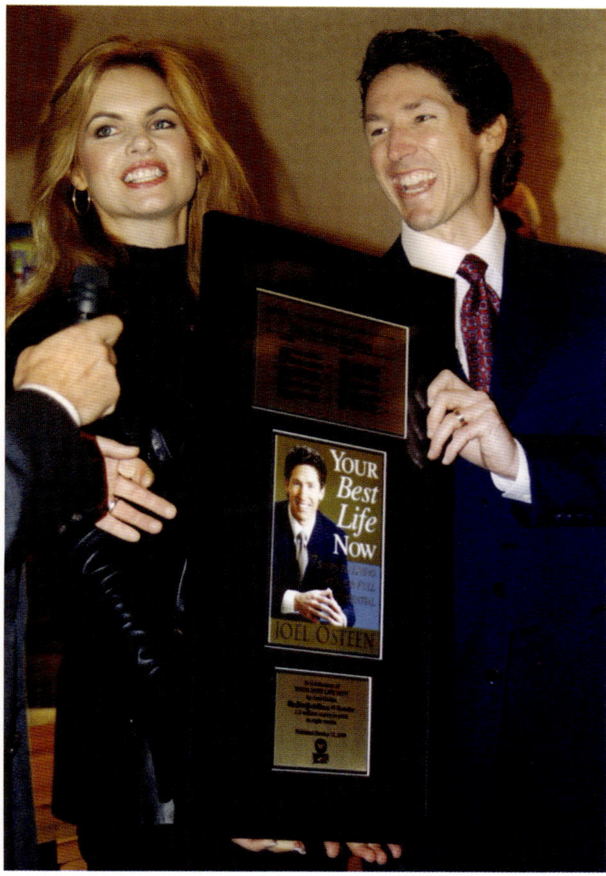

Joel Osteen receiving his #1 Best Seller Award with his wife Victoria

Joel Osteen

Victoria Osteen

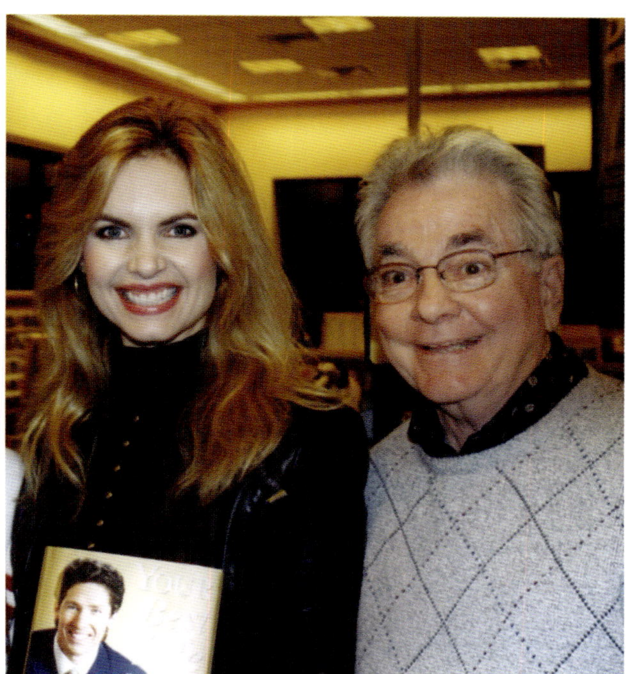

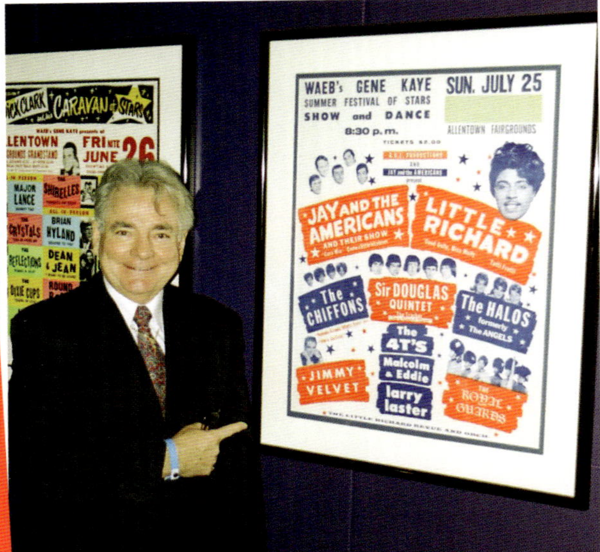

Rock N' Roll Hall of Fame Cleveland, Ohio

"Hey I was on that tour."

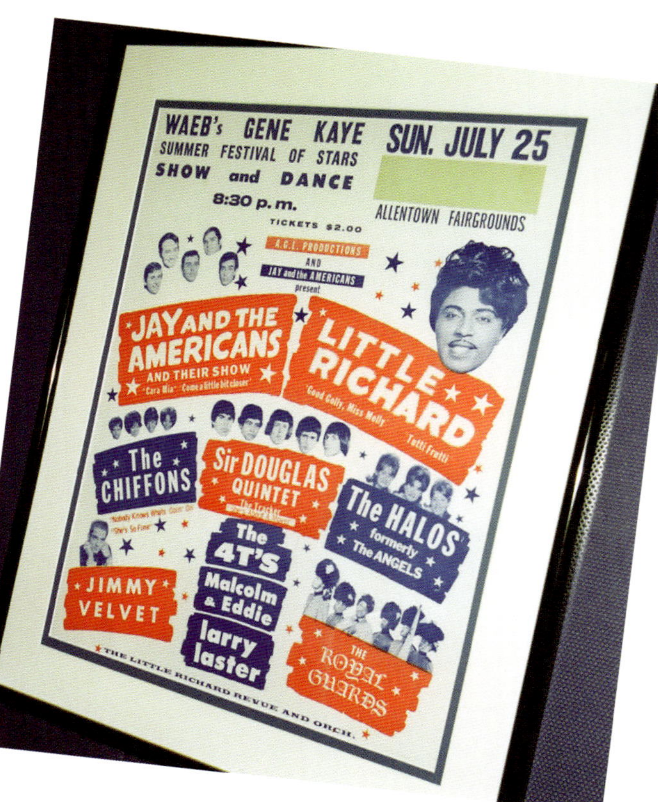

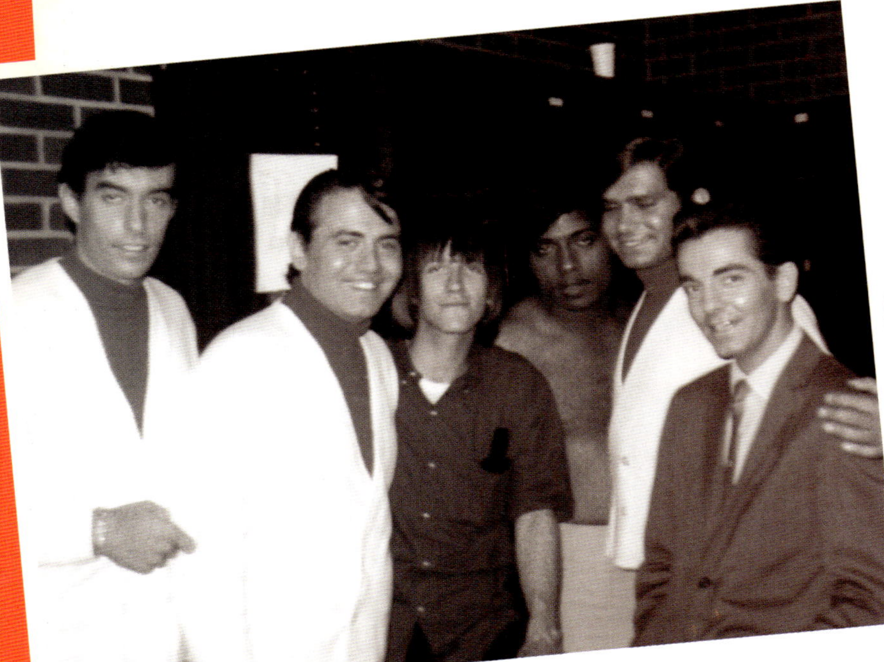

A photo from the tour with Little Richard, Jay and the American's and the Sir Douglas Quintet

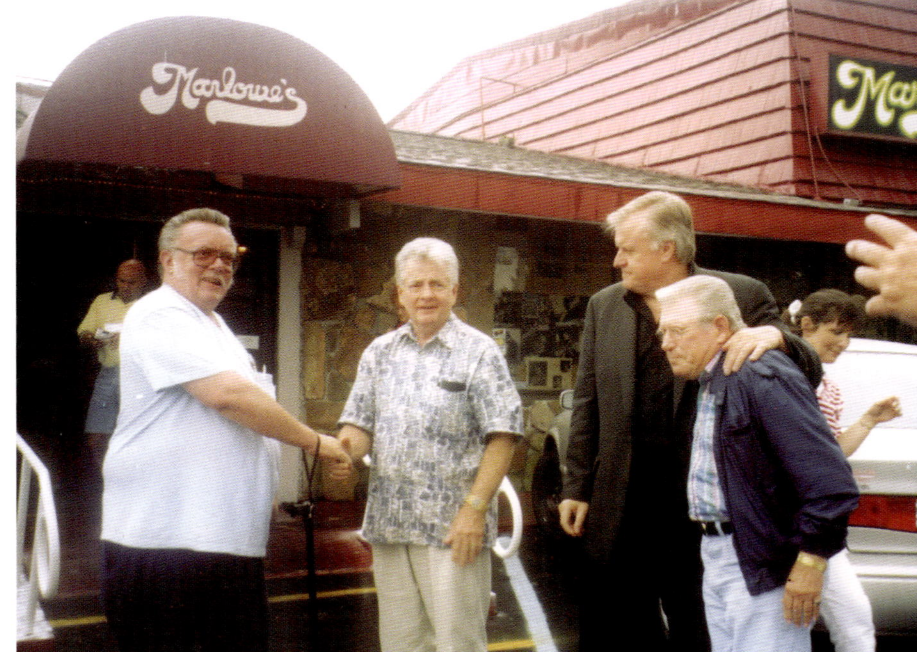

John Wilkinson and myself with Ed Enoch and Charlie Hodge

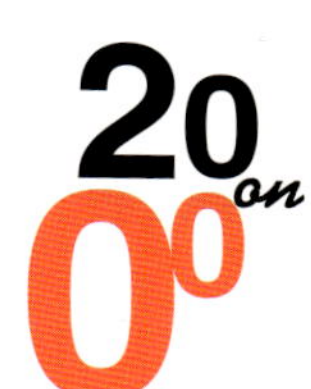

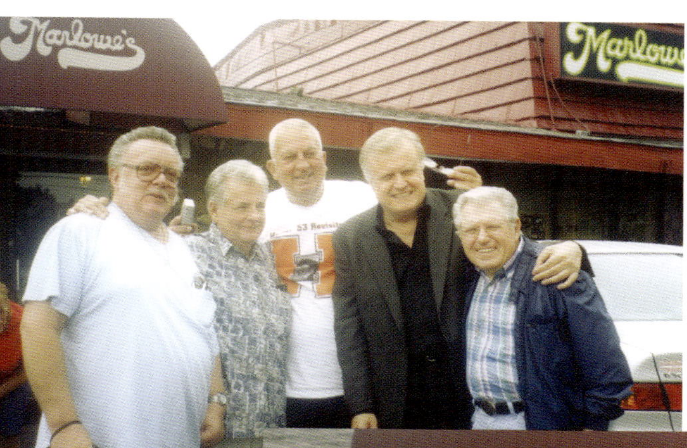

John Wilkinson, Bill Burk, Ed Enoch, Charlie Hodge

and I at our favorite spot in Memphis-Marlowe's

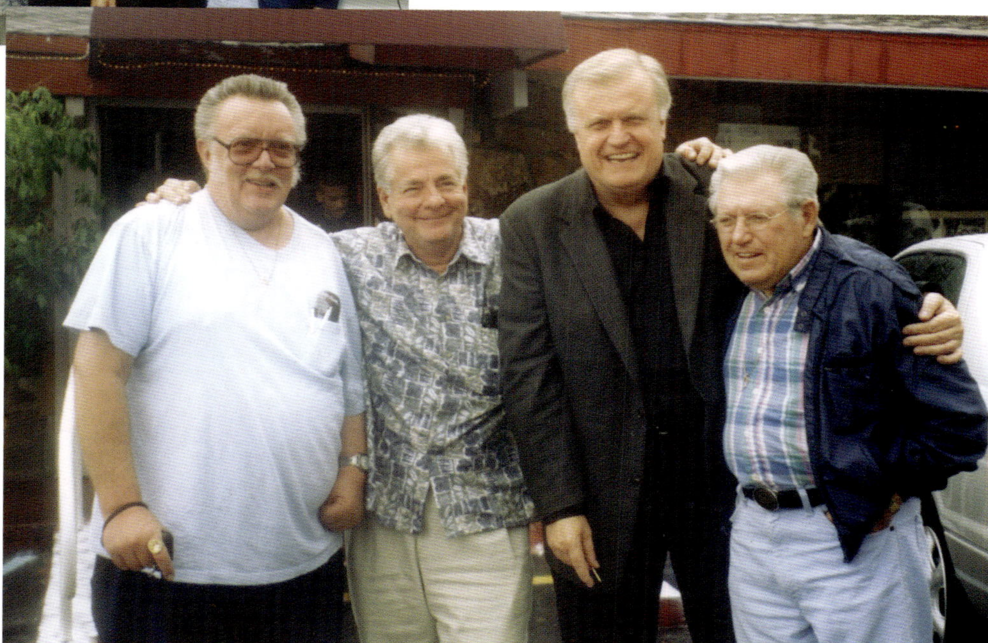

Two of my favorite ladies from the Elvis movies. I've had the pleasure of working with them for the past two years.

Cynthia Pepper

"Kissin' Cousins"

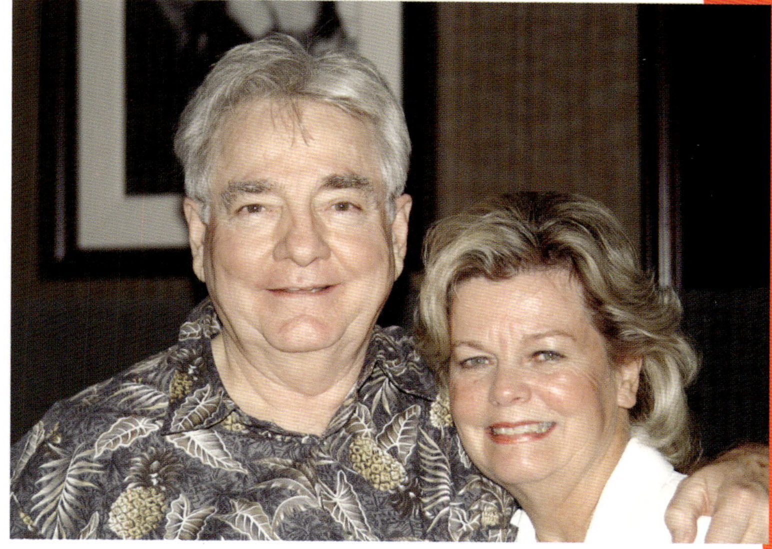

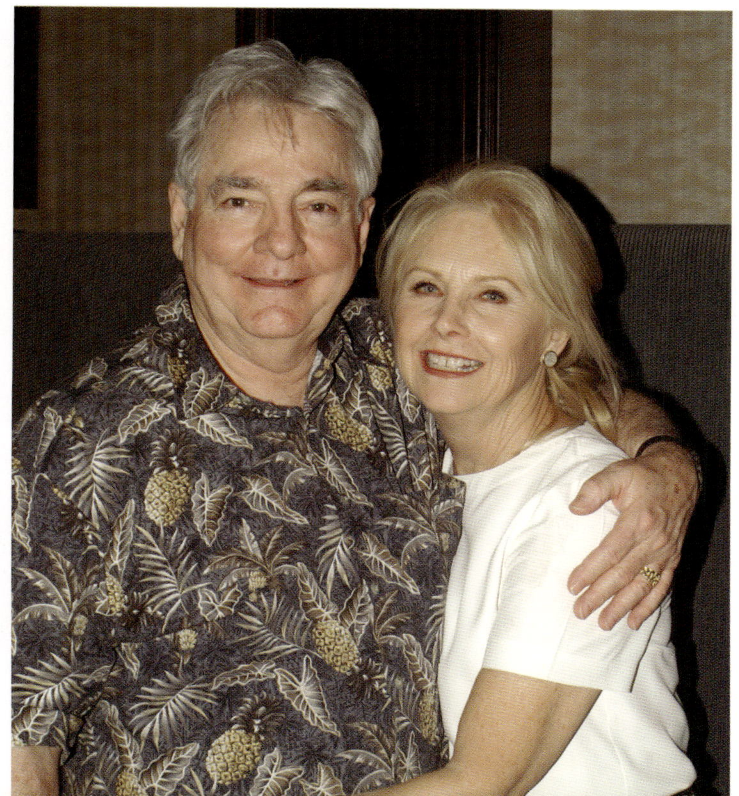

Darlene Tompkins

"Blue Hawaii"

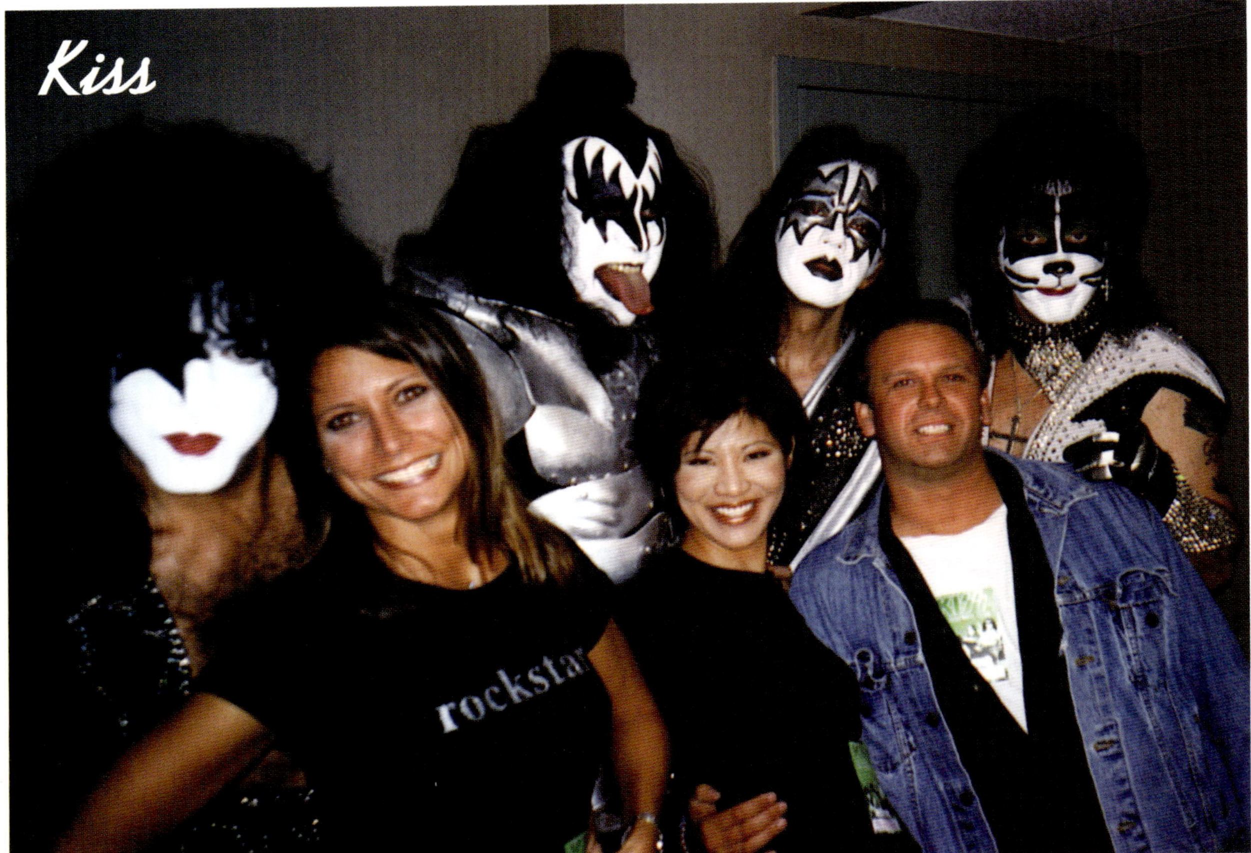

Joanne Petze, Julie Chen, Rocket Roese with Kiss. Julie Chen is now married to CBS President and CEO Les Moonves.

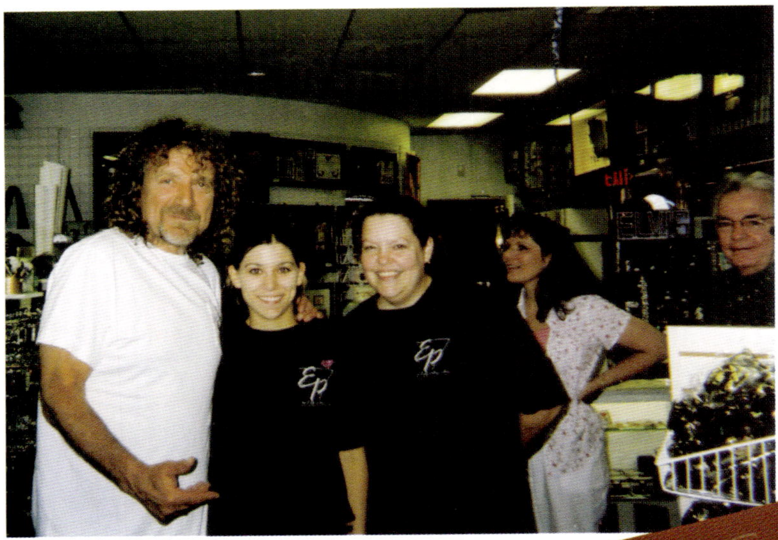

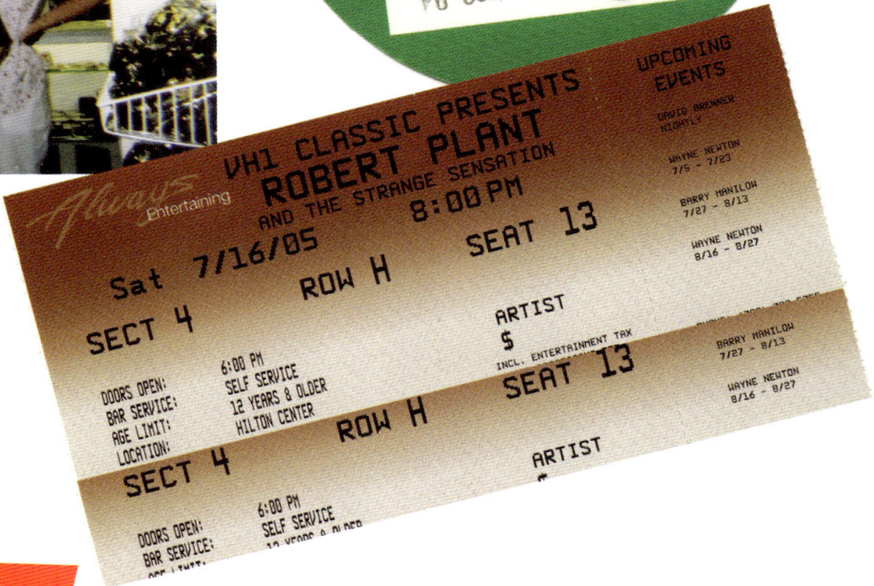

Robert Plant
with Donna Moretti, Jen Thurman, Robin and I

ROBERT PLANT AND THE STRANGE SENSATION
LIVE 2005
GUEST
PRE SHOW/AFTER SHOW
16 JUL 2005

VH1 CLASSIC PRESENTS
ROBERT PLANT
AND THE STRANGE SENSATION
Sat 7/16/05 8:00 PM
SECT 4 ROW H SEAT 13
ARTIST
DOORS OPEN: 6:00 PM
BAR SERVICE: SELF SERVICE
AGE LIMIT: 12 YEARS & OLDER
LOCATION: HILTON CENTER
UPCOMING EVENTS
WAYNE NEWTON 7/5 - 7/23
BARRY MANILOW 7/27 - 8/13
WAYNE NEWTON 8/16 - 8/27

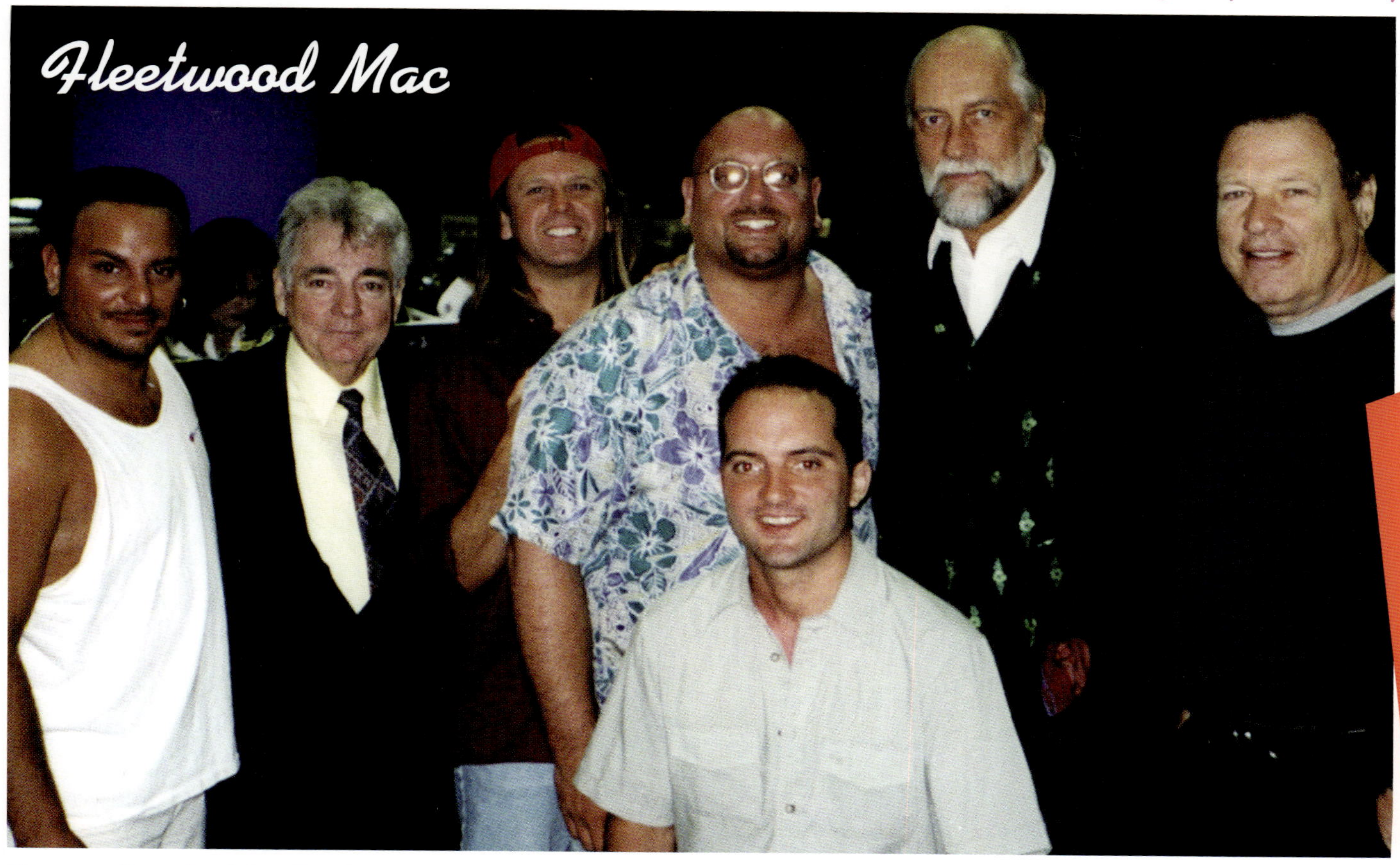

Darren Cuccia, Me, Rocket Roese, Gary Cuccia, Mick Fleetwood and Steve Binder.

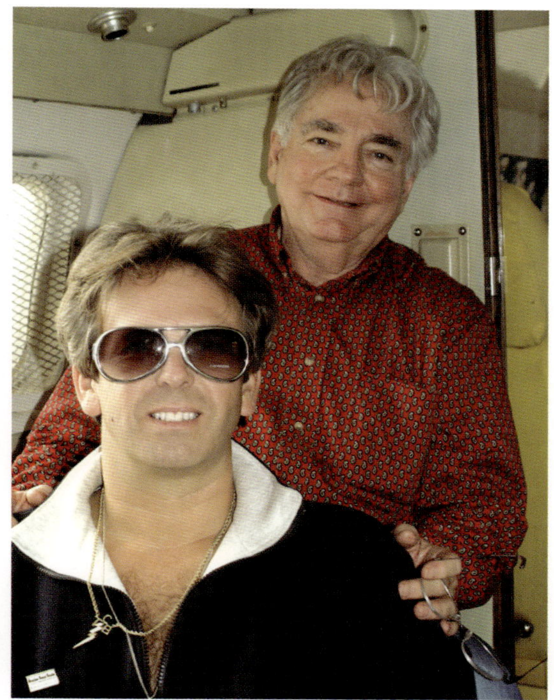

Rocket Roese and I on Hound Dog, Elvis' Lockheed Jet Star

Rocket Roese

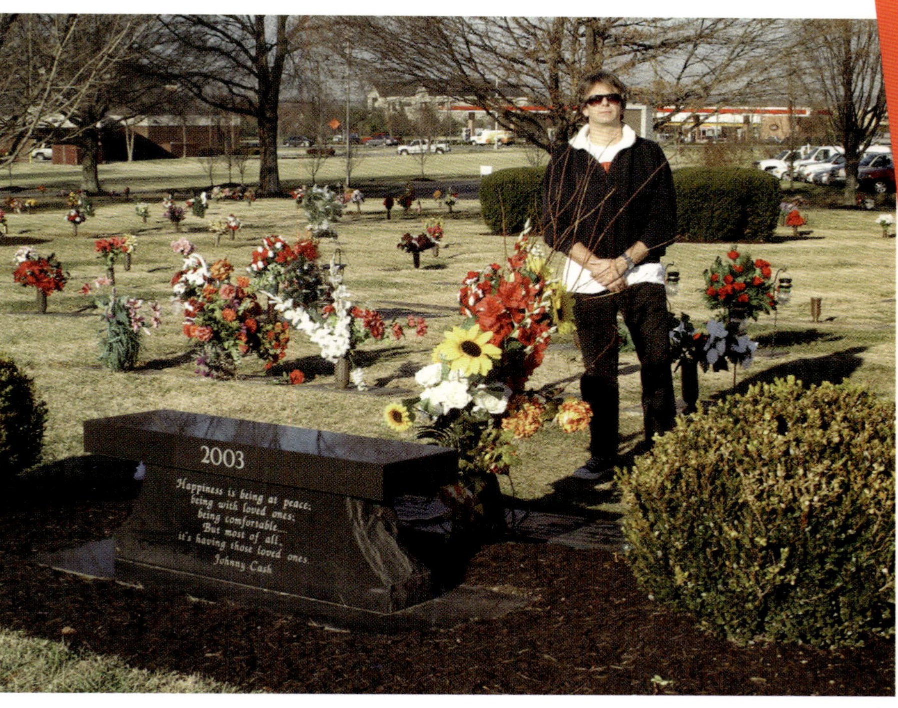

Rocket Roese at Johnny Cash's Grave
Hendersonville, Tennessee

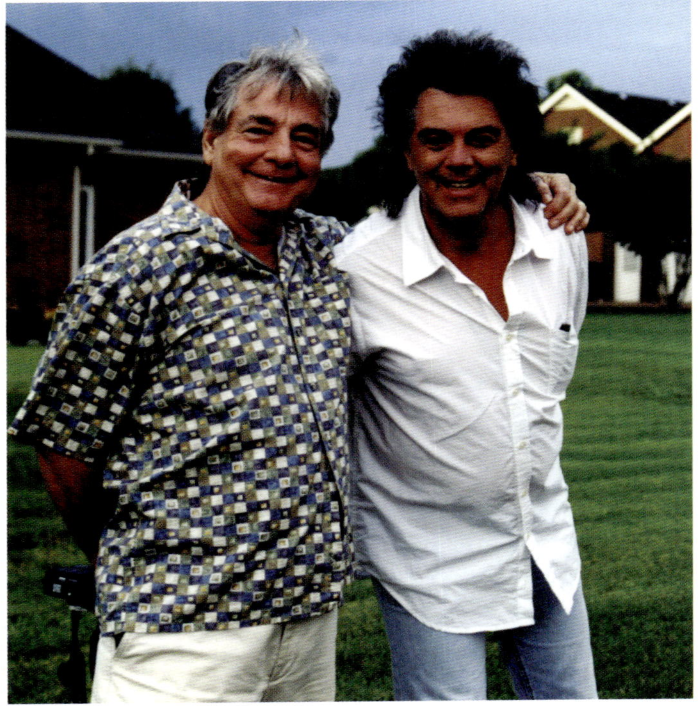

Marty Stuart

My friend and neighbor

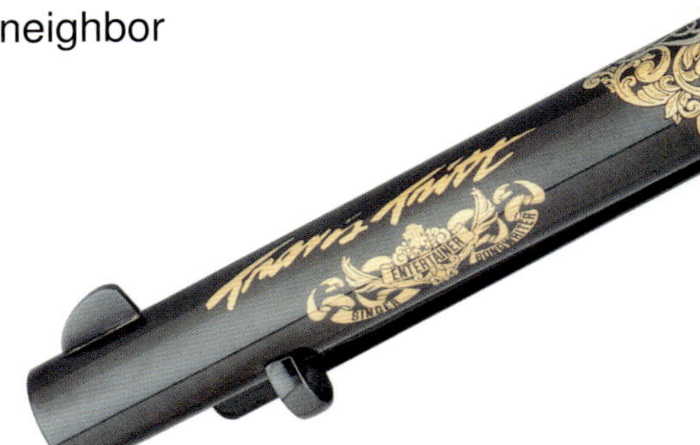

I had the privilege of working with America Remembers in the production of these commemorative firearms honoring Travis Tritt, George Jones and Johnny Cash.

Tricia Yearwood

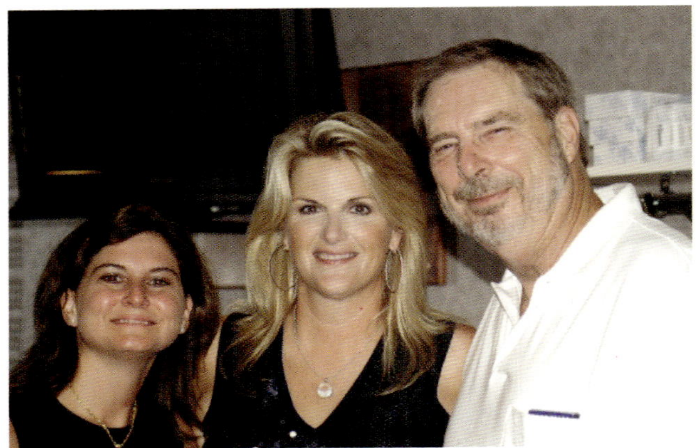

Tricia with Mr. and Mrs. Dick Grob

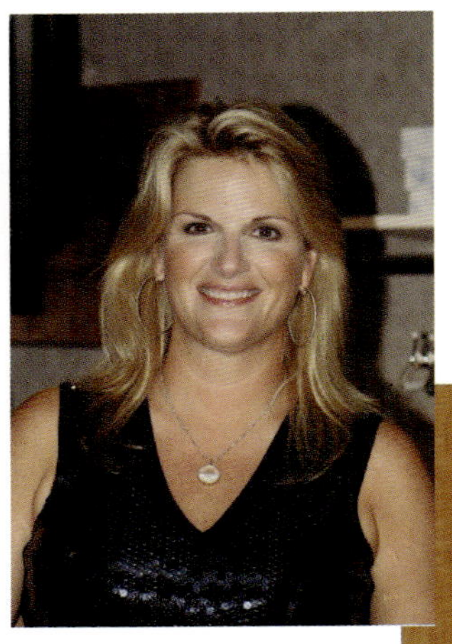

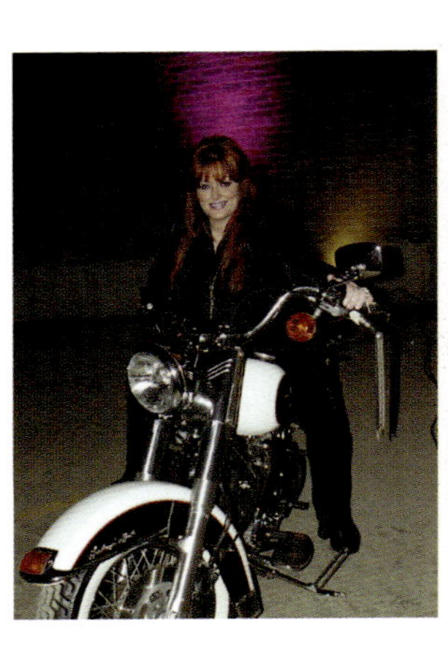

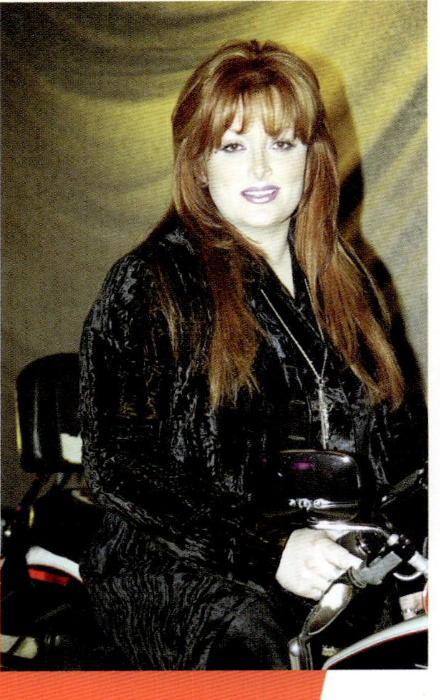

Wynonna

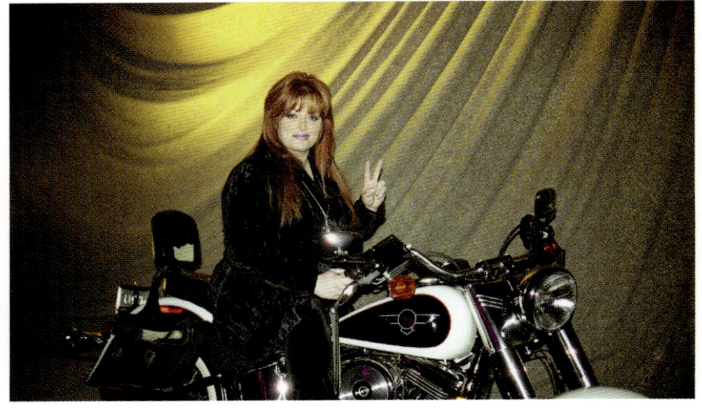

She is such a sweetheart and dear friend, we love her so much.

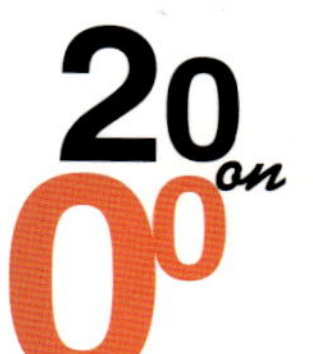

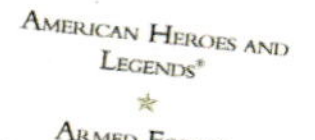

American Heroes and Legends®
★
Armed Forces Commemorative Society®

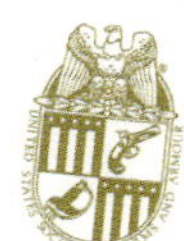

10226 Timber Ridge Drive
★
Ashland, Virginia 23005
★
804-550-9616
Fax 804-550-9603
www.americaremembers.com

America Remembers®
United States Society of Arms and Armour®

Paul J. Warden, *Chairman/President, America Remembers*
Les Line, *Author/Conservationist*
Antique Arms Committee
Michael Korda, *Editor-in-Chief, Simon & Schuster, Inc.*
E. Duston Saunders, *Lt. Col. USAR Ret., College Pistol Coach*
Dale Berry, *Actor/Entertainer*
Jeffery Belcher, *Historical Advisor, United States Society of Arms and Armour*

April 11, 2007

Mr. Jimmy Velvet

Dear Jimmy,

First of all, I want to congratulate you on your upcoming book. With all your years of experience in the entertainment field, I'm sure it will be a great success. And I'm especially excited to see your extensive collection of celebrity photographs, which I know will surely bring back many fond memories for your readers.

I also want to thank you for all the work you've done with America Remembers in the past. Through your assistance, we have been able to produce and issue some very memorable commemorative firearms, honoring such legends as Johnny Cash, Travis Tritt, and George Jones. Jeffrey Belcher and I certainly enjoyed our visit with you in Nashville and our tour of your beautiful museum. We had a wonderful time, and were especially honored to have been able to arrange a meeting with Nancy Jones during our stay. It was a special day that we will never forget.

Again, thank you for all your kind help. I wish you the best of luck with your book and every future endeavor.

Best Wishes,

Paul J. Warden
Paul J. Warden
President

W~sc

HOUSE OF CASH

Dear Friend,

I wanted to tell you personally how excited I am about the Johnny Cash Golden Tribute Texas Paterson Revolver issued by American Heroes and Legends.

These people have a terrific reputation for putting out first quality firearms, and with this one they've really outdone themselves.

When they first suggested a Johnny Cash firearm to me, I said, "Great! Let's issue the Paterson Revolver". This gun played an important part in establishing the legend of Samuel Colt, and you can see for yourself how good-looking it is. It's also very rare to find an original Paterson in good condition, and therefore, very few collectors can actually have one in their collection.

I was once lucky enough to have an original Colt Paterson. I am looking forward to adding this new Paterson to my collection. I assure you this one has everything I loved about the original, plus beautiful gold decorations created especially for this occasion, including the names of eight of my favorite songs on the barrel. The result is a first-class firearm that gets my whole-hearted endorsement.

This is a gun I'm proud to have my name on, and once you display it in your home, you're going to love it as much as I do.

Best Wishes,

Johnny Cash
Johnny Cash

The George Jones single action revolver

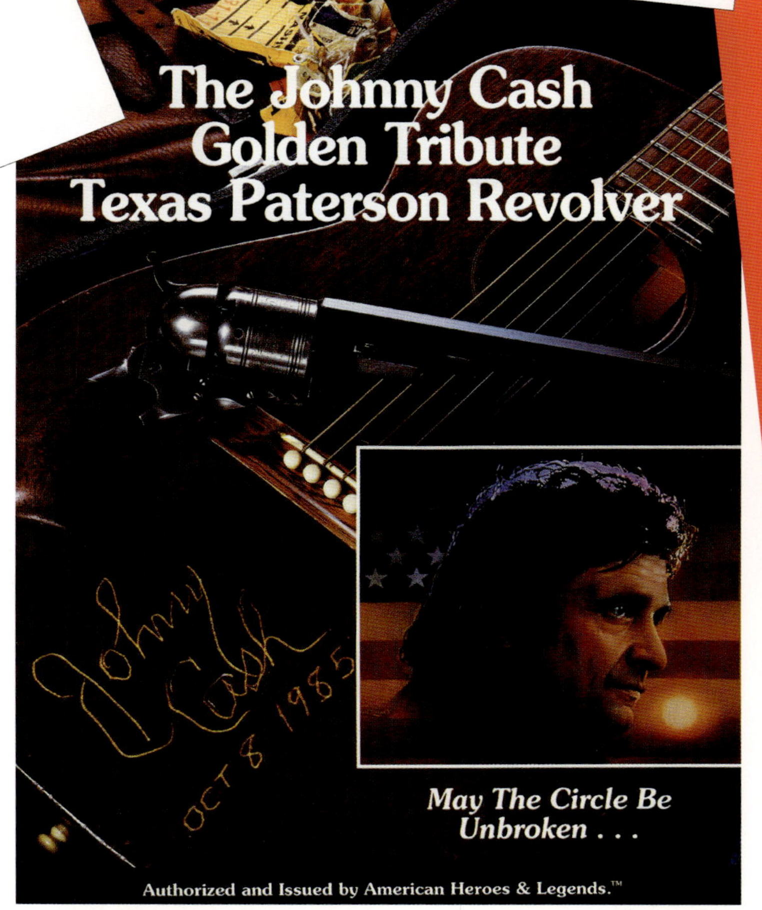

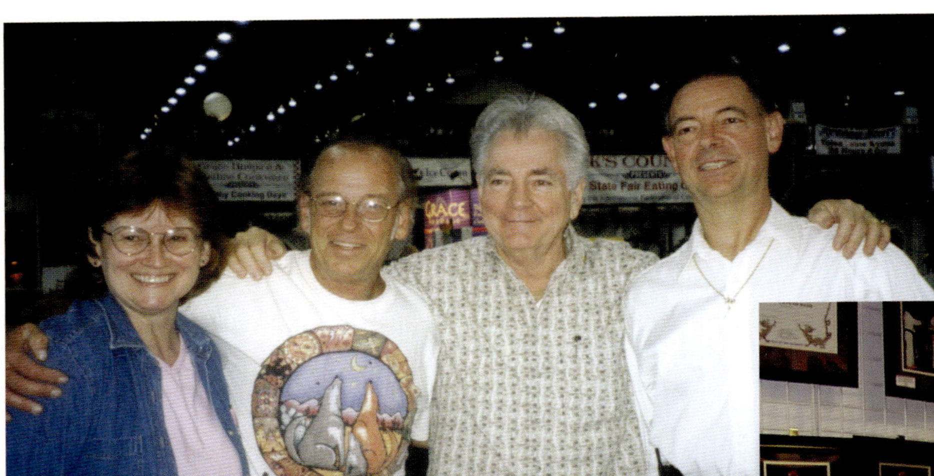

Betty Harper (Elvis Artist), Stanley Oberst, Me and Jerry Osborne

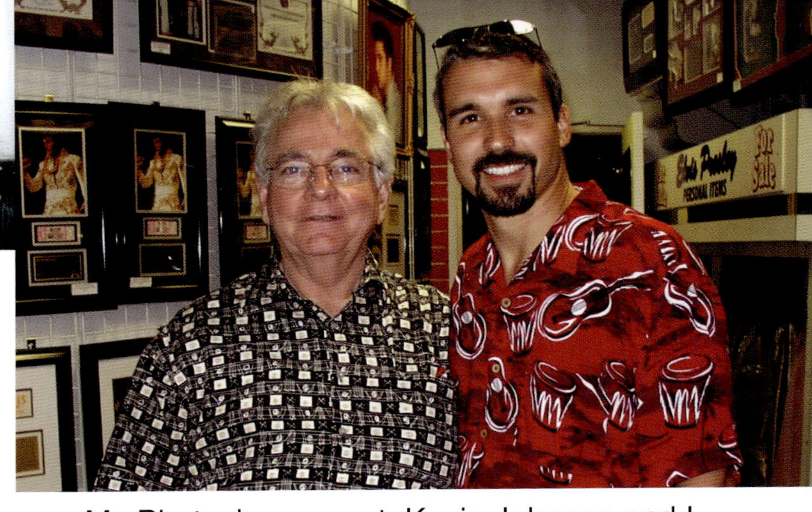

My Photoshop expert, Kevin Johnson and I at the Elvis-A-Rama Museum in Las Vegas.

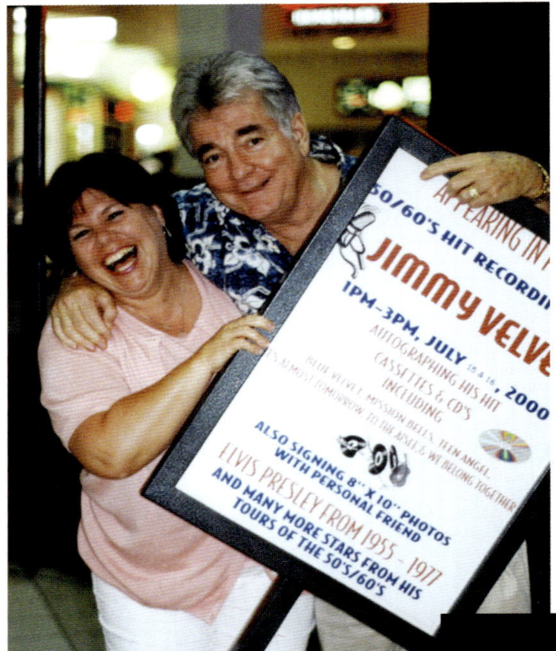

Cheryl Ruby, Robin's best friend who helps her keep it together, while Robin is helping me keep it together!

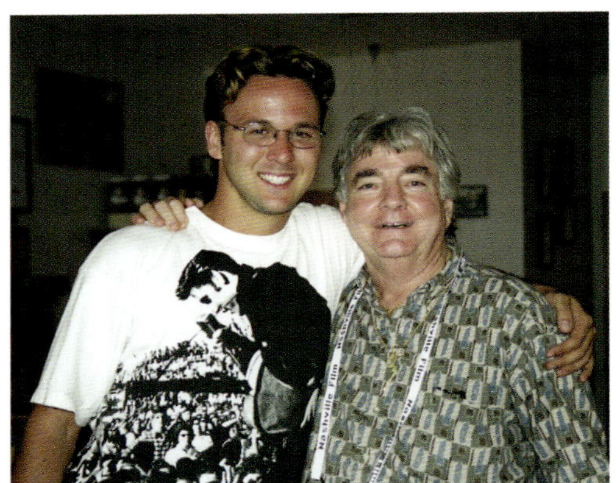

Chad Givens

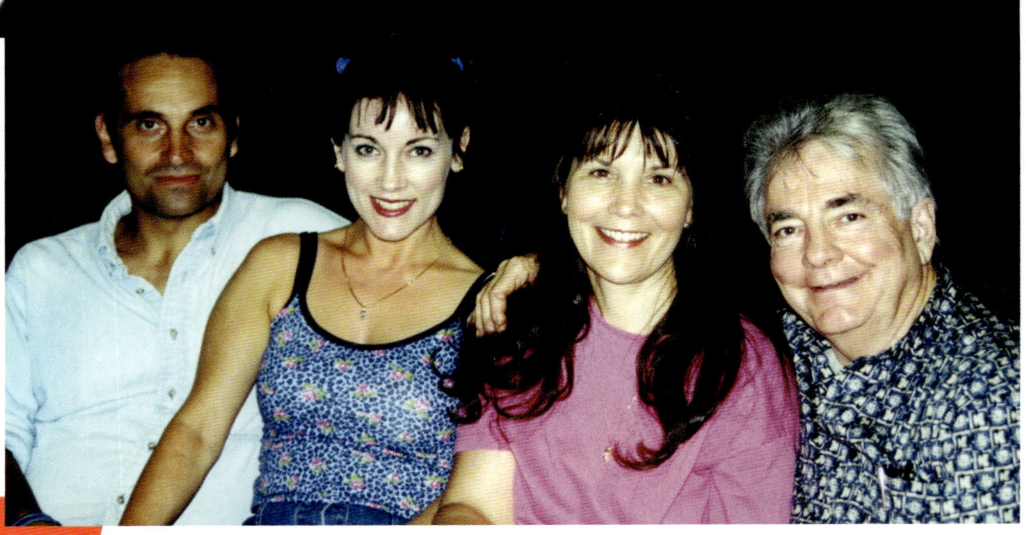

Steven, Kimmy, Robin and I
Our dear friends from "Down Under"

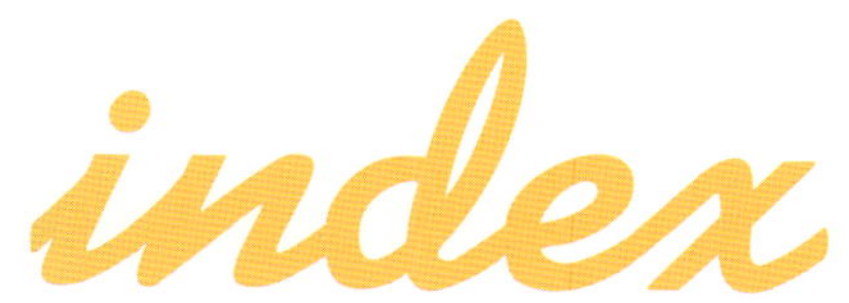

index

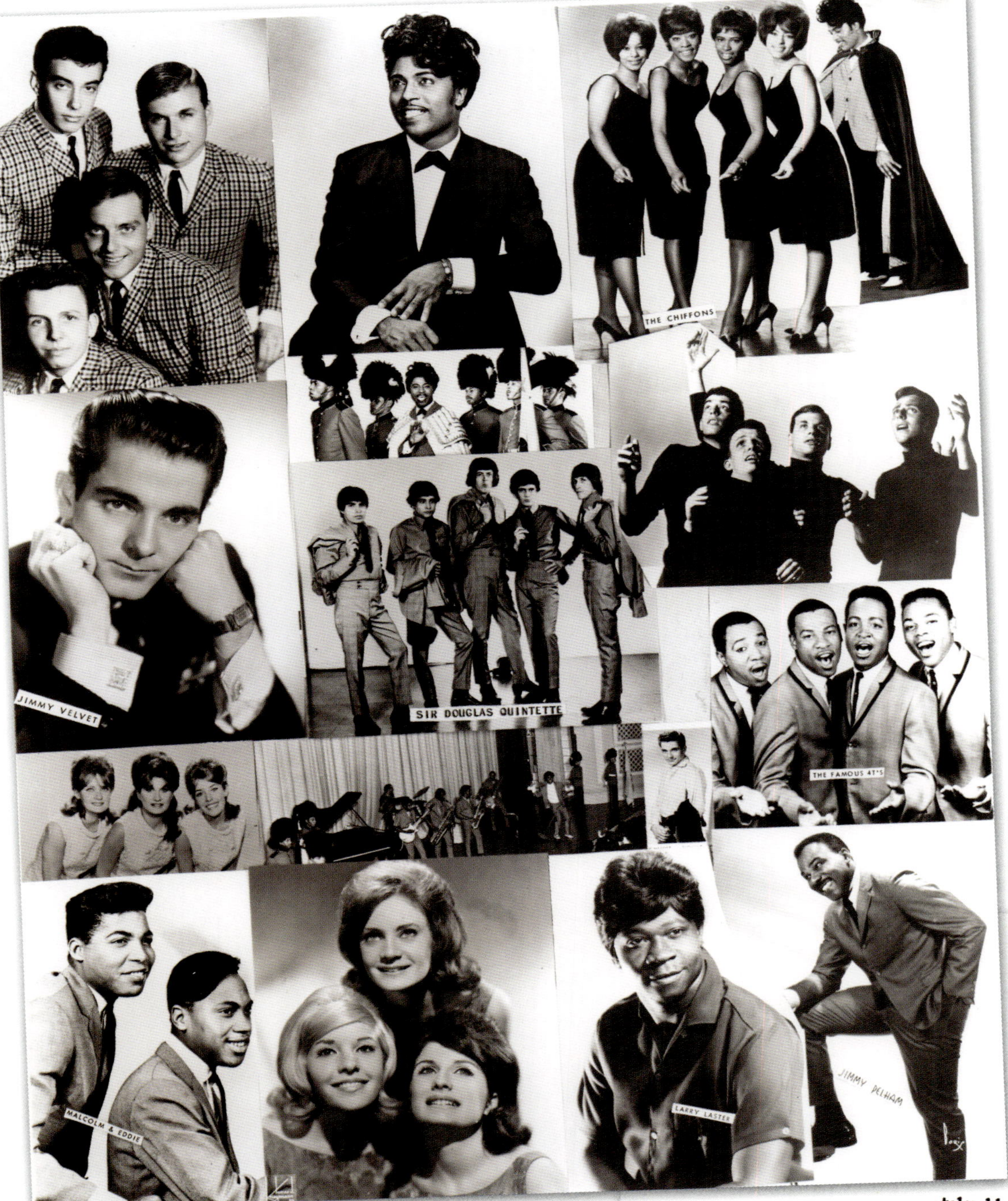

dick clark productions
9125 SUNSET BOULEVARD, LOS ANGELES, CALIFORNIA 90069
CRestview 8-0311

July 11, 1967

Mr. Jimmy Velvet
POB 4045
Huntsville, Ala.

Dear Jimmy:

Please be advised that in regard to

HAPPENING '67

the show will run approximately four hours, and no longer.

If you have any problems with this, please call me at once.

Regards.

Sincerely,

DICK CLARK PRODUCTIONS

Tim Tormey /jk

TIM TORMEY

jk

ELVIS PRESLEY MUSEUM

P.O. BOX 16911 • MEMPHIS, TN. 38116 • (901) 396-6200

"LETTER OF RECOMENDATION"

We, the people who have signed below, do hereby certify that we have known Jimmy Velvet for many years.We have known him as a friend of ours and as a friend of Elvis Presley.

We do at this time further certify that all of us are familiar with most of the items in Jimmy's collection of things that were once owned by Elvis Presley.We have all helped to support Jimmy's Museum by letting him have treasured things that Elvis has given to us through the years to go along with his collection.

To the best of our knowledge, Jimmy now has the largest collection of Authentic Elvis Presley related items in the world.

D.J.FONTANA

ALAN FORTAS

DICK GROB

CHARLIE HODGE

SANDI MILLER

RICHARD DAVIS

BILLY SMITH

JAMES CAUGHLEY

HAROLD LOYD

DONNA KAY EARLY (Pritchett)

MARGIE and SANFORD THOMPSON

MARTY LACKER

Jimmy Velvet, President and Chairman

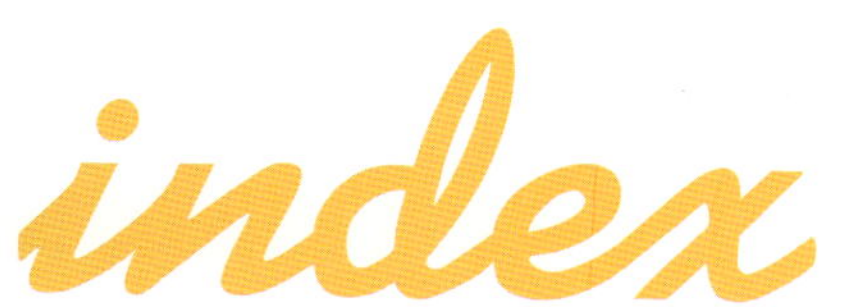

Last Name, First Name	Birth Place and Date		Page #
Laurie, Linda			36
Law. Don			77
Le Doux, Chris	Biloxi, MS	Oct. 2, 1948	183
Leo, Malcom			218, 219
Lettermen: Tony Butala, Donovan Tea, and Mark Preston			245
Lewis, Gary (and The Playboys): Gary, David Walker, David Costell, John West			69, 90
Lewis, Emanuel			163
Lewis, Jerry Lee	Ferriday, LA	Sept. 29, 1935	22, 32-33
Lewis, Jerry	Newark, NJ	Mar. 16, 1926	35
Limbo, Sonny			105
Lindsey, George "Goober"	Jasper, AL	Dec. 17, 1935	122
Lindsey, Mark (Paul Revere and the Raiders)	Caldwell, ID		166
Linkletter, Art	Moose Jaw, Saskatchewan, Canada	July 17, 1912	175
Little Richard, Richard Penniman	Macon, GA	Dec. 5, 1932	90, 223, 270
Little Texas: Del, Porter, Dwayne, Duane, Jeffrey, Timothy			181, 224-226
LL Cool J	St. Albens, Queens, NY	Jan. 14, 1968	163
Lopez, Trini	Dallas, TX	May 15, 1937	122
Loveless, Patty	Pikeville, KY	Jan. 4, 1957	240
Loving, Gene			61, 85
Lucio			182
Lymon, Frankie (and The Teenagers)	Harlem, New York, NY	Sept. 30, 1942-Feb. 27, 1968	23
Lymon, Louis (and the Teenchords)	Harlem, New York		23
Lyn, Rhonda "Priscilla" in "This is Elvis"			142-143
Lynyrd, Skynyrd: Gary Rossington	Jacksonville, FL	Dec. 4, 1951	226
Mandrell, Barbara	Houston, TX	Dec. 25, 1948	161
Mandrell, Louise	Corpus Christie, TX	July 13, 1954	164
Maraquin, Phil			41
Marciano, Rocky	Brockton, MA	Sept. 1, 1923-Aug. 31, 1969	102
Marcucci, Bob	Philadelphia, PA		68
Martin, Claudia			28, 40
Martin, Dean	Steubenville, OH	June 7, 1917-Dec. 25, 1995	28-29
Martin, Dina			40
Martin, Gail			40
Mathers, Jerry "The Beaver"	Sioux City, IA	June 2, 1948	175, 241
Mattea, Kathy	Cross Lanes, WV	June 21, 1959	218
McArthur, James "Dano" "Hawaii Five-O"	Los Angeles, CA	Dec. 8, 1937	148
McBain, Diane	Cleveland, OH	May 18, 1941	125
McBride, Martina	Sharon, KS	July 29, 1966	228, 229
McClain, Charly	Jackson, TN	Mar. 26, 1956	141
McCoy, Neal	Jacksonville, TX	July 30, 1958	185, 238
McCready, Mindy	Ft. Myers, FL	Nov. 30, 1976	253
McDaniel, Mel			253
McDonald, Greg			146, 195
McDowell, Ronnie	Fountain Head, TN	Mar. 26, 1956	201
McEntire, Reba	Cockie, OK	Mar. 28, 1958	242
McGraw, Tim	Delhi, LA	May 1, 1967	248
McKinney, Kurt "General Hospital"	Louisville, KY	Feb. 15, 1962	148
McPhatter, Clyde	Durham, NC	Nov. 15, 1932	21
Medley, Bill (The Righteous Brothers)	Los Angeles, CA	Sept. 19, 1940	57
Mellons, Ken			184
Miller, Roger	Ft. Worth, TX	Jan. 2, 1936-Oct. 25, 1992	80, 162
Mimieux, Yvette			125
Mitchell Hair Products, John Paul			188
Monroe, Marilyn	Los Angeles, CA	June 1, 1926-Aug. 5, 1962	33
Montgomery, Melba			122
Moody Blues: Denny Laine	Birmingham, West Midlands, England	Oct. 29, 1944	255, 262-264
Moore, Scotty	Gadsden, TN	Dec. 27, 1931	43, 54, 92, 105, 141
Morgan, Jane	Newton, MA	Dec. 25, 1920	17
Muhammad Ali, Cassius Clay	Louisville, KY	Jan. 17, 1942	233
Murphy, David Lee	Herin, IL	Jan. 7, 1959	181, 229
Nader, Richard			189
Nelson, Rick	Teaneck, NJ	May 8, 1940-Dec. 31 1985	44, 146
Newland, Pam	Mt. Jackson, VA		50, 53, 56-57, 60, 71, 98
Newton, Wayne	Roanoke, VA	April 3, 1942	220
Nichols, Joe	Rogers, AR	Nov. 26, 1976	238
Noone, Peter (Herman's Hermits)	Manchester, England		111
Norris, Chuck	Ryan, OK	Mar. 10, 1940	165
Oates, John (Hall and Oates)	New York, NY	April 7, 1949	147
Oberst, Stanley			276
Olsson, Nigel (Elton John's drummer)	Wallasey, Maryside, England	Feb. 10, 1941	152
O'Neal, Jimmy			77
O'Neal, Ryan	Los Angeles, CA	April 20, 1941	95
Orlando, Tony	New York, NY	April 3, 1944	236, 248
Orlons: Rosatta Hightower, Shirley Brickley, Marlena Davis, Stephen Caldwell	Philadelphia, PA		60
Osborne, Jerry			276
Osmonds			195
Osteen, Joel and Victoria			269
Owen, Randy			182
Page, Joey			57, 69

RADIO 91-*derful!!*

KDEO "FABULOUS 40"

San Diego's OFFICIAL Top Tune Survey

Week of January 24-30, 1964

This Week	Title	Artist	Last Week
1.	OUT OF LIMITS	The Marketts	1
2.	LOUIE LOUIE	The Kingsmen	2
* 3.	TELL HIM	The Drew-Vells	13
4.	HOOKA TOOKA	Chubby Checker	6
5.	YOU DON'T OWN ME	Leslie Gore	19
6.	ANYONE WHO HAD A HEART	Dionne Warwick	3
7.	I WANT TO HOLD YOUR HAND	Beatles	21
8.	HEY LITTLE COBRA	Ripcords	5
9.	POPSICLES & ICICLES	Murmaids	7
10.	QUICKSAND	Martha & The Vandellas	14
11.	FORGET HIM	Bobby Rydell	10
12.	IN THE SHELTER OF YOUR ARMS	Sammy Davis, Jr.	31
13.	FOR YOU	Ricky Nelson	11
14.	WHAT'S EASY FOR TWO IS SO HARD FOR ONE	Mary Wells	17
15.	THERE I SAID IT AGAIN	Bobby Vinton	12
16.	SURFIN' BIRD	The Trashmen	8
17.	UM, UM, UM	Major Lance	22
*18.	HE WALKS LIKE A MAN	Jody Miller	25
*19.	SOUTHTOWN U.S.A.	The Dixiebelles	27
20.	WHISPERING	April & Nino	9
21.	I WISH YOU LOVE	Gloria Lynne	38
22.	HARLEM SHUFFLE	Bob & Earl	4
*23.	AS USUAL	Brenda Lee	16
24.	A FOOL NEVER LEARNS	Andy Williams	26
25.	LITTLE BOXES	Pete Seeger	37
26.	SINCE I FELL FOR YOU	Lenny Welch	23
*28.	WE BELONG TOGETHER	Jimmy Velvet	30
30.	YOU'RE NO GOOD	Betty Everett	28
31	IT'S ALL IN THE GAME	Cliff Richards	Debut
32.	COMIN' IN THE BACK DOOR	Baja Marimba Band	20
33.	DAISY PETAL PICKIN	Jimmy Gilmer	35
*34.	DRAY CITY	Jan & Dean	33
35.	BYE BYE BARBARA	Johnny Mathis	Debut
36.	SAGINAW MICHIGAN	Lefty Frizzel	39
37.	IF ANYBODY TOLD YOU	Anna King	Debut
*38.	GOOD NEWS	Sam Cooke	Debut
39.	MILLER'S CAVE	Bobby Bare	Debut
40.	HAVE LOVE WILL TRAVEL	Imperialites	Debut

* denotes former disc/overy

D J PERSONAL PICKS

CHUCK DAUGHERTY – What Are We Gonna Do In '64? . . . The Wildcats

NEW YORK RECORD REVIEW

A COMPLETE LISTING OF THE LATEST RELEASES FROM THE FOLLOWING DISTRIBUTORS:

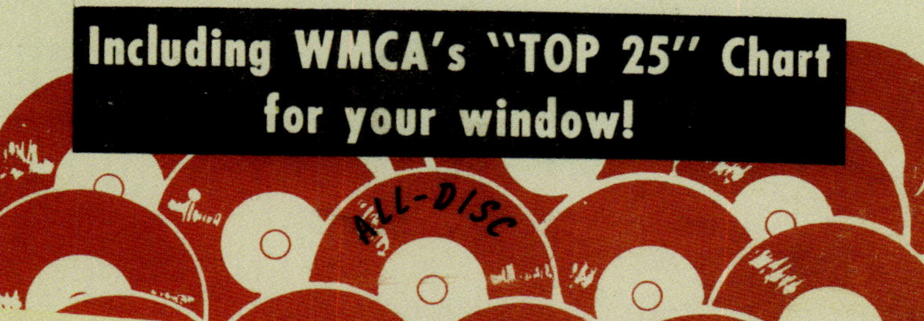

JET RECORD DISTRIBUTING CORP.
40-11 Skillman Ave.
Long Island City, New York
ST 6-0677

A MUST IN THE SUMMER OF HIS YEARS * MILLICENT MARTIN-ABC 10514
(The original as heard on the B.B.C. & NBC, T.V.)

BREAKING BIG WHO CARES FATS DOMINO ABC 10512

BEST SELLING SINGLES

1. LUCKY OLD SUN - Ray Charles - ABC 10509
2. EVERYBODY - Tommy Roe - ABC 10478
3. HARLEM SHUFFLE - Earl & Bob - Marc 104
5. WE BELONG TOGETHER - Jimmy Velvet - ABC 10488
7. SLOWLY LOSING MY MIND - B.B. King - ABC 10486
8. CHEEK TO CHEEK/TEA FOR TWO - Les Dijinns Singers - ABC 10506
9. DADDY'S LITTLE GIRL - Frank Fontaine - ABC 10491
10. I'M WILLING - Earther Doss, Jr. - ABC 10496

NOVEMBER 16, 1963

Wilmington's Authentic Music Survey

WAMS — TOP 30 tunes for the week Featured By "The Fabulous 5"

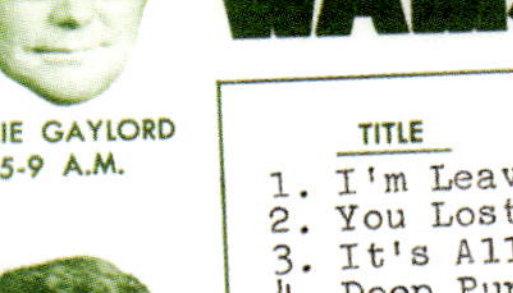

LIE GAYLORD 5-9 A.M.

ROGER HOLMES 9 A.M.-1 P.M.

DEAN TYLER 1-4 P.M.

LEE DAVIS 4-8 P.M.

WILLIE GAYLORD 5-9 A.M.

ROGER HOLMES 9 A.M.-1 P.M.

DEAN TYLER 1-4 P.M.

LEE DAVIS 4-8 P.M.

	TITLE	ARTIST	LAST WEEK
1.	I'm Leaving It Up To You	Dale & Grace	3
2.	You Lost The Sweetest Boy	Mary Wells	2
3.	It's All Right	The Impressions	1
4.	Deep Purple	N.Tempo/A.Stevens	5
5.	Can I Get A Witness	Marvin Gaye	6
6.	Hey Little Girl	Major Lance	8
7.	Wild!	DeeDee Sharp	7
8.	When The Boy's Happy	The Four Pennies	12
10.	We Belong Together	Jimmy Velvet	20
12.	(Down At)Papa Joe's	The Dixiebelles	10
13.	Bossa Nova Baby/Witchcraft	Elvis Presley	14
14.	Little Red Rooster	Sam Cooke	19
15.	Misty	Lloyd Price	9
16.	Dominique	The Singing Nun	--
17.	Crossfire!	The Orlons	13
18.	Talk To Me	Sunny & Sunglows	11
19.	Walking The Dog	Rufus Thomas	22
20.	Workout Stevie, Workout	Little Stevie Wonder	15
21.	The Cheer Leader	Paul Petersen	25
22.	As Long As I Know He's Mine	Marvelettes	23
23.	Have You Heard	The Duprees	27
24.	Midnight Mary	Joey Powers	--
25.	I Adore Him	The Angels	26
26.	31 Flavors	The Shirelles	28
27.	Mr. Cupid	The Vespers	24
28.	She's A Fool	Lesley Gore	--
29.	Baby Don't You Weep	Garnet Mimms	30
30.	Baby I Do Love You	The Galens	--

WAMS PIKS OF THE WEEK

Please-Frank Ifield
The Dictionary Song-Don Robertson
Can't Stop Talking About You-Tobin Matthews
The Nearness of You-Roomates
My Special Angel-Classmen

WAMS SHOWCASE ALBUMS

Blue Gene-Gene Pitney
Wonderful World of Si Zentner

WAMS WAX TO WATCH

Blueberry Hill-Artie & Linda
Does Goodnight Mean Goodbye-Vincent Edwards
A Voice In The Wind-Vic Dana
Somewhere-The Tymes
Dedicate The Blues To Me-Barbara Lynn
Just Loving You-Kim Weston

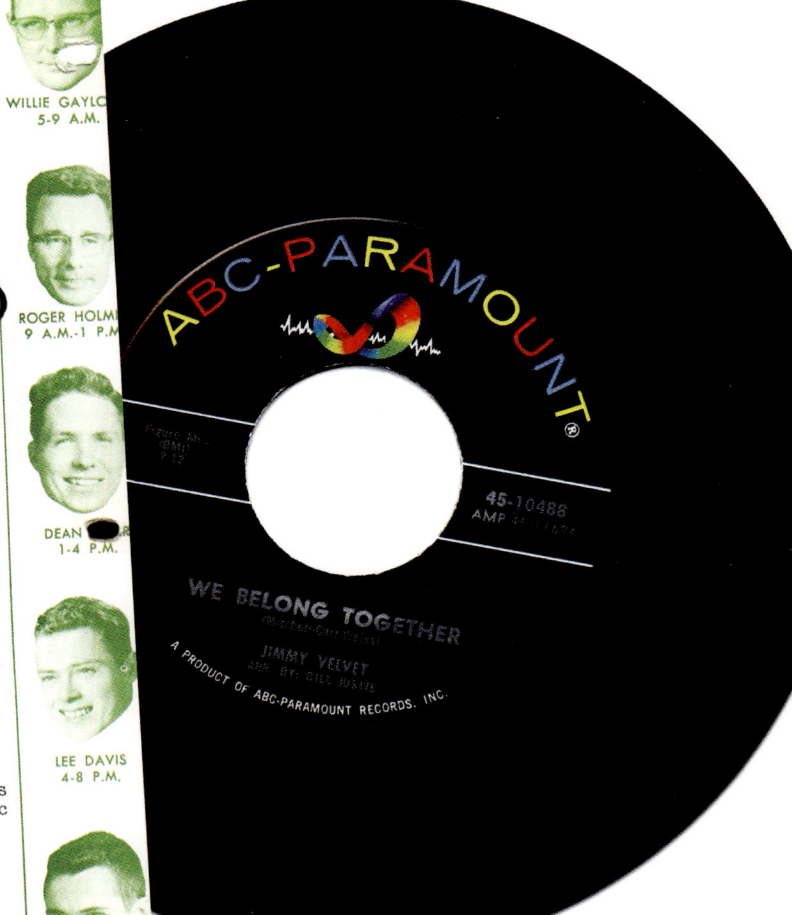

KLUE KLIMBERS

I Can't Help It	Skeeter Davis	RCA
Now that You've Gone	Connie Stevens	Warner
Honest I Do	Sensors	Ty Tex
Stop Th' Music	Sue Thompson	Hickory
It's Almost Tomorrow	Jimmy Velvet	Velvet
Shakin' All Over	Guess Who	Scepter
Catch the Wind	Donovan	Hickory
The Mouse	Soupy Sales	ABC
Time	Jerry Wallace	Mercury
Do the Freddie	Freddie & Dreamers	Mercury
In the Meantime	Georgie Fame	Imperial
Why do I Cry	The Remains	Epic
The Last Thing on my Mind	New Wine Singers	Village Ga
More I Cannot Do	Don Cherry	Monument
Crying in the Chapel	Elvis Presley	RCA
Without You	Matt Monro	Liberty
Come on Over to My Place	Drifters	Atlantic
Queen of the House	Jody Miller	Capitol
Concrete and Clay	Unit Four plus 2	London
You Were Made for Me	Freddie & Dreamers	Tower
The Climb	Kingsmen	Wand
Georgie Porgie ***	Jewel Akins	Era
Wishing it was You ***	Connie Francis	MGM
Voodoo Woman ***	Bobby Goldsboro	UA
Mrs. Jones	The Detergents	Roulette
Keep on Trying ***	Bobby Vee	Liberty
When I Stop Lovin' You	Four Freshmen	Capitol
For Your Love	The Yardbirds	Epic

***Three Star Picks from the KLUE Top Cats...Dave Allen, Phil Ransom, Ken Damon, Wayne McKay ...

Radio Longview
KLUE
Longview, Texas
75603

Jim
Box
Nas

KLUE's IMMEDIATE To

KNBR PLAYLIST

SINGLES

SAN FRANCISCO'S EEST SELLERS — EFFECTIVE MAY 28,1965

1. Hush Hush Sweet Charlotte	Patti Page	2:29	T1/8	S CC
2.*Cast Your Fate	Steve Alaimo	*2:20	6/2	MUAE
3. Walk In The Black Forest	Horst Jankowski	2:50	Inst	U Me
4. Cast Your Fate	Sounds Orch	3:00	Inst	S Pa
5. Engine Engine #9	Roger Miller	2:18	T6/2f	U Sr
6. Catch The Wind	Donovan	2:17	7/4	S Hi
7. Mrs Brown You've Got A Lovely Daughter	Herman's Hermits	2:46	5/5	U Mg
8. Before And After	Chad & Jeremy	2:37	8/5f	S CC
9. I'll Be With You In Appleblossom Time	Wayne Newton	2:23	TO/2	S CA
10. Senorita From Detroit	Jack Nitzsche	2:31	Inst	U RE
11. Please Help Me I'm Falling	Vic Damone	2:05	T1/4	U WE
12. You Were Only Fooling	Vic Damone	2:30	7/5	MUWE
13. A World Of Our Own	The Seekers	2:39	9/4	U CA
14. Seein' The Right Love Go Wrong	Jack Jones	2:31	5/7f	S Ka
15. Summer Sounds	Robert Goulet	2:05	0/7	U Co
16. You've Lost That Lovin' Feeling	Lincolm Mayorga	2:35	Inst	MSCa
17. You'll Never Walk Alone	Gerry & Pacemakers	2:39	0/4	S La
18. I'm The One Who Loves You	Dean Martin	2:24	8/15f	MURe
19. Just Dance On By	Eydie Gorme	2:25	10/4f	U Co
20. It's Almost Tomorrow	Jimmy Velvet	2:35	T1/5	S Ph
21. They Can't Make Her Cry	Nat Cole	2:22	12/6	S Ca
22. Tell Her You Love Her	Frank Sinatra	2:40	T7/0	MURe
23. Bring A Little Sunshine To My Life	Vic Dana	2:31	0/5	MUDo
24. Tears Keep Falling	Jerry Vale	2:18	T1/3	MUCo
25. Too Many Rivers	Brenda Lee	2:46	7/3	MUDe
26. Three O'Clock In The Morning	Lou Rawls	2:47	TO/2	MUCa
27. This Little Bird	Marianne Faithful	2:00	6/6	S IC
28. Get Out Of My Life	Timi Yuro	2:30	0/3	MSMe
29. Let Me Cry On Your Shoulder	Georgia Gibbs	2:23	TO/5	MUBe
30. Mae	Tijuana Brass	2:20	Inst	S A&

MERCURY RECORD PRODUCTIONS, INC.
745 Fifth Avenue · Suite 815 · New York 22, N.Y. · PLaza 9-2727
Cable Address: MERCUCORD NEWYORK

May 11, 1965

Mr. Jimmy Velvet
5504 Hatteras Road
Virginia Beach, Va.

Dear Jimmy:

Enclosed are the contracts I spoke to you about regarding the master purchase and yourself, as an artist. Please check through the contracts and if okay sign and initial where indicated.

The record is doing well and should be a big one. We will keep on it.

Kindest regards,

MERCURY RECORD PRODUCTIONS, INC.

Shelby S. Singleton, Jr.
Vice-President
A&R Division

SSS:car
Encl.

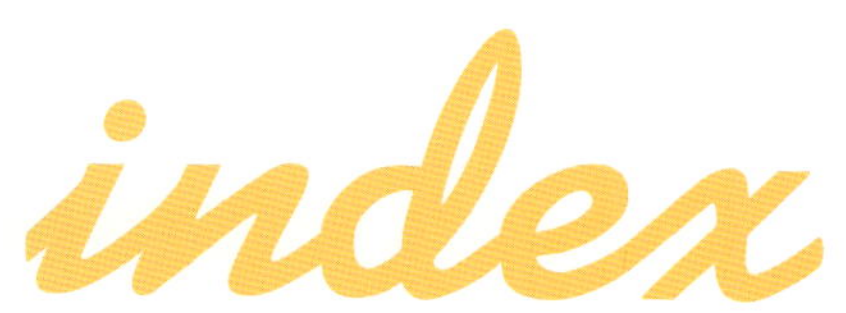

index

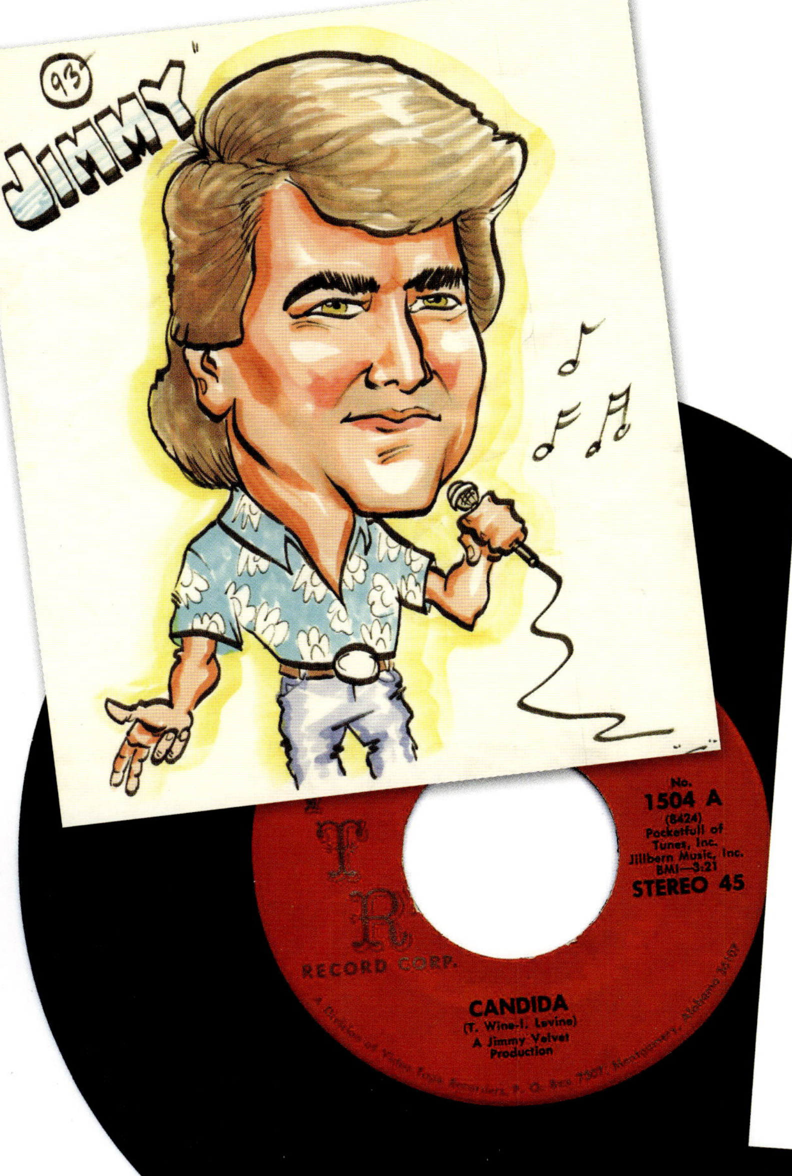

dick clark

September 19, 1989

We can't thank you enough, Jimmy, for your wonderful hospitality during our short stay in Nashville.

Kari and I both really enjoyed your restaurant. It's very special! Thank you, also, for the sweatshirts, caps and souvenirs.

It was nice to meet your wife and daughter. We were happy you brought them along. It'll be interesting to see what direction Candida's life will take her ... she's quite the young woman!

I'm sending along a few things I thought you might enjoy having. If I ever get around to cleaning out the garage and a few closets here at the office, there will be much more!

Again, many thanks for everything. Stopping off in Nashville was the highlight of our trip.

'Look forward to seeing you soon.

Dick

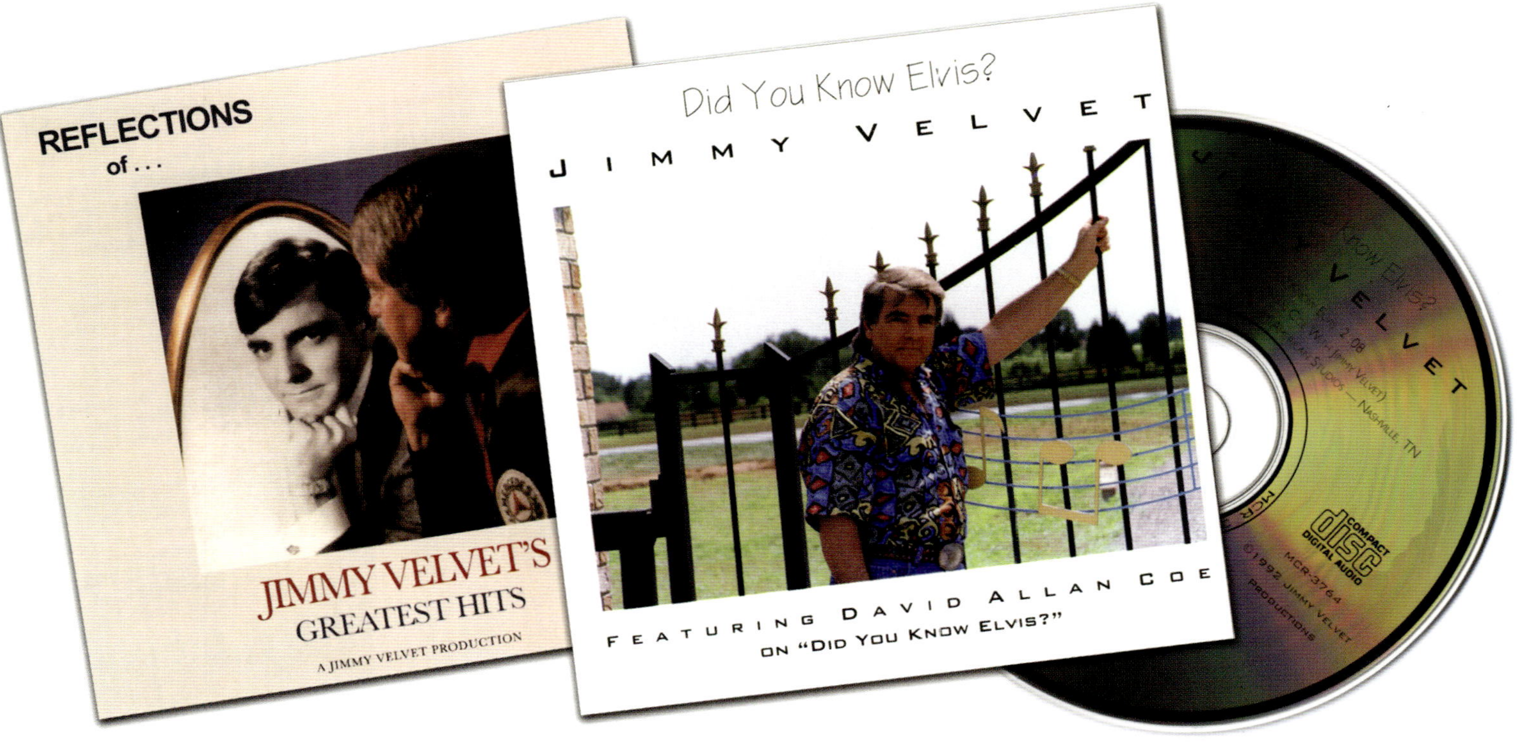

Reflections of...
Jimmy Velvet's Greatest Hits

Blue Velvet
Mission Bell
(You're Mine And) We Belong Together
Roses Are Blue
Teen Angel
It's Almost Tomorrow
Take Me Tonight
Venus
I Won't Be Back This Year
Candida

Did You Know Elvis?
Jimmy Velvet

Did You Know Elvis? *Featuring David Allan Coe*
Things That Make A Woman, A Woman
You Better Move On
It's You
Candida
Blue Velvet
Missing You
Half A Man
I Really Don't Want To Know
Wasted Years

These Jimmy Velvet CDs are available online and can be personally signed by Jimmy Velvet upon request. To purchase your autographed copy, go to: **www.JimmyVelvet.net**